PHILIP'S

STREET ATLAS
Greater Manchester

First published in 1997 by

Philip's, a division of
Octopus Publishing Group Ltd
2-4 Heron Quays, London E14 4JP

Third edition 2004
First impression 2004

ISBN 0-540-08523-5 (pocket)

© Philip's 2004

o|s Ordnance Survey®

This product includes mapping data licensed from
Ordnance Survey® with the permission of the
Controller of Her Majesty's Stationery Office.
© Crown copyright 2004. All rights reserved.
Licence number 100011710.

Printed and bound in Spain
by Cayfosa-Quebecor

Contents

II	**Greater Manchester rail network map**
III	**Key to map symbols**
IV	**Key to map pages**
VI	**Route Planning**
VIII	**Administrative and Postcode boundaries**
1	**Street maps** at 2⅔ inches to 1 mile
138	**Street maps of selected areas** at 5⅓ inches to 1 mile
172	**Index** of towns and villages
173	**Index** of streets, hospitals, industrial estates, railway stations, schools, shopping centres, universities and places of interest

Digital

The exceptio... ...as digital data in TIFF
format, whic... ...ormats.

The index is ... ...a standard database table. It contains all the details
found in the printed index together with the National Grid reference for the map square in which
each entry is named.

For further information and to discuss your requirements, please contact Philip's on
020 7644 6932 or james.mann@philips-maps.co.uk

D1464718

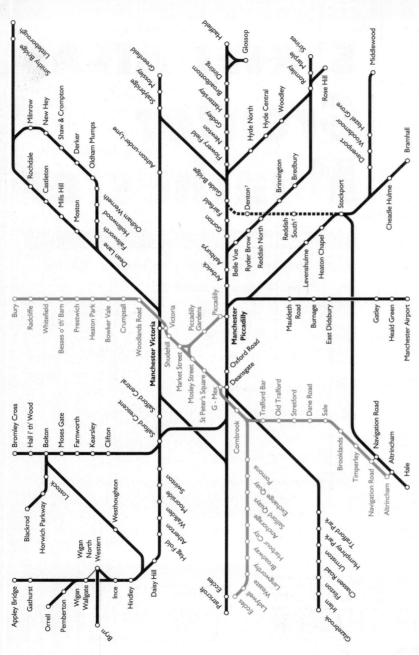

©GMPTE 2003
99/662/0591

KEY

- Rail line in Greater Manchester ticketing area
- Rail line with restricted service
- Metrolink line & stop
- One directional platform (pointing in direction of travel)
- Stations in close proximity
- † Station with restricted service

Motorway with junction number	
Primary route – dual/single carriageway	
A road – dual/single carriageway	
B road – dual/single carriageway	
Minor road – dual/single carriageway	
Other minor road – dual/single carriageway	
Road under construction	
Tunnel, covered road	
Rural track, private road or narrow road in urban area	
Gate or obstruction to traffic (restrictions may not apply at all times or to all vehicles)	
Path, bridleway, byway open to all traffic, road used as a public path	
Pedestrianised area	
DY7 **Postcode boundaries**	
County and unitary authority boundaries	
Railway, tunnel, railway under construction	
Tramway, tramway under construction	
Miniature railway	
Railway station	
Private railway station	
Metro station	
Tram stop, tram stop under construction	
Bus, coach station	

◆	**Ambulance station**
◆	**Coastguard station**
◆	**Fire station**
◆	**Police station**
✚	**Accident and Emergency entrance to hospital**
H	**Hospital**
+	**Place of worship**
i	**Information Centre** (open all year)
P	**Parking**
P&R	**Park and Ride**
PO	**Post Office**
Ă	**Camping site**
⊞	**Caravan site**
▶	**Golf course**
✕	**Picnic site**
Prim Sch	**Important buildings, schools, colleges, universities and hospitals**
River Medway	**Water name**
	River, weir, stream
	Canal, lock, tunnel
	Water
	Tidal water
	Woods
	Built up area
Church	**Non-Roman antiquity**
ROMAN FORT	**Roman antiquity**
87	**Adjoining page indicators and overlap bands** The colour of the arrow and the band indicates the scale of the adjoining or overlapping page (see scales below)
228	

Acad	Academy	Inst	Institute	Recn Gd	Recreation Ground
Allot Gdns	Allotments	Ct	Law Court		
Cemy	Cemetery	L Ctr	Leisure Centre	Resr	Reservoir
C Ctr	Civic Centre	LC	Level Crossing	Ret Pk	Retail Park
CH	Club House	Liby	Library	Sch	School
Coll	College	Mkt	Market	Sh Ctr	Shopping Centre
Crem	Crematorium	Meml	Memorial	TH	Town Hall/House
Ent	Enterprise	Mon	Monument	Trad Est	Trading Estate
Ex H	Exhibition Hall	Mus	Museum	Univ	University
Ind Est	Industrial Estate	Obsy	Observatory	W Twr	Water Tower
IRB Sta	Inshore Rescue Boat Station	Pal	Royal Palace	Wks	Works
		PH	Public House	YH	Youth Hostel

■ The small numbers around the edges of the maps identify the 1 kilometre National Grid lines

■ The dark grey border on the inside edge of some pages indicates that the mapping does not continue onto the adjacent page

The scale of the maps on the pages numbered in blue is 4.2 cm to 1 km • 2⅔ inches to 1 mile • 1:23810	0 ¼ ½ ¾ 1 mile
	0 250m 500m 750m 1 kilometre

The scale of the maps on pages numbered in red is 8.4 cm to 1 km • 5⅓ inches to 1 mile • 1:11900	0 220 yards 440 yards 660 yards ½ mile
	0 125m 250m 375m ½ kilometre

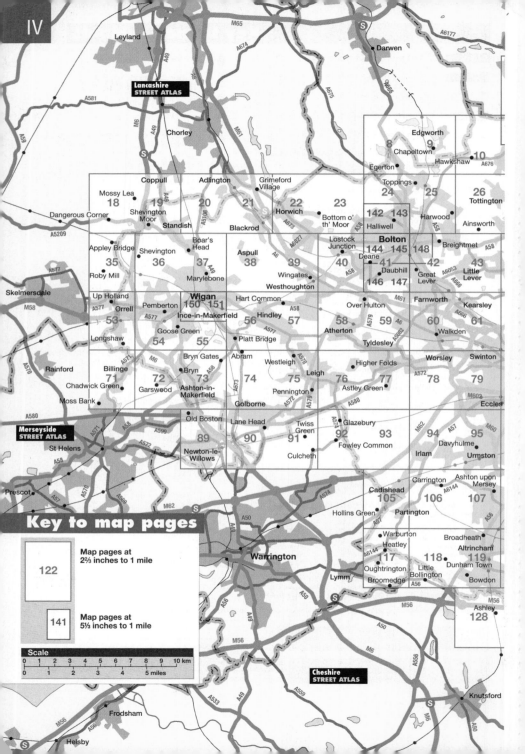

IV

Leyland

M65

Darwen

A6177

Lancashire
STREET ATLAS

A674

A581

A675

A59

Chorley

Edgworth

8 **9** Chapeltown

10

A676

Egerton Hawkshaw

Coppull Adlington Grimeford Village

Toppings

24 **25** **26** Tottington

Mossy Lea

18 **19** **20** **21** **22** Horwich **23** Bottom o' th' Moor

142 143 Harwood Ainsworth

Shevington Moor Standish Blackrod Halliwell

A5209

Dangerous Corner

Appley Bridge Shevington Boar's Head Aspull Lostock Junction **Bolton**

Breightmet A58

35 **36** **37** **38** **39** **40** **144 145 148**

Roby Mill Marylebone Wingates Deane **41** Daubhill **42** **43** Little Lever

Skelmersdale Westhoughton **146 147** Great Lever

M58

Up Holland **Wigan** Hart Common Over Hulton Farnworth Kearsley

Pemberton **150 151** **56** Hindley **57** **58** **59** **60** **61**

53 Orrell Ince-in-Makerfield Atherton Walkden

Longshaw Goose Green Platt Bridge Tyldesley

54 **55** Worsley Swinton

Rainford Billinge Bryn Gates Abram Westleigh Leigh Higher Folds **78** **79**

71 **72** **73** **74** **75** **76** **77** Eccles

Chadwick Green Garswood Bryn Ashton-in-Makerfield Pennington Astley Green

Moss Bank Golborne A580

A580

Merseyside STREET ATLAS Old Boston Lane Head Twiss Green Glazebury

89 **90** **91** **92** **93** **94** **95**

St Helens Newton-le-Willows Culcheth Fowley Common Irlam Davyhulme

Prescot Urmston

Carrington Ashton upon Mersey

Cadishead **105** **106** **107**

Hollins Green Partington

Key to map pages

Warburton Broadheath

Heatley **117** **118** Altrincham **119**

Warrington Oughtrington Little Bollington Dunham Town Bowdon

	Map pages at 2⅔ inches to 1 mile
122	

Lymm Broomedge A56

	Map pages at 5½ inches to 1 mile
141	

Cheshire STREET ATLAS

M56 Ashley

128

Scale

0 1 2 3 4 5 6 7 8 9 10 km

0 1 2 3 4 5 miles

Knutsford

Frodsham

Helsby

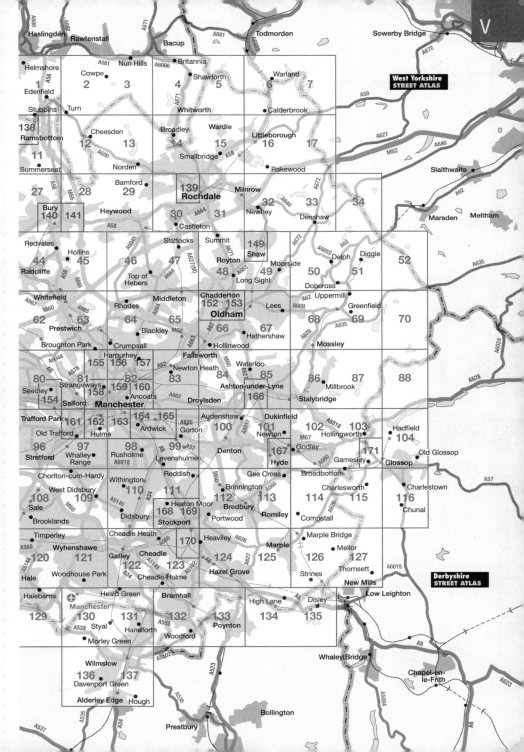

Route Planning

Scale

0 1 2 3 4 5 6 7 8 8 10 km

0 1 2 3 4 5 miles

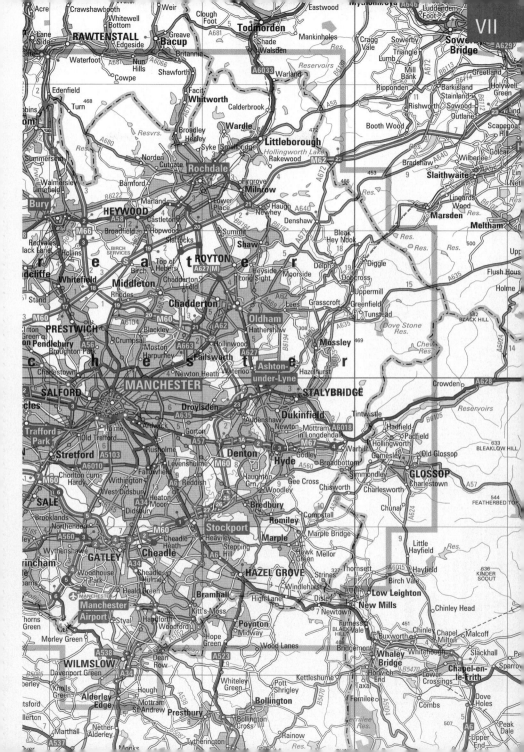

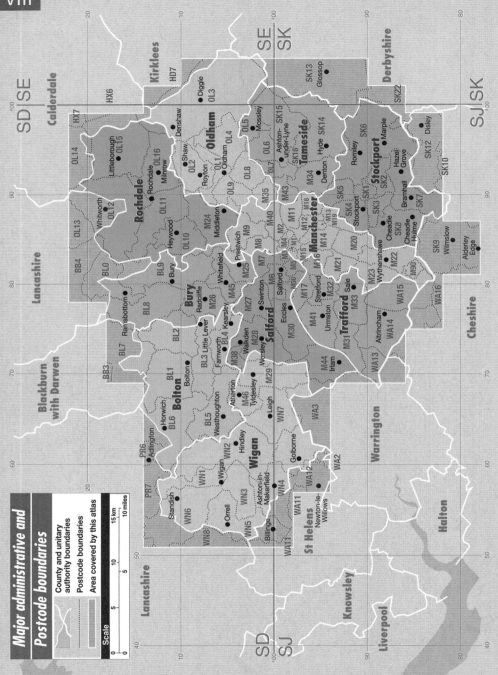

Major administrative and Postcode boundaries

County and unitary authority boundaries

Postcode boundaries

Area covered by this atlas

Scale

| 0 | 5 | 10 | 15 km |
| 0 | 5 | 10 miles |

SD|SE
SE|SK

Calderdale

Kirklees

HD7

Lancashire

Blackburn with Darwen

Derbyshire

SJ|SK

Cheshire

Warrington

Halton

Liverpool

Knowsley

St Helens

Wigan

Bolton

Bury

Rochdale

Oldham

Tameside

Stockport

Manchester

Salford

Trafford

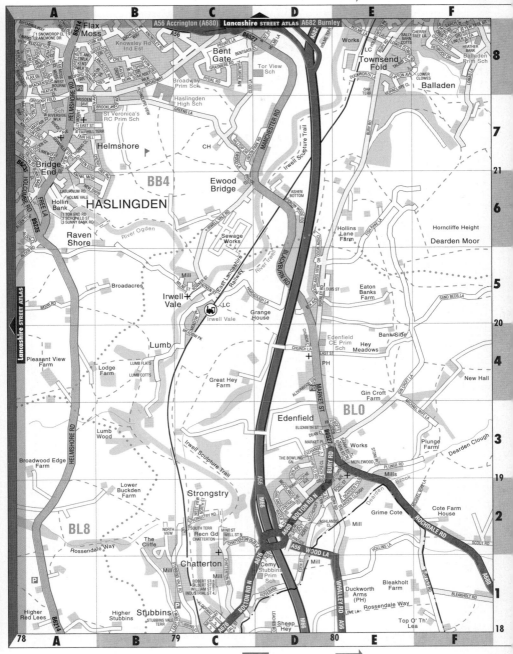

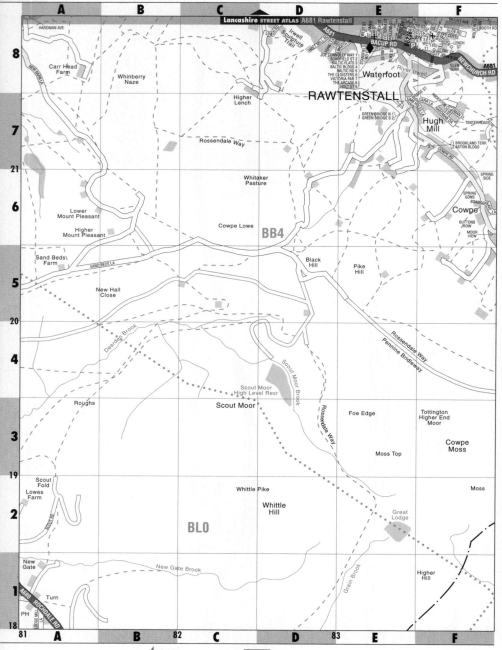

F8
1 IVY ST
2 GEORGE'S ROW
3 PILLING ST
4 SPRING GARDENS ST
5 MARKET ST
6 TENTERFIELD ST
7 YARE ST
8 THORNFIELD AVE
9 WOOD LEA BANK
10 INDUSTRIAL COTTS
11 ASHWORTH ST

Lancashire STREET ATLAS A681 Rawtenstall

HARDMAN AVE

Carr Head
Farm

Whinberry
Naze

Higher
Lench

Irwell
Sculpture
Trail

BACUP RD

JOE CONNOLLY WAY 1
SCHOFIELD ST 2
BALTIC FLATS 3
BALTIC BLDGS 4
BALTIC RD 5
THE CLOISTERS 6
VICTORIA PAR 7
VICTORIA PAR 8
THE ARCADE 8
HOLT ST 9

Waterfoot

River Irwell

RAWTENSTALL

GREEN BRIDGE N 1
GREEN BRIDGE S 2

Hugh
Mill

TENTERMEADS

1 BROOKLAND TERR
2 ASTON BLDGS

Rossendale Way

Whitaker
Pasture

SPRING
SIDE

Lower
Mount Pleasant

Cowpe Lowe

BB4

SPRING
GONS
BOARSGRE

Cowpe

Higher
Mount Pleasant

BUTTONS
ROW
MOOR
VIEW

Sand Beds
Farm

SAND BEDS LA

Black
Hill

Pike
Hill

New Hall
Close

Deardengn Brook

Rossendale Way

Pennine Bridleway

Roughs

Scout Moor
Brook

Scout Moor
High Level Resr

Scout Moor

Rossendale Way

Foe Edge

Tottington
Higher End
Moor

Cowpe
Moss

Moss Top

Scout
Fold

Lowes
Farm

Whittle Pike

Whittle
Hill

BLO

Great
Lodge

Moss

SCOUT RD

New
Gate

New Gate Brook

Grain Brook

Higher
Hill

A680
ROCHDALE RD

Turn

PH

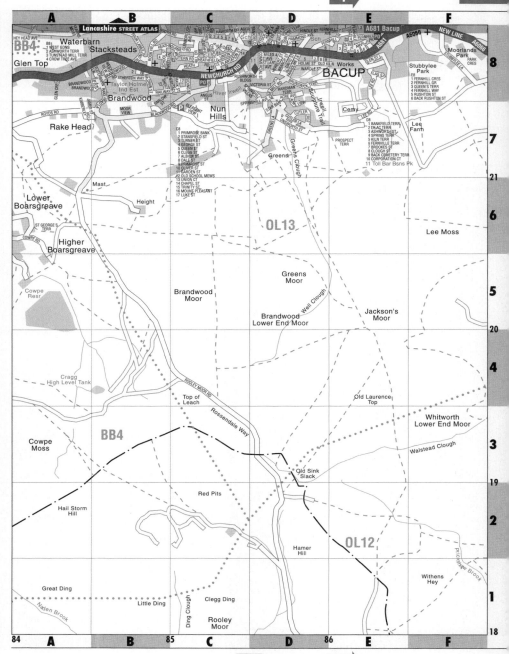

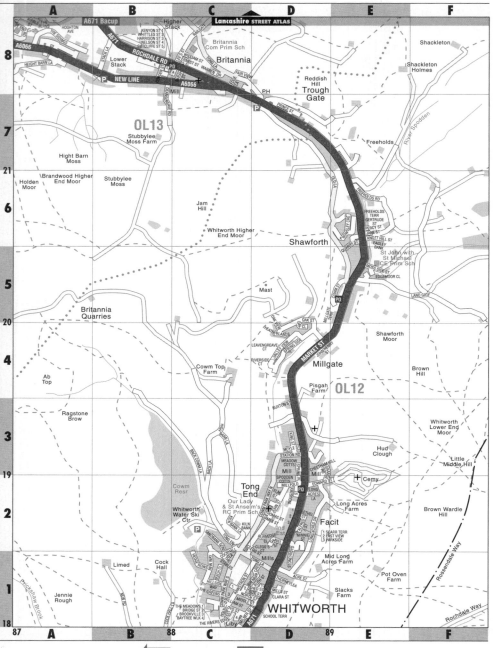

Lancashire STREET ATLAS

A671 Bacup

KENYON ST 1
WHITTLES ST 2
HARRISON ST 3
NELSON ST 4
SUTCLIFFE ST 5

Higher
Stack

Lower
Stack

ROCHDALE RD

NEW LINE

A6066

HEIGHT BARN LA

HOGHTON
AVE

THE PENNS

THE ROW

STACK LA

WILLIAM ST

WARREN DR

FAIR VIEW

Britannia
Com Prim Sch

Britannia

Shackleton

Shackleton
Holmes

Reddish
Hill

Trough
Gate

OL13

Stubbylee
Moss Farm

Hight Barn
Moss

Holden
Moor

Brandwood Higher
End Moor

Stubbylee
Moss

Jam
Hill

Whitworth Higher
End Moor

Freeholds

River Spodden

Shawforth

FREEHOLDS RD

FREEHOLDS
TERR
GERTRUDE
ST
PERCY ST
JANE ST
KNOTT HILL ST

St John with
St Michael
CE Prim Sch

EAGLEY
BANK

MOSS SIDE ST

EDGEMOOR CL

Mast

Britannia
Quarries

LAND GATE

Shawforth
Moor

Brown
Hill

Cowm Top
Farm

LEAVENGREAVE
CT

RIVERSIDE
CT

OAK ST

HEATHERLANDS

MILLGATE RD

MARKET ST

Millgate

OL12

Ab
Top

Ragstone
Brow

Pisgah
Farm

BUXTON ST

Whitworth
Lower End
Moor

Little
Middle Hill

KING ST

HOYLE ST

STATION RD

MEADOW
COTTS

Mill

SPODDEN
COTTS

MILLFOLD

ELM ST

CHEETHAM HILL

Mill

EDWARD ST

LONG
ACRES

Hud
Clough

Cemy

Cowm
Resr

Tong
End

Our Lady
& St Anselm's
RC Prim Sch

Whitworth
Water Ski
Ctr

KILN
BANK

LONG END

BACK CROWN LA

CROWN LA

SANDHAM ST

THOMAS ST

JAMES ST

PURDLEDGE ST

CLEGG'S ST

LONG
ACRES
LA

ETHEL
ST

MINNIE ST

Long Acres
Farm

Facit

1 SCARR TERR
2 EAST VIEW
3 PARKSIDE

Brown Wardle
Hill

Limed

Cock
Hall

HEDGE ROWS

WHIN WAY

SHED ST

ACRE ST

THORNEYLEA

Mid Long
Acres Farm

Pot Oven
Farm

Jennie
Rough

HILLSIDE

THE GREENS

CLARA ST

SCHOOL TERR

Slacks
Farm

WHITWORTH

THE MEADOWS 1
BRIDGE ST 2
BROOKVILLE 3
BAYTREE WLK 4

Lib

THE RIVERS

Rossendale Way

Rochdale Way

Prickshaw Brook

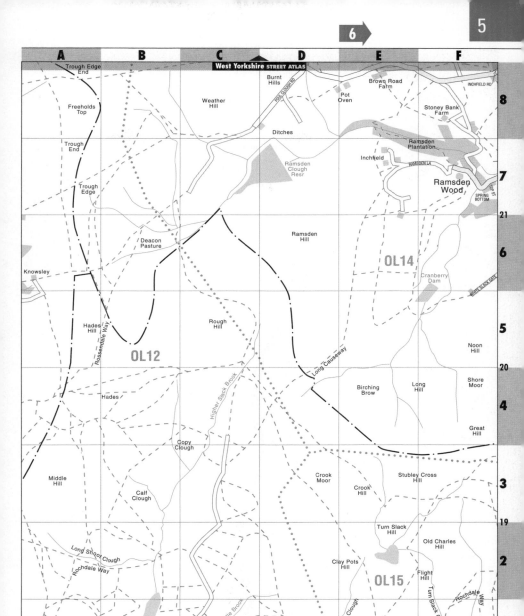

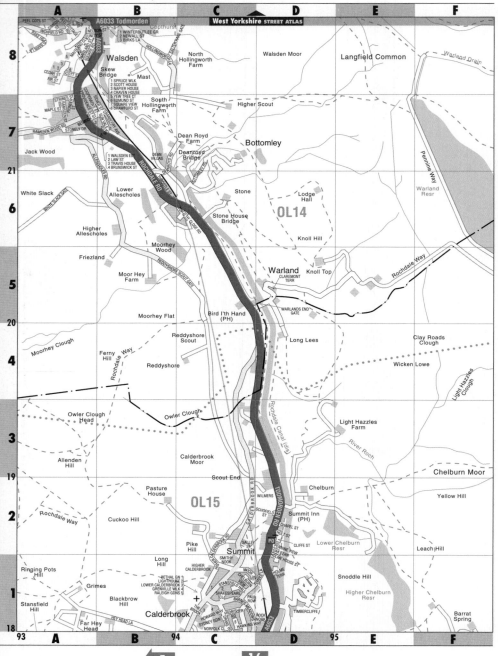

A6033 Todmorden

1 WINTERBUTLEE GR
2 NEWALL ST
3 BIRKS LA

Walsden

Skew Bridge

Mast

1 SPRUCE WLK
2 SCOTT HOUSE
3 NAPIER HOUSE
4 CRAVEN HOUSE
5 YEW TREE CT
6 EDMUND ST
7 SQUARE VIEW
8 BRAWFORD ST

North Hollingworth Farm

South Hollingworth Farm

Walsden Moor

Langfield Common

Warland Drain

Higher Scout

Dean Royd Farm

Bottomley

Deanroyd Bridge

1 WALSDEN EST
2 LAW ST
3 TRAVIS HOUSE
4 BRUNSWICK ST

DEAN VILLAS

Jack Wood

Pennine Way

White Slack

Lower Allescholes

Stone

Lodge Hall

Warland Resr

OL14

Knoll Hill

Higher Allescholes

Stone House Bridge

Moorhey Wood

Friezland

Warland

CLAREMONT TERR

Knoll Top

Rochdale Way

Moor Hey Farm

Bird I'th Hand (PH)

WARLANDS END GATE

Moorhey Flat

Long Lees

Clay Roads Clough

Moorhey Clough

Reddyshore Scout

Wicken Lowe

Ferny Hill

Rochdale Way

Reddyshore

Light Hazzles Clough

Owler Clough Head

Owler Clough

Rochdale Canal (dis)

Light Hazzles Farm

River Roch

Allenden Hill

Calderbrook Moor

Chelburn Moor

Pasture House

Scout End

Chelburn

Yellow Hill

OL15

WILMERS

Rochdale Way

Cuckoo Hill

SCHOFIELD ST

Summit Inn (PH)

CHAPEL ST

Lower Chelburn Resr

Leach Hill

Pike Hill

Summit

CLIFFE ST

Long Hill

SMITHY NOOK

Ringing Pots Hill

Grimes

HIGHER CALDERBROOK

BETHAL GN 1
LIGHTHOUSE 2
LOWER CALDERBROOK 3
GRENVILLE WLK 4
RALEIGH GDNS 5

Snoddle Hill

Higher Chelburn Resr

Stansfield Hill

Blackbrow Hill

Calderbrook

SHAKESPEARE

HOWARD WAY

SYDNEY GDNS

NORFOLK CL

PAUL ROW

TIMBERCLIFFE

Barrat Spring

Far Hey Head

HEY HEAD LA

HAWKINS WAY

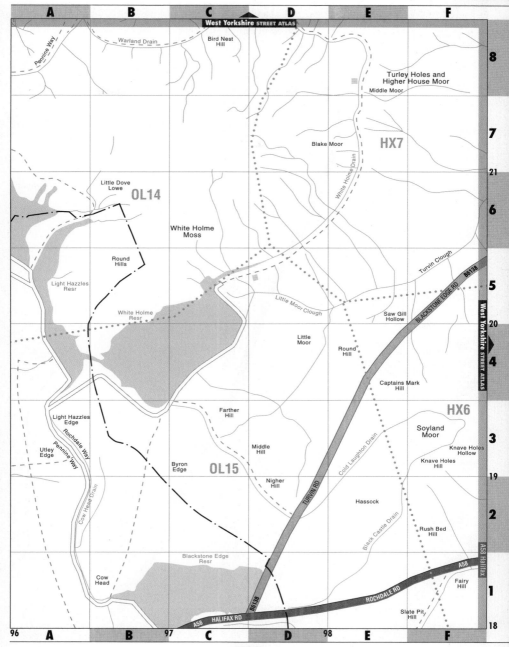

A   B   C   D   E   F

8

Turley Holes and
Higher House Moor

Middle Moor

HX7

Bird Nest
Hill

Warland Drain

Pennine Way

Blake Moor

7

21

Little Dove
Lowe

OL14

White Holme
Moss

6

White Holme Drain

Round
Hills

Light Hazzles
Resr

Turvin Clough

BLACKSTONE EDGE RD

B6138

5

20

White Holme
Resr

Little Moor Clough

Saw Gill
Hollow

Little
Moor

Round
Hill

West Yorkshire STREET ATLAS

4

Light Hazzles
Edge

Rochdale Way

Pennine Way

Farther
Hill

Captains Mark
Hill

HX6

Soyland
Moor

Knave Holes
Hollow

3

Utley
Edge

Middle
Hill

Knave Holes
Hill

19

Cow Head Drain

Byron
Edge

OL15

Nigher
Hill

Cold Laughton Drain

TURVIN RD

Hassock

Black Castle Drain

Rush Bed
Hill

2

Blackstone Edge
Resr

Cow
Head

A58

A58 Halifax

Fairy
Hill

1

B6138

HALIFAX RD

A58

ROCHDALE RD

Slate Pit
Hill

18

96   A   B   97   C   D   98   E   F

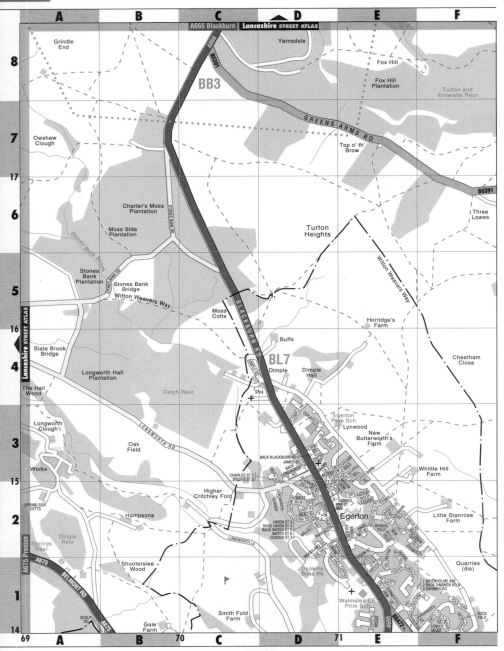

BB3

Grindle
End

Yarnsdale

Fox Hill

Fox Hill
Plantation

Turton and
Entwistle Resr

GREENS ARMS RD

B6391

Owshaw
Clough

Top o' th'
Brow

Three
Lowes

Charter's Moss
Plantation

Moss Side
Plantation

Turton
Heights

STONES BANK RD

Stones Bank Brook

Stones
Bank
Plantation

STONES BANK RD

Stones Bank
Bridge

Witton Weavers Way

Moss
Cotts

Horridge's
Farm

Witton Weavers Way

Lancashire STREET ATLAS

Slate Brook
Bridge

Buffs

Cheetham
Close

BL7

BLACKBURN RD

Longworth Hall
Plantation

Dimple

Dimple
Hall

The Hall
Wood

Delph Resr

PH

Longworth
Clough

LONGWORTH RD

Oak
Field

Egerton
Prim Sch

Lynwood

New
Butterworth's
Farm

Whittle Hill
Farm

Works

BACK BLACKBURN RD E
JAMES ST

Back Blackburn Rd E

SPRING SIDE
COTTS

Charles St 1
Bright St 2

Higher
Critchley Fold

SCHOOL

Little Stanrose
Farm

Hampsons

Egerton

UNION ST 3
BACK UNION ST 4
BACK WATER ST 5
WATER ST 6
COBDEN ST 7

A675 Preston

Dingle
Resr

Springs
Resr

Shooterslee
Wood

LONGWORTH LA

Deakins
Bsns Pk

Quarries
(dis)

BELMONT RD

A675

Smith Fold
Farm

Walmsley CE
Prim Sch

B6472

1 BROOKHOLME AVE
2 BACK DARWEN RD N
3 DARWEN RD

ROCK TERR

LOWER
MEAD

ROCK
FOLD

SCOUT
RD

A675

Gale
Farm

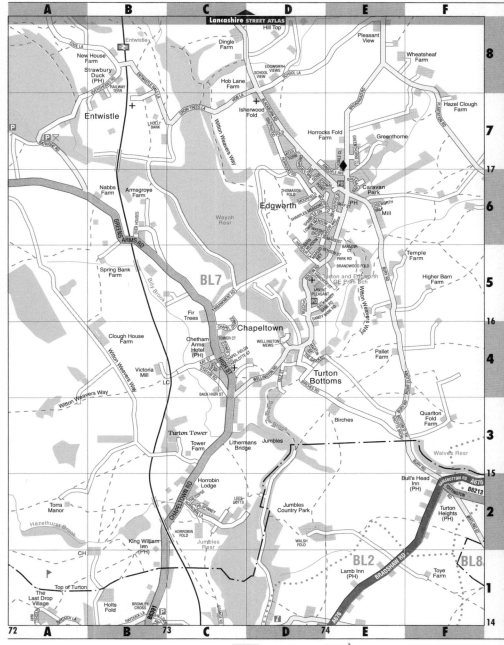

Lancashire STREET ATLAS

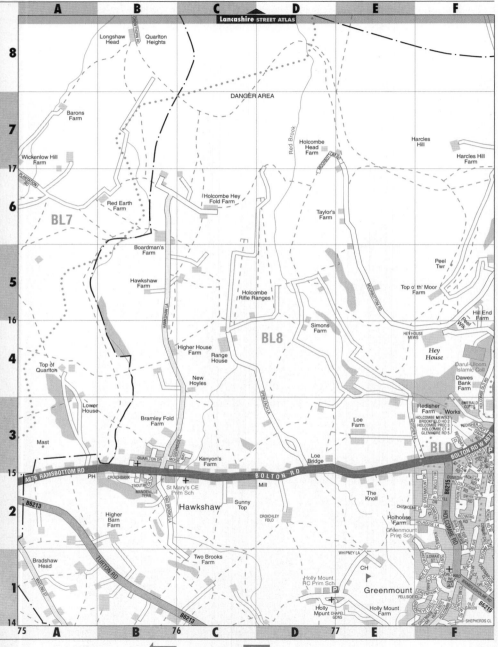

Lancashire STREET ATLAS

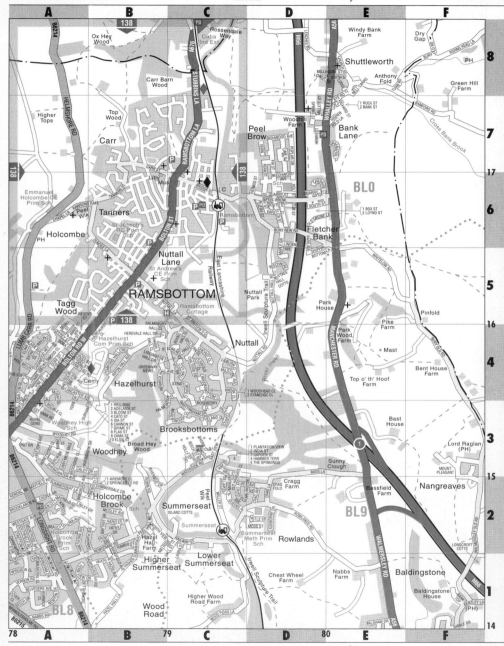

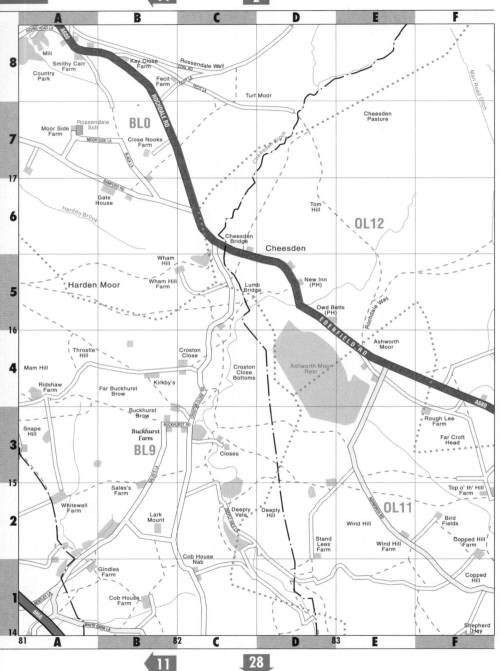

11
2

8

7

17

6

5

16

4

3

15

2

1

14

A B C D E F

RIDING HEAD LA
A680
Mill
Smithy Carr Farm
Country Park
Kay Close Farm
Rossendale Way
COAL RD
Fecit Farm
FECIT LA
Turf Moor

ROCHDALE RD

BLO

Rossendale Sch
Moor Side Farm
MOOR SIDE LA
Close Nooks Farm

BLACK LA

BAMFORD RD
Gate House
Harden Brook

Cheesden Brook

Cheesden Pasture

Tom Hill

OL12

Cheesden Bridge
Cheesden

Wham Hill
Wham Hill Farm
Harden Moor
Lumb Bridge
New Inn (PH)

Owd Betts (PH)

Rochdale Way

EDENFIELD RD

Ashworth Moor

Throstle Hill
Croston Close
Croston Close Bottoms
Ashworth Moor Resr

Mam Hill
Ridshaw Farm
Far Buckhurst Brow
Kirkby's
CROSTON CLOSE RD

Buckhurst Brow
BUCKHURST RD

A680

Rough Lee Farm
Far Croft Head

Snape Hill
Buckhurst Farm
BL9
Closes

Whitewall Farm
Sales's Farm
SALES PA
Lark Mount
Deeply Vale
DEEPLY VALE
Deeply Hill

ASHWORTH RD

OL11

Top o' th' Hill Farm

Wind Hill
Bird Fields
Copped Hill Farm

Gindles Farm
Cob House Nab
Stand Lees Farm
Wind Hill Farm

Copped Hill

HENLEY LA
M66
Cob House Farm
WHITE CARR LA
Shepherd Hey

Man Road Ditch

11
28

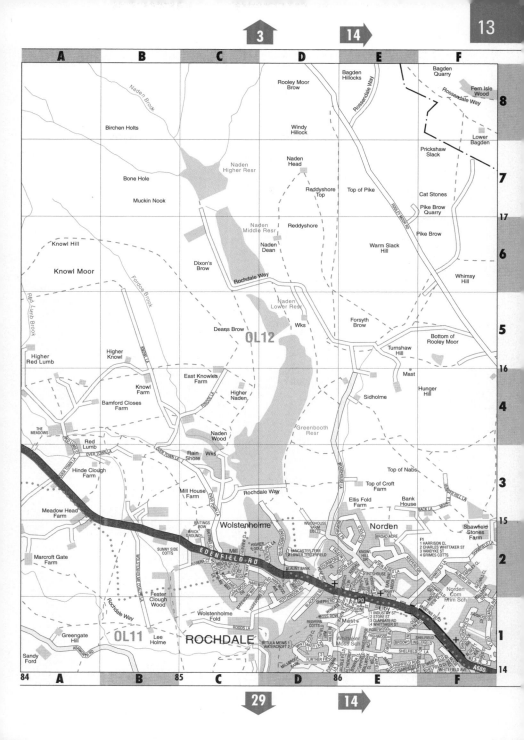

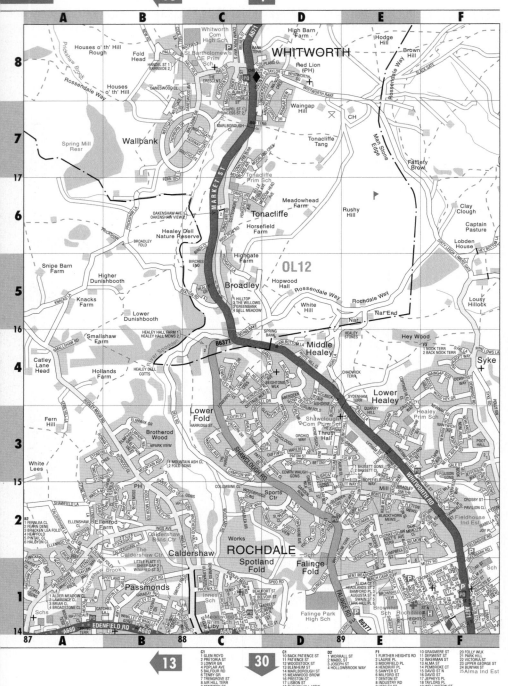

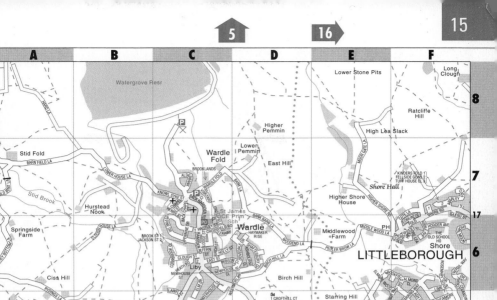

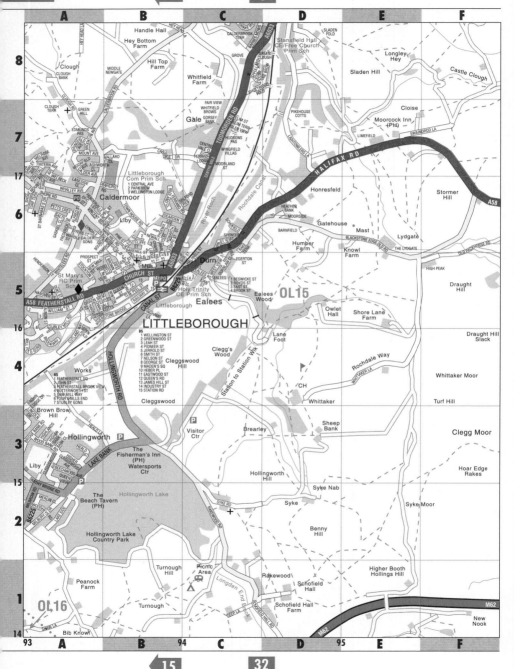

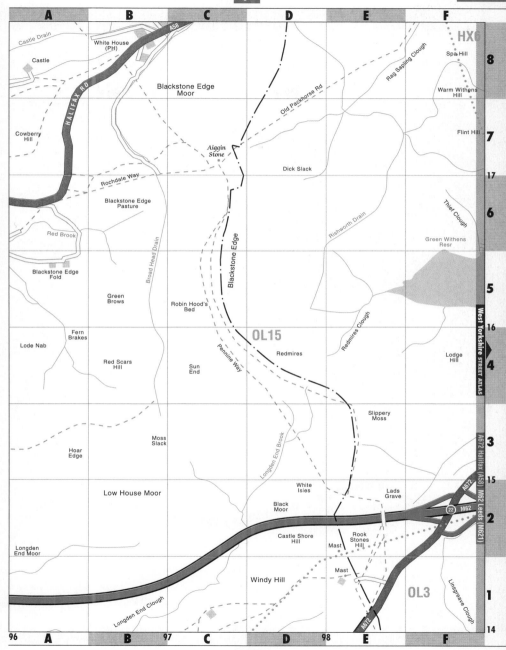

33

HX6

A58

Castle Drain

White House (PH)

Castle

Blackstone Edge Moor

HALIFAX RD

Cowberry Hill

Spa Hill

Rag Sapling Clough

Warm Withens Hill

Old Packhorse Rd

Flint Hill

17

Aiggin Stone

Dick Slack

Rochdale Way

Blackstone Edge Pasture

Thief Clough

6

Broad Head Drain

Rishworth Drain

Green Withens Resr

Red Brook

Blackstone Edge

5

Blackstone Edge Fold

Green Brows

Robin Hood's Bed

Redmires Clough

16

OL15

Fern Brakes

Lode Nab

Pennine Way

Redmires

Lodge Hill

West Yorkshire STREET ATLAS

4

Red Scars Hill

Sun End

Slippery Moss

Moss Slack

Longden End Brook

A672 Halifax (A58) M62 Leeds (M621)

3

Hoar Edge

15

Low House Moor

White Isles

Lads Grave

22 M62

A672

2

Black Moor

Castle Shore Hill

Mast

Rook Stones Hill

Longden End Moor

Mast

OL3

Windy Hill

Linsgreave Clough

1

Longden End Clough

A672

14

96

97

98

A   B   C   D   E   F

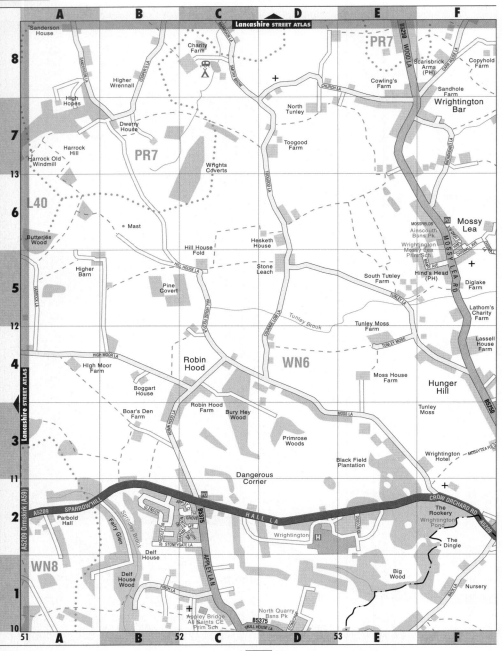

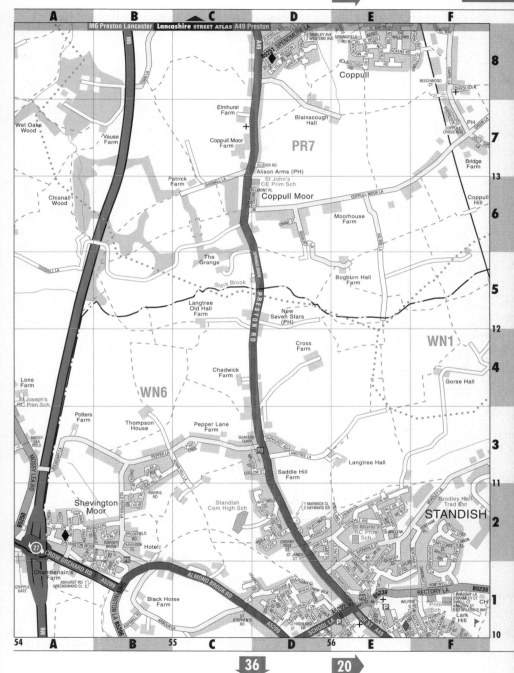

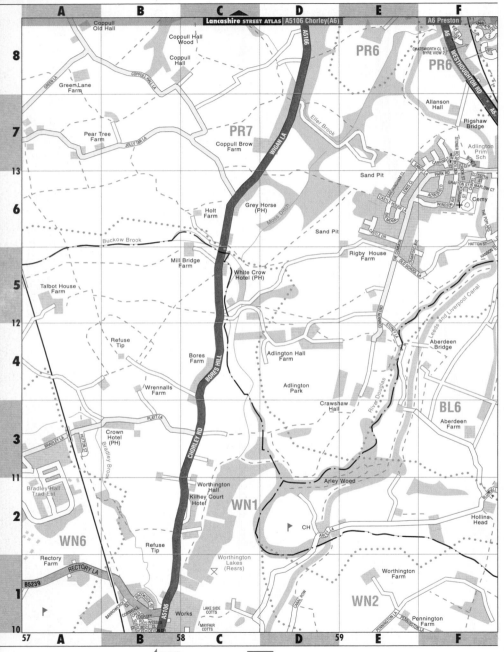

19

Lancashire STREET ATLAS | A5106 Chorley (A6)

A6 Preston

PR6

PR6

CHATSWORTH CL 1
BYRE VIEW 2

WESTHOUGHTON RD

Coppull
Old Hall

Coppull Hall
Wood

Coppull
Hall

Allanson
Hall

Rigshaw
Bridge

GREEN LA

Green Lane
Farm

COPPULL HALL LA

Adlington
Prim
Sch

PR7

Pear Tree
Farm

JOLLY TAR LA

WIGAN LA

Coppull Brow
Farm

Sand Pit

PARK RD

Cemy

Holt
Farm

Grey Horse
(PH)

Moss Ditch

Buckow Brook

Sand Pit

HATTON ST

Mill Bridge
Farm

White Crow
Hotel (PH)

Rigby House
Farm

Leeds and Liverpool Canal

Talbot House
Farm

THE COMMON

OLD SCHOOL LA

Refuse
Tip

Aberdeen
Bridge

Bores
Farm

Adlington Hall
Farm

River Douglas

Wrennalls
Farm

PLATT LA

Adlington
Park

BORES HILL

Crawshaw
Hall

BL6

Aberdeen
Farm

BRADLEY LA

HUTTON RD

Bradley Brook

Crown
Hotel
(PH)

CHORLEY RD

Hollins
Head

Bradley Hall
Trad Est

Worthington
Hall

Arley Wood

Kilhey Court
Hotel

WN1

WN6

Rectory
Farm

RECTORY LA

Refuse
Tip

CH

ARLEY LA

Worthington
Farm

B5239

BARROWDALE

A5106

Worthington
Lakes
(Resrs)

CANAL ROW

WN2

PENNINGTON LA

Pennington
Farm

Works

LAKE SIDE
COTTS

MAYFAIR
COTTS

19 37

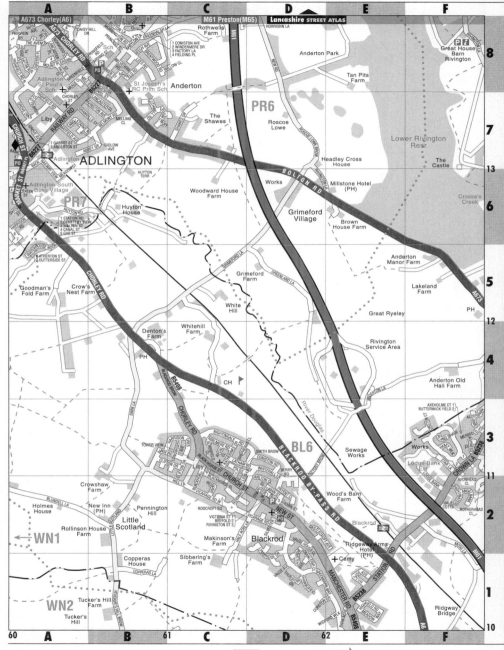

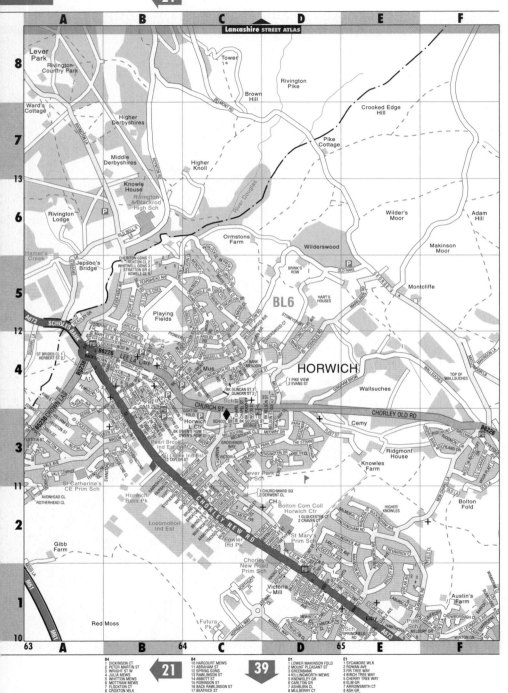

Lancashire STREET ATLAS

21   39

Lancashire STREET ATLAS

BL7

Whimberry Hill

Smithills Moor

Lomax Wifes Farm

Haslam's Farm

Holden's Farm

Gilligant's Farm

COAL PIT RD

Green Nook

Brown Lowe

Chadwick's Close Farm

Sheep Cote Green Farm

Smithills Dean

BL1

NEW COLLIER'S ROW

Cunliffe's Farm

Hampsons Farm

COLLIER'S ROW

COLLIERS ROW RD

Burnt Edge

White Brow

BURNT EDGE LA

Slack Hall

Higher Tongs

Pendlebury's Farm

Walker Fold

Walker Fold Farm

LONGSHAW FOLD RD

Lower Tongs

Mast

EDGE LA

Hole Hill Farm

Little Dakins Farm

Dakin's Brook

BARROW BRIDGE RD

MATCHMOOR LA

Fleet's Moor

Old Harts Farm

WALKER FOLD RD

P

Horwich Moor

Barrow Bridge

Harpers

BL6

Ivy Model Farm

BOTTOM O' TH' MOOR

SHEPHERDS LA

Blundell Arms (PH)

Yate Fold

Harwood's Farm

Johnson Fold Com Prim Sch

CHORLEY OLD RD

Bob's Smithy Inn (PH)

CH

A58

Johnson Fold

Bottom o' th' Moor

B6402

Green Hill

Grundy Fold

MONTSERRAT BROW

MONTSERRAT RD

Colemans

Coal Brow

Rants Farm

Delph Hill

DELPH HILL

PO

Doffcocker

MOSS BANK WAY

Wilson Fold Farm

High Rid Resr

Hawthorn Plantation

OLD KILN RD

Doffcocker Lodge

DOFFCOCKER LA

Fall Birch

High Rid Farm

HIGH RID LA

Old Hall

NEW HALL MEWS

B6402

OLD KILN LA

THORNBECK RD 1
THORNBECK DR 2
BK MARKLAND HILL LA 3
LEVI ST 4
BK MARKLAND HILL LA W 5
BK MARKLAND HILL LA E 6
BK CHORLEY OLD RD 7
HEXHAM AVE 8
BK CHORLEY OLD RD 9
LANDMARK CT 10

66 A B 67 C D 68 E F

E5
1 BK BELMONT RD
2 DURBAN RD
3 BK HAWARDEN ST
4 BK BLACKBURN RD W
5 BK BELMONT RD E
6 BK BROAD O' TH' LA

F6
1 BK PARK VIEW
2 PARK VIEW
3 PARK ROW
4 KELLETT ST
5 WRENBURY DR
6 BRAMLEY RD

7 CRUNDALE RD
8 ASHOVER CL
9 SHARPLES HALL
10 LAKENHEATH CL

F7
1 BRIDGE MILL
2 BROOK MILL

F8
1 BK COX GREEN RD S
2 COX GREEN RD
3 BK COX GREEN RD N
4 BK KING ST N
5 KING ST
6 BK MILL ST N

7 BK MILL ST S
8 SMITH LA
9 MILL ST
10 CONNINGSBY CL

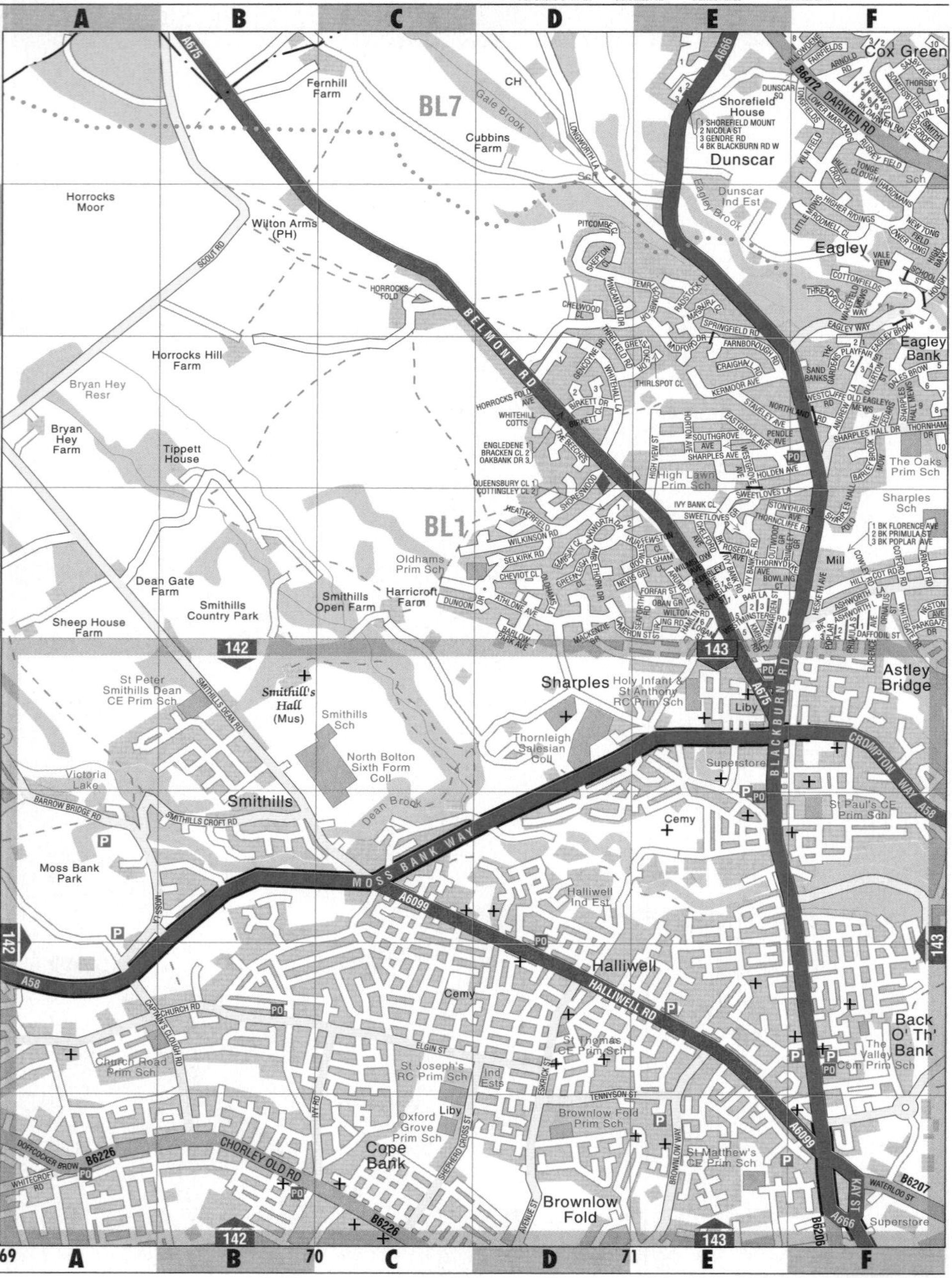

A B C D E F

8
BL7
Fernhill Farm
CH
Gate Brook
Cubbins Farm
Shorefield House
1 SHOREFIELD MOUNT
2 NICOLA ST
3 GENORE RD
4 BK BLACKBURN RD W
Dunscar
Dunscar Ind Est
Cox Green
Darwen Rd

Horrocks Moor
Wilton Arms (PH)
PITCOMB
Dunscar
Eagley

7
HORROCKS FOLD
BELMONT RD
13
Horrocks Hill Farm
Eagley Bank

6
Bryan Hey Resr
Bryan Hey Farm
Tippett House
HORROCKS FOLD
WHITEHILL COTTS
ENGLEDENE 1
BRACKEN CL 2
OAKBANK DR 3
The Oaks Prim Sch
Sharples Sch
1 BK FLORENCE AVE
2 BK PRIMULA ST
3 BK POPLAR AVE

5
QUEENSBURY CL 1
COTTINGLEY CL 2
BL1
Oldhams Prim Sch
Dean Gate Farm
Smithills Open Farm
Harricroft Farm
High Lawn Prim Sch
Mill
Bowling
12
Sheep House Farm
Smithills Country Park
142
143

4
St Peter Smithills Dean CE Prim Sch
Smithill's Hall (Mus)
Smithills Sch
Sharples
Holy Infant & St Anthony RC Prim Sch
Liby
Astley Bridge

Thornleigh Salesian Coll
North Bolton Sixth Form Coll
Superstore
St Paul's CE Prim Sch
CROMPTON WAY
A58

3
Victoria Lake
BARROW BRIDGE RD
SMITHILLS CROFT RD
Smithills
Dean Brook
MOSS BANK WAY
Cemy
143
Moss Bank Park
A6099
Halliwell Ind Est
CHURCH RD
11
142
Halliwell
A58

2
Church Road Prim Sch
Cemy
HALLIWELL RD
St Thomas CE Prim Sch
Back O' Th' Bank
The Valley Prim Sch

ELGIN ST
St Joseph's RC Prim Sch
Ind Est
Brownlow Fold Prim Sch
St Matthew's CE Prim Sch

1
CHORLEY OLD RD
B6226
Cape Bank
Oxford Grove Prim Sch
Liby
A666
B6207
Superstore
WHITECROFT RD
10
142
B6226
Brownlow Fold
143
KAY ST
B6206

69 A B 70 C D 71 E F

For full street detail of the highlighted area see pages 142 and 143.

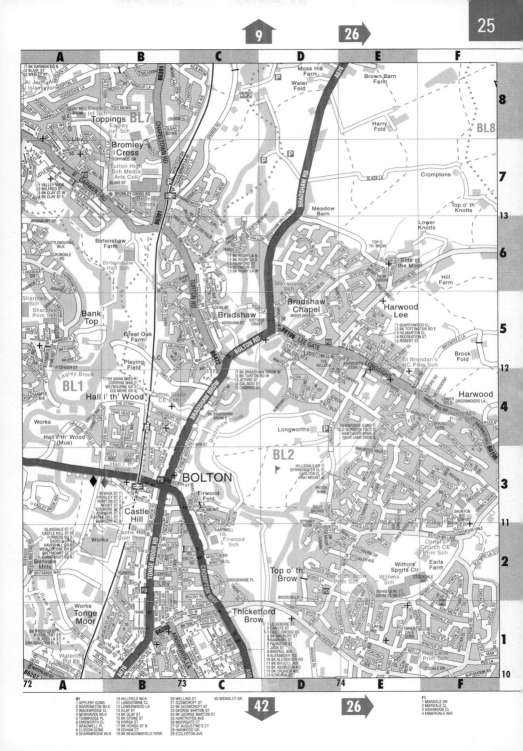

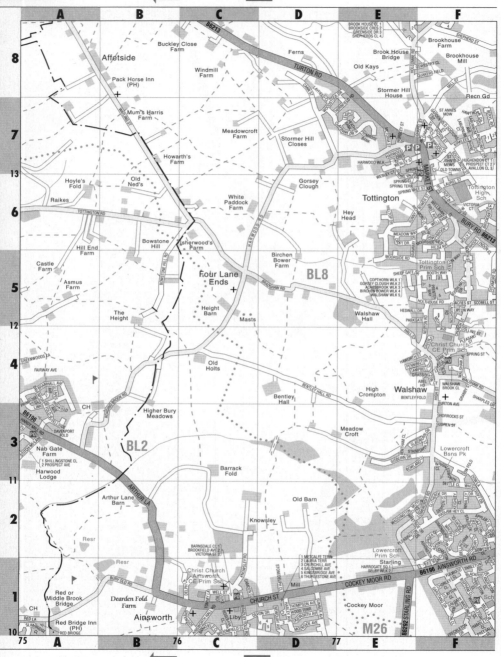

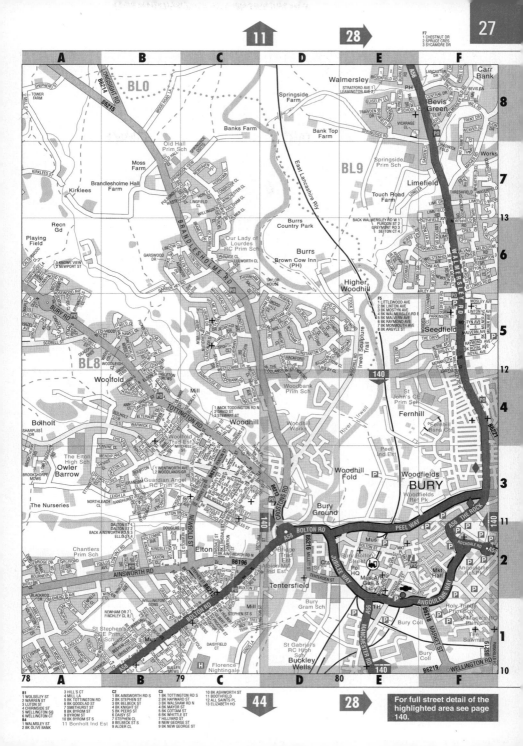

For full street detail of the highlighted area see page 141.

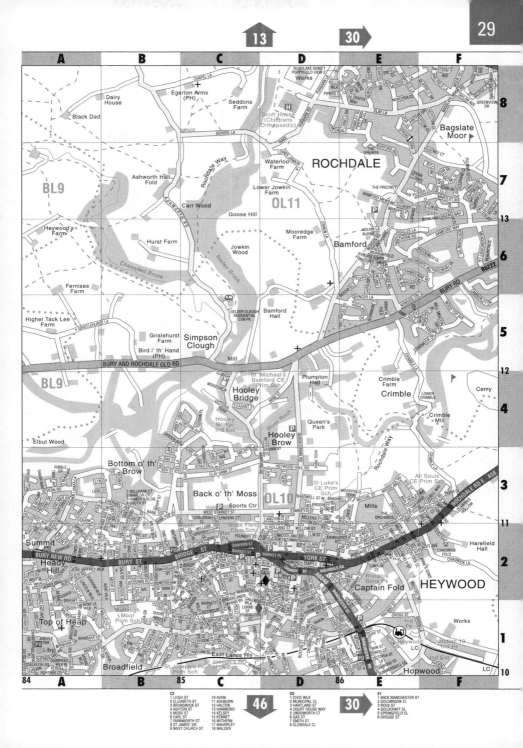

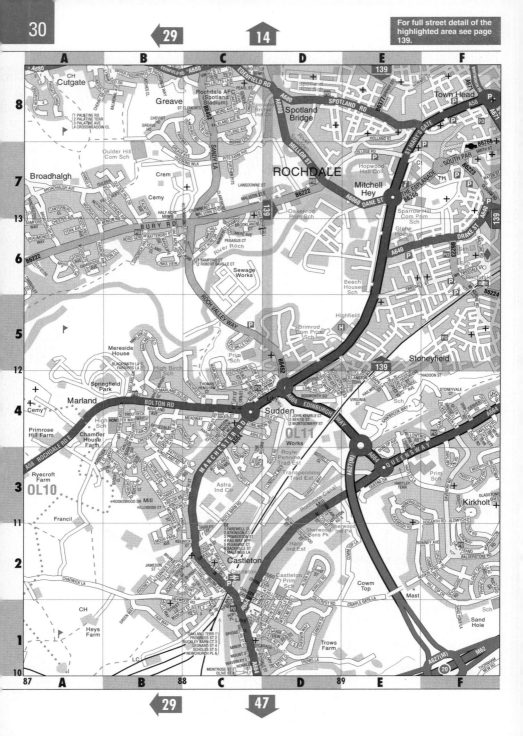

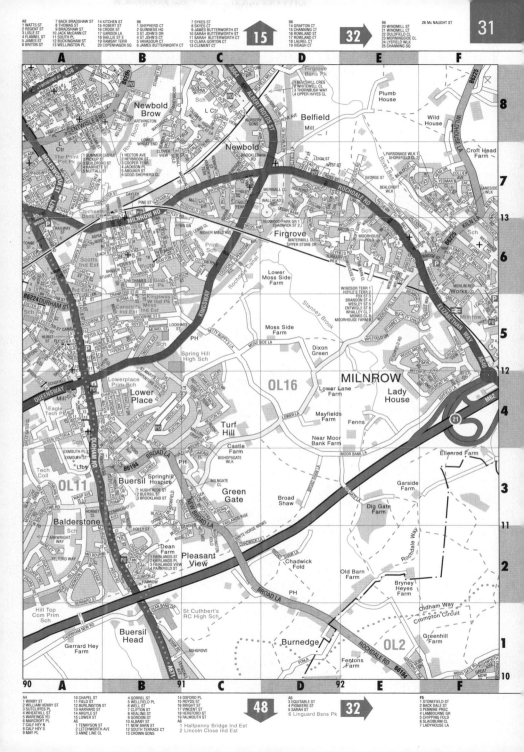

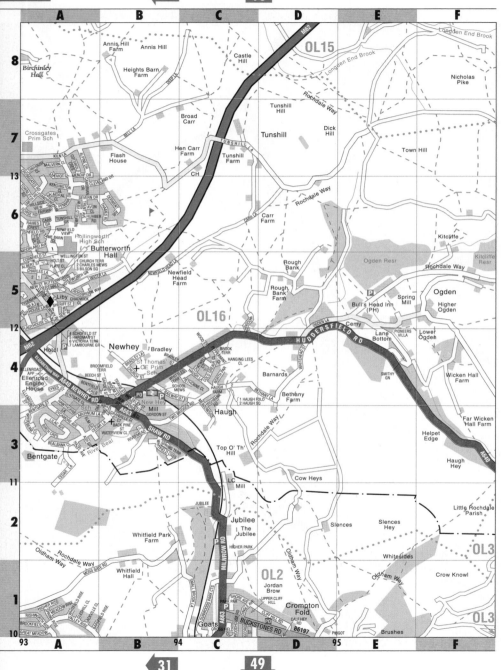

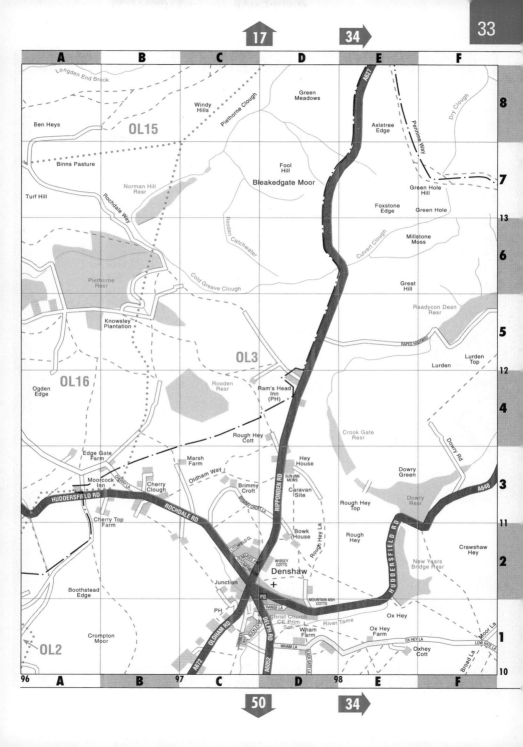

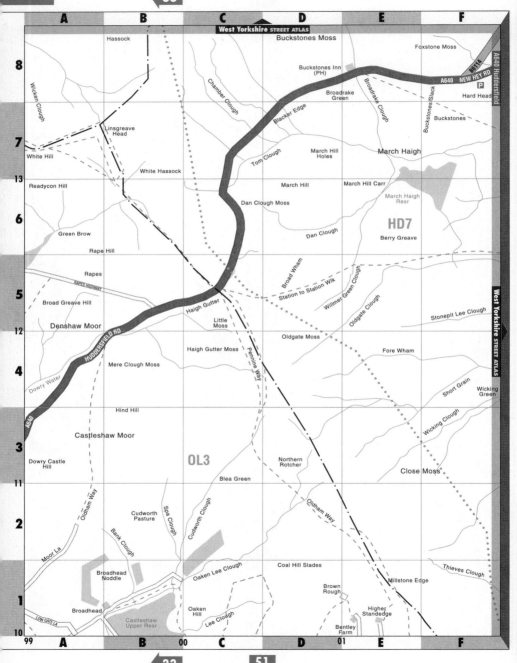

West Yorkshire STREET ATLAS

| | A | B | C | D | E | F |

Buckstones Moss

Hassock

Foxstone Moss

8

Buckstones Inn
(PH)

A640 NEW HEY RD

A640 Huddersfield

Wicken Clough

Chamber Clough

Broadrake
Green

Hard Head

Broadrake Clough

Buckstones/Slack

Buckstones

Linsgreave
Head

Blacker Edge

March Hill
Holes

March Haigh

7

White Hill

White Hassock

Tom Clough

13

Readycon Hill

March Hill

March Hill Carr

March Haigh
Resr

6

Dan Clough Moss

HD7

Green Brow

Dan Clough

Berry Greave

Rape Hill

Rapes

Broad Wham

RAPES HIGHWAY

Station to Station Wlk

Willmer Green Clough

5

Broad Greave Hill

Haigh Gutter

Oldgate Clough

Stonepit Lee Clough

Denshaw Moor

HUDDERSFIELD RD

Little
Moss

12

Oldgate Moss

Fore Wham

4

Dowry Water

Mere Clough Moss

Haigh Gutter Moss

Pennine Way

Short Grain

Wicking
Green

Hind Hill

Wicking Clough

Castleshaw Moor

3

Dowry Castle
Hill

OL3

Northern
Rotcher

Close Moss

11

Blea Green

Oldham Way

Cudworth
Pasture

Spa Clough

Cudworth Clough

Oldham Way

2

Moor La

Bank Clough

Coal Hill Slades

Thieves Clough

Broadhead
Noddle

Oaken Lee Clough

Brown
Rough

Millstone Edge

1

Broadhead

Oaken
Hill

Lee Clough

Higher
Standedge

LOW GATE LA

Castleshaw
Upper Resr

Bentley
Farm

10

West Yorkshire STREET ATLAS

18

36

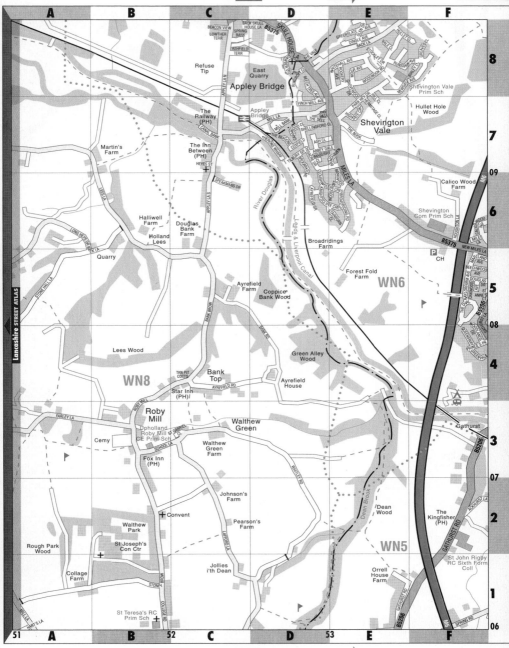

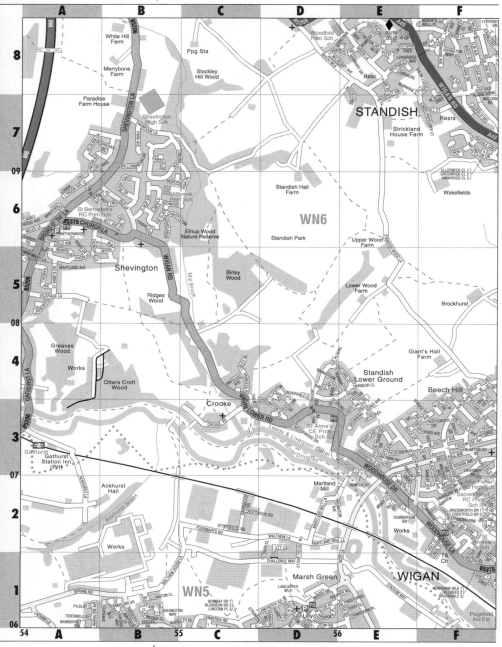

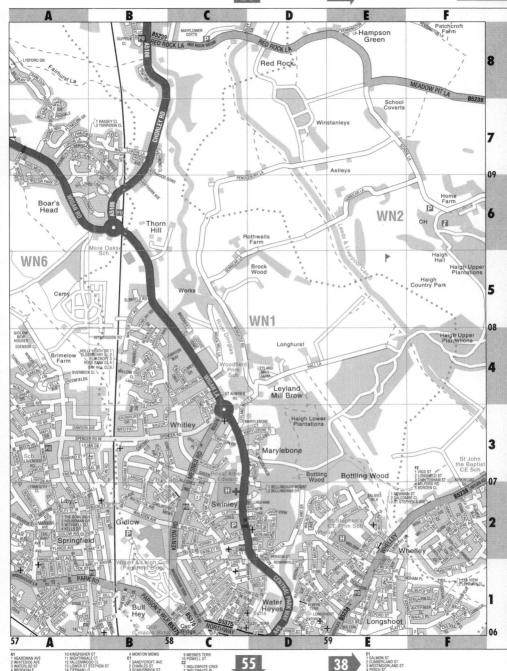

A B C D E F

8
7
09
6
5
08
4
3
07
2
1
06

A B C D E F

57 58 59

A1
1 HEARDMAN AVE
2 WHITESIDE AVE
3 WATERLOO ST
4 BROOKVALE
5 HEDGEMEAD
6 FOSTER ST
7 MEADOW CT
8 BERESFORD ST
9 GORMAN ST

10 KINGFISHER CT
11 NIGHTINGALE CT
12 FALCONWOOD CL
13 LOWER ST STEPHEN ST
14 TIERNAN LO
15 PAGEFIELD CL

B1
1 RIPON AVE
2 PATELEY SQ
3 YEWDALE CRES

4 MONTON MEWS

C1
1 SANDYCROFT AVE
2 CHARLES ST
3 SCARISBRICK ST
4 CLIFTON ST
5 LITTLE LONDON
6 DICCONSON CRES
7 BRICK KILN LA
8 BK MESNES ST

9 MESNES TERR
10 POWELL ST

C2
1 INGLEWHITE CRES
2 INGLEWHITE PL
3 WARNFORD ST
4 EVEREST PL
5 ASHLAND AVE
6 MONUMENT MANSIONS
7 HOLME CT

8 ST MICHAEL'S CT

F2
1 VIGO ST
2 LONGFIELD ST
3 CHELTENHAM ST
4 MILFORD RD
5 BORDEN ST

E1
1 SALMON ST
2 CUMBERLAND ST
3 WESTMOORLAND ST
4 PERCH ST
5 WINDERMERE ST
6 WRIGHT ST
7 SEDWYN ST

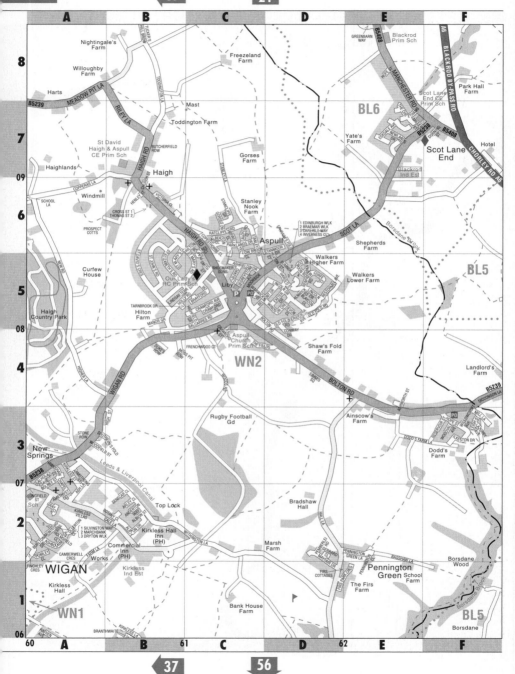

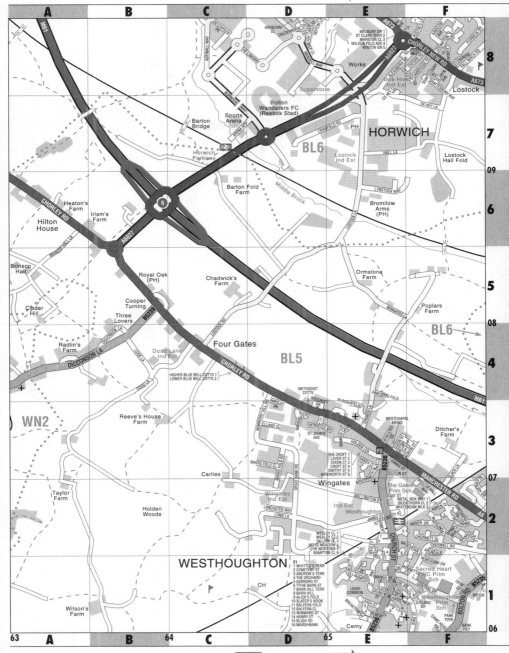

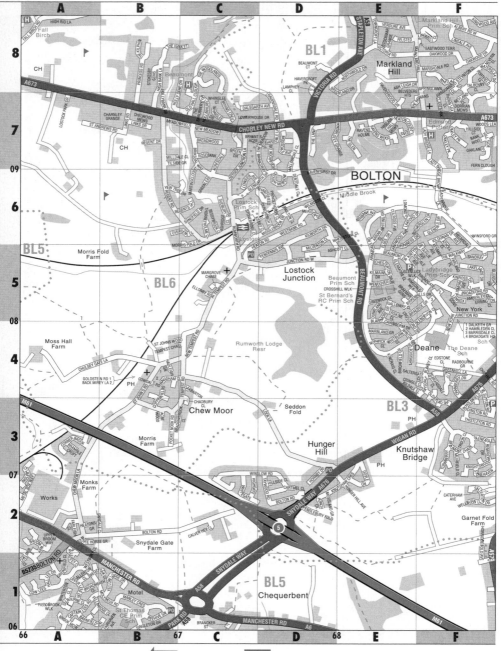

For full street detail of the highlighted area see pages 144, 145, 146 and 147.

41

24
42

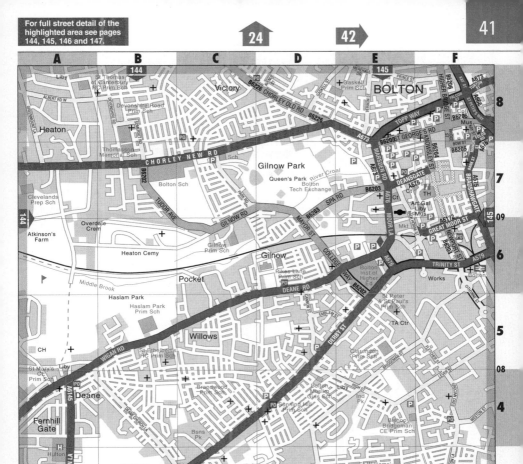

(Map of the Bolton / Breightmet / Farnworth area, showing districts BL2, BL3, BL4, Breightmet, Springfield, Rose Hill, Tonge Fold, Oaken Bottom, Darcy Lever, Burnden, Great Lever, Moses Gate, Harper Green, Clammerclough, Moses Gate Country Park and roads including Bury New Rd, Bury Rd, Radcliffe Rd, Church La, Manchester Rd, St Peter's Way, Bolton Rd, Market St, Gladstone St, A6053, M26.)

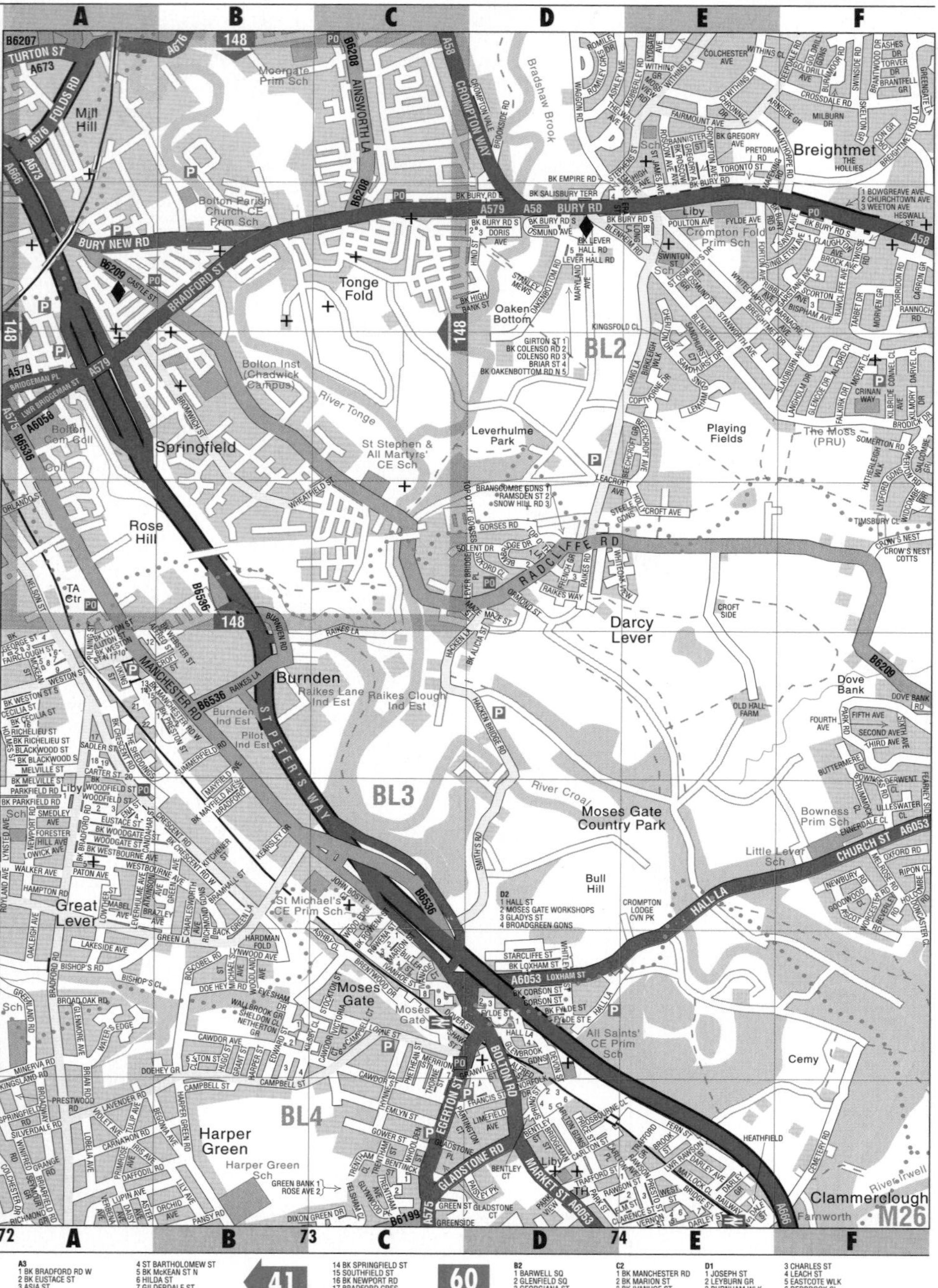

A3
1 BK BRADFORD RD W
2 BK EUSTACE ST
3 ASIA ST
4 BK ENA ST
5 PATON MEWS

A4
1 BK AUGUSTUS ST W
2 BK AUGUSTUS ST
3 AUGUSTUS ST

4 ST BARTHOLOMEW ST
5 BK McKEAN ST N
6 HILDA ST
7 GILDERDALE ST
8 BK McKEAN ST
9 BK WESTON ST N
10 BK MANCHESTER RD S
11 BK VIKING ST N
12 BK ALFRED ST
13 SPRINGFIELD ST

14 BK SPRINGFIELD ST
15 SOUTHFIELD ST
16 BK NEWPORT RD
17 BRADFORD DRES
18 BK BRADFORD RD
19 BK CARTER ST
20 BK DOBIE ST
21 EMBLA WLK
22 BRISCOE MEWS

B2
1 BARWELL SQ
2 GLENFIELD SG
3 GEORGIANA ST
4 VICTORIA ST
5 CLIFTON CT

B4
1 BK SOUTHFIELD ST
2 PRESTON ST

C2
1 BK MANCHESTER RD
2 BK MARION ST
3 BK IVANHOE ST
4 BK MARION ST S
5 CAMPBELL WLK
6 CAWDOR WLK
7 LOMAX ST
8 JENNY LIND CL
9 PENYDARREN VIEW

D1
1 JOSEPH ST
2 LEYBURN GR
3 BURNHAM WLK
4 ASTON GDNS
5 ARNCLIFFE CL
6 BENTHAM CL

E1
1 ENTWISLE ST
2 MOSS ST

3 CHARLES ST
4 LEACH ST
5 EASTCOTE WLK
6 REDBROOK CL
7 LIGHTWOOD CL

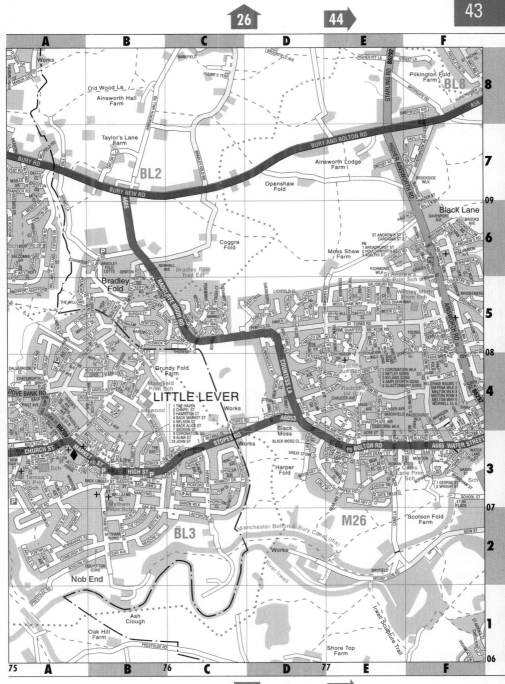

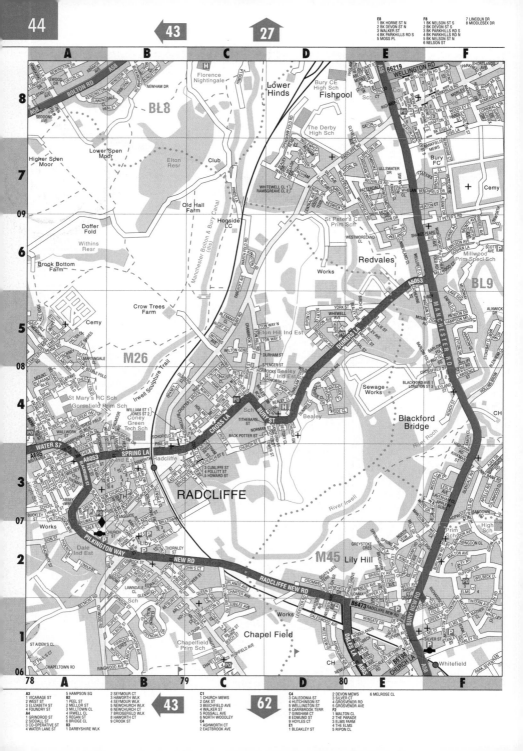

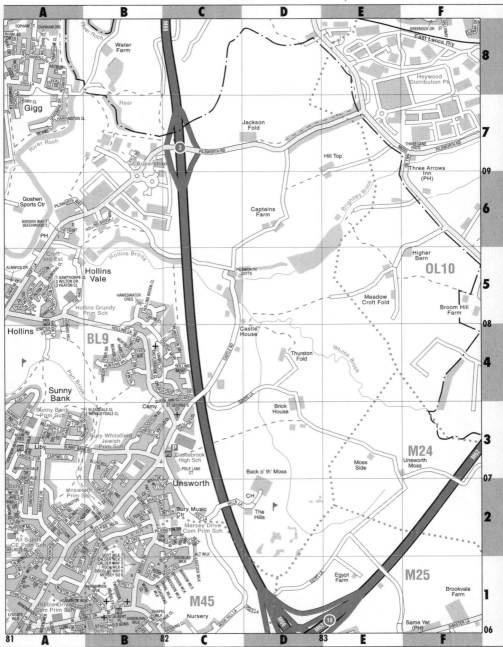

Topham St
Durham Dr
River Roch
Water Farm
RHIWLAS
CORNWALL
Gigg
River Roch
Resr
Goshen Sports Ctr
PILSWORTH RD
Superstore
Hollins Brook
Croft Ind Est
ALNWICK DR
Hollins Vale
Hollins Grundy Prim Sch
HAWESWATER CRES
Hollins
BL9
Sunny Bank
Sunny Bank Prim Sch
Liby
Bury Whitefield Jewish Prim Sch
Castlebrook High Sch
POLE LANE CT
Unsworth Prim Sch
Unsworth
All Saints CE Prim Sch
Bury Music Ctr
Mersey Drive Com Prim Sch
M45
Ribble Drive Com Prim Sch
Nursery

M66
Jackson Fold
Hill Top
Captains Farm
Brightley Brook
Three Arrows Inn (PH)
Higher Barn
OL10
Broom Hill Farm
Meadow Croft Fold
PILSWORTH COTTS
Castle House
Whittle Brook
Thurston Fold
Brick House
Back o' th' Moss
Moss Side
CH
The Hills
M24
Unsworth Moss
Egypt Farm
M25
Brookvale Farm
Same Yet (PH)

East Lancs Rly
GREENOCK DR
Heywood Distribution Pk
THREE LANE ENDS
PILSWORTH RD

M62
M66
M62
78

09
8
7
09
6
5
08
4
3
07
2
1
06

81   82   83
A   B   C   D   E   F

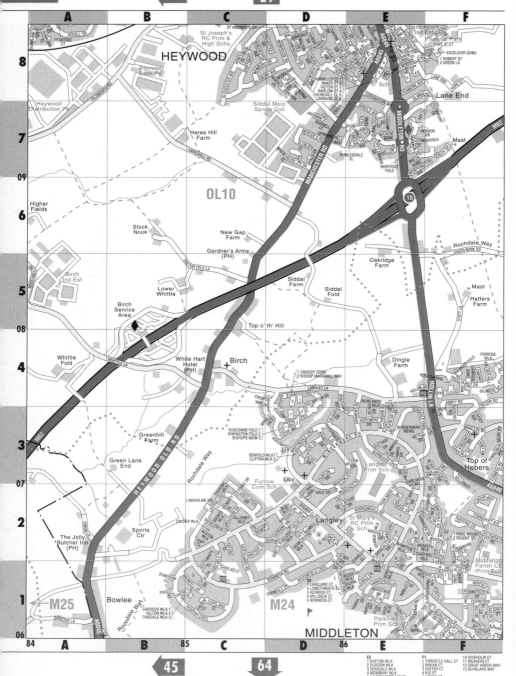

45

29

HEYWOOD

OL10

MIDDLETON

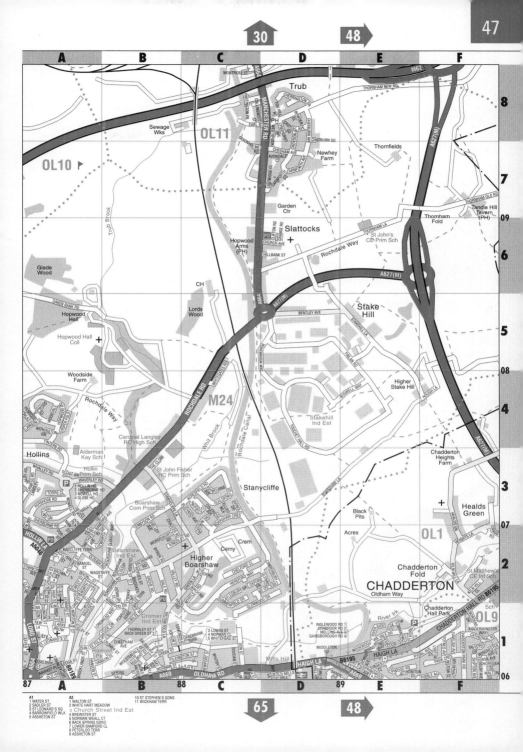

47
31

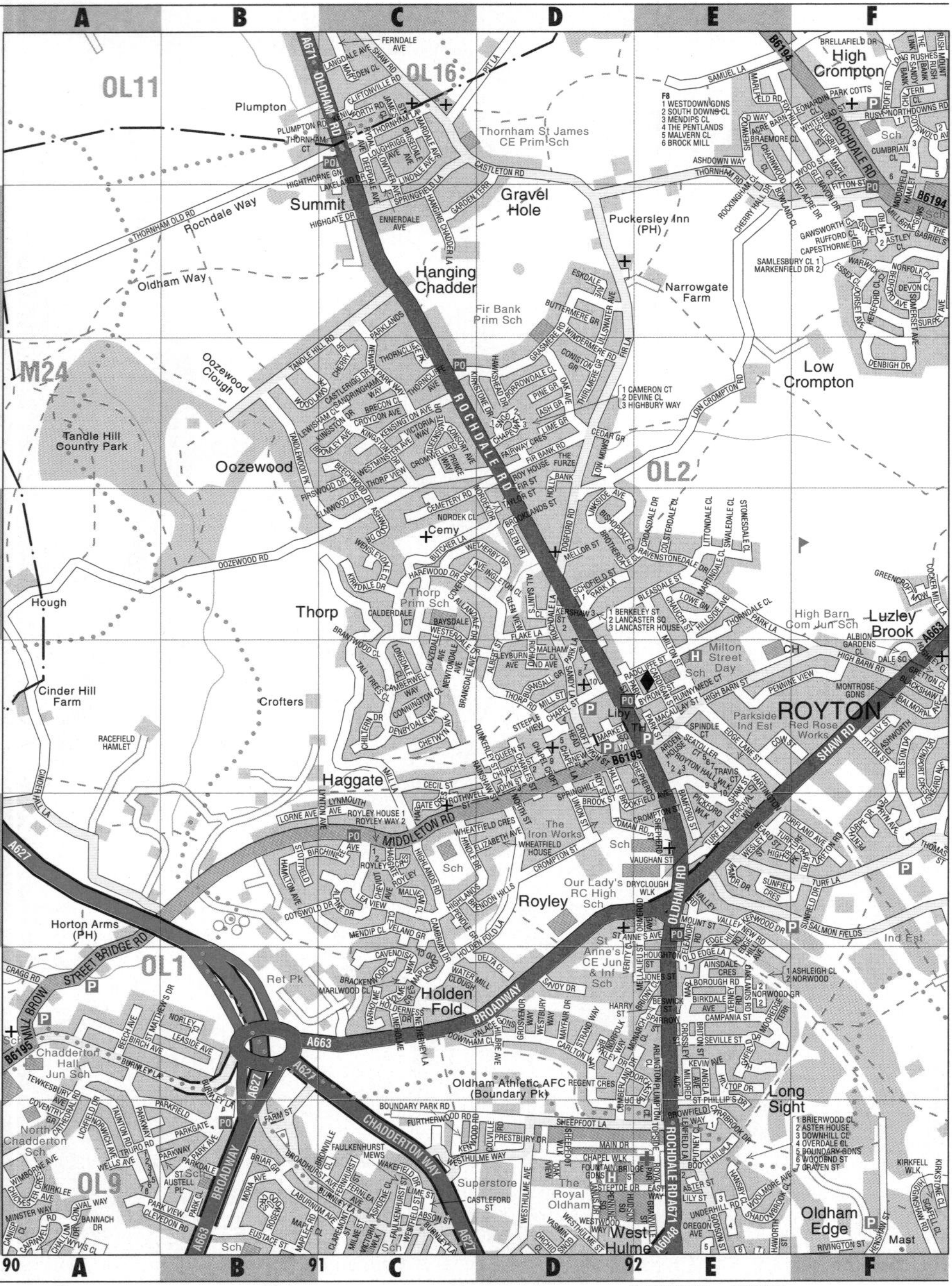
OL11
OL16
OL2
OL1
OL9
M24
Plumpton
Summit
Gravel Hole
Hanging Chadder
Thornham St James CE Prim Sch
Fir Bank Prim Sch
Puckersley Inn (PH)
Narrowgate Farm
High Crompton
Low Crompton
Oozewood Clough
Tandle Hill Country Park
Oozewood
Thorp
Thorp Prim Sch
Hough
Cinder Hill Farm
Crofters
Racefield Hamlet
Haggate
ROYTON
Luzley Brook
High Barn Com Jun Sch
Milton Street Day Sch
Parkside Ind Est
Red Rose Works
The Iron Works
Our Lady's RC High Sch
Royley
Horton Arms (PH)
Ret Pk
Holden Fold
St Anne's CE Jun & Inf Sch
Chadderton Hall Jun Sch
North Chadderton Sch
Oldham Athletic AFC (Boundary Pk)
Long Sight
Superstore
The Royal Oldham
West Hulme
Oldham Edge
Mast
Ind Est
ROCHDALE RD
OLDHAM RD
MIDDLETON RD
BROADWAY
CHADDERTON WAY
SHAW RD
Rochdale Way
Oldham Way
F8
1 WESTDOWN GDNS
2 SOUTH DOWNS CL
3 MENDIPS CL
4 THE PENTLANDS
5 MALVERN CL
6 BROCK MILL
1 CAMERON CT
2 DEVINE CL
3 HIGHBURY WAY
1 BERKELEY ST
2 LANCASTER SQ
3 LANCASTER HOUSE
1 ASHLEIGH CL
2 NORWOOD
1 BRIERWOOD CL
2 ASTER HOUSE
3 DOWNHILL CL
4 OVERDALE CL
5 BOUNDARY GDNS
6 WOODEND ST
7 CRAVEN ST
A B C D E F
8 7 6 5 4 3 2 1
09 08 07 06
90 91 92

A1
1 CAMBORNE WLK
2 PADSTOW PL
3 PENZANCE PL
4 REDRUTH WLK
5 NEWQUAY HO
6 WEYMOUTH HO
7 DUNSTON PL
8 SOMERTON WLK

47
66

D4
1 NORTH ST
2 HOLLY BANK
3 THROSTLE CT
4 SANDY WLK
5 CHURCH WLK
6 YORK SQ
7 CHESTER PL
8 SPRING GDNS
9 ST PAULS HOUSE
10 SPRING GARDEN ST

E4
1 THOMAS HOUSE
2 WESTMORLAND WLK
3 CHARCON WLK
4 APPLEBY WLK
5 TROUTBECK WLK
6 BYRON WLK
7 BOWNESS WLK
8 STAVELY WLK
9 HORDEN WLK
10 BRADBURY WLK

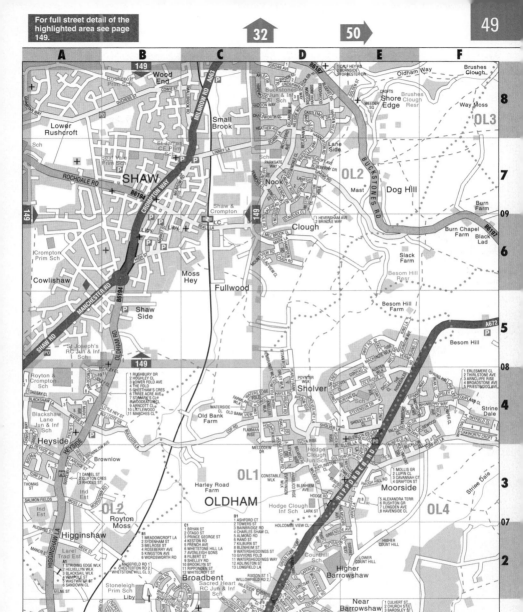

For full street detail of the highlighted area see page 149.

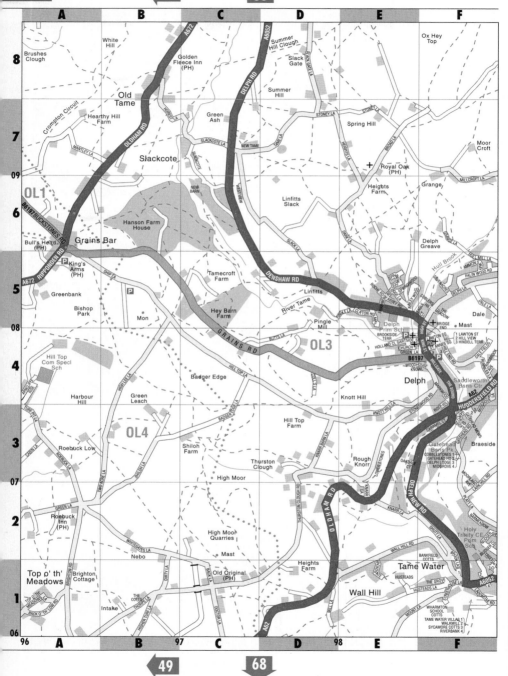

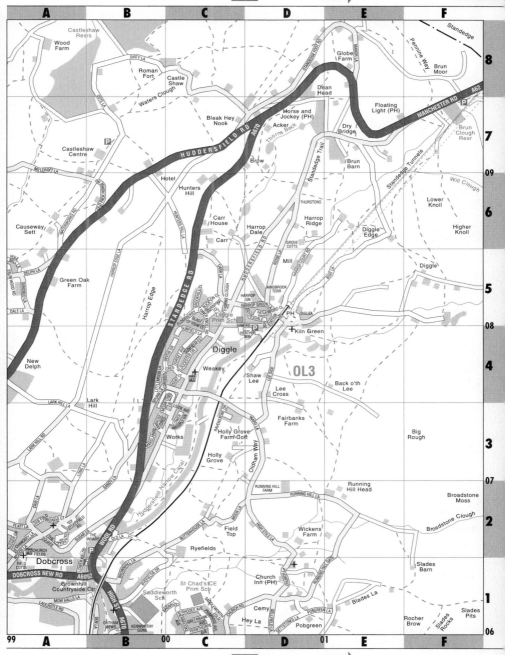

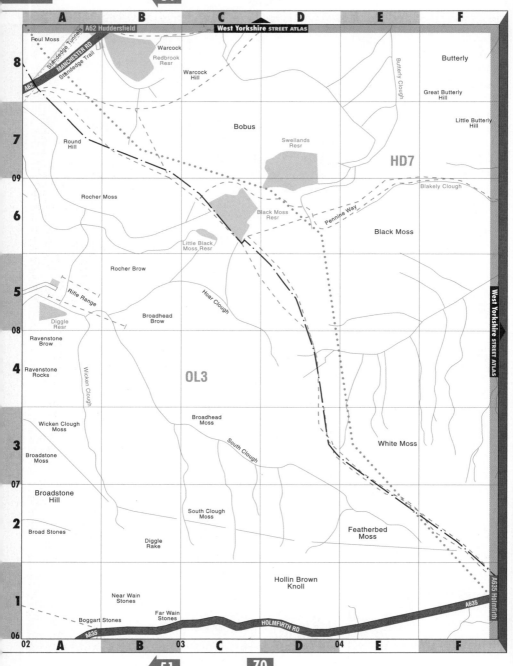

A62 Huddersfield
Foul Moss
Standedge Tunnels
MANCHESTER RD
Standedge Trail
A62

Warcock
Redbrook
Resr
Warcock
Hill

Butterly Clough

Butterly

Great Butterly
Hill

8

Little Butterly
Hill

Bobus

Round
Hill

7

Swellands
Resr

HD7

09

Rocher Moss

Blakely Clough

Black Moss
Resr

Pennine Way

6

Black Moss

Little Black
Moss Resr

Rocher Brow

Rifle Range

Broadhead
Brow

Hoar Clough

5

Diggle
Resr

Ravenstone
Brow

08

Ravenstone
Rocks

4

Wicken Clough

OL3

Broadhead
Moss

White Moss

Wicken Clough
Moss

South Clough

3

Broadstone
Moss

07

Broadstone
Hill

South Clough
Moss

Featherbed
Moss

2

Broad Stones

Diggle
Rake

Hollin Brown
Knoll

1

Near Wain
Stones

A635 Holmfirth

Boggart Stones

Far Wain
Stones

HOLMFIRTH RD

A635

06

A635

West Yorkshire STREET ATLAS

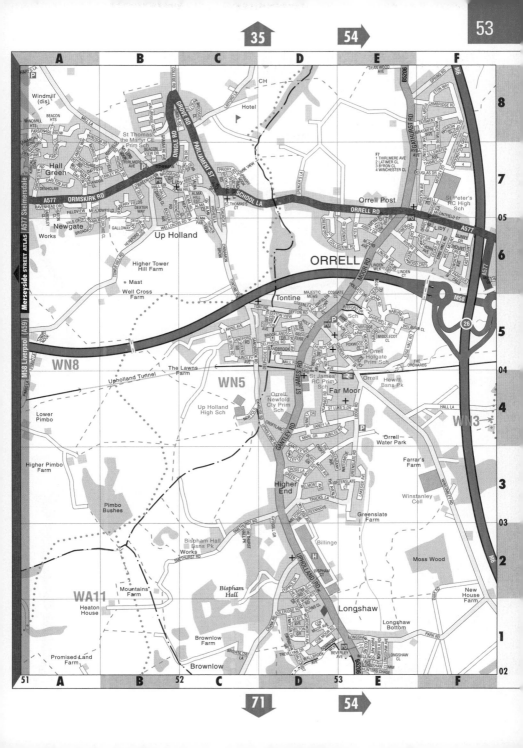

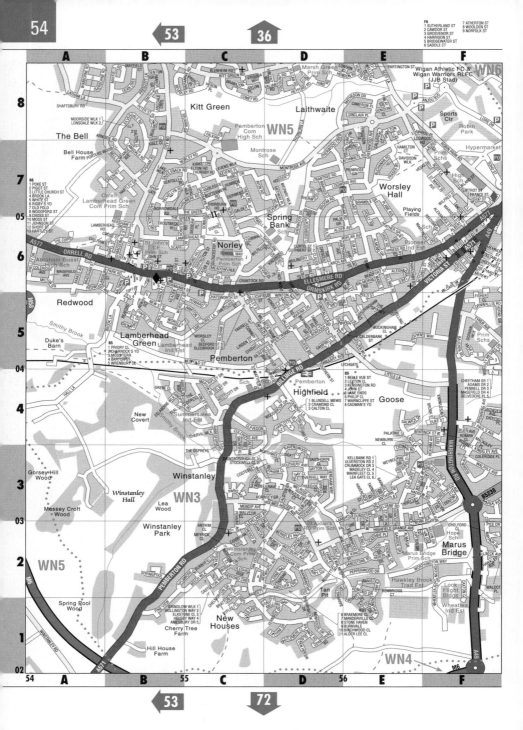

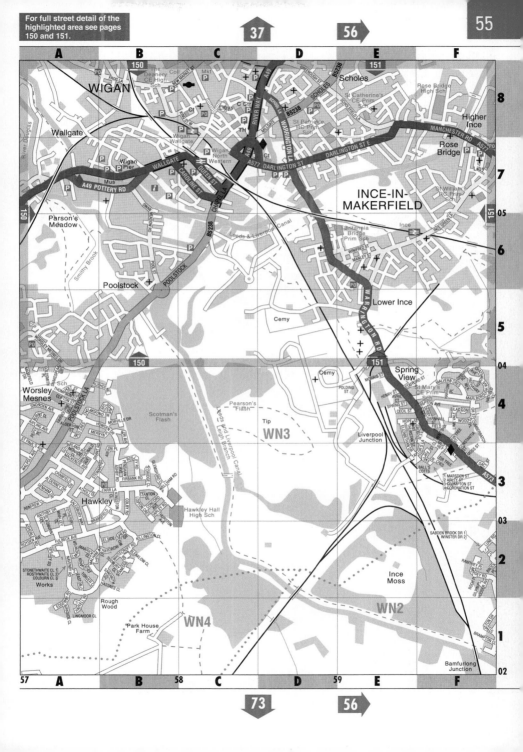

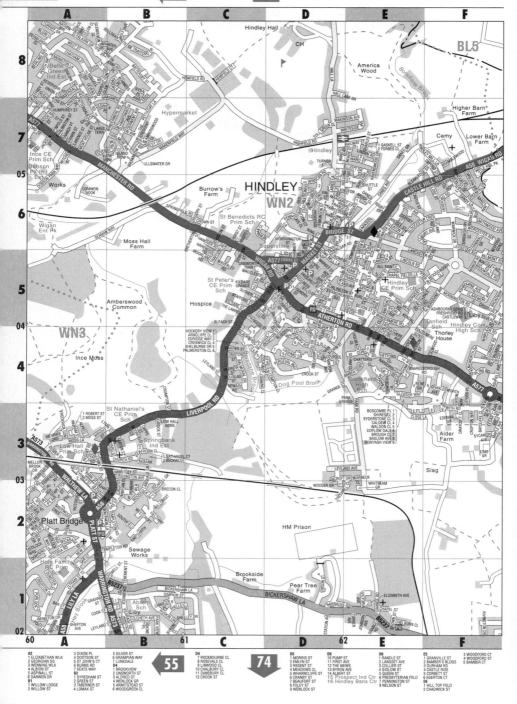

A2
1 ELIZABETHAN WLK
2 GEORGIAN SQ
3 WENNING WLK
4 ALBION ST
5 ASPINALL ST
6 DARWEN DR

B1
1 WILLOW LODGE
2 WILLOW ST

A3
3 DIXON PL
4 DOOTSON ST
5 ST JOHN'S CT
6 BURNS RD
7 KEATS WAY

B2
1 SYHESHAM ST
2 GREEN ST
3 TABERNER ST
4 LOMAX ST

B3
5 SILVER ST
6 GRAMPIAN WAY
7 LUNEDALE

B4
1 BROOKVIEW
2 UNSWORTH ST
3 ALDRED ST
4 WENLOCK GR
5 ARMITSTEAD ST
6 WOODGREEN CL

D4
7 ROCKBOURNE CL
8 ROSEVALE CL
9 LINWOOD CL
10 CHALBURY CL
11 DANEBURY CL
12 CROOK ST

D5
1 MORRIS ST
2 EMLYN ST
3 REGENT ST
4 WHARNCLIFFE ST
5 CRANBY ST
6 BEAUFORT ST
7 FOLEY ST
8 WENLOCK ST

D5
10 PUMP ST
11 FIRST AVE
12 THE MEWS
13 BYRON AVE
14 ALBERT ST
15 Prospect Ind Ctr
16 Hindley Bsns Ctr

D6
1 RANDLE ST
2 LANGSET AVE
3 COLLIER ST
4 GIDLOW ST
5 QUEEN ST
7 PRESBYTERIAN FOLD
8 NELSON ST

E5
1 GRANVILLE ST
2 BAMBER'S BLDGS
3 DURHAM RD
4 CASTLE RISE
5 CORBETT ST
6 EGERTON CT

E6
1 HILL TOP FOLD
2 CHADWICK ST

F3
3 WOODFORD CT
4 WOODFORD ST
5 BAMBER CT

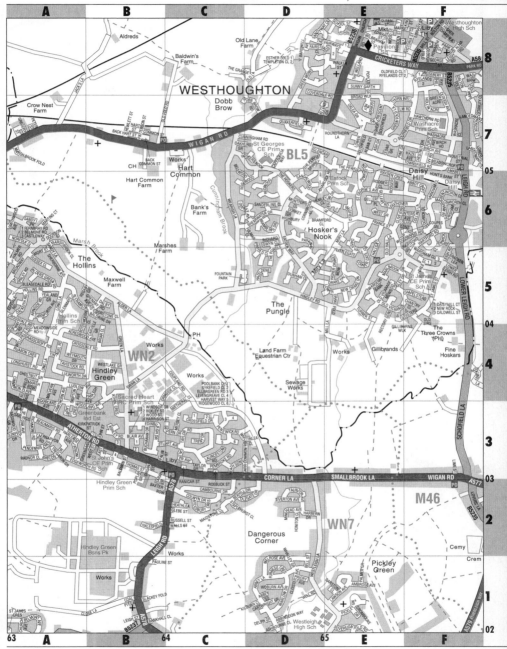

39 58

WESTHOUGHTON

Dobb Brow

Crow Nest Farm

Aldreds

Baldwin's Farm

Old Lane Farm

THE GRANGE

ESTHER FIELD CT 1
TEMPLETON CL 2

CRICKETERS WAY

Westhoughton High Sch

Mkt Pavilion

QUEEN

THE FAIRWAY

Sunny Garth

Broad Wlk

WIGAN RD

Hart Common

Hart Common Farm

Works

CH

BACK HART ST

BACK COMMON ST

CRASHBROOK FOLD

St Georges CE Prim Sch

OAKHURST

CUNNINGHAM RD

BL5

Daisy Hill

Daisy Hill

Peacock Prim Sch

Bank's Farm

Marshes Farm

Marsh Brook

The Hollins

Maxwell Farm

Hollins Prim Sch

Fountain Park

Hosker's Nook

Sanderling Cl

The Pungle

BRAMFORD CL
HIGHBURY

St James CE Prim Sch

The Three Crowns (PH)

Fine Hoskars

Gillibrands

WN2

Hindley Green

Sacred Heart RC Prim Sch

Greenbank Ind Est

Works

Works

PH

Land Farm Equestrian Ctr

Sewage Works

Works

POOLBANK CL 1
SYKEFIELD CL 2
ELLERGREEN RD 3
LEVENGREAVE CL 4
HARVEST WAY 5
RIDGEWOOD CL 6

ATHERTON RD

St John's CE Prim Sch

Hindley Green Prim Sch

CORNER LA

SMALLBROOK LA

WIGAN RD

M46

Hindley Green Bsns Pk

LEIGH RD

Works

Pauline St

WN7

Dangerous Corner

Pickley Green

Hindley Green

St Westleigh High Sch

ST JAMES CRES

Works

Cemy

Crem

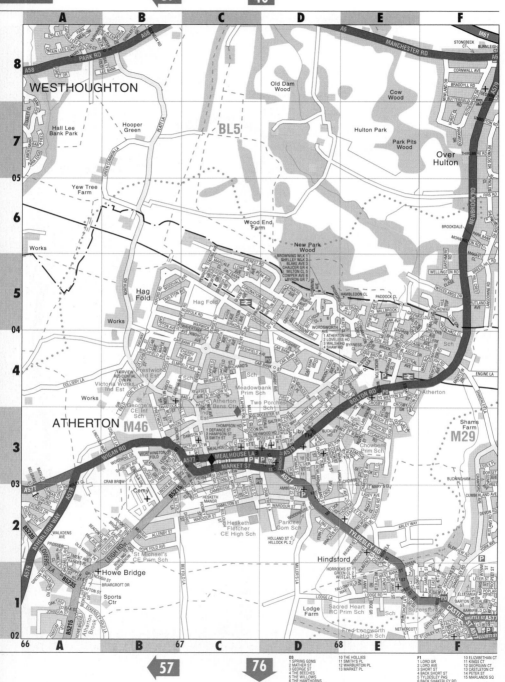

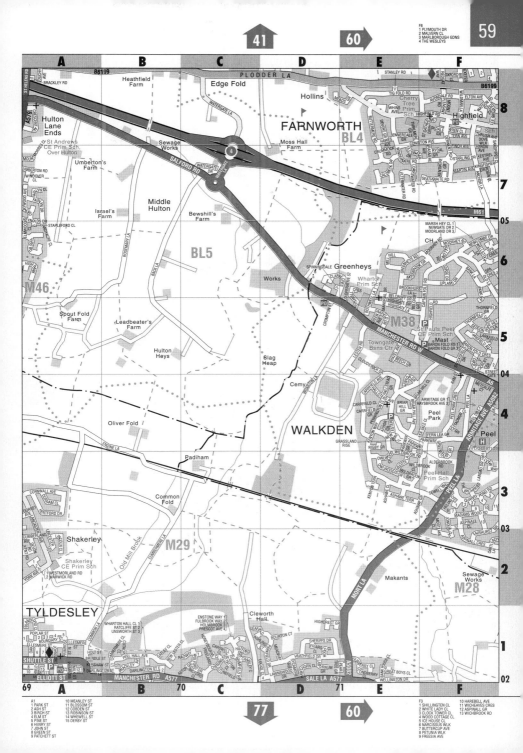

59
42

C8
1 THOMAS GARNET CT
2 PHILIP HOWARD CT
3 SUTHERLAND ST
4 WESTMINSTER WLK
5 LONSDALE GR
6 KENTFORD GR

C8
7 LIDGATE GR
8 ASHLEY GR
9 ALMOND ST
10 ORMROD ST
11 DIXON GREEN DR

D8
1 JANE BARTER HO
2 BARNES HO
3 ELLESMERE WLK
4 WILLOCKSON HO
5 HESKETH WLK

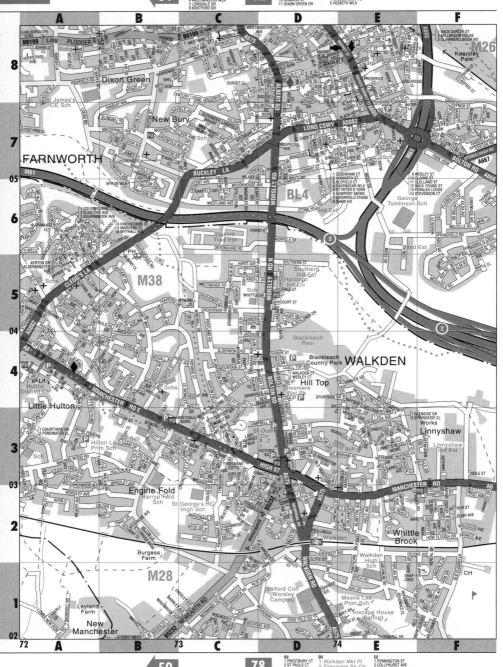

D2
1 PRESTBURY CT
2 ST PAULS CT

D3
1 Walkden Mkt Pl
2 Ellesmere Sh Ctr
3 BRIDGEWATER WLK
4 EDGERTON WLK
5 DAISYFIELD WLK
6 CLOVERFIELD WLK
7 FITCHFIELD WLK

E2
1 PENNINGTON ST
2 COLLYHURST AVE
3 WINDERMERE HOUSE
4 RYDAL HOUSE
5 GRASMERE HOUSE
6 CONISTON HOUSE

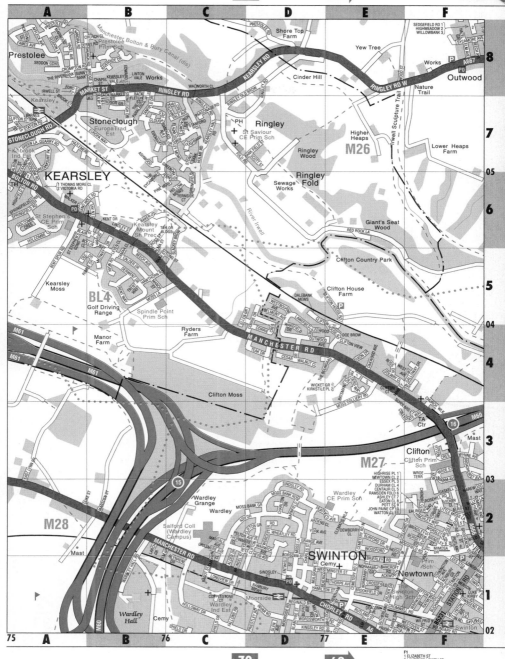

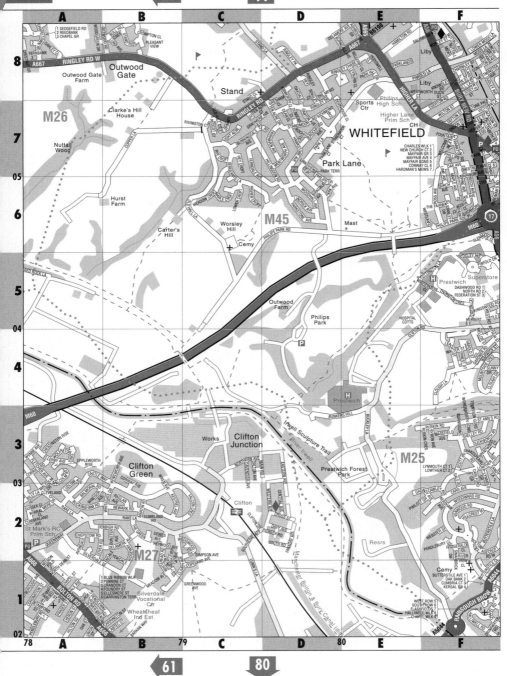

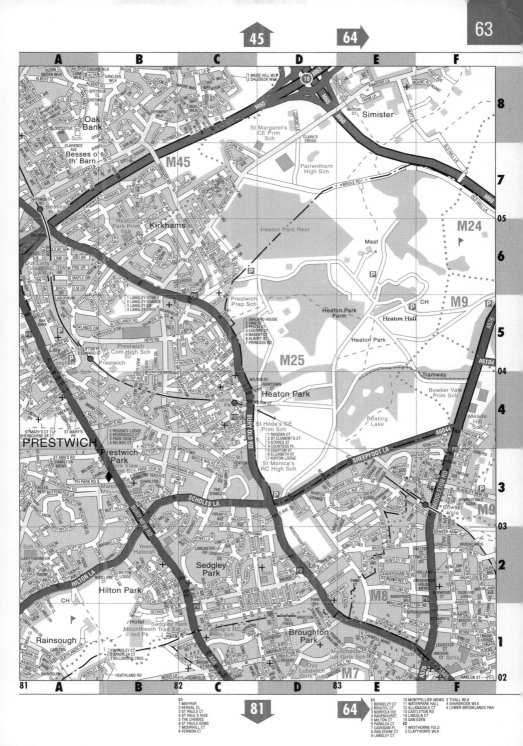

C1
1 MAYFAIR
2 KERSAL CL
3 ST PAULS CT
4 ST PAUL'S RISE
5 THE CHENIES
6 ST PAULS GDNS
7 MOORHILL CT
8 VERNON CT

E1
1 BERKELEY CT
2 BRISTOL CT
3 NORFOLK RD
4 RAVENHURST
5 MILTON CT
6 PARKLEA CT
7 CADOGAN PL
8 INGLEDENE CT
9 LANGLEY CT
10 MONTPELLIER MEWS
11 WATERPARK HALL
12 ALLANDALE CT
13 CASTLETON RD
14 LINCOLN CT
15 GAN EDEN

3 TIXALL WLK
4 SHARBROOK WLK
5 LOWER BROOKLANDS PAR

E2
1 WESTHORNE FOLD
2 CLAYTHORPE WLK

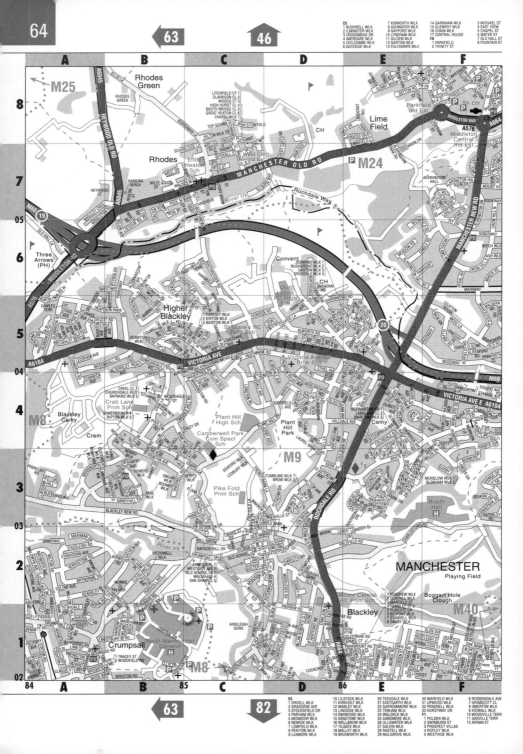

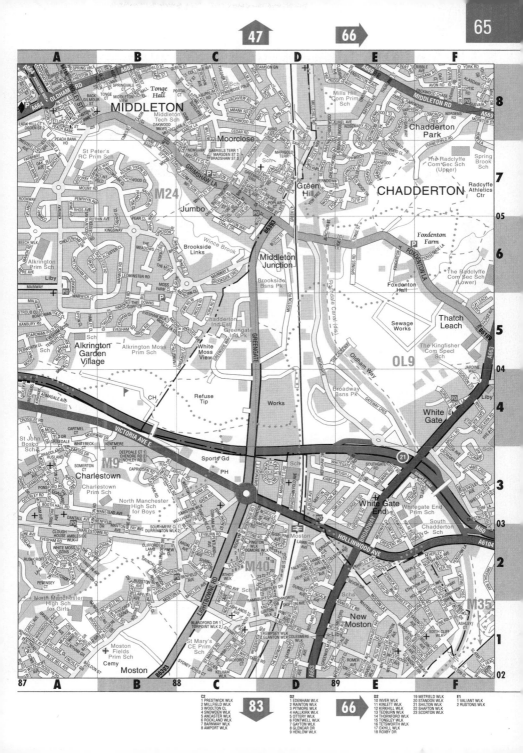

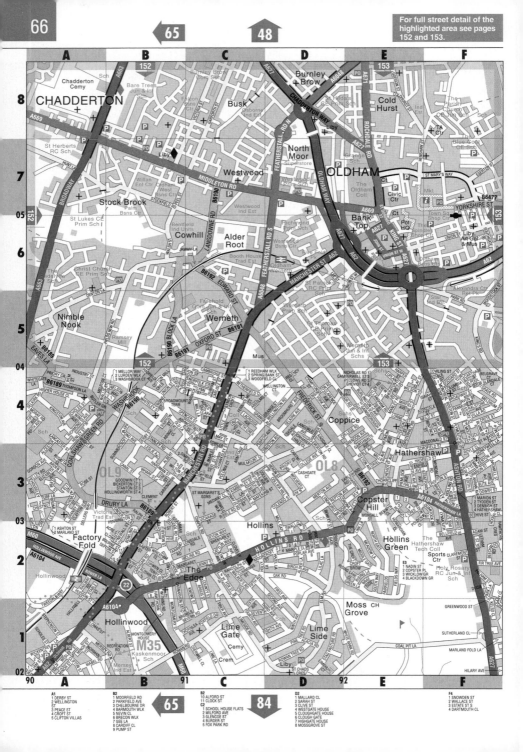

65 48

For full street detail of the highlighted area see pages 152 and 153.

A1	B2	B2	D2	F4
1 DERBY ST	1 MOORFIELD RD	10 ALFORD ST	1 MALLARD CL	1 SNOWDEN ST
2 WELLINGTON ST	2 PARKFIELD AVE	11 CLOCK ST	2 SARAH ST	2 WALLACE ST
3 PEACE ST	3 CHELBOURNE DR	C2	3 CLIVE ST	3 ESTATE ST
4 CROFT ST	4 BARMOUTH WLK	1 SCHOOL HOUSE FLATS	4 WESTGATE HOUSE	4 DARTMOUTH CL
5 CLIFTON VILLAS	5 NEVIN CL	2 MILFORD AVE	5 CLOUGHGATE HOUSE	
	6 BRECON WLK	3 GLENCOE ST	6 CLOUGH GATE	
	7 GEE LA	4 BURDER ST	7 HIGHGATE HOUSE	
	8 CARDIFF CL	5 FOX PARK RD	8 MOSSGROVE ST	
	9 PUMP ST			

65 84

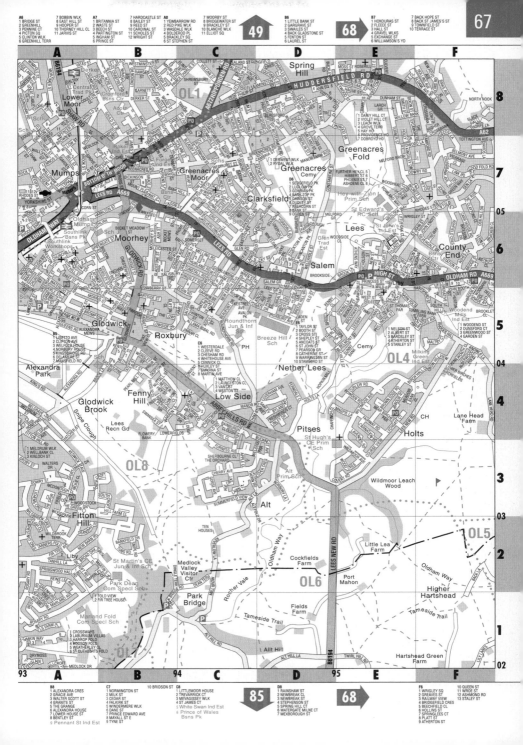

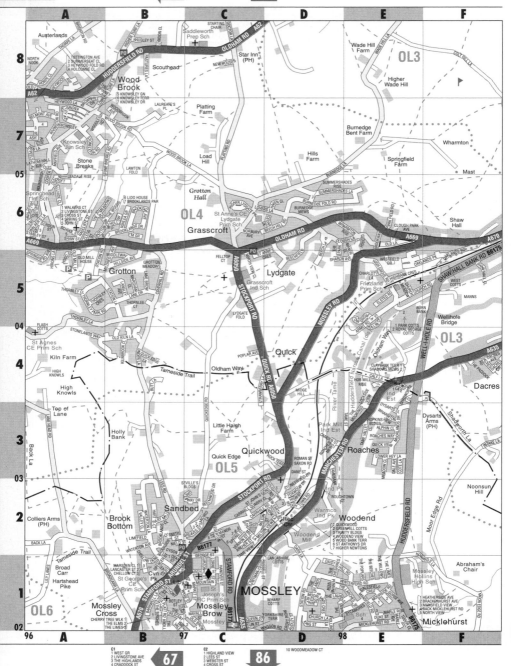

A B C D E F

8

7

05

6

5

04

4

3

03

2

1

02

96 A B 97 C D 98 E F

OL3

OL4

OL5

OL6

OL3

MOSSLEY

Micklehurst

Dacres

Noonsun Hill

Wharmton

Grasscroft

Lydgate

Quick

Grotton

Quickwood

Quick Edge

Sandbed

Brook Bottom

Mossley Cross

Mossley Brow

Woodend

Roaches

Wood Brook

Scouthead

Austerlands

C1
1 WEST GR
2 LIVINGSTONE AVE
3 THE HIGHLANDS
4 CRADDOCK ST
5 CHAPEL CT
6 CHAPEL ST

C2
1 HIGHLAND VIEW
2 LEES ST
3 WEBSTER ST
4 CROSS ST
5 WILD'S SQ
6 QUICKMERE CT
7 SPRING COTTS
8 BACK MILL LA
9 HAWTHORN TERR

10 WOODMEADOW CT

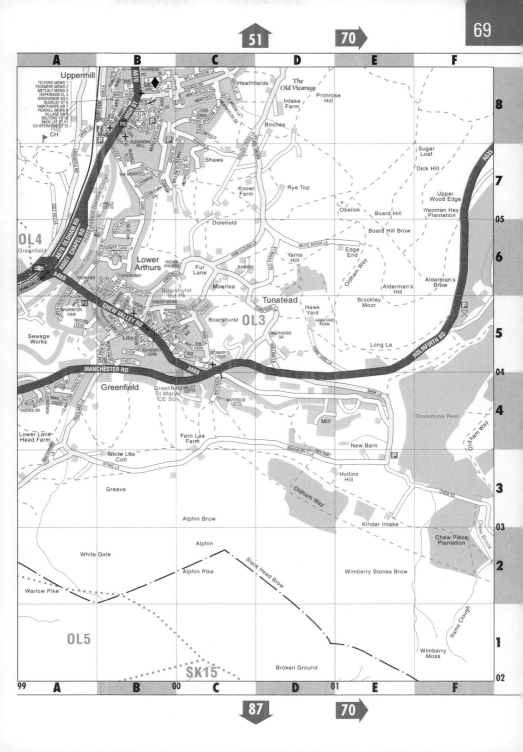

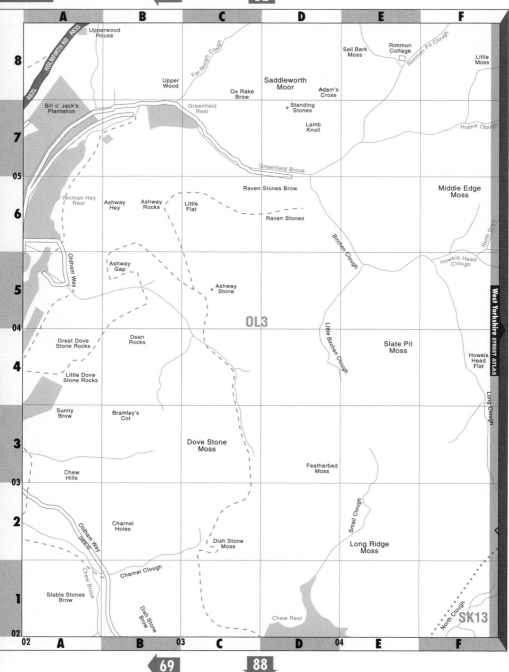

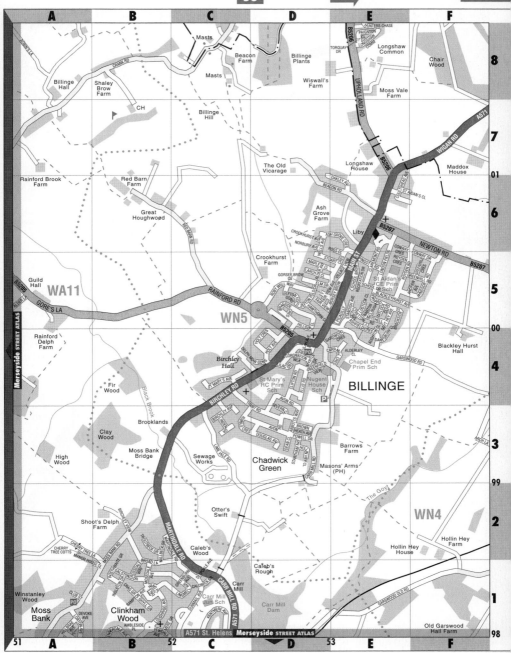

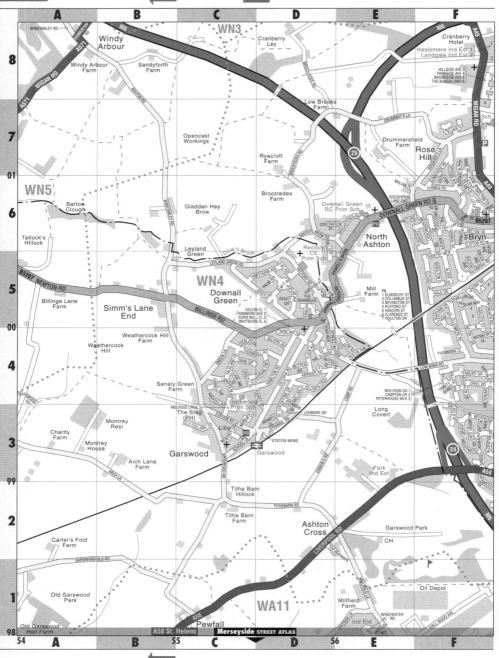

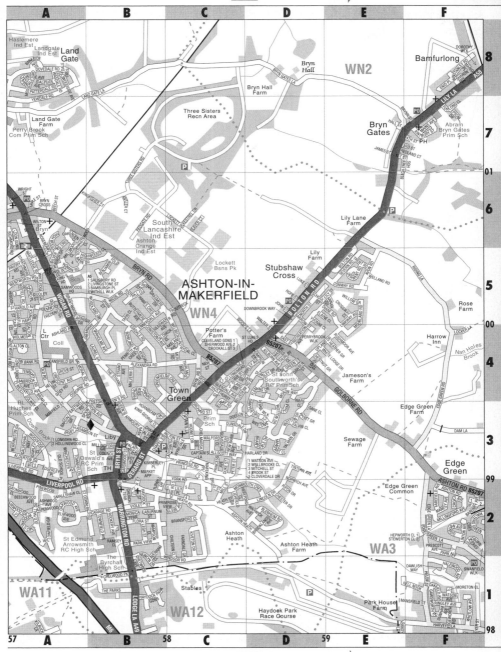

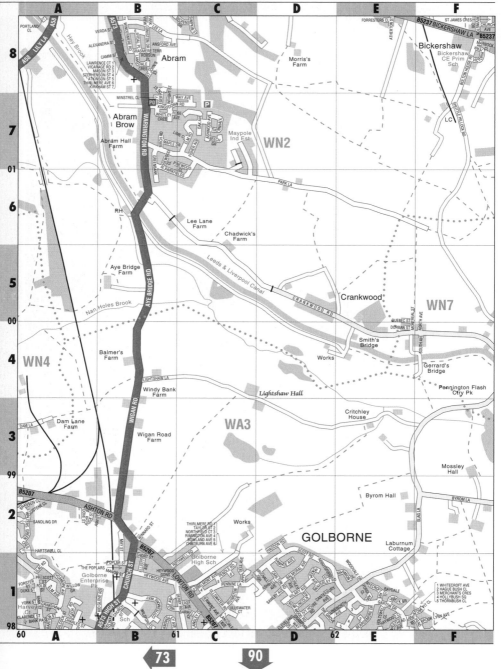

75 58

A B C D E F

8

B5215

HANSON DR
Crab Fold Farm
LEIGH RD
OLD HALL LA
Atherton Brook
Hindsford Brook
Langley Platt La
Sch
KING'S CRES
SQUIRES LA
HANSON ST
ST GEORGE
SCHOOL LA
WAREING ST

M46
Atherton Hall
Atherton Wood
COOLING LA

BLENHEIM ST 1
CROSS ST 2
JAMES ST 3
CHARLESTON CT 4
LUNE ST 5
ST GEORGES CT 6.

7

ORCHARD LA
Leigh
Zoo
Lilford Park
Walmsley Farm
Higher Folds Prim Sch
KENILWORTH
CHEPSTOW GR
Sch
Works
Sports Gd

01

H
THE AVENUE
Bates Farm
Village Inn (PH)
Higher Folds Enterprise Ctr
Gin Pit
NORTH LA

6

HATHAWAY CT
LEIGH
GREEN LA
Higher Folds
SOUTH LA

5

B5215
Mills
St Andrews Dr
WN7
Bedford Lodge
M29

00

A572
P
P
Bedford
MANCHESTER RD
KERFOOT ST
Cemy
A572
RUFFORD
DERSDALE LA
GREEN AVE

4

CHAPEL ST
Bedford Brook
Bedford High Sch
Marsland Green

St Joseph's RC Prim Sch
Acorn Bsns Ctr
Recn Gd
Hooten Gardens
Bridgewater Canal
Great Fold Bridge
Marsland Green Bridge

3

WARRINGTON RD
Siddow Common
Sewage Works
Leigh Bsns Pk
Bedford Hall Meth Prim Sch
Crompton House
Morley's Hall

99

Leigh Commerce Pk
EAST LANCASHIRE RD
A580
Grange Farm

2

Environmental Education Centre
Sandy Pool Farm
Pennington Bridge

1

Hope Carr Nature Reserve
Pennington Brook
Hotel
Grave Oak Farm
Bedford Bridge
Hawk Hurst Farm
WA3
Magpie's Nest
Netherbarrow Farm

98

WA3
A580
Lately Common
A574
Glaze Brook
JENNET'S LA

66 A 67 B C 67 D 68 E F

A4
1 BROWN ST S
2 WHARFDALE
3 RAMSEY ST
4 EAST BRIDGEWATER ST
5 OULTON CL
6 BURWELL CL
7 SIZE HOUSE PL

A5
1 BEDFORD ST
2 BROWN ST N
3 BROWN ST
4 BACK QUEEN ST
5 PRINCESS ST
6 DUKINFIELD ST
7 NOBLE ST
8 WILLIAM ST

B4
1 Waterside Trad Est
2 VILLAGE VIEW
3 WARDS PL
4 LANCASTER CT
5 GEORGIAN CT
6 FARNWORTH ST
7 COSWORTH CL

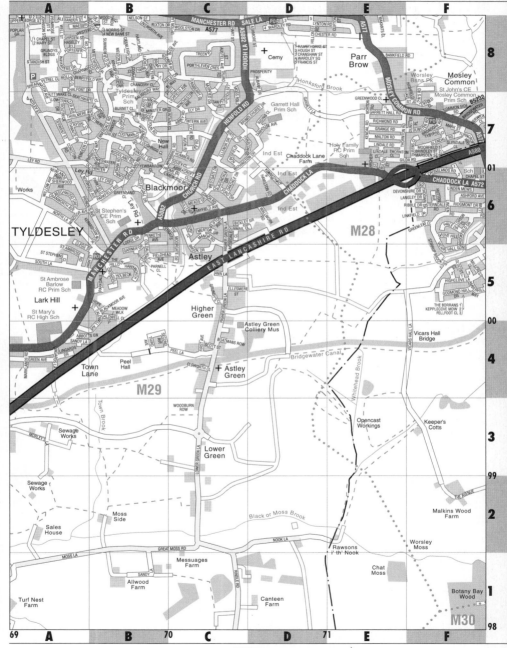

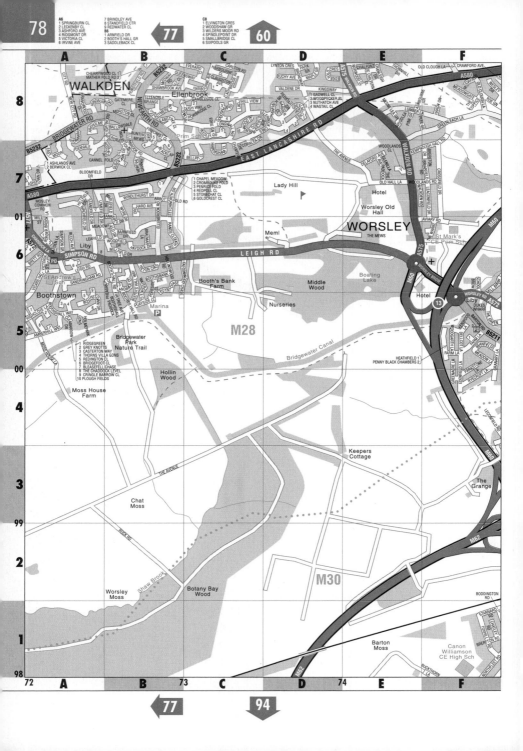

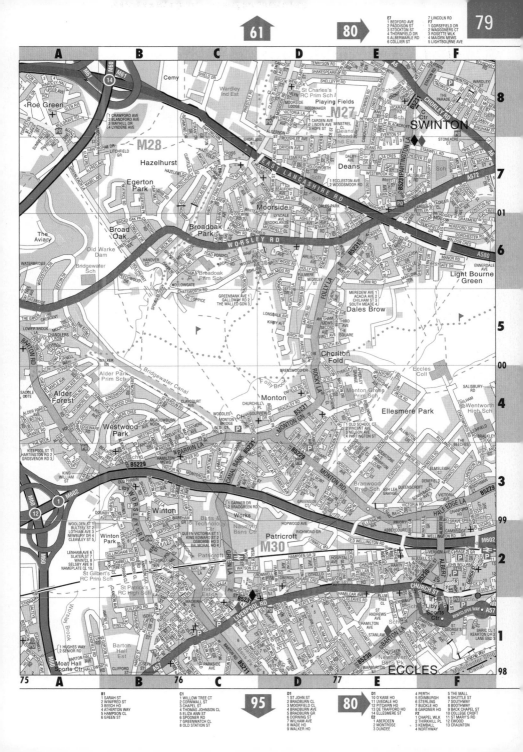

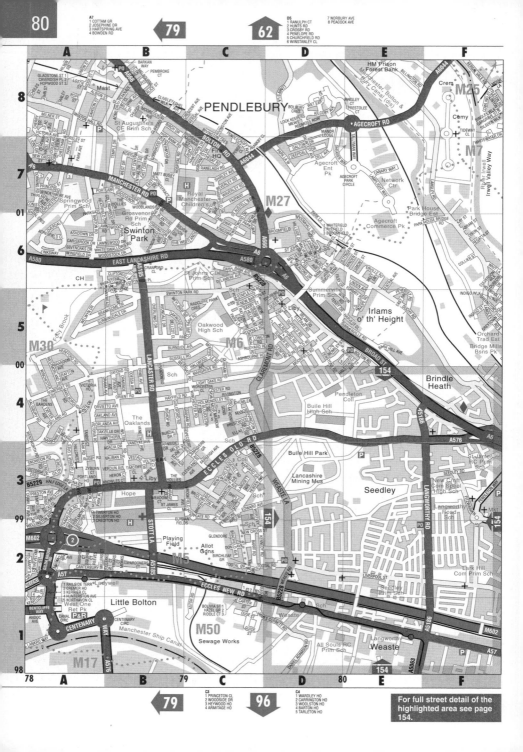

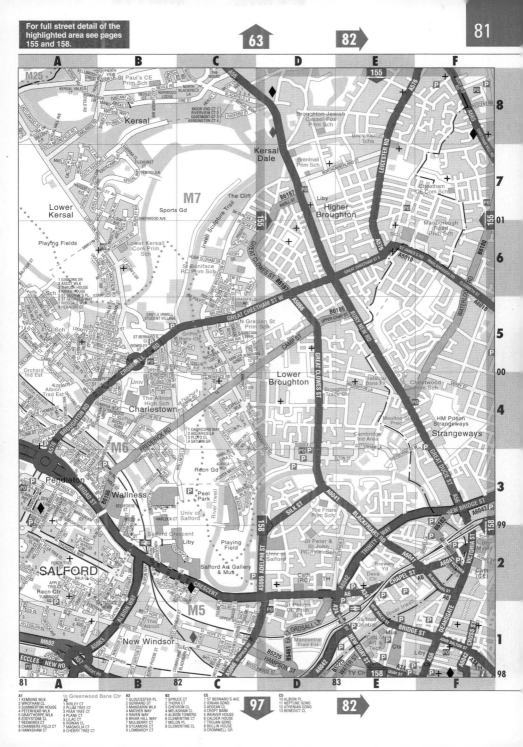

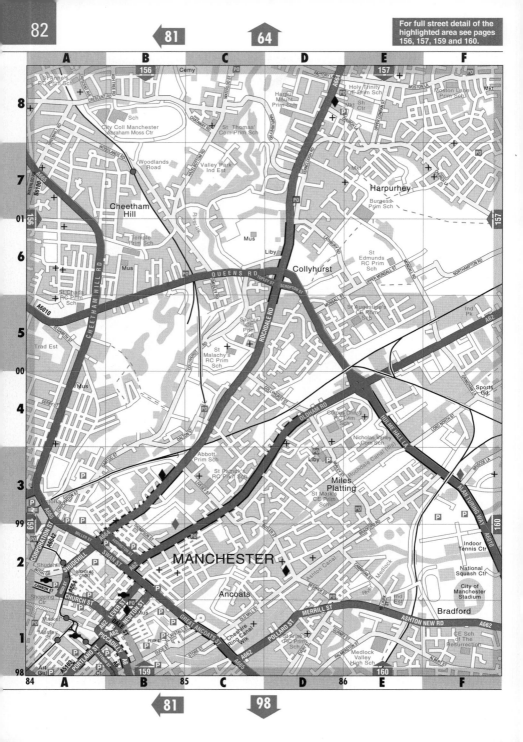

65 84

83

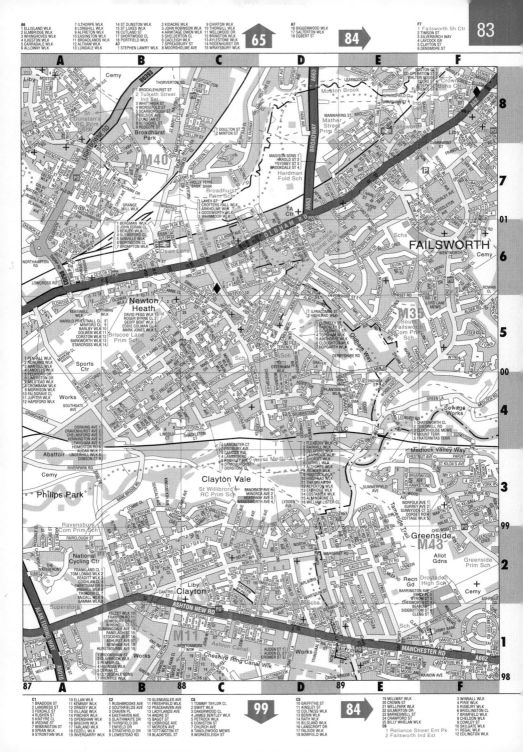

99 84

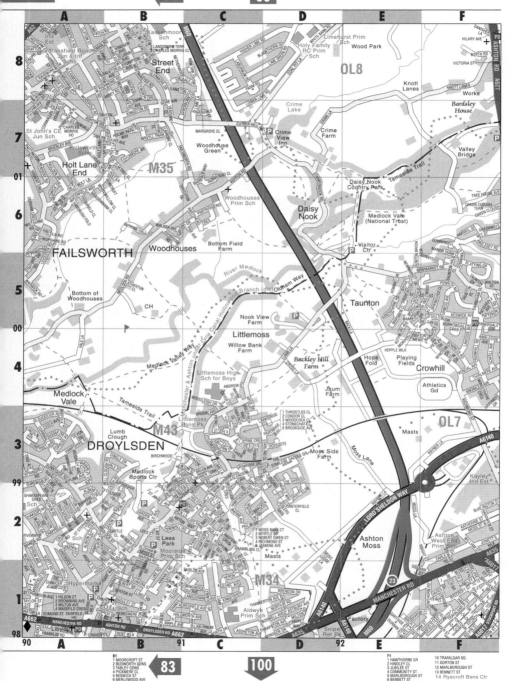

B1
1 MOORCROFT ST
2 BUDWORTH GDNS
3 TABLEY GDNS
4 PICKMERE CL
5 BESWICK ST
6 MERLEWOOD AVE

F1
1 HAWTHORNE GR
2 HINDLEY CL
3 JUBILEE ST
4 COMMUNITY ST
5 MARLBOROUGH ST
6 BENNETT ST
7 FAIRTHORNE GRANGE
8 MASON ST
9 TRAFALGAR SQ
10 TRAFALGAR SQ
11 GORTON ST
12 MARLBOROUGH ST
13 BENNETT ST
14 Ryecroft Bsns Ctr

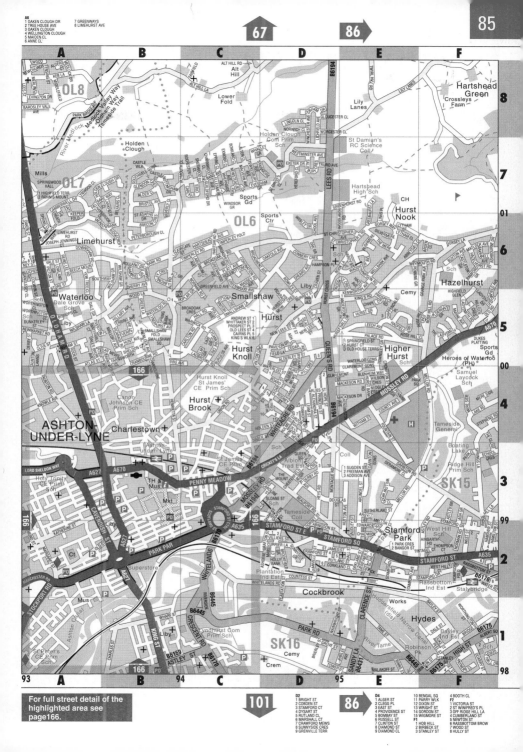

For full street detail of the highlighted area see page 166.

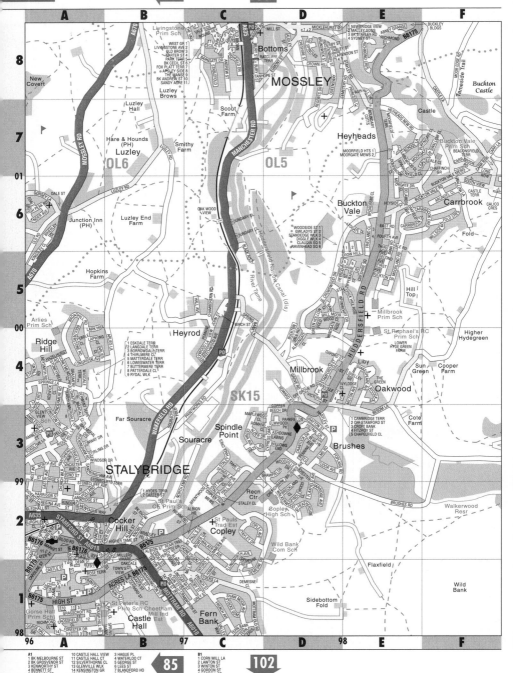

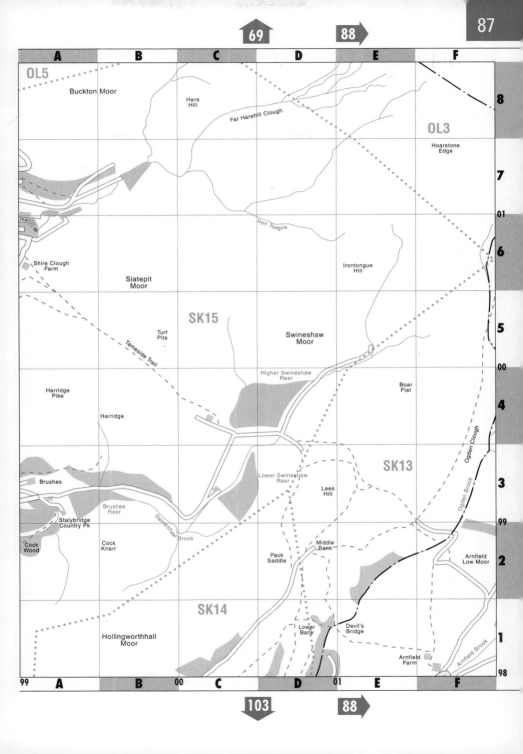

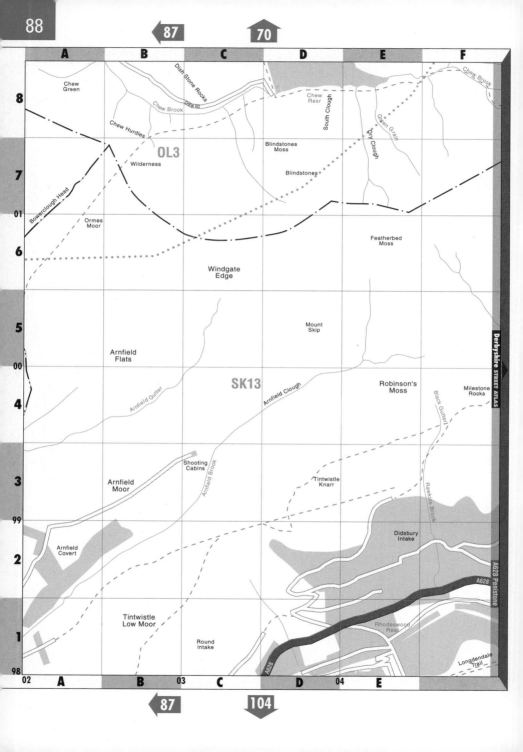

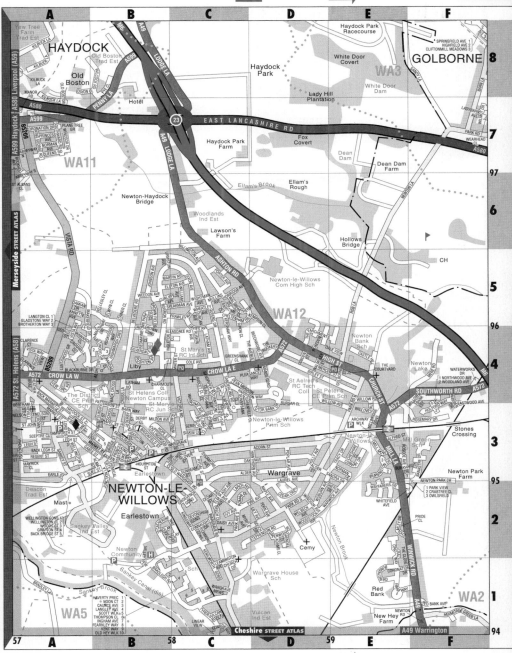

89
74

D8
1 SARSFIELD AVE
2 FOXGLOVE CL
3 GROSVENOR AVE
4 RIDGEWELL AVE

E8
1 TURRET HALL DR
2 ROYSTON CL
3 SANDFIELD CL
4 ARIEL WLK
5 BALLANTYNE WAY
6 BUNTING CL

E7
7 REDSTART CL
8 WILD ARUM CL
9 HUDSON GR
10 STONECHAT CL
11 SPEEDWELL CL
12 LUNEHURST
13 CONINGSBY GDNS

F8
1 SCOTIA WLK
2 TYLER WLK
3 ROBSON WAY
4 HORNCASTLE CL
5 HOPWOOD CL
6 BIRCH TREE RD

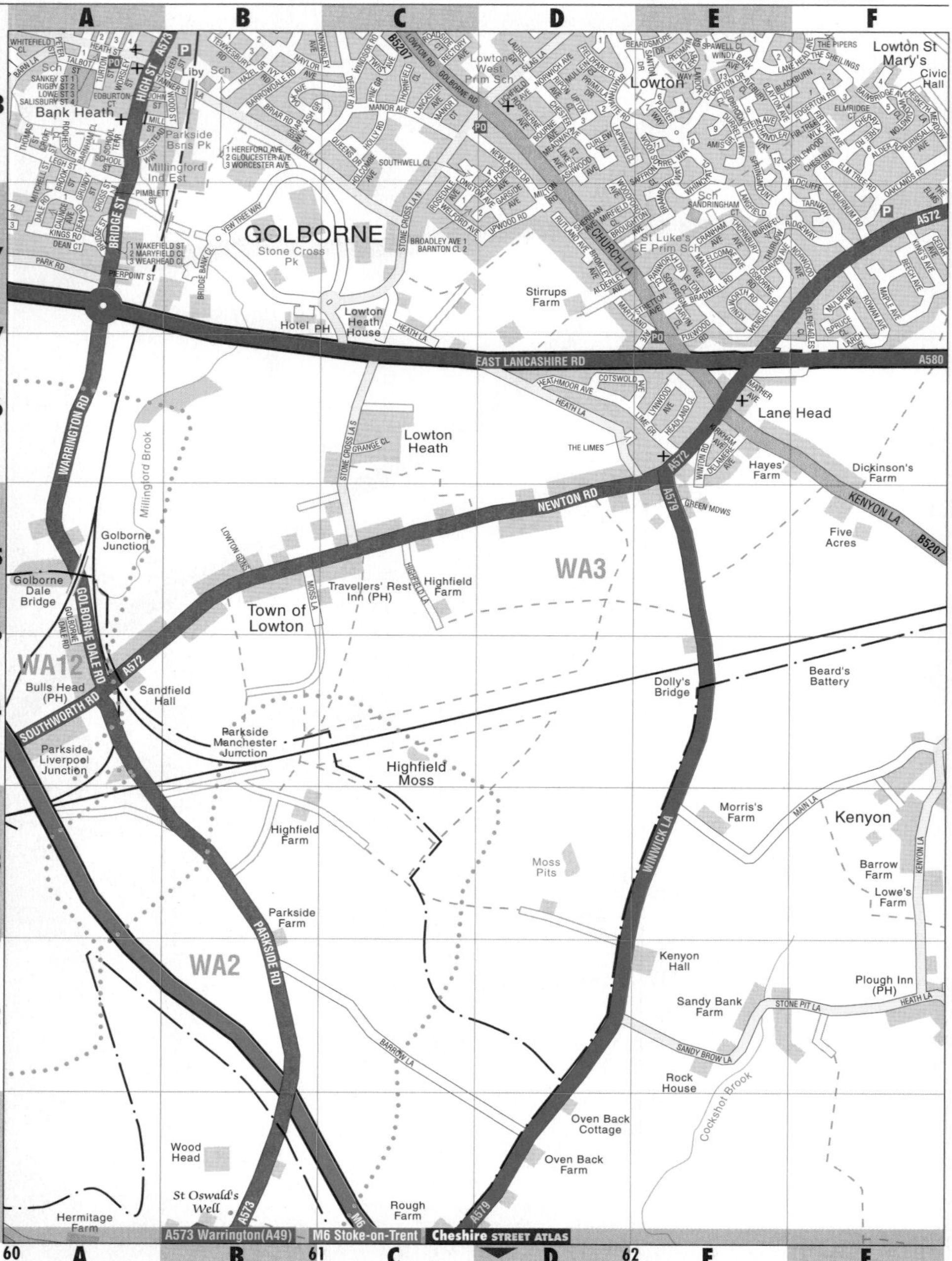

Bank Heath
GOLBORNE
Stone Cross Pk
Lowton West Prim Sch
Lowton
Lowton St Mary's
Civic Hall
Parkside Bsns Pk
Millingford Ind Est
1 HEREFORD AVE
2 GLOUCESTER AVE
3 WORCESTER AVE
SOUTHWELL CL
1 WAKEFIELD ST
2 MARYFIELD ST
3 WEARHEAD CL
PERPOINT ST
St Luke's CE Prim Sch
St Sandringham
Stirrups Farm
Hotel PH
Lowton Heath House
Bradley Ave 1
Barnton Cl 2

EAST LANCASHIRE RD
A580

Lowton Heath
Lane Head
Dickinson's Farm
HEATH MOOR AVE
COTSWOLD
THE LIMES
Hayes' Farm
GREEN MDWS
KENYON LA
B5207

Golborne Junction
NEWTON RD
WA3
Five Acres

Golborne Dale Bridge
WA12
Town of Lowton
Travellers' Rest Inn (PH)
Highfield Farm
Dolly's Bridge
Beard's Battery

Bulls Head (PH)
Sandfield Hall
Parkside Manchester Junction
Highfield Moss
Morris's Farm
Kenyon

Parkside Liverpool Junction
Highfield Farm
Moss Pits
Barrow Farm
Lowe's Farm

WA2
Parkside Farm
Kenyon Hall
Plough Inn (PH)
STONE PIT LA
HEATH LA

Sandy Bank Farm
SANDY BROW LA

Wood Head
BARROW LA
Rock House
Oven Back Cottage
Cookshot Brook

Hermitage Farm
St Oswald's Well
Rough Farm
Oven Back Farm

A573 Warrington (A49)
M6 Stoke-on-Trent
Cheshire STREET ATLAS

89

WARRINGTON RD
HIGH ST
BRIDGE ST
GOLBORNE DALE RD
SOUTHWORTH RD
PARKSIDE RD
A573
A572
A579
WINWICK LA
KENYON LA
MAIN LA
CHURCH LA
LOWTON GDNS
STONE CROSS LA

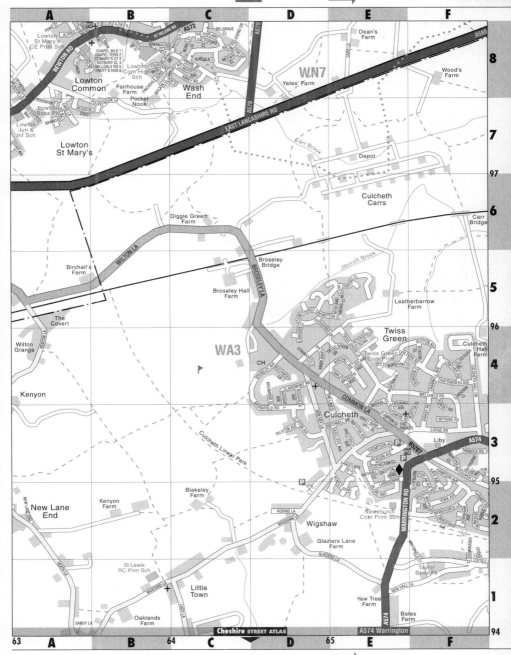

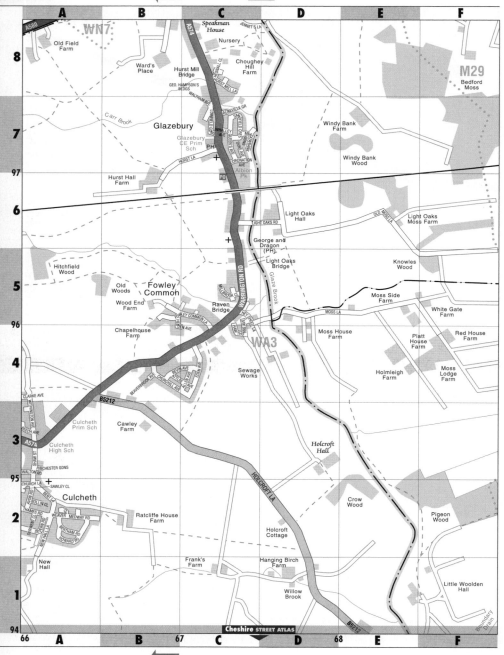

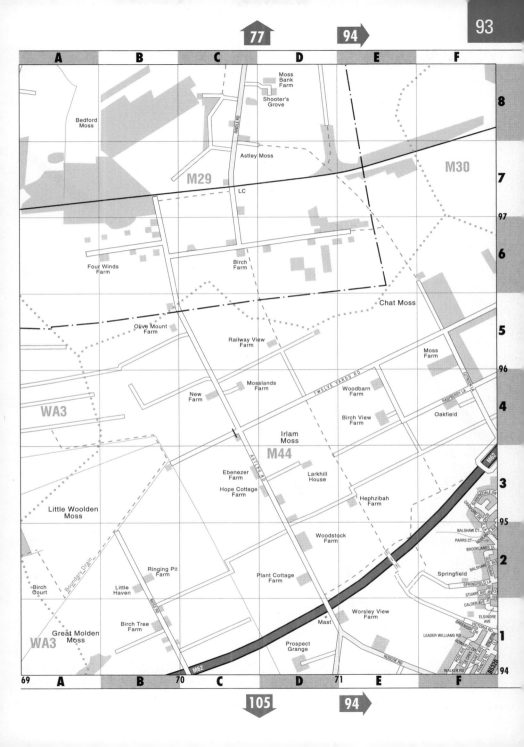

A **B** **C** **D** **E** **F**

8

Bedford
Moss

Moss
Bank
Farm

Shooter's
Grove

Astley Moss

RINDLE RD

M29

M30

7

LC

97

Four Winds
Farm

Birch
Farm

6

Chat Moss

Olive Mount
Farm

5

Railway View
Farm

Moss
Farm

96

WA3

New
Farm

Mosslands
Farm

TWELVE YARDS RD

Woodbarn
Farm

RASPBERRY LA

4

Birch View
Farm

Oakfield

M6

Irlam
Moss

M44

FETTLER RD

Ebenezer
Farm

Larkhill
House

3

Hope Cottage
Farm

Hephzibah
Farm

SUNNINGDALE DR

95

Little Woolden
Moss

Woodstock
Farm

BALSHAW CT.

PARRS CT.

BROOKLANDS CL.

2

Ringing Pit
Farm

Plant Cottage
Farm

Springfield

SPRINGFIELD

STUART AVE.

Boundary Drain

MOSS RD

Birch
Court

Little
Haven

CALDER AVE.

ELSINORE
AVE.

VICTORIA RD

Birch Tree
Farm

Mast

Worsley View
Farm

GREENSIDE DR

LEADER WILLIAMS RD

1

WA3

Great Molden
Moss

Prospect
Grange

ROSCOE RD

WALKER RD

M62

94

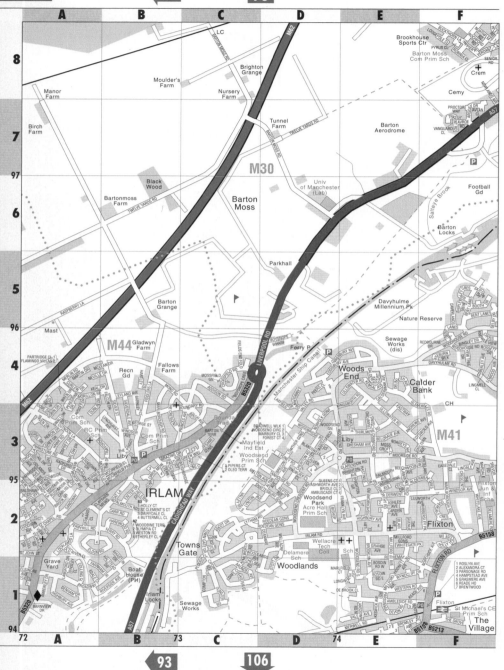

93
78
93
106

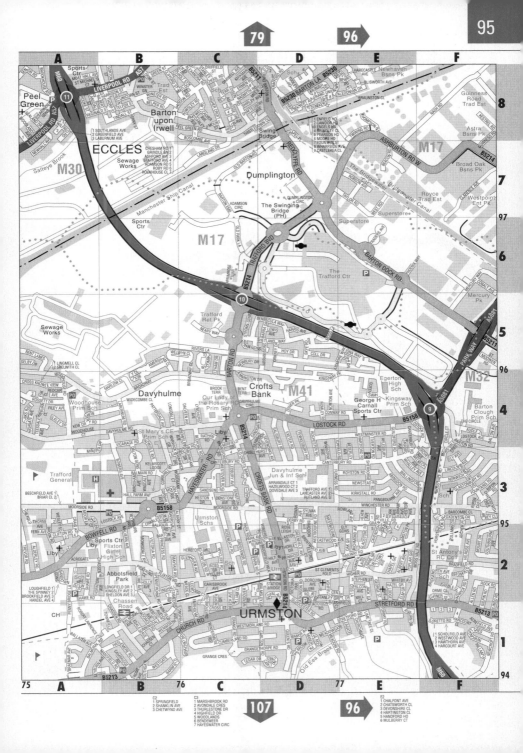

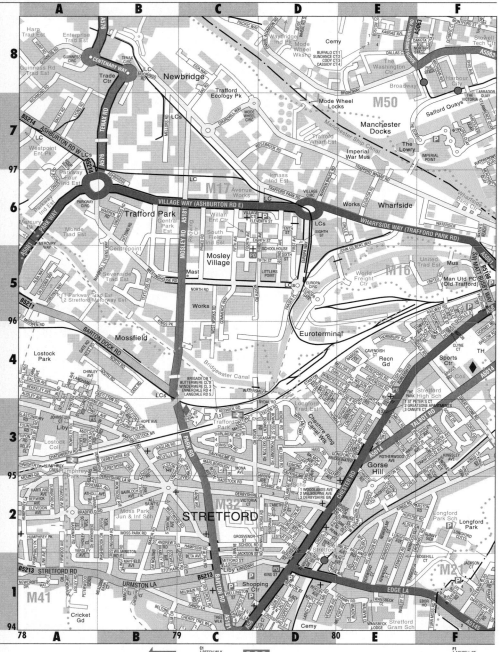

95
80
95
108

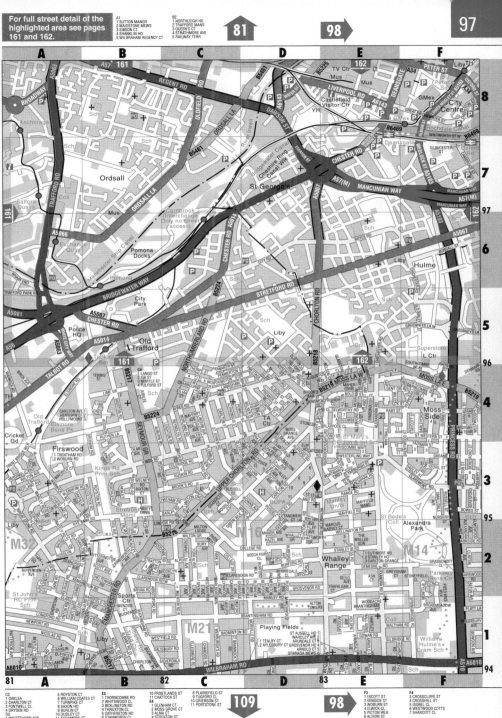

For full street detail of the highlighted area see pages 161 and 162.

81
98

A1
1 SUTTON MANOR
2 MAIDSTONE MEWS
3 SIBSON CT
4 SHANKLIN HO
5 WILBRAHAM REGENCY CT

B2
1 NORTHLEIGH HO
2 TRAFFORD MANS
3 QUEEN'S CT
4 STRATHMORE AVE
5 RAILWAY TERR

109
98

C3
1 OAKLEA
2 CHARLTON CT
3 FONTWELL CL
4 DRYDEN RD
D3
1 WHITETHORN AVE
2 LANSBURY HO
3 YEOMANRY CT
4 CARLTON MANS

5 ROYSTON CT
6 WILLIAM COATES CT
7 TURNIPHLE CT
8 SAXON HO
9 BURLIN CT
10 DUDLEY CT
11 SYCAMORE CT
12 HAZEL CT
13 MAY CT
14 GOODWOOD LODGE

E3
1 THORNCOMBE CL
2 WHITSWOOD CL
3 BEXLINGTON RD
4 THRUXTON CL
5 CATHERSTON RD
6 STANTWORTH CL
7 GROSVENOR
8 ROY GRAINGER CT
9 NELSON MANDELA CT

10 FROSTLANDS ST
11 CHATTOCK ST
E4
1 GLENHAM CT
2 MOSS GROVE CT
3 ALMA CT
4 STOCKTON ST
5 SHOREHAM CL
6 WOODHEAD CL
7 QUANTOCK CL

8 PLAINSFIELD ST
9 TUGFORD CL
10 GRIERSON ST
11 PORTSTONE CL

F3
1 ESCOTT ST
2 KENSIDE ST
3 WOBURN ST
4 ELWICK CL
5 PICTON WLK
6 ALISON ST
F4
1 ORNHILL RD
2 CRICCIETH ST

F4
3 CROSSCLIFFE ST
4 CROSSHILL ST
5 ISOBEL CL
6 WESTWOOD COTTS
7 SHARCOTT CL

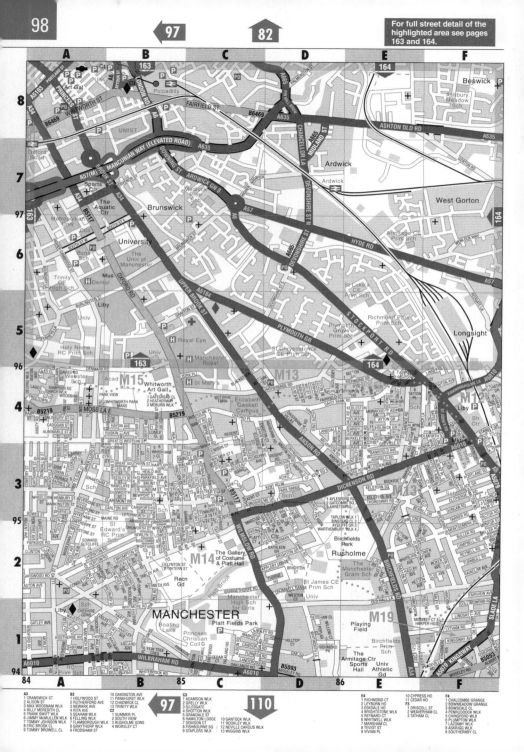

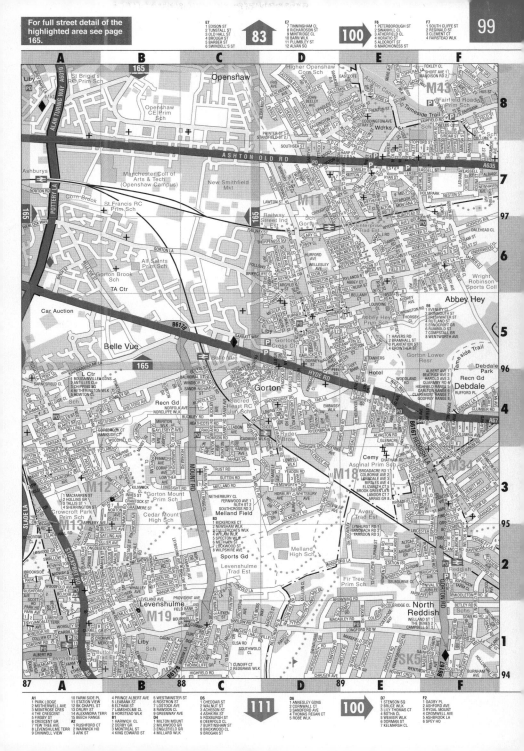

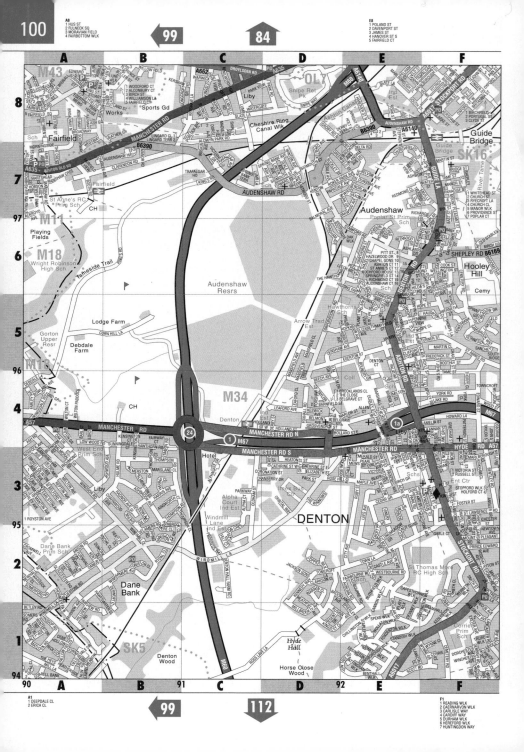

100

A8
1 HUS ST
2 FULNECK SQ
3 MORAVIAN FIELD
4 FAIRBOTTOM WLK

E8
1 POLAND ST
2 DAVENPORT ST
3 JAMES ST
4 HANOVER ST S
5 FAIRFIELD CT

99

84

A1
1 DEEPDALE CL
2 ERICA CL

99

112

F1
1 READING WLK
2 CAERNARVON WLK
3 CARLISLE WAY
4 CARDIFF WAY
5 DURHAM WLK
6 HEREFORD WLK
7 HUNTINGDON WAY

85

102

C8
1 VICTORIA MEWS
2 CONSORT CL

D5
1 SPENCER AVE
2 GLENWOOD AVE
3 BENNET MEWS
4 SACK ST

D8
1 CONCORD WAY
2 SHEPLEY CL
3 JACKSON AVE
4 REECE CT
5 CLAYTON ST
6 PLOUGH ST

E8
1 OLD SCHOOL MEWS
2 OLD CHURCH MEWS
F5
1 GAINSBOROUGH WLK
2 WENTWORTH WLK
3 ST MARYS VIEW

F8
1 CLARENCE HO
2 THE ARCADE
3 CLIFF DALE
4 QUARRY HTS

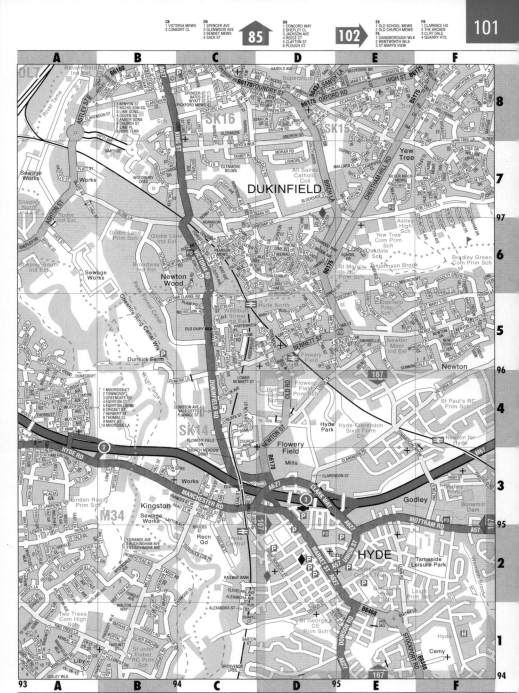

113

102

A1
1 NORTHAMPTON WAY
2 NEWCASTLE WLK
3 NOTTINGHAM WAY
4 OXFORD WLK
5 MAIDSTONE WLK
6 PEMBROKE WAY
7 SHREWSBURY WAY
8 BOSTON WLK
9 WELSHPOOL WAY

10 IPSWICH WLK
11 CHICHESTER WAY
12 STAFFORD WLK
13 TAUNTON WLK
14 CHELMSFORD WLK
15 GAWSWORTH WAY
16 THORSBY WAY
17 HADDON WAY
18 MORTON TERR
19 ADLINGTON WAY

20 PENSHURST WLK
21 HOLKER WAY
22 ARLEY WAY
23 HAREWOOD WLK

A2
1 WITHY TREE GR
2 WOOD HEY GR
3 GARDEN WLK

For full street detail of the
highlighted area see page
167.

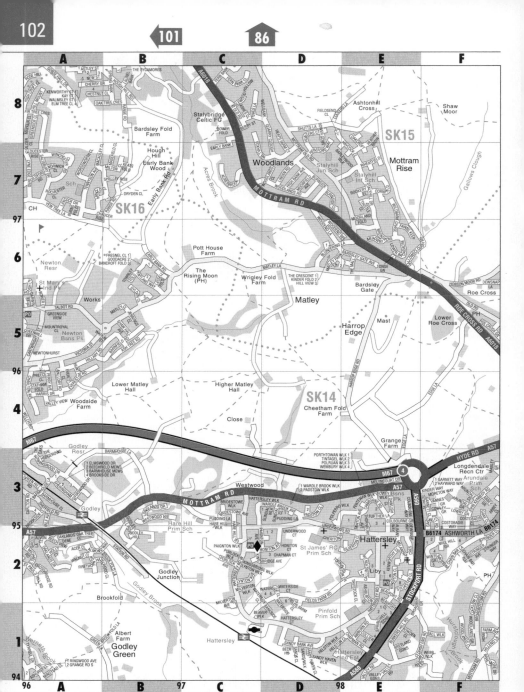

D2
1 ST JAMES' CT
2 UNDERWOOD WLK
3 HONITON WLK
4 WATERSIDE WLK
5 BANKSIDE WLK
6 FIELDS FARM WLK

E1
1 PHILLIP WAY
2 SPRINGWELL WAY
3 BEAUFORT WAY
4 COLLIER WLK

E2
1 BARDSLEY CL
2 THE HATTERSLEY CTR
3 CALLINGTON WLK
4 CALLINGTON CL
5 TAMESIDE CT
6 KINGSTON ARC
7 WORTHINGTON CL
8 SYLVESTER WAY

F2
1 SHELMERDINE CL
2 SLATER WAY
3 MILL HILL WAY
4 WINTERBOTTOM WLK
5 KNOWLE WAY
6 GREEN WAY
7 GREEN WLK
8 ASHWORTH WAY

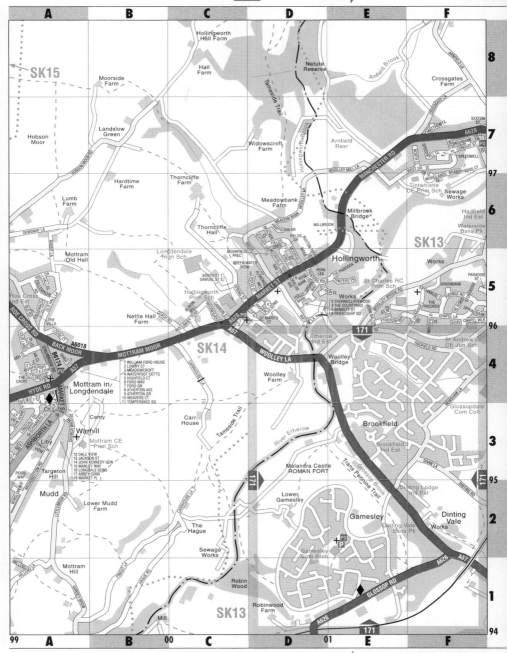

87
104

SK15

Hollingworth
Hall Farm

Hall
Farm

Moorside
Farm

Nature
Reserve

Arnfield Brook

8

Crossgates
Farm

Landslow
Green

Tameside Trail

Hollingworth BROOK

Arnfield
Resr

7

SEXTON
ST

A628

Hobson
Moor

Widowscroft
Farm

CMITHEW CL

SPEEDWELL

97

Hardtime
Farm

Thorncliffe
Farm

Meadowbank
Farm

Manchester Rd

WOOLLEY MILL LA

Tintwhistle
CE Prim Sch

Sewage
Works

Lumb
Farm

6

Millbrook
Bridge

Hadfield
Ind Est

Waterside
Bsns Pk

DEWSNAP LA

Thorncliffe
Hall

MILLBROOK

SK13

Mottram
Old Hall

Longdendale
High Sch

MOORFIELD
PREC

Hollingworth

Works

PARADISE
LA

RABBIT LA

GREEN WATER
MDW

FERN LEA

St Charles RC
Prim Sch

GREENBANK

5

Roe Cross
Ind Est

THE
VILLA

Hollingworth
Prim Sch

Works
3 THORNECLIFFEWOOD
4 THE COURTYARD
5 BENNETT ST
6 FRIENDSHIP SQ

THE
PADDOCK

ROE CROSS RD

Nettle Hall
Farm

St Mary's
CT

96

St Andrew's
CE Jun Sch

BACK MOOR

A6018

MOTTRAM MOOR

SK14

A57

WOOLLEY LA

Etherow
Ind Est

171

HADFIELD RD

HYDE RD

1 WILLIAM FORD HOUSE
2 LOWRY CT
3 MEADOWCROFT
4 WATERFOOT COTTS
5 HIGHFIELD CT
6 FORD WAY
7 FORD GR
8 ATHERTON AVE
9 ATHERTON GR
10 WEAVERS CT
11 TEMPERANCE SQ

Woolley
Farm

Woolley
Bridge

4

Mottram in
Longdendale

Carr
House

Tameside Trail

River Etherow

Brookfield

Glossopdale
Com Coll

ASHWORTH LA

Cemy

Warhill

Brookfield
Ind Est

3

171

Liby

Mottram CE
Prim Sch

12 DALE VIEW
13 JACKSON ST
14 JOHN KENNEDY GDN
15 MANLEY WAY
16 LONGDALE GDNS
17 ABBEY GDNS
18 MARKET PL

Melandra Castle
ROMAN FORT

Trans Pennine Trail

Glossop Brook

Dinting Lodge
Ind Est

95

Targeton
Hill

171

Dinting
Vale

PEARL
WAY

Mudd

Lower Mudd
Farm

The Hague

Lower
Gamesley

Gamesley

Dinting
Vale
Works

2

HILL END

Mottram
Hill

Sewage
Works

Gamesley
Com Prim
Sch

PO
P

A626

A57

Robin
Wood

GLOSSOP RD

1

Mill

SK13

Robinwood
Farm

A626

171

94

115
104

For full street detail of the
highlighted area see page
171.

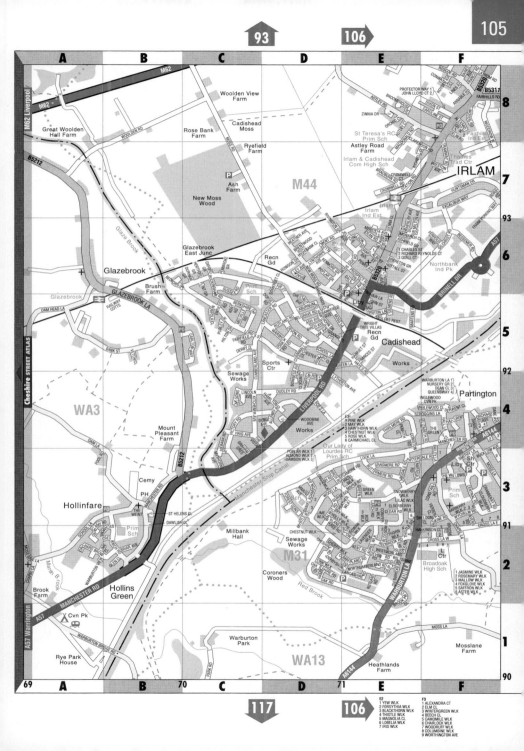

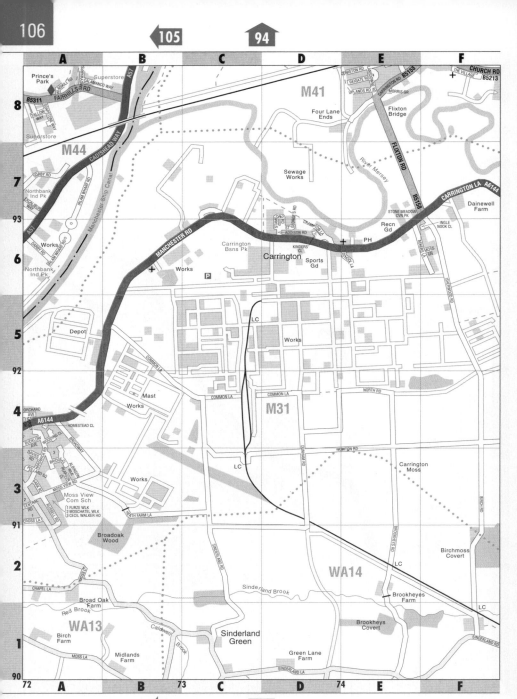

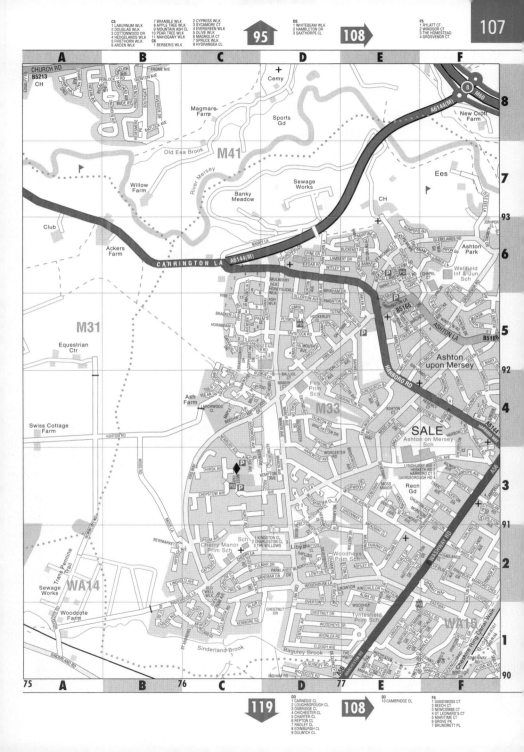

B5
1 RUSSELL PL
2 WILSON ST
3 PARTINGTON PL
4 ORCHARD PL
5 CURZON RD
6 BENBOW ST

107

96

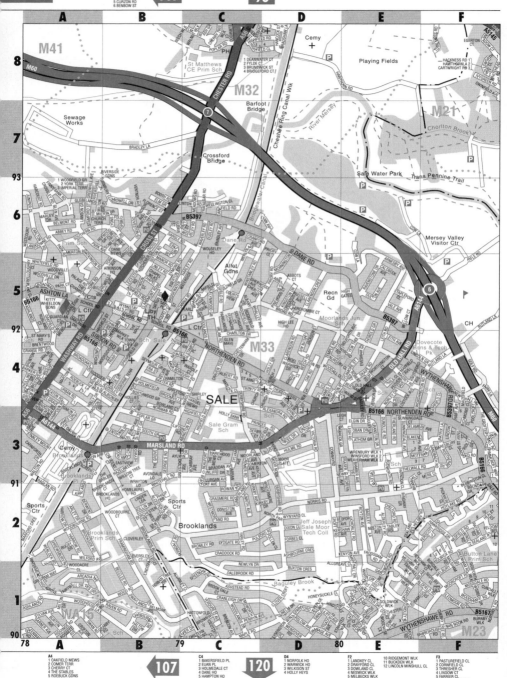

A4
1 OAKFIELD MEWS
2 COMER TERR
3 CHERRY CT
4 THE STABLES
5 ROEBUCK GDNS
6 PALMER ST
7 CHARNLEY CL

C4
1 BAKERSFIELD PL
2 EUAN PL
3 HOLMEDALE CT
4 DANE HO
5 HAMPTON HO

D4
1 NORFOLK HO
2 WARWICK HO
3 WILKISON ST
4 HOLLY HEYS

F2
1 LANDKEY CL
2 DRAYFORD CL
3 DOWLAND CL
4 NESWICK WLK
5 MELBECKS WLK
6 VAWDREY DR
7 HAZELHURST WLK
8 SEDGFIELD WLK
9 MARSETT WLK

10 RIDGEMONT WLK
11 BUCKDEN WLK
12 LINCOLN MINSHULL CL

F3
1 PASTUREFIELD CL
2 CORNFIELD CL
3 THRESHER CL
4 LINDOW CT
5 FARRER CL
6 ROSEWOOD GDNS
7 WOODCHURCH WLK

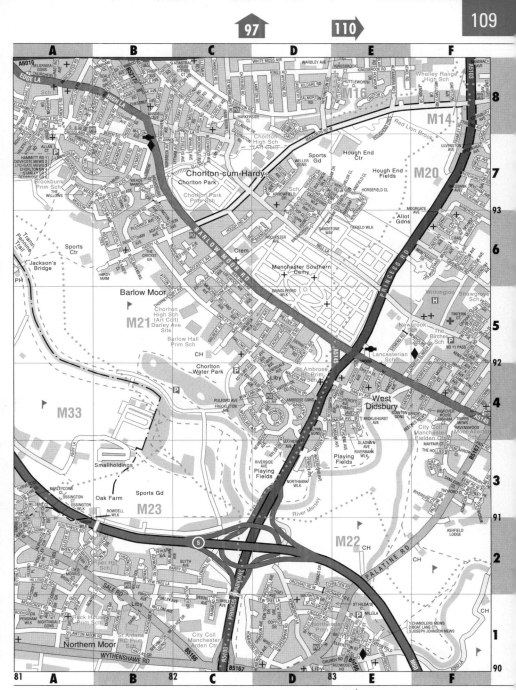

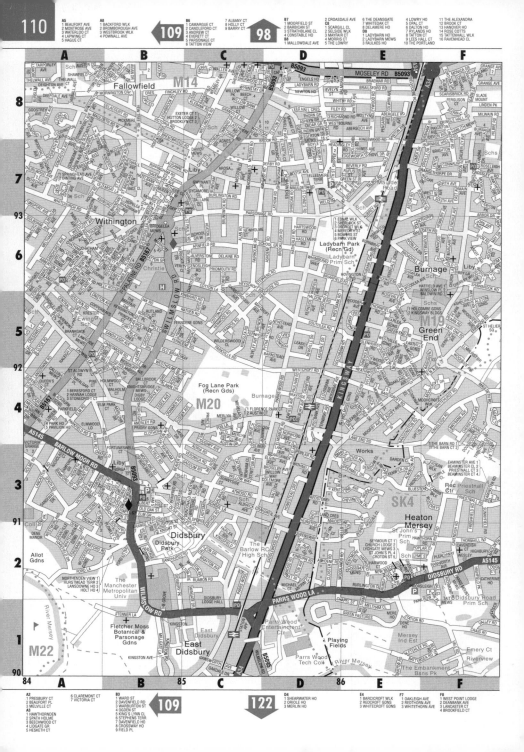

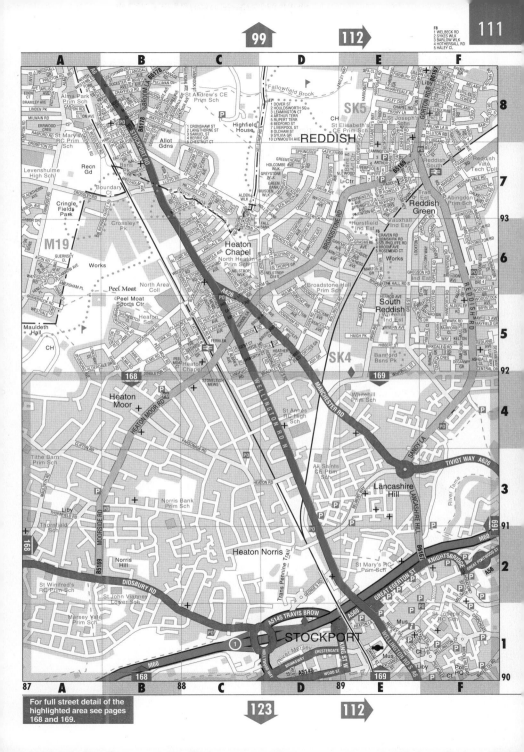

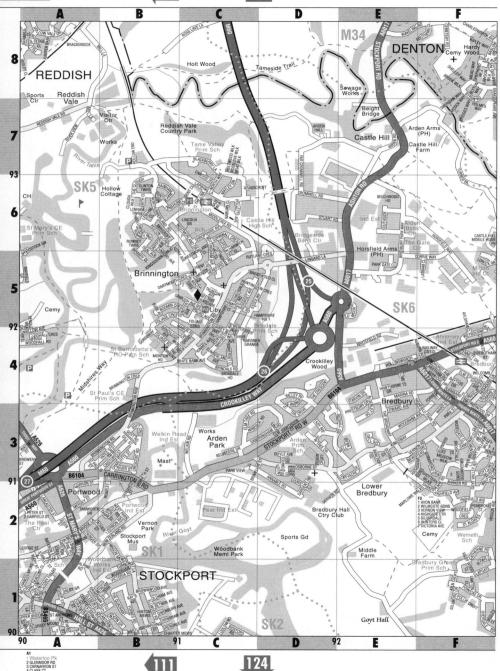

A B C D E F

8
REDDISH

Holt Wood

Tameside Trail

M34

Stockport Rd

DENTON

Cemy
Hardy
Wood

Sports
Ctr

Reddish
Vale

Visitor
Ctr

Reddish Vale
Country Park

Sewage
Works

Beight
Bridge

Arden Arms
(PH)

7

Works

Tame Valley
Prim Sch

Castle Hill

Castle Hill
Farm

93

SK5

Hollow
Cottage

River Tame

Reddish Vale Rd

CH

Arden
Hall

Cromwell Rd

Castle Hill
High Sch

Ashton Rd

Beechwood
Ho

Ind Est

Arden
Bsns
Ctr

Castle Hill
Mobile Home

6

St Mary's CE
Prim Sch

Lincoln
Gn

Bridgeside
Bsns Ctr

Stuart Rd

Southgate

The Gate
Ctr

Corrie Way

Milton
Ind Ct

Brinnington

Rutland Cres

Lingard La

Horsfield Arms
(PH)

Park Gate Ct

5

Cemy

St Bernadette's
RC Prim Sch

Monton
Ho

Hampshire
Rd

Brindale
Prim Sch

Gardner
Grange

25

Crookilley
Wood

SK6

Alvanley
Ind Est

Stockport Rd

A560

92

Woodhall Rd

White Bank Ave

Brindale
Ho

Whitefield Rd

Railway
Cotts

to Bredbury

Sidebotham
St

Welcomb
Cl

4

Midshires Way

Brinnington Cres

St Paul's CE
Prim Sch

26

CROOKILLEY WAY

B6104

Hollingworth

Valley Rd

The Crescent

Hawthorne
Gr

Marina Rd

Bredbury

Tiviot Dr

Edward Ave

A6017

3

A626

M60

B6104

Welkin Road
Ind Est

Works

**Arden
Park**

Stockport Rd W

Arden
Prim
Sch

Kingsway

Meadow
Wlk

Mast

River St

Belvedere Dr

Park View

Doyle Ave

Osborne St

**Lower
Bredbury**

Highfield Ave

Barker Rd

2

Portwood

Carrington Rd

A560

A6 St Mary's Way

1 PETER ST
2 GARFIELD ST
The Peel
Ctr

Tamworth
Gn

Portwood
Ind Est

Pear Ind Est

Vernon
Park

Stockport
Mus

River Goyt

Sports Gd

Bredbury Hall
Ctry Club

Cemy

F3
1 AVON BANK
2 WILMCOTE GDNS
3 VERNON VIEW
4 HIGHGATE CTR
5 SILVERDALE
6 HUNTERS CL
7 VICTORIA AVE

Werneth
Sch

27

George St

Sch

Woodbank
Works
Ind Est

SK1

Woodbank
Meml Park

**Middle
Farm**

Bredbury Green
Prim Sch

1

B5465 Hall St A626

STOCKPORT

Brownwood Ave
Oldham Ave

Belmore Ave

Hinton
Mews

Gwenbury Ave

Grendale Ave

Chaucer Mews

SK2

Goyt Hall

90

90 A B 91 C D 92 E F

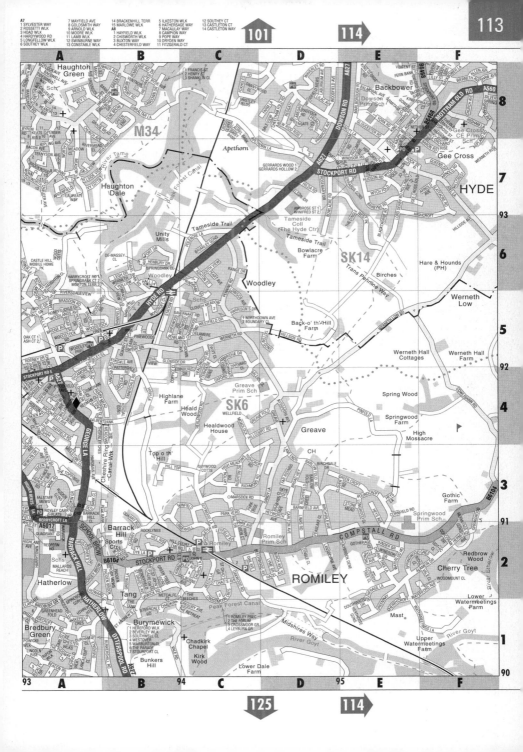

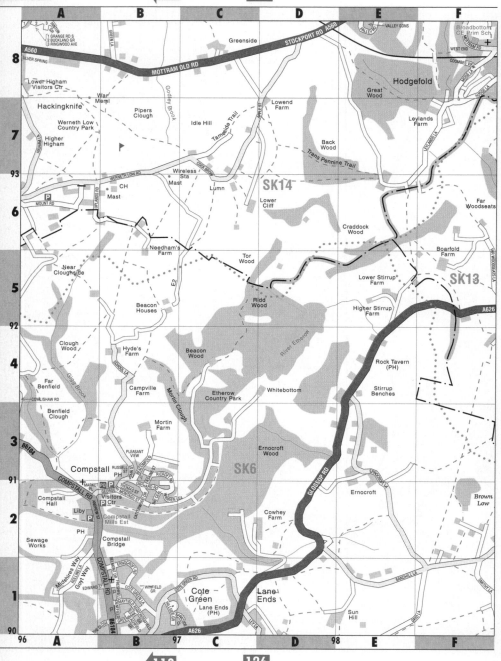

103

116

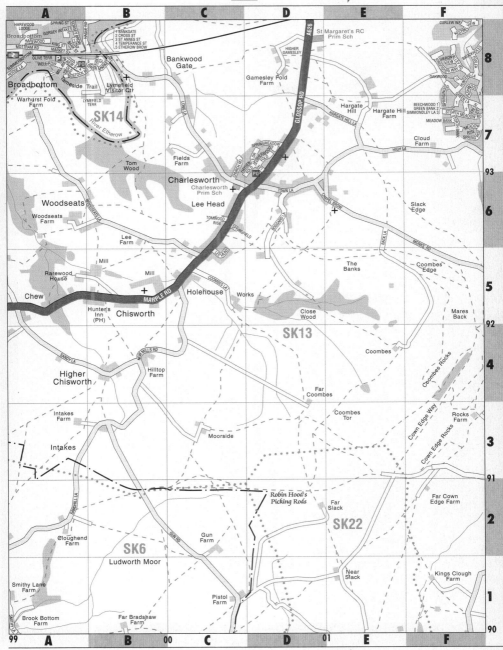

116

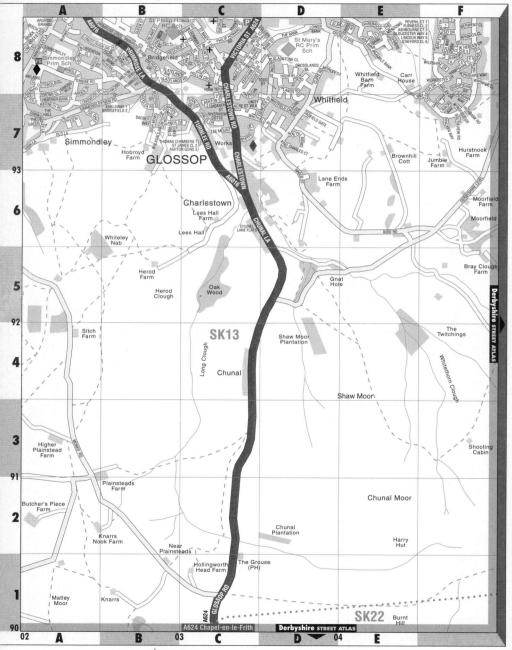

C8
1 LITTLEMOOR CT
2 HADFIELD SQ
3 SEFTON ST
4 HADFIELD PL
5 JAMES ST

GLOSSOP

Simmondley

Whitfield

Charlestown

SK13

Chunal

Shaw Moor

Chunal Moor

SK22

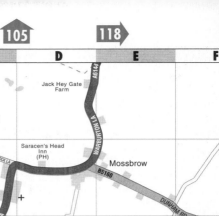

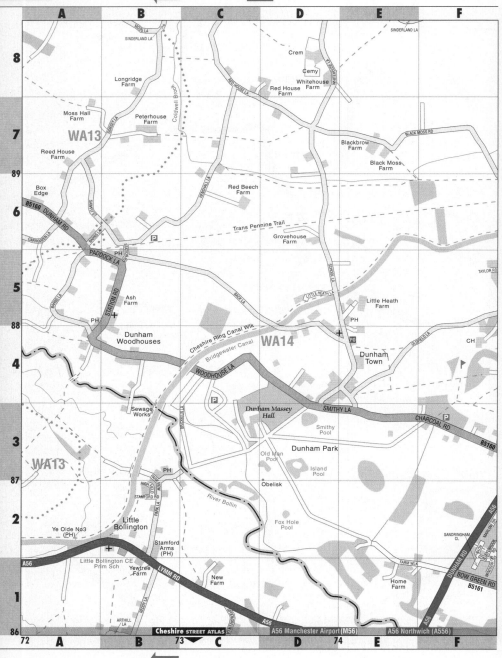

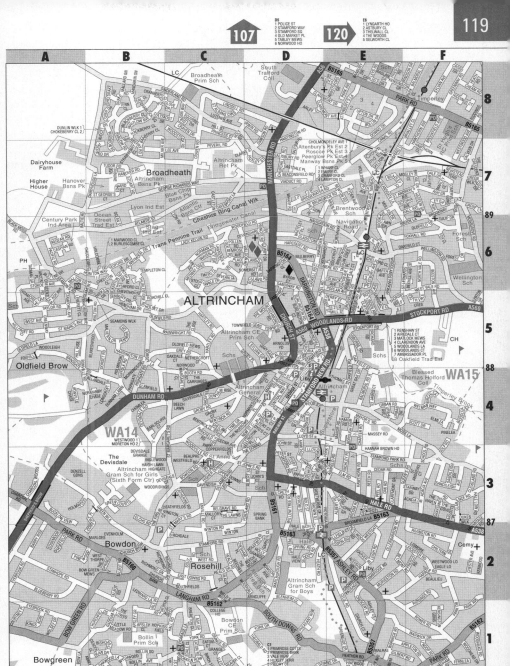

107

120

D5
1 POLICE ST
2 STAMFORD WAY
3 STAMFORD SQ
4 OLD MARKET PL
5 TABLEY MEWS
6 NORWOOD HO

E6
1 LYNGARTH HO
2 ASTBURY CL
3 THELWALL CL
4 THE WOODS
5 SELWORTH CL

Altrincham

WA15

WA14

WA14
WESTWOOD 1
MORETON HO 2

1 WHARF ST
2 EMERY CT
3 STAMFORD CL
4 LAMPTON CL

1 RENSHAW ST
2 AIREDALE CT
3 MATLOCK MEWS
4 CLARENDON AVE
5 WOODLANDS LA
6 WOODLANDS CT
7 AMBASSADOR PL
8 Oakfield Trad Est

CHOLMONDELEY AVE 1
Attenbury's Pk Est 2
Roscoe Pk Est 3
Peerglow Pk Est 4
Manway Bsns Pk 5

Broadheath

Oldfield Brow

Bowdon

Rosehill

Bowgreen

C4
1 STAMFORD GRANGE
2 EASINGWOLD

128

D3
1 ROSTHERNE ST
2 WILLIAM WLK

120

D4
1 GREENWOOD ST
2 THE CAUSEWAY
3 CROSS ST
4 BREWERY ST
5 THE DOME
6 LLOYD SQ
7 OSBOURNE PL

C1
1 PRIMROSE COTTS
2 PRIMROSE BANK
3 VALE MEWS
4 HUXLEY TERR
5 PRIORY CT
6 CHURCH VIEW

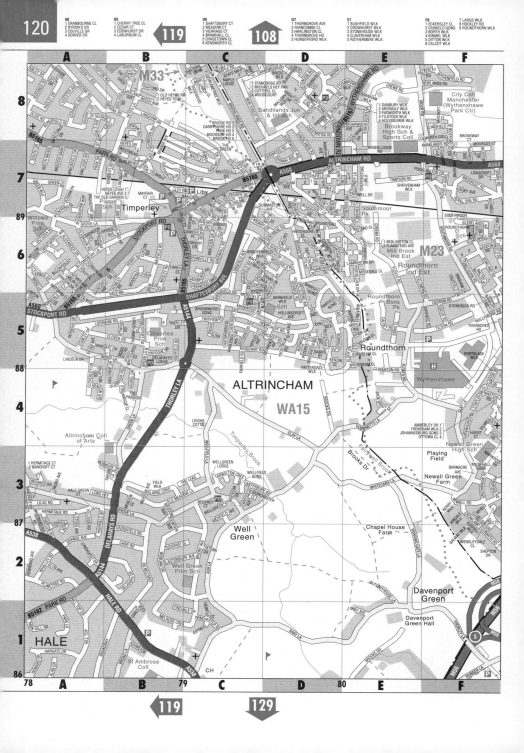

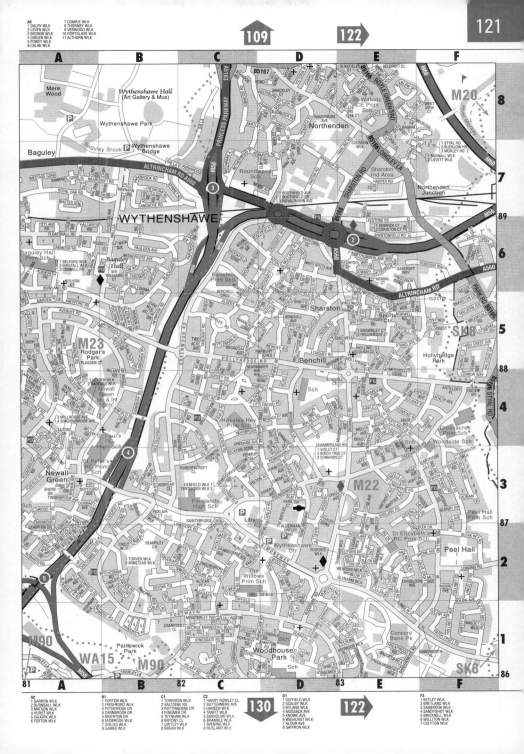

109
122

A5
1 DALRY WLK
2 LEVEN WLK
3 BODMIN WLK
4 DIBDIN WLK
5 FOWEY WLK
6 CALNE WLK

7 COMRIE WLK
8 THORNBY WLK
9 VERWOOD WLK
10 PORTSLADE WLK
11 ALTHORN WLK

Mere Wood

Wythenshawe Hall
(Art Gallery & Mus)

Wythenshawe Park

Baguley Brook

Baguley

Wythenshawe Bridge

ALTRINCHAM RD A560

PRINCESS PARKWAY

M56

B5167

Wythenshawe Hall

Roundwood Sch

Northenden

ROYLE GREEN RD

BELCROFT CL

M60

M20

WEST VIEW

River Mersey

1 STYAL HO
2 BUCKLOW HO
3 MORLEY HO
1 BAGNALL HO
1 LOVETT WLK

Northenden Junction

SHARSTON RD

Sharston Ind Area

HARPER RD

M60

WYTHENSHAWE

1 BOOTHFIELD AVE
2 BOOTHFIELD DR
3 ROYALTHORN AVE

Baguley Hall Prim Sch

1 BELFORD WLK
2 BIRSTALL WLK
3 CONNELL RD

Baguley Hall

SIR WILLIAMS

Benchill Prim Sch

Benchill Cres

Sharston

LEESTONE RD
1 KESWICK CT
2 CONISTON CT
SVENTONFIELD RD

A560

A560

ALTRINCHAM RD

The Old City

SK18

Hollyhedge Park

M23

Rodger's Park

1 LEVEN WLK
2 BARFORD WLK
Newall Green Jun & Inf Sch

3 MILLHOUSE AVE
4 SHADOWBROOK AVE

Luton

St Paul's RC High Sch

HOLLYHEDGE RD

Benchill

1 BROWNLEY CT
2 HOLLYHEDGE CT

Sch

1 CHAMBERLAIN HO
1 VIOLET CT
2 BIRCH TREE CT
3 EDWARDS CT

Crossacres Prim Sch

Woodside Sch

ARTILLERY PL

OGDEN GR

CONNOR WAY

HIGH CREST AVE

SK18

Haveley Hey Prim Sch

M22

Peel Hall Prim Sch

St Peter's RC Prim Sch

Newall Green

St Elizabeth's RC Prim Sch

Peel Hall

Parklands High Sch

Liby

Wythenshawe Ctr

ALDERMAN OATLEY HO

HENFIELD WLK 1
TENTERDEN WLK 2

The Willows Prim Sch

Concord Bsns Pk

M90

WA15

M90

M56

Painswick Park

Woodhouse Park

Sch

SK8

81 A 82 B C 82 D 83 E F 86

A2
1 GARRON WLK
2 BURNSALL WLK
3 MATSON WLK
4 HURST WLK
5 FALKIRK WLK
6 FOXTON WLK

B1
1 PORTON WLK
2 FRESHFORD WLK
3 PETHERIDGE DR
4 DARNBROOK DR
5 BRIERTON DR
6 MIDBROOK WLK
7 SIBLIES WLK
8 GAMES WLK

C1
1 TORRIDON WLK
2 SALTDENE RD
3 ROTTINGDENE DR
4 RINGMER DR
5 TEYNHAM WLK
6 BRYONY CL
7 GRITLEY WLK
8 BREAN WLK

C2
1 HARRY ROWLEY CL
2 BUTTERMERE AVE
3 HANSEN WLK
4 TANPIT WLK
5 SAXHOLME WLK
6 BRAMBLE WLK
7 AVENING WLK
8 RUSLAND WLK

D1
1 SUFFIELD WLK
2 SCALBY WLK
3 BYLAND WLK
4 MOSSACK AVE
5 KNOWE AVE
6 WIGHURST WLK
7 ALTAIR AVE
8 SAFFRON WLK

F3
1 KETLEY WLK
2 BRETLAND WLK
3 SAXBROOK WLK
4 SANDYSHOT WLK
5 BRICKNELL WLK
6 WILLITON WLK
7 COLYTON WLK

130
122

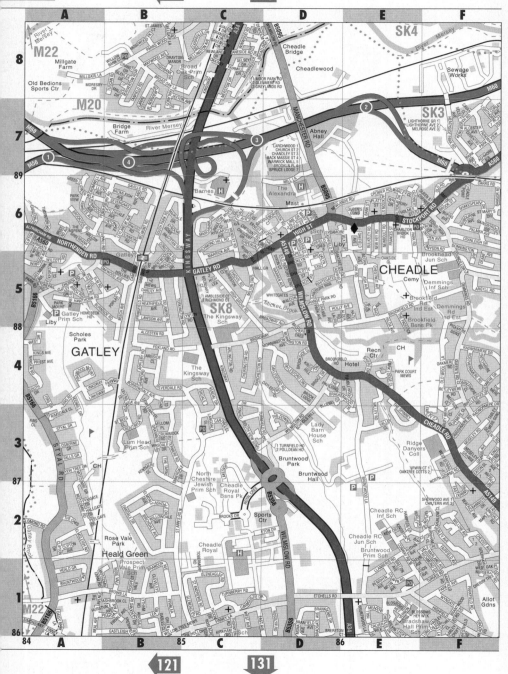

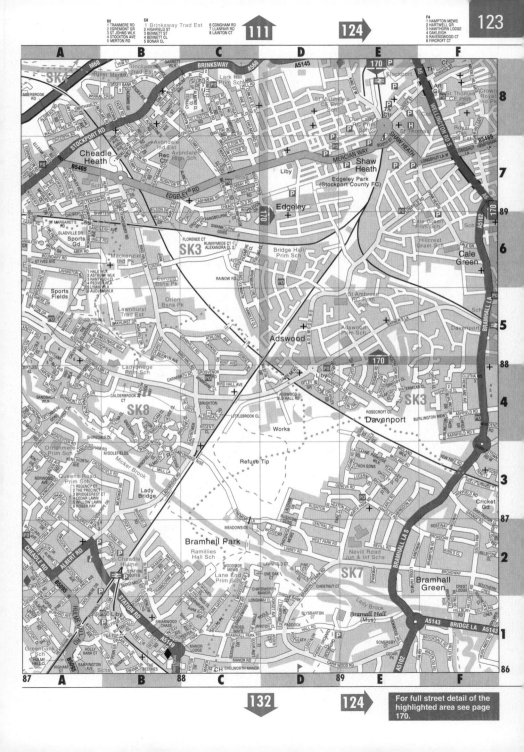

111
124
132
124

For full street detail of the highlighted area see page 170.

123
112

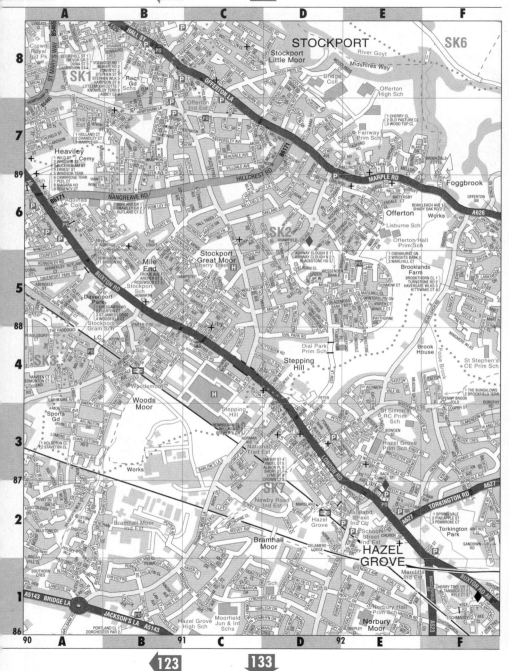

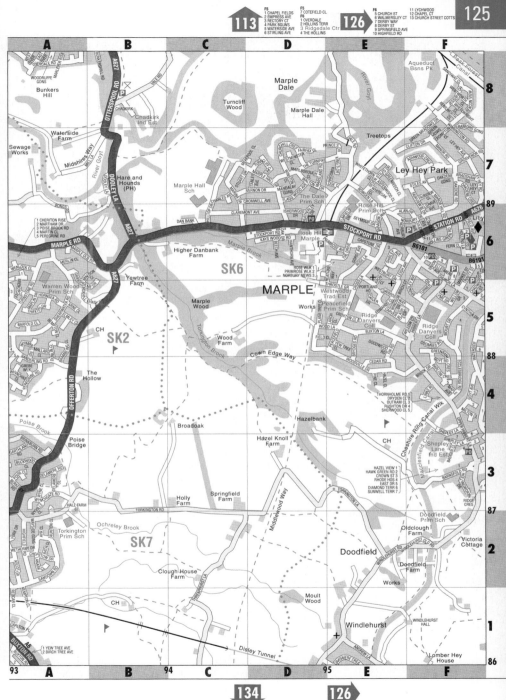

113

126

F5
1 CHAPEL FIELDS
2 EMPRESS AVE
3 RECTORY CT
4 PARK BGLWS
5 WATERSIDE AVE
6 STIRLING AVE

F5
7 COTEFIELD CL

F6
1 OVERDALE
2 HOLLINS TERR
3 Ridgedale Ctr
4 THE HOLLINS

F6
5 CHURCH ST
6 WALMERSLEY CT
7 DERBY WAY
8 DERBY ST
9 SPRINGFIELD AVE
10 HIGHFIELD RD

11 LYCHWOOD
12 CHAPEL CT
13 CHURCH STREET COTTS

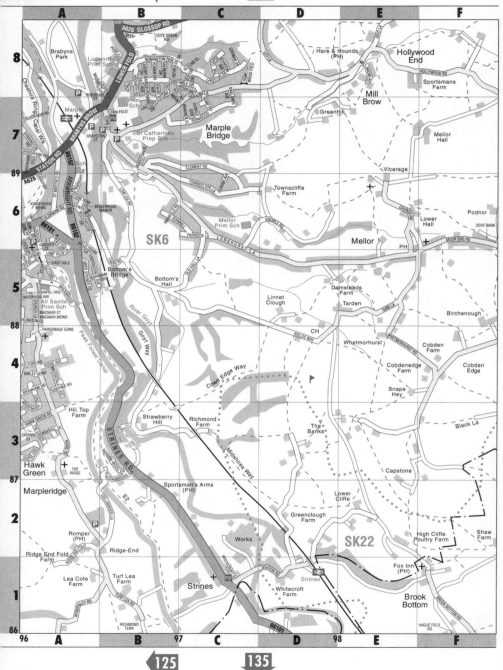

125
114
125
135

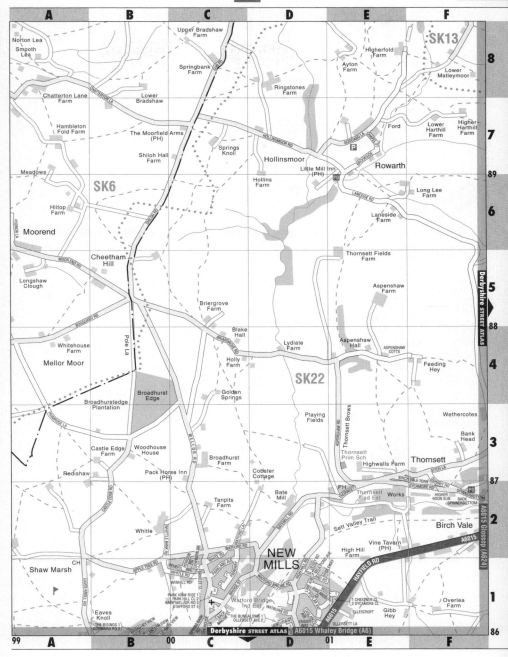

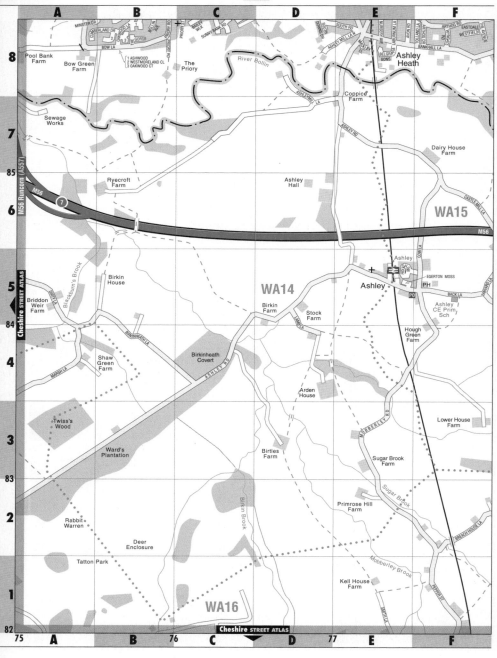

8

7

85

6

5

84

4

3

83

2

1

82

A B C D E F

75 76 77

A **B** **C** **D** **E** **F**

Pool Bank Farm

Bow Green Farm

Bow La

Cumberland Dr

Minster Ct

The Gorse

1 ASHWOOD
2 WESTMORELAND CL
3 OAKWOOD CT

The Priory

Priory Rd

River Bollin

South Rd

South Rd

Kingsway

Nursery Avenue

Ashley Mill La

Belgrave Gdns

Ashley Heath

Bankhall La

Arthog Rd
Westfields
Eastdale Avenue
Av Wymere

Sewage Works

Ashley La

Coppice Farm

Ashley Rd

Dairy House Farm

Ryecroft Farm

Ashley Hall

Castle Mill La

WA15

M56 Runcorn (A557)

M56

7

M56

Briddon Weir Farm

Pexy La

Blackburn's Brook

Birkin House

WA14

Birkin Farm

Stock Farm

Lime La

Ashley

Ashley

Egerton Moss

PH

PO

Ashley CE Prim Sch

Back La

Hanwell La

Hough Green Farm

Marsh La

Shaw Green Farm

Birkinheath La

Birkinheath Covert

Ashley Rd

Arden House

Mobberley Rd

Lower House Farm

Twiss's Wood

Ward's Plantation

Birtles Farm

Sugar Brook Farm

Sugar Brook

Rabbit Warren

Birkin Brook

Primrose Hill Farm

Mobberley Brook

Breach House La

Pepper St

Deer Enclosure

Tatton Park

WA16

Kell House Farm

Smith La

Cheshire STREET ATLAS

Cheshire STREET ATLAS

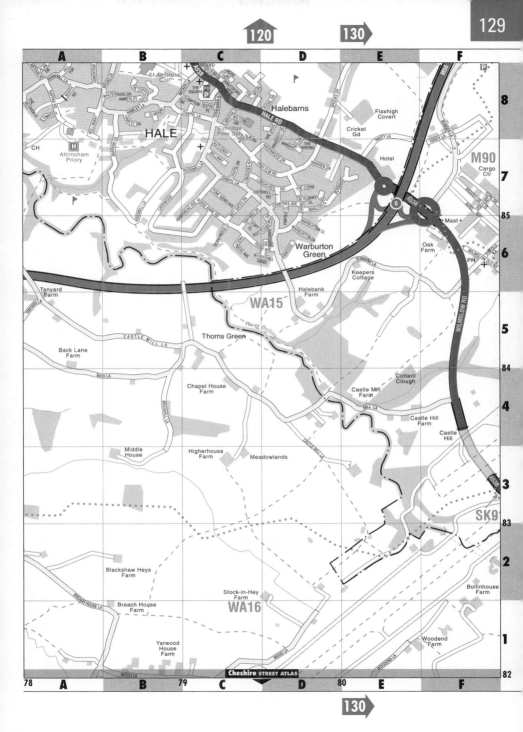

129
121

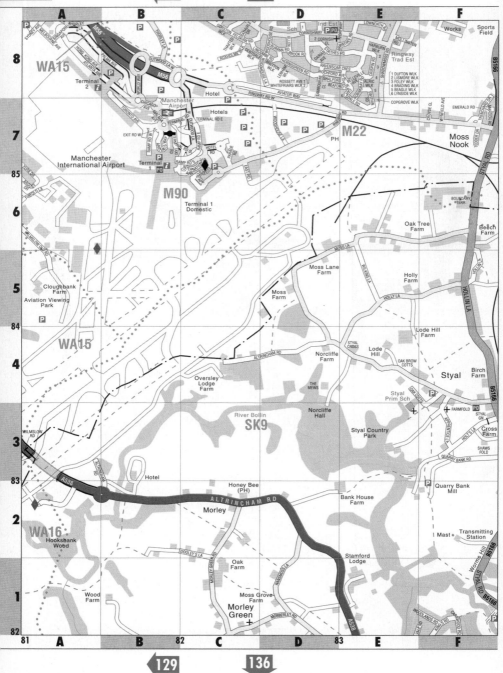

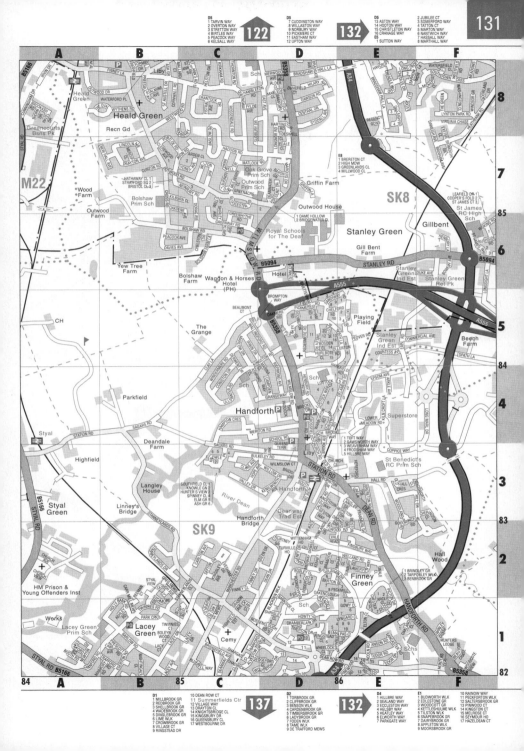

131

D5
1 TARVIN WAY
2 OVERTON WAY
3 STRETTON WAY
4 BIRTLES WAY
5 PEACOCK WAY
6 KELSALL WAY

122

D5
7 CUDDINGTON WAY
8 WILLASTON WAY
9 NORBURY WAY
10 PICKMERE CT
11 EASTHAM WAY
12 UPTON WAY

132

D5
13 ASTON WAY
14 HOOTON WAY
15 CHRISTLETON WAY
16 CRANAGE WAY
E5
1 SUTTON WAY

2 JUBILEE CT
3 SOMERFORD WAY
4 TATTON CT
5 MARTON WAY
6 NANTWICH WAY
7 HASSALL WAY
8 MARTHALL WAY

D1
1 MILLBROOK GR
2 REDBROOK GR
3 SHELLBROOK GR
4 WADEBROOK GR
5 DINGLEBROOK GR
6 LIME WLK
7 CROWBROOK GR
8 VILLAGE CT
9 RINGSTEAD DR
10 DEAN ROW CT
11 Summerfields Ctr
12 VILLAGE WAY
13 DRAYTON CL
14 KNIGHTSBRIDGE CL
15 KINGSBURY DR
16 QUEENSBURY CL
17 WESTBOURNE DR

137

D2
1 TORBROOK GR
2 CLIFFBROOK GR
3 BENSON WLK
4 CARDENBROOK GR
5 TIMBERSBROOK GR
6 LADYBROOK GR
7 ODEN WLK
8 TAME WLK
9 DE TRAFFORD MEWS

132

D4
1 HILLBRE WAY
2 SEALAND WAY
3 ECCLESTON WAY
4 HELSBY WAY
5 HEATLEY WAY
6 ELWORTH WAY
7 PARKGATE WAY

E1
1 BUDWORTH WLK
2 EDLESTONE GR
3 WOODCOTT GR
4 KETTLESHULME WLK
5 TILSTON WLK
6 SNAPEBROOK GR
7 DAIRYBROOK GR
8 APPLETON WLK
9 MOORSBROOK GR
10 RAINOW WAY
11 PECKFORTON WLK
12 SALTERSBROOK GR
13 PINWOOD CT
14 KINGSTON CT
15 MELROSE CT
16 SEYMOUR HO
17 HAZELDEAN CT

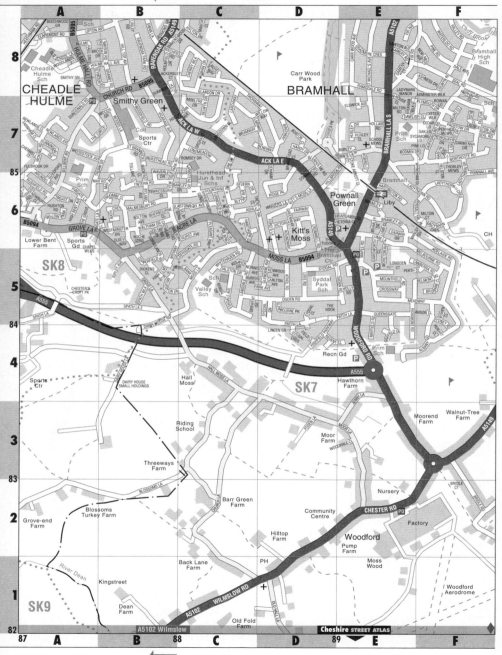

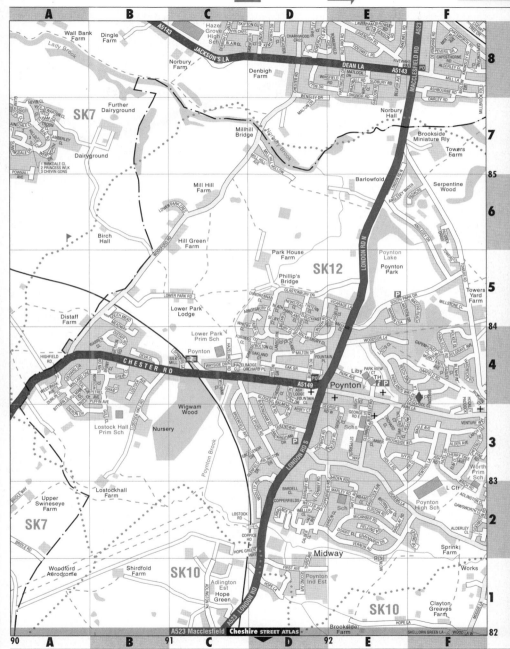

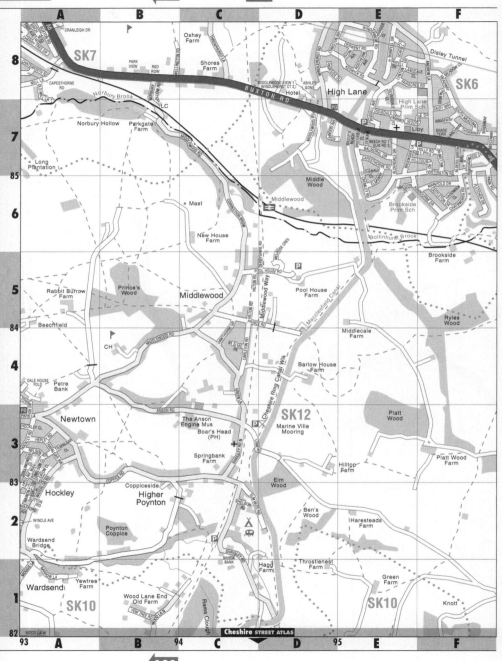

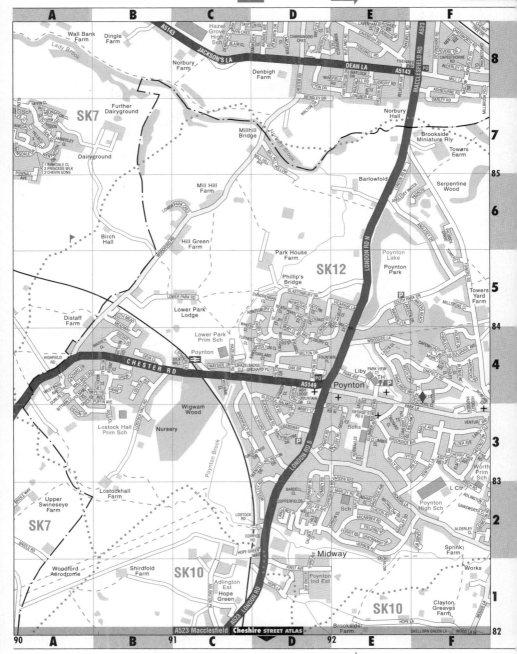

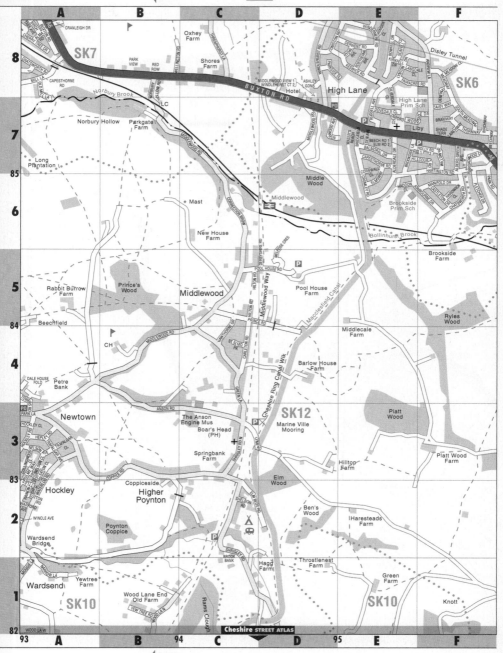

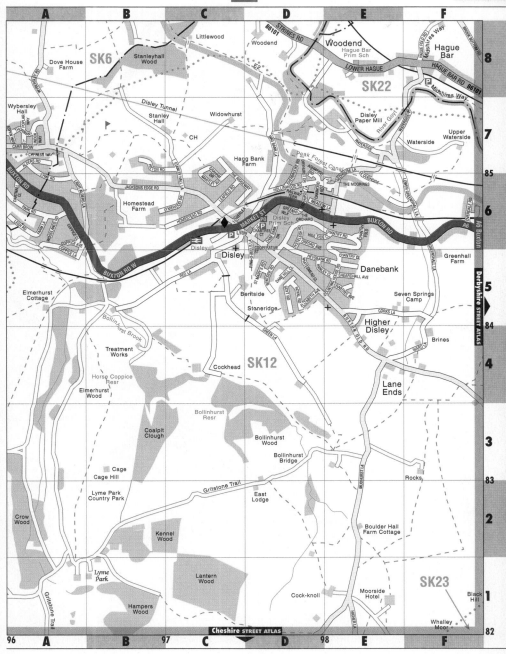

130

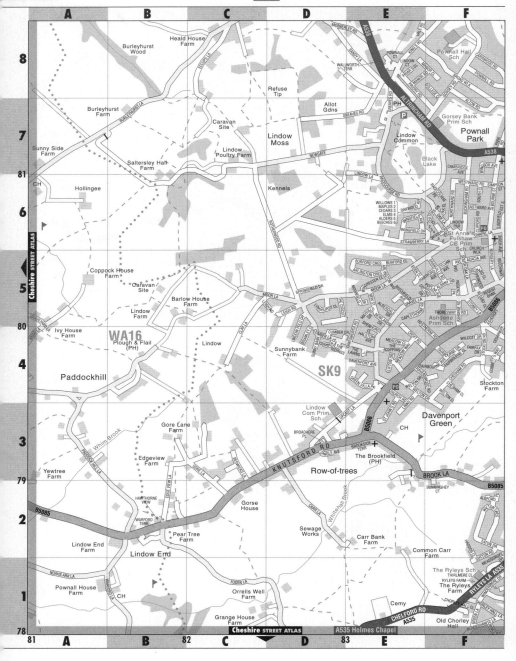

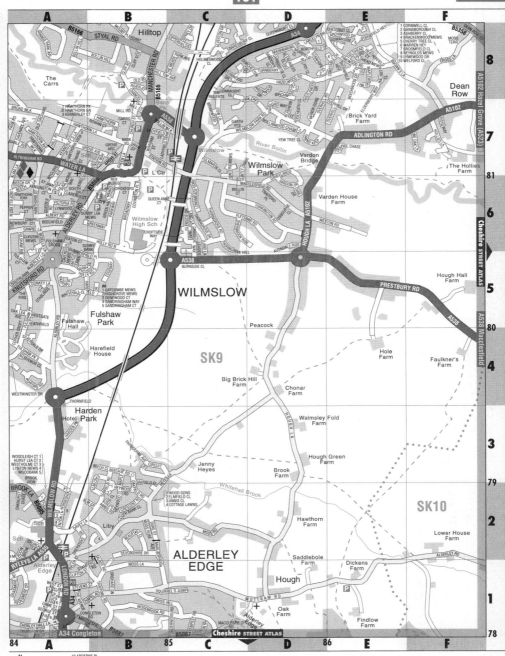

A34

B5166

STYAL RD

Hilltop

The Carrs

MANCHESTER RD

B5166

ALTRINCHAM RD

WATER LA

KNUTSFORD RD

ALDERLEY RD

Wilmslow

Wilmslow Park

Wilmslow High Sch

WILMSLOW

Queen Anne Ct

A6
1 GATCOMBE MEWS
2 HIGHGROVE MEWS
3 DENEWOOD CO
4 SANDRINGHAM WAY
5 SANDRINGHAM CT

Fulshaw Park

Fulshaw Hall

Harefield House

SK9

Thornfield

Harden Park

Hotel

WOODLEIGH CT 1
HURST LEA CT 2
WESTHOLME CT 3
LYNTON MEWS 4
WOODBANK 5
BROOK VIEW

BROOK LA

B5086

WILMSLOW RD

Jenny Heyes

Liby

Sch

Sch

RYLEYS LA A538

Alderley Edge

LONDON RD

A34

ALDERLEY EDGE

CHORLEY HALL

A34 Congleton

B5087

B5087

Dean Row

A5102

Adlington Rd

The Hollies Farm

Brick Yard Farm

Vardon Bridge

Varden House Farm

HOUGH LA

A5102

WESTON RD

Hough Hall Farm

PRESTBURY RD

A538

Faulkner's Farm

Hole Farm

Peacock

Big Brick Hill Farm

Chonar Farm

Walmsley Fold Farm

HOUGH LA

Hough Green Farm

Brook Farm

Whitehall Brook

Hawthorn Farm

SK10

Lower House Farm

Saddlebole Farm

Dickens Farm

Hough

ALDERLEY RD

MOTTRAM RD

Oak Farm

Findlow Farm

Alderley Edge

MACCLESFIELD RD

River Bollin

Cheshire STREET ATLAS

A5102 Hazel Grove (A523)

Cheshire STREET ATLAS

A538 Macclesfield

8
7
81
6
5
80
4
3
79
2
1
78

84 85 86

A B C D E F

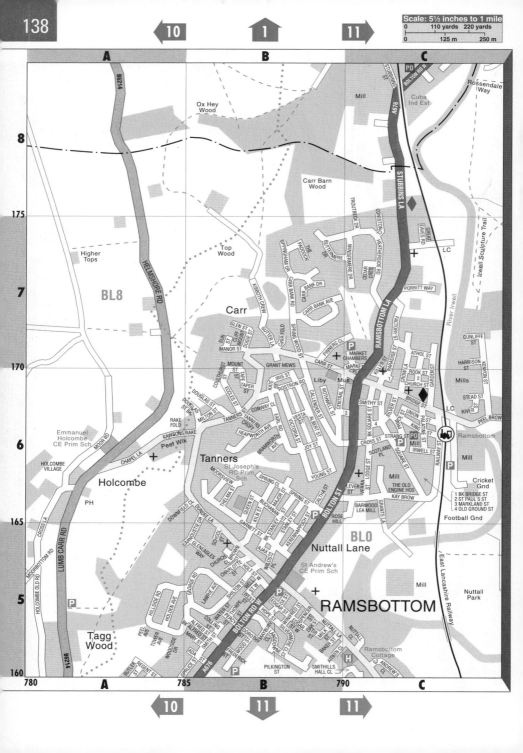

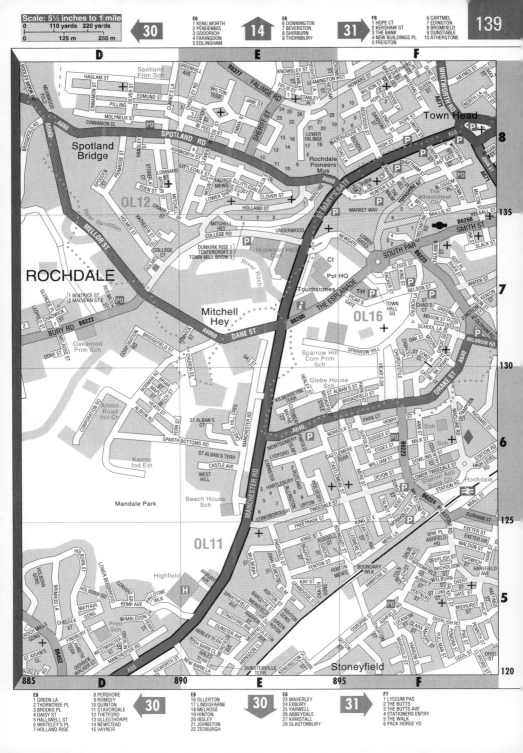

27   27

Scale: 5½ inches to 1 mile
0   110 yards   220 yards
0   125 m   250 m

D   **E**   **F**

THE WOODLANDS
Woodbank Prim Sch
GRANTHAM
BRANDLE WORCESTER AVE
STAFFORD
B6214
4
PROSPECT TERR
LICHFIELD DR
CANTERBURY DR
WOODHILL RD
AVONDALE AVE
MARQUIS ST
VICTORIA AVE
ATHLONE AVE
ARGYLE ST
BK CLIFTON ST
HAMILTON ST
A56
PORTER ST
RAKE ST
BK RAKE ST
St John's CE Prim Sch
BK DENTON ST
DENTON ST
LOUIS AVE
FERNHILL CARAVAN PK
BK ANNE'S ST
HANSON ST
ANNE'S ST
CHESHAM RD
HILTON ST
B6221
Fernhill
Fernhills Bsns Ctr
REGENT ST
BK CANNING ST
CANNING ST
VERNON ST
BK VERNON ST
CATEATON ST
BK CATEATON ST
BIRCH ST
BK BIRCH ST
WALMERSLEY RD
PETER ST
TOPPING ST
FOX ST
Woodhill
B6213
BRANDLESHOLME RD
CROSTONS RD
Works
BL8
Woodhill Works
River Irwell
Irwell Sculpture Trail
GORTON ST
Peel Ind Est
East Lancashire Rly
PARK RD
115
Woodhill Fold
Peel Mills
Woodfields
Woodfields
BURY
BARCROFT RD
MARSDEN ST
BRUNSWICK
BUCKLEY ST
3
WEBB ST
BK CROSTONS RD
Bury Ground
CHAMBERHALL ST
BL9
Works
Woodfields Ret Pk
Moorgate Ret Pk
THE ROCK
BARLOW ST
B6222
110
WOOD ST
A58 BOLTON RD
CARLYLE ST
TANPITS RD
PEEL WAY
SCHOOL BROW
BK PARSONS LA
PARSON ST
THE ROCK
BUTCHER LA
ROCHDALE RD
A58
DERBY ST
Bury Transport Mus
CASTLECROFT MEWS
SANKEY ST
BOLTON ST
CASTLE
THE WYLDE
SOUTH BACK ROCK
NORTH ROCK
SOUTH BACK ROCK
CLERKE ST
CROSS ST
A56
Angouleme Ret Pk
GEORGE ST
FOUNDRY ST
2
MILLETT ST
JUBILEE WAY
BK MILLETT ST
DOCTORS FOLD
PHOENIX ST
IRWELL ST
LOWER BANK ST
Bury Bolton Street
COOPER
PARKS YD
BROAD ST
MARKET ST
UNION ST
EDWIN ST
MILL GATE
MINDEN PAR
MARKET PAR
Kay Garden
Mkt Hall
Mkt
Supermarket
SOUTH CROSS ST
Albion Mill Ind Est
BROOKSMOUTH
Bury Gram Jun Sch
WALSHE
Ct
Pol HQ
REGENCY CHAMBERS
BK PHOENIX ST
BANK ST
BK MARY'S PL
ST MARY'S PL
MOSS ST
Liby Art Gall Mus
PRINCESS PAR
BURY INT
Holy Trinity Prim Sch
SPRING ST
BK SPRING ST E
Tentersfield
TENTERDEN ST
BK SANKEY ST 1
TENTERS ST 2
BK TENTERDEN ST 3
BK TENTERDEN
BK KNOWSLEY ST
HINTWATERSET
HILTON RD
Bury
ANGOULEME WAY
B6218
CECIL ST
FRANK ST
EAST ST
TOWNSIDE ROW
B6213
1
Bury Gram Sch
Irwell Sculpture Trail
BRIDGE RD
Buckley Wells LC
BELLE VUE TERR
MAUDSLEY ST
HOUGHTON ST
BARON
TH
GLENMORE ST
THE SIDINGS
Bury Coll (Woodbury Ctr)
ASHLOR
St Marie's RC Prim Sch
TOWN FIELDS CL
MAXSIDE ROW
MOSS ROW
PARKSIDE WLK
The Sawmill
BROCKLEHURST RD
PARKHILLS RD
St Gabriel's RC High Sch
Buckley Wells
MANCHESTER OLD RD
BARKER ST
BK MANCHESTER OLD RD
BK WELLS ST
WELLS TERR
BRADFORD TERR
MANCHESTER RD
A56
PARLIAMENT ST
SOUTH BANK
WESTMINSTER AVE
WESTGATE AVE
Bury Coll (Peel Ctr)
Bury Coll (Millenium Ctr)
MARKET ST
TOWN HALL WAY
Playing Field
WELLINGTON RD
PILOT ST
B6219

100
795   **D**   800   **E**   805   **F**

44

E2			F3		F4		F4
1 BK BOLTON ST S	2 GEORGIANA ST		1 BK CATEATON ST	8 POWELL CT	1 BK CLIFTON ST		8 BK ROSE BANK
2 BK BROAD ST	3 MARGARET ST		2 CATEATON ST	9 BADGER ST	2 BK PORTER ST		9 BK HILTON ST
3 BK MARKET ST W	4 BK FRANK ST		3 RICHARD BURCH ST		3 BK REGENT ST		10 RUTH ST
4 BK MARKET ST	F2		4 BK HORNBY ST W		4 BK RAVEN ST		11 ST MARK'S SQ
5 BK MANCHESTER RD	1 SOUTH BACK ROCK		5 CHARLES ST		5 RUSSELL ST		12 NEW VERNON ST
F1	2 BEDLAM GN		6 WASHINGTON CT		6 BK HAMILTON ST		
1 BK GEORGIANA ST W	3 TITHEBARN ST		7 BK MOORGATE		7 BK ST ANNE'S ST		

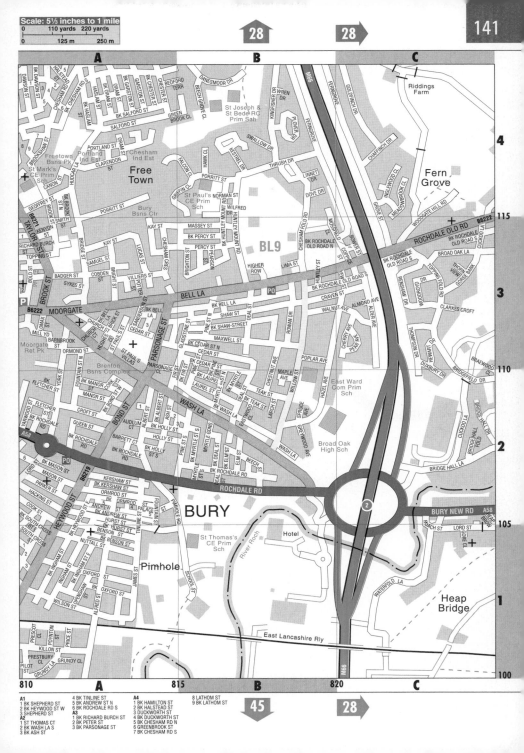

23 24

A **B** **C**

4

St Peter
Smithills
Dean
CE Prim Sch

Smithill's
Hall
(Mus)

Smithills
Country Park

Smithills
Sch

North Bolton
Sixth Form
Coll

115

BRYN LEA
TERR

Victoria Lake

BARROW BRIDGE RD

LIGHTBOUNDS RD

LIMEFIELD D
LIMEFIELD RD
REDCAR RD
JESMOND RD
MYTTON RD
ABERCORN RD
SMITHILLS DEAN RD

Smithills

NEW
SPRINGS

SMITHILLS CROFT RD
WHISTERS HOLLOW
WOODBURN DR
LONGHIRST
LINWOOD
SCHOFIELD DR
ASHINGTON

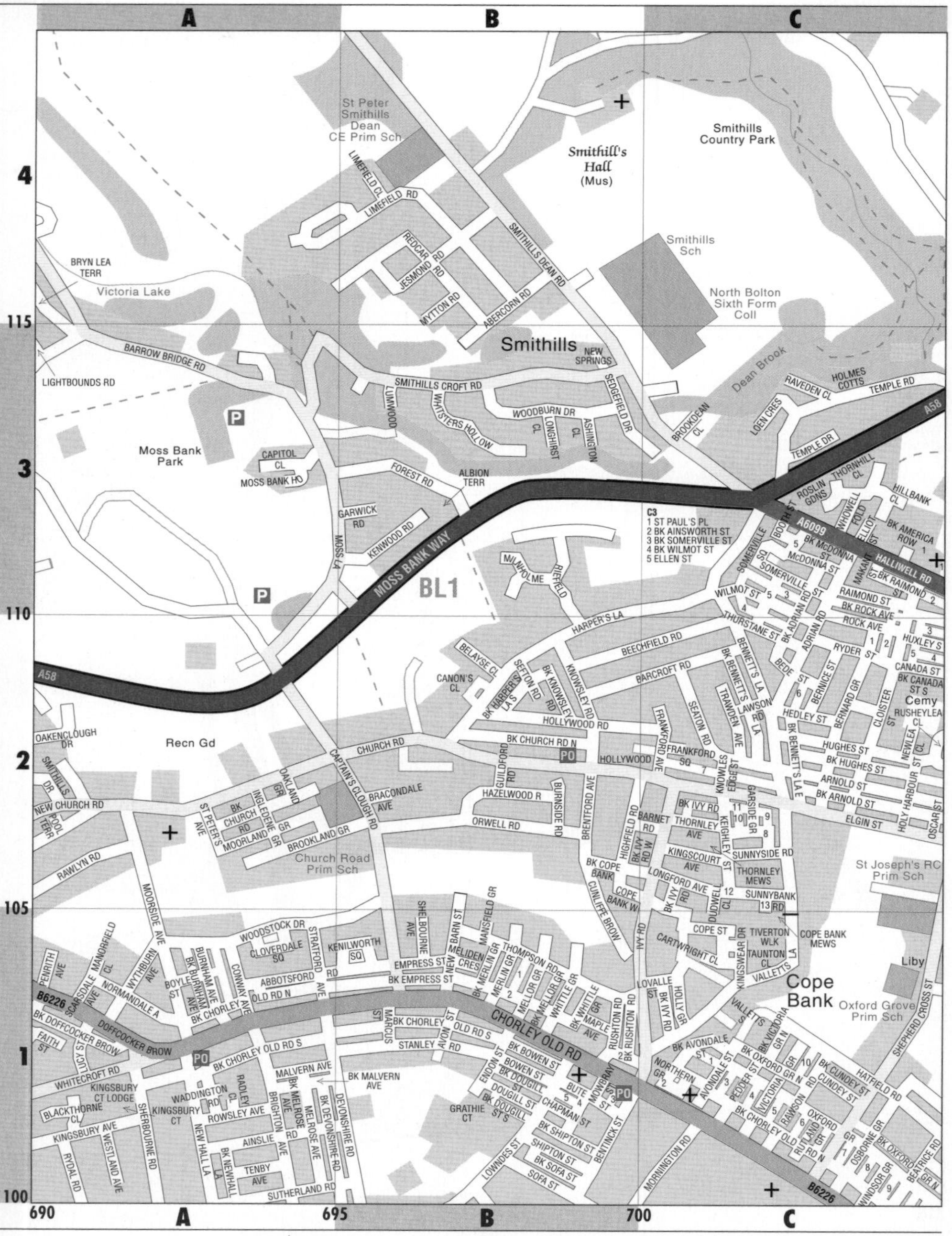

Dean Brook

RAVEDEN CL
LOEN CRES
HOLMES
COTTS
TEMPLE RD

A58

3

Moss Bank
Park

P

CAPITOL
CL

MOSS BANK HO

FOREST RD

ALBION
TERR

BROOKDEAN
CL

TEMPLE DR

C3
1 ST PAUL'S PL
2 BK AINSWORTH ST
3 BK SOMERVILLE ST
4 BK WILMOT ST
5 ELLEN ST

ROSLIN
GDNS
THORNHILL
HILLBANK

A6099

BK AMERICA
ROW

GARWICK
DR

KENWOOD RD

MOSS LA

P

MOSS BANK WAY

BL1

110

A58

MILLWPLME

PURSFIELD

BELAYSE CL
CANON'S
CL

HARPER'S LA

BEECHFIELD RD

SEFTON RD
BK BARNES ST
KNOWLSEY RD
BARCROFT RD
BENNETT'S LA
BK BENNETT'S
ST
TRANTOR AVE

THURSTANE ST
BK ADRIAN ST
BK RAIMOND ST
WILMOT ST
SOMERVILLE ST
MCDONNA ST
BK MCDONNA
RAIMOND ST
BK ROCK AVE
ROCK AVE
HALLIWELL RD
HUXLEY S
BK CANADA
ST S
Cemy
RUSHEYLEA

2

OAKENCLOUGH
DR

Recn Gd

SMITHILLS
DEAN RD

NEW CHURCH RD

RAWLYN RD

BK
CHURCH
RD
ST PETER'S
AVE

MOORLAND GR

INGLEDENE

OAKLAND

CAPTAIN'S CLOUGH RD

BRACONDALE
AVE

BROOKLAND GR

CHURCH RD

Church Road
Prim Sch

HAZELWOOD R

ORWELL RD

GUILFORD

BRENTFORD AVE

BURNSIDE AVE

BK CHURCH RD N

HOLLYWOOD

FRANKFORD

FRANKFORD AVE

SEATON ST

HOLLYWOOD

HEDLEY ST

P

PO

BK CHURCH RD N
BK IVY RD
THORNLEY
AVE
KINGSCOURT
AVE
SUNNYSIDE RD
HIGHFIELD RD
BARNET
GARSIDE GR
KEIGHLEY
BK BENNETT'S LA
HUGHES ST
BK HUGHES
ARNOLD ST
BK ARNOLD ST
ELGIN ST

St Joseph's RC
Prim Sch

105

PERITH
AVE
NORMANDALE A
MANORFIELD
ROSEDALE AVE

BK DOFFCOCKER
WHITECROFT RD
FAITH ST
DOFFCOCKER BROW
B6226

PO

BURNHAM AVE
BK BURNHAM
CONWAY AVE
BK CHORLEY OLD RD N
ABBOTSFORD
BOYLE ST
CLOVERDALE GR
STRATFORD
WOODSTOCK DR

MOORSIDE AVE

KENILWORTH
SQ

MELROSE
AVE
AINSLIE
TENBY
AVE

STANLEY AVE
BK CHORLEY
OLD RD S
MARCUS ST
MANSFIELD GR
MELIDEN
CRES
BK EMPRESS ST
THOMPSON RD
MELLOR GR
MERLIN GR
WHITTLE ST
MAPLE

CHORLEY OLD RD

MALVERN AVE
BK MALVERN
AVE
EASSON
BOWEN ST
DOUGILL ST S
BUTE ST
CHAPMAN ST
SHIPTON ST
BENTINCK ST
LOWNDES
SOFA ST

RUSHTON RD
BK IVY RD
LOVALLE
KINGSWAY
GUNLIFFE BROW
BK COPE
BANK
COPE
BANK W
COPE ST
CARTWRIGHT CL
IVY RD
DUDWELL
TAUNTON
SUNNYBANK
THORNLEY
MEWS
12
SUNNYSIDE RD
13 RD
TIVERTON
WLK
COPE BANK
MEWS

Cope
Bank

AVONDALE
NORTHERN
BK OXFORD GR N
VALLETS
SHEPHERD CROSS ST

Oxford Grove
Prim Sch

Liby

1

KINGSBURY
CT LODGE
KINGSBURY
CT
BLACKTHORNE
CL
KINGSBURY AVE
RYDAL RD
WESTLAND AVE
PYTHA RD
WADDINGTON
RD
ROWSLEY AVE
NEW HALL LA
DEVONSHIRE RD
BRIGHTON
GRATHIE
CT
DOUGILL ST S
CHAPMAN ST
MORNINGTON RD

B6226

BK CHORLEY
OLD RD N
VICTORIA ST
BK OXFORD GR N
OXFORD

100

690 **A** 695 **B** 700 **C**

23 144

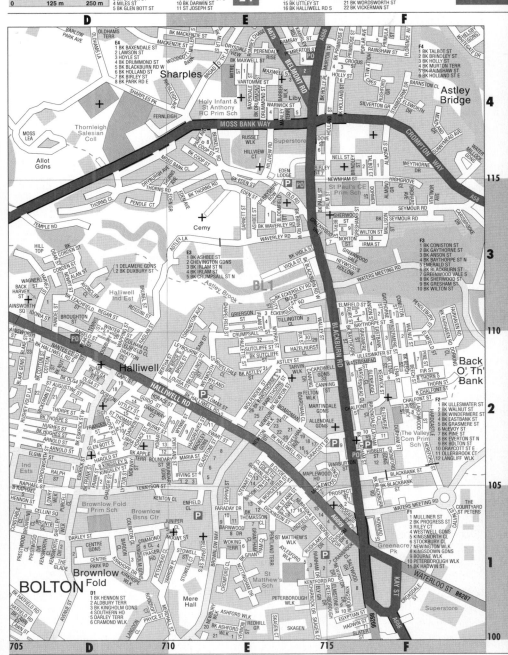

Scale: 5⅓ inches to 1 mile
0   110 yards   220 yards
0   125 m   250 m

D2
1 BK ESKRICK ST
2 BK CHAUCER ST
3 BK LYTTON ST
4 MILES ST
5 BK GLEN BOTT ST

6 BK ESKRICK ST E
7 BK FRANCES ST
8 BK GROVE ST
9 BK ST THOMAS ST E
10 BK DARWIN ST
11 ST JOSEPH ST

24

D2
12 BK BOUNDARY ST
13 HALLIWELL ST
14 BK HAYDN ST
15 BK UTTLEY ST
16 BK HALLIWELL RD S

17 BK ST AUGUSTINE ST
18 BK ESKRICK ST S
19 BK CARL ST
20 BK WAPPING ST
21 BK WORDSWORTH ST
22 BK VICKERMAN ST

23 RUSHEY FOLD CT
24 BK AINSWORTH ST

E4
1 BK BAXENDALE ST
2 LAWSON ST
3 HOYLE ST
4 BK DRUMMOND ST
5 BK BLACKBURN RD W
6 BK HOLLAND ST
7 BK BIRLEY ST
8 BK PARK RD E

'1 DELAMERE GDNS
'2 BK DUXBURY ST

E3
1 BK ASHBEE ST
2 CHEVINGTON GDNS
3 BK IRLAM ST N
4 BK IRLAM ST
5 BK CRUMPSALL ST N

F4
1 BK TALBOT ST
2 BK BRINDLEY ST
3 BK HOLLY ST
4 BK MURTON TERR
5 BK RAINSHAW ST
6 BK HOLLAND ST E

F3
1 BK CONISTON ST
2 BK GAYTHORNE ST
3 BK ANSON ST
4 BK BAYTHORPE ST
5 EMERALD ST
6 BK BLACKBURN ST
7 GREENWOOD VALE S
8 BK SHERWOOD ST
9 BK GRESHAM ST
10 BK WILTON ST

F2
1 BK ULLESWATER ST
2 BK WALNUT ST
3 BK WINDERMERE ST
4 BK EASTBANK ST
5 BK GRASMERE ST
6 McEVOY ST
7 BK PINE ST
8 BK EVERTON ST N
9 BK BOLTON ST
10 DRAYCOTT ST E
11 OLLERBROOK CT
12 LANGLIFF WLK

F1
1 MULLINER ST
2 BK PROGRESS ST
3 RILEY CT
4 WESTWELL GDNS
5 KINGSNORTH CL
6 STOCKBURY CL
7 NEWINGTON WLK
8 KINGSDOWN GDNS
9 BOURNE WLK
10 PETERBOROUGH WLK
11 BK HADWIN ST

D1
1 BK HENNON ST
2 ALDBURY TERR
3 BK KINGHOLM GDNS
4 SOUTHERN HO
5 DARLEY TERR
6 CRAMOND WLK

E1
1 MIDHURST CL
2 RAINHAM GR
3 WOODCHURCH CL
4 WESTMARSH CL
5 MOUNTFIELD WLK
6 BK WOKING GDNS
7 THOMASSON CL

8 ST MATTHEW'S TER
9 FOSTER TERR
10 BARNWOOD CL
11 BARNWOOD CL
12 DICKINSON TER
13 DICKINSON CL
14 HIGHBROOK GR
15 FERNHURST GR

16 GLENTHORNE CL
17 BK NEVADA ST
18 NEVADA ST
19 WORCESTER ST
20 SHAFTSBURY CL
21 FARNHAM CL

E2
1 IRVING HOUSE

2 KEATS WLK
3 TENNYSON WLK
4 BELGRAVE ST
5 BELGRAVE GDNS
6 GLADSTONE CL
7 LONGTOWN GDNS
8 WHITCHURCH GDNS
9 BK HARGREAVES ST

10 BK WYNNE ST
11 BK EWART ST
12 MARSH ST
13 BK STEWART ST
14 BOSTON ST
15 WITNEY CL
16 WATFORD CL
17 WESTWICK TERR

25

18 BENWICK TERR
19 YORK TERR
20 CHESTER WLK
21 HUNTINGDON WLK
22 LANCASTER WLK
23 NEWTON TERR
24 LANCASTER TERR
25 KEMPSTON GDNS

26 WOLFENDEN TERR
27 TANWORTH WLK
28 CHARLOTTE ST
29 HOLYHURST WLK
30 PINEWOOD CL
31 BK WALSHAW ST
32 BK CRUMPSALL ST
33 BK CARDWELL ST

Scale: 5⅓ inches to 1 mile

| 0 | 110 yards | 220 yards |
| 0 | 125 m | 250 m |

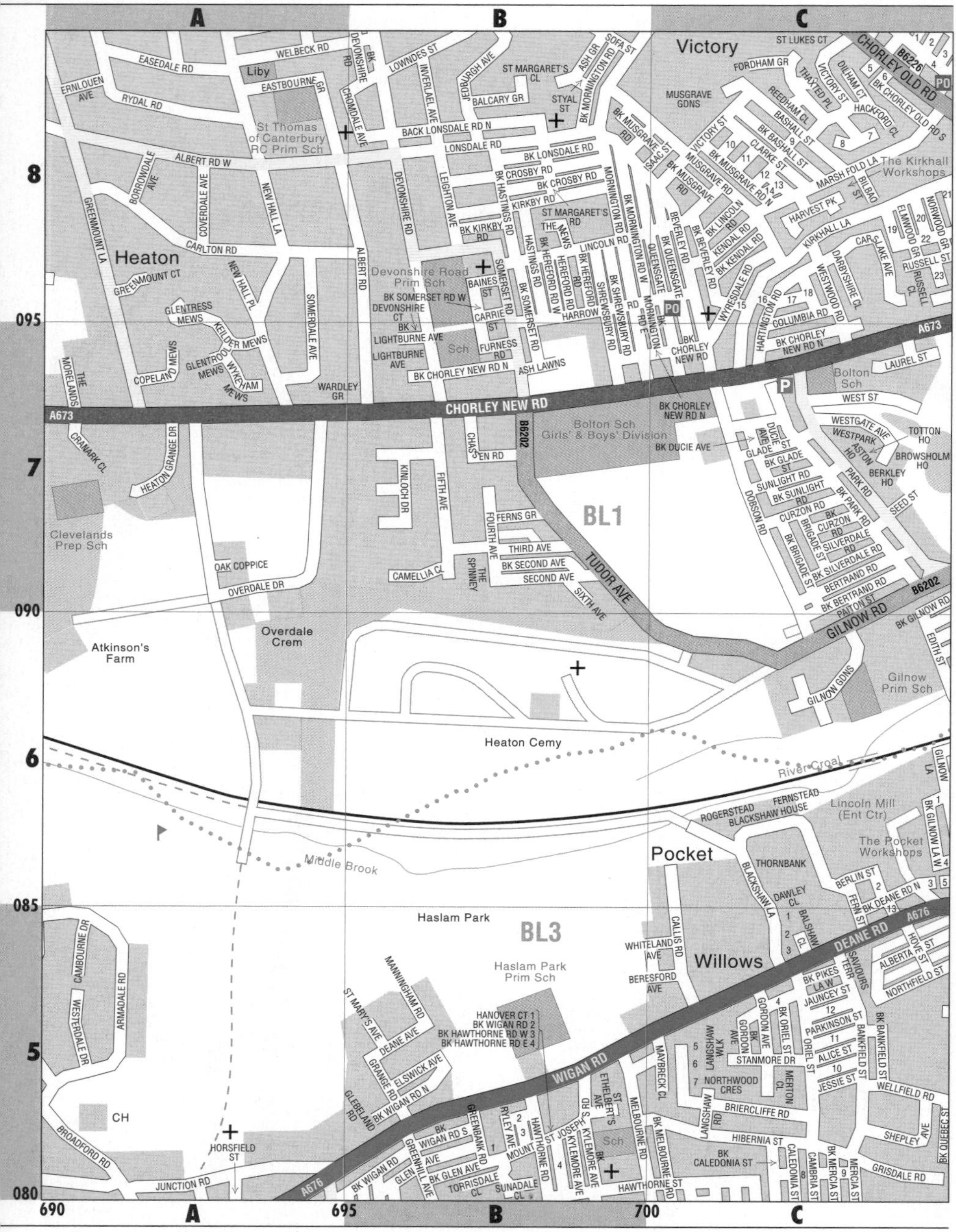

Grid labels

A · B · C

8 · 095 · 7 · 090 · 6 · 085 · 5 · 080

690 · A · 695 · B · 700 · C

Map labels

Victory · St Lukes Ct · CHORLEY OLD RD · PO

Heaton · Liby · St Thomas of Canterbury RC Prim Sch · Devonshire Road Prim Sch

The Kirkhall Workshops

Bolton Sch

Clevelands Prep Sch · Heaton Grange Dr

BL1

Bolton Sch Girls' & Boys' Division

Atkinson's Farm · Overdale Crem

Gilnow Prim Sch

Heaton Cemy · River Croal · Lincoln Mill (Ent Ctr) · The Pocket Workshops

Middle Brook · Pocket

Haslam Park · BL3 · Willows

Haslam Park Prim Sch

CH · Horsfield St

CHORLEY NEW RD · A673

TUDOR AVE · GILNOW RD · B6202

WIGAN RD · A676 · DEANE RD

Street index (bottom)

C5
1 TORBAY CL
2 BLACKSHAW ROW
3 LANGLEY DR
4 BK DEANE RD
5 HEARLESDEN CRES
6 NEASDEN GR
7 COLINDALE CL
8 CAMBRIA SQ
9 NORTHUMBRIA ST
10 BK ALICE ST
11 BK PARKINSON ST
12 BK JAUNCEY ST
13 HOVE ST N

C6
1 BK VINE ST
2 BK FERN ST E
3 WASHINGTON ST
4 RYLEY ST
5 BK GILNOW LA

C8
1 BK BATTENBERG RD
2 BATTENBERG RD
3 BK WALDECK ST
4 BK CHORLEY OLD RD N
5 MOORE'S ST
6 TURK ST
7 CAVENHAM GR
8 METFIELD PL
9 MABEL ST
10 BK VICTORY ST E
11 LONGDEN ST
12 BK LONGDEN ST
13 BK CLARKE ST
14 BK MARSH FOLD LA
15 SCORTON ST
16 BK HARTINGTON RD
17 BK COLUMBIA RD
18 BK WESTWOOD RD
19 BK ELMWOOD GR W
20 BK ELMWOOD GR
21 BK NORWOOD GR
22 BK RUSSELL ST
23 BK RUSSELL CL

Scale: 5⅓ inches to 1 mile
0   110 yards   220 yards
0   125 m   250 m

143

148

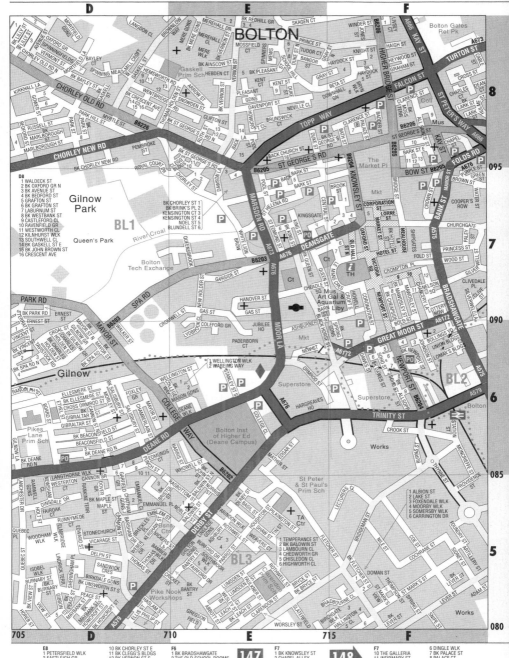

147

148

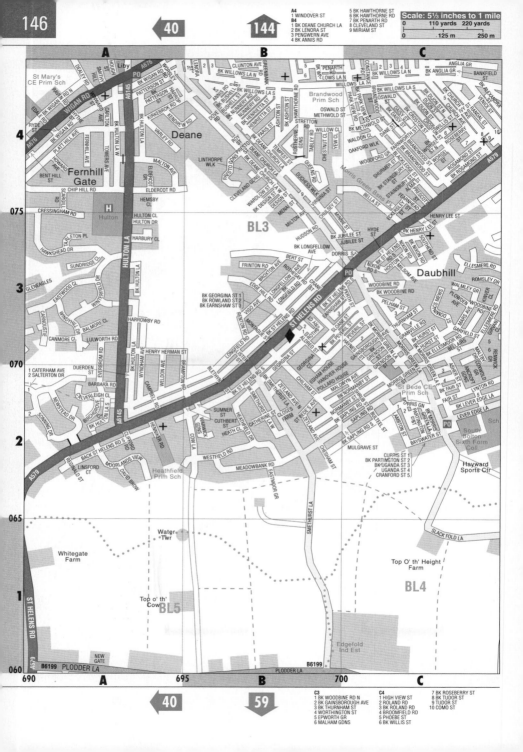

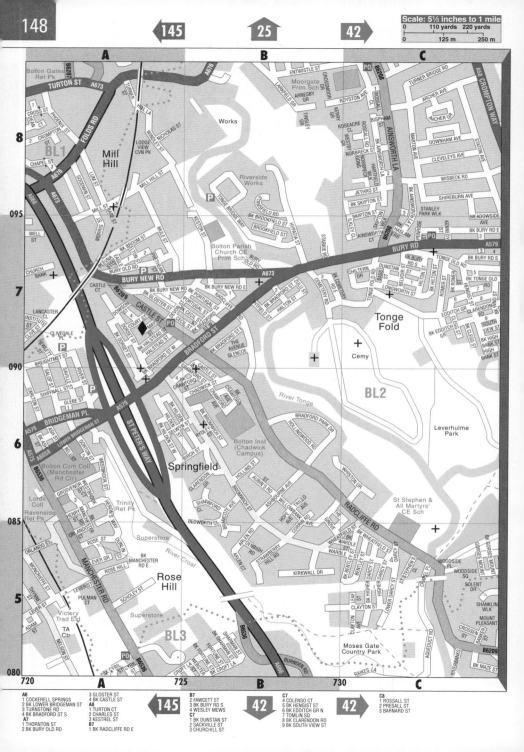

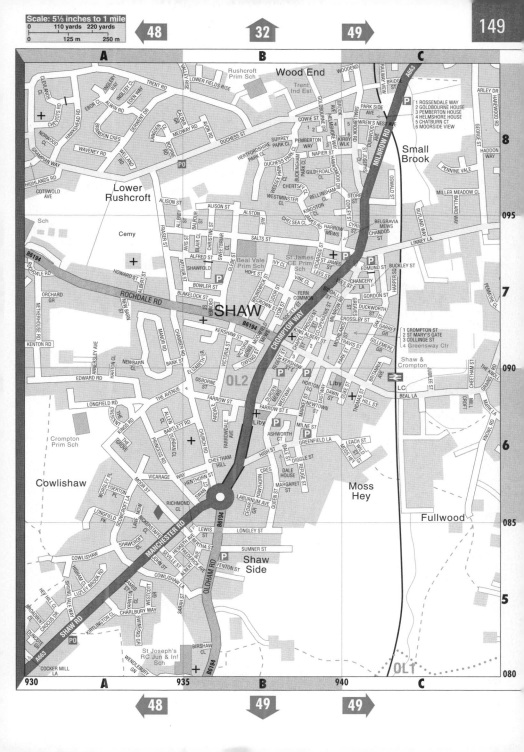

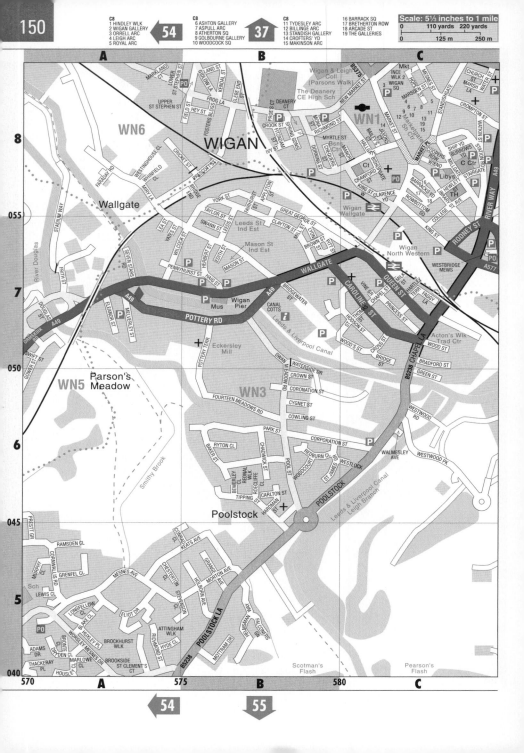

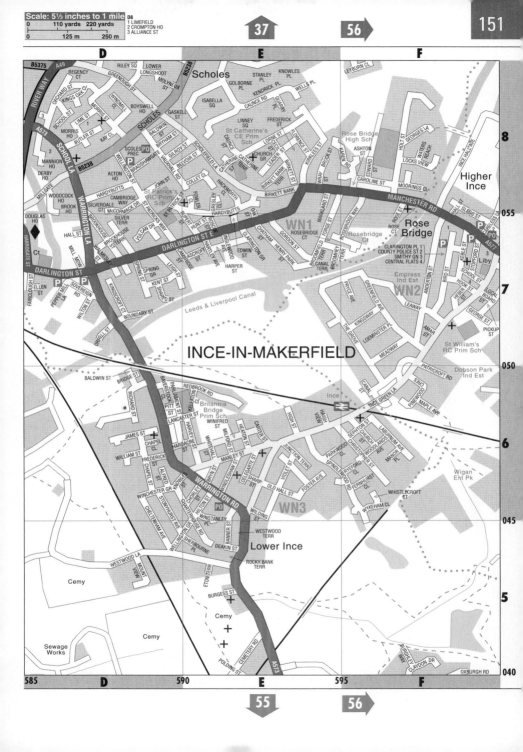

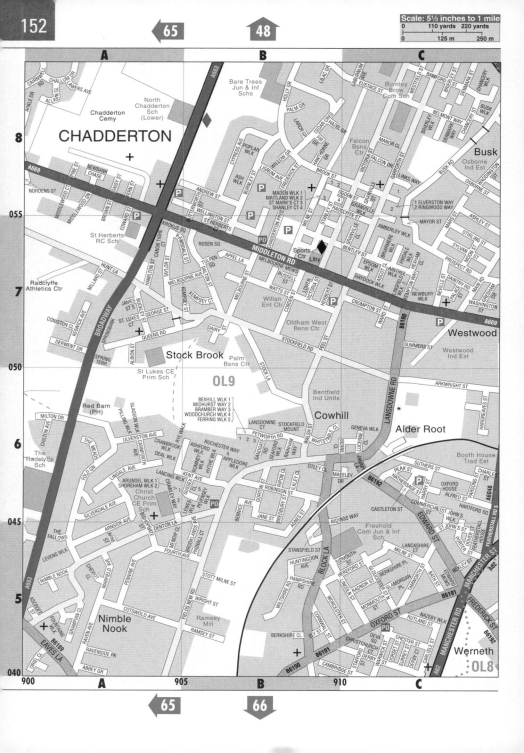

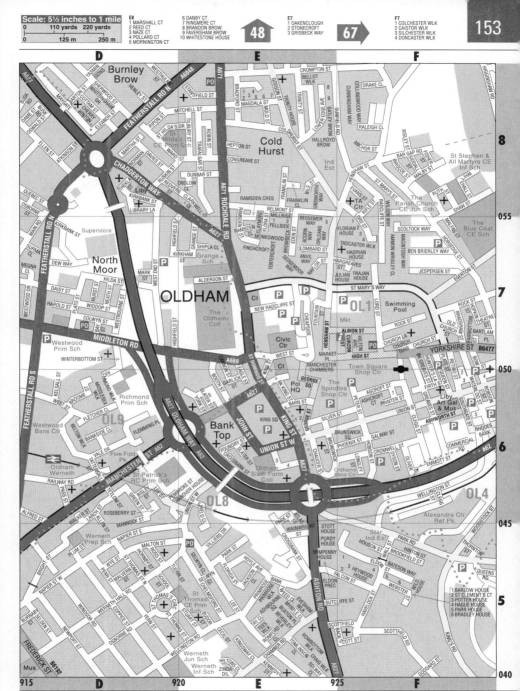

E8
1 MARSHALL CT
2 REED CT
3 NAZE CT
4 POLLARD CT
5 MORNINGTON CT

6 DANBY CT
7 RINGMERE CT
8 BRANDON BROW
9 FAVERSHAM BROW
10 WHITESTONE HOUSE

E7
1 OAKENCLOUGH
2 STONECROFT
3 GRISBECK WAY

F7
1 COLCHESTER WLK
2 CAISTOR WLK
3 SILCHESTER WLK
4 DONCASTER WLK

48

67

E6
1 JACKSON PIT
2 DAVID ST
3 CAVENDISH ST
4 CONNAUGHT ST

66

67

F6
1 HARRISON ST
2 WOOLLACOT ST
3 WALTER ST
4 GREGSON ST
5 MOWBRAY ST

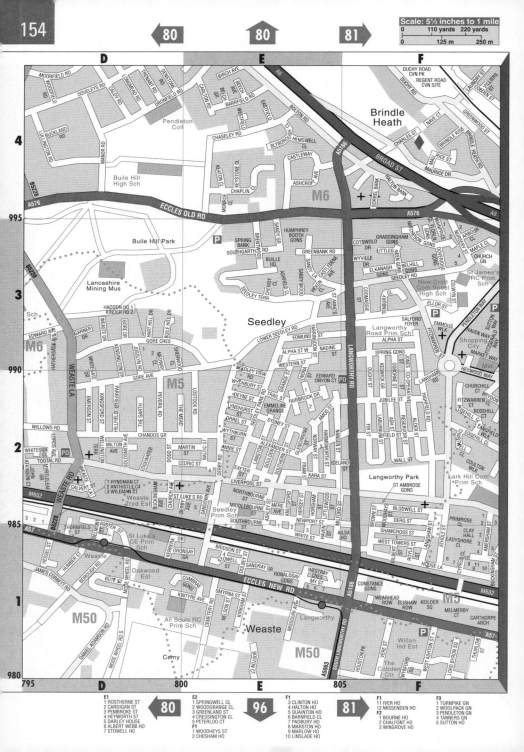

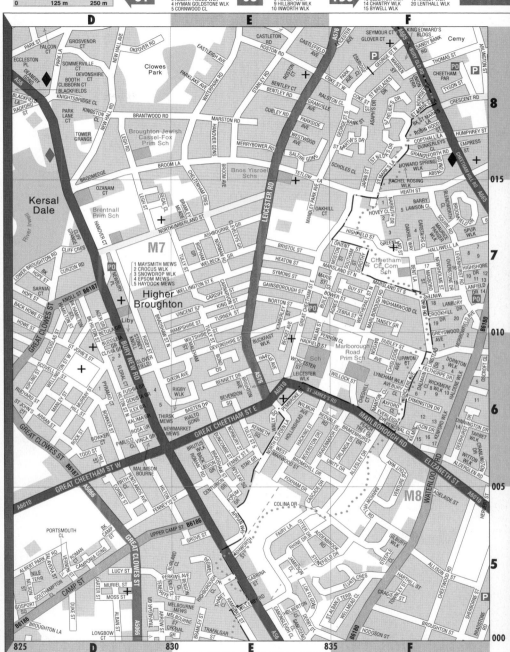

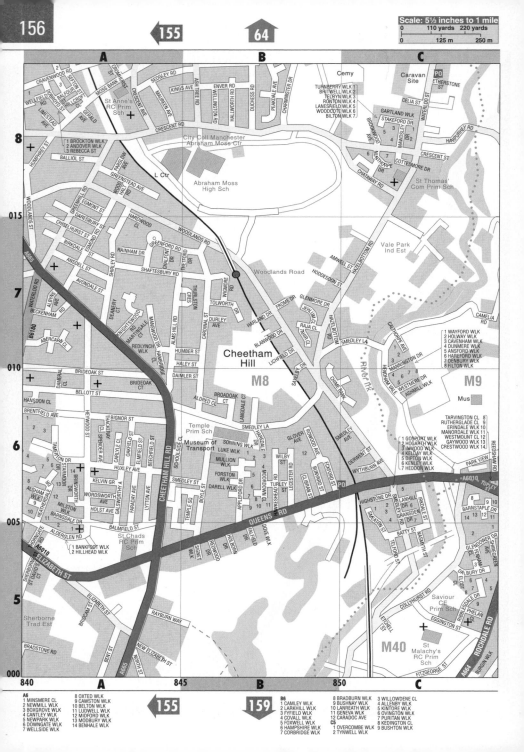

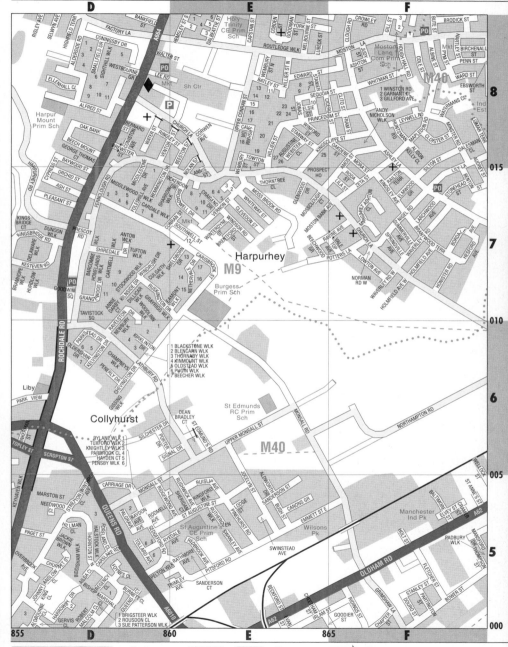

D7
1 BROMWICH DR
2 CLATFORD WLK
3 OAKRIDGE WLK
4 BINDON WLK
5 WATFIELD WLK
6 HOLMFOOT WLK

7 LINSLADE WLK
8 SELWOOD WLK
9 PORTWOOD WLK
10 TREMAIN WLK
11 CALDERBROOK WLK
D8
1 MILLPOOL WLK

2 PATHFIELD WLK
3 MURROW WLK
4 DERVILLE WLK
5 SHAPWICK CL
6 HARROWDENE WLK
7 BRENLEY WLK
8 ROXWELL WLK

9 PORTAL WLK
10 HAYGROVE WLK
11 MAYBROOK WLK
E7
1 WILLOW BANK
2 ORPINGTON RD
3 OSBORNE RD

64

E7
4 ASHGILL WLK
5 GLENPARK WLK
6 DRYGATE WLK
7 BELSYDE WLK
8 NORBET WLK
9 PURTON WLK

83

E7
10 BANKHALL WLK
11 LOWREY WLK
12 DURHAM ST
13 EVANTON WLK
14 MERTON WLK
15 TRONGATE WLK

16 VIEWFIELD WLK
17 FIRDON WLK

Scale: 5½ inches to 1 mile
0 — 110 yards — 220 yards
0 — 125 m — 250 m

E8
1 HERSHAM WLK
2 RADFORD DR
3 MONKWOOD DR
4 LONGDELL WLK
5 ROCKFIELD DR
6 DENESIDE WLK
7 BROWNSON WLK

8 PRIMLEY WLK
9 DARLTON WLK
10 SIMISTER ST
11 THORNSETT CL
12 KINGCOMBE WLK
13 TIPTREE WLK
14 HANSLOPE WLK
15 SWAINSTHORPE DR

160

E8
16 BOOKHAM WLK
17 FARNDALE WLK
18 APPRENTICE CT
19 WADCROFT WLK
20 BRAXTON WLK
21 LODDEN WLK
22 BURNTWOOD WLK

83

E8
23 SALTBURN WLK
24 NAUNTON WLK
25 CROCKER WLK
26 HIGHDOWN WLK
27 ROUNDHAM WLK

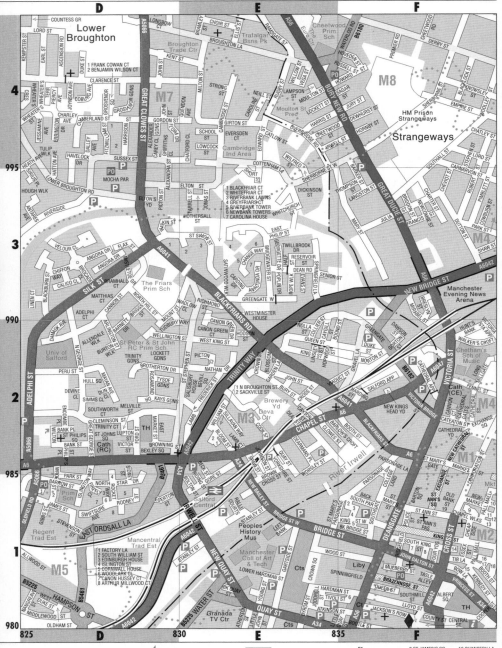

F1
1 BK COLLEGE LAND
2 DUNLOP ST
3 GARDEN LA
4 SMITHY LA
5 BUTTER LA
6 SIDNEY ST
7 BOW ST
8 ST JAMES'S SQ
9 BK POOL FOLD
10 NORFOLK ST
11 KENT ST
12 SUSSEX ST
13 MARSDEN ST
14 TOWN HALL LA
15 CLARENCE ST
16 CHANCERY LA
17 CHANCERY PL
18 BROWN ST
19 HALF MOON ST

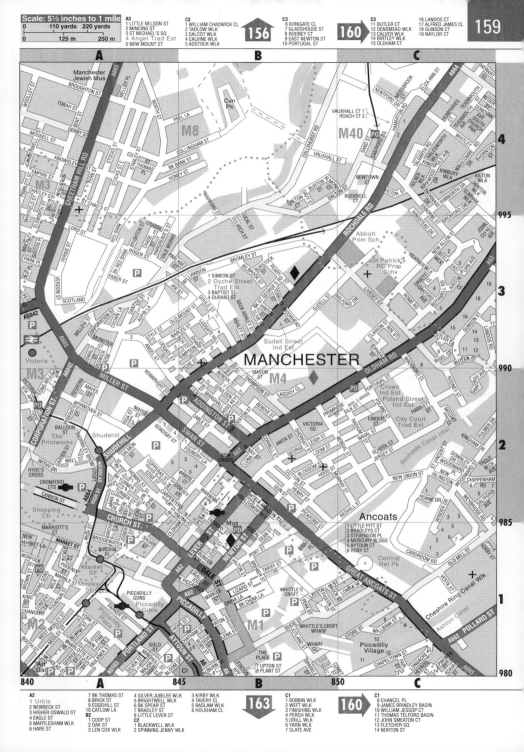

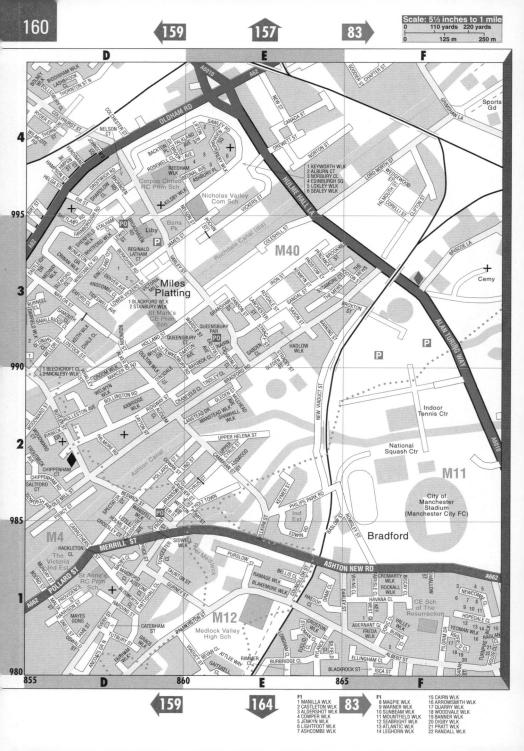

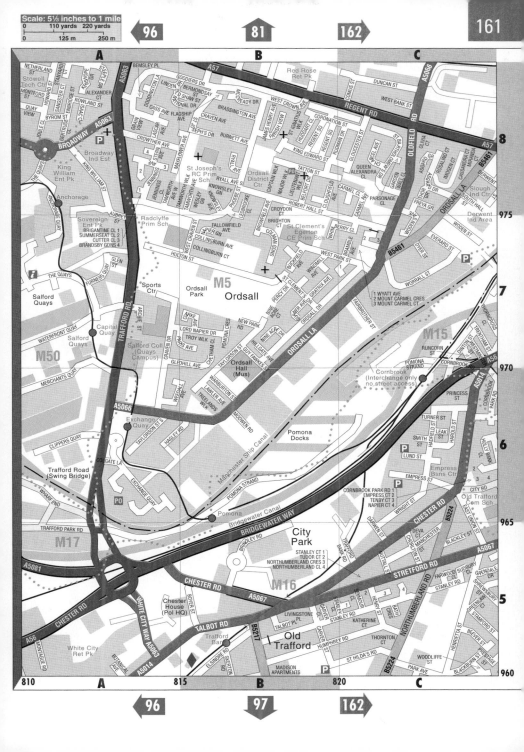

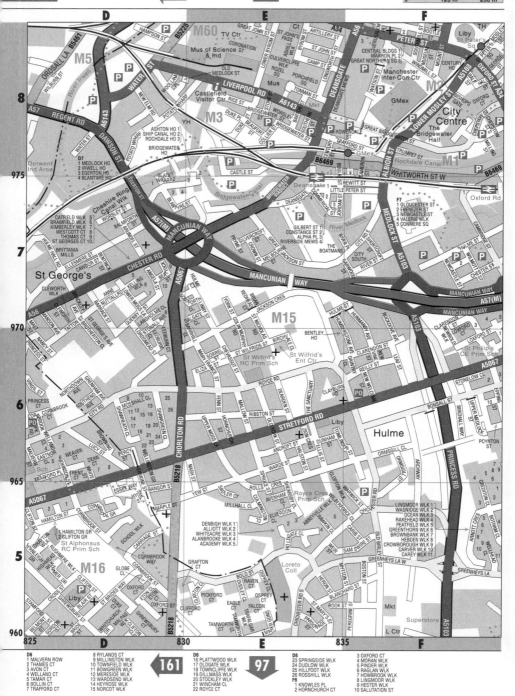

Scale: 5⅓ inches to 1 mile

0   110 yards   220 yards
0   125 m   250 m

D6
1 MALVERN ROW
2 THAMES CT
3 AVON CT
4 WELLAND CT
5 TAMAR CT
6 BOLLIN CT
7 TRAFFORD CT
8 RYLANDS CT
9 MILLINGTON WLK
10 TOWNFIELD WLK
11 BOWGREEN WLK
12 MERESIDE WLK
13 WARDSEND WLK
14 HEYROSE WLK
15 NORCOT WLK

D6
16 PLATTWOOD WLK
17 OLDGATE WLK
18 TOWNCLIFFE WLK
19 DILLMASS WLK
20 STOCKLEY WLK
21 WINCOM CL
22 ROYCE CT

D6
23 SPRINGSIDE WLK
24 DUDLOW WLK
25 HILLFOOT WLK
26 ROSSHILL WLK
F6
1 KNOWLES PL
2 HORNCHURCH CT

3 OXFORD CT
4 MORAN WLK
5 PINDER WLK
6 RAGLAN WLK
7 HOWBROOK WLK
8 LINGMOOR WLK
9 HESTER WLK
10 SALUTATION ST

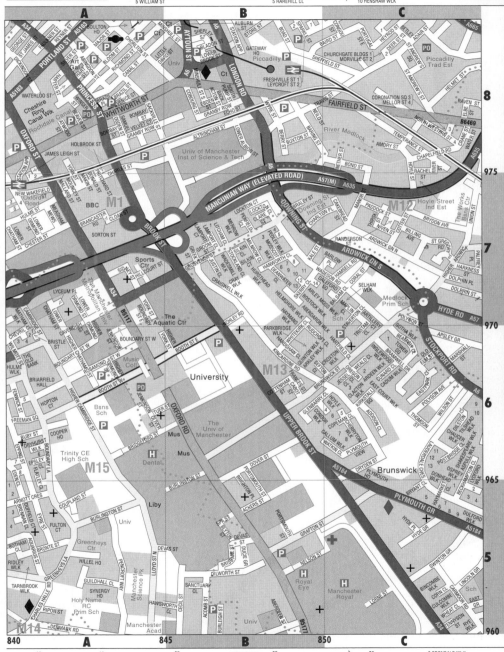

A7
1 CALEY ST
2 WAKEFIELD ST
3 FRANK ST
4 GREAT MARLBOROUGH ST
5 WILLIAM ST

159

B7
1 MANCROFT WLK
2 STATHAM WLK
3 REDMOOR SQ
4 FRANDLEY WLK
5 HAREHILL CL

164

B7
6 EDGEVIEW WLK
7 FULSHAW WLK
8 BLACKHILL CL
9 ELLISBANK WLK
10 HENSHAW WLK

11 BROWNSLOW WLK
12 BANKMILL CL
13 KERFIELD WLK
14 DANEBANK WLK

A5
1 ADMEL SQ
2 HESTER WLK
3 STUDFORTH WLK
4 LONGCRAG WLK

A6
1 CAMBRIDGE HO
2 ELMDALE WLK
3 BROOMWOOD WLK
4 DALESMAN WLK
5 MILLBECK ST
6 MEREDITH CT
7 BRINDLE PL
8 RAIL PL

C5
1 HEATHCLIFFE WLK
2 TORQUAY CL
3 SEVENOAKS WLK
4 WADHURST WLK
5 NAILSWORTH WLK
6 BRIXHAM WLK
7 BEAMINSTER WLK

98

C5
8 WARSTEAD WLK
9 RADLETT WLK

164

C6
1 BELMONT WLK
2 CHAINHURST WLK
3 MALBROOK WLK
4 CUMBRIAN CL
5 LOWNDES WLK
6 ALLERTON WLK
7 HUTTON WLK

8 CRONDALE WLK
9 CONEWOOD WLK
10 JEVINGTON WLK
11 OGBOURNE WLK
12 KINETON WLK
13 MARSHFIELD WLK

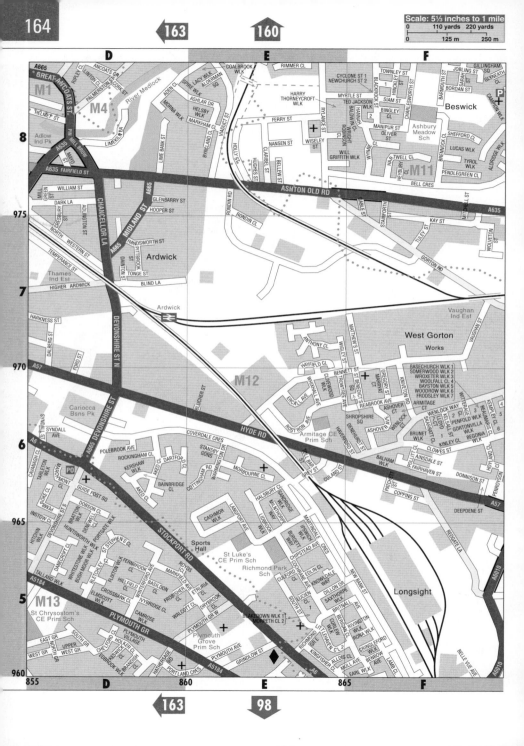

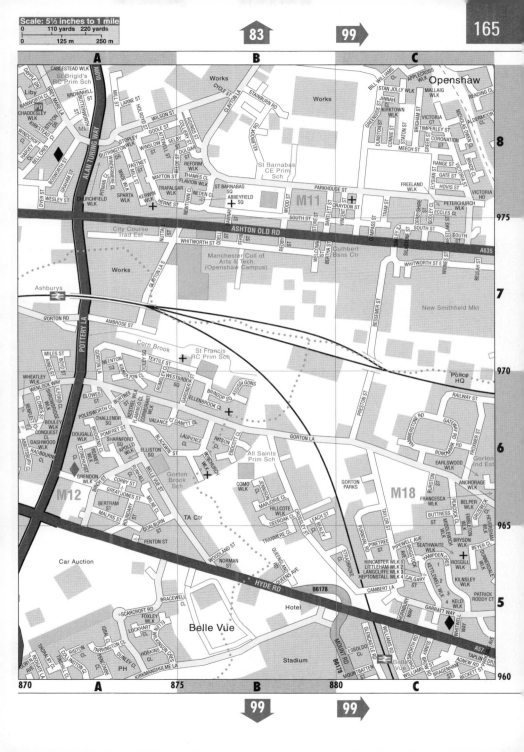

84 85 85

C3
1 FLETCHER ST
2 MULBERRY ST
3 CROSS GLEBE ST
4 ARLINGTON ST
5 SLOANE ST
6 ST MICHAEL'S SQ
7 Stamford Arc
8 OLD SQ

Scale: 5⅓ inches to 1 mile

| 0 | 110 yards | 220 yards |
| 0 | 125 m | 250 m |

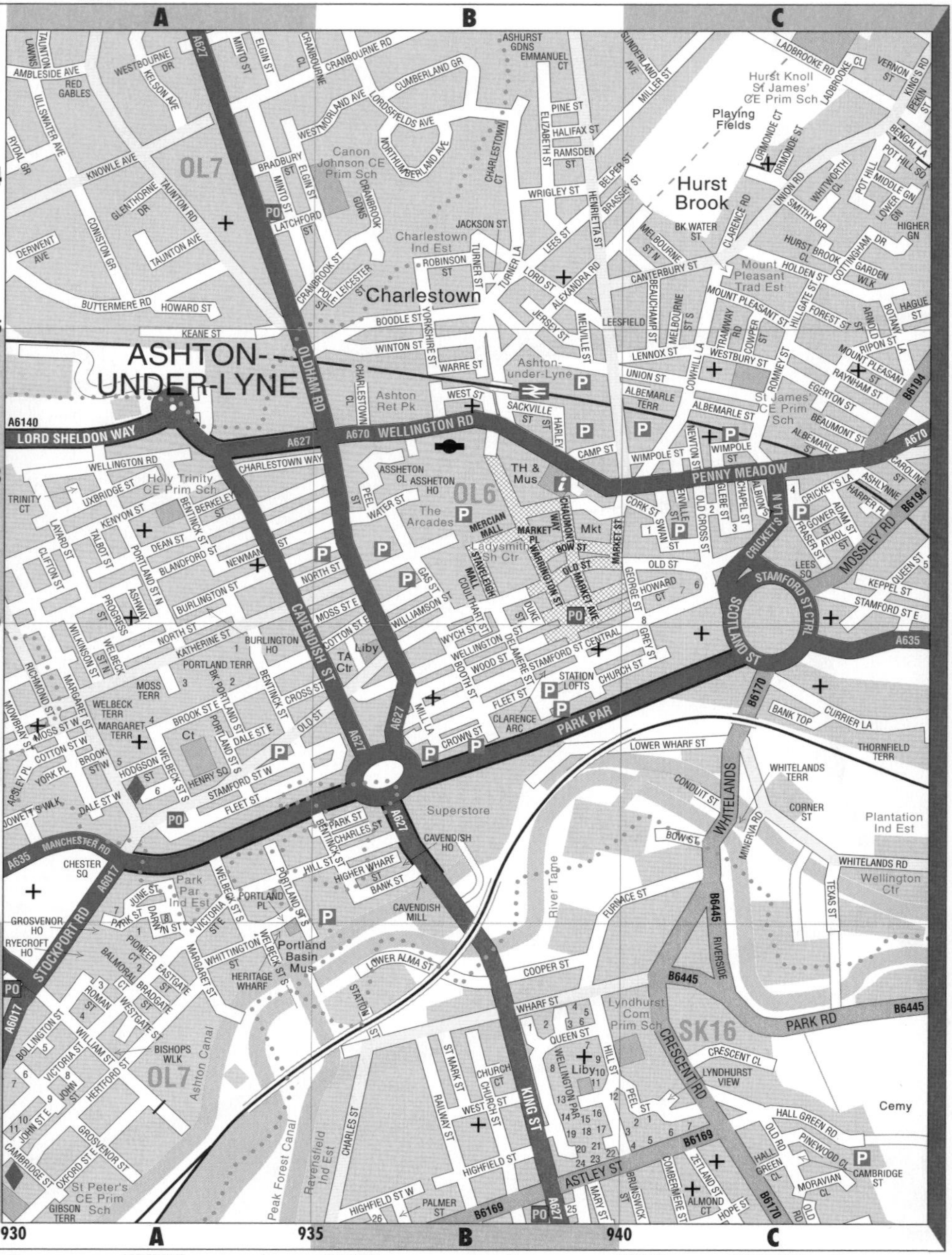

Map labels

OL7
ASHTON-UNDER-LYNE
Charlestown
Hurst Brook
Canon Johnson CE Prim Sch
Charlestown Ind Est
Holy Trinity CE Prim Sch
OL6
The Arcades
MERCIAN HALL
Ladysmith Sh Ctr
STAMFORD ST
TH & Mus
Penny Meadow
Stamford St Ctrl
Ashton Ret Pk
Ashton-under-Lyne
MARKET
Liby
TA Ctr
Superstore
Cavendish Ho
Portland Basin Mus
Heritage Wharf
Cavendish Mill
Park Par Ind Est
Portland Basin Mus
River Tame
Ashton Canal
Peak Forest Canal
Ravensfield Ind Est
SK16
Lyndhurst Com Prim Sch
Plantation Ind Est
Whitelands
Wellington Ctr
St Peter's CE Prim Sch
OL7
St Peter's CE Prim Sch
Cemy
Lord Sheldon Way A6140
Wellington Rd A670
Oldham Rd
Stockport Rd
Manchester Rd A635
Park Par
King St
Astley St
Crescent Rd
Park Rd B6445
Mossley Rd B6194
Hurst Knoll St James' CE Prim Sch
Playing Fields
Mount Holden St Trad Est
Mount Pleasant Trad Est
St James' CE Prim Sch

Index

A1
1 ELLISON HO
2 ALBERT WLK
3 BENJAMIN ST
4 HANOVER CT
5 VICTORIA CT
6 GROSVENOR PL
7 CECIL WLK
8 REDBRICK CT
9 GROSVENOR CT
10 UPTON WLK
11 SOUTHGATE WAY

A2
1 BENTINCK TERR
2 BENTINCK HO
3 PORTLAND HO

B1
1 LYME TERR
2 PICKMERE TERR
4 WELBECK HO
5 MARGARET HO
6 ST PETER'S ST
7 BRADGATE ST
8 GLADSTONE CT

B1
3 WOOLLEY TERR
4 BUDE TERR
5 TATTON TERR
6 BROMPTON TERR
7 QUEEN'S TERR
8 ALDERLEY TERR
9 CHAMPAGNOLE CT
10 GEORGE CT
11 DEAN CT
12 CRESCENT VIEW
13 WELLINGTON TERR
14 KING'S TERR
15 WARWICK TERR
16 EARL TERR
17 DUKE'S TERR
18 TAYLOR TERR
19 PEEL TERR
20 NEWTON TERR
21 COOK TERR
22 DENYER TERR
23 JOHNSTON TERR
24 HATTON TERR
25 DANTY ST
26 GASKELL ST

C1
1 RAVEN TERR
2 PENNINE TERR
3 FRANCIS TERR
4 KENDAL TERR
5 SHAW TERR
6 PLEASANT TERR
7 ASTLEY TERR

84 101

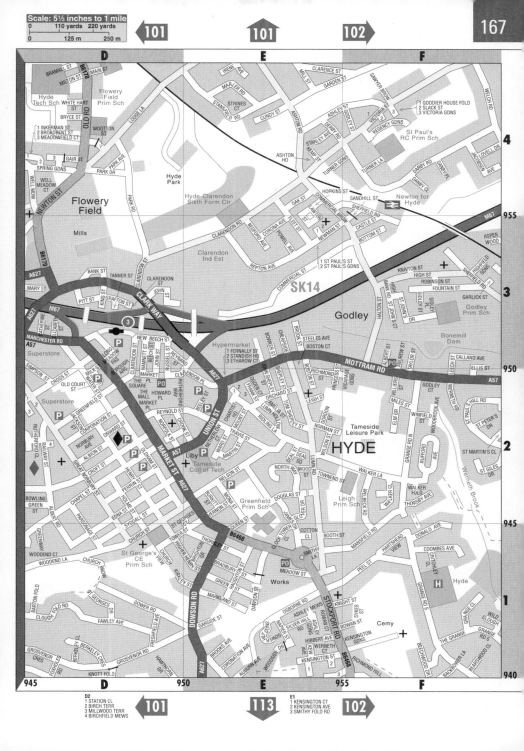

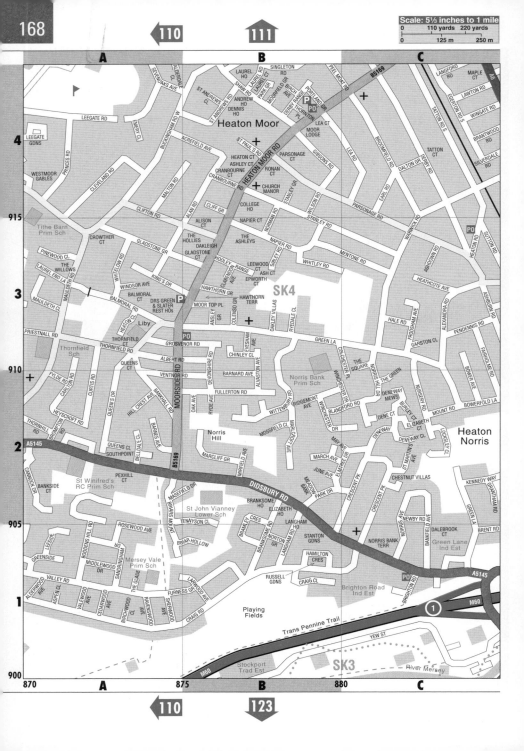

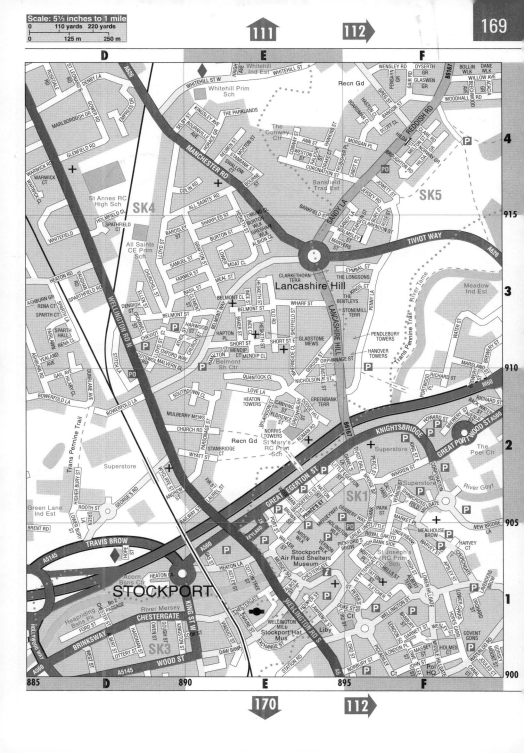

123
E8
1 CHATHAM HO
2 BOWDON HO
3 PEMBROKE HO
4 PALATINE HO

169

5 LANCASTER HO
6 DURHAM HO
7 FRANCES ST
E8

124
F8
1 LOONIES CT
2 JOULES CT
3 OLD GARDENS CL
4 HOLLINGWORTH CL

5 MOTTRAM ST
6 RATCLIFFE ST
7 GROSVENOR ST

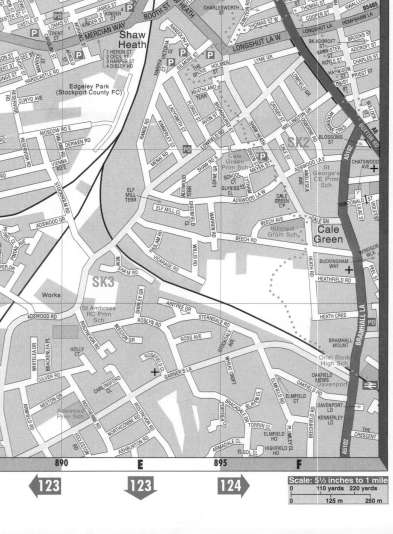

123

123

124

Scale: 5⅓ inches to 1 mile

| 0 | 110 yards | 220 yards |

| 0 | 125 m | 250 m |

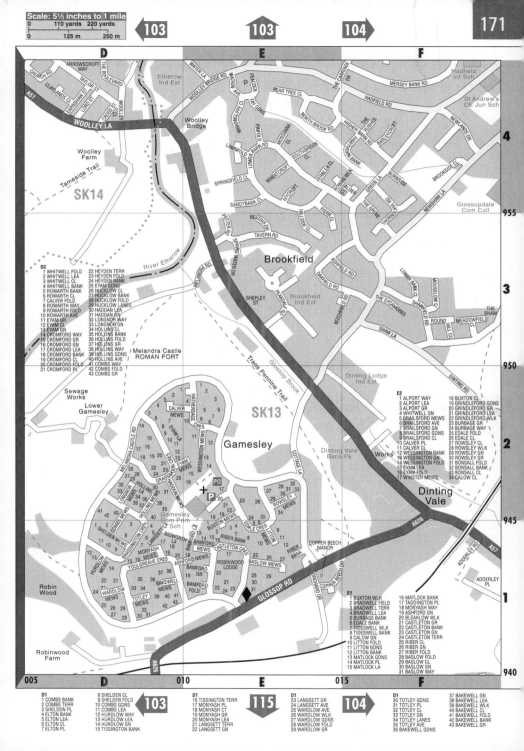

Index

Church Rd **6** Beckenham BR2.......... **53** C6

Place name	**Location number**	**Locality, town or village**	**Postcode district**	**Page and grid square**
May be abbreviated on the map	Present when a number indicates the place's position in a crowded area of mapping	Shown when more than one place has the same name	District for the indexed place	Page number and grid reference for the standard mapping

Public and commercial buildings are highlighted in magenta. Places of interest are highlighted in blue with a star ★

Abbreviations used in the index

Acad	Academy	Comm	Common	Gd	Ground	L	Leisure	Prom	Promenade
App	Approach	Cott	Cottage	Gdn	Garden	La	Lane	Rd	Road
Arc	Arcade	Cres	Crescent	Gn	Green	Liby	Library	Recn	Recreation
Ave	Avenue	Cswy	Causeway	Gr	Grove	Mdw	Meadow	Ret	Retail
Bglw	Bungalow	Ct	Court	H	Hall	Meml	Memorial	Sh	Shopping
Bldg	Building	Ctr	Centre	Ho	House	Mkt	Market	Sq	Square
Bsns, Bus	Business	Ctry	Country	Hospl	Hospital	Mus	Museum	St	Street
Bvd	Boulevard	Cty	County	HQ	Headquarters	Orch	Orchard	Sta	Station
Cath	Cathedral	Dr	Drive	Hts	Heights	Pal	Palace	Terr	Terrace
Cir	Circus	Dro	Drove	Ind	Industrial	Par	Parade	TH	Town Hall
Cl	Close	Ed	Education	Inst	Institute	Pas	Passage	Univ	University
Cnr	Corner	Emb	Embankment	Int	International	Pk	Park	Wk, Wlk	Walk
Coll	College	Est	Estate	Intc	Interchange	Pl	Place	Wr	Water
Com	Community	Ex	Exhibition	Junc	Junction	Prec	Precinct	Yd	Yard

Index of localities, towns and villages

Abram ...74 B8
Abram Brow ...74 B7
Adlington ...21 B7
Ainsworth ...26 B1
Alderley Edge ...137 C2
Altrincham ...119 C5
Appley Bridge ...35 D8
Ashley ...128 E5
Ashton-in-Makerfield ...73 C5
Ashton-under-Lyne ...166 A3
Ashton-under-Lyne ...85 A4
Aspull ...38 D6
Atherton ...58 A3
Bacup ...3 E8
Bickershaw ...74 F8
Billinge ...71 E4
Blackrod ...21 D2
Bolton ...145 E8
Bolton ...41 E8
Boothstown ...78 A5
Bramhall ...132 D8
Bredbury ...112 E4
Brinnington ...112 B5
Broadbottom ...115 A8
Broomedge ...117 C1
Bury ...140 F3
Bury ...27 F3
Carrington ...106 D6
Chadderton ...65 E7
Chapeltown ...9 D4
Charlesworth ...115 C6
Cheadle ...122 E5
Coppull ...19 E8

Culcheth ...91 E3
Delph ...50 E4
Denshaw ...33 D2
Denton ...100 D3
Diggle ...51 C4
Disley ...135 C5
Downall Green ...72 C5
Droylsden ...84 B3
Dukinfield ...101 D7
Eccles ...79 E1
Edenfield ...1 D3
Edgworth ...9 D6
Entwistle ...9 B7
Failsworth ...83 F6
Farnworth ...60 A7
Flixton ...94 F2
Four Gates ...39 C4
Fowley Common ...92 B5
Gamesley ...103 E2
Gamesley ...171 E2
Garswood ...72 C3
Gatley ...122 A4
Glazebury ...92 B7
Glossop ...104 B1
Golborne ...90 B7
Hadfield ...104 B5
Handforth ...131 C4
Haslingden ...1 B6
Hattersley ...102 E2
Hawkshaw ...10 C2
Haydock ...89 A8
Hazel Grove ...124 E2
Heywood ...29 F2

High Lane ...134 E8
Hindley ...56 D6
Hollinfare ...105 A3
Hollingworth ...103 E5
Horwich ...22 D4
Hyde ...101 E2
Hyde ...167 F2
Ince-in-Makerfield ...151 E7
Ince-in-Makerfield ...55 E7
Irlam ...105 F7
Kearsley ...61 A6
Leigh ...75 E6
Lindow End ...136 B2
Little Bollington ...118 B2
Littleborough ...16 B5
Little Lever ...43 C4
Longshaw ...53 E1
Lymm ...117 A3
Manchester ...159 B3
Manchester ...82 C2
Marple ...125 D5
Middleton ...65 B8
Midway ...133 D2
Milnrow ...31 E4
Moorend ...127 A6
Morley Green ...130 C1
Mossbrow ...117 E7
Mossley ...68 C1
Mossy Lea ...18 F6
Mottram-in-Longdendale ...103 A4
Newhey ...32 B4
New Mills ...127 D2

Newton-le-Willows ...89 B2
Oldham ...153 E7
Oldham ...67 E7
Orrell ...53 D6
Over Hulton ...58 F7
Paddockhill ...136 A4
Partington ...105 F4
Pendlebury ...80 C8
Pennington Green ...38 E1
Platt Bridge ...56 A2
Poynton ...133 E4
Prestwich ...63 A4
Radcliffe ...44 C3
Ramsbottom ...11 B5
Ramsbottom ...138 C1
Rawtenstall ...2 E7
Reddish ...111 D8
Rochdale ...139 D7
Rochdale ...30 D7
Romiley ...113 D2
Rowarth ...127 E7
Row-of-trees ...136 D3
Royton ...48 F4
Sale ...108 C4
Salford ...81 A2
Scot Lane End ...38 F7
Shaw ...149 B7
Shaw ...49 B7
Shevington ...36 B5
Shevington Moor ...19 A2
Slattocks ...47 D6
Stake Hill ...47 E5
Stalybridge ...86 B3

Standish ...19 F2
Stockport ...111 D1
Stockport ...169 D1
Stretford ...96 C2
Styal ...130 F4
Swinton ...79 F8
Tintwistle ...104 A7
Trub ...47 D8
Tyldesley ...59 A1
Up Holland ...53 B6
Uppermill ...69 A8
Urmston ...95 D1
Walkden ...60 E4
Walsden ...6 B8
Wardle ...15 D6
Wardsend ...134 A1
Westhoughton ...57 C8
Whitefield ...62 E7
Whitworth ...4 D1
Wigan ...150 B8
Wigan ...55 B8
Wilmslow ...137 C5
Windy Arbour ...72 B8
Woodford ...132 E2
Worsley ...78 E6
Wrightington Bar ...18 F7
Wythenshawe ...121 B6

1st – Alb 173

1
1st St WN2 73 E7

3
3rd St WN2 73 E7

4
4th St WN2 73 F7

A
'A' Ct WN4 73 B2
Abberley Dr M40 65 D2
Abberley Way WN3 54 B4
Abberton Rd M20 110 A6
Abbey Cl
Altrincham WA14 119 B1
Mottram-in-L SK14 102 F3
Radcliffe M26 43 E5
Up Holland WN8 53 C7
Urmston M32 95 F3
Abbey Cres OL10 29 B4
Abbey Ct Manchester M18 99 E6
Poynton SK12 133 D3
Radcliffe M26 43 E4
Stockport SK1 124 B8
Wigan WN5 36 E2
Abbey Dale WN6 35 D7
Abbey Dr Bury BL8 27 A1
Littleborough OL15 15 F3
Orrell WN5 53 E6
Swinton M27 61 E1
Abbey Gdns SK14 103 A3
Abbey Gr Adlington PR6 21 B7
Chadderton OL9 152 A5
Eccles M30 79 E2
Mottram-in-L SK14 102 F3
Stockport SK1 124 B8
Abbey Hey La M11,M18 99 F6
Abbey Hey Prim Sch
M18 99 E5
Abbey Hills Rd OL4,OL8 67 C4
Abbey La WN7 57 D1
Abbey Lawn M16 97 B3
Abbey Rd Cheadle SK8 123 A5
Delph OL3 50 E5
Droylsden M43 83 F3
Failsworth M35 84 B8
Golborne WA3 91 C8
Middleton M24 46 F4
Sale M33 108 A6
Tyldesley M29 77 C7
Abbey Sq WN7 57 D1
Abbey St WN7 75 F6
Abbey Way M26 44 A3
Abbeycourt M30 79 E2
Abbeycroft Cl M29 77 C6
Abbeydale 26 OL12 139 E8
Abbeydale Cl OL6 85 E6
Abbeydale Gdns M28 60 C3
Abbeyfield Sq M11 165 B8
Abbeyfields WN6 36 E2
Abbeystead Ave M21 109 D8
Abbeyville Wlk M15 162 E5
Abbeyway N WA11 89 A7
Abbeyway S WA11 89 A7
Abbeywood Ave M18 99 E4
Abbingdon Way WN7 57 D1
Abbot Croft BL5 57 F6
Abbot's Fold Rd M28 78 B7
Abbots Cl M33 108 D5
Abbots Ct M33 108 D5
Abbotsbury Cl
Manchester M12 165 A6
Poynton SK12 133 D5
Abbotsfield Cl M41 94 D3
Abbotsford Cl WA3 74 D1
Abbotsford Dr M24 46 D4
Abbotsford Gr WA14 119 E8
Abbotsford Prep Sch
M41 95 A2
Abbotsford Rd
Bolton BL1 142 A1
Chadderton OL9 65 E8
Manchester M21 97 B1
Oldham OL1 49 B1
Abbotside Cl M16 97 D3
Abbotsleigh Dr SK7 123 F2
Abbott Com Prim Sch
M40 159 C3
Abbott St Bolton BL3 145 E5
Hindley WN2 56 C6
14 Horwich BL6 22 B4
Rochdale OL11 30 B3
Abbotts Gn M29 77 A4
Abbotts Way WN5 71 D3
Abden St M26 44 A3
Abel Ho BL8 26 F4
Abels La OL3 69 C8
Aber Ave SK2 124 C4
Aber Rd SK8 123 A6
Abercarn Cl M8 156 A7
Abercorn Rd BL1 142 B4
Abercorn St 7 OL4 67 D6
Abercrombie Ct M33 108 D5
Aberdare Wlk 4 M9 64 E5
Aberdaron Wlk M13 163 B7
Aberdeen 1 M30 79 E2
Aberdeen Cres SK3 170 D8
Aberdeen Gdns OL12 14 D4
Aberdeen Gr SK3 170 D8
Aberdeen St M13,M15 163 B5
Aberford Rd M23 121 A5
Abergele Rd M14 110 E8
Abergele St SK2 124 A5
Aberley Fold OL15 15 F7
Abernant Cl M11 160 F1
Abernethy St BL6 22 D2
Abersoch Ave M14 110 E8
Abingdon Ave M45 44 F2
Abingdon Cl Oldham OL9 66 B4
Rochdale OL11 139 E5
Whitefield M45 44 F2
Abingdon Prim Sch SK5 111 F7
Abingdon Rd
Bolton BL2 25 E6
Reddish SK5 111 F7
Stockport SK7 123 E3
Urmston M41 95 E3
Abingdon St
Ashton-u-L OL6 85 D2
Manchester M1 163 A8
Abinger Rd WN4 72 D4
Abinger Wlk M40 83 D4
Abington Dr WN2 56 A1
Abington Rd M33 108 C3
Abney Grange OL5 86 E8
Abney Rd Mossley OL5 86 C8
Reddish SK4 111 C5
Aboukir St OL16 31 B8
Abraham Guest High Sch
WN5 54 A6
Abraham Moss High Sch
M8 156 B8
Abraham St 11 BL6 22 B4
Abram Bryn Gates Prim Sch
WN2 73 F7
Abram CE Prim Sch WN2 56 B1
Abram Cl M14 98 A1
Abram St M6 80 F6
Absalom Dr M8 155 F8
Acacia Ave
Altrincham WA15 119 F3
Cheadle SK8 123 A2
Denton M34 101 A3
Swinton M27 79 E6
Wilmslow SK9 136 F5
Acacia Cres WN6 36 F3
Acacia Dr
Altrincham WA15 119 F3
Salford M6 80 B3
Acacia Gr SK5 169 F4
Acacia Rd OL8 66 D1
Acacias Com Prim Sch
M19 110 F7
Academy Wlk M15 162 E5
Acer Cl Hyde SK14 102 A2
Rochdale OL11 13 D1
Acer Gr M7 155 D7
Acheson St 3 M18 99 D5
Ack La E SK7 132 D7
Ack La W SK8 132 C7
Ackers La M31 106 F6
Ackers St M13 163 B5
Ackersley Ct SK8 132 B8
Ackhurst La WN5 36 A2
Ackroyd Ave M18 99 F6
Ackroyd St M11 99 E7
Ackworth Dr M23 121 A6
Ackworth Rd M27 61 E1
Acme Dr M27 80 B8
Acomb St Manchester M14 98 B4
Manchester M15 163 B5
Acorn Ave Cheadle SK8 122 E5
Hyde SK14 113 E8
Acorn Bsns Ctr
Leigh WN7 76 B4
Stockport SK4 169 D1
Acorn Cl Leigh WN7 75 F3
Manchester M19 110 F8
Whitefield M45 62 F6
Acorn Ct WN7 76 B3
Acorn Ctr OL1 67 B8
Acorn St
Newton-le-W WA12 89 D3
Oldham OL4 67 E6
Acorn Way OL1 153 E7
Acre Ave OL13 3 D8
Acre Barn OL2 48 E8
Acre Cl BL0 1 D3
Acre Field BL2 25 D4
Acre Hall Prim Sch M41 94 D2
Acre La Cheadle SK8 132 C6
Oldham OL1 49 A1
Acre Mill Rd OL13 3 D8
Acre St Denton M34 100 E3
Glossop SK13 116 C7
Oldham OL9 66 B2
Radcliffe M26 43 E3
Whitworth OL12 4 D1
Acre Top Rd M9 64 B5
Acre View OL13 3 D7
Acre Wood BL6 40 B3
Acrefield M33 108 A3
Acrefield Ave
Manchester SK4 168 B4
Urmston M41 95 F1
Acregate M41 95 A2
Acres Ct M22 121 D4
Acres La SK15 86 B1
Acres Rd Gatley SK8 122 A5
Manchester M21 109 B8
Acres St BL8 26 F5
Acresbrook SK15 102 C7
Acresbrook Wlk BL8 26 F5
Acresdale BL6 40 C7
Acresfield
Adlington PR7 20 F6
Tyldesley M29 77 C7
Acresfield Ave M34 84 C1
Acresfield Cl
Blackrod BL6 21 C3
Pendlebury M27 80 A6
Acresfield Rd
Dukinfield SK14 101 F5
Middleton M24 47 C3
Sale WA15 120 A8
Salford M6 80 D5
Walkden M38 60 B4
Acreswood Ave WN2 57 A4
Acreswood Cl PR7 19 E8
Acreville Gr WA3 92 C7
Acton Ave M40 83 B4
Acton Ho WN1 151 D8
Acton Sq M5 81 B2
Acton St Oldham OL1 67 B8
Rochdale OL12 15 A1
Wigan WN1 37 C1
Acton Terr WN1 37 C1
Acton's Walk Trad Ctr
WN3 150 C7
Ada St Manchester M9 64 D1
Ramsbottom BL0 138 B5
Rochdale OL12 15 A2
Adair St Manchester M1 163 C8
Rochdale OL11 30 B2
Adam Cl SK8 123 B4
Adam St Ashton-u-L OL6 166 C3
Bolton BL3 148 A5
Oldham OL8 66 F2
Adams Ave M21 109 B6
Adams Cl
Newton-le-W WA12 89 D2
Poynton SK12 133 E2
Adams Dr WN3 150 A5
Adamson Circ M17 95 C7
Adamson Gdns M20 109 F3
Adamson Rd M30 95 C8
Adamson St
Ashton-in-M WN4 73 A3
Dukinfield SK16 101 C6
Adamson Wlk 1 M14 98 C3
Adastral Ho M21 109 C8
Adcroft St SK1 170 F7
Addenbrook Rd M8 155 E5
Adderley Pl SK13 171 F1
Adderley Rd SK13 171 F1
Addingham Cl M9 64 B5
Addington Rd BL3 40 F3
Addington St M4 159 B2
Addison Ave OL6 85 D3
Addison Cl M13 163 C6
Addison Cres M16 97 B4
Addison Dr M24 47 C3
Addison Rd
Altrincham WA15 119 E2
Carrington M31 106 D6
Irlam M44 94 C4
Stretford M32 96 B3
Urmston M41 95 D1
Adelaide Rd
Bramhall SK7 132 F5
Stockport SK3 170 D7
Adelaide St
5 Adlington PR6 21 A8
Bolton BL3 147 D4
Eccles M30 79 D1
Heywood OL10 29 D2
Manchester M8 155 F5
Middleton M24 65 A8
Ramsbottom BL0 11 A4
Swinton M27 79 D7
Adelaide St E OL10 29 E2
Adelphi Ct M3 158 D3
Adelphi Dr M38 60 B5
Adelphi Gr M38 60 B5
Adelphi St
3 Radcliffe M26 43 F5
Salford M3 158 D2
Standish WN6 19 E2
Aden Cl M12 164 D8
Aden St Oldham OL4 67 D5
Rochdale OL12 15 A1
Adey Rd WA13 117 A5
Adisham Dr BL1 143 F1
Adlington Cl
Altrincham WA15 120 D6
Bury BL8 27 A1
Poynton SK12 133 F2
Adlington Dr M32 96 F4
Adlington Est SK10 133 C1
Adlington Pk SK10 133 C1
Adlington Prim Sch PR7 20 F7
Adlington Rd SK9 137 E7
Adlington South Bsns Village
PR7 21 A6
Adlington St Bolton BL3 147 D3
Manchester M12 164 D8
12 Oldham OL4 49 D1
Adlington St Paul's CE Prim
Sch PR6 21 A7
Adlington Sta PR6 21 A7
Adlington Way 19 M34 101 A1
Adlington Wlk SK1 169 E1
Adlow Ind Pk M12 164 D8
Admel Sq 1 M15 163 A5
Adria Rd M20 110 C3
Adrian Rd BL1 142 C2
Adrian St M40 83 A7
Adrian Terr OL16 31 C7
Adscombe St M16 97 E4
Adshall Rd SK8 123 A5
Adshead Cl M22 121 B3
Adstock Wlk 5 M40 159 C3
Adstone Cl M4 160 D1
Adswood Cl OL4 49 D1
Adswood Gr SK3 170 D6
Adswood La E SK2 170 F6
Adswood La W SK2,SK3 170 F6
Adswood Old Hall Rd
SK8 123 D4
Adswood Prim Sch SK3 170 E5
Adswood Rd SK3,SK8 170 D5
Adswood St M40 160 E2
Adswood Terr SK3 170 E6
Adwell Cl WA3 91 A8
Aegean Cl 3 M7 81 C5
Aegean Rd WA14 119 A6
Affetside Dr BL8 26 E2
Affleck Ave M26 61 A8
Afghan St OL1 67 B8
Agden Brow WA13 117 E1
Agden Brow Pk WA13 117 D1
Agden La WA13 117 E1
Age Croft OL8 67 C3
Agecroft Commerce Pk
M6 80 E6
Agecroft Ent Pk M27 80 E7
Agecroft Park Circ M27 80 E7
Agecroft Rd
Manchester M25,M27 80 E8
Romiley SK6 113 A1
Agecroft Rd E M25 63 A2
Agecroft Rd W M25 63 A2
Ager St OL13 3 C8
Agincourt St OL10 29 B2
Agnes Cl OL9 66 C4
Agnes Ct M14 110 C7
Agnes St Chadderton OL9 152 B6
Manchester M19 99 A2
Salford M7 155 F7
Agnew Pl M6 81 A4
Agnew Rd M18 165 C5
Aigburth Gr SK5 99 E2
Ailsa Cl M40 157 D5
Ailsa Ho M6 154 F1
Aimson Pl WA15 120 C6
Aimson Road E WA15 120 D6
Aimson Road W WA15 120 C7
Aines St M12 165 A7
Aingarth Ho SK15 85 F2
Ainley Rd M22 121 D3
Ainley Wood Delph OL3 50 E5
Dukinfield SK16 101 D7
Ainsbrook Ave OL3 50 F4
Ainsbrook Terr OL3 51 D5
Ainscoughs Ct WN7 75 F4
Ainscouth Bsns Pk WN6 18 F6
Ainscow Ave BL6 39 F8
Ainsdale Ave
Atherton M46 58 C4
Bury BL8 27 B2
Edgworth BL7 9 E6
Manchester M7 63 D1
Ainsdale Cl Bramhall SK7 133 A7
Oldham OL8 66 D4
Ainsdale Cres OL2 48 E2
Ainsdale Dr Gatley SK8 122 B1
Sale M33 107 E2
Whitworth OL12 14 D7
Ainsdale Gr SK5 111 F8
Ainsdale Rd BL3 147 E3
Ainsdale St M12 164 F6
Ainse Rd BL6 21 B3
Ainsford Rd M20 110 D5
Ainsleigh Gdns M9 64 D1
Ainsley Gr M28 60 D2
Ainsley St 11 M40 83 C5
Ainslie Rd BL1 142 A1
Ainsty Rd M14 98 A4
Ainsworth Ave BL6 22 E2
Ainsworth Cl M34 100 B3
Ainsworth Ct BL2 148 C7
Ainsworth Hall Rd BL2 43 B8
Ainsworth La BL2 148 C8
Ainsworth Rd Bury BL8 27 B2
Little Lever BL3 43 B4
Radcliffe M26 43 F5
Ainsworth Sq BL1 143 D3
Ainsworth St Bolton BL1 142 C2
Rochdale OL16 31 A6
Ainthorpe Wlk M40 83 D5
Aintree Ave M33 107 C3
Aintree Cl SK7 124 F2
Aintree Dr OL11 29 E8
Aintree Gr SK3 170 E5
Aintree Rd BL3 43 A3
Aintree St M11 83 B1
Aintree Wlk OL9 152 C7
Air Hill Terr 8 OL12 14 C1
Aire Dr BL2 25 B5
Airedale Cl SK8 122 C6
Airedale Ct WA14 119 E5
Aireworth St BL5 39 F3
Airton Cl M40 159 C3
Airton Pl WN3 55 B3
Aitken Cl BL0 138 B5
Aitken St Haslingden BL0 1 C5
Reddish M19 99 C1
Ajax Dr BL9 45 A4
Ajax St Ramsbottom BL0 138 B5
Rochdale OL11 30 B3
Aked Cl M12 164 D6
Akesmoor Dr SK2 124 C6
Al Jamiah Al Islamiyyah
BL7 25 A8
Alamein Dr SK6 113 F2
Alan Ave M35 83 F5
Alan Dr
Altrincham WA15 120 A1
Marple SK6 125 F6
Alan Rd
Manchester,Heaton Moor
SK4 168 B4
Alan Rd *continued*
Manchester,Withington
M20 110 C6
Alan St BL1 143 D3
Alan Turing Way
Droylsden M11 83 A1
Manchester M11,M40 160 F3
Alanbrooke Wlk M15 162 E5
Alandale Ave M34 100 E7
Alandale Rd SK3 123 C7
Alasdair Cl OL9 65 F8
Alba Cl M30 79 D1
Alba Way M32 96 A5
Alban Ct BL5 57 E7
Alban St M7 155 D5
Albany Ave M11 99 F7
Albany Cl M38 60 B5
Albany Ct
7 Manchester M20 110 B6
Sale M33 108 C5
Urmston M41 95 B3
Albany Dr BL9 44 F7
Albany Gr M29 77 D8
Albany Rd Bramhall SK7 132 F4
Eccles M30 79 B3
Manchester M21 97 B1
Wilmslow SK9 136 F5
Albany Road Trad Ctr
M21 97 B1
Albany St Middleton M24 65 B7
Oldham OL4 49 D1
10 Rochdale OL11 31 A5
Albany Way
Hattersley SK14 102 E2
Salford M6 81 A3
Albemarle Ave M20 110 A6
Albemarle Rd M21 109 A8
Albemarle St
Ashton-u-L OL6 166 C3
Manchester M14 98 A4
Albemarle Terr OL6 166 C3
Alberbury Ave M23 120 D7
Albermarle Rd 5 M27 79 E7
Albert Ave
Dukinfield SK16 101 C6
Manchester M25 63 D1
Reddish M18 99 F4
Shaw OL2 149 B5
Urmston M41 95 E2
Walkden M28 60 C5
Albert Cl Cheadle SK8 123 A2
Whitefield M45 63 A8
Albert Ct WA14 119 D4
Albert Fildes Wlk 3 M8 155 F7
Albert Gdns M40 83 D5
Albert Gr Farnworth BL4 60 D8
Manchester M12 99 A4
Albert Hill St M20 110 B3
Albert Park Rd M7 155 D5
Albert Pl
Altrincham WA14 119 D5
Manchester M13 98 F3
Whitefield M45 45 B1
Albert Rd
Altrincham WA15 119 E3
Bolton BL1 144 B8
Cheadle SK8 123 A2
Eccles M30 79 F2
Farnworth BL4 60 D8
Hyde SK14 167 D2
Manchester M19 99 A1
Sale M33 108 C4
Stockport SK4 168 A3
Whitefield M45 63 A8
Wilmslow SK9 137 A6
Albert Rd E WA15 119 E3
Albert Rd W BL1 40 F8
Albert Royds St OL12,
OL16 15 B2
Albert Sq
Altrincham WA14 119 D3
Manchester M2 158 F1
Stalybridge SK15 85 F1
Albert St Ashton-in-M WN4 73 B3
Bolton BL7 8 D3
Bury BL9 141 A2
Denton M34 100 F3
Droylsden M43 84 B1
Eccles M30 79 F2
Farnworth BL4 60 D7
Farnworth BL4 60 E8
Hadfield SK13 104 A5
Hazel Grove SK7 124 D3
Heywood OL10 29 B2
14 Hindley WN2 56 D5
Horwich BL6 22 B4
Hyde SK14 167 F3
Irlam M44 105 E6
Little Lever BL3 43 B3
Littleborough OL15 16 B5
Manchester M11 160 F1
Middleton M24 65 A8
Milnrow OL16 32 A5
Oldham,Factory Fold OL9 66 B3
Oldham,Hollinwood OL8 66 B1
Oldham,Nether Lees OL4 67 E5
Prestwich M25 63 C4
Ramsbottom BL0 138 B6
Royton OL2 48 D4
Shaw OL2 149 A7
Stockport SK3 169 D1
Whitworth OL12 14 C8
Wigan WN5 54 F6
Albert St W M35 83 D6
Albert Terr SK1 169 F1

Albert Webb Ho 6 M5 154 E1
Albert Wlk 2 OL7 166 A1
Alberta St Bolton BL3 144 C5
Stockport SK1 170 F8
Alberton Cl WN2 38 C6
Albine St M40 157 F8
Albinson Wlk M31 106 A3
Albion Cl SK4 169 E3
Albion Ct BL8 140 D2
Albion Dr Droylsden M43 84 A2
Wigan WN2 38 B2
Albion Fold M43 84 A2
Albion Gardens Cl OL2 48 F4
Albion Gdns SK15 86 B1
Albion Gr M33 108 A4
Albion High Sch The M6 81 B4
Albion Ho SK15 86 C2
Albion Mill SK14 103 C5
Albion Mill Ind Est BL8 140 D2
Albion Pk WA3 92 C7
Albion Pl
Hazel Grove SK7 124 D3
Prestwich M25 63 A4
10 Salford M7 81 C5
Albion Rd Manchester M14 98 C1
Rochdale OL11 139 D6
Albion Road Ind Ctr
OL11 139 D6
Albion St Ashton-u-L OL6 166 C3
7 Bacup OL13 3 C8
Bolton BL3 145 F5
Bury BL8 140 D2
Chadderton OL9 152 A7
Failsworth M35 83 E7
Hyde SK14 167 D2
Kearsley BL4 61 A7
7 Leigh WN7 75 F5
Littleborough OL15 16 A5
Manchester,City Centre
M1 162 F8
Manchester,Old Trafford
M16 97 D4
Oldham OL1 153 F7
Pendlebury M27 80 A8
4 Platt Bridge WN2 56 A2
Radcliffe M26 44 B1
Rochdale OL11 30 D1
Sale M33 108 B4
Stalybridge SK15 86 B2
Westhoughton BL5 39 F3
Wigan WN2 38 B2
Albion Terr BL1 142 B3
Albion The M5 81 B1
Albion Trad Est
Ashton-u-L OL6 85 D3
Salford M6 81 A4
Albion Twrs 5 M5 81 B2
Albion Way M5 81 B1
Alburn Ct M40 160 E4
Albury Dr
Manchester M19 110 D2
Rochdale OL12 13 F2
Albury Way WN2 37 F2
Albyns Ave M8 156 A7
Alcester Ave SK3 122 F7
Alcester Cl Bury BL8 27 B3
Middleton M24 65 B6
Alcester Rd Gatley SK8 122 B4
Sale M33 108 B2
Alcester St OL9 66 A3
Alcester Wlk M9 64 C5
Alconbury Ct M43 100 B8
Alconbury Wlk M9 64 B6
Aldborough Cl M20 110 B6
Aldbourne Cl M40 157 D5
Aldbury Terr 2 BL1 143 D1
Aldcliffe WA3 90 F8
Aldcroft St 5 M18 99 F6
Alden Cl Haslingden BB4 1 A6
Whitefield M45 63 A8
Alden Rd BB4 1 A5
Alden Rise BB4 1 A6
Alden Wlk SK4 111 D7
Alder Ave
Ashton-in-M WN4 72 F5
Billinge WN5 71 D5
Bury BL9 141 C3
Poynton SK12 133 F3
Wigan WN5 54 D6
Alder Cl Ashton-u-L OL6 85 B7
9 Bury BL8 27 C2
Dukinfield SK16 102 A7
Gatley SK8 131 D8
Hadfield SK13 171 F4
Leigh WN7 75 F2
Alder Ct M8 63 F1
Alder Dr
Altrincham WA15 120 E5
Stalybridge SK15 86 C3
Swinton M27 61 C1
Alder Edge 8 M21 96 F1
Alder Forest Ave M30 79 A4
Alder Gr Bolton BL7 25 C6
Denton M34 101 A3
Stockport SK3 123 C8
Stretford M32 96 E2
Alder La Hindley WN2 57 B5
Oldham OL8 66 D2
Alder Lee Cl WN3 54 D1
Alder Meadow Cl OL12 14 A1
Alder Moor Cl M11 99 D8
Alder Park Prim Sch
M30 79 A4
Alder Rd Cheadle SK8 122 E5
Failsworth M35 83 F5
Alder Rd *continued*
Golborne WA3 90 F8
Middleton M24 47 C2
Rochdale OL11 30 D2
Alder St Atherton M46 58 D3
Bolton BL3 147 F3
Eccles M30 79 A4
Newton-le-W WA12 89 C3
Salford M6 154 F2
Alderbank Horwich BL6 21 F3
Wardle OL12 15 C7
Alderbank Cl BL4 60 F6
Alderbrook Rd M38 59 F3
Aldercroft Ave Bolton BL2 25 D1
Wythenshawe M22 121 C2
Alderdale Dr
Droylsden M43 83 E2
High Lane SK6 134 E7
Manchester SK4 111 A5
Alderdale Gr SK9 136 E5
Alderdale Rd SK8 123 C4
Alderfield Ho 5 M21 96 F1
Alderfield Rd M21 96 F1
Alderfold St M46 58 D3
Alderford Par 11 M8 155 F6
Aldergate Gr OL6 85 F5
Alderglen Rd M8 156 A5
Alderley Ave Bolton BL1 24 E5
Golborne WA3 90 D7
Alderley Cl Billinge WN5 71 E5
Hazel Grove SK7 133 F8
Poynton SK12 133 F2
Alderley Dr SK6 112 E3
Alderley Edge* SK9 137 D1
Alderley Edge Prim Sch
SK9 137 A2
Alderley Edge Sch for Girls
SK9 137 A2
Alderley Edge Sta SK9 137 A2
Alderley La WN7 76 B2
Alderley Lo SK9 137 A5
Alderley Rd
Alderley Edge SK10,SK9 137 F2
Hindley WN2 57 A5
Reddish SK5 111 F5
Sale M33 108 E2
Urmston M41 95 A2
Wilmslow SK9 137 A6
Alderley St OL6 85 D5
Alderley Terr 8 SK16 166 B1
Alderman Foley Dr OL12 14 A2
Alderman Gatley Ho
M22 121 D2
Alderman Kay Sch M24 47 A3
Alderman Sq M12 164 E8
Aldermary Rd M21 109 D5
Aldermaston Gr M9 64 B6
Aldermere Cres M41 94 F3
Alderminster Ave M38 60 A5
Alderney Dr WN3 55 A3
Alders SK9 136 F6
Alders Ave M22 121 C5
Alders Ct OL8 85 A8
Alders Green Ave SK6 134 F7
Alders Green Rd WN2 57 A5
Alders Rd
High Lane SK12 135 A7
Wythenshawe M22 121 C5
Alders The WN6 36 D4
Aldersgate Rd
Cheadle SK8 132 C5
Stockport SK2 124 B6
Aldershot Wlk 3 M11 160 F1
Alderside Rd M9 157 D8
Aldersley Ave M9 64 B5
Alderson St Oldham OL9 153 E7
Salford M6 81 A4
Aldersyde St BL3 147 D3
Alderton Dr BL5 57 E6
Alderue Ave M22 121 D6
Alderway BL0 1 C1
Alderwood Ave SK4 168 A1
Alderwood Fold OL4 67 F5
Alderwood Gr BL0 1 D4
Alderwood Wlk 7 M8 155 F6
Aldfield Rd M23 108 F1
Aldford Cl M20 110 C3
Aldford Dr M46 58 E5
Aldford Gr BL2 43 B5
Aldford Pl SK9 136 F2
Aldford Way WN6 36 E8
Aldham Ave M40 83 C4
Aldred Cl M8 156 B6
Aldred St Bolton BL3 146 B3
Eccles M30 79 C1
Failsworth M35 83 E7
3 Hindley WN2 56 D4
Leigh WN7 75 E8
Salford M5 81 B2
Aldridge Cl WN3 55 B3
Aldridge Wlk M11 164 F8
Aldsworth Dr BL3 147 E4
Aldwick Ave M20 110 C3
Aldwinians Cl M34 100 E5
Aldworth Dr M40 157 E5
Aldworth Gr M33 107 D3
Aldwych OL11 30 F3
Aldwych Ave M14 98 B2
Aldwyn Cl M34 100 E5
Aldwyn Cres SK7 124 C2
Aldwyn Park Rd M34 100 C8
Aldwyn Prim Sch M34 84 C1
Alexander Ave M35 84 A8
Alexander Briant Ct BL4 60 C7
Alexander Ct M5 161 A8
Alexander Dr
Altrincham WA15 120 A6
Milnrow OL16 31 F6
Alexander Dr *continued*
Whitefield BL9 45 A2
Alexander Gdns M7 158 D4
Alexander Rd BL2 25 C1
Alexander St
Rochdale OL11 30 B2
Salford M6 154 E2
Tyldesley M29 77 A8
Alexandra Ave
Hyde SK14 101 C2
Manchester M14 97 F2
Whitefield M45 63 A8
Alexandra Cl SK3 123 C6
Alexandra Cres
1 Oldham OL1 67 B8
Wigan WN5 54 E6
Alexandra Ct
1 Partington M31 105 F3
Urmston M41 94 E1
Alexandra Ctr Ret Pk
OL4 153 F6
Alexandra Dr M19 110 F7
Alexandra Gr M44 105 F8
Alexandra Ho 6 OL1 67 B8
Alexandra Hospl The
SK8 122 D6
Alexandra Mews OL4 67 A5
Alexandra Mill OL3 69 B8
Alexandra Park Inf Sch
SK3 123 C7
Alexandra Park Jun Sch
Oldham OL8 67 A5
Stockport SK3 123 C7
Alexandra Rd
Ashton-in-M WN4 73 B4
Ashton-u-L OL6 166 B4
Denton M34 101 A4
Eccles M30 95 C8
Horwich BL6 39 E8
Kearsley BL4 61 A7
Kearsley,Prestolee M26 61 A8
Manchester,Heaton Norris
SK4 168 C3
Manchester,Moss Side M16 97 E4
Oldham OL8 67 A4
Sale M33 108 D3
Walkden M28 60 C5
Alexandra Rd S M16 97 E2
Alexandra St Abram WN2 74 B8
Ashton-u-L OL6 85 D4
9 Bolton BL3 147 D4
Farnworth BL4 60 D7
Heywood OL10 46 E8
Hyde SK14 101 C1
Oldham OL8 67 A5
Salford M7 158 D3
Wigan WN5 54 F6
Alexandra Terr
14 Manchester M19 99 A1
Oldham OL4 49 E3
Alexandra The 11 M14 110 D8
Alexandria Dr BL5 58 B8
Alford Ave M20 110 A8
Alford Cl BL2 42 F6
Alford Rd SK4 111 C6
Alford St 10 OL9 66 B2
Alfred Ave M28 79 A7
Alfred James Cl 17 M40 159 C3
Alfred Morris Ct M23 109 A2
Alfred Rd WA3 91 A8
Alfred St Ashton-u-L OL6 85 D4
Bolton,Burnden BL3 42 B4
Bolton,Egerton BL7 8 D3
Bury BL9 141 A1
Dukinfield SK14 101 C3
Eccles M30 79 D3
Farnworth BL4 42 D2
Ince-in-M WN3 151 D6
Irlam M44 105 E6
Kearsley BL4 60 F8
Littleborough OL15 16 A6
Manchester M9 157 D8
Newton-le-W WA12 89 E3
Oldham OL9 152 C6
Platt Bridge WN2 56 A3
Ramsbottom BL0 138 B5
Shaw OL2 149 B7
9 Tyldesley M29 58 F1
Walkden M28 60 D3
Whitworth OL12 4 D2
Wigan WN1 37 B2
Alfreton Ave M34 113 A8
Alfreton Rd SK2 124 E5
Alfreton Wlk 9 M40 83 A6
Alfriston Dr M23 109 A2
Alger Mews OL6 85 D4
Alger St 1 OL6 85 D4
Algernon Rd M28 60 C4
Algernon St Eccles M30 79 D3
Hindley WN2 56 D5
Swinton M27 79 D8
Wigan WN3 55 A4
Algreave Rd SK3 123 A8
Alice Ingham RC Prim Sch
OL16 15 C2
Alice St Bolton BL3 144 C5
Hyde SK14 113 E7
Pendlebury M27 80 B8
Rochdale OL12 15 B1
Sale M33 108 D4
Alicia Ct OL12 14 E1
Alicia Dr OL12 14 E1
Alick's Fold 9 BL5 39 E1
Alison Ct SK4 168 B3
Alison Kelly Cl M9 157 F8
Alison St
6 Manchester M14 97 F3
2 Manchester M14 98 A3
Alison St *continued*
Shaw OL2 149 B8
Alker Rd M40 160 D3
Alker St WN5 54 F6
Alkrington Cl BL9 45 A2
Alkrington Gn M24 64 F7
Alkrington Hall M24 64 F7
Alkrington Hall Rd N
M24 64 F7
Alkrington Hall Rd S
M24 64 E6
Alkrington Moss Prim Sch
M24 65 B5
Alkrington Park Rd M24 64 E7
Alkrington Prim Sch
M24 65 A6
All Hallows RC High Sch
M6 80 C3
All Saint's CE Prim Sch
M40 83 C5
All Saint's Cl OL2 48 D5
All Saint's Ct M32 96 B2
All Saints Catholic Coll
SK16 101 D7
All Saints CE Prim Sch
Marple SK6 126 A5
Rochdale OL12 15 A2
Stockport SK4 169 D3
Whitefield M45 45 A2
All Saints Gr WN2 56 E5
All Saints Pl 12 BL8 27 C3
All Saints Prim Sch
M18 165 B6
All Saints RC Prim Sch
Golborne WA3 90 B8
Sale M33 107 D6
All Saints Terr OL12 15 B2
All Saints' CE Prim Sch
BL4 42 D2
All Saints' RC Prim Sch
SK13 104 D2
All Saints' Rd SK4 169 E4
All Saints' St Bolton BL1 145 F8
Failsworth M40 83 C5
All Souls CE Prim Sch
OL10 29 F3
All Souls RC Prim Sch
M5 154 D1
Allama Iqbal Rd OL4 67 C5
Allan Ct M21 109 A7
Allan Roberts Cl M9 64 D1
Allan St M29 76 F8
Allanadale Ct 12 M7 63 E1
Allandale WA14 119 B4
Allandale Dr OL2 48 C5
Allandale Rd M19 98 F1
Allanson Rd M22 109 E1
Alldis Cl M12 164 E5
Alldis St SK2 124 B5
Allen Ave
Fowley Common WA3 92 C4
Hyde SK14 113 F8
Allen Cl OL2 149 A6
Allen Ct M34 100 E4
Allen Rd M41 95 F2
Allen St Bury BL8 27 C3
Little Lever BL3 43 A3
Oldham OL8 153 D6
Radcliffe M26 43 F3
Rochdale OL16 31 A5
Allenby Gr BL5 57 D7
Allenby Rd Irlam M44 105 D4
Swinton M27 79 C6
Allenby St Atherton M46 58 B2
Shaw OL2 149 A7
Allenby Wlk 4 M40 156 C5
Allendale Dr BL9 45 A3
Allendale Gdns BL1 143 E2
Allendale Wlk M3 158 D2
Allerby Way WA3 90 E8
Allerdean Wlk SK4 110 F3
Allerford St M16 97 E4
Allerton Cl BL5 40 A1
Allerton Ct 7 BL1 145 E8
Allerton Wlk 6 M13 163 C6
Allescholes Rd OL14 6 B7
Allesley Cl BL5 40 A1
Allesley Dr M7 155 F6
Allgreave Cl M33 108 E1
Alliance St 3 WN1 151 D8
Alligin Cl OL9 152 A8
Allingham St M13 98 E4
Allington OL11 139 E6
Allington Dr M30 79 E4
Alliott Wlk M15 162 E5
Allison Gr M30 79 B1
Allison St M8 155 F5
Allonby Wlk M24 46 C2
Allotment Rd M44 105 D6
Alloway Wlk 6 M40 83 A6
Allscott Way WN4 73 C3
Allsopp St BL3 145 F6
Allwood St M5 158 D1
Alma Cl WN8 53 C7
Alma Ct
3 Manchester M15 97 E4
Up Holland WN8 53 C7
Alma Gr WN3 54 E2
Alma Hill WN8 53 C7
Alma Hill Est WN8 53 C7
Alma Ind Est 25 OL12 14 F1
Alma La SK9 137 A7
Alma Par WN8 53 C7
Alma Park Prim Sch
M19 111 A8
Alma Rd Hazel Grove SK7 134 A8
Manchester,Heaton Moor
SK4 111 B5
Alma Rd *continued*
Manchester,Levenshulme
M19 111 A8
Sale M33 107 E2
Up Holland WN8 53 C7
Westhoughton BL5 57 F8
Alma St Atherton M46 58 C3
Bolton BL3 146 C4
Eccles M30 79 F1
Kearsley BL4 61 B5
Leigh WN7 75 E8
Little Lever BL3 43 B3
Newton-le-W WA12 89 B3
Radcliffe M26 43 F5
13 Rochdale OL12 14 F1
Stalybridge SK15 86 B2
Tyldesley M29 76 F8
Alminstone Cl M40 83 D4
Almond Ave BL9 141 C3
Almond Brook Rd WN6 19 C1
Almond Cl Failsworth M35 83 F6
Littleborough OL15 15 F6
Salford M6 81 B2
Stockport SK3 123 C8
Almond Cres
Rawtenstall BB4 1 F8
Standish WN6 36 F7
Almond Ct SK16 166 C1
Almond Dr M33 107 F6
Almond Gr Bolton BL1 143 F3
Wigan WN5 54 E6
Almond Rd 5 OL4 49 D1
Almond St Bolton BL1 143 F4
9 Farnworth BL4 60 C8
Manchester M40 159 B4
Almond Tree Rd SK8 123 A1
Almond Way SK14 102 A2
Almond Wlk M31 105 D3
Alms Hill Rd M8 156 A7
Alness Rd M16 97 E2
Alnwick Cl WN2 38 D5
Alnwick Dr BL9 45 A5
Alnwick Rd M9 64 D5
Alperton Wlk M40 83 D4
Alpha Court Ind Est
M34 100 C3
Alpha Ct M34 100 C3
Alpha Pl M15 162 E7
Alpha Rd M32 96 C1
Alpha St Manchester M11 99 E7
Salford M6 154 F3
Alpha St W M6 154 E3
Alphagate Dr M34 100 C3
Alphin Cl Mossley OL5 68 E3
Uppermill OL3 69 B5
Alphin Sq OL5 68 D1
Alphingate Cl SK15 86 D4
Alphonsus St M16 97 C4
Alpine Dr Leigh WN7 75 C8
Milnrow OL16 32 A7
Royton OL2 48 C3
Wardle OL12 15 C6
Alpine Rd Stockport SK1 112 A1
Stockport SK1 112 A2
Alpine St Droylsden M11 83 B2
Newton-le-W WA12 89 A3
Alpington Wlk M40 65 C2
Alport Ave M16 97 C2
Alport Gr 3 SK13 171 E2
Alport Lea 2 SK13 171 E2
Alport Way 1 SK13 171 E2
Alresford Rd Middleton M9 64 F5
Salford M6 80 D5
Alric Wlk M22 130 E8
Alsager Cl M21 109 B6
Alsham Wlk M8 156 A6
Alsop Ave M7 81 B7
Alstead Ave WA15 120 A3
Alston Ave Sale M33 107 F3
Shaw OL2 149 B8
Stretford M32 96 B3
Alston Cl SK7 124 A1
Alston Gdns M19 110 F5
Alston Lea M46 58 E4
Alston Rd Manchester M18 99 E5
Wigan WN2 37 F2
Alston St Bolton BL3 147 E3
Bury BL8 27 C4
Alston Wlk M24 46 C2
Alstone Dr WA14 119 A6
Alstone Rd SK4 111 C6
Alt Cl WN7 75 D6
Alt Fold Dr OL8 67 C3
Alt Gr OL6 85 B6
Alt Hill La OL6,OL7 85 C8
Alt Hill Rd OL6 67 C1
Alt La OL8 67 C3
Alt Prim Sch OL8 67 D3
Alt Rd OL6 85 B6
Alt Wlk M45 45 C2
Altair Ave 7 M22 121 D1
Altair Pl M7 81 C4
Altcar Gr SK5 99 E2
Altcar Wlk M22 121 C2
Altham Cl BL9 44 D7
Altham Wlk 12 M40 83 A6
Althorn Wlk 11 M23 121 A5
Althorpe Wlk M40 83 D4
Alton Ave M41 94 D2
Alton Cl Ashton-in-M WN4 73 A4
Ashton-u-L OL6 85 C7
Whitefield BL9 45 A5
Alton Rd SK9 136 F7
Alton Sq M11 99 E7
Alton St OL8 66 F3
Alton Twrs M16 97 D1
Altrincham Bsns Pk
WA14 119 B7

Altrincham CE Prim Sch WA14 119 D5
Altrincham Coll of Arts WA15 120 B3
Altrincham General Hospl WA14 119 D4
Altrincham Gram Sch for Boys WA14 119 D2
Altrincham Gram Sch for Girls WA14 119 C3
Altrincham Gram Sch for Girls (Sixth Form Ctr) WA14 119 B3
Altrincham Prep Sch WA14 119 D2
Altrincham Priory Hospl WA15 129 A7
Altrincham Rd Styal SK9 130 C4
Wilmslow SK9 130 C2
Wythenshawe M23 120 E7
Wythenshawe,Sharston M22 121 E5
Altrincham Ret Pk WA14 119 C7
Altrincham St M1 163 B8
Altrincham Sta WA15 119 D4
Alum Cres BL9 45 A3
Alva Rd OL4 49 D2
Alvan Sq 1 M11 99 E7
Alvanley Cl Sale M33 108 C1
Wigan WN5 36 C1
Alvanley Cres SK3 123 C6
Alvanley Ind Est SK6 112 F4
Alvaston Ave SK4 168 B2
Alvaston Rd M18 99 E4
Alveley Ave M20 110 C5
Alverstone Rd M20 110 C6
Alveston Dr SK9 137 C8
Alvington Gr SK7 124 A1
Alvon Ct SK14 102 A2
Alwin Rd OL2 149 A8
Alwinton Ave SK4 110 E3
Alworth Rd M9 64 D5
Alwyn Cl WN7 75 F1
Alwyn Dr M13 98 E4
Alwyn St WN1 37 D1
Alwyn Terr WN1 37 D1
Amar St WN2 151 F7
Ambassador Pl WA15 119 E5
Amber Gdns
Dukinfield SK16 101 B8
Hindley WN2 56 E4
Amber Gr BL5 39 F2
Ambergate M46 58 D2
Amberhill Way
Boothstown M28 77 F5
Worsley M28 78 A5
Amberley Cl Bolton BL3 40 F5
Wigan WN2 37 F2
Amberley Dr
Altrincham WA15 129 B8
Irlam M44 94 A1
Sale M33 107 E5
Wythenshawe M23 121 A4
Amberley Rd M33 107 E5
Amberley Wlk OL9 152 C7
Amberswood Cl WN2 56 B7
Amberwood OL9 65 E8
Amberwood Dr M23 120 D6
Amblecote Dr E M38 60 A6
Amblecote Dr W M38 60 A6
Ambleside Ince-in-M WN2 56 B7
Stalybridge SK15 86 A3
Wigan WN5 54 C7
Ambleside Ave
Altrincham WA15 120 C5
Ashton-u-L OL7 84 F4
Ambleside Cl Bolton BL2 25 F4
Middleton M24 46 E1
Stalybridge SK15 86 A3
Ambleside Ct SK8 122 C5
Ambleside Pl WA11 71 B1
Ambleside Rd
Reddish SK5 111 F6
Urmston M41 94 E1
Ambleside Wlk M9 65 A2
Amblethorn Dr BL1 24 D5
Ambrose Ave WN7 57 E1
Ambrose Cres OL3 51 B3
Ambrose Dr M20 109 E4
Ambrose Gdns M20 109 E4
Ambrose St Hyde SK14 113 E7
Manchester M12 165 A7
Rochdale OL11 139 F5
Ambuscade Ct M41 94 E2
Ambush St M11 99 F7
Amelia St Denton M34 100 F4
Hyde SK14 167 E2
Amersham Cl M41 95 B5
Amersham Pl M19 111 A6
Amersham St M5 154 F1
Amesbury Dr WN3 54 C2
Amesbury Gr SK5 111 F5
Amesbury Rd M9 64 E4
Amethyst Cl WN2 38 A2
Amherst Rd M14,M20 110 D7
Amis Gr WA3 90 E8
Amlwch Ave SK2 124 D6
Ammon Wrigley Cl OL1 153 F7
Ammon's Way OL3 50 F5
Amory St M12 163 C8
Amos Ave M40 83 C4
Amos St Manchester M9 157 F8
Salford M6 154 E2
Ampleforth Gdns M26 43 E5
Ampney Cl M30 79 B1
Amport Wlk 8 M40 65 C2
Amwell St M8 156 C7
Amy St Middleton M24 47 B1
Rochdale OL12 14 B1
Anaconda Dr M3 158 E3
Ancaster Wlk 5 M40 65 C2
Anchor Cl M19 99 C1
Anchor Ct M8 63 F1
Anchor La BL4,M38 59 F7
Anchor St OL1 153 F8
Anchorage Quay M50 161 A8
Anchorage Rd M41 96 A1
Anchorage Sta M5 161 A8
Anchorage Wlk M18 165 C6
Anchorside Cl M21 109 B7
Ancoats Gr M4 164 D8
Ancoats Gr N M4 160 D1
Ancoats St 5 OL4 67 E6
Ancroft Dr WN2 56 D3
Ancroft Gdns BL3 146 C2
Ancroft St M15 162 E6
Anderton Cl Bury BL8 26 F1
Rawtenstall BB4 2 F7
Anderton Gr OL6 85 E5
Anderton La BL6 21 E4
Anderton Prim Sch PR6 21 B8
Anderton St Adlington PR7 21 A7
Ince-in-M WN2 151 F7
Anderton Way
Handforth SK9 131 D3
Wigan WN2 38 B2
Andoc Ave M30 80 A1
Andover Ave M24 65 C5
Andover Cres WN3 54 D2
Andover Rd WA11 72 E1
Andover St M30 79 C1
Andover Wlk M8 156 A8
Andre St 14 M11 83 C2
Andrew Ave WN5 71 F5
Andrew Cl Radcliffe M26 44 C1
Ramsbottom BL8 10 F1
Andrew Ct 3 M20 110 B6
Andrew Gr SK16 101 D8
Andrew Ho SK4 168 B4
Andrew La Bolton BL1 24 F6
High Lane SK6 134 F8
Andrew Rd M9 64 D1
Andrew St Ashton-u-L OL6 85 D5
Bury BL9 141 A2
Chadderton OL9 152 B8
Droylsden M43 84 C4
Failsworth M35 83 E8
Hyde SK14 167 F3
Middleton M24 65 C7
Mossley OL5 86 C8
Romiley SK6 114 A2
Stockport SK4 169 D2
Andrew's Terr 3 BL5 39 E1
Andrews Ave M41 94 E3
Andy Nicholson Wlk M9 157 F8
Anemone Dr BB4 1 A8
Anerley Rd M20 110 B4
Anfield Cl BL9 45 B3
Anfield Mews SK8 122 F3
Anfield Rd Bolton BL3 147 F2
Cheadle SK8 122 F3
Failsworth M40 65 D1
Sale M33 108 C5
Angel Cl SK16 101 B8
Angel St Denton M34 101 A4
Hazel Grove SK7 124 D3
Manchester M8 159 A3
Angel Trad Est 4 M4 159 A3
Angela Ave OL1,OL2 48 E2
Angela St M15 162 D7
Angelbank BL6 21 F2
Angelico Rise OL1 49 D3
Angelo St BL1 143 D2
Angle St BL2 25 B1
Angler Gr M34 100 F3
Anglers Rest M44 105 E5
Anglesea Ave SK2 170 F6
Anglesey Cl OL7 85 A6
Anglesey Dr SK12 133 F6
Anglesey Gr SK8 123 A6
Anglesey Rd OL7 84 F6
Anglesey Water SK12 133 E6
Angleside Ave M19 110 E4
Anglezarke Rd PR6 21 A7
Anglia Gr BL3 146 C4
Angora Dr M3 158 D3
Angouleme Ret Pk BL9 140 F2
Angouleme Way BL9 140 F1
Angus Ave Heywood OL10 29 A1
Leigh WN7 75 C7
Angus St OL13 3 C8
Aniline St M11 83 B1
Anita St M4 159 B2
Anjou Bvd WN5 54 F8
Ann La M29 77 C5
Ann Sq OL4 67 D8
Ann St Ashton-u-L OL7 100 F8
Denton M34 100 E3
Dukinfield SK14 101 C3
Farnworth BL4 60 E7
Heywood OL10 29 D3
Leigh WN7 75 E8
Reddish SK5 169 E4
Rochdale OL11 139 F6
Annable Rd
Droylsden M43 84 B1
Irlam M44 105 F8
Manchester M18 99 E6
Romiley SK6 112 D3
Annald Sq M43 100 A8
Annan Gr WN4 73 E5
Annan St M34 100 F4
Annandale Gdns WN8 53 A7
Anne Cl 6 OL7 85 A6
Anne Line Cl 3 OL11 31 A5
Anne Nuttall Rd M15 162 D7
Anne St SK16 101 D8
Annecy Cl BL8 27 B4
Annersley Ave OL2 149 A6
Annesley Cres WN3 54 F3
Annesley Gdns 1 M18 99 D6
Annesley Rd M40 65 E1
Annette Ave WA12 89 A5
Annie Darby Ct M9 157 D7
Annie St Ramsbottom BL0 11 A4
Salford M6 154 E2
Annis Cl SK9 137 B2
Annis Rd
Alderley Edge SK9 137 B2
Bolton BL3 146 B4
Annis St M9 157 E7
Annisdale Cl M30 79 B2
Annisfield Ave OL3 69 C5
Anscombe Cl M40 160 D3
Ansdell Ave M21 109 C8
Ansdell Dr M43 83 E2
Ansdell Rd Horwich BL6 22 C4
Reddish SK5 100 A1
Rochdale OL16 31 B4
Wigan WN5 54 D5
Ansdell St M8 156 A7
Ansell Cl M18 99 D6
Anselms Ct OL8 66 C4
Ansford Ave WN2 74 B8
Ansford Wlk M9 156 C6
Ansleigh Ave M8 64 A1
Ansley Gr SK4 168 B3
Anslow Cl M40 157 D5
Anson Ave M27 79 E6
Anson Cl SK7 132 F5
Anson Ct M14 98 D3
Anson Engine Mus The* SK12 134 C3
Anson Pl WN5 54 C8
Anson Rd Handforth SK9 131 E1
Manchester M14 98 D3
Poynton SK12 134 B3
Reddish M34,SK5 100 A2
Swinton M27 79 E6
Anson St Bolton BL1 143 F3
Eccles M30 79 B4
Wigan WN5 54 F7
Answell Ave M8 64 A2
Antares Ave M7 158 D3
Anthistle Ct M5 154 D2
Anthony Cl M12 164 E7
Anthony St OL5 68 B1
Anthorn Rd WN3 54 E3
Antilles Cl M12 99 A4
Antler Ct WN4 73 B6
Anton Wlk M9 157 D7
Antrim Cl
Manchester M19 110 D2
Wigan WN3 54 C2
Anvil Cl WN5 53 D5
Anvil St OL13 3 E8
Anvil Way OL1 153 E7
Apethorn La SK14 113 D7
Apfel La OL9 152 B7
Apollo Ave BL9 44 F3
Apollo Wlk M12 165 A6
Apperley Grange M30 79 E4
Appian Way M7 155 E5
Apple Cl OL8 67 C3
Apple Dell Ave WA3 74 C1
Apple St SK14 114 D7
Apple Tree Ct M5 81 A2
Apple Tree Rd SK22 127 B1
Apple Tree Wlk 8 M33 107 C5
Apple Way M24 65 B6
Appleby Ave
Altrincham WA15 120 C5
Dukinfield SK14 101 C5
Manchester M12 99 A3
Appleby Cl Bury BL8 26 F2
Stockport SK3 170 D5
Appleby Gdns
1 Bolton BL2 25 B1
Whitefield BL9 44 F3
Appleby Lo M14 98 D2
Appleby Rd SK8 122 B4
Appleby Wlk 4 OL2 48 E4
Applecross Wlk M11 165 C8
Appledore Dr Bolton BL2 25 F3
Wythenshawe M23 120 D7
Appledore Wlk OL9 152 B6
Appleford Ave M23 121 A4
Appleford Dr M8 156 B6
Applethwaite WN2 56 B8
Appleton Ct M33 108 B4
Appleton Dr SK13 116 F8
Appleton Gr M33 107 E2
Appleton Rd
Altrincham WA15 119 F1
Reddish SK4 111 D6
Appleton St WN3 150 B8
Appleton Wlk 8 SK9 131 E1
Applewood OL9 65 E7
Appley Bridge All Saints CE Prim Sch WN6 18 C1
Appley Bridge Sta WN6 35 C7
Appley Cl WN6 18 C2
Appley La N WN6 18 C1
Appley La S WN6,WN8 35 C6
Apprentice Ct 18 M9 157 E8
April Cl OL8 67 C4
Apsley Cl WA14 119 B1
Apsley Gr
Altrincham WA14 119 B1
Manchester M12 163 C6
Apsley Pl OL6 166 A2
Apsley Rd M34 100 F4
Apsley Side OL5 86 C8
Apsley St SK1 169 F1
Aquarius La M6 81 C4
Aquarius St M15 163 A5
Aqueduct Bsns Pk SK6 125 F8
Aqueduct Rd BL3 148 C5
Aquinas Coll SK2 124 A6
Aragon Dr OL10 29 C2
Aragon Way SK6 125 E6
Arbor Ave M19 110 F6
Arbor Dr M19 110 F7
Arbor Gr Droylsden M43 83 F3
Walkden M38 59 E4
Arbory Ave M40 83 B7
Arbory Cl WN7 76 C5
Arbour Cl Bury BL9 27 E6
Salford M6 154 F3
Arbour La WN6 19 B1
Arbour Rd OL4 67 E4
Arbroath St M43 83 E1
Arbury Ave Cheadle SK3 123 A7
Rochdale OL11 139 E5
Arcade St 18 WN1 150 C8
Arcade The
Brinnington SK5 112 C5
Rawtenstall BB4 2 E8
2 Stalybridge SK15 101 F8
Arcades The OL6 166 B3
Arcadia Ave M33 108 A1
Arch La WN4 72 B3
Arch St BL1 25 A1
Archer Ave BL2 148 C8
Archer Gr BL2 148 C8
Archer Pk M24 64 E8
Archer Pl M32 95 F3
Archer St Boothstown M28 77 E7
Droylsden M11 83 A2
Leigh WN7 76 B2
Mossley OL5 68 C2
Stockport SK2 124 C5
Archie St M5 161 A7
Archway M15 162 F6
Archway Wlk WA12 89 E3
Arclid Cl SK9 131 E1
Arcon Cl OL16 31 E6
Arcon Dr M16 97 E3
Arcon Pl WA14 119 A6
Ardale Ave M40 65 C2
Ardcombe Ave M9 64 C5
Ardeen Wlk M13 163 C6
Arden Ave M24 65 B5
Arden Bldgs SK3 170 E8
Arden Bsns Ctr SK6 112 E6
Arden Cl Ashton-u-L OL6 85 F6
Bury BL9 44 E8
Gatley SK8 131 C7
Glossop SK13 116 A8
Arden Ct SK7 123 D1
Arden Gr M40 65 C1
Arden Hall SK6 112 D7
Arden Ho OL2 48 E4
Arden Lodge Rd M23 120 E7
Arden Prim Sch SK6 112 D3
Arden Rd SK6 112 E7
Arden St OL9 66 A3
Arden Wlk 6 Sale M33 107 C5
Stockport SK1 169 E1
Ardenfield M34 113 A7
Ardenfield Dr M22 121 E3
Ardens Cl M27 61 D2
Ardent Way M25 63 B1
Ardern Gr SK1 170 F8
Ardern Rd M8 63 F2
Arderne Pl 10 SK9 137 A1
Arderne Rd WA15 120 A8
Ardingly Wlk M23 120 D8
Ardley Rd BL6 22 C4
Ardmore Wlk M22 121 E2
Ardwick Gn N M12 163 C7
Ardwick Gn S M12,M13 163 C7
Ardwick Sta M12 164 D7
Arena App BL6 39 C7
Argo St BL3 147 D4
Argosy Dr Eccles M30 94 F7
Wythenshawe M90 129 F7
Argus St OL8 66 C2
Argyle Ave
Manchester M14 98 E4
Walkden M28 60 C5
Whitefield M45 63 A8
Argyle Cres OL10 29 B1
Argyle Par OL10 29 A1
Argyle St Atherton M46 58 C2
Bury BL9 140 F4
Droylsden M43 84 A1
Hazel Grove SK7 124 E2
Heywood OL10 29 A1
Hindley WN2 56 E5
Manchester M18 99 D5
Mossley OL5 68 C1
Oldham OL1 67 B8
14 Rochdale OL16 31 A4
Swinton M27 79 E7
Wigan WN5 54 F6
Argyll Ave M32 96 B2
Argyll Cl Failsworth M35 84 B7
Garswood WN4 72 C4
Argyll Park Rd M35 84 B7
Argyll Rd Cheadle SK8 122 F5
Oldham OL9 65 F4
Argyll St OL6 85 E3
Ariel Wlk 4 WA3 90 E8
Ark St 3 M19 99 A2
Arkendale Cl M35 84 C7
Arkholme M28 78 A8
Arkholme Wlk M40 83 B7
Arkle Ave SK8,SK9 131 E4
Arkle Dr OL9 65 F8
Arkley Wlk M13 163 B6
Arkwright Dr SK6 126 A6
Arkwright Rd SK6 126 A6
Arkwright St Horwich BL6 22 C2
Oldham OL9 152 C6
Arkwright Way OL11 31 A2
Arlen Ct BL2 148 B5
Arlen Rd BL2 148 B5
Arlen Way OL10 29 B2
Arley Ave Bury BL9 27 F6
Manchester M20 109 F5
Arley Cl Altrincham WA14 119 D8
Dukinfield SK16 101 D6
Wigan WN2 38 B2
Arley Dr Sale M33 108 A2
Shaw OL2 49 D8
Arley Gr SK3 123 D4
Arley Ho M23 121 A4
Arley La WN1,WN2 20 D2
Arley Mere Cl SK8 122 F3
Arley Moss Wlk M13 163 B7
Arley St Ince-in-M WN3 55 F4
Radcliffe M26 44 B1
Arley Way Atherton M46 58 E2
22 Denton M34 101 A1
Arlies Cl SK15 86 A4
Arlies La SK15 86 B4
Arlies Prim Sch SK15 86 A4
Arlies St OL6 85 D4
Arlington Ave
Denton M34 101 A2
Manchester M25 63 B2
Swinton M27 79 D6
Arlington Cl
Ramsbottom BL9 11 C2
Royton OL2 48 E2
Arlington Cres SK9 136 E5
Arlington Dr
Golborne WN7 91 C8
Poynton SK12 133 D3
Stockport SK2 124 A3
Arlington Rd
Cheadle SK8 122 C4
Stretford M32 96 B1
Arlington St
4 Ashton-u-L OL6 166 C3
Bolton BL3 147 F3
Manchester M8 155 F8
Salford M3 158 D2
Arlington Way SK9 136 E5
Arliss Ave M19 111 A8
Arm Rd OL15 15 E4
Armadale Ave M9 65 A4
Armadale Cl SK3 170 F5
Armadale Rd Bolton BL3 40 E5
Dukinfield SK16 101 D7
Armdale Rise OL4 49 E1
Armit Rd OL3 68 E5
Armitage Ave M38 59 F4
Armitage CE Prim Sch M12 164 E6
Armitage Cl Hyde SK14 113 E8
Middleton M24 64 D7
Oldham OL8 66 C3
Armitage Ct M12 164 F6
Armitage Gr M38 59 F4
Armitage Ho 4 M6 80 C3
Armitage Owen Wlk 4 M40 83 A7
Armitage Rd WA14 119 D3
Armitage St M30 79 D1
Armitstead St 5 WN2 56 D4
Armour Pl M9 64 C2
Armoury Bank WN4 73 B3
Armoury St SK3 170 E8
Armstrong Hurst Cl OL12 15 B2
Armstrong St Horwich BL6 22 C2
Wigan WN2 38 A3
Arncliffe WA14 119 D2
Arncliffe Cl
5 Farnworth BL4 42 D1
Hindley WN2 56 C4
Arncliffe Dr M23 121 A3
Arncliffe Rise OL4 50 A4
Arncot Rd BL1 24 F5
Arncott Cl OL2 49 A4
Arne Cl SK2 125 A5
Arne St OL9 152 A5
Arnesby Ave M33 108 E5
Arnesby Gr BL2 148 B8
Arnfield Dr 1 M28 78 B6
Arnfield La SK13 103 F8
Arnfield Rd
Manchester M20 110 C6
Stockport SK3 170 D5
Arnold Ave Heywood OL10 46 E7
Hyde SK14 113 F7
Arnold Cl SK16 102 A7
Arnold Ct M16 97 E1
Arnold Dr Droylsden M43 84 A1
Middleton M24 47 C3
Arnold Rd Bolton BL7 24 F8
Hyde SK14 113 F7
Manchester M16 97 E1
Arnold St Ashton-u-L OL6 166 C3
Bolton BL1 142 C2
Oldham OL1 67 A8
Stockport SK3 170 E7
Arnold Wlk 9 M34 113 A7
Arnolds Yd WA14 119 D5
Arnott Cres M15 162 F5
Arnside Ave
Chadderton OL9 152 A5
Hazel Grove SK7 124 C2
Ince-in-M WN2 56 A7
Reddish SK4 111 E6

Arnside Cl Gatley SK8 .... **122** B4
High Lane SK6 .... **134** E8
Shaw OL2 .... **49** D7
Arnside Dr
Dukinfield SK14 .... **101** C4
Rochdale OL11 .... **29** E5
Salford M6 .... **80** B3
Arnside Gr Bolton BL2 ... **42** E8
Sale M33 .... **108** B6
Arnside Rd Hindley WN2 .. **57** A5
Wigan WN5 .... **54** B8
Arnside St M14 .... **98** B2
Arosa Ct M20 .... **110** C7
Arran Ave Oldham OL8 .... **66** F3
Sale M33 .... **108** C3
Stretford M32 .... **96** A2
Arran Cl BL3 .... **40** E6
Arran Gdns M41 .... **95** C5
Arran Gr M26 .... **43** E5
Arran Rd SK16 .... **101** C7
Arran St
12 Manchester M40 .... **64** F1
Salford M7 .... **155** D6
Arran Wlk OL10 .... **29** A1
Arrandale Ct M41 .... **95** D3
Arras Gr M34 .... **99** F3
Arreton Sq M14 .... **98** D3
Arrivals Way M90 .... **130** B7
Arrow St Bolton BL1 ...... **145** E8
Leigh WN7 .... **76** B3
Salford M7 .... **155** D5
Arrow Trad Est M34 ...... **100** D5
Arrowfield Dr M21 .... **109** D7
Arrowfield Rd M21 .... **109** D7
Arrowhill Rd M21 .... **109** D7
Arrowscroft Way SK14 .... **171** D4
Arrowsmith Ct **7** BL6 ... **22** E1
Arrowsmith Wlk **16** M11 . **160** F1
Arthill La WA14 .... **118** B1
Arthington St OL16 .... **31** B8
Arthog Dr WA15 .... **128** F8
Arthog Rd
Altrincham WA15 .... **128** F8
Manchester M20 .... **110** C3
Arthur Ave M28 .... **60** C5
Arthur La BL2 .... **26** B2
Arthur Millwood Ct M3 .. **158** D1
Arthur Rd M16 .... **97** C3
Arthur St Bury BL8 .... **27** C2
Eccles M30 .... **79** C1
Farnworth BL4 .... **60** D8
Heywood OL10 .... **29** D2
Hindley WN2 .... **56** E5
Hyde SK14 .... **101** C1
Leigh WN7 .... **75** E4
Little Lever BL3 .... **43** B3
Prestwich M25 .... **62** F4
Reddish SK5 .... **111** E7
Rochdale OL12 .... **139** D8
Shaw OL2 .... **149** B7
Swinton M27 .... **79** D7
Walkden M28 .... **60** E1
Walkden M28 .... **60** E1
Arthur Terr **13** SK5 .... **111** E7
Arthurs La OL3 .... **69** B6
Artillery Ct M13 .... **163** C7
Artillery Pl M22 .... **121** F4
Artillery St Bolton BL3 .. **145** F5
Manchester M3 .... **162** E8
Arundale BL5 .... **39** F2
Arundale Ave M16 .... **97** E1
Arundale Cl SK14 .... **102** F3
Arundale Ct M16 .... **97** E1
Arundale Gr SK14 .... **102** F3
Arundale Prim Sch
SK14 .... **102** F3
Arundel Ave
Hazel Grove SK7 .... **133** D8
Prestwich M45 .... **63** B7
Rochdale OL11 .... **30** E4
Urmston M41 .... **94** C1
Arundel Cl
Altrincham WA15 .... **120** C1
Bury BL8 .... **27** C6
Mossley SK15 .... **86** F6
Arundel Dr WN7 .... **75** F6
Arundel Gr SK2 .... **124** B8
Arundel Grange SK13 .... **104** A1
Arundel Rd SK8 .... **132** A6
Arundel St Ashton-u-L OL6 . **85** E3
Bolton BL1 .... **24** E5
Glossop SK13 .... **104** A1
Hindley WN2 .... **56** E5
Manchester M15 .... **68** B1
Mossley OL5 .... **68** B1
Oldham OL4 .... **67** C7
Rochdale OL11 .... **30** E4
Swinton M27 .... **61** C1
Wigan WN5 .... **54** F6
Arundel Wlk OL9 .... **152** A6
Asby Cl M24 .... **46** D2
Ascension Rd M7 .... **158** D4
Ascot Ave Sale M33 ...... **107** D4
Stretford M32 .... **96** F3
Ascot Cl Chadderton OL9 . **152** C7
Rochdale OL11 .... **29** E8
Ascot Dr Atherton M46 ... **58** E4
Hazel Grove SK7 .... **125** A2
Urmston M41 .... **94** C2
Ascot Mdws BL9 .... **141** C4
Ascot Par M19 .... **110** F6
Ascot Rd Failsworth M40 .. **83** B4
Little Lever BL3 .... **42** F3
Ascot Wlk M6 .... **81** A5
Ascroft Ave WN6 .... **36** F3

Ascroft St
Chadderton OL9 .... **152** A5
Oldham OL1 .... **153** F6
Wigan WN1 .... **151** E7
Asgard Dr M5 .... **161** C8
Asgard St M5 .... **161** C8
Ash Ave Altrincham WA14 . **119** A5
Cheadle SK8 .... **122** E5
Irlam M44 .... **105** D5
Newton-le-W WA12 .... **89** C2
Ash Cl Appley Bridge WN6 . **35** D7
Ashton-u-L OL6 .... **85** D5
Mottram-in-L SK14 .... **103** A4
Rochdale OL12 .... **15** C4
Stockport SK2 .... **124** C5
Ash Ct
Manchester,Heaton Moor
SK4 .... **168** B3
Manchester,Whalley Range
M16 .... **97** E2
Romiley SK6 .... **113** A5
Ash Dr M27 .... **61** C2
Ash Gr Altrincham WA15 .. **119** F7
Altrincham,Rosehill WA14 .. **119** C1
Bolton,Harwood BL2 .... **25** F3
Bolton,Victory BL1 .... **144** B8
Bury BL8 .... **27** A5
Droylsden M43 .... **100** A8
Gatley SK8 .... **131** B8
Golborne WA3 .... **90** B8
Handforth SK9 .... **131** C3
8 Horwich BL6 .... **22** E1
Littleborough OL15 .... **15** F5
Manchester M14 .... **98** E4
Marple SK6 .... **125** E5
Newhey OL16 .... **32** A3
Oldham OL4 .... **68** A7
Orrell WN5 .... **53** F6
Prestwich M25 .... **63** A6
Ramsbottom BL0 .... **10** F3
Reddish SK4 .... **111** D5
Royton OL2 .... **48** D6
Stalybridge SK15 .... **85** F3
Standish WN6 .... **36** F8
Stretford M32 .... **108** C8
Swinton M27 .... **79** D5
Walkden M28 .... **60** E1
Westhoughton BL5 .... **57** E7
Ash Grove Cres WN5 ...... **71** E6
Ash Hill Dr OL5 .... **86** E8
Ash La Altrincham WA15 .. **120** C2
Wigan WN2 .... **38** A2
Ash Lawns BL1 .... **144** B7
Ash Lea Grange M30 ...... **79** F3
Ash Leigh Dr BL1 .... **40** E8
Ash Lo SK12 .... **133** D4
Ash Rd Coppull PR7 ...... **19** E8
Droylsden M43 .... **83** F2
Hollinfare WA13 .... **105** A2
Kearsley BL4 .... **60** F5
Partington M31 .... **105** D3
Poynton SK12 .... **133** F3
Reddish M34 .... **99** F3
Ash Sq OL4 .... **67** D8
Ash St Bolton BL2 ...... **148** A6
Bury BL9 .... **141** A2
Denton M34 .... **100** D7
Failsworth M35 .... **83** E8
Golborne WA3 .... **74** B2
Hazel Grove SK7 .... **124** D3
Heywood OL10 .... **29** B3
Manchester M9 .... **157** D7
Middleton M24 .... **65** C8
Oldham OL4 .... **67** B6
Rochdale OL11 .... **30** C2
Salford M6 .... **154** F2
Stockport SK3 .... **123** B8
2 Tyldesley M29 .... **59** A1
Ash Tree Ave M43 .... **83** F2
Ash Tree Dr SK14 .... **101** F5
Ash Tree Rd
Dukinfield SK14 .... **102** B5
Manchester M8 .... **64** A1
Ash Wlk Chadderton OL9 .. **152** B8
Middleton M24 .... **64** F6
Sale M33 .... **107** D5
Ashawe Cl M38 .... **59** F3
Ashawe Gr M38 .... **59** F3
Ashawe Terr M38 .... **59** E3
Ashbank Ave BL3 .... **40** E6
Ashbee St BL1 .... **143** E3
Ashberry Cl SK9 .... **137** D8
Ashborne Ave
Bolton BL2 .... **148** B6
Cheadle SK8 .... **122** F6
Hindley WN2 .... **57** B3
Middleton M24 .... **47** C3
Urmston M41 .... **94** E2
Wigan WN2 .... **38** A2
Ashborne Cres M33 ...... **108** D2
Ashbourne Dr
Ashton-u-L OL6 .... **85** F6
High Lane SK6 .... **134** F6
Ashbourne Gdns WN2 ...... **56** F5
Ashbourne Gr
Salford M7 .... **155** E7
Whitefield M45 .... **45** E1
Worsley M28 .... **78** E8
Ashbourne Rd
Denton M34 .... **100** C2
Eccles M30 .... **79** E1
Hazel Grove SK7 .... **133** F8
Salford M6 .... **80** C5
Stretford M32 .... **96** A3

Ashbourne Sq OL8 .... **153** E5
Ashbourne St OL11 .... **13** E1
Ashbridge M17 .... **96** B6
Ashbridge Rd M35 .... **84** B6
Ashbrook Ave M34 .... **100** B3
Ashbrook Cl Gatley SK8 .. **122** B1
Reddish M34 .... **100** B3
Whitefield M45 .... **63** B8
Ashbrook Cres OL12 ...... **15** C4
Ashbrook Farm Cl SK5 .... **99** F2
Ashbrook Hey La OL12 .... **15** C4
Ashbrook La 5 SK5 ...... **99** F2
Ashbrook Rd OL4 .... **67** F5
Ashbrook St M11 .... **100** A7
Ashburn **11** OL10 .... **29** C2
Ashburn Ave M19 .... **110** F5
Ashburn Cl 2 BL6 .... **22** D1
Ashburn Gr SK4 .... **169** D3
Ashburn Rd SK4 .... **169** D3
Ashburne Ho M14 .... **98** D4
Ashburner St BL1 .... **145** E6
Ashburton Cl SK14 ...... **102** E2
Ashburton Rd SK3 .... **170** E5
Ashburton Rd W W M17,
M41 .... **95** E7
Ashbury Cl BL3 .... **145** E5
Ashbury Meadow Sch
M11 .... **164** F8
Ashbury Pl M40 .... **160** E4
Ashburys Sta M12 ...... **165** A7
Ashby Ave M19 .... **110** E4
Ashby Cl Leigh WN7 ...... **75** C8
Whitefield M45 .... **63** B7
Ashby Rd WN3 .... **55** B3
Ashcombe Dr Bolton BL2 .. **42** A8
Radcliffe M26 .... **43** D5
Ashcombe Wlk **7** M11 ... **160** F1
Ashcott Ave M22 .... **121** D4
Ashcott Cl BL6 .... **40** E5
Ashcroft **6** Rochdale OL12 . **15** C4
Wilmslow SK9 .... **136** F5
Ashcroft Ave M6 .... **154** E4
Ashcroft Ct OL1 .... **153** F6
Ashcroft Rd WN2 .... **56** E4
Ashdale Ave BL3 .... **40** E5
Ashdale Cl Coppull PR7 .. **19** D8
Reddish SK5 .... **111** F5
Ashdale Cres M43 .... **83** F1
Ashdale Dr Gatley SK8 ... **122** B2
Manchester M20 .... **110** D5
Ashdale Rd Hindley WN2 .. **57** A5
Wigan WN3 .... **55** A2
Ashdene Ashton-u-L OL6 .. **85** A2
Rochdale OL12 .... **14** D4
Ashdene Cl
Chadderton OL1,OL9 .... **48** C1
Oldham OL4 .... **67** F7
Ashdene Cres BL2 .... **25** D4
Ashdene Prim Sch SK9 ... **136** F5
Ashdene Rd
Manchester,Heaton Mersey
SK4 .... **110** D2
Manchester,Withington
M20 .... **110** D6
Wilmslow SK9 .... **136** F5
Ashdown Ave
Manchester M9 .... **64** D4
Romiley SK6 .... **113** C5
Ashdown Dr Bolton BL2 ... **25** C3
Pendlebury M27 .... **80** A6
Walkden M28 .... **78** A8
Ashdown Gr M9 .... **64** D4
Ashdown Rd SK4 .... **168** C3
Ashdown Terr M9 .... **64** D4
Ashdown Way OL2 .... **48** E8
Ashdowne Lawns SK15 .... **86** D3
Ashen Bottom BB4 .... **1** C6
Ashes Cl SK15 .... **102** C8
Ashes Dr BL2 .... **42** F8
Ashes La Glossop SK13 .. **104** B2
Milnrow OL16 .... **31** F7
Oldham OL4 .... **67** F6
Stalybridge SK15 .... **102** C8
Ashfell Ct 11 M21 .... **96** F1
Ashfield M34 .... **101** A5
Ashfield Ave
Atherton M46 .... **58** C4
Hindley WN2 .... **56** F4
Rochdale OL11 .... **139** F5
Ashfield Cl Lymm WA13 .. **117** B4
Salford M6 .... **154** E3
Ashfield Cres
Billinge WN5 .... **71** D4
Cheadle SK8 .... **122** D6
Oldham OL4 .... **67** F6
Ashfield Ct M41 .... **95** D1
Ashfield Dr Aspull WN2 .. **38** D6
Failsworth M40 .... **83** D4
Ashfield Gr Bolton BL2 ... **25** A6
Irlam M44 .... **105** C6
Reddish M18 .... **99** F4
Romiley SK6 .... **114** B1
Stockport SK3 .... **123** F4
Wigan WN6 .... **37** A8
Ashfield House Gdns
WN6 .... **36** F8
Ashfield La OL16 .... **31** F4
Ashfield Lo M20 .... **109** F2
Ashfield Park Dr WN5 .... **54** A8
Ashfield Rd Adlington PR6 . **21** B8
Altrincham WA15 .... **119** E4
Cheadle SK8 .... **122** D6
Cheadle SK8 .... **122** D6
Hadfield SK13 .... **171** E3

Ashfield Rd continued
Manchester M13 .... **98** E3
Rochdale OL11 .... **139** F5
Sale M33 .... **108** B5
Stockport SK3 .... **123** F4
Urmston M41 .... **95** D2
Ashfield Sq M43 .... **83** F2
Ashfield St OL8 .... **66** C3
Ashfield Terr WN6 .... **35** C8
Ashfield Valley Prim Sch
OL11 .... **30** E4
Ashford M33 .... **107** C4
Ashford Ave
Boothstown M28 .... **77** F6
Eccles M30 .... **95** C8
Swinton M27 .... **59** F2
Swinton M27 .... **79** C7
Ashford Cl Bolton BL2 .... **25** C4
Bury BL8 .... **27** B1
Handforth SK9 .... **131** C4
Ashford Ct 11 OL4 .... **49** D1
Ashford St 15 SK13 ..... **171** E1
Ashford Mews SK13 ...... **171** E1
Ashford Rd
Manchester M20 .... **110** B7
Reddish SK4 .... **111** D6
Wilmslow SK9 .... **137** A4
Ashford Rise WN1 .... **37** B4
Ashford St OL6 .... **166** B4
Ashford Wlk Bolton BL2 .. **143** E1
Chadderton OL9 .... **152** B6
Ashgate Ave M22 .... **121** E4
Ashgill Wlk 4 M9 .... **157** E7
Ashgrove OL16 .... **31** B1
Ashia Cl OL16 .... **31** B6
Ashill Wlk M13 .... **163** C8
Ashington Cl BL1 .... **142** B3
Ashington Dr BL8 .... **26** F2
Ashington Way WN5 .... **36** B1
Ashkirk St 4 M18 .... **99** D5
Ashland Ave
Ashton-in-M WN4 .... **73** A4
5 Wigan WN1 .... **37** C2
Ashlands BL3 .... **108** A5
Ashlands Ave
Failsworth M40 .... **65** C1
Swinton M27 .... **79** D6
Walkden M28 .... **78** A7
Ashlands Cl BL0 .... **11** D2
Ashlands Dr M34 .... **100** E6
Ashlands Rd WA15 .... **108** A1
Ashlar Dr M12 .... **164** E8
Ashlea Gr OL4 .... **68** B6
Ashleigh Ave SK13 ...... **104** A1
Ashleigh Cl OL2 .... **48** E2
Ashleigh Rd WA15 .... **120** B8
Ashley Ave Bolton BL2 ... **42** D8
Manchester M16 .... **97** D4
Swinton M27 .... **79** D6
Urmston M41 .... **94** E2
Ashley CE Prim Sch
WA15 .... **128** F5
Ashley Cl M40 .... **160** C4
Ashley Court Dr M40,OL9 . **65** F1
Ashley Cres M27 .... **79** D7
Ashley Ct
Altrincham WA15 .... **119** E1
Failsworth M40 .... **65** F1
Manchester SK4 .... **168** B4
Swinton M27 .... **61** F2
Ashley Dr Bramhall SK7 .. **132** C6
Leigh WN7 .... **75** C8
Sale M33 .... **107** E2
Swinton M27 .... **79** D6
Ashley Gdns
High Lane SK6 .... **134** D8
Hyde SK14 .... **167** E1
Ashley Gr 8 BL4 .... **60** C8
Ashley La M9 .... **157** F8
Ashley Mews Hyde SK14 .. **167** E1
Whitefield M45 .... **63** B7
Ashley Mill La N WA14 .. **128** E8
Ashley Mill La S WA14 .. **128** E7
Ashley Rd
Altrincham WA14,WA15 ..... **119** E2
Ashley WA14,WA15,WA16 .... **128** C4
Ashley,Ashley Heath
WA14,WA15 .... **128** C7
Droylsden M43 .... **83** E2
Handforth SK9 .... **131** B1
Hindley WN2 .... **57** B3
Stockport SK3 .... **124** C8
Wilmslow SK9 .... **137** A4
Ashley St Hyde SK14 .... **167** E4
Manchester M4 .... **159** B3
Oldham OL9 .... **152** C7
Salford M6 .... **154** E3
Ashley Sta WA15 .... **128** E5
Ashleymill La WA14 ...... **128** D7
Ashleys Mill SK4 .... **168** B3
Ashling Ct M29 .... **59** D1
Ashlor St BL9 .... **140** E1
Ashlyn Gr M14 .... **110** D8
Ashlyne OL6 .... **166** C3
Ashmeade WA15 .... **120** B1
Ashmill Wlk M9 .... **156** C6
Ashmond **12** OL4 .... **67** F6
Ashmoor Rd M22 .... **121** E1
Ashmoor Wlk M22 .... **121** E1
Ashmore Ave SK3 .... **123** B7
Ashmore St M29 .... **122** F7
Ashmount Dr OL12 .... **14** F2
Ashness Cl BL6 .... **21** F3
Ashness Dr Bolton BL2 ... **25** E1
Bramhall SK7 .... **132** E8
Middleton M24 .... **46** D3
Ashover Ave M12 .... **164** E6
Ashover Cl 8 BL1 .... **24** C6

Ashover Ct M12 .... **164** F6
Ashover St M32 .... **96** E3
Ashridge Cl BL6 .... **40** C6
Ashridge Dr
Dukinfield SK16 .... **101** B7
Eccles M30 .... **95** C8
Ashridge Way WN5 .... **36** B1
Ashstead Rd M33 .... **108** C1
Ashton Ave M14 .... **119** E6
Ashton Cres OL9 .... **66** A2
Ashton Ct Denton M34 ... **100** F6
Sale M33 .... **107** E4
Ashton Field Dr M28 ..... **60** C4
Ashton Gallery 6 WN1 .. **150** C8
Ashton Gdns
Glossop SK13 .... **116** C7
Rochdale OL11 .... **139** E5
Ashton Grange Ind Est
WN4 .... **73** B6
Ashton Heath WN4 .... **73** C2
Ashton Hill La M43 ...... **100** A8
Ashton Ho
Manchester M15 .... **162** E8
Hyde SK14 .... **167** E4
Ashton La Middleton M24 .. **65** A8
Sale M33 .... **107** F5
Ashton New Rd
Droylsden M11,M43 .... **83** C1
Manchester M11 .... **160** F1
Ashton Old Rd
Manchester,Beswick M11,
M12 .... **164** E8
Manchester,Openshaw M11 . **99** D7
Ashton on Mersey Sch
M33 .... **107** F3
Ashton Pl SK7 .... **124** F1
Ashton Rd
Brinnington SK6 .... **112** E6
Carrington M31 .... **106** E3
Denton M34 .... **100** E5
Droylsden M43 .... **84** B1
Dukinfield SK14 .... **101** E5
Golborne WA3 .... **74** A2
Manchester M9 .... **64** D5
Newton-le-W WA12 .... **89** C5
Oldham OL8,OL7 .... **66** F3
Windy Arbour WN4,WN5 ...... **72** B8
Ashton Rd E M35 .... **84** A7
Ashton Rd W M35 .... **83** F7
Ashton St Bolton BL3 ... **146** B4
Chadderton OL9 .... **66** A3
Dukinfield SK16 .... **101** A7
Glossop SK13 .... **116** B8
6 Heywood OL10 .... **29** C2
Little Lever BL3 .... **43** B3
Manchester M9 .... **157** F8
Rochdale OL11 .... **139** E5
Romiley SK6 .... **113** C6
Wigan WN1 .... **151** E8
Ashton West End Prim Sch
OL7 .... **84** F2
Ashton-under-Lyne Sixth
Form Coll OL6 .... **85** E3
Ashton-under-Lyne Sta
OL6 .... **166** B3
Ashurst Ave M11 .... **83** B2
Ashurst Cl Bolton BL2 .... **25** F3
Hyde SK14 .... **102** A1
Ashurst Dr SK3,SK8 ...... **123** B5
Ashurst Gdns OL6 .... **166** B4
Ashurst Rd
Shevington Moor WN6 .... **19** B2
Wythenshawe M22 .... **121** F3
Ashville Terr M40 .... **64** F1
Ashwater Wlk 8 M9 ...... **64** E5
Ashway OL6 .... **166** A3
Ashway Clough N SK2 .... **124** C5
Ashway Clough S SK2 .... **124** D5
Ashwell Ave WA3 .... **74** D1
Ashwell Rd M23 .... **121** B5
Ashwell St BL2 .... **25** B3
Ashwin Wlk 6 M8 .... **155** F6
Ashwood
Altrincham WA14 .... **119** B1
Chadderton OL9 .... **65** E7
Glossop SK13 .... **115** F8
Kearsley M26 .... **61** B7
Ashwood Ave
Abram Brow WN2 .... **74** C7
Ashton-in-M WN4 .... **73** A2
Golborne WA3 .... **90** D8
Manchester M20 .... **109** E4
Ramsbottom BL0 .... **11** C1
Reddish M34 .... **100** B3
Sale M33 .... **107** E3
Walkden M28 .... **60** C5
Ashwood Cres SK6 .... **125** F7
Ashwood Dr M20 .... **109** E5
Ashwood Dr Bury BL8 ..... **27** B6
Littleborough OL15 .... **15** F8
Royton OL2 .... **48** C5
Ashwood Rd SK12 .... **135** D6
Ashworth Ave
Denton M34 .... **100** F7
Little Lever BL3 .... **43** C3
Urmston M41 .... **94** E2
Ashworth Ct
1 Radcliffe M26 .... **44** C4
Shaw OL2 .... **149** B6
Ashworth Gdns OL3 .... **69** B5
Ashworth La Bolton BL1 .. **25** A5

Ashworth La continued
Mottram-in-L SK14 .....102 F2
Ashworth Mews OL10 ....29 A2
Ashworth Rd OL10,OL11 .13 A1
Ashworth St Aspull WN2 ..38 E4
3 Bacup OL13 ....3 D8
Bury BL8 ....27 C3
Denton M34 ....100 E4
Failsworth M35 ....83 D6
Farnworth BL4 ....60 C8
Heywood OL10 ....46 E8
Manchester M7,M8 ....155 E5
Oldham OL1 ....153 F6
Radcliffe M26 ....44 C4
11 Rawtenstall BB4 .....2 F8
Rochdale OL12 ....139 E8
Ashworth Terr
2 Bacup OL13 ....3 B8
Bolton BL2 ....7 E6
Ashworth Way 8 SK14 .102 F2
Asia St 8 BL3 ....42 A3
Askern Ave M22 ......121 D3
Askett CI M40 ....59 C8
Askhigg CI M46 ....76 A8
Askrigg Wlk 8 M13 ...98 F4
Askwith Dr WN2 ......56 F4
Askwith Rd WN2 ......56 F3
Aspell CI M24 ....64 E8
Aspen CI
Altrincham WA15 ......120 E5
Stockport SK4 ....168 A1
Westhoughton BL5 .....39 F2
Aspen Gdns OL12 .....14 A1
Aspen Gn M34 ....101 A2
Aspen Way SK6 ....135 A7
Aspen Wood Dr OL9 ...65 E7
Aspens The SK8 ......122 A6
Aspenshaw Cotts SK22 .127 E4
Aspenshaw Rd SK22 ...127 E3
Aspenwood WN4 ......73 A2
Aspenwood CI SK6 ....125 E7
Aspenwood Dr
Manchester M9 ....64 D2
Sale M33 ....107 C4
Aspin La M4 ....159 A3
Aspinal CI BL6 ....22 D1
Aspinal Prim Sch M18 ..99 E3
Aspinall CI M28 ......59 F2
Aspinall Cres M28 ....59 F2
Aspinall Gr 12 M28 ...59 F3
Aspinall Rd Heywood OL10 .29 E2
Horwich BL6 ....22 D1
Manchester M14 ....98 C3
Middleton M24 ....65 C7
5 Platt Bridge WN2 ....56 A2
Aspinall Way BL6 .....22 C1
Aspland Rd SK14 .....113 F8
Aspull Arc 7 WN1 ....150 C8
Aspull Church Prim Sch
WN2 ....38 C4
Aspull Comm WN7 ....75 C1
Aspull St OL4 ....67 C5
Aspull Wlk M13 ......163 C6
Asquith Rd M19 .....110 F6
Asquith St SK5 ....99 F1
Assheton Ave M34 ....84 C1
Assheton CI
Ashton-u-L OL6 ......166 B3
Newton-le-W WA12 ....89 B4
Assheton Cres M40 ...83 D4
Assheton Ho OL6 .....166 B3
Assheton Rd
Failsworth M40 ....83 D4
Shaw OL2 ....48 F7
Assheton St
5 Middleton M24 ....47 A1
9 Middleton M24 ....47 A2
Assheton Way M24 ....65 A8
Assumption Rd M24 ...46 D1
Astan Ave M43 ....83 D2
Astbury Ave
Droylsden M34 ....84 D1
Manchester M21 ......109 C4
Astbury CI
2 Altrincham WA15 ...119 E6
Bury BL9 ....45 A8
Golborne WA3 ....91 B8
Oldham OL4 ....67 C6
Astbury Cres SK3 ....170 D6
Astbury St M26 ......44 B1
Astbury Wlk SK8 .....123 A5
Aster Ave BL4 ....42 A2
Aster Ho OL1 ....48 E1
Aster St OL1 ....48 E1
Aster Wlk M31 ......105 F2
Astley CI M40 ....48 F7
Astley Ct M44 ....105 E8
Astley Gdns SK16 ....101 B8
Astley Gr SK15 ....85 F3
Astley Green Colliery Mus*
M29 ....77 C4
Astley Hall Dr
Ramsbottom BL0 ......11 C4
Tyldesley M29 ....77 B6
Astley La 8 BL1 ......143 E3
Astley Rd 8 BL2 .....25 E5
Irlam M44 ....93 C3
Stalybridge SK15 ......85 F2

Astley St continued
Stalybridge SK15 ......102 A8
Stockport SK4 ....169 E1
Tyldesley M29 ....77 A7
Astley Terr 7 SK16 ...166 C1
Aston Ave M14 ....98 A2
Aston Bldgs BB4 ......2 F7
Aston CI SK3 ....123 C6
Aston Gdns 8 BL4 ....42 D1
Aston Gr M29 ....59 C1
Aston Ho BL1 ....144 C7
Aston Way 18 SK9 ...131 D5
Astor Rd Manchester M19 .110 E7
Salford M50 ....80 C1
Astra Bsns Pk M17 ...95 F8
Astra Ind Ctr OL11 ...30 C3
Atcham Gr M9 ....64 B6
Athenaeum Art Gall The*
M1 ....163 A8
Athenian Gdns 12 M7 .81 C5
Athens Dr M28 ....60 C2
Athens St SK1 ....124 A8
Athens Way OL4 ......67 E6
Atherfield BL2 ....25 E4
Atherfield CI 8 M18 ..99 F6
Atherleigh Gr M7 .....75 F7
Atherleigh Way WN7 ..75 E5
Atherley Gr OL9 ......65 E4
Atherstone 10 OL12 ..139 F8
Atherstone Ave M8 ...64 A2
Atherstone CI BL8 ....27 C4
Atherton Ave SK14 ..103 A4
Atherton CI M35 ......84 B5
Atherton Gr SK14 ...103 A4
Atherton Green Hall Sch
M46 ....58 F4
Atherton Ho M46 ....58 D8
Atherton La M44 ....105 E5
Atherton Rd WN2 ....56 D5
Atherton Sq 8 WN1 ..150 C8
Atherton St Adlington PR7 .21 A6
Bacup OL13 ....3 C8
Bickershaw WN2 ......74 E8
Eccles M30 ....79 B1
Manchester M3 ....158 E1
Oldham OL4 ....67 E5
Oldham OL4 ....67 F5
9 Oldham OL4 ....67 F6
Stockport SK3 ....170 D8
7 Wigan WN5 ....54 F6
Atherton Sta M46 ....58 E4
Atherton Way Bacup OL13 .3 B8
4 Eccles M30 ....79 C1
Athlone Ave Bolton BL1 .24 D5
Bury BL9 ....140 F4
Cheadle SK8 ....123 C5
Manchester M40 ......83 A8
Athol Cres WN2 ......57 B3
Athol St Ashton-u-L OL6 .166 C1
Eccles M30 ....79 C1
Ramsbottom BL0 ......138 C7
Reddish M18 ....99 E3
Rochdale OL12 ....15 B1
Stockport SK4 ....169 D3
Athole St M5,M6 .....154 F1
Atholl Ave M32 ......96 A2
Atholl CI BL3 ....40 F6
Atholl Dr OL10 ....46 A8
Atholl Gr WN3 ....55 A3
Atkin St M28 ....60 D2
Atkinson Ave BL3 ....42 A4
Atkinson Ho M33 ....108 B3
Atkinson Rd Sale M33 .108 A5
Urmston M41 ....95 D2
Atkinson St Abram WN2 .74 B8
Manchester M3 ....158 E1
Oldham OL9 ....153 D8
2 Rochdale OL11 .....30 C2
Stockport SK1 ....124 A7
Atlanta Ave M90 .....130 A8
Atlantic Bsns Ctr WA14 .119 C7
Atlantic St WA14 ....119 B6
Atlantic Wlk 18 M11 .160 F1
Atlas St Ashton-u-L OL7 .85 A5
Dukinfield SK16 ......101 D8
Oldham OL8 ....153 E6
Atlas Trad Est SK5 ...111 F7
Atlow Dr 8 M23 .....121 B5
Attenbury's La WA14 .119 E8
Attenbury's Pk Est
WA14 ....119 E8
Attercliffe Rd M21 ...109 A7
Attewell St M11 .....165 A8
Attingham Wlk
Denton M34 ....100 E1
Wigan WN3 ....150 A5
Attleboro Rd M40 ....83 A7
Attlee Ave WA3 ......92 C4
Attlee Way M12 .....160 B5
Attwood Rd WA15 ...120 B5
Attwood St M12 .....99 A3
Atwood Rd M20 .....110 C4
Atwood St M1 ....163 A8
Auberge Ho BL3 .....147 D3
Aubrey Rd M14 ......110 F7
Aubrey St Rochdale OL11 .139 F5
Salford M5 ....161 A7
Auburn Ave Hyde SK14 .167 E1
Romiley SK6 ....112 F4
Auburn Dr M41 ......94 F1
Auburn Rd Denton M34 ..100 E2
Manchester M16 ......97 B4
Auburn St Bolton BL3 .147 D4

Auburn St continued
Manchester M1 ....159 B1
Manchester M1 ....163 B8
Auckland Dr M6 ......81 A5
Auckland Rd M19 ....110 F8
Audax Wlk M40 ......83 B4
Auden CI M11 ....83 D1
Auden Ct M11 ....83 D1
Audenshaw Ct M34 ..100 E8
Audenshaw Hall Gr
M34 ....100 B7
Audenshaw Prim Sch
M34 ....100 D7
Audenshaw Rd
Ashton-u-L M34 ......100 E8
Denton M34 ....100 D7
Manchester M34 ......100 E6
Audenshaw St Stephen's CE
Prim Sch M34 ....100 E8
Audlem CI M40 ......160 D2
Audlem Wlk SK8 .....123 A5
Audley Ave M32 ......95 F4
Audley Rd M19 ......110 F8
Audley St Ashton-u-L OL6 .85 E2
Mossley OL5 ....68 D1
Audlum Ct BL9 ......141 A2
Audrey Ave M18 .....99 E5
Audrey St M9 ....157 F7
Aughton CI M5 ......71 E4
Aughton St WN2 .....56 D4
Augusta CI OL12 .....14 E2
Augusta St OL12 .....14 E1
Augustine Webster CI
M9 ....157 E8
Augustus St 8 Bolton BL3 .42 A4
Manchester M3,M8 ...159 A4
Augustus Way M15 ..97 E4
Auriga Wlk M7 ......81 C3
Austell Rd M22 ......121 D1
Austen Ave M20 .....79 D1
Austen Rd M30 ......79 D3
Austen St WN3 ......55 A4
Auster CI M14 ......110 A8
Austin Ave WN4 .....72 E4
Austin Ct M20 ......110 C4
Austin Dr M20 ......110 C4
Austin Gr M19 ......110 F8
Austin's La BL6 .....22 F1
Autumn St M13 .....98 C4
Avallon CI BL8 ......26 F7
Avalon Dr M20 .....122 C8
Avalon Pk OL4 ......67 D6
Avebury CI Golborne WA3 .90 E8
Horwich BL6 ....22 F1
Salford M7 ....81 C5
Avebury Rd M23 ....121 A5
Avenham CI M15 ....162 E5
Avening Wlk 7 M22 .121 C2
Avens Rd M31 ......105 F3
Avenue St Bolton BL1 .143 D1
Stockport SK1 ....169 F2
Avenue The Adlington PR6 .21 A8
Alderley Edge SK9 ...137 A1
Altrincham WA15 ....128 F8
Bolton BL2 ....148 B7
Bury BL9 ....27 F5
Eccles M30 ....79 D3
Gatley SK8 ....122 A1
Hadfield SK13 ....104 A4
Leigh WN7 ....76 A6
Newton-le-W WA12 ...89 D4
Orrell WN5 ....53 D3
Romiley SK6 ....112 D4
Sale M33 ....107 F4
Salford M7 ....81 C5
Shaw OL2 ....149 A6
Urmston M41 ....94 E2
Westhoughton BL5 ....39 F1
Wigan,Standish Lower Ground
WN6 ....36 E4
Wigan,Swinley WN1 ..37 D2
Worsley M28 ....78 B3
Worsley M28 ....78 D7
Averham CI WN4 .....73 B2
Averhill M40 ....88 B8
Averill St M40 ....83 D5
Averon Rise OL4 .....49 D4
Avery Trad Est SK5 ..99 E3
Aveson Ave M21 ....109 B6
Avian Dr M14 ....110 B8
Aviary Rd M28 ....78 F6
Aviary The* M28 ....79 A6
Aviemore CI
Garswood WN4 ....72 D4
Ramsbottom BL0 .....11 A2
Avis St OL2 ....149 B7
Avlan CI M40 ....94 F7
Avocet CI Leigh WN7 ..76 A6
Newton-le-W WA12 ...89 C4
Avocet Dr
Altrincham WA14 ....119 B8
Irlam M44 ....94 A4
Avon 10 OL10 ....29 C2
Avon 1 Sk6 ....112 F3
Avon CI Marple SK6 ..125 E5
Milnrow OL16 ....31 F6
Avon Ct 8 M15 ......162 D6
Avon Dr BL9 ....28 A8
Avon Gdns M19 .....111 A6
Avon Rd
Altrincham WA15 ....128 A3
Ashton-in-W WN4 ....73 A5
Billinge WN5 ....71 D3
Chadderton OL9 .....65 D5
Culcheth WA3 ....92 A2

Avon Rd continued
Gatley SK8 ....131 C7
Heywood OL10 ....29 A2
Kearsley BL4 ....61 B5
Manchester M19 .....111 A6
Shaw OL2 ....149 B8
Tyldesley M29 ....77 C7
Wigan WN5 ....54 C7
Avon St Bolton BL1 ..142 B1
Leigh WN7 ....76 B4
Oldham OL8 ....66 F4
Stockport SK3 ....170 E7
Avonbrook Dr OL9 ...65 F2
Avoncliff CI BL1 .....143 D3
Avoncourt Dr M20 ..110 A4
Avondale Ave Bury BL9 .140 F4
Hazel Grove SK7 .....124 F3
Avondale Cres 2 M41 .95 C3
Avondale Ct OL11 ...47 D7
Avondale Dr
Ramsbottom BL0 .....10 F2
Salford M6 ....80 B5
Tyldesley M29 ....77 C6
Avondale High Sch SK3 .123 B7
Avondale Ind Est SK3 .123 B7
Avondale Lo M33 ...108 B3
Avondale Rd
Farnworth BL4 ....59 F8
Hazel Grove SK7 .....124 F2
Stockport SK3 ....123 C8
Stretford M32 ....96 F4
Whitefield M45 ......44 E1
Wigan WN1 ....37 C1
Avondale Rise SK9 ..137 D6
Avondale St Bolton BL1 .142 C1
Manchester M8 ......156 A7
Standish WN6 ....19 E2
Avonhead CI BL6 ....21 F3
Avonlea Dr M19 ....110 E6
Avonlea Rd Droylsden M43 .83 F2
Sale M33 ....107 D1
Avonleigh Gdns 7 OL1 .49 C1
Avril CI SK5 ....111 F8
Avril Ct WN3 ....55 E4
Avro CI M14 ....98 B1
Avro Ct M20 ....65 D8
Avro Way M90 ......129 F7
Avroe Rd M90 ....94 F7
Awburn Rd SK14 ....102 E1
Axbridge Wlk M40 ..160 D2
Axelholme St BL6 ....21 F3
Axford CI M7 ....155 F6
Axminster Wlk SK7 ..132 E7
Axon Sq M16 ....97 F4
Aycliffe Ave M21 ...109 D5
Aycliffe Gr M13 .....98 E3
Aye Bridge Rd WA3 ..74 B5
Aylesbury Ave
Denton M34 ....100 F1
Urmston M41 ....95 E3
Aylesbury CI M5 .....81 A1
Aylesbury Cres WN2 ..57 C2
Aylesbury Gr M24 ...47 C1
Aylesby Ave M18 ....99 B4
Aylesford Rd M14 ...98 D3
Aylesford Wlk BL1 ..143 E1
Aylestone Wlk 18 M40 .83 A7
Aylsham CI SK6 .....112 F4
Aylsham Mews M27 ..79 D5
Aylwin Dr M33 ......108 C3
Ayr Ave OL8 ....66 F3
Ayr CI SK7 ....125 A2
Ayr Gr OL10 ....29 C3
Ayr St BL2 ....25 C4
Ayrefield Gr WN6 ...35 D6
Ayrefield Rd WN8 ...35 C4
Ayres Rd M16 ....97 C4
Ayrshire Rd M7 .....81 B6
Ayrton Gr M38 ......60 A5
Aysgarth CI
Cheadle SK8 ....122 C6
Droylsden M43 ....99 E5
Romiley SK6 ....112 F4
Aysgarth Gr M33 ...107 D3
Ayshford CI WA14 ..119 C5
Ayton Gr M14 ....98 E4
Aytoun CI M1 ....159 B1
Aytoun St M1 ....159 B1
Azalea Ave M18 .....99 D6

B

Babbacombe Gr M9 ...64 B5
Babbacombe Rd SK2 .124 C6
Babylon La PR6 ......21 B8
Back Abingdon CI BL2 .25 C1
Back Acton St M1 ...163 B8
Back Adrian Rd BL1 .142 C3
Back Adrian Rd E
BL1 ....142 C2
Back Ainscow St BL1 .145 E8
Back Ainsworth La BL2 .25 C1
Back Ainsworth Rd N
Back Ainsworth Rd S 1
.....................27 C2

Back Alexander Rd BL2 ..25 C1
Back Alfred St 12 BL3 ...42 A4
Back Alice St
10 Bolton BL3 ....144 C5
Little Lever BL3 ......43 B3
Back Alicia St BL3 ...42 D5
Back All Saints' St 18
BL1 ....141 A2
Back Alston St BL3 ...147 E3
Back America Row BL1 .142 C3
Back Andrew St BL9 ..141 A2
Back Andrew St N 5
BL9 ....141 A2
Back Anglia Gr BL3 ..146 C4
Back Annis Rd 4 BL3 .146 B4
Back Anson St 3 BL1 .143 F3
Back Apple Terr BL1 ..143 D2
Back Argo St 3 BL3 ..147 D4
Back Argyle St 8 BL9 .27 F5
Back Arlington St BL3 .147 F3
Back Arnold St BL1 ..142 C2
Back Arnold Terr BL1 ..23 F1
Back Ash St Bolton BL2 .148 A6
3 Bury BL9 ....141 A2
Back Ashbee St BL1 ..143 E3
Back Ashford Wlk BL1 .143 E1
Back Ashley St M4 ...159 B3
Back Ashton St BL3 ..146 B4
Back Ashworth La BL1 .24 F5
Back Ashworth St 10 BL8 .27 C3
Back Astley St BL1 ...143 E2
Back Auburn St BL3 ..42 A4
Back Augustus St 2 BL3 .42 A4
Back Augustus St W 7
BL3 ....42 A4
Back Avenue St 3 BL1 ..145 D8
Back Avondale St BL1 ..143 E1
Back Baldwin St BL3 ..145 E5
Back Baldwin St N BL3 .145 E5
Back Banbury St BL2 ..25 C1
Back Bank St M8 .....159 A4
Back Bankfield St BL3 .144 C5
Back Barbara St BL3 ..147 D4
Back Bark St 1 BL1 ..145 E7
Back Bashall St BL1 ..144 C8
Back Battenberg Rd 1
BL1 ....144 C8
Back Baxendale St 1
.....................143 E4
Back Bayley St BL1 ..145 D8
Back Baythorpe St BL1 .143 F2
Back Baythorpe St N 4
BL1 ....143 F2
Back Beaconsfield St
.....................145 D6
Back Beaconsfield Terr 18
.....................25 B1
Back Beatrice St 8 BL9
.....................142 C1
Back Bedford St 4 BL1 .145 D8
Back Beech St BL3 ...143 F2
Back Beechwood St 5
.....................143 F3
Back Belbeck St 3 BL8 .27 C2
Back Bell La Bury BL9 ..141 A3
Bury BL9 ....141 A3
Back Belmont Rd 1 BL1 .24 E5
Back Belmont Rd E 5
.....................24 E5
Back Bennett's La BL1 .142 C2
Back Bennett's La E
.....................142 C2
Back Benson St 3 BL1 .141 A1
.....................142 C2
Back Bentinck St 4
.....................142 B1
Back Bentley St BL2 ..148 C5
Back Bertha St BL1 ..144 C7
Back Beverley Rd BL1 .144 C8
Back Birch St 1 BL9 ..140 F3
Back Birley St 7 BL1 ..143 E4
Back Blackbank St BL1 .143 F3
Back Blackburn Rd E BL7 ..8 D3
Back Blackburn Rd W
Bolton,Dunscar BL7 ...24 E8
5 Bolton,Sharples BL1 .143 E4
4 Bolton,Sharples BL1 ..24 E5
Back Blackburn St 6
.....................143 F3
Back Blackwood St BL3 .42 A4
Back Bolton Rd S
Bury BL8 ....27 C1
Bury BL8 ....27 C2
Back Bolton Rd 9 BL1 .143 F2
Back Bolton St 5 1
.....................140 F2
Back Bond St W BL9 ..141 A2
Back Boundary St 12
BL1 ....143 D2
Back Bowen St 7 BL3 ..42 A3
Back Bowness Rd BL3 .147 D4
Back Bradford Rd
Bolton BL3 ....42 A3
18 Bolton BL3 ....42 A3
Back Bradford Rd W 1
BL3 ....42 A3
Back Bradford St BL2 ..148 B7
Back Bradford St S 4
BL2 ....148 A6

178 Bac – Bac

Back Bradford St W
Bolton BL2 ....148 A7
Bolton BL2 ....148 B7
Back Bradshaw Brow E
BL2 ....25 C4
Back Bradshaw Brow W
BL2 ....25 C4
Back Bradshaw Rd E BL2 .25 D5
Back Bradshaw St 7
OL16 ....31 A8
Back Bradshawgate 1
BL1 ....145 F6
Back Brandon St 3
BL3 ....147 D4
Back Brandon St N BL3 .147 D4
Back Brandon St W 4
BL3 ....147 D4
Back Brandwood St
BL3 ....146 C4
Back Bride St BL3 ....143 E2
Back Bridge St
11 Bolton BL1 ....145 F8
Manchester M3 ....158 F1
New Mills SK22 ....127 C1
Ramsbottom BL0 ....138 C6
Back Bridgeman St BL3 .147 E4
Back Brierley St BL9 ....44 E8
Back Brierley St S BL9 ..44 E8
Back Brigade St BL1 ....144 C7
Back Brindley St 2 BL1 .143 F4
Back Brink's Pl BL1 .....145 E7
Back Bristol Ave BL2 ....25 C1
Back Bristol St BL3 .....145 D5
Back Broach St BL3 .....147 E4
Back Broad o' th' La 6
BL1 ....24 E5
Back Broad St 3 BL9 ...140 E2
Back Bromwich St BL2 ..148 B6
Back Brook St N BL9 ....141 A4
Back Brookfield St BL2 .148 B7
Back Broom St BL2 .....148 A7
Back Brow WN8 ....53 C7
Back Bryce St BL3 ......145 D5
Back Burnaby St BL3 ...145 D5
Back Burnham Ave BL1 .142 A1
Back Bury New Rd BL2 .148 A7
Back Bury New Rd E
BL2 ....148 A7
Back Bury Old Rd 2
BL2 ....148 A7
Back Bury Rd BL2 ....42 E7
Back Bury Rd E BL2 ....148 C7
Back Bury Rd S
Bolton,Breightmet BL2 ..42 F7
3 Bolton,Tonge Fold BL2 .148 C7
Bolton,Tonge Fold BL2 ..148 D7
Back Bushell St BL3 ....146 B4
Back Byrom St 8 BL8 ...27 B4
Back Byrom St S 10 BL8 .27 B4
Back Calder Rd BL3 ....147 E3
Back Caledonia St BL3 .144 C5
Back Calvert Rd 3 BL3 .147 F3
Back Cambridge St OL7 .84 F1
Back Camp St M7 ....155 D5
Back Canada St
4 Bolton BL1 ....142 C4
Horwich BL6 ....22 B3
Back Canada St S BL1 ..142 C2
Back Canning St BL9 ...140 F4
Back Cardwell St 33
BL3 ....143 E2
Back Carl St 18 BL1 ....143 D2
Back Carter St 19 BL3 ..42 A4
Back Castle St
4 Bolton BL2 ....148 A7
Back Cateaton St 1
BL9 ....140 F3
Back Cecil St BL2 ....148 B6
Back Cecilia St BL3 .....42 A4
Back Cedar St BL1 ......141 B3
Back Cedar St N BL9 ...141 B3
Back Cemetery Rd E
BL2 ....148 B7
Back Cemetery Terr 9
OL13 ....3 D8
Back Cestrian St 1 BL1 .147 F3
Back Chalfont St BL1 ...143 F2
Back Chapel St
3 Eccles M30 ....79 F2
Hazel Grove SK7 ....124 E3
Horwich BL6 ....22 C3
Wardle OL12 ....15 C7
Back Chapman St 5
BL1 ....145 F8
Back Charles Holden St
BL1 ....145 D6
Back Chaucer St 2
BL1 ....143 D2
Back Cheapside BL1 ....145 F7
Back Chesham Rd N 5
BL9 ....141 A4
Back Chesham Rd S 7
BL9 ....141 A4
Back Chester St BL9 ...141 A4
Back China La M1 ......159 B1
Back Chorley New Rd
Bolton,Gilnow Park BL1 .145 D8
Back Chorley New Rd N
Bolton BL1 ....144 B7
Bolton BL1 ....144 C7
Back Chorley Old Rd
Bolton BL1 ....142 A1

Back Chorley Old Rd continued
Bolton BL1 ....23 F1
Back Chorley Old Rd N
Bolton,Cope Bank BL1 ...142 C1
Bolton,Doffcocker BL1 ..142 A1
2 Bolton,Doffcocker BL1 .142 B1
4 Bolton,Victory BL1 ...144 C8
Back Chorley Old Rd S
Bolton,Doffcocker BL1 ..142 A1
Bolton,Doffcocker BL1 ..142 B1
Bolton,Doffcocker BL1 ..23 F1
Bolton,Victory BL1 .....144 C8
Back Church Ave BL1 ...145 E7
Back Church St E 10
BL1 ....145 E8
Back Church Ave BL3 ..146 C4
Back Church Rd
1 Bolton,Cope Bank BL1 .142 C2
Bolton,Doffcocker BL1 ..142 A2
Back Church St N
Bolton BL1 ....142 B2
4 Bolton BL1 ....142 C2
Back Church St
Bolton BL1 ....145 E8
Little Lever BL3 ....43 A3
Back Clarendon Rd 8
BL2 ....148 C7
Back Clarke St BL1 .....144 C8
Back Clay St E BL7 .....25 A7
Back Clay St W BL7 ....25 A7
Back Clegg St BL2 .....148 C7
Back Clegg's Bldgs 11
BL1 ....145 E8
Back Clifton St 1 BL9 ..140 F4
Back Cloister St 5 BL1 .142 C2
Back Clyde St BL1 ......143 E2
Back Cobden St BL1 ....143 D3
Back Colenso Rd BL2 ..42 D7
Back College Land 1
M3 ....158 F1
Back College Way BL3 .145 E6
Back Collings St BL1 ...142 C2
Back Columbia Rd 17
BL1 ....144 C8
Back Common St BL5 ..57 B7
Back Coniston St 1
BL1 ....143 F3
Back Coop St BL1 ......143 E4
Back Cope Bank BL1 ...142 B2
Back Cornall St BL3 ....27 C3
Back Corson St BL4 ....42 D2
Back Cottam St 5 BL8 .27 C3
Back Cotton St BL1 ....143 D2
Back Cowm La OL12 ...4 C3
Back Cox Green Rd N 8
BL7 ....24 F8
Back Cox Green Rd S 1
BL7 ....24 F8
Back Crawford Ave BL3 .148 B6
Back Crawford St BL2 .148 B6
Back Crescent Ave BL3 .145 D8
Back Crescent Rd BL3 .42 A4
Back Crescent Rd W BL3 .42 B3
Back Croft La BL3 ......148 B5
Back Cromer Ave BL2 ..25 C1
Back Crosby Rd BL1 ...144 B8
Back Cross La WA12 ...89 B4
Back Croston St BL3 ...144 C5
Back Crostons Rd BL8 .140 D3
Back Crown St BL6 ....22 A4
Back Crumpsall St 32
Back Crumpsall St N 5
BL1 ....143 E2
Back Cundey St BL1 ...142 C1
Back Curzon Rd BL1 ...144 C7
Back Cyril St BL3 ......148 A5
Back Daisy St BL3 .....146 C4
Back Dale St 2 OL16 ..31 F5
Back Darley St BL4 ....60 E8
Back Darwen Rd N
Bolton,Bromley Cross BL7 .25 A7
Bolton,Bromley Cross BL7 .25 B7
Bolton,Cox Green BL7 ..24 F8
Back Darwen Rd S BL7 .25 A7
Back Darwen St 18 BL1 .143 D2
Back Dawes St BL3 ....145 F6
Back Deal St Bolton BL3 .147 F3
Bury BL9 ....141 B2
Back Deane Church La 1
BL3 ....146 B4
Back Deane Church La W
BL3 ....146 B4
Back Deane Rd 4 BL3 .144 C5
Back Deane Rd N
Bolton BL3 ....144 C6
Bolton BL3 ....145 D6
Back Delamere St N BL9 .28 A5
Back Delamere St S BL9 .28 A5
Back Denton St BL9 ...140 F4
Back Derby St
Bolton BL3 ....145 E6
Bolton BL3 ....147 D4
Bury BL9 ....140 F2
Back Design St 1
BL3 ....146 B4
Back Devon St N 2 BL9 .44 E8
Back Devon St S BL9 ...44 E8
Back Devonshire Rd
BL1 ....142 A1
Back Dijon St 1 BL3 ...146 C4
Back Dijon St N BL3 ...146 C4
Back Dobie St 20 BL3 ..42 A4
Back Doffcocker Brow
BL1 ....142 A1
Back Dorset St BL2 ....148 A7
Back Dougill St BL1 ....148 B1
Back Dougill St S BL1 ..142 B1

Back Drake St OL16 ....139 F7
Back Drummond St BL1 .143 E4
Back Duce Ave BL1 ....144 C7
Back Duckworth St 4
BL9 ....141 A4
Back Duncan St
Horwich BL6 ....22 C3
Salford M7 ....81 C7
Back Dunstan St 1 BL2 .148 C7
Back Durham St OL11 ..31 A5
Back Duxbury St BL1 ..143 D3
Back Earnshaw St BL3 .146 B3
Back East St BL9 ....140 F1
Back Eastbank St
BL1 ....143 F2
Back Eckersley Rd BL1 .143 E3
Back Eddith Gr BL2 ....148 C7
Back Eddith Gr N 6
BL2 ....148 C7
Back Eden St BL1 ......143 E3
Back Edgmont Ave BL3 .147 D4
Back Edison St BL9 ....140 F4
Back Elgin St BL1 ......143 D2
Back Ellesmere Rd BL3 .146 C3
Back Ellesmere St BL3 .145 D6
Back Elm St BL9 ....141 B2
Back Elmwood Gr 20
BL1 ....144 C8
Back Elmwood Gr W 19
BL1 ....144 C8
Back Elsworth St M3,
M4 ....159 A4
Back Emmett St BL6 ...22 B3
Back Empire Rd 2 BL2 .42 D7
Back Empress St BL1 ..142 B1
Back Ena St 4 BL3 .....42 A3
Back Ernest St 1 BL3 ..145 D6
Back Eskrick St 5 BL3 .143 D2
Back Eskrick St 6
BL1 ....143 D2
Back Eskrick St S 18
BL1 ....143 D2
Back Eskrick St W BL1 .143 D2
Back Essingdon St BL3 .147 D4
Back Essingdon St S
BL3 ....147 D4
Back Eustace St 2 BL3 .42 A3
Back Euxton St BL3 ...147 D4
Back Everton St N 8
BL1 ....143 F2
Back Ewart St 11 BL1 ..143 E2
Back Fair St BL3 ....146 C2
Back Fairhaven Rd BL1 .143 F3
Back Fenton St BL8 ....27 C3
Back Fern St E 2 BL3 ..144 C6
Back Fir St BL7 ....143 D2
Back Fletcher St
Bury BL9 ....141 A2
Kearsley BL4 ....61 B8
Back Fletcher St S BL3 .145 F5
Back Flora St 1 BL3 ...147 E3
Back Florence Ave BL1 .24 F5
Back Fortune St BL3 ...148 B5
Back Foundry St BL9 ..140 F2
Back Frances St 7 BL1 .143 D2
Back Frank St
Bolton BL1 ....143 D2
3 Bury BL9 ....140 F1
Back Fylde St BL4 .....42 D2
Back Gainsborough Ave 2
BL3 ....146 C3
Back Garside Gr 9 BL1 .142 C2
Back Garston St BL1 ...141 A4
Back Gaskell St BL1 ...145 D8
Back Gaskell St E 14
BL1 ....145 D8
Back Gaythorne St 2
BL1 ....143 D2
Back George Barton St 24
BL3 ....25 B1
Back George St
Bolton BL3 ....42 A4
Horwich BL6 ....22 C3
Manchester M1 ....159 A1
Back Georgiana St W 1
BL9 ....140 F1
Back Georgina St BL3 .146 B3
Back Gibraltar St BL3 ..145 D6
Back Gigg La BL9 ......44 F8
Back Gilmour St M24 ..65 A8
Back Gilnow Gr BL1 ...145 D6
Back Gilnow La 5 BL3 .144 C6
Back Gilnow La W BL3 .144 C6
Back Gilnow Rd BL1 ...144 C7
Back Glade St BL1 .....144 C7
Back Gladstone St 4
OL4 ....67 B6
Back Glen Ave BL3 ....144 B5
Back Glen Bott St 5
BL1 ....143 D2
Back Glenboro Ave BL2 .27 C2
Back Gloster St BL2 ...148 A7
Back Goldsmith St BL3 .147 D4
Back Goodlad St BL8 ..27 B4
Back Gordon Ave BL1 ..144 C5
Back Gorses Mount
BL2 ....148 C5
Back Grafton St 8 BL1 .145 D8
Back Grantham Cl BL1 .143 E1
Back Grasmere St 5
BL1 ....145 D8
Back Greaves St OL1 ..153 F6
Back Green La BL3 ....42 B3
Back Green La S BL3 ..147 F3
Back Green St M24 ....47 B2
Back Greenhalgh St BL3 .43 A3
Back Greenland Rd BL3 .147 F2
Back Gregory Ave BL2 .42 E8
Back Ingham St BL9 ...141 A1

Back Grendon St BL3 ...146 C3
Back Gresham St 9
BL1 ....143 F3
Back Grove St 8 BL1 ...143 D2
Back Hadwin St 11 BL1 .143 F1
Back Halliwell La 8 M8 .155 F7
Back Halliwell Rd BL1 ..143 E2
Back Halliwell Rd S 16
BL1 ....143 D2
Back Halstead St
Bolton BL2 ....148 A7
2 Bury BL9 ....141 A4
Back Hamilton St
6 Bury BL9 ....140 F4
Salford M7 ....155 D7
Back Hampson St M40 .160 D4
Back Hanson St BL9 ...140 F4
Back Hargreaves St 9
BL1 ....143 E2
Back Harper's La S BL1 .142 B2
Back Hart St BL5 ......57 B7
Back Hartington Rd 18
BL1 ....144 C8
Back Harvey St
Bolton BL1 ....143 D3
Bury BL8 ....27 C3
Back Haslam St BL9 ...141 A4
Back Haslam Terr BL2 .148 C7
Back Hastings Rd BL1 .144 B8
Back Hatfield Rd BL1 ..143 D1
Back Hawthorne Rd 8
BL3 ....146 B4
Back Hawthorne Rd E
BL3 ....144 B5
Back Hawthorne Rd W
BL3 ....144 B5
Back Hawthorne St 5
BL3 ....146 B4
Back Haydn St 14 BL1 .143 D2
Back Haydock St BL1 ..143 E2
Back Hayward St 2 BL8 .27 C3
Back Hengist St 5 BL2 .148 C7
Back Hennon St BL1 ...143 D1
Back Henrietta St BL3 .146 B4
Back Henry Lee St BL3 .146 C3
Back Hereford Rd BL1 .144 B8
Back Hereford Rd W
BL1 ....144 B8
Back Heywood St E BL9 .141 A2
Back Heywood St W 2
BL9 ....141 A1
Back High Bank St BL2 .148 C7
Back High St Bolton BL3 .147 D4
Bolton BL3 ....147 E4
Chapeltown BL7 ....9 C4
Heywood OL10 ....29 B2
Back High St S BL3 ....147 E4
Back High St W 2 BL3 .147 E4
Back Higher Darcy St
BL3 ....148 C5
Back Higher Shady La W
BL7 ....25 B7
Back Higher Swan La
BL3 ....147 D3
Back Higher Swan La W
BL3 ....147 D3
Back Hilden St BL2 ....148 A6
Back Hilden St W BL2 .148 A6
Back Hilton St
Bolton BL2 ....148 C7
9 Bury BL9 ....140 F4
Salford M7 ....155 D7
Back Holland St
BL1 ....143 E4
Bolton BL1 ....143 F4
Back Holland St E 6
BL1 ....143 F4
Back Holly Pl BL1 ......143 E4
Back Holly St
Bury BL9 ....143 F4
Back Holly St S BL1 ...141 A2
Back Hope St
7 Oldham OL1 ....67 B7
Salford M7 ....155 D7
Back Hopefield St BL3 .147 D4
Back Horbury St BL8 ..27 C2
Back Hornby St BL9 ...140 F4
Back Hornby St W 4
BL9 ....140 F3
Back Horne St N 1 BL9 .44 F8
Back Horne St S BL9 ..44 E8
Back Horsa St BL2 ....25 B1
Back Horsa St N 17 BL2 .25 B1
Back Hotel St BL1 .....145 F7
Back Hough La E BL7 ..25 A7
Back Howarden St 3
BL1 ....24 E5
Back Howcroft St BL3 .147 D4
Back Howe St M7 .....155 D7
Back Hughes St BL1 ...142 C2
Back Hulbert St BL8 ...27 C1
Back Hulme St Bury BL8 .140 D3
Salford M5 ....81 C1
Back Hulton St
Bolton BL3 ....146 A3
Bolton BL3 ....146 A4
Back Hulton St BL3 ....146 A3
Back Hulton St W BL3 .146 A4
Back Huntley Mount Rd
BL9 ....141 A3
Back Hurst St
BL3 ....146 C3
Bury BL9 ....141 A1
Back Huxley St 3 BL1 .142 C2
Back Ingham St BL9 ...141 A1

Back Ingham St E BL9 .141 A1
Back Irlam St 1 BL1 ...143 E3
Back Irlam St N 3 BL1 .143 E3
Back Ivanhoe St 8 BL3 .42 C2
Back Ivy Bank Rd BL1 .24 E5
Back Ivy Rd Bolton BL1 .142 C1
Bolton BL1 ....142 C2
Back Ivy Rd W BL1 ....142 B2
Back James St BL3 ....43 A3
Back Jauncey St 12 BL3 .144 C5
Back John Brown St 15
BL1 ....145 D8
Back John Cross St 3
BL3 ....147 E4
Back John St BL3 .....145 F6
Back Johnson St BL3 .145 F6
Back Jubilee St BL3 ...146 C3
Back Keighley St 10
BL1 ....142 C2
Back Kendal Rd BL1 ..144 C8
Back Kershaw St BL9 .141 A2
Back King St Bolton BL1 .145 E7
Oldham OL1 ....153 E6
Back King St N 4 BL2 ..24 F8
Back King St S BL3 ....25 D5
Back Kingholm Gdns 3
BL1 ....143 D1
Back Kingsley St BL1 ..143 D2
Back Kirkby Rd BL1 ...144 B8
Back Knight St 8 BL3 ..27 C2
Back Knowsley Rd BL1 .142 B2
Back Knowsley St
1 Bolton BL1 ....145 F7
Bury BL9 ....140 E2
Back Kylemore Ave BL3 .144 B5
Back Latham St Altrincham WA15 .129 B4
Appley Bridge WN6 ...35 E8
Ashton-u-L OL7 ....84 E5
Bolton BL1 ....145 E8
Charlesworth SK13 ...115 E6
Mossley OL5,OL16 ....68 A2
Mottram-in-L SK14 ...103 A4
Oldham OL4 ....50 C1
Over Hulton BL5 ......59 B6
Partington WA14 .....118 C5
Rochdale OL12 ....13 F3
Whitworth OL12 ......4 C3
Back Lark St BL1 ......145 F8
Back Latham St BL1 ...143 F2
Back Lathom St B BL9 .141 A4
Back Lathom St 9 BL1 .141 A4
Back Laurel St BL3 ....141 B2
Back Lawn St BL1 .....143 D1
Back Leach St BL3 ....145 E5
Back Leachfield St BL3 .143 D3
Back Lee Ave BL3 .....147 D3
Back Lee St BL3 ....69 B8
Back Legh St WA12 ...89 A3
Back Lena St BL3 .....143 F2
Back Lenora St 2 BL3 .146 B4
Back Lever Edge La
Bolton,Daubhill BL3 ...146 C2
Bolton,Great Lever BL3 .147 F3
Back Lever Edge La S
BL3 ....147 E3
Back Lever St Bolton BL3 .145 F5
Back Lever St N BL3 ..43 A4
Back Lever St S BL3 ..147 E4
Back Lightburne Ave
BL1 ....144 B7
Back Lilly St BL3 ......145 F6
Back Lincoln Rd BL1 ..144 C8
Back Lindley St BL3 ...43 B3
Back Linton Ave 2 BL9 .27 F5
Back Long La BL2 .....42 E7
Back Longden St 12
BL1 ....144 C8
Back Longfellow Ave
BL3 ....146 B3
Back Longfield Rd BL3 .146 B3
Back Longsight N BL2 .25 C5
Back Longsight S BL2 .25 C5
Back Longworth Rd BL7 .8 D3
Back Lonsdale Rd BL1 .144 B8
Back Lonsdale Rd N
BL1 ....144 B8
Back Lonsdale St 8
BL3 ....27 C2
Back Lord St BL9 .....140 F2
Little Lever BL3 ....43 B3
Back Lower Bridgeman St 2
BL2 ....148 A6
Back Loxham St BL4 ..42 D2
Back Lumsden St BL3 .145 E5
Back Luton St BL3 ....42 A3
Back Lytton St 3 BL1 ..143 D2
Back Mackenzie St BL1 .143 E4
Back Malvern Ave
Bolton BL1 ....142 A1
5 Bury BL9 ....27 F5
Back Manchester Old Rd
BL9 ....140 E1
Back Manchester Rd
Bolton BL2 ....148 A6
6 Bury BL9 ....140 E2
1 Farnworth BL2 ......42 C2
Back Manchester Rd E
BL3 ....148 A5
Back Manchester Rd S 10
BL3 ....42 A4
Back Manchester Rd W
BL3 ....82 A4
Back Manchester St 1
OL10 ....29 E1
Back Manor St N BL2 .142 A4
Back Maple St BL3 ....145 D5
Back Marion St 2 BL3 .42 C2
Back Marion St S 4 BL3 .42 C2

Back Market St
4 Bury BL9 ....140 E2
Hindley WN2 ....56 D5
Kearsley M26 ....61 B8
Leigh WN7 ....75 F5
Little Lever BL3 ....43 B3
Newton-le-W WA12 ......89 A3
Back Market St W 3
BL9 ....140 E2
Back Markland Hill La
BL1 ....23 F1
Back Markland Hill La E
BL1 ....23 F1
Back Markland Hill La W
BL1 ....23 F1
Back Marlborough St
BL1 ....145 D8
Back Marsh Fold La 14
BL1 ....144 C8
Back Mary St 4 BL3 ...145 D5
Back Mason St BL9 ....141 A2
Back Massie St SK8 ...122 D6
Back Mawdsley St BL1 ..145 F7
Back Maxwell St BL1 ...145 E7
Back Maybank St BL3 ...145 D5
Back Mayfield Ave BL3 ...42 B3
Back Mayor St
Bolton BL1 ....145 D6
4 Bury BL8 ....27 C3
Back Mayor St N BL1 ...145 D6
Back Maze St BL3 ......148 C5
Back McDonna St BL1 ...142 C3
Back McKean St BL3 .....42 A4
Back McKean St N 5
BL3 ....42 A4
Back Melbourne Rd
BL3 ....144 C5
Back Mellor Gr BL1 .....142 B1
Back Mellor Gr W 1
BL1 ....142 B1
Back Mellor Rd SK22 ...127 C1
Back Melrose Ave BL1 ..142 A1
Back Melville St BL3 ...142 A3
Back Mercia St BL3 ....144 C5
Back Mere Gdns BL1 ....145 E8
Back Meredith St 6
BL3 ....147 F3
Back Merlin Gr BL8 ....142 B1
Back Merton St BL8 ....140 D2
Back Mesnes St 8 WN1 ..37 C1
Back Methwold St BL3 ...144 C5
Back Micklehurst Rd OL5 ..68 E1
Back Milford Rd BL3 ...147 E3
Back Mill La BL3 ....68 C2
Back Mill St N 6 BL7 ...24 F8
Back Mill St S 7 BL7 ...24 F8
Back Miller St BL1 ....143 E4
Back Miller St N BL1 ..140 D2
Back Milner Ave BL9 ....27 F5
Back Minorca St BL3 ...147 E4
Back Mirey La BL6 ....40 B4
Back Monmouth Ave 7
BL9 ....27 F5
Back Moor SK14 ....103 A4
Back Moorfield Gr BL2 ...25 B1
Back Moorgate 7 BL9 ..140 F3
Back Mornington Rd
BL1 ....144 B8
Back Mornington Rd E
BL1 ....144 C7
Back Mornington Rd W
BL1 ....144 B8
Back Morris Green La
Bolton BL3 ....146 C2
Bolton BL3 ....146 C2
Back Morris Green La E
BL3 ....146 C3
Back Moss Terr BL1 ....145 F8
Back Mostyn Ave 3 BL9 ..27 F5
Back Mowbray St 3
BL1 ....142 B1
Back Murton Terr 4
BL1 ....143 F4
Back Musgrave Rd
Bolton BL1 ....144 B8
Bolton BL1 ....144 C8
Back Musgrave Rd N
BL1 ....144 C8
Back Myrtle St BL9 ....141 B2
Back Myrtle St S BL9 ...141 B2
Back Nebo St BL3 ......147 D4
Back Nelson St BL6 .....22 D3
Back Nelson St N 3 BL9 ..44 F8
Back Nelson St S 1 BL9 ..44 F8
Back Nevada St 17 BL1 ..143 E1
Back New George St W
BL8 ....27 C3
Back Newbold St BL8 ....27 C2
Back Newhall La BL1 ...142 A1
Back Newport Rd 10 BL3 ..42 A4
Back Newport St BL1 ...145 F6
Back Newton St BL1 ...143 E2
Back Nixon Rd BL3 .....146 C3
Back Nook Terr 2 OL12 ...14 F3
Back Normanby St BL3 ..146 C2
Back Norris St BL3 .....43 A3
Back Northern Gr 1
BL1 ....142 C1
Back Northern Gr S 2
BL1 ....142 C1
Back Nunnery Rd BL3 ...146 B4
Back Nut St BL1 ....143 D2
Back o' th' Low Rd OL4 ...49 F1
Back Oak St M26 ....44 C1
Back Oakenbottom Rd N
BL2 ....42 D7
Back Olaf St 11 BL2 ...25 B1
Back Oldham Rd OL16 ....31 A6

Back Olga St BL1 ......143 D2
Back Olga St N BL1 ....143 D2
Back Olive Bank 2 BL8 ..27 B4
Back Oram St BL9 ......141 A4
Back Oriel St BL3 .....144 C5
Back Ormrod St BL1 ....141 A2
Back Osborne Gr 7
BL1 ....122 C1
Back Owen's Row BL6 ....22 C3
Back Oxford Gr N
2 Bolton,Brownlow Fold
BL1 ....145 D8
Bolton,Cope Bank BL1 ...142 C1
Back Oxford St BL9 ....141 A1
Back Packer St 2 BL1 ..142 C2
Back Palace St 7 BL1 ..145 F8
Back Palm St BL3 ......143 E3
Back Park Rd Bolton BL1 ..144 C7
Back Park Rd E 8 BL1 ..145 D7
Back Park St BL1 ......145 D8
Back Park View 1 BL1 ...24 F6
Back Park View N6 BL3 ..146 C4
Back Parkdale BL2 ......25 C1
Back Parkfield Rd
Bolton BL3 ....147 F3
Bolton BL3 ....42 A3
Back Parkhills Rd N 4
BL9 ....44 F8
Back Parkhills Rd S
4 Bury BL9 ....44 E8
3 Bury BL9 ....44 F8
Back Parkinson St 11
BL3 ....144 C5
Back Partington St BL3 ..146 C2
Back Patience St 10
OL12 ....14 C1
Back Patterson St BL3 ..146 A4
Back Peabody St BL3 ...147 E4
Back Peace St BL3 .....145 D5
Back Pedder St 3 BL1 ..142 C1
Back Peers St BL8 ......27 C2
Back Penarth Rd 7
BL3 ....146 B4
Back Pennington Rd
BL3 ....147 F3
Back Percy St BL1 .....141 B3
Back Peter St 2 BL9 ...141 A3
Back Peveril St BL3 ...146 B3
Back Phoenix St BL9 ...140 E2
Back Piccadilly M1 ....159 B1
Back Pikes La W4 BL3 ..144 C5
Back Pine St
7 Bolton BL1 ....143 F2
Bury BL9 ....141 B2
Newhey OL16 ....32 B4
Back Pleasant St BL1 ..158 F8
Back Pool Fold M2 .....158 F3
Back Poplar Ave BL1 ....24 F5
Back Porter St 2 BL9 ..140 F4
Back Portugal St 2 BL8 ..27 C2
Back Potter St M26 .....44 D4
Back Preston St BL3 ....42 B4
Back Primrose St BL1 ..144 C8
Back Primula St BL1 ....24 F5
Back Proctor St BL3 ....27 C1
Back Progress St 2
BL1 ....143 F1
4 Leigh WN7 ....76 A5
Back Queensgate BL1 ..144 C8
Back Queen St
Bolton BL1 ....145 E7
2 Leigh WN7 ....76 A5
Back Radcliffe Rd E 1
BL2 ....148 B7
Back Railway View PR7 ..21 A7
Back Raimond St BL1 ...142 C3
Back Rainshaw St 5
BL1 ....143 F4
Back Rake St BL9 ......140 F4
Back Ramsden Rd OL12 ...15 C7
Back Range St BL3 .....147 D4
Back Raphael St BL1 ...143 E4
Back Rathbone St WA12 ..89 A3
Back Raven St 4 BL9 ...140 F4
Back Rawlinson St 18
BL6 ....22 B4
Back Rawson Rd 5 BL1 ..142 C1
Back Rawson Rd N 10
BL1 ....142 C1
Back Rawsthorne St
BL1 ....143 E2
Back Raymond Ave 6
BL9 ....27 F5
Back Red Bank M4 .....159 A3
Back Redhill Gr BL1 ...145 E8
Back Regent St 3 BL1 ...140 F4
Back Ribblesdale Rd 18
BL3 ....147 D4
Back Richard Burch St 1
BL9 ....141 A3
Back Richelieu St BL3 ...42 A4
Back Rigby La N BL2 ....25 C6
Back Rigby La S BL2 ....25 C6
Back Rishton La
Bolton BL3 ....147 F3
Bolton BL3 ....147 F4
Back Rishton La E BL3 ..147 F3
Back Rochdale Old Rd N
BL9 ....141 B3
Back Rochdale Old Rd S
BL9 ....141 B3
Back Rochdale Old South Rd
BL9 ....28 D3
Back Rochdale Rd
Bury BL9 ....141 A2
Bury BL9 ....141 B2

Back Rochdale Rd S 6
BL9 ....141 A2
Back Rock Ave BL1 .....142 C3
Back Roland Rd 3 BL3 ..146 C4
Back Roman Rd M7 .....155 E6
Back Romer St BL2 .....148 C7
Back Rosamond St BL3 ..146 C4
Back Roscow Ave BL2 ....42 E8
Back Rose Bank 8 BL9 ..140 F4
Back Roseberry St 7
BL3 ....146 C4
Back Rowena St BL3 .....42 C2
Back Rowland St BL3 ...146 B3
Back Roxalina St 5
BL3 ....147 E4
Back Royal Ave BL1 .....27 F5
Back Rudolph St 2 BL3 ..147 F3
Back Rumworth St BL3 ..147 D4
Back Rupert St BL3 ....147 F3
Back Rushton Rd BL1 ...142 B1
Back Rushton St 6 OL13 ...3 E8
Back Russell Cl 2 BL1 ..144 C8
Back Russell St 2 BL1 ..144 C8
Back Rutland Gr 6 BL1 ..142 C1
Back Ryefield St BL1 ...145 A1
Back Salford WN7 ....75 F5
Back Salford St BL9 ...141 A4
Back Salisbury St BL3 ..145 D6
Back Salisbury Terr BL2 ..42 D7
Back Sandon St BL3 ....147 D4
Back Sandon St W 11
BL3 ....147 D4
Back Sankey St BL9 ....140 D2
Back Sapling Rd BL3 ...146 C2
Back Sapling Rd S BL3 ..146 C2
Back Scholes St BL8 ....27 C3
Back School La WN8 .....53 C7
Back Scott St BL3 .....153 F5
Back Scowcroft St 22
BL2 ....25 B1
Back Second Ave BL1 ...144 B7
Back Settle St
Bolton BL3 ....147 E3
Bolton BL3 ....147 F3
Back Settle St N BL3 ...147 E3
Back Seymour Rd BL1 ...143 F3
Back Shakerley Rd 6
M29 ....58 F1
Back Sharman St BL3 ...148 B5
Back Shaw-Street BL1 ..141 B3
Back Shepherd St 1
BL9 ....141 A1
Back Sherwood St 8
BL1 ....143 F3
Back Shipton St BL1 ...142 B1
Back Short St 4 M46 ....58 F1
Back Shrewsbury Rd
BL1 ....144 B8
Back Silver St BL9 ....140 E2
Back Silverdale Rd BL1 ..144 C7
Back Skipton St BL2 ...148 C8
Back Skull House La
WN6 ....35 D8
Back Smethurst La BL3 ..146 B2
Back Smethurst La W
BL3 ....146 B2
Back Sofa St BL1 ......142 B1
Back Soho St BL3 ......145 F6
Back South Par M3 .....158 F1
Back South St BL3 .....147 E3
Back South View St 9
BL2 ....148 C7
Back Southfield St 1
BL3 ....42 B4
Back Spa St BL3 ....145 D6
Back Spa Rd N BL1 .....145 D6
Back Spa Rd W 8 BL1 ...145 D6
Back Spear St 6 M1,M4 ..159 B2
Back Spinnerbottom
SK22 ....127 F2
Back Spring Gdns
Bolton BL1 ....145 F6
6 Middleton M24 ......47 A2
Back Spring St W 6 BL1 ..140 F1
Back Spring St W BL1 ..140 F1
Back Springfield St 14
BL3 ....42 A4
Back Square St BL0 ....138 C6
Back St Ann St BL1 ....143 E1
Back St Anne's St 7
BL9 ....140 F4
Back St Augustine St 17
BL1 ....143 D2
Back St George's Rd
Bolton BL1 ....145 E8
Manchester M4 ....159 B3
Back St George's Rd N
BL1 ....145 E8
Back St Helens Rd
Bolton BL3 ....146 B3
10 Bolton BL3 ....147 D4
Back St Helens Rd S
Bolton BL3 ....146 A4
Bolton BL3 ....146 B2
Bolton BL3 ....146 C3
Back St James's St 8
OL1 ....67 B7
Back St Mark's La M8 ..155 F8
Back St Mary's Pl BL9 ..140 E2

Back St Philip's Ave
BL3 ....147 D4
Back St Thomas St E 9
BL1 ....143 D2
Back Stainsbury St BL3 ..146 C4
Back Stanley St BL3 ...138 B5
Back Stanway Ave 9
BL3 ....145 D6
Back Stephen St 2 BL8 ..27 C2
Back Stewart St 13 BL1 ..27 C2
Back Stone St 15 BL2 ....25 B1
Back Sunlight Rd BL1 ..144 C7
Back Sunning Hill St 12
BL3 ....147 D4
Back Sunnyside Rd 8
BL1 ....142 C2
Back Sutcliffe St BL1 ..143 E2
Back Swan La 15 BL3 ...147 D4
Back Talbot St BL3 ....143 F4
Back Tavistock Rd 3
BL1 ....145 D6
Back Teak St BL9 ......141 B2
Back Tenterden St
Bury BL9 ....140 D2
Back Thicketford Rd BL2 ..25 C1
Back Thicketford Rd W
BL2 ....25 C1
Back Thomas St 7 M4 ..159 A2
Back Thomasson Cl
BL1 ....143 E1
Back Thorn St BL3 .....143 F2
Back Thorns Rd BL1 ....143 E3
Back Thorpe St BL1 ....143 D2
Back Thurnham St
BL3 ....146 C3
Back Tinline St 4 BL9 ..141 A2
Back Tonge Moor Rd
BL2 ....25 B3
Back Tonge Moor Rd E
BL2 ....25 C3
Bolton,Castle Hill BL2 ...25 B2
Bolton,Tonge Moor BL2 ...25 B1
Back Tonge Old Rd BL2 ..148 C2
Back Tottington Rd 5
BL8 ....27 B4
Back Tottington Rd E
BL2 ....25 E5
Back Tottington Rd N
BL8 ....27 C4
Back Tottington St 1
BL8 ....27 C4
Back Tudor St 8 BL3 ...146 C4
Back Turner St M4 .....159 A2
Back Turton Rd E BL2 ...25 C5
Back Turton Rd W BL2 ...25 C4
Back Uganda St BL3 ...146 C2
Back Ulleswater St
BL1 ....143 F2
Back Union Rd BL2 ......25 B1
Back Union St N BL3 .....8 D2
Back Unsworth St
BL3 ....145 D5
Back Uttley St 18 BL1 ..143 D2
Back Venice St BL3 ....147 D4
Back Vernon St
Bolton BL1 ....145 E8
Bury BL9 ....140 F4
Back Vernon St S 12
BL1 ....145 E8
Back Vickerman St 22
BL1 ....143 D2
Back Victoria Gr 4 BL1 ..142 C1
Back Victoria Gr N BL1 ..142 C1
Back Victory St 10
BL1 ....144 C8
Back Viking St N 11 BL3 ..42 A4
Back Vincent St BL1 ...145 D6
Back Vine St 1 BL3 ....144 C6
Back Viola St BL1 .....143 E3
Back Waldeck St 3
BL1 ....144 C8
Back Walmersley Rd E
Bury,Fernhill BL9 .....140 F3
Bury,Fernhill BL9 .....140 F4
4 Bury,Seedfield BL9 ...27 F5
Bury,Seedfield BL9 .....27 F6
Back Walmersley Rd W
Bury,Fernhill BL9 .....140 F4
Bury,Seedfield BL9 .....27 F6
Back Walnut St 2 BL1 ..143 F2
Back Walshaw Rd N
BL8 ....27 C3
Back Walshaw Rd S BL8 ..27 C3
Back Wapping St 20
BL3 ....143 D2
Back Wardle St BL2 ....148 C5
Back Wash La N BL2 ....141 B2
Back Wash La S BL2 ....141 A2
Back Water St Bolton BL2 ..8 D2
Stockport SK1 ....169 F2
Back Waverley Rd BL1 ..143 E3
Back Webster St BL3 ...148 B5
Back Wellington Rd S
BL1 ....44 F8
Back Westbank St BL1 ..140 E1
Back Westbank St 8
BL3 ....145 D8
Back Weston St N 8
BL3 ....42 A4
Back Weston St S BL3 ....42 A4
Back Westwood Rd 18
BL1 ....144 C8
Back Wheatfield St BL8 ..148 C5
Back Whittle St BL1 ....27 C3
Back Whittle St 6 BL8 ...27 C3

Back Wigan Rd BL3 .....146 A4
Back Wigan Rd N
Bolton BL3 ....144 B5
Bolton BL3 ....146 A4
Back Wigan Rd S BL3 ...144 B5
Back Willis St 6 BL3 ...147 D4
Back Willows La 6 BL3 ..147 D4
Back Willows La N
Bolton BL3 ....146 B4
Bolton BL3 ....146 C4
Back Willows La S
Bolton BL3 ....146 A4
Bolton BL3 ....146 C4
Back Wilmot St 4 BL1 ..142 C3
Back Wilton St 10 BL1 ..143 F3
Back Windermere St
BL1 ....143 F2
Back Windsor Gr 8
BL1 ....142 C1
Back Woking Gdns 6
BL1 ....143 E1
Back Wolfenden St 8
BL1 ....143 E2
Back Wood St Bury BL8 ...27 C3
Horwich BL6 ....22 C3
Back Woodbine Rd BL3 ..146 C3
Back Woodbine Rd N 1
BL3 ....146 C3
Back Woodfield St BL3 ...42 A3
Back Woodgate St BL3 ...42 A3
Back Worcester St BL1 ..143 E1
Back Wordsworth St
BL3 ....143 D2
Back Worsel St BL3 ....146 C4
Back Wright St BL6 .....22 B4
Back Wynne St 10 BL1 ..143 E2
Back Yates St BL2 ......25 B1
Back Young St BL4 ......60 E7
Backbower La SK14 .....113 F8
Backford Wlk 8 M20 ...110 A8
Backparsons La BL9 ....140 F3
Backton Pl M40 ....160 D4
Baclaw Cl WN1 ....37 F1
Bacon Ave M34 ....113 A4
**Bacup & Rawtenstall Gram
Sch** BB4 ....2 F8
Bacup Rd BB4,OL13 ......83 A8
Bacup St M40 ....160 D1
Badby Cl SK3 ....170 D5
Badder St BL1 ....145 F8
Bader Dr OL10 ....46 D7
Badger Cl Marple SK6 ..125 F3
Rochdale OL16 ....31 C3
Badger Edge La OL3,OL4 ..50 C3
Badger La
Rochdale,Green Gate OL16 ..31 C3
Rochdale,Pleasant View
OL16 ....31 B2
Badger St Bury BL9 ....141 A3
8 Bury BL9 ....140 F3
Badgers Way SK13 .....116 B7
Badminton Rd M21 ......97 C1
Bag La M46 ....58 C4
Bagnall Cl Rochdale OL12 ..13 F2
Uppermill OL3 ....51 C1
Bagnall Ct M22 ....121 E8
Bagnall Wlk M22 ....121 E8
Bagot St
15 Droylsden M11 ....83 C2
Swinton M27 ....61 C1
Bagshaw La WN2 ....38 E2
Bagshaw St SK14 ......113 E1
Bagslate Moor La OL11 ..29 F8
Bagslate Moor Rd OL11 ..29 F8
Bagstock Ave SK12 ....133 E2
Baguley Cres
Middleton M25 ....64 A7
Stockport SK3 ....170 D6
Baguley Dr BL9 ....45 A2
Baguley Hall Prim Sch
M23 ....121 A6
Baguley La Sale M33 ...108 E2
Sale M33 ....108 E3
Baguley Rd M33 ....108 E4
Baguley St M43 ....84 B1
Baildon Rd OL12 ....14 A1
Baildon St M40 ....65 A1
Bailey Fold BL5 ....58 B8
Bailey La Bolton BL3 ....25 E1
Partington M31 ....105 F3
Wythenshawe M90 ......121 B1
Bailey Rd M17 ....96 A7
Bailey St Droylsden M43 ..84 B1
8 Oldham OL1 ....67 A7
Prestwich M25 ....63 C4
Bailey Wlk WA14 ....128 C8
Bailey's Ct WN1 ....150 C8
Baillie St Radcliffe M26 ..44 C5
Rochdale OL16 ....139 F8
Baillie St E 6 OL16 .....31 A6
Bails The M7 ....81 C6
Bain St M27 ....79 F7
Bainbridge Ave WA3 .....90 F8
Bainbridge Cl M12 .....164 D6
Bainbridge Rd OL4 .....49 E4
Bainburgh Clough OL8 ...67 A4
Baines Ave M44 ....93 F1
Baines St BL1 ....144 B8
Bainton Wlk M9 ....64 C5
Baird St M1 ....163 C8
Baitings Cl OL12 ....13 C2
Baitings Row OL12 ......13 C2
Baker St Heywood OL10 ..46 E8

Baker St continued
Kearsley BL4 ....61 B6
Middleton M24 ....45 B8
Ramsbottom BL0 .....138 B5
Sale WA15 ....120 C7
Stalybridge SK15 ....86 B1
Stockport SK4 ....169 E3
Wigan WN3 ....150 B6
Bakersfield Pl 1 M33 .108 C4
Bakewell Ave
Ashton-u-L OL6 ....85 F6
Denton M34 ....113 A8
Bakewell Bank 12 SK13 .171 D1
Bakewell Cl 40 SK13 .171 D1
Bakewell Dr WN6 ....37 A4
Bakewell Fold 41 SK13 .171 D1
Bakewell Gdns 20 SK13 .171 D1
Bakewell Gn 13 SK13 .171 D1
Bakewell Lea 38 SK13 .171 D1
Bakewell Mews SK13 .171 D1
Bakewell Rd
Droylsden M43 ....83 E2
Eccles M30 ....95 C8
Hazel Grove SK7 ......133 E8
Stretford M32 ....96 A3
Bakewell St
Manchester M18 ....99 C4
Stockport SK3 ....170 D7
Bakewell Wlk 52 SK13 .171 D1
Bala Cl M5 ....81 A2
Balcarres Ave WN1 .....37 E2
Balcarres Rd WN2 ......38 C5
Balcary Gr BL1 ....144 B8
Balcombe Cl BL8 ....27 C7
Balderstone Rd OL11 ...31 A3
Balderstone Tech Coll
OL11 ....31 A3
Baldock Rd M20 ....110 D3
Baldrine Dr WN2 ....57 B5
Baldwin Rd M19 ....110 F6
Baldwin St Bacup OL13 ...3 B8
Bolton BL3 ....145 E5
Hindley WN2 ....57 B3
Ince-in-M WN3 ....151 D6
Wigan,Redwood WN5 ...54 B6
Wigan,Scholes WN1 ...151 D8
Bale St M2 ....162 F8
Balfern Cl 12 BL5 ....39 E1
Balfern Fold 11 BL5 .....39 E1
Balfour Gr SK5 ....111 F8
Balfour Rd
Altrincham WA14 .....119 D7
5 Rochdale OL12 ....14 C1
Urmston M41 ....95 B3
Balfour St 5 Bolton BL3 .145 D6
Manchester M8 ....156 A8
Oldham OL4 ....67 C7
Salford M6 ....81 A6
Shaw OL2 ....149 B7
Balham Wlk M12 ....164 F6
Balholm Ct M20 ....110 B4
Ball St Rochdale OL16 ...31 A8
Wigan WN6 ....36 E2
Ball Wlk SK14 ....102 F1
Ball's Cotts WN3 ....55 F3
Balladen Prim Sch BB4 ...1 F8
Ballantine St M40 ......83 C4
Ballantyne Way 5 WA3 ...90 E8
Ballard Cl OL15 ....16 B7
Ballard Way OL2 ....149 C8
Ballater Ave M41 ....95 A1
Ballater Cl OL10 ....29 B1
Ballater Wlk 1 M8 .....156 B6
Ballbrook Ave M20 ...110 B5
Balleratt St M19 ....99 A1
Balliol Cl SK6 ....113 C4
Balliol Ct M33 ....108 C4
Balliol St Manchester M8 .156 A8
Swinton M27 ....79 E8
Balliol Way WN4 ....72 F4
Balloon St M4 ....159 A2
Balm St BL0 ....11 A4
Balmain Ave M18 ....99 C3
Balmain Rd M41 ....95 B3
Balmer Rd M23 ....121 B4
Balmfield St M8 ....156 A5
Balmforth St M15 ......162 D7
Balmoral PR7 ....20 E6
Balmoral Ave
Cheadle SK8 ....123 A2
Denton M34 ....100 D7
Golborne WA3 ....74 D1
Hyde SK14 ....113 E8
Little Lever BL3 ....43 A3
Rochdale OL11 ....30 B8
Royton OL2 ....48 F4
Stretford M32 ....96 D3
Urmston M41 ....95 D3
Whitefield M45 ....63 A7
Balmoral Cl Horwich BL6 ...22 E2
Milnrow OL16 ....32 A6
Ramsbottom BL8 ....11 A1
Whitefield BL9 ....45 A5
Balmoral Ct
Ashton-u-L OL6 ....166 A1
Manchester SK4 ....168 A3
Balmoral Dr
Altrincham WA14 .....119 F8
Heywood,Broadfield OL10 ...29 E1
Heywood,Top of Heap OL10 ..29 A1
High Lane SK6 ....134 E7
Hindley WN2 ....56 C4
Leigh WN7 ....76 D6

Balmoral Dr continued
Poynton SK12 ....133 D3
Reddish M34 ....100 A3
Stalybridge SK15 ....86 A3
Balmoral Gr SK7 ....124 F3
Balmoral Grange M25 ...63 E3
Balmoral Ho M30 ....79 C2
Balmoral Rd
Altrincham WA14 .....119 E4
Ashton-in-M WN4 ......73 A4
Farnworth BL4 ....60 D7
Manchester,Burnage M14 .110 D8
Manchester,Heaton Mersey
SK4 ....168 A3
Swinton M27 ....62 A2
Urmston M41 ....95 A1
Wigan WN5 ....54 E6
Balmoral St M18 ....99 C4
Balmoral Way SK9 ....137 A6
Balmore Cl BL3 ....146 A3
Balniel Wlk WN1 ....37 E2
Balsam Cl M13 ....163 C7
Balshaw Ave M44 ....93 F2
Balshaw Cl BL3 ....144 C5
Balshaw Ct M44 ....94 A2
Baltic Bldgs BB4 ....2 E8
Baltic Flats BB4 ....2 E8
Baltic Rd
Altrincham WA14 .....119 A6
Rawtenstall BB4 ....2 E8
Baltic St M5 ....154 E2
Baltimore St M40 .....157 F5
Bamber Ave M33 ....108 E3
Bamber Croft BL5 ....39 E3
Bamber Ct 5 WN2 ....56 A6
Bamber St M9 ....64 D5
Bamber Wlk BL3 ....145 D5
Bamber's Bldgs 2 WN2 ...56 F5
6 Oldham OL4 ....43 C5
Bamburgh Cl M26 ......43 C5
Bamburgh Dr OL7 ....84 E5
Bamburgh Pl 3 WN4 ...73 A5
Bamford Ave
Denton M34 ....112 F8
Middleton M24 ....47 E2
Bamford Bsns Pk SK4 ...111 E5
Bamford Cl Bury BL9 ....28 E4
Gatley SK8 ....131 D8
Bamford Dr OL11 ....30 C6
Bamford Fold SK13 ....171 E1
Bamford Gdns WA15 ..120 D6
Bamford Gn SK13 .....171 E1
Bamford Gr
Ashton-u-L OL6 ....85 F6
Manchester M20 ....110 A3
Bamford La SK13 ......171 E1
Bamford Mews
Gamesley SK13 ....171 E1
Rochdale OL11 ....29 E7
Bamford Pl OL12 ....14 E1
Bamford Prim Sch OL11 ..29 F7
Bamford Rd
Heywood OL10 ....29 D3
Manchester M20 ....110 A3
Ramsbottom BL0 ....12 B6
Bamford St
Chadderton OL9 ....152 C8
Droylsden M11 ....83 B2
4 Littleborough OL15 ...15 F5
Royton OL2 ....48 E3
Stockport SK4 ....170 F8
Bamford Way OL11 .....29 F6
Bampton Ave WA11 .....71 B1
Bampton Cl
Stockport SK2 ....124 B7
Westhoughton BL5 ......39 E2
Bampton Rd M22 ....121 D1
Bampton Wlk M24 ....46 E2
Banastre Dr WA12 ......89 F3
Banbury Cl WN7 ....75 E1
Banbury Dr WA14 .....119 E8
Banbury Mews M27 .....61 D1
Banbury Rd
Failsworth M35,M40 ....83 E4
Longshaw WN5 ....53 D2
Middleton M24 ....65 A5
Wythenshawe M22 ...121 D1
Banbury St 5 Bolton BL2 ...25 C1
Stockport SK1 ....169 F1
Bancroft Ave SK8 ......123 A1
Bancroft Cl SK6 ....112 E3
Bancroft Ct WA15 .....120 A3
Bancroft Fold SK14 ...102 B5
Bancroft Rd
Altrincham WA15 .....120 A3
Swinton M27 ....61 E1
Banff Gr OL10 ....29 A1
Banff Rd M14 ....98 C4
Bangor Fold WN7 ....76 C4
Bangor Rd SK8 ....122 F6
Bangor St Ashton-u-L OL6 ...85 E2
Bolton BL1 ....145 E8
Manchester M15 ......162 D5
Reddish SK5 ....169 F4
Rochdale OL16 ....31 B6
Banham Ave WN3 ....54 C3
Banister Way WN3 ....54 E2
Bank Ave WN5 ....53 D5
Bank Barn La OL12 .....15 D6
Bank Bridge Rd M1,M40 ..83 E3
Bank Brow WN8 ....35 C5
Bank Cl OL15 ....16 A3
Bank Field BL5 ....58 A7
Bank Field St M26 ....61 D7
Bank Gr M38 ....59 F6
Bank Hall BL8 ....27 A2
Bank Hey BL5 ....39 F1
Bank Hill St OL4 ....67 C7

Bank Hos WN2 ....75 B8
Bank House Cl M29 .....59 E1
Bank House Rd M9 ......64 C4
Bank La
Pendlebury M6,M27 .....80 D6
Tintwistle SK13 ....104 A7
Uppermill OL3 ....69 E4
Walkden M38 ....59 F6
Wardle OL12 ....15 D7
Bank Mdw BL6 ....22 C4
Bank Pas WA3 ....74 A1
Bank Pl Bury BL8 ....27 C3
Salford M3 ....158 D2
Bank Rd Manchester M8 ...64 A1
Mossley SK15 ....86 E6
Romiley SK6 ....113 B5
Up Holland WN8 ....35 D4
Bank Side BL5 ....58 A7
Bank Side SK5 ....137 B7
Bank St Adlington PR7 ....21 A7
Ashton-u-L OL6 ....166 B2
Bolton BL1 ....145 F7
Bury BL9 ....28 F4
Bury,Walshaw BL8 ......26 F4
Chapeltown BL7 ....9 C4
Cheadle SK8 ....122 C6
Denton,Haughton Green
M34 ....113 B8
Denton,Hooley Hill M34 .100 F8
Droylsden,Clayton M11 ..83 B2
Droylsden,Fairfield M43 .99 F8
Heywood OL10 ....29 B2
Golborne WA3 ....74 A1
Glossop SK13 ....116 D8
Heywood OL10 ....29 B2
Hollinfare WA3 ....105 B5
Hyde SK14 ....167 D3
6 Oldham OL4 ....67 D6
Platt Bridge WN2 ....56 A3
Radcliffe M26 ....44 B2
Ramsbottom BL0 ....11 E7
Rochdale OL12 ....31 A4
Romiley SK6 ....113 B5
Sale M33 ....108 C5
Salford M3 ....158 D2
Salford,Broughton Park
M7 ....155 F8
Shaw OL2 ....149 A4
Whitefield M45 ....44 E1
Wigan WN3 ....54 E6
Bank Terr
7 Hadfield SK13 ....104 A5
Whitworth OL12 ....14 C8
Bank The Glossop SK13 .116 C8
8 Rochdale OL16 ....15 B1
Bank Top Ashton-u-L OL6 .166 C2
Bury BL9 ....11 F1
Heywood OL10 ....29 B3
Bank Top Gr BL1 ....25 A5
Bank Top Pk 4 OL4 .....67 D6
Bank Top St SK19 ....29 B3
Bank Wood BL1 ....145 A7
Bankbottom SK13 ......104 A5
Bankbrook WN6 ....36 D4
Banker St BL3 ....148 C5
Bankes Ave WN5 ....54 A6
Bankfield Ainsworth BL2 ...43 C8
Dukinfield SK14 ....101 D5
Bankfield Cl BL2 ....26 C1
Bankfield Cotts OL3 .....50 F2
Bankfield Dr 6 Oldham OL8 .67 B7
Worsley M28 ....78 B7
Bankfield La OL11 ......29 E8
Bankfield Mews BL9 ....44 F7
Bankfield Rd
Cheadle SK8 ....122 F1
Farnworth BL4 ....60 D6
Romiley SK6 ....113 B5
Sale M33 ....107 E6
Tyldesley M29 ....77 E8
Bankfield St Bacup OL13 ...3 D8
Bolton BL3 ....144 C5
Bolton BL3 ....146 C4
Manchester M9 ....157 D8
Reddish SK4 ....169 F4
Bankfield Terr 1 BL4 ....3 D8
Banks Croft OL10 ....46 D7
Bankfield St
Bankgate SK14 ....115 A8
Bankhall Cl WN2 ....57 B2
Bankhall La WA14,WA15 .128 F8
Bankhall Rd SK4 ....168 A2
Bankhall Wlk 10 M9 ...157 E7
Bankhirst Cl M8 ....64 A1
Bankhouse Rd BL8 ......27 C4
Banklands Cl M44 .....105 D5
Bankley St M19 ....99 A1
Bankmill Cl 12 M13 ....163 B7
Banks Croft OL10 ....46 D7
Banks Ct
Altrincham WA15 .....120 D5
Leigh WN7 ....75 D5
Banks La SK1 ....124 B8
Banks Lane Inf Sch SK1 .124 B8
Banks Lane Jun Sch
SK1 ....124 B8
Bankside
Altrincham WA15 .....129 C6
Hattersley SK14 ....102 D1
Bankside Ave
Ashton-in-M WN4 ....73 A8
Radcliffe M26 ....44 D4

Bankside Ave continued
Uppermill OL3 ....69 C7
Bankside Cl
Handforth SK9 ....131 D1
Oldham OL9 ....153 D6
Romiley SK6 ....114 C1
Bankside Ct
Manchester M12 ....99 A4
Stockport SK4 ....168 A2
Bankside Rd M20 ......122 B7
Bankside Wlk 5 SK14 ..102 D2
Bankswood Cl SK13 ...104 A4
Bankwell St WN6 ....35 C6
Banky La M33 ....107 D6
Bann St SK3 ....170 E8
Bannach Dr OL9 ....48 A1
Bannatyne Cl M40 ......65 E1
Banner Dale Cl M13 ....98 F4
Banner St Hindley WN2 ...57 D5
Ince-in-M WN3 ....151 E5
Banner Wlk 10 M11 ...160 F1
Bannerman Ave M25 ...63 C3
Bannerman Rd M43 .....84 B1
Bannister Dr SK8 ......122 F2
Bannister St Bolton BL2 ..42 E8
Stockport SK1 ....170 F7
Banstead Ave M22 ....121 D7
Bantry Ave M9 ....64 D3
Bantry St Bolton BL3 ...145 E5
4 Rochdale OL12 ....15 A2
Baptist St M4 ....159 B3
Bar Gap Rd OL1 ....153 F8
Bar La BL1 ....24 E5
Bar St WN2 ....56 A1
Bar Terr OL12 ....34 D7
Barathea Cl OL11 ....30 B3
Barbara Rd BL3 ....146 A2
Barbara St BL3 ....147 D4
Barbeck Cl M40 ....160 E3
Barber St
5 Droylsden M11 ....99 E7
Hadfield SK13 ....104 B5
Barber Wlk Bury BL7 .....8 F2
Barberry Cl WA14 ......119 B7
Barberry Wlk M31 .....105 F3
Barbican St 2 M20 ....110 B7
Barbrook Cl WN6 ....19 B2
Barbury Cl WN7 ....75 F7
Barchester Ave BL2 ....25 E1
Barchester Rd SK8 ....122 C4
Barcicroft Rd M19,SK4 .110 E4
Barcicroft Wlk 1 M19 ..110 E4
Barclay Dr M30 ....79 E3
Barclay Rd SK12 ....133 E2
Barclays Ave M6 ....80 D6
Barcliffe Ave M40 ....65 C2
Barclyde St OL11 ......139 E5
Barcombe Cl Oldham OL4 .49 D2
Urmston M32 ....95 F3
Barcombe Wlk M9 .....157 D7
Barcroft Rd BL1 ....142 C2
Barcroft St BL9 ....140 F3
Bardale Gr WN4 ....73 A3
Bardell Cl SK12 ....133 D2
Bardney Ave M33 ....107 E2
Bardon Cl BL1 ....143 D1
Bardon Rd M23 ....120 F6
Bardsea Ave M22 ....121 D1
Bardsley Ave M35 ....83 F7
Bardsley Cl Bolton BL2 ...25 D5
3 Hattersley SK14 ....102 E2
Up Holland WN8 ....53 A7
Bardsley Gate Ave SK15 .102 E6
Bardsley St
Failsworth M40 ....83 D5
Manchester M40 ....47 A1
Oldham,Salem OL4 .....67 E5
Oldham,Watersheddings
OL4 ....49 E1
Oldham,White Gate OL9 .65 F3
Stockport SK4 ....169 D3
Bardsley Vale Ave OL8 ..85 A8
Bardsley St SK14 ....58 D8
Bare St BL1 ....145 F8
Bare Trees Jun & Inf Schs
OL9 ....152 B8
Barehill St OL15 ....16 B6
Barff Rd M5 ....80 C2
Barfold Cl SK2 ....125 A5
Barford Dr WA3 ....91 A8
Barford Gr 6 BL6 ....40 A1
Barford Wlk M23 ....121 A4
Baric Cl M30 ....79 F1
Baring St M1,M12 .....163 B8
Barke St OL15 ....15 F4
Bark St Bolton BL1 .....145 E8
Kearsley BL4 ....61 A8
Bark St E BL1 ....145 F8
Barkan Way M27 ....80 B8
Barke St OL15 ....15 F3
Barker Rd SK6 ....113 F2
Barker St Bury BL9 .....140 E1
Leigh WN7 ....75 C5
Manchester M3 ....158 F3
Barker's La M33 ....108 C4
Barking St M40 ....160 E3
Barkway Rd M32 ....96 A2
Barkwell La OL5 ....86 E6
Barkworth Wlk M40 ....83 B6
Barlborough Rd WN5 ...54 D5
Barlby Wlk M40 ....65 D1
Barlea Ave M40 ....65 D1
Barley Brook Mdw BL1 ..24 F6
Barley Brook St WN6 ...37 B1
Barley Croft SK8 ....122 F1

Barley Croft Rd SK14 ..101 E3
Barley Dr SK7 ....132 E7
Barley Hall St OL10 .....29 E3
Barleycorn Cl M33 ....109 A3
Barleycroft SK14 ....171 F4
Barleycroft St M16 .....97 F4
Barleyfield Wlk M24 ....46 F1
Barleywood Wlk SK15 .102 E7
Barlow Cres SK6 ....125 F4
Barlow Ct Edgworth BL7 ...9 E5
Walkden M28 ....60 E3
Barlow Fold Bury BL9 ...44 F5
Barlow Fold Cl BL9 .....44 F5
Barlow Fold Rd
Reddish SK5 ....111 F8
Romiley SK6 ....113 D3
Barlow Hall Prim Sch
M21 ....109 C5
Barlow Hall Rd M21 ...109 C5
Barlow Ho OL8 ....153 F5
Barlow La M30 ....79 C2
Barlow La N SK5 ....111 F8
Barlow Moor Cl OL12 ...13 E2
Barlow Moor Ct M21 ..109 B5
Barlow Moor Rd M21 .109 C6
Barlow Park Ave BL1 ...24 D5
Barlow Pl M13 ....163 C7
Barlow RC High Sch The
M20 ....110 C2
Barlow Rd
Altrincham WA14 .....119 B7
Dukinfield SK16 ....101 D8
Handforth SK9 ....131 B1
Reddish M19 ....99 C1
Salford M5 ....81 C1
Stretford M16,M32 .....96 F4
Barlow St Bacup OL13 ...3 B7
Bury BL9 ....140 F3
Eccles M30 ....79 D1
Heywood OL10 ....46 E8
Horwich BL6 ....22 C2
Radcliffe M26 ....44 B3
Rochdale OL16 ....31 B1
8 Salford M6 ....80 D4
Barlow Terr M21 ....109 C6
Barlow Wlk 2 SK5 .....111 F8
Barlow Wood Dr SK6 ..126 B3
Barlow's Croft M3 .....158 E2
Barlow's La S SK7 ......124 A1
Barmeadow OL3 ....50 F2
Barmhouse Cl SK14 ...102 A3
Barmhouse La SK14 ...102 B3
Barmhouse Mews SK14 .102 A3
Barmouth St M11 ......164 F8
Barmouth Wlk 4 OL8 ...66 E4
Barmskin La WN6 ....18 C8
Barn Acre BL6 ....21 E1
Barn Cl Glossop SK13 ..116 D7
Urmston M41 ....94 C2
Barn Ct BL2 ....67 E5
Barn Gr M34 ....100 E7
Barn Hill 6 BL5 ....39 E1
Barn Hill Terr 7 BL5 ....39 E1
Barn La WA3 ....89 F8
Barn Mdw BL7 ....9 D5
Barn St Bolton BL3 ....145 E7
Oldham OL1 ....153 E6
Whitefield M45 ....62 E1
Barn Way WA12 ....89 B3
Barn Wlk 10 M11 ....99 F7
Barnaby Rd SK12 ......133 D2
Barnabys Rd BL5 ....39 D3
Barnacre Ave Bolton BL2 ...42 F7
Wythenshawe M23 ...120 F3
Barnard Ave
Manchester SK4 ....168 B2
Prestwich M45 ....63 B7
Barnard Cl OL7 ....84 F4
Barnard Rd M18 ....99 E4
Barnard St 3 BL2 ......148 C8
Barnbrook St BL9 ......141 A3
Barnby St M12 ....99 A3
Barnclose Rd M22 ....121 D1
Barncroft Dr BL6 ....22 F3
Barncroft Gdns M22 ..121 C5
Barncroft Rd BL4 ....60 D8
Barnes Ave SK4 ....168 A2
Barnes Cl Farnworth BL4 ..60 D8
Ramsbottom BL0 ....11 A3
Barnes Ho 2 BL4 ....60 D8
Barnes Hospl SK8 .....122 C6
Barnes Mdws OL15 .....6 C1
Barnes St BL4 ....60 C8
Barnes Terr BL4 ....61 A7
Barnes St 2 M40 ....83 C5
Barnet Rd BL1 ....142 C2
Barnett Ave M16 ....97 F4
Barnett Ct OL10 ....29 C1
Barnett Dr M3 ....158 D2
Barnfield
Littleborough OL15 .....16 D6
Urmston M41 ....95 B1
Barnfield Ave SK6 .....113 D3
Barnfield Cl Bolton BL7 ...8 E2
Radcliffe M26 ....43 E4
6 Salford M5 ....154 F1
Tyldesley M29 ....59 D3
Barnfield Cres M33 ...107 F6
Barnfield Dr
Westhoughton BL5 .....40 A1
Worsley M28 ....78 B6
Barnfield Rd
Dukinfield SK14 ....102 B5
Manchester M19 ......110 E4
Swinton M27 ....61 D2

Barnfield Rd E SK3 ......123 F4
Barnfield Rd W SK3 ......123 D4
Barnfield Rise OL2 ......32 A1
Barnfield St Denton M34 .100 D4
Heywood OL10 ....29 E2
Rochdale OL12 ....14 F2
Barnfield Wlk WA15 ....120 C5
Barngate Dr OL5 ....86 C8
Barngate Rd SK8 ....122 A6
Barngill Gr WN3 ....54 E3
Barnham Cl WA3 ....90 A8
Barnham Wlk M23 ......120 E8
Barnhill Ave M25 ....63 B2
Barnhill Dr M25 ....63 B2
Barnhill Rd M25 ....63 B3
Barnhill St M14 ....97 F4
Barnley Cl M44 ....94 B3
Barns La
Partington WA14 ....118 A5
Partington WA14 ....118 A6
Barns Pl WA15 ....129 C8
Barnsdale Cl BL2 ....26 C1
Barnsdale Dr M8 ....156 A6
Barnsfold Ave M14 ......110 C8
Barnsfold Rd SK6 ....125 F3
Barnside OL12 ....14 B8
Barnside Ave M28 ....60 E3
Barnside Cl BL9 ....27 E8
Barnside Way M35 ....84 C6
Barnsley St
Stockport SK1 ....124 B8
Wigan WN6 ....37 B2
Barnstaple Dr M40 ......156 C6
Barnstead Ave M20 .....110 D5
Barnston Ave M14 ....98 B2
Barnston Cl BL1 ....143 F4
Barnton Cl WA3 ....90 D7
Barnview Dr M44 ....94 A1
Barnway Wlk 7 M40 .....65 C2
Barnwell Ave WA3 ....91 D4
Barnwell Cl M34 ....100 E5
Barnwood Cl 11 BL1 ....143 E1
Barnwood Dr BL1 ....143 E1
Barnwood Rd M23 ......121 A3
Barnwood Terr 10 BL1 ...143 E1
Baron Fold M38 ....60 A5
Baron Fold Cres M38 .....59 F5
Baron Fold Gr M38 ....59 F5
Baron Fold Rd M38 ....59 F5
Baron Gn SK8 ....131 D7
Baron Rd SK14 ....113 F7
Baron St Bury BL9 ......140 D1
Rochdale OL16 ....139 F7
Baron Wlk BL3 ....43 C3
Baroness Gr M7 ....81 C4
Barons Ct M35 ....83 D6
Barr Hill Ave M6 ....80 E5
Barra Dr M41 ....95 D5
Barrack Hill SK6 ....113 A2
Barrack Hill Cl SK6 ......113 A3
Barrack Hill Prim Sch
SK6 ....113 A2
Barrack Sq 16 WN1 .....150 C8
Barrack St M15 ....162 D7
Barracks Rd WN2 ....56 D1
Barracks Yd WN1 ....150 C8
Barrass St M11 ....99 D7
Barratt Gdns M24 ....46 D4
Barrett Ave BL4 ....60 F7
Barrett Ct BL9 ....141 A2
Barrett St OL4 ....67 B5
Barrfield Rd M6 ....154 E4
Barrhill Cl M15 ....162 E6
Barrie St WN7 ....75 D8
Barrie Way BL1 ....25 B4
Barrington Ave
Cheadle SK8 ....123 A1
Droylsden M43 ....83 F1
Barrington Cl
Altrincham WA14 ....119 D6
Wigan WN3 ....54 D2
Barrington Rd WA14 ....119 D5
Barrington St M11 ....83 C2
Barrington Wlk 2 BL2 ....25 B1
Barrisdale Cl BL3 ....40 F5
Barron Mdw WN7 ....75 D7
Barrow Bridge Rd BL1 ..142 A3
Barrow Hill Rd M8 ......155 F5
Barrow La
Altrincham WA15 ....129 B7
Golborne WA2 ....90 C2
Barrow Mdw SK8 ....131 E8
Barrow St
Ashton-in-M WN4 ....73 D5
Salford M3,M5 ....158 D1
Barrowcroft Cl WN1 ......20 B1
Barrowdale Rd WA3 ....90 B8
Barrowdene Ho BL1 ......23 F4
Barrowfield Rd M22 .....121 A2
Barrowfield Wlk 4 M24 ...47 A1
Barrowfields M24 ....47 A2
Barrows Ct 4 BL1 ....145 F6
Barrowshaw Cl M28 ....60 C2
Barrs Fold Cl BL5 ....39 D3
Barrs Fold Rd BL5 ....39 D3
Barrule Ave SK7 ....124 E1
Barry Cres M28 ....60 A3
Barry Ct 9 M20 ....110 B6
Barry Lawson Cl M8 .....155 F7
Barry Rd Reddish SK5 ....111 F5
Wythenshawe M23 ....109 C2
Barry Rise WA14 ....119 A2
Barry St OL1 ....67 B8
Barsham Dr BL3 ....145 D5
Bartlam Pl OL1 ....153 F7
Bartlemore St OL1 ....49 B1
Bartlett Rd OL2 ....149 A6
Bartlett St M11 ....165 B8
Bartley Rd M22 ....121 C8
Barton Ave Urmston M41 ..95 B2
Wigan WN1 ....37 B2
Barton Bsns Pk M30 .....79 C1
Barton Cl SK9 ....131 D2
Barton Clough WN5 ....71 E5
Barton Clough Prim Sch
M32 ....95 F4
Barton Ct SK14 ....101 C1
Barton Dock Rd
Stretford M32 ....96 B4
Urmston M41 ....95 E6
Barton Emb M17 ....95 C7
Barton Fold SK14 ....167 D1
Barton Hall Ave M30 .....79 A1
Barton Hall Est M30 ......79 B1
Barton Ho 4 M6 ....80 C4
Barton La M30 ....79 E1
Barton Moss Com Prim Sch
M30 ....94 F8
Barton Moss Rd M30 .....94 D7
Barton Rd
Dukinfield SK14,SK16 .....101 C6
Eccles M30 ....79 C1
Eccles,Alder Forest M28 ...78 F5
Farnworth BL4 ....60 B7
Manchester SK4 ....110 E1
Middleton M24 ....64 F8
Pendlebury M27 ....80 A6
Stretford M32 ....96 B3
Stretford M32 ....96 C1
Urmston M41 ....95 C5
Barton Sq M2 ....158 F1
Barton St Farnworth BL4 ..60 E7
Golborne WA3 ....74 A1
Manchester M3 ....162 E8
Oldham OL1 ....153 D8
Platt Bridge WN2 ....56 B3
Tyldesley M29 ....58 F1
4 Wigan WN5 ....54 B5
Barton Terr M44 ....94 C3
Barway Rd M21 ....96 F1
Barwell Cl Golborne WA3 ..74 C1
Reddish SK5 ....112 A8
Barwell Rd M33 ....107 E5
Barwell Sq 1 BL4 ....42 B2
Barwick Pl M33 ....108 A4
Barwood Lea Mill BL0 ...138 C6
Basechurch Wlk M12 ...164 F6
Basford Rd M16 ....97 B3
Bashall St BL1 ....144 C8
Basil Ct OL16 ....31 B6
Basil St Bolton BL3 ......145 E5
Manchester M14 ....98 C3
Rochdale OL16 ....31 B6
Stockport SK4 ....169 E3
Basildon Cl M13 ....164 D5
Baslam Wlk 5 M4 ....159 C2
Basle Cl SK7 ....123 E4
Baslow Ave Hindley WN2 ..56 F3
Manchester M19 ....99 C2
Baslow Cl 29 SK13 ......171 E1
Baslow Dr Gatley SK8 ...131 C8
Hazel Grove SK7 ....133 F8
Baslow Fold 28 SK13 ....171 E1
Baslow Gn 30 SK13 .....171 E1
Baslow Gr SK5 ....111 F5
Baslow Mews SK13 .....171 E1
Baslow Rd Denton M34 ..112 F8
Droylsden M43 ....83 E3
Stretford M32 ....96 A3
Baslow St M11 ....160 E2
Baslow Way 31 SK13 .....171 E1
Bass La BL9 ....11 D3
Bass St Bolton BL2 ......148 C7
Dukinfield SK16 ....101 B8
Basset Ave M6 ....81 C5
Bassett Cl OL12 ....14 E3
Bassett Gdns OL12 ....14 E3
Bassett Gr WN3 ....54 C2
Bassett Way OL12 ....14 E2
Basswood Gn WN2 ....57 A3
Basten Dr M7 ....155 E6
Batchelor Cl M21 ....109 E7
Bateman St BL6 ....22 D2
Batemill Rd SK22 ....127 D2
Bates Cl OL11 ....30 D1
Bates St Dukinfield SK16 ..101 C8
Manchester M13 ....98 F4
Bateson Dr OL4 ....67 F6
Bateson St SK1 ....112 A2
Bateson Way OL8 ....153 F5
Bath Cl SK7 ....125 A2
Bath Cres Cheadle SK8 ..132 B6
Manchester M16 ....161 C5
Bath Pl WA14 ....119 D2
Bath St Altrincham WA14 ..119 D2
Atherton M46 ....58 A3
Bolton BL1 ....145 F8
Oldham OL9 ....152 C5
Rochdale OL12 ....15 B1
Wigan WN2 ....37 F2
Batheaston Gr WN7 ....75 D8
Batley St M9 ....157 E8
Batridge Rd BL7 ....9 A7
Batsmans Dr M27 ....61 E4
Battenberg Rd 2 BL1 ...144 C8
Battersbay Gr SK7 ....124 E2
Battersby Ct SK2 ....124 E6
Battersby St Bury BL9 ....28 D3
Droylsden M11 ....99 E7
Ince-in-M WN2 ....56 B8
Leigh WN7 ....76 B4
Rochdale OL11 ....30 B6
Battersea Rd SK4 ....110 F1
Batty St M8 ....156 C5
Baucher Rd WN3 ....54 F5
Baum The OL16 ....139 F8
Baverstock Cl WN3 .....151 D6
Baxendale St BL1 ....143 E4
Baxter Gdns M23 ....121 A7
Baxter Rd M33 ....108 B4
Baxter St Oldham OL8 ....66 B2
Standish WN6 ....19 F1
Baxter's Row WN2 ....57 C2
Bay St Heywood OL10 .....29 B3
Oldham OL9 ....153 D7
Rochdale OL12 ....15 A1
Bay Tree Ave M28 ....79 A5
Baybutt St M26 ....44 C3
Baycliffe Cl WN2 ....56 F3
Baycliffe Wlk 10 M8 .....155 F6
Baycroft Gr M23 ....109 A1
Baydon Ave M7 ....155 F6
Bayfield Gr M40 ....65 A1
Bayle Cl SK14 ....101 E5
Bayley Cl SK14 ....145 D8
Bayley Ct BL1 ....145 D8
Bayley Ind Est SK15 ......85 F1
Bayley St SK15 ....85 F1
Baynard Wlk M9 ....64 B4
Baysdale OL2 ....48 C5
Baysdale Ave BL3 ....40 F4
Bayston Wlk M12 ....164 F6
Bayswater Ave M40 ......83 C4
Bayswater St BL3 ....146 C2
Baythorpe St BL1 ....143 F3
Baytree Ave
Chadderton OL9 ....65 E8
Denton M34 ....101 A4
Baytree Dr SK6 ....112 F4
Baytree Gr BL0 ....11 B2
Baytree La M24 ....65 D8
Baytree Rd WN6 ....36 F2
Baytree Wlk OL12 ....4 C1
Baywood St M9 ....157 D8
Bazaar St M6 ....81 A4
Bazley Rd M22 ....109 D1
Bazley St BL1 ....23 F4
Beacomfold SK6 ....114 B3
Beacon Cl M46 ....58 B2
Beacon Dr M23 ....121 A2
Beacon Gr OL8 ....67 C4
Beacon Hts WN8 ....53 A8
Beacon Rd Billinge WN5 ..71 E6
Leigh WN2 ....75 A8
Romiley SK6 ....113 A1
Shevington Moor WN6 ......19 B2
Urmston M17 ....95 E7
Beacon View
Appley Bridge WN6 ....35 C8
Marple SK6 ....125 F8
Beacon View Dr WN8 .....53 B7
Beacons The WN6 ....35 D7
Beaconsfield M14 ....110 C7
Beaconsfield Rd WA14 ..119 D7
Beaconsfield St BL3 ....145 D6
Beaconsfield Terr SK15 ...86 F7
Beadham Dr M9 ....64 A5
Beadle Ave OL12 ....15 D5
Beaford Cl WN5 ....54 B5
Beaford Dr M22 ....130 E8
Beagle Wlk M22 ....130 E8
Beal Cl SK4 ....110 D3
Beal Cres OL16 ....15 C1
Beal Dr WN2 ....56 A2
Beal La OL2 ....149 C6
Beal Vale Prim Sch OL2 .149 B7
Beal Wlk M45 ....63 C8
Bealbank Cl OL16 ....32 A3
Bealcroft Cl OL16 ....31 E7
Bealcroft Wlk OL16 ....31 E7
Beale Gr M21 ....109 B8
Bealey Ave M26 ....44 E5
Bealey Cl
Manchester M18 ....165 B5
Radcliffe M26 ....44 D4
Bealey Dr BL9 ....44 D7
Bealey Hospl M26 ....44 D4
Bealey Ind Est M26 ....44 D4
Bealey Row M26 ....44 C4
Beaminster Ave SK4 .....110 F3
Beaminster Cl SK4 ......110 F3
Beaminster Ct SK4 ......110 F3
Beaminster Rd SK4 ......110 F3
Beaminster Wlk 7 M13 .163 C5
Beamish Cl M12,M13 ....163 C6
Beamsley Dr M22 ....121 B2
Bean Leach Ave SK2 .....124 F6
Bean Leach Dr SK2 ......124 F6
Bean Leach Rd SK2,SK7 ..124 F5
Beanfields M28 ....78 F5
Beard Rd M18 ....99 C4
Beard St Droylsden M43 ...83 F1
Royton OL2 ....48 E3
Beardsmore Dr WA3 ......74 E1
Beardwood Rd M9 ....64 D4
Bearswood Cl SK14 .....167 F1
Beathwaite Dr SK7 ......123 C1
Beatrice Ave
Cheadle SK8 ....122 F2
Reddish M18 ....99 F4
Beatrice Mews 9 BL6 ....22 B4
Beatrice Rd Bolton BL1 ..142 C1
Swinton M28 ....79 B7
Beatrice St Denton M34 ..100 E3
Farnworth BL4 ....60 C8
17 Horwich BL6 ....22 B4
Rochdale OL11 ....139 D7
Swinton M27 ....61 D1
Beatrice Wignall St
M43 ....100 A8
Beatrix Dr SK13 ....171 E3
Beattock St M15 ....162 D7
Beatty Dr BL5 ....39 E1
Beauchamp St OL6 ......166 C4
Beaufont Dr OL4 ....67 C5
Beaufort Ave
1 Manchester M20 ....110 A5
Sale M33 ....108 C2
Swinton M27 ....79 D7
Beaufort Chase SK9 .....131 F1
Beaufort Cl
Alderley Edge SK9 ....137 B2
Hattersley SK14 ....102 E2
Beaufort Pl 2 M20 ......110 A2
Beaufort Rd
Ashton-u-L OL6 ....85 D3
Hattersley SK14 ....102 E2
Sale M33 ....108 C3
Stockport SK2 ....124 D5
Beaufort St Eccles M30 ....79 B3
7 Hindley WN2 ....56 D5
Manchester M3 ....162 E8
Prestwich M25 ....63 C4
Rochdale OL12 ....14 C1
Wigan WN5 ....54 E6
Beaufort Way 3 SK14 ...102 E1
Beaulieu WA15 ....119 F2
Beauly Cl BL0 ....11 A2
Beaumaris Cl Leigh WN7 ..75 C5
Manchester M12 ....164 F6
Beaumaris Cres SK7 .....124 C1
Beaumaris Rd WN2 ....57 A3
Beaumonds OL11 ....29 F6
Beaumonds Way OL11 ....30 A6
Beaumont Ave BL6 ....22 C4
Beaumont Chase BL3 .....40 F3
Beaumont Cl 2 OL15 ......15 F5
Beaumont Ct Bolton BL1 ..40 D8
Handforth SK9 ....131 C5
Beaumont Dr BL3 ....40 E5
Beaumont Gr WN5 ....54 B8
Beaumont Hospl BL6 ......40 C8
Beaumont Prim Sch BL3 .40 E5
Beaumont Rd
Bolton BL1,BL3,BL6 ....40 E5
Horwich BL6 ....22 C4
Manchester M21 ....109 B7
Beaumont St OL6 ....166 C3
Beaupre WA14 ....119 C3
Beauvale Ave SK2 ....124 C7
Beaver Ct WN4 ....73 C6
Beaver Dr BL9 ....45 B4
Beaver Ho SK1 ....124 B8
Beaver Rd M20 ....110 B3
Beaver Road Prim Sch
M20 ....110 B3
Beaver St M1 ....163 A8
Beaver Wlk SK14 ....102 D1
Beaverbrook Ave WA3 ....92 B4
Bebbington Cl M33 .....108 F3
Bebbington St 7 M11 ....83 C1
Beccles Rd M33 ....108 B1
Beck Gr Shaw OL2 ....49 D8
Walkden M28 ....60 F1
Beck Ho SK14 ....102 D1
Beck St Droylsden M11 ....99 E7
Salford M3 ....158 E1
Beckenham Cl BL8 ....27 B1
Beckenham Rd M8 ......156 A7
Becket Ave M7 ....155 E6
Becket Mdws OL4 ....67 B6
Becket Meadow St OL4 ...67 B6
Beckett Dr WA13 ....117 B8
Beckett St
Manchester M18 ....165 C5
Oldham OL4 ....67 E7
Beckfield Rd M23 ....121 A5
Beckfoot Dr M13 ....98 E3
Beckford St M40 ....157 E5
Beckhampton Cl M13 ...163 C6
Beckley Ave M25 ....63 A2
Beckley Cl OL2 ....49 B4
Beckside Reddish SK5 ....100 A1
Tyldesley M29 ....76 E8
Beckton Gdns M22 ......121 C3
Beckwith WN2 ....56 B3
Becontree Ave M34 ......101 A4
Becontree Dr M23 ....120 E7
Bede St BL1 ....142 C2
Bedells La SK9 ....137 A6
Bedfont Wlk M9 ....64 E1
Bedford Ave Hyde SK14 ..167 E3
Manchester M16 ....97 D2
Sale M33 ....108 D2
Shaw OL2 ....48 F7
1 Swinton M27 ....79 E7
Walkden M28 ....60 C1
Bedford Ct WA15 ....120 C6
Bedford Dr
Altrincham WA15 ....120 C6
Atherton M46 ....58 A1
Bedford Gdns WN2 ....56 F6
Bedford Gn M44 ....105 B6
Bedford Hall Meth Prim Sch
WN7 ....76 C3
Bedford High Sch WN7 ...76 D4
Bedford Pl WN4 ....73 A5
Bedford Rd Eccles M30 ....79 E3
Manchester M16 ....97 A3
Urmston M41 ....95 C4
Bedford St Bolton BL1 ...145 D8
Bolton,Egerton BL7 ....8 D2
Heywood OL10 ....29 E2
1 Leigh WN7 ....76 A5
Prestwich M25 ....63 C5
6 Reddish SK5 ....111 E7
Reddish SK5 ....111 E8
Wigan,Longshoot WN1 .....37 E1
Wigan,Norley WN5 ....54 C5
Bedford Terr Bury BL9 ...141 A4
Haslingden BB4 ....1 A8
Bedlam Gn 2 BL9 ....140 F2
Bedlington Cl M23 ......120 E6
Bednal Ave M40 ....160 E4
Bedwell Cl M16 ....97 F3
Bedworth Cl BL2 ....148 B5
Bee Fold La M46 ....58 C1
Bee Hive Ind Est BL6 .....39 E8
Beech Ave Adlington PR6 ..21 B8
Atherton M46 ....58 E3
Chadderton OL1,OL9 ......48 A2
Culcheth WA3 ....92 A3
Denton M34 ....100 D4
Droylsden M43 ....83 F1
Farnworth BL4 ....60 A8
Gatley SK8 ....122 B5
Glossop SK13 ....116 A8
Golborne WA3 ....90 F7
Hazel Grove SK7 ....124 E2
Horwich BL6 ....22 E1
Irlam M44 ....94 C3
Kearsley BL4 ....61 B5
Little Lever BL3 ....43 B2
Marple SK6 ....125 D6
New Mills SK22 ....127 D1
Oldham OL4 ....67 D8
Radcliffe M26 ....61 F8
Sale WA15 ....120 B8
Salford M6 ....154 E4
Stockport SK2,SK3 ......170 F6
Uppermill OL3 ....69 B6
Urmston M41 ....95 C2
Whitefield M45 ....62 F6
Worsley M28 ....78 A6
Wythenshawe M22 ......121 D8
Beech Cl
Alderley Edge SK9 ....137 B3
Bolton BL2 ....25 C6
Newton-le-W WA12 ....89 C2
4 Partington M31 ....105 F3
Prestwich M25 ....63 C3
Whitworth OL12 ....4 C1
Beech Cres Leigh WN7 ....75 F3
Poynton SK12 ....133 E4
Standish WN6 ....36 E8
Beech Ct
9 Manchester M21 ....96 F1
Manchester,Crumpsall M8 ..63 F1
Manchester,Fallowfield
M14 ....110 C8
2 Sale M33 ....107 F4
Salford M6 ....81 A3
Beech Dr WN7 ....75 F2
Beech Gr
Abram Brow WN2 ....74 C7
Ashton-u-L OL7 ....84 F1
Leigh WN7 ....75 E2
Manchester M14 ....110 D7
Ramsbottom BL8 ....11 A1
Sale M33 ....107 F4
Salford M6 ....154 E4
Stalybridge SK15 ....101 F8
Walkden M38 ....59 E5
Wigan WN6 ....36 E3
Wilmslow SK9 ....137 A6
Beech Grove Cl BL9 .....141 B4
Beech Hall St WN6 ....37 A2
Beech Hill Ave WN6 ......36 F3
Beech Hill Com Prim Sch
WN6 ....37 A3
Beech Hill La WN6 ....36 E3
Beech Hill Rd OL4 ....68 D6
Beech Ho 3 Eccles M30 ...79 B1
Manchester M20 ....109 F4
Beech Holme Gr SK2 ....124 C8
Beech House Sch OL11 .139 E6
Beech Hurst Cl M16 ......97 D2
Beech La Romiley SK6 ...113 C2
Uppermill OL4 ....68 D5
Wilmslow SK9 ....137 A6
Beech Lawn WA14 ......119 C4
Beech Mews
Manchester M21 ....109 A8
Stockport SK2 ....124 A5
Beech Mount
Altrincham WA14 ....119 D2
Ashton-u-L OL7 ....85 A6
Manchester M9 ....157 D8
Beech Range 15 M19 .....99 A1
Beech Rd
Alderley Edge SK9 ....137 B3
Altrincham WA15 ....119 E3
Cheadle SK8 ....123 B1
Golborne WA3 ....74 A1
High Lane SK6 ....134 F7
Manchester M21 ....109 B7
Sale M33 ....108 D4
Stockport SK2,SK3 ......170 F6
Beech St Ashton-in-M WN4 .73 A6
Atherton M46 ....58 E3
Bolton BL1 ....143 F2
Bury BL9 ....141 B2
Eccles M30 ....79 B1
Edgworth BL7 ....9 D5
Failsworth M35 ....83 E8
Hyde SK14 ....167 D3
Middleton M24 ....64 F8
Newhey OL16 ....32 B4
3 Oldham OL1 ....67 A7
Radcliffe M26 ....44 C1
Ramsbottom BL9 ....11 C3
Rochdale OL11 ....139 D6
Swinton M27 ....79 F7
Beech Street Com Prim Sch
M30 ....79 B1
Beech Tree Ave WN6 .....35 D8
Beech Tree Hos WN2 .....73 F7
Beech View SK14 ....102 A2

Beech Wlk Leigh WN7 .....75 E2
Middleton M24 ....65 A6
Standish WN6 ....36 D8
1 Stretford M32 ....96 C1
Wigan WN3 ....54 C2
Beechacre BL0 ....11 D5
Beechcroft M25 ....63 C3
Beechcroft Ave BL2 ....42 E6
Beechcroft Cl M40 .....160 D3
Beechcroft Gr BL2 ....42 E6
Beechdale Cl M40 ....83 C8
Beecher Wlk M9 ....157 D6
Beeches SK9 ....136 F6
Beeches Mews M20 .....109 F4
Beeches The
Altrincham WA14 ....119 C2
4 Atherton M46 ....58 D3
Bolton BL1 ....24 D6
Cheadle SK8 ....123 B1
Eccles M30 ....79 F3
Heywood OL10 ....29 C2
Manchester M20 ....109 F4
Mossley OL5 ....68 E1
Romiley SK6 ....113 B2
Beechey Sq OL1 ....67 A7
Beechfield
Altrincham WA14 ....119 C3
Rochdale OL11 ....29 E6
Sale M33 ....107 F2
Uppermill OL4 ....68 D5
Wilmslow SK9 ....137 A6
Beechfield Ave
Hindley WN2 ....57 A4
3 Radcliffe M26 ....44 C1
Urmston M41 ....95 A3
Walkden M38 ....60 A5
Wilmslow SK9 ....136 E5
Beechfield Cl
5 Oldham OL4 ....67 F6
Rochdale OL11 ....29 E6
Beechfield Dr Bury BL9 ...44 F7
Leigh WN7 ....75 F3
Beechfield Mews SK14 ..102 A3
Beechfield Rd
Bolton BL1 ....142 C2
Cheadle SK8 ....132 B8
Hadfield SK13 ....171 F3
Milnrow OL16 ....31 F4
Stockport SK3 ....170 F5
Swinton M27 ....79 D5
Beechfield St M8 ....156 A6
Beechmill Dr WA3 ....91 E3
Beechpark Ave M22 .....121 C7
Beechurst Rd SK8 ......123 B5
Beechway High Lane SK6 .134 F7
Wilmslow SK9 ....136 F5
Beechwood
Altrincham WA14 ....119 B1
Glossop SK13 ....115 F7
Shaw OL2 ....49 D8
Whitefield BL9 ....45 A6
Beechwood Ave
Ashton-in-M WN4 ....73 A2
Littleborough OL15 ......16 A3
Manchester M21 ....109 C7
Newton-le-W WA12 ....89 D4
Ramsbottom BL0 ....11 D6
Reddish SK5 ....169 F4
Romiley SK6 ....113 D2
Shevington WN6 ....35 F5
Stalybridge SK15 ....86 C4
Urmston M41 ....94 E3
Beechwood Cres
Orrell WN5 ....53 E6
Tyldesley M29 ....77 A6
Beechwood Ct Bury BL8 ..27 A5
Coppull PR7 ....19 F8
3 Manchester M20 .....110 A3
Beechwood Dr
Hyde SK14 ....167 F1
Marple SK6 ....126 A6
Mossley OL5 ....68 C2
Royton OL2 ....48 C6
Sale M33 ....107 C4
Swinton M28 ....79 B6
Wilmslow SK9 ....137 E8
Beechwood Gr
Cheadle SK8 ....132 A8
Manchester M9 ....157 E7
Beechwood Ho SK6 .....112 E6
Beechwood La
Culcheth WA3 ....91 D4
Stalybridge SK15 ....86 C4
Beechwood Manor SK6 .126 A6
Beechwood Rd
Manchester M25 ....63 D3
Oldham OL8 ....66 F2
Beechwood St BL3 .....147 F3
Beede St M11 ....165 B8
Beedon Ave BL3 ....43 A4
Beeford Dr WN5 ....53 E5
Beehive Gn BL5 ....40 B1
Beehive St OL8 ....66 F3
Beeley St Hyde SK14 ....167 E2
Salford M6 ....81 B5
Beenham Cl M33 ....107 C3
Beeston Ave
Altrincham WA15 ....119 F6
Salford M7 ....81 B6
Beeston Cl BL1 ....25 A6
Beeston Gr Leigh WN7 ....76 D7
Prestwich M45 ....63 B7
Stockport SK3 ....170 E5
Beeston Rd
Handforth SK9 ....131 D5
Beeston Rd *continued*
Sale M33 ....107 F4
Beeston St M9 ....157 E8
Beeth St M11 ....99 D7
Beeton Gr M13 ....98 E4
Beever Prim Sch OL1 ....67 A8
Beever St
Manchester M16 ....161 C5
Oldham OL1 ....67 A7
Begley Cl SK6 ....112 F1
Begonia Ave BL4 ....42 B1
Begonia Wlk M12 ....164 F6
Beightons Wlk OL12 .....14 D4
Beis Rochel Sch M8 .....63 F1
Belayse Cl BL1 ....142 B2
Belbeck St BL8 ....27 C2
Belbeck St S 8 BL8 .....27 C2
Belcroft Dr M38 ....59 E6
Belcroft Gr M38 ....59 E5
Belding Ave M40 ....65 F1
Beldon Rd M9 ....64 B4
Belfairs Cl OL7 ....85 B7
Belfield Cl OL16 ....31 C8
Belfield Com Sch OL16 ...31 C8
Belfield La OL16 ....31 C8
Belfield Mill La OL16 ....31 D8
Belfield Old Rd OL16 ....31 C8
Belfield Rd
Manchester,Didsbury M20 .110 B3
Manchester,Sedgley Park M25 ....63 E2
Reddish SK5 ....99 F3
Rochdale OL16 ....31 C8
Belford Ave M34 ....100 A3
Belford Coll OL8 ....66 C4
Belford Dr BL3 ....147 E3
Belford Rd M32 ....96 D3
Belford Wlk M23 ....121 A6
Belfort Dr M5 ....161 B8
Belfry Cl SK9 ....137 D8
Belfry Cres WN6 ....19 F2
Belgate Cl M12 ....99 A4
Belgium St OL11 ....29 E7
Belgrave Ave
Failsworth M35 ....84 B8
Manchester M14 ....98 E3
Marple SK6 ....125 F6
Oldham OL8 ....67 A4
Urmston M41 ....94 E3
Belgrave Bglws M26 .....43 F4
Belgrave Cl Golborne WN7 .91 C8
Radcliffe M26 ....44 A4
Wigan WN3 ....54 D3
Belgrave Cres Eccles M30 .79 F2
Horwich BL6 ....22 D3
Stockport SK2 ....124 B4
Belgrave Ct Denton M34 .100 D4
Oldham OL8 ....66 F4
Belgrave Dr M26 ....44 A4
Belgrave Gdns 5 BL1 ...143 E2
Belgrave Rd
Altrincham WA14 ....119 C3
Failsworth M40 ....65 F1
Irlam M44 ....105 D5
Oldham OL8 ....66 F4
Sale M33 ....108 A4
Belgrave St Atherton M46 .58 A2
4 Bolton BL1 ....143 E2
Denton M34 ....100 D4
Heywood OL10 ....29 C1
Radcliffe M26 ....44 A4
Rochdale OL12 ....14 D1
Belgrave St S BL1 .....143 E1
Belgravia Gdns
Altrincham WA15 ....128 E8
Manchester M21 ....109 A8
Belgravia Mews OL2 ....149 C7
Belhaven Rd M8 ....63 F2
Belhill Gdns M6 ....154 F3
Bell Clough Rd M43 ......84 B3
Bell Cres M11 ....164 F8
Bell La Bury BL9 ......141 B3
Milnrow OL16 ....32 B7
Wigan WN5 ....54 B7
Bell Meadow Dr OL11 ....29 F5
Bell St Bolton BL2 .....148 A6
Droylsden M43 ....84 B2
Hindley WN2 ....56 E6
Leigh WN7 ....57 D1
Oldham OL1 ....67 A7
Rochdale OL16 ....139 F8
Bell Terr M30 ....95 C8
Bella St BL3 ....146 C4
Bellairs St BL3 ....146 C3
Bellamy Ct M18 ....99 E5
Bellamy Dr WN7 ....76 B5
Bellcroft Cl M22 ......121 E8
Belldale Cl SK4 ....168 A2
Belldean WN2 ....56 B8
Belle Green Ind Est WN2 .56 A8
Belle Green La WN2 .....56 A8
Belle Isle Ave OL12 ....14 C6
Belle Vue Ave M12 ....164 F5
Belle Vue St
Manchester M12 ....165 A6
1 Wigan WN5 ....54 D5
Belle Vue Sta M18 .....165 C5
Belle Vue Terr BL9 ....140 E1
Bellerby Cl M45 ....62 E8
Belleville Ave M22 ....130 E8
Bellew St M11 ....164 E8
Bellfield Ave
Cheadle SK8 ....123 B1
Oldham OL8 ....66 F2
Bellingham Ave WN1 .....37 C2
Bellingham Cl Bury BL8 ..26 F2
Shaw OL2 ....149 B8
Bellingham Dr WN1 ......37 D2
Bellingham Mount WN1 ..37 D2
Bellis Cl M12 ....160 E1
Bellot Wlk OL1 ....153 E8
Bellott St M8 ....156 A6
Bellpit Cl M28 ....78 C7
Bells Croft Ave M40 ....83 B7
Bellshill Cres OL16 .....15 C1
Bellwood BL5 ....57 C6
Belmont Ave
Atherton M46 ....58 F4
Denton M34 ....100 D4
Golborne WA3 ....74 C1
Leigh WN2 ....57 A1
Oldham OL4 ....67 F7
Orrell WN5 ....53 D3
Salford M6 ....80 A2
Swinton M27 ....61 D5
Belmont Cl SK4 ....169 E3
Belmont Dr Aspull WN2 ...38 D5
Bury BL8 ....27 A1
Romiley SK6 ....114 B1
Belmont Pl PR7 ....19 C6
Belmont Rd Adlington PR6 .21 B7
Altrincham WA15 ....119 E2
Bolton BL1,BL7 ....24 D6
Bramhall SK7 ....132 F5
Gatley SK8 ....122 B6
Hindley WN2 ....56 F5
Horwich BL6 ....22 C7
Radcliffe M26 ....44 A1
Sale M33 ....108 A6
Belmont Sh Ctr SK4 ....169 E3
Belmont St Eccles M30 ...79 D3
Manchester M16 ....162 D5
Oldham,Cold Hurst OL1 ..153 E8
Oldham,Nether Lees OL4 ..67 E5
Salford M5 ....154 D1
Stockport SK4 ....169 E3
Belmont View BL2 ....25 F4
Belmont Way
Chadderton OL9 ....152 C8
Rochdale OL12 ....14 E2
Stockport SK4 ....169 E3
Belmont Wlk 1 M13 ....163 C6
Belmore Ave M8 ....63 F1
Belmore Rd M33 ....108 B1
Belper Rd Eccles M30 ....95 B8
Manchester SK4 ....110 F1
Belper St OL6 ....166 B4
Belper Way M34 ....113 A8
Belper Wlk M18 ....165 C6
Belroy Ct M25 ....63 B3
Belsay Cl OL7 ....84 F5
Belsay Dr M23 ....121 A4
Belstone Ave M23 ......121 A3
Belstone Cl SK7 ....123 F2
Belsyde Wlk 7 M9 .....157 E7
Belthorne Ave M9 ....65 B2
Belton Ave OL16 ....15 C1
Belton Wlk
10 Manchester M8 ......156 A6
Oldham OL9 ....153 D6
Beltone Cl M32 ....96 B1
Belvedere Ave
Atherton M46 ....58 F4
Ramsbottom BL8 ....11 A1
Reddish SK5 ....99 F2
Belvedere Cl WN7 ....76 D7
Belvedere Ct M25 ....63 A3
Belvedere Dr
Dukinfield SK15,SK16 ...101 E8
Romiley SK6 ....112 C3
Belvedere Hts BL1 ......40 E8
Belvedere Pl 5 WN3 ....54 F5
Belvedere Rd
Adlington PR6 ....21 B8
Ashton-in-M WN4 ....73 C4
Manchester M14 ....110 E8
Newton-le-W WA12 ....89 B5
Salford M6 ....81 A3
Belvedere Rise OL1 .....49 D3
Belvedere Sq M22 .....121 F3
Belvedere St M6 ....81 B3
Belvoir Ave
Hazel Grove SK7 ....133 E8
Manchester M19 ....99 A2
Belvoir Mdws OL16 .....15 E4
Belvoir St Bolton BL2 ..148 C7
Rochdale OL12 ....14 C1
Wigan WN1 ....151 E8
Belvor Ave M34 ....100 E7
Belwood Rd M21 ....109 B7
Bembridge Cl M14 ......98 C3
Bembridge Ct WN3 ......54 E2
Bembridge Dr BL3 ......42 D5
Bembridge Rd M34 .....113 B8
Bempton Cl SK2 ....125 A5
Bemrose Ave WA14 .....119 C6
Bemsley Pl M5 ....161 A8
Ben Brierley Way OL1 ..153 F7
Ben St M11 ....83 B2
Benbecula Way M41 .....95 D5
Benbow Ave M12 ....164 F5
Benbow St 6 M33 .....108 B5
Benbrook Gr SK9 ......131 E2
Bench Carr OL12 ....14 E1
Benchill Ave M22 ......121 D5
Benchill Court Rd M22 ..121 E4
Benchill Cres M22 .....121 C5
Benchill Ct M22 ....121 E4
Benchill Dr M22 ....121 D5
Benchill Prim Sch M22 .121 C6
Benchill Rd M22 ....121 D5
Bendall St M11 ....99 E8
Bendemeer 6 M41 ....95 C3
Bendix St M4 ....159 B2
Benedict Cl 13 M7 ....81 C5
Benedict Dr SK16 ......101 D6
Benfield Ave M40 ....65 C2
Benfield St OL10 ....29 D1
Benfleet Cl M12 ....165 A6
Benfold Wlk M24 ....46 D3
Bengairn Cl WN1 ....37 F1
Bengal La OL6 ....166 C4
Bengal Sq 10 OL6 ....85 D4
Bengal St Leigh WN7 .....75 F5
Manchester M4 ....159 C2
Stockport SK3 ....170 E8
Benhale Wlk 14 M8 ....156 A6
Benham Cl M20 ....110 C3
Benin Wlk 13 M40 ....83 C5
Benjamin Fold WN4 ......73 B5
Benjamin St 3 OL7 ....166 A1
Benjamin Wilson Ct M7 .158 D4
Benmore Cl OL10 ....29 A1
Benmore Rd M9 ....64 F3
Bennet Mews 3 SK14 ...101 D5
Bennet St M26 ....43 D4
Bennett Cl 4 SK3 ......123 C8
Bennett Dr Orrell WN5 ...53 D4
Salford M7 ....155 E6
Bennett Rd M8 ....63 F1
Bennett St
13 Ashton-u-L OL7 ......84 F1
6 Ashton-u-L OL7 ....84 F1
Dukinfield SK14 ....101 D5
Hollingworth SK14 .....103 D5
Manchester M12 ....164 E6
4 Stalybridge SK15 .....86 A1
3 Stockport SK3 ....123 C8
Stretford M32 ....96 C1
Bennett's La BL1 ......142 C2
Benny La M43 ....84 D3
Benson Cl M7 ....155 E5
Benson St Bury BL9 ....141 A1
Edgworth BL7 ....9 E5
Benson Wlk 3 SK9 .....131 D2
Bent Fold Dr BL9 ....45 A1
Bent Hill St BL3 ......146 A4
Bent La Culcheth WA3 ....92 A2
Lymm WA13 ....117 C6
Manchester M8 ....155 F7
Prestwich M25 ....63 C4
Bent Lanes M41 ....94 F5
Bent Spur Rd BL4 ....61 A5
Bent St Farnworth BL4 ...60 E7
Haslingden BB4 ....1 D8
Manchester M3,M8 ......159 A4
Bent Terr M41 ....95 C4
Bentcliffe Way M30 .....80 A1
Bentfield Cres OL16 ....32 A4
Bentfield Ind Units OL9 .152 B6
Bentgate Cl Haslingden BB4 .1 D8
Newhey OL16 ....32 A4
Bentgate St OL16 ....32 A3
Benthall Wlk M34 ......100 E1
Bentham Cl Bury BL8 ....26 E3
6 Farnworth BL4 ....42 D1
Bentham Pl WN6 ....19 F2
Bentham Rd
Culcheth WA3 ....92 A2
Standish WN6 ....19 F2
Bentinck Cl WA14 .....119 C4
Bentinck Ho 2 OL6 ....166 A2
Bentinck Rd WA14 .....119 C4
Bentinck St
Ashton-u-L OL6 ....166 A2
Bolton BL1 ....142 B1
Farnworth BL4 ....42 C1
Manchester M15 ....162 D7
Oldham OL8 ....66 F4
9 Rochdale OL12 ....14 C1
Wigan WN3 ....54 F4
Bentinck Terr 1 OL6 ..166 A2
Bentley Ave M24 ....47 D5
Bentley Cl M26 ....44 D4
Bentley Ct Farnworth BL4 .42 D1
Salford M7 ....155 E8
Bentley Fold BL8 ....26 F4
Bentley Hall Rd BL2,BL8 ..26 D4
Bentley Ho M15 ....162 E6
Bentley La BL9 ....12 A1
Bentley Rd Denton M34 ..100 F3
Manchester M21 ....97 A1
Salford M7 ....155 E8
Bentley St Bolton BL2 ..148 C5
Chadderton OL9 ....152 C7
Farnworth BL4 ....42 D1
8 Oldham OL1 ....67 B8
Rochdale OL12 ....14 E2
Bentleys The SK5 .....169 F3
Bentmeadows OL12 ......14 E1
Benton Dr SK6 ....126 C8
Benton St M9 ....157 F7
Bents Ave Romiley SK6 ..112 F3
Urmston M41 ....94 F1
Bents Farm Cl 1 OL12 ...15 F5
Bentside Rd SK12 .....135 D5
Bentworth Cl BL5 ....57 F6
Benville Wlk M40 ....83 B6
Benwick Terr 18 BL1 ...143 E2
Benyon St OL4 ....67 E6
Berberis Wlk 1 M33 ...107 C6
Beresford Ave BL3 ....144 C5
Beresford Cres
Oldham OL4 ....67 D8
Reddish SK5 ....99 E3
Beresford Ct
4 Alderley Edge SK9 ...137 A1
Manchester M20 ....110 A4
Beresford Rd
Manchester M13 ....98 F3
Stretford M32 ....96 E4
Beresford St
Failsworth M35 ....83 E7
Manchester M14 ....97 F3
Beresford St *continued*
Newhey OL16 ....32 B4
Oldham OL4 ....67 D8
8 Wigan WN6 ....37 A1
Bergman Wlk M40 ....83 B6
Berigan Cl M12 ....164 E5
Berisford Cl WA15 ....119 E7
Berkeley Ave
Manchester M14 ....98 E4
Oldham OL9 ....65 F3
Stretford M32 ....96 A4
Wigan WN3 ....54 D2
Berkeley Cl Golborne WN7 .91 C8
Hyde SK14 ....167 D1
Stockport SK2 ....124 C8
Berkeley Cres
Hyde SK14 ....167 D1
Little Lever M26 ....43 C5
Berkeley Ct 1 M7 ....63 E1
Berkeley Dr OL16 ....31 B4
Berkeley Rd Bolton BL1 .143 E4
Hazel Grove SK7 ....124 F3
Berkeley St
Ashton-u-L OL6 ....166 A3
Royton OL2 ....48 D5
Berkley Ave M19 ....99 A1
Berkley Dr OL2 ....48 D2
Berkley Ho BL1 ....144 C7
Berkley Wlk OL15 ....15 F5
Berkshire Cl OL9 ......152 B5
Berkshire Ct BL9 ....44 F7
Berkshire Dr M44 ......105 C5
Berkshire Pl OL9 ......152 C5
Berkshire Rd M40 ......160 D3
Berlin Rd SK3 ....170 D6
Berlin St BL3 ....144 C6
Bermondsay St M5 .....161 B8
Bernard Gr BL1 ....142 C2
Bernard St Glossop SK13 .104 C1
Manchester M9 ....157 D8
Rochdale OL12 ....14 E3
Berne Ave BL6 ....22 A3
Berne Cl Chadderton OL9 .152 C6
Stockport SK7 ....123 E4
Bernice Ave OL9 ......152 B6
Bernice St BL1 ....142 C2
Berrie Gr M19 ....111 B8
Berriedale Cl M16 ......97 D2
Berrington Gr WN4 ......73 A3
Berry Brow
Failsworth M40 ....83 D4
Uppermill OL3 ....69 B5
Berry Cl SK9 ....137 A5
Berry Sq BL6 ....21 D3
Berry St Eccles M30 .....95 B8
Manchester M1 ....163 B8
Stalybridge SK15 ....102 C8
Swinton M27 ....61 F2
Uppermill OL3 ....69 B5
Berrycroft La SK6 .....113 A3
Berryfold Way M29 ......77 B8
Bert St BL3 ....146 B3
Bertha Rd OL16 ....31 C7
Bertha St Bolton BL1 ...143 D2
Manchester M11 ....165 B7
Shaw OL2 ....149 B5
Bertie St OL11 ....30 D4
Bertram St
Manchester M12 ....165 A6
Newton-le-W WA12 ....89 A4
Sale M33 ....108 E4
Bertrand Rd BL1 ......144 C7
Berwick Ave
Manchester SK4 ....110 E2
Stretford M41 ....96 A2
Whitefield M45 ....63 A7
Berwick Cl
Boothstown M28 ....77 F7
Heywood OL10 ....29 A1
Berwick Pl WN1 ....37 E1
Berwick St OL16 ....31 B6
Berwyn Ave Cheadle SK8 .123 B5
Manchester M9 ....64 C5
Middleton M24 ....65 C8
Berwyn Cl Horwich BL6 ...22 C5
Oldham OL8 ....66 E3
Beryl Ave BL8 ....26 F7
Beryl St BL1 ....143 F3
Besom La SK15 ....86 E3
Bessemer Rd M44 ......105 F6
Bessemer St M11,M18 ..165 C7
Bessemer Way OL1 .....153 E7
Besses o' th' Barn Sta M45 ....63 A7
Bessie's Well Pl WN6 ....36 F8
Bessybrook Cl BL6 ......40 C6
Beswick Dr M35 ....84 A6
Beswick Row M4 ....159 A3
Beswick St
5 Droylsden M43 ....84 B1
Manchester M4 ....160 D2
Royton OL2 ....48 E2
Walsden OL14 ....6 A7
Beswicke Royds St OL16 ..15 C1
Beswicke St
Littleborough OL15 ......16 C5
Rochdale OL12 ....139 E8
Beswicks La SK9 ......136 C3
Beta Ave M32 ....96 C1
Beta St BL1 ....145 F8
Bethal Gn OL15 ....6 C1
Bethany La OL16 ....32 D4
Bethel Ave M35 ....83 E7
Bethel St OL10 ....29 C2
Bethersden Rd WN1 ......37 B4
Bethesda St OL8 ....66 F4
Bethnall Dr M14 ....110 B8
Betjeman Pl OL2 ....49 D8

Betley Rd SK5 ....99 F1
Betley St Heywood OL10 ....29 C1
  Manchester M1 ....163 C8
  Radcliffe M26 ....44 C4
Betlymere Rd SK8 ....122 F4
Betnor Ave SK1 ....112 B1
Betony Cl OL12 ....14 D3
Bets Ct M22 ....121 E7
Bettison Ave WN7 ....76 C3
Bettwood Dr M8 ....63 F2
Betty Nuppy's La OL16 ...31 C5
Betula Gr M7 ....155 D7
Betula Mews OL11 ....13 D1
Betula Ave WN5 ....71 D4
Beulah St M18 ....165 C7
Bevan Cl M12 ....160 E1
Bevendon Sq M7 ....155 E6
Beveridge St M14 ....98 A3
Beverley Ave
  Denton M34 ....101 A2
  Leigh WN7 ....76 A6
  Longshaw WN5 ....53 E1
  Urmston M41 ....95 E3
Beverley Cl M45 ....45 B1
Beverley Pl OL16 ....31 A8
Beverley Rd Bolton BL1 ..144 C8
  Little Lever BL3 ....42 F3
  Pendlebury M27 ....80 C7
  Stockport SK2 ....124 C8
  Wigan WN5 ....54 B8
Beverley St M9 ....64 E1
Beverley Wlk
  Oldham OL8 ....153 E5
  Romiley SK6 ....113 A1
Beverly Cl OL6 ....85 B7
Beverly Rd M14 ....110 E7
Beverston Dr M7 ....155 E6
Bevill Sq M3 ....158 E2
Bevin Ave WA3 ....92 B4
Bevington St ◧ WN4 .....72 F5
Bevis Gn BL9 ....27 F8
Bewerley Cl WN3 ....150 B6
Bewick St BL2 ....25 B3
Bewley Gr WN7 ....76 A6
Bewley St OL8 ....66 D2
Bewley Wlk M40 ....83 A6
Bexhill Ave WA15 ....119 F6
Bexhill Cl BL3 ....43 C3
Bexhill Dr Hindley WN7 ..57 C2
  Manchester M13 ....98 F3
Bexhill Rd SK3 ....123 E4
Bexhill Wlk OL9 ....152 B6
Bexley Cl Glossop SK13 ..104 C3
  Urmston M41 ....95 B4
Bexley Dr Bury BL8 ......27 B1
  Walkden M38 ....60 C4
Bexley Sq M3 ....158 D2
Bexley St Hindley WN2 ...57 B3
  Oldham OL9 ....152 C5
Bexley Wlk M40 ....83 B6
Beyington Rd ◧ M16 .....97 E3
Beyer Cl M18 ....165 C6
Bibby La M19 ....110 F6
Bibby St Bury BL9 ....44 F5
  Dukinfield SK14 ....101 D5
Bibury Ave M22 ....121 B3
Bickerdike Ave M12 ......99 B3
Bickerdike Ct ◧ M11 .....99 B3
Bickershaw CE Prim Sch
  WN2 ....74 F8
Bickershaw Dr M28 ....60 C2
Bickershaw La
  Leigh WN2 ....56 D1
Bickerstaffe Cl OL2 ....149 A5
Bickerton Cl OL9 ....74 A1
Bickerton Dr SK7 ....124 A1
Bickerton Rd WA14 .....119 B6
Bickley Gr M29 ....77 C6
Biddall Dr M23 ....121 B6
Biddisham Wlk
  Manchester M40 ....157 D5
  Manchester M40 ....160 D4
Biddulph Ave SK2 ......124 C5
Wythenshawe M23 ....120 F7
Bideford Dr
  Rochdale OL11 ....30 B3
  Stockport SK2 ....124 C8
Bidford Cl M29 ....59 C1
Bidston Ave M14 ....98 B2
  Shaw OL2 ....49 D6
Bidston Dr SK9 ....131 E2
Bidworth La SK13 ....171 D1
Big Fold BL6 ....21 D2
Biggenwood Wlk ◧ M40 ..83 A7
Biggin Gdns OL10 ....46 E7
Bignor St M8 ....156 A6
Bilbao St BL1 ....144 B8
Bilberry St Rochdale OL16 .31 A6
  Rochdale OL16 ....31 B6
Bickford St M4 ....159 B3
Billey St ◧ 62 F8
Bill Williams Cl M11 ...165 C8
Billberry Cl M45 ....63 B8
Billing Ave M12 ....99 B4
Billinge Arc ◧ WN1 ....150 C8
Billinge St ◧ BL1 ......145 F8
Billinge Hospl WN5 .....51 D2
Billinge Rd
  Garswood WN4 ....72 C5
  Wigan,WN5 ....54 D4
  Wigan WN5 ....54 E6
Billington Ave WA12 ....89 C5
Billington Rd M27 ....80 E8
Billy La M27 ....62 A2

Billy Meredith Cl ◪ M14 .98 A3
Billy Whelan Wlk ◪ M40 .83 C5
Bilsland Wlk ◪ M40 .....83 C5
Bilson Dr SK3 ....123 B7
Bilson Sq OL16 ....32 A5
Bilton Wlk M8 ....156 C8
Binbrook Wlk BL3 ....147 F4
Bincombe Wlk M13 .....165 C5
Bindloss Ave M30 ....80 A3
Bindon Wlk ◪ M9 ....157 D7
Bingham Dr M23 ....120 F6
Bingham St M27 ....79 F8
Bingley Cl M11 ....164 F8
Bingley Dr M41 ....94 F4
Bingley Rd OL16 ....31 C7
Bingley Sq OL16 ....31 C7
Bingley Terr OL16 ....31 C7
Bingley Wlk
  Farnworth BL4 ....60 D7
  Manchester M7 ....80 F8
Binns Nook Rd OL12 .....13 A2
Binns St ◪ M40 ....159 B1
Binns St SK15 ....85 E1
Binsley Cl M44 ....94 A1
Binstead Cl M14 ....98 E3
Birbeck St ◪ SK15 ......85 F1
Birch Ave Bury BL8 ......27 A5
  Chadderton OL1,OL9 .....48 A2
  Failsworth M35 ....83 F5
  Irlam M44 ....105 D5
  Manchester,Heaton Moor
  SK4 ....168 B4
  Manchester,Old Trafford
  M16 ....97 A4
  Middleton M24 ....65 A7
  Oldham OL8 ....66 D2
  Rochdale OL12 ....15 D4
  Romiley SK6 ....113 D2
  Sale M33 ....108 B3
  Salford M6 ....154 E4
  Standish WN6 ....36 F8
  Westhoughton BL5 ....57 F7
  Whitefield M45 ....67 C6
  Wilmslow SK9 ....136 F6
Birch Brook Rd WA13 ...117 C5
Birch Cl OL12 ....14 C4
Birch Cres OL16 ....32 A3
Birch Ct Dukinfield SK16 .101 D8
  Heywood OL10 ....29 E1
  Manchester M13 ....98 E3
  Marple SK6 ....125 E5
Birch Dr Hazel Grove SK7 .124 C2
  Oldham OL4 ....67 F5
  Pendlebury M27 ....80 B8
Birch Gn SK15 ....104 E1
Birch Gr
  Altrincham WA15 ....120 E5
  Denton M34 ....100 E3
  Denton,Hooley Hill M34 .100 F6
  Downall Green WN4 ......72 D5
  Manchester M40 ....98 D3
  Prestwich M25 ....63 A6
  Ramsbottom BL0 ....11 A3
Birch Hall Cl OL4 ....67 F4
Birch Hall La M13 ....98 E3
Birch Hey Cl ◪ OL12 ....15 C4
Birch Hill Cres OL12 ....15 E4
Birch Hill Hospl OL12 ...15 E5
Birch Hill La OL12 ......15 D6
Birch Hill Wlk OL15 .....15 F5
Birch Ho BL5 ....57 E6
Birch Ind Est OL10 ......46 A5
Birch La Dukinfield SK16 .101 D7
Birch Mount OL12 ....15 E4
Birch Polygon M14 ....98 D3
Birch Rd Abram Brow WN2 .74 B7
  Atherton M46 ....58 E3
  Carrington M31,WA14 ...106 F3
  Coppull PR7 ....19 E8
  Gatley SK8 ....122 A5
  Hollinfare WA3 ....105 B2
  Leigh WN7 ....75 F7
  Manchester M8 ....156 B4
  Middleton M24 ....47 C2
  Partington M31 ....105 D3
  Poynton SK12 ....133 F2
  Rochdale OL12 ....15 D5
  Swinton M27 ....79 D5
  Uppermill OL3 ....69 C7
  Walkden M28 ....60 E1
Birch St Ashton-u-L OL7 .100 F8
  Ashton-u-L OL7 ....84 E1
  Bolton BL2 ....148 B6
  Bury BL9 ....140 F3
  Droylsden M43 ....100 E8
  Heywood OL10 ....29 D1
  Hindley WN2 ....56 D5
  Manchester M12 ....165 A6
  Radcliffe M26 ....43 A5
  Stalybridge SK15 ....86 C5
  ◪ Tyldesley M29 ....59 A1
  Wardle OL12 ....15 C6
  Wigan WN6 ....37 A1
Birch Terr ◪ SK14 .....167 D2
Birch Tree Ave SK7 .....134 A8
Birch Tree Cl WA14 ....119 C1
Birch Tree Dr M22 .....121 D3
Birch Tree Rd WA3 ......90 F8
Birch Tree Way ◪ BL6 ...22 E1
Birch Vale Terr SK22 ..127 D2
Birch-Lea Cl BL9 ....44 F7
Birchacre Gr M14 ......110 D7
Birchall Ave WA3 ....91 E4
Birchall Cl SK16 ....101 D6
Birchall Gn SK6 ....113 A5

Birchall Way M15 ....162 F6
Birchdale WA14 ....119 C2
Birchdale Ave SK8 .....122 B2
Birchdale Dr SK6 ....113 D3
Birchen Bower Wlk BL8 ..26 F5
Birchenall St M40 ......157 F8
Birchenlea St OL9 ....66 A3
Birches End OL12 ....14 C5
Birches Rd BL7 ....9 D4
Birches Sch The M20 ...109 F5
  Sale M33 ....107 C5
Birchfield Ashton-u-L OL7 .100 F8
  Bolton BL2 ....25 C6
Birchfield Ave
  Atherton M46 ....58 B4
  Heywood BL9 ....28 E1
Birchfield Dr
  Rochdale OL11 ....30 A1
  Worsley M28 ....78 A7
Birchfield Gr BL3 ....40 E4
Birchfield Mews ◪
  SK14 ....167 D2
Birchfield Rd
  Cheadle SK3 ....123 A7
  Lymm WA13 ....117 B4
Birchfields
  Altrincham WA15 ....119 F1
  Oldham OL4 ....67 F4
  Manchester M13 ....98 E3
Birchfields Prim Sch
  M14,M19 ....98 E1
Birchfields Rd M13,M14 ..98 E2
Birchfield Ct M38 ....60 B4
Birchgate Wlk BL3 .....145 F5
Birchgrove Cl BL3 ......146 A1
Birchin La M4 ....159 A1
Birchin Pl M4 ....159 A1
Birchington Rd M14,
  M20 ....110 A8
Birchinlee Ave OL2 .....48 C3
Birchlea WA15 ....119 F4
Birchleaf Gr M5 ....80 C2
Birchley Ave WN5 ....71 C3
Birchley Rd WN5 ....71 C4
Birchley View WA11 .....71 B2
Birchside Ave SK13 ....104 B2
Birchvale Ave SK6 .....113 D3
Birchvale Cl M15 ......162 E6
Birchway Bramhall SK7 ..132 D7
  High Lane SK6 ....134 F7
Birchwood
  Chadderton OL9 ....65 E7
  Droylsden M43 ....84 B3
Birchwood Cl Leigh WN7 .75 F3
  Stockport SK4 ....168 A1
  Wigan WN3 ....54 D1
Birchwood Dr SK9 ......137 D8
Birchwood Rd M24 ......65 C8
Birchwood Way SK16 ...101 D6
Bird Hall Ave SK8 .....123 C4
Bird Hall La SK3 ....123 B6
Bird Hall Rd SK8 ......123 C5
Bird St WN2 ....74 F8
Birdhall Gr M19 ....111 A8
Birdlip Dr M23 ....121 A3
Birkby Dr M24 ....46 E2
Birkdale Ave
  Atherton M46 ....58 C5
  Royton OL2 ....48 E2
  Whitefield M45 ....62 D6
Birkdale Cl Bramhall SK7 .133 A7
  Dukinfield SK14 ....101 D7
  Heywood OL10 ....46 D8
Birkdale Dr Bury BL8 ....27 B2
  Sale M33 ....107 E2
Birkdale Gdns BL3 .....145 D5
Birkdale Gr Eccles M30 ..79 F2
  Reddish SK5 ....111 F5
Birkdale Rd Reddish SK5 .111 F6
  Rochdale OL16 ....31 C4
Birkdale St M8 ....156 A7
Birkenhills Dr BL3 ......40 E5
Birkett Bank WN1 ......151 B8
Birkett Bank Terr WN1 ..151 B8
Birkett Cl BL1 ....24 D6
Birkett Dr BL1 ....24 D6
Birkett St ◪ WN1 ......151 B8
Birkinbrook Cl M45 .....45 A1
Birkinheath La WA14 ...128 B4
Birkleigh Wlk BL2 ....42 E6
Birks Dr BL9 ....27 B6
Birks La OL14 ....6 B8
Birkside Cl WN3 ....55 A1
Birkworth Ct SK2 ......124 C6
Birley Cl
  Altrincham WA15 ....119 F7
  Appley Bridge WN6 ......35 F8
Birley Ct ◪ M5 ....80 C2
Birley Park ◪ M20 .....109 F3
Birley St Bolton BL1 ...143 E4
  Bury BL9 ....27 F5
  Leigh WN7 ....76 A6
  Newton-le-W WA12 ....89 D4
  Rochdale OL12 ....15 A1
Birling Dr M23 ....121 B6
Birnham Gr OL10 ....29 A1
Birshaw Cl OL2 ....49 B5
Birstall Wlk M23 ....121 A6
Birt St M40 ....160 D4
Birtenshaw Cres BL7 ....25 B7
Birtenshaw Hall Sch BL7 .25 B6
Birtle Rd M29 ....77 F7
Birtle View Sch OL10 ...29 C2
Birtles Ave SK5 ....99 F3
Birtles Cl Cheadle SK8 .123 A5

Birtles Cl continued
  Dukinfield SK16 ....101 D6
Birtles The M22 ....121 D3
Birtles Way ◪ SK9 .....131 D5
Birtlespool Rd SK8 ....122 F4
Birtley Wlk ◪ M40 .....159 C3
Birwood Rd M8 ....64 A3
Biscay Cl M11 ....160 F1
Bishop Bilborrow Meml RC
  Prim Sch M14 ....97 F3
Bishop Bridgeman CE Prim
  Sch BL3 ....147 E4
Bishop Cl M16 ....97 E4
Bishop Marshall Cl
  M40 ....157 D5
Bishop Marshall Way
  M24 ....46 D4
Bishop Rd Salford M6 ....80 B4
  Urmston M41 ....94 D2
Bishop St Middleton M24 .65 D7
  Rochdale OL16 ....15 B1
  Stockport SK1 ....112 A1
Bishop's Cl Bolton BL3 ..42 A2
  Cheadle SK8 ....123 A5
Bishop's Rd BL3 ....42 A2
Bishopbridge Cl BL3 ...147 F4
Bishopdale Cl OL2 ......48 D5
Bishopgate Wigan WN1 ..150 C8
Bishopgate St OL9 .....152 A5
Bishops Cl
  Altrincham WA14 ....119 B1
  Ashton-u-L OL7 ....85 A5
Bishops Gate M2 ....162 F8
Bishops Mdw M24 ....46 D3
Bishops Mews M13 .....107 E6
Bishops Rd M25 ....63 C2
Bishops Wlk OL7 ....166 A1
Bishopsgate Wlk OL16 ...31 C4
Bishopton Cl M19 ....99 C1
Bisley Cl ◪ M40 ....160 A1
Bisley St OL8 ....153 D6
Bismarck St OL4 ....67 A5
Bispham Ave Bolton BL2 .42 F7
  Reddish SK5 ....99 F3
Bispham Cl BL8 ....26 F1
Bispham Gr WN5 ....53 D2
Bispham Gr WN4 ....72 F5
Bispham Rd M7 ....155 E7
Bispham Wlk OL7 ......166 A1
Bittern Cl Poynton SK12 .133 A4
Bittern Dr M43 ....84 C3
Bk Adcroft St SK1 .....170 F7
Bk Alfred St BL0 ....138 B5
Bk Andrew St OL5 ....86 C8
Bk Cecil St OL5 ....86 C8
Bk Chapel St Bury BL8 ..26 F7
  ◪ Manchester M19 ......99 A1
Bk George Church La
  BL3 ....146 B4
Bk Grosvenor St ◪ SK15 .86 A1
Bk Knowl St SK15 ....86 B2
Bk Melbourne St ◪
  SK15 ....86 A1
Bk Portland St OL9 ....166 A2
Bk Stayley Rd OL5 ......86 D8
Bk Water St OL5 ....166 A1
Black Brook Rd SK4 ....111 D7
Black Horse St
  Blackrod BL6 ....21 C3
  Bolton BL1 ....145 E6
  Farnworth BL4 ....60 E7
  Ramsbottom BL0 ....12 B7
Black La Leigh WN7 .....76 D5
Black Moss Cl M26 ....43 D3
Black Moss Rd WA14 ....118 F7
Blackbank St BL1 ......143 F2
Blackberry Cl WA14 ....119 B8
Blackberry Dr WN6 ......36 C4
Blackberry La SK5 .....112 C7
Blackburn Cl WA3 ....90 E8
Blackburn Pl M5 ....81 C1
Blackburn Rd
  Bolton BL1 ....143 F2
  Bolton,Egerton BL7 .....8 C4
  Edenfield BL0,BB4 ....1 D5
  Edgworth BL7 ....9 D7
Blackburn St
  Manchester M16 ....161 C5
  Prestwich M25 ....63 C4
  Radcliffe M26 ....44 A3
  Salford M3 ....158 D3
Blackburne Dr WA12 .....89 A4
Blackcap Cl M28 ....78 B7
Blackcarr Rd M23 ......121 B6
Blackchapel Dr OL16 ....31 B3
Blackcroft Cl M27 ......80 A6
Blackden Wlk SK9 ......131 D1
Blackdown Gr OL8 ....66 E3
Blackfield La M7 ....81 C8
Blackford Rd M19 .....111 A7
Blackford Wlk M40 .....157 D6
Blackfriars Rd M3 .....158 E3
Blackfriars St M3 .....158 F2
Blackhill Cl ◪ M13 ....163 B7
Blackhorse Ave BL6 .....21 C2
Blackhorse Cl BL6 ......21 C3
Blackleach Ctry Pk*
  M28 ....60 D4
Blackleach Dr M28 ......60 D5
Blackledge Cl WN5 ......53 E5

Blackledge St BL3 .....146 C4
Blackley Cl BL9 ....45 A2
Blackley New Rd M9,M25 .64 B3
Blackley Park Rd M9 ....64 D1
Blackley St
  Manchester M16 ....161 C5
  Middleton M24 ....64 B7
Blackleyhurst Ave WN5 ..71 E5
Blacklock St M3,M8 ....158 F4
Blackmoor Ave M29 ......77 B5
Blackpits Rd OL11 ......13 D1
Blackpool St ◪ M11 ....83 C2
Blackrock OL5 ....86 C6
Blackrock St M11 ......164 F8
Blackrod Brow BL6 ......21 B4
Blackrod By-Pass Rd
  BL6 ....21 D2
Blackrod Dr BL8 ....26 F1
Blackrod Ind Est BL6 ...38 E7
Blackrod Prim Sch BL6 ..38 E8
Blackrod Sta BL6 ....21 E2
Blacksail Wlk ◪ OL1 ...49 A1
Blackshaw Ho BL3 ......144 C6
Blackshaw La
  Alderley Edge SK9 .....136 F1
  Bolton BL3 ....144 C6
  Royton OL2 ....49 A4
Blackshaw Lane Jun & Inf
  Sch OL2 ....49 A4
Blackshaw Prim Sch BL3 .143 A6
Blackshaw Row ◪ BL3 ..144 C5
Blackshaw St SK3 ......170 E8
Blacksmith La OL11 .....30 B4
Blacksmiths Fold M46 ...58 E3
Blackstock St M13 ......98 C4
Blackstone Ave OL16 ....31 C8
Blackstone Edge Old Rd
  OL15 ....16 E6
Blackstone Edge Rd HX6,
  HX7 ....7 F5
Blackstone Ho SK2 ....124 D5
Blackstone Rd SK2 ....124 D5
Blackstone Wlk M9 ....157 D6
Blackthorn Ave
  Manchester M19 ....111 A7
  Wigan WN6 ....36 F3
Blackthorn Cl OL12 .....14 E2
Blackthorn Mews OL12 ..14 E2
Blackthorn Rd OL8 ......84 C8
Blackthorn Wlk ◪ BL1 ..105 E2
Blackthorne Cl BL1 ....142 A1
Blackthorne Dr M33 ...107 D2
Blackthorne Rd SK14 ...113 E7
Blackwell Wlk ◪ M4 ...159 C2
Blackwood Dr WN3 .....165 A6
Blackwood Dr M23 .....120 D8
Blackwood Rd OL13 ......3 B7
Bladen Cl SK8 ....123 A4
Bladon St M1 ....163 B8
Blainscough Rd PR7 .....19 E8
Blair Ave Hindley WN2 ..57 B3
  Urmston M41 ....60 B4
  Walkden M38 ....60 B4
Blair Cl Hazel Grove SK7 .133 C8
  Sale M33 ....107 C1
  Shaw OL2 ....149 B7
Blair La BL2 ....25 D1
Blair Rd M16 ....97 B1
Blair St Bolton BL7 .....25 A8
  Kearsley BL4 ....61 B6
  Manchester M16 ....162 D5
  Rochdale OL12 ....14 D1
Blairhall Ave M40 ......83 A7
Blairmore Dr BL3 ....40 E5
Blake Cl WN4 ....72 B8
Blake Dr SK2 ....124 E7
Blake Gdns BL1 ....143 D2
Blake St
  Bolton,Bromley Cross BL7 .25 A7
  Bolton,Halliwell BL1 ...143 D2
  Rochdale OL16 ....31 A8
Blakeborough Ho ◪
  M46 ....58 D3
Blakedown Wlk M12 ....164 E5
Blakefield Dr M28 ......60 E1
Blakelock St OL2 ......149 B7
Blakemere Ave M33 ....108 E3
Blakemere Cl M45 ......44 E1
Blakeswell Cl M41 ......94 D3
Blakewood Cl WA14 ....119 B5
Blakey Cl BL3 ....40 F4
Blakey St M12 ....99 A4
Blanchard St M15 .....162 E5
Blanche St OL12 ....15 A2
Blanche Wlk ◪ M40 ....83 E7
Bland Cl M35 ....83 E7
Bland Rd M25 ....63 B2
Bland St M16 ....97 E4
Blandford Ave M28 ......79 A8
Blandford Cl Bury BL8 ..27 D5
  Tyldesley M29 ....59 A1
Blandford Ct SK15 ......86 A3
Blandford Dr M40 ......157 D6
Blandford Ho ◪ SK15 ...65 C2
Blandford Rd Eccles M30 .79 B2
  Salford M6 ....154 E4
  Stockport SK4 ....168 C2
Blandford Rise BL6 .....22 F1
Blandford St
  Ashton-u-L OL6 ....166 A3
  Stalybridge SK15 ....86 A2
Blanefield Cl M21 .....109 E7

Blantyre Ave M28 ... 60 E2
Blantyre Ho 4 M15 ... 162 D7
Blantyre Rd M27 ... 80 B6
Blantyre St Eccles M30 ... 79 A3
Hindley WN2 ... 56 E6
Manchester M15 ... 162 D7
Swinton M27 ... 61 D1
Blanwood Dr M8 ... 156 B7
Blaven Cl SK3 ... 170 F5
Blaydon Cl WN2 ... 38 D5
Blazemoss Bank SK2 ... 124 D5
Bleach St WN2 ... 56 C4
Bleackley St BL8 ... 27 C4
Bleadale Cl SK9 ... 131 D1
Bleak Hey Rd M22 ... 121 F2
Bleak St BL2 ... 25 B2
Bleakholt Rd BL0 ... 1 F1
Bleakledge Gr WN2 ... 56 F7
Bleakley St 1 M45 ... 44 E1
Bleaklow Cl WN3 ... 55 B2
Bleaklow Wlk 20 SK13 ... 171 E1
Bleasby St OL4 ... 67 C7
Bleasdale Cl Horwich BL6 ... 39 F8
Whitefield BL9 ... 45 A3
Bleasdale Rd Bolton BL1 ... 23 F2
Newton-le-W WA12 ... 89 C4
Wythenshawe M22 ... 121 A2
Bleasdale St OL2 ... 48 E5
Bleasedale Rd WN2 ... 57 A5
Bleasefell Chase M28 ... 78 A5
Bleatarn Rd SK1 ... 124 B7
Bledlow Cl M30 ... 79 E3
Blencarn Wlk M9 ... 157 D6
Blendworth Cl M8 ... 155 F7
Blenheim Ave M16 ... 97 D2
Blenheim Cl
Altrincham WA14 ... 119 D2
6 Hadfield SK13 ... 104 A5
Heywood OL10 ... 29 E2
Poynton SK12 ... 133 F4
Whitefield BL9 ... 45 A5
Wilmslow SK9 ... 137 D7
Blenheim Dr WN7 ... 76 E7
Blenheim Rd
Ashton-in-M WN4 ... 73 D2
Bolton BL2 ... 42 E6
Cheadle SK8 ... 123 B2
Manchester M16 ... 97 A3
Wigan WN5 ... 54 C8
Blenheim St
8 Oldham OL4 ... 49 D1
13 Rochdale OL12 ... 14 C1
Tyldesley M29 ... 76 F8
Blenheim Way OL6 ... 85 E4
Blenliem Ave OL1 ... 49 D3
Blenmar Cl M26 ... 44 C5
Bleriot St BL3 ... 147 D3
Blessed Thomas Holford Coll
WA15 ... 119 E4
Bletchley Cl M13 ... 164 D5
Bletchley Rd SK4 ... 110 E1
Blethyn St BL3 ... 146 B2
Blewberry Cl WN7 ... 75 F7
Bligh Rd 15 BL5 ... 39 E1
Blinco Rd M41 ... 95 F1
Blind La M12 ... 164 D7
Blindsill Rd BL4 ... 60 B7
Blissford Cl WN2 ... 56 D4
Blisworth Ave M30 ... 95 E8
Blisworth Cl M4 ... 160 D1
Blithfield Wlk M34 ... 100 E2
Block La OL9 ... 152 B5
Blocksage St SK16 ... 101 D7
Blodwell St M5,M6 ... 154 F2
Blofield Ct BL4 ... 60 D7
Blomley St OL11 ... 30 C2
Bloom St Manchester M1 ... 163 A8
Ramsbottom BL0 ... 11 A4
Salford M3 ... 158 E2
Stockport SK3 ... 170 D8
Bloomfield Dr
Whitefield BL9 ... 45 B3
Worsley M28 ... 78 A7
Bloomfield Rd BL4 ... 60 D6
Bloomfield St BL1 ... 143 E3
Bloomsbury Gr WA15 ... 120 A6
Bloomsbury La WA15 ... 120 A6
Blossom Pl OL16 ... 139 F8
Blossom Rd M31 ... 105 E2
Blossom St
Manchester M4 ... 159 B2
Salford M3 ... 158 E2
11 Tyldesley M29 ... 59 A1
Blossoms Hey SK8 ... 122 E1
Blossoms Hey Wlk SK8 ... 122 E1
Blossoms La SK7 ... 132 B2
Blossoms St SK2 ... 170 F7
Bloxham Wlk M9 ... 64 F3
Blucher St Ashton-u-L OL7 ... 85 A6
Manchester M12 ... 164 E6
Salford M5 ... 81 C1
Blue Bell Ave
Manchester M40 ... 65 A1
Wigan WN6 ... 36 F4
Blue Chip Bsns Pk
WA14 ... 119 C7
Blue Coat CE Sch The
OL1 ... 153 F7
Blue Ribbon Wlk M27 ... 62 A1
Bluebell Ave BB4 ... 1 A8
Bluebell Cl SK14 ... 101 F5
Bluebell Dr OL11 ... 30 B3
Bluebell Gr SK8 ... 122 D4
Bluebell Way SK9 ... 131 C1
Blueberry Dr OL2 ... 49 D7
Blueberry Rd WA14 ... 119 A2
Bluefields OL2 ... 49 D8
Bluestone Dr SK4 ... 110 E3
Bluestone Rd
Manchester M40 ... 83 A8
Reddish M34 ... 100 A2
Blundell Cl BL9 ... 45 B3
Blundell La BL6 ... 21 A2
Blundell Mews WN3 ... 54 D4
Blundell St BL1 ... 145 E7
Blundering La SK15 ... 102 D6
Blunn St OL8 ... 66 F4
Blyborough Cl M6 ... 154 E4
Blyth Ave
Littleborough OL15 ... 15 F3
Wythenshawe M23 ... 109 C2
Blyth Cl WA15 ... 120 D6
Blythe Ave SK7 ... 132 C6
Blyton St M15 ... 163 B5
Blyton Way M34 ... 112 F8
Bnos Yisroel Schs M7 ... 155 E8
Boad St M1 ... 163 B8
Boar Green Cl M40 ... 83 C7
Board St Ashton-u-L OL6 ... 85 D4
Bolton BL3 ... 145 D6
Boardale Dr M24 ... 46 E1
Boardman Cl BL1 ... 143 E2
Boardman Fold Cl M24 ... 65 A5
Boardman Fold Rd M24 ... 65 A5
Boardman La M24 ... 64 C8
Boardman Rd M8 ... 63 F2
Boardman St
Blackrod BL6 ... 21 D2
Bolton BL1 ... 143 E2
Eccles M30 ... 79 E1
Hyde SK14 ... 167 D2
Boars Head Ave WN6 ... 37 A7
Boarsgreave La BB4 ... 2 F6
Boarshaw Clough M24 ... 47 B2
Boarshaw Clough Way
M24 ... 47 B2
Boarshaw Com Prim Sch
M24 ... 47 B3
Boarshaw Cres M24 ... 47 C3
Boarshaw Ind Est M24 ... 47 B2
Boarshaw La M24 ... 47 D3
Boarshaw Rd M24 ... 47 B2
Boarshurst Ind Pk OL3 ... 69 B6
Boarshurst La OL3 ... 69 C5
Boat La Diggle OL3 ... 51 E5
Irlam M44 ... 94 B2
Wythenshawe M22 ... 109 E1
Boat Lane Ct M22 ... 109 E1
Boatmans Row M29 ... 77 C4
Boatmans The M15 ... 162 E7
Bob Massey Cl M11 ... 83 C1
Bob's La M44 ... 105 D4
Bobbin Wlk
1 Manchester M4 ... 159 C1
7 Oldham OL1 ... 67 A6
Bodden St WA3 ... 75 A1
Boddens Hill Rd SK4 ... 168 A1
Boddington Rd M30 ... 79 A1
Bodiam Rd BL8 ... 10 F2
Bodley St M11 ... 83 C2
Bodmin Cl OL2 ... 49 A3
Bodmin Cres SK5 ... 112 B5
Bodmin Dr Bramhall SK7 ... 132 E7
Platt Bridge WN2 ... 56 A1
Bodmin Rd Sale M33 ... 107 D5
Tyldesley M29 ... 77 C8
Bodmin Wlk 3 M23 ... 121 A5
Bodney Wlk M9 ... 64 B3
Bogburn La PR7 ... 19 D6
Boggard La SK13 ... 115 D6
Boggard Rd SK6 ... 127 A5
Bognor Rd SK3 ... 123 E4
Bolam Cl M23 ... 108 F1
Boland Dr M14 ... 110 D8
Bolbury Cres M27 ... 80 D8
Bold St Altrincham WA14 ... 119 D3
Bolton BL1 ... 145 F6
Bury BL9 ... 141 A3
Leigh WN7 ... 75 F5
Leigh WN7 ... 75 F6
Manchester,Moss Side M16 ... 97 E4
Manchester,Old Trafford
M15 ... 162 E5
Swinton M27 ... 61 F2
Wigan WN5 ... 54 E5
Bolderod Pl 4 OL1 ... 67 A8
Bolderstone Pl SK2 ... 124 E4
Bolderwood Dr WN2 ... 56 D4
Bolesworth Cl M21 ... 108 F8
Boleyn Ct OL10 ... 29 C1
Boleyn Wood Ct SK9 ... 131 B1
Bolholt Terr BL8 ... 27 B4
Bolivia St M5 ... 80 C2
Bollin Ave WA14 ... 119 B1
Bollin Cl Culcheth WA3 ... 92 A2
Kearsley BL4 ... 61 B6
Lymm WA13 ... 117 A4
Bollin Ct
Altrincham WA14 ... 119 B1
6 Manchester M15 ... 162 D6
Wilmslow SK9 ... 137 C6
Bollin Dr
Altrincham WA14 ... 119 E8
Lymm WA13 ... 117 A4
Sale M33 ... 108 B2
Bollin Hill SK9 ... 137 B8
Bollin Ho 8 M7 ... 81 C5
Bollin Prim Sch WA14 ... 119 B1
Bollin Sq WA14 ... 119 B1
Bollin Way M45 ... 45 C2
Bollin Wlk Reddish SK5 ... 169 F4
Whitefield M45 ... 45 C2
Wilmslow SK9 ... 137 C7
Bollings Yd BL1 ... 145 F6
Bollington Rd
Manchester M40 ... 160 D2
Reddish SK4 ... 111 D5
Bollington St OL7 ... 166 A1
Bollinway WA15 ... 129 A8
Bollinwood Chase SK9 ... 137 D7
Bolney St WN2 ... 38 A3
Bolney Wlk M40 ... 160 D4
Bolshaw Farm La SK8 ... 131 C6
Bolshaw Prim Sch SK8 ... 131 B7
Bolshaw Rd SK8 ... 131 C6
Bolton Ave Cheadle SK8 ... 132 B6
Manchester M19 ... 110 D2
Bolton Boys' Division Jun
Dept BL1 ... 144 C7
Bolton Cl Golborne WA3 ... 91 B8
Poynton SK12 ... 133 D4
Prestwich M25 ... 62 F2
Bolton Com Coll (Manchester
Rd Ctr) BL2 ... 148 A6
Bolton Com Coll, Horwich Ctr
BL6 ... 22 D2
Bolton Gates Ret Pk
BL1 ... 145 F8
Bolton House Rd WN2 ... 74 F8
Bolton Inst (Chadwick
Campus) BL2 ... 148 B6
Bolton Inst of H Ed (Deane
Campus) BL3 ... 145 E6
Bolton Metropolitan Coll
BL1 ... 145 F8
Bolton Mus, Art Gal &
Aquarium* BL1 ... 145 F7
Bolton Muslim Girls Sch
BL3 ... 147 D4
Bolton Old Rd M46 ... 58 E3
Bolton Parish Church CE
Prim Sch BL2 ... 148 B7
Bolton Rd
Adlington BL6,PR6 ... 21 D6
Ashton-in-M WN2,WN4 ... 73 D5
Aspull WN2 ... 38 D4
Atherton M46 ... 58 E4
Bolton,Bradshaw BL2 ... 25 C5
Bolton,Hunger Hill BL3 ... 40 D2
Bury BL8,BL9 ... 27 C1
Edgworth BL7 ... 9 D5
Farnworth BL4 ... 42 D2
Kearsley BL4 ... 60 F7
Pendlebury M27 ... 80 C7
Radcliffe M26 ... 43 E3
Ramsbottom BL8 ... 10 D2
Rochdale OL11 ... 30 B4
Salford M6 ... 80 E5
Swinton M27 ... 62 A1
Walkden M28 ... 60 D4
Westhoughton BL5 ... 39 F1
Bolton Rd N BL0 ... 1 D2
Bolton Rd W BL0 ... 11 A4
Bolton Royal Infmy BL1 ... 145 D7
Bolton Sch Girls' & Boys'
Division BL1 ... 144 B7
Bolton Sq WN1 ... 37 E1
Bolton St Bury BL9 ... 140 E2
Downall Green WN4 ... 72 D5
Oldham OL4 ... 67 B6
Radcliffe M26 ... 43 F3
Ramsbottom BL0 ... 138 B6
Reddish SK5 ... 111 E7
Salford M3 ... 158 E1
Bolton Sta BL3 ... 145 F6
Bolton Tech Exchange
BL1 ... 145 D7
Bolton Wanderers FC
(Reebok Stad) BL6 ... 39 D7
Boltons Yd OL3 ... 69 B8
Bombay Rd
Stockport SK3 ... 123 C7
Wigan WN5 ... 36 C1
Bombay St
5 Ashton-u-L OL6 ... 85 D4
Manchester M1 ... 163 A8
Bonar Cl 5 SK3 ... 123 C8
Bonar Rd SK3 ... 123 C8
Boncarn Dr M23 ... 121 A4
Bonchurch Wlk M18 ... 165 B6
Bond Cl BL6 ... 22 C3
Bond Sq M7 ... 155 E6
Bond St Bury BL9 ... 141 A2
Denton M34 ... 100 F3
Edenfield BL0 ... 1 E2
Leigh WN7 ... 75 F5
Manchester M12 ... 163 C8
Rochdale OL12 ... 15 A2
Stalybridge SK15 ... 86 A3
Tyldesley M46 ... 58 F1
Bond's La PR7 ... 20 F7
Bondmark Rd M18 ... 165 C6
Bongs Rd SK2,SK6 ... 125 A6
Bonhill Wlk M11 ... 83 B2
Bonholt Ind Est 11 BL8 ... 27 B4
Bonington Rise SK6 ... 126 B8
Bonis Cres SK2 ... 124 C4
Bonny Brow St M24 ... 64 B7
Bonnyfield SK6 ... 113 B2
Bonnywell Rd WN7 ... 75 F3
Bonsall Bank 32 SK13 ... 171 E2
Bonsall Cl 33 SK13 ... 171 E2
Bonsall Fold 31 SK13 ... 171 E2
Bonsall St M15 ... 162 F6
Bonscale Cres M24 ... 46 E3
Bonville Chase WA14 ... 119 A4
Bonville Rd WA14 ... 119 A4
Boodle St OL6 ... 166 B4
Bookham Wlk 16 M9 ... 157 E8
Boond St Manchester M4 ... 160 D1
Salford M3 ... 158 E2
Boonfields BL7 ... 25 A8
Boot La BL1 ... 23 E1
Booth Ave M14 ... 110 D7
Booth Bridge Cl M24 ... 64 C7
Booth Cl Bury BL8 ... 27 A5
4 Stalybridge SK15 ... 85 F1
Booth Clibborn Ct M7 ... 155 D8
Booth Ct BL4 ... 60 D8
Booth Dr M41 ... 94 F5
Booth Hall Dr BL8 ... 26 F5
Booth Hall Hospl M9 ... 64 F3
Booth Hall Rd M9 ... 65 A3
Booth Hill La OL1 ... 48 E1
Booth House Trad Est
OL9 ... 152 C6
Booth Rd
Altrincham WA14 ... 119 C4
Bacup OL13 ... 3 B8
Droylsden M34 ... 100 A7
Handforth SK9 ... 131 A1
Little Lever BL3 ... 43 B2
Manchester M16 ... 97 C3
Sale M33 ... 108 B6
Booth St Ashton-u-L OL6 ... 166 B2
Bolton BL1 ... 142 C3
Bury BL8 ... 26 F5
Denton M34 ... 100 F5
Failsworth M35 ... 83 E7
Hollingworth SK14 ... 103 C5
Hyde SK14 ... 167 E1
Manchester M2 ... 158 F1
Middleton M24 ... 65 D6
Oldham,Bank Top OL9 ... 153 E6
2 Oldham,Lees OL4 ... 67 E6
Rawtenstall BB4 ... 2 E8
Salford M3 ... 158 F2
Stalybridge SK15 ... 101 F8
Stockport SK3 ... 170 E7
Booth St E M13 ... 163 B6
Booth St W M13,M15 ... 163 A6
Booth Way BL8 ... 26 F5
Booth's Brow Rd WN4 ... 72 D6
Booth's Hall M28 ... 78 B5
Booth's Hall Gr 2 M28 ... 78 B6
Booth's Hall Rd M28 ... 78 B6
Booth's Hall Way M28 ... 78 B6
Boothby Rd M27 ... 61 E1
Boothby St SK2 ... 124 C4
Boothcote M34 ... 100 D6
Boothfield 11 Bury BL8 ... 27 C3
Eccles M30 ... 79 A3
Boothfield Ave M22 ... 121 D6
Boothfield Dr M22 ... 121 D6
Boothfield Rd M22 ... 121 D6
Boothman Ct M30 ... 79 F3
Boothroyden Cl M24 ... 64 C7
Boothroyden Rd
Manchester M24,M9 ... 64 C6
Middleton M24 ... 64 C7
Boothroyden Terr M9 ... 64 C6
Boothsbank Ave M28 ... 78 B6
Boothshall Paddock M28 ... 78 B5
Boothshall Way M28 ... 78 A5
Boothstown Dr M28 ... 78 A5
Boothstown Meth Prim Sch
M28 ... 77 F6
Boothway 8 M30 ... 79 F2
Bootle St M2 ... 162 F8
Bor Ave WN3 ... 55 B4
Bordale Ave M9 ... 157 F7
Bordan St M11 ... 164 F8
Borden Cl 5 WN2 ... 37 F2
Borden Way BL9 ... 45 A6
Border Brook La M28 ... 78 A6
Bordesley Ave M38 ... 60 A6
Bordley Wlk M23 ... 108 E1
Bordon Rd SK3 ... 123 B7
Bores Hill WN1 ... 20 C4
Boringdon Cl M40 ... 83 B6
Borland Ave M40 ... 65 D1
Borough Arc SK14 ... 167 D2
Borough Ave
Radcliffe M26 ... 44 D5
Swinton M27 ... 62 A1
Borough Rd
Altrincham WA15 ... 119 E4
Salford M50 ... 154 D1
Borough St 5 SK15 ... 86 A1
Borrans The M28 ... 77 F5
Borron Rd WA12 ... 89 B5
Borron St SK1 ... 112 A2
Borrowdale Ave
Bolton BL1 ... 144 A8
Gatley SK8 ... 122 B4
Borrowdale Cl OL2 ... 48 D6
Borrowdale Cres
Ashton-u-L OL7 ... 84 F4
Manchester M20 ... 109 E4
Borrowdale Dr
Rochdale OL11 ... 30 C4
Whitefield BL9 ... 45 A3
Borrowdale Rd
Middleton M24 ... 46 E2
Stockport SK2 ... 124 B6
Wigan WN5 ... 54 B7
Borrowdale Terr SK15 ... 86 A4
Borsdane Ave WN2 ... 56 F5
Borsden St M27 ... 61 D2
Borth Ave SK2 ... 124 C7
Borth Wlk 3 M23 ... 120 F6
Borwell St M18 ... 99 D5
Boscobel Rd BL3 ... 42 B2
Boscombe Ave M30 ... 95 C8
Boscombe Dr SK7 ... 124 C1
Boscombe Pl WN2 ... 56 E4
Boscombe St
Manchester M14 ... 98 B2
Reddish SK5 ... 99 F2
Boscow Rd BL3 ... 43 A2
Bosden Ave SK7 ... 124 F3
Bosden Cl Handforth SK9 ... 131 D5
Stockport SK1 ... 170 F8
Bosden Fold SK1 ... 170 F8
Bosden Hall Rd SK7 ... 124 E3
Bosdenfold Rd SK7 ... 124 E3
Bosdin Rd E M41 ... 94 E1
Bosdin Rd W M41 ... 94 E1
Bosley Ave M20 ... 110 A8
Bosley Cl SK9 ... 131 D2
Bosley Dr SK12 ... 134 A3
Bosley Rd SK3 ... 123 A8
Bossall Ave M9 ... 64 E4
Bossington Cl SK2 ... 124 C8
Bostock Rd SK14 ... 115 A8
Bostock Wlk M13 ... 163 B7
Boston Cl Bramhall SK7 ... 132 D7
Culcheth WA3 ... 91 F4
Failsworth M35 ... 83 F8
Boston Ct Hyde SK14 ... 167 E3
Salford M50 ... 96 E8
Boston Gr WN7 ... 75 E8
Boston St 14 Bolton BL1 ... 143 E2
Hyde SK14 ... 167 E2
Manchester M15 ... 162 F5
Oldham OL8 ... 66 F4
Boston Wlk 8 M34 ... 101 A1
Boswell Ave M34 ... 84 D1
Boswell Pl WN3 ... 54 F3
Boswell Way M24 ... 47 E4
Bosworth Cl M45 ... 63 C8
Bosworth Sq OL11 ... 30 D4
Bosworth St Horwich BL6 ... 22 B4
Manchester M11 ... 165 A8
Rochdale OL11 ... 30 D4
Botanical Ave M16 ... 161 A5
Botany Cl Heywood OL10 ... 29 B2
Wigan WN2 ... 38 B2
Botany La OL6 ... 166 C3
Botany Rd Eccles M30 ... 79 A4
Romiley SK6 ... 113 A6
Botesworth Cl WN2 ... 57 A4
Botesworth Gn OL16 ... 32 A5
Botha Cl 4 M11 ... 99 D7
Botham Cl M15 ... 162 F5
Bothwell Rd M40 ... 159 C3
Botley St OL5 ... 68 B1
Bottesford Ave M20 ... 109 F5
Bottom o' th' Knotts Brow
BL7 ... 9 E3
Bottom o' th' Moor
Horwich BL6 ... 23 A3
Oldham OL1,OL4 ... 67 B7
Bottom O'Th Moor BL2 ... 25 D2
Bottom St SK14 ... 167 F3
Bottomfield Cl OL1 ... 49 A1
Bottomley Rd OL14 ... 6 C6
Bottomley Side M9 ... 64 C2
Bougainvillea Gdns M12 ... 99 A4
Boughey St WN7 ... 75 E5
Boulden Dr BL8 ... 27 C5
Boulder Dr M23 ... 121 A2
Boulderstone Rd SK15 ... 86 A4
Boulevard The
Hazel Grove SK7 ... 124 E2
Hollingworth SK14 ... 171 D4
Manchester M20 ... 109 F6
Bouley Wlk M12 ... 165 A6
Boulton Ho M1 ... 163 A8
Boundary Cl Mossley OL5 ... 86 C6
Romiley SK6 ... 113 C5
Boundary Cotts SK15 ... 86 E7
Boundary Ct
Cheadle SK8 ... 122 C5
Manchester SK4 ... 111 A7
Boundary Dr BL2 ... 43 A5
Boundary Gdns
Bolton BL1 ... 143 E2
Oldham OL1 ... 48 E1
Boundary Gr M33 ... 108 F2
Boundary La
Manchester M15 ... 163 A6
Shevington Moor WN6 ... 19 A3
Boundary Park Rd OL1 ... 48 C1
Boundary Rd
Cheadle SK8 ... 123 A6
Irlam M44 ... 94 C3
Swinton M27 ... 61 F1
Boundary St Bolton BL1 ... 143 D2
Leigh WN7 ... 76 B4
Littleborough OL15 ... 16 B6
Manchester M12 ... 165 A6
Rochdale OL11 ... 139 F5
Tyldesley M29 ... 59 A1
Wigan WN1 ... 151 D7
Boundary St E M1, M13 ... 163 A7
Boundary St W M15 ... 163 A6
Boundary Terr SK9 ... 130 F6
Boundary The M27 ... 61 E4
Boundary Trad Pk M44 ... 94 C3
Boundary Wlk OL11 ... 139 E5
Boundry Gn M34 ... 100 E4
Bourdon St M40 ... 160 D3
Bourget St M7 ... 155 F8
Bournbrook Ave M38 ... 60 A6
Bourne Ave Golborne WA3 ... 90 D8
Swinton M27 ... 79 F7
Bourne Dr M40 ... 65 B1
Bourne Ho 1 M6 ... 154 F2
Bourne Rd OL2 ... 149 A8
Bourne St Oldham OL9 ... 66 B2
Stockport SK4 ... 169 E4
Wilmslow SK9 ... 136 F6
Bourne Wlk 9 BL1 ... 143 F1
Bournelea Ave M19 ... 110 F6
Bourneville Dr BL8 ... 27 A2
Bournville Ave SK4 ... 169 E4

Bournville Gr M19 .....99 C1
Bourton Cl BL8 .....27 B3
Bourton Ct M29 .....59 D1
Bourton Dr M18 .....99 B4
Bow Green Mews WA14 .119 B2
Bow Green Rd WA14 .....119 A1
Bow La Altrincham WA14 .128 B8
  Heywood OL10 .....29 D2
  Manchester M2 .....158 F1
Bow Rd WN7 .....76 B3
Bow St Ashton-u-L OL6 .166 B3
  Bolton BL1 .....145 F7
  Dukinfield OL6,SK16 .....166 D2
  7 Manchester M2 .....158 F1
  Oldham OL1 .....153 F7
  Rochdale OL11 .....30 D3
  Stockport SK3 .....123 C8
Bowden Cl Culcheth WA3 .91 F4
  Hattersley SK14 .....102 E1
  Leigh WN7 .....76 C2
  Trub OL11 .....47 D8
Bowden La SK6 .....125 E7
Bowden Rd
  Glossop SK13 .....104 C3
  4 Pendlebury M27 .....80 A7
Bowden St Denton M34 .100 E3
Bowden Ave WA14 .....124 E3
Bowdon Ave M41 .....97 F1
Bowdon CE Prim Sch
  WA14 .....119 C1
Bowdon Ho 2 SK3 .....170 E8
Bowdon Prep Sch
  WA14 .....119 C2
Bowdon Rd WA14 .....119 C1
Bowdon Rise WA14 .....119 C2
Bowdon St SK3 .....170 E8
Bowen Cl SK7 .....132 F5
Bowen St BL1 .....142 B1
Bower Ave
  Hazel Grove SK7 .....124 D1
  Rochdale OL12 .....15 D4
  Stockport SK4 .....168 C2
Bower Ct SK14 .....169 D2
Bower Fold SK15 .....102 C8
Bower Gdns SK15 .....102 D8
Bower Gr SK15 .....86 C2
Bower La OL9 .....66 A2
Bower Rd WA15 .....119 F1
Bower St Bury BL9 .....141 C3
  Failsworth M40 .....83 A5
  Oldham OL1 .....67 B8
  Radcliffe SK5 .....99 F2
  Salford M7 .....155 F7
Bower Terr M3 .....84 C3
Bowerfield Ave SK7 .133 D8
Bowerfield Cres SK7 .133 E8
Bowerfold La SK4 .....169 D2
Bowers Ave M41 .....95 B3
Bowers St M14 .....110 E7
Bowery Ave SK8 .....131 F6
Bowes Cl BL8 .....27 B5
Bowes M14 .....97 F3
Bowfell Dr SK6 .....134 E8
Bowfell Gr M9 .....64 B4
Bowfell Rd M41 .....95 B2
Bowfield Wlk 18 M40 .83 C5
Bowgreave Ave BL2 .....42 F7
Bowgreen Wlk 11 M15 .162 D6
Bowker Ave M34 .....113 B8
Bowker Bank Ave M8 .....63 F2
Bowker Cl OL11 .....13 E1
Bowker M7 .....155 D6
Bowker St Haslingden BL0 .....1 C5
  Hyde SK14 .....167 D3
  Radcliffe M26 .....44 A3
  Salford M7 .....155 D6
  Walkden M28 .....60 B3
Bowker Vale Gdns M9 .63 F3
Bowker Vale Prim Sch
  M8 .....63 F4
Bowker Vale Sta M8 .....63 F3
Bowkers Row 12 BL1 .145 F7
Bowlacre Rd SK14 .....113 D7
Bowland Ave
  Ashton-in-M WN4 .....73 B4
  Golborne WA3 .....74 C1
  Reddish M18 .....100 A4
Bowland Cl
  Ashton-u-L OL6 .....85 C7
  Bury BL8 .....26 F3
  Shaw OL2 .....48 E7
  Stockport SK2 .....124 E5
Bowland Dr M33 .....108 B4
Bowland Gr BL11 .....23 E2
Bowland Gr OL16 .....31 F4
Bowland Rd
  Glossop SK13 .....116 A8
  Reddish M34 .....100 B3
  Romiley SK6 .....113 B5
  Wythenshawe M23 .....121 A6
Bowles Cl BL9 .....45 A2
Bowler St
  Manchester M19 .....111 B8
  Shaw OL2 .....149 B7
Bowlers Wlk OL22 .....14 F2
Bowley Ave M22 .....121 B2
Bowling Cl BL1 .....24 E5
Bowling Gn The BL0 .....1 C5
Bowling Green Row M46 .58 B2
Bowling Green St
  Heywood OL10 .....29 D2
  Hyde SK14 .....167 D2
Bowling Green Way OL11 .14 C7
Bowling Rd M18 .....99 E3
Bowling St OL9 .....66 B2
Bowlings The WN6 .....37 A2
Bowman Cres OL6 .....85 D3
Bowmead Wlk 8 M8 .....155 F6

Bowmeadow Grange 2
  M12 .....98 F4
Bowmont Cl SK8 .....123 A4
Bowness Ave
  Cheadle SK8 .....123 B1
  Irlam M44 .....105 D4
  Reddish SK4 .....111 E6
  Rochdale OL12 .....14 C1
Bowness Ct 5 M24 .....46 D2
Bowness Dr M33 .....107 F5
Bowness Pl WN2 .....56 B8
Bowness Prim Sch BL3 .....42 F3
Bowness Rd
  Altrincham WA15 .....120 D5
  Ashton-u-L OL7 .....84 F4
  Bolton BL3 .....147 D4
  Little Lever BL3 .....42 F4
  Middleton M24 .....46 D3
Bowness St Droylsden M11 .99 F7
  Stretford M32 .....96 E3
Bowness Wlk 7 OL2 .....48 E4
Bonring St M7 .....81 C5
Bowscale Cl 3 M13 .....164 D6
Bowstone Hill Rd BL2,BL8 .26 B5
Box St Littleborough OL15 .....16 A5
  Ramsbottom BL0 .....11 D6
Box Wlk M31 .....105 C3
Boxgrove Rd M33 .....107 F5
Boxgrove Wlk 8 M8 .....156 A6
Boxhill Dr M23 .....109 A1
Boxtree Ave M18 .....99 D4
Boyd Cl WN6 .....19 F1
Boyd St M12 .....165 A7
Boyd's Wlk SK16 .....101 C7
Boydell St WN7 .....75 F6
Boydell's Hos WN2 .....75 B8
Boyer St M16 .....161 B5
Boyle St Manchester M8 .....158 C6
Boysnope Cres M30 .....94 C4
Boysnope Wharf M30 .....94 D4
Boyswell Ho WN1 .....151 D8
Brabant Rd SK8 .....123 B2
Brabazon Pl WN5 .....54 C8
Brabham Cl M21 .....109 B8
Brabyns Ave SK6 .....113 D3
Brabyns Brow SK6 .....126 A7
Brabyns Rd SK14 .....113 E7
Brabyns Sch SK6 .....126 B7
Bracadale Dr SK3 .....170 F5
Bracewell Cl M12 .....165 A8
Bracken Ave M28 .....60 E3
Bracken Cl Bolton BL1 .....24 D6
  Droylsden M43 .....84 D2
  Heywood OL10 .....46 D8
  Hollingworth SK14 .....103 D6
  Marple SK6 .....126 C7
  Oldham OL4 .....67 F6
  Sale M33 .....107 C5
Bracken Dr M23 .....121 B5
Bracken Gr BB4 .....1 A8
Bracken Lea BL5 .....57 F5
Bracken Lea Fold 3
  OL12 .....14 B2
Bracken Rd Atherton M46 .58 D2
  Leigh WN7 .....75 B5
Bracken Way SK13 .....116 F7
Brackenfield Wlk WA15 .120 D6
Brackenhill Terr 14
  M34 .....113 A7
Brackenhurst Ave OL5 .....68 E1
Brackenlea Dr M9 .....64 C2
Brackenlea Pl SK3 .....170 D5
Brackenside SK15 .....112 A8
Brackenwood Cl OL11 .....48 C2
Brackenwood Dr SK8 .....122 E4
Brackenwood Mews
  SK9 .....137 E8
Brackley Ave Irlam M44 .105 D6
  Manchester M15 .....162 D7
  Tyldesley M29 .....59 B1
Brackley Dr M24 .....65 A5
Brackley Lo M30 .....79 F3
Brackley Rd Eccles M30 .....79 D4
  Over Hulton BL5 .....58 A4
  Reddish SK4 .....111 D5
Brackley Sq 5 OL1 .....67 A8
Brackley St Farnworth BL4 .60 D8
  9 Oldham OL1 .....67 A8
  Walkden M28 .....60 C4
Bracondale Ave BL1 .....142 B2
Braconbate Cl BL3 .....145 F5
Bradburn Ave 4 M30 .....79 D1
Bradburn Cl 8 M30 .....79 D1
Bradburn Gr 5 M30 .....79 D1
Bradburn Rd M44 .....105 E2
Bradburn St M30 .....79 D1
Bradburn Wlk 8 M8 .....156 B6
Bradbury Ave WA14 .....119 A5
Bradbury St
  Ashton-u-L OL7 .....166 A4
  Hyde SK14 .....167 E1
  Radcliffe M26 .....44 A2
Bradbury Wlk 10 OL2 .....48 E4
Bradbury's La OL3 .....69 D3
Bradda Mount SK7 .....124 A2
Braddan Ave M33 .....108 C3
Bradden Cl M5 .....81 A1
Braddocks Cl OL12 .....15 D4
Braddon Ave M41 .....95 D2
Braddon Rd SK6 .....113 A5
Braddon St 1 M11 .....83 E2
Braddyll Rd BL5 .....58 F8
Brade Cl M11 .....165 C8
Bradfield Ave M6 .....80 C2
Bradfield Cl SK5 .....99 E2
Bradfield Rd M32,M41 .....96 A2

Bradford Ave BL3 .....42 B3
Bradford Cres 17 BL3 .....42 A4
Bradford Ct M40 .....65 C1
Bradford Park Dr BL2 .148 B6
Bradford Rd
  Bolton BL3,BL4 .....42 A2
  Eccles M30 .....79 E4
  Manchester M40 .....160 E2
  9 Rochdale OL16 .....31 A8
Bradford St Bolton BL2 .148 B7
  Farnworth BL4 .....60 D7
  Oldham OL1 .....153 E8
  Wigan WN3 .....150 C7
Bradford Terr BL9 .....140 C1
Bradgate Ave SK8 .....122 D1
Bradgate Cl M22 .....121 E2
Bradgate Rd
  Altrincham WA14 .....119 A5
  Sale M33 .....108 A3
Bradgate St
  Ashton-u-L OL7 .....166 A1
  7 Ashton-u-L OL7 .....166 A2
Bradgreen Rd M30 .....79 C3
Brading Wlk M22 .....130 E8
Bradleigh Rd WA12 .....89 B1
Bradley Ave M7 .....158 B3
Bradley Cl WA15 .....119 E7
Bradley Dr BL9 .....45 A5
Bradley Fold SK15 .....86 B2
Bradley Fold Cotts BL2 .43 B6
Bradley Fold Rd BL2 .....43 C7
Bradley Fold Trad Est
  BL2 .....43 C6
Bradley Green Com Prim Sch
  SK14 .....101 F6
Bradley Green Rd SK14 .101 F6
Bradley Hall Trad Est
  WN6 .....20 A2
Bradley Ho OL8 .....153 F5
Bradley La
  Little Lever BL2,M26 .....43 B5
  Newhey OL16 .....32 B4
  Newton-le-W WA5,WA12 .....89 A1
  Sale M32,M33 .....108 B7
  Standish WN6 .....19 F2
Bradley Smithy Cl OL12 .14 E2
Bradley St
  7 Manchester M1 .....159 B2
  Newhey OL16 .....32 B4
Bradleys Ct M1 .....159 B1
Bradney Cl M9 .....64 B4
Bradnor Rd M22 .....121 D7
Bradshaw Ave
  Failsworth M35 .....83 E5
  Manchester M20 .....110 B7
  Whitefield M45 .....44 E2
Bradshaw Brow BL2 .....25 C4
Bradshaw Cl WN6 .....19 D1
Bradshaw Cres SK6 .....126 A7
Bradshaw Fold Ave M40 .65 D3
Bradshaw Hall Fold BL2 .25 D6
Bradshaw St
  Atherton M46 .....58 D3
  Farnworth BL4 .....60 D7
  Heywood OL10 .....29 E2
  Middleton M24 .....65 C7
  Oldham OL1 .....153 F7
  Radcliffe M26 .....43 F3
  9 Rochdale OL16 .....31 A8
  Salford M7 .....155 E6
Bradshaw St N M7 .....155 D7
Bradshawgate
  Bolton BL1,BL3 .....145 F7
  Leigh WN7 .....75 F5
  Wigan WN1 .....150 C8
Bradshawgate Sh Arc 7
  WN7 .....75 F5
Bradstock Rd M16 .....97 E3
Bradstone Rd M8 .....156 A5
Bradwell Ave
  Manchester M20 .....109 F6
  Stretford M32 .....96 A3
Bradwell Dr SK8 .....131 C7
Bradwell Field 4 SK13 .171 E1
Bradwell Lea 4 SK13 .....171 E1
Bradwell Pl 7 BL2 .....25 B1
Bradwell Rd
  Golborne WA3 .....90 E2
  Hazel Grove SK7 .....133 E8
Bradwell Terr 3 SK13 .171 E1
Bradwell Wlk M41 .....94 D3
Brady St WN1 .....151 F8
Brady St BL0 .....22 A4
Brae Side OL8 .....66 E2
Braeburn Ct WN7 .....75 D5
Braemar Ave
  Stretford M32 .....96 A2
  Urmston M41 .....95 A1
Braemar Dr BL3 .....107 C2
Braemar Gdns BL3 .....40 E5
Braemar La M28 .....78 B6

Braemar Rd
  Hazel Grove SK7 .....124 F3
  Manchester M14 .....110 E8
Braemar Wlk WN2 .....38 D5
Braemore Cl Shaw OL2 .....48 E8
  Wigan WN3 .....54 D2
Braemore Dr
  Broadbottom SK14 .....102 F1
  Bury BL9 .....28 D2
Braeside Cl SK2 .....124 F6
Braeside Cres WN5 .....71 D5
Braeside Gr BL3 .....40 F5
Braewood Cl BL9 .....28 D2
Bragenham St M18 .....165 C5
Braidhaven WN6 .....35 E7
Brailsford Ave 6 SK13 .171 E2
Brailsford Cl 9 SK13 .171 E2
Brailsford Gdns 8
  SK13 .....171 E2
Brailsford Mews 5
  SK13 .....171 E2
Brailsford Rd Bolton BL2 .25 C3
  Manchester M14 .....110 E8
Braintree Rd M22 .....130 E8
Braithwaite WN6 .....36 A6
Braithwaite Rd
  Golborne WA3 .....90 D8
  Middleton M24 .....46 D4
Brakehouse Cl OL16 .....31 E6
Brakenhurst Dr M7 .....155 F6
Brakesmere Gr M28 .....60 A4
Bramall St M12 .....163 B7
Bramall Ct SK13 .....103 F7
Bramall Dr BL9 .....28 D2
Bramber Way OL3 .....152 B6
Bramble Ave Oldham OL4 .49 D1
  Salford M5 .....161 C7
Bramble Cl OL15 .....15 F5
Bramble Croft BL6 .....40 A3
Bramble Gr WN5 .....54 E7
Bramble Wlk
  7 Sale M33 .....107 C5
  9 Wythenshawe M22 .....121 C2
Brambles The WN4 .....72 D5
Bramblewood
  Chadderton OL9 .....65 E8
  Hindley WN2 .....56 F7
Brambling Cl
  Droylsden M34 .....84 C2
  Hazel Grove SK12 .....125 A5
Brambling Dr BL5 .....57 D6
Brambling Way WA3 .....90 E7
Bramcote Ave
  Bolton BL2 .....148 B6
  Wythenshawe M23 .....121 B6
Bramdean Ave BL2 .....25 E5
Bramfield Wlk M15 .....162 D7
Bramford Cl BL5 .....57 E6
Bramhall Ave BL2 .....26 A4
Bramhall Cl
  18 Altrincham WA15 .....120 D6
  Dukinfield SK16 .....101 D6
  Milnrow OL16 .....31 E5
  Sale M33 .....108 A3
Bramhall Ct M20 .....158 D3
Bramhall Ctr The SK7 .132 E6
Bramhall High Sch SK7 .132 F8
Bramhall La SK2,SK3 .....170 F5
Bramhall La S
  Bramhall SK7 .....132 E7
  Stockport SK3,SK7 .....123 E2
Bramhall Moor Ind Est
  SK7 .....124 B2
Bramhall Moor La SK7 .124 C2
Bramhall Mount SK2 .....170 F5
Bramhall Park Rd SK7,
  SK8 .....123 D2
Bramhall Sta SK7 .....132 E6
Bramhall St Bolton BL3 .42 B3
  Manchester M18 .....99 E5
Bramham Rd SK6 .....126 A4
Bramhope Wlk M9 .....157 D7
Bramley Ave
  Manchester M19 .....111 A8
  Stretford M32 .....96 B1
Bramley Cl Bramhall SK7 .132 E6
  Swinton M27 .....79 B6
  Wilmslow SK9 .....136 D4
Bramley Cres SK4 .....168 B1
Bramley Ct WN6 .....19 E1
Bramley Dr Bramhall SK7 .132 E6
  Bury BL8 .....27 C6
Bramley Meade M7 .....155 E6
Bramley Rd Bramhall SK7 .132 E6
  Rochdale OL11 .....29 E8
Bramley St M7 .....155 E5
Bramwell Ave M9 .....64 C8
Bramworth Ave BL0 .....138 B6
Brancaster Dr WA3 .....91 A7
Brancaster Rd M1 .....163 B8
Branch Cl BL8 .....140 D3
Branch Rd OL15 .....15 F1
Branch St Bacup OL13 .....3 D8

Branch St *continued*
  Ince-in-M WN2 .....56 A7
Brancker St BL5 .....40 C1
Brandish Cl M13 .....164 D5
Brandle Ave BL8 .....27 C4
Brandlehow Dr M44 .....46 C2
Brandlesholme Rd BL8 .....27 C6
Brandon Ave Gatley SK8 .122 B1
  Reddish M34 .....99 F3
  Salford M30 .....80 A5
  Wythenshawe M22 .....121 C8
Brandon Brow 8 OL1 .153 E8
Brandon Cl Bury BL8 .....27 D5
  Handforth SK9 .....131 D2
  Up Holland WN8 .....53 A7
Brandon Cres OL2 .....149 A8
Brandon Rd M6 .....80 B5
Brandon St
  2 Bolton BL3 .....147 D4
  Milnrow OL16 .....31 D6
Brandram Rd M25 .....63 D4
Brandreth Pl WN6 .....19 F1
Brandsby Gdns M5 .....161 A8
Brandwood OL1 .....153 D6
Brandwood Ave M14 .....109 D4
Brandwood Cl M28 .....78 A8
Brandwood Fold BL7 .....9 E5
Brandwood Pk OL13 .....3 B8
Brandwood Prim Sch
  BL3 .....146 C4
Brandwood Rd BL3 .....146 C4
Branfield Ave WA15 .....122 D1
Brankgate St M20 .....110 A5
Branksome Ave M25 .....63 B4
Branksome Dr
  Cheadle SK8 .....122 D1
  Manchester M9 .....64 B6
  Salford M6 .....80 B5
Branksome Ho SK4 .....168 B2
Branksome Rd SK4 .....168 B1
Bransby Ave M9 .....64 E4
Branscombe Dr M33 .107 C5
Branscombe Gdns BL3 .42 D5
Bransdale Ave OL2 .....48 C4
Bransdale Cl BL3 .....40 F4
Bransdale Dr WN4 .....73 D3
Bransdale Rd WN3 .....55 B3
Bransford Cl WN4 .....73 C2
Bransford Rd
  Droylsden M11 .....99 F8
  Urmston M41 .....95 C3
Branson Cl WA3 .....74 A2
Branson St M4,M40 .....160 D2
Branston Rd M40 .....65 D2
Brantfell Gr BL2 .....42 F8
Branthwaite WN2 .....38 B1
Brantingham Ct M16 .....97 E1
Brantingham Rd M16,
  M21 .....97 D1
Brantwood Cl 2 OL2 .....48 C4
Brantwood Dr BL2 .....42 F8
Brantwood Rd
  Cheadle SK8 .....122 F1
  Manchester SK4 .....168 C4
  Salford M7 .....155 D8
Brantwood Terr M9 .....157 F7
Branwood Prep Sch M30 .79 C3
Broadlands Rd M28 .....65 A3
Brassey St
  Ashton-u-L OL6 .....166 B4
  Middleton M24 .....47 A1
Brassington Ave
  Manchester M21 .....109 B7
  Salford M5 .....161 B8
Brassington Cres SK13 .171 D1
Brassington Rd SK4 .....110 E4
Brathay Cl Bolton BL2 .....25 F2
  Prestwich M45 .....63 C8
Bratton Cl WN3 .....54 C2
Bratton Wlk M13 .....164 E6
Brattray Dr M24 .....46 E3
Braunston Cl M30 .....95 E8
Braxton Wlk 20 M9 .....157 E8
Bray Ave M30 .....79 B3
Bray Cl BL8 .....122 E2
Braybrook Dr BL1 .....40 D7
Brayford Dr WN2 .....38 C5
Brayford Rd M22 .....121 D1
Brayshaw Cl OL10 .....29 C1
Brayside Rd M19,M20 .....110 D4
Braystan Gdns SK8 .....122 B6
Brayston Fold M24 .....64 C8
Brayton Ave
  Manchester M20 .....110 C2
  Sale M33 .....107 C6
Brazennose St M2 .....158 F1
Brazil Pl M1 .....163 A8
Brazil St M1 .....163 A8
Brazley Ave Bolton BL3 .42 A4
  Horwich BL6 .....22 C1
Breach House La WA16 .129 A1
Bread St M18 .....99 E6
Breaktemper BL5 .....39 E1
Bream Wlk 8 M22 .....121 C1
Brearley St OL13 .....3 D8
Breaston Ave M20 .....122 C1
Brechin Wlk 18 M11 .....83 C1
Breck Rd M30 .....79 E2
Breckland Cl SK15 .....86 D2
Breckland Dr BL1 .....40 D8
Breckles Pl BL3 .....145 D5

Brecon Ave Cheadle SK8 ..**122** E1
Denton M34 ....**100** F1
Manchester M19 ....**110** F7
Urmston M41 ....**94** D3
Brecon Cl
Platt Bridge WN2 ....**56** B2
Poynton SK12 ....**133** F4
Royton OL2 ....**48** C6
Brecon Cres OL6 ....**85** B6
Brecon Dr Bury BL9 ....**44** E7
Hindley WN2 ....**57** A3
Brecon Wlk 6 OL8 .....**66** B2
Bredbury Dr BL4 ....**60** E8
Bredbury Gn SK6 ....**113** A1
Bredbury Green Prim Sch
SK6 ....**112** F1
Bredbury Park Way SK6 .**112** E6
Bredbury Rd M14 ....**98** B2
Bredbury St
Chadderton OL9 ....**152** B6
Dukinfield SK14 ....**101** D5
Bredbury Sta SK6 ....**112** F4
Brede Wlk M23 ....**120** D8
Bredon Way OL8 ....**66** E3
Breeze Hill WN6 ....**37** B7
Breeze Hill Rd
Oldham OL4 ....**67** D5
Over Hulton M46 ....**58** F5
Breeze Hill Sch OL4 ......**67** D5
Breeze Mount M25 ......**63** C3
Breightmet Dr BL2 ......**42** E7
Breightmet Fold La BL2 .**42** F8
Breightmet St BL2 ......**148** A7
Brellafield Dr OL2 ......**48** F8
Brenbar Cres OL12 ......**4** D1
Brenchley Dr M23 ....**109** A2
Brencon Ave M23 ....**108** C1
Brendall Cl SK2 ....**125** A5
Brendon Ave
Manchester M40 ....**83** A7
Reddish SK5 ....**111** F6
Brendon Cl SK13 ....**116** A8
Brendon Dr M34 ....**84** D1
Brendon Hills OL2 ......**48** D3
Brenley Wlk 7 M9 ......**157** D8
Brennan Cl M15 ....**163** A5
Brennan Cr OL8 ....**66** C2
Brennock Cl M11 ....**164** F8
Brent Cl Little Lever BL2 .**43** B5
Poynton SK12 ....**133** B4
Brent Moor Rd SK7 .....**124** A3
Brent Rd Stockport SK4 ..**168** C1
Wythenshawe M23 ....**109** A2
Brentbridge Rd M14 .....**110** B8
Brentfield Ave M8 ......**156** A6
Brentford Ave BL1 ......**142** B2
Brentford Rd SK5 ....**111** F6
Brentford St M9 ....**157** E7
Brentnall Prim Sch M7 ..**155** D7
Brentnall St M7 ....**157** F7
Brentnor Rd M40 ....**65** C3
Brenton Ave M33 ....**108** A4
Brentwood Sale M33 ....**108** A4
Salford M6 ....**154** E3
Urmston M41 ....**94** F1
Wigan WN5 ....**54** D5
Brentwood Ave
Altrincham WA14 ....**119** E7
Irlam M44 ....**105** D6
Swinton M28 ....**79** B6
Urmston M41 ....**95** D2
Brentwood Cl
Brinnington SK5 ....**112** D5
Littleborough OL15 ......**15** F3
Stalybridge SK15 ....**86** A2
Brentwood Cres WA14 ..**119** E6
Brentwood Ct M25 ......**62** F3
Brentwood Dr Eccles M30 .**79** D4
Farnworth BL3,BL4 ......**42** C2
Gatley SK8 ....**122** B5
Brentwood Rd
Adlington PR6 ....**21** B8
Swinton M27 ....**79** D6
Brentwood Sch WA14 .....**119** F7
Brentwood St M16 ......**97** F3
Brereton Cl WA14 ....**119** C1
Brereton Ct SK8 ....**122** E1
Brereton Dr M28 ....**78** F7
Brereton Gr M44 ....**105** E6
Brereton Rd Eccles M30 ..**78** F1
Handforth SK9 ....**131** E3
Breslyn St M3 ....**158** F3
Bretherton Row 7
WN1 ....**150** C8
Bretherton St M9 ....**56** C6
Brethren's Ct M43 ......**100** A8
Bretland Gdns SK14 ....**102** E1
Bretland Wlk 2 M22 ....**121** F3
Breton Ho SK2 ....**124** B6
Bret Rd M28 ....**77** F6
Brett St M22 ....**109** E1
Brettargh St M6 ....**81** A4
Bretton Wlk M22 ....**121** F3
Brewer's Gn SK7 ....**124** D3
Brewerton Rd OL4 ......**67** A6
Brewery La WN7 ....**76** A5
Brewery St
4 Altrincham WA14 .....**119** D4
Stockport SK1 ....**169** E3
Brewery Yd M3 ....**158** E2
Brewster St
Manchester M9 ....**157** D8
Middleton M24 ....**47** A2

Brewster St continued
4 Middleton M24 ....**47** A2
Brian Ave M43 ....**84** C3
Brian Rd BL4 ....**42** A1
Brian Redhead Ct M15 ..**162** E7
Brian St OL11 ....**30** B2
Briar Ave
Hazel Grove SK7 ....**124** F2
Hollinfare WA3 ....**105** B2
Oldham OL4 ....**49** D1
Briar Cl Ashton-in-M WN4 .**73** A4
Hindley WN2 ....**57** A2
Rochdale OL12 ....**14** A1
Sale M33 ....**107** C4
Urmston M41 ....**95** A3
Briar Cres M22 ....**121** E5
Briar Gr Chadderton OL9 .**48** B1
Leigh WN7 ....**75** E8
Romiley SK6 ....**113** A5
Briar Hill Ave M38 .....**59** E4
Briar Hill Cl M38 ....**59** E4
Briar Hill Gr M38 ....**59** E4
Briar Hill Way 6 M6 ....**81** A3
Briar Hollow SK4 ....**168** B1
Briar Lea Cl BL3 ....**147** E3
Briar Rd Golborne WA3 ..**90** B8
Wigan WN5 ....**54** E7
Briar St Bolton BL2 .....**42** D7
Rochdale OL11 ....**139** D6
Briar Wlk WA3 ....**90** B8
Briarcroft Dr M46 ......**58** A1
Briardene M34 ....**100** F3
Briardene Gdns M22 ....**121** E4
Briarfield BL7 ....**8** D2
Briarfield Hall M1 ......**163** A6
Briarfield Rd
Altrincham WA15 ....**120** C6
Cheadle SK8 ....**123** B3
Farnworth BL4 ....**42** A1
Manchester M19,M20 .....**110** D6
Reddish SK4 ....**111** E6
Uppermill OL3 ....**51** A2
Worsley M28 ....**78** F7
Briargrove Rd SK6,SK22 .**127** D4
Briarlands Ave M33 .....**107** F2
Briarlands Cl SK7 ....**132** D6
Briarlea Gdns M19 ......**110** E5
Briarley Gdns SK6 ......**113** C6
Briarly WN6 ....**37** A7
Briarmere Wlk OL9 .....**152** C7
Briars Mount SK4 ....**168** A2
Briars Pk SK7 ....**123** C1
Briarstead Cl SK7 ....**132** D7
Briarwood Bolton BL2 ...**25** B1
Wilmslow SK9 ....**137** C7
Briarwood Ave
Droylsden M43 ....**83** F3
Wythenshawe M23 ....**120** E8
Briarwood Chase SK8 ...**123** B1
Briarwood Cres SK6 ....**126** A3
Briary Dr M29 ....**77** B8
Brice St SK16 ....**101** B8
Brick Ground OL12 .....**13** C2
Brick Kiln La 4 WN1 ....**37** C1
Brick St Bury BL9 ....**141** A3
8 Manchester M4 ....**159** A2
Brickbridge Rd SK6 .....**126** A5
Brickfield St
Hadfield SK13 ....**104** B5
Rochdale OL16 ....**15** B2
Brickhill La WA15 ......**129** B4
Brickkiln La WA14 ......**118** C3
Brickkiln Row WA14 ....**119** C1
Brickley St M3,M4 ......**159** A3
Bricknell Wlk 5 M22 ....**121** F3
Bridcam St M8 ....**156** A5
Briddon St M3 ....**158** F3
Bride St BL1 ....**143** E2
Brideoak St M8 ....**156** A6
Brideoake St M8 ....**156** A6
Brideoake St Leigh WN7 .**76** B4
Oldham OL4 ....**67** E8
Bridestowe Ave SK14 ...**102** C3
Bridestowe Wlk SK14 ...**102** C3
Bridge Ave SK6 ....**113** A5
Bridge Bank Cl WA3 ....**90** B7
Bridge Bank Rd OL15 ...**16** A3
Bridge Cl Lymm WA13 ..**117** B4
Partington M31 ....**106** A3
8 Radcliffe M26 ....**44** B2
Bridge Coll SK2 ....**124** D8
Bridge Dr Cheadle SK8 ..**122** D4
Handforth SK9 ....**131** D3
Bridge End Delph OL3 ...**50** F4
Wigan WN5 ....**150** B8
Bridge End Cl BB4 ......**1** A7
Bridge Gr WA15 ....**119** F7
Bridge Hall Dr BL9 ......**141** C2
Bridge Hall Fold BL9 ....**141** C2
Bridge Hall La BL9 ......**28** D2
Bridge Hall Prim Sch
SK3 ....**170** D6
Bridge La SK7 ....**123** F1
Bridge Mill 1 BL7 ......**24** F7
Bridge Mills Bsns Pk M6 .**80** F5
Bridge Rd Bury BL9 .....**140** D1
Sale M23 ....**120** C7
Bridge St Bolton BL1 ....**145** F7
Bury BL9 ....**141** A3
Denton M34 ....**100** E4
Denton,Guide Bridge M34 .**100** F7
Droylsden M43 ....**99** E8
Dukinfield SK16 ....**101** A6
Farnworth BL4 ....**42** E1
Golborne WA3 ....**90** A7
Haslingden BB4 ....**1** C6
Heywood OL10 ....**29** C2
Hindley WN2 ....**56** E6

Bridge St continued
Horwich BL6 ....**22** C4
Ince-in-M WN3 ....**151** D6
Kearsley M26 ....**61** B8
Manchester M3 ....**158** E1
Middleton M24 ....**65** A8
Milnrow OL16 ....**31** F6
New Mills SK22 ....**127** C1
Newton-le-W WA12 ......**89** B3
Oldham,Lower Moor OL1 ..**67** A6
Oldham,County End OL4 ..**67** F6
1 Oldham,Lower Moor OL1 .**67** A6
Oldham,West Hulme OL1 ..**48** D1
Pendlebury M27 ....**80** A8
Ramsbottom BL0 ....**138** C6
Rawtenstall BB4 ....**2** E7
Rochdale,Castleton OL11 ..**30** C1
Rochdale,Hurstead OL12 ..**15** C3
Shaw OL2 ....**149** C8
Stalybridge SK15 ....**85** F1
Stockport SK1 ....**169** F2
Uppermill OL3 ....**69** B7
Whitworth OL12 ....**4** C1
Wigan WN3 ....**150** C7
Bridge St W M3 ....**158** E1
Bridge Trad Est BL8 .....**140** D2
Bridge's St M46 ....**58** B2
Bridgecrest Ct SK8 .....**123** A2
Bridgefield SL13 ....**116** B8
Bridgefield Ave SK9 ....**131** C1
Bridgefield Cres 4 OL4 .**67** F6
Bridgefield Dr BL9 ......**28** D2
Bridgefield St
Radcliffe M26 ....**44** B3
Rochdale OL11 ....**139** D7
Stockport SK1 ....**169** E2
Bridgefield Wlk 7 M26 ..**44** B3
Bridgefold Rd OL11 .....**139** D8
Bridgefoot Cl M28 ......**78** A5
Bridgeford St M32 ......**108** D8
Bridgeford St M13,M15 ..**163** A6
Bridgehall Dr WN8 ......**53** B7
Bridgelea Mews M20 ....**110** B6
Bridgelea Rd M20 ......**110** B6
Bridgeman Pl BL2 ......**148** A8
Bridgeman St Bolton BL3 .**145** F5
Farnworth BL4 ....**42** D1
Bridgeman Terr WN1 ....**37** C1
Bridgemere Cl M26 .....**43** F5
Bridgend Cl Cheadle SK8 .**123** C4
Manchester M12 ....**165** A6
Bridgenorth Ave M41 ...**95** F2
Bridgenorth Dr OL15 ...**15** F3
Bridges Ave BL9 ....**44** F6
Bridges Ct 5 BL3 ....**145** F6
Bridges Way M34 ......**112** F7
Bridgeside Bsns Ctr
SK6 ....**112** D6
Bridgewater Bsns Pk
WN7 ....**75** F4
Bridgewater Cl SK8 .....**131** D7
Bridgewater Ct M32 ....**96** E3
Bridgewater Ctr The
M41 ....**95** F2
Bridgewater Ho M15 ....**162** D8
Bridgewater Park Nature
Trail* M28 ....**78** B5
Bridgewater Pl M4 ......**159** A1
Bridgewater Prim Sch
M38 ....**60** B4
Bridgewater Rd
Altrincham WA14 ....**119** D7
Pendlebury M27 ....**80** B7
Walkden,Ellenbrook M28 ..**78** A8
Walkden,Engine Fold M28 .**60** D2
Bridgewater Sch M28 ....**79** A6
Bridgewater St
2 Bolton BL1 ....**145** D6
Eccles M30 ....**79** B2
Farnworth BL4 ....**60** E8
Hindley WN2 ....**56** E6
Manchester M3 ....**162** E8
8 Oldham OL1 ....**67** A8
Sale M33 ....**108** B3
Salford M5 ....**158** E3
Stretford M32 ....**96** E2
Walkden M38 ....**60** B4
Wigan WN3 ....**150** B7
5 Wigan,Worsley Hall
WN5 ....**54** F6
Bridgewater Viaduct
M15,M3 ....**162** E7
Bridgewater Way M15,
M16 ....**161** B5
Bridgewater Wlk 8 M28 .**60** D3
Bridgfield Cl SK6 ....**134** E7
Bridgnorth Rd M9 ......**64** A3
Bridle Cl Droylsden M43 ..**84** E2
Urmston M41 ....**94** E2
Bridle Ct SK7 ....**132** F2
Bridle Fold M26 ....**44** A4
Bridle Rd Prestwich M25 .**63** E7
Woodford SK7 ....**132** F2
Bridle Way SK7 ....**133** A2
Bridlington Ave M6 .....**80** C2
Bridlington Cl 6 M40 ...**83** C6
Bridport Ave M40 ......**83** D8
Bridson La BL2 ....**25** C2
Bridson St Oldham OL4 ..**67** C7
Salford M5 ....**154** E1
Brief St BL2 ....**148** B8
Brien Ave WA14 ....**119** E7
Briercliffe Cl M18 ......**99** D6
Briercliffe Rd BL3 ......**144** C5
Brierfield Ave M46 .....**58** C4
Brierfield Dr BL9 ....**27** E8
Brierholme Ave BL7 ....**8** E1

Brierley Ave
Failsworth M35 ....**84** A7
Whitefield M45 ....**44** E2
Brierley Cl Ashton-u-L OL6 .**86** A6
Denton M34 ....**100** E1
Brierley Dr M24 ....**65** A7
Brierley Rd M27 ....**61** E1
Brierley St Bury BL9 ....**44** E8
Chadderton OL9 ....**152** C8
Heywood OL10 ....**29** D2
Oldham OL8 ....**66** F3
Stalybridge SK16 ....**85** D1
Brierley Wlk OL9 ....**152** C8
Brierton Dr 5 M22 .....**121** B1
Brierwood Cl OL1 ......**48** E1
Briery Ave BL2 ....**25** D6
Brigade Dr M32 ....**96** C3
Brigade St BL1 ....**144** C7
Brigadier Cl M20 ....**110** B6
Brigantine Cl M5 ......**161** A8
Briggs Cl M33 ....**107** C1
Briggs Fold BL7 ....**8** E2
Briggs Fold Cl BL7 .....**8** E2
Briggs Fold Rd BL7 .....**8** E2
Briggs Rd M32 ....**96** F4
Briggs St Leigh WN7 ....**75** E7
Salford M3 ....**158** D3
Brigham St M11 ....**165** C8
Bright Rd M30 ....**79** E2
Bright St
Ashton-u-L OL6 ....**85** D2
Bolton BL9 ....**8** D2
Bury BL9 ....**141** A3
Chadderton OL9 ....**66** A4
Droylsden M43 ....**84** B1
Leigh WN7 ....**75** E7
Oldham OL8 ....**153** D5
Radcliffe M26 ....**44** C4
7 Rochdale OL16 ....**31** A5
Brighton Ave Bolton BL1 .**142** A1
Manchester M19 ....**110** F7
Reddish SK5 ....**99** F2
Salford M7 ....**155** E6
Urmston M41 ....**94** E3
Brighton Cl SK8 ....**123** C4
Brighton Ct
Manchester M14 ....**98** D2
Salford M5 ....**161** B7
Brighton Gr Hyde SK14 ..**98** D2
Manchester M14 ....**98** D2
Sale M33 ....**108** B5
Urmston M41 ....**94** E3
Brighton Pl M13 ....**163** B6
Brighton Range M18 ....**99** F4
Brighton Rd Oldham OL4 .**50** A1
Stockport SK4 ....**168** C1
Brighton Road Ind Est
SK4 ....**168** C1
Brighton St Bury BL9 ....**141** B3
Manchester M4 ....**159** A3
Brightstone Wlk 4 M13 .**98** E4
Brightwater Cl BL6 .....**21** F2
Brightwater Ct M45 ....**63** A8
Brightwell Wlk 5 M4 ...**159** B2
Brignall Gr WA3 ....**74** D1
Brigsteer Wlk M40 .....**157** D5
Brigstock Ave M18 .....**165** C5
Briksdal Way BL6 ......**40** C7
Brimelow St SK6 ....**112** D3
Brimfield Ave M27 .....**59** C1
Brimfield Wlk 7 M40 ...**83** C6
Brimmy Croft La OL3 ...**33** C3
Brimpton Wlk 13 M8 ...**155** F6
Brimrod Com Prim Sch
OL11 ....**139** D5
Brimrod La OL11 ....**139** D5
Brimscombe Ave M22 ..**121** C2
Brindale Ho SK5 ....**112** C4
Brindale Prim Sch SK5 ..**112** C4
Brindale Rd SK5 ....**112** C4
Brindle Rise M6 ....**154** F4
Brindle Heath Ind Est
M6 ....**81** A4
Brindle Heath Rd M6 ...**154** F4
Brindle Pl 7 M15 ....**163** A6
Brindle Rise M6 ....**154** F4
Brindle St Hindley WN2 ..**56** F6
Tyldesley M29 ....**59** A1
Brindley Ave
Manchester M9 ....**64** B5
Marple SK6 ....**125** F5
Sale M33 ....**108** C6
7 Worsley M28 ....**78** A6
Brindley Cl Atherton M46 .**58** A2
Eccles M30 ....**95** D8
Farnworth BL4 ....**60** B8
Brindley Gr SK9 ....**131** E2
Brindley Ho M5 ....**161** B5
Brindley St Bolton BL1 ..**143** F4
Boothstown M28 ....**77** F6
Eccles M30 ....**79** B2
Horwich BL6 ....**22** C2
Swinton M27 ....**61** F2
Walkden M28 ....**60** D2
Wigan WN5 ....**54** C5
Brinell Dr M44 ....**105** F6
Brink's Row BL6 ....**22** D5
Brinkburn Rd SK7 ......**125** A3
Brinklow Cl M11 ....**99** E7
Brinks La BL2 ....**43** A6
Brinkshaw Ave M22 ....**121** E2
Brinksway Bolton BL1 ...**40** D7
Stockport SK3 ....**123** C8
Brinksway Trad Est **1**
SK3 ....**123** C8

Brinksworth Cl BL2 .....**43** A8
Brinnington Cres SK5 ...**112** B4
Brinnington Rd
Brinnington SK5 ....**112** C4
Stockport SK1 ....**112** A3
Brinnington Rise SK1,
SK5 ....**112** B4
Brinnington Sta SK5 ....**112** C6
Brinsop Hall La BL5 ....**39** A6
Brinsop Sq M12 ....**165** B6
Brinston Wlk 12 M40 ...**83** A7
Brinsworth Dr M8 ......**156** A6
Briony Ave WA15 ....**120** C2
Briony Cl OL2 ....**48** E2
Brisbane Cl SK7 ....**132** F5
Brisbane St M13,M15 ...**163** B5
Brisco Wlk M24 ....**46** C2
Briscoe La M40 ....**83** B4
Briscoe Lane Prim Sch
M40 ....**83** B5
Briscoe Mews 22 BL3 ...**42** A4
Briscoe St OL1 ....**153** F8
Bristle Hall Way BL5 ....**39** F2
Bristol Ave Ashton-u-L OL6 .**85** B7
Bolton BL2 ....**25** C1
Manchester M19 ....**111** B8
Bristol Cl SK8 ....**131** C7
Bristol St 2 M7 ....**63** E1
Bristol St M7 ....**155** E7
Bristowe St M11,M43 ...**83** D3
Britain St BL9 ....**44** F5
Britannia Ave OL2 .....**149** C6
Britannia Bridge Prim Sch
WN3 ....**151** E6
Britannia Cl M26 ....**44** A3
Britannia Com Prim Sch
OL13 ....**4** C8
Britannia Mill Ind Est
OL10 ....**29** C2
Britannia Rd Sale M33 ..**108** C5
Wigan WN5 ....**54** B8
Britannia St
Ashton-u-L OL7 ....**100** F8
Heywood OL10 ....**29** B2
1 Oldham OL1 ....**67** A7
Salford M6 ....**81** A5
Britannia Way Bolton BL1 .**25** A2
Haslingden BB4 ....**1** A8
Brittnall Ave M12 ......**164** F5
Briton St
6 Rochdale OL16 ....**31** A8
Royton OL2 ....**48** E2
Brittania Mills M15 .....**162** D7
Britwell Wlk M8 ....**156** C8
Brixham Dr M33 ....**107** D6
Brixham Rd M16 ....**97** B4
Brixham Wlk
Bramhall SK7 ....**132** E7
6 Manchester M13 ......**163** C5
Brixton Ave M20 ....**110** A6
Brixton Wlk 19 M9 .....**64** E3
Broach St BL3 ....**147** E4
Broad Acre OL12 ....**13** E2
Broad Hey SK6 ....**113** D3
Broad Ing OL12 ....**14** C1
Broad La
Altrincham WA15 ....**120** B1
Billinge WA11 ....**71** B1
Delph OL3 ....**50** E7
Rochdale,Buersil OL16 ...**31** B3
Rochdale,Burnedge OL16 .**31** D2
Broad Lea M41 ....**95** C3
Broad o' th' La
Bolton BL1 ....**143** E4
Shevington WN6 ....**36** A6
Broad Oak Bsns Pk M17 ..**95** F7
Broad Oak Cl 4 PR6 ....**21** A8
Broad Oak Cres OL8 ....**67** A2
Broad Oak High Sch
BL9 ....**141** B2
Broad Oak La Bury BL9 ..**28** D3
Manchester M20 ....**122** B8
Manchester M20 ....**122** C8
Broad Oak Pk Eccles M30 .**79** D4
Swinton M28 ....**79** B6
Broad Oak Prim Sch
M20 ....**122** C8
Broad Oak Rd BL3 ......**42** A2
Broad Oak Terr BL9 ....**28** E3
Broad St M6 ....**108** D5
Broad Shaw La
Rochdale,Burnedge OL16 .**31** D3
Rochdale,Green Gate OL16 .**31** D3
Broad St Bury BL9 ......**140** E2
Middleton M24 ....**64** C7
Salford M6 ....**154** F4
Broad Wlk
Westhoughton BL5 ......**57** E7
Wilmslow SK9 ....**136** F8
Broadacre
Shevington Moor WN6 ...**19** B2
Stalybridge SK15 ....**102** E6
Up Holland WN8 ....**53** A6
Broadacre Pl SK9 ....**136** D3
Broadacre Rd M18 .....**99** E3
Broadbent Ave
Ashton-u-L OL6 ....**86** E6
Dukinfield SK16 ....**101** D8
Broadbent Cl
Mossley SK15 ....**86** A6
Royton OL2 ....**149** A5
Broadbent Dr BL9 ......**27** F6
Broadbent Fold Prim Sch
SK16 ....**102** A7
Broadbent Gr SK14 .....**102** E1

Broadbent Rd OL1 . . . . .49 C1
Broadbent St Hyde SK14 .167 D4
Swinton M27 . . . . .79 D7
Broadbottom CE Prim Sch
SK14 . . . . .114 F8
Broadbottom Rd SK14 .103 A3
Broadbottom Sta SK14 . .115 A8
Broadcarr La OL5 . . . . .68 B1
Broadfield Cl M34 . . . . . . .101 A2
Broadfield Dr OL15 . . . . .15 F3
Broadfield Gr SK5 . . . . .99 E3
Broadfield Prim Sch OL8 .66 F4
Broadfield Rd
  Manchester M14 . . . . .98 A3
  Reddish SK5 . . . . .99 E3
Broadfield St
  Heywood OL10 . . . . .29 B1
  Rochdale OL16 . . . . .139 F6
Broadfield Stile OL16 . .139 E6
Broadford Rd BL3 . . . . .40 F5
Broadgate Bolton BL3 . . . .40 F5
  Middleton M24,OL9 . . . . . . .65 D5
  Uppermill OL3 . . . . .50 E1
Broadgate Ho BL3 . . . . .40 F5
Broadgreen Gdns ☐ BL4 .42 D2
Broadhalgh Ave OL11 . . . .30 A7
Broadhalgh Rd OL11 . . . . .30 A6
Broadhaven Rd M40 . . . .160 D3
Broadhead Rd BL7 . . . . .9 E7
Broadhead Wlk M45 . . . . . .45 B1
Broadheath Cl BL5 . . . . .40 A1
Broadheath Prim Sch
  WA14 . . . . .119 C8
Broadhey View SK22 . .127 B1
Broadhill Rd
  Manchester M19 . . . . .110 E6
  Stalybridge SK15 . . . . .86 A5
Broadhurst M34 . . . . .101 A5
Broadhurst Ave
  Chadderton OL1 . . . . .48 C1
  Culcheth WA3 . . . . .91 F2
  Swinton M27 . . . . .61 F3
Broadhurst Ct ☐ BL3 .147 D4
Broadhurst Gr OL6 . . . . .85 C6
Broadhurst La WN6 . . . . . . .18 F7
Broadhurst Prim Sch
  M40 . . . . .83 C7
Broadhurst St
  ☐ Bolton BL3 . . . . .147 D4
  ☐ Radcliffe M26 . . . . .43 F5
  Stockport SK3 . . . . .170 F7
Broadlands WN6 . . . . .36 B6
Broadlands Rd M28 . . . . .79 C6
Broadlands Wlk ☐☐ M40 .83 A6
Broadlea Gr OL12 . . . . .14 C2
Broadlea Rd M19 . . . . .110 E5
Broadley Ave
  Golborne WA3 . . . . .90 C7
  Wythenshawe M22 . . . . . . .121 D4
Broadley Fold OL12 . . . .14 B6
Broadmeadow BL7 . . . . . .25 B8
Broadmeadow Ave M16 .97 F1
Broadmoss Dr M9 . . . . .65 A3
Broadmoss Rd M9 . . . . . . .65 A3
Broadmount Terr M9 . . . . .66 B4
Broadoak Ave
  Boothstown M28 . . . . .77 F7
  Wythenshawe M22 . . . . . . .121 C5
Broadoak Cres OL6 . . . . . .85 B5
Broadoak Ct M8 . . . . .156 B6
Broadoak Dr M22 . . . . . . .121 D5
Broadoak High Sch
  M31 .105 F2
Broadoak Prim Sch
  Ashton-u-L OL6 . . . . .85 C6
  Rochdale OL11 . . . . .29 E6
  Stockport SK7 . . . . .123 F2
Broadoak Rd
  Ashton-u-L OL6 . . . . .85 C6
  Rochdale OL11 . . . . .29 E6
  Stockport SK7 . . . . .123 F2
  Wythenshawe M22 . . . . . . .121 D4
  Wythenshawe M22 . . . . . . .121 D4
Broadoak St M35 . . . . .83 D3
Broadoaks Rd Sale M33 .108 A4
  Urmston M41 . . . . .95 B1
Broadriding Rd WN6 . . . .35 E6
Broadstone Ave OL4 . . . .49 F4
Broadstone Cl
  Prestwich M25 . . . . .63 A3
  Rochdale OL12 . . . . .14 A3
Broadstone Hall Prim Sch
  SK4 . . . . .111 D6
Broadstone Hall Rd N
  SK4 . . . . .111 D6
Broadstone Hall Rd S
  SK4,SK5 . . . . .111 E6
Broadstone Rd Bolton BL2 .25 D5
  Reddish SK4,SK5 . . . . .111 D6
Broadwalk M6 . . . . .81 A3
Broadway
  Altrincham WA15 . . . . .120 B1
  Chadderton,Stock Brook
    OL9 . . . . .152 A7
  Chadderton,White Gate End
    M40,OL9 . . . . .65 E2
  Cheadle SK8 . . . . .122 C4
  Droylsden M43 . . . . .100 A8
  Dukinfield SK14,SK16 . . . .101 B5
  Failsworth M35,M40 . . . . . .83 E8
  Farnworth BL4 . . . . .42 A1
  Haslingden BB4 . . . . .1 B8
  Hindley WN2 . . . . .57 A5
  Horwich BL6 . . . . .22 D3
  Irlam M44 . . . . .94 A1
  Over Hulton M46 . . . . .58 F5
  Partington M31 . . . . .106 A4
  Royton OL1,OL2 . . . . .48 D2

Broadway continued
  Sale M33 . . . . .108 A5
  Salford M50 . . . . .96 E8
  Stockport SK7 . . . . .124 C7
  Stockport,Bramhall Green
    SK7 . . . . .123 F2
  Urmston M41 . . . . .95 B4
  Walkden M28 . . . . .60 D1
  Wilmslow SK9 . . . . .137 B6
Broadway Ave M22 . . . .122 D5
Broadway Bsns Pk OL9 . .65 E4
Broadway Cl M41 . . . . .95 C5
Broadway Cres BB4 . . . . . . .1 A8
Broadway Ind Est
  Dukinfield SK16 . . . . .101 B6
  Salford M50 . . . . .161 A8
Broadway N M43 . . . . .100 A8
Broadway Prim Sch BB4 . .1 C8
Broadway St OL8 . . . . .66 F4
Broadway Sta M50 . . . . . . .96 F8
Broadway The M46 . . . . .112 E3
Broadwell Dr Leigh WN7 . .75 E1
  Manchester M9 . . . . .157 E7
Broadwood BL6 . . . . .40 C7
Broadwood Cl SK6 . . . . . .134 F7
Brocade Cl M3 . . . . .158 D3
Broche Cl OL11 . . . . .30 B3
Brock Ave BL2 . . . . .42 F7
Brock Cl M11 . . . . .99 D7
Brock Dr SK8 . . . . .132 B8
Brock Mill ☐ OL2 . . . . .48 F8
Brock Mill La WN1 . . . . . . .37 C4
Brock Pl WN2 . . . . .55 F2
Brock St Manchester M1 .159 B1
  Wigan WN1 . . . . .151 E8
Brockenhurst Dr BL2 . . . .25 F3
Brockford Dr M9 . . . . .64 E5
Brockholes SK13 . . . . .115 F8
Brockhurst Wlk WN3 . . . .150 A5
Brocklebank Rd
  Manchester M14 . . . . .110 D8
  Rochdale OL16 . . . . .31 D7
Brocklehurst Ave BL9 .140 F1
Brocklehurst St M9,M40 . .83 A8
Brockley Ave M14 . . . . .98 B2
Brockstedes Ave WN4 . . .72 E6
Brockton Wlk M8 . . . . .156 A8
Brocstedes Rd WN4 . . . . .72 D7
Brockton Ct M7 . . . . .63 E4
Brodick Dr BL2 . . . . .42 F6
Brodick St M40 . . . . .157 F8
Brodie Cl M30 . . . . .79 B2
Brogan St ☐ M18 . . . . . . .99 D5
Brogden Ave WA3 . . . . .91 E4
Brogden Dr SK8 . . . . .122 B5
Brogden Gr M33 . . . . .108 A3
Brogden Terr M33 . . . . . . .108 A3
Bromborough Ave ☐
  M20 .110 A8
Bromfield ☐ OL9 . . . . .139 F8
Bromfield Ave M9 . . . . .64 D1
Bromleigh Ave SK8 . . . . .122 B6
Bromley Ave
  Golborne WA3 . . . . .90 D7
  Royton OL2 . . . . .48 C6
  Urmston M41 . . . . .94 E1
Bromley Cl WN2 . . . . .38 A2
Bromley Cres OL6 . . . . . . .85 B6
Bromley Cross Rd BL7 . .25 B7
Bromley Cross Sta BL7 . .25 B7
Bromley Dr WN7 . . . . .75 D8
Bromley Rd M33 . . . . .108 C2
Bromley St
  Chadderton OL9 . . . . .66 A3
  Manchester M4 . . . . .159 B3
  Manchester M4,M40 . . . . .159 B3
Bromlow St M11 . . . . .83 C1
Brompton Ave M35 . . . . . .84 B8
Brompton Rd
  Manchester M14 . . . . .98 B2
  Stockport SK4 . . . . .168 A2
  Urmston M41 . . . . .95 F3
Brompton St OL4 . . . . .67 A5
Brompton Terr ☐ SK16 .166 B1
Brompton Way SK9 . . . . .131 C5
Brompton Wlk M40 . . . . . .83 B6
Bromsgrove Ave M30 . . . .79 B2
Bromshill Dr M7 . . . . .155 E6
Bromwich St Bolton BL2 .148 B6
Bronington Cl M22 . . . . . .121 E7
Bronte Ave BL9 . . . . .44 F6
Bronte Cl Bolton BL1 . . . .143 D1
  Oldham OL1 . . . . .49 D4
  Rochdale OL12 . . . . .14 A4
  Wigan WN3 . . . . .150 A5
Bronte St M15 . . . . .163 A5
Bronville Cl OL1 . . . . .48 C1
Brood Ford Cl OL10 . . . . . .28 F1
Brook Ave
  Altrincham WA15 . . . . .119 E6
  Droylsden M43 . . . . .83 E1
  Handforth SK9 . . . . .131 D4
  Manchester M19 . . . . .99 B2
  Reddish SK4 . . . . .111 D5
  Shaw OL2 . . . . .149 B8
  Swinton M27 . . . . .79 F7
Brook Bank Bolton BL2 . .25 D3
  Poynton SK12 . . . . .134 C2
Brook Bottom Rd SK22 .126 F1
Brook Cl
  Altrincham WA15 . . . . .119 E6
  Whitefield M45 . . . . .63 B8
Brook Ct
  ☐☐ Manchester M14 . . . . . .110 D8

Brook Ct continued
  Prestwich M25 . . . . .63 C1
Brook Dale Ct M33 . . . . .108 C1
Brook Dr Marple SK6 . . . .125 F4
  Tyldesley M29 . . . . .77 C5
  Whitefield M45 . . . . .63 B8
Brook Fm Cl M31 . . . . . .105 E2
Brook Fold La SK14 . . . .102 B2
Brook Gdns Bolton BL2 . .25 E4
Brook Green La M34 . . . . .29 C2
Brook Gr M44 . . . . .94 A2
Brook Green La M34 . . . .99 F3
Brook Hey Cl OL12 . . . . . .15 D4
Brook Ho Sale WA15 . . . .120 C7
Wigan WN1 . . . . .151 D8
Brook House Cl
  Bolton BL2 . . . . .25 E3
  Bury BL8 . . . . .26 E8
Brook La
  Alderley Edge SK9 . . . . . . .136 F3
  Altrincham WA15 . . . . .119 E6
  Oldham,Alexandra Park OL8 .67 B4
  Oldham,Salem OL4 . . . . . . .67 E6
  Rochdale OL16 . . . . .31 B3
  Uppermill OL3 . . . . .50 F2
  Whitefield BL9 . . . . .45 A4
  Wigan WN5 . . . . .54 B5
Brook Lo SK8 . . . . .122 D4
Brook Lynn Ave WA3 . . . .74 F1
Brook Mdw
  Glossop SK13 . . . . .104 E1
  Westhoughton BL5 . . . . .40 A1
Brook Mill ☐ BL7 . . . . .24 F7
Brook Rd Cheadle SK8 . .122 D6
  Manchester M14 . . . . .110 D7
  Reddish SK4 . . . . .111 C5
  Urmston M41 . . . . .95 A2
Brook St Ashton-in-M WN4 .73 C2
  Atherton M46 . . . . .58 B3
  Bolton BL1 . . . . .145 F7
  Bury BL9 . . . . .141 A3
  Chadderton OL9 . . . . .152 B8
  Cheadle SK8 . . . . .122 D4
  Failsworth M35 . . . . .83 D6
  Farnworth BL4 . . . . .42 E1
  ☐ Glossop SK13 . . . . .104 C1
  Golborne,Aspull Common
    WA3 . . . . .75 A1
  Golborne,Bank Heath WA3 .90 A8
  Hazel Grove SK7 . . . . .124 E2
  Hyde SK14 . . . . .167 E3
  Ince-in-M WN2 . . . . .56 A7
  Kearsley M26 . . . . .61 A7
  Littleborough OL15 . . . . .16 C5
  Manchester M1 . . . . .163 A7
  Oldham OL1 . . . . .67 A7
  Radcliffe M26 . . . . .44 B3
  Royton OL2 . . . . .48 D3
  Sale M33 . . . . .108 C5
  Swinton M27 . . . . .79 D8
  Wardle OL12 . . . . .15 C6
  Westhoughton BL5 . . . . .39 F1
  Wigan WN1 . . . . .54 F4
Brook St E OL6 . . . . .166 A2
Brook St W OL6 . . . . .166 A2
Brook Terr
  Manchester M13 . . . . .98 F3
  Newhey OL16 . . . . .32 C4
  Urmston M41 . . . . .95 C4
Brook The OL5 . . . . .6 C1
Brook View WN5 . . . . .137 A3
Brook Wlk M34 . . . . .112 F8
Brook's Bar M16 . . . . .97 D4
Brook's Pl ☐ OL12 . . . . .139 E8
Brook's Rd M16 . . . . .97 C3
Brookash Rd M22 . . . . . .131 A8
Brookbank Cl M24 . . . . . .65 B7
Brookbottom Rd M26 . . . .43 F6
Brookburn Prim Sch
  M21 .109 A7
Brookburn Rd M21 . . . . .109 A7
Brookcot Rd M23 . . . . . . .120 F7
Brookcroft Ave M22 . . . .121 D5
Brookcroft Rd M22 . . . . .121 D5
Brookdale
  Over Hulton M46 . . . . .58 F6
  Rochdale OL11 . . . . .30 C6
Brookdale Ave
  Denton M34 . . . . .101 B2
  Denton,Audenshaw M34 .100 F7
  Failsworth M40 . . . . .83 D4
  Marple SK6 . . . . .126 A4
Brookdale Cl Bolton BL1 .143 F2
  Romiley SK6 . . . . .112 F3
Brookdale Cotts SK2 . .124 F7
Brookdale Rd
  Bramhall SK7 . . . . .123 F1
  Hindley WN2 . . . . .56 F5
  Wythenshawe SK8 . . . . . . .121 F5
Brookdale Rise SK7 . . . .123 F1
Brookdale St M35 . . . . . . .83 E7
Brookdean Cl BL1 . . . . . .142 C3
Brookdene Rd
  Manchester M19 . . . . .110 E6
  Whitefield BL9 . . . . .45 A2
Brooke Dean Com Sch
  SK9 .131 D4
Brooke Dr SK9 . . . . .131 D4
Brooke Way SK9 . . . . .131 D4
Brookes St ☐☐ Bacup OL13 . .3 D8
  Middleton M24 . . . . .47 B2
Brookfield Atherton M46 . .58 B2
  Prestwich M25 . . . . .63 B4
  Shaw OL2 . . . . .32 A1
Brookfield Ave
  Ainsworth BL2 . . . . .26 C1
  Ainsworth BL2 . . . . .43 D8
  Altrincham WA15 . . . . .119 F8

Brookfield Ave continued
  Manchester M21 . . . . .109 C7
  Poynton SK6 . . . . .133 C3
  Romiley SK6 . . . . .113 A4
  Royton OL2 . . . . .48 D3
  Salford M6 . . . . .80 C3
  Salford M5 . . . . .80 C3
  Stockport SK1 . . . . .124 A7
  Urmston M41 . . . . .95 A2
Brookfield Bsns Pk SK8 .122 E5
Brookfield Cl SK1 . . . . . .124 A7
Brookfield Cres SK8 . . . .122 D4
Brookfield Ct ☐ M19 . . . .110 F8
Brookfield Dr
  Altrincham WA15 . . . . .120 A7
  Boothstown M28 . . . . .77 F6
  Littleborough OL15 . . . . .15 F6
  Swinton M27 . . . . .61 E1
Brookfield Gdns M22 . . .121 C6
Brookfield Gr OL6 . . . . . . .85 D2
Brookfield High Sch
  WN2 .56 E4
Brookfield Ho
  Cheadle SK8 . . . . .122 D4
  Ramsbottom BL0 . . . . .10 F3
Brookfield Ind Est SK13 .171 E2
Brookfield Rd Bury BL9 . .27 E8
  Cheadle SK8 . . . . .122 E5
  Culcheth WA3 . . . . .91 D3
  Eccles M30 . . . . .79 B4
  Manchester M8 . . . . .64 A1
  Shevington Moor WN6 . . . . .19 B2
  Up Holland WN8 . . . . .53 B7
Brookfield Rd Ind Est
  SK8 .122 F5
Brookfield St Bolton BL2 .148 B7
  Leigh WN7 . . . . .76 A6
  Newton-le-W WA12 . . . . .89 C3
  Oldham OL8 . . . . .153 F5
Brookfield Terr SK7 . . . .124 F4
Brookfold M35 . . . . .83 E8
Brookfold Rd SK4 . . . . . .111 D6
Brookhead Ave M20 . . . .109 F7
Brookhead Dr SK8 . . . . .123 A6
Brookhead Jun Sch
  SK8 .122 F5
Brookhey Ave BL3 . . . . . .147 F3
Brookheys Rd M31,
  WA3 . . . . .106 A2
Brookhill Cl OL3 . . . . .51 C5
Brookhill St M40 . . . . .160 E3
Brookhouse Ave
  Eccles M30 . . . . .95 A8
  Farnworth BL4 . . . . .60 C6
Brookhouse Sports Ctr
  M30 . . . . .94 F8
Brookhouse Terr WN1 . .151 D7
Brookhurst La M18 . . . . . .59 E6
Brookhurst Rd M18 . . . . . .99 D4
Brookland Ave
  Denton M34 . . . . .100 D2
  Farnworth BL4 . . . . .60 C7
  Hindley WN2 . . . . .56 D5
Brookland Gr BL1 . . . . . .142 A2
Brookland Rd WN1 . . . . . .37 B3
Brookland Terr BB4 . . . . . .2 F7
Brooklands Horwich BL6 .22 C3
  Wardle OL12 . . . . .15 C7
Brooklands Ave
  Ashton-in-M WN4 . . . . .73 D2
  Atherton M46 . . . . .58 D4
  Chadderton OL9 . . . . .152 B5
  Haslingden BB4 . . . . .1 B7
  Leigh WN7 . . . . .75 E3
  Manchester M24,M40 . . . .110 A6
Brooklands Cl
  Denton M34 . . . . .100 D4
  Irlam M44 . . . . .93 F2
  Mossley OL5 . . . . .68 B2
  Reddish SK4 . . . . .111 D5
Brooklands Cres M33 . .108 B3
Brooklands Dr
  Droylsden M43 . . . . .84 C3
  Glossop SK13 . . . . .116 B7
  Oldham OL4 . . . . .68 B6
  Orrell WN5 . . . . .53 D5
Brooklands Ho M33 . . . .108 B2
Brooklands Par OL4 . . . .68 B6
Brooklands Pl M33 . . . . .108 A3
Brooklands Prim Sch
  M33 .108 A2
Brooklands Rd
  Hazel Grove SK7 . . . . .124 E1
  Manchester M25,M8 . . . . . .63 E2
  Ramsbottom BL0 . . . . .11 A2
  Reddish SK5 . . . . .99 E2
  Sale M33 . . . . .108 A2
  Swinton M27 . . . . .79 E6
  Up Holland WN8 . . . . .53 D7
Brooklands Sta M33 . . . .108 A3
Brooklands Station App
  M33 .108 A2
Brooklawn Dr
  Manchester M20 . . . . .110 B4
  Prestwich M25 . . . . .63 C6

Brooklyn Ave
  Littleborough OL15 . . . . .16 A7
  Manchester M16 . . . . .97 C2
  Rochdale OL16 . . . . .15 E4
  Urmston M41 . . . . .94 E3
Brooklyn Cres SK8 . . . . .122 D5
Brooklyn Ct M14 . . . . . . .110 C7
Brooklyn Rd
  Cheadle SK8 . . . . .122 D5
  Stockport SK2 . . . . .124 C6
Brooklyn St Bolton BL1 . .143 E1
  ☐☐ Oldham OL1 . . . . .49 C1
Brooks Ave
  Hazel Grove SK7 . . . . .124 D3
  Hyde SK14 . . . . .167 E1
  Radcliffe M26 . . . . .43 F6
Brooks Dr
  Altrincham M23,WA15 . . . .120 D6
  Altrincham,Halebarns
    WA15 . . . . .129 D8
  Failsworth M35 . . . . .83 E6
Brooks End OL11 . . . . .13 E1
Brooks St ☐ WN7 . . . . . . .75 E8
Brooks St SK1 . . . . .170 F7
Brooksbottom Cl BL0 . . .11 C4
Brookshaw St Bury BL9 . .141 A4
  Droylsden M11 . . . . .83 C2
Brookside Glossop SK13 .116 B8
  Mossley OL5 . . . . .68 B2
  Oldham OL4 . . . . .67 D6
  Rowarth SK22 . . . . .127 E2
  Wigan WN3 . . . . .150 A5
Brookside Ave
  Ashton-in-M WN4 . . . . .72 F8
  Droylsden M43 . . . . .84 C3
  Farnworth BL4 . . . . .60 C7
  Oldham OL4 . . . . .68 B6
  Poynton SK12 . . . . .133 E3
  Stockport SK2 . . . . .124 F7
Brookside Bsns Pk M24 .65 D6
Brookside Cl
  Atherton M46 . . . . .58 E4
  Billinge WN5 . . . . .71 E5
  Bolton BL2 . . . . .25 D5
  Cheadle SK8 . . . . .122 D4
  Hadfield SK14 . . . . .171 F4
  Hyde SK14 . . . . .102 A3
  Ramsbottom BL0 . . . . .11 A3
Brookside Cres Bury BL8 .26 E8
  Middleton M24 . . . . .65 C6
  Walkden M28 . . . . .60 E3
Brookside Ct M19 . . . . . . .99 A2
Brookside Dr Hyde SK14 .102 A3
  Manchester M7 . . . . .63 D1
Brookside La SK6 . . . . . .134 E7
Brookside Miniature Rly*
  SK12 . . . . .133 F7
Brookside Prim Sch
  SK6 .134 E6
Brookside Rd Bolton BL2 . .42 D8
  Gatley SK8 . . . . .122 A6
  Manchester M40 . . . . .65 A1
  Sale M33 . . . . .108 A2
  Standish WN1 . . . . .20 B1
Brookside Terr Delph OL4 .50 E4
  Wigan WN3 . . . . .136 E3
Brookside Wlk M26 . . . . .43 F7
Brooksmouth BL8 . . . . . .140 D2
Brookstone Cl M21 . . . . .109 D6
Brookthorn Cl SK2 . . . . .124 F5
Brookthorpe Ave M19 . .110 E6
Brookthorpe Rd BL8 . . . .27 A3
Brookvale ☐ WN6 . . . . . .37 A1
Brookview ☐ WN6 . . . . . .56 D4
Brookville OL12 . . . . .4 C1
Brookwater Cl BL8 . . . . . .26 F6
Brookway
  Altrincham WA15 . . . . .119 F7
  Littleborough OL15 . . . . .16 A4
  Oldham OL4 . . . . .67 E5
  Uppermill OL4 . . . . .68 E6
Brookway Cl M19 . . . . . .110 E4
Brookway M23 . . . . .120 F7
Brookway High Sch & Sports
  Coll M23 . . . . .120 E7
Brookwood Ave
  Manchester M8 . . . . .156 C6
  Sale M33 . . . . .107 E3
Brookwood Cl M34 . . . . .113 A7
Broom Ave Leigh WN7 . . .75 E7
  Manchester M19 . . . . .111 B8
  Salford M7 . . . . .155 E8
Broom La
  Manchester M19 . . . . .111 B8
  Salford M7 . . . . .155 D8
Broom Rd
  Altrincham WA15 . . . . .119 E3
  Partington M31 . . . . .105 F2
  Wigan WN5 . . . . .54 D7
Broom St Bury BL8 . . . . .140 D2
  Newhey OL16 . . . . .32 B4
  Swinton M27 . . . . .79 F7
Broom Way BL5 . . . . .40 A2
Broome St OL9 . . . . .153 D6
Broomedge M7 . . . . .155 D8
Broomehouse Ave M44 .105 E8
Broomfield M6 . . . . .80 D6
Broomfield Cl
  Ainsworth BL2 . . . . .26 C1
  Reddish SK5 . . . . .111 F6
  Wilmslow SK9 . . . . .137 E8

Broomfield Cres
Middleton M24 ....46 D1
Stockport SK2 ....124 A4
Broomfield Dr
Manchester M8 ....155 F7
Reddish SK5 ....111 F6
Broomfield La WA15 ....119 E3
Broomfield Pl WN6 ....19 E1
Broomfield Rd
4 Bolton BL3 ....146 C4
Manchester SK4 ....168 C4
Standish WN6 ....19 E2
Broomfield Sq OL11 ....139 F5
Broomfield Terr
Newhey OL16 ....32 B4
Wigan WN1 ....151 E7
Broomfields M34 ....101 A5
Broomflat Cl WN6 ....19 E1
Broomgrove La M34 ....101 A4
Broomhall Rd
Manchester M9 ....64 B5
Pendlebury M27 ....80 D6
Broomhey Ave WN1 ....37 C4
Broomhey Terr WN1 ....151 E7
Broomhill Dr SK7 ....123 D1
Broomholme WN6 ....35 D7
Broomhurst Ave OL8 ....66 D4
Broomstair Rd M34 ....100 F6
Broomville Ave M33 ....108 B4
Broomwood Gdns
WA15 ....120 C5
Broomwood Prim Sch
WA15 ....120 D5
Broomwood Rd WA15 ....120 C5
Broomwood Wlk 3
M15 ....163 A6
Broseley Ave
Culcheth WA3 ....91 D4
Manchester M20 ....110 D3
Broseley La WA3 ....91 D5
Broseley Rd M16 ....97 A2
Brosscroft SK13 ....104 A6
Brosscroft Cl SK13 ....104 A6
Brosscroft Village SK13 .104 A6
Brotherdale Cl OL2 ....48 D5
Brotherod Hall Rd OL12 ....14 C2
Brotherton Cl M15 ....162 D6
Brotherton Dr M3 ....158 D2
Brotherton Way WA12 ....89 B4
Brough Cl WN2 ....56 E3
Brough St 4 M11 ....99 E7
Brougham St M28 ....60 C3
Broughton Ave
Golborne WA3 ....90 D7
Walkden M38 ....60 B4
Broughton Cl M24 ....46 D2
Broughton Jewish Cassel-Fox Prim Sch
M7 ....155 D8
Broughton La
Salford M7 ....155 D5
Salford M7,M8 ....158 E4
Broughton Rd
Reddish SK5 ....169 F4
Salford M6 ....81 A4
Broughton Rd E M6 ....81 B4
Broughton St Bolton BL1 .143 D2
Manchester M8 ....159 A4
Broughton Trade Ctr
M7 ....158 E4
Broughville Dr M20 ....122 C8
Brow Ave M24 ....65 C6
Brow St OL11 ....31 A4
Brow Wlk M9 ....64 D3
Browbeck OL1 ....153 E7
Browfield Ave M5 ....161 B8
Browfield Way OL1 ....48 E1
Browmere Dr M20 ....110 A4
Brown Bank Rd OL15 ....15 F3
Brown Edge Rd OL4 ....67 E4
Brown Heath Ave WN5 ....71 D3
Brown La SK8 ....122 B1
Brown Lodge Dr OL15 ....15 F3
Brown Lodge St OL15 ....15 F3
Brown St
3 Alderley Edge SK9 ....137 A1
Altrincham WA14 ....119 D3
Blackrod BL6 ....21 D2
Bolton BL1 ....145 F7
Chadderton OL9 ....152 A8
Failsworth M35 ....83 E7
Heywood OL10 ....29 D3
Ince-in-M WN2 ....56 A7
3 Leigh WN7 ....76 A5
Leigh,Bickershaw WN2 ....56 E1
Littleborough OL15 ....16 B5
Manchester M2 ....159 A1
Middleton M24 ....47 A2
Oldham OL1 ....67 A7
Radcliffe M26 ....43 F6
Ramsbottom BL0 ....138 B5
Salford M6 ....154 F1
Stockport SK1 ....169 E2
Tyldesley M29 ....76 F7
Wigan WN3 ....150 B7
Brown St N 2 WN7 ....76 A5
Brown St S 1 WN7 ....76 A4
Brown's La SK9 ....137 E8
Brownacre St M20 ....110 B6
Brownbank Wlk M15 ....162 F5
Browncross St M3 ....158 E1
Brownhill Countryside Ctr*
OL3 ....51 B1
Brownhill Dr OL4 ....68 A7
Brownhill La OL3 ....51 B1
Brownhill Sch OL12 ....14 E1
Brownhill St M11 ....165 A8
Brownhill View OL12 ....14 E1
Brownhills Cl BL8 ....27 A5
Browning Ave
Atherton M46 ....58 D5
Droylsden M43 ....84 A1
Wigan WN3 ....54 F4
Browning Cl BL1 ....143 D1
Browning Gr WN6 ....36 E3
Browning Rd
Middleton M24 ....47 B2
Oldham OL1 ....49 B1
Reddish SK5 ....99 E2
Swinton M27 ....79 E8
Browning St Leigh WN7 ....75 D6
Manchester M15 ....162 D6
Salford M3 ....158 D2
Browning Wlk M46 ....58 D5
Brownlea Ave SK16 ....101 C7
Brownley Court Rd
M22 ....121 D5
Brownley Ct M22 ....121 E5
Brownley Rd M22 ....121 E4
Brownlow Ave
Ince-in-M WN2 ....56 B7
Royton OL2 ....49 A3
Brownlow Bsns Ctr BL1 .143 D1
Brownlow Cl SK12 ....133 E2
Brownlow Fold Prim Sch
BL1 ....143 D1
Brownlow La WN5 ....53 C1
Brownlow Rd BL6 ....22 C5
Brownlow Way BL1 ....143 E1
Brownmere WN6 ....36 F2
Browns Rd BL2 ....43 B6
Brownside Cl OL16 ....15 C3
Brownslow Wlk 11 M13 .163 B7
Brownson Wlk 7 M9 ....157 E8
Brownsville Rd SK4 ....111 C5
Brownville Gr SK16 ....101 E7
Brownwood Ave SK1 ....112 B1
Brownwood Cl M33 ....108 C1
Brows Ave M23 ....109 A2
Browsholm Ho BL1 ....144 C7
Broxton Ave Bolton BL3 ....146 B3
Orrell WN5 ....53 F7
Broxton St M40 ....160 F3
Broxwood Cl 8 M18 ....99 D5
Bruce St OL11 ....30 C4
Bruce Wlk 2 M11 ....99 D7
Brundage Rd M22 ....121 D2
Brundrett Pl 7 M33 ....107 F4
Brundrett St SK1 ....124 A8
Brundrett's Rd M21 ....109 B8
Brunel Ave M5 ....81 B1
Brunel Cl M32 ....96 E2
Brunel St Bolton BL1 ....143 D3
Horwich BL6 ....22 C2
Brunet Wlk M12 ....164 F6
Brunstead Cl M23 ....120 D6
Brunswick Ave BL6 ....22 E2
Brunswick Ct BL1 ....145 E8
Brunswick Rd
Altrincham WA14 ....119 D7
Manchester M20 ....110 C7
Brunswick Sq OL1 ....153 F6
Brunswick St Bury BL9 ....140 F3
Dukinfield SK16 ....101 C8
3 Heywood OL10 ....29 C2
Leigh WN7 ....76 A4
Manchester M13 ....163 B6
Mossley OL5 ....86 D8
Oldham OL1 ....153 E6
Rochdale OL16 ....31 A8
Shaw OL2 ....149 B7
Stretford M32 ....108 D8
Walsden OL14 ....6 A7
Brunswick Terr OL13 ....3 D8
Brunt St M14 ....98 B3
Brunton Rd SK5 ....111 F6
Bruntwood Ave SK8 ....122 A1
Bruntwood La
Cheadle SK8 ....122 E1
Cheadle,Cheadle Hulme
SK8 ....122 E2
Bruntwood Prim Sch
SK8 ....122 E2
Brushes Ave SK15 ....86 D3
Brushes Rd SK15 ....86 E2
Brussels Rd SK3 ....170 D6
Bruton Ave M32 ....96 B1
Brutus Wlk M7 ....155 E6
Bryan Rd M21 ....97 B2
Bryan St 1 OL4 ....49 C1
Bryant Cl M13 ....163 C5
Bryant's Acre BL1 ....40 D7
Bryantsfield BL1 ....40 D6
Bryce St Bolton BL3 ....145 E5
Hyde SK14 ....167 D4
Brydges Rd SK6 ....125 E5
Brydon Ave M12 ....163 C7
Brydon Cl M6 ....154 F2
Bryham St WN1 ....151 D8
Bryn Cross WN4 ....73 A6
Bryn Dr SK5 ....111 F5
Bryn Gates La WN2 ....73 D8
Bryn Lea Terr BL1 ....142 A4
Bryn Rd WN4 ....73 B5
Bryn Rd S WN4 ....73 C4
Bryn St Ashton-in-M WN4 ....73 B3
Ince-in-M WN3 ....151 E6
Bryn St Peter's CE Prim Sch
WN4 ....72 F6
Bryn Sta WN4 ....73 A6
Bryn Wlk BL1 ....145 F8
Bryndale Gr M33 ....107 F1
Brynden Ave M20 ....110 C5
Brynford Ave M9 ....64 A5
Bryngs Dr BL2 ....25 F4
Brynhall Cl M26 ....43 E5
Brynheys Cl M38 ....60 A5
Brynn St WN2 ....73 F7
Brynorme Rd M8 ....64 A2
Brynton Rd M13 ....98 E2
Bryone Dr SK2 ....124 B5
Bryony Cl Orrell WN5 ....53 D5
Walkden M28 ....60 D5
6 Wythenshawe M22 ....121 C1
Bryson Wlk M18 ....165 C5
Buchan St M11 ....83 B2
Buchanan Dr WN2 ....57 B3
Buchanan Rd WN5 ....54 E7
Buchanan St Leigh WN7 ....75 E5
Ramsbottom BL0 ....138 B5
Swinton M27 ....61 F1
Buck La M33 ....107 E6
Buck St WN7 ....75 F4
Buckden Rd SK4 ....111 D7
Buckden Wlk 11 M23 ....108 F2
Buckfast Ave
Haydock WA11 ....89 A7
Oldham OL8 ....67 D3
Buckfast Cl
Altrincham WA15 ....120 B2
Cheadle SK8 ....132 B6
Manchester M21 ....97 B1
Poynton SK12 ....133 D5
Buckfast Rd
Middleton M24 ....46 F3
Sale M33 ....107 E6
Buckfast Wlk M7 ....155 E6
Buckfield Ave M5 ....161 B7
Buckhurst Rd
Manchester M19 ....99 A1
Ramsbottom BL9 ....12 C3
Buckingham Ave
Denton M34 ....101 B2
Horwich BL6 ....22 E2
Salford M6 ....154 D2
Whitefield M45 ....63 A7
Buckingham Cl WN5 ....54 E5
Buckingham Dr Bury BL8 ....44 B8
Dukinfield SK16 ....101 F7
Buckingham Park Cl
OL2 ....149 B8
Buckingham Pl
Manchester M21 ....97 B1
Tyldesley M29 ....58 F3
Buckingham Rd
Cheadle SK8 ....123 A3
Droylsden M43 ....83 E1
Irlam M44 ....105 C6
Manchester M21 ....97 B1
Manchester,Heaton Chapel
SK4 ....111 C6
Manchester,Heaton Moor
SK4 ....111 B5
Manchester,Hilton Park
M25 ....63 C2
Poynton SK12 ....133 D3
Sale WA14 ....107 F1
Stalybridge SK15 ....86 A3
Stretford M32 ....96 F4
Swinton M27 ....62 A2
Wilmslow SK9 ....136 F6
Buckingham Rd W SK4 .168 A4
Buckingham St
12 Rochdale OL16 ....31 A8
Salford M5 ....154 F1
Stockport SK2 ....124 A6
Buckingham Way
Altrincham WA15 ....120 A7
Stockport SK2 ....170 F6
Buckland Ave M9 ....64 A3
Buckland Dr WN5 ....36 B1
Buckland Gr SK14 ....114 A8
Buckland Rd M6 ....154 D4
Buckle Ho 7 M30 ....79 E2
Buckley Ave M18 ....99 C4
Buckley Barn Ct OL11 ....30 C1
Buckley Bldgs OL5 ....86 E8
Buckley Brook St OL12 ....15 B2
Buckley Chase OL16 ....31 E5
Buckley Cl SK14 ....113 E7
Buckley Dr Denshaw OL3 ....33 C1
Romiley SK6 ....113 A1
Buckley Farm La OL12 ....15 B3
Buckley Fields OL12 ....15 A2
Buckley Hall Ind Est
OL12 ....15 B3
Buckley Hill La OL16 ....31 E5
Buckley Ho M46 ....58 D3
Buckley La Farnworth BL4 ....60 C7
Prestwich M25 ....62 E3
Rochdale OL12 ....15 B3
Buckley Rd
Manchester M18 ....99 C4
Oldham OL4 ....67 D8
Rochdale OL12 ....15 B2
Buckley Sq BL4 ....60 C6
Buckley St Bury BL9 ....140 F3
Chadderton OL9 ....152 A7
Denton M34 ....100 D7
Droylsden M43 ....84 A1
Heywood OL10 ....29 E3
Manchester M11 ....99 E7
Oldham OL4 ....67 E5
Radcliffe M26 ....44 A3
Reddish SK5 ....99 E2
Rochdale OL16 ....31 A8
Shaw OL2 ....149 C7
Stalybridge SK15 ....101 F8
Uppermill OL3 ....69 B8
Wigan WN6 ....37 B2
Buckley St W WN6 ....37 A2
Buckley Terr OL12 ....15 B3
Buckley View OL12 ....15 B3
Bucklow Ave
Manchester M14 ....98 B1
Partington M31 ....105 F4
Bucklow Cl
Broadbottom SK14 ....102 F1
Oldham OL4 ....49 E4
Bucklow Dr M22 ....121 E8
Bucklow Gdns WA13 ....117 A4
Bucklow Ho M22 ....121 F7
Bucklow View WA14 ....119 A3
Bucknell Ct M40 ....159 C4
Buckstones Jun & Inf Sch
OL2 ....49 D8
Buckstones Rd OL1,OL2 ....49 E7
Buckthorn Cl
Altrincham WA15 ....120 E5
Manchester M21 ....109 D6
Westhoughton BL5 ....39 F2
Buckthorn La M30 ....94 F8
Buckton Cl OL3 ....51 C5
Buckton Dr SK15 ....86 E5
Buckton Vale Mews SK15 .86 F7
Buckton Vale Prim Sch
SK15 ....86 F7
Buckton Vale Rd
Mossley,Carrbrook SK15 ....86 F6
Mossley,Millbrook SK15 ....86 D4
Buckwood Cl SK7 ....125 A3
Buddleia Gr M7 ....155 D6
Bude Ave
Brinnington SK5 ....112 B5
Tyldesley M29 ....77 C8
Urmston M41 ....107 B8
Bude Cl SK7 ....132 F7
Bude Terr 4 SK16 ....166 B1
Bude Wlk M23 ....121 B5
Budsworth Ave M20 ....110 B7
Budworth Gdns 2 M43 ....84 B1
Budworth Rd M33 ....108 E3
Budworth Wlk 1 SK9 ....131 E1
Buer Ave WN3 ....54 F4
Buersil Ave OL16 ....31 B4
Buersil St OL16 ....31 B3
Buerton Ave M9 ....64 A5
Buffalo Ct M50 ....96 E8
Buffoline Trad Est M19 ....99 B1
Bugle St M1 ....162 E8
Buile Dr M9 ....64 F4
Buile Hill Ave M38 ....60 B5
Buile Hill Dr M5 ....154 D3
Buile Hill Gr M38 ....60 B5
Buile Hill High Sch M6 .154 D4
Buile St M7 ....155 E7
Buille Ho M6 ....154 E3
Bulford Ave M22 ....121 B2
Bulkeley Rd Cheadle SK8 .122 E6
Handforth SK9 ....131 D3
Poynton SK12 ....133 E3
Bulkeley St SK3 ....170 D8
Bull Hill Cres M26 ....62 B8
Bullcote Gn OL2 ....49 B4
Bullcote La OL1,OL2 ....49 B4
Bullcroft Dr M29 ....77 C6
Buller Mews BL8 ....27 B1
Buller Rd M13 ....98 F2
Buller St Bury BL8 ....27 C1
Droylsden M43 ....100 B8
Farnworth BL3 ....42 C2
Oldham OL4 ....67 D8
Bullfinch Dr BL9 ....28 B5
Bullfinch Wlk M21 ....109 D7
Bullock St SK1 ....170 F7
Bullough Moor Prim Sch
OL10 ....29 B1
Bullough St Atherton M46 .58 C2
Atherton M46 ....58 C3
Bullows Rd M38 ....59 F6
Bullrush Cl M28 ....60 D5
Bulteel St Bolton BL3 ....146 C2
Boothstown M28 ....77 E7
Eccles M30 ....79 B3
Wigan WN5 ....54 D6
Bulwer St OL16 ....31 A8
Bungalow Rd WA12 ....89 E1
Bungalows The
Ashton-in-M WN4 ....72 F7
Hazel Grove SK7 ....124 F4
New Mills SK22 ....127 D1
Bunkers OL3 ....69 C6
Bunkers Hill M45 ....62 D3
Bunkers Hill Rd SK14 ....102 E1
Bunkershill Rd SK6 ....113 B1
Bunsen St M1 ....159 B1
Bunting Cl 6 WA3 ....90 E8
Bunting Mews M28 ....78 B8
Bunyan Cl OL1 ....49 E4
Bunyan St 24 OL12 ....14 F1
Bunyard St M8 ....156 B6
BUPA Hospl Manchester
M16 ....97 D3
Burbage Bank 5 SK13 ....171 E1
Burbage Gr 23 SK13 ....171 E2
Burbage Rd M23 ....121 A2
Burbage Way 24 SK13 ....171 E2
Burbridge Cl M11 ....160 E1
Burchall Field OL16 ....31 B7
Burdale Dr M6 ....80 B4
Burdale Wlk M23 ....108 F1
Burder St 4 OL8 ....66 C2
Burdett Ave OL12 ....13 F1
Burdett Way M12 ....164 E5
Burdith Ave M14 ....98 A2
Burdon Ave M22 ....121 E3
Burford Ave
Bramhall SK7 ....132 D5
Manchester M16 ....97 D2
Burford Ave *continued*
Urmston M41 ....95 E4
Burford Cl SK9 ....136 E5
Burford Cres SK9 ....136 E5
Burford Dr Bolton BL3 ....145 E5
Manchester M16 ....97 D2
Swinton M27 ....61 E2
Burford Gr M33 ....107 E1
Burford La WA13 ....117 C2
Burford Rd M16 ....97 D2
Burford Wlk M16 ....97 D2
Burgess Ave OL6 ....85 C5
Burgess Dr M35 ....83 F7
Burgess Prim Sch M9 ....157 E7
Burgess St WN3 ....151 E5
Burghley Ave OL4 ....67 D6
Burghley Cl
Little Lever M26 ....43 B5
Stalybridge SK15 ....86 A2
Burghley Dr M26 ....43 B5
Burghley Way WN3 ....151 F5
Burgin Wlk M40 ....156 C5
Burgundy Dr BL8 ....26 F7
Burke St BL1 ....143 D2
Burkhardt Dr WA12 ....89 E3
Burkitt St SK14 ....167 E2
Burland Cl M7 ....155 D5
Burland St WN5 ....54 F7
Burleigh Cl SK7 ....124 A1
Burleigh Ct M32 ....96 E4
Burleigh Mews M21 ....109 B6
Burleigh Rd M32 ....96 E4
Burleigh St M15 ....163 B5
Burlescombe Cl WA14 ....119 B6
Burley Ave WA3 ....74 D1
Burley Cres WN3 ....54 C2
Burley Ct SK4 ....168 C2
Burleyhurst La SK9,
WA16 ....136 B7
Burlin Ct 9 M16 ....97 D3
Burlington Ave OL8 ....66 E4
Burlington Cl SK4 ....110 E2
Burlington Ct WA14 ....119 D5
Burlington Dr SK3 ....123 F4
Burlington Gdns SK3 ....123 F4
Burlington Ho OL6 ....166 A3
Burlington Mews SK3 ....123 F4
Burlington Rd
Altrincham WA14 ....119 D5
Eccles M30 ....79 E4
Manchester M20 ....110 C7
Burlington St
Ashton-u-L OL6,OL7 ....166 A3
Hindley WN2 ....56 D5
Hindley WN2 ....56 E5
Manchester M13,M15 ....163 B5
Manchester M15 ....163 A5
12 Rochdale OL11 ....31 A4
Burlton Gr WN2 ....38 A2
Burman St M11,M43 ....99 F7
Burn Bank OL3 ....68 F5
Burnaby St Bolton BL3 ....145 D5
Oldham OL8 ....153 D5
Rochdale OL11 ....30 C4
Burnage Ave M19 ....110 F8
Burnage Hall Rd M19 ....110 F7
Burnage High Sch For Boys
M19 ....110 E5
Burnage La M19 ....110 F4
Burnage Range M19 ....99 A1
Burnage Sta M20 ....110 D4
Burnaston Gr WN5 ....54 D5
Burnbray Ave M19 ....110 E6
Burnby Wlk M23 ....108 F1
Burndale Dr BL9 ....45 A3
Burnden Ind Est BL3 ....42 B4
Burnden Rd BL3 ....148 B5
Burnden Way BL6 ....39 C7
Burnedge Cl OL12 ....4 D2
Burnedge Fold Rd OL4 ....68 D6
Burnedge La OL4 ....68 D7
Burnedge Mews OL4 ....68 D6
Burnell Cl M40 ....160 D3
Burnell Ct OL10 ....46 D7
Burneside Cres M24 ....46 E3
Burnet Cl Rochdale OL16 ....31 C4
Tyldesley M29 ....77 B7
Burnett Ave M5 ....161 B8
Burnett Cl M40 ....157 D5
Burnfell WA3 ....90 E7
Burnfield Rd
Manchester M18 ....99 D3
Reddish SK5 ....99 F3
Burnham Ave Bolton BL1 .142 A1
Reddish SK5 ....99 F1
Burnham Cl Cheadle SK8 .122 F2
Culcheth WA3 ....91 E4
Burnham Dr
Manchester M19 ....110 F8
Urmston M41 ....95 C3
Burnham Gr WN2 ....37 F2
Burnham Rd M34 ....100 A3
Burnham Wlk 3 BL4 ....42 D1
Burnhill Ct WN6 ....36 E8
Burnleigh Ct BL5 ....58 F8
Burnley Brow Com Sch
OL9 ....152 C8
Burnley La
Chadderton OL1,OL9 ....48 A2
Chadderton,Busk OL9 ....48 C1
Burnley Rd Bury BL9 ....27 E8
Edenfield BL0 ....1 D5
Burnley Rd E BB4 ....2 E8
Burnley St
Chadderton OL9 ....152 B8
Failsworth M35 ....84 A8
Burnmoor Rd BL2 ....42 F8
Burns Ave Atherton M46 ....58 D5

Burns Ave *continued*
Bury BL9 . . . . .44 F6
Cheadle SK8 . . . . .122 F6
Leigh WN7 . . . . .75 C8
Swinton M27 . . . . .61 D1
Burns Cl Ashton-in-M WN4 . .72 F6
Longshaw WN5 . . . . .53 D1
Manchester M11 . . . . .160 F1
Oldham OL1 . . . . .49 E5
Wigan WN3 . . . . .55 A4
Burns Cres SK2 . . . . .124 E7
Burns Ct OL11 . . . . .29 E6
Burns Fold SK16 . . . . .102 A7
Burns Gdns M25 . . . . .62 F3
Burns Gr M43 . . . . .84 A2
Burns Rd 6 Abram WN2 . . .56 B1
Denton M34 . . . . .113 A7
Walkden M38 . . . . .60 B5
Burns St Bolton BL3 . . . . . .145 F6
Heywood OL10 . . . . .29 E1
Burnsall Ave
Golborne WA3 . . . . .90 F8
Whitefield M45 . . . . .62 D8
Burnsall Gr OL2 . . . . .48 D4
Burnsall Wlk 2 M22 . . . .121 A2
Burnside
Altrincham WA15 . . . . .129 D7
Edenfield BL0 . . . . .1 D2
Hadfield SK14 . . . . .171 F4
Shaw OL2 . . . . .49 D8
Stalybridge SK15 . . . . .102 D7
Burnside Ave
Reddish SK4 . . . . .111 E6
Salford M6 . . . . .80 B5
Burnside Cl
Heywood OL10 . . . . .29 D1
Radcliffe M26 . . . . .43 F7
Romiley SK6 . . . . .112 F3
Stalybridge SK15 . . . . .102 D7
Tyldesley M29 . . . . .77 B7
Wilmslow SK9 . . . . .137 C6
Burnside Dr M19 . . . . .110 F7
Burnside Rd Bolton BL1 . . .142 B2
Gatley SK8 . . . . .122 B5
Rochdale OL16 . . . . .31 C6
Burnt Edge La BL6 . . . . . . .23 B5
Burnthorp Ave M9 . . . . .64 B3
Burnthorpe Cl OL11 . . . . . .29 E6
Burntwood Wlk 22 M9 . . .157 E8
Burnvale WN3 . . . . .54 D2
Burran Rd M22 . . . . .130 D8
Burrington Dr WN7 . . . . . .75 D7
Burrows Ave M21 . . . . . . .109 C6
Burrows Yd WN1 . . . . . . .150 C8
Burrs Cl BL8 . . . . .27 C6
Burrs Ctry Pk BL8 . . . . .27 D6
Burrs Lea Cl BL9 . . . . .27 E6
Burrswood Ave BL9 . . . . . .27 F6
Bursar Cl WA12 . . . . .89 D4
Burslem Ave M20 . . . . . . .110 A8
Burstead St M18 . . . . .99 E7
Burstock St M4 . . . . .159 B3
Burston St M18 . . . . .165 C6
Burtinshaw St 7 M18 . . . .99 D5
Burton Ave
Bury BL8 . . . . .26 F4
Manchester M20 . . . . .110 B6
Sale WA15 . . . . .108 A1
Burton Cl WA3 . . . . .91 F3
Burton Dr SK12 . . . . .133 D4
Burton Gr M28 . . . . .79 C8
Burton Rd M20 . . . . .110 A6
Burton St
Manchester M40 . . . . .159 B4
Middleton M24 . . . . .64 F8
Oldham OL4 . . . . .67 E5
Stockport SK4 . . . . .169 E3
Burton Wlk Salford M3 . . .158 D2
Stockport SK4 . . . . .169 E3
Burtonwood Ct M24 . . . . . .46 F1
Burtree St M12 . . . . .165 A6
Burwell Ave PR7 . . . . .19 D8
Burwell Cl Bolton BL3 . . . .147 D4
Glossop SK13 . . . . .116 A8
6 Leigh WN7 . . . . .76 A4
Rochdale OL12 . . . . .14 D4
Burwell Gr M23 . . . . .120 F7
Bury & Bolton Rd M26 . . . .43 E7
Bury & Rochdale Old Rd
BL9,OL10 . . . . .29 B5
Bury Art Gall & Mus★
BL9 . . . . .140 E2
Bury Ave M16 . . . . .97 C2
Bury Bolton Street Sta★
BL9 . . . . .140 E2
Bury Bsns Ctr BL9 . . . . . .141 A4
Bury CE High Sch BL9 . . . .44 D8
Bury Coll (Millenium Ctr)
BL9 . . . . .140 F1
Bury Coll (Peel Ctr)
BL9 . . . . .140 E1
Bury Coll (woodbury Ctr)
BL9 . . . . .140 E1
Bury FC (Gigg La) BL9 . . . .44 F7
Bury Gram Jun Sch BL9 .140 D2
Bury Gram Sch BL9 . . . . .140 D2
Bury Intc BL9 . . . . .140 E2
Bury New Rd
Ainsworth BL2,M26 . . . . . . .43 B7
Bolton BL1,BL2 . . . . .148 A7
Bury BL9 . . . . .141 C2
Heywood BL9,OL10 . . . . . . .28 E2
Prestwich M25 . . . . .63 B3
Ramsbottom BL0 . . . . .11 D6
Salford M7,M8,M25 . . . . . .155 E5
Whitefield M45 . . . . .62 F7
Bury Old Rd
Ainsworth BL2 . . . . .26 B1
Bolton BL2 . . . . .148 A7
Bury Old Rd *continued*
Bolton BL2 . . . . .148 B7
Edenfield BL0 . . . . .1 F1
Heywood BL9,OL10 . . . . . . .28 E1
Prestwich M25,M45,M7,M8 .63 C4
Ramsbottom BL9 . . . . .11 F4
Bury Pl M11 . . . . .83 C2
Bury RC Prep Sch BL9 . . . .44 E8
Bury Rd Bolton BL2 . . . . . . .42 D7
Bury BL8 . . . . .27 A5
Edenfield BL0 . . . . .1 D3
Edgworth BL7 . . . . .9 E5
Radcliffe BL9,M26 . . . . .44 C5
Rawtenstall BB4 . . . . .1 E7
Rochdale OL11 . . . . .30 B6
Bury St Heywood OL10 . . . . .29 B2
Mossley OL5 . . . . .86 C8
Radcliffe M26 . . . . .44 D4
Reddish SK5 . . . . .169 F3
Salford M3 . . . . .158 E2
Bury Sta BL9 . . . . .140 E2
Bury Transport Mus★
BL9 . . . . .140 E2
Bury Whitefield Jewish Prim
Sch BL9 . . . . .45 B3
Bush Moor Wlk M13 . . . . .164 D5
Bush St M40 . . . . .157 E5
Bushell St BL3 . . . . .146 B4
Bushey Dr M23 . . . . .121 A5
Busheyfield Cl SK14 . . . . .101 D5
Bushfield Wlk 1 M23 . . .120 E7
Bushgrove Wlk M9 . . . . . . .64 D5
Bushnay Wlk 9 M8 . . . . .156 B6
Bushnell Wlk 1 M9 . . . . . .64 E5
Bushton Wlk 9 M40 . . . . .156 C5
Busk Rd OL9 . . . . .152 C8
Busk Wlk OL9 . . . . .152 C8
Butcher La
Bury BL9 . . . . .140 F2
Royton OL2 . . . . .48 C5
Wythenshawe M23 . . . . . . .120 D7
Butcherfield Row WN2 . . . .38 B7
Butchers La WN4 . . . . .73 B3
Bute Ave OL8 . . . . .66 F3
Bute St Bolton BL1 . . . . . . .142 B1
Glossop SK13 . . . . .104 E3
Manchester M40 . . . . .157 F8
Salford M5,M50 . . . . .154 D1
Butler Ct 11 M40 . . . . .159 C3
Butler Gn OL9 . . . . .66 A4
Butler La M4,M40 . . . . . . .159 C3
Butler St
Manchester M4,M40 . . . . . .160 D2
Ramsbottom BL0 . . . . .138 A5
Wigan WN1 . . . . .151 D8
Butley St SK7 . . . . .124 E4
Butman St M18 . . . . .99 F6
Butt Hill Ave M25 . . . . .63 B3
Butt Hill Ct M25 . . . . .63 B3
Butt Hill Dr M25 . . . . .63 B3
Butt Hill Rd M25 . . . . .63 B3
Butt La OL4 . . . . .68 B4
Butter La 5 M3 . . . . .158 F1
Buttercup Ave 7 M28 . . . .59 F3
Buttercup Cl M46 . . . . .58 D5
Buttercup Dr Oldham OL4 .49 D2
Rochdale OL11 . . . . .30 B3
Stockport SK3 . . . . .170 D5
Butterfield Cl SK8 . . . . . .123 B1
Butterfield Rd BL5 . . . . . . .58 F8
Butterhouse La OL3 . . . . . .51 C2
Butterley Cl SK16 . . . . . . .101 F7
Buttermere Ave
Ashton-in-M WN4 . . . . .73 B5
Heywood OL10 . . . . .46 D8
Swinton M27 . . . . .79 F6
2 Wythenshawe M22 . . . . .121 C2
Buttermere Cl
Little Lever BL3 . . . . .42 F4
Stretford M32 . . . . .96 C3
Buttermere Dr
Altrincham WA15 . . . . .129 D6
Middleton M24 . . . . .46 E2
Ramsbottom BL0 . . . . .138 B7
Buttermere Gr OL2 . . . . . .48 D7
Buttermere Rd
Ashton-u-L OL7 . . . . .166 A4
Farnworth BL4 . . . . .59 E8
Gatley SK8 . . . . .122 B3
Oldham OL4 . . . . .67 D8
Partington M31 . . . . .105 E3
Wigan WN5 . . . . .54 C7
Buttermere Terr SK15 . . . .86 A3
Buttermill Cl 4 M44 . . . . .94 B3
Butterstile Ave M25 . . . . . .62 F1
Butterstile La M25 . . . . . . .63 A3
Butterstile Prim Sch
M25 . . . . .63 A2
Butterwick Cl M12 . . . . .99 B3
Butterwick Field BL6 . . . . .21 F3
Butterworth Hall OL16 . . . .32 A5
Butterworth La M40,OL9 . .65 E2
Butterworth St
Chadderton OL9 . . . . .152 B8
4 Littleborough OL15 . . . . .16 A5
Manchester M11 . . . . .165 A8
Middleton M24 . . . . .65 C7
Radcliffe M26 . . . . .44 B4
Butterworth Way OL3 . . . .69 B5
Butteryhouse La WA15 . . .120 E2
Button Hole OL2 . . . . .49 D7
Button La M23 . . . . .109 A2
Button La Prim Sch
M23 . . . . .108 F2
Buttons Row BB4 . . . . .2 F6
Buttress St M18 . . . . .165 C6
Butts Ave WN7 . . . . .76 C3
Butts Ave The 3 OL16 . . .139 F7
Butts Ct WN7 . . . . .76 A4
Butts La OL3 . . . . .50 D4
Butts St WN7 . . . . .76 B3
Butts The 2 OL16 . . . . . .139 F7
Buxted Rd OL1 . . . . .49 B1
Buxton Ave Ashton-u-L OL6 .85 F6
Manchester M20 . . . . .109 F6
Buxton Cl Atherton M46 . . . .58 E4
18 Gamesley SK13 . . . . . . .171 E2
Buxton Cres
Rochdale OL16 . . . . .31 B4
Sale M33 . . . . .108 D1
Buxton La Droylsden M43 . .83 E1
Marple SK6 . . . . .125 E5
Buxton Mews SK13 . . . . . .171 E2
Buxton Old Rd SK12 . . . . .135 E4
Buxton Pl OL8 . . . . .153 E5
Buxton Rd Disley SK12 . . .135 E6
High Lane SK6,SK7,SK12 . .134 D8
Stockport SK2 . . . . .124 B5
Stretford M32 . . . . .96 A3
Buxton Rd W SK12 . . . . . .135 B5
Buxton St Bury BL8 . . . . . . .27 C2
Gatley SK8 . . . . .122 A5
Hazel Grove SK7 . . . . .124 D3
Heywood OL10 . . . . .29 D1
Manchester M1 . . . . .163 B8
Whitworth OL12 . . . . .4 D3
Buxton Terr SK14 . . . . . . .103 D5
Buxton Way 3 M34 . . . . .113 A8
Buxton Wlk 1 SK13 . . . . .171 E1
Bycroft Wlk M40 . . . . .83 D4
Bye Rd BL0 . . . . .11 E8
Bye St M34 . . . . .100 F7
Byfield Rd M22 . . . . .121 C4
Byfleet Cl WN3 . . . . .54 C1
Byland Ave Cheadle SK8 . .132 B6
Oldham OL4 . . . . .67 D4
Byland Cl BL1 . . . . .143 E2
Byland Gdns M26 . . . . .43 E5
Byland Wlk 3 M22 . . . . . .121 D1
Bylands Cl SK12 . . . . .133 D4
Bylands Fold SK16 . . . . . .101 D6
Byley Rise WN6 . . . . .36 E8
Byng Ave M44 . . . . .105 D4
Byng St Farnworth BL4 . . . .60 D8
Heywood OL10 . . . . .46 E8
Byrchall High Sch The
WN4 . . . . .73 B1
Byrcland Cl M12 . . . . .164 E8
Byre Cl M23 . . . . .109 A3
Byre View PR6 . . . . .20 F8
Byrness Cl M46 . . . . .58 E4
Byrom Ave M19 . . . . .99 C1
Byrom Ct M43 . . . . .83 F1
Byrom La WA3 . . . . .74 F2
Byrom St
Altrincham WA14 . . . . .119 D3
9 Bury BL8 . . . . .27 B4
Manchester M3 . . . . .162 E8
Manchester,Old Trafford
M16 . . . . .97 D4
Salford M5 . . . . .161 A8
Byron Ave Droylsden M43 . .84 A2
13 Hindley WN2 . . . . .56 D5
Prestwich M25 . . . . .62 F3
Radcliffe M26 . . . . .43 E4
Swinton M27 . . . . .79 E8
Byron Cl Abram WN2 . . . . . .56 B1
3 Orrell WN5 . . . . .53 F7
Wigan WN6 . . . . .36 E3
Byron Cres PR7 . . . . .19 F8
Byron Ct WA14 . . . . .119 D6
Byron Dr SK8 . . . . .122 F6
Byron Gr Atherton M46 . . . .58 D5
Leigh WN7 . . . . .75 E7
Reddish SK5 . . . . .99 E1
Byron Rd Denton M34 . . . .112 F8
Middleton M24 . . . . .47 B2
Ramsbottom BL8 . . . . .10 F2
Stretford M32 . . . . .96 F3
Byron St Eccles M30 . . . . . .79 D2
Leigh WN7 . . . . .75 F7
Oldham OL8 . . . . .66 B2
Royton OL2 . . . . .48 E4
Byron Street Inf Sch OL2 .48 E4
Byron Wlk Farnworth BL4 . .60 B6
6 Royton OL2 . . . . .48 E4
Byron's Dr 2 WA15 . . . . .120 A6
Byrth Rd OL8 . . . . .84 F8
Bywell Wlk 15 M8 . . . . . . .155 F7

C

'C' Ct WN4 . . . . .73 B2
Cabin La OL4 . . . . .50 A3
Cable St Bolton BL1 . . . . . .145 F8
Manchester M4 . . . . .159 B2
Cablestead Wlk M11 . . . . .165 A8
Cabot Pl SK5 . . . . .169 F4
Cabot St M13 . . . . .163 B6
Caddington Rd M21 . . . . .109 C8
Cadishead Prim Sch
M44 . . . . .105 E6
Cadishead Way M41,M44 . .94 C2
Cadleigh Wlk 6 M40 . . . . .83 A7
Cadman Gr WN2 . . . . .56 D4
Cadman's Yd 8 WN5 . . . . .54 D5
Cadmium Wlk M18 . . . . . . .99 C4
Cadnam Dr M22 . . . . .121 F3
Cadogan Dr WN3 . . . . .54 D2
Cadogan Pl 7 M7 . . . . .63 E1
Cadogan St M14 . . . . .98 A4
Cadum Wlk M13 . . . . .163 C6
Caen Ave M40 . . . . .65 C3
Caernarvon Cl BL8 . . . . . . .10 F1
Caernarvon Dr SK7 . . . . .124 C1
Caernarvon Rd WN2 . . . . . .57 A3
Caernarvon Way 2
M34 . . . . .100 F1
Caesar St OL11 . . . . .31 A2
Cairn Dr Rochdale OL11 . . . .29 E6
Salford M6 . . . . .81 C5
Cairn Wlk 15 M11 . . . . . . .160 F1
Cairngorm Dr BL3 . . . . .40 E5
Cairns Pl OL6 . . . . .85 D5
Cairnwell Rd OL9 . . . . .65 F8
Caister Ave M45 . . . . .63 A7
Caister Cl M41 . . . . .94 C1
Caistor Cl M16 . . . . .109 E8
Caistor St SK1 . . . . .112 B3
Caistor Wlk 2 OL1 . . . . . .153 F7
Caithness Cl M23 . . . . . . .121 A4
Caithness Dr BL3 . . . . .40 E6
Caithness Rd OL11 . . . . . . .29 E5
Cakebread St M12 . . . . . .163 C7
Calamanco Way M44 . . . .106 A8
Calbourne Cres M12 . . . . . .99 B3
Calcot Wlk 6 M23 . . . . . .120 F6
Calcutta Rd SK3 . . . . .123 C7
Caldbeck Ave Bolton BL1 . . .23 F1
Sale M33 . . . . .108 E5
Caldbeck Cl WN4 . . . . .73 B4
Caldbeck Dr
Farnworth BL4 . . . . .59 E7
Middleton M24 . . . . .46 E2
Caldbeck Gr WA11 . . . . . . .71 C1
Caldecott Rd M9 . . . . .64 A5
Calder Ave Hindley WN2 . . .57 C3
Irlam M44 . . . . .93 F1
Littleborough OL15 . . . . . . .16 A7
Wythenshawe M22 . . . . . . .121 D8
Calder Cl Bury BL9 . . . . . . .28 A8
Poynton SK12 . . . . .133 D2
Reddish SK5 . . . . .112 A4
Calder Cres M45 . . . . .45 B2
Calder Dr Kearsley BL4 . . . .61 B5
Platt Bridge WN2 . . . . .56 A2
Swinton M27 . . . . .61 E1
Walkden M28 . . . . .60 B2
Calder Gdns OL15 . . . . . . .16 A6
Calder Gr OL2 . . . . .149 B8
Calder Ho 6 M7 . . . . .81 C5
Calder Pl WN5 . . . . .54 C7
Calder Rd BL3 . . . . .147 E3
Calder St OL16 . . . . .15 B2
Calder Way M45 . . . . .45 B2
Calder Wlk
Middleton M24 . . . . .46 C2
Whitefield M45 . . . . .45 B2
Calderbank Ave M41 . . . . .94 E4
Calderbank St WN5 . . . . . .54 E5
Calderbeck Way M22 . . . .121 E6
Calderbrook Ct SK8 . . . . .123 B4
Calderbrook Dr SK8 . . . . .123 A4
Calderbrook Rd OL15 . . . . . .6 C2
Calderbrook Terr OL15 . . . .16 C8
Calderbrook Way OL4 . . . .67 B5
Calderbrook Wlk 11 M9 .157 D7
Calderburn Cl BL6 . . . . . . .39 D8
Caldercourt M41 . . . . .94 E4
Calderdale Ct OL2 . . . . . . .48 C5
Caldershaw Bsns Ctr
OL12 . . . . .14 B2
Caldershaw Ctr The
OL12 . . . . .14 B2
Caldershaw La OL12 . . . . .14 A2
Caldershaw Prim Sch
OL12 . . . . .14 A1
Caldershaw Rd OL11,
OL12 . . . . .14 A1
Caldervale Ave M21 . . . . .109 C4
Calderwood Cl BL8 . . . . . .27 A6
Caldew Cl WN2 . . . . .56 E4
Caldey Rd M23 . . . . .120 E5
Caldford Cl WN2 . . . . .38 C6
Caldon Cl M30 . . . . .95 D8
Caldwell Ave M29 . . . . .77 B4
Caldwell Cl M29 . . . . .77 B5
Caldwell St BL5 . . . . .57 F5
Caldy Dr BL0 . . . . .11 A3
Caldy Rd Handforth SK9 . . .131 D3
Salford M6 . . . . .154 D4
Cale Gn SK2 . . . . .170 F6
Cale Green Ct SK2 . . . . . .170 F6
Cale Green Prim Sch
SK3 . . . . .170 F6
Cale La WN2 . . . . .38 B2
Cale St SK2 . . . . .170 F6
Caleb Cl M29 . . . . .58 F1
Caledon Ave M40 . . . . .83 A8
Caledonia St
Bolton BL3 . . . . .144 C5
3 Radcliffe M26 . . . . .44 C4
Caledonia Way M32 . . . . . .96 A5
Caledonian Dr M30 . . . . . . .95 E8
Caley St Bolton BL1 . . . . . . .23 F2
1 Manchester M1 . . . . .163 A7
Calf Hey OL15 . . . . .15 F6
Calf Hey Cl M26 . . . . .43 D3
Calf Hey N 7 OL11 . . . . . . .31 A4
Calf Hey Rd OL2 . . . . .49 D8
Calf Hey S 8 OL11 . . . . . .31 A4
Calf La OL3,OL5 . . . . .68 E4
Calgarth Dr M24 . . . . .46 D3
Calgary St M18 . . . . .165 C5
Calico Cl M3 . . . . .158 D3
Calico Cres SK15 . . . . .86 F6
Calico Wood Ave WN6 . . . .35 F6
Callaghan Wlk OL10 . . . . . .29 C1
Calland Ave SK14 . . . . . . .167 F3
Callander Ct WN5 . . . . .54 E8
Callander Sq OL10 . . . . . . .28 F1
Callender St BL0 . . . . .138 B6
Calliards Rd OL16 . . . . .15 E4
Callingdon Rd M21 . . . . . .109 D5
Callington Cl 4 SK14 . . . .102 E2
Callington Dr SK14 . . . . . .102 E2
Callington Wlk 3 SK14 . .102 E2
Callis Rd BL3 . . . . .144 C5
Callum Wlk M13 . . . . .163 C6
Calluna Mews M20 . . . . . .110 A4
Calne Wlk 6 M23 . . . . . . .121 A5
Calow Cl 34 SK13 . . . . . . .171 E2
Calow Dr WN7 . . . . .76 C3
Calow Gn 9 SK13 . . . . . . .171 E1
Caltha St BL0 . . . . .138 B6
Calthorpe Ave M9 . . . . . . .156 C7
Calton Ave M7 . . . . .81 A7
Calve Croft Rd M22 . . . . .121 F2
Calveley Wlk WN6 . . . . .36 E8
Calver Ave M30 . . . . .95 C8
Calver Cl
11 Gamesley SK13 . . . . . . .171 E2
Urmston M41 . . . . .94 D3
Calver Fold 7 SK13 . . . . .171 D2
Calver Hey Cl BL5 . . . . . . .40 C2
Calver Mews SK13 . . . . . .171 D2
Calver Pl 10 SK13 . . . . . . .171 E2
Calver Wlk Cheadle SK8 . .122 E1
Denton M34 . . . . .113 A8
13 Manchester M40 . . . . . .159 C3
Calverhall Way WN4 . . . . . .73 A3
Calverleigh Cl BL3 . . . . . .146 A2
Calverley Ave M19 . . . . . .110 F7
Calverley Cl 3 SK9 . . . . .137 C8
Calverley Way OL12 . . . . . .14 E4
Calverly Rd SK8 . . . . .123 A5
Calvert Rd BL3 . . . . .147 F3
Calvert St M5 . . . . .154 D2
Calverton Dr M40 . . . . .83 C7
Calvin St BL1 . . . . .143 F1
Calvine Wlk 4 M40 . . . . . .159 C3
Camargue Ct 1 M20 . . . . .110 B6
Cambeck Cl M45 . . . . .45 B1
Cambeck Wlk M45 . . . . .45 A1
Cambell Rd M30 . . . . .79 B2
Camberley Cl
Bramhall SK7 . . . . .133 A7
Bury BL8 . . . . .27 A5
Camberley Dr OL11 . . . . . . .29 F5
Camberly Dr OL11 . . . . .29 F6
Cambert La
Manchester M18 . . . . .99 D5
Manchester,Belle Vue
M18 . . . . .165 C5
Camberwell Cres WN2 . . . .37 F1
Camberwell Dr OL7 . . . . . .85 A7
Camberwell Park Com Specl
Sch M9 . . . . .64 C4
Camberwell St
Manchester M3,M8 . . . . . .159 A4
Oldham OL8 . . . . .66 E4
Camberwell Way OL2 . . . . .48 C4
Cambo Wlk SK4 . . . . .110 F3
Camborne Rd SK14 . . . . . .102 E3
Camborne St M14 . . . . .98 B3
Camborne Wlk 1 OL9 . . . .48 A1
Cambourne Dr
Bolton BL3 . . . . .144 A5
Hindley WN2 . . . . .57 C2
Cambrai Cres M30 . . . . . . .79 A4
Cambria Sq 8 BL3 . . . . . .144 C5
Cambria St Bolton BL3 . . .144 C5
Oldham OL4 . . . . .67 D7
Cambrian Cres WN3 . . . . . .54 C2
Cambrian Dr
Milnrow OL16 . . . . .32 A6
Royton OL2 . . . . .48 C3
Cambrian Rd SK3 . . . . . . .123 C8
Cambrian St M11,M40 . . .160 E2
Cambridge Ave
Manchester M16 . . . . .97 C2
Rochdale OL11 . . . . .30 A6
Wilmslow SK9 . . . . .136 F7
Cambridge Cl
Farnworth BL4 . . . . .147 F1
10 Sale M33 . . . . .107 D3
Cambridge Dr
Little Lever BL3 . . . . .43 B4
Reddish M34 . . . . .100 A3
Romiley SK6 . . . . .113 C5
Cambridge Gr Eccles M30 . .79 F2
Whitefield M45 . . . . .63 A7
Cambridge Ho 1 M1 . . . .163 A6
Cambridge Ind Area
M7 .158 E4
Cambridge Rd
Altrincham WA15 . . . . .119 E2
Droylsden M43 . . . . .83 F3
Failsworth M35 . . . . .83 F5
Gatley SK8 . . . . .122 B5
Horwich BL6 . . . . .39 F8
Manchester M9 . . . . .64 D1
Orrell WN5 . . . . .53 F8
Reddish SK4 . . . . .111 C5
Urmston M41 . . . . .95 B1
Cambridge St
Ashton-u-L OL7 . . . . .84 F1
Atherton M46 . . . . .58 C2
Dukinfield SK16 . . . . .166 C1
Manchester M1,M15 . . . . . .162 F7
Oldham OL9 . . . . .66 C4
Salford M7 . . . . .158 E4
Stalybridge SK15 . . . . .86 A2
Stockport SK2 . . . . .124 A6
Wigan WN1 . . . . .151 D7
Cambridge Terr
Stalybridge SK15 . . . . .86 D4

Cambridge Terr continued
  Stockport SK2 ....124 A6
Cambridge Way WN1 ....151 D8
Camdale Wlk **9** M8 .....155 F6
Camden Ave M40 ....83 C4
Camden Cl BL2 ....26 C1
Camden St OL5 ....68 D3
Camelia Rd M9 ....156 C7
Camellia Cl BL1 ....144 B7
Cameron Cl OL2 ....48 D6
Cameron Pl WN5 ....54 E8
Cameron St Bolton BL1 ..143 D4
  Bury BL8 ....27 C2
  Leigh WN7 ....75 D7
  Manchester M1 ....162 F8
Camley Wlk **1** M8 ....156 B6
Camm St WN2 ....74 B8
Camms View BB4 ....1 A8
Camomile Wlk **5** M31 ...105 F3
Camp Rd WN4 ....72 E4
Camp St Ashton-u-L OL6 ...166 B3
  Bury BL8 ....27 C3
  Manchester M3 ....162 E8
  Salford M7 ....155 D5
Campania St OL2 ....48 E2
Campbell Cl BL8 ....26 F4
Campbell Ct BL4 ....42 C2
Campbell Rd Bolton BL3 ..146 A2
  Manchester M13 ....98 F2
  Sale M33 ....107 F3
  Swinton M27 ....79 E6
Campbell St
  Farnworth BL4 ....42 B1
  Reddish SK5 ....99 F1
  Rochdale OL12 ....14 C2
  Wigan WN5 ....54 D5
Campbell Way M28 ....60 D3
Campbell Wlk **5** BL4 ....42 C2
Campden Way SK9 ......131 D4
Campion Dr BB4 ....1 A8
Campion Gr WN4 ....72 F4
Campion Way
  8 Denton M34 ....113 A8
  Rochdale OL12 ....14 C3
Campion Wlk M11 ......164 F8
Camponia Gdns M7 .....155 D5
Camrose Wlk M13 ......164 D5
Cams Acre Cl M26 ....43 E3
Cams La M26 ....43 E2
Cams Lane Prim Sch
  M26 ....43 F3
Canaan WA3 ....91 C8
Canada St Bolton BL1 ...142 C2
  Horwich BL6 ....22 B3
  Manchester M40 ....160 E4
  Stockport SK2 ....124 A6
Canal Bank
  Appley Bridge WN6 ......35 C7
  Eccles M30 ....79 C3
Canal Bridge La M43 ....83 E1
Canal Circ M50 ....80 A1
Canal Cotts WN3 ....135 B7
Canal Rd WA14 ....119 E8
Canal Row WN2 ....20 D1
Canal Side M30 ....79 C3
Canal St Adlington PR7 ...21 A6
  Droylsden M43 ....84 A1
  Dukinfield SK14 ....101 C3
  Heywood OL10 ....46 F8
  Ince-in-M WN2 ....151 F6
  Leigh WN7 ....75 F4
  Littleborough OL15 .....16 B5
  Manchester M1 ....163 A8
  Marple SK6 ....126 A6
  Oldham OL9 ....66 B3
  Rochdale OL11 ....31 A5
  Salford M5 ....81 C1
  Stalybridge SK15 ....86 A1
  Stockport SK1 ....170 F8
  Wigan WN6 ....36 F2
Canal Terr WN1 ....151 E7
Canalside Ind Est OL16 ..31 B5
Canary Way M27 ....80 C2
Canberra Rd
  Bramhall SK7 ....132 F5
  Wigan WN5 ....36 C1
Canberra St M11 ....83 C2
Candahar St BL3 ....42 A3
Candleford Cl **2** M20 ...110 B6
Candleford Pl SK2 ....124 E4
Candleford Rd M20 .....110 B6
Candlestick Pk BL9 ......28 D4
Canisp Cl OL9 ....48 A1
Canley Cl SK1 ....170 F8
Canmore Cl BL3 ....146 A3
Cann St BL8 ....26 D8
Cannel Fold M28 ....78 B7
Canning Cl WN2 ....56 C4
Canning Dr BL1 ....143 E2
Canning St Bolton BL1 ...143 F2
  Bury BL9 ....140 F4
  Stockport SK4 ....169 E2
Cannock Dr SK4 ....168 F2
Cannon Gr M4 ....158 F2
Cannon Gr BL3 ....145 D5
Cannon St Atherton M46 ..58 D3
  Bolton BL3 ....145 D5
  Eccles M30 ....79 E1
  Hollingworth SK14 ....103 C5
  Manchester M4 ....159 A2
  Oldham OL9 ....153 F5
  Radcliffe M26 ....43 F5
  Ramsbottom BL0 ....11 A4
  Salford M3 ....158 D3
Cannon St N BL3 ....145 D6

Cannon Wlk M34 ....100 E2
Canon Burrows CE Prim Sch
  OL7 ....85 A5
Canon Cl WN6 ....19 F2
Canon Dr WA14 ....119 B1
Canon Flynn Ct OL16 ....31 C7
Canon Green Cl M3 .....158 E2
Canon Green Dr M3 .....158 E2
Canon Hussey Ct M3 ...158 D1
Canon Johnson CE Prim Sch
  OL7 ....166 B4
Canon Slade CE Sch BL2 ..25 C4
Canon St Bury BL9 ......141 A4
  Rochdale OL16 ....15 B1
Canon Tighe Ct OL9 ....152 A7
Canon Williamson CE High
  Sch M30 ....78 F1
Canon's Cl BL1 ....142 B2
Canons Gr M40 ....157 E5
Canonsleigh Cl M8 .....155 C5
Canonsway M27 ....79 E8
Cansfield Gr WN4 ....73 A4
Cansfield High Specialist
  Language Coll WN4 ......73 A4
Canterbury Ave WA3 ....74 D1
Canterbury Cl
  Atherton M46 ....58 E4
  Dukinfield SK16 ....101 D6
  Rochdale OL11 ....30 A7
Canterbury Cres M24 ...47 D2
Canterbury Dr Bury BL8 ..140 D4
  Manchester M25 ....63 C2
Canterbury Gdns M5 .....80 A2
Canterbury Gr BL3 ......147 D3
Canterbury Pk M20 .....109 F3
Canterbury Rd
  Altrincham WA15 ......120 C3
  Stockport SK1 ....112 B1
  Urmston M41 ....95 D3
Canterbury St OL6 ......166 C4
Canterfield Cl M43 ....84 D2
Cantley Wlk **8** M8 ....156 A6
Cantrell St M11 ....83 B2
Canute Ct M32 ....96 E3
Canute Rd M32 ....96 E3
Canute St Bolton BL2 .....25 C1
  Radcliffe M26 ....43 E3
Cape St M14 ....110 C7
Capella Wlk M7 ....81 C4
Capenhurst Cl
  Poynton SK12 ....133 F4
  Wythenshawe M23 .....120 F4
Capesthorne Cl SK7 ....133 F8
Capesthorne Dr OL2 .....48 F7
Capesthorne Rd
  Altrincham WA15 ......120 D6
  Dukinfield SK16 ....101 D6
  Hazel Grove SK7 ....133 F8
  High Lane SK6 ....134 E7
  Wilmslow SK9 ....136 E5
Capesthorne Wlk M34 ..100 E2
Capital Quay M50 ....161 A2
Capital Rd M11 ....99 F7
Capitol Cl BL1 ....142 A3
Cappadocia Way BL5 ....57 D7
Capps St WN6 ....56 B3
Capricorn Rd M9 ....65 B3
Capricorn Way M6 ....81 C4
Capstan St M9 ....157 E8
Capstone Dr SK6 ....125 E6
Captain Clarke Rd SK14 ..101 C5
Captain Fold Rd M38 ....59 F6
Captain Lees Gdns BL5 ..58 B7
Captain Lees Rd BL5 .....40 A1
Captain St BL6 ....22 B4
Captain Wlk M6 ....161 B8
Captain's Clough Rd
  BL1 ....142 B2
Capton Cl **1a** WN4 ....73 C3
Capton Cl SK7 ....124 A2
Car Bank Ave M46 ....58 D4
Car Bank Cres M46 .....58 D4
Car Bank Sq M46 ....58 D4
Car Bank St M46 ....58 D4
Car St WN2 ....56 A2
Caradoc Ave **12** M8 .....156 B6
Carawood Cl M9 ....55 D7
Carberry Rd M18 ....99 D5
Cardale Wlk M9 ....157 D7
Carden Ave Swinton M27 ..79 F7
  Urmston M41 ....94 E2
Cardenbrook Gr **4** SK9 ..131 D2
Carder Cl M27 ....79 F7
Carders Ct WN7 ....75 A5
Cardew Ave M22 ....121 F4
Cardiff Cl **8** OL8 ....66 B2
Cardiff St M7 ....155 E4
Cardiff Wlk **4** M34 .....100 F1
Cardigan Dr BL9 ....28 A1
Cardigan Rd OL8 ....66 B2
Cardigan St Radcliffe M26 ..43 F6
  Rochdale OL12 ....14 F1
  Royton OL2 ....48 E4
  2 Salford M6 ....80 A3
Cardigan Terr M14 ....97 F4
Cardinal Langley RC High
  Sch M24 ....47 B4
Cardinal Mews M24 ......46 D2
Cardinal St
  Manchester M8 ....156 B7
  10 Oldham OL1 ....67 A7
Carding Gr M3 ....158 E3
Cardinal Ave M9 ....64 F4
Cardus St M19 ....99 A1
Cardwell Gdns BL1 ......143 E2
Cardwell Rd M30 ....79 A1
Cardwell St OL8 ....66 B3
Careless La WN2 ....151 F7

Carey Cl Salford M7 .....158 D4
  Wigan WN3 ....54 D2
Carey Wlk M15 ....162 F5
Carfax Fold OL12 ....14 B2
Carfax St M18 ....99 D5
Cargate Wlk **14** M8 .....155 F6
Carib St M15 ....162 F5
Carill Ave M40 ....65 A1
Carill Dr M14 ....110 D8
Carina Pl M7 ....81 C4
Cariocca Bsns Pk
  Manchester,Ardwick M12 ..164 D6
  Manchester,Miles Platting
  M40 ....160 D3
Carisbrook Ave
  Prestwich M25,M45 .....63 A6
  Urmston M41 ....95 C2
Carisbrook Dr M27 ....80 A6
Carisbrook St M9 ....157 E7
Carisbrooke Ave SK7 ...124 D1
Carisbrooke Dr BL1 ....143 E3
Carisbrooke Rd WN7 ....76 D6
Carl St BL1 ....143 D2
Carlburn St M11 ....83 D2
Carleton Rd SK12 ....134 C4
Carley Gr M9 ....64 B4
Carlford Gr M25 ....62 F3
Carlin St SK3 ....170 E8
Carlin Gate WA15 ....120 A6
Carling Dr M22 ....121 E2
Carlingford Cl SK3 ......170 E5
Carlisle Cl Little Lever BL3 ..43 A2
  Prestwich M45 ....63 A8
  Romiley SK6 ....113 A1
Carlisle Cres OL6 ....85 C7
Carlisle Dr
  Altrincham WA14 ......119 E8
  Irlam M44 ....94 A2
Carlisle Pl **3** PR6 ....21 A8
Carlisle St
  11 Alderley Edge SK9 ..137 A1
  Bolton BL3 ....147 D4
  Hindley WN2 ....56 E6
  Salford M7 ....158 E4
  Stalybridge SK15 ....86 A1
  Stockport SK3 ....170 D7
  Swinton M27 ....61 F2
  Wigan WN5 ....54 D6
Carlisle Way Aspull WN2 ..38 D5
  3 Denton M34 ....101 B1
Carloon Rd M23 ....109 B1
Carlow Dr M22 ....121 E2
Carlton Ave Bolton BL3 ..146 A4
  Bramhall SK7 ....132 D5
  Cheadle SK8 ....122 F3
  Handforth SK9 ....131 C2
  Manchester M14 ....98 B3
  Manchester,Old Trafford
  M16 ....97 B4
  Oldham OL4 ....49 D1
  Prestwich M25 ....63 E2
  Romiley SK6 ....113 D2
  Up Holland WN8 ....53 A7
  Whitefield M45 ....44 D1
Carlton Cl
  Ashton-in-M WN4 ....73 A5
  Blackrod BL6 ....21 D2
  Bolton BL2 ....25 E3
  Walkden M28 ....60 C1
Carlton Cres
  Stockport SK1 ....112 A2
  Urmston M41 ....95 D1
Carlton Ct
  Altrincham WA15 ......120 B1
  Manchester M25 ....63 A1
Carlton Dr Gatley SK8 ...122 A6
  Prestwich M25 ....63 E2
Carlton Gdns BL4 ....42 D1
Carlton Grange M43 ....97 E2
Carlton Mans **4** M16 ....97 D3
Carlton Pl Farnworth BL4 ..42 D1
  Hazel Grove SK7 ....125 A1
Carlton Range M18 ....99 F4
Carlton Rd
  Altrincham WA15 ......120 B2
  Ashton-u-L OL6 ....85 C5
  Bolton BL1 ....144 A8
  Golborne WA3 ....74 D1
  Hyde SK14 ....102 A3
  Lymm WA13 ....117 B5
  Manchester,Heaton Moor
  SK4 ....168 A2
  Manchester,Whalley Range
  M16 ....97 D3
  Sale M33 ....108 A6
  Salford M6 ....154 E4
  Walkden M28 ....60 C1
Carlton St Bolton BL2 ...148 A6
  Bury BL9 ....44 F8
  Eccles M30 ....79 D3
  Farnworth BL4 ....42 D1
  Manchester M16 ....97 C4
Carlton Way Irlam M44 ..105 C5
  Royton OL1,OL2 ....48 D2
Carlyle Cl M8 ....156 A6
Carlyle Gr WN7 ....75 C8
Carlyle St BL9 ....140 F4
Carlyn Ave M33 ....108 D4
Carmel Ave M5 ....161 C8
Carmel Cl M5 ....161 C8
Carmel Ct M9 ....64 E1
Carmenna Dr SK7 ....133 D6
Carmichael Cl **6** M31 ..105 E3
Carmichael St SK3 .....170 D8

Carmine Fold M24 ....46 F2
Carmona Dr M25 ....63 A4
Carmona Gdns M7 ....63 C1
Carmoor Rd M13 ....163 C5
Carna Rd SK5 ....99 E2
Carnaby St M9 ....64 F1
Carnarvon St
  Manchester M3 ....158 F3
  Oldham OL8 ....66 B2
  Salford M7 ....155 E7
  3 Stockport SK1 ......112 A1
Carnation Rd
  Farnworth BL4 ....42 A1
  Oldham OL4 ....67 E4
Carnegie Ave M19 ....99 B1
Carnegie Cl **1** M33 .....107 D3
Carnegie Dr WN4 ....73 A5
Carnforth Ave
  Chadderton OL9 ....152 A6
  Hindley WN2 ....57 A5
  Trub OL11 ....47 D7
Carnforth Dr
  Ramsbottom BL0,BL8 ....11 A2
  Sale M33 ....108 A3
Carnforth Rd
  Cheadle SK8 ....123 C4
  Reddish SK4 ....111 D7
  Carrock Wlk M24 ....46 B1
Carnforth St M14 ....98 B3
Carnoustie M33 ....146 A3
Carnoustie Cl
  Failsworth M40 ....83 C7
  Wilmslow SK9 ....137 D8
Carnoustie Dr
  Gatley SK8 ....122 C1
  Ramsbottom BL0 ....138 B5
Carnwood Cl M40 ....83 D4
Carolina Ho M3 ....158 E3
Caroline St
  Ashton-u-L OL6 ....166 C3
  Bolton BL3 ....147 D4
  Irlam M44 ....94 D1
  Salford M7 ....158 E4
  Stalybridge SK15 ....86 A1
  Stockport SK3 ....170 D7
  Wigan WN3 ....150 C7
Carpenters La M4 ....159 A2
Carpenters Way OL16 ....31 B4
Carpenters Wlk M43 .....83 F1
Carr Ave M25 ....62 F2
Carr Bank SK13 ....116 E8
Carr Bank Ave
  Manchester M9 ....63 F3
  Ramsbottom BL0 ....138 B7
Carr Bank Dr BL0 ....138 B7
Carr Bank Rd BL0 ....138 B7
Carr Brook Dr M46 ....58 E4
Carr Brow SK6 ....134 E7
Carr Cl SK1 ....124 B8
Carr Common Rd WN2 ...57 D3
Carr Fold BL0 ....138 B7
Carr Gr OL16 ....32 A6
Carr House La WN6 ....18 F8
Carr House Rd OL4 ......67 F6
Carr La Alderley Edge SK9 ..136 D2
  Diggle OL3 ....51 C5
  Golborne WA3 ....91 A7
  Leigh WN7 ....91 E8
  Milnrow OL16 ....32 C6
  Mossley SK15 ....86 F7
  Rawtenstall BB4 ....2 F7
  Uppermill OL3 ....69 B7
  Wigan WN3 ....55 B3
Carr Mill Cres WN5 ......71 E4
Carr Mill Jun Sch WN1 ..71 C1
Carr Mill Mews SK9 .....131 B1
Carr Rd Altrincham WA15 ..120 B2
  Irlam M44 ....94 B2
Carr Rise SK15 ....86 F7
Carr St Ashton-u-L OL6 ..85 D5
  Hindley WN2 ....56 D6
  Leigh WN7 ....75 C5
  Ramsbottom BL0 ....138 B7
Carr Wood Ave SK7 .....132 E8
Carr Wood Rd SK7 ......123 E1
Carradale Dr M33 ....107 C5
Carradale Wlk **5** M40 ...83 A6
Carradon Dr WN6 ....19 E1
Carrbrook Cl SK15 ....86 F6
Carrbrook Cres SK15 ...86 F6
Carrbrook Dr OL1 ....48 E1
Carrbrook Rd SK15 ......86 F7
Carrbrook Terr **6** M26 ..44 C4
Carrfield Ave
  Altrincham WA15 ......120 D6
  Stockport SK3 ....124 A4
  Walkden M38 ....59 E4
Carrfield Cl M38 ....59 E4
Carrfield Gr M38 ....59 E4
Carrgate Rd M44 ....101 B1
Carrgreen Cl M19 ....110 F5
Carrgreen La WA13 ....117 F6
Carrhill Quarry OL5 .....68 C2
Carrhill Rd OL5 ....68 C2
Carrhouse La
  Hollingworth SK14 ....103 C4
  Mottram-in-L SK14 ....103 C2
Carriage Dr
  Littleborough OL15 .....16 B7
  Manchester M40 ....157 D5
Carriage Dr The SK13 ..103 F5
Carriage St M16 ....162 D5
Carriages The WA14 ....119 C4

Carrick Gdns
  Middleton M24 ....46 F4
  Wythenshawe M22 .....121 D4
Carrie St BL1 ....144 B8
Carrigart M25 ....63 B3
Carrill Gr M19 ....99 A1
Carrill Gr E M19 ....99 A1
Carrington Bsns Pk
  M31 ....106 C6
Carrington Cl OL16 ....15 D3
Carrington Dr BL3 .....145 F5
Carrington Field St **1** SK1 ..124 A7
Carrington Gr WN7 ......75 F7
Carrington Ho **2** M6 ....80 C4
Carrington La
  Carrington M31,M33 ...107 C6
  Sale M33 ....107 E5
Carrington Rd
  Adlington PR7 ....20 F7
  Flixton M41 ....106 E8
  Manchester M14 ....98 C1
  Stockport SK1 ....112 C1
Carrington St Leigh WN7 ..75 F7
  Oldham OL9 ....66 B3
  Swinton M27 ....62 B1
Carrington Terr M27 .....62 A1
Carmel Ct OL3 ....50 F3
  Carrock Wlk M24 ....46 B1
Carron Ave M9 ....64 F1
Carron Gr BL2 ....42 F7
Carrs Ave SK3,SK8 .....123 A6
Carrs Ct SK9 ....137 B7
Carrs Rd SK8 ....122 F6
Carrsfield Rd M22 ......121 E6
Carrs Dr M40 ....43 E5
Carrsvale Ave M41 ......95 B3
Carrswood Rd M23 .....120 D8
Carruthers Cl OL10 ......29 F3
Carruthers St M4 ....160 D1
Carwood Hey BL0 ....11 A4
Carwood Rd SK9 ....136 F8
Carsdale Rd M22 ....130 E8
Carslake Ave BL1 ....144 C8
Carslake Rd M40 ....157 D5
Carson Rd M19 ....111 A8
Carstairs Ave SK2 ......124 A4
Carstairs Cl M8 ....155 F7
Carswell Cl M29 ....59 C1
Carter Cl M34 ....100 F2
Carter Pl SK14 ....101 D5
Carter St Bolton BL3 ....42 A4
  Dukinfield SK14 ....60 E7
  Ince-in-M WN3 ....151 E6
  Mossley OL5 ....86 C8
  Salford,Lower Broughton
  M7 ....155 D5
  Salford,Weaste M50 ....80 C1
  Stalybridge SK15 ....86 D8
Carthage St OL8 ....66 F4
Carthorpe Arch M5 .....154 F1
Cartleach Gr M28 ....60 A2
Cartleach La M28 ....60 A2
Cartmel **6** OL12 ....139 F8
Cartmel Ave Milnrow OL16 ..31 F4
  Reddish SK4 ....111 E6
  Wigan WN1 ....37 B3
Cartmel Cl Bolton BL3 ..40 D2
  Gatley SK8 ....122 C3
  Hazel Grove SK7 ....124 C3
  Oldham OL8 ....66 D3
  Whitefield BL9 ....45 A3
Cartmel Cres Bolton BL2 ..25 C2
  Failsworth OL9 ....65 F2
Cartmel Ct M9 ....65 A4
Cartmel Dr WA15 ....120 D6
Cartmel Gr M28 ....60 B7
Cartmel Wlk
  Manchester M9 ....157 D7
  Middleton M24 ....46 F2
Cartridge Cl M22 ....121 F3
Cartridge St OL10 ....29 C2
Cartwright Cl BL1 ......142 C1
Cartwright Gr WN7 ......57 D1
Cartwright Rd M21 ....108 F8
Cartwright St
  Denton M34 ....100 F6
  Dukinfield SK14 ....102 A5
Carver Ave M25 ....63 C5
Carver Cl M16 ....161 B5
Carver Dr SK6 ....113 A2
Carver Rd
  Altrincham WA15 ......119 E2
  Marple SK6 ....125 C5
Carver St M16 ....161 B5
Carver Wlk M15 ....162 F5

Carville Gr WN2 ....57 B4
Carville Rd M9 ....65 C4
Carwood Gr BL6 ....22 D3
Cascade Dr M7 ....155 E5
Cashgate Ct OL4 ....49 F1
Cashmere Rd SK3 ....123 C7
Cashmore Dr WN2 ......56 D2
Cashmore Wlk M12 ....164 E6
Caspian Rd
  Altrincham WA14 ......119 A6
  Manchester M9 ....65 B3
Cass Ave M5 ....161 A8
Cassandra Ct M5 ....161 C8
Cassidy Cl M4 ....159 B2
Cassidy Dr M50 ....99 E8
Cassius Wlk M7 ....81 C4
Casson Gate OL12 ......14 E1
Casson St M35 ....83 F7
Casterton Way M28 .....78 A5
Castle Ave Denton M34 ..100 E2
  Rochdale OL11 ....139 E6

Castle Cl M43 . . . . .84 B2
Castle Cres BL6 . . . . .22 C5
Castle Croft BL2 . . . . .25 E3
Castle Ct Ashton-u-L OL6 . . .85 B7
 Bolton BL2 . . . . .148 A7
Castle Dr PR7 . . . . .20 E6
Castle Edge Rd SK22 . . . .127 B2
Castle Farm Dr SK2 . . . . .124 B5
Castle Farm La SK2 . . . . . .124 C5
Castle Gr Leigh WN7 . . . . . .76 D6
 Ramsbottom BL0 . . . . .11 A2
Castle Hill SK15 . . . . .86 B1
Castle Hall Ct SK15 . . . .86 A1
Castle Hall View SK15 .86 A1
Castle Hey Cl BL9 . . . . .45 C3
Castle Hill Glossop SK13 . .104 E2
 Newton-le-W WA12 . . . . . . .89 E4
Castle Hill Com Prim Sch
 BL2 .25 E2
Castle Hill Cres OL11 . . . .139 E6
Castle Hill High Sch
 SK5 . . . . .112 C6
Castle Hill Mobile Home Pk
 SK6 . . . . .113 A6
Castle Hill Pk WN2 . . . . . . .56 F7
Castle Hill Rd Bury BL9 . . .28 D5
 Hindley WN2 . . . . .56 E6
 Manchester M25 . . . . .63 D2
Castle Hill St Bolton BL2 . .25 B2
 Bolton BL1 . . . . .25 B3
Castle Hill St Philip's CE Prim
 Sch WN2 . . . . .56 F6
Castle House La PR7 . . . . .20 E6
Castle Irwell Student Village
 M6 .81 B5
Castle La OL5,SK15 . . . . . . .86 F8
Castle Mews BL4 . . . . .60 D7
Castle Mill La WA15 . . . . .129 B5
Castle Rd BL9 . . . . .45 C4
Castle Rise M40 . . . . . . .63 D2
Castle Shaw Rd SK2 . . . . .124 E5
Castle St Bolton BL2 . . . . . .148 A7
 Bury BL9 . . . . .140 E2
 Eccles M30 . . . . .79 F2
 Farnworth BL4 . . . . .60 D7
 Hadfield SK13 . . . . .104 A4
 Hyde SK14 . . . . .167 F3
 Manchester M3 . . . . .162 E8
 Middleton M24 . . . . .65 D7
 Ramsbottom BL9 . . . . .11 D2
 Stalybridge SK15 . . . . .86 A1
 Stockport SK3 . . . . .170 E8
 Tyldesley M29 . . . . .58 F1
Castle Terr SK15 . . . . .86 F6
Castle Way M27 . . . . .62 A3
Castle Yd SK1 . . . . .169 F2
Castlebrook Cl BL9 . . . . . . .45 B4
Castlebrook High Sch
 BL9 .45 C3
Castlecroft Ave BL6 . . . . . .21 D2
Castlecroft Mews BL9 . . .140 E2
Castlecroft Rd BL9 . . . . . .140 E3
Castledene Ave M6 . . . . . .154 E3
Castlefield Ave M7 . . . . . .155 E8
Castlefield Visitor Ctr*
 M3 .162 E8
Castleford Cl BL1 . . . . .145 D8
Castleford St OL1 . . . . .48 C1
Castleford Wlk M21 . . . . .109 D7
Castlemere Cl WN3 . . . . . . .54 D1
Castlemere Dr OL2 . . . . . . .49 D8
Castlemere Rd M9 . . . . . . .64 C3
Castlemere St OL11 . . . . . .139 F6
Castlemere Terr OL11 . . .139 F6
Castlemill St OL1 . . . . .67 B7
Castlemoor Ave M7 . . . . . . .81 B8
Castlerea Cl M30 . . . . .95 D8
Castlerigg Cl SK4 . . . . .111 D7
Castlerigg Dr
 Middleton M24 . . . . .46 C2
 Royton OL2 . . . . .48 C6
Castleton Ave M32 . . . . .96 B3
Castleton Bank SK13 .171 C1
Castleton Cres SK13 . . . . .171 C1
Castleton Ct
  Denton M34 . . . . .113 A8
  Tyldesley M29 . . . . .58 F1
Castleton Gn SK13 . . . .134 F6
Castleton Gn SK13 . . . .171 C1
Castleton Gr
 Ashton-u-L OL6 . . . . .85 F6
  Gamesley SK13 . . . . . . .171 C1
Castleton Prim Sch OL11 .30 D2
Castleton Rd
 Hazel Grove SK7 . . . . .124 E1
  Manchester M7 . . . . .63 E1
 Royton OL2,OL16 . . . . .48 D8
 Salford M7 . . . . .155 E8
 Stretford M32 . . . . .96 B4
Castleton Rd S OL11 . . . . . .30 D3
Castleton St
 Altrincham WA14 . . . . .119 C7
 Bolton BL2 . . . . .25 B2
 Oldham OL9 . . . . .152 C6
Castleton Sta OL11 . . . . . . .30 C2
Castleton Terr SK13 . . .171 C1
Castleton Way
  Denton M34 . . . . .113 A8
 Wigan WN3 . . . . .54 C2
Castleton Wlk M11 . . . .160 F1
Castleway
 Altrincham WA15 . . . . .129 C7
 Hindley WN2 . . . . .57 A5
 Rochdale OL11 . . . . .30 B1
 Salford M6 . . . . .154 E4
Castlewood Gdns SK2 . . .124 C5

Castlewood Rd M7 . . . . .81 A8
Castlewood Sq BL2 . . . . . . .25 C1
Catchdale Cl M9 . . . . .64 C5
Catches Cl OL11 . . . . .30 B8
Catches La OL11 . . . . .14 B1
Cateaton St Bury BL9 .140 F3
 Manchester M3 . . . . .158 F2
Caterham Ave BL3 . . . . . . .146 A3
Catford La SK4 . . . . .160 D1
Catesby Rd M16 . . . . .97 D3
Catfield Wlk M15 . . . . .162 D7
Catford Rd M23 . . . . .120 F5
Cathedral App M3 . . . . . . .158 F2
Cathedral Cl OL11 . . . . . . .101 D6
Cathedral Gates M4 . . . . .158 F2
Cathedral Rd OL9 . . . . .48 A1
Cathedral St M4 . . . . .158 F2
Cathedral Yd M3 . . . . .158 F2
Catherine Ho SK4 . . . . .110 F2
Catherine Rd
 Altrincham WA14 . . . . .119 C3
 Manchester M7,M8 . . . . . . .63 E1
 Romiley SK6 . . . . .112 F2
 Swinton M27 . . . . .79 C7
Catherine St Bolton BL3 . .146 B2
 Bury BL9 . . . . .44 E6
 Eccles M30 . . . . .79 B3
 Hazel Grove SK7 . . . . .124 E3
 Hyde SK14 . . . . .167 D3
 Leigh WN7 . . . . .75 F6
 Manchester M11 . . . . .99 E7
  Oldham OL4 . . . . .67 E6
 Wigan WN1 . . . . .151 E8
Catherine St E Bl6 . . . . . . .22 B5
Catherine St W Bl6 . . . . . . .22 B5
Catherine Terr WN1 . . . . .151 E8
Catherine Way WA12 . . . . .89 B2
Catherston Rd M16 . . . .97 E3
Cathrine St E M34 . . . . . . .100 D3
Cathrine St W M34 . . . . . .100 D3
Catlow La M 159 A2
Catlow St M7 . . . . .158 E4
Cato St M7 . . . . .11 A4
Caton Cl BL9 . . . . .44 E8
Caton Dr M46 . . . . .76 A8
Caton St OL16 . . . . .139 F6
Catterall Cres BL2 . . . . .25 C6
Catterick Ave
 Manchester M20 . . . . .110 C3
 Sale M33 . . . . .107 C2
Catterick Dr BL3 . . . . .43 A3
Catterick Rd M20 . . . . .110 C3
Catterwood Dr SK6 . . . . . .114 B2
Cattlin Way OL8 . . . . .66 C2
Caunce Ave Golborne WA3 .90 A7
 Newton-le-W WA12 . . . . . . .89 C1
Caunce Rd WN1 . . . . .151 E8
Caunce St WN1 . . . . .151 E8
Causeway Head BB4 . . . . . .1 A8
Causeway The
  Altrincham WA14 . . . . . .119 D4
 Oldham OL9 . . . . .65 E5
Causewood Cl OL4 . . . . .49 E4
Causey Dr M24 . . . . .46 D3
Cavalier St M40 . . . . .160 D2
Cavan Cl SK3 . . . . .122 F7
Cavanagh Cl M13 . . . . .164 D6
Cavannah Ct OL11 . . . . .49 E3
Cavell St M1 . . . . .159 B1
Cavell Way M5 . . . . .81 A1
Cavendish Ave
 Manchester M20 . . . . .109 F6
 Swinton M27 . . . . .62 C3
Cavendish Ct
 Manchester,Broughton Park
 M7 .63 D1
 Manchester,Heaton Mersey
 SK4 . . . . .110 F2
 Stretford M32 . . . . .96 E4
Cavendish Dr WN3 . . . . . .147 D3
Cavendish Gdns BL3 . . . .147 D3
Cavendish Gr M30 . . . . .79 E3
Cavendish Ho OL7 . . . . . . .166 B2
Cavendish Mews SK9 . . . .137 A6
Cavendish Mill OL6 . . . . . .166 B2
Cavendish Pl
 Droylsden M11 . . . . .83 A2
 Pendlebury M27 . . . . .80 A8
Cavendish Rd
 Altrincham WA14 . . . . .119 C3
 Eccles M30 . . . . .79 E4
 Hazel Grove SK7 . . . . .133 E8
 Manchester,Broughton Park
 M7 .63 D1
 Manchester,Heaton Mersey
 SK4 . . . . .110 F2
 Manchester,Withington
 M20 . . . . .109 F6
 Rochdale OL11 . . . . .30 E3
 Stretford M32 . . . . .96 E4
 Swinton M28 . . . . .79 B6
 Urmston M41 . . . . .95 E2
Cavendish Road Prim Sch
 M20 . . . . .110 A5
Cavendish St
 Ashton-u-L OL6 . . . . .166 A2
 Leigh WN7 . . . . .75 F7
 Manchester M15 . . . . .163 A6
  Oldham OL8 . . . . .153 E6
Cavendish Way OL1 . . . . . .48 C2
Cavenham Gr BL1 . . . .144 C8
Cavenham Wlk M9 . . . . . . .156 C7
Caversham Dr M9 . . . . . . .157 E8
Cawdor Ave BL4 . . . . .42 C2
Cawdor Ho M24 . . . . .65 D7
Cawdor Pl WA15 . . . . .120 C6
Cawdor Rd M14 . . . . .98 C1

Cawdor St Eccles M30 . . . .79 C1
 Farnworth BL4 . . . . .42 C1
 Hindley WN2 . . . . .56 E5
 Leigh WN7 . . . . .75 F4
 Manchester M15 . . . . .162 D7
 Swinton M27 . . . . .79 D8
 Walkden M28 . . . . .60 E2
  Wigan WN5 . . . . .54 F6
Cawdor Wlk BL4 . . . . . .42 C2
Cawley Ave Culcheth WA3 .91 E4
 Prestwich M25 . . . . .62 F2
Cawley Terr M9 . . . . .64 A5
Cawood Sq SK5 . . . . .112 C6
Cawston Wlk M8 . . . . .156 A6
Caxton Cl WN3 . . . . .54 F7
Caxton Rd M14 . . . . .110 B8
Caxton St Heywood OL10 . .29 D2
 Rochdale OL11 . . . . .30 C1
 Salford M3 . . . . .158 E2
Caxton Way M5 . . . . .81 B1
Caygill St M3 . . . . .158 F2
Caythorpe St M14 . . . . .98 A3
Cayton St M12 . . . . .99 A3
CE Sch of the Resurrection
 M11 . . . . .160 F1
Ceal The SK6 . . . . .114 B2
Cecil Ave Sale M33 . . . . . .107 F3
 Wigan WN6 . . . . .37 A2
Cecil Dr M41 . . . . .94 E2
Cecil Gr M18 . . . . .99 D5
Cecil Rd
 Altrincham WA14 . . . . .119 E2
 Eccles M30 . . . . .79 D3
 Manchester M9 . . . . .64 D5
 Stretford M32 . . . . .96 C1
Cecil St Ashton-u-L OL7 . . .84 F1
 Bolton BL2 . . . . .148 B7
 Bury BL9 . . . . .140 F1
 Dukinfield SK16 . . . . .101 C8
 Ince-in-M WN3 . . . . .53 E4
 Leigh WN7 . . . . .76 A4
 Littleborough OL15 . . . . . . .15 F5
 Manchester M15 . . . . .163 B5
 Mossley OL5 . . . . .86 C8
 Oldham OL8 . . . . .153 E5
 Rochdale OL11 . . . . .139 F5
 Royton OL2 . . . . .48 C4
 Stalybridge SK15 . . . . .86 B1
 Stockport SK3 . . . . .170 E7
 Walkden M28 . . . . .60 D3
 Wigan WN1 . . . . .151 E8
Cecil Walker Ho M31 . . . .106 A1
Cecil Wlk OL7 . . . . . . .166 A1
Cecilia St BL3 . . . . .42 A4
Cedar Ave
 Altrincham WA14 . . . . .119 C4
 Ashton-u-L OL6 . . . . .85 D5
 Atherton M46 . . . . .58 B4
 Hazel Grove SK7 . . . . .124 E2
 Heywood OL10 . . . . .29 C3
 Hindley WN2 . . . . .56 F3
 Horwich BL6 . . . . .22 E1
 Little Lever BL3 . . . . .43 B2
 Stalybridge SK15 . . . . .86 C3
 Standish WN6 . . . . .36 B4
 Whitefield M45 . . . . .62 F6
Cedar Bank Cl OL16 . . . . . .31 D7
Cedar Cl Glossop SK13 . . .104 B2
 Poynton SK12 . . . . .133 E3
Cedar Cres
 Chadderton OL9 . . . . .152 B8
 Newton-le-W WA12 . . . . . . .89 D2
 Ramsbottom BL0 . . . . .138 C7
Cedar Ct
  Altrincham WA15 . . . . . .120 B5
 Culcheth WA3 . . . . .91 F1
 Manchester M14 . . . . .98 C1
Cedar Dr Swinton M27 . . . .61 D4
 Urmston M41 . . . . .95 C1
 Wigan WN1 . . . . .37 D2
Cedar Gr Denton M34 . . . .100 E3
 Downall Green WN4 . . . . . .72 D5
 Farnworth BL4 . . . . .60 B8
 Manchester M14 . . . . .110 D8
 Manchester,Heaton Chapel
 SK4 . . . . .111 C5
 Orrell WN5 . . . . .53 F6
 Prestwich M25 . . . . .63 A6
 Royton OL2 . . . . .48 D6
 Shaw OL2 . . . . .149 B6
 Stalybridge SK16 . . . . .101 F8
 Westhoughton BL5 . . . . . . .57 E5
Cedar Ho M14 . . . . .98 C1
Cedar La Newhey OL16 . . . .32 A3
 Uppermill OL4 . . . . .68 D6
Cedar Lawn SK8 . . . . .123 A2
Cedar Lo SK7 . . . . .132 F7
Cedar Mews OL7 . . . . .85 B5
Cedar Mount High Sch
 M18 .99 C3
Cedar Pk SK7 . . . . .123 E1
Cedar Pl M7 . . . . .81 C4
Cedar Rd
 Altrincham WA14 . . . . .119 E3
 Failsworth M35 . . . . .152 A8
 Leigh WN7 . . . . .75 E8
 Marple SK6 . . . . .125 E4
 Middleton M24 . . . . .65 C8
 Partington M31 . . . . .105 E3
 Sale M33 . . . . .107 D6
 Stockport SK2 . . . . .123 E1
Cedar St Ashton-u-L OL6 . .85 D4
 Bolton BL3 . . . . .141 A3
 Bury BL9 . . . . .141 B3
 Dukinfield SK14 . . . . .101 E5

Cedar St continued
 Newton-le-W WA12 . . . . . . .89 C2
  Oldham OL4 . . . . .67 C7
 Rochdale OL12 . . . . .14 F1
 Walsden OL14 . . . . .6 A8
Cedarfield Rd WA13 . . . . .117 B4
Cedars SK9 . . . . .136 F6
Cedars Rd M22 . . . . .121 D3
Cedars The Bolton BL1 . .24 F6
 Manchester SK4 . . . . .111 C5
Cedarway SK9 . . . . .136 F5
Cedarwood Ave SK4 . . . . .168 A1
Cedric Rd Manchester M8 . .63 E2
 Oldham OL4 . . . . .67 D7
Cedric St M5 . . . . .154 E2
Celandine Cl OL15 . . . . .15 F6
Celandine Wlk WN3 . . . . . .54 B4
Celia St M8 . . . . .156 C8
Cellini Sq BL1 . . . . .143 D1
Celtic St SK1 . . . . .124 A8
Cemetery Rd N M27 . . . . . .61 E2
Cemetery Rd S M27 . . . . . .61 E1
Cemetery St
 Middleton M24 . . . . .47 A1
 Radcliffe M26 . . . . .43 F4
Cemetery View PR7 . . . . . .21 A6
Cennick Cl OL4 . . . . . . .67 C6
Centaur Cl M27 . . . . .61 F2
Centaur Way M8 . . . . .155 F7
Centenary Circ M50 . . . . . .80 B1
Centenary St BL3 . . . . .147 F4
Centenary Way
 Eccles M17 . . . . .96 B8
 Salford M17,M50 . . . . .80 A1
Central Ave Atherton M46 . .58 E4
 Bury BL9 . . . . .44 D7
 Edenfield BL0 . . . . .1 C4
 Farnworth BL4 . . . . .60 B8
 Leigh WN7 . . . . .76 C3
 Littleborough OL15 . . . . . . .16 B6
 Manchester M19 . . . . .99 A1
 Pendlebury M6 . . . . .80 E6
 Sale M33 . . . . .107 D1
 Swinton M27 . . . . .62 B2
 Uppermill OL3 . . . . .69 B5
 Walkden M28 . . . . .60 C5
Central Bldgs M2 . . . . .162 F8
Central Dr Bury BL9 . . . . . .27 F8
 Gatley SK8 . . . . .131 D8
 Manchester M8 . . . . .64 B1
 Pendlebury M27 . . . . .80 D7
 Reddish SK5 . . . . .111 F5
 Romiley SK6 . . . . .113 C3
 Shevington WN6 . . . . .36 B6
 Stockport SK7 . . . . .123 D2
 Urmston M41 . . . . .95 E2
Central Store SK13 . . . .104 C1
 Central Trad Pk OL11 . . . .67 A8
Central Way
 Altrincham WA14 . . . . .119 D4
 Newton-le-W WA12 . . . . . . .89 E2
Centre Ct WN7 . . . . .75 B1
Centre Gdns BL1 . . . . .143 D1
Centre Park Rd BL1 . . . . .143 D1
Centre The WN7 . . . . .76 E6
Centre Vale OL15 . . . . .16 C7
Centrepoint M17 . . . . .96 B5
Centurion Gr M7 . . . . .155 E6
Century Ho M22 . . . . .162 F8
Century Lo BL4 . . . . .60 C8
Century Park Ind Area
 WA14 . . . . .119 A6
Century St M3 . . . . .162 E8
Cestrian St BL3 . . . . .147 F3
Ceylon St Failsworth M40 . .83 A6
 Oldham OL8 . . . . .66 D3
Chadbury Cl BL6 . . . . .40 C3
Chadderton Dr BL9 . . . . . . .45 A2
Chadderton Hall Jun Sch
 OL9 .47 F1
Chadderton Hall Rd OL1,
 OL9 .47 F1
Chadderton Ind Est M24 . .65 C5
Chadderton Park Rd OL9 .47 F1
Chadderton Prec OL9 . . . .152 B7
Chadderton Rd M4 . . . . . . .159 B2

Chadderton Way
 Oldham OL1,OL9 . . . . .153 D8
 Oldham OL1,OL9 . . . . .48 C1
Chaddesley Wlk M11 . . . .165 A8
Chaddock La
 Boothstown M28 . . . . .77 F6
 Tyldesley M29,M29 . . . . . . .77 D6
Chaddock Level The M28 .78 A5
Chadkirk SK6 . . . . .125 B8
Chadkirk Chapel* SK6 . . .113 C1
Chadkirk Ind Est SK6 . . . .125 B8
Chadkirk Rd SK6 . . . . .113 B1
Chadvil Rd SK8 . . . . .122 C5
Chadwell Rd SK2 . . . . .124 E7
Chadwick Cl
 Handforth SK9 . . . . .131 C1
  Manchester M14 . . . . . . .98 B3
Chadwick Fold Bury BL9 . .27 F7
 Heywood OL10 . . . . .29 F2
Chadwick Hall Rd OL11 . . .30 B6
Chadwick La
 Rochdale,Castleton OL10,
 OL11 . . . . .30 A2
 Rochdale,Pleasant View
 OL16 . . . . .31 C2
Chadwick Rd Eccles M30 . .79 E2
 Urmston M41 . . . . .95 F2
Chadwick St
 Ashton-u-L OL6 . . . . .85 E2
 Bolton BL2 . . . . .148 B6
 Bury BL9 . . . . .28 E4
 Glossop SK13 . . . . .116 B8
  Hindley WN2 . . . . .56 E6
 Leigh WN7 . . . . .75 F6
 Little Lever BL3 . . . . .43 B3
 Marple SK6 . . . . .125 F5
 Milnrow OL16 . . . . .31 D7
 Rochdale OL11 . . . . .139 D7
 Stockport SK1 . . . . .170 F8
 Swinton M27 . . . . .79 F8
 Wigan WN3 . . . . .150 B6
Chadwick Terr OL12 . . . . . .14 D4
Chaffinch Cl
 Droylsden M43 . . . . .84 C3
 Oldham OL4 . . . . .67 D4
 Wythenshawe M22 . . . . . .121 F5
Chaffinch Dr BL9 . . . . .141 C4
Chain Bar La SK14 . . . . . . .86 E7
Chain Bar La SK14 . . . . . .102 F2
Chain Rd M9 . . . . .64 D5
Chain St M1 . . . . .159 A1
Chain Wlk M9 . . . . . . .163 C6
Chainhurst Wlk M13 .163 C6
Chalbury Cl WN2 . . . . .56 D4
Chalcombe Grange
 M12 .98 F4
Chale Cl M40 . . . . .160 D3
Chale Dr M24 . . . . .65 C6
Chale Gn BL2 . . . . .25 E3
Chalfont Ave M41 . . . . .95 E2
Chalfont Cl OL8 . . . . .67 B4
Chalfont Dr
 Manchester M8 . . . . .156 A7
 Tyldesley M29 . . . . .77 A8
 Walkden M28 . . . . .78 E8
Chalfont Ho M6 . . . . . . .154 F2
Chalfont St BL1 . . . . .143 F2
Chalford Rd M23 . . . . .121 A4
Challenge Way WN5 . . . . . .36 D1
Challenor Sq M12 . . . . . . .165 A6
Challum Dr OL9 . . . . .152 A8
Chamber Hall Cl OL8 . . . . .66 D4
Chamber House Dr OL11 . .30 B3
Chamber House Farm*
 OL10 . . . . .30 A4
Chamber Rd Oldham OL8 . .66 D4
 Shaw OL2 . . . . .149 A7
Chamberhall St BL9 . . . . .140 E3
Chamberlain Dr SK9 . . . . .131 D1
Chamberlain Ho M22 . . . .121 E4
Chamberlain Rd SK15 . . . .86 C5
Chamberlain St BL3 . . . . .145 D6
Chambers Ct SK14 . . . . . .103 A3
Chambers Field Ct
 M5 .81 A1
Chambers The M33 . . . . . .108 A5
Champagnole Ct
 SK16 . . . . .166 B1
Champneys Wlk M9 . . . . .157 D6
Chancel Ave M5 . . . . .161 C8
Chancel Cl SK16 . . . . .101 C6
Chancel La SK9 . . . . .137 B8
Chancel Mews SK1 . . . . . .112 A1
Chancel Pl
  Manchester M1 . . . . .159 C1
 Rochdale OL16 . . . . .139 F7
Chancellor La M12 . . . . . . .164 D7
Chancery Cl M29 . . . . .77 B8
Chancery La Bolton BL1 . .145 F7
  Manchester M3 . . . . .158 F1
 Shaw OL2 . . . . .149 C7
 Uppermill OL3 . . . . .51 A2
Chancery Pl M1 . . . . . .158 F1
Chancery Wlk OL9 . . . . . .152 C8
Chandler Way M29 . . . . . . .90 E8
 Oldham OL4 . . . . .67 C6
Chandlers Mews M22 . . . .109 E1
Chandlers Row M5 . . . . . . .79 A5
Chandley Ct SK1 . . . . .124 A7
Chandley St SK8 . . . . .122 D6
Chandos Gr M5 . . . . .154 D2

Chandos Rd
Manchester M21 . . . .**97** C1
Manchester,Heaton Chapel
SK4 . . . .**111** C6
Manchester,Hilton Park
M25 . . . . .63 B2
Chandos Rd S M21 . . . . .**109** C8
Chandos St OL2 . . . .**149** C7
Change Way M3 . . . .**158** E3
Channing Ct 15 OL16 . . . . .31 B6
Channing Sq 22 OL16 . . . . .31 B6
Chanters Ave M46 . . . . . . .58 E3
Chanters The M28 . . . . . . .78 C7
Chantlers Ave BL8 . . . . . . .27 A1
Chantlers Prim Sch BL8 . . .27 A2
Chantry Cl Disley SK12 . . .**135** E5
Reddish M45 . . . .**111** E7
Westhoughton BL5 . . . . .57 F5
Chantry Fold SK12 . . . . . .**135** E6
Chantry Rd SK12 . . . .**135** E6
Chantry Wlk
Ashton-in-M WN4 . . . .**72** F5
14 Manchester M8 . . . .**155** F7
Chapel Alley 2 BL1 . . . .**145** F7
Chapel Brow
Charlesworth SK13 . . . .**115** E6
Tintwistle SK13 . . . .**104** A7
Chapel Cl
Dukinfield SK16 . . . .**101** D8
Ince-in-M WN3 . . . .**151** D6
Whitefield BL9 . . . . .45 B4
Chapel Croft OL2 . . . .**48** D4
Chapel Ct
Altrincham WA14 . . . .**119** D4
Hyde SK14 . . . .**101** C1
12 Marple SK6 . . . .**125** F6
5 Mossley OL5 . . . . .68 C1
Sale M33 . . . .**107** E6
Wilmslow SK9 . . . .**137** A6
Chapel Dr
Altrincham WA15 . . . .**129** C7
Ashton-u-L OL6 . . . . .85 E5
Chapel End Prim Sch
WN5 . . . . .71 E4
Chapel Field Rd M34 . . . .**100** F3
Chapel Fields
Chapeltown BL7 . . . . .9 C4
1 Marple SK6 . . . .**125** F5
Chapel Fields La WN2 . . . .36 E5
Chapel Gate OL16 . . . . .31 F6
Chapel Gdns Denton M34 .**100** F6
Ramsbottom BL8 . . . . .10 E1
Chapel Gn M34 . . . .**100** F7
Chapel Gr Radcliffe M26 . . .62 A8
Urmston M41 . . . . .95 E2
Chapel Grange BL7 . . . . . . .9 C4
Chapel Green Rd WN2 . . . .56 E5
Chapel Hill OL15 . . . . .16 B5
Chapel Ho SK5 . . . .**111** E8
Chapel Hos SK6 . . . .**126** A5
Chapel La
Altrincham WA15 . . . .**129** C7
Coppull PR7 . . . . .19 F8
Hadfield SK13 . . . .**103** F5
Hollinfare WA3 . . . .**105** A2
Manchester M9 . . . . .64 C3
Partington M31 . . . .**105** F2
Ramsbottom BL8 . . . .**138** A6
Rochdale OL11 . . . . .29 C8
Royton OL2 . . . . .48 D4
Sale M33 . . . .**107** E6
Stretford M32 . . . . .96 C1
Wilmslow SK9 . . . .**137** A6
Chapel Mdw M28 . . . . .78 B7
Chapel Pl
Ashton-in-M WN4 . . . . .73 B3
Bolton BL2,BL3 . . . .**148** C5
Urmston M41 . . . . .95 D8
Chapel Rd
Alderley Edge SK9 . . . .**137** A1
Irlam M44 . . . . .94 A2
Manchester M25 . . . . .63 A1
Oldham OL8 . . . . .66 C2
Sale M33 . . . .**108** B5
Swinton M27 . . . . .79 C7
Uppermill OL3 . . . . .69 A6
Wythenshawe M22 . . . .**121** D8
Chapel St Adlington PR7 . . .20 F6
7 Alderley Edge SK9 . . . . .**137** A1
Ashton-in-M WN4 . . . . .73 B3
Ashton-u-L OL6 . . . .**166** C3
Atherton M46 . . . . .58 D3
14 Bacup OL13 . . . . .3 C8
Blackrod BL6 . . . . .21 D2
Bolton BL1 . . . .**145** F8
Bolton,Egerton BL7 . . . . .8 D3
Boothstown M28 . . . . .77 F6
Bury BL9 . . . .**140** F2
Bury,Tottington BL8 . . . . . . .26 F7
Cheadle SK8 . . . .**122** D5
Denton M34 . . . .**100** F6
Droylsden M43 . . . . .84 B1
Dukinfield SK16 . . . .**101** B8
3 Eccles M30 . . . . .79 C1
Farnworth BL4 . . . . .60 E8
Glossop SK13 . . . .**104** C1
Hazel Grove SK7 . . . .**124** E3
Heywood OL10 . . . . .29 D2
Hindley WN2 . . . . .56 D5
Horwich BL6 . . . . .22 C3
Hyde SK14 . . . .**167** D2
Ince-in-M WN3 . . . .**151** D6
Kearsley M26 . . . . .61 B8

Chapel St continued
Leigh WN7 . . . . .76 B4
Leigh,Bickershaw WN2 . . . . .56 E1
Little Lever BL3 . . . . .43 B3
Littleborough OL15 . . . . .6 D2
Manchester,Heaton Mersey
SK4 . . . .**110** D2
Manchester,Levenshulme
M19 .99 B1
12 Middleton M24 . . . . .46 F1
6 Mossley OL5 . . . . .68 C1
Newton-le-W WA12 . . . . .89 B3
Oldham OL4 . . . . .67 E6
Platt Bridge WN2 . . . . .56 B2
Prestwich M25 . . . . .63 A4
10 Rochdale OL11 . . . . .31 A4
Romiley SK6 . . . .**113** B5
Rowarth SK22 . . . .**127** E7
Royton OL2 . . . . .48 D4
Salford M3 . . . .**158** E2
Shaw OL2 . . . .**149** B7
Stalybridge SK15 . . . . .86 A2
Swinton M27 . . . . .62 A1
Tyldesley M29 . . . . .77 A8
Uppermill OL3 . . . . .69 B8
Wardle OL12 . . . . .15 C7
Whitworth OL12 . . . . .14 C8
Wigan WN3 . . . .**150** C7
Wigan,Lamberhead Green
WN5 . . . . .54 B5
Wigan,Lamberhead Green
WN5 . . . . .54 B6
Wigan,Whelley WN2 . . . . . . .38 A2
Chapel Street Prim Sch
M19 .99 B1
Chapel Terr WA3 . . . . .91 B8
Chapel View SK16 . . . . . .**101** C8
Chapel Way PR7 . . . . .19 F8
Chapel Wlk 1 Eccles M30 .79 F2
Golborne WA3 . . . . .91 B8
Hadfield SK13 . . . .**103** E5
Middleton M24 . . . . .64 C7
Oldham OL1 . . . . .48 D1
Prestwich M25 . . . . .62 F1
Whitefield M45 . . . . .45 A1
Chapel Wlks
Cheadle SK8 . . . .**132** B6
Manchester M2 . . . .**158** F1
Sale M33 . . . .**108** B5
Chapelfield M26 . . . . .44 C1
Chapelfield Cl SK15 . . . . . .86 D4
Chapelfield Dr M28 . . . . . . .60 B3
Chapelfield Prim Sch
M26 .44 C1
Chapelfield Rd M12 . . . . . .**163** C8
Chapelfield St BL1 . . . . . .**143** E3
Chapelhill Dr M9 . . . . .64 C3
Chapelstead BL5 . . . . .57 F5
Chapeltown Rd
Chapeltown BL7 . . . . .9 C2
Radcliffe M26 . . . . .62 A8
Chapeltown St M1 . . . . . .**159** C1
Chapelway Gdns OL2 . . . . .48 D6
Chaplin Cl M6 . . . .**154** E4
Chapman Ct SK14 . . . .**102** D2
Chapman Mews M18 . . . . . .99 D5
Chapman Rd SK14 . . . . . .**102** E1
Chapman St Bolton BL1 . . .**142** B1
Manchester M18 . . . . .99 D5
Chappell Rd M43 . . . . .84 A2
Chapter St M40 . . . .**160** F4
Charcoal Rd WA14 . . . . . .**118** F3
Charcoal Woods WA14 . . .**118** F3
Charcon Wlk 3 OL2 . . . . . .48 E4
Chard Dr M22 . . . .**121** D1
Chard St M26 . . . . .44 C1
Chardin Ave SK6 . . . .**126** C8
Charges St OL7 . . . . .84 F1
Chariot St M11 . . . . .99 D8
Charity St WN7 . . . . .75 C5
Charlbury Ave
Manchester M25 . . . . .63 E3
Reddish SK5 . . . .**111** E8
Charlbury Way OL2 . . . . . .**149** A5
Charlecote Rd SK12 . . . . .**133** F4
Charles Ave
Droylsden M34 . . . .**100** A7
Tyldesley M29 . . . . .77 B8
Walkden M28 . . . . .60 C2
Charles Ct
Altrincham WA15 . . . .**120** B6
Bolton BL1 . . . .**145** F8
Charles Halle Rd M15 . . . .**163** A5
Charles Holden St BL1 . . .**145** D6
Charles La Glossop SK13 . .**104** E3
Milnrow OL16 . . . . .32 A5
Charles Mews OL16 . . . . . .32 A5
Charles Morris Cl M35 . . . .84 B8
Charles Morris Ho M35 . . .84 A7
Charles Shaw Cl 4 OL4 . . .49 D1
Charles St
Ashton-u-L OL7 . . . .**166** B2
Bolton,Egerton BL7 . . . . .8 D2
2 Bolton,Mill Hill BL1 . . . . .**148** A8
5 Bury BL9 . . . .**140** F3
Denton M34 . . . .**100** F5
Droylsden M43 . . . . .83 E1
Dukinfield SK16 . . . .**166** B1
6 Farnworth BL4 . . . . .42 E1
Farnworth BL4 . . . . .42 E1
Glossop SK13 . . . .**104** C1
Golborne WA3 . . . . .74 A1
Hazel Grove SK7 . . . .**124** D3
Heywood OL10 . . . . .46 E8
Hindley WN2 . . . . .56 D5
Ince-in-M WN2 . . . . .56 A7
Irlam M44 . . . .**105** E6
Leigh WN7 . . . . .76 A5
Leigh WN7 . . . . .76 A6

Charles St continued
Littleborough OL15 . . . . .16 A5
Manchester M1 . . . .**163** A8
Oldham OL2 . . . .**152** C6
Royton OL2 . . . . .48 D4
Salford M6 . . . .**154** F4
Stockport SK1 . . . .**124** A7
Swinton M27 . . . . .61 D2
Tyldesley M29 . . . . .58 F1
Whitefield M45 . . . . .62 F7
2 Wigan WN1 . . . .**151** D7
Charles Whittaker St 2
OL12 . . . . .13 F1
Charles Wlk M45 . . . . .62 F7
Charleston Cl M33 . . . . . .**107** D2
Charleston Ct M30 . . . . . . .79 D2
Charleston Sq M41 . . . . . . .95 B3
Charleston St OL8 . . . . . . .66 F4
Charlestown SK13 . . . .**116** C7
Charlestown Cl OL6 . . . . .**166** B3
Charlestown Com Prim Sch
M6 . . . . .81 B4
Charlestown Ct OL6 . . . . .**166** B4
Charlestown Ind Est
OL6 . . . .**166** B4
Charlestown Prim Com Sch
M9 . . . . .65 B3
Charlestown Rd
Glossop SK13 . . . .**116** C7
Manchester M9 . . . . .64 E2
Charlestown Rd E SK2 . . .**124** A3
Charlestown Rd W SK3 . .**123** F3
Charlestown Way OL6 . . .**166** A3
Charlesworth Ave
Bolton BL3 . . . . .42 B3
Denton M34 . . . .**112** F8
Hindley WN2 . . . . .56 F4
Charlesworth Prim Sch
SK13 . . . .**115** C6
Charlesworth St
Manchester M11 . . . .**164** F8
Stockport SK1,SK3 . . . .**170** F7
Charley Ave M7 . . . .**158** D4
Charlock Ave BL5 . . . . .57 E6
Charlock Cl WN7 . . . . .75 F3
Charlotte La OL4 . . . . .68 E5
Charlotte Pl WA15 . . . .**119** F7
Charlotte St
28 Bolton BL1 . . . .**143** E2
Chapeltown BL7 . . . . .9 C4
Cheadle SK8 . . . .**122** D5
Manchester M1,M2 . . . .**159** A1
Ramsbottom BL0 . . . .**138** B5
Rochdale OL16 . . . . .31 B3
Stockport SK1 . . . .**112** B3
Charlton Ave
Dukinfield SK14 . . . .**102** A4
Eccles M30 . . . . .79 D1
Prestwich M25 . . . . .63 B3
Charlton Brook Ho SK8 . .**122** E6
Charlton Ct
2 Manchester M16 . . . . .97 C3
Prestwich M25 . . . . .63 B3
Charlton Dr Sale M33 . . . .**108** C4
Swinton M27 . . . . .61 D2
Charlton Pl M12 . . . .**163** B7
Charlton Rd M19 . . . . .99 B1
Charminster Dr M8 . . . . . .**156** B8
Charmouth Cl WA12 . . . . . .89 B4
Charmouth Wlk M22 . . . . .**121** F3
Charnley Cl
Manchester M40 . . . .**160** E3
7 Sale M33 . . . .**108** A4
Charnley Grange BL6 . . . . .40 B7
Charnley St M45 . . . . .62 F8
Charnock Dr BL1 . . . .**143** E1
Charnock Rd WA3 . . . . .91 F3
Charnock St WN2 . . . . .56 B1
Charnock's Yd 2 WN5 . . . .54 B5
Charnville Rd SK8 . . . .**121** F5
Charnwood Ave M34 . . . . .**100** B3
Charnwood Cl
Ashton-u-L OL6 . . . . .85 C7
Shaw OL2 . . . . .48 E8
Tyldesley M29 . . . . .77 B8
Walkden M28 . . . . .60 C2
Charnwood Cres SK7 . . . .**133** D8
Charnwood Rd
Manchester M9 . . . . .64 D5
Romiley SK6 . . . .**113** C5
Wilmslow SK9 . . . .**137** D6
Charter Ave M26 . . . . .44 C2
Charter Cl 3 M33 . . . .**107** D3
Charter Ho M30 . . . . .79 F1
Charter Rd WA15 . . . .**119** E4
Charter St
Manchester M3 . . . .**158** F3
Rochdale OL16 . . . . .31 B4
Charterhouse Rd WN3 . . .**151** E6
Chartist Ho SK14 . . . .**167** E2
Chartwell Cl M5,M6 . . . . .**154** F2
Chartwell Dr M23 . . . .**120** E7
Chase St M4 . . . .**159** A3
Chase The M28 . . . . .79 A5
Chasefield WA14 . . . .**119** A2
Chaseley Rd
Rochdale OL12 . . . .**139** E8
Salford M6 . . . .**154** F3
Chasetown Cl 5 M23 . . . .**120** D6
Chassen Ave M41 . . . . .95 B2
Chassen Cl M41 . . . . .95 B1
Chassen Rd Bolton BL1 . . .**144** B7
Urmston M41 . . . . .95 B1
Chassen Road Sta M41 . . .95 B1
Chataway Rd M8 . . . .**156** C8

Chatburn Ave
Golborne WA3 . . . . .74 C1
Trub OL11 . . . . .47 D8
Chatburn Ct Culcheth WA3 .91 F2
Shaw OL2 . . . .**149** C8
Chatburn Gdns OL10 . . . . .28 F2
Chatburn Rd Bolton BL1 . . .23 F3
Manchester M21 . . . .**109** C8
Chatburn Sq OL11 . . . . . . .47 D8
Chatcombe Rd M22 . . . . . .**121** A2
Chatfield Rd M21 . . . .**109** B8
Chatford Cl M7 . . . .**158** E4
Chatham Ct M20 . . . .**110** A6
Chatham Gdns BL3 . . . . . .**145** D5
Chatham Gr M20 . . . .**110** A6
Chatham Ho 1 SK3 . . . . . .**170** E8
Chatham Pl 2 BL3 . . . . . .**145** D5
Chatham Rd
Manchester M16 . . . . .97 C3
Reddish M18 . . . . .99 E3
Chatham St Hyde SK14 . . .**113** E7
Ince-in-M WN2 . . . . .56 B8
Leigh WN7 . . . . .75 F7
Manchester M1 . . . .**159** B1
Stockport SK3 . . . .**170** D8
Wigan WN1 . . . .**151** E2
Chatley Rd M30 . . . . .78 F1
Chatley St M3,M4 . . . .**159** A4
Chatswood Ave SK2 . . . . .**170** F6
Chatsworth Ave
Culcheth WA3 . . . . .91 F4
Ince-in-M WN3 . . . . .55 F4
Prestwich M25 . . . . .63 B4
Chatsworth Cl
Altrincham WA15 . . . .**120** C5
Ashton-in-M WN4 . . . . .72 F4
Droylsden M43 . . . . .83 E3
Shaw OL2 . . . . .49 D8
2 Urmston M41 . . . . .95 E2
Whitefield BL9 . . . . .45 A5
Chatsworth Cres M32 . . . .95 F3
Chatsworth Ct
Adlington PR6 . . . . .20 F8
Stockport SK2 . . . .**124** A5
Leigh WN7 . . . . .76 E7
Chatsworth Gr
Little Lever BL3 . . . . .43 A4
Manchester M16 . . . . .97 D2
Chatsworth Manor SK7 . .**123** C2
Chatsworth Mews SK7 . . .**123** D2
Chatsworth Rd
Droylsden M43 . . . . .83 E2
Eccles M30 . . . . .79 F4
Hazel Grove SK7 . . . .**133** F8
High Lane SK6 . . . .**134** F6
Manchester M18 . . . .**165** C5
Radcliffe M26 . . . . .43 D5
Stretford M32 . . . . .96 A3
Swinton M28 . . . . .79 C5
Wilmslow SK9 . . . .**136** E4
Chatsworth St
Oldham OL4 . . . . .67 C5
Rochdale OL16 . . . . .14 E3
Wigan WN5 . . . . .54 C5
Chatteris Cl WN2 . . . . .56 E4
Chatterton Cl M20 . . . . . .**110** C6
Chatterton La SK6 . . . . . .**127** B8
Chatterton Old La BL0 . . . .1 C2
Chatterton Rd BL0 . . . . .1 C1
Chattock Cl 11 M16 . . . . . .97 E3
Chatton Cl BL8 . . . . .26 F2
Chatwell Cl OL16 . . . . .32 C4
Chatwood Rd M40 . . . . . . .65 E2
Chaucer Ave
Denton M34 . . . .**113** A7
Droylsden M43 . . . . .84 A1
Radcliffe M26 . . . . .43 E4
Reddish SK5 . . . . .99 D8
Chaucer Gr Atherton M46 . .58 D5
Leigh WN7 . . . . .75 D8
Chaucer Mews SK1 . . . . .**112** B1
Chaucer Pl Abram WN2 . . .56 B1
Wigan WN1 . . . . .37 C3
Chaucer Rd M24 . . . . .47 B2
Chaucer Rise SK16 . . . . . .**102** A7
Chaucer St Bolton BL1 . . . .**143** D2
Oldham OL1 . . . .**153** E6
Rochdale OL11 . . . . .30 C2
Royton OL2 . . . . .48 E5
Chaucer Wlk M13 . . . .**163** C6
Chaumont Way OL6 . . . . .**166** B3
Chauncy Rd M40 . . . . .83 E8
Chaytor Ave M40 . . . . .83 B7
Cheadle Coll SK8 . . . .**132** B7
Cheadle Heath Prim Sch
SK3 . . . .**123** A7
Cheadle Hulme Sch
SK8 . . . .**132** A8
Cheadle Hulme Sta SK8 . .**123** B2
Cheadle Old Rd SK3 . . . . .**123** C7
Cheadle Point SK8 . . . . . .**122** F6
Cheadle Prim Sch SK8 . . .**122** D6
Cheadle RC Inf Sch SK8 . .**122** E2
Cheadle RC Jun Sch
SK8 . . . .**122** E2
Cheadle Rd SK8 . . . .**132** F3
Cheadle Royal Bsns Pk
SK8 . . . .**122** C2
Cheadle Royal Hospl
SK8 . . . .**122** C2
Cheadle St M11 . . . . .99 D8
Cheadle Wood SK8 . . . . . .**131** E8
Cheam Rd WA15 . . . .**119** F8
Cheap Side M24 . . . . .47 A2

Cheapside Hyde SK14 . . . .**167** E3
Manchester M2 . . . .**158** F1
Oldham OL1 . . . .**153** E7
Cheapside Sq 8 BL1 . . . .**145** F7
Cheddar St 1 M18 . . . . . . .99 D5
Chedlee Dr SK8 . . . .**131** E8
Chedlin Dr M23 . . . .**121** A4
Chedworth Cres M38 . . . . .60 A6
Chedworth Dr M23 . . . . . .**121** B6
Chedworth Gr BL3 . . . . . .**145** E5
Cheeryble St M11,M43 . . . .99 F7
Cheesden Wlk M45 . . . . . . .45 C1
Cheetham Ave M24 . . . . . . .47 B1
Cheetham CE Com Sch
M8 . . . .**155** F7
Cheetham Fold Rd
SK14 . . . .**113** D8
Cheetham Gdns 7 SK15 . .86 B1
Cheetham Gr 1 WN3 . . . . .54 F5
Cheetham Hill Shaw OL2 . .**149** B6
Whitworth OL12 . . . . .4 D3
Cheetham Hill Rd
Dukinfield SK15,SK16 . . . . .**101** C3
Manchester M8,M4 . . . .**159** A3
Manchester,Cheetham Hill
M8 . . . .**155** F6
Cheetham Mill Ind Est
SK15 . . . . .86 B1
Cheetham Pk M8 . . . .**155** F8
Cheetham Pl SK6 . . . .**112** F4
Cheetham Rd M27 . . . . . . .80 A7
Cheetham St
Failsworth M35 . . . . .84 A8
Manchester M40 . . . .**157** E5
Middleton M24 . . . . .64 A1
Oldham OL1 . . . . .67 B7
Radcliffe M26 . . . . .44 C4
Rochdale OL16 . . . .**139** F8
Shaw OL2 . . . .**149** C6
Cheetham's Cres OL2 . . . . .49 A4
Cheethams The BL6 . . . . . .38 E7
Cheetwood Prim Sch
M8 . . . .**158** E4
Cheetwood Rd M8 . . . . . .**155** F5
Cheetwood St M8 . . . .**158** E4
Chelbourne Dr 3 BL8 . . . .66 B2
Chelburn Cl Leigh WN7 . . .56 E1
Stockport SK2 . . . .**124** D5
Chelburn View OL15 . . . . . .6 C1
Cheldon Wlk 8 M40 . . . . . .83 C6
Chelford Ave Bolton BL1 . . .24 C5
Golborne WA3 . . . . .90 D8
Chelford Cl
Altrincham WA15 . . . .**119** C6
Manchester M13 . . . .**164** D5
Middleton M24 . . . . .47 C2
Wigan WN3 . . . . .54 F2
Chelford Dr Swinton M27 . .61 E2
Tyldesley M29 . . . . .77 C6
Chelford Gr SK3 . . . .**170** D5
Chelford Rd
Alderley Edge SK9 . . . .**136** E1
Handforth SK9 . . . .**131** D5
Manchester M16 . . . . .97 C3
Sale M33 . . . .**108** E2
Chell St M13 . . . . .98 F4
Chellow Ct OL5 . . . . .68 B1
Chellow Dene OL5 . . . . . . .68 B1
Chelmarsh Ave WN4 . . . . . .73 C3
Chelmer Cl BL5 . . . . .40 A1
Chelmer Gr OL10 . . . . .29 A3
Chelmorton Gr WN3 . . . . . .54 C2
Chelmsford Ave M40 . . . . . .83 B4
Chelmsford Dr WN3 . . . . . .35 A1
Chelmsford Mews M7 . . . . .37 C2
Chelmsford Rd SK3 . . . . . .**123** C8
Chelmsford St OL8 . . . . . .**153** E5
Chelmsford Wlk 14 M34 .**101** A1
Chelsea Ave M26 . . . . .43 D4
Chelsea Cl OL2 . . . .**149** B7
Chelsea Rd Bolton BL3 . . .**147** D3
Failsworth M40 . . . . .83 C5
Urmston M41 . . . . .94 C1
Chelsea St Bury BL9 . . . . . .44 F4
Rochdale OL11 . . . .**139** D5
Chelsfield Gr M21 . . . .**109** D8
Chelston Ave M40 . . . . .65 C1
Chelston Dr Gatley SK8 . . .**131** C6
Haslingden BB4 . . . . .1 A7
Chelt Wlk M22 . . . .**121** B2
Cheltenham Ave WN3 . . . .**151** D5
Cheltenham Cres M7 . . . .**155** E7
Cheltenham Dr
Longshaw WN5 . . . . .53 D2
Newto-le-W WA12 . . . . .89 C5
Sale M33 . . . .**108** C4
Cheltenham Gn M24 . . . . . .65 A6
Cheltenham Rd
Cheadle SK3 . . . .**123** A7
Manchester M21 . . . . .97 B2
Middleton M24 . . . . .65 A6
Cheltenham St
Oldham OL1 . . . . .49 B1
Rochdale OL11 . . . . .30 D4
Salford M6 . . . . .81 A4
3 Wigan WN2 . . . . .37 F2
Chelwood Cl Bolton BL1 . . .24 D7
Droylsden M43 . . . . .84 C2
Chelwood Mews BL6 . . . . . .40 B7
Chelwood Pk WA12 . . . . . . .73 B1
Chelworth Manor SK7 . . .**123** C1
Chemical St WA12 . . . . . . .89 B3
Chendre Cl M27 . . . . .61 F2
Chendre Rd M9 . . . . .65 A4
Cheney Cl M11 . . . . .99 D7
Chenies The 8 M7 . . . . . . .63 C1
Chepstow Ave M33 . . . . . .**107** C3
Chepstow Cl OL11 . . . . . . .29 F8

Chepstow Dr
Hazel Grove SK7 . . . . .125 A2
Oldham OL1 . . . . .49 B1
Chepstow Gr WN7 . . . . .76 E7
Chepstow Rd
Manchester M21 . . . . .97 A1
Swinton M27 . . . . .62 A2
Chepstow St M1,M2 . . . . . .162 F8
Chepstow St S M1 . . . . . . .162 F8
Chequers Rd M21 . . . . .109 B8
Chequers St WN1 . . . . .150 B8
Cherington Cl
Handforth SK9 . . . . .131 F3
Wythenshawe M23 . . . . .109 B2
Cherington Dr M29 . . . . . . .59 C1
Cherington Rd SK8 . . . . . . .122 C4
Cheriton Ave M33 . . . . . . .108 C5
Cheriton Cl SK14 . . . . .102 D2
Cheriton Dr BL2 . . . . .42 E6
Cheriton Gdns BL2 . . . . . . .22 B5
Cheriton Rd M41 . . . . .94 D3
Cheriton Rise SK2 . . . . . . .125 A6
Cherrington Dr OL11 . . . . .47 D8
Cherry Ave Ashton-u-L OL6 .85 D6
Bury BL9 . . . . .141 C3
Oldham OL8 . . . . .67 C3
Cherry Cl Bury BL9 . . . . .45 A7
Stockport SK2 . . . . .124 E7
Cherry Cres BB4 . . . . .1 F8
Cherry Ct M33 . . . . .108 A4
Cherry Dr M27 . . . . .80 A8
Cherry Gr Leigh WN7 . . . . .75 F8
Rochdale OL11 . . . . .30 A8
Royton OL2 . . . . .48 C6
Stalybridge SK15 . . . . .102 A8
Wigan WN6 . . . . .36 F3
Cherry Hall Dr OL2 . . . . . . .48 E7
Cherry Hinton OL11 . . . . .153 D8
Cherry Holt Ave SK4 . . . .110 F4
Cherry La
Denshaw OL16,OL3 . . . . .33 B3
Sale M33 . . . . .107 D8
Cherry Manor Prim Sch
M33 . . . . .107 C2
Cherry Orchard Cl SK7 . .123 D1
Cherry St M25 . . . . .63 C5
Cherry Tree Ave
Farnworth BL4 . . . . .60 A8
Poynton SK12 . . . . .133 F3
Cherry Tree Cl
[1] Altrincham WA15 . . . . . . .120 B5
Romiley SK6 . . . . .113 E2
Wilmslow SK9 . . . . .137 E8
Cherry Tree Cotts WA11 . .71 A2
Cherry Tree Ct
[8] Salford M6 . . . . .81 A2
Standish WN6 . . . . .19 D2
Stockport SK2 . . . . .124 C4
Cherry Tree Dr SK7 . . . . .134 A8
Cherry Tree Gr
Atherton M46 . . . . .58 C4
Leigh WN7 . . . . .75 D6
Cherry Tree Hospl SK2 . .124 C5
Cherry Tree La
Billinge WN5 . . . . .71 A2
Bury BL8 . . . . .27 C1
Rawtenstall BB4 . . . . .1 F8
Romiley SK6 . . . . .113 E2
Stockport SK2 . . . . .124 C5
Cherry Tree Prim Sch
BL4 . . . . .59 E8
Cherry Tree Rd
Cheadle SK8 . . . . .123 A1
Golborne WA3 . . . . .90 F8
Wythenshawe M23 . . . . .108 F1
Cherry Tree Way
Bolton BL2 . . . . .25 C5
Haslingden BB4 . . . . .1 B7
[5] Horwich BL6 . . . . .22 E1
Cherry Tree Wlk
Mossley OL5 . . . . .68 B1
Stretford M32 . . . . .96 C1
Cherry Wlk Cheadle SK8 . .132 C8
Partington M31 . . . . .105 D5
Cherrybrook Dr WN3 . . . . .54 D1
Cherrycroft SK6 . . . . .113 E1
Cherryton Wlk M13 . . . . .163 C6
Cherrywood OL9 . . . . .65 D7
Cherrywood Ave BL5 . . . . .59 A7
Cherrywood Cl M28 . . . . . .60 B1
Chertsey Cl Droylsden M18 .99 E5
Shaw OL2 . . . . .149 B8
Chervil Cl M14 . . . . .110 C8
Chervil Wlk WN3 . . . . .54 C4
Cherwell Ave OL10 . . . . . . .29 B3
Cherwell Cl Aspull WN2 . . . .38 C6
Cheadle SK8 . . . . .132 D8
Oldham OL8 . . . . .66 C1
Whitefield M45 . . . . .63 A8
Cherwell Rd BL5 . . . . .39 F2
Cheryl's Bank SK13 . . . . . .116 B8
Chesham Ave Bolton BL1 .143 E2
Trub OL11 . . . . .47 D7
Urmston M41 . . . . .94 E3
Wythenshawe M22 . . . . .121 C4
Chesham Cl
Hadfield SK13 . . . . .104 B5
Wilmslow SK9 . . . . .136 F4
Chesham Cres BL9 . . . . . . .141 A3
Chesham Fold Rd BL9 . . .141 B4
Chesham Ho [6] M5 . . . . . .154 F1
Chesham Ind Est BL9 . . . .141 A4
Chesham Pl WA14 . . . . .119 C2
Chesham Prim Sch BL9 . . .28 A5
Chesham Rd Bury BL9 . . . . .28 A5
Eccles M30 . . . . .95 C8
[3] Oldham OL4 . . . . .67 C6
Wilmslow SK9 . . . . .136 F4

Chesham St BL3 . . . . .146 B2
Cheshill Ct M7 . . . . .155 F6
Cheshire Cl
Newton-le-W WA12 . . . . .89 E3
Stretford M32 . . . . .96 B1
Cheshire Ct BL0 . . . . .11 D6
Cheshire Gdns M14 . . . . . . .98 A1
Cheshire Rd Mossley SK15 .86 E5
Partington M31 . . . . .105 D2
Cheshire Sq SK15 . . . . .86 E5
Cheshire St OL5 . . . . .86 D8
Cheshires The OL5 . . . . . . .68 D1
Chesney Ave OL9 . . . . .65 E2
Chesshyre Ave M4 . . . . . . .160 D1
Chessington Rise M27 . . . .62 A3
Chester Ave
Altrincham WA15 . . . . .119 F2
Dukinfield SK16 . . . . .101 E7
Golborne WA3 . . . . .90 D8
Little Lever BL3 . . . . .43 B4
Rochdale OL11 . . . . .30 A6
Sale M33 . . . . .107 B1
Stalybridge SK15 . . . . .86 D3
Urmston M41 . . . . .95 E3
Whitefield M45 . . . . .63 A7
Chester Cl Handforth SK9 .131 E2
Irlam M44 . . . . .105 D5
Little Lever BL3 . . . . .43 B4
Chester Cres BB4 . . . . .1 B8
Chester Dr
Ashton-in-M WN4 . . . . .73 D2
Ramsbottom BL0 . . . . .11 A4
Chester Pl Adlington PR6 . .21 A8
[7] Royton OL2 . . . . .48 D4
Chester Rd
Hazel Grove SK7 . . . . .124 D1
Manchester,City Park M15,
M16 .161 B5
Manchester,St George's
M15 .162 D7
Poynton SK12 . . . . .133 B4
Stretford M16,M32 . . . . .96 E1
Tyldesley M29 . . . . .77 D8
Woodford SK7 . . . . .132 E2
Chester Sq OL7 . . . . .166 A2
Chester St Bury BL9 . . . . . .141 A4
Denton M34 . . . . .100 F2
Leigh WN7 . . . . .75 F5
Manchester M1 . . . . .163 A7
Oldham OL9 . . . . .152 C5
Prestwich M25 . . . . .63 A5
Stockport SK3 . . . . .169 D1
Swinton M27 . . . . .79 F7
Tyldesley M46 . . . . .58 B5
Chester Wlk [20] BL1 . . . . .143 E2
Chester Wlks SK6 . . . . . . .113 A1
Chester's Croft Pk SK8 . .132 A5
Chesterfield Gr OL6 . . . . . .85 D3
Chesterfield Rd OL4 . . . . . .67 B6
Chesterfield Way [4]
M34 . . . . .113 A8
Chestergate SK1,SK3,
SK4 . . . . .169 E1
Chesterton Cl WN3 . . . . . .150 A5
Chesterton Dr BL3 . . . . .40 E5
Chesterton Gr M43 . . . . . . .84 A2
Chesterton Rd
Oldham OL1 . . . . .49 B2
Wythenshawe M23 . . . . .120 D8
Chestnut Ave
Atherton M46 . . . . .58 C4
Bury BL9 . . . . .141 B2
Bury,Tottington BL8 . . . . .27 A5
Cheadle SK8 . . . . .122 E5
Droylsden M43 . . . . .83 E3
Irlam M44 . . . . .105 D5
Leigh WN7 . . . . .75 F3
Manchester M21 . . . . .109 B8
Walkden M28 . . . . .60 D2
Whitefield M45 . . . . .62 F7
Chestnut Cl Bolton BL3 . . .146 B4
New Mills SK22 . . . . .127 E1
Oldham OL4 . . . . .67 B8
Stalybridge SK15 . . . . .102 A8
Wilmslow SK9 . . . . .137 E8
Chestnut Cres OL8 . . . . . . .67 A2
Chestnut Ct
Manchester M19 . . . . .111 B8
Stockport SK7 . . . . .123 D2
Chestnut Dr [1] Bury BL9 . .27 F6
Leigh WN7 . . . . .75 F2
Poynton SK12 . . . . .133 F3
Rawtenstall BB4 . . . . .1 F8
Sale M33 . . . . .107 D1
Westhoughton BL5 . . . . .57 F7
Chestnut Dr S WN7 . . . . . .75 F1
Chestnut Fold M26 . . . . . . .44 A4
Chestnut Gdns
Denton M34 . . . . .100 E2
Heywood OL10 . . . . .29 C1
Chestnut La
Ashton-in-M WN4 . . . . .73 D4
Failsworth M35 . . . . .83 F6
Golborne WA3 . . . . .90 D8
Hindley WN2 . . . . .57 A4
Radcliffe M26 . . . . .62 A8
Chestnut La WN7 . . . . .75 F2
Chestnut Rd Eccles M30 . . .79 A4
Wigan WN1 . . . . .37 E2
Chestnut St OL9 . . . . .152 C5
Chestnut Villas SK4 . . . . .168 C2
Chestnut Way OL15 . . . . . . .15 F6
Chestnut Wlk
Partington M31 . . . . .105 D2
[4] Partington M31 . . . . .105 E3

Chetham Cl M5 . . . . .161 B7
Chetham's Sch of Music
M3 . . . . .158 F2
Chetwode Ave WN4 . . . . . . .73 B1
Chetwyn Ave Bolton BL2 . . .25 A7
Royton OL2 . . . . .48 C4
Chetwynd Ave M33 . . . . . . .95 C2
Chetwynd Cl [8] M41 . . . . . .95 C2
Chevassut St M15 . . . . . . .162 E6
Chevin Gdns SK7 . . . . .133 A7
Chevington Dr
Manchester,Collyhurst M9 . .157 D6
Manchester,Heaton Mersey
SK4 . . . . .110 E3
Chevington Gdns [2]
BL1 . . . . .143 E3
Cheviot Ave Cheadle SK8 .122 F2
Oldham OL8 . . . . .66 E3
Royton OL2 . . . . .48 C3
Cheviot Cl Bolton BL1 . . . . .24 D5
Bury BL8 . . . . .27 B4
Chadderton OL9 . . . . .152 A5
Horwich BL6 . . . . .22 B5
Middleton M24 . . . . .65 D8
Milnrow OL16 . . . . .32 A7
Ramsbottom BL0 . . . . .11 C4
Salford M6 . . . . .154 E3
Stockport SK4 . . . . .169 C3
Wigan WN3 . . . . .54 C2
Cheviot Ct OL8 . . . . .66 E3
Cheviot Ho OL11 . . . . .30 B8
Cheviot Rd SK7 . . . . .124 B1
Cheviot St M3 . . . . .158 F3
Cheviots Rd OL2 . . . . .149 A8
Chevithorne Cl WA14 . . . .119 B5
Chevril Cl M15 . . . . .162 A6
Chevron Cl Rochdale OL11 . .30 B3
[8] Salford M6 . . . . .81 B2
Chevron Pl WA14 . . . . .119 D7
Chew Brook Dr OL3 . . . . . .69 B5
Chew Moor La BL5,BL6 . . . .40 A2
Chew Rd OL3 . . . . .70 A2
Chew Vale
Dukinfield SK16 . . . . .101 F7
Uppermill OL3 . . . . .69 B5
Chew Valley Rd OL3 . . . . . .69 B5
Chicago Ave M90 . . . . .130 B7
Chichester Ave M46 . . . . . . .58 A2
Chichester Bsns Ctr
OL16 . . . . .31 A7
Chichester Cl
Littleborough OL15 . . . . .15 F3
[4] Sale M33 . . . . .107 D3
Stockport SK9 . . . . .48 A1
Chichester Cres OL9 . . . . . .48 A1
Chichester Rd
Manchester M15 . . . . .162 F5
Romiley SK6 . . . . .113 C2
Chichester Rd S M15 . . . .162 E5
Chichester St OL16 . . . . . . .31 B7
Chichester Way [11] M34 .101 A1
Chidlow Ave M20 . . . . .110 A7
Chidwall Rd M22 . . . . .121 B2
Chief St OL4 . . . . .67 A6
Chiffon Way M3 . . . . .158 D3
Chigwell Cl M22 . . . . .121 E5
Chilcombe Wlk [5] M9 . . . .64 E5
Chilcote Ave M33 . . . . .107 E4
Childwall Cl BL3 . . . . .147 E2
Chilgrove Ave BL6 . . . . .21 D1
Chilham Rd Eccles M30 . . . .79 F4
Walkden M28 . . . . .60 E2
Chilham St Bolton BL3 . . . .146 B2
Swinton M27 . . . . .79 E6
Wigan WN5 . . . . .54 B6
Chillingham Dr WN7 . . . . . .76 C4
Chillington Wlk M34 . . . . .100 E1
Chilmark Dr M23 . . . . .121 A6
Chiltern Ave Atherton M46 .58 F5
Cheadle SK8 . . . . .122 F2
Urmston M41 . . . . .94 F3
Chiltern Cl
Ashton-in-M WN4 . . . . .73 C2
Horwich BL6 . . . . .22 C5
Ramsbottom BL0 . . . . .11 C4
Shaw OL2 . . . . .48 F8
Walkden M28 . . . . .78 E8
Chiltern Dr
Altrincham WA15 . . . . .119 F2
Bolton BL2 . . . . .148 C7
Bury BL8 . . . . .27 B4
Royton OL2 . . . . .48 C4
Stockport SK2 . . . . .124 B4
Swinton M27 . . . . .79 F6
Wigan WN3 . . . . .54 D2
Chiltern Gdns M33 . . . . . .108 C1
Chiltern Rd Culcheth WN3 . .11 C4
Ramsbottom BL0 . . . . .11 C4
Chiltern Way M29 . . . . .77 B8
Chilton Ave OL9 . . . . .152 A6
Chilton Cl WN7 . . . . .75 F7
Chilton Dr M24 . . . . .65 C7
Chilworth St M14 . . . . .98 B3
Chime Bank M8 . . . . .156 B6
Chimes Rd WN4 . . . . .72 F6
China La [1] Bolton BL1 . . .145 F8
Manchester M1 . . . . .159 B1
Chingford Wlk [5] M13 . . . .98 F4
Chinley Ave
Manchester M40 . . . . .83 A8
Stretford M32 . . . . .96 A4
Chinley Cl
Manchester SK4 . . . . .168 B3
Sale M33 . . . . .108 D3
Stockport SK7 . . . . .123 E3
Chinley St M6 . . . . .81 B5
Chinnor Cl WN7 . . . . .75 F7
Chinwell View [9] M19 . . . .99 A1

Chip Hill Rd BL3 . . . . .146 A4
Chippendale Pl OL6 . . . . . . .85 E5
Chippenham Ave SK2 . . . .124 D7
Chippenham Ct M8 . . . . . .160 D1
Chippenham Rd M4 . . . . . .160 D2
Chipping Fold [5] OL16 . . . .31 F5
Chipping Rd BL1 . . . . .23 E2
Chipping Sq M12 . . . . .99 A4
Chipstead Ave M12 . . . . . .164 E5
Chirmside St [5] BL8 . . . . . .27 B1
Chirton Wlk [9] M40 . . . . . .83 A1
Chisacre Dr WN6 . . . . .35 D7
Chiseldon Ave M22 . . . . . .121 E2
Chiselhurst St M8 . . . . . . .156 A7
Chisholm Cl WN6 . . . . .19 B2
Chisholm Ct [10] M24 . . . . .46 F1
Chisholm St M11 . . . . .99 D7
Chisholme Cl BL8 . . . . .10 F2
Chisledon Ave M7 . . . . . . .155 F6
Chisledon Cl BL3 . . . . .145 E5
Chislehurst Ave M41 . . . . . .95 D3
Chislehurst Cl BL8 . . . . .27 B1
Chisnall Ave WN6 . . . . .18 F6
Chisnall La Coppull PR7 . . . .19 C6
Wrightington Bar WN6 . . . . . . .19 A5
Chiswell St WN5 . . . . .54 C5
Chiswick Dr M26 . . . . .43 B5
Chiswick Rd M20 . . . . .110 C3
Chisworth Cl Leigh WN7 . . .75 E7
Stockport SK7 . . . . .123 A1
Chisworth St BL2 . . . . .25 B3
Chisworth Wlk [2] M34 . . .113 A8
Choir St M7 . . . . .158 E4
Chokeberry Cl WA14 . . . . .119 B8
Cholmley Dr WA12 . . . . .89 E2
Cholmondeley Ave
WA14 .119 E8
Cholmondeley Rd M6 . . . . .80 C4
Cholmlea WA14 . . . . .119 B4
Cholmlea Manor M6 . . . . . .80 C4
Choral Gr M7 . . . . .155 D5
Chorley Cl BL8 . . . . .26 F1
Chorley Hall Cl SK9 . . . . . .136 F1
Chorley Hall La SK9 . . . . .137 A1
Chorley New Rd
Bolton BL1,BL6 . . . . .40 C7
Horwich BL6 . . . . .22 C2
Chorley New Road Prim Sch
BL6 . . . . .22 B2
Chorley Old Rd
Bolton,Cope Bank BL1 . . . . .142 B1
Bolton,Doffcocker BL1,BL6 . .23 C3
Chorley Rd
Adlington BL6,PR7 . . . . .21 B5
Adlington PR6 . . . . .21 A8
Four Gates BL1,BL6 . . . . .39 C4
Sale M33 . . . . .108 E2
Standish WN1 . . . . .20 C3
Swinton M27 . . . . .79 F8
Chorley St Adlington PR6 . . .21 B8
Bolton BL1 . . . . .145 E7
Ince-in-M WN3 . . . . .151 B6
Stretford M32 . . . . .96 F5
Chorley Wood Ave M19 . .110 F6
Chorlton CE Prim Sch
M21 . . . . .109 A8
Chorlton Dr SK8 . . . . .122 E6
Chorlton Fold M30 . . . . .79 D4
Chorlton Gn M21 . . . . .109 A8
Chorlton Gr SK1 . . . . .124 B7
Chorlton High Sch (Art Coll)
M21 . . . . .109 D7
Chorlton High Sch (Art Coll)
Darley Ave Site M21 . . . . . .109 C5
Chorlton Park Prim Sch
M21 . . . . .109 C6
Chorlton Pl M21 . . . . .97 B1
Chorlton Rd M15,M16 . . . .162 D6
Chorlton St
Manchester M1 . . . . .163 A8
Manchester,Old Trafford
M16 .161 C5
Chorlton Water Pk M21 . . .109 C4
Chowbent Cl M46 . . . . .58 E3
Chowbent Prim Sch M46 . .58 E3
Chretien Rd M22 . . . . .109 E2
Christ Church Ainsworth CE
Prim Sch BL2 . . . . .26 C1
Christ Church CE Prim Sch
Bury BL9 . . . . .26 F4
Chadderton OL9 . . . . .152 A6
Denshaw OL3 . . . . .33 D1
Eccles M30 . . . . .79 D2
Leigh WN7 . . . . .75 F4
Christ Church Cl BL2 . . . . . .25 F2
Christ Church CE Prim Sch
BL2 . . . . .25 F2
Christ the King RC Prim Sch
Failsworth M40 . . . . .83 C5
Walkden M28 . . . . .60 E3
Christ's Church CE Prim Sch
BL2 . . . . .25 F2
Christchurch Ave M5 . . . . . .81 B2
Christchurch Ct M5 . . . . . . .152 B3
Christchurch Rd M33 . . . . .107 C5
Christie Hospl & Holt Radium
Inst M20 . . . . .110 B6
Christie Rd M32 . . . . .96 E2
Christie St OL2 . . . . .149 B7
Christine St OL2 . . . . .149 B7
Christleton Ave SK4 . . . . . .111 F6
Christleton Way [15] SK9 .131 D5
Christopher Acre OL11 . . . .13 E1
Christopher St
Failsworth M40 . . . . .83 D4
Ince-in-M WN3 . . . . .151 F6
Salford M5 . . . . .81 B1
Chronnell Dr BL2 . . . . .42 E8

Chudleigh Cl
Altrincham WA14 . . . . .119 B6
Stockport SK7 . . . . .124 A3
Chudleigh Rd M8 . . . . .64 A2
Chulsey Gate La BL6 . . . . . .40 A4
Chulsey St BL3 . . . . .146 B4
Chunal La SK13 . . . . .116 C6
Chunal Lane Flats SK13 . .116 C6
Church Ave
Bickershaw WN2 . . . . .74 F8
Bolton BL3 . . . . .146 C4
Denton M34 . . . . .113 A8
[7] Failsworth M40 . . . . .83 C5
Handforth SK9 . . . . .131 F2
Hyde SK14 . . . . .113 F8
Leigh WN2 . . . . .74 A8
Salford M6 . . . . .154 D2
Slattocks OL11 . . . . .47 D6
Church Bank
Altrincham WA14 . . . . .119 B2
Bolton BL1 . . . . .148 A7
Church Brow
Altrincham WA14 . . . . .119 B2
Hyde SK14 . . . . .167 D1
Mottram-in-L SK14 . . . . .103 A3
Church Cl Denton M34 . . . .100 F7
Glossop SK13 . . . . .104 E2
Handforth SK9 . . . . .131 D3
Kearsley M26 . . . . .61 B8
Ramsbottom BL0 . . . . .138 B5
Church Croft BL9 . . . . .45 C4
Church Ct
Altrincham WA15 . . . . .119 E1
Bury BL9 . . . . .141 A3
Dukinfield SK16 . . . . .166 B1
Edenfield BL0 . . . . .1 D4
Church Dr
Newton-le-W WA12 . . . . .89 C1
Orrell WN5 . . . . .53 D5
Prestwich M25 . . . . .63 A4
Church Field Lt M26 . . . . . .43 F1
Church Fields OL3 . . . . .51 A2
Church Fold PR7 . . . . .19 F8
Church Gn Lymm WA13 . . .117 B8
Radcliffe M26 . . . . .44 D4
Salford M6 . . . . .154 F3
Church Gr SK7 . . . . .124 E2
Church La
Alderley Edge SK9 . . . . .137 A2
Bramhall SK7 . . . . .132 C2
Culcheth WA3 . . . . .91 F3
Edenfield BL0 . . . . .1 D4
Golborne WA3 . . . . .90 D7
Manchester,Broughton Park
M7 . . . . .63 C1
Manchester,Harpurhey
M40,M9 . . . . .157 F2
Manchester,Harpurhey M9 .157 E8
Marple SK6 . . . . .125 F5
Mossley OL5 . . . . .68 D1
Oldham OL1 . . . . .153 F7
Prestwich M25 . . . . .63 A4
Rochdale OL16 . . . . .139 F7
Romiley SK6 . . . . .113 C2
Sale M33 . . . . .107 E6
Shevington WN6 . . . . .36 A6
Uppermill OL3 . . . . .51 D1
Westhoughton BL5 . . . . .39 E3
Whitefield M45 . . . . .44 E1
Wrightington Bar WN6 . . . . . .18 D8
Church Lo SK4 . . . . .110 E2
Church Manor SK4 . . . . . . .168 B4
Church Mdw
Dukinfield SK14 . . . . .101 C3
Whitefield BL9 . . . . .45 C4
Church Mdws Bolton BL2 . .25 F3
Uppermill OL3 . . . . .68 C5
Church Meadow Gdns
SK14 .101 C3
Church Mews
Denton M34 . . . . .100 E3
[1] Radcliffe M26 . . . . .44 C1
Church Pl OL10 . . . . .29 D2
Church Rd Bolton BL1 . . . . .142 B2
Charlesworth SK13 . . . . .115 C7
Cheadle SK8 . . . . .132 B8
Eccles M30 . . . . .79 F2
Farnworth BL4 . . . . .60 E8
Gatley SK8 . . . . .122 A5
Handforth SK9 . . . . .131 D3
Hollingworth SK14 . . . . .171 D4
Kearsley M26 . . . . .61 A8
Middleton M24 . . . . .65 D7
Moorend SK6 . . . . .126 E6
Platt Bridge WN2 . . . . .56 B3
Ramsbottom BL0 . . . . .11 B8
Rochdale OL16 . . . . .31 B6
Sale M33 . . . . .108 A4
Stockport SK4 . . . . .169 E2
Tyldesley M29 . . . . .77 C6
Uppermill,Lydgate OL3 . . . . . .68 E5
Urmston M41 . . . . .95 C1
Walkden M28 . . . . .59 F6
Wythenshawe M22 . . . . .109 E1
Church Rd E M33 . . . . .108 D4
Church Rd W M33 . . . . . . .108 D4
Church Road Prim Sch
BL1 . . . . .142 B2
Church St Adlington PR7 . . .21 A7
Ainsworth BL2 . . . . .26 D1
Altrincham WA14 . . . . .119 D5

Church St continued
Ashton-u-L OL6 ....166 B2
Aspull WN2 ....38 B6
Atherton M46 ....58 D3
Bacup OL13 ....3 C8
Blackrod BL6 ....21 C2
Bolton BL2 ....25 D5
Bury BL9 ....141 A3
Bury,Walshaw BL8 ....26 F5
Cheadle SK8 ....122 D6
Delph OL3 ....50 E4
Denton M34 ....100 F7
Droylsden M43 ....84 B1
Dukinfield SK16 ....166 B1
Eccles M30 ....79 F2
Failsworth M35 ....83 F8
Farnworth BL4 ....60 E7
Farnworth BL4 ....60 E8
Glossop SK13 ....104 D2
Golborne WA3 ....74 B1
Hadfield SK13 ....104 A4
Heywood OL10 ....29 D2
Hindley WN2 ....56 D5
Horwich BL6 ....22 C3
Hyde SK14 ....167 D1
Ince-in-M WN3 ....151 F6
Leigh WN7 ....75 F5
Little Lever BL3 ....42 F3
Littleborough OL15 ....16 B5
Manchester M14 ....159 A2
5 Marple SK6 ....125 F6
Marple SK6 ....126 A5
Middleton M24 ....47 A2
Newton-le-W WA12 ....89 E4
Oldham OL1 ....153 F7
Oldham,Salem OL4 ....67 E5
Orrell WN5 ....53 E5
Pendlebury M27 ....80 B8
Radcliffe M26 ....44 B2
Rawtenstall BB4 ....2 E8
Rochdale,Greengate OL16 .15 D3
Rochdale,Mitchell Hey
OL12 ....139 E7
Romiley SK6 ....113 A5
Royton OL2 ....48 D4
Stalybridge SK15 ....86 A2
Standish WN6 ....19 E1
Stockport SK4 ....92 B5
Stretford M32 ....96 C1
Swinton M27 ....79 E8
Tintwistle SK13 ....104 A7
Up Holland WN8 ....53 C7
Westhoughton BL5 ....39 E2
Whitworth OL12 ....14 C8
Wigan WN1 ....150 C8
Wigan,Norley WN5 ....54 B6
Wilmslow SK9 ....137 B7
Church St E Oldham OL4 ..67 E8
Radcliffe M26 ....44 C3
Church St S SK13 ....104 E2
Church St W M26 ....44 B3
Church Stile OL16 ....139 F7
Church Street Cotts **18**
SK6 ....125 F6
Church Street Ind Est **3**
M24 ....47 A2
Church Terr
Ashton-in-M WN4 ....73 B2
Handforth SK9 ....131 D4
Milnrow OL16 ....32 A5
Oldham OL1 ....153 F7
Sale M33 ....108 A6
Church View
6 Altrincham WA14 .....119 C1
Handforth SK9 ....131 A2
Hyde SK14 ....167 D1
Irlam M44 ....94 A2
Lymm WA13 ....117 B4
Mottram-in-L SK14 ....103 A3
Rochdale OL12 ....13 E2
Church Wlk
Farnworth BL4 ....60 C8
5 Royton OL2 ....48 D4
Stalybridge SK15 ....86 A3
Swinton M27 ....64 F4
Wilmslow SK9 ....136 F6
Churchbank SK15 ....86 D2
Churchdale Rd M9 ....64 B4
Churchfield
Manchester M21 ....109 A8
Shevington WN6 ....36 A5
Churchfield Rd 6 M6 ....80 D5
Churchfield Wlk M11 ....165 A8
Churchfields
Altrincham WA14 ....119 B1
Denton M34 ....100 E7
Sale M33 ....107 D6
Churchgate Bolton BL1 ..145 F7
Stockport SK1 ....169 F1
Urmston M41 ....13 D2
Churchgate Bldgs M1 ....163 C8
Churchill Ave
Ainsworth BL2 ....26 D1
Fowley Common WA3 ....92 B4
Manchester M16 ....97 D2
Churchill CI OL10 ....46 E8
Churchill Cres
Marple SK6 ....125 D7
Reddish SK5 ....99 E1
Churchill Ct M6 ....154 F2
Churchill Dr BL3 ....43 C3
Churchill Pl M30 ....79 C4
Churchill Rd WA14 ....119 D7

Churchill St
3 Bolton BL2 ....148 C7
Oldham OL4 ....67 A6
Rochdale OL11,OL12 ......14 C1
Stockport SK4 ....169 D3
Churchill St E OL4 ....67 A6
Churchill Way
Salford M5,M6 ....81 A2
Stretford M17 ....96 C7
Churchlands La WN6 ....19 F1
Churchley CI SK3 ....123 A6
Churchley Rd SK3 ....123 A7
Churchside BL4 ....60 B7
Churchside CI M9 ....64 D2
Churchstoke Wlk M23 ...120 E7
Churchston Ave SK7 ....124 A2
Churchtown Ave M42 ....42 F7
Churchward Sq BL6 ......22 C2
Churchwood Rd M20 ....110 B3
Churchwood View
WA13 ....117 A2
Churnet St M40 ....157 D5
Churnett CI BL5 ....39 F2
Churning Terr M44 ....94 B3
Churston Ave M9 ....64 E4
Churton Ave
Manchester M14 ....98 B2
Sale M33 ....107 F3
Churton Gr WN6 ....19 B2
Churton Rd M18 ....99 C2
Churwell Ave SK4 ....110 F4
Cicero St Manchester M9 .157 F8
Oldham OL1 ....49 A1
Cinder Hill La M24,OL1,
OL2 ....48 A3
Cinder St M4 ....159 C2
Cinnabar Dr M24 ....46 F2
Cinnamon Ave WN2 ......52 F4
Cinnamon Brow WN8 ....53 C6
Cinnamon CI OL12 ......139 D8
Cinnamon St OL12 ......139 D8
Cipher St M4 ....159 C3
Circle Ct M32 ....95 F4
Circle S M17 ....96 E6
Circle The M32 ....95 F4
Circuit The
Alderley Edge SK9 ....137 B3
Cheadle SK8 ....132 A7
Manchester M20 ....110 B5
Stockport SK3 ....123 A6
Wilmslow SK9 ....136 D5
Circular Rd Denton M34 .100 E1
Manchester,Hilton Park
M25 ....63 B2
Manchester,Withington
M20 ....110 B5
Cirencester CI M38 ....60 A6
Ciss La M41 ....95 E2
Citrus Way M6 ....81 A2
City Ave M34 ....100 E2
City Coll Manchester
(Wythenshawe Pk Ctr)
M23 ....120 F8
City Coll Manchester
Abraham Moss Ctr M8 ..156 B8
Ctr M23 ....109 C1
City Coll Manchester Fielden
Ctr M20 ....109 F4
City Course Trad Est
M11 ....165 A7
City Court Trad Est M4 ..159 C2
City of Manchester Stadium
(Manchester City FC)
M11 ....160 F2
City Rd Manchester M15 .162 D6
Walkden M28 ....29 A8
Wigan WN5 ....54 B7
City Rd E M15 ....162 F7
City S M15 ....162 D6
City Wlk M27 ....80 B8
Civic Wlk 1 OL10 ....29 D2
Clacton Wlk M13 ....163 C6
Clague St M11 ....83 A2
Claife Ave M40 ....65 B2
Clandon Ave M30 ....79 B1
Clanwood Dr WN3 ....54 E2
Clap Gate La WN3 ....54 E3
Clapgate SK6 ....112 F1
Clapgate Rd OL11 ....13 E1
Clapham St M40 ....83 C8
Clara Gorton Ct 12 OL16 .31 B6
Clara St Oldham OL9 .....66 C4
Rochdale OL11 ....139 F5
Whitworth OL12 ....4 D1
Clare Ave SK9 ....137 C3
Clare CI BL8 ....27 D5
Clare Ct Farnworth BL4 ..147 F1
4 Stockport SK3 ....123 A1
Clare Rd Manchester M19 .111 A8
Reddish SK5 ....169 F4
Clare St Denton M34 ....100 E4
Manchester M1 ....163 B7
Salford M5 ....81 C1
Clarebank M40 ....40 F7
Claremont Ave
Altrincham WA14 ....119 E8
Hindley WN2 ....56 F5
Manchester,Heaton Chapel
SK4 ....111 C5
Manchester,Withington'
M20 ....110 A5
Marple SK6 ....125 C6
Claremont Ct 6 M20 ....110 A3
Claremont Dr
Altrincham WA14 ....119 E8
Walkden M38 ....60 B5
Claremont Gdns OL6 .....85 E5

Claremont Gr
Altrincham WA15 ....119 E3
Manchester M20 ....110 A3
Claremont Prim Sch
M14 ....98 A3
Claremont Range M18 ...99 F4
Claremont Rd
Billinge WN5 ....71 E5
Cheadle SK8 ....132 A8
Culcheth WA3 ....91 D4
Manchester M14 ....98 B3
Manchester M16 ....97 F3
Milnrow OL16 ....31 F5
Rochdale OL11 ....30 C7
Sale M33 ....108 B5
Salford M6 ....80 D5
Stockport SK2 ....124 B4
Claremont St
Ashton-u-L OL6 ....85 D4
Chadderton OL9 ....48 C1
Failsworth M35 ....83 F8
Oldham OL8 ....66 F2
Claremont Terr OL14 ......6 D5
Clarence Arc OL6 ....166 B2
Clarence Ave Oldham OL8 .66 D4
Urmston M17 ....95 F7
Whitefield M45 ....63 A7
Clarence Ct
14 Bolton BL1 ....145 E8
Newton-le-W WA12 ....89 A4
Wilmslow SK9 ....137 A6
Clarence Ho 1 SK15 ....101 F8
Clarence Rd
Altrincham WA15 ....119 F3
Ashton-u-L OL6 ....85 D4
Manchester,Heaton Chapel
SK4 ....111 C5
Manchester,Longsight M13 .98 E4
Swinton M27 ....79 C7
Clarence St
6 Ashton-in-M WN4 .....72 F5
Bolton BL1 ....145 F8
Farnworth BL4 ....42 E1
Golborne WA3 ....74 A1
Hyde SK14 ....167 E4
Ince-in-M WN2 ....56 A7
Leigh WN7 ....76 B4
15 Manchester M3 ......158 F1
Rochdale OL12 ....14 D2
Royton OL2 ....49 A3
Salford M7 ....158 D4
Stalybridge SK15,SK16 ...85 E1
Tyldesley M46 ....58 E2
Clarence Yd WN1 ....150 C8
Clarendon Ave
Altrincham WA15 ....119 C5
Manchester M16 ....168 B3
Clarendon Cres
Eccles M30 ....79 D3
Sale M33 ....108 D5
Clarendon Fields Prim Sch
SK16 ....101 B8
Clarendon Gr BL2 ....148 B6
Clarendon Ind Est SK14 .167 E3
Clarendon Pl SK14 ......167 E2
Clarendon Prim Sch
BL3 ....145 E5
Clarendon Rd
Bolton BL2 ....148 C7
Denton M34 ....101 B2
Droylsden M34 ....100 B7
Eccles M30 ....79 F3
Hazel Grove SK7 ....124 F3
Hyde SK14 ....167 E3
Irlam M44 ....94 E3
Manchester M16 ....97 D2
Sale M33 ....108 D4
Swinton M27 ....79 F8
Urmston M41 ....94 E3
Clarendon Rd W M21 ...109 B2
Clarendon Recn Ctr M5 .81 A2
Clarendon Road Com Prim
Sch M30 ....79 F3
Clarendon St Bolton BL3 .145 E5
Bury BL9 ....141 A4
Dukinfield SK16 ....101 A8
Dukinfield SK16 ....101 D8
Hyde SK14 ....167 D3
Manchester M15 ....162 F7
Mossley OL5 ....86 D8
Reddish SK5 ....169 F3
Rochdale OL16 ....31 B4
Whitefield M45 ....62 F8
Claribel St M11 ....164 E8
Claridge Rd M21 ....97 A1
Clarington Gr WN1 ......151 E7
Clarington Pl WN1 ....151 F7
Clarion St M4 ....159 C3
Clark Ave M18 ....99 C5
Clark Way SK14 ....167 E5
Clark's Cross M25 ....63 D8
Clark's Hill M25 ....63 A4
Clarke Ave Culcheth WA3 .92 A4
Salford M5 ....161 B7
Clarke Brow M24 ....47 A1
Clarke Cres
Altrincham WA15 ....120 B3
Walkden M38 ....59 E6
Clarke St
Altrincham WA14 ....119 D7
Ashton-u-L OL7 ....166 A1
Bolton BL1 ....144 C8
Farnworth BL4 ....60 E7
Heywood OL10 ....29 D2
Leigh WN7 ....75 E4
Rochdale OL12 ....14 D3
Clarke's La OL12 ....139 D8
Clarkes Croft BL9 ....141 C3

Clarkethorn Terr SK5 ....169 E3
Clarksfield Prim Sch
OL4 ....67 C6
Clarksfield Rd OL4 ....67 C6
Clarksfield St OL4 ....67 C6
Clarkson CI Denton M34 .100 D2
Middleton M24 ....64 C7
Clarkwell CI OL1 ....153 E8
Clatford Wlk 2 M9 ......157 D7
Claude Ave M27 ....79 D8
Claude Rd M21 ....109 B7
Claude St Eccles M30 ....79 B3
Manchester M8 ....64 A1
Swinton M27 ....79 D8
Wigan WN5 ....54 D6
Claudia Sq SK15 ....85 D1
Claughton Ave Bolton BL2 .42 F7
Walkden M28 ....78 C8
Claughton Rd BL8 ....26 F5
Claverham Wlk 2 M23 ..120 E7
Claverton Rd M23 ....120 E5
Claxton Ave M9 ....64 D3
Clay Bank M43 ....83 F1
Clay Bank St OL10 ....29 C3
Claybank Dr BL8 ....26 E7
Claybank Terr OL5 ....68 E4
Claybar Dr M30 ....79 E3
Claybarn Mews M44 .....94 B2
Claybridge CI WN5 ....36 B1
Claybrook Wlk M11 ......83 A1
Clayburn Rd M15 ....162 E6
Claycourt Ave M30 ....79 B4
Claydon Dr
Ince-in-M WN3 ....151 F5
Little Lever M26 ....43 C5
Clayfield Dr OL11 ....29 F8
Claygate Dr M9 ....64 D5
Clayhill Gr WA3 ....91 B8
Clayhill Wlk M9 ....64 E1
Claylands CI SK14 ....171 D4
Claymere Ave OL11 ......29 E8
Claymore St BL3 ....148 A5
Claymore St Bolton BL3 .147 F3
Droylsden M18 ....99 E6
Claypool Prim Sch BL6 ..22 F1
Claypool Rd BL6 ....22 E1
Claythorpe Wlk 2 M8 ...63 E3
Clayton Ave Bolton BL3 .148 C5
Golborne WA3 ....90 E8
Manchester M20 ....110 B4
Rawtenstall BB4 ....1 E8
Clayton CI Bury BL8 ......26 F1
Manchester M15 ....162 E5
Clayton Hall Rd M11 .....83 D2
Clayton Ho WN7 ....75 C5
Clayton La M11 ....83 B1
Clayton La S M11,M12 ..165 A7
Clayton St Bolton BL3 ...148 C5
Chadderton OL9 ....66 A3
Denton M34 ....100 F2
Droylsden M11 ....83 F1
5 Failsworth M35 ....83 F7
Rochdale OL12 ....15 B2
Wigan WN3 ....150 B7
Claytonbrook Rd M11 ...83 D1
Claytons CI OL4 ....67 B6
Cleabarrow Dr M28 ....78 A5
Cleadon Ave M18 ....99 C4
Cleadon Dr S BL8 ....27 C5
Cleavley St M30 ....79 B2
Clee Ave M13 ....98 F2
Cleethorpes Ave M9 .....64 B3
Cleeve Rd 2 Oldham OL4 .67 A6
Manchester M23 ....109 A2
Cleeve Way SK8 ....132 B6
Clegg Hall Rd OL15,OL16 .15 E1
Clegg Pl 2 OL6 ....85 D4
Clegg St 6 Bacup OL13 ..3 C8
Bolton BL2 ....148 C7
Droylsden M43 ....83 F1
Littleborough OL15 ....15 F7
Milnrow OL16 ....32 A5
Oldham OL4 ....153 F6
Oldham,Grotton OL4 ....68 A6
Romiley SK6 ....112 F3
Tyldesley M29 ....77 A5
Whitefield M45 ....62 F7
Whitworth OL12 ....4 C2
Clegg's Bldgs M15 ......145 E8
Clegg's La M38 ....60 A5
Cleggswood Ave OL15 ...16 A3
Clematis Wlk M27 ....61 E1
Clement Ave M46 ....58 A2
Clement Ct
1 Droylsden M11 ....99 F7
18 Rochdale OL16 ....31 B6
Clement Rd SK6 ....126 C7
Clement Royds St OL12 .139 E8
Clement Scott CI M9 .....64 E3
Clement St Oldham OL9 ..66 B3
Stockport SK4 ....169 E3
Clementina St OL12 ......14 F1
Clementine CI 3 M6 ......81 B2
Clementine St 6 M6 ......81 B2
Cleminson St M3 ....158 D2
Clemshaw CI OL10 ....29 C1

Clerewood Ave SK8 ......131 B7
Clerke St BL9 ....140 F2
Clerks Ct M5 ....80 B2
Clevedon Ave M41 ....96 A2
Clevedon Dr WN3 ....54 D4
Clevedon Rd OL9 ....48 B1
Clevedon St M9 ....157 E7
Cleveland Ave
Hyde SK14 ....101 C2
Manchester M19 ....99 B2
Salford M6 ....80 C3
Wigan WN3 ....54 C3
Cleveland CI
Ramsbottom BL0 ....11 C3
Swinton M27 ....62 A2
Cleveland Dr
Ashton-in-M WN4 ....73 C4
Golborne WA3 ....74 D1
Milnrow OL16 ....32 A6
Cleveland Gdns
Ashton-in-M WN4 ....73 C4
Bolton BL3 ....146 B4
Cleveland Gr OL2 ....48 C3
Cleveland Rd
Altrincham WA15 ....119 F3
Manchester M8 ....64 A1
Manchester SK4 ....168 A4
Manchester,Crumpsall M8 ..64 B2
Rochdale OL16 ....31 B3
Cleveland St 8 BL3 ......146 B4
Clevelands Prep Sch
BL1 ....144 A7
Cleveleys Ave
Bolton BL2 ....148 C8
Bury BL9 ....44 E7
Gatley SK8 ....122 B1
Manchester M21 ....109 C7
Rochdale OL16 ....31 B3
Cleveleys Gr M7 ....155 E7
Cleves Ct OL10 ....29 C1
Cliff Ave 1 SK4 ....168 B4
Cliff Dale 3 SK15 ....101 F8
Cliff Gr SK4 ....168 B4
Cliff Grange M7 ....155 D7
Cliff Hill Rd OL2 ....32 D1
Cliff Mount BL0 ....138 B7
Cliff Rd Bury BL9 ....44 F5
Wilmslow SK9 ....137 B8
Cliff Side SK9 ....137 B8
Cliff St OL16 ....31 B3
Cliffbrook Gr 2 SK9 .....131 D2
Cliffdale Dr M8 ....64 A1
Cliffe Rd SK13 ....116 D8
Cliffe St OL15 ....6 D2
Cliffmere CI SK8 ....122 F3
Clifford Ave
Altrincham WA15 ....120 B6
Denton M34 ....100 E5
Clifford Ct M15 ....162 E5
Clifford Lamb CI M9 ......65 B2
Clifford Rd Bolton BL3 ...146 A2
Poynton SK12 ....133 D3
Wilmslow SK9 ....136 F6
Clifford St Eccles M30 ....95 B8
Leigh WN7 ....76 B4
Pendlebury M27 ....80 B8
Rochdale OL11 ....139 F5
Clifton Ave
Altrincham WA15 ....119 E5
Culcheth WA3 ....91 D3
Eccles M30 ....79 D3
Gatley SK8 ....122 A2
Manchester M14 ....110 D8
2 Oldham OL4 ....67 B5
Tyldesley M29 ....77 C6
Clifton CI Heywood OL10 .29 C1
2 Manchester M16 .....168 C3
Oldham OL4 ....67 B5
Clifton Cres Royton OL2 .49 A3
Wigan WN1 ....37 C2
Clifton Ct
5 Farnworth BL4 ....42 B2
Swinton M27 ....61 F3
Clifton Ctry Pk*
M26&M27 ....61 E5
Clifton Dr Blackrod BL6 ..21 C3
Gatley SK8 ....122 A6
Gatley,Heald Green SK8 ..122 A2
Marple SK6 ....125 E6
Swinton M27 ....61 D2
Swinton,Clifton Junction
M27 ....61 D2
Wilmslow SK9 ....136 E4
Clifton Gr
Manchester M16 ....162 D5
Swinton M27 ....61 D2
Clifton Holmes OL3 ....61 E5
Clifton House Rd M27 ....61 E4
Clifton Lo SK2 ....124 A5
Clifton Park Rd SK2 .....124 A5
Clifton Pl M25 ....63 A5
Clifton Prim Sch M27 ....61 F3
Clifton Rd
Ashton-in-M WN4 ....72 F6
Billinge WN5 ....71 D4
Eccles M30 ....79 D3
Leigh WN7 ....75 E2
Manchester,Chorlton-cum-Hardy
M21 ....109 C8
Manchester,Heaton Moor
SK4 ....168 A4

Clifton Rd *continued*
Prestwich M25 ..62 E4
Sale M33 ..108 B3
Slattocks OL11 ..47 D6
Urmston M41 ..95 A2
Clifton St
Alderley Edge SK9 ..137 A1
Ashton-u-L OL6 ..166 A3
Bolton BL1 ..145 E8
Bury BL9 ..140 F4
Failsworth M35 ..66 A1
Farnworth BL4 ..42 B2
Kearsley BL4 ..60 F7
Leigh WN7 ..75 D5
Manchester,Old Trafford M16 ..162 D5
Manchester,Philips Park M40 ..160 F4
Milnrow OL16 ..31 F6
7 Rochdale OL11 ..31 A5
Tyldesley M29 ..77 E8
4 Wigan,Water Heyes WN1 ..37 C1
Wigan,Worsley Mesnes WN3 ..55 A4
Clifton Sta M27 ..62 C2
Clifton View M27 ..61 E4
Clifton Villas 5 M35 ..66 A1
Clifton Wlk M24 ..46 D3
Cliftonmill Mdw WA3 ..89 F8
Cliftonville Dr M6,M27 ..80 B6
Cliftonville Rd OL16 ..48 C8
Clinton Ave M14 ..98 A2
Clinton Gdns M14 ..98 A2
Clinton Ho 3 M5 ..154 F1
Clinton St 7 OL6 ..85 D4
Clinton Wlk 5 OL4 ..67 A6
Clippers Quay M50 ..161 A6
Clipsley Cres OL4 ..49 F4
Cliston Wlk SK7 ..124 A2
Clitheroe Cl OL10 ..29 D3
Clitheroe Dr BL8 ..26 F2
Clitheroe Rd M13 ..98 F3
Clito St M9 ..157 F8
Clive Ave M45 ..44 E1
Clive Rd Failsworth M35 ..83 E6
Westhoughton BL5 ..57 E6
Clive St Ashton-u-L OL7 ..85 A5
Bolton BL2 ..148 A7
Manchester M4 ..159 B3
3 Oldham OL8 ..66 D2
Clivedale Pl BL1 ..145 F7
Cliveley Wlk M27 ..80 B8
Clively Ave M27 ..62 C1
Clivewood Wlk M12 ..164 E6
Clivia Gr M7 ..155 D6
Cloak St M1 ..163 A7
Clock House Ave M43 ..83 E3
Clock St 11 OL9 ..66 B2
Clock Tower Cl
Hyde SK14 ..167 E1
3 Walkden M28 ..59 F3
Clockhouse Mews M43 ..83 E3
Clod La BB4 ..1 C8
Cloister Ave WN7 ..57 D1
Cloister Cl SK16 ..101 C6
Cloister Rd SK4 ..110 D2
Cloister St Bolton BL1 ..142 C2
Manchester M9 ..157 F8
Cloisters The
Cheadle SK8 ..123 A5
Rawtenstall BB4 ..2 E8
Rochdale OL16 ..15 B1
Sale M33 ..108 D4
Westhoughton BL5 ..57 E5
Clondberry Cl M29 ..59 E1
Clopton Wlk M15 ..162 E5
Close La Hindley WN2 ..56 E3
Leigh WN2 ..57 B1
Close St WN2 ..56 F6
Close The
Altrincham WA14 ..119 C5
Bolton BL2 ..25 B3
Bury BL8 ..27 C5
Denton M34 ..100 D4
Middleton M24 ..47 B3
Newton-le-W WA12 ..89 E1
Over Hulton M46 ..58 F5
Romiley SK6 ..114 B1
Stalybridge SK15 ..85 F4
Closebrook Rd WN5 ..54 D6
Closes Farm BL3 ..146 B2
Clothorn Rd M20 ..110 B4
Cloudberry Wlk M31 ..105 F3
Cloudstock Gr M38 ..59 E5
Clough Ave
Handforth SK9 ..131 B2
Marple SK6 ..126 C6
Sale M33 ..107 D1
Westhoughton BL5 ..57 F7
Clough Bank
Littleborough OL15 ..16 A8
Manchester M9 ..64 D2
Clough Cl OL4 ..68 E6
Clough Dr M25 ..62 F4
Clough End Rd SK14 ..102 F1
Clough Fold Kearsley M26 ..61 B7
Westhoughton BL5 ..57 F8
Clough Fold Rd SK14 ..167 D1
Clough Gate Hyde SK14 ..113 F8
6 Oldham OL8 ..66 D2
Clough Gr
Ashton-in-M WN4 ..72 F5
Whitefield M45 ..44 D2
Clough Ho M9 ..65 A2
Clough House Dr WN7 ..76 B5
Clough House La OL12 ..15 B6
Clough La Heywood OL10 ..29 C4

Clough La *continued*
Prestwich M25 ..62 F4
Uppermill OL4 ..68 E6
Clough Mdw Bolton BL1 ..40 D6
Romiley SK6 ..113 C5
Clough Meadow Rd M26 ..43 E3
Clough Park Ave OL4 ..68 E6
Clough Rd Droylsden M43 ..84 B2
Failsworth M35 ..84 A6
Littleborough OL15 ..16 A7
Manchester M9 ..64 F1
Middleton M24 ..47 A2
Shaw OL2 ..49 D6
Clough Side
Manchester M9 ..64 F1
Marple SK6 ..126 C7
Clough St 8 Bacup OL13 ..3 D8
Failsworth M40 ..83 C4
Kearsley BL4 ..60 F7
Middleton M24 ..47 B2
Radcliffe M26 ..44 C1
Wardle OL12 ..15 C6
Clough Terr OL15 ..16 A7
Clough The
Brinnington SK5 ..112 B6
Garswood WN4 ..72 D4
Clough Top Rd M9 ..65 A2
Clough Wlk SK5 ..112 B6
Cloughbank M26 ..61 C7
Cloughfield Ave M5 ..161 B8
Cloughgate Ho 5 OL8 ..66 D2
Cloughs Ave OL9 ..65 D8
Cloughside SK12 ..135 E6
Cloughton Wlk M40 ..83 D5
Cloughwood Cres WN6 ..35 D6
Clovelly Ave Leigh WN7 ..75 F8
Oldham OL8 ..66 C2
Clovelly Rd
Manchester M21 ..109 C8
Stockport SK2 ..124 C8
Swinton M27 ..79 C6
Clovelly St Failsworth M40 ..83 D5
Rochdale OL11 ..30 B3
Clover Ave SK3 ..170 D5
Clover Cres OL8 ..67 C3
Clover Croft M33 ..108 D1
Clover Hall Cres OL16 ..15 C1
Clover Rd
Altrincham WA15 ..120 B5
Romiley SK6 ..113 E3
Clover St Rochdale OL12 ..139 E8
Wigan WN6 ..37 B2
Clover View OL16 ..31 C7
Cloverbank Ave M19 ..110 D4
Cloverdale Dr WN4 ..73 C2
Cloverdale Sq BL1 ..142 A1
Cloverfield Wlk 6 M28 ..60 D3
Cloverlea Prim Sch WA15 ..120 B5
Cloverley M33 ..108 B2
Cloverley Dr WA15 ..120 A4
Clowes St
Manchester M12 ..164 F6
Oldham OL9 ..66 B2
Salford M3 ..158 E2
Club St Billinge WA11 ..71 A1
Droylsden M11 ..99 F7
Clumber Cl SK12 ..133 E3
Clumber Rd
Poynton SK12 ..133 E3
Reddish M18 ..99 F4
Clunton Ave BL3 ..146 B4
Clutha Rd SK3 ..123 F4
Clwyd Ave SK3 ..170 D7
Clyde Ave M45 ..62 F6
Clyde Ct OL16 ..31 B6
Clyde Rd
Manchester M20 ..110 A5
Radcliffe M26 ..43 F5
Stockport SK3 ..123 C7
Tyldesley M29 ..77 C7
Clyde St Ashton-u-L OL7 ..100 F8
Bolton BL1 ..143 E2
Leigh WN7 ..76 B4
Oldham OL1 ..49 C1
Clyde Terr M26 ..43 F5
Clydesdale Gdns M11 ..83 A1
Clydesdale Rise OL3 ..51 D5
Clydesdale St OL8 ..66 E4
Clyne Ct M32 ..96 F4
Clyne St M32 ..96 F5
Clysbarton Ct SK7 ..123 D1
Co-operation St M35 ..83 F8
Co-operative St
Hazel Grove SK7 ..124 E3
5 Leigh WN7 ..75 D5
Oldham OL4 ..67 F5
3 Radcliffe M26 ..44 A4
Salford M6 ..154 F2
Shaw OL2 ..149 B7
Uppermill OL3 ..69 B8
Walkden M38 ..59 E5
Coach House Dr WN6 ..36 B6
Coach La OL11 ..29 E5
Coach Rd
Hollingworth SK14 ..103 B5
Tyldesley M29 ..77 C6
Coach St M46 ..58 D3
Coal Pit La Atherton M46 ..58 B3
Atherton M46 ..58 B4
Leigh,Tamer Lane WN2 ..57 B1
4 Leigh,Westleigh WN7 ..75 E8
Oldham OL8 ..66 E1
Coal Pit Rd BL1 ..23 D7
Coal Rd BL0 ..12 C8
Coalbrook Wlk M12 ..164 E8
Coalburn St M12 ..165 A6
Coalshaw Green Rd OL9 ..66 A3

Coatbridge St M11 ..83 C1
Cob Hall Rd 6 M32 ..96 C1
Cob Moor Ave WN5 ..53 D1
Cob Moor Rd WN5 ..53 D1
Cobal Ct SK2 ..124 A5
Cobalt Ave M41 ..95 F6
Cobb Cl M8 ..63 E3
Cobbett's Way SK9 ..136 F4
Cobble Bank M9 ..64 D3
Cobblestones OL3 ..50 F3
Cobden Ctr The M50 ..154 F1
Cobden St
2 Ashton-u-L OL6 ..85 D2
Bacup OL13 ..4 B8
Bolton,Egerton BL7 ..8 D2
Bolton,Halliwell BL1 ..143 D3
Bury BL9 ..141 A3
Chadderton OL9 ..152 B7
Heywood OL10 ..29 D1
Manchester M9 ..64 E1
Newton-le-W WA12 ..89 D4
Oldham OL4 ..49 D1
Radcliffe M26 ..43 F6
Salford M6 ..81 A4
12 Tyldesley M29 ..59 A1
Coberley Ave M41 ..94 F4
Cobham Ave Bolton BL3 ..147 D3
Manchester M40 ..65 C2
Coblers Hill OL3 ..50 F5
Cobourg St M1 ..163 B8
Coburg Ave M7 ..158 D4
Cochrane Ave M12 ..164 E5
Cochrane St BL3 ..145 F5
Cock Brow SK14 ..114 C7
Cock Clod St M26 ..44 C3
Cock Hall La OL12 ..14 C8
Cockcroft Rd M5 ..81 B2
Cockcroft St M9 ..64 D1
Cocker Hill SK15 ..86 B2
Cocker Mill La OL2 ..48 F5
Cocker St M38 ..60 A4
Cockerell Springs 1 BL2 ..148 A6
Cockers La SK15 ..102 D8
Cockey Moor Rd BL2,BL8 ..26 E1
Cockhall La OL12 ..4 C1
Coconut Gr M6 ..81 B2
Codale Dr BL2 ..25 F1
Coddington Ave M11 ..99 E8
Code La BL5 ..39 B4
Cody Ct M50 ..96 E8
Coe St BL3 ..145 F5
Coghlan Cl M11 ..83 B2
Coin St OL2 ..48 E4
Cojeton Ho M9 ..64 F5
Coke St M7 ..155 F8
Coke St W M7 ..155 F8
Colborne Ave Eccles M30 ..79 B2
Reddish SK5 ..99 F3
Romiley SK6 ..113 C2
Colbourne Ave M8 ..63 F1
Colbourne Gr SK14 ..102 E3
Colbourne Way SK14 ..102 E3
Colburn Cl WN3 ..55 A2
Colby Rd WN3 ..55 B3
Colby Wlk M40 ..83 A7
Colchester Ave
Bolton BL2 ..42 E8
Manchester M25 ..63 C2
Colchester Cl M23 ..108 E1
Colchester Dr BL4 ..42 A1
Colchester Pl SK4 ..168 C3
Colchester St M40 ..160 D4
Colchester Wlk 1 OL1 ..153 F7
Colclough Cl M40 ..83 B6
Cold Greave Cl OL16 ..32 C4
Coldalhurst La M29 ..77 B5
Coldfield Dr M23 ..120 F6
Coldhurst St OL1 ..153 E8
Coldstone Dr WN4 ..72 D4
Coldstream Ave M9 ..64 D4
Cole Ave WA12 ..89 C4
Cole St M40 ..157 F8
Colebrook Dr M40 ..83 A6
Colebrook Rd WA15 ..120 A6
Coleby Ave
Manchester M16 ..97 C4
Wythenshawe M22 ..121 F1
Coleclough Pl WA3 ..91 F4
Coledale Dr M24 ..46 C2
Coleford Gr BL1 ..145 E6
Colemore Ave M20 ..110 D3
Colenso Ct 4 BL2 ..148 C7
Colenso Gr SK4 ..168 B3
Colenso Rd BL2 ..42 D7
Colenso St OL8 ..66 D3
Coleport Cl SK8 ..123 A1
Coleridge Ave
Middleton M24 ..47 C3
Radcliffe M26 ..43 E4
Wigan WN5 ..54 A6
Coleridge Cl SK5 ..99 E1
Coleridge Pl WN3 ..54 F3
Coleridge Rd
Littleborough OL15 ..15 F2
Longshaw WN5 ..53 D1
Manchester M16 ..97 C3
Oldham OL1 ..49 E4
Ramsbottom BL8 ..10 F2
Reddish SK5 ..99 E1
Coleridge Way SK5 ..99 E1
Colerne Way WN3 ..54 D2
Colesbourne Cl M38 ..60 A6
Coleshill Rise WN3 ..54 C2
Coleshill St M40 ..160 E3
Colesmere Wlk M40 ..65 D1
Colgate Cres M14 ..110 B8
Colgate La M5 ..161 A6

Colgrove Ave M40 ..65 C2
Colin Murphy Rd M15 ..162 E6
Colin Rd SK4 ..169 E4
Colin St WN1 ..37 D1
Colina Dr M7 ..155 E5
Colindale Ave M9 ..64 E4
Colindale Cl 7 BL3 ..144 C5
Colinton Cl BL1 ..143 D1
Colinwood Cl BL9 ..44 F3
Coll Dr M41 ..95 D5
Coll's La OL3 ..50 D4
Collard St M46 ..58 B4
College Ave
Droylsden M43 ..99 F8
Oldham OL8 ..66 D3
Wigan WN1 ..150 C8
College Cl Bolton BL3 ..145 E6
Stockport SK2 ..124 A6
Wilmslow SK9 ..136 F8
College Croft 10 M30 ..79 F2
College Ct OL12 ..139 D7
College Dr M16 ..97 C2
College Ho
Altrincham WA14 ..119 C1
Manchester SK4 ..168 B4
College Land M3 ..158 F1
College Rd
Manchester M16 ..97 D2
Oldham OL8 ..66 E4
Rochdale OL12 ..139 E7
Salford M30 ..80 A2
Up Holland WN8 ..53 B8
College St WN7 ..76 A5
College Way BL3 ..145 E6
Collegiate Way M27 ..61 F3
Collen Cres BL8 ..27 C6
Collet Cl WN1 ..151 E8
Collett St OL1 ..67 C8
Colley St Rochdale OL16 ..15 B1
Stretford M32 ..96 F5
Collie Ave M6 ..81 C5
Collier Ave OL16 ..31 F7
Collier Brook Ind Est M46 ..58 C3
Collier Cl SK14 ..102 E1
Collier Ct M19 ..99 A1
Collier Hill OL8 ..66 D3
Collier Hill Ave OL8 ..66 C3
Collier St Glossop SK13 ..116 C8
3 Hindley WN2 ..56 D6
Manchester,Charlestown M6 ..80 F6
Manchester,City Centre M3 ..162 E8
Salford M3 ..158 E2
6 Swinton M27 ..79 E7
Collier Wlk 4 SK14 ..102 E1
Collier's Row BL1 ..23 E5
Colliers Cl WN7 ..75 E2
Colliers Row Rd BL1 ..23 E5
Colliery La M46 ..58 A4
Colliery St Droylsden M11 ..83 A1
Manchester M11 ..165 B8
Collin Ave M18 ..99 C4
Colling Cl M44 ..94 A1
Colling St BL0 ..138 B5
Collingburn Ave M5 ..161 B7
Collingburn Ct M5 ..161 B7
Collinge Ave M24 ..65 C8
Collinge St Bury BL8 ..27 B4
Heywood OL10 ..29 C2
Middleton M24 ..65 D7
Platt Bridge WN2 ..56 A2
Shaw OL2 ..149 B7
Collingham St M8 ..159 B4
Collings St BL1 ..143 E2
Collington Cl M12 ..165 A5
Collingwood Ave M43 ..83 E3
Collingwood Cl SK12 ..134 A3
Collingwood Dr M27 ..80 B7
Collingwood Rd
Manchester M19 ..98 F1
Newton-le-W WA12 ..89 B3
Collingwood St
Standish WN6 ..19 E1
Trub OL11 ..47 D8
Collingwood Way
Oldham OL1 ..153 F8
Westhoughton BL5 ..39 E1
Collins La BL5 ..57 F6
Collins St BL8 ..26 F4
Collisdene Rd WN5 ..53 E6
Collop Dr OL10 ..46 E7
Collyhurst Ave 2 M28 ..60 E2
Collyhurst Rd M40 ..156 C5
Collyhurst St M40 ..160 D4
Colman Gdns M5 ..161 B7
Colmore Dr M9 ..65 A4
Colmore Gr BL2 ..25 B4
Colmore St BL2 ..25 B3
Colnbrook WN6 ..19 B1
Colne St OL11 ..30 D1
Colonial Rd SK2 ..124 A6
Colshaw Cl E M26 ..43 F4
Colshaw Cl S M26 ..43 F4
Colshaw Dr SK9 ..131 D2
Colshaw Rd M23 ..121 A4
Colson Dr M24 ..64 F7
Colsterdale Cl OL2 ..48 E5
Colt Hill La Uppermill OL3 ..68 F8
Uppermill OL3 ..69 A6
Coltishall Ho SK8 ..123 A5
Coltness Wlk 12 M40 ..83 C5
Coltsfoot Cl WN7 ..76 B5
Coltsfoot Dr WA14 ..119 B8
Columbia Ave M18 ..99 F4
Columbia Rd BL1 ..144 C8
Columbia St OL8 ..66 F4

Columbine Cl OL12 ..14 C3
Columbine St M11 ..99 D7
Columbine Wlk 8 M31 ..105 F3
Columbus St 2 WN4 ..72 F5
Colville Dr BL8 ..27 B1
Colville Gr
3 Altrincham WA15 ..120 A6
Sale M33 ..107 E1
Colville Rd OL1 ..48 D1
Colwell Ave M32 ..96 B1
Colwell Wlk M9 ..64 B5
Colwick Ave WA14 ..119 E6
Colwith Ave BL2 ..25 E1
Colwood Wlk 15 M8 ..155 F6
Colwyn Ave
Manchester M14 ..110 E8
Middleton M24 ..65 A6
Colwyn Cres SK5 ..111 F5
Colwyn Dr WN2 ..57 C2
Colwyn Gr M46 ..58 C5
Colwyn Rd Bramhall SK7 ..132 F8
Cheadle SK8 ..122 E1
Swinton M27 ..79 C6
Colwyn St Ashton-u-L OL7 ..85 A6
Oldham OL9 ..153 D7
Rochdale OL11 ..30 B2
Salford M6 ..154 F3
Colyton Wlk 7 M22 ..121 F3
Combe Cl M11 ..83 B3
Combermere Ave M20 ..110 A7
Combermere Cl
Cheadle SK8 ..122 F4
Tyldesley M29 ..59 B1
Combermere St SK16 ..166 C1
Combs Bank 1 SK13 ..171 D1
Combs Fold 42 SK13 ..171 D2
Combs Gdns 10 SK13 ..171 D1
Combs Gr 43 SK13 ..171 D2
Combs Lea 11 SK13 ..171 D1
Combs Mews SK13 ..171 D1
Combs Terr 2 SK13 ..171 D1
Combs Way 41 SK13 ..171 D2
Comer Terr 2 M33 ..108 A4
Comet Rd WN5 ..54 C8
Comet St M1 ..159 B1
Commerce Way M17 ..96 C5
Commercial Ave SK8 ..131 F5
Commercial Brow SK14 ..167 E4
Commercial Rd
Hazel Grove SK7 ..124 E3
Oldham OL1 ..153 F6
Commercial St Bacup OL13 ..3 D8
Hyde SK14 ..167 E3
Manchester M15 ..162 E7
Oldham OL9 ..152 C6
Commodore Pl WN5 ..36 E1
Common End PR7 ..20 E5
Common La Culcheth WA3 ..91 E4
Leigh WN7 ..75 B4
Partington M31 ..106 B5
Partington M31 ..106 D4
Tyldesley M29 ..59 A1
Common Nook WN2 ..56 A6
Common Side Rd M28 ..77 F7
Common St BL5 ..57 B7
Common The PR7 ..20 E5
Commonwealth Cl WN7 ..76 B3
Community St 4 OL7 ..84 F1
Como St 10 BL3 ..146 C4
Como Wlk M18 ..165 B6
Compass St M11 ..165 C7
Compstall Ave M14 ..98 B1
Compstall Gr 7 M18 ..99 E6
Compstall Mills Est SK6 ..114 B2
Compstall Rd SK6 ..113 E2
Compton Cl Hindley WN2 ..56 D4
Urmston M41 ..94 C1
Compton Dr M23 ..121 A2
Compton St 6 SK15 ..86 B1
Compton Way
Middleton M24 ..65 C6
Shaw OL2 ..149 B6
Comrie Wlk 7 M23 ..121 A5
Comus St M5 ..161 C8
Concert La M2 ..159 A1
Concord Ave WN3 ..55 B3
Concord Bsns Pk M22 ..121 E1
Concord Pl M6 ..81 A5
Concord Way 1 SK16 ..101 D8
Condor Cl M43 ..84 C3
Condor Pl M6 ..81 A5
Condor Wlk M13 ..163 B6
Conduit St
Ashton-u-L OL6 ..166 C2
Oldham OL1 ..49 E3
Tintwistle SK13 ..103 F7
Conewood Wlk 9 M13 ..163 C6
Coney Gr M23 ..121 A7
Coney Green Tech Sch M26 ..44 B4
Coneymead SK15 ..86 A4
Congham Rd 6 SK3 ..123 C8
Congleton Ave M14 ..98 A2
Congleton Rd SK9 ..137 A1
Congou St M1 ..163 C8
Congreave St OL1 ..153 E8
Congresbury Rd WN7 ..75 D7
Conifer Wlk Leigh WN7 ..75 B5
Partington M31 ..105 E3
Coningsby Dr M9 ..157 D8
Coningsby Gdns 13 WA3 ..90 E8
Conisber Cl BL7 ..8 E1
Conisborough OL11 ..139 E6
Conisborough Pl M45 ..63 B7

Coniston Ave
Adlington PR6 . . . . .21 B8
Atherton-in-M WN4 . . . . . .73 B4
Atherton M46 . . . . .58 D5
Dukinfield SK14 . . . . .101 C4
Farnworth BL4 . . . . .59 F8
Ince-in-M WN2 . . . . .56 B7
Manchester M9 . . . . .157 D8
Oldham OL8 . . . . .66 D4
Orrell WN5 . . . . .53 F7
Sale M33 . . . . .108 C2
Walkden M38 . . . . .60 A4
Whitefield M45 . . . . .62 F8
Wigan WN1 . . . . .37 C3
Coniston Cl
Chadderton OL9 . . . . .152 A7
Little Lever BL3 . . . . .43 A4
Ramsbottom BL0 . . . . . . .138 C7
Reddish M34 . . . . .100 B2
Coniston Ct M22 . . . . . . .121 E6
Coniston Dr Abram WN2 . . .74 B8
Bury BL9 . . . . .44 E7
Handforth SK9 . . . . .131 C4
Middleton M24 . . . . .46 F2
Stalybridge SK15 . . . . .86 A3
Coniston Gr
Ashton-u-L OL7 . . . . .166 A4
Heywood OL10 . . . . .46 D8
Royton OL2 . . . . .48 D8
Walkden M38 . . . . .60 A4
Coniston Ho 6 M28 . . . . . .60 E2
Coniston Park Dr WN6 . . .37 A6
Coniston Blackrod BL6 . .21 D3
Flixton M41 . . . . .106 E8
Gatley SK8 . . . . .122 B5
High Lane SK6 . . . . .134 D8
Hindley WN2 . . . . .56 E4
Partington M31 . . . . .105 E4
Reddish SK5 . . . . .111 F6
Stretford M32 . . . . .96 C3
Swinton M27 . . . . .79 F1
Tyldesley M29 . . . . .77 A7
Coniston St Bolton BL1 . .143 F3
6 Failsworth M40 . . . . . . .83 C5
Leigh WN7 . . . . .75 E5
Salford M6 . . . . .81 B4
Coniston Wlk WA15 . . . . .120 D5
Conival Way OL9 . . . . .48 A1
Conmere Sq 8 M15 . . . . . .162 F7
Connaught Ave
Manchester M19 . . . . .110 F7
Rochdale OL16 . . . . .31 B3
Whitefield M45 . . . . .62 F8
Connaught Cl SK9 . . . . . .137 C8
Connaught Dr WA12 . . . . .89 C2
Connaught Sq BL2 . . . . . .25 B2
Connaught St Bury BL8 . . .27 B1
4 Oldham OL8 . . . . .153 E6
Connel Cl BL2 . . . . .42 F6
Connell Rd M23 . . . . .121 A6
Connell Way OL10 . . . . . . .29 F3
Connery Cres OL6 . . . . . . .85 D6
Connie St M11 . . . . .165 C8
Conningsby Cl 10 BL7 . . . .24 F8
Connington Ave M9 . . . . . .64 D1
Connington Cl OL2 . . . . . . .48 C4
Connor Way SK8 . . . . .121 F4
Conquest Cl M12 . . . . . . .165 A6
Conrad Cl Oldham OL1 . . . .49 E4
Wigan WN3 . . . . .150 A5
Conran St M9 . . . . .157 E7
Consett Ave M23 . . . . . . .121 A6
Consort Cl 8 SK16 . . . . . .101 C6
Consort Pl WN14 . . . . . . .119 B3
Constable Cl BL1 . . . . . . .143 D1
Constable Dr Marple SK6 .126 B8
Wilmslow SK9 . . . . .137 E8
Constable Ho 4 M20 . . . .110 E7
Constable St M18 . . . . . . .99 E6
Constable Wlk M34 . . . . . .113 A7
Constance Gdns M5 . . . . .154 F1
Constance Rd
Bolton BL3 . . . . .146 C4
Partington M31 . . . . .105 F3
Constance St M15 . . . . . .162 C6
Constantia St WN3 . . . . . .55 F3
Constantine Ct M6 . . . . . . .81 B3
Constantine Rd OL16 . . . .139 F7
Constantine St OL4 . . . . . .67 D7
Consul St M22 . . . . .109 E1
Convamore Rd SK7 . . . . . .132 D7
Convent Gr OL11 . . . . . . .139 D5
Convent St OL8 . . . . .67 C4
Conway Ave Bolton BL1 . .142 A1
Irlam M44 . . . . .105 F8
Swinton M27 . . . . .62 B3
Whitefield M45 . . . . .62 F7
Conway Cl Heywood OL10 . .29 A3
Leigh WN7 . . . . .76 E7
Manchester M16 . . . . .97 A3
Middleton M24 . . . . .65 A7
Ramsbottom BL0 . . . . . . .138 B6
Whitefield M45 . . . . .62 F7
Conway Cres Billinge WN5 .71 E6
Ramsbottom BL0 . . . . .10 F2
Conway Ctr The SK5 . . . . .169 E4
Conway Dr
Altrincham WA15 . . . . . . .120 C6
Aspull WN2 . . . . .38 D5
Billinge WN5 . . . . .71 F5
Bury BL9 . . . . .28 D2
Hazel Grove SK7 . . . . . . .124 C1
Newton-le-W WA12 . . . . . .89 E3
Stalybridge SK15 . . . . .86 A3

Conway Gr OL9 . . . . .47 F1
Conway Rd
Ashton-in-M WN4 . . . . . . .73 E5
Cheadle SK8 . . . . .122 E2
Hindley WN2 . . . . .56 F4
Sale M33 . . . . .108 A3
Urmston M41 . . . . .95 D4
Conway St Farnworth BL4 .60 D7
Reddish SK5 . . . . .169 E4
Wigan WN5 . . . . .54 C5
Conyngham Rd M14 . . . . . .98 D3
Cook St Abram WN2 . . . . . .56 B1
Bury BL9 . . . . .141 A2
Denton M34 . . . . .100 F6
Eccles M30 . . . . .79 C2
Leigh WN7 . . . . .75 F5
Oldham OL4 . . . . .67 C7
Rochdale OL16 . . . . .15 B1
Salford M3 . . . . .158 E2
Stockport SK3 . . . . .169 E1
Cook Terr
21 Dukinfield SK16 . . . . . .166 B1
Rochdale OL16 . . . . .15 B1
Cooke St Ashton-in-M WN4 .72 F6
Denton M34 . . . . .100 F3
Dukinfield SK14 . . . . .101 F5
Farnworth BL4 . . . . .60 C7
Hazel Grove SK7 . . . . . . .124 D3
Horwich BL6 . . . . .22 D4
Cooling La M29,WN7 . . . . .76 E8
Coomassie St
Heywood OL10 . . . . .29 C1
Radcliffe M26 . . . . .44 A3
Salford M6 . . . . .154 F3
Coombe Cl M29 . . . . .77 B8
Coombes Ave Hyde SK14 .167 F1
Marple SK6 . . . . .125 F5
Coombes La SK13 . . . . . . .115 C5
Coombes St SK2 . . . . .124 B5
Coombes View SK14 . . . .114 E4
Coop St Bolton BL1 . . . . . .143 E4
1 Manchester M4 . . . . . . .159 B2
Wigan WN1 . . . . .37 D1
Cooper Fold M24 . . . . .47 A4
Cooper Ho M15 . . . . .163 A6
Cooper La Manchester M9 .64 D5
Middleton M24 . . . . .46 F3
Cooper St Bury BL9 . . . . . .140 E2
Dukinfield SK16 . . . . .166 B1
Glossop SK13 . . . . .104 B1
Hazel Grove SK7 . . . . . . .124 F3
Horwich BL6 . . . . .22 B4
Manchester M2 . . . . .158 F1
Oldham OL4 . . . . .68 A7
Rochdale OL12 . . . . .15 D4
Stockport SK1 . . . . .170 F7
Stretford M32 . . . . .96 D1
Cooper Terr OL16 . . . . . . .31 B8
Cooper's Fold SK8 . . . . . .131 F6
Cooper's La PR7 . . . . .18 B8
Cooper's Row BL1 . . . . . .145 F7
Cooperative St
Disley SK12 . . . . .135 D6
Walsden OL14 . . . . .6 A7
Coopers Glen WN2 . . . . . .56 A8
Coopers Row WN1 . . . . . .150 C8
Coopers Wlk OL16 . . . . . .15 C2
Coops Foyer & Coops Bsns
Ctr WN1 . . . . .150 B8
Cop Rd OL1 . . . . .49 C4
Copage Dr SK6 . . . . .113 A4
Cope Bank 12 BL1 . . . . . .142 C2
Cope Bank Mews BL1 . . .142 C1
Cope Bank W BL1 . . . . . .142 B2
Cope Cl M11 . . . . .99 E7
Cope St BL1 . . . . .142 C1
Copeland Ave M27 . . . . . . .62 C1
Copeland Cl M24 . . . . .46 C1
Copeland Dr WN6 . . . . . . .19 F1
Copeland Mews BL1 . . . . .144 A2
Copeland St SK14 . . . . . .101 D5
Copeman Cl M13 . . . . . . .163 C6
Copenhagen Sq OL16 . .31 A8
Copenhagen St
Failsworth M40 . . . . .83 A6
Rochdale OL16 . . . . .31 A8
Copesthorne Cl WN2 . . . . .38 C6
Copgrove Rd M21 . . . . . . .109 B7
Copgrove Wlk M22 . . . . . .130 E7
Copley Ave SK15 . . . . .86 C2
Copley High Sch SK15 . . . .86 D2
Copley Park Mews SK15 . . .86 C2
Copley Rd M21 . . . . .97 A2
Copley St OL2 . . . . .149 C8
Coplow Dale WN2 . . . . .56 F3
Copper Beech Dr
Gamesley SK13 . . . . .171 E1
Stalybridge SK15 . . . . .86 D3
Copper Beech Manor
SK13 . . . . .171 E1
Copper La M45 . . . . .62 B7
Copperas Cl WN6 . . . . .36 B7
Copperas La Aspull WN2 . .38 A6
Blackrod BL6 . . . . .21 B1
Droylsden M43 . . . . .159 A2
Copperas St M4 . . . . .159 A2
Copperbeech Cl M22 . . . .109 E1
Copperbeech Dr WN6 . . . .37 B7
Copperfield WN1 . . . . .37 C2
Copperfield Rd
Cheadle SK8 . . . . .132 B5
Poynton SK12 . . . . .133 D2
Copperfields Bolton BL6 . .40 B3
Poynton SK12 . . . . .133 D2
Wilmslow SK9 . . . . .137 C8
Copperfields Ct WA14 . . .119 C3
Copperways M20 . . . . . . .110 B5

Coppice Ave
High Lane SK12 . . . . .135 A6
Sale M33 . . . . .107 D2
Coppice Cl
High Lane SK12 . . . . .135 A6
Romiley SK6 . . . . .113 B4
Coppice Dr
Longshaw WN5 . . . . .53 D2
Whitworth OL12 . . . . .14 D7
Wigan WN3 . . . . .54 F2
Wythenshawe M22 . . . . . .109 D1
Coppice Ho SK12 . . . . . . .133 D2
Coppice Inf Sch OL8 . . . . .66 E4
Coppice Jun Sch OL8 . . . .66 E4
Coppice La SK12 . . . . .135 A5
Coppice Rd SK12 . . . . . . .134 B3
Coppice St BL9 . . . . .141 C3
Coppice The
Altrincham WA15 . . . . . . .129 B8
Bolton BL2 . . . . .25 D5
Manchester M9 . . . . .65 A2
Middleton M24 . . . . .65 B5
Prestwich M25 . . . . .63 A4
Ramsbottom BL0 . . . . .11 A4
Swinton M28 . . . . .79 C5
Worsley M28 . . . . .78 F8
Coppice Way SK9 . . . . . . .131 E3
Coppice Wlk M34 . . . . . . .100 D2
Copping St M12 . . . . .164 F6
Coppingford Cl OL12 . . . . .14 A2
Coppins The SK9 . . . . . . .136 E4
Coppleridge Dr M8 . . . . . .64 A2
Copplestone Ct M27 . . . . .61 C1
Copplestone Dr M33 . . . .107 C5
Coppull Cross Rds PR7 . .19 F7
Coppull Hall La PR7 . . . . . .20 B8
Coppull La WN1 . . . . .37 D2
Coppull Moor La PR7 . . . .19 E6
Copse Ave M22 . . . . .121 E3
Copse Dr BL9 . . . . .27 F6
Copse The
Altrincham WA15 . . . . . . .129 D7
Chapeltown BL7 . . . . .9 C2
Marple SK6 . . . . .126 C8
Newton-le-W WA12 . . . . . .89 B4
Wigan WN5 . . . . .54 A6
Copse Wlk OL15 . . . . .15 F5
Copson St M20 . . . . .110 B7
Copster Ave OL8 . . . . .66 E3
Copster Pl 2 OL8 . . . . .66 E3
Copsterhill Rd OL8 . . . . . .66 E4
Copthall La M8 . . . . .155 F8
Copthorn Wlk BL8 . . . . . . .26 F5
Copthorne Cl OL10 . . . . . .46 D8
Copthorne Cres M13 . . . . .98 E3
Copthorne Dr BL2 . . . . . . .42 E6
Copthorne Dr OL9 . . . . . . .65 F8
Coptrod Head Cl OL12 . . . .14 F4
Coral Ave SK8 . . . . .123 A1
Coral Gr WN7 . . . . .75 E4
Coral St Manchester M13 .163 C7
Wigan WN6 . . . . .37 A3
Coralin Way WN4 . . . . .72 F7
Coram St M18 . . . . .99 F6
Corbar Rd SK2 . . . . .124 B5
Corbett St 5 WN2 . . . . . . .56 E5
Corbett St Droylsden M11 . .83 A1
Rochdale OL16 . . . . .31 B8
Corbett Way OL3 . . . . .33 C1
Corbridge Wlk 7 M8 . . . .156 B6
Corby St M12 . . . . .165 A6
Corcoran Cl OL10 . . . . .29 A1
Corcoran Dr SK6 . . . . .113 F2
Corda Ave M22 . . . . .121 D8
Corday La M25 . . . . .63 D8
Cordingley Ave M43 . . . . . .99 F8
Cordova Ave M34 . . . . .99 F3
Corelli St M40 . . . . .160 F4
Corfe Cl Aspull WN2 . . . . . .38 D5
Urmston M41 . . . . .94 C1
Corfe Cres SK7 . . . . .124 B1
Corhampton Cres M46 . . . .58 E5
Corinth Wlk M28 . . . . .60 D2
Corinthian Ave M7 . . . . . . .81 C5
Cork St Ashton-u-L OL6 . .166 C3
Bury BL9 . . . . .141 A2
Manchester M12 . . . . .164 D8
Corkland Cl OL6 . . . . .85 E2
Corkland Rd M21 . . . . . . .109 C8
Corkland St OL6 . . . . .85 E2
Corks La SK12 . . . . .135 E5
Corley Ave SK3 . . . . .122 F7
Cormallen Gr M35 . . . . . . .84 A7
Cormorant Cl M28 . . . . . . .60 C3
Cormorant Wlk M12 . . . . .165 A6
Corn M13 . . . . .163 C5
Corn Hey Rd M33 . . . . . . .107 C2
Corn Hill La M34 . . . . .100 B5
Corn Mill Cl
Garswood WN4 . . . . .72 C8
Rochdale OL12 . . . . .15 C4
Corn Mill La 1 SK15 . . . . .86 B1
Corn St Failsworth M35 . . .83 C6
Glossop SK13 . . . . .104 C1
Leigh WN7 . . . . .75 D5
Oldham OL4 . . . . .67 A7
Cornall St SK16 . . . . .27 C3
Cornbrook M15 . . . . .162 D6
Wardle OL12 . . . . .15 C6
Westhoughton BL5 . . . . . . .39 D3
Cornbrook Cl M15 . . . . . .162 D8
Cornbrook Gr M16 . . . . . .162 D5
Cornbrook Park Rd
M15 . . . . .162 E6
Cornbrook Rd M15 . . . . . .161 C6
Cornbrook St M16 . . . . . .162 D5

Cornbrook Sta (Interchange
only no street access)
M15 . . . . .161 C6
Cornbrook Way M16 . . . .162 D5
Cornelian Gr WN4 . . . . . . .72 F5
Cornell St M4 . . . . .159 B2
Corner Brook BL6 . . . . . . .40 A3
Corner Croft SK9 . . . . . . .137 A4
Corner Ct SK8 . . . . .122 F6
Corner La WN7 . . . . .57 D3
Corner St OL6 . . . . .166 C2
Cornergate BL5 . . . . .57 E5
Cornet St M7 . . . . .155 D5
Cornfield SK15 . . . . .102 E7
Cornfield Cl Bury BL9 . . . . .27 F7
2 Sale M33 . . . . .108 F3
Cornfield Dr M22 . . . . .121 C3
Cornfield Rd SK6 . . . . . . .113 E3
Cornfield St OL16 . . . . .32 A5
Cornford Ave M18 . . . . . . .99 B3
Cornhill Ave M41 . . . . .95 B3
Cornhill Rd M41 . . . . .95 B3
Cornhill St OL1 . . . . .49 D2
Cornish Cl M22 . . . . .130 D8
Cornish Way OL2 . . . . .49 A4
Cornishway M22 . . . . .130 D8
Cornishway Ind Est
M22 . . . . .130 D8
Cornlea Dr M28 . . . . .78 C7
Cornwall Ave
Manchester M19 . . . . .111 B8
Over Hulton BL5 . . . . .58 F8
Tyldesley M29 . . . . .59 A3
Cornwall Cl SK6 . . . . .134 E7
Cornwall Cres
Brinnington SK5 . . . . .112 C6
Diggle OL3 . . . . .51 B4
Standish WN1 . . . . .20 B1
Cornwall Ct 2 M18 . . . . . .99 D6
Cornwall Dr Bury BL9 . . . . .45 A8
Hindley WN2 . . . . .56 F6
Cornwall Ho M3 . . . . .158 D1
Cornwall Pl WN5 . . . . .54 C6
Cornwall Rd
Droylsden M43 . . . . .84 A3
Gatley SK8 . . . . .131 B8
Irlam M44 . . . . .105 D5
Cornwall St
2 Eccles M30 . . . . .79 C1
Manchester M11,M18 . . .99 D7
Oldham OL9 . . . . .152 A8
Cornwallis Rd WN3 . . . . . .150 A5
Cornwell St SK9 . . . . .137 D8
Cornwood Cl 3 M8 . . . . . .155 F7
Corona Ave Hyde SK14 . .167 E3
Oldham OL8 . . . . .66 E4
Coronation Ave
Atherton M46 . . . . .58 C5
Dukinfield SK16 . . . . .101 F6
Glazebury WA3 . . . . .92 C7
Heywood OL10 . . . . .46 A4
Hyde SK14 . . . . .167 E1
Coronation Dr
Haydock WA11 . . . . .89 A7
Leigh WN7 . . . . .76 E6
Newton-le-W WA12 . . . . . .89 E1
Coronation Gdns M26 . . . .43 E4
Coronation Rd
Ashton-u-L OL6 . . . . .85 C6
Droylsden M43 . . . . .83 F3
Failsworth M35 . . . . .83 E4
Radcliffe M26 . . . . .43 E4
Wigan WN1 . . . . .36 D3
Coronation Sq
Little Lever BL3 . . . . .43 A3
Manchester M1,M12 . . . .163 C8
Coronation St
Bolton BL1 . . . . .145 F7
Denton M34 . . . . .100 D3
Downall Green WN4 . . . . . .72 D6
Ince-in-M WN3 . . . . .55 F3
Manchester M11 . . . . .165 C8
Reddish SK5 . . . . .169 E4
Salford M5 . . . . .161 B8
Swinton M27 . . . . .62 A1
Wigan WN3 . . . . .150 B6
Coronation Wlk
Billinge WN5 . . . . .71 D4
Radcliffe M26 . . . . .43 E5
Corporation Rd
Denton M34 . . . . .100 D5
Eccles M30 . . . . .79 F1
Rochdale OL11 . . . . .139 D6
Rochdale OL11 . . . . .139 D7
Corporation St
Bolton BL1 . . . . .145 F7
Manchester M4 . . . . .158 F2
Middleton M24 . . . . .65 A8
Stalybridge SK15 . . . . .86 A1
Stockport SK1 . . . . .169 F2
Wigan WN3 . . . . .150 B6
Corpus Christ RC Prim Sch
M40 . . . . .160 D4
Corpus Christi RC Prim Sch
M40 . . . . .160 D4
Corran Cl M30 . . . . .79 B2
Corranstone Cl BL6 . . . . . .22 B3
Correction Brow SK12 . . .134 C6
Corrie Cl M34 . . . . .101 D4
Corrie Cres SK14 . . . . . . .102 F5
Corrie Dr BL4 . . . . .60 E7
Corrie Prim Sch M34 . . . .100 F1
Corrie Rd M27 . . . . .62 A3
Corrie St M38 . . . . .60 A4
Corrie Way SK6 . . . . .112 F5
Corrigan St M18 . . . . .99 E6

Corrin Rd BL2 . . . . .148 B5
Corring Way BL1 . . . . .25 B4
Corringham Rd M19 . . . . .111 C7
Corriss Ave M9 . . . . .64 A5
Corry St OL10 . . . . .29 E2
Corsey Rd WN2 . . . . .56 E4
Corsock Dr WN1 . . . . .37 E1
Corson St BL4 . . . . .42 D2
Corston Gr BL6 . . . . .21 D1
Corston Wlk M40 . . . . .83 B6
Corwen Ave M9 . . . . .157 E8
Corwen Cl OL8 . . . . .66 B2
Cosgate Cl WN5 . . . . .53 D5
Cosgrove Cres M35 . . . . . .83 E5
Cosgrove Rd M35 . . . . .83 E5
Cosham Rd M22 . . . . .121 F3
Costabeck Wlk M40 . . . . . .83 D4
Costessey Way WN1 . . . . . .54 C3
Costobadie Cl SK14 . . . . .102 F3
Costobadie Way SK14 . . .102 F3
Cosworth Cl 2 WN7 . . . . . .76 B4
Cotaline Cl OL11 . . . . .30 B3
Cote Green La SK6 . . . . . .114 B1
Cote Green Rd SK6 . . . . .114 C1
Cote La Delph OL3 . . . . . . .51 B7
Littleborough OL15 . . . . . .115 F6
Mossley OL5 . . . . .68 E3
Cotefield Ave BL3 . . . . . . .147 F3
Cotefield Cl 7 SK6 . . . . . .125 F5
Cotefield Rd M22 . . . . . . .121 C2
Cotford Rd BL1 . . . . .24 F5
Cotman Dr SK6 . . . . .126 C8
Cotswold Ave
Chadderton OL9 . . . . .152 A5
Golborne WA3 . . . . .90 D6
Hazel Grove SK7 . . . . . . .124 B1
Shaw,High Crompton OL2 . .48 F8
Shaw,Lower Rushcroft
OL2 . . . . .149 A8
Urmston M41 . . . . .94 F3
Wigan WN5 . . . . .54 B5
Cotswold Cl
Glossop SK13 . . . . .116 A8
Prestwich M25 . . . . .63 C5
Ramsbottom BL0 . . . . .11 C4
Cotswold Cres Bury BL8 . .27 B3
Milnrow OL16 . . . . .32 A7
Cotswold Dr Horwich BL6 . .22 C5
Royton OL2 . . . . .48 B3
Salford M6 . . . . .154 F3
Cotswold Rd SK4 . . . . . . .169 D3
Cottage Croft BL2 . . . . . . .25 D5
Cottage Gdns SK6 . . . . . .112 D3
Cottage Gr SK9 . . . . .136 F5
Cottage La SK13 . . . . .171 E2
Cottage Lawns SK9 . . . . .137 B2
Cottage Wlk
Droylsden M43 . . . . .83 F3
Rochdale OL12 . . . . .14 C4
Cottam Cres SK6 . . . . . . .126 B8
Cottam Gr 1 M27 . . . . .80 A7
Cottam St Bury BL8 . . . . . .27 C3
Oldham OL1 . . . . .153 D8
Cottenham La M7 . . . . . . .158 E4
Cottenham St M13 . . . . . .163 B6
Cotter St M12 . . . . .163 C7
Cotterdale Cl M16 . . . . . . .97 D2
Cotterill Ct M23 . . . . .120 C8
Cotterill St M6 . . . . .81 B2
Cottesmore Cl OL12 . . . . .14 C6
Cottesmore Dr M8 . . . . . .156 C8
Cottesmore Gdns WA15 .129 C8
Cottesmore Way WA3 . . . .74 B1
Cottingham Dr OL6 . . . . . .166 C4
Cottingham Rd M12 . . . . .164 E6
Cottingley Cl BL1 . . . . .24 D5
Cotton Cl SK14 . . . . .167 E1
Cotton Fold OL16 . . . . .31 C5
Cotton Hill M20 . . . . .110 C6
Cotton La M20 . . . . .110 C6
Cotton Mill Cres OL9 . . . . .66 B4
Cotton St Bolton BL1 . . . .143 D2
Leigh WN7 . . . . .75 D5
Manchester M4 . . . . .159 B2
Cotton St E OL6 . . . . .166 B2
Cotton St W OL6 . . . . . . .166 A2
Cotton Tree Cl OL6 . . . . . .67 E8
Cotton Tree St SK4 . . . . .169 E1
Cottonfield Rd M20 . . . . .110 C6
Cottonfields BL7 . . . . .24 F7
Cottonwood Dr 3 M33 . .107 C5
Cottrell Rd WA15 . . . . . . .129 D7
Cotts The OL4 . . . . .50 B1
Coucill Sq BL4 . . . . .60 E8
Coulsden Dr M9 . . . . .64 D3
Coulthart St OL6 . . . . .166 B3
Coulthurst St BL0 . . . . . . .138 B6
Coulton Cl OL1 . . . . .67 A8
Coulton Wlk M6 . . . . .154 F2
Coultshead Ave WN5 . . . . .71 E6
Council Ave WN4 . . . . .73 B3
Councillor La SK8 . . . . . . .123 A4
Councillor St M12 . . . . . . .160 E1
Count St OL16 . . . . .31 A5
Countess Ave SK8 . . . . . .131 E5
Countess Gr M7 . . . . .158 D4
Countess La M26 . . . . .43 D4
Countess Pl M25 . . . . .63 C4
Countess Rd M20 . . . . . . .110 B3
Countess St
Ashton-u-L OL6 . . . . .85 D2
Stockport SK2 . . . . .170 F5
Counthill Dr M8 . . . . .63 E2
Counthill Rd OL4 . . . . .49 D1
Counthill Sch OL4 . . . . . . .49 D2
Counting House Rd
SK12 . . . . .135 E5
County Ave OL6 . . . . .85 E4

County Police St WN2 ..151 F7
County Rd M28 ....60 A4
County St Manchester M2 .158 F1
Oldham OL8 ....66 C2
Coupes Gn BL5 ....57 F6
Coupland Cl Oldham OL4 .49 F4
Coupland Rd WN2 ....57 C4
Coupland St M15 ......163 A5
Courage Low La WN6 ...18 D5
Courier Pl WN5 ....36 E1
Courier St M18 ....99 F6
Course View OL4 ....67 E3
Court Dr M40 ....83 E4
Court House Way 4
OL10 ....29 D2
Court St Bolton BL2 ..148 A7
Uppermill OL3 ....69 B8
Courtfield Ave M9 .....64 D4
Courthill St SK1 .....124 A8
Courtney Gn SK9 .....131 D2
Courtney Pl WA14 ....119 A1
Courts View M33 .....108 C5
Courtyard Dr M28 .....60 A3
Courtyard St Peters The
BL1 ....143 F1
Courtyard The
Hollingworth SK14 ...103 D5
Newton-le-W WA12 ....89 E4
Cousin Fields BL7 ....25 C7
Covall Wlk 4 M8 ....156 B6
Cove The WA15 ......119 F3
Covell Rd SK12 ......133 D5
Coventry Ave SK3 ...123 C4
Coventry Gr OL9 ......48 A1
Coventry Rd M26 ......43 F5
Coventry St OL11 ...139 F6
Coverdale Ave
Bolton BL1 ....144 A8
Royton OL2 ....48 C5
Coverdale Cl OL10 ....29 C1
Coverdale Cres M12 ..164 E6
Coverdale Rd BL5 .....57 D8
Coverham Ave OL4 ....67 D4
Coverhill Rd OL4 .....68 B5
Covert Rd Oldham OL4 .67 D3
Wythenshawe M22 ....121 E5
Coverts The WN6 ......36 F7
Covington Pl SK9 ....137 B6
Cow La Ashley WA15 ..128 F6
Bolton BL3 ....146 B2
Failsworth M35 ....83 E7
Oldham OL4 ....67 C7
Sale M33 ....108 C5
Salford M5 ....81 C1
Stockport SK2,SK7 ...124 D4
Wilmslow SK9 ....137 C7
Cow Lees BL5 ....40 A1
Cowbrook Ave SK13 ..104 F1
Cowburn Dr SK22 ....127 C1
Cowburn St
Heywood OL10 ....29 E1
Hindley WN2 ....56 F6
1 Leigh WN7 ....75 D5
Manchester M3 ......158 F3
Cowdals Rd BL6 ....40 B4
Cowesby St M14 ......98 A3
Cowhill La OL6 ......166 C3
Cowie St OL2 ....149 B8
Cowley Gr SK14 .....102 F3
Cowley Rd BL1 ....24 F5
Cowley St 8 M40 ....83 C6
Cowling St Manchester M7 .80 F8
Oldham OL8 ....66 F4
Wigan WN3 ....150 B6
Cowlishaw OL2 ......149 A5
Cowlishaw La OL2 ...149 A5
Cowlishaw Rd SK14,SK6 .113 F4
Cowm Park Way N OL12 .4 C1
Cowm St OL12 ....4 E5
Cowm Top La OL11 ...30 E2
Cowpe Rd BB4 ....2 F7
Cowper Ave M46 ......58 D5
Cowper St
Ashton-u-L OL6 ......166 C3
Leigh WN7 ....75 D5
Middleton M24 ....65 D8
Cowper Wlk 4 M11 ..160 F1
Cox Green Cl BL7 .....8 D3
Cox Green Rd
2 Bolton,Cox Green BL7 .24 F8
Bolton,Egerton BL7 ...8 E2
Cox Way M46 ....58 D3
Coxfield WN6 ....35 D7
Coxton Rd M22 ......121 E1
Coxwold Gr BL3 .....146 C2
Crab Brow M46 ....58 A3
Crab La M9 ....64 B4
Crab Lane Prim Sch M9 .64 B4
Crab Tree La M46 ....58 D2
Crabbe St M4 ....159 A3
Crabtree Ave
Altrincham WA15 .....129 D7
Disley SK12 ....135 E5
Crabtree Ct WA12 ...109 B3
Crabtree Ct SK12 ...135 D6
Crabtree La M11 ......83 D1
Crabtree Rd Oldham OL1 .67 B8
Wigan WN5 ....54 D7
Craddock Rd M33 ...108 C2
Craddock St 4 OL5 ..68 C1
Cradley Ave M11 .....99 D8
Crag Ave BL9 ....11 D2
Crag Fold BL9 ....11 D2
Crag Gr WA11 ....71 B1

Crag La BL9 ....11 D2
Crag Rd OL1 ....48 A2
Cragie St M 155 F5
Cragside Way SK9 ...137 C6
Craig Ave Bury BL8 ..27 B1
Urmston M41 ....95 A3
Craig Cl SK4 ....168 B1
Craig Cl Manchester M18 .99 C4
Stockport SK4 ......168 B1
Craig Wlk OL8 .....153 E5
Craigend Dr M9 ....157 E2
Craighall Ave M19 .110 F8
Craighall Rd BL1 ...24 E6
Craiglands OL16 .....31 B2
Craigmore Ave M20 .110 A6
Craignair Ct M27 ....80 C7
Craigslands Ave M40 .83 A6
Craigwell Ave M20 .110 D3
Craigwell Rd M25 ...63 E2
Craigwell Wlk M13 .163 B7
Crail Pl OL10 ....29 B2
Cramer St M40 .....157 F5
Crammond Cl M40 ...83 D6
Cramond Cl BL1 ....143 D1
Cramond Wlk 6 BL1 .143 D1
Crampton Dr WA15 .129 C8
Crampton La M31 ...106 D6
Cranage Rd M19 ....111 B8
Cranage Way 16 SK9 .131 D5
Cranark Cl BL1 ....144 A7
Cranberry Ave
Walsden OL14 ....6 B7
Wigan WN6 ....36 F3
Cranberry Cl WA14 .119 B8
Cranberry Dr Bolton BL3 .40 F4
Denton M34 ....100 D3
Cranberry Rd M31 ..105 F3
Cranberry St OL4 ...67 B6
Cranborne Ct Horwich BL6 .22 F1
Standish WN6 ....19 D1
Cranbourne Cl
1 Altrincham WA15 .120 A6
Ashton-u-L OL7 ....166 A4
Cranbourne Rd
Ashton-u-L OL7 ....166 B4
Manchester,Chorlton-cum-Hardy
M21 ....109 B8
Manchester,Heaton Moor
SK4 ....168 B4
Cranbourne St M5 ...81 C1
Cranbourne Terr OL6 .85 B5
Cranbrook Ave WN4 .73 A4
Cranbrook Cl BL1 ..143 F1
Cranbrook Dr M25 ..63 C2
Cranbrook Gdns OL7 .166 A4
Cranbrook Rd Eccles M30 .79 F4
Reddish M18 ....99 F3
Cranbrook St
Ashton-u-L OL7 ....166 B4
Oldham OL4 ....67 C6
Radcliffe M26 ....44 C5
Cranbrook Way WN3 .54 D3
Cranbrook Wlk OL9 .152 A6
Cranby St 6 WN2 ...56 D5
Crandon Cl M27 .....62 A1
Crandon Dr M20 ...122 C8
Crane St Bolton BL3 .146 B3
Coppull PR7 ....19 D6
Cranefield Pl M12 .163 C8
Craneshill Cl M22 .121 C1
Cranfield Cl M40 ..160 D2
Cranfield Rd Horwich BL6 .39 F7
Wigan WN3 ....55 A3
Cranford Ave
Manchester M20 ....110 D4
Sale M33 ....108 C6
Stretford M32 ....96 F3
Whitefield M45 ......44 E2
Cranford Cl Salford M27 .80 B6
Whitefield M45 ......44 E2
Cranford Dr M44 ....93 F3
Cranford Gdns
Marple SK6 ....125 F8
Urmston M41 ....94 E3
Cranford Ho M30 ....79 F3
Cranford Rd
Handforth SK9 .....131 A1
Urmston M41 ....94 E3
Cranford St BL3 ...146 B4
Cranham Ave WA3 ...90 E7
Cranham Cl Bury BL8 .27 B3
Walkden M38 ....60 A6
Cranham Rd M22 ...121 A2
Crank Rd WA11,WN5 .71 B8
Crankwood Rd WN2,WN7 .74 D5
Cranleigh WN6 ....37 A8
Cranleigh Ave SK4 .110 F4
Cranleigh Cl Blackrod BL6 .21 D1
Oldham OL4 ....49 E1
Cranleigh Dr
Cheadle SK8 ....122 F6
Hazel Grove SK7 ...134 A8
Sale M33 ....108 C6
Tyldesley M29 ......77 B8
Walkden M38 ....78 E8
Wythenshawe M23,M33 .108 C1
Cranlington Dr M8 .155 F6
Cranmer Ct OL10 ....29 C1
Cranmer Rd M20 ...122 C1
Cranmere Ave M19 ..99 C2
Cranmere Dr M33 ..107 D2
Cranshaw St M29 ...77 D8
Cranstal Dr WN2 ...57 A5

Cranston Dr
Manchester M20 ....122 B8
Sale M33 ....108 E3
Cranston Gr SK8 ...121 F5
Cranswick St 1 M14 .98 A3
Crantock Dr Gatley SK8 .131 C8
Stalybridge SK15 ....86 D3
Crantock Rd WN5 ...54 C6
Crantock St M12 ....99 B3
Cranwell Ave WA3 ...91 F4
Cranwell Dr M19 ...110 E4
Cranworth Ave M29 .77 A6
Cranworth St SK15 ..86 B1
Craston Rd M13 .....98 E2
Craunton 8 M30 ....79 F2
Craven Ave Golborne WA3 .90 F7
Salford M5 ....161 B8
Craven Ct BL6 ....22 D2
Craven Dr
Altrincham WA14 ...119 C8
Salford M5 ....161 A7
Craven Gdns OL11 .139 E5
Craven Ho OL14 ......6 A8
Craven Pl Bolton BL1 .23 E2
3 Droylsden M11 ...83 C2
Craven Rd
Altrincham WA14 ...119 C7
1 Reddish SK5 .....111 F6
Craven St Ashton-u-L OL6 .85 D5
Bury BL9 ....141 C3
Oldham OL1 ....48 E1
Salford M5 ....81 C1
Craven St E BL6 .....22 D2
Craven Terr M33 ...108 C4
Cravenhurst Ave M40 .83 B4
Cravenwood Com Prim Sch
M8 ....164 A1
Cravenwood Rd M8 .156 A8
Crawford Ave
Adlington PR7 ....20 E5
Aspull WN2 ....38 C5
Bolton BL2 ....148 B6
Tyldesley M29 ......58 F2
Worsley M28 ....79 A8
Crawford Cl WN2 ....38 C5
Crawford Mews 7 OL6 .85 D2
Crawford Sq OL10 ...29 A1
Crawford St
Ashton-u-L OL6 .....85 D2
Aspull WN2 ....38 C4
24 Failsworth M40 .83 C5
Rochdale OL16 ....31 B6
Walsden OL14 ....6 B8
Wigan WN1 ....150 C8
Crawley Ave Salford M30 .80 A3
Wythenshawe M22 ..121 E3
Crawley Cl M29 .....59 C1
Crawley Gr SK2 ....124 B6
Crawley Way OL9 ..152 A6
Cray The OL16 .....31 C6
Cray Wlk M13 .....163 B7
Craydon St M11 ...165 C8
Crayfield Rd M19 ..111 B8
Crayford Rd M40 ...83 B4
Creaton Way M24 ..46 D4
Creden Ave M22 ...121 F3
Crediton Cl
Altrincham WA14 ..119 B6
Manchester M15 ...162 F5
Crediton Dr Bolton BL2 .43 A7
Platt Bridge WN2 ...56 A1
Crediton Ho M6 ....80 A3
Creel Cl M9 ....64 B4
Cremer St M40 ......80 A2
Cresbury St M12 ..164 D8
Crescent M5 ....81 C2
Crescent Ave
Ashton-in-M WN4 ...73 A4
Bolton BL1 ....145 D8
Farnworth BL4 ......42 E7
Manchester,Crumpsall M8 .156 A8
Manchester,Hilton Park
M25 ....63 B2
Over Hulton BL5 .....59 A8
Pendlebury M27 .....80 B8
Crescent Cl
Dukinfield SK16 ...166 C1
Stockport SK3 ....124 A5
Crescent Ct
6 Manchester M21 ..96 F1
Sale M33 ....108 B3
Crescent Dr
Manchester M18 ....64 B1
Walkden M38 ....59 D6
Crescent Gr
Cheadle SK8 ....122 C6
Manchester,Hilton Park
M25 ....63 B2
6 Manchester,Levenshulme
M19 ....99 C1
Crescent Park SK4 .168 B4
Crescent Range M14 .98 C3
Crescent Rd
Alderley Edge SK9 .137 B2
Altrincham,Ashley Heath
WA15 ....119 E1
Altrincham,Oldfield Brow
WA14 ....119 A6
Bolton BL3 ....42 B3
Cheadle SK8 ....122 C6
Dukinfield SK16 ...166 C1
Failsworth OL9 .....65 E2
Kearsley M26 ....61 B6
Manchester M8 ....156 A8
Rochdale OL11 ......30 B4
Stockport SK4 ....112 B3

Crescent St M8 ....156 C8
Crescent The
Altrincham,Oldfield Brow
WA14 ....119 A5
Altrincham,Timperley
WA15 ....119 D4
Bolton,Bromley Cross BL7 .25 A7
Bolton,Harwood BL2 .25 F4
Cheadle SK8 ....122 D6
Droylsden M43 .....83 F1
Horwich BL6 ....22 E1
Ince-in-M WN2 .....56 B7
Irlam M44 ....94 B3
Little Lever BL3 ...43 B2
4 Manchester M19 .99 A1
Middleton M24 .....64 E8
Mossley OL5 ....68 B1
Prestwich M25 .....63 B4
Radcliffe M26 ......43 D5
Romiley SK6 ......112 D4
Shaw OL2 ....149 A6
Stalybridge SK15 .102 D6
Stockport SK3 ....124 A4
Urmston M41 ....94 F3
Westhoughton BL5 .57 E7
Whitworth OL12 ....14 C8
Wigan WN5 ....54 D6
Worsley M28 ....79 A8
Crescent View 12 SK16 .166 B1
Crescent Way SK3 .124 A5
Cresgarth Ho SK3 .124 A4
Cressell Pk WN6 ...19 B1
Cressfield Way M21 .109 D7
Cressingham Rd
Bolton BL3 ....146 A4
Stretford M32 ......96 B2
Cressington Cl 4 M5 .154 E2
Cresswell Gr M20 .110 A5
Crest Lo SK7 ......123 F2
Crest St M4 ....159 A4
Crest The M43 ....100 A7
Crestfield Gr WN6 .36 F2
Crestfold M38 .....60 A4
Crestwood Ave WN3 .54 F3
Crestwood Wlk M40 .156 C6
Creswick Cl WN2 ...56 C4
Crete St OL8 ......153 F5
Crewe Rd M23 ....120 E8
Crib Fold OL3 .....51 A2
Crib La OL3 ....51 A2
Criccieth Ave WN2 .38 D5
Criccieth Rd SK3 .123 A7
Criccieth St 8 M16 .97 F4
Cricket Gr The M21 .109 B6
Denton M34 ....101 A4
Wigan WN6 ....150 B8
Cricket View OL16 .31 F5
Cricket's La N OL6 .85 D3
Cricket's La N OL6 .85 D3
Cricketers Way BL5 .57 F8
Cricketfield La M28 .60 C3
Cricklewood Rd M22 .121 C2
Crimble La OL10,OL11 .29 F3
Crimble St OL12 ..139 D8
Crimbles St OL14 ..67 E8
Crime La OL8 ......44 D4
Crimsworth Ave M16 .97 B2
Crinan Sq OL10 ....28 F1
Crinan Way BL2 ....42 F6
Crinan Wlk M40 ..160 D3
Cringle Barrow Cl M28 .78 A5
Cringle Cl BL3 ....40 F4
Cringle Dr SK8 ...122 C8
Cringle Hall Rd M19 .110 F8
Cringle Rd M19 ...111 C7
Cringleford Wlk M12 .164 F5
Crippen St M46 ...58 A1
Cripple Gate WN6 .19 A2
Cripple Gate La OL11 .30 E1
Crispin Rd M22 ..130 E8
Critchley Cl SK14 .167 F1
Criterion St SK5 ..99 F2
Croal Ave WN2 ....56 A2
Croal Wlk M45 ....45 B1
Croasdale Ave 2 M14 .110 B8
Croasdale Dr OL2 .48 E5
Croasdale St BL1 .143 F1
Crocker Wlk 25 M9 .157 E8
Crocus Dr OL2 ...149 A5
Crocus St BL1 ...143 F4
Crocus Wlk M7 ..155 D6
Croft Acres BL0 ...1 D2
Croft Ave Atherton M46 .58 D2
Golborne WA3 ......73 F2
Middleton M25 .....63 F8
Orrell WN5 ....53 D5
Croft Bank
Manchester M18 ....99 D5
4 Salford M7 .....155 D5
Stalybridge SK15 ..86 D4
Croft Brow OL8 ...66 E2
Croft Dr BL8 ......26 E6
Croft Gate BL2 ....25 E4
Croft Gates Rd M24 .64 D7
Croft Gr M38 ....59 F5
Croft Head Cl OL2 .48 D4
Croft Head Rd OL16 .31 F7
Croft Hill Rd M40 .65 A1
Croft La Bolton BL3 .148 B5
Radcliffe M26 ......43 A5
Whitefield BL9 .....45 A5
Croft Manor SK13 .104 E1
Croft Pl M29 ......76 F8
Croft Rd Cheadle SK8 .123 B2

Croft Rd continued
Sale M33 ....108 D2
Wilmslow SK9 .....136 E4
Croft Row OL5 .....68 D1
Croft Side BL3 ....42 E5
Croft Sq OL12 .....15 C3
Croft St Bolton BL3 .42 B4
Bury BL9 ....141 A2
Droylsden M11 .....83 B1
4 Failsworth M35 .66 A1
Golborne WA3 ......90 A8
Hyde SK14 ....167 D2
Rochdale OL12 .....15 C3
Salford M7 ....81 C5
Stalybridge SK15 ..86 B2
Walkden M38 ....59 F5
Westhoughton BL5 .39 E3
Croft The 8 Bolton BL1 .145 F8
Hadfield SK13 .....14 A8
Mottram-in-L SK14 .103 A4
Oldham OL8 ....66 E2
Orrell WN5 ....53 D3
Stockport SK2 ...124 B6
Westhoughton BL5 .39 E3
Whitefield BL9 ....45 A6
Crofters Brook M26 .44 C4
Crofters Gn SK9 ..136 F6
Crofters Hall Wlk M40 .83 B7
Crofters The M33 .108 F3
Crofters Wlk BL2 ..25 C6
Croft Fold 10 M11 .160 C8
Crofthill Ct BL2 ..25 D4
Croftlands Orrell WN5 .53 D4
Ramsbottom BL0 ....11 A3
Croftlands Rd M22 .121 E4
Croftleigh Cl M45 .44 E2
Crofton Ave WA15 .120 A8
Crofton Gdns WA3 .91 E3
Crofton St
Manchester M14 ....98 B3
Manchester,Old Trafford
M16 ....97 D4
Oldham OL8 ....66 F3
Crofts OL2 ....149 A6
Crofts Bank Rd M41 .95 D3
Croftside Ave M28 .60 E3
Croftside Cl M28 ..60 E3
Croftside Gr M28 ..60 E3
Croftside Way SK9 .137 C6
Croftwood Sq WN5 .36 C2
Croichbank BL8 ....10 B2
Croichly Fold BL8 .10 D2
Cromar Rd SK7 ...124 F3
Cromarty Ave OL9 .65 F3
Cromarty Sq OL10 .28 F1
Cromarty Wlk M11 .160 F1
Crombie Dr M7 ...155 C7
Crombouke Dr WN7 .57 E1
Crombouke Fold M28 .78 B7
Cromdale Ave
Bolton BL1 ....144 B8
Hazel Grove SK7 ..124 F3
Cromedale Cres WN6 .37 A7
Cromer Ave Bolton BL2 .25 C1
Manchester M20 ...110 B6
Reddish M34 ......100 A3
Cromer Rd Bury BL8 .27 D5
Cheadle SK8 ......122 E6
Sale M33 ....108 B2
Wigan WN3 ....54 E5
Cromer St Droylsden M11 .83 D1
Middleton M24 .....47 B1
Rochdale OL12 ....139 E8
Shaw OL2 ....149 B7
Stockport SK1 ...112 A2
Cromford Ave M32 .96 B3
Cromford Bank 18 SK13 .171 D2
Cromford Bsns Ctr OL1 .67 B8
Cromford Cl Bolton BL1 .143 E1
19 Gamesley SK13 .171 D2
Cromford Cts M4 .159 A2
Cromford Dr WN5 ..54 B5
Cromford Fold 20 SK13 .171 D2
Cromford Gdns BL1 .143 F2
Cromford Gr 18 SK13 .171 D2
Cromford Lea 17 SK13 .171 D2
Cromford Pl 21 SK13 .171 D2
Cromford St OL1 ...67 B8
Cromford Way 19 SK13 .171 D2
Cromhurst St M8 ..156 A8
Cromley Rd
High Lane SK6 ....134 E6
Stockport SK2 ...124 A3
Crompton Ave Bolton BL2 .42 E8
Rochdale OL16 .....31 B3
Marple SK6 ....125 F7
Radcliffe M26 ......62 B8
Crompton Ct SK8 .123 B1
Crompton Fold Prim Sch
BL2 ....42 E7
Crompton Ho 2 WN1 .151 D8
Crompton House CE Sch
OL2 ....48 F7
Crompton Lodge Cvn Pk
BL3 ....42 E7
Crompton Pl Bolton BL1 .145 F7
Radcliffe M26 ......44 B3
Crompton Prim Sch
OL2 ....149 A6
Crompton Rd Horwich BL6 .39 F8
Kearsley M26 ......61 A8

Crompton Rd continued
Manchester M19 ....111 A7
Crompton St
Ashton-u-L OL6 ....85 E4
Bolton BL1 ....148 A8
Bury BL9 ....140 E2
Chadderton OL9 ....152 C7
Farnworth BL4 ....60 E7
Ince-in-M WN3 ....55 F3
Oldham OL1 ....153 E8
Platt Bridge WN2 ....56 B3
Royton OL2 ....48 D3
Royton OL2 ....48 E3
Shaw OL2 ....149 B7
Swinton M27 ....149 D8
Walkden,Greenheys M38 ...59 D5
Walkden,Whittle Brook M28 .60 F2
Wigan WN1 ....150 C8
Crompton Vale BL2 ....42 D8
Crompton Way Bolton BL2 .25 C2
Shaw OL2 ....149 B7
Cromwell Ave
Gatley SK8 ....122 A6
Manchester M16 ....97 C2
Marple SK6 ....125 D7
Reddish SK5 ....100 A2
Cromwell Cl WA12 ....89 A4
Cromwell Ct M44 ....105 E7
Cromwell Gr
Manchester M19 ....99 B1
❼ Salford M7 ....81 C5
Cromwell Range M14 ....98 D2
Cromwell Rd
Bramhall SK7 ....132 D6
Brinnington SK6 ....112 D6
Eccles M30 ....79 D2
Irlam M44 ....105 E7
Prestwich M25 ....63 C4
Royton OL2 ....48 C6
Salford M6 ....81 B5
Stretford M32 ....96 F2
Swinton M27 ....61 E1
Whitefield M45 ....44 D2
Cromwell St Bolton BL1 ...145 E7
Heywood OL10 ....29 D1
Oldham OL1 ....153 F6
Stockport SK4 ....169 D3
Crondale Wlk BL3 ....163 C6
Crondall St M14 ....98 A3
Cronkeyshaw Ave OL12 ....14 E2
Cronkeyshaw Rd OL12 .....14 F1
Cronshaw St M19 ....111 B8
Crook St Adlington PR7 ...20 F7
Bolton BL3 ....145 F6
❼ Hindley WN2 ....56 D4
Hyde SK14 ....167 E2
❿ Radcliffe M26 ....44 B3
❿ Rochdale OL16 ....31 A8
Wigan WN1 ....150 B8
Crookall St WN4 ....73 C4
Crooke Rd WN6 ....36 C3
Crookhill Dr M8 ....155 F7
Crookhurst Ave WN5 ....71 D6
Crookilley Way SK1,SK6 ...112 C4
Croom Wlk M40 ....160 D2
Cropton Way WN2 ....56 F3
Crosby Ave M46 ....60 F2
Crosby Gr M46 ....58 E4
Crosby Rd Bolton BL1 ....148 B8
Failsworth M40 ....83 D5
Radcliffe M26 ....43 E7
❸ Salford M6 ....80 D5
Crosby St Atherton M46 ...58 E4
❶ Rochdale OL12 ....15 A2
Stockport SK2 ....170 F7
Crosfield Ave BL9 ....11 C2
Crosfield Gr M18 ....99 D4
Cross Ave M25 ....63 A6
Cross Cliffe
Glossop SK13 ....116 E8
Hyde SK14 ....116 E8
Cross Field Cl OL2 ....32 C1
Cross Glebe St ❸ OL6 ...166 C3
Cross Gr WA15 ....119 F8
Cross Keys St M4 ....159 B2
Cross La Droylsden M43 ...84 D4
Manchester M18 ....99 D5
Marple SK6 ....125 E5
Newton-le-W WA12 ....89 B4
Orrell WN5 ....53 D3
Radcliffe M26 ....44 C4
Ramsbottom BL8 ....138 A6
Salford M5,M6 ....81 B2
Wilmslow SK9 ....137 F8
Cross La E M31 ....105 F3
Cross La W M31 ....105 F2
Cross Lees OL12 ....15 A3
Cross Ormrod St BL3 ....145 D6
Manchester M21 ....109 B8
Cross Rise SK13 ....116 E8
Cross St
❸ Altrincham WA14 ....119 D4
Ashton-u-L OL6 ....166 A2
Aspull WN2 ....38 B6
Atherton M46 ....58 D4
Bolton BL1 ....145 F8
Bolton,Eagley BL7 ....25 A7
Bury BL9 ....140 F2
Denton M34 ....100 E5
Farnworth BL4 ....60 D8
❶ Glossop SK13 ....104 C1
Golborne WA3 ....90 A7
Hadfield SK13 ....104 A4

Cross St continued
Heywood OL10 ....29 E1
Hindley WN2 ....56 D5
Hollingworth SK14 ....171 D4
Hyde SK14 ....167 D2
Ince-in-M WN3 ....55 E4
Kearsley BL4 ....61 B6
Leigh WN7 ....76 A4
Little Lever BL3 ....43 B3
Manchester M2 ....158 F1
Manchester,Old Trafford
M16 ....162 D5
❾ Middleton M24 ....46 F1
Middleton M25 ....64 F8
Milnrow OL16 ....31 D7
❹ Mossley OL5 ....68 C1
Mottram-in-L SK14 ....115 B8
Oldham,County End OL4 ...68 A6
Oldham,Mumps OL4 ....67 B7
❸ Oldham,Salem OL4 ......67 E6
Radcliffe M26 ....44 B3
Ramsbottom BL0 ....138 C6
Rochdale OL11 ....30 C2
Sale M33 ....108 B6
Salford M3 ....158 E2
Stalybridge SK15 ....86 D4
Standish WN6 ....19 E1
Stretford M32 ....96 D2
Swinton,Clifton Junction
M27 ....62 D2
Swinton,Hazelhurst M28 ...79 C7
Tyldesley M29 ....76 F8
Urmston M41 ....95 C1
Whitefield M45 ....44 E1
Wigan WN3 ....150 C7
❼ Wigan,Lamberhead Green
WN5 ....54 B6
Cross The ❸ SK13 ....104 A5
Crossacres Prim Sch
M22 ....121 E3
Crossacres Rd M22 ....121 E3
Crossbank Ave OL4 ....67 F7
Crossbank Cl M13 ....164 D5
Crossbank St
Oldham OL8 ....153 E5
Oldham OL8 ....153 E6
Crossbank Way M24 ....46 F1
Crossbridge Rd SK14 .....102 A2
Crossbrook Way OL16 ......32 A5
Crossby Cl M9 ....64 F5
Crosscliffe St ❸ M16 ......97 F4
Crossdale Rd Bolton BL2 ...42 F8
Hindley WN2 ....57 A5
Manchester M9 ....64 F4
Crossdale Way WA11 ......71 B1
Crossefield Rd SK8 ....123 A3
Crossen St BL3 ....148 C5
Crossfell Ave M9 ....64 E5
Crossfield Ave WA3 ....91 F2
Crossfield Cl
Denton M34 ....101 A2
Stalybridge SK15 ....86 A1
Wardle OL12 ....15 C6
Crossfield Dr
Hindley WN2 ....57 C3
Radcliffe M26 ....43 E3
Swinton M27 ....61 E1
Worsley M28 ....78 B7
Crossfield Gr
Romiley SK6 ....114 B1
Stockport SK2 ....124 B4
Crossfield Pl OL11 ....31 A5
Crossfield Rd
Altrincham WA15 ....120 B2
Handforth SK9 ....131 D4
Irlam M30 ....94 C4
Wardle OL12 ....15 C6
Crossfield St ❺ BL9 ......44 F4
Crossfields BL7 ....25 C8
Crossford Dr BL3 ....40 E4
Crossford St M32 ....96 D1
Crossgate Ave M22 ....121 D6
Crossgate La SK13 ....103 F7
Crossgate Mews SK4 .....110 E2
Crossgates Prim Sch
OL16 ....32 A7
Crossgates Rd OL16 ....32 A6
Crossgill M29 ....77 B5
Crosshill St ❹ M16 ....97 F4
Crosshill Wlk BL3 ....40 E5
Crossings The WA12 .....89 C3
Crossland Rd
Droylsden M43 ....84 B2
Manchester M21 ....109 A8
Crosslands M25 ....63 A3
Crosslands Cl SK13 ....116 D8
Crosslands Rd M28 ....77 F6
Crosslee Com Prim Sch
M9 ....64 F4
Crosslee Rd M9 ....64 A4
Crossley Cres OL6 ....85 E5
Crossley Pk M19 ....111 B6
Crossley Rd
Manchester M19,SK4 ......111 A3
Sale M33 ....108 A6
Crossley St
Little Lever BL3 ....43 A3
Manchester M18 ....165 A6
Milnrow OL16 ....31 E6
Royton OL2 ....48 E2
Shaw OL2 ....149 C7
❸ Stalybridge SK15 ....86 A2
Crossmead Dr ❸ M9 .....64 E5
Crossmeadow Cl OL11 ....30 A8
Crossmoor Cres SK6 ......113 C1
Crossmoor Dr BL2 ....148 B8
Crossmoor Gr SK6 ....113 C2
Crosswaite Rd SK2 ....124 E6

Crossway Bramhall SK7 ...132 E5
Manchester M20 ....110 B3
Stockport SK2 ....124 A4
Crossway Cl WN4 ....73 C5
Crossway Ho ❽ M20 .....110 B3
Crossway Rd M33 ....107 F1
Crossways Bramhall SK7 ..132 E5
Oldham OL8 ....67 A1
Croston Ave PR6 ....21 A8
Croston Cl SK9 ....137 C1
Croston Close Rd BL9,
OL12 ....12 C4
Croston St Bolton BL3 ....146 C4
Hindley WN2 ....56 C6
Croston Wlk M11 ....160 E1
Crostons Rd BL8 ....140 D3
Croton St SK4 ....110 E2
Croughton Cl M11 ....99 D7
Crow Hill SK15 ....86 E5
Crow Hill N M24 ....64 F7
Crow Hill S M24 ....64 F6
Crow Hill View OL4 ....67 F5
Crow La OL6 ....138 C6
Crow La E WA12 ....89 C4
Crow La W WA12 ....89 A4
Crow Orchard Rd WN6 ....19 A1
Crow Tree Ave ❹ OL13 ...3 B8
Crow Trees La BL7 ....9 C7
Crow Wood Rd
Edenfield BB4 ....1 D6
Golborne WA3 ....74 D1
Crow's Nest BL3 ....42 F5
Crow's Nest Cotts BL3 ...42 F5
Crowbank Wlk M40 ....83 A5
Crowborough Cl BL6 ....22 F1
Crowborough Wlk M15 ...162 F5
Crowbrook Gr ❼ SK9 .....131 D1
Crowcroft Park Prim Sch
M12 ....99 A3
Crowcroft Rd M12,M13 ...99 A3
Crowden Rd M40 ....65 B2
Crowhill Rd OL7 ....84 F4
Crowhurst Dr WN1 ....37 B3
Crowhurst Wlk ❸ M23 ...120 E7
Crowland Gdns SK8 ......132 B6
Crowland Rd M23 ....120 D7
Wythenshawe M23 ....120 F3
Crowley La OL4 ....49 D1
Crowley Rd
Altrincham WA15 ....120 B6
Manchester M9 ....157 F8
Crown Bsns Ctr M35 ....83 F8
Crown Cl SK7 ....124 D3
Crown Fields Cl WA12 .....89 B5
Crown Gdns Edgworth BL7 ..9 D6
Newton-le-W WA12 ....89 B4
Crown La M9 ....157 F8
Crown Gr WN7 ....76 D6
Crown Hill OL5 ....68 D8
Crown Ind Est
Altrincham WA14 ....119 E7
Manchester M4 ....159 C2
Crown La Horwich BL6 .....22 E4
Manchester M4 ....159 A3
Crown Mews SK2 ....124 C4
Crown Park Dr WA12 ......89 B5
Crown Passages WA15 ...119 E2
Crown Point M7 ....9 D6
Crown Point Ave M40 .....83 C5
Crown Rd OL10 ....29 B2
Crown Royal Ind Pk
SK1 ....124 A8
Crown Sq M3 ....158 E1
Crown St Ashton-u-L OL6 .166 B2
Atherton M46 ....58 B3
Bolton BL1 ....145 F7
Denton M34 ....100 E4
Failsworth M35 ....43 B3
❷❹ Failsworth,Newton Heath
M40 ....83 C5
Hindley WN2 ....56 C6
Manchester M15 ....162 E7
Marple SK6 ....125 F3
Newton-le-W WA12 ....89 A5
Rochdale OL16 ....31 B5
Romiley SK6 ....113 A3
Salford M3 ....158 E2
Shaw OL2 ....150 B6
Wigan WN3 ....150 B6
Crowndale M7 ....9 D7
Crowneast St OL11 ....30 C7
Crowngreen Rd M30 ....79 E1
Crownhill Rd M43 ....84 A2
Crowsdale Pl SK2 ....124 E4
Crowshaw Dr OL12 ......14 F1
Crowswood Dr SK15 ......86 D5
Crowther Ave M5 ....161 A8
Crowther Ct
Manchester SK4 ....168 A3
❺ Rochdale OL16 ....15 C4
Crowther Dr WN3 ....54 E1
Crowther St
Littleborough OL15 ....15 E4
Manchester M18 ....99 E5
Rochdale OL16 ....31 B4
Crowthorn Dr M23 ....121 A2
Crowthorn Rd
Ashton-u-L OL7 ....84 F1
Edgworth BL7 ....10 B8
Reddish SK4 ....111 D7
Croxden Ave M33 ....107 D2
Croxdale Cl OL7 ....84 E5
Croxdale Wlk M9 ....64 D5
Croxton Ave OL16 ....31 B8
Croxton Cl Marple SK6 ...126 E5
Sale M33 ....107 D2

Croxton Wlk
❽ Horwich BL6 ....22 B4
Manchester M13 ....163 C6
Croyde Cl Bolton BL2 ......25 F3
Wythenshawe M22 ....130 F7
Croydon Ave Leigh WN7 ...75 F8
Croydon Ave
Royton OL2 ....48 C6
Trub OL11 ....47 D8
Croydon Ct M5 ....161 B8
Croydon Dr M40 ....83 C4
Croydon Sq OL11 ....47 D8
Crummock Dr
Middleton M24 ....46 E3
Wigan WN3 ....54 F3
Crummock Rd
Farnworth BL4 ....59 E7
Gatley SK8 ....122 B3
Crumpsall La ❼ M8 ....64 A1
Crumpsall Lane Prim Sch
M8 ....64 A1
Crumpsall St BL1 ....143 E3
Crumpsall Sta M8 ....64 A1
Crumpsall Vale M9 ....64 C2
Crumpsall Way M8 ....64 B1
Crundale Rd ❼ BL1 ....24 F6
Cruttenden Rd SK2 ....124 D4
Cryer St M43 ....84 C4
Cuba Ind Est BL0 ....138 C8
Cuba St M7 ....65 C8
Cubley Rd M7 ....155 E8
Cuckoo Gr M25 ....64 A1
Cuckoo La Bury BL9 ......141 C2
Bury BL9 ....141 C3
Prestwich M25 ....64 A1
WA14 ....119 D3
Cuddington Ave M20 .....110 A8
Cuddington Cres SK3 ....170 D6
Cuddington Way ❼
Sale M33 ....131 D5
Cudworth Rd M9 ....64 A5
Cuerdon Wlk M22 ....121 E8
Culand St M24 ....65 E7
Culbert Ave M20 ....110 C3
Culchetch Ave SK6 ....125 F6
Culchetch Ave WN2 ....56 B1
Culcheth Hall Dr WA3 .....91 F4
Culcheth Hall Sch
WA14 ....119 D3
Culcheth High Sch WA3 ..92 A3
Culcheth La M40 ....83 C4
Culcheth Prim Sch WA3 ..92 A2
Culcheth Rd WA14 ....119 F3
Culcombe Wlk M13 ....163 C5
Culcross Ave WN3 ....54 C4
Culford Cl M12 ....164 E5
Culgaith Wlk M9 ....157 D7
Culham Cl BL1 ....143 D2
Culholm Rd M22 ....130 F8
Cullen Gr M9 ....64 F3
Cullercoats Wlk ❸ M12 ..99 B3
Culmere Rd M22 ....121 D1
Culmington Cl M15 ....162 E5
Culross Ave Bolton BL3 ...40 E6
Failsworth M40 ....65 F1
Culver Rd SK3 ....170 D5
Culvercliffe Wlk M3 ....162 E8
Culverden Wlk M6 ....80 F6
Culvert St Oldham OL4 ....67 E8
Rochdale OL16 ....31 B2
Wigan M6 ....37 A3
Culverwell Dr M5 ....81 B2
Culzean Cl WN7 ....76 C4
Cumber Cl SK9 ....136 D4
Cumber Dr SK9 ....136 D4
Cumber La SK9 ....136 D4
Cumberbatch Pl WN3 .....55 F4
Cumberland Ave
Brinnington SK6 ....112 C4
Dukinfield SK16 ....101 E8
Heywood OL10 ....29 A2
Irlam M44 ....105 C5
Swinton M27 ....61 F2
Tyldesley M29 ....58 F2
Cumberland Cl BL9 ....44 E6
Cumberland Gr
Altrincham WA14 ....128 B8
Royton OL1,OL2 ....48 D2
Cumberland Gr OL7 ......166 B4
Cumberland Rd
Atherton M46 ....58 F4
Manchester M9 ....157 D7
Partington M31 ....105 E2
Rochdale OL11 ....30 F2
Sale M33 ....108 C2
Urmston M41 ....95 C1
Cumberland St
Salford M7 ....158 D4
❹ Salford M7 ....158 D4
Wigan WN1 ....37 E1
Cumbermere La M29 ......59 B2
Cumbrae Gdns M5 ....154 E1
Cumbrae Rd M19 ....99 C1
Cumbria Ct M25 ....62 F1
Cumbria Wlk M6 ....81 B4
Cumbrian Cl
Manchester M13 ....163 C6
Platt Bridge WN2 ....56 B2
Shaw OL2 ....48 F8
Cummings St OL8 ....66 C2
Cunard Cl M13 ....163 C6
Cundall Wlk M23 ....108 F1
Cundey St Bolton BL1 ....144 C4
Cundiff Ct M19 ....99 C1
Cundiff Rd M21 ....109 B6
Cundy St SK14 ....167 E4
Cunliffe Ave
Newton-le-W WA12 ....89 B5
Ramsbottom BL0 ....11 A4

Cunliffe Brow BL1 ....142 B1
Cunliffe Ct WN7 ....75 A4
Cunliffe Dr Sale M33 .....108 C3
Shaw OL2 ....49 D7
Cunliffe St
Dukinfield SK14 ....101 C4
Leigh WN7 ....75 C5
Radcliffe M26 ....44 C3
Ramsbottom BL0 ....138 C7
Stockport SK3 ....123 C8
Cunningham Dr
Gatley M22 ....131 A8
Whitefield BL9 ....45 B2
Cunningham Rd BL5 ......57 D7
Cunningham Way OL11 ..153 F8
Curate Ct SK1 ....112 A1
Curate St SK1 ....112 A1
Curlew Cl OL11 ....29 F7
Curlew Dr M44 ....94 A4
Curlew Rd OL4 ....67 E4
Curlew Way SK13 ....115 F8
Curlew Wlk M12 ....164 E5
Currier La OL6 ....85 D2
Curteis St BL6 ....22 B4
Curtels Cl M28 ....79 C7
Curtis Gr SK13 ....104 A5
Curtis Rd
Manchester SK4 ....168 A2
Reddish M19 ....99 C1
Wigan WN5 ....54 D6
Curven Edge BB4 ....1 A7
Curzon Ave M14 ....98 E4
Curzon Dr WA15 ....120 B6
Curzon Gn SK2 ....124 D7
Curzon Mews SK9 ....137 A5
Curzon Rd Ashton-u-L OL6 .85 D4
Bolton BL1 ....144 C7
Gatley SK8 ....131 A8
Poynton SK12 ....133 E2
Rochdale OL11 ....30 F2
❺ Sale M33 ....108 B5
Salford M7 ....155 D7
Stockport SK2 ....124 D7
Stretford M32 ....96 A4
Curzon St Mossley OL5 ...68 C1
Oldham OL1 ....153 F7
Cut La OL12 ....13 F1
Cutacre Cl M29 ....59 B1
Cutgate Cl M23 ....108 E1
Cutgate Rd OL12 ....14 B1
Cuthbert Ave M19 ....111 B8
Cuthbert Bsns Ctr M11 ..165 C7
Cuthbert Ho M16 ....97 E2
Cuthbert Mayne Ct
OL16 ....139 E6
Cuthbert Rd SK8 ....122 E6
Cuthbert St Bolton BL3 ...146 B2
Wigan WN5 ....54 D6
Cuthill Wlk M40 ....83 D4
Cutland St ❶❸ M40 ....83 A6
Cutland Way M14 ....16 A4
Cutler Cres OL13 ....3 D7
Cutler Hill Rd M35 ....84 C7
Cutler La OL13 ....3 D7
Cutnook La M44 ....94 A3
Cutter Cl M5 ....161 A8
Cycle St M11 ....165 B8
Cyclone St M11 ....164 F8
Cygnet St WN3 ....150 B6
Cygnus Ave M7 ....81 B3
Cymbal Ct SK5 ....169 F3
Cynthia Dr SK6 ....125 F5
Cypress Ave OL9 ....152 B8
Cypress Cl SK3 ....123 C8
Cypress Gdns OL16 ....31 D7
Cypress Gr Denton M34 ..101 A3
Kearsley BL4 ....60 F7
Cypress Ho ❿ M14 ....98 E4
Cypress Oaks SK15 ....86 D3
Cypress Rd Droylsden M43 .84 F3
Eccles M30 ....79 A4
Oldham OL4 ....67 D8
Wigan WN5 ....54 D6
Cypress St
Manchester M9 ....157 D7
Middleton M24 ....65 C8
Cypress Way SK6 ....135 A7
Cypress Wlk ❷ M33 .....107 C6
Cyprus Cl Oldham OL4 ....67 D6
Salford M5 ....154 F1
Cyprus St M32 ....96 D2
Cyril St Bolton BL3 ....148 A5
Manchester M14 ....98 B3
Shaw OL2 ....149 C7
Cyrus St M40 ....160 E2

D

D'Olivera Ct ❼ M24 ....46 E2
Daccamill Dr M27 ....79 F6
Dacre Ave M16 ....97 B2
Dacre Cl M24 ....46 B1
Dacre Rd OL11 ....30 F4
Dacres Ave OL3 ....68 F4
Dacres Dr OL3 ....68 F4
Dacres Rd OL3 ....68 F4
Daffodil Cl Haslingden BB4 ..1 A8
Rochdale OL12 ....14 D3
Daffodil Rd BL4 ....42 A1
Daffodil St BL1 ....143 E2
Dagenham Rd M14 ....98 C4
Dagmar St M28 ....60 C4
Dagnall Ave M21 ....109 B6
Dahlia Cl OL12 ....14 D3
Dailton Rd WN8 ....53 A7
Daimler St M8 ....156 B6

Dain Cl SK16 101 D8
Daine Ave M23 109 B1
Dainton St M12 164 D7
Daintry Cl M15 162 F6
Daintry Rd OL9 152 C7
Dairy House La SK7 132 B4
Dairy House Rd SK7 132 B5
Dairy House Small Holdings
SK7 132 B4
Dairy St OL9 152 B7
Dairydale Cl 3 M44 94 B3
Dairyground Rd SK7 132 F7
Dairyhouse La WA14 119 B7
Daisy Ave Farnworth BL4 42 A1
Manchester M13 98 E4
Newton-le-W WA12 89 C2
Daisy Bank
Failsworth M40 83 D5
Hyde SK14 113 C8
Daisy Bank Ave M27 80 C6
Daisy Bank La SK8 122 A1
Daisy Bank Mill Cl WA3 91 E3
Daisy Bank Rd M14 98 D4
Daisy Hall Dr BL5 57 E5
Daisy Hill Ct OL4 67 E8
Daisy Hill Dr PR6 21 A8
Daisy Hill Rd OL5 68 D1
Daisy Hill Sta BL5 57 F6
Daisy Mews SK3 123 D4
Daisy Nook Ctry Pk*
OL8 84 E6
Daisy Rd WN5 54 E6
Daisy St Bolton BL3 146 C4
6 Bury BL8 27 C2
Chadderton OL9 152 A8
Oldham OL9 153 D7
4 Rochdale OL12 139 E8
Stockport SK1,SK2 170 F7
Daisy Way SK6 134 F7
Daisybank Cl WN2 56 D5
Daisybank Villas M14 98 D4
Daisyfield Cl M22 121 C1
Daisyfield Ct BL8 27 C1
Daisyfield Wlk 5 M28 60 D3
Daisyhill Cl M33 108 E4
Daisyhill Ct BL5 57 F5
Dak Wlk M34 100 E6
Dakerwood Cl 3 M40 83 C5
Dakins Rd WN7 76 B3
Dakley St M11 165 C7
Dakota Ave M50 96 F8
Dakota S M50 96 F8
Dalbeatie Rise WN1 37 F1
Dalbeattie St M9 64 E1
Dalberg St M12 164 D7
Dalbury Dr M40 156 C5
Dalby Ave M27 79 E7
Dalby Gr SK1 112 A1
Dalby Rd WN2 57 B5
Dale Ave Bramhall SK7 132 F8
Eccles M30 79 C3
Mossley OL5 68 E3
Dale Brook Ave SK16 101 D6
Dale Fields OL3 50 F4
Dale Gr Altrincham WA15 119 F7
Ashton-u-L OL7 85 A5
Irlam M44 105 E6
Leigh WN7 75 C4
Dale Grove Sch OL7 85 A5
Dale Ho OL2 149 B6
Dale House Fold SK12 134 A4
Dale Ind Est M26 44 A2
Dale La OL3 50 F5
Dale Lee BL5 58 A8
Dale Prim Sch The SK6 125 D7
Dale Rd Golborne WA3 90 A7
Marple SK6 125 E7
Middleton M24 47 B2
Dale Sq OL2 48 F4
Dale St Ashton-u-L OL6 86 A6
8 Bacup OL13 3 C8
Bury BL8 27 C4
Farnworth BL4 42 E1
Ince-in-M WN3 55 F3
Leigh WN7 75 C5
Manchester M1 159 B1
Middleton M24 65 B7
Milnrow OL16 31 F6
Ramsbottom BL0 1 C1
Rochdale OL16 31 C7
Shaw OL2 149 B6
Stalybridge SK15 85 F1
Stockport SK3 170 D7
Swinton M27 79 E6
Westhoughton BL5 57 F5
Whitefield M45 44 E1
Dale St E Ashton-u-L OL6 166 A2
Horwich BL6 22 D2
Dale St W Ashton-u-L OL6 166 A2
Horwich BL6 22 D2
Dale View Denton M34 113 A7
Hyde SK14 113 D8
Littleborough OL15 15 F2
Mottram-in-L SK14 103 A3
Newton-le-W WA12 89 E4
Dalebank M46 58 C5
Dalebank Mews M27 61 D5
Dalebeck Cl M45 63 C8
Dalebeck Wlk M45 63 C8
Dalebrook Ct SK4 168 C1
Dalebrook Rd M33 108 C1
Dalecrest WN5 53 D1
Daleford Sq M13 163 C7
Dalegarth Ave BL1 40 C7
Dalehead Cl M18 99 F6
Dalehead Dr OL2 49 D7
Dalehead Gr WN7 75 C4
Dalehead Pl WA11 71 B1
Dales Ave Manchester M8 63 F2
Whitefield M45 44 D1
Dales Brow Bolton BL1 24 F6
Swinton M27 79 E6
Dales Brow Ave OL7 85 A5
Dales Gr M28 60 F1
Dales La M45 44 E1
Dales Park Dr M27 79 D6
Dalesbrook Cl BL3 43 A4
Dalesfield Cres OL5 68 E1
Dalesford Cl WN7 91 C8
Daleside Ave WN4 73 A8
Dalesman Cl M9 157 F8
Dalesman Wlk 4 M15 163 A6
Daleswood Ave M45 44 D1
Dalham Ave M9 65 A2
Dalkeith Ave SK5 111 F7
Dalkeith Gr BL3 40 F5
Dalkeith Rd Hindley WN2 57 A5
Reddish SK5 111 F7
Dalkeith Sq OL10 29 A1
Dallas Ct M50 96 E8
Dalley Ave M7 158 D4
Dallimore Rd M23 120 E6
Dalmahoy Cl M40 83 C8
Dalmain Cl M8 155 F6
Dalmeny Terr OL11 30 F4
Dalmorton Rd M21 109 D8
Dalny St M19 99 B1
Dalry Wlk 1 M23 121 A5
Dalrybrook Gr 7 SK9 131 E1
Dalston Ave M35 84 B8
Dalston Dr Billinge WA11 71 B1
Bramhall SK7 132 C5
Manchester M20 110 C2
Dalston Gr WN3 54 D3
Dalton Ave
Manchester M14 98 A2
Milnrow OL16 31 D7
Stretford M32 96 A4
Swinton M27 62 C3
Whitefield M45 63 A7
Dalton Cl Milnrow OL16 31 D7
Ramsbottom BL0 11 A4
Wigan WN5 54 B7
Dalton Ct M40 159 B4
Dalton Dr Pendlebury M27 80 D7
Wigan WN3 54 E2
Dalton Fold BL5 57 F8
Dalton Gdns M41 95 B3
Dalton Gr
Ashton-in-M WN4 73 A4
Manchester SK4 168 C4
Dalton Ho 6 M14 110 D8
Dalton Rd Manchester M9 64 D5
Middleton M24 64 B7
Dalton St Bury BL8 27 B2
Chadderton OL9 152 B7
Eccles M30 79 D3
Failsworth M35 83 E8
Manchester M4,M40 159 B4
Oldham OL1 67 B7
Sale M33 108 C6
Daltry St OL1 67 A8
Dalveen Ave M41 95 C4
Dalveen Dr WA15 119 F7
Dalwood Cl WN2 56 F4
Dalymount Cl BL2 25 B2
Dam Head Dr M9 64 E3
Dam Head La WA3 105 A5
Dam La Ashton-in-M WN4 73 F3
Hollinfare WA3 105 A4
Damask Ave M3 158 D2
Dame Hollow SK8 131 D7
Dame St OL9 153 D8
Dameny Ct SK7 132 E8
Dameral Cl M8 156 A6
Damery Rd SK7 132 E8
Damian Dr WA12 89 A5
Damien St M12 99 B2
Dams Head Fold BL5 39 F1
Damson Gn M24 65 D8
Damson Wlk M31 105 D3
Dan Bank SK6 125 C6
Danbury Wlk M23 120 D8
Danby Cl SK14 167 F4
Danby Ct 6 OL1 153 E8
Danby Pl SK14 167 F4
Danby Rd Bolton BL3 147 E3
Hyde SK14 167 F4
Danby Wlk M9 64 E1
Dane Ave Cheadle SK3 123 A8
Partington M31 105 F4
Dane Bank M24 65 B7
Dane Bank Dr SK12 135 D6
Dane Bank Prim Sch
SK5 100 A2
Dane Cl SK7 123 D3
Dane Dr SK9 137 D6
Dane Hill Cl SK12 135 D5
Dane Ho 4 M33 108 C4
Dane Mews M33 108 B4
Dane Rd Reddish M34 100 A2
Sale M33 108 D5
Dane Road Sta M33 108 C6
Dane St Bolton BL3 146 C4
Manchester M11 99 E7
Mossley OL5 68 D3
6 Oldham OL4 67 C7
Rochdale OL11 139 E7
Dane Wlk SK5 169 F4
Danebank Mews M34 100 B2
Danebank Wlk 14 M13 163 B7
Danebridge Cl BL4 60 E8
Danebury Cl 11 WN2 56 D4
Danecroft Cl M13 164 D5
Danefield Ct SK8 131 D8
Danefield Rd M33 108 C6
Daneholme Rd M19 110 E5
Danes Ave WN2 56 E6
Danes Brook Cl WN2 56 E6
Danes Gn WN2 56 E7
Danes Rd M14 98 D2
Danesbury Cl WN5 71 E4
Danesbury Rd BL2 25 B4
Danesbury Rise SK8 122 D5
Daneshill M25 63 B6
Danesmoor Dr BL9 141 B4
Danesmoor Rd M20 110 B5
Danesway Adlington PR7 20 F8
Manchester M25 63 D2
Pendlebury M27 80 C6
Wigan WN1 37 B3
Danesway Ct BL1 143 D2
Daneswood Ave
Manchester M9 64 F4
Whitworth OL12 14 C8
Daneswood Cl OL12 14 C8
Danett Cl M12 165 B6
Danforth Gr M19 111 B8
Daniel Adamson Ave
M31 105 D3
Daniel Adamson Rd
Salford M50 154 D1
Stretford M50 96 D8
Daniel Ct M31 105 F4
Daniel Fold OL12 14 B2
Daniel St
Hazel Grove SK7 124 E2
Heywood OL10 29 B2
Oldham OL1 67 C8
Royton OL2 49 A3
Whitworth OL12 4 D2
Daniel's La SK1 169 F2
Danisher La OL8 84 F8
Dannywood Cl SK14 113 C8
Danson St M40 160 E3
Dantall Ave M9 65 A3
Dante Cl M6,M30 80 A4
Danty St 25 SK16 166 B1
Dantzic St M4 159 A3
Danwood Cl M34 101 B1
Dapple Gr M11 165 A8
Darbishire St BL1 25 A1
Darby La WN2 56 D6
Darby Rd M44 106 A6
Darbyshire Cl BL1 144 C8
Darbyshire Ho WA15 120 C7
Darbyshire St M26 44 A3
Darbyshire Wlk 1 M26 44 B3
Darcy St BL2 148 C5
Darcy Wlk M14 98 A4
Darden Cl SK4 110 E3
Darell Wlk M8 156 B6
Daresbury Ave
Altrincham WA15 119 E5
Urmston M41 94 E4
Daresbury Cl Sale M33 108 F3
Stockport SK3 170 D5
Wilmslow SK9 137 C8
Daresbury Rd M21 96 F1
Daresbury St M8 156 A7
Darfield Wlk M40 160 D3
Dargai St M11 83 D1
Dargle Rd M33 108 B6
Darian Ave M22 130 D8
Daric Cl WN7 75 C1
Dark La Blackrod BL6 21 B3
Delph OL3 50 E6
Manchester M12 164 D8
Mossley OL5 68 D2
Uppermill OL3 69 A8
Darlbeck Wlk M21 109 C5
Darley Ave Eccles M30 95 C8
Farnworth BL4 42 E1
Gatley SK8 122 B5
Manchester M21 109 C5
Darley Gr BL4 42 E1
Darley Ho 5 M5 154 E1
Darley Rd
Hazel Grove SK7 133 F7
Manchester M16 97 C3
Rochdale OL11 30 F4
Wigan WN3 55 B3
Darley St Bolton BL1 143 D1
Farnworth BL4 60 E8
Horwich BL6 22 B5
Manchester M11 160 F1
Sale M33 108 B4
Stretford M32 96 E4
Darley Terr 5 BL1 143 D1
Darlington Cl BL8 27 B5
Darlington Rd
Manchester M20 110 A6
Rochdale OL11 30 F3
Darlington St
Ince-in-M WN2 56 A7
Tyldesley M29 59 A1
Wigan WN1 151 D7
Darlington St E
Tyldesley M29 59 B1
Wigan WN1 151 E7
Darliston Ave M9 64 A5
Darlton Wlk 9 M9 157 E8
Darnall Ave M14 110 A8
Darnbrook Dr 4 M22 121 B1
Darncombe Cl M16 97 F4
Darnhall St WN3 55 F4
Darnhill Com Sch OL10 28 F1
Darnley Ave M28 60 C1
Darnley St M16 97 D4
Darnton Gdns OL6 85 E3
Darnton Rd OL6,SK15 85 E3
Darran Ave WN3 54 F3
Darras Rd M18 99 C3
Dart Cl OL9 65 F8
Dartford Ave
Brinnington SK5 112 B6
Eccles M30 79 B2
Dartford Cl M12 164 D6
Dartford Rd M41 95 C1
Dartington Cl
Altrincham M23 120 D6
Stockport SK7 123 F2
Dartmouth Cl 4 OL8 66 F4
Dartmouth Cres SK5 112 C5
Dartmouth Rd
Manchester M21 109 C8
Whitefield M45 63 A7
Dartnall Cl SK12 135 A6
Darton Ave M40 160 E3
Darul-Uloom Islamic Coll
BL8 10 F4
Darvel Ave WN4 72 C4
Darvel Cl BL2 42 F6
Darwell Ave M30 95 C8
Darwen Dr 6 WN2 56 A2
Darwen Rd BL7 25 A7
Darwen St M16 161 C5
Darwin Gr SK7 132 E6
Darwin St Ashton-u-L OL7 166 A2
Bolton BL1 143 D2
Dukinfield SK14 102 A5
Oldham OL4 67 C5
Dashwood Rd M25 62 F5
Dashwood Wlk M12 165 A6
Datchett Terr OL11 30 F4
Dauntesy Ave M27 80 D7
Davehall Ave SK9 137 A7
Davenfield Gr M20 110 B3
Davenfield Ho 7 M20 110 B3
Davenfield Rd 2 M20 110 B3
Davenham Rd
Handforth SK9 131 D4
Reddish SK5 99 F2
Sale M33 107 F6
Davenhill Rd M19 111 A8
Davenport Ave
Manchester M20 110 B7
Radcliffe M26 43 F6
Wilmslow SK9 136 E4
Davenport Dr SK6 113 B6
Davenport Fold BL2 26 A3
Davenport Fold Rd BL2 26 A4
Davenport Gdns 9 BL1 145 E8
Davenport La WA14 119 C7
Davenport Lo SK3 170 F5
Davenport Park Rd SK2 124 A5
Davenport Rd SK7 124 D2
Davenport St
2 Ashton-u-L M34 100 E8
Bolton BL1 145 E8
Droylsden M43 83 E1
Davenport Sta SK3 170 F5
Daventry Rd
Manchester M21 109 D8
Rochdale OL11 30 F3
Davey La SK9 137 B2
Daveyhulme St OL12 15 B1
Daveylands Urmston M41 94 F5
Wilmslow SK9 137 D7
David Brow BL3 146 A2
David Cl M34 101 A1
David Lewis Cl OL16 31 C6
David Mews M14 110 C7
David Pegg Wlk M40 83 B5
David St Bacup OL13 3 D8
Bury BL8 27 C4
Denton M34 101 A2
2 Oldham OL1 153 E6
Reddish SK5 111 E8
16 Rochdale OL12 14 F1
David St N 15 OL12 14 F1
David's Farm Cl M24 65 C7
David's Rd M43 83 E2
Davids La OL4 67 F7
Davidson Dr M24 65 B6
Davidson Wlk WN5 54 E7
Davies Ave Gatley SK8 131 B6
Newton-le-W WA12 89 C4
Davies Rd
Partington M31 106 A3
Romiley SK6 112 D3
Davies Sq M14 98 A4
Davies St Ashton-u-L OL7 84 F1
Kearsley BL4 61 A7
Oldham OL1 153 D8
Platt Bridge WN2 56 A2
Davis St M30 79 F1
Davy Ave M27 62 D2
Davy St M40 159 B4
Davyhulme Circ M41 95 C4
Davyhulme Jun & Inf Sch
M41 95 D3
Davyhulme Rd
Stretford M32 96 C3
Urmston,Calder Bank M41 94 F4
Urmston,Davyhulme M41 95 B4
Davyhulme Rd E M32 96 D3
Daw Bank SK3 169 E1
Dawber Delph WN6 35 D8
Dawber St WN4 73 D4
Dawes St BL3 145 F6
Dawley Cl
Ashton-in-M WN4 73 A3
Bolton BL3 144 C6
Dawlish Ave
Brinnington SK5 112 C5
Chadderton OL9 47 F1
Cheadle SK8 131 F7
Droylsden M43 83 E1
Dawlish Cl Bramhall SK7 132 E7
Hattersley SK14 102 E3
Hollinfare WA3 105 B3
Dawlish Rd
Manchester M21 109 C8
Sale M33 107 E5
Dawlish Way WA3 73 F1
Dawn St OL2 149 B6
Dawnay St M11 165 B7
Dawnwood Sq WN5 36 C2
Dawson Ave WN6 37 A3
Dawson La BL1 145 E7
Dawson Rd
Altrincham WA14 119 D8
Gatley SK8 131 D8
Dawson St Atherton M46 58 C3
Bury BL9 141 A4
Heywood OL10 29 C2
Hyde SK14 167 E1
Manchester M3,M15 162 D8
5 Oldham OL4 67 D6
Oldham OL4 67 E5
Pendlebury M27 80 A8
Rochdale OL12 139 F8
Salford M3 158 F2
Stockport SK1 112 B3
Day Dr M35 83 F6
Day Gr SK14 103 A3
Dayfield WN8 53 B7
Daylesford Cl SK8 122 D4
Daylesford Cres SK8 122 D4
Daylesford Rd SK8 122 D4
De Brook Cl M41 94 E1
De Quincey Cl WA14 107 D1
De Quincey Rd WA14 107 D1
De Trafford Dr WN2 56 B8
De Trafford Ho 13 M30 79 D1
De Trafford Mews 9
SK9 131 D2
De Traffords The M44 94 B3
De-Massey Cl SK6 113 B6
Deacon Ave M27 61 E1
Deacon Cl WA14 119 B1
Deacon St OL16 15 B1
Deacon Trad Est WA12 89 A2
Deacons Cl SK1 112 A1
Deacons Cres BL8 27 A5
Deacons Dr M6 80 D6
Deakin St WN3 151 E5
Deakins Bsns Pk BL7 8 D1
Deal Ave SK5 112 B6
Deal Cl M40 83 D5
Deal Sq SK14 167 E2
Deal St Bolton BL3 147 F3
Bury BL9 141 B2
Hyde SK14 167 E2
Salford M3 158 E2
Deal Wlk OL9 152 A6
Dealey Rd BL3 146 A4
Dean Ave Failsworth M40 83 B6
Manchester M16 97 B3
Dean Bank Dr OL16 31 B1
Dean Bradley Ct M40 157 E6
Dean Brook Cl M40 83 B7
Dean Cl Billinge WN5 71 D3
Edenfield BL0 1 D3
Farnworth BL4 59 F8
Handforth SK9 131 C1
Partington M31 105 F4
Up Holland WN8 53 C7
Whitefield M45 62 D7
Dean Cres WN5 54 B8
Dean Ct Bolton BL1 148 A8
11 Dukinfield SK16 166 B1
Golborne WA3 90 A7
Manchester M15 162 D6
Rochdale OL11 30 F4
Dean Dr Altrincham WA14 119 B1
Handforth SK9 131 D2
Dean La Failsworth M40 83 B6
Hazel Grove SK7 133 E8
Dean Lane Sta M40 83 B6
Dean Mdw WA12 89 C4
Dean Moor Rd SK7 124 A1
Dean Rd Golborne WA3 90 A7
Handforth SK9 131 E3
Haslingden BB4 1 B8
Irlam M44 105 E6
Reddish M18 99 E4
Salford M3 158 E3
Dean Row Ct 10 SK9 131 D1
Dean Row Jun Sch SK9 131 E1
Dean Row Rd SK9 137 F8
Dean St Ashton-u-L OL6 166 A3
Failsworth M35 83 E7
Manchester M1 159 B1
Mossley OL5 68 B1
Radcliffe M26 43 F3
Rochdale OL16 15 B1
Stalybridge SK15 86 A1
Dean Terr OL6 67 C2
Dean Villas OL14 6 B7
Dean Wlk M24 46 D2
Dean Wood Ave WN5 53 E8
Deanbank Ave 2 M19 110 F8
Deane Ave
Altrincham WA15 120 A5
Bolton BL3 144 B5
Cheadle SK8 122 F5
Deane Church La BL3 146 B4
Deane Rd BL3 145 D6
Deane Sch The BL3 40 F4
Deane Wlk BL3 145 E6
Deanery CE High Sch The
WN1 150 B8
Deanery Ct
Manchester M8 156 A7
Wigan WN1 150 B8

Deanery Gdns M7 ....155 D8
Deanery Way SK1 ....169 F2
Deanroyd Rd OL14 ....6 B7
Deans Prim Sch The
 M27 ....79 E8
Deans Rd M27 ....79 E7
Deans Road Ind Est M27 .79 E7
Deanscourt Ave M27 ......79 E8
Deansgate Bolton BL1 ...145 E7
 Hindley WN2 ....56 E6
 Manchester M2,M3 ....158 F1
 Manchester M3 ....162 F7
 Radcliffe M26 ....44 B3
Deansgate La WA14,
 WA15 ....119 E7
Deansgate Mews M3 ......162 E8
Deansgate Sta M3 ....162 E8
Deansgate The 6 M14 ....110 C8
Deansgreave Rd OL13 ......4 B7
Deanshut Rd BL8 ....67 A2
Deansway M27 ....79 E8
Deanswood Dr M9 ....64 A5
Deanway CT M13 ....163 B7
Deanwater Ct
 Gatley SK8 ....131 D7
 Stretford M32 ....108 C8
Deanway Handforth SK9 ..131 C1
 Manchester M40 ....83 A8
 Urmston M41 ....94 D2
 Deanway Trad Est SK9 ..131 D3
Dearden Ave M38 ....60 A5
Dearden Clough BL0 ....1 E2
Dearden Fold BL0 ....1 E2
Dearden St
 Little Lever BL3 ....43 A4
 Littleborough OL15 ....16 B6
 12 Stalybridge SK15 ....86 A2
Deardens Fold BL8 ....27 C1
Deardens St BL8 ....27 C1
Dearmans Pl M3 ....158 E2
Dearne Dr M22 ....96 E2
Dearnley CI OL15 ....15 E4
Debdale La Reddish M18 ...99 F4
 Tyldesley M29 ....76 F4
Deben CI WN6 ....19 D1
Debenham Ave M40 ....83 C4
Debenham Ct BL4 ....60 D7
Debenham Rd M32 ....96 A2
Dee Ave WA15 ....120 D5
Dee Dr BL4 ....61 B5
Dee Rd M29 ....77 C7
Deep La
 Littleborough OL15 ....16 C1
 Milnrow OL15,OL16 ....32 B8
Deepcar St M19 ....99 A2
Deepdale Leigh WN7 ....76 C3
 Oldham OL4 ....67 D6
Deepdale Ave
 Billinge WA11 ....71 C1
 Manchester M14 ....110 A8
 Rochdale OL16 ....31 C6
 Royton OL2 ....48 F4
Deepdale CI 1 SK5 ....100 A1
Deepdale Ct M9 ....65 B3
Deepdale Dr M27 ....80 D7
Deepdale Rd BL2 ....25 F1
Deepdene St M12 ....164 F6
Deeping Ave M16 ....97 D2
Deeplish Com Prim Sch
 OL11 ....31 A5
Deeplish Rd OL11 ....139 F5
Deeplish St OL11 ....139 F5
Deeply Vale La BL9,OL11 .12 C2
Deer St M1 ....163 C8
Deeracre Ave SK2 ....124 C6
Deerfold CI 6 M18 ....99 D5
Deerhurst Dr M8 ....155 F6
Deeroak CI M18 ....165 B6
Deerpark Rd M16 ....97 E3
Deerwood Gdns WN1 ......37 B7
Defence St 7 BL3 ....145 D6
Defiance St M46 ....58 C3
Deganwy Gr SK5 ....111 F5
Degas CI M7 ....81 B8
Deighton Ave M14 ....110 A8
Deighton CI WN5 ....53 E6
Deighton Rd M14 ....110 B8
Delafield Ave M12 ....99 A2
Delafield Ave M28 ....78 E7
Delaford CI SK3 ....123 E4
Delaford Wlk M40 ....83 D4
Delahayes Lo WA15 ....120 B5
Delahays Dr WA15 ....120 B2
Delahays Range M18 ......99 F4
Delahays Rd WA15 ....120 B2
Delaine Rd M20 ....110 C6
Delamer Rd WA14 ....119 E2
Delamere Ave
 Golborne WA3 ....90 E6
 Sale M33 ....108 A2
 Salford M6 ....80 C6
 Shaw OL2 ....49 D8
 Stretford M32 ....96 D2
 Swinton M27 ....61 E8
 Whitefield M45 ....62 E8
Delamere CI
 Hazel Grove SK7 ....125 A3
 Mossley SK15 ....86 E6
 Romiley SK6 ....113 C5
Delamere Gdns BL1 ....143 D3
Delamere Rd 8 M14 ......110 C8
Delamere Lo SK7 ....124 D2
Delamere Rd Gatley SK8 .122 B5
 Handforth SK9 ....131 E4

Delamere Rd continued
 Hazel Grove SK7 ....125 A3
 Manchester M19 ....99 B1
 Reddish M34 ....100 B2
 Rochdale OL16 ....31 C4
 Stockport SK2 ....124 B4
 Urmston M41 ....94 F2
Delamere Sch M41 ....94 D2
Delamere St
 Ashton-u-L OL6 ....166 B2
 Bury BL9 ....28 A5
 Droylsden M11 ....99 F7
 6 Oldham OL8 ....67 B5
Delamere Way WN8 ....53 A7
Delaunays Rd
 Manchester M8 ....64 B2
 Sale M33 ....107 F4
Delaware Wlk M9 ....157 D7
Delbooth Ave M41 ....94 E4
Delegarte St WN3 ....151 E6
Delfhaven Ct WN6 ....37 A7
Delft Wlk M6 ....81 A5
Delfur Rd M22 ....132 F7
Delhi Rd M44 ....105 F8
Delhi Ho SK4 ....168 B4
Dell Ave Pendlebury M27 ..80 D7
 Wigan WN6 ....36 E3
Dell CI OL4 ....67 F5
Dell Gdns OL12 ....14 B2
Dell Mdw OL12 ....14 C5
Dell Rd OL12 ....14 B3
Dell Side SK6 ....112 E3
Dell Side Way OL12 ....14 C2
Dell St BL2 ....25 C5
Dell The
 Appley Bridge WN6 ....35 D7
 Bolton BL2 ....25 E2
 Up Holland WN8 ....53 B7
Dellar St OL12 ....14 C1
Dellcot CI
 Manchester M25 ....63 D2
 Salford M6 ....80 B5
Dellcot La M28 ....78 F5
Dellhide CI OL4 ....68 A6
Delliside Gr M28 ....60 E3
Delph Ave BL7 ....8 D3
Delph Brook Way BL7 ....8 D2
Delph Gr WN7 ....57 D1
Delph Hill BL1 ....23 E2
Delph Hill CI BL1 ....23 E2
Delph La Ainsworth BL2 ....26 C1
 Delph OL3 ....50 F5
Delph Lodge OL3 ....50 C8
Delph Mdw Gdns WN5 .....71 D4
Delph New Rd OL3 ....50 E2
Delph Prim Sch OL3 ....50 C8
Delph Rd OL3 ....50 C8
Delph St Bolton BL3 ....145 D5
 Milnrow OL16 ....31 F6
 Wigan WN6 ....37 B1
Delphi Ave M28 ....60 D2
Delphside CI WN5 ....53 D5
Delphside Rd WN5 ....53 D5
Delside Ave M40 ....83 A8
Delta CI OL2 ....48 D2
Delta Rd M34 ....83 A7
Delvino Wlk M14 ....98 A4
Delwood Gdns M22 ....121 D3
Demesne CI SK15 ....86 C1
Demesne Cres SK15 ....86 C1
Demesne Dr SK15 ....86 C1
Demesne Rd M16 ....97 E2
Demmings Inf Sch SK8 ..122 F5
Demmings Rd SK8 ....122 F5
Demmings Rd Ind Est
 SK8 ....122 F5
Dempsey Dr BL9 ....45 B2
Den Hill Dr OL4 ....67 F6
Den La Oldham OL4 ....67 F6
 Uppermill OL3 ....69 B8
Denbigh CI SK7 ....133 C8
Denbigh Dr OL2 ....48 F6
Denbigh PI M5 ....161 A8
Denbigh PI M5 ....81 A2
Denbigh Rd Bolton BL2 ..148 B5
 Denton M34 ....100 E6
 Swinton M27 ....62 B2
Denbigh St Mossley OL5 ..86 D8
 Oldham OL8 ....66 F3
Denbridge Wlk M12 ....97 F3
Denbury Dr WA14 ....119 B5
Denbury Gn SK7 ....124 A1
Denbury Wlk M9 ....156 C6
Denby La WA3 ....90 C8
Denby Rd SK16 ....101 C7
Denbydale Way OL2 ....48 F4
Dencombe St M12,M13 ....98 F4
Dene Bank BL2 ....25 C5
Dene Brow M34 ....113 B8
Dene Ct M34 ....168 C2
Dene Dr M24 ....64 F7
Dene Gr WN7 ....75 B4
Dene Ho SK4 ....110 E1
Dene Hollow SK5 ....100 A1
Dene Manor M20 ....110 A2
Dene Pk M20 ....110 A2
Dene Rd M20 ....110 A2
Dene Rd W M20 ....109 F3
Dene St 5 Bolton BL2 .....25 C5
Dene Wlk M22 ....109 F3
Denefield CI SK6 ....114 B1
Denefield PI M30 ....79 F3
Deneford Rd M20 ....122 A8
Denehurst Rd OL11 ....30 C8
Denehurst St M12 ....164 F6
Denes The SK5 ....99 F1

Deneside Cres SK7 ....124 F3
Deneside Wlk 6 M9 ....157 E8
Denesway M33 ....107 E3
Deneway Bramhall SK7 ...132 D7
 High Lane SK6 ....134 F8
 Stockport SK4 ....168 C2
Deneway CI SK4 ....168 C2
Deneway Mews SK4 ....168 C2
Denewell CI M13 ....164 D6
Denewood CI 3 SK9 ....137 A6
Denford CI WN3 ....54 F3
Denham CI BL1 ....25 A5
Denham Dr
 Bramhall SK7 ....132 D7
 Irlam M44 ....94 A1
 Wigan WN3 ....55 A3
Denham St
 Manchester M13 ....98 D4
 Radcliffe M26 ....43 F6
Denholm Rd M20 ....122 C6
Denholme WN8 ....53 A7
Denholme Rd OL11 ....30 F4
Denhurst Rd OL15 ....16 B6
Denis Ave M16 ....97 E2
Denison Ct 7 M14 ....98 C3
Denison Rd
 Hazel Grove SK7 ....133 D8
 Manchester M14 ....98 C3
Deniston Rd SK4 ....111 B5
Denman Wlk 12 M8 ....155 F6
Denmark Rd
 Manchester M14,M15 ......98 A4
 Sale M33 ....108 B6
Denmark St
 Altrincham WA14 ....119 D4
 Chadderton OL9 ....152 C8
 Oldham OL4 ....31 A8
 Rochdale OL16 ....31 A8
Denmark Way OL9 ....152 C8
Denmore Rd M40 ....65 D3
Dennington Dr M41 ....95 C4
Dennis Ho SK4 ....168 B4
Denison Ave M20 ....110 B7
Dennison Rd SK8 ....132 B8
Denshaw Ave M34 ....100 D5
Denshaw CI M19 ....110 E3
Denshaw Rd OL3 ....50 D5
Densmead Wlk 12 M40 ..159 C3
Densmore St 6 M35 ....83 F7
Denson Rd WA15 ....120 B8
Denstone Ave Eccles M30 .79 E3
 Sale M33 ....107 E3
 Urmston M41 ....95 C3
Denstone Cres BL2 ....25 D2
Denstone Rd Reddish SK5 .99 F1
 Salford M6 ....80 D5
 Urmston M41 ....95 C3
Denstone Wlk 15 M9 ....64 E3
Dent CI SK5 ....112 C6
Dental Hospl M13,M15 ...163 A6
Dentdale CI BL1 ....24 D6
Dentdale Wlk M22 ....130 C8
Denton CI M34 ....100 E5
Denton Gr WN5 ....54 B8
Denton La OL9 ....152 A5
Denton Rd Denton M34 ...100 E6
 Little Lever BL2 ....43 B6
Denton St Bury BL9 ....140 F4
 Heywood OL10 ....29 C1
 Handforth SK9 ....131 C5
 Kearsley BL4 ....61 B5
Denton Sta M34 ....100 C4
Denton West End Prim Sch
 M34 ....100 A3
Denver Ave M40 ....160 D3
Denver Dr 4 WA15 ....120 A6
Denver Rd OL11 ....30 F4
Denville Cres M22 ....121 E3
Denver Terr 22 SK16 ......166 B1
Denzell Gdns WA14 ....119 A3
Depleach Rd SK8 ....122 D5
Deptford Ave M23 ....121 A3
Deramore CI OL6 ....85 E3
Deramore St M14 ....98 B3
Derby Ave M5 ....154 E2
Derby CI Irlam M44 ....105 C5
 Newton-le-W WA12 ....89 B3
Derby Ct Oldham OL9 .....152 C5
 Sale M33 ....108 C3
Derby Gr 2 M19 ....99 B1
Derby High Sch The BL9 ..44 D8
Derby Ho WN1 ....151 D8
Derby PI PR6 ....21 A8
Derby Range SK4 ....168 B4
Derby Rd Ashton-u-L OL6 ..85 D3
 Golborne WA3 ....90 C8
 Hyde SK14 ....167 E4
 Kearsley M26 ....61 A8
 Manchester M14,M20 .....110 D7

Derby St continued
 Ince-in-M WN3 ....55 F4
 Leigh WN7 ....76 A4
 Manchester M8 ....158 F4
 8 Marple SK6 ....125 F6
 Mossley OL5 ....86 D8
 Newton-le-W WA12 ....89 B3
 Oldham OL9 ....66 B4
 Oldham,Werneth OL9 .....152 C5
 Prestwich M25 ....63 A4
 Ramsbottom BL0 ....11 D6
 Rochdale OL11 ....31 A5
 Stockport SK3 ....170 D8
 18 Tyldesley M29 ....59 A1
 Westhoughton BL5 ....39 F1
Derby St W WN7 ....75 F4
Derby Terr M34 ....100 F8
Derby Way 7 SK6 ....125 F6
Derbyshire Ave M32 ....96 B3
Derbyshire Cres M32 ......96 B3
Derbyshire Gn M32 ....96 D2
Derbyshire Gr M32 ....96 B3
Derbyshire La W M32 ......96 C2
Derbyshire Level SK13 ...116 F6
Derbyshire Rd
 Failsworth M40 ....83 D4
 Partington M31 ....105 E2
 Poynton SK12 ....134 D5
 Sale M33 ....108 C4
 Wigan WN3 ....54 D1
Derbyshire Rd S M33 .....108 D2
Derbyshire Row BL1 ....143 B1
Derbyshire St M11 ....165 C7
Dereham CI BL8 ....27 D5
Dereham Way WN3 ....54 D3
Derg St M6 ....154 F1
Derker St OL1 ....67 B8
Derker St OL1 ....67 A8
Dermot Murphy CI M20 ..109 F6
Dernford Ave M19 ....110 F5
Derngate Dr WN6 ....37 A7
Derrick Walker Ct OL11 ..139 D5
Derry Ave M22 ....121 E4
Derville Wlk 4 M9 ....157 D8
Derwen St SK3 ....170 E7
Derwent Ave
 Altrincham WA15 ....120 D5
 Ashton-u-L OL7 ....166 A4
 Droylsden M43 ....83 E1
 Gatley SK8 ....74 C1
 Heywood OL10 ....46 D8
 Ince-in-M WN2 ....56 B7
 Manchester M21 ....109 D6
 Milnrow OL16 ....32 B6
 Whitefield M45 ....63 C8
Derwent CI Culcheth WA3 .91 E3
 Glossop SK13 ....116 F8
 Horwich BL6 ....22 C2
 Leigh WN7 ....75 E3
 Little Lever BL3 ....42 F4
 Partington M31 ....109 D5
 Walkden M28 ....60 B2
 Whitefield M45 ....63 B8
Derwent Dr
 Bramhall SK7 ....132 C5
 Bury BL9 ....44 D7
 Derwent CI SK9 ....152 A7
 Handforth SK9 ....131 C5
 Kearsley BL4 ....61 B5
 Littleborough OL15 ....15 F2
 Sale M33 ....108 A2
 Shaw OL2 ....49 D8
Derwent Ind Area M5 .....162 D8
Derwent PI WN5 ....54 C7
Derwent Rd
 Ashton-in-M WN4 ....73 E5
 Farnworth BL4 ....59 F7
 High Lane SK6 ....134 E8
 Hindley WN2 ....56 E5
 Middleton M24 ....46 E3
 Orrell WN5 ....53 F8
 Stretford M32 ....96 D3
 Urmston M41 ....94 E2
Derwent Terr SK15 ....86 A4
Derwent Way WN7 ....75 B1
Derwent Wlk Oldham OL7 .67 D7
 Whitefield M45 ....63 B8
Desford Ave M16,M21 .....97 C1
Design Sta 3 M3 ....158 E2
Desmond Rd M22 ....121 E4
Desmond St M46 ....58 A2
Dettingen St M6 ....80 B5
Deva Cl Hazel Grove SK7 .124 D1
 Poynton SK12 ....133 B4
Deva Ct M16 ....161 C5
Deva Ctr M3 ....158 E2
Deva Sq OL9 ....152 B5
Devaney Wlk M34 ....100 E1
Devas St M13,M15 ....163 A6
Deverill Ave M18 ....99 F4
Devine CI Royton OL2 ......48 D6
 Salford M3 ....158 D2
Devisdale Ct M14 ....119 C3
Devisdale Grange WA14 ..119 B4
Devisdale Rd WA14 ....119 B4
Devoke Ave Billinge WA11 .71 A1
 Walkden M28 ....60 A1
Devoke Gr BL4 ....59 E8
Devoke Rd M22 ....121 B2

Devon Ave
 Manchester M19 ....110 F8
 Up Holland WN8 ....53 B6
 Whitefield M45 ....44 E1
Devon CI Aspull WN2 ....38 D5
 Brinnington SK5 ....112 C4
 Little Lever BL3 ....43 B4
 Salford M6 ....80 A3
 Shaw OL2 ....48 F7
 Wigan WN5 ....54 C6
Devon Cres BB4 ....1 B8
Devon Dr Ainsworth BL2 ..26 D1
 Diggle OL3 ....51 C4
 Standish WN1 ....20 B1
Devon Mews 2 M45 ....44 E1
Devon Rd Droylsden M43 ..84 A3
 Failsworth M35 ....83 E6
 Irlam M44 ....105 D5
 Partington M31 ....105 E2
 Tyldesley M29 ....59 A2
 Urmston M41 ....94 E1
Devon St Bolton BL2 ......148 A1
 Bury BL9 ....42 D2
 Farnworth BL4 ....42 D2
 Hindley WN2 ....56 E5
 Leigh WN7 ....76 E4
 Oldham OL9 ....66 C4
 Rochdale OL11 ....139 F6
 Swinton M27 ....61 F2
Devon Way OL8 ....66 C2
Devonport Cres OL2 ....48 F4
Devonshire CI
 Heywood OL10 ....29 A1
 3 Urmston M41 ....95 E2
Devonshire Ct
 Bolton BL1 ....144 B7
 Salford M7 ....155 D8
 Stockport SK3 ....124 A5
Devonshire Dr
 Alderley Edge SK9 ....137 B2
 Boothstown M28 ....77 F6
Devonshire Gdns WA12 ...89 C2
Devonshire Park Rd
 SK2 ....124 A5
Devonshire PI
 Atherton M46 ....58 D4
 Prestwich M25 ....63 A5
Devonshire Rd
 Altrincham WA14 ....119 D6
 Atherton M46 ....58 C5
 Bolton BL1 ....144 B8
 Eccles M30 ....79 E2
 Hazel Grove SK7 ....133 F8
 Manchester,Chorlton-cum-Hardy
 M21 ....109 C8
 Manchester,Heaton Norris
 SK4 ....168 B3
 Rochdale OL11 ....30 F2
 Salford M6 ....80 A3
 Walkden M28 ....60 C6
Devonshire Road Prim Sch
 BL1 ....144 B8
Devonshire St
 Manchester M12 ....164 D6
 Salford M7 ....155 E6
Devonshire St E M35 ....83 E5
Devonshire St N M12 .....164 D7
Devonshire St S M13 .....164 D5
Dew Meadow CI OL12 ......14 E2
Dewar CI M11 ....83 A1
Dewberry CI Swinton M27 .61 E2
 Tyldesley M29 ....59 E1
Dewberry Fields WN8 ......53 B7
Dewes Ave M27 ....62 B2
Dewey St M11 ....99 D7
Dewhirst Rd OL12 ....14 F4
Dewhirst Way OL12 ....14 F4
Dewhurst Clough Rd BL7 ...8 D2
Dewhurst Ct BL7 ....8 D3
Dewhurst Rd BL2 ....25 E3
Dewhurst St
 Heywood OL10 ....29 E2
 Manchester M8 ....158 F4
Dewint Ave SK6 ....126 B8
Dewsnap CI SK16 ....101 C6
Dewsnap La
 Dukinfield SK16 ....101 D6
 Mottram-in-L SK14 ....103 A6
Dewsnap Way SK14 ....102 E2
Dexter Rd M9 ....64 A5
Dexter Way WN8 ....53 B6
Deyne Ave
 Manchester M14 ....98 C4
 Prestwich M25 ....63 B4
Deyne St M6 ....154 E2
Dial CI BL4 ....42 D2
Dial Park Prim Sch SK2 ..124 D4
Dial Park Rd SK2 ....124 D4
Dial Rd Altrincham WA15 .129 C8
 Stockport SK2 ....124 A5
Dialstone La SK2 ....124 C6
Diamond CI 9 OL6 ....85 D4
Diamond St
 Leigh WN7 ....75 B4
 Stockport SK3 ....124 A6
 Wigan WN6 ....37 A3
Diamond Terr SK6 ....125 F3
Diane Rd WN4 ....73 C4
Dibden Wlk 4 M23 ....121 A5
Dicconson Cres 6 WN1 ...37 C1
Dicconson La BL5,WN2 ....39 A4
Dicconson St WN1 ....37 C1
Dicconson Terr WN1 ....37 C1
Dicken Gn OL11 ....30 F4
Dicken Green La OL11 .....30 F4
Dickens CI SK8 ....132 B5

Dickens Dr WN2 ....74 C8
Dickens La SK12 .....133 E2
Dickens Pl WN3 ......54 F4
Dickens Rd Coppull PR7 ..19 E8
Eccles M30 ....79 D1
Dickens St Heywood OL10 ..29 B2
Oldham OL1 ....49 E4
Dickenson Rd M13,M14 ..98 E3
Dickenson St WN2 .....56 E4
Dickinson Cl 19 BL1 ..143 E1
Dickinson Ct 1 BL1 ...62 A2
Dickinson St Bolton BL1 .143 E1
Manchester M1 ......163 A8
Oldham OL4 ....67 B7
Salford M3 ....158 E3
Dickinson St W BL6 .....22 B4
Dickinson Terr 12 BL1 .143 E1
Dickson St W BL6 ......22 A4
Didcot Rd M22 .....121 C1
Didley Sq M12 .....165 A7
Didsbury CE Prim Sch
M20 ....110 B3
Didsbury Gr WN2 .....56 D5
Didsbury Lodge Hall
M20 ....110 C1
Didsbury Pk M20 ....110 B2
Didsbury Rd SK4 ....168 B2
Didsbury Road Prim Sch
SK4 ....110 F2
Dig Gate La OL16 ......31 E3
Digby Lo M20 ....110 B4
Digby Rd OL11 ....30 F4
Digby Wlk 20 M11 ....160 F1
Diggle St Shaw OL2 ...149 B6
Wigan WN6 ....37 A1
Diggle Wlk SK15 ......86 E6
Diggles La OL11 ......29 E6
Diglands Ave SK22 ...127 D1
Diglands Cl SK22 ....127 D1
Diglea OL3 ....51 D5
Dijon St BL3 ....146 C4
Dilham Ct BL1 ......144 C8
Dillicar Wlk M9 ....157 D7
Dillmass Wlk 19 M15 ..162 D6
Dillon Dr M12 .....164 E5
Dilston Cl M13 ....163 C6
Dilworth Cl OL10 .....29 A2
Dilworth Ct SK2 ....124 E5
Dilworth St M13,M15 .163 B5
Dimple Pk BL7 ....8 D3
Dimple Rd BL7 ....8 C4
Dingle Ave
Appley Bridge WN6 ....35 E8
Denton M34 ....101 B2
Row-of-trees SK9 ....136 D2
Shaw OL2 ....32 C1
Up Holland WN8 ......53 C8
Dingle Bank Rd SK7 ..123 D1
Dingle Dr M43 ....84 B3
Dingle Gr SK8 .....121 F6
Dingle Rd Middleton M24 ..64 F6
Up Holland WN8 ......53 B7
Dingle Terr OL6 .....67 B2
Dingle The Bramhall SK7 ..123 C1
Hyde SK14 ....113 E7
Dingle Wlk 6 Bolton BL1 ..145 F8
Wigan WN6 ....36 D4
Dinglebrook Gr 5 SK9 .131 D1
Dinglewood SK7 .....123 C1
Dinmor Rd M22 .....121 D1
Dinmore Ct SK2 ....124 D5
Dinnington Dr M8 ...155 F6
Dinorwic Cl M8 ....156 A6
Dinsdale Cl M40 ...160 D2
Dinsdale Dr BL3 ...145 D5
Dinslow Wlk 18 M8 ..155 F7
Dinting Ave M20 ...110 A7
Dinting CE Prim Sch
SK13 ....104 A1
Dinting La SK13 ....104 A1
Dinting Lane Trad Est
SK13 ....104 A1
Dinting Lodge Ind Est
SK13 ....171 F2
Dinting Rd SK13 ....104 B2
Dinting Sta SK13 ...104 A2
Dinting Vale SK13 ..104 A1
Dinting Vale Bsns Pk
SK13 ....171 F2
Dinton St M15 .....161 C7
Dipton Wlk M9 .....156 C6
Dirty La Ashley WA14 .128 A5
Delph OL3 ....51 B6
Oldham OL4 ....50 B1
Dirty Leech OL12 ....14 F6
Disley Ave M20 ....109 F6
Disley Ho SK3 .....170 E7
Disley Prim Sch SK12 .135 D6
Disley St OL11 ......30 C4
Disley St SK12 ....135 C6
Disley Wlk M34 ....101 A1
Distaff Rd SK12 ...133 B4
District CE Prim Sch The
WA12 ....89 A4
Ditton Mead Cl OL12 ..15 B2
Ditton Wlk 5 M23 ..120 F6
Division St Bolton BL3 .147 F4
Rochdale OL12 ......15 B2
Dixey St BL6 ....22 A3
Dixon Ave
Newton-le-W WA12 ....89 C5
Salford M7 ....155 E6
Shevington WN6 ......36 A5
Dixon Cl Haydock WA11 ..89 A8
Sale M33 ....108 D2

Dixon Closes OL11 .....29 E7
Dixon Ct Cheadle SK8 .122 D5
Westhoughton BL5 .....39 E3
Dixon Dr Shevington WN6 ..36 A5
Swinton M27 ....61 E4
Dixon Green Dr 11 BL4 ..60 E7
Dixon Pl 3 WN2 ......56 B1
Dixon Rd M34 ......101 B1
Dixon St
12 Ashton-u-L OL6 ....85 D4
Failsworth M40 ......83 B6
Horwich BL6 ....22 B3
Irlam M44 ....105 F8
Manchester M6 ......80 F6
Middleton M24 ......47 A2
Oldham OL4 ....67 E8
Rochdale OL11 ......30 D4
Westhoughton BL5 .....39 E3
Dob Brook Cl M35,M40 ..83 C6
Dob Hedge Cl WA15 ..129 C6
Dobbin Dr OL11 ......30 F3
Dobbinetts La M23,
WA15 ....120 E4
Dobcross Cl M13 ......99 A2
Dobcross New Rd OL3 ..51 A1
Dobhill St BL4 ......60 D8
Dobroyd Ho OL4 .....67 E8
Dobroyd St M8 .....156 A8
Dobson Cl
Appley Bridge WN6 ....18 E2
Manchester M13 ....164 D6
Dobson Ct M40 ......83 B4
Dobson Park Ind Est
WN2 ....151 F6
Dobson Park Way WN2 ..56 A6
Dobson Pk Ind Est WN2 ..56 A7
Dobson Rd BL1 .....144 C7
Dobson St BL1 .....143 D2
Doctor Fold La OL10 ..46 C5
Doctor La OL4 ......50 C1
Doctors La M45 ....140 D2
Doctors Nook WN7 ....75 F5
Dodd Croft OL16 .....31 B3
Dodd La BL5 ....39 B4
Dodd Lane Ind Est BL5 ..39 C4
Dodd St M5 ....154 D2
Dodd's Farm La WN2 ..38 E3
Doddington La M45 .161 A8
Doddington Wlk M34 .100 E1
Dodge Fold SK2 ....124 E6
Dodge Hill SK4 ....169 E2
Dodgson St OL16 .....31 A6
Dodhurst Rd WN2 ....56 F6
Dodson Cl WN4 ....73 C4
Doe Brow M27 ....61 C4
Doe Hey Gr BL4 .....42 B2
Doe Hey Rd BL3 .....42 B2
Doefield Ave M28 ....78 C8
Doeford Cl WA3 .....91 E5
Doffcocker Brow BL1 .142 A1
Doffcocker La BL1 ..142 B2
Dogford Rd OL2 .....48 D5
Dolbey St M5 ......154 E1
Dolman Wlk 4 M8 ..155 F6
Dolphin Pl M12 ....163 C7
Dolphin St M12 ....163 C7
Dolwen Wlk M40 ......83 B6
Doman St BL3 .....145 F5
Dombey Rd SK12 ....133 D2
Dome The 5 WA14 ..119 D4
Domestic App M90 ..130 C6
Domett St M9 ....64 C2
Dominic Cl M23 ....108 E1
Don Ave M6 ....80 D7
Don St Bolton BL3 ..147 D3
Middleton M24 ......47 C1
Dona St SK1 ....124 A8
Donald Ave SK14 ...167 F1
Donald St M1 ......163 A7
Doncaster Ave M20 .110 A7
Doncaster Cl BL3 ....43 F2
Doncaster Wlk 8 OL1 ..153 F7
Donhead Wlk M13 ..163 C6
Donington Gdns M28 ..60 D3
Donkey La SK9 .....137 A5
Donleigh St M35 .....83 D6
Donnington 6 OL11 .139 E6
Donnington Ave SK8 .122 F6
Donnington Cl WN7 ...75 E1
Donnington Rd
Droylsden M18 ....99 E5
Little Lever M26 ......43 C5
Donnison St M12 ...164 F6
Donovan Ave M40 ..159 C4
Doodfield Prim Sch
SK6 ....125 F2
Doodson Ave M44 ....94 A2
Doodson Sq BL4 .....60 D8
Dooley La SK2,SK6 ..125 B7
Dooley's La SK9 ...130 C2
Dootson St 4 Abram WN2 ..56 B1
Hindley WN2 ....57 A6
Dora St BL0 ....11 A4
Dorac Ave SK8 ....131 C7
Dorchester Ave
Bolton BL2 ....25 E1
Denton M34 ....100 F1
Manchester M25 ......63 C2
Urmston M41 ....95 F3
Dorchester Cl
Altrincham WA15 ...120 C3
Wilmslow SK9 .....137 D8
Dorchester Ct
Bramhall SK8 ......123 B1
Sale M33 ....108 B2
Dorchester Dr Royton OL2 ..48 E2

Dorchester Dr continued
Sale M23 ....108 E1
Dorchester Gr OL10 ..46 D8
Dorchester Par SK7 .124 B1
Dorchester Rd
Hazel Grove SK7 ....124 B1
Swinton M27 ....79 F6
Up Holland WN8 ......53 A7
Dorclyn Ave M41 .....95 D2
Dorfield Cl SK6 ....112 E3
Doric Ave SK6 .....112 D2
Doric Cl M11 ......160 F1
Doric Gn WN5 ....53 D3
Doris Ave BL2 ......42 D7
Doris Rd SK3 ......123 C8
Doris St M24 ....47 A2
Dorket Gr BL5 ......40 E2
Dorking Ave M40 ....83 B4
Dorking Cl Bolton BL1 .143 F2
Stockport SK1 .....124 B7
Dorlan Ave M18 .....99 F4
Dorland Gr SK2 ....124 B7
Dorman St 6 M11 ....99 D7
Dorman St BL1 .....143 E2
Dorney St BL3 ......99 D5
Dorning Rd M27 .....80 A7
Dorning St Bury BL8 ..27 B4
6 Eccles M30 ......79 D1
Kearsley BL4 ......60 F8
1 Leigh WN7 ......75 E5
Scot Lane End BL6 ...38 F7
Dornton Wlk M8 ....155 F6
Dorothy Gr WN7 .....75 E4
Dorothy Rd SK7 ....124 F3
Dorothy St
Ramsbottom BL0 ....138 B5
Salford M7 ....155 F7
Dorothy Wlk WN7 ....73 F8
Dorrian Mews BL1 ....40 F7
Dorrington Rd
Cheadle SK3 ....123 A7
Sale M33 ....107 F4
Dorris St Bolton BL3 .146 C3
Manchester M19 ....111 B8
Dorrit Cl SK12 ....133 E2
Dorset Ave Bramhall SK7 ..123 D1
Brinnington SK5 ....112 C5
Cheadle SK8 ....123 C5
Diggle OL3 ....51 C4
Droylsden M34 .....100 C8
Farnworth BL4 ......60 C8
Manchester M14 .....98 A2
Shaw OL2 ....48 F7
Tyldesley M29 ......59 D3
Dorset Cl Farnworth BL4 ..60 C8
Heywood OL10 ......29 A1
Wigan WN5 ....54 C6
Dorset Dr Bury BL9 ...45 A8
Haslingden BB4 ......1 A8
Dorset Rd
Altrincham WA14 ...119 B5
Atherton M46 ......58 C5
Droylsden M43 ......83 F3
Failsworth M35 .....83 F6
Irlam M44 ....105 D5
Reddish M19 ....99 C1
Standish WN1 ....37 D1
Dorset St Ashton-u-L OL6 ..85 D2
Bolton BL2 ....148 A2
Hindley WN2 ....56 E6
Leigh WN7 ....76 D4
Oldham OL9 ....152 C5
Stretford M32 ......96 D1
Swinton M27 ....79 D7
Dorsey St M4 ......159 B2
Dorstone Cl
Failsworth M40 ......83 C4
Hindley WN2 ....57 B5
Dorwood Ave M9 .....64 C5
Dotterel Cl WN7 .....76 C6
Dougall Wlk M12 ...165 A6
Doughty Ave M30 ....79 F3
Dougill St BL1 ....142 B1
Douglas Ave Billinge WN5 ..71 D3
Bury BL8 ....27 B2
Horwich BL6 ....22 C6
Stretford M32 ......96 D3
Up Holland WN8 ......53 B7
Douglas Bank Dr WN6 ..36 F2
Douglas Cl Horwich BL6 ..22 C5
Whitefield M45 .....45 C2
Douglas Dr Orrell WN5 ..53 F7
Walkden M38 ....59 E5
Douglas Gn M6 ......81 A5
Douglas Ho WN1 ....151 D7
Douglas Pk M46 .....58 E2
Douglas Rd Atherton M46 ..58 E2
Hazel Grove SK7 ....124 C3
Leigh WN7 ....75 C7
Shevington Moor WN6 ..19 F8
Stockport SK3 .....123 E4
Swinton M28 ....79 C7
Wigan WN1 ....37 D1
Douglas Sq OL10 .....28 F1
Douglas St Ashton-u-L OL6 ..85 D3
Atherton M46 ......58 E3
Bolton BL1 ....143 A4
Failsworth M35 .....84 A7
Hindley WN2 ....56 C4
Hyde SK14 ....167 E2
Oldham OL9 ....66 A4
Pendlebury M27 ......80 A7
Ramsbottom BL0 ....138 B6
Salford M7 ....155 D6

Douglas St continued
Wigan WN5 ....150 A7
Douglas St Back BL0 .138 B6
Douglas Way M45 ....45 C1
Douglas Wlk
8 Sale M33 ....107 C5
Whitefield M45 .....45 C2
Doulton St M40 .....83 C8
Dounby Ave M30 .....79 B3
Douro St M40 ......157 F5
Douthwaite Dr SK6 ..113 E1
Dove Bank Rd SK6 ..126 F6
Dove Bank Rd BL3 ....43 A4
Dove Dr Bury BL9 ...141 B4
Irlam M44 ....94 A3
Dove Rd BL3 ....146 B4
Dove St Bolton BL1 .143 E2
Golborne WA3 ....74 A2
Oldham OL4 ....67 C6
Rochdale OL11 ....139 D7
Dove Wlk Farnworth BL4 ..59 F8
Manchester M8 .....156 B5
Dovebrook Cl SK15 ...86 E7
Dovecote M41 ......84 D3
Dovecote Bsns & Tech Pk
M33 ....108 F4
Dovecote Cl BL7 .....25 B8
Dovecote La Oldham OL4 ..67 F7
Walkden M38 ....59 E3
Dovecote Mews M21 ..109 A8
Dovedale Ave
Droylsden M43 ......83 E2
Eccles M30 ....79 E3
Manchester,Sedgley Park
M25 ....63 E3
Manchester,Withington
M20 ....110 A7
Urmston M41 ....95 D3
Dovedale Cl SK6 ...134 E7
Dovedale Cres WN4 ...73 A8
Dovedale Ct
Glossop SK13 ......104 F1
8 Middleton M24 ...46 E2
Dovedale Dr
Standish WN6 ....19 E2
Wardle OL12 ....15 D6
Dovedale Rd
Ashton-in-M WN4 ....73 A8
Bolton BL2 ....25 F1
Stockport SK2 .....124 D7
Dovedale St M35 .....83 E7
Dovehouse Cl M45 ...62 D7
Doveleys Rd M6 ....154 D4
Dovenby Fold WN2 ...56 B7
Dover Cl BL8 ....11 A1
Dover Gr BL3 .....145 D5
Dover Pk M41 ......95 D4
Dover Rd M27 ....62 A2
Dover St Eccles M30 ..79 B2
Farnworth BL4 ......42 D2
Manchester M13 ....163 B6
Oldham OL9 ....152 C5
1 Reddish SK5 ....111 E7
Rochdale OL16 ......15 B2
Dovercourt Ave SK4 .110 F4
Doveridge Gdns M6 ..154 F3
Doveston Rd M33 ...108 B6
Dovestone Cres SK16 .101 F7
Dovestone Wlk M40 ...65 E1
Dovey Cl M27 ....79 F5
Dow Fold BL8 ....26 F3
Dow La BL8 ....26 F3
Dow St SK14 ....101 D5
Dowland Cl 3 M23 ..108 F2
Dowling St OL11 ...139 F6
Downall Green RC Prim Sch
WN4 ....72 C6
Downall Green Rd WN4 ..72 D6
Downbrook Way WN4 ..73 D5
Downes Way M22 ...121 E6
Downesway SK9 ....136 F1
Downfield Cl BL0 ..138 B6
Downfields SK5 ....100 A1
Downgate Wlk 6 M8 ..156 A6
Downgreen Rd BL2 ...25 E3
Downham Chase WA15 ..120 B6
Downham Cres M25 ...63 F3
Downham Gdns M25 ...63 E3
Downham Gr M25 .....63 E3
Downham Rd
Heywood OL10 ......29 A2
Reddish SK4 ....111 D5
Downham Wlk
Longshaw WN5 ......53 D1
Wythenshawe M23 ...120 E8
Downhill Cl OL1 .....48 E1
Downing St
Ashton-u-L OL7 .....84 F6
Platt Bridge WN2 ....56 C2
Downing Cl
Ashton-u-L OL7 .....84 F6
5 Leigh WN7 ......75 F5
Manchester M1,M12,M13 .163 B7
Downing Street Ind Est
M12 ....163 B7
Downley Cl OL12 .....14 E2
Downley Dr M4 .....159 C2
Downs The
Altrincham WA14 ...119 D3
Cheadle SK8 ....122 D3

Downs The continued
Middleton M24 ......65 B5
Prestwich M25 ......63 A2
Wigan WN3 ....54 C4
Downshaw Rd OL7 ....85 A6
Downton Ave WN2 ....56 D4
Dowry Rd OL4 ....67 F7
Dowson Cl OL4 ......67 A3
Dowson Prim Sch SK14 ..113 E8
Dowson Rd SK14 ...113 E8
Dowson St BL2 .....148 A7
Doyle Ave SK6 ....112 D3
Doyle Cl OL1 ....49 E4
Doyle Rd BL3 ....40 E2
Drake Ave Farnworth BL4 ..60 D7
Irlam M44 ....105 E6
Drake Cl OL1 ......153 F8
Drake Ct SK5 ......169 E4
Drake Hall BL5 .....57 E5
Drake Rd
Altrincham WA14 ...119 B8
Littleborough OL15 ...6 C1
Drake St Atherton M46 ..58 C2
Rochdale OL11,OL16 ..139 F6
Draycott Cl WN2 ....56 F3
Draycott St BL1 ...143 E2
Draycott St E 8 BL1 .143 E2
Drayfields M43 ......84 D2
Drayford Cl 2 M23 .108 F2
Drayton Ave SK8 ...131 B7
Drayton Cl Bolton BL1 .143 D2
Sale M33 ....107 D2
16 Handforth SK9 ..131 D1
Drayton Gr WA15 ...120 A5
Drayton Manor M20 .122 B8
Drayton Wlk M16 ...162 D5
Dresden St M40 .....83 C8
Drewett St M40 ....160 E4
Dreyfus Ave M11 ....83 C2
Driffield St Eccles M30 ..95 C8
Manchester M14 .....98 A3
Drill Wlk 5 M4 ....159 C1
Drinkwater Rd M25 ...62 F1
Driscoll St 1 M13 ...98 F3
Drive The
Altrincham WA15 ...129 D8
Brinnington SK5 ....112 C4
Broomedge WA13 ...117 D1
Bury BL9 ....27 F5
Cheadle SK8 ....123 C4
Edenfield BL0 ....1 D3
Hazel Grove SK7 .....75 F3
Manchester,Broughton Park
M7 ....63 C1
Manchester,Didsbury M20 .110 C4
Marple SK6 ....125 E6
Prestwich M25 ......63 B4
Romiley SK6 ....112 D3
Sale M33 ....107 E1
Droitwich Rd M40 ..160 D4
Dronfield Rd Salford M6 .154 D4
Wythenshawe M22 ...121 D8
Droughts La M25 ....63 E8
Drovers Wlk SK13 ..104 D1
Droxford Ct SK9 ...137 B6
Droxford Gr M46 ....58 C5
Droylsden High Sch M43 ..83 F2
Droylsden
Droylsden M34 .....100 C8
Failsworth M40 ......83 D5
Drs Green & Slater Rest Hos
SK4 ....168 A3
Druid St M6 ....168 A3
Druids Cl BL7 ....8 D3
Drummer's La WN4 ...72 E7
Drummond Sq WN5 ...54 E7
Drummond St BL1 ..143 E4
Drummond Way WN7 ..76 B5
Drury La WN7 ....99 A1
Drury St 18 M19 ....99 A1
Dryad Cl M27 ....61 F2
Drybrook Cl M13 ...164 E5
Dryburgh Ave BL1 ..143 D4
Dryclough Wlk OL2 ..48 E3
Dryden Ave
Ashton-in-M WN4 ....72 F6
Cheadle SK8 ....122 F6
Swinton M27 ....79 D7
Dryden Cl
Dukinfield SK16 ...102 B7
Marple SK6 ....125 F4
Dryden Rd 4 M16 ...97 C3
Dryden St M13 ....163 C6
Dryden Way 10 M34 .113 A8
Dryfield La BL8 .....22 A5
Drygate Wlk 6 M9 ..157 E7
Dryhurst Cl SK12 ..135 D6
Dryhurst Wlk 8 M15 .163 A5
Drymoss OL8 ....67 A1
Drysdale View BL1 .143 E4
Dryton Wlk M28 .....38 A2
Drywood Ave M28 ...79 A5
Ducal St M4 ....159 B4
Duchess Park Cl OL2 ..48 D4
Duchess Rd M8 ....156 B8
Duchess St M40 ...149 B8
Duchess Wlk BL3 ..146 B4
Duchy Ave
Over Hulton BL5 .....59 A8
Walkden M28 ....78 D8
Duchy Bank M6 .....80 D6
Duchy Rd M6 ....80 C5

Duchy Road Cvn Pk M6 .154 F4
Duchy St Salford M6 ....154 F3
 Stockport SK3 ....170 D7
Ducie Av BL1 ....144 C7
Ducie Gr M13 ....163 B5
Ducie St Manchester M1 .159 B3
 Oldham OL4 ....66 F2
 Radcliffe M26 ....43 F5
 Whitefield M45 ....62 F8
Duckshaw La BL4 ......60 D8
Duckworth La BB4 ......1 C8
Duckworth Rd M25 ......62 F3
Duckworth St
 3 Bury BL9 ....141 A4
 Shaw OL2 ....149 C7
Duddon Ave M43 ......25 F1
Duddon Cl Standish WN6 ..36 F7
 Whitefield M45 ....63 C8
Duddon Wlk 2 M24 ....46 E2
Dudley Ave Bolton BL2 ..25 C1
 Whitefield M45 ....62 F8
Dudley Cl M15 ....162 E5
Dudley Ct 10 M16 ......97 D3
Dudley Rd Irlam M44 ..105 D4
 Manchester M16 ......97 D3
 Sale M33 ....108 C6
 Sale,Timperley WA15 ..120 B7
 Swinton M27 ....61 F1
Dudley St
 Ashton-u-M WN4 ......73 A5
 Denton M34 ....100 E4
 Eccles M30 ....79 C1
 6 Oldham OL4 ....67 D6
 Salford M7 ....155 F6
Dudlow Wlk 24 M15 ..162 D6
Dudwell Cl BL1 ....142 C2
Duerden St BL3 ....146 A2
Duffield Ct M15 ....163 A5
Duffield Gdns M9 ......64 F5
Duffield Rd Middleton M9 .64 F5
 Salford M6 ....80 D5
Duffins Cl OL12 ....14 C8
Dufton Wlk
 1 Middleton M24 ......46 E2
 Wythenshawe M22 ....130 E8
Dugdale Ave M9 ......64 E4
Dugie St BL0 ....138 B7
Duke Ct M16 ....162 D5
Duke of Norfolk CE Prim Sch
 Glossop SK13 ....104 D1
 Glossop,Old Glossop SK13 .104 E2
Duke Pl M3 ....162 E8
Duke Rd Ainsworth BL2 ..26 C1
 Dukinfield SK14 ......101 F5
Duke St
 Alderley Edge SK9 ....137 B2
 Ashton-in-M WN4 ......73 C3
 Ashton-u-L OL6 ......166 B3
 Bolton BL1 ....145 E8
 Denton M34 ....100 E3
 Eccles M30 ....79 C4
 Failsworth M35 ....84 A8
 Golborne WA3 ....74 A1
 Heywood OL10 ....29 B2
 Leigh WN7 ....76 A4
 Littleborough OL15 ....16 A5
 Manchester M3 ......162 E8
 Mossley OL5 ....68 E1
 Newton-le-W WA12 ....89 B3
 Platt Bridge WN2 ......56 A3
 Radcliffe M26 ....43 A4
 Ramsbottom BL0 ......11 A4
 Rawtenstall BB4 ......2 C2
 Rochdale OL12 ....14 F1
 Salford M3 ....158 F2
 Salford,Lower Broughton
  M7 ....155 D5
 Salford,Lower Broughton
  M7 ....158 D4
 Shaw OL2 ....149 C6
 Stalybridge SK15 ......85 F1
 Stockport SK1 ....169 F1
 Tyldesley M29 ....77 C6
 Walkden M38 ....60 A5
 Walkden,Linnyshaw M28 ..61 A2
 Wigan,Goose WN3 ....54 F4
 Wigan,Swinley WN1 ....37 C2
Duke St N BL1 ....145 E8
Duke's Row WN7 ......38 B4
Duke's Ter 17 SK16 ..166 B1
Dukefield St M22 ......121 E8
Dukes Ave BL3 ....146 A5
Dukes Fold SK13 ......116 B7
Dukes Platting OL6 ....85 F5
Dukes St SK13 ....116 C5
Dukes Wharf M28 ......78 C5
Dukes Wlk WA15 ......119 F3
Dukesgate Prim Sch
 M38 ....60 A4
Dukinfield Rd SK14 ..101 C4
Dukinfield St 6 WN7 ..76 A5
Dulford Wlk M13 ....163 C5
Dulgar St M11 ....165 B8
Dulverton Gdns BL3 ..43 B2
Dulverton St M40 ......83 B6
Dulwich Cl 9 M33 ..107 D3
Dulwich St M4 ....159 B3
Dumbarton Cl SK5 ....111 F6
Dumbarton Dr OL10 ....46 A8
Dumbarton Gr WN6 ....36 E2
Dumbarton Rd
 Heywood OL10 ....29 A1
 Reddish SK5 ....111 F6

Dumbell St M27 ....61 F2
Dumber La M33 ....107 F6
Dumers Cl M26 ....44 D4
Dumers Cl b M9,M26 ..44 E5
Dumfries Ave OL3 ....33 C2
Dumfries Dr OL3 ......33 C2
Dumfries Hollow OL10 ..29 F3
Dumfries Wlk OL10 ....29 A1
Dumplington Circ M41 ..95 D7
Dun Cl M3 ....158 D2
Dunbar Ave M23 ......121 A3
Dunbar Dr BL3 ....147 E3
Dunbar Gr OL10 ....45 F8
Dunbar St OL1 ....153 E8
 Stockport SK4 ....169 D2
Dunblane Cl WA3 ......72 C4
Dunblane Gr OL10 ......46 A8
Duncan Ave WA12 ......89 C5
Duncan Pl WN5 ....54 E7
Duncan Rd M13 ....98 F3
Duncan St
 Dukinfield SK16 ......101 C6
 Horwich BL6 ....22 C3
 Salford,Higher Broughton
  M7 ....81 C6
Dunchurch Cl BL6 ......40 D6
Dunchurch Rd M33 ..107 E4
Dunchurch Cl SK7 ....124 A3
Duncombe Dr M40 ....83 B7
Duncombe Rd BL3 ....147 E2
Duncombe St M7 ......155 E6
Duncote Gr OL2 ......149 A5
Dundee Cl 3 M30 ......79 C2
Dundee Cl OL10 ....28 F1
Dundee La BL0 ....138 B6
Dundonald Rd
 Cheadle SK8 ....132 A7
 Manchester M20 ......110 C3
Dundonald St SK2 ....170 F6
Dundraw Cl M24 ......46 B1
Dundrennan Cl SK12 ..133 D5
Dunecroft M34 ....101 A4
Dunedin Dr M6 ....80 F6
Dunedin Rd BL8 ....10 F2
Dunelm Dr M33 ......108 D1
Dunham Ave WA3 ......72 F1
Dunham Cl BL5 ....57 D5
Dunham Gr WN7 ......76 C2
Dunham Lawn WA14 ..119 B4
Dunham Massey Hall*
 WA14 ....118 D3
Dunham St OL4 ......118 D3
Dunham Rd
 Altrincham WA14 ....119 B4
 Altrincham,Bowgreen
  WA14 ....118 F1
 Carrington M31 ......106 D3
 Dukinfield SK16 ......101 D6
 Mosstow WA13 ......117 E2
Dunham Rise WA14 ..119 C4
Dunham St
 Manchester M15 ....162 E6
 Oldham OL4 ....67 E8
 Royton OL2 ....48 D4
Dunkerleys Cl M8 ....155 F8
Dunkery Rd M22 ......121 D1
Dunkirk Cl M34 ......100 A2
Dunkirk La SK14 ......101 B4
Dunkirk Rd M45 ......44 F1
Dunkirk Rise OL12 ..139 E7
Dunkirk St M43 ....84 B1
Dunley Cl M12 ......165 A5
Dunlin Ave WA12 ......89 C4
Dunlin Cl Bolton BL2 ..148 A5
 Hazel Grove SK12 ....125 A5
 Poynton SK12 ....133 A4
 Rochdale OL11 ....29 F7
Dunlin Dr M44 ....94 A3
Dunlin Gr WN7 ....76 B5
Dunlin Wlk WA14 ....119 B8
Dunlop Av OL11 ......30 E4
Dunlop St 2 M3 ......158 F1
Dunmail Ave WA11 ....71 C1
Dunmail Cl M24 ......46 D2
Dunmere Wlk M23 ..109 D7
Dunmore Rd SK8 ....122 B6
Dunmow Ct SK2 ......124 E5
Dunmow Wlk M23 ..109 A2
Dunne La SK13 ......104 B1
Dunnerdale Wlk M18 ..165 C5
Dunnisher Rd M23 ..121 B5
Dunnock Cl SK2 ......124 F5
Dunollie Rd M33 ....108 E3
Dunoon Cl OL10 ......29 A1
Dunoon Dr BL1 ......24 C5
Dunoon Rd Aspull WN2 ..38 D5
 Reddish SK5 ....111 F7
Dunoon Wlk M9 ......157 D7
Dunrobin Cl OL10 ....46 A8
Dunscar Cl M45 ......62 D7
Dunscar Ind Est BL7 ..24 E7
Dunscar Sq BL7 ......24 F8
Dunscore Rd WN3 ....54 E3
Dunsdale Dr WN4 ....73 C3
Dunsfold Dr M23 ....120 D8
Dunsford Ct OL4 ......67 E8
Dunsley Ave M40 ......65 D2
Dunsmore Cl M16 ....97 E4

Dunsop Dr BL1 ....23 F3
Dunstable M19 ....99 B1
Dunstable St 2 OL12 ..139 F8
Dunstable St M19 ....99 B1
Dunstall Rd M22 ....121 E5
Dunstan Ct M40 ....83 A8
Dunstan St BL2 ......148 C7
Dunstan Ave M34 ....100 E7
Dunster Ave
 Brinnington SK5 ......112 C5
 Manchester M9 ....64 E4
 Rochdale OL11 ......139 E5
 Swinton M27 ....62 B2
Dunster Cl
 Hazel Grove SK7 ....124 C1
 Platt Bridge WN2 ......56 A1
Dunster Dr M41 ....94 C1
Dunster Pl M28 ....77 F7
Dunster Rd M28 ....77 F7
Dunsters Ave BL8 ......27 C5
Dunsterville Terr OL11 .139 E5
Dunston Pl 7 OL9 ......48 A1
Dunston St M11 ......165 C8
Dunton Gn SK5 ......112 B6
Dunton Twrs SK5 ....112 B6
Dunvegan Rd SK7 ....124 F1
Dunwood Ave OL2 ..149 C8
Dunwoods Park Courts
 OL2 ....32 C1
Dunworth St M14 ......98 B3
Durant St M4 ....159 B3
Durban Cl OL2 ......149 A6
Durban Rd 2 BL1 ......24 E5
Durban St Ashton-u-L OL7 .84 E1
 Atherton M46 ....58 A2
 Golborne WN2,WN7 ..74 E4
 Oldham OL8 ....66 C3
 Rochdale OL11 ....30 C2
Durden Mews OL2 ..149 B6
Durham Ave M41 ......95 E3
Durham Cl
 Dukinfield SK16 ......101 D6
 Little Lever BL3 ......43 B4
 Romiley SK6 ....113 A1
 Swinton M27 ....61 F2
 Tyldesley M29 ....59 A3
Durham Cres M35 ....84 A6
Durham Dr Ashton-u-L OL6 .85 D8
 Bury BL9 ....45 A3
 Ramsbottom BL0 ......11 B3
Durham Gr M44 ....94 A1
Durham Ho 6 SK3 ....170 E8
Durham Rd
 Handforth SK9 ......131 D5
 3 Hindley WN2 ......56 D5
 5 Salford M6 ....80 C4
Durham St Bolton BL1 ..143 F2
 Droylsden M43 ......100 A8
 12 Manchester M9 ..157 E7
 Oldham OL9 ....66 A4
 Radcliffe M26 ....44 B3
 Reddish SK5 ....99 E2
 Rochdale OL11 ....31 A5
 Wigan WN1 ....37 E1
Durham Wlk
 5 Denton M34 ......100 F1
 Heywood OL10 ....29 A2
Durley Ave
 Manchester M8 ......156 B7
 Sale WA15 ....120 B7
Durn St OL16 ....16 C6
Durnford Ave M41 ....96 A2
Durnford Cl OL12 ......13 D2
Durnford St M24 ......65 A4
Durnford Wlk M22 ..121 B3
Durnlaw Cl OL15 ......16 C5
Durrell Way WA3 ......90 E8
Durrington Wlk M40 ..65 C3
Dursley Dr WN4 ......73 D4
Dutton Gr WN7 ......76 C2
Dutton St M3 ....158 F3
Duty St BL1 ....143 E3
Duxbury Ave Bolton BL2 .25 E5
 Little Lever BL3 ......43 B4
Duxbury Dr BL9 ......141 C2
Duxbury St BL1 ......143 D2
Duxford Lo M8 ....63 F2
Duxford Wlk M40 ......65 C3
Dyche St M4 ....159 B3
Dyche Street Trad Est
 M4 ....159 B3
Dye House La
 New Mills SK22 ......127 C1
 Rochdale OL16 ....15 C3
Dyer St Golborne WA3 ..73 F1
 Manchester M11 ....165 A8
 Salford M5 ....161 C7
Dyers Cl WA13 ......117 A4
Dyers Ct OL15 ....16 A6
Dyers La WA13 ......117 A4
Dymchurch Ave M26 ..61 C7
Dymchurch St M40 ....83 C4
Dysart St
 4 Ashton-u-L OL6 ....85 D2
 Stockport SK1 ......124 B5
Dysarts Cl OL5 ....68 E3
Dyserth Gr SK5 ......169 F4
Dyson Cl BL4 ....60 D8
Dyson Gr OL4 ....67 F8
Dyson St Farnworth BL4 ..60 D7
 Mossley OL5 ....68 E1
 Oldham OL1 ....153 F6
Dystelegh Rd SK12 ..135 D6

E

Eades St M6 ....81 A3

Eadington St M8 ......64 A1
Eafield Ave OL16 ......31 F7
Eafield Cl OL16 ....31 F7
Eafield Rd
 Littleborough OL15 ..15 E3
 Rochdale OL16 ....15 C1
Eagar St M40 ....83 C6
Eagle Ct Delph OL3 ....50 F5
 Salford M15 ....162 E5
Eagle Dr M6 ....81 A5
Eagle Lo WA15 ......119 F2
Eagle St Bolton BL2 ..148 A7
 4 Manchester M4 ..159 A2
 Oldham OL9 ....153 E6
 Rochdale OL16 ....31 A6
Eagles Nest M25 ......63 A3
Eagley Bank OL12 ......4 E6
Eagley Brook Way BL1 ..25 A3
Eagley Brow BL1 ......24 F7
Eagley Dr BL8 ....27 A1
Eagley Inf Sch BL7 ....25 A8
Eagley Jun Sch BL7 ..25 B8
Eagley Way BL1,BL7 ..24 F7
Ealand Chase BL6 ....21 F3
Ealees OL15 ....16 C5
Ealees Rd OL15 ......16 C5
Ealing Ave M14 ....98 C2
Ealing Pl M19 ....111 A6
Ealing Rd SK3 ......170 D8
Ealinger Way M27 ....61 F2
Eames Ave M26 ....61 A8
Eamont Wlk M9 ......157 D7
Earby Gr M9 ....64 F3
Earl Rd
 Handforth SK8,SK9 ..131 E5
 Manchester SK4 ....168 C4
 Ramsbottom BL0 ......138 B6
Earl St Atherton M46 ..58 B2
 Bury BL9 ....140 F2
 6 Heywood OL10 ......29 C2
 Ince-in-M WN2 ....56 A7
 Leigh WN7 ....76 A4
 Mossley M25 ....68 B1
 Prestwich M25 ......63 C8
 Ramsbottom BL0 ......11 D6
 Reddish M34 ....100 A4
 Sale M33 ....108 C5
 Salford M7 ....158 D4
 Stockport SK3 ......170 E8
 Trub OL11 ....47 D8
 Wigan WN1 ....37 C1
Earl Terr 16 SK16 ..166 B1
Earl Wlk M12 ......164 F5
Earl's Lo M35 ....83 D6
Earle Rd SK7 ....123 E3
Earle St Ashton-u-L OL7 .84 F2
 Newton-le-W WA12 ..89 A3
Earlesdon Cres M38 ..60 A5
Earlestown Sta WA12 ..89 B3
Earlham St M18 ......99 C6
Earlsfife Ct WA14 ..119 B4
Earlston Ave M34 ....100 A3
Earlsway M33 ....116 B8
Earlswood Rd OL8 ....66 E3
Earlswood Wlk
 Bolton BL1 ....147 F4
 Manchester M18 ....165 C6
Early Bank SK15 ....102 C7
Early Bank Rd SK14,
 SK15,SK16 ....102 B6
Earnshaw Ave
 Rochdale OL12 ....14 D3
 Stockport SK1 ......112 B1
Earnshaw Cl Bolton BL3 .146 B3
 Hollingworth SK14 ..171 D4
Easby Cl Cheadle SK8 .132 B6
 Poynton SK12 ......133 D4
Easby Rd M24 ....46 E3
Easedale Cl M41 ......94 F3
Easedale Rd BL1 ....144 A8
Easington Wlk 10 M40 ..83 A6
Easingwold 2 WA14 ..119 C4
East Ave Gatley SK8 ..131 D8
 Golborne WA3 ....74 C1
 Leigh WN7 ....76 C3
 Manchester M19 ....110 F7
 Stalybridge SK15 ......86 A3
 Whitefield M45 ....44 E2
East Bond St WN7 ....76 A5
East Bridgewater St 4
 WN7 ....76 A4
East Central Dr M27 ..80 B7
East Court Wlk M13 ..163 C6
East Cres M24 ....64 F7
East Crompton St George's
 CE Sch OL2 ....49 D7
East Crompton St James CE
 Prim Sch OL2 ......149 B7
East Didsbury Sta M20 .110 C1
East Downs Rd
 Altrincham WA14 ....119 C2
 Cheadle SK8 ....131 A3
East Dr Marple SK6 ..125 F3
 Pendlebury M27 ......80 B7
 Whitefield BL9 ....45 B4
East Gate St OL16 ..139 F8
East Gr M13 ....164 D5
East Grange M11 ......83 C3
East Hill St 8 OL1 ....67 A6
East Lancashire Rd
 Haydock WA11,WA12,WA3 .89 C7
 Leigh WA3,WN7,M29 ..76 D2
 Pendlebury M6,M27 ..80 A2
 Swinton M27,M28 ......79 D7
 Tyldesley M28,M29 ....77 C5

East Lancashire Rd continued
 Worsley M28 ....78 D7
East Lancashire Rly* BB4,
 BL0 ....1 C5
East Lancs Rly* Bury BL8 .27 D6
 * Heywood OL10 ......29 C1
East Lea M34 ....101 A2
East Lynn Dr M28 ......61 A3
East Market St M3 ..158 D2
East Meade Bolton BL3 .147 E2
 Manchester,Chorlton-cum-Hardy
  M21 ....109 B7
 Manchester,Sedgley Park
  M25 ....63 D2
 Swinton M27 ....79 E6
East Moor M28 ....78 A7
East Mount WN5 ......53 F6
East Newton St 9 M4 ..159 C3
East Ordsall La M3,M5 .158 D1
East Over SK6 ......125 A8
East Park Cl M13 ....163 C6
East Philip St M3 ....158 E3
East Rd Manchester M12 .99 B4
 Manchester M18 ......99 B4
 Mossley SK15 ....86 E6
 Stretford M32 ....96 B4
 Wythenshawe M90 ..130 C7
East St Ashton-in-M WN4 .73 D4
 8 Ashton-u-L OL6 ....73 D4
 Bury BL9 ....140 F1
 Denton M34 ....100 F7
 Edenfield BL0 ....1 D4
 Haslingden BB4 ......1 A7
 Hindley WN2 ....57 B3
 Littleborough OL15 ..16 C5
 Milnrow OL16 ....31 D7
 Radcliffe M26 ....44 B3
 Rochdale OL16 ....31 A8
 Tyldesley M46 ....58 F1
 Wardle OL12 ....15 C6
East Union St M16 ..161 C6
East Vale SK6 ......126 A5
East View
 4 Middleton M24 ......64 F8
 Ramsbottom,Brooksbottoms
  BL9 ....11 C3
 Ramsbottom,Chatterton BL0 .1 C1
 Whitworth OL12 ......4 D2
East Ward Com Prim Sch
 BL9 ....141 B2
East Way Bolton BL1 ..25 B3
 Oldham OL10 ....48 E1
East Wlk BL7 ....8 D2
Eastbank St BL1 ....143 F2
Eastbourne Gr BL1 ..144 A8
Eastbourne St
 Oldham OL8 ....67 B4
 Rochdale OL11 ......139 F5
Eastbrook Ave 2 M26 ..44 C4
Eastburn Ave M40 ..159 C3
Eastchurch Cl BL4 ....60 D7
Eastcombe Ave M7 ....81 B7
Eastcote Ave M11 ....99 E8
Eastcote Rd SK5 ......111 F5
Eastdale Av M15 ....128 F8
Eastdale Pl WA14 ..119 C2
Easterdale OL4 ....67 C6
Eastern Ave M27 ......62 D3
Eastern By-Pass
 Droylsden M11 ....99 D8
 Manchester M11 ......99 D8
Eastern Circ M19 ....111 A6
Eastfield M6 ....154 E4
Eastfield Ave
 Manchester M40 ....160 E3
 Middleton M24 ....65 A7
Eastfields M26 ....43 E5
Eastford Sq M40 ....159 C4
Eastgarth WN2 ....56 B2
Eastgate Wlk 21 M9 ..64 E3
Eastgate Wlk 21 M9 ..14 C7
Eastgate St OL7 ....166 A1
Eastgrove Ave BL1 ....24 E6
Eastham Ave Bury BL9 ..27 F6
 Manchester M14 ......98 B1
Eastham Way
 11 Handforth SK9 ..131 D5
 Walkden M38 ....60 B5
Easthaven Ave 4 M11 ..83 C2
Eastholme Dr M19 ..111 B7
Easthope Cl M20 ....110 B7
Eastlands Rd M9 ....64 E5
Eastleigh Ave M7 ..155 E8
Eastleigh Cres WN7 ..76 B3
Eastleigh Dr M40 ..160 D3
Eastleigh Gr 2 BL1 ..145 E8
 Manchester M25 ......63 E3
Eastleigh Rd Gatley SK8 .122 B1
 Manchester M25 ......63 E3
Eastmoor Dr M40 ....83 D4
Eastmoor Gr BL3 ..146 B2
Eastnor Cl M15 ......162 D6
Easton Cl Middleton M24 .65 C7
 Wigan WN3 ....55 A2
Easton Dr SK8 ....123 A5
Easton Rd M43 ....83 F3
Eastpark Cl M13 ....163 C6
Eastry Ave SK5 ......112 B6
Eastview WA3 ....108 B3
Eastville Gdns M19 ..110 E5
Eastward Ave SK9 ..136 F6
Eastway Middleton M24 ..46 F1
 Sale M33 ....107 C1
 Urmston M41 ....94 B2
Eastwell Rd
 Ashton-in-M WN4 ....73 A3
 Wigan WN6 ....36 F3

Eastwood M14 ....98 C1
Eastwood Ave
Droylsden M43 ....83 E1
Failsworth M40 ....65 F1
Newton-le-W WA12 ....89 F3
Urmston M41 ....95 D2
Walkden M28 ....60 A2
Eastwood Cl Bolton BL3 ..146 A3
Bury BL9 ....141 B2
Eastwood Gr WN7 ....75 D5
Eastwood Rd M40 ....65 E1
Eastwood St Denton M34 .100 D7
11 Littleborough OL15 ....16 B5
Eastwood Terr BL1 ....40 E8
Eatock Prim Sch BL5 ....57 E6
Eatock St WN2 ....56 B3
Eatock Way BL5 ....57 D6
Eaton Cl Cheadle SK8 ....122 F3
Dukinfield SK16 ....101 C6
Poynton SK12 ....134 A3
Swinton M27 ....61 F2
Eaton Ct
Altrincham WA14 ....119 C1
Wilmslow SK9 ....137 A6
Eaton Dr
Alderley Edge SK9 ....136 F2
Ashton-u-L OL7 ....84 F4
Sale WA15 ....120 A8
Eaton Rd
Altrincham WA14 ....119 C1
Manchester M8 ....63 F1
Sale M33 ....108 A4
Eaton St WN2 ....56 E6
Eaves Knoll Rd SK22 ....127 A1
Eaves La OL9 ....152 A5
Ebbdale Cl SK1 ....124 A8
Ebberstone St M14 ....98 A2
Ebden St M1 ....163 B8
Ebenezer St
Glossop SK13 ....116 D7
2 Manchester M15 ....162 F7
Ebnal Wlk M14 ....110 D7
Ebor Cl OL2 ....149 A8
Ebor Ho M21 ....96 F1
Ebor Rd M22 ....121 E4
Ebor St OL15 ....16 B5
Ebsworth St M40 ....157 F8
Ebury St M26 ....43 F3
Eccles Cl M11 ....165 C8
Eccles Coll M30 ....79 F4
Eccles New Rd M5,M50 ...80 C2
Eccles Old Rd M6,M30 ...80 C3
Eccles Rd Swinton M27 ....79 F6
Wigan WN5 ....36 B1
Eccles St BL0 ....138 B6
Eccles Sta Eccles M30 ....79 F1
Eccles M30 ....79 F2
Ecclesbridge Rd SK6 ....125 F4
Eccleshall St M11 ....83 C1
Eccleston Ave
29 Bolton BL2 ....25 B1
Manchester M14 ....98 B1
Swinton M27 ....79 D7
Eccleston Cl BL8 ....27 A1
Eccleston Pl M7 ....155 D8
Eccleston Rd SK3 ....123 E4
Eccleston St
Failsworth M35 ....84 A8
Wigan WN1 ....37 C1
Eccleston Way 3 SK9 ....131 D4
Eccups La SK9 ....136 C8
Echo St M1 ....163 B8
Eckersley Cl 1 M23 ....120 F6
Eckersley Fold La M46 ....58 A1
Eckersley Mill WN3 ....150 B7
Eckersley Rd BL1 ....143 E3
Eckersley St Bolton BL3 ..146 C4
Wigan WN1 ....37 E1
Eckford St M8 ....156 B6
Eclipse Cl OL16 ....31 C7
Edale Ave
Denton,Audenshaw M34 ..100 D7
Denton,Haughton Green
M34 ....112 F8
Manchester M40 ....83 A8
Reddish SK5 ....100 A1
Urmston M41 ....95 B1
Edale Bank 6 SK13 ....171 E1
Edale Cl
Altrincham WA14 ....119 C1
Atherton M46 ....58 C3
26 Gamesley SK13 ....171 E2
Gatley SK8 ....131 D7
Hazel Grove SK7 ....124 E1
Irlam M44 ....94 A1
Edale Cres SK13 ....171 E1
Edale Dr WN6 ....19 E2
Edale Fold 25 SK13 ....171 E2
Edale Gr Ashton-u-L OL6 ....86 A6
Sale M33 ....107 E2
Edale Rd Bolton BL3 ....146 A4
Farnworth BL4 ....60 C7
Leigh WN7 ....76 C4
Stretford M32 ....96 B3
Edale St M6 ....81 B5
Edbrook Wlk M13 ....164 D5
Edburton Ct WA3 ....90 A8
Eddie Colman Cl M40 ....83 B5
Eddisbury Ave
Manchester M20 ....109 F8
Urmston M41 ....94 D4
Eddisford Dr WA3 ....91 D4
Edditch Gr BL2 ....148 C7
Eddleston St WN4 ....72 F6
Eddystone Cl 6 M5 ....81 A1
Eden Ave Bolton BL1 ....143 E3
Edenfield BL0 ....1 D3
Fowley Common WA3 ....92 C4
Eden Ave *continued*
High Lane SK6 ....134 E7
Eden Bank WN7 ....76 B6
Eden Cl Heywood OL10 ....29 A3
Manchester M15 ....163 A6
Stockport SK1 ....124 A8
Wilmslow SK9 ....136 E5
Eden Ct Edenfield BL0 ....1 D2
Manchester M19 ....111 A8
Eden Gr Bolton BL1 ....143 E3
Leigh WN7 ....75 C5
Eden Lo BL1 ....143 E3
Eden Pl SK8 ....122 D6
Eden St Bolton BL1 ....143 E3
Bury BL9 ....140 F2
Edenfield BL0 ....1 D1
Oldham OL1 ....153 E7
Rochdale OL12 ....139 D8
Eden Way OL2 ....149 A8
Edenbridge Dr M26 ....61 B7
Edenbridge Rd
Cheadle SK8 ....123 B4
Failsworth M40 ....83 B4
Edendale Dr M22 ....121 D1
Edenfield Ave M21 ....109 D4
Edenfield CE Prim Sch
BL0 ....1 D4
Edenfield La M28 ....78 F4
Edenfield Rd
Manchester M25 ....63 E2
Rochdale OL11,OL12 ....13 C2
Edenfield St OL11,OL12 ....14 C1
Edenhall Ave M19 ....110 F8
Edenhall Gr WN2 ....56 F3
Edenham Wlk 1 M40 ....65 D2
Edenhurst Dr 3 WA15 ....120 B5
Edenhurst Rd SK2 ....124 B6
Edensor Cl WN6 ....37 A4
Edensor Dr WA15 ....120 C3
Edenvale M28 ....78 A7
Edgar St Bolton BL3 ....145 E6
Ramsbottom BL0 ....138 B5
Rochdale OL16 ....15 C2
Edgar St W BL0 ....138 B5
Edgbaston Dr M16 ....97 A3
Edge Fold Cres M28 ....78 D8
Edge Fold Rd M28 ....60 D1
Edge Gn M28 ....78 C8
Edge Green La WA3 ....73 F2
Edge Green Rd WN4 ....73 F4
Edge Green St WN4 ....73 D4
Edge Hall Rd WN5 ....53 E5
Edge Hill Ave OL2 ....48 E3
Edge Hill Rd Bolton BL3 ..146 B3
Royton OL2 ....48 E3
Edge La Bacup OL13 ....4 C8
Bolton BL1,BL6 ....23 C5
Droylsden M11,M43 ....83 D2
Entwistle BL7 ....9 A8
Mottram-in-L SK14 ....102 F4
Stretford M21,M32 ....96 E1
Edge Lane Rd OL1 ....67 A8
Edge Lane St OL2 ....48 E4
Edge St M4 ....159 A2
Edge View OL1 ....47 E1
Edge View La SK9 ....136 B2
Edgedale Ave M19 ....110 E5
Edgefield Ave M9 ....64 E4
Edgefold Ind Est BL4 ....146 B1
Edgehill Chase SK9 ....137 E7
Edgehill Cl M5 ....154 F2
Edgehill Ct M32 ....96 E1
Edgehill Rd M6 ....80 C3
Edgehill St 9 M4 ....159 A2
Edgeley Fold SK3 ....123 C7
Edgeley Park (Stockport
County FC) SK3 ....170 E7
Edgeley Rd
Stockport SK3 ....123 B7
Urmston M41 ....107 A8
Edgemoor WA14 ....119 A2
Edgemoor Cl Oldham OL4 ....49 D1
Radcliffe M26 ....43 E5
Whitworth OL12 ....4 E5
Edgemoor Dr OL11 ....29 F5
Edgerley Pl WN4 ....73 A3
Edgerton Rd WA3 ....90 F8
Edgerton Wlk 4 M28 ....60 D3
Edgeview Wlk 6 M13 ....163 B7
Edgeware Ave M25 ....63 F4
Edgeware Gr WN3 ....54 D3
Edgeware Rd Eccles M30 ..79 A4
Failsworth OL9 ....65 E3
Edgewater M5 ....154 D2
Edgeway SK9 ....137 B5
Edgeway Rd WN3 ....55 A1
Edgewood WN6 ....36 A5
Edgeworth Ave BL2 ....26 D1
Edgeworth Dr Bury BL8 ....27 A1
Manchester M14 ....110 E7
Edgeworth Rd
Golborne WA3 ....73 F1
Hindley WN2 ....57 A3
Edgeworth Vale BL7 ....9 E6
Edgmont Ave BL3 ....147 D4
Edgware Rd M40 ....83 B4
Edgworth Cl OL10 ....29 A2
Edgworth Views BL7 ....9 D8
Edilom Rd M8 ....63 E2
Edinburgh 5 M30 ....79 E2
Edinburgh Cl
Cheadle SK8 ....122 F6
Ince-in-M WN2 ....56 A8
8 Sale M33 ....107 D3
Edinburgh Dr
Hindley WN2 ....57 B3
Romiley SK6 ....113 C4
Wigan WN5 ....54 D5
Edinburgh Ho M3 ....158 D1
Edinburgh Rd BL3 ....43 A2
Edinburgh Sq M40 ....160 E4
Edinburgh Way OL11 ....30 D4
Edinburgh Wlk WN2 ....38 D5
Edington 7 OL12 ....139 F8
Edison Rd M30 ....95 C8
Edison St 1 M11 ....99 E7
Edith Ave M14 ....98 A3
Edith Cavell Cl M11 ....83 C1
Edith Cliff Wlk M40 ....65 F1
Edith St Bolton BL1 ....144 C6
Farnworth BL4 ....60 D7
Oldham OL8 ....66 F3
Ramsbottom BL0 ....11 E8
Wigan WN3 ....150 B7
Edlestone Gr 2 SK9 ....131 E1
Edlin Cl M12 ....164 E5
Edlingham 5 OL11 ....139 E6
Edlington Wlk 12 M40 ....83 C6
Edmonds St M24 ....47 B1
Edmonton Ct SK2 ....124 A4
Edmonton Rd
Failsworth M40 ....83 A4
Stockport SK2 ....124 A4
Edmund Cl SK4 ....169 E4
Edmund Dr WN7 ....75 C5
Edmund Potter Hospl
BL1 ....40 F7
Edmund St Droylsden M43 ....84 A1
Failsworth M35 ....83 F8
Milnrow OL16 ....31 F6
8 Radcliffe M26 ....44 C4
Rochdale OL12 ....139 D8
Salford M6 ....154 E3
Shaw OL2 ....149 C7
Walsden OL14 ....6 A8
Edmunds Ct BL3 ....145 D6
Edmunds Fold OL15 ....15 F6
Edna Rd WN7 ....75 C7
Edna St SK14 ....167 D2
Edridge Way WN2 ....56 C4
Edson Rd M9 ....63 F3
Edstone Cl BL3 ....40 F4
Edward Ave
Littleborough OL15 ....15 F3
Manchester M21 ....109 A8
Romiley SK6 ....112 E3
Salford M5,M6 ....80 C3
Edward Charlton Rd M16,
M21 ....97 A2
Edward Ct WA14 ....119 B7
Edward Dr WN4 ....73 B4
Edward Mews OL9 ....152 C5
Edward Onyon Ct M5 ....154 E2
Edward Rd
Manchester M9 ....64 D5
Shaw OL2 ....149 A6
Edward St Ashton-u-L OL6 ..85 E2
Bolton BL3 ....145 D5
Bury BL9 ....140 F1
Chadderton OL9 ....152 A8
Denton M34 ....100 F4
Denton,Audenshaw M34 ..100 D7
Droylsden M43 ....100 A8
Dukinfield SK16 ....101 C6
Farnworth BL4 ....42 B2
Glossop SK13 ....104 C1
Horwich BL6 ....22 A3
Hyde SK14 ....101 C3
Kearsley M26 ....61 B8
Leigh WN7 ....76 A4
Manchester M9 ....157 E8
Middleton M24 ....47 A1
Oldham OL9 ....152 C5
Prestwich M25 ....63 A5
Radcliffe M26 ....44 B2
Rochdale,Newbold Brow
OL16 ....31 A8
Rochdale,Wuerdle OL12 ....15 D4
Romiley SK6 ....114 B1
Sale M33 ....108 E4
Salford M7 ....158 E4
Stockport SK1 ....170 F8
Westhoughton BL5 ....57 E8
Whitworth OL12 ....4 D2
Wigan,Rose Bridge WN1 ..151 F8
Wigan,Swinley WN1 ....37 C2
Edward Sutcliffe Cl M14 ..98 A2
Edwards Cl SK6 ....125 E5
Edwards Ct M22 ....121 D3
Edwards Dr M45 ....63 B8
Edwards Way SK6 ....125 E5
Edwin Rd M11 ....160 E1
Edwin St Bury BL9 ....140 E2
Stockport SK1 ....124 B8
Wigan WN1 ....151 E7
Edwin Waugh Gdns OL12 ..14 D3
Edzell Wlk 18 M11 ....83 C1
Eeasbrook M41 ....95 D1
Egbert St 18 M40 ....83 A7
Egerton Ave WA13 ....117 C8
Egerton Cl OL10 ....29 D1
Egerton Cres
Heywood OL10 ....29 C1
Manchester M20 ....110 B7
Egerton Ct Denton M34 ....101 A4
6 Hindley WN2 ....56 E5
Manchester M14 ....98 C4
Stockport SK3 ....124 A4
Stretford M21 ....108 F8
Egerton Dr
Altrincham WA15 ....120 A3
Sale M33 ....108 B5
Egerton Gr M28 ....60 D3
Egerton High Sch M41 ....95 E4
Egerton Ho 3 M15 ....162 D7
Egerton Lo Bolton BL7 ....8 E1
Egerton Lo *continued*
Denton M34 ....101 A4
Egerton Mews
Droylsden M43 ....100 A8
Manchester M14 ....110 D8
Egerton Moss WA15 ....128 E5
Egerton Park Arts Coll
M34 ....100 E4
Egerton Pk M28 ....79 B7
Egerton Pl OL2 ....149 A6
Egerton Prim Sch BL7 ....8 D3
Egerton Rd
Altrincham WA15 ....120 A2
Eccles M30 ....79 D4
Handforth SK9 ....131 B1
Manchester M14 ....110 D8
Stockport SK3 ....124 A4
Walkden M28 ....60 D3
Whitefield M45 ....62 F7
Egerton Rd N
Manchester M16,M21 ....97 C1
Manchester,Heaton Chapel
SK4 ....111 C5
Egerton Rd S
Manchester,Chorlton-cum-Hardy
M21 ....109 C8
Manchester,Heaton Moor
SK4 ....168 C4
Egerton St
Abram Brow WN2 ....74 B7
Ashton-u-L OL6 ....166 C3
Denton M34 ....100 E5
Droylsden M43 ....84 B1
Eccles M30 ....79 B2
Farnworth BL4 ....42 C1
Heywood OL10 ....29 C1
Littleborough OL15 ....16 C5
Manchester M15 ....162 D7
Middleton M24 ....64 C7
Mossley OL5 ....68 C2
Oldham OL1 ....67 A8
Prestwich M25 ....63 C4
Salford M3 ....158 D1
Egerton Terr M14 ....110 D7
Egerton Vale BL7 ....8 D2
Eggar Cl M29 ....77 B7
Eggington St M40 ....156 C5
Egham Ct 18 BL2 ....25 B1
Egham Ho BL3 ....146 B2
Egmont St
Manchester M8 ....156 A8
Mossley OL5 ....86 D8
Pendlebury M6 ....80 E6
Egremont Ave M20 ....110 A7
Egremont Cl M45 ....45 A1
Egremont Ct M7 ....81 C8
Egremont Gr 2 SK3 ....123 B8
Egremont Rd OL16 ....31 F4
Egret Dr M44 ....94 A3
Egypt La M25 ....45 D1
Egyptian St BL1 ....143 F1
Ehlinger Ave SK13 ....104 A5
Eida Way M17 ....96 C8
Eight Acre M45 ....62 C7
Eighth Ave OL8 ....66 D1
Eighth St M17 ....96 D6
Eileen Gr M14 ....98 C2
Eileen Gr W M14 ....98 B2
Elaine Ave M9 ....65 B2
Elaine Cl WN4 ....73 D5
Elbain Wlk M40 ....83 C5
Elbe St M12 ....163 C8
Elberton Wlk 13 M8 ....155 F7
Elbow St M19 ....99 A1
Elbut La BL9 ....28 F5
Elcho Rd WA14 ....119 B3
Elcombe Ave WA3 ....90 E7
Elcot Cl M40 ....156 C5
Elder Cl SK2 ....124 D8
Elder Gr M40 ....65 F2
Elder Rd OL4 ....67 E6
Elder St OL16 ....31 B5
Elderberry Cl Diggle OL3 ....51 C5
Wigan WN1 ....37 B4
Elderberry Way SK9 ....137 E8
Elderberry Wlk M31 ....105 E3
Eldercot Gr BL3 ....146 A4
Eldercot Rd BL3 ....146 A4
Eldercroft Rd WA15 ....120 D5
Elderfield Dr SK6 ....112 F4
Eldermount Rd M9 ....64 D2
Elderwood OL9 ....65 E7
Eldon Cl M34 ....100 E7
Eldon Gdns WN4 ....73 A6
Eldon Pl M30 ....79 C1
Eldon Prec OL8 ....153 E5
Eldon Rd Irlam M44 ....94 A2
Stockport SK3 ....123 C7
Eldon St Bolton BL2 ....25 B2
Bury BL9 ....140 F4
Leigh WN7 ....75 D6
Oldham OL8 ....153 F5
Eldridge Dr M40 ....83 A5
Eleanor Rd
Manchester M21 ....109 A8
Royton OL2 ....48 E3
Eleanor St Bolton BL1 ....25 A5
Oldham OL1 ....153 D8
Wigan WN3 ....150 A7
Electo St M11 ....99 E7
Elevator Rd M17 ....96 E6
Eleventh St M17 ....96 D6
Elf Mill Cl SK3 ....170 E6
Elf Mill Terr SK3 ....170 E6
Elford Gr M18 ....100 A4
Elgar St M12 ....99 A4
Elgin Ave Garswood WN4 ....72 D4
Manchester M20 ....110 D3
Elgin Cl WN2 ....56 A8
Elgin Dr M33 ....108 E3
Elgin Rd Dukinfield SK16 ..101 C6
Oldham OL4 ....67 C5
Elgin St Ashton-u-L OL7 ..166 A4
Bolton BL1 ....142 C2
Stalybridge SK15 ....86 B1
Elgol Cl SK3 ....170 F5
Elgol Dr BL3 ....40 E6
Elham Cl M26 ....61 C7
Eli St OL9 ....66 A3
Elim St OL15 ....16 C7
Elim Terr OL15 ....16 C7
Eliot Dr WN3 ....150 A5
Eliot Rd M30 ....79 D1
Elishaw Row M5 ....154 F1
Eliza Ann St
5 Eccles M30 ....79 C1
Manchester M40 ....159 C4
Eliza St Manchester M15 ..162 E6
Ramsbottom BL0 ....11 D6
Elizabeth Ave
Chadderton OL9 ....66 A3
Denton M34 ....100 E5
Disley SK12 ....135 D5
Leigh WN2 ....56 E1
Royton OL2 ....48 D3
1 Stalybridge SK15 ....86 A2
Stockport SK1 ....170 F8
Elizabeth Cl M32 ....96 D2
Elizabeth Ct
Manchester M14 ....110 D7
Reddish M18 ....99 F3
Stockport SK4 ....168 C2
Elizabeth Dr BB4 ....1 A8
Elizabeth Gr OL2 ....149 B7
Elizabeth Ho 13 Bury BL8 ..27 C3
Stockport SK4 ....168 B2
Elizabeth Rd M31 ....105 F4
Elizabeth Slinger Rd
M20 ....109 F5
Elizabeth St
Ashton-u-L OL6 ....166 B4
Atherton M46 ....58 D3
Denton M34 ....100 D3
Edenfield BL0 ....1 D3
2 Heywood OL10 ....29 C2
Hyde SK14 ....167 D3
Ince-in-M WN2 ....56 B8
Leigh WN7 ....76 B3
Manchester M8 ....156 A5
Prestwich M25 ....63 C4
3 Radcliffe M26 ....44 A3
Rochdale OL11 ....30 C3
1 Swinton M27 ....61 F1
Whitefield M45 ....62 F7
Elizabethan Ct 10 M29 ....58 F1
Elizabethan Dr WN3 ....55 E4
Elizabethan Way OL16 ....31 F5
Elizabethan Wlk 1 WN2 ..56 A2
Elkanagh Gdns M6 ....154 F3
Elkstone Ave M38 ....60 A6
Elkstone Cl WN3 ....54 C2
Elkwood Cl WN1 ....37 B4
Elladene Pk M21 ....109 C8
Ellan Wlk 10 M11 ....83 C1
Ellanby Cl M14 ....98 B3
Elland Cl
Westhoughton BL5 ....39 D3
Whitefield BL9 ....45 B2
Ellaston Dr M41 ....95 D2
Ellastone Rd M6 ....80 C4
Ellbourne Rd M9 ....64 A3
Ellen Brook Rd M22 ....130 D8
Ellen Gr BL4 ....61 C5
Ellen St 5 Bolton BL1 ....142 C3
Droylsden M43 ....100 B8
Oldham OL9 ....153 D8
Stockport SK4 ....169 D3
Wigan WN1 ....151 D7
Ellen Wilkinson Cres
M12 ....165 A5
Ellenbrook Cl M12 ....165 B6
Ellenbrook Com Prim Sch
M28 ....78 C8
Ellenbrook Rd M28 ....78 B7
Ellendale Grange M28 ....78 B8
Ellenhall Cl M9 ....157 D8
Ellenor Dr M29 ....77 C7
Ellenroad App OL16 ....32 A4
Ellenroad Engine Ho*
OL16 ....32 A4
Ellenroad St OL16 ....32 A4
Ellenrod Dr OL12 ....14 A2
Ellenrod La OL12 ....14 A2
Ellenshaw Cl OL12 ....14 A2
Elleray Cl BL3 ....43 C3
Elleray Rd Middleton M9 ....64 F5
Salford M6 ....80 D5
Ellerbeck Cl Bolton BL2 ....25 C5
Standish WN6 ....36 F7
Ellerbeck Cres M28 ....78 C8
Ellerby Ave M27 ....62 A3
Ellergreen Rd WN2 ....57 C3
Ellerslie Ct M14 ....98 C4
Ellescroft SK22 ....127 E1
Ellesmere Ave
Ashton-u-L OL6 ....85 C7
Eccles M30 ....79 E2
Marple SK6 ....125 F6
Walkden M28 ....60 C3
Ellesmere Cl SK16 ....101 E8
Ellesmere Dr SK8 ....123 A5
Ellesmere Gdns BL3 ....147 D3

Ellesmere Rd
Altrincham WA14 . . . .**119** E6
Ashton-in-M WN4 . . . .**72** F4
Bolton BL3 . . . .**146** C3
Cheadle SK3 . . . .**123** A7
Culcheth WA3 . . . .**91** E3
Eccles M30 . . . .**79** C3
Manchester M21 . . . .**97** C1
Wigan WN5 . . . .**54** D6
Ellesmere Rd N SK4 . . . .**111** C5
Ellesmere Rd S M21 . . . .**109** C8
Ellesmere Ret Pk M28 . . . . . .**60** D4
Ellesmere Sh Ctr ☑ M28 . . . . .**60** D3
Ellesmere St Bolton BL3 . . . .**145** D6
🖪 Eccles M30 . . . .**79** D1
Failsworth M35 . . . .**83** F8
Farnworth BL4 . . . .**60** D8
Leigh WN7 . . . .**75** F4
Manchester M15 . . . .**162** D7
Rochdale OL11 . . . .**139** F5
Swinton,Clifton Green M27 . . . .**62** A1
Swinton,Deans M27 . . . .**79** D7
Tyldesley M29 . . . .**59** A1
Tyldesley,Higher Green
M29 . . . .**77** C5
Walkden M38 . . . .**60** D7
Ellesmere Terr M14 . . . .**110** D7
Ellesmere Wlk 🖪 BL4 . . . . . .**60** D8
Ellingham Cl M11 . . . .**160** F1
Elliot Sq 🔟 OL1 . . . .**67** A8
Elliot St Bolton BL1 . . . .**142** C3
Oldham OL4 . . . .**67** E6
Elliot Wlk M24 . . . .**47** C3
Elliott Ave
Dukinfield SK14 . . . .**101** D5
Golborne WA3 . . . .**74** B1
Elliott Dr Hindley WN2 . . . .**56** E7
Sale M33 . . . .**107** E4
Elliott St Farnworth BL4 . . . . .**60** C7
Rochdale OL12 . . . .**31** A8
Tyldesley M29 . . . .**76** F8
Ellis Cres M28 . . . .**60** B3
Ellis Dr M8 . . . .**64** B1
Ellis Fold OL12 . . . .**13** E2
Ellis Rd M46 . . . .**44** A8
Ellis St Bury BL8 . . . .**27** B2
Hyde SK14 . . . .**167** F2
Manchester M15 . . . .**162** E6
Wigan WN1 . . . .**37** E1
Ellisbank Wlk 🖪 M13 . . . . . .**163** B7
Ellisland Wlk 🔟 M40 . . . .**83** A6
Ellison Cl SK14 . . . .**103** D5
Ellison Ho 🔟 OL7 . . . .**166** A1
Ellison St SK13 . . . .**104** D3
Elliston Sq M12 . . . .**165** A6
Ellonby Rise BL6 . . . .**40** C5
Ellor St Salford M5 . . . .**81** B2
Salford,Seedley M6 . . . .**154** F3
Ellwood Rd SK1 . . . .**112** B1

Elm Ave
Donwald Green WN4 . . . .**72** D5
Golborne WA3 . . . .**74** A1
Newton-le-W WA12 . . . .**89** C2
Radcliffe M26 . . . .**61** F8
Standish WN6 . . . .**36** F8
Wigan WN5 . . . .**54** E6
Elm Beds Rd SK12 . . . .**134** C2
Elm Cl Mottram-in-L SK14 .**103** A4
🖪 Partington M31 . . . .**105** F3
Poynton SK12 . . . .**133** F3
Elm Cres
Alderley Edge SK9 . . . .**137** B3
Worsley M28 . . . .**79** A7
Elm Croft WN1 . . . .**37** B4
Elm Ct SK1 . . . .**124** B8
Elm Dr Billinge WN5 . . . .**71** D5
Denton M34 . . . .**100** D4
Stretford M32 . . . .**108** C8
Elm Gr Alderley Edge SK9 .**137** B2
Ashton-u-L OL6 . . . .**85** C5
Bolton BL7 . . . .**25** A8
Denton M34 . . . .**100** D5
Droylsden M43 . . . .**83** D2
Farnworth BL4 . . . .**60** C6
Glossop SK13 . . . .**104** C2
Handforth SK9 . . . .**131** C3
🖪 Horwich BL6 . . . .**22** E1
Hyde SK14 . . . .**167** F2
Manchester M20 . . . .**110** B3
Newhey OL16 . . . .**32** A3
Oldham OL4 . . . .**68** B6
Prestwich M25 . . . .**63** A6
Rochdale OL11 . . . .**139** E5
Sale M33 . . . .**108** B6
Swinton M27 . . . .**61** B2
Urmston M41 . . . .**95** E2
Wardle OL12 . . . .**15** C6
Elm Ho M16 . . . .**97** D3
Elm Park Ct M20 . . . .**110** B4
Elm Rd Abram Brow WN2 . . . .**74** C7
Altrincham WA15 . . . .**119** E3
High Lane SK6 . . . .**134** F7
Hollinfare WA3 . . . .**105** A2
Kearsley BL4 . . . .**60** F5
Little Lever BL3 . . . .**43** B2
Manchester M20 . . . .**110** A4
Oldham OL8 . . . .**66** D2
Westhoughton BL5 . . . .**57** F7
Elm Rd S SK2 . . . .**123** A7
Elm St Bury BL9 . . . .**141** B2
Eccles M30 . . . .**79** D1

Elm St continued
Edenfield BL0 . . . .**1** E3
Failsworth M35 . . . .**83** F8
Farnworth BL4 . . . .**42** E1
Heywood OL10 . . . .**29** D2
Leigh WN7 . . . .**75** F3
Middleton M24 . . . .**65** C8
Platt Bridge WN2 . . . .**56** A2
Ramsbottom BL0 . . . .**11** D6
Rochdale OL12 . . . .**14** F1
Romiley SK6 . . . .**112** F4
Swinton M27 . . . .**61** E1
🖪 Tyldesley M29 . . . .**59** A1
Whitworth OL12 . . . .**4** D2
Elm Tree Cl
Failsworth M35 . . . .**84** B7
Stalybridge SK15 . . . .**102** A8
Elm Tree Dr
Dukinfield SK16 . . . .**101** F7
Wythenshawe M22 . . . .**121** D3
Elm Tree Rd
Golborne WA3 . . . .**90** F8
Romiley SK6 . . . .**112** C3
Elm Wood Prim Sch M24 . . .**65** C8
Elmbank Ave M20 . . . .**109** E4
Elmbank Rd M24 . . . .**65** C8
Elmbridge Wlk
Bolton BL3 . . . .**145** D5
🖪 Manchester M40 . . . .**83** A6
Elmdale Ave SK8 . . . .**122** B2
Elmdale Wlk 🖪 M15 . . . .**163** A6
Elmfield WN6 . . . .**36** B6
Elmfield Ave
Atherton M46 . . . .**58** C4
Wythenshawe M22 . . . .**121** E8
Elmfield Cl SK9 . . . .**137** B2
Elmfield Ct SK3 . . . .**170** F5
Elmfield Dr SK6 . . . .**125** E6
Elmfield Ho SK3 . . . .**170** F5
Elmfield Rd
Alderley Edge SK9 . . . .**137** B2
Droylsden M43 . . . .**100** C8
Stockport SK3 . . . .**170** F5
Wigan WN1 . . . .**37** B5
Elmfield St Bolton BL1 . . . . .**143** F2
Manchester M8 . . . .**156** A6
Elmgate Gr M19 . . . .**99** A1
Elmham Wlk M40 . . . .**159** C4
Elmhow Gr WN3 . . . .**55** A2
Elmhurst Dr M19 . . . .**110** F5
Elmlea Ave WA15 . . . .**119** F4
Elmley Cl SK2 . . . .**125** A5
Elmore Wood OL15 . . . .**15** E6
Elmpark Gate OL12 . . . .**14** B3
Elmpark Gr OL12 . . . .**14** B3
Elmpark Vale OL12 . . . .**14** B3
Elmpark View OL12 . . . .**14** B3
Elmpark Way OL12 . . . .**14** B3
Elmridge WN7 . . . .**76** B6
Elmridge Ct WA3 . . . .**90** F8
Elmridge Dr WA15 . . . .**129** C8
Elmridge Prim Sch
WA15 . . . .**129** C8
Elms SK9 . . . .**136** F6
Elms Bank Com High Specl
Sch M45 . . . .**44** F2
Elms Cl M45 . . . .**44** F2
Elms Farm 🖪 M45 . . . .**44** F2
Elms Rd Manchester SK4 . . .**111** B5
Stalybridge SK15 . . . .**86** D3
Whitefield M45 . . . .**44** F1
Elms St M45 . . . .**44** F1
Elms The Golborne WA3 . . . . . .**90** F7
Mossley OL5 . . . .**68** B3
Rochdale OL15 . . . .**15** E4
🖪 Whitefield M45 . . . .**44** F2
Elmsbury St 🔟 WN4 . . . .**72** F5
Elmscott Wlk M13 . . . .**164** D5
Elmsdale Ave M9 . . . .**64** D5
Elmsfield Ave OL11 . . . .**13** E1
Elmsleigh Ct M30 . . . .**79** F3
Elmsleigh Rd SK8 . . . .**122** A2
Elmsmere Rd M20 . . . .**110** D4
Elmstead Ave M20 . . . .**110** A6
Elmsted Cl SK8 . . . .**123** B3
Elmstone Gr BL1 . . . .**143** F1
Elmsway
Altrincham WA15 . . . .**129** B8
Bramhall SK7 . . . .**132** C7
High Lane SK6 . . . .**134** E6
Elmswood Ave M14 . . . .**97** F2
Elmswood Dr SK14 . . . .**102** A3
Elmsworth Ave M19 . . . .**99** B1
Elmton Rd M9 . . . .**64** F1
Elmtree Dr SK4 . . . .**168** C2
Elmwood M33 . . . .**107** C4
Elmwood Ave WN4 . . . .**73** A2
Elmwood Cl BL5 . . . .**59** A6
Elmwood Ct M32 . . . .**108** C8
Elmwood Dr OL2 . . . .**48** C5
Elmwood Gr Bolton BL1 . . . .**144** C8
Farnworth BL4 . . . .**60** C6
Manchester M9 . . . .**157** F7
Elmwood Lo M20 . . . .**110** A4
Elmwood Pk SK15 . . . .**86** D3
Elnup Ave WN6 . . . .**36** D4
Elnup Wood Nature
Reserve* WN6 . . . .**36** C6
Elsa Rd M19 . . . .**99** C1
Elsdon Dr Atherton M46 . . . . . .**58** E4
🖪 Manchester M18 . . . .**99** D6
Elsdon Gdns 🖪 BL2 . . . .**25** B1
Elsdon Rd M13 . . . .**98** F2
Elsfield Cl BL1 . . . .**143** D2
Elsham Cl BL1 . . . .**143** E1
Elsham Gr M28 . . . .**60** B3
Elsham Gdns M18 . . . .**99** B4
Elsie St Farnworth BL4 . . . .**60** C7

Elsie St continued
Manchester M9 . . . .**157** E8
Ramsbottom BL0 . . . .**11** A4
Elsinore Ave M44 . . . .**94** A1
Elsinore Bsns Pk M16 . . . . . .**97** A4
Elsinore Cl M35 . . . .**84** B7
Elsinore Rd M16 . . . .**97** A4
Elsinore St BL2 . . . .**25** B3
Elsma Rd M40 . . . .**83** E4
Elsmore Rd M14 . . . .**110** A8
Elson Dr SK14 . . . .**113** D7
Elson St BL8 . . . .**27** B4
Elstead Gr WN4 . . . .**72** D4
Elstead Wlk M9 . . . .**64** A3
Elsted Rd OL3 . . . .**68** E5
Elston Ave M40 . . . .**83** C5
Elstree Ave M40 . . . .**83** B4
Elstree Ct M41 . . . .**95** D2
Elswick Ave Bolton BL3 . . . .**144** B5
Bramhall SK7 . . . .**132** E7
Manchester M21 . . . .**109** D4
Elsworth Cl M26 . . . .**44** B1
Elsworth Dr BL1 . . . .**143** F4
Elsworth St M3 . . . .**159** A4
Elterwater Cl BL8 . . . .**27** B4
Elterwater Rd BL4 . . . .**59** E7
Eltham Ave SK2 . . . .**124** C5
Eltham Cl WN4 . . . .**73** D3
Eltham Dr M41 . . . .**95** C5
Eltham St 🔟 M19 . . . .**99** A2
Elton Ave Farnworth BL4 . . . . .**59** F8
Manchester M19 . . . .**111** A8
Elton Bank 🖪 SK13 . . . .**171** D1
Elton Brook Cl BL8 . . . .**27** C3
Elton Cl
🖪 Gamesley SK13 . . . .**171** D1
Golborne WA3 . . . .**90** E7
Handforth SK9 . . . .**131** E1
Whitefield M45 . . . .**63** A8
Elton Com Prim Sch BL8 . . . .**27** C4
Elton Dr 🖪 M11 . . . .**83** C2
Elton High Sch The BL8 . . . . .**27** A4
Elton Ho WN5 . . . .**54** D7
Elton Lea 🖪 SK13 . . . .**171** D1
Elton Pl 🔟 SK13 . . . .**171** D1
Elton Rd M33 . . . .**107** E2
Elton St Bolton BL2 . . . .**148** A7
Rochdale OL11 . . . .**139** A6
🖪 Salford M7 . . . .**158** E3
Stretford M32 . . . .**96** F5
Elton Vale Rd BL8 . . . .**27** B2
Elton's Yd M7 . . . .**158** D3
Elvate Cres M8 . . . .**155** F5
Elverdon Cl M15 . . . .**162** E5
Elverston St M22 . . . .**109** E1
Elverston Way OL9 . . . .**152** C8
Elvey St M40 . . . .**157** F5
Elvington Cl WN5 . . . .**36** B1
Elvington Cres 🔟 M28 . . . . . .**78** C8
Elvira Cl M35 . . . .**84** B7
Elworth Ave M19 . . . .**111** A8
Elwick Cl 🖪 M16 . . . .**97** F3
Elworth Way 🖪 SK9 . . . .**131** D4
Elworthy Gr WN1 . . . .**37** E2
Elwyn Ave M22 . . . .**121** D7
Ely Ave M32 . . . .**95** F3
Ely Cl M28 . . . .**78** B8
Ely Cres M35 . . . .**83** F5
Ely Dr Bury BL8 . . . .**140** D4
Tyldesley M29 . . . .**77** C7
Ely Gdns M41 . . . .**95** E2
Ely Gr BL1 . . . .**143** E1
Ely St OL9 . . . .**152** B5
Elysian Fields M6 . . . .**80** C3
Elysian St M11 . . . .**99** E7
Embankment Bsns Pk The
SK4 . . . .**110** F1
Embankment Rd BL7 . . . .**9** C5
Embassy Wlk M18 . . . .**99** D4
Ember St M11 . . . .**83** D2
Embla Wlk 🗗 BL3 . . . .**42** A4
Emblem St BL3 . . . .**145** D5
Embleton Cl BL2 . . . .**25** E1
Embleton Wlk M18 . . . .**165** C6
Embsay Cl BL1 . . . .**24** D5
Emerald Ave WN7 . . . .**75** E4
Emerald Cotts BL8 . . . .**10** F3
Emerald Ct OL1 . . . .**49** E3
Emerald Rd M22 . . . .**130** F7
Emerald St 🖪 Bolton BL1 . . .**143** F3
Denton M34 . . . .**100** E3
Wigan WN6 . . . .**37** A3
Emerson Ave M30 . . . .**80** A3
Emerson Dr M24 . . . .**46** F1
Emerson St Salford M5 . . . . .**154** D2
Swinton M27 . . . .**61** F1
Emery Ave M21 . . . .**109** C6
Emery Cl
Altrincham WA14 . . . .**119** D7
Manchester SK4 . . . .**168** A4
Emily Beavan Cl M11 . . . .**83** B1
Emily Pl M43 . . . .**83** F1
Emley St M19 . . . .**99** B1
Emlyn Gr SK8 . . . .**123** A6
Emlyn St Farnworth BL4 . . . . . .**42** C1
🖪 Hindley WN2 . . . .**56** D5
Swinton M27 . . . .**79** D8
Walkden M28 . . . .**60** D3
Emma St Oldham OL8 . . . .**66** F3
Rochdale OL12 . . . .**139** E8
Emmanuel Christian Sch
OL12 . . . .**14** D2
Emmanuel Cl BL3 . . . .**145** D5
Emmanuel Ct WN3 . . . .**54** D3
Emmanuel Holcombe CE
Prim Sch BL8 . . . .**138** A4
Emmanuel Pl BL3 . . . .**145** D5

Emmeline Grange M6 . . . .**154** E2
Emmett St BL6 . . . .**22** B3
Emmett St E M40 . . . .**157** E5
Emmett Cl OL10 . . . .**29** C2
Emmott St OL1 . . . .**153** F6
Emmous Wlk M6 . . . .**154** F3
Empire Rd Bolton BL2 . . . .**42** E7
Dukinfield SK16 . . . .**101** C6
Empire St M3,M48 . . . .**158** F4
Empress Ave 🖪 SK5 . . . . . .**125** C5
Empress Bsns Ctr M16 . . . . .**161** C6
Empress Ct M15 . . . .**161** C6
Empress Dr Leigh WN7 . . . . . .**76** B6
Reddish SK4 . . . .**169** D4
Empress Ind Est WN2 . . . . . .**151** F7
Empress St Bolton BL1 . . . . .**143** A2
Manchester,City Park M16 . . .**161** A6
Manchester,Crumpsall M8 . . .**155** F8
Emsworth Cl 🖪 BL2 . . . .**25** B1
Emsworth Dr M33 . . . .**108** C1
Ena Cres WN7 . . . .**75** C7
Ena St Bolton BL3 . . . .**42** A3
Oldham OL1 . . . .**49** A1
Enbridge St M5 . . . .**161** A8
Encombe Pl M3 . . . .**158** D2
Endcott Cl M18 . . . .**165** B6
Enderby Rd M40 . . . .**65** C1
Ending Rake OL12 . . . .**14** C4
Endon Dr M21 . . . .**109** F8
Endon St BL1 . . . .**142** B1
Endsleigh Gdns 🔟 WN7 . . . .**75** F5
Endsleigh Rd M20 . . . .**110** C6
Endsley Ave M28 . . . .**60** C1
Energy St M40 . . . .**160** E3
Enfield Ave
Manchester M19 . . . .**111** A6
Oldham OL8 . . . .**66** E3
Enfield Cl Bolton BL1 . . . .**143** E1
Bury BL9 . . . .**44** F5
Eccles M30 . . . .**95** D8
Rochdale OL11 . . . .**29** E8
Enfield Dr 🔟 M11 . . . .**83** C2
Enfield Gr WN7 . . . .**76** B6
Enfield Ho M30 . . . .**95** D8
Enfield Rd Eccles M30 . . . .**79** D4
Swinton M27 . . . .**79** E6
Enfield St Hyde SK14 . . . .**113** E7
Walkden M28 . . . .**60** A5
Wigan WN5 . . . .**54** C5
Enford Ave M22 . . . .**121** A2
Engell Cl M18 . . . .**99** D5
Engels Ho Eccles M30 . . . .**95** D8
Manchester M14 . . . .**110** D8
Engine Fold Rd M28 . . . .**60** A3
Engine La M29 . . . .**59** B8
Engine St OL10 . . . .**64** B4
Engineer St 🔟 WN2 . . . .**56** A7
Engledene BL1 . . . .**24** D6
Englefield Gr 🖪 M18 . . . .**99** D4
English Martyrs' RC Prim Sch
M41 . . . .**95** A2
English St WN7 . . . .**76** A4
Enid Cl M7 . . . .**155** D5
Enid Pl WN2 . . . .**73** F8
Ennerdale Ave
Ashton-in-M WN4 . . . .**73** B5
Billinge WA11 . . . .**71** B1
🖪 Bolton BL2 . . . .**25** F1
Manchester M21 . . . .**109** D4
Royton OL2 . . . .**48** C7
Swinton M27 . . . .**79** F6
Ennerdale Cl BL3 . . . .**42** F3
Ennerdale Dr Gatley SK8 . . .**122** B3
Sale,Ashton upon Mersey
M33 . . . .**107** E5
Sale,Timperley WA15 . . . .**120** A8
Whitefield BL9 . . . .**45** A2
Ennerdale Gdns BL2 . . . .**25** E1
Ennerdale Gr
Ashton-u-L OL7 . . . .**84** F5
Farnworth BL4 . . . .**59** E8
Ennerdale Pl WN2 . . . .**56** B8
Ennerdale Rd
Hindley WN2 . . . .**56** E5
Leigh WN7 . . . .**76** C4
Middleton M24 . . . .**46** F2
Partition M31 . . . .**105** E3
Rochdale OL11 . . . .**30** B4
Romiley SK6 . . . .**113** B4
Stockport SK1 . . . .**124** B7
Stretford M32 . . . .**96** C3
Tyldesley M29 . . . .**77** B7
Ennerdale Terr SK15 . . . .**86** A3
Ennis Cl M23 . . . .**120** E5
Ennismore Ave M5,M30 . . . . . .**80** A2
Ensor Way SK22 . . . .**127** D1
Enstone Dr M40 . . . .**65** D1
Enstone Way M29 . . . .**59** C1
Enterprise Pk BL6 . . . .**39** C8
Enterprise Trad Est
Manchester M18 . . . .**99** E6
Stretford M31 . . . .**96** A8
Enterprise Way M41 . . . .**91** A7
Enticott Rd M44 . . . .**105** C5
Entwisle Ave M41 . . . .**95** B4
Entwisle Rd OL16 . . . .**31** A8
Entwisle Row M41 . . . .**60** D8
Entwisle St
🔟 Farnworth BL4 . . . .**42** E1
Milnrow OL16 . . . .**31** E6
Swinton M27 . . . .**61** D1
Entwistle Gr WN7 . . . .**76** C3
Entwistle Hall La BL7 . . . .**9** B8
Entwistle St BL2 . . . .**148** B8
Entwistle St M26 . . . .**44** A3
Enver Rd M8 . . . .**156** B8
Enville Rd
Altrincham WA14 . . . .**119** C3

Enville Rd continued
Manchester M40 . . . .**65** B1
Pendlebury M6 . . . .**80** E6
Enville St Ashton-u-L OL6 . . .**166** C3
Denton M34 . . . .**100** F7
Manchester M9 . . . .**64** D3
Envoy Cl WN5 . . . .**36** E1
Enys Wlk M6 . . . .**81** A5
Ephraim's Fold WN2 . . . .**38** D6
Epping Cl Ashton-u-L OL6 . . . .**85** C7
Chadderton OL9 . . . .**47** F4
Epping Dr M33 . . . .**107** C5
Epping Rd M34 . . . .**100** B3
Epping Wlk M15 . . . .**163** A6
Eppleworth Rise M27 . . . .**62** A3
Epsley Cl M15 . . . .**163** A6
Epsom Ave
Hand'forth SK8,SK9 . . . .**131** E4
Manchester M19 . . . .**110** F6
Sale M33 . . . .**107** C2
Epsom Cl
Hazel Grove SK7 . . . .**124** F3
Rochdale OL11 . . . .**29** F8
Epsom Croft PR6 . . . .**21** B7
Epsom Dr WN2 . . . .**73** F7
Epsom Mews M7 . . . .**155** D6
Epsom Wlk OL9 . . . .**152** C7
Epworth Ct SK4 . . . .**168** B3
Epworth Gr 🖪 BL3 . . . .**146** C3
Epworth St M4 . . . .**159** C1
Equitable St Milnrow OL16 . . .**31** F5
Oldham OL4 . . . .**67** D8
🖪 Rochdale OL11 . . . .**31** A6
Era St Bolton BL2 . . . .**42** E7
Sale M33 . . . .**108** B4
Ercall Ave M12 . . . .**164** E6
Eric Brook Cl 🖪 M14 . . . .**98** A3
Eric Bullows Cl M22 . . . .**121** C1
Eric St Littleborough OL15 . . . .**16** A6
Oldham OL4 . . . .**67** C6
Erica Ave OL4 . . . .**49** F4
Erica Cl 🖪 SK5 . . . .**100** A1
Erica Dr M19 . . . .**110** E4
Erica Wlk WN7 . . . .**75** B5
Erin St M11 . . . .**99** E7
Erindale Wlk M40 . . . .**156** C6
Erith Cl SK5 . . . .**112** B6
Erith Rd OL4 . . . .**67** C6
Erlesmere Ave M34 . . . .**101** A4
Erlesmere Cl OL4 . . . .**49** F4
Erlington Ave M16 . . . .**97** B2
Ermen Rd M30 . . . .**95** C8
Ermington Ct OL10 . . . .**29** C1
Ermington Dr M8 . . . .**155** F6
Emeley Cl M12 . . . .**99** B3
Ernest St Bacup OL13 . . . .**4** C8
Bolton BL1 . . . .**145** D7
Cheadle SK8 . . . .**122** C6
Prestwich M25 . . . .**62** F4
Stockport SK3 . . . .**123** E4
Ernest Terr OL12 . . . .**15** B1
Ernlouen Ave BL1 . . . .**144** A8
Ernocroft Gr SK6 . . . .**114** E3
Ernocroft La SK6 . . . .**115** A1
Ernocroft Rd SK6 . . . .**114** B1
Erradale Cres WN3 . . . .**54** D2
Errington Cl SK2 . . . .**124** E6
Errington Dr M7 . . . .**158** D4
Errol Ave M9 . . . .**64** A5
Errwood Cres M19 . . . .**111** A8
Errwood Rd M19 . . . .**111** A7
Erskine Cl BL3 . . . .**40** E5
Erskine Pl WN2 . . . .**56** B1
Erskine Rd Manchester M9 . . .**64** E1
Partington M31 . . . .**105** F3
Erskine St
Manchester M15 . . . .**162** D6
Romiley SK6 . . . .**114** B3
Erwin St M40 . . . .**83** B6
Escott St 🖪 M16 . . . .**97** F3
Esher Dr M23,M33 . . . .**108** C1
Esk Ave BL0 . . . .**1** D5
Esk Cl M41 . . . .**95** A4
Eskdale SK8 . . . .**122** C4
Eskdale Ave Bolton BL2 . . . . .**25** F2
Bramhall SK7 . . . .**132** C5
Manchester M20 . . . .**110** A7
Rochdale OL11 . . . .**30** B4
Romiley SK6 . . . .**113** B5
Royton OL2 . . . .**48** D7
Scot Lane End BL6 . . . .**38** D5
Uppermill OL3 . . . .**69** B5
Wigan WN3 . . . .**37** B3
Eskdale Cl BL9 . . . .**45** A3
Eskdale Dr
Altrincham WA15 . . . .**120** C7
Middleton M24 . . . .**46** F3
Eskdale Ho 🖪 M13 . . . .**98** E4
Eskdale Mews OL3 . . . .**69** B5
Eskdale Rd
Ashton-in-M WN4 . . . .**73** B4
Hindley WN2 . . . .**56** E5
Eskdale Terr SK15 . . . .**86** A4
Eskrick St BL1 . . . .**143** D2
Eskrigge Cl M7 . . . .**155** F8
Esmond Rd M8 . . . .**156** A7
Esmont Dr M24 . . . .**46** E3
Esplanade The OL16 . . . .**139** E7
Essex Ave Droylsden M43 . . . .**84** A3
Heywood BL9 . . . .**27** A6
Manchester M20 . . . .**110** B4
Stockport SK3 . . . .**123** B8
Essex Cl Failsworth M35 . . . . .**83** F5

Essex Cl *continued*
Shaw OL2 48 F7
Essex Dr BL9 45 A8
Essex Gdns M44 105 C4
Essex Pl Swinton M27 61 F2
Tyldesley M29 58 F3
Essex Rd Brinnington SK5 112 C5
Reddish M18 99 F4
Standish WN1 37 B8
Essex St Horwich BL6 22 D1
Manchester M2 158 F1
Rochdale OL11 139 F6
Wigan WN1 37 E1
Essex Way M15,M16 162 D5
Essingdon St BL3 147 D4
Essington Wlk M34 100 E1
Essoldo Cl M18 165 C5
Est Bank Rd BL0 11 A3
Estate St OL8 66 F4
Estate St S 3 OL8 66 F4
Estcourt Prep Sch for Girls
OL8 66 D4
Esther Fold BL5 57 E8
Esther St OL4 67 D7
Esthwaite Dr M29 77 A7
Eston St M13 98 D4
Estonfield Dr M41 95 F2
Eswick St M11 83 C1
Etchell St M40 156 C5
Etchells Prim Sch SK8 122 C1
Etchells Rd SK8 122 D1
Etchells St SK1 169 F1
Etharow Ct SK14 167 E2
Ethel Ave Manchester M9 64 D5
Pendlebury M27 80 B8
Ethel Ct OL16 31 B6
Ethel St Bolton BL3 145 D6
Oldham OL8 66 F3
Rochdale OL16 31 B6
Whitworth OL12 4 D2
Ethel Terr M19 99 A1
Etherley Cl 4 M44 94 A2
Etherow Ave
Failsworth M40 65 F2
Romiley SK6 113 E2
Etherow Brow SK14 115 B8
Etherow Ctry Pk SK6 114 C4
Etherow Ctry Pk Visitors
Ctr* SK6 114 B2
Etherow Ind Est SK13 171 D3
Etherow Way SK13 103 E5
Etherstone St Leigh WN7 75 E4
Manchester M8 156 C8
Eton Ave OL8 66 E3
Eton Cl Manchester M16 162 D5
Rochdale OL11 30 B6
Eton Ct M16 162 D5
Eton Dr SK8 122 D2
Eton Hill Ind Est M26 44 C5
Eton Hill Rd M26 44 C5
Eton Pl M26 43 F3
Eton St WN7 75 F3
Eton Terr WN3 151 E5
Eton Way WN5 53 F8
Eton Way N M26 44 C5
Eton Way S M26 44 D5
Etruria Cl M13 164 E5
Ettington Cl BL8 27 A3
Ettrick Cl M11 99 D7
Euan Pl 2 M33 108 C4
Euclid Cl M11 160 E1
Euro Ctr The M8 158 E4
Europa Bsns Pk SK3 123 B6
Europa Circ M17 96 D5
Europa Gate M17 96 D5
Europa Trad Est M26 61 B7
Europa Way Cheadle SK3 123 B6
Kearsley M26 61 B7
Stretford M17 96 D5
Eustace St Bolton BL3 42 A3
Chadderton OL9 152 C8
Euston Ave M9 65 A3
Euxton Cl BL8 27 A1
Eva Rd SK3 123 A7
Eva St Leigh WN7 75 C7
Manchester M14 98 C3
Rochdale OL12 15 A2
Evan Cl WN6 36 D4
Evan St M40 157 E5
Evans Cl M20 110 A3
Evans Rd M30 79 A1
Evans St Ashton-u-L OL6 85 D4
Horwich BL6 22 D4
Leigh WN7 75 F5
Middleton M24 65 B8
Oldham OL1 153 F8
Salford M3 158 E3
Evanstone Cl BL6 22 B3
Evanton Wlk 13 M9 157 E7
Eve St OL8 66 F2
Evelyn St
Manchester M14 110 D8
Oldham OL1 49 B1
Evenholm WA14 119 B2
Evening St M35 83 F8
Evenley Cl 1 M18 99 E6
Everard Cl M28 78 C8
Everard St M5 161 C7
Everbrom Rd BL3 146 A3
Everdingen Wlk OL1 49 D3
Everest Ave OL7 85 B5
Everest Cl SK14 102 A4
Everest Pl 4 WN1 37 C2
Everest Rd Atherton M46 58 C5
Dukinfield SK14 102 A4
Everest St OL11 31 A2
Everett Ct 4 M20 110 B6
Everett Rd M20 110 B6
Everglade OL8 67 A1
Evergreen Wlk 4 M33 107 C6
Everleigh Cl BL2 25 E5
Everleigh Dr M7 155 F6
Eversden Ct M7 158 E4
Eversley Ct M33 108 B2
Eversley Rd M20 110 A3
Everton Rd Oldham OL8 66 D3
Reddish SK5 99 F2
Everton St
Downall Green WN4 72 D5
Swinton M27 79 E8
Every St Bury BL9 140 F4
Manchester M4 160 D1
Ramsbottom BL0 11 D6
Evesham Ave
4 Hadfield SK13 104 A5
Manchester SK4 168 B3
Wythenshawe M23 120 D7
Evesham Cl
11 Bolton BL3 145 D6
Leigh WN7 75 E1
Middleton M24 65 B5
Evesham Dr
Farnworth BL3,BL4 42 B2
Handforth SK9 131 C2
Evesham Gdns M24 65 A5
Evesham Gr
Ashton-u-L OL6 85 C7
Sale M33 108 E4
Evesham Rd Cheadle SK8 123 A4
Manchester M9 65 A2
Middleton M24 65 B5
Evesham Wlk
10 Bolton BL3 145 D6
Middleton M24 65 B5
Oldham OL8 153 E5
Eveside Cl SK8 123 B4
Evington Ave M11 100 A7
Ewan St M18 99 D6
Ewart Ave M5 81 A1
Ewart St BL1 143 E2
Ewhurst Ave M27 79 D6
Ewing Cl M8 64 A1
Ewing Sch M20 110 A5
Ewood 12 Eccles M30 79 F2
Oldham OL8 85 A8
Ewood Dr BL8 44 A8
Ewood La BB4 1 C7
Exbourne Rd M22 121 C1
Exbridge Wlk M40 83 D4
Exbury 24 OL12 139 E8
Exbury St M14 110 D7
Excalibur Way M44 105 F7
Excelsior Gdns OL10 46 F8
Excelsior Terr OL15 15 F3
Exchange Quay M5 161 A6
Exchange Quay Sta M5 161 A6
Exchange Sq M4 158 F2
Exchange St
9 Bolton BL1 145 F7
Edenfield BL0 1 D3
Manchester M2 158 F1
5 Oldham OL4 67 B7
Stockport SK3 169 E1
Exeter Ave Bolton BL2 25 B2
Denton M34 100 F1
Farnworth BL4 59 F8
Radcliffe M26 43 E5
Salford M30 80 A4
Exeter Cl Cheadle SK8 131 F8
Dukinfield SK16 101 D6
Exeter Ct
Manchester M14 110 C7
3 Middleton M24 46 F1
Exeter Dr Ashton-u-L OL6 85 D7
Aspull WN2 38 D5
Irlam M44 94 B2
Exeter Gr OL11 139 F5
Exeter Rd
Brinnington SK5 112 C5
Hindley WN2 56 E5
Urmston M41 95 D4
Exeter St Rochdale OL11 139 F5
Salford M6 154 E2
Exeter Wlk SK7 132 F7
Exford Ave WN3 55 B4
Exford Cl
Manchester M40 160 D3
Reddish SK5 111 F6
Exford Dr BL2 43 A6
Exhall Cl M38 60 A6
Exit Rd W M90 130 B7
Exmoor Cl OL6 85 C7
Exmouth Ave SK5 112 C5
Exmouth Pl OL16 31 A4
Exmouth Rd M33 107 D5
Exmouth Sq OL16 31 A3
Exmouth St OL16 31 A3
Eyam Cl 12 SK13 171 D2
Eyam Fold 16 SK13 171 E2
Eyam Gdns 25 SK13 171 D2
Eyam Gn 13 SK13 171 D2
Eyam Gr
11 Gamesley SK13 171 D2
Stockport SK2 124 D5
Eyam La SK13 171 D2
Eyam Lea 15 SK13 171 E2
Eyam Mews SK13 171 D2
Eyam Rd SK7 124 E1
Eyebrook Rd WA14 119 A2
Eyet St WN7 75 E5
Eynford Ave SK5 112 B6
Eyre St M15 163 A5

F

Faber St M4 159 A3
Factory Brow
Blackrod BL6 21 D3
Middleton M24 64 C7
Factory Hill BL6 22 D4
Factory La Adlington PR6 21 B8
Manchester M9 64 D1
Salford M3 158 D1
Factory St Middleton M24 64 F8
Radcliffe M26 44 B3
Ramsbottom BL0 138 C7
Tyldesley M29 58 F1
Factory St E M46 58 C3
Factory St W M46 58 C3
Faggy La WN3 150 C7
Failsworth Ind Est 2
M40 83 C6
Failsworth Rd M35 84 C7
Failsworth Sch M35 84 A7
Failsworth Sch (Lower)
M35 83 F7
Failsworth Sh Ctr 1 M35 83 F7
Failsworth Sta M35 83 E8
Fair Acres BL2 25 E3
Fair Hill BB4 1 A7
Fair Oak Rd M19 110 F5
Fair St Bolton BL3 146 C2
Manchester M1 159 C1
Swinton M27 62 A1
Fair View Bacup OL13 4 C8
Billinge WN5 71 D5
Littleborough OL15 16 C7
Fair View Ave WN5 71 D5
Fair Way OL11 30 B1
Fairacres WN6 19 B1
Fairacres Rd SK6 134 E8
Fairbairn St BL6 22 B3
Fairbank M43 99 F8
Fairbank Ave M14 98 B4
Fairbank Dr M24 46 D2
Fairbottom St OL1 153 F7
Fairbottom Wlk 4 M43 100 A8
Fairbourne Ave
Alderley Edge SK9 137 B3
Wigan WN3 55 A4
Wilmslow SK9 136 F4
Fairbourne Cl SK9 136 F4
Fairbourne Dr
Sale WA15 108 B1
Wilmslow SK9 136 F4
Fairbourne Rd
Denton M34 100 E2
Reddish M19 99 C1
Fairbrook Dr M6 154 E2
Fairbrother St M5 161 C7
Fairburn Cl M41 95 A4
Fairclough St Bolton BL3 42 A4
Droylsden M11 83 A2
Hindley WN2 56 D6
Newton-le-W WA12 89 B3
Wigan WN1 151 D7
Faircroft Cl SK2 124 E7
Fairfax Ave
Altrincham WA15 120 A6
Manchester M20 110 B4
Fairfax Cl SK6 125 D7
Fairfax Dr
Littleborough OL15 15 F3
Wilmslow SK9 136 F4
Fairfax Rd M25 63 A5
Fairfield OL6 85 C8
Fairfield Ave
Cheadle SK8 122 F2
Droylsden M43 100 A7
Platt Bridge WN2 56 A3
Romiley SK6 113 A4
Wigan WN5 54 D5
Fairfield Com Prim Sch
BL9 28 D3
Fairfield Ct
Droylsden M43 100 A8
Manchester M14 98 D4
Fairfield Dr BL9 28 D3
Fairfield General Hospl
BL9 28 E4
Fairfield High Sch for Girls
M43 100 A8
Fairfield Ho M43 84 A1
Fairfield Rd
Altrincham WA15 120 C5
Droylsden M43 99 F8
Farnworth BL4 60 C7
Irlam M44 105 C5
Middleton M24 46 E1
Fairfield Road Prim Sch
M43 99 F8
Fairfield Sq M43 100 A8
Fairfield St
Manchester M1,M12 163 C8
Salford M6 80 E5
Wigan WN5 54 D5
Fairfield Sta M34 100 A7
Fairfield View M34 100 A7
Fairfields Bolton BL7 24 F8
Oldham OL8 66 E2
Fairford Cl SK5 111 F5
Fairford Dr BL3 145 E5
Fairford Way
Reddish SK5 111 F5
Wilmslow SK9 137 D7
Fairham Wlk M12 160 D1
Fairhaven Ave
Manchester M21 109 B8
Westhoughton BL5 58 B8
Whitefield M45 62 D7
Fairhaven Cl SK7 132 F8
Fairhaven Cvn Pk SK14 101 C2
Fairhaven Rd BL1 143 F3
Fairhaven St M12 164 F6
Fairhill Terr BB4 1 A7
Fairhills Ind Est M44 105 F8
Fairhills Rd M44 106 A8
Fairholme Ave
Ashton-in-M WN4 73 B4
Urmston M41 95 C1
Fairholme Rd
Manchester,Heaton Norris
SK4 168 C3
Manchester,Withington
M20 110 C6
Fairhope Ave M6 80 C3
Fairhurst Ave WN6 19 D3
Fairhurst Dr M28 59 F2
Fairhurst St Leigh WN7 75 E5
Wigan WN3 150 B8
Fairisle Cl M11 160 F1
Fairlands Pl OL11 31 B2
Fairlands Rd Bury BL9 27 F6
Sale M33 107 F2
Fairlands St OL11 31 B2
Fairlands View OL11 31 B2
Fairlawn SK4 169 D3
Fairlawn Cl M14 98 A4
Fairlea M34 101 A2
Fairlea Ave M20 110 C2
Fairlee Ave M34 84 C1
Fairleigh Ave M6 80 C3
Fairless Rd M30 79 D1
Fairlie Ave BL3 40 F5
Fairlie Dr WA15 120 B8
Fairlyn Cl BL5 59 A7
Fairlyn Dr BL5 59 A7
Fairman St M16 97 F3
Fairmead Rd M23 109 C1
Fairmile Dr M20 122 C8
Fairmount Ave BL2 42 E8
Fairmount Rd M27 79 C6
Fairoak Ct BL3 145 D5
Fairstead Cl BL5 57 D8
Fairstead Wlk 4 M11 99 F7
Fairthorne Grange 7
OL7 84 F1
Fairview Ave
Manchester M19 98 F2
Reddish M34 100 A1
Fairview Cl
Ashton-in-M WN4 73 B4
Chadderton OL9 65 F8
Marple SK6 125 F7
Rochdale OL12 13 C2
Fairview Dr
Adlington PR6,PR7 20 F8
Marple SK6 125 F7
Fairview Rd
Altrincham WA15 120 C5
Reddish M34 100 A1
Fairview Residential Cvn Pk
M46 58 B4
Fairway Bramhall SK7 132 D6
Droylsden M43 100 A8
Gatley SK8 122 B4
Manchester M25 63 D2
Milnrow OL16 32 A6
Pendlebury M27 80 C7
Whitworth OL12 14 C7
Fairway Ave Bolton BL2 26 A4
Wythenshawe M23 120 D7
Fairway Cres OL2 48 D6
Fairway Ct M34 100 B4
Fairway Dr M33 107 E2
Fairway Prim Sch SK2 124 E7
Fairway Rd Oldham OL4 67 E4
Whitefield BL9 45 A3
Fairway The
Failsworth M40 83 C8
Stockport SK2 124 D7
Fairways BL6 22 C3
Fairways Cl SK13 104 F1
Fairways The
Garswood WN4 72 D2
Westhoughton BL5 57 E8
Whitefield M45 62 F6
Fairwood Rd M23 120 D7
Fairy La Manchester M8 155 E5
Wythenshawe M23 109 A3
Fairy St BL8 27 C2
Fairywell Cl SK9 131 D1
Fairywell Dr M33 108 A1
Fairywell Rd WA15 120 C7
Faith St Bolton BL1 142 A1
Leigh WN7 75 C5
Falcon Ave M41 95 E2
Falcon Bsns Ctr OL9 152 C8
Falcon Cl Bury BL9 141 B4
Leigh WN7 76 B5
Rochdale OL12 13 E2
Falcon Cres M27 62 C2
Falcon Ct
Manchester M15 162 E5
Salford M7 155 D8
Falcon Dr
Chadderton OL9 152 C8
Irlam M44 94 B4
Middleton M24 46 E3
Walkden M38 60 A5
Falcon St Bolton BL1 145 F8
Oldham OL8 153 F5
Falconers Gn WN3 150 B5
Falconwood Chase M28 78 C6
Falconwood Cl 12 WN6 37 A1
Falfield Dr M8 156 B5
Falinge Fold OL12 14 D1
Falinge Mews OL12 139 E8
Falinge Park High Sch
OL12 14 D1
Falinge Rd OL12 14 E1
Falkirk Dr Bolton BL2 42 F6
Ince-in-M WN2 56 A8
Falkirk Gr WN5 54 C8
Falkirk St 4 OL4 67 C7
Falkirk Wlk 5 M23 121 A2
Falkland Ave
Manchester M40 160 D4
Rochdale OL11 30 C8
Falkland Cl OL4 49 E4
Falkland Dr WN4 72 C4
Falkland Ho M14 98 C1
Falkland Rd BL2 43 A7
Fall Bank SK4 111 D6
Fall Birch Hospl BL6 23 A1
Fall Birch Rd BL6 39 F8
Fallons Rd M28 61 C1
Fallow Cl BL5 39 E2
Fallow Fields Dr SK5 100 A1
Fallowfield Ave M5 161 B7
Fallowfield Dr OL12 14 D2
Fallowfield Sh Ctr M14 98 E1
Fallowfield Way M46 58 E1
Fallows The OL9 152 A5
Falls Gr SK8 122 A3
Falmer Cl Bury BL8 27 C6
Droylsden M18 99 F6
Falmer Dr M22 121 D1
Falmouth Ave Sale M33 107 D5
Urmston M41 94 E3
Falmouth Cres SK5 112 C5
Falmouth Rd M44 94 B2
Falmouth St
Manchester M40 160 F4
Oldham OL8 66 F4
19 Rochdale OL11 31 A5
Falsgrave Cl M40 83 A5
Falshaw Dr BL9 11 E1
Falside Wlk 17 M40 83 C5
Falstaff Mews SK6 113 A3
Falston Ave M40 65 D2
Falstone Ave BL0 11 C4
Falstone Cl WN3 54 E2
Falterley Rd M23 120 F8
Fancroft Rd M22 121 C5
Fane Wlk M9 64 B3
Far Cromwell Rd SK6 112 D7
Far Hey Cl M26 43 E3
Far La M18 99 D4
Far Ridings SK6 113 D3
Far Woodseats La SK14 114 F5
Faraday Ave
Manchester M8 156 A6
Swinton M27 62 D2
Faraday Dr BL1 143 E1
Faraday Rd WN6 150 A8
Faraday Rise OL12 14 B1
Faraday St M1 159 B1
Farcroft Ave M26 44 C6
Farcroft Cl M23 120 F8
Fardale OL2 149 B6
Farden Dr M23 120 D8
Fardon Cl WN3 54 F3
Farefield Ave WA3 73 F2
Farewell Cl 1 OL11 30 C2
Farholme OL1 48 C2
Farholme La OL13 3 D8
Faringdon 4 OL11 139 E6
Faringdon Wlk BL3 145 E5
Farland Pl BL3 40 F5
Farlands Dr M20 122 B7
Farlands Rise OL16 31 C3
Farleigh Cl BL5 40 A2
Farley Ave M18 100 A4
Farley Ct SK8 122 F3
Farley La WN8 35 A3
Farley Rd M33 108 C2
Farley Way SK5 99 E1
Farm Ave Adlington PR6 21 A8
Stretford M32 96 A4
Farm Cl Bury BL8 26 F6
Reddish SK4 111 C6
Farm La Eccles M28 78 F5
High Lane SK12 135 A6
Hyde SK14 113 D8
Middleton M25 63 E8
Wigan WN2 38 A2
Farm Meadow Rd WN5 53 E5
Farm Rd OL8 84 C8
Farm Side Pl 10 M19 99 A1
Farm St
Chadderton OL1,OL9 48 B1
Failsworth M35 83 E6
Heywood OL10 46 E8
Farm Way WA12 89 E1
Farm Wlk
Altrincham WA14 118 E1
Littleborough OL15 15 F5
Rochdale OL16 15 C1
Farm Yd M19 99 A1
Farman St BL3 147 D3
Farmer St SK4 169 E3
Farmers Cl M33 109 A3
Farmfield M33 107 E6
Farmfold SK9 130 F3
Farmlands Wlk OL1 49 C4
Farmside Ave M44 94 A3
Farmstead Cl M35 84 C6
Farmway M24 65 A7
Farn Ave SK5 99 F2
Farnborough Ave OL4 67 D6
Farnborough Rd
Bolton BL1 24 E6

Farnborough Rd continued
Manchester M40 ......160 D3
Farncombe Cl 2 M23 ..120 D7
Farndale Gr WN4 ......73 C2
Farndale Sq M38 ......60 C3
Farndale Wlk 17 M9 ..157 E8
Farndon Ave SK7 ......124 F4
Farndon Cl M33 ......108 E3
Farndon Dr WA15 ......120 A6
Farndon Rd SK5 ......99 E2
Farnham Ave M9 ......64 D5
Farnham Cl
21 Bolton BL1 ......143 E1
Cheadle SK8 ......132 A7
Leigh WN7 ......75 F6
Farnham Dr M44 ......94 B1
Farnhill Wlk M23 ......108 E1
Farnley Cl OL12 ......13 F2
Farnsfield WN1 ......37 F1
Farnsworth Ave OL7 ...85 B5
Farnsworth Cl OL7 ...85 B5
Farnworth Dr M41 ......72 C8
7 Heywood OL10 ......29 C2
6 Leigh WN7 ......76 B4
Farnworth St Bolton BL3 .146 C4
Farnworth Sta BL4 ......42 E1
Farr Cl WN3 ......54 F5
Farr St SK3 ......170 D8
Farrand Rd OL8 ......66 B2
Farrant Rd M12 ......99 A4
Farrar Rd M43 ......99 F8
Farrell St Salford M7 .158 E3
Wigan WN5 ......54 C5
Farrer Rd M13 ......98 F3
Farrier Cl 11 M33 ......108 E3
Farrier's Croft WN6 ...36 E3
Farriers La OL11 ......30 B4
Farringdon Dr M26 ......43 E4
Farringdon St M6 ......154 E3
Farrington Ave M20 ...110 A7
Farrow Dr M30 ......79 B4
Farrow St OL2 ......149 B6
Farrow St E OL2 ......149 B6
Farrowdale Ave OL2 ..149 B6
Farsley Pk BL5 ......39 D4
Farwood Cl M16 ......161 C5
Fastnet St M11 ......165 A8
Fatherford Cl OL3 ......51 D5
Faulkenhurst Mews OL1 ..48 C1
Faulkenhurst St OL1,OL9 .48 C1
Faulkes Ho 3 M14 ......110 D8
Faulkner Dr WA15 ......120 B5
Faulkner Rd M32 ......96 A2
Faulkner St Bolton BL3 .145 E5
Manchester M1 ......163 A8
Rochdale OL16 ......139 F7
Fauvel Pl SK13 ......104 C1
Fauvel Rd SK13 ......104 C1
Faversham Brow 9
OL15 ......16 A5
Faversham St M40 ......83 B7
Fawborough Rd M23 ..108 F1
Fawcett St 2 BL2 ......148 B7
Fawcetts Fold BL5 ......39 E4
Fawley Ave SK14 ......167 D1
Fawley Gr M22 ......121 D4
Fawns Keep
Stalybridge SK15 ......102 E6
Wilmslow SK9 ......137 D7
Fay Ave M9 ......65 B2
Fay Gdns SK13 ......171 E4
Faywood Dr SK6 ......126 A6
Fearn Dene 2 OL12 ...14 B2
Fearn St OL10 ......29 C2
Fearney Side BL3 ......42 F3
Fearnham Cl WN7 ......75 E1
Fearnhead Ave BL6 ...22 B5
Fearnhead Cl BL4 ......60 E8
Fearnhead St BL3 ......146 C4
Fearnley Way WA12 ...89 C1
Fearns Moss OL13 ......3 B6
Feathersfall Brook View 3
OL15 ......16 A5
Featherstall Ho OL9 ..152 C5
Featherstall Rd OL15 .16 A5
Featherstall Rd N OL1,
OL9 ......153 D8
Featherstall Rd S OL9 .153 D6
Featherstall Rd 1 OL15 ..16 A5
Fecit La BL0 ......12 C8
Federation St
Manchester M4 ......159 A2
Prestwich M25 ......62 F5
Feldom Rd M23 ......108 F2
Fell St Bury BL8 ......27 C2
Leigh WN7 ......75 B4
Fellbridge Cl BL5 ......40 B1
Fellbrigg St M18 ......99 C3
Fellfoot Cl M28 ......77 F5
Felling Wlk 6 M14 ....98 B3
Fellpark Rd M23 ......109 A2
Fells Gr M28 ......60 F1
Fellside Bolton BL2 ....26 A4
Oldham OL1 ......153 E7
Wigan WN1 ......37 D2
Fellside Cl BL8 ......10 F1
Fellside Gdns OL15 ...15 F7
Fellside Gn WN15 ......86 A3
Felltop Cl OL4 ......68 C5
Felltop Dr M9 ......112 A8
Felsham Cl BL4 ......42 C1
Felskirk Rd M22 ......130 C8
Felsted BL1 ......40 E8
Felt Cl M34 ......100 C2
Felthorpe Dr M8 ......155 F6

Felton Ave M22 ......121 D3
Felton Cl BL9 ......45 A5
Felton Wlk BL1 ......143 E2
Fence St SK2 ......124 D4
Fencegate Ave SK4 ...111 D5
Fenchurch Ave M40 ...83 C2
Fencot Dr M12 ......99 A4
Fenella St M13 ......98 E4
Fenham Cl M40 ......156 C5
Fenmore Ave M18 ......99 B3
Fenn St M15 ......162 E6
Fennel St M4 ......158 F2
Fenners Cl BL3 ......147 D3
Fenney St M7 ......155 D5
Fenney St E M7 ......155 E6
Fenside Rd M22 ......121 E5
Fenstock Wlk M40 ......83 D4
Fentewan Wlk SK14 ..102 E3
Fenton Mews OL11 ...139 F5
Fenton St Bury BL8 ......27 C3
Manchester M12 ......165 A5
5 Oldham OL4 ......67 B6
Rochdale OL11 ......139 E5
Shaw OL2 ......149 B5
Fenton Way M17 ......96 F1
Fenwick Cl BL5 ......57 F6
Fenwick Dr SK4 ......110 E3
Fenwick St
Manchester M15 ......163 A6
Rochdale OL12 ......139 E7
Ferdinand St M40 ......160 D4
Fereday St M28 ......60 D4
Ferguson Ct M19 ......110 F8
Ferguson Gdns OL12 ...14 F3
Ferguson Rise WN5 ...54 E8
Ferguson Way OL4 ......49 D1
Fern Ave
Newton-le-W WA12 ......89 D2
Urmston M41 ......95 A2
Fern Bank Failsworth M40 .83 C7
Stalybridge SK15 ......86 C1
Fern Bank Cl SK15 ...102 C8
Fern Bank Dr M23 ...120 E8
Fern Bank St SK14 ...113 E8
Fern Cl Atherton M46 ...58 D2
Marple SK6 ......125 F6
Middleton M24 ......65 D8
Shevington WN6 ......36 A6
Fern Clough BL1 ......40 F7
Fern Comm OL2 ......149 B7
Fern Cres SK15 ......86 C1
Fern Hill La OL12 ......14 A3
Fern Ho M23 ......121 A4
Fern Isle Cl OL12 ......14 B6
Fern Lea WA14 ......103 D5
Fern Lea Gr M38 ......59 F4
Fern Lea St BB4 ......2 C8
Fern St Bolton BL3 ...144 C6
Bury BL9 ......140 F3
Chadderton OL9 ......152 A8
Farnworth BL4 ......42 E1
Manchester M8,M8 ...159 A4
11 Rochdale OL11 ......31 A4
Romiley SK6 ......113 A3
Salford M6 ......154 F2
Wigan WN6 ......37 A3

Fernhurst Rd M20 ......110 C5
Fernhurst St OL1,OL9 ...48 C1
Fernie St M4 ......159 A3
Fernilee Cl SK22 ......127 C1
Fernlea Altrincham WA15 .119 F1
Gatley SK8 ......122 A3
Manchester SK4 ......111 C5
Fernlea Ave OL1 ......48 C1
Fernlea Cl Hadfield SK13 ..171 E4
1 Rochdale OL11 ......14 B2
Fernlea Cres M27 ......79 E7
Fernlea Gr M44 ......72 C5
Fernlea Lo BL4 ......60 A7
Fernleaf St M14 ......98 A4
Fernleigh BL1 ......143 E4
Fernleigh Ave M19 ......99 C1
Fernleigh Dr M16 ......162 D5
Fernley Ave M34 ......101 A2
Fernley Rd SK2 ......124 B6
Ferns Gr BL1 ......144 B7
Ferns The OL13 ......4 A8
Fernside M26 ......61 C6
Fernside Ave M20 ......110 D5
Fernside Ct M26 ......61 C6
Fernside Gr Walkden M28 .60 A8
Wigan WN3 ......54 D1
Fernside Way OL12 ......14 A1
Fernstead BL3 ......144 C6
Fernstone Cl BL6 ......22 A3
Fernthorpe Ave OL3 ...51 C1
Fernview Dr BL0 ......11 A1
Fernville Terr 8 OL13 ...3 D8
Fernwood SK6 ......126 C7
Fernwood Ave M18 ......99 D3
Fernwood Gr SK9 ......137 C8
Ferrand Lodge OL15 ...16 C7
Ferrand Rd OL15 ......16 B6
Ferring Wlk M15 ......162 E6
Ferris St M11 ......99 D8
Ferrous Way M44 ......105 F6
Ferryhill Rd M44 ......94 B2
Fettler Cl M27 ......79 F7
Fewston Cl BL1 ......24 E5
Fiddlers La M44 ......94 B3
Fiddlers Lane Com Prim Sch
M44 ......94 B3
Field Bank Gr M19 ......99 C1
Field Cl Bramhall SK7 .132 D4
Marple SK6 ......125 D5
Field Cotts OL5 ......51 A2
Field House La SK6 ...126 A6
Field La OL6 ......85 D5
Field Pl 9 M20 ......110 B3
Field Rd Milnrow OL16 ...31 D7
Sale M33 ......107 E6
Field St Droylsden M43 ..99 F8
Dukinfield SK14 ......101 D5
Failsworth M35 ......83 E7
Hindley WN2 ......56 E4
Ince-in-M WN3 ......56 A8
Manchester M18 ......99 E6
11 Rochdale OL11 ......31 A4
Romiley SK6 ......113 A3
Salford M6 ......154 F2
Wigan WN6 ......37 A3
Field Vale Dr SK5 ......100 A1
Fieldbrook Wlk BL5 ......40 A1
Fieldcroft OL11 ......30 B7
Fielden Ave M21 ......97 B1
Fielden Ct M21 ......109 D5
Fielden Rd M20 ......109 F4
Fielden St OL15 ......16 B4
Fielders Way M27 ......61 E4
Fieldfare Ave M40 ......83 B4
Fieldfare Way OL7 ......85 B7
Fieldhead Ave Bury BL8 ..27 A2
Rochdale OL11 ......30 B7
Tyldesley M29 ......77 B5
Fieldhead Mews SK7 ..132 E5
Fieldhead Rd SK9 ......137 E8
Fieldhouse Ind Est OL12 ..14 F2
Fieldhouse Rd OL12 ...14 F2
Fielding Ave SK12 ...133 E2
Fielding Pl PR6 ......21 B8
Fielding St Eccles M30 ..79 C1
Middleton M24 ......47 A2
Fields Cres SK14 ......103 D6
Fields End Fold M30 ...94 C4
Fields Farm Cl SK14 ..102 D1
Fields Farm Rd SK14 ..102 D2
Fields Farm Wlk 6
SK14 ......102 D2
Fields Gr SK14 ......103 D5
Fields New Rd OL9 ....152 B5
Fields The Aspull WN2 ...38 C4
Standish WN6 ......36 F8
Fields Way OL8 ......66 E2
Fieldsend Cl SK15 ...102 D8
Fieldsend Dr WN7 ......91 C8
Fieldvale Rd M33 ......107 E1
Fieldview WN8 ......53 A7
Fieldway Platt Bridge WN2 ..56 B2
Rochdale OL16 ......31 B3
Fife Ave OL9 ......66 A4
Fifield Cl OL8 ......67 A3
Fifth Ave Bolton BL1 ...144 B7
Bury BL9 ......28 D4
Droylsden M11 ......83 C2
Dukinfield SK16 ......101 B8
Little Lever BL3 ......42 F4
Oldham OL8 ......66 C2
Stretford M17 ......96 C6
Fifth St Bolton BL1 ......23 F4

Fifth St continued
Stretford M17 ......96 D5
Filbert St 8 OL1 ......49 C1
Filby Wlk M24 ......160 E4
Fildes St M24 ......65 D7
Filey Ave Manchester M16 .97 D2
Urmston M41 ......95 A4
Filey Dr M6 ......80 D6
Filey Rd Manchester M14 .110 D8
Stockport SK2 ......124 C2
Filey St OL16 ......15 C3
Filton Ave 8 BL3 ......145 D5
Filton Wlk M9 ......156 C6
Finance St OL15 ......15 F4
Finborough Cl M16 ....97 E4
Finch Ave BL4 ......59 F7
Finch La BL4 ......18 B1
Finch Mill Ave WN6 ...35 D7
Finchale Dr WA15 ...120 D7
Finchcroft OL1 ......153 E7
Finchdale Gdns WA3 ..91 B8
Finchley Ave M40 ......83 C4
Finchley Cl BL8 ......27 B1
Finchley Cres WN2 ...38 A2
Finchley Rd Gr M40 ...65 A1
Finchley Rd
Altrincham WA15 ......119 E3
Manchester M14 ......110 B8
Finchwood Rd M22 ...121 E5
Findlay Cl WA12 ......89 C2
Findlay St WN7 ......75 E5
Findon Rd M23 ......121 A6
Finger Post BL3 ......43 A4
Finghall Rd M41 ......95 B2
Finishing Wlk 3 M4 ..159 C1
Finlan Rd M24 ......47 E5
Finland Rd SK3 ......170 D7
Finlay Ct WN5 ......54 E8
Finlay St OL4 ......60 D8
Finney Cl SK9 ......131 C2
Finney Dr Handforth SK9 .131 C2
Manchester M21 ......109 A7
Finney La SK8 ......122 C1
Finney St BL3 ......147 F4
Finningley Rd M9 ......64 B3
Finny Bank Rd M33 ...108 A6
Finsbury Ave M40 ......83 C4
Finsbury Cl OL8 ......67 B4
Finsbury Rd SK5 ......111 E8
Finsbury St OL11 ......139 D5
Finsbury Way SK9 ...131 E2
Finstock Cl M30 ......79 B1
Fintry Gr M30 ......79 D1
Fir Ave SK7 ......132 E8
Fir Bank Prim Sch OL2 .48 D7
Fir Bank Rd OL2 ......48 D6
Fir Cl SK12 ......133 E3
Fir Gr Chadderton OL9 .152 B8
Manchester M19 ......99 A1
Wigan WN6 ......37 A3
Fir La OL2 ......48 D6
Fir Rd Bramhall SK7 ...132 E8
Denton M34 ......101 A3
Farnworth BL4 ......60 B8
Marple SK6 ......125 E5
Swinton M27 ......79 E6
Fir St Bolton BL3 ......143 F2
Bury BL9 ......141 A2
Eccles M30 ......79 D1
Heywood OL10 ......29 E1
Irlam M44 ......105 D6
Manchester,Miles Platting
M40 ......160 D4
2 Manchester,Old Trafford
M16 ......97 C4
Radcliffe M26 ......44 B2
Ramsbottom BL0 ......11 D7
Royton OL2 ......48 D5
Salford M6 ......154 F2
Stockport SK4 ......169 E2
Walsden OL14 ......6 A8
Fir Tree Ave
Golborne WA3 ......90 F8
Oldham OL8 ......67 A2
Worsley M28 ......78 B5
Fir Tree Cl SK16 ......101 F8
Fir Tree Cres
Ince-in-M WN3 ......55 F3
Stalybridge SK15 ......101 F8
Fir Tree Dr
Dukinfield SK14 ......101 E5
Ince-in-M WN3 ......55 F3
Fir Tree Ho OL8 ......67 A2
Fir Tree La SK16 ......101 F8
Fir Tree Prim Sch SK5 .99 E2
Fir Tree St WN3 ......55 F4
Fir Tree Way 3 BL6 ...22 F1
Fir Tree Wlk WA3 ......90 F8
Firbank Rd Wigan WN3 .55 B3
Wythenshawe M23 ...121 B4
Firbarn Cl OL16 ......31 D7
Firbeck Dr M4 ......160 D2
Fircroft WN6 ......19 A2
Fircroft Ct 2 SK3 ...123 F4
Fircroft Rd OL8 ......67 A2
Firdale Ave M40 ......65 E1
Firdale Wlk OL9 ......152 C7
Firdon Wlk 17 M9 ...157 E7
Fire Station Sq M5 ...81 C2
Firecrest Cl M28 ......78 B8
Firefly Cl M3 ......162 E8
Firethorn Ave M19 ...110 F6
Firethorn Cl BL5 ......39 F2
Firethorn Dr SK14 ...102 A2
Firethorn Wlk 5 M33 .107 C5
Firfield Gr M28 ......60 F3
Firgrove Ave OL16 ......31 D8
Firgrove Bsns Pk OL16 .31 D8

Firgrove Gdns OL16 ......31 D8
Firs Ave Ashton-u-L OL6 ..85 B5
Failsworth M35 ......83 E7
Manchester M16 ......97 B2
Firs Cl SK8 ......122 A3
Firs Cotts WN2 ......38 B1
Firs Gr SK8 ......122 A4
Firs La WN7 ......75 C5
Firs Park Cres WN7 ...38 D1
Firs Prim Sch M33 ...107 A4
Firs Rd Gatley SK8 ...122 A4
Over Hulton BL5 ......59 A6
Sale M33 ......107 C4
Firs The Altrincham WA14 .119 B3
Wilmslow SK9 ......137 A5
Firs Way SK3 ......107 C3
Firsby Ave SK6 ......112 F4
Firsby St M19 ......99 A1
Firsby St 5 M19 ......99 A1
First Ave Atherton M46 ..58 D4
Bury BL9 ......26 F6
Droylsden M11 ......83 D2
11 Little Lever BL3 ......43 A4
Mossley SK15 ......86 D2
Oldham OL8 ......66 D2
Poynton SK12 ......133 D1
Stretford M17 ......96 D6
Swinton M27 ......79 D5
Tyldesley M29 ......77 C4
Wigan WN6 ......37 A2
First St BL1 ......23 F4
Firswood Dr Hyde SK14 .102 A3
Royton OL2 ......48 C6
Swinton M27 ......79 E6
Firswood Mount SK8 ..122 A4
Firth Cl M7 ......155 D6
Firth St OL1 ......153 E6
Firtree Ave M33 ......107 C4
Firvale Ave SK8 ......122 B1
Firvale Cl WN7 ......75 C5
Firwood Ave
Farnworth BL4 ......60 C7
Stretford M41 ......96 A1
Stretford M41 ......96 A2
Firwood Cl SK2 ......124 C8
Firwood Cres M26 ......44 B1
Firwood Gr
Ashton-in-M WN4 ......73 A2
Bolton BL2 ......25 E2
Firwood La BL2 ......25 E3
Firwood Manor Prep Sch
OL9 ......48 B1
Firwood Pk OL9 ......65 B8
Firwood Sch BL2 ......25 C2
Firwood Stables BL2 ..25 C3
Fish Rake La BL0,BB4 ...1 E6
Fishbourne Sq 8 M14 ..98 C3
Fishbrook Ind Est BL4 ..61 A7
Fisher Ave WN2 ......74 C7
Fisher Cl WN3 ......54 F5
Fisher Dr WN5 ......53 E7
Fisher St OL1 ......153 F8
Fisherfield OL12 ......13 F1
Fishermore Rd M41 ...94 E2
Fishwick St OL16 ......31 A6
Fistral Ave SK8 ......131 C8
Fistral Cres SK15 ......86 D3
Fitchfield Wlk 7 M28 ..60 D3
Fitton Ave M21 ......109 B6
Fitton Hill Rd OL8 ......67 A4
Fitton St Rochdale OL16 .31 A6
Royton OL2 ......48 F4
Fitzadam St WN1 ......150 B8
Fitzalan St OL13 ......104 C1
Fitzgeorge St M40 ...156 C5
Fitzgerald Cl M25 ......62 F2
Fitzgerald Ct 11 M34 .113 A8
Fitzgerald Way M6 ...154 F3
Fitzhugh St BL1 ......25 A5
Fitzroy St Ashton-u-L OL7 .100 F8
Droylsden M43 ......100 B8
Stalybridge SK15 ......86 D4
Fitzwarren Ct M6 ......154 F2
Fitzwarren St M6 ......154 F3
Fitzwilliam St M7 ......158 D4
Five Fold OL9 ......153 D6
Five Quarters M26 ......43 E5
Fiveways Par SK7 ......133 E8
Flag St OL13 ......3 E8
Flagcroft Dr M23 ......121 B5
Flagg Wood Ave SK6 ..125 D7
Flagship Ave M5 ......161 B8
Flake La OL2 ......48 D5
Flamborough Wlk 7
M14 ......98 B3
Flamingo Cl M12 ......165 A6
Flamingo Villas M44 ...94 A3
Flamstead Ave M20 ..120 E6
Flannel St 8 OL12 ......31 A8
Flapper Fold La M46 ..58 C3
Flash Cotts OL4 ......68 A4
Flash St M40 ......83 C6
Flashfields M25 ......62 F1
Flatley Cl M15 ......163 A5
Flavion Wlk M11 ......165 B8
Flax Cl BB4 ......1 A8
Flax Moss Cl BB4 ......1 A8
Flax St Ramsbottom BL0 .11 A4
Salford M3 ......158 D3
Flaxcroft Rd M22 ......121 B3
Flaxfield Ave SK15 ...86 D2
Flaxman Rise OL1 ......49 C4
Flaxpool Cl M16 ......97 E4

Fla – Fro 207

Flaxwood Wlk M22 ...121 B3
Fleece St 2 Oldham OL4 ...67 B7
Rochdale OL16 ...139 F7
Fleeson St M14 ...98 C3
Fleet St Ashton-u-L OL6 ...166 B2
Droylsden M18 ...99 F6
Horwich BL6 ...22 D3
Hyde SK14 ...167 E3
Oldham OL4 ...67 C7
Wigan WN5 ...54 B6
Fleetwood Dr WA12 ...89 B4
Fleetwood Rd M28 ...60 A3
Fleming Cl OL12 ...15 D5
Fleming Dr WN4 ...73 D4
Fleming Rd M22 ...121 D2
Flemish Rd M34 ...101 B2
Flemming Pl OL9 ...153 D6
Fletcher Ave
Atherton M46 ...58 D5
Swinton M27 ...62 A3
Fletcher Cl Heywood OL10 ...29 D2
Oldham OL9 ...153 D6
Fletcher Dr
Altrincham WA14 ...119 C1
High Lane SK12 ...134 F6
Fletcher Fold Rd BL9 ...44 F6
Fletcher Moss Botanical & Parsonage Gdns* M20 ...110 B1
Fletcher Sq 13 M1 ...159 C1
Fletcher St
1 Ashton-u-L OL6 ...166 C3
Atherton M46 ...58 C3
Bolton BL3 ...145 E5
Bury BL9 ...141 A2
Farnworth BL4 ...60 D8
Little Lever BL3 ...43 B3
Manchester M40 ...157 F5
Radcliffe M26 ...44 C4
Rochdale OL11 ...31 A5
Stockport SK1 ...169 F1
Fletcher's Rd OL15 ...15 E3
Fletsand Rd SK9 ...137 D6
Fletton Cl OL12 ...14 E2
Fletton Mews OL12 ...14 E2
Flexbury Wlk M40 ...83 D4
Flint Cl Droylsden M11 ...83 B2
Hazel Grove SK7 ...124 C1
Flint Gr M44 ...105 C6
Flint St Droylsden M43 ...84 B2
Oldham OL1 ...67 C8
Stockport SK3 ...170 E7
Flitcroft Ct BL3 ...147 F4
Flixton Girls' High Sch M41 ...95 A2
Flixton Inf Sch M41 ...94 F3
Flixton Jun Sch M41 ...94 F2
Flixton Rd
Carrington M31 ...106 E7
Flixton M41 ...94 F1
Urmston M41 ...95 B2
Flixton Sta M41 ...94 F1
Flixton Wlk M13 ...164 D5
Floats Rd
Wythenshawe M23 ...120 E4
Wythenshawe M23 ...120 E6
Floatshall Rd M23 ...121 A6
Flockton Ave WN6 ...36 D4
Flockton Ct 7 BL6 ...22 B4
Flora Dr M7 ...158 D4
Flora St Ashton-in-M WN4 ...73 B2
Bolton BL3 ...147 E4
Manchester M9 ...64 C3
Oldham OL1 ...153 E7
Floral Ct M7 ...155 D6
Florence Ave BL1 ...24 F5
Florence Ct SK3 ...123 B6
Florence Nightingale Hospl BL8 ...27 C1
Florence Park Ct M20 ...110 C4
Florence St Bolton BL3 ...147 D4
Droylsden M43 ...100 B8
Eccles M30 ...79 B1
Failsworth M35 ...83 F8
Sale M33 ...108 B6
Stockport SK4 ...169 E2
Wigan WN1 ...151 E8
Florence Way SK14 ...103 D5
Florian Ho OL1 ...153 F7
Florida St OL8 ...153 E5
Florist St SK3 ...170 E7
Florin Gdns M6 ...154 F3
Flowery Bank OL8 ...67 B4
Flowery Field SK2 ...124 A3
Flowery Field Gn SK14 ...101 C4
Flowery Field Prim Sch SK14 ...167 D4
Flowery Field Sta SK14 ...101 D5
Floyd Ave M21 ...109 C5
Floyer Rd M9 ...64 E5
Foden La
Alderley Edge SK9 ...136 C1
Bramhall SK7 ...132 D3
Foden Wlk 7 SK9 ...131 D2
Fog La M19,M20 ...110 C4
Fold Ave M43 ...84 B2
Fold Cres SK15 ...86 F6
Fold Gdns OL12 ...14 B3
Fold Gn OL9 ...152 A6
Fold Mews SK7 ...124 E3
Fold Rd M26 ...61 C7
Fold St Bolton BL1 ...145 F7
Bury BL9 ...140 D2
Golborne WA3 ...74 A1
Heywood OL10 ...29 E3
Manchester M40 ...83 A8
Fold The Manchester M9 ...64 D3
Royton OL2 ...49 A4
Fold The *continued*
Urmston M41 ...95 A3
Fold View Bolton BL7 ...8 E1
Oldham OL8 ...67 A2
Folds BL6 ...21 C3
Folds Rd BL1,BL2 ...148 A8
Foleshill Ave M9 ...157 D7
Foley Gdns OL10 ...46 E7
Foley St 8 WN2 ...56 D5
Foley Wlk M22 ...130 E8
Foliage Cres SK5 ...112 B5
Foliage Gdns SK5 ...112 C5
Foliage Rd SK5 ...112 B4
Folkestone Rd M11 ...83 D2
Folkestone Rd E M11 ...83 D2
Folkestone Rd W M11 ...83 C2
Follows St M18 ...99 D6
Folly La M27 ...79 D6
Folly Wlk 20 OL12 ...14 F1
Fonthill Gr M33 ...107 F1
Fontwell Cl
3 Manchester M16 ...97 C3
Standish WN6 ...19 F1
Fontwell La OL1 ...49 A1
Fontwell Rd BL3 ...43 A2
Fontwell Wlk 6 M40 ...65 D2
Foot Mill Cres OL12 ...14 D2
Foot Wood Cres OL12 ...14 D2
Footman Cl M29 ...77 B7
Forber Cres M18 ...99 D3
Forbes Cl Sale M33 ...108 D2
Stockport SK1 ...124 B8
Forbes Pk SK7 ...132 D7
Forbes Rd SK1 ...112 B1
Forbes St SK6 ...112 F4
Ford Gdns OL11 ...30 B6
Ford Gr SK14 ...103 A4
Ford La Manchester M20 ...110 A2
Salford M6 ...81 A4
Wythenshawe M20,M22 ...109 F1
Ford Lo M20 ...110 B2
Ford St Dukinfield SK16 ...101 C6
Kearsley M26 ...61 A8
Manchester M12 ...164 D7
Salford M3 ...158 D2
Stockport SK3 ...169 D1
Ford Way SK14 ...103 A4
Ford's La SK7 ...132 D6
Fordbank Rd M20 ...110 A2
Fordham Gr BL1 ...144 C8
Fordland Cl WA3 ...74 E1
Fordoe La OL12 ...13 C4
Fordyce Way WN2 ...56 A8
Foreland Cl M40 ...157 D5
Forest Ave WN6 ...36 F3
Forest Cl SK16 ...101 C6
Forest Ct M41 ...94 D3
Forest Dr
Altrincham WA15 ...119 F6
Sale M33 ...107 E2
Shevington Moor WN6 ...19 A2
Westhoughton BL5 ...58 A8
Forest Gate Com Prim Sch M31 ...105 D3
Forest Gdns M31 ...105 D3
Forest Range M19 ...99 A1
Forest Rd BL1 ...142 B3
Forest Sch WA15 ...119 F6
Forest St Ashton-u-L OL6 ...166 C4
Eccles M30 ...79 A4
Oldham OL8 ...66 F2
Forest View OL12 ...14 D2
Forest Way BL7 ...25 C6
Forester Dr SK15 ...86 A1
Forester Hill Ave
Bolton BL3 ...147 F3
Bolton,Great Lever BL3 ...42 A3
Forester Hill Cl BL3 ...147 F3
Forfar St BL1 ...24 E5
Forge Ind Est OL4 ...67 B7
Forge St Oldham OL4 ...67 B7
Wigan WN1 ...151 E7
Formby Ave Atherton M46 ...58 D4
Manchester M21 ...109 D7
Formby Dr SK8 ...131 B8
Formby Rd M6 ...80 E5
Forres Gr WN4 ...72 D4
Forrest Rd M34 ...101 B1
Forrester Dr OL2 ...49 D8
Forrester St M28 ...79 A8
Forresters Cl WN2 ...74 E8
Forshaw Ave M18 ...99 F6
Forshaw St M34 ...100 D4
Forster St WA3 ...74 A1
Forston Wlk M8 ...156 B6
Forsyth St OL12 ...13 E2
Forsythia Wlk 2 M31 ...105 E2
Fort Rd M25 ...63 D2
Fortescue Rd SK2 ...124 D7
Forth Pl M26 ...43 F5
Forth Rd M26 ...43 F5
Forth St WN7 ...76 C4
Forton Ave BL2 ...42 E7
Forton Rd WN3 ...54 F2
Fortran Cl M5 ...81 A1
Fortrose Ave M9 ...64 B3
Fortuna Gr M19 ...110 F8
Fortune St BL3 ...148 B5
Fortuneswell Ct M20 ...110 B3
Fortyacre Dr SK6 ...112 E3
Forum Gr M7 ...155 E5
Forum The SK6 ...113 C2
Fosbrook Ave M20 ...110 C4
Foscarn Dr M23 ...121 B5
Fossgill Ave BL2 ...25 C5
Foster Ave WN3 ...151 E6
Foster Ct BL9 ...28 D4
Foster La BL2 ...25 F1
Foster St Denton M34 ...100 F3
Oldham OL4 ...67 C7
Radcliffe M26 ...43 F3
Salford M5 ...154 D1
6 Wigan WN6 ...37 A1
Foster Terr 9 BL1 ...143 E1
Fosters Bldgs WN6 ...150 B8
Fotherby Dr M9 ...64 D3
Fotherby Pl WN3 ...55 A3
Foul Clough Rd OL14 ...5 D8
Foulds Ave BL8 ...27 B2
Foundry La
Manchester M4 ...159 B2
Wigan WN3 ...54 D4
Foundry St Bolton BL3 ...145 F5
Bury BL9 ...140 F2
Dukinfield SK16 ...101 D8
Heywood OL10 ...29 C2
Hindley WN2 ...56 D5
Leigh WN7 ...76 B4
Little Lever BL3 ...43 A3
Newton-le-W WA12 ...89 B3
Oldham OL8 ...153 E6
4 Radcliffe M26 ...44 A3
Swinton M27 ...62 A1
Fountain Ave WA15 ...120 B2
Fountain Cl SK12 ...133 D4
Fountain Gdns OL1 ...48 D1
Fountain Pk BL5 ...57 C5
Fountain Pl
Poynton SK12 ...133 D4
Whitefield M45 ...62 F7
Fountain St
Ashton-u-L OL6 ...85 E4
Bury,Elton BL8 ...27 C2
Bury,Pimhole BL9 ...141 A2
Eccles M30 ...95 D8
Hyde SK14 ...167 F3
Manchester M2 ...159 A1
Middleton M24 ...65 A8
Oldham OL1 ...153 E7
Fountain St N BL9 ...141 A3
Fountains Ave BL2 ...25 C1
Fountains Cl M29 ...77 C7
Fountains Rd
Cheadle SK8 ...132 C6
Urmston M32 ...95 F3
Fountains Wlk
Chadderton OL9 ...152 A5
Dukinfield SK16 ...101 C6
Golborne WA3 ...91 B8
Four Lane Ends BL2 ...25 E4
Four Lanes SK14 ...103 A4
Four Lanes End Rd OL13 ...3 B8
Four Lanes Way OL11 ...13 C2
Four Stalls End 6 OL15 ...16 A5
Four Yards M2 ...158 F1
Fouracres Rd M23 ...121 A5
Fourmarts Rd WN5 ...36 C2
Fourteen Meadows Rd WN3 ...150 B6
Fourth Ave Bolton BL1 ...144 B7
Bury BL9 ...28 D4
Chadderton OL9 ...152 A5
Droylsden M11 ...83 C3
Little Lever BL3 ...42 F4
Mossley SK15 ...86 E6
Oldham OL8 ...66 C1
Stretford M17 ...96 C6
Swinton M27 ...79 D5
Fourth St BL1 ...23 F3
Fourways M17 ...96 A7
Fowey Wlk
Hattersley SK14 ...102 E3
5 Wythenshawe M23 ...121 A5
Fowler Ave M18 ...99 F7
Fowler Cl WN1 ...151 E8
Fowler Ind Pk BL6 ...22 C2
Fowler St OL8 ...66 C3
Fowley Common La WA3 ...92 C5
Fownhope Ave M33 ...107 F3
Fownhope Rd M33 ...107 F3
Fox Bank Ct SK3 ...170 D8
Fox Bench Cl SK7 ...132 C6
Fox Cl WA15 ...119 F6
Fox Hill OL2 ...48 E8
Fox Hill Rd OL11 ...47 D8
Fox Park Rd 5 OL8 ...66 C2
Fox Platt Rd OL5 ...68 B1
Fox Platt Terr OL5 ...86 C8
Fox St Bury BL9 ...140 F3
Eccles M30 ...79 F2
Heywood OL10 ...29 C2
Horwich BL6 ...22 C2
Oldham OL8 ...66 C2
Rochdale OL16 ...15 B1
Stockport SK3 ...170 D8
Foxall Cl M24 ...64 C7
Foxall St M24 ...64 C7
Foxbank St M13 ...98 E4
Foxbench Wlk M21 ...109 D6
Foxcroft St OL15 ...15 F5
Foxdale Cl BL7 ...9 E7
Foxdale St 3 M11 ...83 C1
Foxdene Gr WN3 ...54 E2
Foxdenton Dr M32 ...95 F3
Foxdenton Hall* M24 ...65 E6
Foxdenton La M24,OL9 ...65 F6
Foxdenton Wlk M34 ...100 E1
Foxendale Wlk BL3 ...145 F5
Foxfield Cl BL8 ...27 B5
Foxfield Dr OL8 ...66 C1
Foxfield Gr WN6 ...36 B6
Foxfield Rd M23 ...121 A3
Foxfold Cl M28 ...77 F7
Foxford Wlk M22 ...121 E2
Foxglove Cl
2 Golborne WA3 ...90 D8
Foxglove Cl *continued*
Standish WN6 ...19 D2
Foxglove Ct OL12 ...14 D3
Foxglove Dr
Altrincham WA14 ...119 C8
Bury BL9 ...28 D3
Foxglove La SK15 ...86 A3
Foxglove Wlk M31 ...105 F2
Foxhall Rd
Altrincham WA15 ...119 F6
Denton M34 ...100 D4
Foxham Dr M7 ...155 E6
Foxhill WA14 ...119 A5
Foxhill Chase SK2 ...125 A5
Foxhill Dr SK15 ...102 C7
Foxhill Rd M30 ...78 F1
Foxholes Cl OL12 ...15 A1
Foxholes Rd Horwich BL6 ...22 D4
Hyde SK14 ...113 C8
Rochdale OL12 ...15 A2
Foxlair Ct M22 ...121 B3
Foxlair Rd M22 ...121 B3
Foxland Rd SK8 ...122 B4
Foxlea SK13 ...115 F8
Foxley Cl Droylsden M43 ...99 E8
Lymm WA13 ...117 A2
Foxley Gr BL3 ...145 D6
Foxley Hall Mews WA13 ...117 A1
Foxley Wlk M12 ...165 A5
Foxton St M24 ...64 C7
Foxton Wlk 6 M23 ...121 A2
Foxwell Wlk 5 M8 ...156 B6
Foxwood Cl WN5 ...53 E5
Foxwood Dr OL5 ...68 D2
Foxwood Gdns M19 ...110 E5
Foy St WN4 ...73 B3
Foynes Cl M40 ...157 D5
Fram St Manchester M9 ...157 F8
Salford M6 ...154 E2
Framingham Rd M33 ...108 B2
Framley Rd M20,M21 ...109 F7
Frampton Cl M24 ...65 B7
France St Hindley WN2 ...56 D6
Westhoughton BL5 ...57 E6
Wigan WN5 ...54 F7
Frances Ave SK8 ...122 A6
Frances Pl M46 ...58 A2
Frances St Bolton BL1 ...143 D2
Cheadle SK8 ...122 E6
Dukinfield SK14 ...101 C3
Irlam M44 ...105 E5
Manchester M13 ...163 B6
Oldham OL1 ...49 B1
Rochdale OL16 ...15 D4
7 Stockport SK1,SK3 ...170 E8
Frances St W SK14 ...101 C3
Francesca Wlk M18 ...165 C6
Francis Ave Eccles M30 ...79 E2
Walkden M28 ...60 F2
Francis Rd Irlam M44 ...93 F1
Manchester M20 ...110 C5
Francis St Denton M34 ...113 B8
Eccles M30 ...79 D3
Failsworth M35 ...83 F7
Farnworth BL4 ...42 D1
Hindley WN2 ...56 E5
Leigh WN7 ...75 E7
Manchester M3 ...158 F3
Tyldesley M29 ...77 D8
Francis Terr 3 SK16 ...166 C1
Frandley Wlk 4 M13 ...163 B7
Frank Cowan Ct M7 ...158 D4
Frank Fold OL10 ...29 A2
Frank Perkins Way M44 ...105 F7
Frank St Bolton BL1 ...143 D2
Bury BL9 ...140 F1
Failsworth M35 ...83 E7
Hyde SK14 ...167 E2
3 Manchester M1 ...163 A7
Salford M6 ...81 A4
Frank Swift Wlk 5 M14 ...98 A3
Frankby Cl M27 ...80 C7
Frankford Ave BL1 ...142 C2
Frankford Sq BL1 ...142 C2
Frankland Cl M11 ...83 B2
Franklin Cl Oldham OL1 ...153 E8
Reddish M34 ...100 A2
Franklin Rd M43 ...84 A1
Franklin St Eccles M30 ...79 D2
Oldham OL1 ...153 E8
Rochdale OL16 ...31 B5
Franklyn Ave M41 ...94 E2
Franklyn Rd M18 ...99 E6
Frankton Rd M45 ...62 F7
Franton Rd M11 ...83 B2
Fraser Ave M33 ...108 E3
Fraser Ho BL1 ...143 D1
Fraser Pl M17 ...96 D5
Fraser Rd Manchester M8 ...63 F1
Wigan WN5 ...54 E7
Fraser St Ashton-u-L OL6 ...166 C3
Rochdale OL16 ...31 B4
Shaw OL2 ...149 A7
Swinton M27 ...62 A1
Fraternitas Terr M43 ...83 E3
Frawley Ave WA12 ...89 C5
Freckleton Ave M21 ...109 C4
Freckleton Dr BL8 ...43 F8
Freckleton St WN1 ...37 C2
Fred Longworth High Sch M29 ...58 E1
Fred Tilson Cl M14 ...98 A3
Freda Wlk M11 ...160 F1
Frederica Gdns WN2 ...56 A3
Frederick Ave OL2 ...149 B5
Frederick Ct BL4 ...60 E8
Frederick Rd M6,M7 ...81 B4
Frederick St
Ashton-in-M WN4 ...73 A5
Ashton-u-L OL6 ...85 E2
Chadderton OL9 ...152 B8
Denton M34 ...100 F5
Farnworth BL4 ...60 D8
Hindley WN2 ...56 D5
Ince-in-M WN3 ...151 D6
Littleborough OL15 ...16 A6
Oldham OL8 ...66 D4
Ramsbottom BL0 ...138 B5
Salford M3 ...158 E2
Wigan WN1 ...151 E8
Free La BB4 ...1 A6
Freehold Com Jun & Inf Sch OL9 ...152 C5
Freehold St OL11 ...139 E5
Freeholds Rd OL12 ...4 E6
Freeholds Terr OL12 ...4 E6
Freeland Wlk M11 ...165 C8
Freelands M29 ...59 C1
Freeman Ave OL6 ...85 D3
Freeman Rd SK16 ...101 C7
Freeman Sq M15 ...163 A6
Freemantle St SK3 ...170 D8
Freesia Ave 9 M28 ...59 F3
Freestone Cl BL8 ...140 D3
Freetown SK13 ...116 C7
Freetown Bsns Pk BL9 ...141 A4
Freetown Cl M14 ...98 A4
Freetrade St OL11 ...139 E6
Freiston 5 OL12 ...139 F8
Fremantle Ave M18 ...99 D3
French Ave
5 Oldham OL1 ...49 C1
Stalybridge SK15 ...86 C1
French Barn La M9 ...64 C3
French Gr BL3 ...42 D5
French St Ashton-u-L OL6 ...85 D4
Stalybridge SK15 ...86 C1
Frenches Ct OL3 ...69 A6
Frenchwood Ct WN2 ...38 C4
Frensham Wlk M23 ...120 F4
Fresca Rd OL1 ...49 D4
Fresh Ct SK13 ...115 F7
Freshfield SK8 ...131 B8
Freshfield Ave
Atherton M46 ...58 C4
Bolton BL3 ...147 D2
Bolton BL3 ...147 F2
Hyde SK14 ...167 D1
Prestwich M25 ...63 C6
Freshfield Cl
Failsworth M35 ...84 A6
Romiley SK6 ...114 B1
Freshfield Gr BL3 ...147 F2
Freshfield Rd
Hindley WN2 ...56 F5
Manchester SK4 ...110 F3
Wigan WN3 ...54 E3
Freshfield Wlk 11 M11 ...83 C2
Freshfields M26 ...43 D5
Freshford Wlk 2 M22 ...121 B1
Freshpool Way M22 ...121 E6
Freshville St M1 ...163 B8
Freshwater Dr M34 ...113 B8
Freshwater St 3 M18 ...99 E6
Freshwinds Ct OL4 ...67 D4
Fresnel Cl SK14 ...102 B6
Frew Cl M9 ...65 B2
Frewland Ave SK3 ...123 F4
Freya Gr M5 ...161 C8
Friar's Cl SK9 ...136 E8
Friar's Rd M33 ...108 B4
Friarmere Rd OL3 ...50 E5
Friars Cl
Altrincham WA14 ...119 B1
Tyldesley M29 ...59 D1
Friars Cres OL11 ...30 F2
Friars Ct M5 ...81 B2
Friars Prim Sch The M3 ...158 D3
Friendship Ave M18 ...99 E4
Friendship Sq SK14 ...103 D5
Frieston Rd WA14 ...119 E8
Friezland Cl SK15 ...86 E6
Friezland La OL3 ...69 A4
Friezland Prim Sch OL3 ...68 E5
Frimley Gdns M22 ...121 D3
Frinton Ave M40 ...65 D3
Frinton Cl M33 ...107 F1
Frinton Rd BL3 ...146 B3
Frith Rd M20 ...110 C5
Frith St WN5 ...150 A7
Frobisher Cl M13 ...164 D5
Frobisher Pl SK5 ...169 E4
Frobisher Rd OL15 ...6 C1
Frodsham Ave SK4 ...168 C3
Frodsham Cl WN6 ...36 D3
Frodsham Rd M33 ...108 E2
Frodsham St 9 M14 ...98 B3
Frodsham Way SK9 ...131 E4
Frodsley Wlk M12 ...164 F6
Frog La WN1,WN6 ...150 B8
Frogley St BL2 ...25 B3
Frogmore Ave SK14 ...113 E7
Frome Ave Stockport SK2 ...124 C5
Urmston M41 ...95 B1
Frome Cl M29 ...77 C6
Frome Dr M8 ...156 B7
Frome St OL4 ...67 C6
Frost St Manchester M4 ...160 D1
Oldham OL8 ...66 E4
Frostlands St 10 M16 ...97 E3
Froxmer St M18 ...165 C6

Fryent Cl BL6 ....21 D2
Fulbeck Ave WN3 ....55 A2
Fulbrook Dr SK8 ....132 A6
Fulbrook Way M29 ....59 C1
Fulford St M16 ....97 C4
Fulham Ave M40 ....83 B5
Fulham St OL4 ....67 C6
Full Pot La OL11 ....29 E8
Fullerton Rd SK4 ....168 B2
Fulmar Cl Poynton SK12 .....133 A4
Westhoughton BL5 ....57 D6
Fulmar Dr
  Hazel Grove SK2 ....124 F5
  Sale M33 ....107 C2
Fulmar Gdns OL11 ....29 F7
Fulmards Cl SK9 ....137 C7
Fulmead Wlk **16** M8 ....155 F6
Fulmer Dr M4 ....159 C2
Fulmere Ct M27 ....79 D6
Fulneck Sq **2** M43 ....100 A8
Fulshaw Ave SK9 ....137 A6
Fulshaw Cross SK9 ....137 A5
Fulshaw Ct SK9 ....137 A5
Fulshaw Pk SK9 ....137 A5
Fulshaw Pk S SK9 ....137 A4
Fulshaw Wlk **7** M13 ....163 B7
Fulstone Mews SK2 ....124 B6
Fulthorpe Wlk **16** M9 ......64 E5
Fulton Ct M15 ....163 A5
Fulwell Ave M46 ....76 E8
Fulwood Ave M9 ....64 F4
Fulwood Cl BL8 ....26 F1
Fulwood Rd WA3 ....90 E7
Furbarn La OL11 ....29 D8
Furbarn Rd OL11 ....29 D8
Furlong Cl WN2 ....73 F7
Furlong Rd M22 ....121 B3
Furnace St
  Dukinfield SK16 ....166 B2
  Hyde SK14 ....101 C4
Furness Ave
  Ashton-u-L OL7 ....84 F5
  Bolton BL2 ....25 B2
  Heywood OL10 ....29 C3
  Littleborough OL15 ....16 A6
  Oldham OL8 ....67 C3
  Whitefield M45 ....63 A8
Furness Cl Glossop SK13 .....116 F8
  Milnrow OL16 ....31 E6
  Poynton SK12 ....133 D4
Furness Cres WN7 ....57 D1
Furness Gr SK4 ....168 A1
Furness Quay M50 ....161 A7
Furness Rd Bolton BL1 ....144 B7
  Cheadle SK8 ....132 C6
  Manchester M14 ....98 C1
  Middleton M24 ....47 A3
  Urmston M41 ....95 D3
Furness Sq BL2 ....25 B2
Furnival Cl M34 ....100 A2
Furnival Rd M18 ....165 C5
Furnival St Leigh WN7 ....75 F7
  Reddish SK5 ....99 F2
Furrow Com Sch M24 ....46 D2
Further Field OL11 ....13 D1
Further Heights Rd **1**
  OL12 ....14 F1
Further Hey Cl OL4 ....67 E7
Further La SK14 ....102 E3
Further Pits OL11 ....30 C7
Furtherwood Rd OL1 ....48 C1
Furze Ave BL5 ....57 F7
Furze La OL4 ....49 D1
Furze The OL2 ....49 D1
Furze Wlk M31 ....106 A3
Furzegate OL16 ....31 C3
Fushia Gr M7 ....155 D6
Futura Pk BL6 ....22 C1
Fyfield Wlk **18** M8 ....156 B6
Fylde Ave Bolton BL2 ....42 E7
  Gatley SK8 ....131 C8
Fylde Ct SK3 ....108 C8
Fylde Rd M24 ....168 A2
Fylde St BL4 ....42 D2
Fylde St E BL4 ....42 D2

G

Gabbot St PR7 ....21 A7
Gable Ave SK9 ....137 A7
Gable Ct M34 ....100 F2
Gable Dr M24 ....46 E1
Gable St Bolton BL2 ....25 B1
  Manchester M11 ....164 F8
  Newton-le-W WA12 ....89 B3
Gables The M33 ....108 F3
Gabriels Terr M24 ....65 C7
Gabriels The OL2 ....48 F7
Gadbury Ave M46 ....58 B3
Gaddum Rd
  Altrincham WA14 ....119 B1
  Manchester M20 ....110 C3
Gadwell Cl M28 ....78 D8
Gail Ave SK4 ....169 D2
Gail Cl Alderley Edge SK9 ...137 B2
  Failsworth M35 ....83 E5
Gainford Ave SK8 ....122 B4
Gainford Gdns M40 ....65 A5
Gainford Rd SK5 ....99 F1
Gainford Wlk BL3 ....147 E4
Gainsborough Ave
  Bolton BL3 ....146 C3
  Manchester M20 ....110 C5
  Marple SK6 ....126 B8

Gainsborough Ave continued
  Oldham OL8 ....66 E4
  Stretford M32 ....96 F3
Gainsborough Cl
  Wigan WN3 ....54 D3
  Wilmslow SK9 ....137 D8
Gainsborough Dr
  Cheadle SK8 ....122 F6
  Rochdale OL11 ....30 E3
Gainsborough Ho M33 ....107 F3
Gainsborough Rd
  Chadderton OL9 ....47 E1
  Droylsden M34 ....84 D1
  Ramsbottom BL0 ....11 B1
Gainsborough St M7 ....155 E7
Gainsborough Wlk
  Denton M34 ....100 E1
  1 Dukinfield SK14 ....101 F5
Gair Rd SK5 ....169 F4
Gair St SK14 ....167 D8
Gairloch Ave M32 ....96 B2
Gaitskell Cl M12 ....160 E1
Galbraith Rd M20 ....110 C3
Gale Dr M24 ....46 D2
Gale Rd M25 ....63 A2
Gale St Heywood OL10 ....29 B2
  Rochdale OL12 ....14 F3
Gales Terr OL11 ....139 E5
Galgate Cl Bury BL8 ....26 F1
  Manchester M15 ....162 E7
Galindo St M12 ....87 D1
Galland St OL4 ....67 D7
Galleria The **10** BL1 ....145 F7
Galleries The **19** BL1 .....150 C8
Gallery of Costume & Platt
  Hall The* M14 ....98 C2
Galloway Cl Bolton BL3 ....40 E5
  Heywood OL10 ....29 A2
Galloway Dr Swinton M27 .....61 F4
  Up Holland WN8 ....53 B6
Galloway Rd M27 ....79 D6
Gallowsclough Rd SK15 ....102 E6
Galsworthy Ave M8 ....156 A6
Galvin Rd WN1 ....37 A4
Galway St OL1 ....153 F6
Galway Wlk M23 ....120 F2
Galwey Gr WN1 ....37 C4
Gamble St WN7 ....76 A5
Gambleside Cl M28 ....78 B8
Gambrel Bank Rd OL6 ....85 B6
Gambrel Gr OL6 ....85 B6
Game St OL4 ....67 C5
Games Wlk **8** M22 ....121 B1
Gamesley Com Prim Sch
  SK13 ....171 E2
Gamma Wlk M11 ....83 B2
Gan Eden **17** M7 ....63 E1
Gandy La OL12 ....14 D4
Gantley Ave WN5 ....53 D3
Gantley Cres WN5 ....53 D3
Gantley Rd WN5 ....53 D4
Gantock Wlk **10** M14 ....98 C3
Ganton Ave M45 ....62 D7
Garbrook Ave M9 ....64 C5
Garden Ave
  Droylsden M43 ....84 B2
  Stretford M32 ....96 D3
Garden City BL0 ....11 A2
Garden Cl OL15 ....15 F2
Garden La
  Altrincham WA14 ....119 D5
  3 Manchester M3 ....158 F1
  17 Rochdale OL16 ....31 A8
  Salford M3 ....158 E2
  Worsley M28 ....78 A6
Garden Row
  Heywood OL10 ....29 C4
  Rochdale OL12 ....14 D2
Garden St **11** Bacup OL13 ...3 C8
  Bury BL8 ....26 F7
  Denton M34 ....100 F6
  Eccles M30 ....79 E1
  Farnworth BL4 ....60 E8
  Heywood OL10 ....29 C2
  Hyde SK14 ....167 E4
  Manchester M4 ....159 A2
  Newhey OL16 ....32 B4
  Oldham,County End OL4 ....67 F5
  Oldham,Mumps OL1 ....67 A7
  Ramsbottom BL0 ....138 C6
  Ramsbottom,Brooksbottoms
  BL9 ....11 C3
  Stockport SK2 ....124 C5
  Tyldesley M29 ....77 A8
Garden Terr OL12 ....11 E3
Garden Wall Cl M5 ....161 C8
Garden Way OL15 ....15 F2
Garden Wlk
  Ashton-u-L OL6 ....166 C4
  3 Denton M34 ....101 A2
Gardens The Bolton BL1 ....24 F6
  Edgworth BL7 ....9 E4
  Salford M3 ....80 A4
Garden Grange SK5 ....112 C4
Gardner Ho **8** M30 ....79 E2
Gardner Rd M25 ....62 F4
Gardner St
  Manchester M12 ....165 B6
  Salford M6 ....81 A3
Garfield Ave M19 ....99 B1
Garfield Cl OL11 ....113 B1
Garfield Gr **3** BL3 ....145 D5
Garfield St Bolton BL3 ....146 C3
  Stockport SK1 ....112 A2
Garforth Ave M4 ....159 C2
Garforth Cres M43 ....84 C3
Garforth St OL9 ....152 C8

Gargrave Ave BL1 ....23 F2
Gargrave St
  Manchester M7 ....80 F8
  2 Oldham OL4 ....67 B6
Garland Rd M22 ....121 E3
Garlick St Hyde SK14 ....167 F3
  Manchester M18 ....99 D5
  Oldham OL9 ....153 E6
Garnant Cl M9 ....157 F8
Garner Ave WA15 ....108 A1
Garner Cl WA14 ....119 D2
Garner Dr Eccles M30 ....79 C3
  Salford M5 ....154 D3
Garnet St SK14 ....167 E2
Garner's La SK3 ....170 E5
Garnett Cl SK14 ....102 F3
Garnett Rd SK14 ....102 F3
Garnett St Bolton BL1 ....143 E3
  Oldham OL1 ....67 B8
  Ramsbottom BL0 ....138 B5
  Stockport SK1 ....169 F1
Garnett Way SK14 ....102 F3
Garnham Wlk **14** M9 ....64 E5
Garratt Way M18 ....165 C5
Garret Gr OL2 ....149 C7
Garrett Hall Prim Sch
  M29 ....77 D7
Garrett Hall Rd M28 ....77 E7
Garrett La M28,M29 ....77 D7
Garrett Wlk SK3 ....123 C8
Garron Wlk **1** M22 ....121 A2
Garrowmore Wlk **22** M9 ...64 E3
Garsdale La BL1 ....40 D7
Garside Ave WA3 ....90 D7
Garside Cl Bolton BL1 ....142 C2
Garside Hey Rd BL8 ....27 B6
Garside St Bolton BL1 ....145 E7
  Denton M34 ....100 F2
  Hyde SK14 ....167 E1
Garstang Ave BL2 ....42 F7
Garstang Dr BL8 ....26 F1
Garston Ave M46 ....58 B5
Garston Cl Leigh WN7 ....57 E1
  Manchester M14 ....110 A1
Garston St BL9 ....141 A4
Garswood Cres WN5 ....71 E4
Garswood Dr BL8 ....27 B6
Garswood Old Rd WA11,
  WN4 ....71 E1
Garswood Prim Sch
  WN4 ....72 C4
Garswood Rd Billinge WN5 ...71 F4
  Bolton BL3 ....147 E2
  Garswood WA11,WN4 ....72 C3
  Manchester M14 ....98 A2
Garth Ave WA15 ....73 B3
Garswood Sta WN4 ....72 D3
Garth Ave WA15 ....119 E6
Garth Hts SK6 ....137 C7
  Stockport SK2 ....124 C7
  Wythenshawe M22 ....121 D4
Garth The M5 ....154 E2
Garthland Rd SK7 ....124 F3
Garthmere Rd M46 ....58 F5
Garthorne Cl M16 ....97 D4
Garthorp Rd M23 ....108 E1
Garthwaite Ave OL4 ....66 E4
Gartland Wlk M8 ....156 C8
Garton Ave WA3 ....74 E1
Garton Wlk **8** M9 ....64 E5
Gartside Cl Ashton-u-L OL7 ...84 F1
  Delph OL3 ....50 E4
  Manchester M3 ....158 E1
  Oldham OL4 ....67 B5
Garwick Rd BL1 ....142 B3
Garwood St M15 ....162 F7
Gas St Adlington PR7 ....21 A6
  Ashton-u-L OL6 ....166 B3
  Bolton BL1 ....145 E7
  Farnworth BL4 ....60 D8
  6 Heywood OL10 ....29 D2
  Hollingworth SK14 ....103 D5
  Leigh WN7 ....75 F5
  Platt Bridge WN2 ....139 E2
  Stockport SK4 ....169 E1
Gascoyne St M14 ....98 B3
George Leigh St M4 ....159 B2
George Mann Cl M22 ....121 C1
George Rd BL0 ....138 B5
George Richards Way
  WA14 ....119 C7
George Sq OL1 ....153 E6
George St
  Alderley Edge SK9 ....137 A1
  Altrincham WA14 ....119 D4
  Ashton-in-M WN4 ....73 C4
  Ashton-u-L OL6 ....166 C3
  3 Atherton M46 ....58 D3
  3 Bacup OL13 ....3 C8
  Bury BL9 ....140 F2
  Chadderton OL9 ....152 A7
  Denton M34 ....101 A3
  Failsworth M35 ....83 F8
  Farnworth BL4 ....60 B7
  Glossop SK13 ....116 C8
  Heywood OL10 ....29 B3
  Hindley WN2 ....56 E5
  Horwich BL6 ....22 C3
  Ince-in-M WN3 ....151 D8
  Irlam M44 ....105 E7
  8 Littleborough OL15 ......16 B5
  Manchester,City Centre
  M1 ....163 A8
  Manchester,Hilton Park
  M25 ....63 B1

Gatehead Croft OL3 ....50 F3
Gatehead Ho OL3 ....50 F3
Gatehead Mews OL3 ....50 F3
Gatehead Rd OL3 ....50 F3
Gatemere Cl M28 ....78 B8
Gates Prim Sch The BL5 ....46 C2
Gatesgarth Rd M24 ....46 C2
Gateshead Cl M14 ....98 B4
Gateside Wlk **6** M9 ....64 E5
Gateway Cres OL9 ....65 E4
Gateway Ho M1 ....163 B8
Gateway Ind Est M1 ....159 B1
Gateway Rd M18 ....99 A5
Gateways The M27 ....61 F1
Gathill Cl SK8 ....122 F1
Gathurst La WN5,WN6 ....36 A4
Gathurst Rd WN5 ....53 E8
Gathurst St M18 ....99 E6
Gathurst Sta WN5 ....36 A3
Gatley Ave M14 ....98 A1
Gatley Brow OL1 ....153 E8
Gatley Gn SK8 ....122 A5
Gatley Prim Sch SK8 ....122 A5
Gatley Rd Cheadle SK8 ......122 A5
  Sale M33 ....108 E3
Gatley Sta SK8 ....122 B5
Gatling Ave M12 ....99 B2
Gatwick Ave M23 ....121 B6
Gavel Wlk M24 ....46 E1
Gavin Ave M5 ....81 A1
Gawsworth Ave M20 ....110 C1
Gawsworth Cl
  Altrincham WA15 ....120 D6
  Bramhall SK7 ....132 E6
  Hadfield SK13 ....104 A5
  Poynton SK12 ....133 F2
Gawsworth Mews SK8 ....122 B5
Gawsworth Pl M22 ....121 F1
Gawsworth Rd
  Golborne WA3 ....73 F1
  Sale M33 ....108 E1
Gawsworth Way
  13 Denton M34 ....101 A1
  Handforth SK9 ....131 E4
Gawthorpe Cl BL9 ....45 A5
Gawthorpe Cl SK9 ....124 C2
Gaydon Rd M33 ....107 D4
Gayford Wlk **3** M9 ....64 E5
Gaythorn St M5 ....81 C1
Gaythorne St BL1 ....143 F3
Gayton Cl WN3 ....54 D3
Gayton Wlk **7** M40 ....65 D2
Gaywood Wlk M40 ....156 C6
Gee Cross Fold SK14 ....113 E7
Gee Cross Holy Trinity CE
  Prim Sch SK14 ....113 E8
  7 Oldham OL1 ....66 B2
Gee St SK3 ....170 D7
Gelder Clough Residential
  Cvn Pk OL10 ....29 C5
Gellert Pl BL5 ....57 E6
Gellert Rd BL5 ....57 E6
Gellfield La OL3 ....51 D1
Gemini Rd M6 ....81 C4
Gencoyne Dr BL1 ....24 D6
Gendre Rd BL7 ....8 B2
Geneva Rd SK7 ....123 E3
Geneva Terr OL11 ....30 C8
Geneva Wlk
  Chadderton OL9 ....152 C6
  11 Manchester M8 ....156 B6
Genista Gr M7 ....155 D6
Geo Hampson's Bldgs
  WA3 ....92 C8
Geoff Bent Wlk M40 ....83 B5
Geoffrey St Bury BL9 ....141 A4
  Over Hulton BL5 ....58 F8
  Ramsbottom BL0 ....11 A4
George Barton St **28** BL2 ...25 B3
George Cl SK16 ....166 B1
George H Carnall Sports Ctr
  M41 ....95 A5
George La SK6 ....113 A4

George St continued
  Milnrow OL16 ....31 E7
  Mossley OL5 ....68 C1
  Newton-le-W WA12 ....89 A4
  Oldham OL1 ....153 E6
  Radcliffe M26 ....43 F3
  Rochdale,Greengate OL16 .....15 D3
  Rochdale,Newbold Brow
  OL16 ....31 A8
  Romiley SK6 ....114 B2
  Shaw OL2 ....149 C8
  5 Stalybridge SK15 ....86 A2
  Stockport SK1 ....112 A2
  Urmston M41 ....95 B2
  Westhoughton BL5 ....57 F8
  Whitefield M45 ....44 E1
  Whitworth OL12 ....14 C8
George St E SK1 ....124 B8
George St N M7 ....155 F8
George St W SK1 ....124 B8
George Terr WN5 ....53 D5
George Thomas Ct M9 ....157 D8
George Tomlinson Sch
  BL4 ....60 E6
George's La SK12 ....133 E3
George's La BL6 ....22 E5
George's Rd Sale M33 ....108 B3
  Stockport SK4 ....169 D2
George's Rd E SK12 ....133 E3
George's Rd W SK12 ....133 E3
George's Row **4** BB4 ....2 F8
George's St M4 ....151 F8
Georgette Dr M3 ....158 E3
Georgian Ct **5** Leigh WN7 ...76 B4
  12 Tyldesley M29 ....58 F1
Georgian Sq **2** WN2 ....56 A2
Georgiana St
  2 Bolton BL4 ....140 F1
  3 Farnworth BL4 ....42 B2
Georgina Ct BL3 ....146 B3
Georgina St BL3 ....146 B3
Gerald Ave M8 ....156 A8
Gerald Rd M6 ....81 B5
Gerard St M4 ....73 B3
Gerard La M9 ....99 F6
Gerrard Ave WA15 ....120 A8
Gerrard Cl WN2 ....38 C2
Gerrard Rd WN5 ....71 F1
Gerrard St Farnworth BL4 .....60 E8
  Leigh WN7 ....75 F5
  Rochdale OL11 ....31 A2
  Stalybridge SK15 ....86 B1
  5 Westhoughton BL5 ....39 E1
Gerrards Cl M44 ....94 A2
Gerrards Gdns SK8 ....113 C4
Gerrards Hollow SK14 ....113 D7
Gerrards Wood SK14 ....113 D7
Gertrude Cl M5 ....161 B4
Gertrude St OL12 ....4 E6
Gervis Cl M40 ....157 D5
Ghyll Gr Billinge WA11 ....71 B1
  Walkden M28 ....60 E2
Giants Hall Rd WN6 ....56 E1
Gib Field M46 ....58 B4
Gib Fold M46 ....58 D4
Gib La M23 ....121 B7
Gibb La SK6 ....126 E5
Gibb Rd M28 ....79 B7
Gibbon Ave M22 ....121 D1
Gibbon St Bolton BL3 ....145 D5
  Droylsden M11 ....83 A2
Gibbon's Rd WN4 ....72 D3
Gibbs St M5 ....158 D1
Gibraltar La M34 ....113 B8
Gibraltar St Bolton BL3 ....145 D6
  Oldham OL4 ....67 B5
Gibsmere Cl M23,WA15 ....120 D6
Gibson Ave M18 ....99 F6
Gibson Gr M28 ....60 A3
Gibson La M28 ....60 A3
Gibson Pl M4 ....159 A3
Gibson St Bolton BL2 ....25 C1
  Leigh WN2 ....56 D1
  Oldham OL4 ....67 C6
  Rochdale OL16 ....31 C8
Gibson Terr OL7 ....166 A1
Gibson Way WA14 ....119 C8
Gibsons Rd SK4 ....168 B4
Gibwood Rd M22 ....121 C8
Gidlow Ave Adlington PR6 .....21 A7
  Wigan WN6 ....37 A2
Gidlow La Wigan WN6 ....150 B8
  Wigan,Springfield WN6 ....37 A2
Gidlow New Hos WN4 ....72 C4
Gidlow St **4** Hindley WN2 ...56 D6
  Manchester M18 ....99 F6
Gifford Ave M9 ....64 F4
Gifford Pl WN2 ....56 F4
Gifford Wlk SK7 ....124 A2
Gigg La M9 ....44 F8
Gilbert Rd WA15 ....119 E1
Gilbert St Eccles M30 ....95 B8
  Leigh WN7 ....76 A4
  Manchester M15 ....162 E7
  Ramsbottom BL0 ....1 C1
  Salford M6 ....154 F1
  Walkden M28 ....60 D1
Gilbertbank SK6 ....113 B4
Gilderdale Cl OL2 ....48 E4
Gilderdale Way OL16 ....31 B2
Gilchrist Rd M44 ....94 B1
Gilda Brook Rd M30 ....80 A2
Gilda Cres M30 ....80 A3
Gilda Rd M28 ....77 F7
Gilded Hollins Com Sch
  WN7 ....75 C1
Gilden Wlk **11** M9 ....64 E5

Gildenhall M35 ....84 A7
Gilderdale Cl OL2 ....149 B8
Gilderdale St **7** BL3 .....42 A4
Gildersdale Dr M9 ....64 C6
Gildridge Rd M16 ....97 E1
Giles St M12 ....99 A4
Gilesgate **8** M14 ....98 C3
Gill Ave WN6 ....36 B6
Gill St Manchester M9 ...64 F1
  Stockport SK1 ....112 B3
Gillan Rd M8 ....37 B3
Gillbent Rd SK8 ....132 A7
Gillbrook Rd M20 ....110 B2
Gillbrow Cres WN1 ....37 F1
Gillemere Gr OL2 ....149 C7
Gillers Gn M28 ....60 C3
Gillford Ave M9 ....157 F8
Gilliburns Wlk BL5 ....57 F5
Gillingham Rd M30 ....79 B2
Gillingham Sq M11 ....164 F8
Gillwood Dr SK6 ....112 F1
Gilman Cl M9 ....64 C2
Gilman St M9 ....64 C2
Gilmerton Dr **22** M40 .....83 C5
Gilmore Dr M25 ....63 B5
Gilmore St SK3 ....170 E7
Gilmour St M24 ....65 A8
Gilmour Terr M9 ....64 F1
Gilnow Gdns BL1 ....144 C6
Gilnow Gr BL1 ....145 D6
Gilnow La BL3 ....145 D6
Gilnow Prim Sch BL1 ....144 C6
Gilnow Rd BL1 ....144 C6
Gilpin Pl WN2 ....55 F2
Gilpin Rd M41 ....95 F2
Gilpin Wlk M24 ....46 E1
Gilroy St WN1 ....151 D8
Giltbrook Ave M40 ......160 D4
Gilwell Dr M23 ....120 F4
Gilwood Gr M24 ....46 F4
Gin Croft La BL0 ....1 E4
Gingham Brow BL6 ....22 E4
Gingham Ct **7** M26 ....44 C4
Gingham Pk M26 ....43 C5
Gipsy La BL0 ....124 C6
Girton Ave WN4 ....72 F4
Girton St Bolton BL2 .....42 D7
  Salford M7 ....158 E4
Girton Wlk M40 ....65 D1
Girvan Ave M40 ....65 D2
Girvan Cl BL3 ....146 C8
Girvan Cres WN4 ....72 D4
Girvan Wlk OL10 ....28 F1
Gisborn Dr M6 ....81 A5
Gisburn Ave Bolton BL1 ..23 E2
  Golborne WA3 ....73 F2
Gisburn Dr BL8 ....26 E3
Gisburn Rd OL11 ....31 A3
Gisburne Ave M40 ....65 D2
Gissing Wlk M9 ....157 D6
Givendale Dr M8 ....64 A2
Givvons Fold **10** OL4 .....49 D1
Glabyn Ave BL6 ....39 F8
Gladden Hey Dr WN3 .....54 A1
Glade Brow OL4 ....68 A6
Glade St BL1 ....144 C7
Glade The Bolton BL1 ...143 D1
  Shevington WN6 ....36 B6
  Stockport SK4 ....168 A1
Gladeside Rd M22 ....121 C4
Gladewood Cl **1** SK9 ....137 C8
Gladstone Cl
  8 Bolton BL1 ....143 E2
  Glossop SK13 ....116 D8
Gladstone Cres OL11 .....31 A3
Gladstone Ct
  8 Ashton-u-L OL7 .....166 A2
  Farnworth BL4 ....42 C1
  Manchester,Heaton Moor
  SK4 ....168 B3
  Manchester,Old Trafford
  M15 ....97 E4
Gladstone Gr SK4 ....168 A3
Gladstone Mews SK4 ....169 E3
Gladstone Pl BL4 ....42 C1
Gladstone Rd
  Altrincham WA14 ......119 D6
  Eccles M30 ....79 E2
  Farnworth BL4 ....42 D1
  Urmston M41 ....95 E2
Gladstone St Bolton BL1 .143 E2
  Bury BL9 ....141 B3
  Glossop SK13 ....116 D8
  Hadfield SK13 ....104 A4
  Oldham OL4 ....67 B6
  Pendlebury M27 ....80 B8
  Stockport SK2 ....124 C4
Gladstone St W BL5 ......59 E1
Gladstone Terrace Rd
  OL3 ....69 A4
Gladstone Way WA12 .....89 B4
Gladville Dr SK8 ....123 A6
Gladwyn Ave M20 ....109 E4
Gladys St
  3 Farnworth BL4 ......42 D2
  Manchester M16 ....97 C4
Glaisdale OL4 ....67 D6
Glaisdale Cl
  Ashton-in-M WN4 ....73 C3
  Bolton BL2 ....25 B2
Glaisdale St BL2 ....25 D1
Glaister La BL2 ....25 D1
Glamis Ave Droylsden M43 .83 B3
  Heywood OL10 ....46 F8
  Stretford M32 ....96 A2
Glamis Cl WN7 ....76 D6
Glamorgan Pl OL9 ....152 C5
Glandon Dr SK8 ....132 C8

Glanford Ave M9 ....64 A3
Glanton Wlk M40 ....65 D1
Glanvor Rd SK3 ....123 C8
Glass St BL4 ....60 E7
Glassbrook St WN6 ....37 A1
Glasshouse St **7** M4 ....159 C3
Glasson Wlk OL9 ....152 A6
Glastonbury **8** OL12 ....139 E8
Glastonbury Ave
  Altrincham WA15 ......120 B2
  Cheadle SK8 ....132 C6
  Golborne WA3 ....91 C8
Glastonbury Dr SK12 ...133 D5
Glastonbury Gdns M26 ...43 E5
Glastonbury Rd
  Tyldesley M29 ....77 B7
  Urmston M32 ....95 F3
Glaswen Gr SK5 ....169 F4
Glaze Wlk M45 ....45 C2
Glazebrook Cl OL10 ......29 C1
Glazebrook La WA3 .....105 B5
Glazebrook Sta WA3 ....105 B5
Glazebury CE Prim Sch
  WA3 ....92 C7
Glazebury Dr
  Westhoughton BL5 ......39 F2
  Wythenshawe M23 .....121 B5
Glazedale Ave OL2 ....48 C5
Glaziers La WA3 ....91 D2
Gleave St **12** Bolton BL1 .145 F8
  Sale M33 ....108 B6
Gleaves Ave BL2 ....42 A4
Gleaves Rd M30 ....79 E1
Glebe Ave WN4 ....73 C2
Glebe Cl WN6 ....19 F1
Glebe End St WN6 ......150 B8
Glebe Ho M24 ....47 A2
Glebe House Sch OL16 ..139 E6
Glebe La OL1 ....49 E4
Glebe Rd Standish WN6 ..19 F1
  Urmston M41 ....95 D2
Glebe St Ashton-u-L OL6 166 C3
  Bolton BL2 ....148 A6
  Chadderton OL9 ....66 A3
  Hindley WN2 ....57 C2
  Leigh WN7 ....75 F6
  Radcliffe M26 ....44 B3
  Shaw OL2 ....149 B7
  Stockport SK1 ....112 A1
  Westhoughton BL5 ......39 E1
Gleben Rd BL3 ....144 B5
Glebelands Rd
  Prestwich M25 ....63 B5
  Sale M33 ....108 A6
  Wythenshawe M23 .....120 F6
Gleden St
  Manchester M40 ....160 E2
  Manchester M40 ....160 E3
Gledhall St SK15 ....86 A2
Gledhill Ave M5 ....161 B7
Gledhill Cl OL2 ....32 A1
Gledhill St M20 ....110 B7
Gledhill Way BL2 ....9 A1
Glegg St WN2 ....151 F8
Glemsford Cl
  Failsworth M40 ....83 B6
  Wigan WN3 ....55 B3
Glen Ave Bolton BL3 ....144 B5
  Kearsley BL4 ....61 B6
  Manchester M9 ....64 E1
  Sale M33 ....108 A6
  Swinton M27 ....79 D8
  Worsley M28 ....79 A8
Glen Bott St BL1 ....143 D2
Glen Cl WA3 ....105 B2
Glen Cres OL13 ....3 A8
Glen Dr WN6 ....35 E8
Glen Gdns OL12 ....14 C1
Glen Gr Middleton M24 ..65 C7
  Royton OL2 ....48 D5
Glen Maye BL3 ....108 C4
Glen Rd Oldham OL4 .....67 C6
  Rawtenstall BB4 ....2 F8
Glen Rise WA15 ....120 A5
Glen Royd **8** OL12 ....14 C1
Glen St Bacup OL13 ......3 E8
  Ramsbottom M26 ......138 B7
  Salford M50 ....161 A1
Glen Terr BB4 ....2 F8
Glen The Bolton BL1 .....40 E7
  Middleton M24 ....65 B6
Glen Trad Est OL4 ....67 D6
Glen View
  Littleborough OL15 ....16 C7
  Royton OL2 ....48 D5
Glenacre Gdns M18 ......99 E3
Glenarm Wlk M22 ....121 E2
Glenart M30 ....79 E3
Glenavon Dr
  Rochdale OL12 ....14 D3
  Shaw OL2 ....48 F8
Glenbarry Cl M13 ......163 B6
Glenbarry St M12 ......164 D8
Glenbeck Cl BL6 ....22 C1
Glenbeck Rd M45 ....44 E1
Glenboro Ave BL8 ....27 C2
Glenborough Ave OL13 ....3 C8
Glenbourne Pk SK7 .....132 D5
Glenbranter Ave WN2 ....56 A8
Glenbrook Gdns BL4 .....42 D2
Glenbrook Hill SK13 ....104 C2
Glenbrook Rd M9 ....64 A5
Glenburn St BL3 ....147 D3
Glenby Ave M22 ....121 F3
Glencar OL12 ....57 D7
Glencar Dr **8** M40 ....65 D2
Glencastle Rd M18 ......99 C4

Glencoe BL2 ....148 B7
Glencoe Cl OL10 ....28 F1
Glencoe Dr Bolton BL2 ...42 F6
  Sale M33 ....107 C2
Glencoe Pl OL11 ....139 D7
Glencoe St **3** OL8 ....66 C2
Glencross Ave M21 ......97 A2
Glendale M27 ....62 B2
Glendale Ave
  Ashton-in-M WN4 ....73 C4
  Manchester M19 ....110 F6
  Whitefield BL9 ....44 F3
Glendale Cl
  Boothstown M28 ....77 F7
  8 Heywood OL10 ....29 D2
Glendale Ct OL8 ....66 F4
Glendale Dr BL3 ....40 F6
Glendale Rd
  Boothstown M28 ....77 F7
  Salford M30 ....80 A3
Glenden Foot OL12 ....14 D2
Glendene Ave
  Bramhall SK7 ....132 D5
  Droylsden M43 ....84 C3
Glendevon Cl Bolton BL3 .40 F5
  Ince-in-M WN2 ....56 A8
Glendevon Pl M45 ....63 B7
Glendinning St M6 ......154 E2
Glendon Cres OL6 ....85 B7
Glendon Ct OL11 ....49 E4
Glendore M5 ....80 C2
Glendower Dr M40 ......156 C5
Gleneagles BL3 ....40 F3
Gleneagles Ave
  10 Droylsden M11 ......83 C2
  Heywood OL10 ....46 D8
Gleneagles Cl
  Bramhall SK7 ....133 A7
  Gatley SK8 ....131 C7
  Hyde SK14 ....114 F8
  Wilmslow SK9 ....137 D8
Gleneagles Rd
  Gatley SK8 ....122 C1
  Urmston M41 ....94 F3
Glenfield WN2 ....56 A8
Glenfield Ave BL0 ......138 B6
Glenfield Cl OL4 ....67 D6
Glenfield Dr SK12 ......133 D3
Glenfield Rd SK4 ....169 D4
Glenfield Sq **8** BL4 ......42 B2
Glenfyne Rd M6 ....80 D5
Glengarth OL3 ....69 A2
Glengarth Dr BL1,BL6 ....40 C6
Glenham Ct **8** M15 ......97 E4
Glenhaven Ave M41 ......95 C2
Glenholme Rd SK7 ......132 D7
Glenhurst Rd M19 ......110 E5
Glenilla Ave M20 ....122 B8
Glenluce Wlk BL3 ....40 E5
Glenmay Gr WN2 ....57 A5
Glenmere Cl M25 ....62 F6
Glenmere Rd M20 ......122 C8
Glenmoor Rd **2** SK1 ....112 A1
Glenmore Ave
  Farnworth BL3,BL4 .....42 A2
  Manchester M20 ....109 E4
Glenmore Cl Bolton BL3 .40 F5
  Rochdale OL11 ....29 E5
Glenmore Dr
  Failsworth M9 ....84 B8
  Manchester M8 ....156 B7
Glenmore Gr SK16 .....101 C8
Glenmore Rd BL0 ....10 F7
Glenmore St BL9 ....140 E1
Glenolden St M11 ....83 D2
Glenpark WN7 ....76 B6
Glenpark Wlk **16** M7 ...157 E7
Glenridding Cl OL1 .....49 A1
Glenridge Cl BL1 ....143 F2
Glenroy Wlk **15** M9 ......64 E5
Glensdale Dr M40 ....65 E1
Glenshee Dr BL3 ....40 F5
Glenside Ave M18 ....99 D3
Glenside Dr Bolton BL3 .147 F2
  Romiley SK6 ....113 B5
  Wilmslow SK9 ....137 C6
Glenside Gdns M35 ......84 B7
Glenside Gr M28 ....60 E3
Glent View SK15 ....86 A2
Glenthorn Ave M9 ......157 E8
Glenthorn Gr SK6 ....64 D6
Glenthorne St **16** BL1 ..143 E1
Glentress Mews BL1 ....144 A8
Glentrool Mews BL1 ....144 A7
Glenvale Cl M26 ....101 B8
Glenville Way M34 ......101 A2
Glenville Wlk **15** SK15 ...86 A1
Glenwood Ave **2** SK14 ..101 D5
Glenwood Cl M26 ....44 B2
Glenwood Dr
  Manchester M9 ....157 E7
  Middleton M24 ....47 C1
Glenwood Gr SK2 ....124 B4
Glenwyn Ave M9 ....64 E4
Globe Cl M16 ....162 D5
Globe Ind Est M26 ......44 B3
Globe La Boiton BL2 ......8 D3
  Dukinfield SK16 ......101 B7
Globe Lane Ind Est
  SK16 ....101 B6
Globe Lane Prim Sch
  SK16 ....101 B6
Globe Pk SK16 ....31 B6
Globe Sq SK16 ....101 A7

Glodwick OL4 ....67 B6
Glodwick Inf Sch OL4 ....67 B5
Glodwick Rd OL4 ....67 B6
Glossop Brook Rd SK13 .104 B1
Glossop Heritage Ctr*
  SK13 ....104 C1
Glossop Rd
  Charlesworth SK13 ....115 D7
  Romiley SK6,SK13 ......114 D3
  Rowarth SK13,SK22 ....116 C1
Glossop Sta SK13 .....104 C1
Glossop Way WN2 ....56 E4
Glossopbrook Bsns Pk
  SK13 ....104 C1
Glossopdale Com Coll
  Glossop SK13 ....104 C2
  Hadfield SK13 ....104 A4
Gloster St **8** BL2 ....148 A7
Gloucester Ave
  Golborne WA3 ....90 B8
  Heywood OL10 ....46 C8
  Horwich BL6 ....22 D2
  Manchester M19 ....111 B8
  Marple SK6 ....125 F6
Gloucester Cl OL6 ....85 D8
Gloucester Cres WN2 ....56 E6
Gloucester Ct BL6 ....22 D2
Gloucester Dr Diggle OL3 .51 C4
  Sale M33 ....107 D4
Gloucester Pl
  Atherton M46 ....58 D4
  1 Salford M6 ....81 A3
Gloucester Rd
  Droylsden M43 ....84 A3
  Gatley SK8 ....131 C7
  Hyde SK14 ....114 A8
  Middleton M24 ....65 B6
  Poynton SK12 ....133 D4
  Reddish M34 ....100 A3
  Salford M6 ....80 C4
  Urmston M41 ....95 D1
  Wigan WN5 ....54 C6
Gloucester Rise SK16 ...102 A7
Gloucester St
  Atherton M46 ....58 D3
  1 Manchester M1 .....162 F7
  Salford,Ordsall M5 ...161 C8
  Salford,Pendleton M6 .81 A4
  Stockport SK3 ....170 D7
  Stretford SK16 ....102 A7
Gloucester St N OL9 ...152 C5
Gloucester Way SK13 ...116 B8
Glover Ave M8 ....156 B6
Glover St M6 ....154 E3
Glover Dr SK14 ....167 E2
Glover Field M7 ....155 D6
Glover Pl PR7 ....19 D7
Glover St Horwich BL6 ...22 B4
  Leigh WN7 ....75 C8
  Newton-le-W WA12 .....89 C3
Glyn Ave WA15 ....120 A3
Glyneath Cl M11 ....164 F8
Glyniss Cl SK3 ....170 F6
Glynn Gdns M20 ....109 D4
Glynne St BL4 ....60 C8
Glynrene Dr M27 ....61 C1
Glynwood Pk BL4 ....42 C1
GMex Sta M1 ....162 F8
Goadsby St M4 ....159 A2
Goats Gate Terr M45 ....44 D2
Godbert Ave M21 ....109 C5
Goddard La
  Hadfield SK13 ....104 A6
  Rowarth SK22 ....127 E2
Goddard St OL8 ....66 E4
Godfrey Ave M43 ....83 D3
Godfrey Ermen Meml CE
  Prim Sch M30 ....95 C8
Godfrey Range M18 ......99 F4
Godfrey Rd M6 ....80 C5
Godlee Dr M27 ....79 E7
Godley Cl M18 ....99 A4
Godley Ct SK14 ....167 F2
Godley Hill SK14 ......102 B3
Godley Hill Rd SK14 ...102 B3
Godley Prim Sch SK14 .167 F3
Godley St SK14 ....167 F4
Godmond Hall Dr M28 ...77 F5
Godson St OL1 ....48 E1
Godward Rd SK22 ......127 B1
Godwin St M18 ....99 E6
Goit Pl OL16 ....139 F7
Golborne Ave M20 .....109 F7
Golborne Dale Rd WA3,
  WA12 ....90 A5
Golborne Enterprise Pk
  WA3 ....74 A1
Golborne Gallery **9**
  WN1 ....150 C8
Golborne Jun & Inf Sch
  WA3 ....90 A8
Golborne St WA12 ....89 C4
Golborne High Sch
  WA3 ....74 C1
Golbourne St Thomas' CE Jun
  & Inf Sch WA3 ....74 B1
Gold St M1 ....159 A1
Goldbourne Ho OL2 ....149 B8
Goldcraft Cl **2** OL10 ....29 E1
Goldcraft Cl **4** OL10 ....29 E1

Goldcrest Cl Walkden M28 .78 B7
  Wythenshawe M22 .....121 F5
Golden St Eccles M30 ....79 D1
  Shaw OL2 ....49 E8
Goldenhill Ave M11 ......83 C3
Goldenways WN1 ....37 C2
Goldfinch Dr BL9 ....141 C4
Goldfinch Way M43 ......84 C3
Goldie Ave M22 ....121 F2
Goldrill Ave BL2 ....42 F8
Goldsmith Ave
  Oldham OL1 ....49 E4
  Salford M5 ....154 D2
Goldsmith Pl WN3 ....55 A4
Goldsmith Rd SK5 ....99 E1
Goldsmith St BL3 ......147 D4
Goldsmith Way **8** M34 ..113 A7
Goldstein Rd BL6 ....40 B4
Goldsworth Rd OL1 ......49 E3
Goldsworthy Rd M41 ....94 E2
Golf Rd Altrincham WA15 .119 F3
  Sale M33 ....108 C4
Golfview Dr M30 ....79 D4
Gooch Dr WA12 ....89 D2
Gooch St BL6 ....22 C2
Good Shepherd Cl OL16 ..31 B8
Goodacre SK14 ....102 B6
Gooden St OL10 ....29 E1
Goodier House Fold
  SK14 ....167 F4
Goodier St
  Manchester M40 ....160 F4
  Sale M33 ....108 A4
Goodier View SK14 .....101 F5
Goodiers Dr M5 ....161 B8
Goodison Cl BL9 ....45 E4
Goodlad St BL8 ....27 B4
Goodman St M9 ....64 E1
Goodrich **8** OL11 ....139 E6
Goodridge Ave M22 ....121 C1
Goodshaw Rd M28 ....78 C8
Goodwill Cl M27 ....79 F7
Goodwin Ct OL9 ....66 C3
Goodwin St M9 ....157 D7
Goodwood Ave
  Sale M33 ....107 C4
  Wythenshawe M23 .....120 D7
Goodwood Cl BL3 ....42 F3
Goodwood Cres WA15 ..120 C6
Goodwood Dr Oldham OL1 .49 B1
  Pendlebury M27 ....80 B7
Goodwood Lo **14** M6 .....97 E5
Goodworth Wlk M40 .....83 B7
Goole St M11 ....165 A8
Goose Cote Hill BL7 ......8 E1
Goose Gn WA14 ....119 D4
Goose La OL12 ....139 F8
Goosetrey Cl SK9 ....131 E1
Goostrey Ave M20 ......110 A8
Gordon Ave Bolton BL3 .144 C5
  Chadderton OL9 ....66 A3
  Garswood WN4 ....72 E4
  Hazel Grove SK7 ......124 D3
  Manchester M19 ....111 B8
  Oldham OL4 ....67 C6
Gordon Cl WN5 ....54 E8
Gordon Pl M20 ....110 B5
Gordon Rd Eccles M30 ...79 D3
  Sale M33 ....108 B6
  Swinton M27 ....79 C6
Gordon St
  14 Ashton-u-L OL6 .....85 D4
  Bury BL9 ....140 E3
  Droylsden M18 ....99 E6
  Hyde SK14 ....167 E2
  Manchester M16 ....162 D5
  Newhey OL16 ....32 B3
  Oldham,County End OL4 .68 A6
  Oldham,White Gate OL9 .65 F4
  9 Rochdale OL11 ......31 A5
  Salford M7 ....158 D4
  7 Stalybridge SK15 ....86 B1
  Stockport SK4 ....169 E3
  Wigan WN1 ....151 E2
Gordon Terr **2** SK15 .....86 A2
Gordon Way OL10 ....28 F1
Gordonstoun Cres WN5 ..53 F7
Gore Ave Failsworth M35 .84 B7
  Salford M5 ....154 D2
Gore Cl BL9 ....141 C1
Gore Cres M5 ....154 D3
Gore Dr M5 ....154 D3
Gore La SK9 ....136 C3
Gore St Manchester M1 .159 B1
  Salford,Pendleton M6 .81 A3
  Wigan WN5 ....54 E6
Gore's La WA11 ....71 A5
Gorebrook Ct M12 ....99 A4
Goreable Ave M18 ....99 F4
Gorelan Rd M18 ....99 D6
Goring Ave M18 ....99 D6
Gorman St **8** WN6 ....37 A1
Gorman Wlk WN3 ....54 F5
Gorrel St OL11 ....31 A5
Gorrells Cl OL11 ....30 D3
Gorrells Way OL11 ......30 D3

Gorse Ave Droylsden M43 ..84 C2
Marple SK6 ....125 E6
Mossley OL5 ....68 E1
Oldham OL8 ....67 C3
Stretford M32 ....96 F3
Gorse Bank BL9 ....141 C3
Gorse Bank Rd WA15 ...129 C7
Gorse Cres M32 ....96 F3
Gorse Dr Stretford M32 ....96 F3
Walkden M38 ....59 F6
Gorse Gr BB4 ....1 A8
Gorse Hall Cl SK16 ....101 F7
Gorse Hall Dr SK15 ....85 F1
Gorse Hall Prim Sch
SK15 ....86 A1
Gorse Hall Rd SK16 .....101 F7
Gorse La M32 ....96 F3
Gorse Rd Milnrow OL16 ....32 A6
Swinton M27 ....79 E6
Walkden M28 ....60 E2
Gorse Sq M31 ....105 D3
Gorse St Oldham OL9 ......65 F4
Stretford M32 ....96 E3
Gorse The WA14 ....128 B8
Gorse Way SK13 ....116 F7
Gorse Wlk WN7 ....75 B5
Gorsefield Cl M26 ....44 A4
Gorsefield Dr 1 M27 ......79 F7
Gorsefield Hey SK9 .....137 E8
Gorsefield Prim Sch M26 .44 A4
Gorselands SK8 ....132 B5
Gorses Dr WN2 ....38 C6
Gorses Mount BL2 ......148 C5
Gorses Rd BL2,BL3 ....42 D5
Gorseway SK5 ....112 B4
Gorsey Ave M22 ....121 C4
Gorsey Bank Prim Sch
SK9 ....136 F7
Gorsey Bank Rd SK3 ....123 B8
Gorsey Brow Billinge WN5 .71 E5
Mottram-in-L SK14 ....103 A1
Romiley SK6 ....113 A2
Shevington Moor WN6 .....19 B2
Stockport SK1 ....112 A1
Gorsey Brow Cl WN5 ......71 D5
Gorsey Clough Wlk BL8 ...26 F5
Gorsey Dr M22 ....121 C4
Gorsey Hey BL5 ....57 E7
Gorsey Hill St OL10 ......29 D1
Gorsey Intakes SK14 ....115 A8
Gorsey La
Altrincham WA14 ....119 B5
Ashton-u-L OL6 ....85 F6
Partington WA13 ....118 B7
Gorsey Mount St SK1 ...112 A1
Gorsey Rd Wilmslow SK9 .136 F8
Wythenshawe M22 ....121 C4
Gorsey Way OL6 ....85 E6
Gorseyfields M43 ....100 A8
Gorsley Bank OL15 ....16 C7
Gorston Wlk M22 ....130 C8
Gort Cl BL9 ....45 A1
Gorton Brook Sch M12 ..165 A6
Gorton Cres M34 ....100 C2
Gorton Cross Ctr M18 ....99 D5
Gorton Fold BL6 ....22 C3
Gorton Gr M28 ....60 C5
Gorton Ind Est M18 .....165 C6
Gorton La M12,M18 ......165 B6
Gorton Mount Prim Sch
M18 ....99 C3
Gorton Parks M18 ......165 C6
Gorton Rd
Manchester M11,M12 .....164 F7
Reddish SK5 ....99 F2
Gorton St
11 Ashton-u-L OL7 ....84 F1
Bolton BL2 ....148 A6
Chadderton OL9 ....152 B6
Eccles M30 ....79 B1
Farnworth BL4 ....60 B7
Heywood OL10 ....29 E2
Manchester M40 ....159 C4
Salford M3 ....158 F2
Gorton Sta M18 ....99 D6
Gortonvilla Wlk M12 ....164 F6
Gosforth Cl Bury BL8 .....27 C5
Oldham OL1 ....49 A1
Gosforth Wlk M23 ....108 F1
Goshen La BL9 ....44 F6
Gosport Sq M7 ....155 D5
Gosport Wlk M8 ....156 C6
Goss Hall St OL4 ....67 C6
Gotha Wlk M13,M13 .....163 C6
Gotherage Cl SK6 ....113 E2
Gotherage La SK6 ......113 E2
Gothic Cl SK6 ....113 F2
Gough St Heywood OL10 ...29 E2
Stockport SK3 ....169 D1
Gould St Denton M34 ....100 E3
Manchester M4 ....159 B3
Oldham OL1 ....67 B8
Goulden Rd M20 ....110 A5
Goulden St
Manchester M4 ....159 B2
Salford M6 ....154 E2
Goulder Rd M18 ....99 E3
Gourham Dr SK8 ....122 F2
Govan St M22 ....109 E1
Gowan Dr M24 ....46 D1
Gowan Rd M16 ....97 E1
Gowanlock's St BL1 .....143 E2
Gower Ave SK7 ....124 C3
Gower Ct SK14 ....113 E8
Gower Hey Gdns SK14 ..167 E1
Gower Rd Hyde SK14 ....167 D1
Reddish SK4 ....169 D4
Gower St Ashton-u-L OL6 .166 C3
Bolton BL1 ....145 D8
Farnworth BL4 ....42 C1
Leigh WN7 ....75 E4
Oldham OL1 ....67 A7
Swinton M27 ....62 A1
Wigan WN5 ....150 A7
Gowerdale Rd SK5 ......112 C5
Gowers St OL16 ....31 B8
Gowran Pk 3 OL4 ....67 D6
Gowy Cl SK9 ....131 E1
Goya Rise OL1 ....49 D4
Goyt Ave SK6 ....125 F4
Goyt Cres Romiley SK6 ...112 F3
Stockport SK1 ....112 B3
Goyt Hey Ave WN5 ....71 E5
Goyt Rd Disley SK12 .....135 D5
Marple SK6 ....125 F4
Stockport SK1 ....112 B3
Goyt Valley Rd SK6 .....112 F3
Goyt Valley Wlk SK6 ....112 F3
Goyt Wlk M45 ....45 B2
Grace St Horwich BL6 ....22 B3
Leigh WN7 ....75 C5
6 Rochdale OL12 ....15 A2
Grace Wlk M4 ....160 D1
Gracie Ave 2 OL1 ....67 B8
Gradwell St SK3 ....170 D8
Grafton Ave M30 ....80 A4
Grafton Ct
Manchester M15 ....162 E5
14 Rochdale OL16 ....31 B6
Grafton St Adlington PR7 ...20 F6
Altrincham WA14 ....119 D4
Ashton-u-L OL6 ....85 D2
Atherton M46 ....58 A1
5 Bolton BL1 ....145 D8
Bury BL9 ....44 F8
Failsworth M35 ....84 A8
Hyde SK14 ....167 D3
Manchester M13 ....163 B5
Newton-le-W WA12 ....89 B3
Oldham OL1 ....49 E4
Rochdale OL16 ....31 B6
Stalybridge SK15 ....86 D3
Stockport SK4 ....169 E3
Graham Ave WN6 ....18 C2
Graham Cres M44 ......105 C3
Graham Dr SK12 ....135 C6
Graham Rd Salford M6 ....80 C4
Stockport SK1 ....124 C8
Graham St Ashton-u-L OL7 .84 F1
Bolton BL1 ....145 F8
Manchester M11 ....165 A8
Platt Bridge WN2 ....56 A1
Grain View M5 ....161 A8
Grainger Ave M12 ....99 A3
Grains Rd Delph OL3,OL4 ..50 C4
Shaw OL1,OL2 ....49 D7
Gralam Cl M33 ....108 E1
Grammar School Rd
Lymm WA13 ....117 A2
Oldham OL8 ....66 B2
Grampian Cl OL9 ....152 A5
Grampian Way
Golborne WA3 ....74 D1
6 Platt Bridge WN2 ....56 B2
Shaw OL2 ....149 A8
Granada Mews M16 ......97 E1
Granada Rd M34 ....100 A3
Granada Studios* M3 162 E8
Granada TV Ctr M3 .....158 E1
Granary La M28 ....78 F5
Granary Way M33 ....107 F2
Granby Rd Cheadle SK8 ..132 B8
Sale WA15 ....108 A1
Stockport SK2 ....124 B5
Stretford M32 ....96 E1
Swinton M27 ....79 C7
Granby Row M1 ....163 A8
Granby St Bury BL8 ....26 F4
Chadderton OL9 ....66 A3
Grand Union Way M30 ....95 D8
Grandale St 5 M14 ....98 C3
Grandidge St OL11 .....139 E5
Granford Cl WA14 ......119 D7
Grange PR7 ....19 D8
Grange Ave
Altrincham WA15 ....120 A2
Cheadle SK8 ....122 F3
Denton M34 ....101 B2
Eccles M30 ....79 D4
Little Lever BL3 ....43 C3
Milnrow OL16 ....31 F4
Oldham OL8 ....66 C4
Reddish SK4 ....111 D5
Sale WA15 ....120 B7
Stretford M32 ....96 D2
Swinton M27 ....61 D2
Urmston M41 ....94 E2
Wigan,Poolstock WN3 ...150 B5
Wigan,The Bell WN5 ....54 B7
Grange Cl Golborne WA3 ...90 C6
Hyde SK14 ....167 F1
Grange Cres M41 ....95 C1
Grange Ct
Altrincham WA14 ....119 C1
Oldham OL8 ....66 D4
Grange Dr Eccles M30 ....79 D4
Manchester M9 ....64 F3
Grange Gr M45 ....62 F8
Grange La Delph OL3 ......50 F6
Manchester M20 ....110 B2
Grange Manor BL7 ....25 C8
Grange Mill Wlk M40 .....83 B7
Grange Park Ave
Ashton-u-L OL6 ....85 F6
Cheadle SK8 ....122 D5
Wilmslow SK9 ....137 A8
Grange Park Rd
Bolton BL7 ....25 C7
Cheadle SK8 ....122 D5
Grange Pl M44 ....105 E5
Grange Rd
Altrincham WA14 ....119 C1
Ashton-in-M WN4 ....72 F6
Bolton,Bromley Cross BL7 ..25 C8
Bolton,Deane BL3 ....144 B5
Boothstown M28 ....77 E7
Bury BL8 ....27 B2
Eccles M30 ....79 A4
Farnworth BL4 ....42 A1
Leigh WN2 ....56 E1
Manchester M21 ....97 A2
Sale M33 ....108 A4
Sale,Timperley WA15 ....120 B7
Slattocks OL11 ....47 D6
Stockport SK7 ....123 F3
Urmston M41 ....95 C1
Whitworth OL12 ....4 D3
Grange Rd N SK14 ......167 F2
Grange Rd S SK14 ......102 A1
Grange Sch
Manchester M14 ....98 D3
Oldham OL9 ....153 E7
Grange St Failsworth M35 .83 D6
Hindley WN2 ....56 E4
Leigh WN7 ....75 E3
Oldham OL9 ....153 E7
Salford M6 ....154 E2
Grange The Hyde SK14 ...167 F1
Manchester M14 ....98 C2
5 Oldham OL1 ....67 B8
Westhoughton BL5 ....57 D8
Grange Wlk M24 ....46 C2
Grangeforth Rd M8 .....155 F8
Grangepark Rd M9 ....65 A3
Grangethorpe Dr M19 ...110 F7
Grangethorpe Rd
Manchester M14 ....98 C2
Urmston M41 ....95 D1
Grangeway SK9 ....131 D4
Grangewood BL7 ....25 C7
Grangewood Dr M9 .....157 D7
Granite St 4 OL1 ....67 B8
Gransden Dr M8 ....156 C6
Granshaw St M40 ....160 E3
Gransmoor Ave M11 ....99 F7
Gransmoor Rd M11,M43 ...99 F7
Grant Cl M9 ....64 D2
Grant Mews BL0 ....138 B7
Grant Rd WN3 ....55 A3
Grant St Farnworth BL4 ....42 B2
Rochdale OL11 ....30 D2
Grantchester Pl BL4 ....147 F1
Grantchester Way BL2 ....25 E1
Grantham Cl BL1 ....143 E1
Grantham Dr BL8 ....140 D4
Grantham Gr WN2 ....37 F2
Grantham Rd SK4 ......168 C2
Grantham St
Manchester M14 ....98 B3
Oldham OL4 ....67 A5
Grantley St WN4 ....73 A5
Grants La BL0 ....138 C6
Grantwood WN4 ....73 A5
Granville Ave
Manchester M16 ....97 C2
Salford M7 ....155 E8
Granville Cl OL9 ....152 C7
Granville Ct
Manchester M16 ....97 C3
Newhey OL16 ....32 B3
Granville Gdns M20 .....110 A2
Granville Rd
Altrincham WA15 ....120 C6
Bolton BL3 ....146 C3
Cheadle SK3,SK8 ....123 C5
Droylsden M34 ....84 B1
Manchester M14 ....110 C8
Urmston M41 ....95 E3
Wilmslow SK9 ....136 F5
Granville St Adlington PR6 .21 A7
Ashton-u-L OL6 ....85 D2
Chadderton OL9 ....152 C8
Eccles M30 ....79 D3
Farnworth BL4 ....42 D2
Haslingden BB4 ....1 A7
1 Hindley WN2 ....56 E5
Leigh WN7 ....75 F7
Oldham OL1 ....48 E1
Walkden M28 ....60 D4
Granville Wlk OL9 ......152 C8
Grasdene Ave 2 M9 ......64 E3
Grasmere Ave
Farnworth BL4 ....59 F7
Heywood OL10 ....46 D8
Hindley WN2 ....56 E4
Ince-in-M WN2 ....56 B7
Little Lever BL3 ....43 A4
Orrell WN5 ....53 F8
Reddish SK4 ....111 E6
Swinton M27 ....61 C2
Up Holland WN8 ....53 B7
Urmston M41 ....94 E1
Whitefield M45 ....62 C7
Grasmere Cl SK15 ....86 A4
Grasmere Cres
Bramhall SK7 ....132 E8
Eccles M30 ....79 B4
High Lane SK6 ....125 E1
Grasmere Dr
Ashton-in-M WN4 ....73 B5
Grasmere Dr continued
Bury BL9 ....45 A7
Grasmere Gr OL7 ....84 F4
Grasmere Ho 5 M28 .....60 E2
Grasmere Rd
Alderley Edge SK9 ....137 A1
Altrincham WA15 ....120 C6
Gatley SK8 ....122 B3
Haslingden BB4 ....1 C8
Oldham OL4 ....67 C7
Partington M31 ....105 E3
Royton OL2 ....48 D6
Sale M33 ....108 C2
Stretford M32 ....96 D3
Swinton M27 ....79 F6
Wigan WN5 ....54 C7
Grasmere St Bolton BL1 ..143 F2
Leigh WN7 ....75 E5
Manchester M12 ....99 B3
10 Rochdale OL12 ....14 F1
Grasmere Terr WN2 ....74 B8
Grasmere Wlk M24 ....46 F2
Grason Ave SK9 ....131 C1
Grass Mead M34 ....113 B8
Grasscroft SK5 ....112 C6
Grasscroft Cl M14 ....97 F2
Grasscroft Ind Sch OL4 ..68 C5
Grasscroft Rd
Hindley WN2 ....57 A4
Stalybridge SK15 ....86 A1
Grassfield Ave M7 ....81 C6
Grassholme Dr SK2 .....125 A5
Grassingham Gdns M6 ..154 F3
Grassington Ave M40 ....65 A1
Grassington Ct BL8 ....26 F4
Grassington Dr BL9 ......28 D1
Grassington Pl BL2 ....25 A1
Grassland Rise M38 ......59 E4
Grassmoor Cres SK13 ...171 D2
Grathie Ct BL1 ....142 B1
Grathome Wlk BL3 ......147 E3
Gratrix Ave M5 ....161 B7
Gratrix La M33 ....108 F3
Gratrix St M18 ....99 E4
Gratten Ct M28 ....60 C4
Grave Oak La WN7 ....76 B1
Gravel Bank Rd SK6 .....113 B6
Gravel La Salford M3 ....158 F2
Wilmslow SK9 ....136 E5
Gravel Wlks 4 OL4 ....67 B7
Gravenmoor Dr M7 ......155 E6
Graver La Failsworth M40 ..83 D5
Failsworth M40 ....83 E4
Graves St M26 ....43 F6
Graveyard La WA16 .....136 A5
Gray Cl
Mottram-in-L SK14 ....102 F3
Wigan WN2 ....38 A2
Gray St BL1 ....145 E8
Gray St N BL1 ....145 E8
Graymar Rd M38 ....60 A4
Graymarsh Dr SK12 .....133 E2
Grayrigg Wlk M9 ....157 D7
Graysands Rd WA15 .....119 F3
Grayson Ave M45 ....63 B8
Grayson Rd M38 ....60 B4
Grayson Way OL3 ....69 B6
Grayson's Cl WN1 ....37 C1
Grayston Ct SK6 ....126 B7
Graythorp Wlk 8 M14 .....98 B3
Graythorpe Wlk 5 M5 ....81 A1
Graythwaite Rd BL1 ......23 F2
Grazing Dr M44 ....94 B3
Greame St M14,M16 ....98 A3
Great Acre WN1 ....37 D1
Great Ancoats St M1,
M4 ....159 C1
Great Arbor Way 12 M24 ..46 F1
Great Bank Rd BL5 ....39 D3
Great Bent Cl OL12 ....15 D4
Great Boys Cl M29 ....59 E1
Great Bridgewater St
M1,M3 ....162 F8
Great Cheetham St E
M7 ....155 E7
Great Cheetham St W
M7 ....81 C5
Great Clowes St M7 ....155 D5
Great Ducie St M3 ......158 F3
Great Eaves Rd BL0 ....138 C7
Great Egerton St SK1,
SK4 ....169 E2
Great Flatt OL12 ....14 B1
Great Gable Cl OL1 ......67 A8
Great Gates Cl OL11 .....31 A4
Great Gates Rd OL11 .....31 A3
Great George St
Rochdale OL16 ....139 F7
Salford M3 ....158 D2
Wigan WN3 ....150 B7
Great Hall Cl M26 ....44 A4
Great Heaton Cl M24 ....64 C7
Great Holme BL3 ....147 F4
Great House Barn
Rivington* BL6 ....21 F8
Great Howarth OL12 ......15 B4
Great Jackson St M15 ..162 E7
Great John St M3 ....162 E8
Great Jones St M12 ....165 A6
Great Lee OL12 ....14 D3
Great Lee Wlk OL12 .....14 D2
Great Marlborough St 4
M1 ....163 A7
Great Marld Cl BL1 ......23 F2
Great Mdw OL2 ....31 F1
Great Moor Inf Sch SK2 .124 B4
Great Moor Jun Sch
SK2 ....124 B4
Great Moor St
Bolton BL1 ....145 F6
Stockport SK2 ....124 B5
Great Moss Rd M29 ....77 C2
Great Newton St M40 ....83 C5
Great Norbury St SK14 ..167 D2
Great Northern Sq M2 ..162 F8
Great Oak Dr WA15 .....119 E4
Great Portwood St SK1 ..169 F2
Great Southern St M14 ...98 B3
Great Stone Cl M26 ......43 D3
Great Stone Rd
Manchester M16,M21,M32 ..97 A3
Stretford M16,M32 ....96 F3
Great Stones Cl BL7 ....8 E2
Great Underbank SK1 ...169 F1
Great Western St M14 ...98 B4
Greater Manchester Exhib
Ctr (GMex)* M2,M3 ..162 F8
Greatfield Rd M22 ......121 B4
Greatstone Apartments
M32 ....96 E3
Greave SK6 ....113 D4
Greave Ave OL11 ....30 B7
Greave Fold SK6 ....113 D4
Greave Ho OL11 ....30 B8
Greave Prim Sch SK6 ...113 D4
Greave Rd SK1,SK2 .....124 C8
Greaves Ave M35 ....83 E6
Greaves Cl WN6 ....35 F8
Greaves Rd SK9 ....136 E7
Greaves St Mossley OL5 ...68 C2
Oldham OL1 ....153 F6
2 Oldham,County End OL4 ..67 F6
Shaw OL2 ....149 C7
Grebe Cl Poynton SK12 ...133 B4
Wigan WN3 ....54 B4
Grebe Wlk SK2 ....125 A4
Grecian Cres BL3 ....147 F4
Grecian St M7 ....81 C5
Grecian St N M7 ....81 C5
Grecian Terr M7 ....81 C5
Gredle Cl M41 ....95 F2
Greeba Rd M23 ....120 E6
Greek St Manchester M1 ..163 B7
Stockport SK1,SK3 ......170 E8
Green Acre BL5 ....57 F7
Green Ave Bolton BL3 .....42 B3
Swinton M27 ....79 F7
Tyldesley M29 ....77 A4
Walkden M38 ....59 E5
Green Bank Bacup OL13 ....3 D8
Bolton BL2 ....25 E3
Farnworth BL4 ....42 C1
Glossop SK13 ....115 F7
Reddish SK4 ....111 D7
Green Booth Cl SK16 ....101 F7
Green Bridge Cl OL11 ....30 F4
Green Bridge N BB4 ....2 E7
Green Bridge S BB4 ....2 E7
Green Brook Cl BL9 .....141 A4
Green Cl Gatley SK8 .....122 A6
Tyldesley M46 ....58 E1
Green Clough OL15 ....16 C8
Green Common La BL5 ...58 B7
Green Courts WA14 .....119 B3
Green Croft SK6 ....113 E3
Green Ct WN7 ....75 B1
Green Dr
Altrincham WA15 ....120 A7
Bolton BL6 ....40 C7
Handforth SK9 ....131 D2
Manchester M19 ....98 F1
Green End M34 ....113 B8
Green End Prim Sch
M19 ....110 F5
Green End Rd M19 ......110 E5
Green Fold M18 ....99 F6
Green Fold La BL5 ....57 E7
Green Fold Sch BL4 ......59 F8
Green Gables Cl SK8 ....122 B1
Green Grove Bank OL16 ...15 D3
Green Hall Cl M46 ....58 F5
Green Hall Mews SK9 ...137 B6
Green Hayes Ave WN1 ....37 C3
Green Hill OL15 ....16 A7
Green Hill Rd SK14 .....102 A3
Green Hill St SK3 ......170 D7
Green Hill Terr SK3 ....170 D7
Green Hollow Fold SK15 .86 D5
Green La
Alderley Edge SK9 ....136 F1
Altrincham WA15 ....120 B4
Ashton-u-L OL6 ....85 B5
Bolton BL3 ....42 B2
Coppull PR7 ....20 A8
Delph OL3 ....50 E4
Disley SK12 ....135 D4
Eccles M30 ....79 C2
Failsworth M35 ....83 F4
Glossop SK13 ....115 F7
Golborne WA3 ....75 A2
Hadfield SK14 ....171 F4
Hazel Grove SK7 ....124 D3
Heywood OL10 ....29 F1
Hindley WN2 ....57 B4
Hollingworth SK14 ....103 D6
Horwich BL6 ....22 B5
Hyde,Godley SK14 ....102 A1
Hyde,Godley Green SK14 ..102 A2
Irlam M44 ....105 E5
Kearsley BL4 ....61 A7
Leigh WN7 ....76 C6
Manchester,Gorton M18 ...99 D6
Manchester,Heaton Norris
SK4 ....168 B3
Middleton,Green Hill M24 ...65 D7

Green La *continued*
Middleton,Higher Boarshaw
M24 ....47 C2
Oldham,Moss Grove OL8 ....66 E2
Oldham,Top o' th' Meadows
OL4 ....50 A2
Orrell WN5 ....53 D3
Poynton SK12 ....134 C4
❶ Rochdale OL12 ....139 E8
Romiley SK6 ....113 B2
Sale M33 ....107 E6
Standish WN6 ....36 E8
Stockport SK4 ....168 C2
Stockport SK4 ....169 D1
Whitefield M45 ....44 F1
Wilmslow SK9 ....137 B7
Green La N WA15 ....120 B5
Green Lane Ind Est SK4 ...168 C1
Green Mdw OL12 ....15 D4
Green Mdws
Golborne WA3 ....90 E5
Marple SK6 ....125 F7
Westhoughton BL5 ....57 F8
Green Meadows Dr SK6 .125 F8
Green Meadows Wlk
M22 ....121 E1
Green Park View OL1 ....49 D2
Green Pastures SK4 .....110 E1
Green Rd M31 ....105 E3
Green Royde OL11 ......139 E5
Green St Adlington PR6 ...21 B8
❺ Alderley Edge SK9 ...137 A1
Bolton BL1 ....145 F7
Bury,Walshaw BL8 ....26 F4
Bury,Woolfold BL8 ....27 B4
Eccles M30 ....95 B8
Edenfield BL0 ....1 E3
Hyde SK14 ....167 E1
Manchester M14 ....110 C7
Middleton M24 ....47 B1
Oldham OL8 ....153 D6
❷ Platt Bridge WN2 ......56 B2
Radcliffe M26 ....44 A3
Stockport SK3 ....170 F6
Stretford M32 ....108 C8
❽ Tyldesley M29 ......59 A1
Tyldesley,Hindsford M46 ...58 E1
Wigan WN3 ....150 C6
Green The Cheadle SK8 ..131 F8
Glossop SK13 ....116 A7
Handforth SK9 ....131 E3
Marple SK6 ....126 A3
Oldham OL8 ....67 A3
Partington M31 ....105 F4
Ramsbottom BL8 ....10 F1
Rochdale OL11 ....30 B3
Sale WA15 ....120 C7
Stalybridge SK15 ....86 E4
Stockport SK4 ....168 C2
Swinton M27 ....62 B2
Wigan WN5 ....54 B6
Wigan WN5 ....54 C7
Wilmslow SK9 ....78 E5
Green Tree Gdns SK6 ...113 B2
Green View WA11 ......117 B5
Green Villa Pk SK9 ....136 E4
Green Water Mdw SK14 .103 D5
Green Way Bolton BL1 ....25 B4
❻ Mottram-in-L SK14 ....102 F2
Rochdale OL11 ....30 B1
Green Way Cl BL1 ......25 B4
Green Wlk
Altrincham,Bowdon WA14 ..119 B3
Altrincham,Timperley
WA15 ....120 A7
Gatley SK8 ....122 A6
Manchester M16 ....97 C2
❼ Mottram-in-L SK14 ...102 F2
Partington M31 ....105 E3
Stretford M32 ....96 B2
Green Wlks 63 C3
Wigan WN1 ....37 D1
Greenacre Cl BL0 ......11 E7
Greenacre La M28 ......78 F4
Greenacre Pk BL1 ......35 F7
Greenacres Edgworth BL7 ..9 E6
Lymm WA13 ....117 A4
Greenacres Cl WA3 ......91 B8
Greenacres Ct ❸ OL12 ..15 D4
Greenacres Dr M19 ......110 E4
Greenacres Jun & Inf Sch
OL4 ....67 C7
Greenacres Rd OL4 ......67 D7
Greenall St WN4 ......73 B5
Greenbank
Gatley SK8 ....122 A5
Hadfield SK13 ....103 F5
Hindley WN2 ....57 B3
❸ Horwich BL6 ....22 D1
Whitworth OL12 ....14 C5
Greenbank Ave
Gatley SK8 ....122 A5
Manchester SK4 ....110 E2
Orrell WN5 ....53 D3
Swinton M27 ....79 D6
Uppermill OL3 ....51 C1
Greenbank Cres SK6 ...125 F5
Greenbank Dr OL5 ......68 D2
Greenbank Ind Est WN2 ...57 B3
Greenbank Prim Sch
OL12 ....14 F1
Greenbank Rd
Bolton BL3 ....144 B5
Bolton BL3 ....146 B4
Gatley SK8 ....122 A6
Radcliffe M26 ....44 A5

Greenbank Rd *continued*
Rochdale OL12 ....14 F2
Rochdale OL12 ....15 A2
Romiley SK6 ....114 B1
Sale M33 ....107 E5
Salford M6 ....154 E3
Greenbank Sch SK8 ...123 A1
Greenbank Terr
Middleton M24 ....47 C1
Stockport SK4 ....169 E2
Greenbarn Way BL6 ......21 D1
Greenbeech Cl SK6 ......125 E7
Greenbooth Rd OL11,
OL12 ....13 D2
Greenbridge La OL3 ......69 B5
Greenbrook St ❻ BL1 ...141 A4
Greenbrow Inf Sch M23 .120 F3
Greenbrow Rd M23 ......121 A4
Greenburn Ave WA11 ...71 C6
Greenburn Dr BL2 ......25 E2
Greencourt Dr M38 ......59 F3
Greencourts Bsns Pk
M22 ....131 A8
Greencroft Mdw OL2 ......48 F5
Greencroft Rd M30 ......79 B4
Greencroft Way OL12 ...15 D3
Greendale M46 ....58 E4
Greendale Cres WN7 ......76 C4
Greendale Dr
Manchester M9 ....64 E3
Radcliffe M26 ....44 B1
Greenfield Gr M34 ....113 B8
Greenfield Prim Sch OL3 ...69 B6
Greenfield Prim Sch
SK14 ....167 E2
Greenfield Ave
Altrincham WA15 ....120 C6
Bury BL8 ....27 A1
Newton-le-W WA12 ....89 C4
Stockport SK3 ....170 E6
Westhoughton BL5 ....40 A1
Greenfield Cl OL10 ......29 D1
Greenfield La
Rochdale,Greengate OL15 ..15 D3
Rochdale,Lower Place OL11 ..31 A4
Shaw OL2 ....149 B6
Greenfield Prim Sch
SK14 ....167 E2
Greenfield Rd
Adlington PR6 ....21 A8
Atherton M46 ....58 E5
Walkden M38 ....60 A4
Greenfield St
Denton M34 ....100 D7
Hadfield SK13 ....104 A6
Hyde SK14 ....167 D2
Rochdale OL11 ....31 A4
Greenfield St Mary's CE Sch
OL3 ....69 C4
Greenfield Sta OL3 ....69 A6
Greenfield View WN5 ...71 C6
Greenfields WN6 ....37 A4
Greenfields Cl M29 ......56 F6
Greenfields Cres WN4 ...73 B4
Greenfold Rd BL4 ......60 B7
Greenfold Way WN7 ......76 A3
Greenford Cl
Cheadle SK8 ....123 B4
Orrell WN5 ....53 D6
Greenford Rd M8 ......156 A7
Greengate
Altrincham WA15 ....129 D7
Hyde SK14 ....113 D8
Middleton OL9,M9,M40 ...65 C5
Salford M3 ....158 F2
Greengate Cl OL12 ......15 D3
Greengate E M40 ......65 D3
Greengate Ind Pk M24 ...65 C5
Greengate La Bolton BL2 ...42 F8
Prestwich M25 ....63 A4
Greengate Rd M34 ......101 A4
Greengate St OL4 ......67 B6
Greengate W M3 ......158 E3
Greenhalgh La PR6 ......21 C8
Greenhalgh Moss La BL8 ..27 B5
Greenhalgh St
Failsworth M35 ....83 C6
Stockport SK4 ....169 E2
Greenham Rd M23 ......108 F2
Greenhaven WN8 ......53 B7
Greenheys M34 ....60 F3
Greenhead Fold SK6 ...113 A1
Greenhead Wlk BL3 ......147 E3
Greenhey WN5 ....54 C3
Greenheys Bolton BL2 ...25 E1
Droylsden M43 ....84 A2
Greenheys Cres BL8 ......10 F1
Greenheys Ctr M15 ...163 A5
Greenheys La M15 ......163 A5
Greenheys La W M15 ...162 F5
Greenheys Rd M38 ......59 E6
Greenhill ❷ Oldham OL1 ...67 A5
Prestwich M25 ....63 A4
Greenhill Ave Bolton BL3 .144 B5
Farnworth BL4 ....60 C6
Rochdale OL12 ....139 E8
Sale M33 ....108 A6
Shaw OL2 ....149 A6
Greenhill Cotts OL5 ......68 D2
Greenhill La BL3 ......40 F4
Greenhill Prim Sch
Bury BL8 ....26 F1
Oldham OL4 ....67 A5

Greenhill Rd
Altrincham WA15 ....120 C6
Billinge WN5 ....71 F5
Bury BL8 ....27 A1
Manchester M8 ....156 A8
Middleton M24 ....65 D7
Greenhill Terr
Middleton M24 ....65 C7
❻ Oldham OL1 ....67 A6
Greenhill Wlk SK12 ...135 D6
Greenholm Cl M40 ......65 D1
Greenhow St ❷ M43 ...99 F8
Greenhurst Cres OL8 ...82 A2
Greenhurst La OL6 ......85 E6
Greenhurst Rd OL6 ......85 D7
Greenhythe Rd SK8 ...131 C6
Greening Rd M19 ......99 B2
Greenland Ave WN6 ......19 E1
Greenland Cl M29 ......77 B6
Greenland La PR6 ......21 D5
Greenland Rd Bolton BL3 .147 F2
Farnworth BL3,BL4 ....42 A2
Tyldesley M29 ....77 B6
Greenland St
Manchester M8 ....155 F7
❸ Salford M6 ....154 E2
Greenlands Cl ❸ SK8 ...131 E8
Greenlaw Ct M16 ......161 C5
Greenlea Ave M18 ......99 D3
Greenlea Cl WN5 ......53 D5
Greenleach La M28 ......79 A7
Greenleaf Cl M28 ......77 F6
Greenleas BL6 ....40 C6
Greenlees St OL12 ......139 F8
Greenleigh Cl BL1 ......24 D5
Greenmans La OL3 ......69 A3
Greenmount Cl BL8 ......10 F2
Greenmount Ct BL1 ......144 A8
Greenmount Dr
Heywood OL10 ....46 F7
Ramsbottom BL8 ....10 F2
Greenmount La BL1 ......144 A8
Greenmount Pk BL4 ......61 A7
Greenmount Prim Sch
BL8 ....10 F2
Greenoak M26 ....61 C6
Greenoak Dr Sale M33 ...108 C1
Walkden M28 ....60 C5
Greenock Cl BL3 ......40 E5
Greenock Dr OL10 ......28 F1
Greenough St
Atherton M46 ....58 A1
Wigan WN1 ....151 D8
Greenpark Cl BL8 ......10 F1
Greenpark Rd M22 ......109 D1
Greenrigg Cl WN6 ......36 F3
Greenroyd Ave BL2 ......25 E2
Greens Arms Rd BB3,BL7 ..8 E7
Greens La Bacup OL13 ...3 D7
Haslingden BL4 ....1 C7
Greens The
Altrincham WA14 ....129 D7
Whitworth OL12 ....4 D1
Greenshall La SK12 ...135 F5
Greenside Cl Leigh WN7 ...76 B5
Newton-le-W WA12 ....89 C4
Rochdale OL11 ....29 F7
Greenside Ainsworth BL2 ...26 C1
Farnworth BL4 ....42 C1
Stockport SK4 ....168 A1
Worsley M28 ....79 A5
Greenside Ave
Kearsley BL4 ....60 F6
Oldham OL4 ....49 E2
Greenside Cl
Dukinfield SK16 ....102 A8
Hawkshaw BL8 ....10 B3
Greenside Cres M43 ......83 F2
Greenside Dr OL10 ......79 D3
Greenside Dr
Altrincham WA14 ....119 E1
Bury M43 ....26 F8
Irlam M44 ....93 F1
Greenside La M43 ......83 F3
Greenside Prim Sch M43 .83 F2
Greenside St M11 ......165 C8
Greenside View SK14 ...102 A5
Greenslate Ave WN6 ...36 A5
Greenslate Ct WN5 ......53 E3
Greenslate Rd WN5 ......53 E3
Greensmith Way BL5 ......39 E3
Greenson Dr M24 ......64 E7
Greenstead Ave M8 ......156 A8
Greenstone Ave BL6 ......22 B3
Greenstone Dr M6 ......80 F5
Greensward Cl WN6 ......19 B1
Greensway Ctr OL2 ......149 B7
Greenthorn Wlk M15 ...162 F5
Greenthorne Ave SK4 ...111 D7
Greenthorne Cl BL7 ......9 E7
Greenvale Rochdale OL11 ...29 D8
Shevington WN6 ....35 F4
Greenvale Dr SK8 ......122 C6
Greenview Dr
Manchester M20 ....122 C8
Rochdale OL11 ....29 D8
Greenwatch Cl ❼ M30 ...79 C1
Greenway
Altrincham WA14 ....119 A5
Ashton-in-M WN4 ....73 A4
Bramhall SK7 ....132 D6
Horwich BL6 ....22 F3
Hyde SK14 ....167 D1
Middleton M9 ....64 F5
Romiley SK6 ....113 E1
Shaw OL2 ....31 F1

Greenway *continued*
Wilmslow SK9 ....137 B6
Wythenshawe M22 ....121 E8
Greenway Ave ❾ M19 ...99 B1
Greenway Cl Bury BL8 ...27 B3
Sale M33 ....107 E2
Greenway Dr OL5 ......68 C2
Greenway Mews BL0 ...11 C4
Greenway Rd
Altrincham WA15 ....119 F8
Gatley SK8 ....131 C6
Greenways
❼ Ashton-u-L OL7 ......85 A6
Failsworth M40 ....65 D1
Leigh WN7 ....76 B6
Orrell WN5 ....53 D3
Standish WN6 ....37 A6
Greenwich Cl
Failsworth M40 ....83 D4
Rochdale OL11 ....29 F6
Greenwood Ave
Ashton-u-L OL6 ....85 C6
Horwich BL6 ....22 D1
Stockport SK2 ....124 C6
Swinton M27 ....62 B1
Walkden M28 ....60 C3
Wigan WN5 ....54 E7
Greenwood Bsns Ctr ❿
M5 ....81 A1
Greenwood Cl
Altrincham WA15 ....120 D5
Boothstown M28 ....77 E7
Culcheth WA3 ....91 F1
Greenwood Dr
Newton-le-W WA12 ....89 D2
Wilmslow SK9 ....137 D8
Greenwood Gdns M16 ...112 F3
Greenwood La BL6 ......22 E1
Greenwood Rd
Standish WN6 ....19 E2
Wythenshawe M22 ....121 C5
Greenwood St
❶ Altrincham WA14 ....119 D4
Farnworth BL4 ....60 D8
❷ Littleborough OL15 ...16 B5
Oldham,County End OL4 ...67 F5
Oldham,Fitton Hill OL8 ...66 F1
Oldham,Greenacres OL4 ...67 C8
Rochdale OL16 ....139 F7
Salford M6 ....81 A4
Greenwood Vale BL1 ...143 E3
Greenwood Vale S ❼
BL1 ....143 F3
Greenwoods La BL2 ......25 F4
Greer St M11 ....165 C8
Greetland Dr M9 ......64 F4
Greg Mews SK9 ......131 B2
Greg St SK5 ....111 E5
Gregge St
❻ Heywood,Hopwood OL10 .29 E1
Heywood,Lane End OL10 ...46 C7
Gregory Ave Atherton M46 .58 C5
Bolton BL2 ....42 E8
Romiley SK6 ....113 C1
Gregory Fold BB4 ......1 A7
Gregory St
Dukinfield SK14 ....101 E5
Hindley WN2 ....56 C6
Leigh WN7 ....75 E4
Manchester M12 ....164 F6
Oldham OL8 ....66 E3
Westhoughton BL5 ....57 A7
Gregory Way SK5 ......111 F6
Gregorys Row SK3 ......75 A1
Gregson Field BL3 ......147 E4
Gregson Rd SK5 ......111 E6
Gregson St ❸ OL1 ...153 F6
Grelly Wlk ❷ M14 ......98 C3
Grenaby Ave WN2 ......57 B5
Grendale Ave
Hazel Grove SK7 ....124 E1
Stockport SK1 ....112 B1
Grendale Dr M16 ......161 C5
Grendon Ave OL8 ......66 F3
Grendon St BL3 ......146 C3
Grendon Wlk M12 ......165 A6
Grenfel Cl WN3 ......150 A5
Grenfell Rd M20 ......110 B3
Grenham Ave M15 ......162 D6
Grenville Rd SK7 ......124 D3
Grenville St
Dukinfield SK16 ....101 C8
Stalybridge SK15 ....86 D4
Stockport SK3 ....170 D8
Grenville Terr ❾ OL6 ...85 D2
Grenville Wlk OL15 ......6 C1
Gresford Cl M21 ....108 F8
Gresham Cl M45 ......62 D7
Gresham Dr OL9 ......152 C7
Gresham St Bolton BL3 .143 F3
Denton M34 ....100 F4
Gresham Way M33 ......108 A1
Gresley Ave BL6 ......169 E3
Gresley Ave BL6 ......22 B3
Gresley Cl WN1 ......151 E8
Gresty Ave M22 ......130 F7
Greswell Prim Sch M34 .100 E2
Greswell St M34 ......100 F4
Greta Ave SK8 ......131 C6
Gretna Rd M46 ......58 A1
Gretton Cl M13 ......99 E4
Gretton Cl OL2 ......48 F4
Greville St M13 ......98 E4
Grey Cl SK6 ....113 A4
Grey Knotts M28 ......78 A5
Grey Mare La M11 ......83 A1
Grey Rd Altrincham WA14 .119 C5

Grey Rd *continued*
Ashton-in-M WN4 ....73 A4
Grey St Ashton-u-L OL6 ...166 C2
Denton M34 ....100 D3
Manchester M12 ....164 E6
Middleton M24 ....46 F1
Prestwich M25 ....63 C4
Radcliffe M26 ....44 B3
Stalybridge SK15 ....86 C1
Greyfriars WN4 ......72 F6
Greyfriars Ct M3 ......158 E3
Greyfriars Rd M22 ......121 B2
Greyhound Dr M6 ......81 C5
Greylag Cres M28 ......78 D8
Greylands Cl M33 ......107 F4
Greylands Rd M20 ......122 C8
Greymont Rd BL9 ......27 F6
Greyson St M16 ......97 E2
Greystoke Ave
Altrincham WA15 ....120 D5
Reddish M19 ....99 C1
Sale M33 ....108 B3
Greystoke Cres M45 ...44 E2
Greystoke Dr
Alderley Edge SK9 ....137 A2
Bolton BL1 ....24 E5
Middleton M24 ....46 D2
Greystoke La M35 ......83 D6
Greystoke St SK1 ......112 A1
Greystone Ave
Aspull WN2 ....38 C5
Manchester M21 ....109 F8
Greystone Wlk SK4 ......111 D7
Greyswood Ave BL9 ...141 B2
Grid La SK6 ....114 F1
Grierson St Bolton BL1 ...143 E3
❿ Manchester M16 ....97 E4
Griffe La BL9 ....45 D4
Griffin Cl M7 ....81 C5
Griffin Bsns Ctr M7 ...81 C5
Griffin Gr M19 ....111 A8
Griffin La SK8 ....131 D7
Griffin Rd M35 ......83 D6
Griffin St M7 ....81 C6
Griffiths Cl M7 ......158 D4
Griffiths St ❸ M40 ......83 C5
Grime St BL0 ......11 A4
Grimeford La BL6,6.PR6 ...21 C5
Grimes Cotts ❹ OL12 ...13 F1
Grimes St 13 F1
Grimscott Cl M9 ......64 F1
Grimshaw Ave M35 ......84 A8
Grimshaw Cl SK6 ......113 A4
Grimshaw La
Manchester M40 ....160 F4
Middleton M24 ....65 C7
Grimshaw St
Failsworth M35 ....83 E8
Golborne WA3 ....74 A1
Stockport SK1 ....112 A1
Grimstead Cl M23 ......120 E6
Grindall Ave M40 ......65 B2
Grindle Gn M30 ......95 C8
Grindleford Gdns ❿
SK13 ....171 E2
Grindleford Gr ❷ SK13 .171 E2
Grindleford Lea ❷❶
SK13 ....171 E2
Grindleford Wlk
❷❷ Gamesley SK13 ....171 E2
Manchester M21 ....109 D5
Grindley Ave M21 ......109 D5
Grindlow St M13 ......164 D5
Grindlow Wlk WN3 ......54 C2
Grindon Ave M7 ......81 A7
Grindrod St ❸ M26 ......44 A4
Grindsbrook Rd M26 ...43 F7
Grinton Ave M13 ......98 F2
Grisbeck Way BL0 ......153 E7
Grisdale Dr M24 ......46 E2
Grisdale Rd BL3 ......144 C5
Grisedale Ave OL2 ......48 C8
Grisedale Ct M9 ......65 A4
Grisedale Rd OL11 ......30 B4
Gristlehurst La BL9,OL10 .29 A5
Gritley Wlk ❼ M22 ......121 C1
Grizebeck Cl M18 ......99 C4
Grizedale Cl Bolton BL1 ...23 F2
Mossley SK15 ....86 F7
Grizedale Dr WN2 ......56 A7
Grizedale Rd SK6 ......113 B4
Groby Cl WA14 ....119 C4
Groby Pl WA14 ....119 D5
Groby Rd
Altrincham WA14 ....119 C4
Denton M34 ....100 F4
Manchester M21 ....109 B8
Groby Rd N M34 ......100 D8
Groby St Oldham OL8 ...67 A3
Stalybridge SK15 ....86 C1
Groom St M1 ....163 B7
Grosvenor Ave
❸ Golborne WA3 ....90 D8
❺ Whitefield M45 ....44 E1
Grosvenor Ct
❾ Ashton-u-L OL7 ....166 A1
Cheadle SK8 ....122 D6
❼ Manchester M16 ....97 E3
❹ Sale M33 ....107 F5

Grosvenor Ct continued
Salford M7 .....155 D8
Grosvenor Dr
Poynton SK12 .....133 D3
Walkden M28 .....60 C5
Grosvenor Gdns
Newton-le-W WA12 .....89 C2
Salford M7 .....158 D4
9 Stalybridge SK15 .....86 A1
Wythenshawe M22 .....121 E6
Grosvenor Ho
Ashton-u-L OL7 .....166 A1
Manchester M16 .....97 E1
Grosvenor House Mews
M5 .....63 F2
Grosvenor House Sq 8
SK15 .....86 A1
Grosvenor Pl 6 OL7 OL4 .....166 A1
Grosvenor Rd
Altrincham WA14 .....119 E5
Cheadle SK8 .....123 C4
Eccles M30 .....79 A3
Hyde SK14 .....167 D1
Leigh WN7 .....75 D6
Manchester,Heaton Moor
SK4 .....168 B3
Manchester,Whalley Range
M16 .....97 D2
Marple SK6 .....125 F7
Pendlebury M27 .....80 B7
Sale M33 .....107 F6
Urmston M41 .....95 C2
Walkden M28 .....60 C5
4 Whitefield M45 .....44 E1
Grosvenor Rd Prim Sch
M27 .....80 B7
Grosvenor Sq Sale M33 .108 A4
Salford M7 .....158 D4
Uppermill OL3 .....69 B8
Grosvenor St
Ashton-u-L OL7 .....166 A1
Ashton-u-L OL7 .....84 F1
Bolton BL2 .....148 A6
Bury BL9 .....44 F8
Denton M34 .....100 F4
Hazel Grove SK7 .....124 D3
Heywood OL10 .....29 C1
Hindley WN2 .....56 D5
Kearsley BL4 .....60 F7
Little Lever BL3 .....43 B4
Manchester M1 .....163 B7
Prestwich M25 .....63 C4
Radcliffe M26 .....43 F4
Rochdale OL11 .....30 C1
5 Stalybridge SK15 .....86 A1
7 Stockport SK1 .....170 F8
Stretford M32 .....96 D2
Swinton M27 .....61 F2
3 Wigan WN5 .....54 F6
Grosvenor Way
Horwich BL6 .....22 C3
Royton OL1,OL2 .....48 D2
Grotton Hollow OL4 .....68 A6
Grotton Mdws OL4 .....68 B5
Grouse St OL12 .....14 F1
Grove OL15 .....16 C8
Grove Arc SK9 .....137 A2
Grove Ave Adlington PR6 ..21 A7
Failsworth M35 .....83 E5
Wilmslow SK9 .....137 B7
Grove Cl M14 .....98 C2
Grove Cotts OL3 .....51 D6
Grove Cres PR6 .....21 A7
Grove Ct M33 .....108 D4
Grove Hill M28 .....77 F6
Grove La
Altrincham,Timperley
WA15 .....120 A6
Altrincham,Well Green
WA15 .....120 B3
Cheadle SK8 .....132 A6
Manchester M20 .....110 B3
Standish WN6 .....36 F8
Grove Pk 6 M33 .....107 F4
Grove Pl WN6 .....36 F8
Grove Rd
Altrincham WA15 .....119 E3
Middleton M24 .....47 B2
Stalybridge SK15 .....86 D4
Up Holland WN8 .....53 C8
Uppermill OL3 .....69 B7
Grove St Ashton-in-M WN4 .73 A4
Ashton-u-L OL7 .....84 E5
Bolton BL1 .....143 D2
Bury BL9 .....141 C3
Droylsden M43 .....99 F8
Farnworth BL4 .....60 E8
Hazel Grove SK7 .....124 E3
Heywood OL10 .....29 E2
Leigh WN7 .....76 B4
Oldham OL1 .....67 B7
Rochdale OL11 .....139 E5
Salford M7 .....155 E5
Stalybridge SK16 .....85 D1
Uppermill OL3 .....69 B5
Wilmslow SK9 .....137 B7
Grove Terr 7 OL7 .....67 E8
Grove The
Appley Bridge WN6 .....18 C2
Bolton BL2 .....148 B5
Cheadle SK8 .....132 A6
Golborne WA3 .....74 D1
Hadfield SK14 .....171 F4
Ince-in-M WN2 .....151 F7

Grove The continued
Little Lever BL3 .....43 B3
Manchester M20 .....110 B1
Sale M33 .....108 B3
Shaw OL2 .....149 A6
Stockport SK2 .....170 E7
Uppermill OL3 .....50 F1
Urmston M41 .....94 F1
Grove Way SK9 .....137 B2
Grovehurst M27 .....79 C6
Grovewood Cl OL7 .....84 E5
Grovewood Dr WN6 .....35 E8
Grundey St SK7 .....124 E2
Grundy Ave M25 .....62 F2
Grundy Cl BL9 .....141 A1
Grundy La BL9 .....141 A1
Grundy Rd BL4 .....60 E7
Grundy St Bolton BL3 .147 D4
Golborne WA3 .....90 A7
Heywood OL10 .....46 E8
Manchester SK4 .....110 E2
Walkden M28 .....60 F2
Grundy's Cl M12 .....77 C5
Grundys Bldgs M29 .....77 A8
Gt Western St 4 M14 ..97 F4
**Guardian Angel's RC Prim
Sch** A3 .....27 B3
Guardian Cl OL12 .....15 D5
Guardian Ct M33 .....108 A5
Guernsey Cl M11 .....111 A6
Guest Rd M25 .....63 A6
Guest St WN7 .....76 B5
Guide Bridge Mills Ind Est
OL7 .....100 E8
Guide Bridge Sta M34 .100 F8
Guide La M34 .....100 F7
Guide Post Sq M13 .164 D6
Guide St M50 .....80 C1
Guido St BL1 .....143 E2
Guild Ave M28 .....60 D2
Guild St BL7 .....25 B7
Guildford Ave SK8 .132 A6
Guildford Cl 1 .....124 B7
Guildford Cres WN6 ....36 F3
Guildford Dr OL6 .....85 C7
Guildford Gr M24 .....47 C3
Guildford Rd Bolton BL1 ..143 D2
Dukinfield SK16 .....102 A7
Manchester M19 .....99 B2
Salford M6 .....80 B4
Urmston M41 .....95 E4
Guildford St OL16 .....31 A7
Guildhall Cl M15 .....163 A5
Guildford Rd M30 .....79 B1
Guinness Circ M17 .....96 A8
Guinness Ho 2 OL16 .....31 B6
Guinness Rd M17 .....96 A8
Guinness Road Trad Est
M17 .....95 F8
Guiseley Cl BL9 .....27 E8
Guil Cl SK12 .....133 B3
Gullane Cl M40 .....83 C7
Gulvain Pl OL9 .....65 F8
Gun Rd SK13,SK6 .....115 C2
Gun St M4 .....159 B2
Gunson Ct 8 M40 .....159 C3
Gunson St M40 .....159 C3
Gunters Ave BL5 .....57 F6
Gurner Ave M5 .....161 B7
Gurney St M4 .....160 D1
Gutter End BL9 .....140 F2
Gutter La BL0 .....138 B7
Guy Fawkes St M5 .....161 B7
Guy St M7 .....155 F7
Guywood Cotts SK6 .113 C3
Guywood La SK6 .....113 C3
Gwelo St M11 .....83 A2
Gwenbury Ave SK1 .....112 B1
Gwendor Ave M8 .....63 F2
Gwladys St SK15 .....86 E6
Gwynant Pl M20 .....110 C7
Gylden Cl SK14 .....102 B5
Gypsy La OL11 .....30 C3
Gypsy Wlk SK2 .....124 C6
Gyte's La M19 .....99 C2

H

Habergham Cl M28 .....78 C7
Hackberry Cl WA14 .119 B8
Hacken Bridge Rd BL3 ..42 D4
Hacken La BL3 .....42 C4
Hackford Cl Bolton BL1 ..144 C8
Bury BL8 .....27 D5
Hacking St Bury BL8 ....141 A2
Prestwich M25 .....63 A4
Hackle St M11 .....83 C2
Hackleton Cl M4 .....160 D1
Hackness Rd M21 .....108 F8
Hackney Ave M40 .....83 C4
Hackney Cl M26 .....44 A5
Hackwood Wlk 16 M8 ..155 F7
Hackworth Cl WN1 .....151 E8
Hadbutt La M29 .....76 F4
Haddan Gn 3 SK13 ..171 D2
Haddan Lea 3 SK13 ..171 D2
Haddington Dr M9 .....64 E3
Haddon Ave M40 .....65 F1
Haddon Cl
Alderley Edge SK9 .....136 F2
High Lane SK6 .....134 E6
Rochdale OL11 .....45 A5
Haddon Gr
Altrincham WA15 .....119 F7
Reddish SK5 .....111 E7

Haddon Gr continued
Sale M33 .....108 A4
Haddon Hall Rd M43 ....83 E2
Haddon Ho M5 .....154 D3
Haddon Mews SK13 .171 D2
Haddon Rd Eccles M30 ..95 C8
Gatley SK8 .....131 C7
Golborne WA3 .....74 D2
Hazel Grove SK7 .....124 E1
Manchester M21 .....109 D5
Swinton M28 .....79 C6
Wigan WN3 .....54 E3
Haddon St
5 Ashton-in-M WN4 ....72 F5
Rochdale OL11 .....30 E4
Salford M6 .....81 B5
Stretford M32 .....96 D4
Haddon Way
17 Denton M34 .....101 A1
Shaw OL2 .....149 C8
Hadfield Cl M14 .....98 D3
Hadfield Cres OL6 .....66 B4
Hadfield Inf Est SK13 ..103 F6
Hadfield Inf Sch SK13 ..103 F5
Hadfield Pl 3 SK13 ..116 C8
Hadfield Sq 2 SK13 ..116 C8
Hadfield St
Dukinfield SK16 .....101 A7
Manchester M16 .....161 C8
Oldham OL8 .....66 F3
Salford M7 .....155 E6
Hadfield Sta SK13 .....104 A5
Hadfields Ave SK14 ..103 D5
Hadleigh Cl BL1 .....144 C8
Hadleigh Gr BL6 .....40 B4
Hadley Ave M13 .....98 E2
Hadley Cl SK8 .....122 F1
Hadley St M6 .....81 B5
Hadlow Gn SK5 .....112 B6
Hadlow Wlk M40 .....160 E3
Hadrian Ho OL1 .....153 F7
Hadwin St BL1 .....143 F1
Hafton Rd M7 .....81 B6
Hag Bank La SK12 .....135 D7
Hag Fold Sta M46 .....58 C5
Haggate OL2 .....48 C3
Haggate Cres OL2 .....48 C3
Hagley Rd M5 .....161 A6
Hags The BL9 .....45 C3
Hague Bar Prim Sch
SK22 .....135 E8
Hague Bar Rd SK22 ..135 E8
Hague Bush Cl WA3 ....74 E1
Hague Ct 5 M20 .....110 A5
Hague Fold Rd SK22 ..135 F8
Hague Ho OL8 .....153 F5
Hague Pl 3 SK15 .....86 A2
Hague Rd
Manchester M20 .....110 A5
Mottram-in-L SK13,SK14 ..103 B1
Hague St Ashton-u-L OL6 ..85 D4
Glossop SK13 .....116 D6
Oldham OL4 .....67 E8
Haig Ave M44 .....105 F1
Haig Ct BL8 .....27 B1
Haig Rd Aspull WN2 ....38 A7
Bury BL8 .....27 B1
Stretford M32 .....96 D3
Haig St WN3 .....150 B7
Haigh Ave SK4 .....111 E5
Haigh Ctry Pk* WN2 ..37 F5
Haigh Hall Cl BL0 .....11 B4
Haigh La Oldham OL9 ..47 E1
Haigh Lawn WA14 .....119 B3
Haigh Pk SK4 .....111 E5
Haigh Rd WN2 .....38 C6
Haigh St Bolton BL1 ..145 F8
Rochdale OL11 .....31 A5
Haigh View
Ince-in-M WN3 .....151 E6
Wigan WN1 .....37 D2
Haile St BL0 .....11 A4
Haile Dr M28 .....77 F6
Hailsham Cl BL8 .....27 C7
Hailwood St OL11 .....30 E4
Halcyon Cl 2 OL12 ..114 B2
Haldane Wlk M8 .....155 F6
Haldon Rd M20 .....110 D5
Hale Ave SK12 .....133 D2
Hale Cl WN7 .....76 A4
Hale Ct WA14 .....119 D2
Hale Gr WN4 .....72 D3
Hale Green Ct WA15 ..120 A3
Hale La M35,M40 .....83 E8
Hale Low Rd WA15 ..119 E3
Hale Prep Sch WA15 ..119 E3
Hale Rd Altrincham WA15 ..120 E1
Manchester M16 .....168 C3
Hale View WA14 .....119 D2
Hale Wlk SK8 .....123 A5
Halebank Ave M20 ..109 F4
Hales Cl M43 .....83 F3
Halesden Rd SK4 .....111 B5
Halesfield Rd WN7 .....57 B2
Halesworth Wlk M40 ..159 C4
Halewood Ave WA3 ....73 F1
Haley Cl 6 SK5 .....111 F8
Haley St M8 .....156 B7
Half Acre M26 .....43 F6
Half Acre Dr OL11 .....30 D6
Half Acre La Blackrod BL6 ..21 C7
Rochdale OL11 .....30 D6
Half Acre Mews OL11 ..30 B6
Half Acre Rd OL11 .....30 B6
Half Edge La M30 .....79 F3

Half Moon La SK2 .....124 E6
Half Moon St 10 M2 ..158 F1
Half St M3 .....158 E3
Halfacre Rd M22 .....121 C4
Halford St WN4 .....83 C8
Halfpenny Bridge Ind Est 1
OL11 .....31 A6
Halifax Rd
Littleborough OL15 .....16 D7
Rochdale OL12 .....15 C2
Halifax St OL6 .....166 B4
Haliwell St OL15 .....16 B8
Hall Ave Altrincham WA15 ..119 F7
Manchester M14 .....98 D3
Sale M33 .....107 E6
Stalybridge SK15 .....86 D5
Hall Bank M30 .....79 F3
Hall Cl Mottram-in-L SK14 ..103 A5
Shevington WN6 .....36 A6
Hall Coppice The BL7 ....8 E1
Hall Dr Middleton M24 ....64 F7
Hall Farm Ave M41 .....95 B3
Hall Farm Cl SK7 .....125 A3
Hall Fold OL12 .....14 C8
Hall Gdns OL12 .....14 C8
Hall Gn WN8 .....53 B7
Hall Gr Cheadle SK8 ..122 C6
Manchester M14 .....98 D3
Hall Green Cl
Dukinfield SK16 .....166 C1
Up Holland WN8 .....53 B7
Hall Green Rd SK16 ..166 C1
Hall House La WN7 .....76 C4
Hall i' th' Wood La
Bolton,Castle Hill BL1,BL2 ..25 B3
Bolton,Bromley Cross BL1 ..25 A4
Hall i' th' Wood Sta BL2 ..25 B3
Hall i'th'Wood (Mus)*
BL1 .....25 A4
Hall La Appley Bridge WN6 ..18 D2
Bolton BL3,BL4 .....42 E3
Farnworth BL4 .....42 D2
Horwich BL6 .....39 E7
Orrell WN5 .....53 F4
Partington M31 .....105 F4
Pennington Green WN2 ..38 B7
Romiley SK6 .....113 B6
Wigan,Leyland Mill Brow
WN1 .....37 D4
Wythenshawe M23 .....121 B6
Hall Lane Gr WN2 .....56 D8
Hall Lee Dr BL5 .....40 A1
Hall Mdw SK8 .....122 E1
Hall Meadow Rd SK13 ..104 D2
Hall Moss La SK7 .....132 C4
Hall Moss Rd M9 .....65 A3
Hall Pool Dr SK2 .....124 E2
Hall Rd Altrincham WA14 ..119 C1
Ashton-u-L OL6 .....85 C5
Bramhall SK7 .....123 D1
Handforth SK9 .....131 E3
Manchester M14 .....98 D3
Wilmslow SK9 .....137 A7
Hall St Ashton-in-M WN2 ..73 E7
Ashton-u-L OL6 .....85 E2
Bury,Walshaw BL8 .....26 E4
Bury,Woodhill BL8 .....27 C4
Cheadle SK8 .....122 D6
Denton SK14 .....101 B3
Failsworth M35 .....83 D6
1 Farnworth BL4 .....60 E8
Heywood OL10 .....29 E1
Ince-in-M WN2 .....151 F8
Manchester M2 .....162 F8
Middleton M24 .....65 A8
3 Oldham OL4 .....67 B7
Radcliffe M26 .....43 F6
Ramsbottom BL9 .....11 C2
Royton OL2 .....48 D4
Stockport SK1 .....112 A2
Swinton M27 .....61 F2
Whitworth OL12 .....14 C8
Wigan WN1 .....151 D7
Hall The SK13 .....116 A7
Hall Wood Ave WA11 ..72 F1
Hall's Ct 8 SK13 .....104 C1
Hallam Rd M40 .....83 B5
Hallam St Radcliffe M26 ..44 D4
Stockport SK2 .....124 A6
Hallas Gr M23 .....109 B1
Hallbottom St SK14 ..101 F5
Hallbridge Gdns WN8 ..53 B8
Hallcroft M31 .....105 E4
Hallcroft Gdns OL16 ....31 E6
Hallgate
Westhoughton BL5 .....57 E5
Wigan WN1 .....150 C8
Hallgate Dr SK8 .....122 A3
Hallgate Rd SK1 .....124 B8
Halliday Ct 4 OL15 ....15 E4
Halliday Rd M40 .....83 A4
Halliford Rd M40 .....83 A6
Hallington Cl BL3 .....145 F5
Halliwell Ave OL8 .....66 B3
Halliwell Ind Est BL1 ..143 D3
Halliwell La M8 .....155 F7
Halliwell Rd Bolton BL1 ..143 E2
Prestwich M25 .....62 F1
Halliwell St
18 Bolton BL1 .....143 D2
Milnrow OL16 .....31 E7
Oldham OL9 .....66 A2
5 Rochdale OL12 .....139 E8
Halliwell St W 17 M8 ..155 F7

Halliwell Wlk M25 .....62 F1
Hallkirk Wlk 4 M40 ....65 D2
Hallows Ave M21 .....109 C5
Hallows Farm Ave OL12 ..14 D2
Hallroyd Brow OL1 .....153 E8
Halls Cotts OL3 .....69 B7
Halls Way OL3 .....69 B6
Hallstead Ave M38 .....59 E4
Hallstead Gr M38 .....59 E4
Hallsville Rd M19 .....99 C1
Hallsworth Rd M30 .....79 A1
Hallview Way M28 .....59 F3
Hallwood Ave M6 .....80 C5
Hallwood Rd
Handforth SK9 .....131 D2
Wythenshawe M23 .....121 A6
Hallworth Ave M43 .....84 C1
Hallworth Rd M8 .....156 B8
Hallworthy Cl WN7 .....75 B1
Halmore Rd M40 .....160 D2
Halsall Cl BL9 .....27 F6
Halsall Dr BL3 .....147 E2
Halsbury Cl M12 .....164 E6
Halsey Cl OL9 .....65 E2
Halsey Wlk 2 M8 .....155 F7
Halshaw La BL4 .....60 F7
Halsmere Dr M9 .....64 E3
Halstead Ave
Manchester M21 .....109 A7
Salford M6 .....80 E5
Halstead Dr M44 .....94 B1
Halstead Gr Leigh WN7 ..76 B5
Wythenshawe SK8 .....131 B7
Halstead St Bolton BL2 ..148 A7
Bury BL9 .....141 A4
Halstock Wlk BL9 .....28 A5
Halstock Wlk M40 .....157 D5
Halston St M15 .....162 E6
Halstone Ave SK9 .....136 E4
Halter Cl M26 .....44 A5
Halton Ho M22 .....121 C2
Halton Bank M6 .....154 F4
Halton Dr WA15 .....108 B1
Halton Ho 4 M5 .....154 F1
Halton Rd M11 .....83 C2
Halton St Bolton BL2 ..148 B4
Hyde SK14 .....167 F3
Halvard Ave BL9 .....27 F6
Halvard Ct BL9 .....27 F6
Halvis Gr M16 .....97 B3
Hambledon Cl BL3 .....40 F5
Hambledon Cl M46 .....58 E5
Hambleton Cl BL8 .....26 F1
Hambleton Dr 2 M33 ..107 D5
Hamblett St WN7 .....75 B5
Hambridge Cl M8 .....156 A7
Hamel St Bolton BL2 ..147 E3
Dukinfield SK14 .....167 F3
Hamer Com Prim Sch
OL16 .....15 B2
Hamer Dr M16 .....162 D5
Hamer Hall Cres OL12 ..15 B1
Hamer Hill M9 .....64 C3
Hamer St Bolton BL2 ..25 B1
Heywood OL10 .....29 B2
Radcliffe M26 .....44 C4
Ramsbottom BL0 .....11 B2
Hamer's Bldg OL10 .....29 B2
Hamerton Rd M40 .....159 C4
Hamilcar Ave M30 .....79 E1
Hamilton Ave Eccles M30 ..79 E1
Irlam M44 .....105 D4
Royton OL2 .....48 E8
Hamilton Cl Bury BL8 ....27 B3
Prestwich M25 .....63 A3
Hamilton Cres SK4 .....168 B1
Hamilton Ct
Little Lever BL3 .....43 B3
Sale M33 .....108 B4
Wigan WN5 .....54 E8
Hamilton Gr M16 .....162 D5
Hamilton Lo 6 M14 ....98 C3
Hamilton Mews
Eccles M30 .....79 E3
Prestwich M25 .....63 A3
Hamilton Rd
Garswood WN4 .....72 D4
Hindley WN2 .....56 F4
Manchester M13 .....98 F3
Prestwich M25 .....63 A3
Tyldesley M29 .....77 D6
Whitefield M45 .....62 E8
Hamilton Sq 169 E3
Wigan WN5 .....54 E8
Hamilton St
Ashton-u-L OL7 .....84 F1
Atherton M46 .....58 C2
Bolton BL1 .....24 E5
Bury BL9 .....140 F4
Chadderton OL9 .....152 A7
Eccles M30 .....79 B3
Leigh WN7 .....75 D6
Manchester M16 .....167 B7
Salford M7 .....155 D7
Stalybridge SK15 .....85 F2
Swinton M27 .....61 D1
Hamilton Way OL10 ....28 E1
Hamlet Dr M33 .....107 E6
Hamlet The BL6 .....40 B8
Hammer Terr BL9 .....11 C3
Hammerstone Rd M18 ..165 C6
Hammett Rd M21 .....109 A8
Hammond OL16 .....29 C2
Hammond Ave Bacup OL13 ..3 D8

Hammond Ave *continued*
Reddish SK4 111 E5
Hamnet Cl BL1 25 A5
Hamnett St
Droylsden M11,M43 83 D1
Hyde SK14 167 D3
Hamon Rd WA15 119 E4
Hampden Cres M18 165 C5
Hampden Gr M30 79 D2
Hampden Pl WN5 36 D1
Hampden Rd
Prestwich M25 63 C4
Sale M33 108 A3
Shaw OL2 49 D6
Hampden St
Heywood OL10 29 D1
Rochdale OL11 139 F6
Hampshire Cl
Brinnington SK5 112 C5
Bury BL9 45 A8
Glossop SK13 116 F8
Hampshire Ho SK5 112 C5
Hampshire Rd
Brinnington SK5 112 C5
Chadderton OL9 152 B5
Droylsden M43 84 A3
Partington M31 105 D2
Hampshire St M7 155 E7
Hampshire Wlk 6 M8 156 B6
Hampson Ave WA3 91 F3
Hampson Cl
Ashton-in-M WN4 73 B2
5 Eccles M30 79 B1
Hampson Cres SK9 131 C4
Hampson Fold M26 43 F4
Hampson Mill La BL9 44 F5
Hampson Pl OL6 85 E6
Hampson Rd
Ashton-u-L OL6 85 E6
Stretford M32 96 C2
Hampson Sq 5 M26 44 A4
Hampson St Atherton M46 58 C3
Droylsden M43 84 A2
Eccles M30 79 B1
Horwich BL6 22 B4
Manchester M5 162 D8
Manchester,Miles Platting M40 160 D4
Radcliffe M26 44 A3
Sale M33 108 D4
Salford M3,M5 158 D1
Stockport SK1 124 B8
Swinton M27 62 A1
Hampstead Ave M41 94 E1
Hampstead Dr
Stockport SK2 124 C5
Whitefield M45 44 E1
Hampstead La SK2 124 C5
Hampstead Rd WN6 19 D1
Hampsted Ho SK2 124 C5
Hampton Gr Bury BL9 27 F6
Cheadle SK8 122 E2
Leigh WN7 76 E7
Sale WA14 107 F1
Hampton Ho 5 M33 108 C4
Hampton Mews 1 SK3 123 F4
Hampton Rd Bolton BL3 42 A3
Failsworth M35 84 B8
Irlam M44 105 D4
Stretford M21 96 F1
Urmston M41 95 D2
Hampton St OL8 66 D4
Hamsell Rd M13 163 C7
Hanborough Ct M29 76 F8
Hancock Cl M14 98 B3
Hancock St M32 108 D8
Hand La Leigh WN7 75 E1
Leigh WN7 75 E2
Handel Ave M41 95 A2
Handel Mews M33 108 C4
Handel St Bolton BL1 143 D3
Whitworth OL12 14 B8
Handford Ho 5 M41 95 E2
Handforth Gr M13 98 E2
Handforth Rd
Handforth SK9 131 E1
Reddish SK5 111 F5
Handforth Sta SK9 131 D3
Handley Ave M14 98 B1
Handley Cl SK3 123 C5
Handley Rd SK7 123 E3
Handley St Bury BL9 44 F8
Rochdale OL12 139 D8
Hands La OL11 30 A7
Handsworth St M12 164 D7
Hanging Birch M24 64 B7
Hanging Chadder La OL2 48 C7
Hanging Lees Cl OL16 32 C4
Hani Ct M8 63 F1
Hani Wells Bsns Pk M19 111 B7
Hankinson Cl M31 105 E2
Hankinson Way M6 81 A3
Hanley Cl Disley SK12 135 D5
Middleton M24 65 A5
Hanlith Mews M19 110 F8
Hanlon St
Manchester M8 156 A8
Manchester,Crumpsall M8 63 F1
Hanmer St WN2 56 D5
Hannah Baldwin Cl M11 164 F8
Hannah Brown Ho WA15 119 E3
Hannah Lo M20 110 A4
Hannah St M12 99 A2
Hannerton Rd OL2 49 D7
Hannet Rd M22 121 D2
Hanover Bsns Pk WA14 119 B7
Hanover Cres M14 98 D4
Hanover Ct
4 Ashton-u-L OL7 166 A1
Bolton BL3 144 B5
Salford M7 155 D7
Swinton M28 79 B6
Hanover Gdns M7 155 E8
Hanover Ho Bolton BL3 146 B2
13 Manchester M14 110 D8
Oldham OL8 153 D6
Hanover Rd
Altrincham WA14 119 B7
Hindley WN2 56 C6
Hanover St Bolton BL1 145 E7
Leigh WN7 76 A6
Littleborough OL15 16 A5
Manchester M4 159 A2
Mossley OL5 68 C1
Rochdale OL11 30 C2
Stalybridge SK15 85 F2
Hanover St N M34 100 E8
Hanover St S 4 M34 100 E8
Hanover Twrs SK5 169 F3
Hansby Cl OL1 48 E1
Hansdon Cl M8 156 A6
Hansen Wlk 3 M22 121 C2
Hansham Wlk M23 108 E1
Hanslope Wlk 14 M9 157 E8
Hansom Dr M46 58 A1
Hanson Cl M24 47 A1
Hanson Dr M46 76 A8
Hanson Mews SK1 112 B2
Hanson Pk M24 47 A1
Hanson Rd M40 83 B7
Hanson St Adlington PR7 20 F5
Bury BL9 140 F4
Middleton M24 47 A1
Oldham OL4 67 C7
Hanstock Cl WN5 53 E5
Hanwell Cl WN7 75 E1
Hanworth Cl M13 163 B7
Hapsford Wlk M40 83 A5
Hapton Ave M32 96 D1
Hapton Pl SK4 169 E3
Hapton St M19 99 A1
Harbern Cl M30 79 D4
Harbern Dr WN7 57 D2
Harbord St M24 65 A8
Harboro Ct M33 107 F3
Harboro Gr M33 107 F4
Harboro Rd M33 107 E4
Harboro Way M33 107 F4
Harbour City Sta M50 96 F8
Harbour Farm Rd SK14 101 E5
Harbour La Edgworth BL7 9 D5
Milnrow OL16 31 F5
Harbour La N OL16 31 F6
Harbourne Ave M28 78 C8
Harbourne Cl M28 78 C8
Harbrook Gr WN2,WN7 75 C8
Harburn Wlk M22 130 E8
Harbury Cl Bolton BL3 146 A3
Wigan WN6 36 F2
Harbury Cres M22 121 C5
Harbury Wlk WN6 36 F2
Harcles Dr BL0 11 B2
Harcombe Rd M20 110 C6
Harcourt Ave M41 95 F1
Harcourt Cl M41 95 F1
Harcourt Ind Ctr M28 60 D5
Harcourt Mews 10 BL6 22 B4
Harcourt Rd
Altrincham WA14 119 D6
Sale M33 108 A6
Harcourt St Oldham OL1 67 B8
Reddish SK5 111 F8
Stretford M32 96 E3
Walkden M28 60 D5
Hard La OL12 15 A8
Hardacre St WN3 151 D6
Hardberry Pl SK2 124 E6
Hardcastle Ave M21 109 C6
Hardcastle Cl BL2 25 C6
Hardcastle Gdns BL2 25 C6
Hardcastle Rd SK3 170 D7
Hardcastle St Bolton BL1 143 F2
Oldham OL1 153 F7
7 Oldham,Mumps OL1 67 A7
Harden Dr BL2 25 D2
Harden Hills OL2 49 D8
Harden Pk SK9 137 A3
Hardfield Rd M24 65 B5
Hardfield St OL10 29 D2
Hardicker St M19 111 B7
Hardie Ave BL4 60 B7
Harding St Adlington PR6 21 B8
Dukinfield SK14 101 D5
Manchester M4 160 D1
Salford M3 158 F2
Salford,Pendleton M6 81 A4
Stockport SK1 112 B1
Hardman Ave
Manchester M25 63 D2
Rawtenstall BB4 2 A8
Romiley SK6 113 A3
Hardman Cl Radcliffe M26 43 F6
Rawtenstall BB4 2 F7
Hardman Dr BB4 2 F7
Hardman Fold BL3 42 B2
Hardman Fold Sch M35 83 D7
Hardman La M35 83 E8
Hardman Rd SK5 111 F8
Hardman St Bury BL9 140 F4
Failsworth M35 83 D7
Farnworth BL4 60 E7
Heywood OL10 29 D2
Manchester M3 158 E1
Milnrow OL16 32 A5
Hardman St *continued*
Oldham OL9 66 B3
Radcliffe M26 43 F6
Stockport SK3 169 D1
Stockport SK3 170 D8
Wigan WN3 150 B6
Hardman Terr OL13 3 D8
Hardman's La BL7 24 F8
Hardman's Mews M45 62 F6
Hardman's Rd M45 62 F6
Hardmans BL7 24 F7
Hardon Gr M13 98 F2
Hardrow Cl WN3 55 B2
Hardrush Fold M35 84 A6
Hardshaw Cl M13 163 B6
Hardsough La BL0 1 D5
Hardwick Cl
High Lane SK6 134 F6
Little Lever M26 43 B5
Hardwick Rd
Ashton-in-M WN4 73 A5
Partington M31 106 A3
Hardwick St OL7 84 F2
Hardwicke Rd SK12 133 F4
Hardwicke St OL11 30 E4
Hardwood Cl M8 156 A7
Hardy Ave M21 109 A8
Hardy Cl Rochdale OL11 30 F3
Westhoughton BL5 39 E3
Hardy Dr
Altrincham WA15 119 F7
Bramhall SK7 132 D7
Hardy Farm M21 109 B6
Hardy Gr Swinton M27 79 D5
Worsley M28 78 F8
Hardy La M21 109 B6
Hardy Mill Prim Sch BL2 25 F4
Hardy Mill Rd Bolton BL2 25 F4
Bolton BL2 26 A3
Hardy St Ashton-u-L OL6 85 E6
Eccles M30 79 B1
Oldham OL4 67 A6
Wigan WN6 37 A1
Hardybutts Wigan WN1 151 D8
Wigan WN1 151 E8
Hardywood Rd 4 M34 113 A7
Hare Dr BL9 45 B4
Hare Hill Prim Sch SK14 102 C3
Hare Hill Rd
Hattersley SK14 102 C2
Littleborough OL15 16 B6
Hare Hill Wlk SK14 102 C3
Hare St
6 Manchester M4 159 A2
Rochdale OL11 139 F5
Rochdale OL11 31 A6
Harebell Ave 10 M28 59 F3
Harebell Cl OL12 14 D3
Harecastle Ave M30 95 E8
Haredale Dr M8 156 B6
Harefield Ave OL11 139 F5
Harefield Dr
Heywood OL10 29 F2
Manchester M20 110 A2
Wilmslow SK9 137 B5
Harefield Rd SK9 131 E4
Hareford Wlk M9 156 C6
Harehill Cl 5 M13 163 B7
Hareshill Rd OL10 46 C7
Harewood SK13 115 A8
Harewood Ave
Rochdale OL11 13 D2
Sale M33 107 D3
Harewood Cl OL11 13 D2
Harewood Ct M33 108 C3
Harewood Dr
Rochdale OL11 13 C2
Royton OL2 48 C5
Harewood Gr SK5 111 E8
Harewood Lodge SK13 115 A8
Harewood Rd
Hindley WN2 56 C5
Irlam M44 94 B2
Rochdale OL11 13 D2
Shaw OL2 49 D8
Harewood Way
Rochdale OL11 13 C2
Swinton M27 61 F2
Harewood Wlk 23 M34 101 A1
Harford Cl SK7 124 A1
Hargate Ave OL12 14 A2
Hargate Cl BL9 11 C2
Hargate Dr
Altrincham WA15 120 A1
Irlam M44 94 A3
Hargate Hill La SK13 115 E7
Hargrave Cl M9 64 C6
Hargreave's St M4 159 A3
Hargreaves Ho BL3 145 E6
Hargreaves Rd WA15 120 C6
Hargreaves St
Bolton BL1 143 E2
Oldham OL1 153 F7
Oldham,Alder Root OL9 152 C6
Rochdale OL11 30 C4
Harkerside Cl M21 109 C8
Harkness St M12 164 D7
Harland Dr
Ashton-in-M WN4 73 C3
Manchester M8 156 B7
Harland Way OL12 14 B2
Harlea Ave WN2 57 A3
Harlech Ave Hindley WN2 57 B4
Prestwich M25,M45 63 B7
Harlech Dr SK7 124 D1
Harlech St WN4 72 F5
Harleen Gr SK2 124 D7
Harley Ave Ainsworth BL2 26 D1
Bolton BL2 25 E3
Manchester M14 98 E3
Harley Ct M24 46 F1
Harley Hall Royal Northern Coll of Music M16 97 E1
Harley Rd Middleton M24 46 F1
Sale M33 108 C5
Harley St Ashton-u-L OL6 166 B3
Manchester M11 99 D8
Harling Rd M22 121 E7
Harlington Cl 3 M23 120 D7
Harlock Ct M6 81 B3
Harlow Dr M18 99 D3
Harlyn Ave SK7 132 F7
Harmer Cl M40 83 B5
Harmol Gr OL7 84 F6
Harmony St Milnrow OL16 31 F6
Oldham OL4 67 A6
Harmsworth Dr SK4 111 B5
Harmsworth St M6 154 E2
Harmuir Cl WN6 36 E4
Harold Ave
Ashton-in-M WN4 73 A5
Dukinfield SK16 101 D8
Reddish M18 99 F4
Harold Lees Rd OL10 29 F3
Harold Priestnall Cl M40 83 B6
Harold St Aspull WN2 38 D5
Bolton BL1 143 D2
Failsworth M35 83 E7
Manchester M16 161 C6
Middleton M24 46 E1
Oldham OL9 153 D7
Prestwich M25 62 F4
Rochdale OL16 15 C2
Stockport SK1 124 B8
Haroldene St BL2 25 B2
Harp Ind Est OL11 30 D2
Harp Rd M17 96 A8
Harp St M11 99 E7
Harp Trad Est M17 96 A8
Harper Ct SK3 170 E7
Harper Fold Rd M26 43 E3
Harper Green Rd BL3,BL4 42 B1
Harper Green Sch BL4 42 B1
Harper Ho M19 98 F1
Harper Pl OL6 166 C3
Harper Rd M22 121 E7
Harper Sq OL2 149 C7
Harper St Farnworth BL4 42 B2
Hindley WN2 56 C4
Oldham OL8 66 E4
Rochdale OL11 139 E5
Stockport SK3 170 E7
Wigan WN1 151 E7
Harper's La BL1 142 B2
Harpford Cl BL2 43 A5
Harpford Dr BL2 43 A5
Harptree Gr WN7 75 D7
Harpur Mount Prim Sch M9 157 D8
Harpurhey Rd M8,M9 157 D8
Harridge Ave
Rochdale OL12 14 C3
Stalybridge SK15 86 D2
Harridge St OL12 14 C3
Harridge The OL12 14 C3
Harrier Cl Leigh WN7 76 B5
Walkden M28 78 D8
Wythenshawe M22 121 E5
Harriet St Irlam M44 105 E5
Walkden M28 60 D3
Harriett St
Manchester M4 159 C2
Rochdale OL16 31 A7
Harringay Rd M40 83 B5
Harrington Cl BL9 45 A7
Harrington Rd WA14 119 B5
Harrington St M18 99 E5
Harris Ave Reddish M34 100 B3
Urmston M41 95 D5
Harris Cl Heywood OL10 28 E1
Reddish M34 100 B3
Harris Dr Dukinfield SK14 102 A4
Whitefield BL9 45 B2
Harris Rd WN6 19 B3
Harris St Bolton BL3 145 E6
Manchester M8 158 E4
Harrison Ave M19 99 B2
Harrison Cl 1 OL12 13 F1
Harrison Cres BL6 21 C3
Harrison Rd PR7 21 A6
Harrison St Bacup OL13 4 B8
Eccles M30 95 B8
Hindley WN2 57 B3
Horwich BL6 22 B4
Hyde SK14 113 F8
Manchester M4 160 D1
1 Oldham OL1 153 F6
Ramsbottom BL0 138 C7
Salford M7 158 D4
Stalybridge SK15 86 A2
Stockport SK1,SK2 170 F7
Walkden M38 60 A4
4 Wigan WN5 54 F6
Harrison Way WA12 89 C4
Harrison's Dr SK6 113 C5
Harrock La WN6 18 A5
Harrogate Ave M25 63 D2
Harrogate Cl M11 99 E7
Harrogate Dr SK5 111 E8
Harrogate Rd SK5 99 E1
Harrogate Sq BL8 26 F1
Harrogate St WN1 151 D7
Harrop Court Rd OL3 51 D5
Harrop Edge La OL3 51 B5
Harrop Edge Rd SK14, SK15 102 E4
Harrop Fold OL8 67 A1
Harrop Fold Sch M28 60 B3
Harrop Gn OL3 51 D5
Harrop Green La OL3 51 D5
Harrop Rd WA15 119 F2
Harrop St Bolton BL3 146 A4
Droylsden M18 99 F6
10 Stalybridge SK15 86 A2
Stockport SK1 124 A7
Walkden M28 60 B3
Harrow Ave
Manchester M19 111 A6
Oldham OL8 66 E3
Rochdale OL11 30 A6
Harrow Cl Bury BL9 44 F5
Orrell WN5 53 F8
Harrow Cres WN7 75 F3
Harrow Dr M33 108 A2
Harrow Mews OL2 149 B7
Harrow Pl WN3 55 F4
Harrow Rd Bolton BL1 144 B8
Sale M33 108 A2
Wigan WN5 36 D1
Harrow St Manchester M8 64 B1
Rochdale OL11 31 B2
Harrowby Ct BL4 60 B8
Harrowby Dr M40 157 D5
Harrowby Fold BL4 60 C8
Harrowby La BL4 60 C8
Harrowby Rd
Bolton,Doffcocker BL1 23 F2
Bolton,Fernhill Gate BL3 146 A3
Swinton M27 79 E7
Harrowby St
Farnworth BL4 60 C8
Wigan WN5 54 E6
Harrowdene Wlk 6 M9 157 D8
Harry Hall Gdns M7 81 C3
Harry Pigott Ave M40 83 A7
Harry Rd SK5 111 F8
Harry Rowley Cl 1 M22 121 C2
Harry St Oldham OL9 152 C6
Rochdale OL11 30 B3
Royton OL2 48 E2
Harry Thorneycroft Wlk M11 164 E8
Harry's Ct 3 WN7 75 D5
Harrycroft Rd SK6 113 B5
Harrytown SK6 113 A2
Harrytown RC High Sch SK6 113 A2
Harswell Cl WN5 53 E5
Hart Ave Droylsden M43 84 B1
Sale M33 108 F3
Hart Ct OL5 68 B2
Hart Dr BL9 45 B4
Hart Hill Dr M5 154 D3
Hart Mill Cl OL5 68 B2
Hart Rd M14 98 B1
Hart St Altrincham WA14 119 E5
Droylsden M43 84 B1
Manchester M1 159 A1
Tyldesley M29 77 C8
Westhoughton BL5 57 B7
Hart's Houses BL6 22 D5
Harter St M1 163 A8
Hartfield Cl M13 163 C6
Hartfield Wlk BL2 148 C8
Hartford Ave
Heywood OL10 29 B3
Reddish SK4 111 D6
Wilmslow SK9 136 F5
Hartford Cl OL10 29 B3
Hartford Gdns WA15 120 D5
Hartford Gn BL5 57 F6
Hartford Rd Sale M33 107 D2
Urmston M41 95 E4
Westhoughton BL5 57 F6
Hartford Sq OL9 152 C6
Hartford St M34 100 E5
Harthill St M8 155 F5
Hartington Cl 4 M41 95 E2
Hartington Ct OL2 48 E4
Hartington Dr
Droylsden M11 83 B3
Hazel Grove SK7 133 E8
Standish WN6 36 F7
Hartington Rd
Altrincham WA14 119 D8
Bolton BL1 144 C8
Bramhall SK7 132 E6
Eccles M30 79 A3
Gatley SK8 131 D8
High Lane SK12,SK6 134 F7
Manchester M21 109 B8
Stockport SK2 124 D5
Hartington St M14 97 F3
Hartis Ave M7 155 E6
Hartland Ave M41 96 A2
Hartland Cl
Poynton SK12 133 D5
Stockport SK2 124 C8
Tyldesley M29 77 B8
Hartland St 3 OL10 29 D2
Hartlebury OL11 139 E6
Hartlepool Cl M14 98 B3
Hartley Ave
Manchester M25 63 D3
Wigan WN1 151 E7
Hartley Gr Irlam M44 94 B4
Wigan WN5 54 B7
Hartley Hall Gdns M16 97 E1
Hartley La OL11 30 E3

Hartley Rd
Altrincham WA14 ....**119** C5
Manchester M21 ....**97** A1
Hartley St Heywood OL10 ..**29** D2
Horwich BL6 ....**22** B3
Littleborough OL15 ....**16** A5
Manchester M40 ....**157** F8
Milnrow OL16 ....**31** D7
Rochdale OL12 ....**14** B1
Stalybridge SK15 ....**86** D3
Stockport SK3 ....**170** D8
Wardle OL12 ....**15** C6
IG Wigan WN5 ....**54** B6
Hartley Terr
Rochdale OL11 ....**30** E3
Wigan WN3 ....**150** C7
Harton Ave M18 ....**99** C3
Harton Cl OL2 ....**149** A6
Hartridge Cl BL5 ....**57** F6
Harts Farm Mews WN7 ..**75** F7
Hartshead Ave
Ashton-u-L OL6 ....**85** C6
Stalybridge SK15 ....**86** A3
Hartshead Cl M11 ....**100** A7
Hartshead Cres M35 .....**84** B6
Hartshead High Sch OL6 ..**85** E7
Hartshead Rd OL6 ....**85** C6
Hartshead St OL4 ....**67** F5
Hartshead View SK14 ...**167** F1
Hartsop Dr M24 ....**46** C2
Hartspring Ave [27] M27 ..**80** A7
Hartswell Cl WA3 ....**74** A2
Hartswood Cl M34 ....**101** A4
Hartswood Rd M20 ......**110** D6
Hartwell Cl Bolton BL2 ....**25** C3
Manchester M11 ....**164** F8
Hartwell Gr [2] SK3 ......**123** F4
Harty Ho M30 ....**79** E2
Harvard Cl SK6 ....**113** C5
Harvard Gr M6 ....**80** C3
Harvard St [16] OL11 ......**31** A4
Harvest Cl Salford M6 ....**80** E5
Wythenshawe M33 ....**109** A3
Harvest Pk BL1 ....**144** C8
Harvest Way WN2 ....**57** C3
Harvey Cl M11 ....**165** A8
Harvey Ct Golborne WN7 ..**75** B1
Golborne,Bank Heath WA3 ..**74** A1
Stockport SK1 ....**169** F1
Harvey La WA3 ....**73** F1
Harvey St Bolton BL1 ......**143** D3
Bury BL8 ....**27** C3
Ince-in-M WN3 ....**151** E6
Rochdale OL12 ....**15** B2
Stockport SK1 ....**169** F1
Harvin Gr M34 ....**101** A2
Harwich Cl
Brimington SK5 ....**112** C6
II Manchester M19 ....**99** B1
Harwin Cl OL12 ....**14** D3
Harwood Cres BL8 ....**26** E7
Harwood Ct
Manchester SK4 ....**110** E2
Salford M6 ....**81** B4
Harwood Dr BL8 ....**27** A1
Harwood Gdns OL10 .....**29** D1
Harwood Gr [28] BL2 ......**25** B1
Harwood Mdw BL2 ....**25** F3
Harwood Meadows Prim Sch
BL2 ....**25** F3
Harwood Park Prim Sch
OL10 ....**29** D1
Harwood Rd Bury BL2,BL8 ..**26** C6
Manchester,Burnage M19 ..**110** E6
Manchester,Heaton Mersey
SK4 ....**110** E2
Harwood St
Littleborough OL15 ....**15** F5
Stockport SK4 ....**169** E3
Harwood Vale BL2 ....**25** E3
Harwood Vale Ct BL2 .....**25** E3
Harwood Wlk BL8 ....**26** E7
Haseldine St WN4 ....**72** F6
Haseley Cl Little Lever M26 ..**43** B5
Poynton SK12 ....**133** G5
Tyldesley M29 ....**77** A8
Hasguard Cl BL1 ....**40** F8
Haskoll St BL6 ....**22** D1
Haslam Brow BL9 ....**44** E8
Haslam Ct M7 ....**63** D1
Haslam Hall Mews BL1 ..**40** E2
Haslam Hey Cl BL8 ....**26** F2
Haslam Park Prim Sch
BL3 ....**144** B5
Haslam Rd SK3 ....**170** A6
Haslam St Bolton BL3 ....**145** D5
Bury BL9 ....**44** A1
Manchester M24 ....**65** C7
Rochdale OL12 ....**139** D8
Haslemere Ave WA15 ....**129** C6
Haslemere Dr SK8 ....**122** B3
Haslemere Ind Est WN4 ..**73** A8
Haslemere Rd
Manchester M20 ....**110** D6
Urmston M41 ....**95** B1
Haslingden High Sch BB4 ..**1** B8
Haslington Rd M22 ....**121** E2
Hasper Ave M20 ....**110** A7
Hassal St M26 ....**44** E5
Hassall Ave M20 ....**109** F7
Hassall St [5] SK6 ....**85** B1
Hassall Way [8] SK9 ......**131** E5
Hassnes Ct WN5 ....**55** B2
Hassop Ave M7 ....**81** A7
Hassop Cl M11 ....**160** E1

Hassop Rd SK5 ....**100** A1
Hastings Ave
Manchester M21 ....**109** A8
Prestwich M45 ....**63** B7
Hastings Cl Bramhall SK8 ..**123** C2
Prestwich M45 ....**63** B7
Stockport SK1 ....**124** B7
Hastings Dr M41 ....**94** E3
Hastings Rd Bolton BL1 ..**144** B8
Eccles M30 ....**79** A4
Prestwich M25 ....**63** C5
Hastings St OL11 ....**139** F5
Haston Cl SK5 ....**169** F4
Hasty La
Altrincham WA15 ....**129** E8
Manchester M90 ....**130** A8
Wythenshawe WA15 ....**129** F8
Hatchett Rd M22 ....**121** E1
Hatchmere Cl WA15 .....**120** D6
Hatchmere Rd SK8 ......**122** F4
Hatfield Ave M19 ....**110** F6
Hatfield Cl WN3 ....**55** F1
Hatfield Rd BL1 ....**142** C1
Hatford Cl M29 ....**59** C1
Hathaway Cl SK8 ....**131** B7
Hathaway Dr WN7 ....**76** B6
Hathaway Dr BL1 ....**25** A5
Hathaway Gdns SK6 .....**112** F3
Hathaway Rd BL9 ....**45** A3
Hathaway Wlk WN3 ......**55** F4
Hatherleigh Wlk BL2 ....**42** F6
Hatherley Rd M20 ....**110** D6
Hatherlow SK6 ....**113** A1
Hatherlow Hts SK6 ......**113** A1
Hatherlow La SK7 ....**124** D2
Hatherop Cl M30 ....**79** B1
Hathersage Ave M5,M6 ..**154** D3
Hathersage Cres SK13 ..**171** E2
Hathersage Dr SK13 .....**116** F8
Hathersage Rd M13 ......**98** B4
Hathersage St OL9 ......**152** C6
Hathersage Way [6]
M34 ....**113** B8
Hathershaw OL8 ....**66** F3
Hathershaw La OL8 ....**66** F3
Hathershaw Tech Coll The
OL8 ....**66** F2
Hatro Ct M41 ....**96** A1
Hatter St M4 ....**159** B2
Hattersley Ctr The [2]
SK14 ....**102** E2
Hattersley Ind Est SK14 ..**102** E1
Hattersley Rd E SK14 ....**102** C2
Hattersley Rd W SK14 ...**102** C2
Hattersley Sta SK14 ......**102** D3
Hattersley Wlk SK14 ....**102** C3
Hatton Ave Atherton M46 ..**58** D5
Salford M7 ....**158** D3
Hatton Gr BL1 ....**23** A1
Hatton St Adlington PR7 ..**20** F6
Manchester M12 ....**99** A3
Stockport SK1 ....**170** F8
Hatton Terr [24] SK16 ...**166** B1
Hattonfold M33 ....**108** C1
Hattons Ct M32 ....**96** C3
Hattons Rd M17 ....**96** B6
Haugh Farm OL16 ....**32** C4
Haugh Fold OL16 ....**32** C4
Haugh Hill Rd OL4 ....**49** E3
Haugh La OL16 ....**32** C4
Haugh Sq OL16 ....**32** C4
Haughton Cl SK6 ....**113** A6
Haughton Dr M22 ....**109** D1
Haughton Green Rd
M34 ....**113** B8
Haughton Hall Rd M34 ..**113** B8
Haughton St Denton M34 ..**100** F5
Hyde SK14 ....**167** E1
Havana Cl M11 ....**160** F1
Have Ct M6 ....**154** F1
Haveley Hey Prim Sch
M22 ....**121** C4
Haveley Rd M22 ....**121** C5
Havelock Dr M7 ....**158** D4
Havelock St OL8 ....**153** F5
Haven Cl
Hazel Grove SK7 ....**124** C1
Radcliffe M26 ....**43** D5
Uppermill OL4 ....**68** D6
Haven Dr M43 ....**83** E2
Haven La OL4 ....**49** E3
Haven St M6 ....**154** E1
Haven The
Altrincham WA15 ....**119** F3
Little Lever BL3 ....**43** B3
Havenbrook Gr BL0 ......**11** A3
Havenscroft Ave M30 ...**95** D8
Havenside Cl OL4 ....**49** E3
Havenwood Rd WN1 .....**37** B4
Havercroft Cl WN3 ....**54** E3
Havercroft Pk BL1 ....**40** D8
Haverfield Rd M9 ....**64** E3
Haverford St M12 ....**164** F6
Havergate Wlks SK2 .....**124** B6
Haverhill Gr BL2 ....**25** B2
Havers Rd M18 ....**99** E5
Haversham Rd M8 ....**63** E2
Haverty Prec WA12 ....**89** B1
Havisham Cl BL6 ....**40** B4
Haw Clough La OL3 ......**69** C6
Hawarde Cl WA12 ....**89** A4
Hawarden Ave M16 ....**97** C2
Hawarden Rd WA14 .....**119** D6
Hawarden St BL1 ....**24** E5
Haweswater Ave
Hawes Green WN4 ....**25** E4
Swinton M27 ....**79** F6

Hawes Cl Bury BL8 ....**27** B5
Stockport SK2 ....**124** A6
Hawes Cres WN4 ....**73** B5
Haweswater Ave
Ince-in-M WN2 ....**56** B7
Tyldesley M29 ....**77** B7
Haweswater Cl M34 .....**100** A2
Haweswater Cres BL9 ....**45** B5
Haweswater Dr M24 ......**46** E2
Haweswater Mews [3]
M24 ....**46** E2
Hawfinch Gr M28 ....**78** D8
Hawick Gr OL10 ....**28** E1
Hawk Cl BL9 ....**141** B4
Hawk Green Rd SK6 .....**126** A3
Hawk Rd M44 ....**94** A3
Hawk Yard La OL3 ....**69** D5
Hawke St SK15 ....**86** C1
Hawker Ave BL3 ....**147** D3
Hawkeshead Rd M8 .....**156** B6
Hawkhurst Rd M13 ....**98** F3
Hawkhurst St Leigh WN7 ..**76** B4
Leigh WN7 ....**76** C5
Hawkins St SK5 ....**169** E4
Hawkins Way OL15 ....**6** C1
Hawkley Ave WN3 ....**54** F2
Hawkley Brook Trad Est
WN3 ....**54** E2
Hawkley Hall High Sch
WN3 ....**55** C3
Hawkridge Cl BL5 ....**57** F6
Hawkridge Dr M23 ....**108** F2
Hawkrigg Cl WN2 ....**38** A3
Hawkshaw Cl WN2 ....**38** A3
Hawkshaw Gr [9] M5 .....**81** A1
Hawkshaw La BL8 ....**10** B5
Hawkshaw St BL6 ....**22** D3
Hawkshead Dr
Bolton BL3 ....**146** A3
Middleton M24 ....**46** E1
Royton OL2 ....**48** D6
Hawkshead Rd
Glossop SK13 ....**104** C3
Shaw OL2 ....**149** A8
Hawksheath Cl BL7 ....**8** E1
Hawksley Ind Est OL8 ....**66** C3
Hawksley St Horwich BL6 ..**22** D2
Oldham OL8 ....**66** C3
Hawksmoor Dr OL2 ....**149** A8
Hawkstone Ave
Droylsden M43 ....**83** E3
Whitefield M45 ....**62** D7
Hawkstone Cl BL2 ....**25** E3
Hawkswick Dr M23 ......**109** A2
Hawksworth M29 ....**77** B5
Hawkyard Farm OL8 .....**69** D5
Hawley Dr WA15 ....**129** A8
Hawley Gn OL12 ....**14** D2
Hawley La WA15 ....**129** B8
Hawley St M19 ....**111** B8
Haworth Ave BL0 ....**11** A2
Haworth Cl BL9 ....**44** F6
Haworth Ct [8] M26 ......**44** B3
Haworth Dr M Bacup OL13 ..**3** C8
Haworth Rd M18 ....**99** D4
Haworth St Bury BL8 ......**26** F4
Edgworth BL7 ....**9** D5
Hindley WN2 ....**57** A4
Oldham OL1 ....**48** E1
Radcliffe M26 ....**44** B3
Haworth Wlk [3] M26 .....**44** B3
Hawsworth Cl M15 ......**163** B5
Hawthorn Ave
Altrincham WA15 ....**119** F8
Bury BL8 ....**27** C4
Downall Green WN4 ....**72** D5
Eccles M30 ....**79** D8
Edenfield BL0 ....**1** D2
Hindley WN2 ....**57** A4
Marple SK6 ....**125** D6
Newton-le-W WA12 ....**89** D3
Orrell WN5 ....**53** F6
Radcliffe M26 ....**44** B1
Ramsbottom BL0 ....**11** A2
Standish WN1 ....**37** B6
Urmston M41 ....**95** F1
Walkden M28 ....**60** E1
Wigan WN5 ....**54** D6
Wilmslow SK9 ....**137** A7
Hawthorn Bank BL2 ......**25** E4
Hawthorn Cl
Altrincham WA15 ....**119** F7
Wilmslow SK9 ....**137** A7
Tyldesley M29 ....**59** D1
Hawthorn Cres Bury BL8 ..**26** F7
Oldham OL8 ....**66** D2
Shaw OL2 ....**149** B6
Hawthorn Dr Irlam M44 ..**105** D3
Manchester M19 ....**110** F7
Pendlebury M27 ....**80** C7
Salford M6 ....**80** B4
Stalybridge SK15 ....**101** F8
Hawthorn Gn SK9 ....**137** A7
Hawthorn Gr
Bramhall SK7 ....**132** C6
Huddersfield SK14 ....**103** D6
Hyde SK14 ....**167** D1
Manchester SK4 ....**168** B3
Wilmslow SK9 ....**137** A7
Hawthorn La Sale M33 ..**107** C6
Stretford M21 ....**108** B8
Wilmslow SK9 ....**137** A7
Hawthorn Rd
Altrincham WA15 ....**119** E3

Hawthorn Rd continued
Droylsden M43 ....**84** C2
Failsworth M40 ....**65** F1
Gatley SK8 ....**122** A5
Kearsley BL4 ....**61** B5
Manchester SK4 ....**110** F2
Oldham OL8 ....**66** B1
Reddish M34 ....**100** B4
Rochdale OL11 ....**29** C6
Stretford M21,M32 ....**108** E8
Westhoughton BL5 ....**57** F7
Hawthorn Rd S M43 ......**84** C2
Hawthorn St Denton M34 ..**100** E6
Manchester M18 ....**99** E5
Wilmslow SK9 ....**137** A6
Hawthorn View SK9 .....**137** A7
Hawthorn Wlk
Littleborough OL15 ....**15** F5
[3] Partington M31 ....**105** E3
Wilmslow SK9 ....**137** A7
Hawthornden [1] M20 ...**110** A3
Hawthorne Ave
Farnworth BL4 ....**60** B8
Fowley Common WA3 ....**92** C5
Horwich BL6 ....**22** E1
Hawthorne Dr M28 ....**79** A7
Hawthorne Gr
[1] Ashton-u-L OL6 ....**84** F1
Chadderton OL9 ....**152** B8
Leigh WN7 ....**75** E7
Romiley SK6 ....**112** E4
Hawthorne La OL16 ....**32** A3
Hawthorne Rd BL3 ....**146** B4
Hawthorne St BL3 ....**144** C5
Hawthorne View WA16 ..**136** B2
Hawthorns Com Sch
M34 ....**100** E5
Hawthorns The
[6] Atherton M46 ....**58** D3
Denton M34 ....**100** E5
Hawthorpe Gr OL3 ....**69** B8
Haxby Rd M18 ....**99** D3
Haxey Wlk BL6 ....**21** F3
Haxworth Wlk SK7 ......**124** A2
Hay Ho OL4 ....**67** E8
Hayburn Rd M23 ....**121** B7
Hayburn Rd SK2 ....**124** C8
Haycock Cl SK15 ....**102** E3
Haycroft SK8 ....**131** E8
Hayden Cl
[4] Glossop SK13 ....**104** C1
Manchester M40 ....**157** D5
Hayden Fold SK13 ....**115** D7
Haydn Ave M14 ....**98** B4
Haydock Ave M33 ....**107** B2
Haydock Cl M32 ....**96** F4
Haydock Dr
Altrincham WA15 ....**120** B5
Hazel Grove SK7 ....**124** F2
Worsley M28 ....**78** B6
Haydock La
Ashton-in-M WA11 ....**72** E1
Bolton BL7 ....**25** A8
Bolton BL7 ....**9** B1
Haydock Lane Ind Est
WA11 ....**72** E1
Haydock Mews M7 ......**155** D6
Haydock Park Gdns
WA12 ....**73** B1
Haydock Park Race Course
WA12 ....**73** D1
Haydock St
Ashton-in-M WN4 ....**73** B2
Bolton BL1 ....**145** F8
Newton-le-W WA12 ....**89** A3
Wilmslow SK9 ....**137** C4
Hay's Rd M44 ....**105** E5
Hayes Row WA3 ....**75** A1
Hayes St Leigh,Plank WN7 ..**75** A4
Leigh,Westleigh WN7 ....**75** C7
Hayeswater Circ [7] M41 ..**95** C3
Hayeswater Rd M41 ....**95** C3
Hayfield Rd WN3 ....**55** A1
Hayfield Cl
Romiley SK6 ....**113** A4
Tyldesley M29 ....**77** C6
Hayfield Cl
Manchester M12 ....**164** E7
Middleton M24 ....**47** C3
Oldham OL4 ....**49** F4
Ramsbottom BL0 ....**11** A2
Hayfield Rd
New Mills SK22 ....**127** E1
Romiley SK6 ....**113** A4
Salford M6 ....**80** B4
Stalybridge SK13 ....**108** B5
Hayfield Wlk
Altrincham WA15 ....**120** C6
[1] Denton M34 ....**100** F5
Haygrove Wlk [10] M9 ..**157** D8
Hayle Rd OL1 ....**49** D4
Hayley St M12,M13 ....**98** E4
Hayling Rd M33 ....**107** E5
Haymaker Rise OL12 .....**15** D6
Hayman Ave WN7 ....**75** D7
Haymans Wlk M13 ....**163** B6
Haymarket Cl M13 ....**163** C5
Haymarket St BL9 ....**140** E2
Haymarket The BL9 .....**140** E2
Haymill Ave M38 ....**60** A6
Haymond Cl M7 ....**81** A5
Haynes St Bolton BL3 ...**146** C3
Rochdale OL12 ....**139** F8
Haysbrook Ave M28 ......**60** A4

Haysbrook Cl OL7 ....**85** A7
Hayside Way BL9 ....**140** F1
Haythorp Ave M22 ....**121** E3
Hayward Ave BL3 ....**43** C3
Hayward Gr WN6 ....**19** D2
Hayward Sch BL3 ....**147** D2
Hayward St BL8 ....**27** C3
Hayward Way SK14 ......**102** F3
Haywards Cl SK13 ....**104** C3
Haywood Cl WA3 ....**74** E1
Haywood Gdns BL3 ....**147** E4
Haywood Park View
BL3 ....**147** E4
Hazel Ave Ashton-u-L OL6 ..**85** E6
Bury BL9 ....**141** B2
Bury,Tottington BL8 ....**27** A5
Cheadle SK8 ....**122** E5
Kearsley M26 ....**61** A8
Manchester M16 ....**97** D2
Newhey OL16 ....**32** A3
Pendlebury M27 ....**80** A7
Ramsbottom BL0 ....**11** B1
Romiley SK6 ....**113** D2
Sale M33 ....**108** B3
Walkden M38 ....**59** E5
Westhoughton BL5 ....**57** F7
Wigan WN6 ....**37** A3
Hazel Cl Droylsden M43 ..**84** C2
Marple SK6 ....**125** E4
Hazel Ct [5] M16 ....**97** D3
Hazel Dr Gatley M22 .....**131** A8
Poynton SK12 ....**133** F3
Stockport SK2 ....**124** D6
Hazel Gr Chadderton OL9 ..**152** B8
Poynton SK12 ....**133** F3
Hazel Grove High Sch
SK7 ....**133** C8
Hazel Grove Prim Sch
SK7 ....**124** E3
Hazel Grove Sta SK7 .....**124** D2
Hazel Hall La BL0 ....**11** B1
Hazel La OL8 ....**66** D2
Hazel Mount BL7 ....**8** E2
Hazel Rd
Altrincham WA14 ....**119** D6
Atherton M46 ....**58** C4
Cheadle SK8 ....**123** B1
Middleton M24 ....**47** B2
Whitefield M45 ....**63** B8
Hazel St Denton M34 ....**100** E6
Hazel Grove SK7 ....**124** E3
Ramsbottom BL0 ....**11** A4
Hazel View SK6 ....**125** F3
Hazel Wlk M31 ....**105** E3
Hazel-Dene Cl BL9 ....**44** F7
Hazelbadge Cl SK12 ....**133** C4
Hazelbadge Rd SK12 ...**133** C4
Hazelbank Ave M20 ....**110** B3
Hazelbottom Rd M8 ....**156** C7
Hazeldean Rd SK9 ....**137** D5
Hazeldene Rd M40 ....**65** E1
Hazelfields M28 ....**79** C7
Hazelhurst Cl Bolton BL1 ..**143** E2
Ramsbottom BL0 ....**11** B4
Hazelhurst Com Prim Sch
BL0 ....**11** A4
Hazelhurst Dr M24 ....**46** A4
Hazelhurst Fold M28 .....**79** C7
Hazelhurst Rd
Ashton-u-L OL6 ....**85** F6
Bolton BL1 ....**142** B2
Hazel Grove SK7 ....**124** A4
Stockport SK2 ....**124** A4
Wigan WN1 ....**37** B4
Wilmslow SK9 ....**137** D8
Hazlehurst Wk WA4 ....**73** C4
Hazlemere BL4 ....**61** A7
Headen Ave WN5 ....**53** A2
Headingley Dr M16 ....**97** A3
Headingley Rd M14 ......**110** D7
Headingley Way BL3 ....**147** D3
Headland Cl WA3 ....**90** E6
Headlands Dr M25 ....**63** A1
Headlands Rd SK7 ....**123** F1
Headlands St OL12 ....**14** D3
Heady Hill Ct OL10 ....**29** A2
Heady Hill Rd OL10 ....**29** A2
Heald Ave M14 ....**98** B3
Heald Cl
Altrincham WA14 ....**119** C2
Littleborough OL15 ....**16** A3
Rochdale OL12 ....**14** C3
Heald Dr
Altrincham WA14 ....**119** C2
Rochdale OL12 ....**14** C3

Heald Gr Gatley SK8 .....122 A1
Manchester M14 ....98 B4
Heald Green Sta M22 ...131 A8
Heald La OL15 ....16 A3
Heald Pl M14 ....98 B3
Heald Place Prim Sch
M14 ....98 B3
Heald Rd WA14 ....119 C2
Healds Gn OL1 ....47 F3
Healdwood Rd SK6 .....113 C4
Healey Ave Heywood OL10 .29 E3
Rochdale OL12 ....14 D4
Healey Cl Salford M7 ......81 C8
Wythenshawe M23 ....108 F2
Wythenshawe M23 ....109 A2
Healey Dell Cotts OL12 ...14 B4
Healey Dell Nature Reserve*
OL12 ....14 B6
Healey Gr OL12 ....14 C5
Healey Hall Farm OL12 ...14 C4
Healey Hall Mews OL12 ..14 C4
Healey La OL12 ....14 E3
Healey Prim Sch OL12 ....14 E3
Healey St OL16 ....139 E6
Healey Stones OL12 ......14 E4
Healing St 8 OL11 ....31 A5
Heanor Ave M34 ....113 A8
Heap Bridge Village Prim Sch
BL9 ....28 D1
Heap Brow BL9 ....28 D1
Heap Rd OL12 ....13 D2
Heap St Bolton BL3 ......147 E4
Heywood BL9 ....28 D1
Oldham OL4 ....67 C7
Radcliffe M26 ....44 B3
Whitefield M45 ....62 F7
Heape St OL11 ....30 C1
Heapfold 4 OL12 ....14 B2
Heaplands BL8 ....10 F1
Heapriding Bsns Pk
SK4 ....169 D1
Heaps Farm Ct SK15 ....102 D7
Heapworth Ave BL0 .....138 B6
Heapy Cl BL8 ....26 F1
Heardman Ave 1 WN6 ...37 A1
Hearlesden Cres 5 BL3 .144 C5
Heath Ave
Ramsbottom BL0 ....11 B1
Salford M7 ....81 C4
Urmston M41 ....95 E3
Heath Cl BL3 ....146 B2
Heath Cres SK2 ....170 F5
Heath Farm La M31 .....106 B3
Heath Gdns WN2 ....57 C3
Heath Hill Dr OL13 ....3 C8
Heath La Culcheth WA3 ....91 A1
Golborne WA3 ....90 F2
Leigh WN7 ....75 B5
Heath Rd
Altrincham,Rosehill WA14 .119 D2
Altrincham,Timperley
WA15 ....119 F8
Ashton-in-M WN4 ....73 C2
Glossop SK13 ....104 D2
Stockport SK2,SK3 ......170 F6
Wardle OL12 ....15 C6
Heath St Ashton-in-M WN4 .73 C2
Golborne WA3 ....90 A8
Manchester M8 ....155 F7
Rochdale OL11 ....139 D6
Heath The Ashton-u-L OL7 ..85 A7
Middleton M24 ....65 B6
Heath View M7 ....81 A8
Heathbank Rd
Cheadle SK8 ....131 F8
Manchester M9 ....64 C5
Stockport SK3 ....123 B7
Heathbourne Rd OL13 .....3 C8
Heathcliffe Wlk 1 M13 .163 C5
Heathcote Ave SK4 .....168 C3
Heathcote Gdns SK6 ....113 E1
Heathcote Rd M18 ....99 C4
Heather Ave
Droylsden M43 ....84 C2
Irlam M44 ....105 D6
Shaw OL2 ....49 D8
Heather Bank Bury BL8 ...26 E7
Littleborough OL15 ......16 D6
Rawtenstall BB4 ....1 F8
Heather Bank Cl SK13 ...116 A7
Heather Brae WA12 ......89 A4
Heather Brow SK15 .....102 E7
Heather Cl Haslingden BB4 ..1 A8
Heywood OL10 ....46 D8
Horwich BL6 ....22 B4
Oldham OL4 ....49 E1
Heather Ct SK4 ....111 D5
Heather Gr
Ashton-in-M WN4 ....73 E4
Droylsden M43 ....100 B8
Hollingworth SK14 .....103 D6
Leigh WN7 ....75 E7
Wigan WN5 ....54 E6
Heather Lea M34 ....101 A2
Heather Rd WA14,WA15 ..119 E1
Heather St M11 ....83 B2
Heather Way Diggle OL3 ...51 C4
Marple SK6 ....125 E6
Heather Wlk M31 ....105 E3
Heatherdale Dr M8 .....156 A6
Heatherfield Bolton BL1 ...24 D5
Edgworth BL7 ....9 E6
Heatherfield Ct SK9 ....137 E8
Heatherlands OL12 ....4 D4
Heatherlea Cl WN8 ......53 C7
Heathers The SK2 ......124 B4
Heatherside Reddish SK5 .100 A1
Stalybridge SK15 ....86 D2
Heatherside Ave OL5 .....68 E1
Heatherside Rd BL0 ....138 C7
Heatherway
Manchester M14 ....98 B4
Sale M33 ....107 D5
Heathfield Bolton BL2 .....25 F3
Eccles M28 ....78 F5
Farnworth BL4 ....42 E1
Wilmslow SK9 ....137 A5
Heathfield Ave Bacup OL13 ..3 C8
Denton M34 ....100 D1
Gatley SK8 ....122 B5
Manchester SK4 ....111 C5
Heathfield Cl M33 ......108 F4
Heathfield Dr Bolton BL3 .146 B2
Pendlebury M27 ....80 A7
Tyldesley M29 ....59 D1
Heathfield Prim Sch
BL3 ....146 A2
Heathfield Rd Bacup OL13 ..3 C8
Stockport SK2 ....170 F6
Whitefield BL9,M45 ......44 F3
Heathfield St M40 ....83 C5
Heathfields WA14 ......119 C3
Heathfields Rd OL3 ......69 C8
Heathfields Sq OL3 ......69 C8
Heathland Rd M7,M25 ....81 B8
Heathland Terr SK3 .....170 E7
Heathlands Dr M25 ......63 A1
Heathlea WN2 ....57 C2
Heathmoor Ave WA3 .....90 D6
Heathside Gr M28 ....60 E3
Heathside Park Rd SK3 .122 F7
Heathside Rd
Cheadle SK3 ....123 A7
Manchester M20 ....110 D6
Heathway Ave M11 ....83 D2
Heathwood OL3 ....69 C8
Heathwood Rd M19 ......110 E4
Heatley Cl Lymm WA13 ...117 A5
Reddish M34 ....100 B2
Heatley Rd OL16 ....31 D6
Heatley Way 5 SK9 .....131 D4
Heaton Ave
Bolton,Doffcocker BL1 ......23 F1
Bolton,Harwood Lee BL2 ....25 E5
Farnworth BL4 ....60 C8
Little Lever BL3 ....43 A4
Stockport SK7 ....123 E3
Heaton Chapel Sta SK4 .111 C5
Heaton Cl
Manchester SK4 ....168 A3
Up Holland WN8 ....53 A7
Whitefield BL9 ....45 A5
Heaton Court Gdns BL1 ..40 E7
Heaton Ct Bury BL9 ......44 E7
Manchester SK4 ....168 B4
Prestwich M25 ....63 C3
Heaton Dr BL9 ....45 A5
Heaton Fold BL9 ....44 E8
Heaton Grange Dr BL1 ..144 A7
Heaton Hall* M25 ....63 E5
Heaton La SK4 ....169 E1
Heaton Moor Rd SK4 ....168 B4
Heaton Mount BL1 ....23 F1
Heaton Park Prim Sch
M45 ....63 B6
Heaton Park Rd M9 ......64 B5
Heaton Park Rd W M9 ...64 A5
Heaton Park Sta M25 .....63 C4
Heaton Pk* M25 ....63 E5
Heaton Rd Bolton BL6 .....40 D6
Little Lever BL2 ....43 B5
Manchester,Heaton Norris
SK4 ....168 C3
Manchester,Withington
M20 ....110 C6
Heaton Sch SK4 ....111 B5
Heaton St Aspull WN2 .....38 D5
Denton M34 ....100 D3
Ince-in-M WN3 ....151 E6
Middleton M24 ....64 B7
Milnrow OL16 ....32 A5
Prestwich M25 ....63 C4
Salford M7 ....155 E7
Standish WN6 ....19 E1
Wigan WN1 ....37 C2
Heaton Twrs SK4 ....169 E2
Heatons Gr BL5 ....40 A2
Heaviley Gr Horwich BL6 ...22 A5
Stockport SK2 ....124 A6
Hebble Butt Cl OL16 .....31 E6
Hebble Cl BL2 ....25 B5
Hebburn Dr BL8 ....27 C5
Hebden Ave
Fowley Common WA3 ......92 B5
Romiley SK6 ....113 A4
Salford M5,M6 ....80 C3
Hebden Ct BL1 ....145 E8
Hebden Dr SK13 ....116 F8
Hebden Wlk M15 ....162 F5
Hebdon Cl WN4 ....73 A5
Heber Pl 10 OL15 ....16 B5
Heber St Ince-in-M WN2 ..151 F7
Radcliffe M26 ....44 A3
Hebron St OL2 ....49 A3
Hector Ave OL16 ....31 B8
Hector Rd Manchester M13 .98 F3
Wigan WN5 ....36 D1
Heddles Ct WN7 ....75 E4
Heddon Cl SK4 ....110 E3
Heddon Wlk M8 ....156 C6
Hedge Rows OL12 ....4 C1
Hedgelands Wlk 4
M33 ....107 C5
Hedgemead 5 WN6 ....37 A1
Hedgerows The SK14 ...102 A3
Hedges St M35 ....84 A8
Hedley St BL1 ....142 C2
Hedley Wlk 8 M8 ....155 F7
Heeley St WN1 ....37 B2
Heginbottom Cres OL6 ...85 C5
Height Barn La OL13 ......4 A8
Heights Ave OL12 ....14 E2
Heights Cl OL12 ....14 E2
Heights Ct OL12 ....14 E1
Heights La Chadderton OL1 .47 F2
Delph OL3 ....50 E7
Rochdale OL12 ....14 E1
Heights The BL6 ....22 D1
Helen St Ashton-in-M WN4 .73 A4
Eccles M30 ....95 B8
Farnworth BL4 ....60 D7
Golborne WA3 ....73 F1
Salford M7 ....81 C5
Helena St M6 ....80 C5
Helensville Ave M6 ......80 F5
Helga St M40 ....160 D4
Helias Cl M28 ....59 F3
Hell Nook WA3 ....73 F1
Helmclough Way M28 .....78 B8
Helmet St M1,M12 ......163 C8
Helmsdale M28 ....60 C2
Helmsdale Ave BL3 ......40 F6
Helmsdale Cl BL0 ....11 A4
Helmshore Ave OL4 ......49 E3
Helmshore Ho OL2 ......149 B8
Helmshore Prim Sch BB4 ..1 A7
Helmshore Rd
Haslingden BB4 ....1 A7
Ramsbottom BL0,BL8,BB4 ....1 A3
Helmshore Way OL2 .....149 B8
Helmshore Wlk M13 ....163 B7
Helmsman Way WN3 .....150 B5
Helsby Cl OL4 ....68 A6
Helsby Gdns BL1 ....143 F4
Helsby Rd M33 ....108 E2
Helsby Way
4 Handforth SK9 ....131 D4
Wigan WN3 ....54 C2
Helsby Wlk M12 ....164 E8
Helston Cl Bramhall SK7 ..132 F7
Hattersley SK14 ....102 D1
Irlam M44 ....94 B2
Helston Dr OL2 ....48 F4
Helston Gr SK8 ....131 C8
Helston Way M29 ....77 C8
Helston Wlk SK14 ......102 D1
Helton Wlk M24 ....46 C1
Helvellyn Dr M24 ....46 D2
Helvellyn Rd WN5 ....54 B7
Helvellyn Wlk 2 OL1 .....49 A1
Hembury Ave M19 ....110 F6
Hembury Cl M24 ....47 B2
Hemfield Ct WN2 ....56 C8
Hemfield Rd WN2 ....56 C8
Hemley Cl BL5 ....57 E6
Hemlock Ave OL8 ....66 E3
Hemming Dr M30 ....79 E1
Hemmington Dr M9 .....157 D7
Hemmons Rd M12 ....99 B3
Hempcroft Rd WA15 .....120 D5
Hempshaw La SK1,SK2 ..124 B7
Hemsby Cl BL3 ....146 A4
Hemsley St M9 ....64 E1
Hemsley St S M9 ....64 E1
Hemswell Cl M6 ....154 E4
Hemsworth Rd
Bolton BL1 ....145 D8
Manchester M18 ....99 D3
Henbury Dr SK6 ....113 B6
Henbury La SK8 ....131 F6
Henbury Rd SK9 ....131 D4
Henbury St
Manchester M14 ....98 A3
Stockport SK2 ....124 C4
Henderson Ave 3 M27 ....61 F1
Henderson St
Littleborough OL15 ......16 A5
Manchester M19 ....111 B8
Rochdale OL12 ....15 B2
Henderville St OL15 .....16 A6
Hendham Cl SK7 ....124 A2
Hendham Dr WA14 ......119 B5
Hendham Vale M9 ......156 C6
Hendon Dr Bury BL9 ......44 F5
Cheadle SK3 ....123 A7
Hendon Gr Heywood OL10 .46 E7
Leigh WN7 ....75 F8
Hendon Rd
Manchester M9 ....64 D4
Wigan WN5 ....54 E8
Hendon St WN7 ....75 F8
Hendriff Pl 4 OL12 ......14 F1
Henfield Wlk M22 ......121 C3
Henfold Rd M29 ....77 C7
Hengist St Bolton BL2 ...148 C7
Manchester M18 ....99 D4
Henley Ave Cheadle SK8 ..122 F2
Irlam M44 ....105 E6
Manchester M16 ....97 B3
Henley Cl BL8 ....44 B8
Henley Dr
Altrincham WA15 ....119 F7
Ashton-u-L OL7 ....84 F4
Henley Gr BL3 ....147 D3
Henley Pl M19 ....111 A6
Henley St Aspull WN2 ....38 B6
Chadderton OL9 ....66 A4
Oldham OL1 ....153 D8
9 Rochdale OL12 ....14 F1
Henley Terr OL11 ......139 E5
Henlow Wlk 9 M40 ......65 D2
Henniker Rd BL3 ....146 A2
Henniker St M27 ....79 E6
Hennon St BL1 ....143 D1
Henrietta St
Ashton-u-L OL6 ....166 B4
Bolton BL3 ....146 B4
Leigh WN7 ....75 F5
Manchester M16 ....161 C5
Henry Herman St BL3 ...146 A3
Henry Lee St BL3 ......146 C3
Henry Park St WN1 .....151 E7
Henry Sq OL6 ....166 A2
Henry St Bolton BL2 ....148 A6
Denton M34 ....113 B8
Droylsden M43 ....84 A1
Eccles M30 ....79 C1
Failsworth M35 ....83 F7
Glossop SK13 ....104 C1
Hyde SK14 ....167 D2
Ince-in-M WN3 ....55 E4
Leigh WN7 ....76 A3
Leigh WN7 ....76 A4
Littleborough OL15 ......15 F3
Manchester M4 ....159 B2
Manchester,Old Trafford
M16 ....161 C5
Middleton M24 ....64 F8
Prestwich M25 ....63 C5
Ramsbottom BL0 ....11 D7
Rochdale OL11 ....139 F6
Stockport SK1 ....124 B8
6 Tyldesley M29 ....59 A1
Wardle OL12 ....15 C7
14 Westhoughton BL5 ....39 E1
Henshall La WA14 ......118 C6
Henshaw Ct M16 ....97 B4
Henshaw La OL9 ....65 F2
Henshaw St Oldham OL1 .153 E7
Oldham OL1 ....153 F8
Stretford M32 ....96 D2
Henshaw Wlk 10 M13 ...163 B7
Henson Gr WA15 ....120 A4
Henthorn St OL2 ....149 B6
Henton Wlk M40 ....159 C4
Henwick Hall Ave BL0 ....11 B4
Henwood Rd M20 ....110 C5
Hepley Rd SK12 ....134 A3
Hepple Cl SK4 ....110 F3
Hepple Wlk OL7 ....84 E5
Heppleton Rd M40 ....65 D2
Hepton St OL1 ....153 E8
Heptonstall Wlk M18 ...165 C5
Hepworth Cl WN3 ....73 F2
Hepworth St SK14 ......113 E7
Heraldic Ct M6 ....81 A4
Herbert St Bacup OL13 .....3 D8
Chadderton OL9 ....152 B7
Denton M34 ....101 A4
Droylsden M43 ....83 F1
Horwich BL6 ....22 B4
Little Lever BL3 ....43 B3
Manchester M8 ....155 F5
Oldham OL4 ....49 D1
Prestwich M25 ....62 F4
Radcliffe M26 ....43 F5
Stockport SK3 ....170 D7
Stretford M32 ....96 D2
Westhoughton BL5 ....39 E2
Wigan WN3 ....150 B7
Hereford Ave WA3 ....90 B8
Hereford Cl
Ashton-in-M WN4 ....73 C2
Ashton-u-L OL6 ....85 D7
Shaw OL2 ....48 F7
Hereford Cres BL3 ......43 A4
Hereford Dr Bury BL9 ....44 F8
Handforth SK9 ....131 E3
Manchester M25 ....63 C2
Swinton M27 ....79 F6
Hereford Gr
Up Holland WN8 ....53 B6
Urmston M41 ....95 C2
Hereford Rd Bolton BL1 ..144 B8
Brinnington SK5 ....112 C5
Cheadle SK8 ....123 A4
Hindley WN2 ....56 F6
Salford M30 ....80 A5
Hereford St Bolton BL1 ..143 F2
Oldham OL9 ....152 C5
18 Rochdale OL11 ....31 A5
Sale M33 ....108 B4
Hereford Way
Middleton M24 ....47 C2
Stalybridge SK15 ......102 D7
Hereford Wlk
6 Denton M34 ....100 F1
Romiley SK6 ....113 A1
Herevale Grange M28 ....78 B7
Herevale Hall Dr BL0 ....11 B4
Heristone Ave M34 .....100 F3
Heritage Gdns M20 .....110 B2
Heritage Wharf OL7 ....166 A1
Herle Dr M22 ....121 C1
Hermitage Ave SK6 .....113 F2
Hermitage Cl WN6 ....35 E7
Hermitage Ct WA15 .....120 A3
Hermitage Gdns SK6 ....113 F2
Hermitage Rd
Altrincham WA15 ....120 A3
Manchester M8 ....64 A1
Hermon Ave OL8 ....66 E4
Herne St M11 ....165 A8
Heron Ave
Dukinfield SK16 ....101 E7
Farnworth BL4 ....59 F7
Heron Ct Salford M6 .....80 B3
Stockport SK3 ....170 E7
Heron Dr Droylsden M34 ...84 C1
Irlam M44 ....94 A3
Poynton SK12 ....133 A3
Wigan WN3 ....54 E2
Heron Pl WN5 ....54 C8
Heron St
Manchester M15 ....162 E5
Oldham OL8 ....66 D3
Stockport SK3 ....170 D7
Swinton M27 ....62 A1
Heron View SK13 ....115 F8
Heron's Way BL2 ....148 A6
Herondale Cl M40 ....83 B5
Herons Wharf WN6 ......35 D7
Herries St OL6 ....85 D4
Herristone Rd M8 ....64 A2
Herrod Ave SK4 ....111 E5
Herschel St M40 ....83 A8
Hersey St M6 ....154 E2
Hersham Wlk 1 M9 .....157 E8
Hertford Dr M29 ....59 A3
Hertford Gr M44 ....105 C6
Hertford Rd M9 ....64 D1
Hertford St OL7 ....166 A1
Hertfordshire Park Cl
OL2 ....149 B8
Hesford Ave M9 ....157 F7
Hesketh Ave Bolton BL1 ...24 F5
Manchester M20 ....110 A3
Shaw OL2 ....149 B5
Hesketh Ct Atherton M46 ..58 C3
5 Manchester M20 ......110 A3
Hesketh Dr WN6 ....19 A2
Hesketh Fletcher CE High
Sch M46 ....58 C2
Hesketh Manor M46 .....58 C3
Hesketh Meadow La
WA3 ....90 F8
Hesketh Rd Rochdale OL16 .31 C7
Sale M33 ....107 F3
Hesketh St Atherton M46 ..58 D4
Leigh WN7 ....75 D5
Stockport SK4 ....169 E3
Wigan WN5 ....54 F7
Hesketh Wlk
5 Farnworth BL4 ....60 D8
Middleton M24 ....46 E2
Hesnall Cl WA3 ....92 C8
Hessel St M50 ....154 D1
Hester Wlk 2 M15 ......163 A5
Heston Ave M13 ....98 F2
Heston Dr M41 ....95 C3
Heswall Ave Culcheth WA3 .91 E4
Manchester M20 ....110 B7
Heswall Dr BL8 ....26 F5
Heswall Rd SK5 ....99 F1
Heswall St BL2 ....42 F7
Hetherington Wlk M12 ...99 A4
Hethorn St M40 ....83 C5
Hetton Ave M13 ....98 E2
Heversham Ave OL2 ......49 D7
Heversham Wlk M18 ....165 C6
Hewart Cl M40 ....159 C4
Hewart Dr BL9 ....141 C3
Hewitt Ave M34 ....99 F3
Hewitt Bsns Pk WN5 .....53 E4
Hewitt St M15 ....162 F7
Hewlett Rd M21 ....97 A1
Hewlett St Bolton BL2 ...148 A7
Westhoughton BL5 ....57 B7
Wigan WN1 ....150 C8
Hexham Ave Bolton BL1 ...23 F1
Wigan WN3 ....54 F4
Hexham Cl Atherton M46 ..58 E4
Chadderton OL9 ....152 C7
Sale M33 ....107 D3
Stockport SK2 ....124 E5
Hexham Rd M18 ....99 C3
Hexon Cl M6 ....154 E3
Hey Bottom La OL12 .....15 A6
Hey Cres OL4 ....67 F7
Hey Croft M46 ....62 C7
Hey Head Ave BB4 ....3 A8
Hey Head La OL15 ....6 B1
Hey Hill Cl OL2 ....149 A5
Hey House Mews BL8 .....10 F4
Hey Shoot La WA3 ....92 C5
Hey St Ince-in-M WN3 ....55 F3
Rochdale OL16 ....31 B8
Wigan WN6 ....150 B8
Hey Top OL3 ....69 D3
Hey Willow BL7 ....25 C6
Hey-with-Zion Prim Sch
OL4 ....67 E7
Heybrook Cl M45 ....63 C8
Heybrook Prim Sch OL12 .15 A1
Heybrook Rd M23 ....121 B5
Heybrook St OL16 ....31 B8
Heybrook Wlk M45 ....63 C8
Heybury Cl M11 ....164 F8
Heycrofts View BL0 ......1 E3
Heyden Bank 24 SK13 ...171 D2
Heyden Fold 23 SK13 ...171 D2
Heyden Terr 22 SK13 ...171 D2
Heyes Ave WA15 ....120 B7
Heyes Dr WA15 ....120 B7
Heyes La
Alderley Edge SK9 .....137 B3
Sale WA15 ....120 B8
Heyes Lane Jun & Inf Sch
WA15 ....120 B8
Heyes Leigh WA15 ......120 B7
Heyes Rd WN5 ....53 E6
Heyes St WN6 ....35 C7
Heyes Terr WA15 ....120 B8
Heyford Ave M40 ....65 D2
Heyford Rd WN5 ....54 D8
Heyheads New Rd SK15 ...86 E7
Heyland Rd M23 ....121 A6

Heyridge Dr M22 ....**109** D1
Heyrod St
  Manchester M1 ....**163** C8
  Mossley SK15 ....**86** D5
Heyrose Wlk 14 M15 ...**162** D6
Heys Ave Romiley SK6 ...**113** E3
  Swinton M27 ....**61** D2
  Wythenshawe M23 ......**109** A1
Heys Cl N M27 ....**61** C2
Heys La Heywood OL10 ...**29** A1
  Romiley SK6 ....**113** E3
Heys Prim Sch The OL6 ...**85** D3
Heys Rd Ashton-u-L OL6 ...**85** D3
  Prestwich M25 ....**63** B5
Heys St BL8 ....**140** D2
Heys The Prestwich M25 ...**63** B5
  Reddish SK5 ....**100** A1
Heys View M25 ....**63** B4
Heysbank Rd SK12 .....**135** D5
Heyscroft Rd
  Manchester,Heaton Mersey
  SK4 ....**168** A2
  Manchester,Withington
  M20 ....**110** C6
Heysham Ave M20 ......**109** F7
Heysham Rd WN5 ....**54** B7
Heysham Wlk M23 .....**108** F1
Heyside OL2 ....**49** A3
Heyside Ave OL2 ....**49** A3
Heyside Cl SK15 ....**86** E6
Heythrop Cl M45 ....**44** E1
Heywood Ave
  Golborne WA3 ....**74** B1
  Oldham OL4 ....**68** A8
  Swinton M27 ....**62** B2
Heywood Cl SK9 ....**137** B2
Heywood Com High Sch
  OL10 ....**28** E1
Heywood Ct M25 ....**64** A7
Heywood Distribution Pk
  BL9,OL10 ....**45** F8
Heywood Fold Rd OL4 ...**67** F7
Heywood Gdns
  Golborne WA3 ....**74** B1
  Prestwich M25 ....**63** B4
Heywood Gr M33 ......**108** B6
Heywood Hall Rd OL10 ...**29** D3
Heywood Ho
  Atherton M46 ....**58** C3
  Oldham OL8 ....**153** F5
  Salford M6 ....**80** C3
Heywood La OL4 ....**68** A7
Heywood Old Rd M24,
  OL10 ....**46** B3
Heywood Rd
  Alderley Edge SK9 ......**137** B2
  Prestwich M25 ....**63** C7
  Rochdale OL11 ....**30** C1
  Sale M33 ....**108** B3
Heywood St Bolton BL1 ...**145** F8
  Bury BL9 ....**141** A2
  Little Lever BL3 ....**43** B3
  Manchester M8 ....**156** A6
  Oldham OL4 ....**67** E8
  Swinton M27 ....**79** E8
Heywood Sta OL10 .....**29** E1
Heywood Way M6 .....**154** F3
Heywood's Hollow BL1 ...**143** F3
Heyworth St 4 M5 .....**154** E1
Hibbert Ave Denton M34 ...**100** E5
  Hyde SK14 ....**167** E1
Hibbert Cres M35 ......**84** A6
Hibbert La SK6 ....**125** F5
Hibbert St Bolton BL1 ...**143** F2
  Manchester M14 ....**98** C3
  Oldham OL4 ....**67** A7
  Reddish SK4,SK5 ....**111** E5
Hibernia St BL3 ....**144** C5
Hibernia Way M32 .....**96** A5
Hibson Ave OL12 ......**13** E2
Hibson Cl OL12 ....**15** C6
Hic Bibi La PR7 ....**19** A6
Hicken Pl SK14 ....**101** F5
Hickenfield Rd SK14 ...**101** F5
Hickton Dr WA14 ......**119** B6
Hieland Rd WN1 ......**37** E2
Higginshaw La OL2 .....**49** A2
Higginshaw Rd WN5 ...**111** E8
Higginson St WN7 ......**76** A5
Higgs Cl OL4 ....**67** D7
High Ash Gr M34 ......**100** D7
High Ave BL2 ....**42** E7
High Bank
  Altrincham WA14 ....**119** D5
  Bolton BL7 ....**24** F7
  Manchester M18 ....**99** E5
  Over Hulton M46 ....**59** A6
High Bank Ave SK15 ...**102** D7
High Bank Cl M44 ......**105** D6
High Bank Cres M25 ...**63** C3
High Bank Gr M25 ....**63** C3
High Bank La BL6 ......**40** B8
High Bank Rd
  Droylsden M43 ....**99** F8
  Hyde SK14 ....**167** F3
  Pendlebury M27 ....**80** B7
High Bank Side SK1 ....**169** F1
High Bank St BL2 ......**148** C7
High Barn Cl OL11 .....**139** E5
High Barn Com Jun Sch
  OL2 ....**48** E4
High Barn La OL12 .....**4** C3

High Barn Rd
  Middleton M24 ....**65** A7
  Royton OL2 ....**48** F4
High Barn St OL2 ......**48** E4
High Beeches BL2 ......**43** B5
High Beeches Cres WN4 ...**73** A6
High Bent Ave SK8 .....**132** A6
High Birch Sch OL11 ...**30** B4
High Crest Ave SK8 ....**121** F5
High Croft Cl SK16 ....**102** A8
High Elm Dr WA15 .....**129** C8
High Elm Rd WA15 .....**129** D7
High Elms BL8 ....**132** B5
High Field WA14 ......**118** B2
High Gates M33 ......**108** C5
High Grove Rd
  Cheadle SK8 ....**122** C5
  Uppermill OL4 ....**68** E5
High Hill Rd SK22 .....**127** D1
High Hurst Cl M24 .....**64** C7
High Knowls OL4 ......**68** A4
High La Glossop SK13 ...**115** F7
  Romiley SK6 ....**113** B4
High Lane Prim Sch
  SK6 ....**134** F8
High Lawn Prim Sch BL1 ...**24** E6
High Lea SK8 ....**122** C5
High Lee M33 ....**108** C4
High Lee La OL4 ......**50** B4
High Legh Rd M11 .....**99** D8
High Level Rd OL11 ....**31** A6
High Mdw 2 SK8 .....**131** E8
High Mdws Bolton BL7 ...**25** B8
  Glossop SK13 ....**116** E7
  Romiley SK6 ....**113** C3
High Moor Cres OL4 ...**49** E1
High Moor La WN6 .....**18** B4
High Mount BL2 ......**25** E3
High Peak OL15 ....**16** F5
High Peak Rd
  Ashton-u-L OL6 ....**86** A6
  Whitworth OL12 ....**14** C6
High Peak St M40 .....**83** B6
High Pk WN6 ....**36** C6
High Rid La BL6 ....**23** B1
High St Altrincham WA14 ...**119** D4
  Bolton BL3 ....**147** E4
  Bury BL8 ....**26** F4
  Chapeltown BL7 ....**9** C4
  Cheadle SK8 ....**122** D6
  Delph OL3 ....**50** F5
  Droylsden M43 ....**84** B1
  Golborne WA3 ....**90** A8
  Hazel Grove SK7 ....**124** F2
  Heywood OL10 ....**29** B2
  Horwich BL6 ....**22** B4
  Hyde SK14 ....**167** F3
  Ince-in-M WN3 ....**151** E6
  Leigh WN7 ....**76** A5
  Little Lever BL3 ....**43** B3
  5 Littleborough OL15 ...**15** F5
  Manchester M1,M4 .....**159** A1
  Middleton M24 ....**47** A1
  Middleton M24 ....**47** A2
  Mossley OL5 ....**68** B1
  Newton-le-W WA12 .....**89** D4
  Oldham OL1 ....**153** F7
  Oldham,Lees OL4 ......**67** E6
  Rochdale OL12 ....**139** F8
  Royton OL2 ....**48** D4
  Stalybridge SK15 ......**85** F1
  Stalybridge SK15 ......**86** A1
  Standish WN6 ....**19** E1
  Stockport SK1 ....**169** F1
  Tyldesley M29 ....**58** F1
  Tyldesley,Lark Hill M29 ...**77** B5
  Uppermill OL3 ....**69** B8
  Walkden M28 ....**60** D2
  Wigan,New Springs WN2 ...**38** B3
  Wigan,Swinley WN1 .....**37** D2
High St E SK13 ....**104** D1
High St W SK13 ....**104** B1
High Stile La OL4 ......**51** D2
High Stile St BL4 ......**60** E7
High View St
  Bolton,Daubhill BL1 .....**24** E6
  1 Bolton,Willows BL3 ...**146** C4
High Wood Fold SK6 ...**126** C8
Higham Cl OL2 ....**149** A5
Higham La SK14 ......**114** A7
Higham St SK8 ....**123** A2
Higham View M6 ......**81** A3
Highbank SK13 ....**103** F7
Highbank Cres OL4 ....**68** E5
Highbank Dr M20 .....**122** B8
Highbank Rd
  Glossop SK13 ....**116** F7
  Newhey OL16 ....**32** C4
  Whitefield BL9 ....**44** F3
Highbridge Cl BL2 .....**43** A6
Highbrook Gr 14 BL1 ...**143** E1
Highbury SK4 ....**110** F2
Highbury Ave Irlam M44 ...**94** A1
  Urmston M41 ....**94** E2
Highbury Cl BL5 ....**57** D6
Highbury Rd
  Manchester M16 ....**97** E1
  Reddish SK4 ....**111** C6
Highbury Way OL2 .....**48** D6
Highclere Ave M7,M8 ...**155** F6
Highclere Rd M8 ......**63** F2
Highcliffe Ct SK6 .....**126** D7
Highcliffe Rd M9 ......**64** A3
Highclove La M28 .....**77** F5
Highcrest Gr M29 .....**59** D1

Highcroft SK14 ....**113** F6
Highcroft Ave M20 ....**109** E4
Highcroft Rd SK6 .....**113** C3
Highcroft Way OL12 ...**14** F4
Highdales Rd M23 .....**121** B5
Highdown Wlk 26 M9 ...**157** E8
Higher Ainsworth Rd
  M26 ....**43** E7
Higher Ardwick M12 ...**163** C7
Higher Arthurs OL3 ....**69** A6
Higher Bank Rd OL15 ...**16** A3
Higher Barlow Row SK1 ...**170** F8
Higher Barn BL6 ......**22** F3
Higher Bents La SK6 ...**113** A3
Higher Blue Bell Cotts
  BL5 ....**39** C4
Higher Bridge St BL1 ...**145** F8
Higher Bury St SK4 ...**169** D2
Higher Calderbrook Rd
  OL15 ....**6** C2
Higher Cambridge St
  M15 ....**163** A6
Higher Carr La OL3 ....**69** B7
Higher Chatham St
  M15 ....**163** A6
Higher Cleggswood Ave
  OL15 ....**16** A3
Higher Count Hill OL4 ...**49** E2
Higher Croft Eccles M30 ...**95** C8
  Whitefield M45 ....**62** C6
Higher Cross La OL3 ...**69** C8
Higher Crossbank OL4 ...**67** F8
Higher Damshead BL5 ...**57** F8
Higher Darcy St BL2 ...**148** C5
Higher Dean St M26 ...**43** E3
Higher Dinting SK13 ...**104** A2
Higher Downs WA14 ...**119** C3
Higher Drake Mdw BL5 ...**57** E5
Higher Dunscar BL7 ....**8** E1
Higher Fold La BL0 ....**11** E7
Higher Folds Enterprise Ctr
  WN7 ....**76** E6
Higher Folds Prim Sch
  WN7 ....**76** D7
Higher Fullwood OL1 ...**49** D4
Higher Gamesley SK13 ...**115** D8
Higher Gn
  Ashton-u-L OL6 ....**166** C4
  Salford M6 ....**154** F4
Higher Green La M29 ...**77** C6
Higher Henry St SK14 ...**167** E1
Higher Hillgate SK1,SK2 ...**170** F8
Higher House OL9 .....**66** A4
Higher Kinders OL3 ...**69** C6
Higher Knowles BL6 ...**22** E2
Higher La Aspull WN2 ...**38** A4
  Disley SK12 ....**135** E1
  Lymm WA13 ....**117** B1
  Up Holland WN8 ....**53** C7
  Whitefield M45 ....**62** E8
Higher Lane Prim Sch
  M45 ....**62** F7
Higher Lime Rd OL8 ...**84** C8
Higher Lo OL11 ....**13** D2
Higher Lomax La OL10 ...**29** A3
Higher Lydgate Pk OL4 ...**68** B3
Higher Market St BL4 ...**60** E8
Higher Moulding BL7 ...**28** E5
Higher Newtons OL5 ...**68** D2
Higher Noon Sun SK22 ...**127** F2
Higher Openshaw Com Sch
  M11 ....**99** D8
Higher Ormond St M13,
  M15 ....**163** A6
Higher Oswald St 3
  M4 ....**159** A2
Higher Pit La M26 .....**43** E8
Higher Pk OL2 ....**32** C2
Higher Rd M41 ....**95** E2
Higher Ridings BL7 ....**24** F7
Higher Rise OL2 ......**32** A1
Higher Row BL9 ......**141** B3
Higher Shady La BL7 ...**25** C7
Higher Shore Rd OL15 ...**15** E7
Higher Southfield BL5 ...**57** F7
Higher Summerseat BL0 ...**11** B2
Higher Swan La BL3 ...**147** D3
Higher Tame St SK15 ...**86** B2
Higher Turf La OL4 ....**50** B1
Higher Turf Pk OL2 ....**48** E3
Higher View WN8 .....**53** C6
Higher Wharf St OL6,
  OL7 ....**166** B2
Higher Wheat La OL16 ...**31** C8
Higher Wood St M24 ...**46** F1
Higher York St M13 ...**163** B6
Highfield Sale M33 ....**108** C3
  Wigan WN3 ....**54** D4
Highfield Ave
  Atherton M46 ....**58** E5
  Bolton BL2 ....**26** A3
  Boothstown M28 ......**77** F7
  Golborne WA3 ....**89** F8
  Heywood OL10 ....**29** A2
  Leigh WN7 ....**76** C3
  Radcliffe M26 ....**44** C1
  Romiley SK6 ....**112** F2
  Shevington WN6 ....**36** A6
  Wigan WN1 ....**37** E1
Highfield Cl Adlington PR6 ...**21** A7
  Dukinfield SK14 ....**101** F6
  Stockport SK3 ....**123** F4
  Stretford M32 ....**108** C8
Highfield Cres SK9 ....**131** C1
Highfield Dr Eccles M30 ...**79** D3

Highfield Dr continued
  Farnworth BL4 ....**60** A7
  Middleton M24 ....**64** F7
  Mossley OL5 ....**86** C8
  Pendlebury M27 ....**80** C7
  Royton OL2 ....**48** C2
  Standish WN6 ....**36** F7
  4 Urmston M41 ....**95** C3
Highfield Est SK9 .....**131** C1
Highfield Gdns
  Hollingworth SK14 .....**103** D5
  Hyde SK14 ....**167** F3
Highfield Glen OL6 ....**85** F5
Highfield Gr WN2 .....**38** C5
Highfield Grange Ave
  WN3 ....**54** E2
Highfield Rd M45 ....**170** F5
Highfield La
  Golborne WA3 ....**90** C5
  Whitefield M45 ....**44** F3
Highfield Park Rd SK6 ...**112** F3
Highfield Parkway SK7 ...**132** D4
Highfield Pl SK4 ......**110** F2
Highfield Pl
  Prestwich M25 ....**63** A5
  Reddish M18 ....**99** F4
Highfield Prim Sch
  Farnworth BL4 ....**60** A8
  Urmston M41 ....**95** F2
Highfield Private Hospl
  OL11 ....**139** E5
Highfield Range M18 ...**99** F4
Highfield Rd
  Adlington PR6 ....**21** A7
  Altrincham WA15 ......**120** B5
  Altrincham,Well Green
  WA15 ....**120** A3
  Blackrod BL6 ....**21** E1
  Bolton BL1 ....**142** B2
  Cheadle SK8 ....**122** F1
  Eccles M30 ....**79** D4
  Edenfield BL0 ....**11** D3
  Farnworth BL4 ....**60** A8
  Glossop SK13 ....**116** D8
  Hazel Grove SK7 ......**125** A2
  Hindley WN2 ....**56** D7
  10 Marple SK6 ....**125** F6
  Marple,Marple Bridge SK6 ...**126** B6
  Milnrow OL16 ....**32** A6
  Poynton SK12 ....**133** A4
  Prestwich M25 ....**63** A5
  Reddish M19 ....**99** C1
  Rochdale OL11 ....**13** E1
  Salford M6 ....**154** F2
  Stockport SK7 ....**123** F3
  Stretford M32 ....**108** C8
  Walkden M38 ....**59** F5
Highfield Rd N PR6 ...**21** A8
Highfield St Denton M34 ...**100** E5
  Denton M34 ....**100** F6
  Dukinfield SK16 ....**101** A8
  Kearsley BL4 ....**61** A6
  Manchester M7,M8 .....**155** F7
  Middleton M24 ....**65** B8
  Oldham OL9 ....**153** D7
  2 Stockport SK3 .....**123** C8
Highfield St Matthews CE
  Prim Sch WN3 ....**54** C4
Highfield St W SK16 ...**166** B1
Highfield Terr
  Ashton-u-L OL7 ....**85** A7
  Manchester M9 ....**157** D8
Highgate
  Altrincham WA14 ......**119** B3
  Bolton BL3 ....**40** C2
Highgate Ave M41 .....**95** A4
Highgate Cres
  Appley Bridge WN6 .....**35** E7
  Manchester M18 ....**99** D3
Highgate Ctr 4 SK6 ...**112** F3
Highgate Dr Royton OL2 ...**48** C2
  Walkden M38 ....**59** E5
Highgate Ho 7 OL6 ...**166** C3
Highgate La Walkden M38 ...**59** E5
  Whitworth OL12 ....**14** C5
Highgate Rd
  Altrincham WA14 ......**119** B4
  Up Holland WN8 ....**53** B2
Highgrove WA15 ......**108** A1
Highgrove Cl BL1 .....**143** F3
Highgrove Mews 2
  SK9 ....**137** A6
Highgrove The BL1 ....**23** D1
Highland Ave SK6 .....**113** A2
Highland Lo WN6 .....**19** D1
Highland Rd Bolton BL2 ...**25** C8
  Horwich BL6 ....**22** E1
Highland View 1 OL5 ...**68** C2
Highland Wlk M35 .....**83** D6
Highlands
  Littleborough OL15 .....**16** A3
  Royton OL2 ....**48** C3
Highlands Dr SK2 .....**124** F6
Highlands Rd
  Hazel Grove SK2 ......**124** F6
  Rochdale OL11 ....**29** E5
  Royton OL2 ....**48** C3
  Shaw OL2 ....**48** C8
Highlands The 3 OL3 ...**68** C1
Highmarsh Cres WA12 ...**89** B4
Highmead St M18 .....**99** D5
Highmead Wlk M16 ...**162** D5
Highmeadow
  Radcliffe M26 ....**43** F1
  Up Holland WN8 ....**53** A6
Highmoor View OL4 ...**49** E1
Highmore Dr M9 ......**64** E3
Highnam Wlk M22 ....**121** A1

Highover Ho M20 ....**109** F4
Highrise Pl M27 ......**61** F2
Highshore Dr M8 .....**155** C6
Highstone Dr M8 .....**156** C6
Highstones SK13 .....**104** F2
Highthorne Gn OL2 ...**48** C8
Highview SK13 ....**116** A7
Highview Wlk M9 .....**64** E3
Highwood OL11 ......**13** E1
Highwood Cl
  8 Bolton BL2 ....**25** F1
  Glossop SK13 ....**116** B8
Highwoods Cl WN4 ....**73** B5
Highworth Cl BL3 ....**145** E5
Highworth Dr M40 ....**65** D2
Higson Ave Eccles M30 ...**95** C8
  Manchester M21 ....**109** B7
  Romiley SK6 ....**113** B4
Hilary Ave Atherton M46 ...**58** C5
  Gatley SK8 ....**131** D8
  Golborne WA3 ....**74** D1
  Oldham OL8 ....**66** C3
Hilary Cl SK4 ....**169** D2
Hilary Gr BL4 ....**60** D7
Hilary Rd M22 ....**121** C1
Hilary St OL11 ....**30** D1
Hilbre Ave OL1 ......**48** D2
Hilbre Rd M19 ....**110** F8
Hilbury Ave M9 ......**64** D1
Hilda Ave Bury BL8 ...**26** F6
  Cheadle SK8 ....**122** E6
Hilda Gr SK5 ....**169** F4
Hilda Rd SK14 ....**113** D7
Hilda St 6 Bolton BL3 ...**42** A4
  Heywood OL10 ....**29** D3
  Leigh WN7 ....**75** D6
  Oldham OL9 ....**153** D7
  Reddish SK5 ....**169** F4
Hilden Ct M16 ....**97** D4
Hilden St Bolton BL2 ...**148** A6
  4 Leigh WN7 ....**75** E5
Hilditch Cl M23 .....**121** B6
Hildyard St WN5 .....**54** F6
Hiley Rd M30 ....**79** A1
Hilgay Cl WN3 ....**54** D3
Hill Bank Cl SK15 ....**86** D5
Hill Cot Rd BL1 ......**35** E8
Hill Cot Rd BL1 ......**143** E8
Hill Court Mews SK6 ...**113** B2
Hill Cres Leigh WN7 ...**75** C8
  Manchester M9 ....**64** A3
Hill Crest M46 ......**58** F5
Hill Crest Ave Leigh WN7 ...**75** C8
  Manchester SK4 ......**168** A2
Hill Dr SK9 ....**131** E3
Hill End Rd OL3 .....**50** F4
Hill Farm Cl OL8 ....**67** B3
Hill House Fold La WN6 ...**18** C5
Hill House La WN6 ...**18** C5
Hill La Blackrod BL6 ...**21** C2
  Bolton BL2 ....**148** A8
  Manchester M9 ....**64** C4
Hill Mount SK16 .....**102** A8
Hill Rise
  Altrincham WA14 .....**119** A5
  Ramsbottom BL0 ......**11** A3
  Romiley SK6 ....**113** B2
Hill Side BL1 ....**40** F7
Hill Side Cl SK12 ....**135** E6
Hill St Altrincham WA14 ...**119** C8
  Ashton-u-L OL6,OL7 ...**166** B3
  Bury BL8 ....**26** F4
  Dukinfield SK16 ....**166** B1
  Heywood OL10 ....**29** C2
  Hindley WN2 ....**56** D6
  Hyde SK14 ....**113** F8
  Leigh WN7 ....**75** E5
  Manchester M20 ......**110** B7
  Middleton M24 ....**47** A3
  Oldham OL4 ....**67** B7
  Radcliffe M26 ....**44** B3
  Ramsbottom BL9 ......**11** C3
  Rochdale OL16 ....**31** A2
  Romiley SK6 ....**113** B2
  Salford M7 ....**155** D6
  Shaw OL2 ....**149** C6
  Wigan WN6 ....**37** A7
Hill Top Altrincham WA15 ...**120** A1
  Bolton BL3 ....**143** D3
  Little Lever BL3 ....**43** A4
  Over Hulton M46 ......**58** F5
  Romiley SK6 ....**113** B3
Hill Top Ave Cheadle SK8 ...**132** B8
  Prestwich M25 ....**63** B4
  Wilmslow SK9 ....**137** B8
Hill Top Com Prim Sch
  OL11 ....**31** A1
Hill Top Com Specl Sch
  OL4 ....**50** A4
Hill Top Dr
  Altrincham WA15 .....**120** A1
  Rochdale OL11 ....**30** F2
Hill Top Fold 1 WN2 ...**56** C5
Hill Top La OL3 ......**50** C4
Hill Top Rd M28 .....**60** D4
Hill View Digle OL3 ...**50** F4
  Stalybridge SK15 .....**102** E6
Hill View Cl OL1 .....**49** C2
Hill View Dr PR7 .....**19** D8
Hill's Ct 3 BL8 ......**27** B4
Hillam Cl M41 ....**95** F1
Hillary Ave Ashton-u-L OL7 ...**85** B5
Hillary Rd SK14 .....**102** A5
Hillbank WN6 ....**37** A7
Hillbank Cl BL1 ......**142** C3

Hillbank St OL11 .... 47 D6
Hillbeck Cres WN4 .... 72 D4
Hillbrae Ave WA11 .... 71 A1
Hillbre Way SK9 .... 131 E4
Hillbrook Ave M40 .... 65 B2
Hillbrook Rd
 Bramhall SK7 .... 132 D6
 Stockport SK1 .... 124 C8
Hillbrow Wlk 9 M8 .... 155 F7
Hillbury Rd SK7 .... 123 F1
Hillcote Wlk M18 .... 165 B6
Hillcourt Rd
 High Lane SK6 .... 134 F7
 Romiley SK6 .... 113 C4
Hillcourt St M1 .... 163 A7
Hillcrest Hyde SK14 .... 113 F7
 Middleton M24 .... 46 F3
 Platt Bridge WN2 .... 56 B2
Hillcrest Ave SK9 .... 80 A3
Hillcrest Ave OL10 .... 29 A3
Hillcrest Cres OL10 .... 29 A3
Hillcrest Dr Denton M34 .... 101 B1
 Reddish M19 .... 111 C2
Hillcrest Gram Sch SK3 .... 170 F6
Hillcrest Rd
 Prestwich M25 .... 62 F2
 Rochdale OL11 .... 30 D1
 Stockport,Bramhall Green
  SK7 .... 123 F1
 Stockport,Stockport Great Moor
  SK2 .... 124 C2
 Tyldesley M29 .... 77 D8
Hillcroft Oldham OL8 .... 67 A1
 Stockport SK2 .... 124 E6
Hillcroft Cl M8 .... 156 A8
Hillcroft Rd WA14 .... 119 A5
Hilldale Ave M9 .... 64 E4
Hilldean WN8 .... 53 C8
Hillel Ho M15 .... 163 A5
Hillend SK14 .... 103 A1
Hillend La SK14 .... 103 A1
Hillend Rd M23 .... 109 A2
Hillfield M5 .... 154 D2
Hillfield Cl M13 .... 164 D5
Hillfield Dr Bolton BL2 .... 25 B1
 Worsley M28 .... 78 A7
Hillfoot Wlk 28 M15 .... 162 D6
Hillgate Ave M5 .... 161 B7
Hillgate St OL6 .... 166 C4
Hillhead Wlk M8 .... 156 A5
Hillhouse Ct OL12 .... 30 B3
Hillier St M9 .... 157 E8
Hillier St N M9 .... 157 E8
Hillingdon Cl OL8 .... 84 B8
Hillingdon Dr M9 .... 65 B2
Hillingdon Rd
 Stretford M32 .... 96 E2
 Whitefield M45 .... 62 D7
Hillington Rd Sale M33 .... 107 F5
 Stockport SK3 .... 123 C8
Hillkirk Dr OL12 .... 14 C3
Hillkirk St M11 .... 160 E1
Hillman Cl M40 .... 157 D5
Hillock The Bolton BL2 .... 25 D5
 Tyldesley M29 .... 77 B5
Hillreed WN6 .... 36 F1
Hills La BL9 .... 45 C2
Hillsborough Dr BL9 .... 45 B2
Hillsdale Gr BL2 .... 25 E3
Hillside WA13 .... 117 E1
Hillside
 Ashton-in-M WN4 .... 72 F8
 Atherton M46 .... 58 E4
 Blackrod BL6 .... 21 E1
 Bolton BL7 .... 9 D2
 Diggle OL3 .... 51 C3
 Farnworth BL4 .... 22 C4
 Horwich BL6 .... 22 C4
 Hyde SK14 .... 113 F6
 Mossley SK15 .... 86 F6
 Oldham,Clarksfield OL4 .... 67 C7
 Oldham,Grotton OL4 .... 68 B5
 Royton OL2 .... 48 E5
 Salford M7 .... 81 A8
 Shaw OL2 .... 49 D8
 Walkden M28 .... 60 C4
 Whitefield M45 .... 44 E2
Hillside Cl Billinge WN5 .... 71 D5
 Bolton,Harwood Lee BL2 .... 25 E5
 Bolton,Hunger Hill BL3 .... 40 D2
 Bramhall SK7 .... 133 A7
 Hadfield SK14 .... 171 E3
 Manchester M40 .... 65 A1
 Wigan WN3 .... 54 D3
Hillside Cres
 Ashton-u-L OL6 .... 85 F5
 Bury BL9 .... 27 F6
 Horwich BL6 .... 22 C4
Hillside Ct BL1 .... 40 F7
Hillside Dr Middleton M24 .... 47 B1
 Pendlebury M27 .... 80 D6
Hillside Gr SK6 .... 114 B1
Hillside Rd
 Altrincham WA15 .... 120 A3
 Hyde SK14,SK6 .... 113 D5
 Ramsbottom BL0 .... 138 A5
 Stockport SK2 .... 124 D7
Hillside St 5 BL3 .... 145 F7
Hillside View
 Denton M34 .... 113 A7
 Milnrow OL16 .... 32 A6
Hillside Way OL12 .... 4 C1
Hillside Wlk OL12 .... 14 D4
Hillspring Rd OL4 .... 68 A6
Hillstone Ave OL12 .... 14 D4
Hillstone Cl BL8 .... 10 F2

Hilltop OL12 .... 14 C5
Hilltop Ave
 Manchester M9 .... 64 D3
 Whitefield M45 .... 63 B8
Hilltop Ct Manchester M14 .... 98 D1
 Manchester,Crumpsall M8 .... 63 F2
Hilltop Dr Bury BL8 .... 26 E6
 Haslingden BB4 .... 1 C7
 Marple SK6 .... 125 C7
 Royton OL2 .... 48 E2
Hilltop Gr M45 .... 63 B8
Hilltop Rd SK13 .... 104 B2
Hillview Ct BL1 .... 143 E4
Hillview Rd Bolton BL1 .... 143 E4
 Reddish M34 .... 100 A1
Hillwood Ave M8 .... 63 F2
Hillwood Dr SK13 .... 116 F8
Hilly Croft BL7 .... 24 F8
Hillyard St 2 BL8 .... 27 C3
Hilmarton Cl BL2 .... 25 E5
Hilrose Ave M41 .... 95 F2
Hilson Ct M43 .... 84 A1
Hilton Arc OL1 .... 153 F7
Hilton Ave Horwich BL6 .... 22 A3
 Urmston M41 .... 95 D2
Hilton Bank M28 .... 60 B3
Hilton Cl WN7 .... 76 A5
Hilton Cres
 Ashton-u-L OL6 .... 85 C5
 Manchester M25 .... 63 B2
 Worsley M28 .... 78 B6
Hilton Ct SK4 .... 168 C3
Hilton Dr Irlam M44 .... 105 C5
 Manchester M25 .... 63 B2
Hilton Fold La M24 .... 47 B1
Hilton Gr Poynton SK12 .... 133 D4
 Walkden M28 .... 60 B3
Hilton La Prestwich M25 .... 63 A2
 Walkden M28 .... 60 B2
Hilton La Prim Sch M28 .... 60 B3
Hilton Lo M25 .... 63 B2
Hilton Pl WN2 .... 38 C6
Hilton Rd Bury BL9 .... 140 F2
 Disley SK12 .... 134 C5
 Poynton SK12 .... 134 C5
 Stockport SK7 .... 123 F1
 Wythenshawe M22 .... 121 E5
Hilton Sq M27 .... 62 A1
Hilton St Ashton-in-M WN4 .... 73 C3
 Bolton BL2 .... 148 C7
 Bury BL9 .... 141 C4
 Dukinfield SK14 .... 101 F5
 Ince-in-M WN3 .... 151 E6
 Manchester M1 .... 159 B2
 Manchester M1,M4 .... 159 B2
 Salford M7 .... 155 D5
 Stockport SK3 .... 170 D8
 Wigan WN1 .... 37 D1
Hilton St N M7 .... 155 D6
Hilton Wlk M24 .... 64 C8
Hiltons Cl OL8 .... 153 E5
Hiltons Farm Cl M34 .... 100 E6
Himley Rd M11 .... 83 C2
Hinchcombe Cl M38 .... 60 A6
Hinchley Rd M9 .... 65 C3
Hinchley Way M27 .... 61 F1
Hinckley St M11 .... 164 F8
Hind Hill St OL10 .... 29 D1
Hind Rd WN5 .... 54 D8
Hind St BL2 .... 148 C7
Hind's Head Ave WN6 .... 18 F6
Hindburn Cl M45 .... 45 B1
Hindburn Dr M28 .... 78 A8
Hindburn Wlk M45 .... 45 B1
Hinde St M40 .... 83 A8
Hindell Terr OL3 .... 50 F4
Hindhead Wlk M40 .... 83 D4
Hindle Dr OL2 .... 48 C3
Hindle St Bacup OL13 .... 3 D8
 Radcliffe M26 .... 44 A3
Hindles Cl M46 .... 58 A1
Hindley All Saints CE Prim
 Sch WN2 .... 56 E5
Hindley Ave M22 .... 121 B2
Hindley Bsns Ctr 18 WN2 .... 56 D5
Hindley Cl 2 OL7 .... 84 F1
Hindley Com High Sch
 WN2 .... 56 F5
Hindley Green Bsns Pk
 WN2 .... 57 B2
Hindley Green Prim Sch
 WN2 .... 57 B3
Hindley Jun & Inf Sch
 WN2 .... 56 E5
Hindley Mill La WN2 .... 56 F7
Hindley Rd BL5,WN2 .... 57 D5
Hindley St Ashton-u-L OL7 .... 84 F1
 Stockport SK1 .... 170 F8
Hindley Sta WN2 .... 56 D7
Hindley Wlk 1 WN1 .... 150 C8
Hinds La Bury BL8 .... 27 C1
 Bury BL8,BL9 .... 44 C7
Hindsford CE Prim Sch
 M46 .... 58 E1
Hindsford St M46 .... 58 E1
Hinkler Ave BL3 .... 147 E3
Hinstock Cres M18 .... 99 D5
Hinton 16 OL12 .... 14 C5
Hinton 2 OL11 .... 29 E6
Hinton Cl OL11 .... 29 E6
Hinton Gr SK14 .... 114 A8
Hinton Mews M41 .... 112 B1
Hinton St Manchester M4 .... 159 B3
 Oldham OL8 .... 153 F5
Hipley Cl SK6 .... 113 A5
Hirons La OL4 .... 68 A5

Hirst Ave M28 .... 60 C5
Hitchen Cl SK16 .... 101 F7
Hitchen Dr SK16 .... 101 F7
Hitchin Wlk M13 .... 164 D5
Hive St OL8 .... 66 B2
HM Prison Strangeways
 M3,M8 .... 158 F4
Hoad Wlk 3 M34 .... 113 A7
Hoade St WN2 .... 56 E7
Hob Hey La WA3 .... 91 D3
Hob Hill SK15 .... 85 F1
Hob Hill Mdws SK13 .... 116 F7
Hob La BL7 .... 9 C7
Hob Mill Rise OL5 .... 68 E4
Hobart Cl SK7 .... 132 F4
Hobart St Bolton BL1 .... 143 D2
 Manchester M18 .... 99 E5
Hobby Gr WN7 .... 76 B5
Hobson Cres M34 .... 100 E6
Hobson Ct M34 .... 100 E6
Hobson Moor Rd SK14,
 SK15 .... 103 A7
Hobson St
 Droylsden M11 .... 100 A1
 Failsworth M35 .... 83 D6
 Oldham OL1 .... 153 F6
 Reddish SK5 .... 99 F2
Hockenhull Cl M22 .... 121 E2
Hockerley La M33 .... 107 D5
Hockery View WN2 .... 56 C4
Hockley Cl SK12 .... 134 A3
Hockley Paddock SK12 .... 133 F3
Hockley Rd
 Poynton SK12 .... 134 A3
 6 Wythenshawe M23 .... 120 F6
Hodder Ave
 Littleborough OL15 .... 15 F6
 Platt Bridge WN2 .... 55 F2
Hodder Bank SK2 .... 124 E5
Hodder Cl WN5 .... 54 D7
Hodder Way M45 .... 63 C8
Hoddesdon St M8 .... 156 B7
Hodge Clough Inf Sch
 OL1 .... 49 D3
Hodge Clough Jun Sch
 OL1 .... 49 D3
Hodge Clough Rd OL1 .... 49 D3
Hodge La
 Mottram-in-L SK14 .... 114 F8
 Salford M5,M6 .... 154 F1
Hodge Rd Oldham OL1 .... 49 D3
 Walkden M28 .... 60 D2
Hodge St M9 .... 64 F1
Hodges St WN6 .... 37 A8
Hodgson Dr WA15 .... 120 A8
Hodgson St
 Ashton-u-L OL6 .... 166 A2
 Manchester M8 .... 155 F5
Hodnet Dr WN4 .... 73 C3
Hodnet Wlk M34 .... 100 E1
Hodnett Ave M41 .... 94 E1
Hodson Fold OL8 .... 67 A1
Hodson Rd M27 .... 61 E2
Hodson St Salford M3 .... 158 E2
 Wigan WN3 .... 150 C7
Hogarth Rd Marple SK6 .... 126 B8
 Rochdale OL11 .... 30 F3
Hogarth Rise OL1 .... 49 D4
Hogarth Wlk M8 .... 156 C6
Hoghton Ave OL13 .... 4 A8
Holbeach Cl Bury BL8 .... 27 D5
 Hindley WN2 .... 56 E4
Holbeck M29 .... 77 B5
Holbeck Ave OL12 .... 14 C4
Holbeck Cl BL6 .... 39 D8
Holbeck Gr M14 .... 98 E4
Holberton Cl M8 .... 155 E5
Holborn Cl SK7 .... 124 A3
Holborn Ave
 Failsworth M35 .... 84 B7
 Leigh WN7 .... 75 F8
 Radcliffe M26 .... 43 D4
 Wigan WN3 .... 150 B5
Holborn Dr M8 .... 159 C8
Holborn Gdns OL11 .... 139 D5
Holborn Sq OL11 .... 139 D5
Holborn St OL11 .... 139 D5
Holbrook Ave M38 .... 60 A6
Holbrook St M1 .... 163 A8
Holcombe Bury BL8 .... 27 B2
 Grasmere WA3 .... 90 E8
Holcombe Brook Prim Sch
 BL0 .... 11 A2
Holcombe Cl
 Altrincham WA14 .... 119 B6
 Kearsley BL4 .... 61 A6
 Oldham OL4 .... 67 F7
 Salford M6 .... 81 A2
Holcombe Cres BL0 .... 61 A6
Holcombe Gdns WN9 .... 110 E5
Holcombe Lee BL0 .... 11 A4
Holcombe Mews BL0 .... 1 A5
Holcombe Old Rd BL8 .... 138 A5
Holcombe Prec BL0 .... 10 F3
Holcombe Rd
 Haslingden BB4 .... 1 A6
 Little Lever BL3 .... 42 F3
 Manchester M14 .... 110 E7
 Ramsbottom BL0 .... 10 F5
Holcombe View Cl OL4 .... 49 D2
Holcombe Village BL8 .... 138 A6
Holcombe Wlk SK4 .... 111 D7
Holcroft La WA3 .... 92 D2
Holden Ave Bolton BL1 .... 24 E6
 Bury BL9 .... 28 E4
Holden Fold OL2 .... 48 E5
Holden Fold La OL2 .... 48 D5
Holden Rd WN7 .... 76 A1
Holden St OL11 .... 139 A5

Holden Brook Cl WN7 .... 76 B5
Holden Clough Com Prim
 Sch OL6 .... 85 D7
Holden Clough Dr OL7 .... 85 B7
Holden Fold La OL1,OL2 .... 48 D3
Holden Lea BL5 .... 39 E3
Holden Rd Leigh WN7 .... 76 B5
 Manchester M7 .... 63 D1
Holden St Adlington PR7 .... 20 F7
 Ashton-u-L OL6 .... 166 C4
 Oldham OL8 .... 66 F3
 8 Rochdale OL12 .... 15 A2
Holden Wlk WN5 .... 54 E5
Holder Ave BL3 .... 43 B5
Holderness Dr OL1 .... 48 C2
Holdgate Cl M15 .... 162 E5
Holding St WN2 .... 56 D6
Holdsworth St M27 .... 79 D7
Hole House Fold SK6 .... 113 B2
Holebottom OL6 .... 85 C6
Holford Ave M14 .... 98 B2
Holford Ct M34 .... 100 F3
Holford Way WA12 .... 89 F3
Holford Wlk OL16 .... 31 B7
Holgate Dr WN5 .... 53 E6
Holgate St OL4 .... 49 E1
Holhouse La BL8 .... 10 F2
Holiday La SK2 .... 124 F7
Holkar Mdws BL7 .... 25 B8
Holker Cl
 Manchester M13 .... 164 D5
 Poynton SK12 .... 133 F4
Holker Way 21 M34 .... 101 A1
Holkham Cl 6 M4 .... 159 C2
Holland Ave SK15 .... 86 A2
Holland Cl OL3 .... 50 E4
Holland Ct Manchester M8 .... 63 F2
 Radcliffe M26 .... 44 C4
 Stockport SK1 .... 124 A7
Holland Gr OL6 .... 85 B6
Holland Rd Bramhall SK7 .... 132 E7
 Manchester M8 .... 63 F2
Holland Rise 8 OL12 .... 139 E8
Holland St Bolton BL1 .... 143 F4
 Denton M34 .... 100 F3
 Heywood OL10 .... 29 D2
 Manchester M40 .... 160 D3
 Radcliffe M26 .... 44 C4
 Rochdale,Wuerdle OL16 .... 15 D4
 Salford M6 .... 81 A5
Holland St E M34 .... 100 F4
Holland St W M34 .... 100 E4
Holland Wlk M6 .... 81 A5
Hollies Ct M33 .... 108 B4
Hollies Dr SK6 .... 126 A5
Hollies La SK9 .... 137 F7
Hollies The
 10 Atherton M46 .... 58 D3
 Bolton BL2 .... 42 F8
 Gatley SK8 .... 122 B5
 Manchester,Heaton Moor
  SK4 .... 168 B3
 Manchester,West Didsbury
  M20 .... 109 F3
 Pendlebury M27 .... 80 B7
 Salford M6 .... 80 B8
Hollin Ave SK5 .... 99 F3
Hollin Bank SK4 .... 111 D7
Hollin Cres OL3 .... 68 E5
Hollin Cross La SK13 .... 116 C8
Hollin Dr M24 .... 46 F4
Hollin Hey WN5 .... 71 D3
Hollin Hey Rd BL1 .... 23 E3
Hollin House La M27 .... 47 A3
Hollin La
 Middleton M24,OL10 .... 46 F4
 Rochdale OL11 .... 29 E6
 Styal SK9 .... 130 F5
Hollin Prim Sch M24 .... 47 A3
Hollinbrook WN6 .... 36 E2
Hollinbury Ave M22 .... 121 F1
Hollinbush St M22 .... 121 F2
Hollington Way M33 .... 54 C2
Hollingwood Cl WN4 .... 73 A3
Hollingworth Ave M40 .... 65 F2
Hollingworth Cl 4 SK1 .... 170 F8
Hollingworth Dr SK6 .... 125 F3
Hollingworth High Sch
 OL16 .... 32 A6
Hollingworth La OL14 .... 15 F8
Hollingworth Lake Ctry Pk*
 OL15 .... 16 C3
Hollingworth Lake Ctry Pk
 Visitor Ctr* OL15 .... 16 C3
Hollingworth Lake Water
 Sports Ctr* OL15 .... 16 B3
Hollingworth Prim Sch
 SK14 .... 103 C5
Hollingworth Rd
 Littleborough OL15 .... 16 B4
 Romiley SK6 .... 112 E4
Hollingworth St OL9 .... 66 B3
Hollinhall St OL4 .... 67 C7
Hollinhey Terr SK14 .... 103 C5
Hollinhurst Dr BL6 .... 40 C7
Hollinhurst Rd M26 .... 44 C1
Hollins Ave
 13 Gamesley SK13 .... 171 D2
 Hyde SK14 .... 113 E7
 Oldham OL4 .... 67 F8
Hollins Brook 35 SK13 .... 171 D2
Hollins Brook Cl BL9 .... 45 B5
Hollins Brook Way BL9 .... 45 B6
Hollins Brow BL9 .... 44 F4

Hollins Cl
 34 Gamesley SK13 .... 171 D2
 Garswood WN4 .... 72 D4
 Tyldesley M29 .... 77 A8
 Whitefield BL9 .... 45 B4
Hollins Com Prim Sch
 WN2 .... 57 A5
Hollins Fold 38 SK13 .... 171 D2
Hollins Gdns 36 SK13 .... 171 D2
Hollins Grn M24 .... 47 A3
Hollins Gr
 37 Gamesley SK13 .... 171 D2
 Manchester M12 .... 99 A3
 Sale M33 .... 108 A4
Hollins Green St Helens CE
 Prim Sch WA3 .... 105 B2
Hollins Green Rd SK6 .... 125 F6
Hollins Grundy Prim Sch
 BL9 .... 45 A5
Hollins Ind Pk BL9 .... 104 B5
Hollins La Edenfield BL0 .... 1 A6
 Gamesley SK13 .... 171 D2
 Marple SK6 .... 125 F6
 Marple,Marple Bridge SK6 .... 126 C8
 Mossley OL5 .... 68 D1
 Uppermill OL3 .... 69 D5
 Whitefield BL9 .... 45 B4
Hollins Mews
 Gamesley SK13 .... 171 D2
 Whitefield BL9 .... 45 C4
Hollins Mount SK6 .... 126 B8
Hollins Rd Hindley WN2 .... 57 A5
 Oldham,Greenacres Fold
  OL4 .... 67 F8
 Oldham,Hollins OL8 .... 66 D2
Hollins St Bolton BL2 .... 148 B6
 6 Oldham OL4 .... 67 F6
 Stalybridge SK15 .... 101 F8
 Walsden OL14 .... 6 B8
Hollins Terr 2 SK6 .... 125 F6
Hollins Tce 8 SK6 .... 125 F6
Hollins Way 38 SK13 .... 171 D2
Hollins Wlk M22 .... 121 D2
Hollinsclough Cl M22 .... 121 E5
Hollinscroft Ave WA15 .... 120 D5
Hollinshead M7 .... 155 E6
Hollinsmoor Rd SK6,
 SK22 .... 127 D7
Hollinswood Rd
 Bolton BL2 .... 148 B6
 Worsley M28 .... 78 B6
Hollinwood Ave M40,OL9 .... 65 E2
Hollinwood La SK6 .... 126 B2
Hollinwood Rd SK12 .... 135 D6
Hollinwood Sta OL9 .... 66 A2
Hollow End SK5 .... 112 B7
Hollow Mdws M26 .... 61 C6
Hollow The SK8 .... 122 C1
Hollow Vale Dr SK5 .... 112 A8
Hollow Vale Rd SK5 .... 99 F1
Holloway Dr M27,M28 .... 61 C1
Hollowbrook Way 4
 OL12 .... 14 D2
Hollowell La BL6 .... 22 D1
Hollowfield OL11 .... 13 D1
Hollowgate M30 .... 79 B1
Hollows The SK8 .... 122 C1
Hollowspell OL12 .... 15 C3
Holly Ave Cheadle SK8 .... 122 D5
 Newton-le-W WA12 .... 89 D3
 Urmston M41 .... 95 B2
 Walkden M28 .... 60 D2
Holly Bank Ashton-u-L OL6 .... 85 B7
 Entwistle BL7 .... 9 B2
 Failsworth M40 .... 83 C7
 Glossop SK13 .... 116 E8
 Hollingworth SK14 .... 103 D5
 2 Royton OL2 .... 48 D4
 Royton OL2 .... 48 D3
 Sale M33 .... 108 C3
Holly Bank Cl M15 .... 161 C6
Holly Bank Rd SK9 .... 123 A1
Holly Cl WA15 .... 120 A6
Holly Ct Hyde SK14 .... 102 A2
 1 Irlam M44 .... 94 B3
 8 Manchester M20 .... 110 B6
 Stockport SK3 .... 170 E5
Holly Dene Dr BL6 .... 40 B7
Holly Dr M33 .... 108 A4
Holly Fold M45 .... 44 F1
Holly Gr Bolton BL1 .... 142 C1
 Chadderton OL9 .... 152 B8
 Denton M34 .... 101 A3
 Dukinfield SK15 .... 101 E8
 Farnworth BL4 .... 60 A8
 Leigh WN7 .... 75 E7
 Oldham OL4 .... 67 E7
 Sale M33 .... 108 D4
Holly Grange
 Altrincham WA14 .... 119 D2
 Stockport SK7 .... 123 F3
Holly Bank Dr Ty WN1 .... 37 B4
Holly Heys 4 M33 .... 108 D4
Holly House Dr M41 .... 94 F2
Holly La Oldham OL4 .... 66 C2
Holly Mill Cres SK9 .... 130 E5
Holly Mount M24 .... 1 A7
Holly Mount RC Prim Sch
 BL8 .... 10 D1
Holly Oak Gdns OL10 .... 29 C1
Holly Rd Aspull WN2 .... 38 B5
 Bramhall SK7 .... 132 E5
 Golborne WA3 .... 90 C8

Holly Rd *continued*
High Lane SK6 ....134 F7
Lymm WA13 ....117 B5
Poynton SK12 ....133 E3
Reddish SK4 ....111 C5
Swinton M27 ....79 D6
Wigan WN5 ....54 E6
Holly Rd N SK9 ....137 B6
Holly Rd S SK9 ....137 B5
Holly Royde Cl M20 ....110 B6
Holly St Bolton BL1 ....143 F4
Bury BL9 ....141 A2
Bury,Tottington BL8 ....26 F6
Droylsden M43 ....83 D2
Manchester M11 ....108 B7
Ramsbottom BL9 ....11 C3
Stockport SK1 ....112 B1
Wardle OL12 ....15 C6
Holly Wlk M31 ....105 D3
Hollybank M43 ....84 C3
Hollybank Dr BL6 ....40 B7
Hollybank Rise SK16 ....101 F8
Hollybank St M26 ....43 F3
Hollybush Sq WA3 ....74 E1
Hollybush St M18 ....99 E6
Hollycroft Ave Bolton BL2 ..42 E5
Wythenshawe M22 ....121 D6
Hollyedge Dr M25 ....63 A2
Hollyhedge Ave M22 ....121 D5
Hollyhedge Court Rd
M22 ....121 E5
Hollyhedge Rd M22,M23 ...121 C5
Hollyhey Dr M23 ....109 C2
Hollyhouse Dr SK6 ....113 A5
Hollyhurst M28 ....79 B6
Hollymount M16 ....97 B4
Hollymount Ave SK2 ....124 C5
Hollymount Dr
Oldham OL4 ....49 E3
Stockport SK2 ....124 C5
Hollymount Gdns SK2 ......124 D5
Hollymount Rd SK2 ....124 D5
Hollythorn Ave SK8 ....132 C7
Hollyway M22 ....121 E8
Hollywood
Altrincham WA14 ....119 D2
Bolton BL1 ....142 B2
Hollywood Rd
Bolton BL1 ....142 B2
Moorend SK6 ....126 F8
Hollywood Twrs SK3 ....170 D8
Hollywood Way SK3,SK4 ...169 D1
Holm Ct M6 ....81 A3
Holmbrook M29 ....59 C1
Holmcroft Rd M18 ....99 D3
Holmdale Ave M19 ....110 E5
Holme Ave Bury BL8 ....27 C5
Wigan WN5 ....37 C2
Holme Cres OL1 ....48 C2
Holme **7** WN1 ....37 C2
Holme House St OL15 ....6 D1
Holme La Haslingden BB4 ...1 D8
Rawtenstall BB4 ....1 E8
Holme Park Way SK3 ....84 B7
Holme Rd M20 ....110 A3
Holme St Bacup OL13 ....3 D8
Hyde SK14 ....167 D2
Holme Terr Haslingden BB4 ...1 D8
Littleborough OL15 ....6 D1
Wigan WN1 ....37 B3
Holme Vale BB4 ....1 A6
Holmebrook Dr BL6 ....22 D1
Holmedale Ct 8 M33 ....108 C4
Holmefield M33 ....108 B4
Holmepark Gdns M28 ....78 A5
Holmes Cotts BL1 ....142 C3
Holmes Ct SK1 ....169 F1
Holmes House Ave WN3 .....54 D3
Holmes Rd OL12 ....139 D7
Holmes St Bolton BL2 ....42 A4
Cheadle SK8 ....122 E6
Rochdale,Greengate OL12 ...15 C3
Rochdale,Spotland Bridge
OL12 ....139 D7
Stockport SK2 ....170 E7
Holmes Way M34 ....112 E7
Holmeswood Cl SK9 ....137 C8
Holmeswood Pk BB4 ....1 E8
Holmeswood Rd BL3 ....147 D2
Holmfield Ave
Manchester,Harpurhey M9 .157 F7
Manchester,Sedgley Park
M25 ....63 C3
Holmfield Ave W M9 ....157 F7
Holmfield Cl SK4 ....169 D3
Holmfield Dr SK8 ....132 B8
Holmfield Gn BL3 ....40 F4
Holmfirth Rd OL3 ....70 A8
Holmfirth St M13 ....98 F4
Holmfoot Wlk 6 M9 ....157 D7
Holmlea Rd M43 ....83 E2
Holmleigh Ave M9 ....64 E1
Holmpark Rd M11 ....99 F7
Holmrook WA14 ....119 B5
Holmsfield Cl WN2 ....38 A2
Holmside Gdns M19 ....110 E4
Holmwood WA14 ....119 A3
Holmwood Cl WA14 ....73 A5
Holmwood Ct M20 ....110 B4
Holmwood Rd M20 ....110 B5
Holroyd St
Manchester M11 ....165 A8
Rochdale OL16 ....31 A7
Holset Dr WA14 ....119 B5

Holset Wlk SK7 ....124 A2
Holst Ave M8 ....156 A6
Holstein Ave OL12 ....14 D4
Holt Ave WN5 ....71 D4
Holt Cres WN5 ....71 C4
Holt Ho M20 ....110 B2
Holt La M35 ....84 B7
Holt Lane Mews M35 ....84 B7
Holt Mill Rd BB4 ....2 D8
Holt St Altrincham WA14 ...119 C8
Ashton-u-L M34 ....100 E8
Bolton BL5 ....64 D8
Eccles M30 ....95 C8
Hindley WN2 ....56 C5
Leigh WN7 ....75 E7
Littleborough OL15 ....6 D2
Manchester M40 ....157 F5
Milnrow OL16 ....32 A5
Oldham OL4 ....49 C1
Orrell WN5 ....53 D5
Ramsbottom BL0 ....11 D6
Rawtenstall BB4 ....2 E8
Stockport SK1 ....170 F8
Swinton M27 ....61 F2
Tyldesley M29 ....59 A1
Whitworth OL12 ....14 C1
Wigan,Scholes WN1 ....151 F8
Wigan,Springfield WN6 ......36 F2
Wigan,Worsley Mesnes
WN3 ....55 A4
Holt St W BL0 ....138 B5
Holt Town M4,M40 ....160 E2
Holt's La SK5 ....130 F3
Holt's Terr OL12 ....14 E2
Holtby St M9 ....64 E1
Holthouse Rd BL8 ....26 F5
Holton Way WN3 ....54 E1
Holts La OL4 ....49 D2
Holtswell Cl WA3 ....74 E1
Holtwood Wlk SK5 ....112 C7
Holway Wlk M9 ....156 C7
Holwick Rd M23 ....108 F2
Holwood Dr M16 ....109 E8
Holy Cross & All Saints RC
Sch M30 ....95 D8
Holy Cross Coll BL9 ....44 E8
Holy Family RC Inf Sch
WN2 ....38 A2
Holy Family RC Prim Sch
Boothstown M28 ....77 E7
Oldham OL8 ....84 D8
Platt Bridge WN2 ....56 A1
Rochdale OL11 ....31 A2
Sale M33 ....108 E4
Holy Harbour St BL1 ....142 C2
Holy Inf & St Anthony RC
Prim Sch BL1 ....143 E4
Holy Name RC Prim Sch
M15 ....163 A5
Holy Rosary RC Jun & Inf Sch
OL8 ....66 F2
Holy St OL16 ....31 B2
Holy Trinity CE Dobcross
Prim Sch OL3 ....50 F2
Holy Trinity CE Prim Sch
Ashton-u-L OL6 ....166 A3
Littleborough OL15 ....16 B5
Manchester M9 ....157 E8
Holy Trinity Prim Sch
BL9 ....140 F1
Holy Trinity Stacksteads CE
Prim Sch OL13 ....3 C8
Holybourne Wlk M23 ....120 D8
Holybrook Dene SK6 ....113 E2
Holyhurst Wlk 29 BL1 ......143 E2
Holyoak St M40 ....83 C6
Holyoake Rd M28 ....60 E2
Holyoake St M43 ....84 C2
Holyrood Cl Leigh WN7 ......76 E7
Prestwich M25 ....63 C6
Holyrood Ct M25 ....63 C6
Holyrood Dr
Prestwich M25 ....63 C6
Swinton M27 ....79 D7
Holyrood Gr M25 ....63 C6
Holyrood Rd M25 ....63 C5
Holyrood St
Failsworth M40 ....83 E4
Oldham OL1 ....49 A1
Holywood St **1** M14 ....98 B3
Home Dr M24 ....64 F7
Home Farm Ave SK14 ....102 F1
Homebeck Ho SK8 ....122 A5
Homebury Dr M11 ....83 B2
Homelands Cl M33 ....107 F2
Homelands Rd M33 ....107 E2
Homelands Wlk M9 ....157 D7
Homelaurel Ho M22 ....108 B2
Homer Dr SK6 ....126 B8
Homer St M26 ....43 E3
Homerton Rd M40 ....83 B4
Homestead Cl M31 ....106 A4
Homestead Cres M19 ....110 D3
Homestead Gdns OL12 ......15 D4
Homestead Rd SK12 ....135 C6
Homestead The **3** M40 ....107 F5
Homewood Ave M22 ....109 D1
Homewood Rd M22 ....109 C1
Honduras St **1** OL4 ....67 B7
Honeychurch Cl OL2 ....25 D5
Honey St M8 ....159 B4
Honeybourne Cl M29 ....59 C1
Honeysuckle Ave WN6 ....36 F3
Honeysuckle Cl
Romiley SK6 ....113 A5
Sale M23 ....108 D1
Honeysuckle Dr SK15 ....86 C2
Honeysuckle Way OL12 ......14 D3

Honeysuckle Wlk M33 ......107 D6
Honeywell La OL8 ....66 F3
Honeywood Cl BL0 ....11 A3
Honford Rd M22 ....121 C4
Hong Kong Ave M90 ....130 A8
Honister Dr M24 ....46 F2
Honister Rd
Manchester M9 ....157 F7
Wigan WN5 ....54 B6
Honister Way OL11 ....30 B4
Honiton Ave SK14 ....102 D2
Honiton Cl
Chadderton OL9 ....47 E1
Heywood OL10 ....46 C8
Hindley WN7 ....57 D2
Honiton Ct SK14 ....102 D2
Honiton Dr BL2 ....43 A6
Honiton Gr M26 ....43 D4
Honiton Way WA14 ....119 B6
Honiton Wlk **3** SK14 ....102 D2
Honor St M13 ....98 F3
Hood Cl M29 ....59 D1
Hood Gr WN7 ....76 B3
Hood Sq OL4 ....68 A5
Hood St M4 ....159 B2
Hook St WN2 ....151 F7
Hoole Cl SK8 ....123 A5
Hooley Bridge Ind Est
OL10 ....29 C4
Hooley Range SK4 ....168 B3
Hooper St
Manchester M12 ....164 D8
10 Oldham OL4 ....67 A6
Stockport SK1,SK4 ....169 E1
Hooten La WN7 ....76 C3
Hooton St Bolton BL3 ....146 C3
Manchester M40 ....160 F3
Hooton Way **14** SK9 ....131 D5
Hopcroft Cl M9 ....64 B6
Hope Ave
Bolton,Harwood Lee BL2 ...25 E5
Bolton,Springfield BL2 .....148 B6
Handforth SK9 ....131 C3
Stretford M32 ....96 B3
Walkden M38 ....60 C4
Hope Carr La WN7 ....76 B2
Hope Carr Rd Leigh WN7 ...76 A3
Leigh WN7 ....76 B3
Hope Carr Way WN7 ....76 A3
Hope Cres WN6 ....36 B6
Hope Ct **11** OL12 ....139 F8
Hope Fold Ave M46 ....58 B2
Hope Green Way SK10 ......133 D2
Hope Hey La M38 ....59 F5
Hope High Sch M6 ....80 C4
Hope Hospl M6 ....80 B3
Hope La Leigh WA3,WN7 ....76 C3
Midway SK10 ....133 D1
Wardsend SK10 ....133 E1
Hope Park Cl M25 ....63 B3
Hope Park Rd M25 ....63 B3
Hope Pl OL11 ....30 C1
Hope Rd Manchester M14 ...98 D4
Prestwich M25 ....63 A2
Sale M33 ....108 B4
Hope Sch WN3 ....54 F2
Hope St Adlington PR6 ......21 B8
Ashton-in-M WN4 ....73 D5
Ashton-u-L OL6 ....85 D4
Aspull WN2 ....38 F3
Denton M34 ....100 F5
Dukinfield SK16 ....101 B8
Eccles M30 ....79 F2
Glossop SK13 ....104 E2
Hazel Grove SK7 ....124 D3
Heywood OL10 ....46 F8
Hindley WN2 ....56 D6
Horwich BL6 ....22 B4
Ince-in-M WN3 ....55 E4
Leigh WN7 ....75 F6
Manchester M1 ....159 A1
Newton-le-W WA12 ....89 B3
Oldham OL1 ....67 B7
Prestwich M27 ....80 A8
Ramsbottom BL0 ....138 B5
Rochdale OL12 ....15 A1
Salford,Higher Broughton
M7 ....155 D7
Salford,New Windsor M5 ....81 C1
Scot Lane End BL6 ....38 E8
Shaw OL2 ....49 E4
Stockport SK4 ....169 D1
Swinton M27 ....79 D7
Tyldesley M29 ....77 B5
Walkden M38 ....60 A4
Wigan WN1 ....150 C8
Hope St **5** M14 ....98 B3
Hope Terr Stockport SK3 .170 E8
Dukinfield SK16 ....101 B8
Hopecourt Cl M6 ....80 B4
Hopedale Cl M11 ....160 F1
Hopedale Rd SK5 ....111 F6
Hopefield Rd WA13 ....117 B4
Hopefield St BL3 ....147 D4
Hopefold Dr M28 ....60 A3
Hopelea St M20 ....110 B7
Hopes Carr SK1 ....169 F1
Hopgarth Wlk M40 ....83 D5
Hopkin Ave OL1 ....67 B8
Hopkin Mill OL4 ....67 D4
Hopkin St OL1 ....153 F7
Hopkins Bldgs OL5 ....68 E3
Hopkins Field WN1 ....119 B1
Hopkins St Hyde SK14 ......167 E4
Manchester M12 ....99 A3
Hopkinson Ave M34 ....100 E5
Hopkinson Cl OL3 ....69 B8
Hopkinson Rd M9 ....64 D5

Hoppet La M43 ....84 C2
Hopton Ave M22 ....121 F3
Hopton Ct M15 ....163 A6
Hopwood Ave Eccles M30 ..79 D3
Heywood OL10 ....46 D8
Horwich BL6 ....22 C4
Hopwood Cl
5 Golborne WA3 ....90 F8
Whitefield BL9 ....44 F3
Hopwood Com Prim Sch
OL10 ....46 E8
Hopwood Ct
Heywood OL10 ....46 E8
Middleton M24 ....47 A4
Hopwood Hall Coll
Middleton M24 ....47 A5
Rochdale OL12 ....139 E7
Hopwood Rd M24 ....47 A4
Hopwood St
Failsworth M40 ....83 B6
Pendlebury M27 ....80 A8
Salford M3 ....158 E2
Horace Barnes Cl M14 ....98 A3
Horace Gr SK4 ....169 E4
Horace St BL1 ....143 D2
Horatio St **4** M18 ....99 F6
Horbury Ave M18 ....99 E5
Horbury Dr BL8 ....27 C2
Horden Wlk **9** OL2 ....48 E4
Hordern Cl SK13 ....104 A4
Horeb St BL3 ....145 D5
Horest La OL3 ....50 B7
Horley Cl BL8 ....27 C7
Hornbeam Cl
Altrincham WA15 ....120 E5
Sale M33 ....107 C5
Hornbeam Cres WN4 ....73 B3
Hornbeam Ct M6 ....81 A3
Hornbeam Rd M19 ....110 E8
Hornby Ave M9 ....64 E5
Hornby Dr BL3 ....40 D3
Hornby Rd M26 ....96 B4
Hornby Rd M16,M32 ....96 F4
Hornby St Bury BL9 ....140 F4
Heywood OL10 ....29 D2
Manchester M8 ....158 F4
Middleton M24 ....65 A8
Oldham OL8 ....153 D5
Wigan WN1 ....37 C2
Horncastle Cl Bury BL8 ......27 D5
4 Golborne WA3 ....90 F8
Horncastle Rd M40 ....65 B1
Hornchurch Ct
Heywood OL10 ....46 E7
2 Manchester M15 ....162 F6
Hornchurch St M15 ....162 E6
Horncliffe Cl BB4 ....1 B8
Horncliffe View BB4 ....1 B8
Horne Dr M4 ....159 C2
Horne Gr WN3 ....54 F5
Hornet St BL9 ....44 E8
Hornet Cl OL11 ....31 A3
Hornsea Cl Bury BL8 ....26 F2
Chadderton OL9 ....47 F1
Hornsea Rd SK2 ....125 B5
Hornsea Wlk M11 ....83 A1
Hornsey Gr WN3 ....54 D3
Horridge Ave M12 ....89 C5
Horridge Fold BL7 ....8 E3
Horridge Fold Ave BL5 ....40 F2
Horridge St BL8 ....27 B4
Horrobin Fold BL7 ....9 C2
Horrobin La Adlington PR6 ..21 C8
Chapeltown BL7 ....9 C2
Horrocks Fold BL1 ....24 C7
Horrocks Fold Ave BL1 ....24 D6
Horrocks Rd BL2 ....25 A6
Horrocks St Leigh WN7 ......75 A4
Radcliffe M26 ....44 C4
Tyldesley M46 ....58 E1
Horsa St **16** BL2 ....25 B1
Horsedge St OL1 ....153 F7
Horsefield Ave OL12 ....14 C6
Horsefield Cl M21 ....109 E7
Horseforth La OL3 ....69 A4
Horseshoe La
Alderley Edge SK9 ....137 A2
Bolton BL7 ....25 A8
Oldham OL8 ....65 F6
Horsfield St BL3 ....144 A5
Horsfield Way SK6 ....112 F6
Horsham Ave SK7 ....124 C1
Horsham Cl Bury BL8 ....27 C1
Westhoughton BL5 ....57 F6
Horsham Gr WN2 ....37 F2
Horsham St M6 ....54 E2
Horstead Wlk **8** M19 ....99 A2
Horton Ave BL1 ....24 E6
Horton Mill Prim Sch
OL4 ....67 B6
Horton Rd M14 ....98 A2
Horton Sq OL2 ....49 B6
Horton St Stockport SK1 ...124 A7
Wigan WN6 ....37 A3
Hortree Rd M32 ....96 E2
Hortus St **11** BL2 ....22 B2
Horton Mill Prim Sch
OL4 ....67 B6
Horwich Bsns Pk BL6 ....22 B2
Horwich Heritage Ctr*
BL6 ....22 C3
Horwich L Ctr* BL6 ....22 C3
Horwich Parish CE Prim Sch
BL6 ....22 C4
Horwich Parkway Sta
BL6 ....39 C2
Horwood Cres M20 ....110 D5
Hoscar Dr M19 ....110 F7
Hoskers Nook BL5 ....57 D7
Hoskers The BL5 ....57 D6
Hoskins Cl M12 ....165 A5

Hospital Ave M30 ....79 E2
Hospital Cotts M25 ....62 E5
Hospital Rd Bolton BL7 ....25 A8
Pendlebury M27 ....80 B7
Hotel Rd M90 ....130 C7
Hotel St Bolton BL1 ....145 F7
Horwich BL6 ....22 C4
Newton-le-W WA12 ....89 B3
Hothersall Rd **4** SK5 ....111 F8
Hothersall St M7 ....158 E3
Hotspur Cl M14 ....110 A8
Hough Cl Oldham OL8 ....66 F3
Oldham OL8 ....67 A2
Hough End Ave M21 ....109 C6
Hough Fold Way BL2 ....25 E6
Hough Gn WA15 ....128 E5
Hough Hall Rd M40 ....157 F8
Hough Hill Rd SK15 ....102 B8
Hough La
Alderley Edge SK9 ....137 D3
Bolton BL7 ....24 F7
Dukinfield SK14 ....101 F6
Stake Hill M24 ....47 F4
Tyldesley M29 ....77 C8
Hough Rd M20 ....110 A3
Hough St Bolton BL3 ....146 A4
Tyldesley M29 ....77 D8
Hough Wlk M7 ....158 D3
Houghend Cres M21 ....109 E8
Houghton Ave
Oldham OL8 ....66 D2
Wigan WN5 ....36 F2
Houghton Cl
Newton-le-W WA12 ....89 B3
Rochdale OL16 ....31 C6
Houghton La
Shevington WN6 ....35 F6
Swinton M27 ....79 D5
Houghton Rd M8 ....64 A1
Houghton St Bolton BL3 ...145 E5
Bury BL9 ....140 E1
Leigh WN7 ....75 F6
Newton-le-W WA12 ....89 B3
Pendlebury M27 ....80 D6
Royton OL2 ....48 E2
Houghwood Grange
WN4 ....72 F3
Houldsworth Ave WA14 ....119 E7
Houldsworth Mill Bsns & Art
Ctr SK4,SK5 ....111 E7
Houldsworth Sq 2 SK5 ...111 E7
Houldsworth St
Manchester M1 ....159 B2
2 Radcliffe M26 ....43 F5
Reddish SK5 ....111 E7
Houseley Ave OL9 ....66 F3
Houseman Gr WN6 ....37 A2
Housley Cl WN3 ....150 A5
Houson St OL8 ....153 F5
Houston Pk M50 ....154 F1
Hove Cl BL8 ....10 F1
Hove Dr M14 ....110 E7
Hove St BL3 ....144 C5
Hove St N **13** BL3 ....144 C5
Hoveden St M8 ....158 F4
Hovey Cl M8 ....155 F7
Hovingham St OL16 ....31 B8
Hovington Gdns M19 ....110 E6
Hovis St M11 ....165 C8
How Clough Cl M28 ....60 F2
How Clough Dr M28 ....60 F2
How Lea Dr BL9 ....27 F8
Howard Ave Bolton BL3 ....146 A4
Cheadle SK8 ....123 A1
Eccles M30 ....79 D3
Kearsley BL4 ....60 F7
Lymm WA13 ....117 B4
Reddish SK4 ....111 C6
Howard Cl Glossop SK13 ..104 A2
Romiley SK6 ....113 A2
Howard Ct OL6 ....166 C3
Howard Dr WA15 ....120 A1
Howard Hill BL9 ....45 A5
Howard La M34 ....100 F4
Howard Pl Hyde SK14 ....167 D2
Rochdale OL16 ....139 F8
Howard Rd Culcheth WA3 ...92 A2
Wythenshawe M22 ....109 D1
Howard Spring Wlk M8 ....155 F8
Howard St
Ashton-u-L OL7 ....166 A4
Bolton BL1 ....143 F1
Denton M34 ....100 E5
Glossop SK13 ....104 C1
Manchester M8 ....158 F4
Oldham OL4 ....49 E1
Radcliffe M26 ....44 B3
Rochdale OL12 ....139 F8
Salford M5 ....154 D2
Shaw OL2 ....49 A7
Stalybridge SK15 ....86 D4
Stockport SK1 ....169 F2
Stretford M32 ....96 D2
Wigan WN5 ....54 C5
Howards La OL5 ....6 C1
Howard's La OL5 ....68 E1
Howardian Cl OL8 ....66 E2
Howards La WN5 ....53 F7
Howarth Ave M46 ....79 C7
Howarth Cl M11 ....83 A1
Howarth Cross St OL16 ......31 C5
Howarth Ct SK2 ....124 B5
Howarth Dr M44 ....93 F1
Howarth Farm Way OL12 ...15 C3
Howarth Gn OL12 ....15 C3
Howarth Sq OL16 ....31 A8
Howarth St Farnworth BL4 ..60 D7
Leigh WN7 ....76 B4

Howarth St *continued*
Littleborough OL15 16 B6
Manchester M16 97 C4
Westhoughton BL5 57 F8
Howbridge Cl M28 78 C8
Howbro Dr OL7 84 E5
Howbrook Wlk 7 M15 162 F6
Howcroft Cl BL1 145 E8
Howcroft St BL3 145 D5
Howden Cl SK5 99 E2
Howden Dr WN3 55 B4
Howden Rd
Manchester M9 64 C5
New Mills SK22 127 C1
Howe Bridge Cl M46 58 A1
Howe Dr BL0 11 B2
Howe St Ashton-u-L OL7 100 F8
Salford M7 155 D7
Howell Croft N 7 BL1 145 F7
Howell Croft S BL1 145 F7
Howell's Yd 6 BL1 145 F7
Howells Ave M33 108 B5
Howgill Cres OL8 66 E3
Howgill St M11 83 D1
Howsin Ave BL2 25 B4
Howton Cl M12 99 A4
Howty Cl SK9 131 D1
Hoxton Cl SK6 113 A4
Hoy Dr M41 95 D5
Hoylake Cl Failsworth M40 83 D8
Leigh WN7 75 D2
Hoylake Rd
Stockport SK3 123 B8
Wythenshawe M33 108 F2
Hoyland Cl M12 164 F6
Hoyle Ave OL8 153 E5
Hoyle St Bacup OL13 3 E8
3 Bolton BL1 143 E4
Manchester M12 163 C8
Radcliffe M26 44 C1
Whitworth OL12 4 D3
Hoyle Street Ind Est
M12 163 C7
Hoyle Wlk M13 163 C6
Hoyle's Terr OL16 31 E6
Hoyles Ct 9 M26 44 C4
Hubert Worthington Ho 8
SK9 137 A1
Hucclecote Ave M22 121 C2
Hucklow Ave M23 121 A2
Hucklow Bank 27 SK13 171 D2
Hucklow Cl 26 SK13 171 D2
Hucklow Fold 28 SK13 171 D2
Hucklow Lanes 29 SK13 171 D2
Hudcar La BL9 141 A4
Huddart Cl M5 161 B8
Huddersfield Rd
Denshaw OL3 33 E2
Diggle OL3 51 C7
Diggle OL3 51 D5
Newhey OL16,OL3 32 D5
Oldham OL1,OL4 67 D8
Stalybridge OL5,SK15 86 E4
Hudson Gr 9 WA3 90 E8
Hudson Rd Bolton BL3 146 B3
Hyde SK14 113 E7
Hudson Sq OL1 48 D1
Hudson St OL9 66 A2
Hudsons Pas OL15 16 C7
Hudsons Wlk OL11 30 C7
Hudswell Cl M45 62 E8
Hugh Lupus St BL1 25 A5
Hugh Oldham Dr M7 81 C6
Hugh St Glossop SK13 104 B1
Rochdale OL16 31 A8
Hughendon Ct BL8 26 F7
Hughes Ave BL6 22 A4
Hughes Cl Bury BL9 141 A3
Failsworth M35 83 E8
Hughes St Bolton BL1 142 C2
Bolton BL1 143 D2
Manchester M11 164 E8
Hughes Way M30 79 A1
Hughley Cl OL2 49 A4
Hughtrede St OL16 31 B3
Hugo St Farnworth BL4 42 B2
Manchester M40 83 A7
Rochdale OL11 30 D2
Hulbert St Bury BL8 27 C1
Middleton M24 47 B1
Hull Mill La OL3 50 F5
Hull Sq M3 158 D2
Hullet Cl WN6 35 E8
Hully St 8 SK15 85 F2
Hulme Court Prep Sch
OL8 66 D4
Hulme Ct M15 162 E7
Hulme Dr WA15 120 C7
Hulme Gr WN7 75 C6
Hulme Gram Sch for Boys
OL8 66 D4
Hulme Gram Sch for Girls
OL8 66 D4
Hulme Hall Ave SK8 132 B8
Hulme Hall Cl SK8 123 A1
Hulme Hall Cres SK8 132 A8
Hulme Hall La M40 160 E4
Hulme Hall Rd
Cheadle SK8 123 A1
Manchester M15 162 D7
Hulme Hall Schs SK8 123 A1
Hulme Pl M5 81 C2
Hulme Rd Bolton BL2 25 E5
Kearsley M26 61 C7
Leigh WN7 75 C6
Reddish,Dane Bank M34 100 B3
Reddish,Heaton Chapel
SK4 111 D6
Hulme Rd *continued*
Sale M33 108 D3
Hulme St Ashton-u-L OL6 85 D4
Bolton BL1 145 F8
Bury BL8 140 D3
Manchester M1,M15 162 F7
Oldham OL8 66 E4
Salford M5 81 C1
Stockport SK1 124 B7
Hulme Wlk M15 163 A6
Hulme's Terr BL2 43 C8
Hulmes Rd M35,M40 83 E5
Hulton Ave M28 60 B3
Hulton Cl BL3 146 A3
Hulton District Ctr M28 60 A4
Hulton Dr BL3 146 A3
Hulton Hospl BL3 146 A3
Hulton La BL3 146 A3
Hulton St Denton M34 100 E4
Failsworth M35 83 E7
Manchester M16 97 E4
Salford M5 161 A7
Humber Dr BL9 27 F7
Humber Pl WN5 54 C7
Humber Rd Milnrow OL16 32 A6
Tyldesley M29 77 C7
Humber St
Manchester M8 156 B7
Salford M50 154 D1
Humberstone Ave M15 162 F6
Hume St Manchester M19 111 B8
Rochdale OL16 31 A5
Humphrey Booth Gdns
M6 154 E3
Humphrey Cres M41 96 A2
Humphrey La M41 96 A2
Humphrey Park Sta M32 96 A3
Humphrey Pk M41 96 A2
Humphrey Rd M16 161 B5
Humphrey St
Ince-in-M WN2 56 A7
Manchester M8 155 F8
Humphries Ct M40 159 C4
Huncoat Ave SK4 111 D5
Huncote Dr M9 64 E1
Hunger Hill Ave BL3 40 E2
Hunger Hill La OL12 13 F3
Hungerford Wlk 5
M23 120 D7
Hunmanby Ave M15 162 F7
Hunstanton Dr BL8 27 D5
Hunston Rd M33 107 F2
Hunt Ave OL7 85 B5
Hunt Fold Dr BL8 10 F1
Hunt La OL9 152 A7
Hunt Rd SK14 102 A5
Hunt St Atherton M46 58 D3
Manchester M9 64 D1
Wigan WN1 151 E7
Hunt's Bank
Manchester M3 158 F2
Westhoughton BL5 57 F6
Hunter Dr M26 44 A5
Hunter Rd WN5 36 E1
Hunter's La Oldham OL1 153 F7
Rochdale OL12,OL16 139 F8
Hunter's View SK9 131 C3
Hunters Chase WN5 53 E1
Hunters Cl Handforth SK9 131 F1
6 Romiley SK6 112 F3
Hunters Ct SK15 102 D8
Hunters Gn BL0 10 F3
Hunters Hill BL9 45 B4
Hunters Hill La OL3 51 C6
Hunters La Glossop SK13 115 F8
Rochdale OL16 139 F8
Hunters Lodge SK9 131 F1
Hunters Mews Sale M33 108 A5
Wilmslow SK9 137 C7
Hunterston Ave M30 80 A2
Huntingdon Ave OL9 152 B5
Huntingdon Cres SK5 112 C5
Huntingdon Way 7
M34 100 F1
Huntingdon Wlk 21 BL1 143 E2
Huntington Ave M20 110 A7
Huntley Mount Rd BL9 141 B3
Huntley Rd Manchester M8 63 E2
Stockport SK3 123 B7
Huntley St BL9 141 B3
Huntly Chase SK9 137 C7
Huntly Way OL10 28 E1
Huntroyde Ave 25 BL2 25 B1
Hunts Rd 2 M6 80 D5
Huntsham Cl WA14 119 B6
Huntsman Dr M44 105 F7
Huntsman Rd M9 157 F8
Huntsworth Wlk M13 164 D5
Hurdlow Ave M7 81 A7
Hurdlow Gn 14 SK13 171 D1
Hurdlow Lea 13 SK13 171 D1
Hurdlow Mews SK13 171 D1
Hurdlow Way 12 SK13 171 D1
Hurdlow Wlk M9 157 D7
Hurdsfield Rd SK2 124 D4
Hurford Ave M18 99 D6
Hurlbote Cl SK9 131 D5
Hurley Dr SK8 122 E2
Hurlston Rd BL3 147 D2
Hurst Ave Cheadle SK8 132 C6
Sale M33 107 C3
Hurst Bank Rd OL6 85 E4
Hurst Brook Cl OL6 166 C4
Hurst Cl BL5 58 F7
Hurst Cross OL6 85 D5
Hurst Ct Ashton-u-L OL6 85 E5
Wythenshawe M23 120 F4
Hurst Gr OL6 85 E5
Hurst Green Cl BL8 43 F8
Hurst Hall Dr OL6 85 E5
Hurst Hill Cres OL6 85 D4
Hurst Knoll St James' CE
Prim Sch OL6 166 C4
Hurst La WA3 92 C7
Hurst Lea Ct SK9 137 A2
Hurst Mdw Ashton-u-L OL6 85 D5
Rochdale OL16 31 C3
Hurst Mill La WA3 92 C8
Hurst Rd SK13 104 F1
Hurst St Bolton BL3 146 C3
Bury BL9 141 A2
Hindley WN2 56 C6
Leigh WN7 76 B3
Oldham OL9 153 D7
Reddish SK5 111 E7
Rochdale OL11 31 A5
Walkden M28 60 D6
Hurst Wlk 4 M22 121 A2
Hurstbank Ave M19 110 D4
Hurstbourne Ave M11 83 B2
Hurstbrook Cl SK13 104 F1
Hurstbrook Dr M32 95 F2
Hurstead 2 OL12 15 D4
Hurstead Gn 8 OL12 15 D4
Hurstead Rd OL16 31 F6
Hursted Rd OL16 31 F6
Hurstfield Ind Est SK4,
SK5 111 E6
Hurstfield Rd M28 78 B8
Hurstfold Ave M19 110 D3
Hursthead Inf Sch SK8 132 C6
Hursthead Jun Sch SK8 132 C7
Hursthead Rd SK8 132 B7
Hursthead Wlk M13 163 B7
Hurstmead Terr M20 110 B2
Hurstvale Ave SK8 122 B1
Hurstville Rd M21 109 B6
Hurstway Dr 33 M9 64 E3
Hurstwood BL1 24 E5
Hurstwood Cl OL8 67 C4
Hurstwood Rd SK2 124 F6
Hus St 1 M43 100 A8
Huskisson Way WA12 89 B4
Husteads OL3 50 E1
Husteads La OL3 50 F1
Hutchins La OL4 49 D1
Hutchinson Rd OL11 13 D2
Hutchinson St
4 Radcliffe M26 44 C4
Rochdale OL11 30 C6
Hutchinson Way M26 44 A3
Huttock End La OL13 3 D8
Hutton Ave Ashton-u-L OL6 85 E3
Boothstown M28 77 F6
Hutton Cl WA3 91 E5
Hutton Lo M14 110 C7
Hutton St WN1 20 A3
Hutton Wlk 7 M13 163 C6
Huxley Ave M8 156 A6
Huxley Cl SK7 132 E7
Huxley Dr SK7 132 E7
Huxley Pl WN3 150 A5
Huxley St
Altrincham WA14 119 D7
Bolton BL1 142 C2
6 Oldham OL4 67 C6
Huxley Terr 4 WA14 119 C1
Huxton Gn SK7 124 A2
Huyton Rd BL6,PR7 21 A6
Huyton Terr PR6 21 B6
Hyacinth Cl SK3 170 D5
Hyatt Cres WN6 19 C3
Hyde Central Sta SK14 101 C2
Hyde Cl WN3 150 A5
Hyde Dr M28 60 C2
Hyde Fold Cl M19 110 F6
Hyde Gr Manchester M13 163 C5
Sale M33 108 B4
Walkden M28 60 C2
Hyde Ho SK4 111 C5
Hyde Hospl SK14 167 F1
Hyde North Sta SK14 101 C5
Hyde Pl M13 163 C5
Hyde Rd Denton M34 101 A3
Manchester,Gorton M12,
M18 99 D4
Manchester,West Gorton
M12 164 E6
Oldham M24 65 E6
Romiley SK14,SK6 113 B5
Walkden M28 60 C2
Hyde Sq M24 46 E1
Hyde St Bolton BL3 146 C3
Droylsden M43 84 C4
Dukinfield SK16 101 D8
Manchester M16 162 D5
Hyde Tech Sch SK14 167 D4
Hyde's Cross M4 159 A2
Hyde-Clarendon Sixth Form
Ctr SK14 167 E4
Hydes Terr SK15 86 B2
Hydon Brook Wlk OL11 30 C4
Hydra Cl M7 81 C3
Hydrangea Cl 8 M33 107 C6
Hyldavale Ave SK8 122 B6
Hylton Dr Ashton-u-L OL7 84 F5
Cheadle SK8 132 C8
Hyman Goldstone Wlk 4
M8 155 F7
Hyndman Ct M5 154 D2
Hypatia St BL2 148 B7
Hythe Cl M14 98 C3
Hythe Rd SK3 123 B8
Hythe St BL3 146 A4
Hythe Wlk OL9 152 B6

I

Ibberton Wlk 8 M9 64 F1
Ibsley 20 OL12 139 E8
Ice House Cl 5 M28 59 F3
Iceland St M6 154 F2
Idonia St BL1 143 D3
Ifco Ctr M14 98 C3
Ilex Gr M7 155 D6
Ilford St M11 83 B2
Ilfracombe Rd SK2 124 D8
Ilfracombe St M40 83 D6
Ilk St M11 83 B2
Ilkeston Dr WN2 38 F3
Ilkeston Wlk
5 Denton M34 113 A8
4 Manchester M40 83 A6
Ilkley Cl Bolton BL2 148 C7
Chadderton OL9 152 B6
Ilkley Cres SK5 111 E8
Ilkley Dr M41 95 A4
Ilkley St M40 83 A8
Illingworth Ave SK15 86 C2
Illona Dr M7 81 A8
Ilminster OL11 139 E6
Ilminster Wlk 2 M9 64 E5
Ilthorpe Wlk 7 M40 83 A6
Imex Bsns Pk M13 98 F3
Imex Bus Ctr M34 100 D3
Imogen Ct M5 161 C8
Imperial Dr WN7 76 D6
Imperial Point M50 96 F7
Imperial Terr M33 108 A4
Imperial War Mus* M17 96 E7
Ina Ave BL1 23 F1
Ince CE Prim Sch WN2 56 A7
Ince Cl Manchester M20 110 B7
Stockport SK4 169 E3
Ince Green La WN2,WN3 151 F6
Ince Hall Ave WN2 151 F8
Ince St SK4 169 E3
Ince St Mary's CE Prim Sch
WN3 55 F4
Ince Sta WN3 151 F6
Ince Wlk WN1 150 C8
Inchcape Dr M9 64 B4
Inchfield Cl OL11 29 E8
Inchfield Rd
Manchester M40 65 B1
Walsden OL14 6 A8
Inchley Rd M13 163 B7
Inchwood Mews OL4 49 E4
Incline Rd OL8 66 C2
Independent St BL3 43 A3
India St BL9 11 C3
Indigo St M6 80 F5
Indigo Wlk M6 80 F5
Industrial Cotts 10 BB4 2 F8
Industrial St
Ramsbottom BL0 1 C1
Westhoughton BL5 57 F7
Industry Rd 8 OL12 14 F1
Industry St
Chadderton OL9 66 A4
14 Littleborough OL15 16 B5
Rochdale OL11 13 E1
Whitworth OL12 4 D2
Infant St M25 63 C4
Infirmary St 11 BL1 145 F7
Ingersol Rd BL6 22 E1
Ingham Ave WA12 89 C1
Ingham Brow BL6 22 F4
Ingham Rd WA14 107 D1
Ingham St Bury BL9 141 A1
Failsworth M40 83 E4
Leigh WN7 75 E8
5 Oldham OL1 67 A7
Inghams La OL15 16 B5
Inghamwood Cl M7 155 F7
Ingle Dr SK2 124 C7
Ingle Nook Cl M31 106 F6
Ingle Rd SK8 123 A6
Ingleby Ave M9 64 F4
Ingleby Cl Shaw OL2 149 A8
Standish WN6 19 D2
Westhoughton BL5 40 A3
Ingleby Ct M32 96 E1
Ingleby Way OL2 149 A8
Ingledene Ave M7 63 E1
Ingledene Ct 8 M7 63 E1
Ingledene Gr BL1 142 A2
Inglefield OL11 13 F1
Inglehead Cl M34 101 A2
Inglenook Ct M46 76 A8
Ingles Fold M28 78 B7
Inglesham Cl Leigh WN7 75 E1
Wythenshawe M23 121 B6
Ingleton Ave M8 64 B2
Ingleton Cl Bolton BL2 25 D4
Cheadle SK8 122 C6
Newton-le-W WA12 89 B4
Royton OL2 48 D5
Ingleton Dr WA11 71 B1
Ingleton Mews BL8 27 B4
Ingleton Rd SK3 123 C7
Inglewhite Ave WN1 37 C2
Inglewhite Cl BL9 44 D7
Inglewhite Cres 1 WN1 37 C2
Inglewhite Pl 2 WN1 37 C2
Inglewood WA14 119 B3
Inglewood Ave WN1 151 E7
Inglewood Cl
Ashton-u-L OL7 84 F5
Bury BL9 141 C4
Partington M31 105 F4
Inglewood Cvn Pk M31 105 F4
Inglewood Hollow SK15 102 C8
Inglewood Rd M24 47 E1
Inglewood Wlk M13 163 C6
Inglis St OL15 16 B6
Ingoe Cl OL10 29 F3
Ingoldsby Ave M13 98 D4
Ingram Dr SK4 110 E3
Ingram St
Platt Bridge WN2 56 A3
Wigan WN6 36 F2
Ings Ave OL12 14 B2
Ings La OL12 14 C2
Ink St OL16 139 F7
Inkerman St Hyde SK14 167 D4
Manchester M40 157 D6
12 Rochdale OL12 14 F1
Inman St Bury BL9 44 E8
Denton M34 100 F3
Innes Sch OL12 14 C1
Innes St M12 99 B3
Innis Ave M40 83 C5
Inscape House Salford
M28 60 E1
Institute St BL1 148 A7
Instow Cl Chadderton OL9 47 F1
Manchester M13 164 D6
Intake La OL3 69 B3
International App M90 130 C7
Invar Rd M27 61 D1
Inver Wlk 10 M40 65 D2
Inverbeg Dr BL2 43 A7
Invergarry Wlk 19 M11 83 C1
Inverlael Ave BL1 144 B8
Inverness Ave M9 65 A4
Inverness Cl WN2 38 D5
Inverness Rd SK16 101 C7
Inward Dr WN6 36 A5
Inwood Wlk M8 156 C6
Inworth Cl BL5 57 F6
Inworth Wlk 10 M8 155 F7
Iona Pl BL2 25 C2
Iona Way M41 95 E5
Ionian Gdns 2 M7 81 C5
Ipswich St OL11 139 F5
Ipswich Wlk
10 Denton M34 101 A1
Manchester M12 164 E5
Iqbal Cl M12 165 A5
Irby Wlk SK8 123 A4
Ireby Cl M24 46 C2
Iredale Cres WN6 36 F7
Iredine St 6 M11 83 C1
Irene Ave SK14 101 E5
Iris Ave Farnworth BL4 42 A1
Kearsley BL4 60 F5
Manchester M11 99 D8
Iris St Oldham OL8 66 F3
Ramsbottom BL0 138 B6
Iris Wlk 7 M31 105 E2
Irk St M4 159 A3
Irk Vale Dr OL1,OL9 47 E1
Irk Wlk M45 45 B2
Irkdale St M8 156 C6
Irlam & Cadishead Com High
Sch M44 105 E7
Irlam Ave M30 79 D1
Irlam Endowed Prim Sch
M44 94 A2
Irlam Ind Est M44 105 E7
Irlam Prim Sch M44 94 A1
Irlam Rd Sale M33 108 C4
Urmston M41 94 D2
Irlam Sq M6 80 D5
Irlam St Bolton BL1 143 E3
Manchester M40 157 E5
Irlam Sta M44 105 E7
Irlam Wharf Rd M44 106 A6
Irma St BL1 143 F3
Irmass Ind Est M17 96 D6
Iron St Denton M34 100 F3
Horwich BL6 22 C2
Manchester M40 160 E3
Iron Works The OL2 48 D3
Irvin Dr M22,SK8 131 A8
Irvin St M40 83 C6
Irvine Ave 6 M28 78 A6
Irvine St WN7 75 F6
Irving Cl SK2 124 A3
Irving Ho 1 BL1 143 E2
Irving St Bolton BL1 143 E2
Oldham OL8 66 B2
Irwell Ave Eccles M30 79 F1
Walkden M38 60 B4
Irwell Cl 4 M26 44 B2
Irwell Gr M30 79 F1
Irwell Ho 2 M15 162 D7
Irwell Park High Sch M6 81 A5
Irwell Pl Eccles M30 79 F1
Salford M5 81 C2
Wigan WN5 54 C6
Irwell Rd WN5 53 F7
Irwell St Bury BL9 140 E2
Kearsley M26 61 A8
Manchester M7,M8 158 E4
Radcliffe M26 44 B2
Ramsbottom BL0 138 C6
Salford M3 158 E1
Irwell Vale Rd BB4,BL0 1 C6
Irwell Vale Sta BL0 1 C5
Irwell Wlk OL8 66 C3
Irwin Ct SK8 122 F3
Irwin Dr SK9 131 C5
Irwin Rd WA14 119 D8
Irwin St M34 100 E3
Isa St BL0 11 A4
Isaac Cl M5 161 A8

Isaac St BL1 ....144 C8
Isabella Cl M16 ....97 C4
Isabella Sq WN1 ....151 E8
Isabella St OL12 ....15 A2
Isaiah St OL8 ....66 F4
Isca St M11 ....160 F1
Isel Wlk M24 ....46 D2
Isherwood Dr SK6 ....125 D6
Isherwood Fold BL7 ....9 D7
Isherwood Rd M31 ....106 F6
Isherwood St
 Heywood OL10 ....29 E1
 Leigh WN7 ....75 E8
 Rochdale OL11 ....31 A6
Isis Cl M7 ....81 A8
Island Cotts BL9 ....11 C2
Island Row WN2 ....56 B7
Islington Rd SK2 ....124 C4
Islington St M3 ....158 D1
Islington Way M3 ....158 D1
Isobel Cl Eccles M30 ....79 B1
 Manchester M16 ....97 F4
Isobel Wlk BL4 ....145 D5
Ivanhoe Ave WA3 ....74 D1
Ivanhoe Ct BL3,BL4 ....42 C2
Ivanhoe St
 Farnworth BL3,BL4 ....42 C2
 Oldham OL1 ....49 C1
Iveagh Ct 16 OL16 ....31 B6
Ivor St OL11 ....30 B3
Ivy Ave WA12 ....89 C2
Ivy Bank Cl BL1 ....24 E5
Ivy Bank Rd BL1 ....24 E5
Ivy Cl Droylsden M43 ....83 F3
 Shaw OL2 ....149 B7
Ivy Cotts Denton M34 ....113 A7
 Rawtenstall BB4 ....2 F8
Ivy Dr M24 ....64 F6
Ivy Farm Gdns WA3 ....91 D4
Ivy Gr Farnworth BL4 ....60 B8
 Kearsley BL4 ....60 F7
 Walkden M28 ....59 F4
Ivy House Rd WA3 ....74 D1
Ivy Rd Bolton BL1 ....142 B1
 Bury BL9 ....27 B2
 Golborne WA3 ....90 B8
 Poynton SK12 ....133 E3
 Westhoughton BL5 ....57 F7
Ivy St Ashton-in-M WN4 ....73 B3
 Bolton BL3 ....146 C4
 Eccles M30 ....79 D1
 Manchester M40 ....83 A8
 Ramsbottom BL0 ....10 F3
 Rawtenstall BB4 ....2 F8
 Wigan WN1 ....150 B8
Ivy Wlk M31 ....105 D3
Ivybridge Cl M13 ....164 D5
Ivycroft SK13 ....171 E4
Ivydale Dr WN7 ....76 C5
Ivygreen Dr OL4 ....67 F6
Ivygreen Rd M21 ....109 A8
Ivylea Rd M19 ....110 E4
Ivylodge Cl SK15 ....86 E4

J

Jack Brady Cl M23 ....120 E4
Jack La Droylsden M43 ....84 B2
 Droylsden M43 ....84 C2
 Urmston M41 ....95 E2
Jack McCann Ct 10 OL16 ....31 A4
Jack St BL2 ....25 C1
Jack Taylor Ct OL12 ....15 B1
Jack's La BL5 ....57 A8
Jackdaw Rd BL8 ....10 F2
Jackie Brown Wlk M40 ....157 D5
Jackman Ave OL10 ....46 D5
Jackson Ave
 Culcheth WA3 ....91 E3
 3 Dukinfield SK16 ....101 D8
Jackson Cl
 Altrincham WA15 ....120 C7
 Bury BL8 ....27 B3
 Oldham OL8 ....153 E5
Jackson Cres WN5 ....162 E7
Jackson Ct
 Manchester M21 ....96 F1
 Urmston M41 ....95 A3
Jackson Gdns M34 ....100 D2
Jackson Pit 1 OL1 ....153 E6
Jackson Pl OL16 ....31 B8
Jackson St
 Ashton-u-l OL6 ....166 B4
 Cheadle SK8 ....122 E6
 Failsworth M35 ....83 D6
 Farnworth BL4 ....60 D8
 Glossop SK13 ....116 C7
 Hadfield SK13 ....104 C5
 Hyde SK14 ....167 D2
 Ince-in-M WN2 ....56 A7
 Kearsley BL4 ....60 F7
 Middleton M24 ....65 A8
 Mottram-in-L SK14 ....103 A3
 Oldham,County End OL4 ......67 F6
 Oldham,Greenacres Moor
 OL4 ....67 B7
 Radcliffe M26 ....44 B1
 Rochdale OL16 ....31 B6
 Sale M33 ....108 D5
 Stretford M32 ....96 C1
 Walkden M28 ....60 C4
 Wardle OL12 ....15 C6

 Whitefield M45 ....62 F7
Jackson's La SK7 ....133 C8
Jackson's Row M2 ....158 F1
Jacksons Edge Rd SK12 ....135 B6
Jacob St WN2 ....53 D6
Jacobite Cl M7 ....63 C1
Jacobsen Ave SK14 ....167 F4
Jaffrey St 2 WN7 ....75 E5
James Andrew St M24 ....47 B1
James Bentley Wlk 4
 M40 ....83 C5
James Brindley Basin 9
 M1 ....159 C1
James Brindley Com Prim
 Sch M28 ....60 C1
James Butterworth Ct 6
 OL16 ....31 B6
James Butterworth St 9
 OL16 ....31 B6
James Cl SK16 ....101 E8
James Cnr M34 ....167 E2
James Dr SK14 ....167 E2
James Henry Ave M5 ....161 B8
James Hill St 18 OL15 ....16 B5
James Leech St SK1,SK3 .....170 E8
James Leigh St M1 ....163 A8
James Pl Coppull PR7 ....19 E8
 Standish M6 ....19 D2
James Rd OL2 ....149 B7
James Sq WN6 ....19 D2
James St Ashton-in-M WN2 ...73 E7
 8 Ashton-u-l M34 ....100 E8
 Bacup OL13 ....3 B7
 Bolton BL7 ....9 D2
 Bury BL9 ....141 A1
 Denton M34 ....101 A4
 Droylsden M43 ....83 F3
 Dukinfield SK15,SK16 ....101 E8
 Failsworth M40 ....84 A7
 4 Glossop SK13 ....116 C8
 Heywood OL10 ....29 D3
 Horwich BL6 ....21 F3
 Ince-in-M WN3 ....151 D6
 Kearsley BL4 ....60 F8
 Little Lever BL3 ....43 B3
 Manchester M40 ....160 D3
 Prestwich M25 ....63 A5
 Radcliffe M26 ....44 B2
 4 Rochdale,Dearnley OL15 ...15 E4
 Rochdale,Hurstead OL12 .....15 C4
 8 Rochdale,Newbold Brow
 OL12 ....31 A8
 Romiley SK6 ....113 A5
 Royton OL2 ....149 A5
 Sale M33 ....108 D4
 Salford M3 ....158 D1
 Stockport SK3 ....170 E7
 Tyldesley M29 ....76 F8
 Westhoughton BL5 ....39 E2
 Whitworth OL12 ....14 A2
James St N M26 ....44 B2
James St S M26 ....44 B2
James's St OL1 ....49 D1
Jameson St OL11 ....30 B2
Jamieson Cl M8 ....155 E5
Jammy La OL9 ....152 C6
Jane Barter Ho 1 BL4 ....60 E7
Jane St Chadderton OL9 ......152 B6
 Rochdale OL12 ....139 E8
 Whitworth OL12 ....14 A1
Janus Dr OL1 ....48 D1
Japan St M7 ....155 F7
Jardine Way OL9 ....65 F4
Jarvis St 11 Oldham OL4 ....67 A6
 Rochdale OL12 ....14 F1
Jasmine Ave M43 ....84 C2
Jasmine Cl M23 ....108 E1
Jasmine Rd WN5 ....54 D7
Jasmine Wlk M31 ....105 F2
Jason St M4 ....159 B3
Jauncey St WN1 ....144 C5
Jaxons Ct WN1 ....150 C8
Jayton Ave M20 ....122 B8
Jean Ave WN7 ....75 E2
Jean Cl M19 ....99 A2
Jedburgh Ave BL1 ....144 B8
Jeff Joseph Sale Moor Tech
 Coll M33 ....108 D2
Jefferson Way OL12 ....14 F3
Jeffrey St WN2 ....56 A8
Jeffrey Wlk OL10 ....29 A2
Jeffreys Dr SK16 ....101 D8
Jehlum Cl M8 ....156 B7
Jellicoe Ave M44 ....105 E6
Jenkinson St
 Hindley WN2 ....56 D6
 Manchester M13,M15 ....163 A6
Jenkyn Wlk 6 M11 ....160 F1
Jennet Hey WA3 ....72 F6
Jennet's La WA3 ....73 C1
Jennings Ave M5 ....161 A8
Jennings Ct
 Dukinfield SK14 ....102 B5
 Salford M6 ....161 A8
Jennings St SK3 ....170 D7
Jennison Cl M18 ....165 B6
Jenny Beck Gr BL3 ....147 E4
Jenny La SK7 ....132 E4
Jenny Lind Cl BL4 ....60 D8
Jenny St OL8 ....66 C2
Jepheys Pl 17 OL12 ....14 F1
Jepheys St OL12 ....14 F1
Jepson St SK2 ....124 A6
Jericho Rd BL9 ....28 E4
Jermyn St OL12 ....31 A8
Jerrold St 8 OL15 ....16 B5
Jersey Cl M19 ....110 F7

Jersey Rd SK5 ....169 F4
Jersey St Ashton-u-l OL6 .....166 B4
 Manchester M4 ....159 C2
Jerusalem Pl M2 ....162 F8
Jesmond Ave M25 ....63 B2
Jesmond Dr BL8 ....27 D5
Jesmond Gr SK8 ....132 B8
Jesmond Rd BL1 ....142 B4
Jesmond Wlk M9 ....64 D5
Jespersen St OL1 ....153 F7
Jessamine Ave M7 ....158 D4
Jessel Cl M13 ....163 C6
Jessica Way WN7 ....75 B4
Jessie St Bolton BL3 ....144 C5
 Failsworth M40 ....83 A6
Jessop Dr SK6 ....125 F8
Jessop Forge BL3 ....43 A3
Jessop St M18 ....99 D5
Jethro St
 Bolton,Bradshaw BL2 ....25 C4
 Bolton,Tonge Fold BL2 ......148 C8
Jetson St M18 ....99 F6
Jevington Wlk 10 M13 ....163 C6
Jimmy McMullen Wlk 6
 M14 ....98 A3
Jinnah Cl
 Manchester M11 ....165 C8
 Oldham OL4 ....67 C5
Jo St M5 ....81 A1
Joan St M40 ....83 A7
Jobling St M11 ....164 F8
Jocelyn St M40 ....157 E1
Joddrell St M3 ....158 E1
Joe Connolly Way BB4 ....2 E8
Joel La SK14 ....113 F7
Johannesburg Gdns
 M23 ....120 F4
John Ashworth St OL12 ....15 B1
John Atkinson Ct M5 ....154 D2
John Ave SK8 ....122 E5
John Beeley Ave M11 ....99 D8
John Booth St OL4 ....67 F5
John Boste Ct BL3 ....42 C3
John Clynes Ave M40 ....145 E8
John Clynes Ave M40 ....159 C3
John Cross St BL3 ....147 E4
John Dalton St
 Hadfield SK13 ....103 E5
 Manchester M2 ....158 F1
John Foran Cl M40 ....83 B6
John Gilbert Way OL12 ....15 C4
John Henry St OL12 ....4 D4
John Heywood St M11 ....83 B2
John Howarth Countryside
 Visitor Ctr* M35 ....84 E6
John Kemble Ct OL11 ....30 C4
John Kennedy Gdn
 SK14 ....103 A3
John Kennedy Rd SK14 ....102 F3
John Knott St OL4 ....67 F6
John Lee Fold M24 ....47 A1
John Lloyd Ct M44 ....105 F8
John Roberts Cl OL11 ....139 E5
John Robinson Wlk 8
 M40 ....83 A7
John Shepley St SK14 ....167 E2
John Smeaton Ct 12
 M1 ....159 C1
John St Altrincham WA14 ....119 D4
 Ashton-in-M WN4 ....73 D5
 Ashton-u-l OL7 ....166 A1
 Bolton BL7 ....25 A7
 Bury BL9 ....140 F3
 Denton M34 ....100 F4
 Droylsden M43 ....83 F3
 Eccles M30 ....79 B1
 Failsworth M35 ....65 F1
 Farnworth BL4 ....60 E8
 Glossop SK13 ....116 C8
 Golborne WA3 ....90 A8
 Hazel Grove SK7 ....124 D3
 Heywood OL10 ....29 D3
 Heywood OL10 ....29 D3
 Hindley WN2 ....56 D6
 Hyde SK14 ....167 D3
 Irlam M44 ....105 E5
 Leigh WN7 ....75 F5
 Little Lever BL3 ....43 B3
 Marple SK6 ....126 A5
 Middleton M25 ....63 E8
 Oldham,Bank Top OL8 ....153 E6
 Oldham,County End OL4 ......68 A6
 Pendlebury M27 ....80 A8
 Rochdale OL16 ....15 C3
 Romiley SK6 ....113 C2
 Romiley,Bredbury SK6 ....113 A4
 Romiley,Compstall SK6 .....114 B3
 Royton OL2 ....149 A4
 Sale M33 ....158 E2
 Salford,Lower Broughton
 M7 ....158 D4
 Shaw OL2 ....149 A5
 Stalybridge SK15 ....86 C5
 Stockport SK1 ....169 F1
 7 Tyldesley M29 ....76 E5
 Walkden M28 ....60 D4
 Wigan,Pemberton WN5 ....54 D5
 Wigan,Scholes WN1 ....151 D8
John St E OL7 ....100 F8
John St W OL7 ....100 F8
John William St
 Droylsden M11 ....83 C1
 Eccles M30 ....79 F2
John's Pl SK6 ....113 C2

Johnny King Cl M40 ....157 D5
Johns Cl M21 ....109 B8
 Newton-le-W WA12 ....89 B5
 Oldham OL1 ....49 E5
Johnson Ave Leigh WN2 ....56 E1
Johnson Cl WN7 ....75 B4
Johnson Fold Ave BL1 ....23 E2
Johnson Fold Com Prim Sch
 BL1 ....23 F3
Johnson Gr M24 ....64 E8
Johnson St Atherton M46 .....58 A1
 Bolton BL1 ....145 F6
 Manchester M15 ....162 D6
 Pendlebury M27 ....80 D6
 Radcliffe M26 ....44 B1
 Salford M3 ....158 E2
 Tyldesley M29 ....59 A1
 11 Wigan WN5 ....54 B6
Johnson Terr 22 SK16 ....166 B1
Johnson's Sq M40 ....160 D4
Johnsonbrook Rd SK14,
 SK16 ....101 D5
Johnston 21 OL12 ....139 E8
Johnston Ave OL15 ....15 F3
Johnstone Ct M32 ....96 A3
Join Rd M33 ....108 B5
Joiner St Manchester M4 ....159 A1
 Salford M5 ....81 C1
Jolly Brows BL2 ....25 D3
Jolly Tar La PR7 ....20 B7
Jonas St Manchester M9 .....157 E8
 Salford M7 ....158 E3
Jonathan Cl BB4 ....1 A8
Jones Sq SK1 ....124 A7
Jones St Bolton BL1 ....145 F8
 Hadfield SK13 ....104 A5
 Horwich BL6 ....22 B4
 Oldham OL8 ....153 F6
 Radcliffe M26 ....44 B4
 Rochdale OL16 ....31 A6
 Royton OL2 ....48 E2
 Salford M6 ....154 F2
Jonquil Dr M28 ....59 F3
Jopson St M24 ....47 B1
Jordan Ave OL2 ....48 D4
Jordan St Glossop SK13 .....104 E1
 Manchester M15 ....162 F7
Joseph Jennings Ct OL7 ......85 A6
Joseph Johnson Mews
 M22 ....109 E1
Joseph St Eccles M30 ....79 B1
 Reddish SK5 ....169 F4
 4 Farnworth BL4 ....42 D1
 Littleborough OL15 ....16 B6
 Marple SK6 ....126 A6
 Middleton M24 ....46 F1
 Radcliffe M26 ....44 C1
 8 Rochdale OL12 ....14 D2
 Royton OL2 ....48 E4
Josephine Dr 2 M27 ....80 A7
Joshua La M24 ....65 D7
Josslyn Rd M5 ....154 D3
Joule Cl M5 ....161 A8
Joule St M9 ....64 E2
Joules Ct 8 SK1 ....170 F8
Jowett St Oldham OL1 ....49 C1
 Reddish SK5 ....169 F4
Jowett's Wlk OL7 ....84 F2
Jowkin La OL11 ....29 D6
Joy Pl OL12 ....14 F2
Joy St 5 Ramsbottom BL0 ...138 B6
 Rochdale OL12 ....14 F2
Joyce St M40 ....83 B7
Joynson Ave M7 ....158 D4
Joynson St M33 ....108 B5
Jubilee Cl M30 ....32 C2
Jubilee Ave Orrell WN5 ....53 D4
 Radcliffe M26 ....44 C1
 Stalybridge SK15 ....85 E1
Jubilee Cl M30 ....79 D3
Jubilee Cotts M28 ....60 C3
Jubilee Ct
 2 Handforth SK9 ....131 E5
 Manchester M16 ....97 B4
 Salford M6 ....99 F2
Jubilee Ho BL1 ....145 E6
Jubilee Rd M24 ....47 B1
Jubilee St
 3 Ashton-u-l OL7 ....84 F1
 Bolton BL3 ....146 C3
 Salford M6 ....154 F2
Jubilee Terr M24 ....47 B2
Jubilee Way BL9 ....140 D2
Judith St OL12 ....14 C3
Judson Ave M21 ....109 C6
Judy St M9 ....157 F8
Julia St Horwich BL6 ....22 B4
 Manchester M3 ....158 F4
 Rochdale OL12 ....139 E8
Julian Ho OL1 ....111 B8
Julius St M19 ....111 B8
Jumbles Ctry Pk* BL2 ....9 D2
Junction 19 Ind Pk OL10 .....29 F1
Junction Alley OL16 ....31 A6
Junction La WA12 ....89 B3
Junction Rd Bolton BL3 ......144 A5
 Stockport SK1,SK2 ....170 F7
Junction Rd W BL6 ....40 D5
Junction St
 Dukinfield SK14 ....101 C5
 Middleton M24 ....65 D6
 Oldham OL8 ....153 F5
Junction Terr WN3 ....151 E6
June Ave Leigh WN7 ....75 C6
 Stockport WN3 ....168 B2
June St OL7 ....166 A2
Juniper Bank SK5 ....112 A8

Juniper Cl Bolton BL1 ....143 E1
 Oldham OL4 ....49 F4
 Sale M33 ....108 A6
Juniper Dr Hindley WN2 ....57 A3
 Milnrow OL16 ....31 D7
Jupiter Gr WN3 ....54 E2
Jupiter Wlk M40 ....83 A5
Jura Cl SK16 ....101 D8
Jura Dr M41 ....95 E5
Jura Gr OL10 ....29 B1
Jurby Ave M9 ....64 D4
Jury St Leigh WN7 ....75 E7
 Manchester M8 ....158 F4
Justene Cl WA3 ....74 A2
Justin Cl M13 ....163 B7
Jutland Ave OL11 ....30 C8
Jutland Gr BL5 ....39 F1
Jutland St M1 ....159 B1

K

Kale St M13 ....163 B7
Kalima Gr M7 ....155 D6
Kane Ct WA3 ....75 A1
Kansas Ave M50 ....154 E2
Kara St M6 ....154 E2
Karen Rd WN1 ....151 F8
Karmo Ind Est OL11 ....139 D6
Kaskenmoor Sch OL8 ....66 B1
Kate St BL0 ....138 B6
Kathan Cl OL16 ....31 B7
Katherine Ct M16 ....161 C5
Katherine Rd SK2 ....124 C5
Katherine St OL6 ....166 A2
Kathkin Ave M8 ....64 B2
Kathleen Gr M14 ....98 D2
Kathleen St OL12 ....139 D7
Kay Ave SK4 ....112 D3
Kay Brow Heywood OL10 .....29 B2
 Ramsbottom BL0 ....138 C6
Kay Cl WN1 ....151 D8
Kay Garden Sh Ctr BL9 ......140 E2
Kay St Atherton M46 ....58 D2
 Bolton BL1 ....145 F8
 Bury BL9 ....141 A3
 Chapeltown BL7 ....9 C4
 Heywood OL10 ....29 C2
 Little Lever BL3 ....43 A3
 Manchester,Charlestown
 M6 ....80 F6
 Manchester,West Gorton
 M11 ....164 F7
 Ramsbottom BL9 ....11 C3
 Rochdale OL11 ....139 E5
 Stalybridge SK15 ....102 A8
 18 Stalybridge SK15 ....86 A1
Kay's Ave SK1 ....112 B2
Kaye Ave WA3 ....91 F3
Kayfields BL2 ....25 E4
Kayley Ind Est OL7 ....84 F3
Kays Gdns M3 ....158 D2
Kays Wood Rd SK6 ....125 D6
Keadby Cl M30 ....95 E8
Keal Dr M44 ....94 B4
Kean Pl M30 ....79 D1
Keane St M29 ....58 F1
Keane St OL7 ....166 A3
Kearsley Dr BL3 ....42 B3
Kearsley Hall Rd M26 ....61 D8
Kearsley Mount Sh Prec
 BL4 ....61 B6
Kearsley Rd Kearsley M26 ....61 D8
 Manchester M8 ....64 A2
Kearsley St Eccles M30 ....79 B2
 Leigh WN7 ....75 D5
 Wigan WN6 ....37 B1
Kearsley Sta BL4 ....61 A7
Kearsley Vale M26 ....61 A7
Kearsley West Prim Sch
 BL4 ....60 E7
Kearton Dr M30 ....80 A1
Keary Cl M18 ....99 D6
Keats Ave Denton M34 ....113 A8
 Droylsden M43 ....84 A2
 Longshaw WN5 ....53 D1
 Rochdale OL12 ....14 A1
 Wigan,Poolstock WN3 ....150 B8
 Wigan,Standish Lower Ground
 WN6 ....36 E3
Keats Cl M46 ....58 E5
Keats Cres M26 ....43 E4
Keats Fold SK16 ....102 B7
Keats Mews M23 ....120 C8
Keats Rd Eccles M30 ....79 D1
 Oldham OL1 ....49 B1
 Ramsbottom BL8 ....10 F1
Keats St WN7 ....75 D7
Keats Way 7 WN2 ....56 B1
Keats Wlk 2 BL1 ....143 E2
Keb La OL8 ....85 A8
Keble Ave OL8 ....66 C8
Keble Gr WN7 ....75 C8
Keble St WN2 ....151 F7
Kedington Cl M40 ....156 C5
Kedleston Ave M14 ....98 E4
Kedleston Gn SK2 ....124 D7
Kedleston Wlk M34 ....100 F1
Keele Cl SK2 ....124 B6
Keele Wlk M40 ....159 C3
Keeley Cl M40 ....83 C4
Keepers Dr OL12 ....13 E2
Keighley Ave M43 ....84 A3
Keighley Cl BL8 ....26 F2
Keighley St BL1 ....142 C2
Keilder Mews BL1 ....144 A7
Keilder Sq M5 ....154 F1

Keith Dr SK3 . . . . .123 B7
Keith Wlk M40 . . . . .160 D3
Kelboro Ave M34 . . . . .100 D7
Kelbrook St SK2 . . . . .124 E5
Kelbrook Rd M11 . . . . .165 B8
Kelby Ave M23 . . . . .121 B7
Keld Cl BL8 . . . . .27 B5
Keld Wlk M18 . . . . .165 C5
Kelday Wlk M8 . . . . .156 C6
Kelfield Ave M23 . . . . .109 A2
Kelham Wlk M40 . . . . .65 C1
Kellaton Cl WN3 . . . . .151 E6
Kellbank Rd WN3 . . . . .54 E3
Kellbrook Cres
  Manchester M7 . . . . .63 B1
  Salford M7 . . . . .81 A8
Kellet Wlk M11 . . . . .83 B2
Kellett Cl WN5 . . . . .36 D1
Kellett St **4** Bolton BL1 . . .24 F6
  Rochdale OL16 . . . . .31 B8
Kelling Wlk M15 . . . . .162 D7
Kells Gr WN6 . . . . .37 A2
Kelmarsh Dr M41 . . . . .99 D7
Kelmscott Lodge M41 . . . . .95 B3
Kelsall Cres SK3 . . . . .170 D6
Kelsall Dr
  Altrincham WA15 . . . . . . .120 C6
  Droylsden M43 . . . . .83 F3
Kelsall Rd SK8 . . . . .123 A5
Kelsall St
  Manchester M12 . . . . .164 F6
  Oldham OL9 . . . . .153 D6
  Rochdale OL16 . . . . .139 F8
  Sale M33 . . . . .108 B4
Kelsall Way **6** SK9 . . . . . .131 D5
Kelsey Wlk M9 . . . . .64 B5
Kelso Cl OL8 . . . . .66 F1
Kelso Gr WN7 . . . . .56 D4
Kelson Ave OL7 . . . . .166 A4
Kelstern Ave M13 . . . . .98 E3
Kelstern Sq M13 . . . . .98 E3
Kelton Cl SK5 . . . . .111 F5
Kelverlow St OL4 . . . . .67 C6
Kelvin Ave Middleton M24 . .64 B6
  Sale M33 . . . . .107 E4
Kelvin Cl WN4 . . . . .72 D4
Kelvin Gr Manchester M8 . .156 A6
  Wigan WN3 . . . . .54 F2
Kelvin St Ashton-u-L OL7 . .100 F8
  Manchester M4 . . . . .159 A2
Kelvindale Dr WA15 . . . . . .120 C7
Kelvington Dr M9 . . . . .157 D6
Kelway Terr WN1 . . . . .37 D1
Kelwood Ave BL9 . . . . .28 D5
Kemball **3** M30 . . . . .79 F2
Kemble Ave M23 . . . . .109 C1
Kemble Cl BL6 . . . . .22 B5
Kemmel Ave M22 . . . . .121 E5
Kemmay Wlk **11** M11 . . . . .83 C1
Kemp Ave OL11 . . . . .139 D5
Kemp Rd SK6 . . . . .126 C2
Kemp St Hyde SK14 . . . . . .167 E4
  Middleton M24 . . . . .64 F8
Kempley Cl M12 . . . . .164 F6
Kempnough Hall Rd M28 . . .78 D7
Kempsey Cl OL9 . . . . .152 B7
Kempsey St OL9 . . . . .152 B7
Kempsey Wlk M40 . . . . .65 D1
Kempsford Cl M23 . . . . . . .121 B6
Kempster St M7 . . . . .158 D4
Kempton Ave
  Little Lever BL3 . . . . .43 A2
  Sale M33 . . . . .107 D3
Kempton Cl
  Droylsden M43 . . . . .84 C2
  Hazel Grove SK7 . . . . . . .125 A1
  Newton-le-W WA12 . . . . . .89 D5
Kempton Rd M19 . . . . .111 A8
Kempton Way OL9 . . . . . . .152 C7
Kemsing Wlk M5 . . . . .81 A1
Kenchester Ave M11 . . . . . .99 D8
Kendal Ave Ashton-u-L OL7 .84 F4
  Denton M34 . . . . .101 A1
  Dukinfield SK14 . . . . .101 C5
  Rochdale OL12 . . . . .13 E3
  Sale M33 . . . . .108 C3
  Urmston M41 . . . . .94 E4
Kendal Cl
  Altrincham WA15 . . . . . . .120 D5
  Heywood OL10 . . . . .46 E8
Kendal Dr Bramhall SK7 . . .132 C5
  Bury BL9 . . . . .44 D7
  Gatley SK8 . . . . .122 C4
  Shaw OL2 . . . . .49 D7
Kendal Gdns SK6 . . . . .113 B4
Kendal Gr
  Ashton-in-M WN4 . . . . . . .73 B4
  Leigh WN7 . . . . .75 D5
  Walkden M28 . . . . .60 F2
  Whitefield M45 . . . . .62 F8
Kendal Rd Bolton BL1 . . . .144 C8
  Boothstown M28 . . . . .77 E7
  Hindley WN2 . . . . .56 A7
  Ince-in-M WN2 . . . . .56 A7
  Ramsbottom BL0 . . . . .11 A2
  Salford M6 . . . . .80 C5
  Stretford M32 . . . . .96 D3
Kendal Rd W BL0 . . . . .10 F2
Kendal St WN6 . . . . .150 B8
Kendal Terr **8** SK16 . . . . . .166 C1
Kendal Wlk M24 . . . . .46 E1
Kendall Rd M9 . . . . .63 F3
Kendon Gr M34 . . . . .100 E3
Kendrew Rd BL3 . . . . .146 A4
Kendrew Wlk M9 . . . . .64 E1

Kendrick Pl WN1 . . . . .151 E8
Kenford Dr WN3 . . . . .54 E2
Kenford Wlk M8 . . . . .155 F6
Kenhall Rd WN7 . . . . .76 C4
Kenilworth Ave
  Chadderton OL9 . . . . .47 E1
  Cheadle SK8 . . . . .123 A3
  Handforth SK9 . . . . .131 D3
  Manchester M20 . . . . . . .109 F5
  Swinton M27 . . . . .62 B3
  Whitefield M45 . . . . .63 A7
Kenilworth Cl
  Marple SK6 . . . . .125 F8
  Oldham OL4 . . . . .67 F5
  Radcliffe M26 . . . . .43 F6
Kenilworth Dr
  Hazel Grove SK7 . . . . . . .133 D8
  Hindley WN2 . . . . .56 F4
  Leigh WN7 . . . . .76 E7
Kenilworth Gdns WA12 . . . .89 C1
Kenilworth Gr M34 . . . . . . .100 C8
Kenilworth Rd
  Cheadle SK8 . . . . .122 F7
  Golborne WA3 . . . . .90 E7
  Royton OL16 . . . . .48 C8
  Sale M33 . . . . .107 E4
  Urmston M41 . . . . .94 C2
Kenilworth Sq BL1 . . . . . . .142 B1
Kenion Rd OL11 . . . . .30 B6
Kenion St OL16 . . . . .139 F7
Kenley Dr OL10 . . . . .46 F7
Kenley Wlk M8 . . . . .156 C6
Kenmay Ave BL3 . . . . .146 A3
Kenmere Gr M40 . . . . .65 B1
Kenmor Ave BL8 . . . . .27 A1
Kenmore Ave M45 . . . . .63 B8
Kenmore Dr WA15 . . . . . . .120 B3
Kenmore Gr
  Garswood WN4 . . . . .72 D4
  Irlam M44 . . . . .105 D6
Kenmore Rd Sale M33 . . . .107 C1
  Whitefield M45 . . . . .63 B8
  Wythenshawe M22 . . . . . .121 D7
Kenmore Way M45 . . . . .63 B8
Kennard Cl M9 . . . . .64 F1
Kennard Pl WA14 . . . . .119 E6
Kennedy Cl WN6 . . . . .36 F8
Kennedy Dr
  Little Lever BL3 . . . . .43 C3
  Whitefield M45 . . . . .45 B2
Kennedy Rd Salford M5 . . . .80 C2
  Tyldesley M28,M29 . . . . . .77 D6
Kennedy St Bolton BL2 . . .148 C1
  Manchester M2 . . . . .158 F1
  Oldham OL8 . . . . .153 E5
Kennedy Way
  Denton M34 . . . . .100 C2
  Stockport SK4 . . . . .168 C2
Kennerley Ct
  Stockport SK2 . . . . .124 A5
  Wilmslow SK9 . . . . .137 A7
Kennerley Lo SK2 . . . . .170 F5
Kennerley's La SK9 . . . . . .137 A7
Kennet **16** OL10 . . . . .29 C2
Kennet Cl Handforth SK9 . .131 D2
  Westhoughton BL5 . . . . . .39 E1
Kennet Way WN7 . . . . .75 F7
Kenneth Ave WN7 . . . . .75 F8
Kenneth Collis Ct M22 . . . .121 C3
Kenneth Gr WN7 . . . . .75 D6
Kenneth Sq M7 . . . . .155 E6
Kennett Dr SK6 . . . . .112 F4
Kennett Rd M23 . . . . .121 A3
Kenninghall Rd M22 . . . . . .121 D3
Kennington Ave M40 . . . . . .83 B4
Kennington Fold BL3 . . . . .147 D3
Kenny Cl OL4 . . . . .67 D5
Kenside St **2** M16 . . . . .97 F3
Kensington Ave
  Ashton-u-L OL6 . . . . .85 E4
  Chadderton OL9 . . . . .65 E8
  2 Hyde SK14 . . . . .167 E1
  Manchester M14 . . . . .98 D4
  Radcliffe M26 . . . . .43 D4
  Royton OL2 . . . . .48 C6
Kensington Cl
  Milnrow OL16 . . . . .32 A6
  Ramsbottom BL8 . . . . .11 A1
Kensington Ct
  Bolton BL1 . . . . .145 E7
  1 Hyde SK14 . . . . .167 E1
  Reddish M34 . . . . .100 B4
  Salford M7 . . . . .81 C8
  Wilmslow SK9 . . . . .137 A6
Kensington Dr Bury BL8 . . .44 A8
  Horwich BL6 . . . . .22 D3
  Leigh WN7 . . . . .76 E7
  Salford M5 . . . . .154 D3
Kensington Gdns
  Altrincham WA14 . . . . . . .119 F1
  Hyde SK14 . . . . .167 F1
Kensington Gr
  Altrincham WA14 . . . . . . .119 E8
  Reddish M34 . . . . .100 B4
  14 Stalybridge SK15 . . . . .86 A1
Kensington Rd
  Failsworth M35 . . . . .84 B8
  Manchester M21 . . . . .97 B2
  Oldham OL8 . . . . .66 D4
  Stockport SK3 . . . . .123 B7
  3 Wigan WN5 . . . . .54 D5
Kensington St
  Bolton BL1 . . . . .145 E7
  Hyde SK14 . . . . .167 E1
  Manchester M14 . . . . .98 A3
  Rochdale OL11 . . . . .30 E5

Kensington The M20 . . . . .110 B5
Kensington Mdw M8 . . . . . .63 F2
Kensworth Cl
  6 Altrincham M23 . . . . . .120 D6
  Bolton BL1 . . . . .143 D1
Kensworth Dr BL1 . . . . . . .143 D1
Kent Ave Chadderton OL9 . .152 B6
  Cheadle SK8 . . . . .123 C5
  Droylsden M43 . . . . .83 E1
  Platt Bridge WN2 . . . . . . .56 A2
Kent Cl Diggle OL3 . . . . . . .51 C4
Kent Dr Bury BL9 . . . . .45 A8
  Kearsley BL4 . . . . .61 B6
Kent Gr M35 . . . . .83 E6
Kent Rd Atherton M46 . . . . .58 C4
  Glossop SK13 . . . . .104 D1
  Irlam M44 . . . . .105 C5
  Partington M31 . . . . .105 E2
  Reddish M34 . . . . .100 A2
  Stockport SK3 . . . . .123 B8
  Tyldesley M29 . . . . .59 A2
Kent Rd E M14 . . . . .98 D3
Kent Rd W M14 . . . . .98 D3
Kent St Bolton BL1 . . . . . . .145 E8
  Manchester M14 . . . . .98 C3
  Leigh WN7 . . . . .76 E4
  11 Manchester M2 . . . . .158 F1
  Oldham OL8 . . . . .66 F4
  Rochdale OL11 . . . . .139 F6
  Salford M7 . . . . .158 D4
  Swinton M27 . . . . .61 F2
  Wigan WN1 . . . . .151 D7
Kent Way WA12 . . . . .89 C1
Kent Wlk Haslingden BB4 . . .1 A8
  Heywood OL10 . . . . .29 A1
  Heywood OL10 . . . . .29 B2
Kentford Dr M40 . . . . .159 C4
Kentford Gr **6** BL4 . . . . . . .60 C8
Kentford Rd BL1 . . . . .143 F1
Kentmere Ave
  Billinge WA11 . . . . .71 C1
  Rochdale OL12 . . . . .15 B3
Kentmere Cl SK8 . . . . .122 B3
Kentmere Ct M9 . . . . .65 B4
Kentmere Dr
  Middleton M24 . . . . .46 E3
  Tyldesley M29 . . . . .77 B7
Kentmere Gr BL4 . . . . .59 F7
Kentmere Rd
  Altrincham M23,WA15 . . .120 D6
  Bolton BL2 . . . . .25 F1
  Dukinfield SK14 . . . . .110 E2
  High Lane SK6 . . . . .135 A6
Kenton Ave M18 . . . . .99 C3
Kenton Cl Bolton BL1 . . . . .143 D1
  Denton M34 . . . . .100 D7
Kenton Rd OL2 . . . . .149 A7
Kenton St OL8 . . . . .66 F3
Kentsford Dr M26 . . . . .43 B5
Kentstone Ave SK4 . . . . . . .110 E3
Kentucky St OL4 . . . . .67 C6
Kentwell Cl SK16 . . . . .101 B7
Kenwick Dr M40 . . . . .65 E2
Kenwood Ave
  Altrincham WA15 . . . . . . .119 F2
  Bramhall SK7 . . . . .132 D5
  Gatley SK8 . . . . .122 A6
  Leigh WN7 . . . . .76 C5
  Manchester M19 . . . . . . .110 F8
Kenwood Cl Leigh WN7 . . . .76 C4
  Stretford M32 . . . . .96 E2
Kenwood Ct M32 . . . . .96 E1
Kenwood La M28 . . . . .78 F5
Kenwood Rd Bolton BL1 . . .142 B3
  Oldham OL1 . . . . .48 C1
  Reddish SK5 . . . . .99 E2
  Stretford M32 . . . . .96 E1
Kenworthy Ave OL6 . . . . . . .85 D5
Kenworthy Cl SK14 . . . . . .102 E2
Kenworthy Gdns OL3 . . . . . .51 B1
Kenworthy La M22 . . . . . . .109 D1
Kenworthy St
  Rochdale OL16 . . . . .31 C7
  Stalybridge SK15 . . . . . . .102 A8
Kenworthy Terr OL16 . . . . . .31 C7
Kenwright St M4 . . . . .159 A2
Kenwyn St M40 . . . . .160 E3
Kenyon Ave
  Dukinfield SK16 . . . . .101 E7
  Oldham OL8 . . . . .66 F3
  Sale M33 . . . . .108 A1
Kenyon Cl SK14 . . . . .101 F5
Kenyon Fold OL11 . . . . .29 E5
Kenyon Gr M38 . . . . .59 E4
Kenyon La Culcheth WA3 . . .91 A3
  Golborne WA3 . . . . .90 F3
  Golborne WA3 . . . . .90 F5
  Manchester M40 . . . . .83 A8
  Middleton M24 . . . . .65 C8
  Prestwich M25 . . . . .63 B6
Kenyon Rd Little Lever BL2 . .43 B5
  Standish WN6 . . . . .19 D2
  Wigan WN1 . . . . .37 C2
Kenyon St
  Ashton-u-L OL6 . . . . .166 B3
  Bacup OL13 . . . . .4 B8
  Bury BL9 . . . . .141 A3
  Droylsden M18 . . . . .99 F6
  Dukinfield SK16 . . . . .101 B8
  Heywood OL10 . . . . .29 C2
  Leigh WN7 . . . . .75 D8
  Radcliffe M26 . . . . .44 B2
  Ramsbottom BL0 . . . . . . .138 C6
Kenyon Terr M38 . . . . .59 E4
Kenyon Way Bury BL8 . . . . .26 F5
  Walkden M38 . . . . .59 E4
Keppel Rd M21 . . . . .97 B1

Keppel St OL6 . . . . .166 C3
Kepplecove Mdw M28 . . . . .77 F5
Kepwick Dr M22 . . . . .121 E1
Kerans Dr BL5 . . . . .39 E1
Kerenhappuch St BL0 . . . .138 B6
Kerfield Wlk **12** M13 . . . . .163 B7
Kerfoot Cl M22 . . . . .121 E8
Kerfoot St WN7 . . . . .76 C4
Kermishaw Nook M29 . . . . .77 B8
Kermoor Ave BL1 . . . . .24 E6
Kerne Gr M23 . . . . .109 A1
Kerr St M9 . . . . .64 D3
Kerrera Dr M5 . . . . .154 D1
Kerridge Dr SK6 . . . . .112 F4
Kerrier Cl M30 . . . . .80 A2
Kerris Cl M22 . . . . .121 E1
Kerry Gr BL2 . . . . .148 B8
Kerry Wlk M23 . . . . .120 F3
Kersal Ave
  Pendlebury M27 . . . . .80 C8
  Walkden M38 . . . . .60 B4
Kersal Bank M7 . . . . .81 C8
Kersal Bar M7 . . . . .81 C8
Kersal Cl Manchester M25 . .63 A1
  2 Prestwich M7 . . . . .63 C1
Kersal Crag M7 . . . . .63 C1
Kersal Dr WA15 . . . . .120 C7
Kersal Hall Ave M7 . . . . . . .81 A8
Kersal Rd M25,M7 . . . . .63 A1
Kersal Vale Ct M7 . . . . .80 E8
Kersal Vale Rd M7,M25 . . . .80 F8
Kersal Way M7 . . . . .81 B7
Kerscott Rd M23 . . . . .108 F2
Kersh Ave M19 . . . . .111 B8
Kershaw Ave
  Little Lever BL3 . . . . .43 A4
  Prestwich M25 . . . . .62 F2
  Sale M33 . . . . .108 E2
Kershaw Bsns Ctr BL3 . . . .145 D5
Kershaw Dr M24 . . . . .64 F8
Kershaw Gr M34 . . . . .100 C8
Kershaw La M34 . . . . .100 C8
Kershaw Rd M35 . . . . .83 F7
Kershaw St
  Ashton-u-L OL7 . . . . .100 F8
  Bolton BL3 . . . . .145 D5
  Bolton,Bradshaw BL2 . . . .25 C5
  Bury BL9 . . . . .141 A2
  Droylsden M43 . . . . .83 F1
  Heywood OL10 . . . . .29 B2
  2 Rochdale OL12 . . . . . .139 F8
  Royton OL2 . . . . .48 D5
  Shaw OL2 . . . . .149 B7
  Tyldesley M29 . . . . .59 A1
  Wigan WN5 . . . . .54 B6
Kershaw St E OL2 . . . . . . .149 B7
Kershaw Wlk M12 . . . . .164 D6
Kershope Gr M5 . . . . .161 A8
Kersley St OL4 . . . . .67 B6
Kerswell Wlk M40 . . . . .83 A6
Kerwin Wlk M11 . . . . .165 A8
Kerwood Dr OL2 . . . . .48 E3
Kesteven Rd M9 . . . . .157 D7
Keston Ave Droylsden M43 . .83 E1
  Manchester M9 . . . . .65 A3
Keston Cres SK5 . . . . .112 B6
Keston Rd **4** OL1 . . . . .49 C1
Kestor St BL2 . . . . .148 B7
Kestrel Ave
  Droylsden M34 . . . . .84 C1
  Farnworth BL4 . . . . .59 F7
  Oldham OL4 . . . . .67 C5
  Swinton M27 . . . . .61 F1
  Walkden M38 . . . . .60 A5
Kestrel Cl Marple SK6 . . . .126 A3
  Prestwich M25 . . . . .63 B6
Kestrel Dr
  Ashton-in-M WN4 . . . . . . .73 C6
  Bury BL9 . . . . .141 B4
  Irlam M44 . . . . .94 A3
Kestrel Rd M17 . . . . .95 F8
Kestrel St **3** BL1 . . . . .148 A8
Kestrel Way SK13 . . . . .115 F8
Kestrel Wlk M12 . . . . .165 A6
Keswick Ave
  Ashton-u-L OL7 . . . . .84 F5
  Chadderton OL9 . . . . . . .152 A7
  Denton M34 . . . . .100 D4
  Dukinfield SK14 . . . . .101 C4
  Gatley SK8 . . . . .122 B4
  Hyde SK14 . . . . .167 A3
  Manchester M13 . . . . . . .164 D5
  Stalybridge SK15 . . . . . . .86 A4
Keswick Cl
  3 Middleton M24 . . . . . . .46 D2
  Wythenshawe M22 . . . . . .121 C2
  Bury BL9 . . . . .44 E6
Keswick Dr Bramhall SK7 . .132 C5
Keswick Gr M6 . . . . .154 F2
Keswick Pl WN2 . . . . .56 A7
Keswick Rd
  Altrincham WA15 . . . . . . .120 C6
  High Lane SK6 . . . . .134 F7
  Reddish SK4 . . . . .111 D7
  Stretford M32 . . . . .96 C3
  Walkden M38 . . . . .60 A5
  Rochdale OL11 . . . . .30 C2
Ketley Wlk **1** M22 . . . . . . .121 F3
Kettering Rd M19 . . . . .111 A8
Kettleshulme Way SK12 . . .134 A3
Kettleshulme Wlk **4**
  SK9 . . . . .131 E1

Kettlewell Wlk M18 . . . . . .165 C5
Ketton Cl M11 . . . . .99 E7
Keverlow La OL8 . . . . .67 C2
Kevin Ave OL2 . . . . .48 E2
Kevin Cl SK2 . . . . .124 B4
Kevin St M19 . . . . .111 B8
Kew Ave SK14 . . . . .167 E1
Kew Dr Cheadle SK8 . . . . .122 E2
  Urmston M41 . . . . .95 A4
Kew Gdns M40 . . . . .65 E1
Kew Rd Failsworth M35 . . . .84 A8
  Oldham OL4 . . . . .67 C6
  Rochdale OL11 . . . . .31 A3
Key Ct M34 . . . . .113 A8
Key West Cl M11 . . . . .160 F1
Keyhaven Wlk M40 . . . . . . .157 D5
Keymer St M11 . . . . .160 E2
Keynsham Rd M11 . . . . .83 B3
Keystone Cl M6 . . . . .154 E4
Keyworth Wlk M40 . . . . . . .160 E1
Khartoum St
  Droylsden M11 . . . . .83 D2
  Manchester M16 . . . . .97 D4
Kibbles Brow BL7 . . . . .9 A8
Kibboth Crew BL0 . . . . . . .138 B7
Kibworth Cl M45 . . . . .62 D8
Kibworth Wlk **7** M9 . . . . . . .64 E5
Kid Glove Rd WA3 . . . . .74 B1
Kidacre St **4** M46 . . . . .46 F1
Kidacre Wlk **8** M40 . . . . . . .83 A7
Kidd Rd SK13 . . . . .116 E6
Kidderminster Way OL9 . . . .47 F1
Kidwall Wlk **9** M9 . . . . .64 F1
Kiel Cl M30 . . . . .95 E8
Kielder Cl WN4 . . . . .72 F7
Kielder Hill M24 . . . . .46 F4
Kilbride Ave BL2 . . . . .42 F6
Kilbuck La WA11 . . . . .89 A8
Kilburn Ave
  Ashton-in-M WN4 . . . . . . .73 D4
  Manchester M9 . . . . .64 D5
Kilburn Cl Gatley SK8 . . . .131 B7
  Leigh WN7 . . . . .57 D1
Kilburn Dr WN6 . . . . .36 A7
Kilburn Gr WN3 . . . . .54 D3
Kilburn Rd Orrell WN5 . . . . .53 F5
  Radcliffe M26 . . . . .43 E4
Kilburn St **8** OL1 . . . . .49 D1
Kilcoby Ave M27 . . . . .80 D8
Kildale Cl BL3 . . . . .40 E4
Kildare Cres OL11 . . . . .30 F2
Kildare Grange WN2 . . . . . .56 C5
Kildare Rd
  Manchester M21 . . . . . . .109 D8
  Swinton M27 . . . . .79 E6
Kildare St Farnworth BL4 . . .60 C7
  Hindley WN2 . . . . .56 D6
  Wigan WN3,WN5 . . . . . . .54 F6
Kildonan Dr BL3 . . . . .40 F6
Killer St BL0 . . . . .138 C6
Killington Dr BL3 . . . . .42 F6
Killingworth Mews **4**
  BL6 . . . . .22 D1
Killon St BL9 . . . . .141 A1
Kilmaine Dr BL3 . . . . .40 E5
Kilmarsh Wlk **7** M8 . . . . . .155 F7
Kilmington Dr M8 . . . . .156 A6
Kilmory Dr BL2 . . . . .42 F6
Kilmory Fold SK13 . . . . . . .104 E3
Kiln Bank OL12 . . . . .4 C2
Kiln Bank La OL12 . . . . .4 C2
Kiln Brow BL7 . . . . .25 C8
Kiln Croft SK6 . . . . .112 F1
Kiln Croft La SK9 . . . . .131 E4
Kiln Field BL7 . . . . .24 F8
Kiln Hill Cl OL1 . . . . .47 F2
Kiln Hill La OL1 . . . . .47 F2
Kiln St Little Lever BL3 . . . . .43 A3
  Ramsbottom BL0 . . . . . . .138 B5
Kiln Terr **5** OL13 . . . . .3 D8
Kiln Wlk OL12 . . . . .14 E2
Kilnbrook Cl OL4 . . . . .68 B4
Kilner Cl BL9 . . . . .45 B4
Kilner Wlk M40 . . . . .159 C4
Kilnerdeyne Terr OL16 . . . .139 F6
Kilnhurst Wlk **12** BL1 . . . .145 D8
Kilnside Dr M9 . . . . .157 D7
Kilnsley Wlk M18 . . . . .165 C5
Kilnwick Cl M18 . . . . .99 B3
Kilphin The BL6 . . . . .21 C3
Kilrush Ave M30 . . . . .95 D8
Kilsby Cl Bolton BL6 . . . . . .40 C6
  Farnworth BL4 . . . . .42 C2
Kilsby Wlk M40 . . . . .160 D4
Kilshaw St WN1 . . . . .37 F1
Kilton Wlk M40 . . . . .159 C4
Kilvert Dr M33 . . . . .107 F5
Kilworth Ave M33 . . . . .107 F3
Kilworth Dr BL6 . . . . .40 C6
Kilworth St OL11 . . . . .139 F5
Kimberley Ave SK6 . . . . . .113 C2
Kimberley Pl WN4 . . . . .73 C3
Kimberley Rd BL1 . . . . .24 E5
Kimberley St
  Oldham OL8 . . . . .66 C3
  Salford M7 . . . . .155 E7
  Stockport SK3 . . . . .170 E7
Kimberley Wlk M15 . . . . . .162 D7
Kimberly St WN6 . . . . .37 A1
Kimble Cl BL8 . . . . .10 F2
Kimbolton Cl M12 . . . . .165 A6
Kinburn Rd M19 . . . . .110 D2

Kinbury Wlk M40 ....159 C4
Kincardine Rd M13 ....163 B6
Kincraig Cl Bolton BL3 ....40 E4
Droylsden M11 ....83 C1
Kinder Ave Ashton-u-L OL6 .86 A6
Oldham OL4 ....67 D5
Kinder Cl SK13 ....116 A8
Kinder Ct SK3 ....170 E7
Kinder Dr SK6 ....126 A6
Kinder Fold SK15 ....102 D6
Kinder Gr
Ashton-in-M WN4 ....72 F6
Romiley SK6 ....113 E2
Kinder Ho M5 ....154 D3
Kinder Mews OL3 ....69 B5
Kinder St Stalybridge SK15 .86 A2
Stockport SK3 ....170 E7
Kinder Way Middleton M24 .46 F2
Mottram-in-L SK14 ....102 F3
Kinders Cl M31 ....106 D6
Kinders Cres OL3 ....69 B5
Kinders Fold OL15 ....15 F7
Kinders La OL3 ....69 B6
Kinderton Ave M20 ....110 B7
Kineton Wlk 12 M13 ....163 C6
King Albert St OL2 ....149 B7
King Charles Ct SK13 ...116 D7
King David High Sch The
M8 ....63 F1
King David Jun & Inf Schs
M8 ....63 F1
King Edward Ave SK13 ..104 D1
King Edward Ct SK14 ....113 F8
King Edward Rd SK14 ...113 E8
King Edward St
Eccles M30 ....79 C2
4 Manchester M19 ....99 B1
Salford M5 ....161 B8
King Edward's Bldgs
M7 ....155 F8
King George Cl WN4 ....73 B3
King George Rd
Haydock WA11 ....89 A7
Hyde SK14 ....113 E8
King La Oldham OL1 ....49 E4
Oldham OL1 ....49 E5
King Sq OL8 ....153 E6
King St Bolton BL1 ....145 E7
Bolton,Bradshaw Chapel
BL2 ....25 D5
5 Bolton,Cox Green BL7 ...24 F8
Delph OL3 ....50 F4
Denton M34 ....100 F3
Denton,Hooley Hill M34 ..100 F6
Droylsden M43 ....100 A8
Dukinfield SK16 ....101 C7
Eccles M30 ....79 F1
Failsworth M35 ....83 D6
Farnworth BL4 ....60 D8
Glossop SK13 ....116 C8
Heywood OL10 ....29 D1
Hindley WN2 ....56 D6
Hollingworth SK14 ....103 D5
Horwich BL6 ....22 A4
Hyde SK14 ....167 D3
Ince-in-M WN2 ....56 A7
Leigh WN7 ....75 F4
Manchester M2 ....158 F1
Middleton M24 ....47 A1
Mossley OL5 ....68 D1
Mottram-in-L SK14 ....115 A8
Newton-le-W WA12 ....89 B3
Oldham OL8 ....153 E6
Radcliffe M26 ....44 B2
Ramsbottom BL0 ....138 C6
Rawtenstall BB4 ....2 E8
Rochdale OL16 ....139 F7
Salford M3 ....158 E2
Salford,Higher Broughton
M7 ....155 E7
Salford,Irlams o' th' Height
M6 ....80 D5
8 Stalybridge SK15 ....86 A2
Stretford M32 ....96 D1
Westhoughton BL5 ....39 F1
Whitworth OL12 ....4 D3
Wigan WN1 ....150 C7
King St E Rochdale OL11 ..139 F6
Stockport SK1 ....169 F2
King St S OL11 ....139 E5
King St W
Manchester M3 ....158 F1
Stockport SK3 ....169 E1
Wigan WN1 ....150 C8
King William Ent Pk
M50 ....161 A8
King William St
Eccles M30 ....79 A3
Salford M50 ....161 A8
Tyldesley M29 ....76 F8
King's Ave WA3 ....90 F7
King's Cl Droylsden M18 ...99 F6
Stockport SK7 ....123 F2
King's Cres M46 ....76 E8
King's Dr
Manchester SK4 ....168 A3
Marple SK6 ....125 E7
Middleton M24 ....64 D8
King's Gdns WN7 ....76 C5
King's Lynn Cl 5 M20 ...110 B3
King's Rd
Ashton-in-M WN4 ....73 A5
Ashton-u-L OL6 ....85 E5
Manchester M25 ....63 C2
Oldham OL8 ....153 F5
King's Rd *continued*
Reddish M34 ....100 B6
Rochdale OL16 ....31 B5
Romiley SK6 ....113 A3
Wilmslow SK9 ....136 E8
King's Terr 14 SK16 ....166 B1
Kingcombe Wlk 12 M9 ...157 E8
Kingfisher Ave M34 ....84 C1
Kingfisher Cl M12 ....164 E5
Kingfisher Com Specl Sch
The OL9 ....65 F5
Kingfisher Ct
Ashton-in-M WN4 ....73 B6
Rochdale OL12 ....15 C4
10 Wigan WN6 ....37 A1
Kingfisher Dr Bury BL9 ..141 B4
Farnworth BL4 ....59 F7
Kingfisher Mews SK6 ...126 A6
Kingfisher Rd SK2 ....124 F5
Kingfisher Way SK13 ....115 F8
Kingham Dr M4 ....159 C2
Kingholm Gdns BL1 ....143 D1
Kingmoor Ave M26 ....44 B4
Kings Acre WA14 ....119 A1
Kings Ave Gatley SK8 ...122 A4
Manchester M8 ....156 B8
Whitefield M45 ....44 E2
Kings Cl Prestwich M25 ...63 C5
Wilmslow SK9 ....137 A6
Kings Cres M16 ....97 B3
Kings Ct Glossop SK13 ...116 C8
Stockport SK5 ....169 F3
11 Tyldesley M29 ....58 F1
Kings Dr SK8 ....123 A3
Kings Gr Rochdale OL12 ...15 C4
Stretford M32 ....96 F3
Kings La M32 ....96 F3
Kings Oak Cl WN1 ....151 D8
Kings Pk M17 ....96 B4
Kings Rd Cheadle SK8 ...123 A3
Failsworth OL9 ....65 E3
Golborne WA3 ....90 A7
Hazel Grove SK7 ....124 E3
Irlam M44 ....105 E6
Manchester,Chorlton-cum-Hardy
M21 ....109 D8
Manchester,Firswood M16 ..97 B3
Sale M33 ....107 F4
Shaw OL2 ....149 A6
Stretford M32 ....96 E2
Kings Road Prim Sch
M16 ....97 A3
Kings Terr M32 ....96 F3
Kings Wlk M43 ....100 A8
Kings' Wlk OL6 ....85 D5
Kingsbridge Ave
Ainsworth BL2 ....26 D1
Hattersley SK14 ....102 C2
Kingsbridge Cl SK6 ....125 E7
Kingsbridge Ct M9 ....157 D7
Kingsbridge Dr SK16 ....101 B7
Kingsbridge Rd
Manchester M9 ....157 D7
5 Oldham OL8 ....67 B5
Kingsbridge Wlk SK14 ..102 C2
Kingsbrook Ct M21 ....109 E8
Kingsbrook Rd M16,M21 .109 E8
Kingsbury Ave BL1 ....142 A1
Kingsbury Ct BL1 ....142 A1
Kingsbury Ct Lo BL1 ....142 A1
Kingsbury Dr 15 SK9 ....131 D1
Kingsbury Rd M11 ....83 C2
Kingscliffe St M9 ....157 E8
Kingscourt Ave BL1 ....142 C2
Kingscroft Ct WN1 ....151 D7
Kingsdale Rd M18 ....100 A4
Kingsdown Cres WN1 ....37 C4
Kingsdown Dr BL1 ....143 F1
Kingsdown Gdns 8 BL1 .143 F1
Kingsdown Rd
Abram Brow WN2 ....74 B7
Wythenshawe M22 ....121 C1
Kingsdown Wlk SK5 ....112 B5
Kingsfield Dr M20 ....110 C2
Kingsfield Way M29 ....77 B8
Kingsfold Ave M40 ....159 C4
Kingsfold Cl BL2 ....42 E6
Kingsford St M5 ....154 D2
Kingsgate BL1 ....145 E7
Kingsgate Rd M22 ....121 C1
Kingshill Ct WN6 ....36 F7
Kingshill Rd M21 ....109 A8
Kingshill Sch M29 ....76 F8
Kingsholme Rd M22 ....121 C2
Kingsland Cl M40 ....160 D3
Kingsland Rd
Cheadle SK3 ....123 A7
Farnworth BL4 ....42 A1
Rochdale OL11 ....30 B3
Kingslea PR7 ....20 F8
Kingslea Rd M20 ....110 C5
Kingsleigh Rd SK4 ....110 F4
Kingsley Ave
Handforth SK9 ....131 C2
Manchester M9 ....157 F7
Salford M7 ....81 B7
Stockport SK4 ....169 E4
Stretford M32 ....96 F3
Urmston M41 ....95 B2
Whitefield M45 ....63 B8
Wigan WN3 ....54 F3
Kingsley Cl Ashton-u-L OL6 .86 A5
Denton M34 ....100 D1
Kingsley Dr Cheadle SK8 .123 A3
Oldham OL4 ....67 E7
Kingsley Gr M34 ....100 C8
Kingsley Rd
Altrincham WA15 ....120 B7
Kingsley Rd *continued*
Hindley WN2 ....56 F5
Middleton M24 ....47 B2
Oldham OL4 ....67 C6
Swinton M27 ....61 D1
Walkden M28 ....60 C4
Wythenshawe M22 ....121 D8
Kingsley St Bolton BL1 ...143 D2
Bury BL8 ....27 B2
Leigh WN7 ....75 C7
Kingsmead Mews M9 ....64 C5
Kingsmede WN1 ....37 D3
Kingsmere Ave M19 ....98 F1
Kingsmill Ave M19 ....111 B8
Kingsmoor Fields SK13 .104 D3
Kingsmoor Rd SK13 ....104 D2
Kingsneath Ave M11 ....83 B3
Kingsnorth Cl 5 BL1 ...143 F1
Kingsnorth Rd M41 ....94 E4
Kingston Arc 6 SK14 ...102 E2
Kingston Ave Bolton BL2 ..25 C1
Chadderton OL9 ....66 A4
Manchester M20 ....110 B1
5 Oldham OL1 ....49 B1
Kingston Cl Bury BL8 ....44 B8
Hattersley SK14 ....102 E2
Sale M33 ....107 D2
Salford M7 ....155 D8
Shaw OL2 ....149 B8
Wigan WN3 ....55 B3
Kingston Cres BB4 ....1 A7
Kingston Ct
14 Handforth SK9 ....131 E1
Manchester M20 ....110 B1
Kingston Dr Royton OL2 ..48 C6
Sale M33 ....108 D5
Urmston M41 ....107 B8
Kingston Gdns SK14 ....101 B3
Kingston Gr M9 ....64 F4
Kingston Hill SK8 ....122 D4
Kingston Pl SK8 ....122 E2
Kingston Rd
Failsworth M35 ....84 B7
Handforth SK9 ....131 D5
Manchester M20 ....110 B1
Radcliffe M26 ....44 C6
Kingston St SK3 ....169 D1
Kingsway
Altrincham WA14 ....119 D5
Cheadle M20,SK8 ....122 C6
Dukinfield SK16 ....101 E7
Gatley SK8 ....122 C4
Ince-in-M WN2 ....151 F7
Kearsley BL4 ....60 F6
Manchester M14,M19,
M20 ....110 D4
Middleton M24 ....65 B6
Newton-le-W WA12 ....89 C2
Pendlebury M27 ....80 C6
Rochdale OL16 ....31 C5
Romiley SK6 ....112 E3
Stockport SK7 ....123 F2
Stretford M32 ....96 C1
Walkden M28 ....78 D8
Wigan WN1 ....37 D2
Kingsway Ave M19 ....98 F1
Kingsway Bldgs M19 ....110 E5
Kingsway Cl OL8 ....153 E5
Kingsway Cres M19 ....110 E5
Kingsway Pk M41 ....95 D4
Kingsway Prim Sch M41 ..95 E4
Kingsway Sch WN1 ....37 C1
Kingsway Sch The SK8 ..122 C4
Kingsway W Ind Pk OL16 .31 B5
Kingswear Dr BL1 ....142 C1
Kingswood Gr SK5 ....99 F1
Kingswood Rd Eccles M30 .79 B4
Manchester M14 ....110 E8
Middleton M24 ....46 F3
Prestwich M25 ....62 F5
Kingthorpe Gdns BL3 ....147 F4
Kingwood Ave BL1 ....40 F8
Kingwood Cres WN5 ....54 D6
Kinlet Rd WN3 ....54 C4
Kinlett Wlk 11 M40 ....65 D2
Kinley Cl M12 ....164 F6
Kinloch Dr BL1 ....144 B7
Kinloch St Droylsden M11 ..83 A2
Oldham OL8 ....67 A4
Kinmel Ave SK5 ....112 C4
Kinmel Wlk 4 M23 ....120 F6
Kinmount Wlk M9 ....157 D6
Kinnaird Cres SK1 ....124 B8
Kinnaird Rd M20 ....110 C5
Kinnerly Gr M28 ....60 A1
Kinniside Cl WN3 ....55 A2
Kinross Ave
Garswood WN4 ....72 C4
Stockport SK2 ....124 A3
Kinross Cl BL0 ....11 A2
Kinross Dr BL3 ....40 F5
Kinross Rd M14 ....98 E3
Kinsale Wlk M23 ....120 F3
Kinsey Ave M23 ....120 F7
Kinsley Dr M28 ....60 C2
Kintbury St WN2 ....73 F7
Kintore Ave SK7 ....124 F3
Kintore Wlk 5 M40 ....156 C5
Kintyre Ave M5 ....154 E1
Kintyre Cl 5 M11 ....83 C1
Kintyre Dr BL3 ....40 E5
Kinver Cl BL3 ....146 C3
Kinver Rd M40 ....65 C2
Kipling Ave Denton M34 ..113 A7
Droylsden M43 ....84 A3
Wigan WN3 ....55 A4
Kipling Cl SK2 ....124 E7
Kipling Gr WN7 ....75 D7
Kipling Rd OL1 ....49 B2
Kipling St M7 ....155 D6
Kippax St M14 ....98 B3
Kirby Ave Atherton M46 ...58 C5
Failsworth OL9 ....65 D3
Swinton M27 ....79 D5
Kirby Rd WN7 ....75 E5
Kirby Wlk
3 Manchester M4 ....159 C2
Shaw OL2 ....149 B8
Kiribati Way WN7 ....75 E6
Kirk Rd M19 ....111 B7
Kirk St M18 ....99 D5
Kirkbank St Oldham OL9 .153 D7
Oldham OL9 ....153 D8
Kirkbeck WN7 ....76 C3
Kirkburn View BL8 ....27 C5
Kirkby Ave
Manchester M40 ....83 B7
Sale M33 ....108 C2
Kirkby Cl BL9 ....44 E7
Kirkby Dr M33 ....108 D2
Kirkby Rd Bolton BL1 ....144 B8
Culcheth WA3 ....91 F3
Kirkdale Ave M40 ....65 D2
Kirkdale Dr OL2 ....48 C5
Kirkdale Gdns WN8 ....53 A7
Kirkebrok Rd BL3 ....146 A4
Kirkfell Dr High Lane SK6 .134 E8
Tyldesley M29 ....77 B7
Kirkfell Wlk OL1 ....48 F1
Kirkgate Cl 6 M40 ....159 C3
Kirkhall La Bolton BL1 ...144 C8
Leigh WN7 ....75 F6
Kirkhall Wkshps The
BL1 ....144 C8
Kirkham Ave
Golborne WA3 ....90 E6
Manchester M18 ....99 D6
Kirkham Cl M34 ....100 F3
Kirkham Rd Gatley SK8 ...131 C8
Leigh WN7 ....75 D2
Kirkham St Abram WN2 ...74 B8
Bolton BL2 ....25 C1
Oldham OL9 ....153 E7
Salford M5 ....154 E1
Walkden M38 ....60 A5
Kirkhaven Sq M40 ....160 E4
Kirkhill Wlk 12 M40 ....65 D2
Kirkholt Wlk 11 M9 ....64 E3
Kirkhope Dr BL1 ....143 D1
Kirkhope Wlk BL1 ....143 D1
Kirklands Bolton BL2 ....25 D2
Sale M33 ....108 A2
Kirklee Ave OL9 ....48 A1
Kirklee Rd OL11 ....30 D2
Kirklees St Bury BL8 ....26 F7
Wigan WN1 ....151 E8
Kirklees Wlk M45 ....63 B8
Kirkless Ind Est WN2 ....38 B1
Kirkless La WN2 ....38 B1
Kirkless St WN2 ....38 A3
Kirkless Villas WN2 ....38 A2
Kirkley St SK14 ....167 E1
Kirklinton Dr M9 ....157 D6
Kirkman Ave M30 ....95 C8
Kirkman Cl M18 ....99 D4
Kirkman St BL9 ....44 F3
Kirkmanshulme La M12,
M18 ....165 B5
Kirkpatrick St WN2 ....57 B3
Kirkstall 27 OL12 ....139 E8
Kirkstall Ave
Heywood OL10 ....29 C3
Littleborough OL15 ....16 A7
Kirkstall Cl SK12 ....133 D4
Kirkstall Gdns M26 ....43 E5
Kirkstall Rd Middleton M24 .46 F3
Urmston M41 ....95 E3
Kirkstall Sq M13 ....163 C6
Kirkstead Cl M11 ....165 A8
Kirkstead Rd SK8 ....132 C6
Kirkstead Way WA3 ....90 A8
Kirkstile Cres WN3 ....54 E2
Kirkstile Pl M27 ....61 E4
Kirkstone WN5 ....54 C7
Kirkstone Ave M28 ....60 F1
Kirkstone Cl OL1 ....48 F1
Kirkstone Dr
Middleton M24 ....46 E2
Royton OL2 ....48 D6
Kirkstone Rd
Dukinfield SK14 ....101 C5
Failsworth M40 ....65 C2
Kirktown Wlk M11 ....165 C8
Kirkwall Dr BL2 ....148 B5
Kirkway Manchester M9 ...65 A4
Middleton M24 ....65 A7
Rochdale OL11 ....30 F2
Kirkwood Cl WN2 ....37 F2
Kirkwood Dr M40 ....159 C4
Kirtley Ave M30 ....79 D3
Kirtlington Cl OL2 ....149 A5
Kirton Lo M25 ....63 C4
Kirton Wlk M9 ....64 C5
Kitchen St 14 OL16 ....31 A8
Kitchener Ave M44 ....105 C4
Kitchener St Bolton BL3 ...42 B3
Bury BL8 ....27 B1
Kite Gr WN7 ....76 B5
Kitepool St M30 ....79 A3
Kitt Green Rd WN5 ....54 C8
Kitt's Moss La SK7 ....132 D6
Kitter St OL12 ....15 C3
Kittiwake Cl M29 ....77 A7
Kittiwake Ct SK2 ....124 F5
Kitty Wheeldon Gdns
M33 ....108 A5
Kiveton Cl M28 ....60 C2
Kiveton Dr WN4 ....73 C2
Knacks La OL12 ....14 A5
Knaresborough Cl SK5 ...99 E1
Knaresborough Rd WN2 ..56 E4
Knarr Barn La OL3 ....50 D3
Knarr La OL3 ....50 E2
Kneller Wlk OL1 ....49 D4
Knight Cres M24 ....46 D3
Knight St Ashton-u-L OL7 ...84 F2
Bolton BL1 ....145 F8
Bury BL8 ....27 C2
Hyde SK14 ....167 E1
Manchester M20 ....110 B2
Knight's Cl M25 ....63 B5
Knightley Wlk M40 ....157 D5
Knights Ct M5 ....80 A2
Knightsbridge SK1 ....169 F2
Knightsbridge Cl
14 Handforth SK9 ....131 D1
Salford M7 ....155 D8
Knightsbridge Mews
M20 ....110 B4
Knightscliffe Cres WN6 ..35 D6
Knightshill Cres WN6 ....37 A1
Knightswood BL3 ....40 F3
Knightswood Rd M8 ....156 A7
Kniveton Rd M12 ....164 F6
Knivton St SK14 ....167 F3
Knob Hall Gdns M23 ....120 F3
Knole Ave SK12 ....133 F4
Knoll St Rochdale OL11 ....30 C2
Salford M7 ....155 D7
Knoll The Mossley OL5 ....68 B1
Shaw OL2 ....149 C6
Knott Fold SK14 ....167 D1
Knott Hill La OL3 ....50 E3
Knott Hill St OL12 ....4 E6
Knott La Bolton BL1 ....23 F2
Hyde SK14 ....113 E8
Knott Lanes OL8 ....84 F8
Knott's Hos WN7 ....91 B8
Knotts Brow BL7 ....9 F4
Knowe Ave 5 M22 ....121 D1
Knowl Cl Ramsbottom BL0 ..11 C4
Reddish M34 ....100 B2
Knowl Hill Dr OL12 ....13 E2
Knowl La OL12 ....13 B5
Knowl Mdw BB4 ....1 A6
Knowl Rd Milnrow OL16 ...31 D6
Shaw OL2 ....149 C6
Knowl St Oldham OL8 ....66 C2
Stalybridge SK15 ....86 B2
Knowl Syke St OL12 ....15 C7
Knowl Top La OL3 ....69 D7
Knowl View Bury BL8 ....27 A6
Littleborough OL15 ....15 F2
Knowldale Way M12 ....164 E5
Knowle Ave OL7 ....166 A4
Knowle Dr M25 ....63 A2
Knowle Gn SK9 ....131 C3
Knowle Pk SK9 ....131 C3
Knowle Rd SK6 ....126 D6
Knowle Way 5 SK14 ....102 F2
Knowles Ave WN3 ....54 F4
Knowles Ct M6 ....80 B3
Knowles Edge St BL1 ...142 C2
Knowles Pl
1 Manchester M15 ....162 F6
Wigan WN1 ....151 E8
Knowles St Bolton BL1 ....25 A1
Ince-in-M WN3 ....151 D6
Radcliffe M26 ....44 A4
Knowls La OL4 ....67 F5
Knowls The OL8 ....66 C1
Knowlsley Grange BL1 ...40 D7
Knowsley OL4 ....68 A7
Knowsley Ave
Atherton M46 ....58 C4
Golborne WA3 ....74 B1
Oldham OL4 ....68 A7
Salford M5 ....161 B8
Urmston M41 ....95 C4
Knowsley Cres
Stockport SK1 ....124 B8
Whitworth OL12 ....4 E6
Knowsley Dr Leigh WN7 ...75 E2
Oldham OL4 ....68 A7
Swinton M27 ....79 D5
Knowsley Gn Oldham OL4 ..68 A7
Salford M5 ....161 B8
Knowsley Gr 5 BL6 ....22 D1
Knowsley Jun Sch OL4 ...68 A7
Knowsley Park Way BB4 ..1 B8
Knowsley Rd
Ainsworth BL2 ....26 C1
Bolton BL1 ....142 B2
Haslingden BB4 ....1 B8
Hazel Grove SK7 ....133 F8
Stockport SK1 ....124 B8
Whitefield M45 ....62 F8
Wigan WN6 ....37 A3
Knowsley Rd Ind Est BB4 ..1 B8
Knowsley St Bolton BL1 ..145 F7
Bury BL9 ....140 E1
Leigh WN7 ....75 D5
Manchester M8 ....159 A4
Rochdale OL12 ....139 E8
Knowsley Terr
Oldham OL4 ....68 A7
Stockport SK1 ....124 B8
Knutsford Ave
Manchester M16 ....97 D3
Reddish SK4 ....111 D7
Sale M33 ....108 E4
Knutsford Rd
Manchester M18 ....99 C4
Row-of-trees SK9,WA16 ..136 D3

Knutsford St M6 ....154 E2
Knutsford View WA15 ...129 C8
Knutshaw Cres BL3 ....40 E2
Knypersley Ave SK2 ...124 C7
Krester Ct M20 .....110 A5
Krokus Sq OL9 .....152 A7
Kyle Ct SK7 ......124 F1
Kyle Rd SK7 ......124 F1
Kylemore Ave BL3 .....144 B5
Kylemore Pl BL4 ......60 C7
Kynder St M34 ......100 F3

L

Labrador Quay M50 ....96 F7
Labtec St M27 ......62 B1
Laburnum Ave
Ashton-u-L OL6 .....85 C6
Atherton M46 ......58 E3
Bury BL8 ....26 C1
Chadderton OL9 .....46 A1
Droylsden M34 .....84 C1
Eccles M30 ......95 A8
Failsworth M35 .....83 F6
Hyde SK14 ......113 D8
Ince-in-M WN3 .....151 F6
Leigh WN7 ......75 E8
Shaw OL2 ....149 B6
Stalybridge SK15,SK16 ..101 F8
Swinton M27 ......79 E6
Whitefield M45 .....62 F7
Laburnum Cl ■ WA15 ..120 B5
Laburnum Ct BL8 .....26 F7
Laburnum Dr
Whitefield M45 .....45 A1
Wigan WN6 ......37 A4
Laburnum Gr Horwich BL6 .22 E1
Prestwich M25 .....63 A5
Tyldesley M29 .....59 D1
Laburnum La
Altrincham WA15 ....128 E8
Newhey OL16 ......32 A3
Laburnum Pk BL2 .....25 B5
Laburnum Rd
Farnworth BL4 .....60 B8
Golborne WA3 .....90 F7
Haslingden BB4 .....1 A7
Irlam M44 ....105 D5
Manchester M18 .....99 D4
Middleton M24 .....65 C8
Oldham OL8 ......84 C8
Reddish M34 ......99 F3
Urmston M41 ......95 B4
Walkden M28 ......60 E1
Laburnum St
Ashton-in-M WN4 ....73 B2
Atherton M46 .....58 E3
■ Bolton BL1 ......147 F4
Salford M6 ....154 F2
Laburnum Terr OL11 ...30 E4
Laburnum Villas OL8 ...67 A1
Laburnum Way
Littleborough OL15 ....15 F5
Stockport SK3 .....123 B5
Laburnum Wlk ■ M33 ..107 C5
Lacerta Mews M7 .....81 E3
Lacey Ave SK9 .....131 B1
Lacey Ct SK9 .....131 B1
Lacey Gn SK9 .....131 B1
Lacey Gr SK9 .....131 C1
Lacey Green Prim Sch
SK9 ....131 B1
Lackford Dr M40 ....159 C4
Lacrosse Ave OL8 ....66 C4
Lacy Ct SK9 ......131 B1
Lacy Gr M32 ......96 D1
Lacy St Stockport SK1 ...170 F8
Stretford M32 .....96 D1
Lacy Wlk M12 .....164 E8
Ladbrooke Cl OL16 ...166 C4
Ladbrooke Rd OL6 ....85 C5
Ladcastle Rd OL3 .....69 A7
Ladhill La OL3 ......69 B5
Ladies La WN2 .....56 D6
Lady Barn House Sch
SK8 ....122 D3
Lady Bridge Brow BL1 ..40 F7
Lady Bridge La BL1,BL3 ..40 F7
Lady Harriet Wlk M28 ...60 C3
Lady Kelvin Rd WA14 ..119 C6
Lady La Culcheth WA3 ...91 C1
Wigan WN3 ......54 E3
Lady Rd OL4 ......67 E6
Ladybarn Ave WA3 ....89 F7
Ladybarn Cres
Bramhall SK7 .....132 F6
Manchester M14 ....110 D7
Ladybarn Ho ■ M14 ...110 D8
Ladybarn La M14 ....110 D8
Ladybarn Mews M7 ...132 E8
Ladybarn Mews ■ M14 .110 D8
Ladybarn Prim Sch
M20 ....110 D6
Ladybarn Rd M14 ....110 D8
Ladybower SK8 .....123 C4
Ladybridge Ave M28 ...78 C8
Ladybridge Com Prim Sch
BL3 ....40 F5
Ladybridge Prim Sch
SK8 ....123 B4
Ladybridge Rd SK8 ...123 B3
Ladybridge Rise SK8 ..123 C3
Ladybrook Ave WA15 ..120 B8
Ladybrook Gr ■ SK9 ..131 D2
Ladybrook Prim Sch
SK7 ....132 F7
Ladybrook Rd SK7 ...123 C1
Ladyfield St SK9 ....137 B7

Ladyfield Terr SK9 ....137 C7
Ladyhill View M28 ....78 C8
Ladyhouse Cl OL16 ....32 A5
Ladyhouse La OL16 ....32 A5
Ladylands Ave ■ M11 ..83 C2
Ladymere Dr M28 ....78 B8
Ladys Cl SK12 .....133 E4
Ladyshore Cl M6 ....154 F1
Ladyshore Rd BL3 .....43 C2
Ladysmith Ave
Ashton-in-M WN4 ....73 C3
Bury BL9 ....28 A5
Ladysmith Dr OL6 ....85 F5
Ladysmith Rd
Ashton-u-L OL6 .....85 F5
Manchester M20 ....110 C3
Stalybridge SK15 ....86 A4
Ladysmith Sh Ctr OL6 ..85 F5
Ladysmith St Oldham OL8 .66 C3
Stockport SK3 .....170 E7
Ladysmith The OL6 ....85 F5
Ladythorn Ave SK6 ...126 A5
Ladythorn Cres SK7 ..132 F6
Ladythorn Ct M25 ....63 A2
Ladythorn Gr SK7 ...132 F6
Ladythorn Rd SK7 ...132 E6
Ladythorne Ave M25 ...63 A2
Ladythorne Dr M25 ...63 A2
Ladywell Ave M38 ....60 A5
Ladywell Cl SK7 ....124 A2
Ladywell Gr M38 ....60 A5
Ladywell Sta M5 .....80 A2
Ladywood Sch BL4 ....60 A6
Lafford La WN8 .....35 C2
Lagos Cl M14 ......98 A4
Laindon Rd M13,M14 ...98 E4
Lainton Ct ■ SK3 ...123 C8
Laithwaite Rd WN5 ...54 E7
Lake Bank OL15 .....16 A3
Lake Dr M24 ......46 F2
Lake Rd Denton M34 ..100 F4
Stalybridge SK15 .....85 F4
Stretford M17 .....96 C7
Lake Side Bury BL9 ....44 F5
Leigh WN7 ......75 D6
Littleborough OL15 ....16 A3
Lake Side Cotts WN1 ...20 C1
Lake St Bolton BL3 ...145 F5
Leigh WN7 ......76 A6
Stockport SK2 .....124 B5
Lake View M9 .....65 A2
Lake Wlk WN5 .....54 E7
Lakeland Ave WN4 ....73 C4
Lakeland Cres BL9 ....44 E6
Lakeland Ct ■ M24 ....46 D2
Lakeland Dr OL2 .....48 C8
Lakelands Dr BL3 ....40 F5
Lakenheath Cl ■ BL1 ..24 F6
Lakenheath Dr BL1 ...25 A6
Lakers Dr WN5 .....53 E6
Lakes Rd Dukinfield SK16 ..101 C8
Marple SK6 ......126 B5
Lakes Terr WN2 .....56 A7
Lakeside Gatley SK8 ..122 C3
Hadfield SK13 .....104 A6
Prestwich M7 .....63 D1
Lakeside Ave
Ashton-u-L OL7 .....84 F4
Bolton BL3 ......42 A2
Orrell WN5 ......53 E3
Walkden M28 .....60 D5
Lakeside Cl M18 .....99 F6
Lakeside Dr SK12 ....133 E5
Lakeside Gn SK2 ....124 C6
Lakeside Way BL9 ...140 F1
Lakin St M40 ......83 A7
Laleham Gn SK7 ....123 D3
Lamb Cl M12 ......164 F5
Lamb Ct M3 ......158 E2
Lamb La Ashley WA14 ..128 D4
Salford M3 ......158 E2
Lamb St WN1 ......37 E1
Lamb Wlk ■ M34 ....113 A7
Lambarde Ho WN5 ....54 B6
Lamberhead Ind Est
WN5 ....54 B5
Lamberhead Rd WN5 ..54 C6
Lambert Dr M33 ....107 E6
Lambert St OL7 ....100 F8
Lamberton Dr M23 ...120 E6
Lambeth Ave M35 ....84 B8
Lambeth Cl BL6 .....22 D3
Lambeth Gr SK6 ....113 A5
Lambeth Rd
Failsworth M40 .....83 C4
Reddish SK5 ......111 F7
Lambeth St M46 .....58 B3
Lambeth Terr OL11 ...139 D5
Lambgates SK13 ....104 A5
Lambley Cl WN7 ....75 D8
Lambourn Cl Bolton BL3 .145 F5
Poynton SK12 .....133 D4
Lambourn Rd M41 ....94 D4
Lambourne Cl M22 ...130 D8
Lambourne Gr ■ OL16 ..31 F5
Lambrook Wlk M40 ...83 D4
Lambs Fold SK4 ....111 D5
Lambton Rd
Manchester M21 ....109 D8
Swinton M28 ......79 C7
Lambton St Bolton BL3 .146 C2
Eccles M30 ......79 B3
Wigan WN5 ......54 D5
Lamburn Ave M40 ....65 D2
Lamorna Cl M7 .....81 B7
Lamphey Cl BL1 .....40 D8
Lamplight Way M27 ...80 E7

Lamport Cl M1 .....163 B7
Lamport Ct M1 .....163 B7
Lampson St M8 .....158 E4
Lampton Cl WA14 ....119 D7
Lamsholme Cl ■ M19 ..99 A2
Lanark Ave M22 ....121 E8
Lanark Cl
Hazel Grove SK7 ....125 A2
Heywood OL10 .....28 F1
Lanbury Dr M8 .....155 F7
Lancashire Cotts OL5 ...68 D1
Lancashire Ct OL9 ...152 C5
Lancashire Fusiliers
Regimental Mus* BL8 **27** B1
Lancashire Hill SK4,SK5
SK5 ....169 E3
Lancashire Mining Mus*
M5 ....154 D3
Lancashire Rd M31 ...105 E2
Lancaster Ave
Atherton M46 .....58 E2
Failsworth M35 .....83 E7
Golborne WA3 .....90 C8
Haslingden BB4 .....1 B8
Horwich BL6 ......22 D2
Middleton M24 .....65 C7
Ramsbottom BL0 .....11 A4
Stalybridge SK15 ....86 A3
Tyldesley M29 .....59 A3
Urmston M41 ......95 E3
Whitefield M45 .....63 A7
Lancaster Cl
Adlington PR6 .....21 B7
Bolton BL2 ......148 A7
Hazel Grove SK7 ....133 D8
Romiley SK6 ......113 A1
Lancaster Ct
Failsworth M40 .....83 C4
■ Leigh WN7 ......76 B4
■ Manchester M19 ..110 F8
Little Lever BL3 .....43 B4
Manchester M25 ....63 C2
Lancaster Ho Royton OL2 .48 D5
■ Stockport SK3 ...170 E8
Lancaster PI PR6 ....21 A8
Lancaster Rd
Denton M34 ......100 F1
Droylsden M43 .....83 F3
Handforth SK9 ....131 E1
Hindley WN2 ......56 F5
Irlam M44 ......105 D5
Manchester M20 ....110 A3
Salford M6 ......80 B4
Wigan WN5 ......36 D1
Lancaster Sq OL2 ....48 D5
Lancaster St
Chadderton OL9 .....66 A3
■ Manchester M9 ...151 D6
Mossley OL5 ......68 B1
Radcliffe M26 .....43 E3
Stockport SK1 .....112 A2
Lancaster Terr
■ Bolton BL1 .....143 E2
Rochdale OL11 .....13 D2
Lancaster Way BL5 ....39 C2
Lancaster Wlk
■ Bolton BL1 .....143 E2
Wigan WN5 ......36 D1
Lancasterian Sch M20 .109 E4
Lance Wood Pl WN5 ...54 D6
Lancelot Rd M22 ....121 F2
Lancelyn Dr SK9 ....137 D8
Lanchester Dr BL3 ...145 D5
Lanchester St M40 ....83 A5
Lancing Ave M20 ....110 D3
Lancing Wlk OL9 ....152 A6
Land Gate OL12 .....4 F5
Land Gate La WN4 ....73 B8
Land La SK9 ......137 C6
Land St M46 ......150 B8
Landau Dr M28 .....59 F3
Landcross Rd M14 ....98 C1
Landedmans BL5 .....58 A7
Landells Wlk M40 ....83 A5
Landers Gdns M25 ....63 C3
Landgate Ind Est WN4 .73 A8
Landkey Cl ■ M23 ...108 F2
Landmark Ct BL1 ....23 F1
Landor Cl WA3 .....90 E8
Landor Ct M34 .....99 F3
Landore Cl M26 .....44 B4
Landos Ct ■ M40 ...159 C3
Landos Rd M40 ....159 C3
Landrace Dr M28 .....78 B6
Lands End Rd M24 ....64 B7
Landsberg Rd M35 ....84 B8
Landsberg Terr M35 ...84 B8
Landseer Dr SK6 ....126 B7
Landseer St OL4 .....67 A5
Landside WN7 .....75 F7
Lane Brow OL4 .....68 B5
Lane Dr OL4 ......68 B5
Lane End Eccles M30 ...79 F1
Heywood OL10 .....14 F1
Lane End Cl M35 .....84 A6
Lane End Prim Sch SK8 .123 C2
Lane End Rd Bacup OL13 ..4 A8
■ Wigan WN5 .....54 D5
Lane Ends Romiley SK6 ..113 B3
Lane Head Rd
Mossley OL4,OL5 ....68 A3
Oldham OL4 ......68 A3
Lane Mdw OL2 ....149 A6
Lane The BL1 ......40 D7
Lanegate SK14 .....113 D8

Lanesfield Wlk M8 ...156 C8
Laneside Ave OL2 ....49 D7
Laneside Cl OL15 .....16 A6
Laneside Dr SK7 ....124 A1
Laneside Rd
Manchester M20 ....122 C8
Rowarth SK22 .....105 B8
Lanfield Dr M8 .....156 C8
Lanfield Dr M8 .....155 F7
Langcliff Wlk ■ BL1 ..143 F2
Langcliffe Cl WA3 .....91 E3
Langcliffe Wlk M18 ...165 C5
Langcroft Dr ■ M40 ...83 C5
Langdale Ave
Golborne WA3 .....74 C1
Ince-in-M WN2 .....56 B8
Manchester M19 ....111 B8
Oldham OL8 ......66 D4
Royton OL16 ......48 C8
Wigan WN1 ......37 B3
Langdale Cl
Altrincham WA15 ...119 E5
Denton M34 ......100 E1
Gatley SK8 ......122 C3
High Lane SK6 .....134 E8
Langdale Cres
Adlam WN2 ......74 B8
Wigan WN5 ......54 B8
Langdale Ct M8 ....156 B6
Langdale Dr
Middleton M24 .....46 F3
Walkden M28 .....60 F1
Whitefield BL9 .....45 A3
Langdale Gr WN2 ....56 B2
Langdale Rd
Bramhall SK7 .....132 C5
Hindley WN2 ......56 E5
Manchester M14 ....98 D4
Partington M31 ....105 E3
Reddish SK4 ......111 B4
Romiley SK6 ......113 B4
Sale M33 ....107 E1
Stretford M32 .....96 C3
Langdale St Bolton BL3 .147 E3
Farnworth BL4 .....60 E8
Leigh WN7 ......75 E5
Langdale Terr SK15 ...86 A4
Langden Cl Culcheth WA3 .91 D4
Shaw OL2 ....149 A8
Langdon Cl BL1 ....143 D1
Langdon Coll M7 .....63 F1
Langfield Ave M14 ....97 D3
Langfield Cres M43 ...84 C2
Langfield Wlk M6 ...154 F2
Langford Dr Irlam M44 ..94 A1
Leigh WN7 ......75 E2
Langford Rd
Manchester,Heaton Moor
SK4 ....168 C4
Manchester,Withington
M20 ....110 A6
Langford St M34 ....100 F3
Langham Cl BL1 .....25 A5
Langham Ct
Manchester M20 ....109 F4
Stretford M32 .....96 A4
Langham Gr WA15 ...120 B8
Langham Ho SK4 ....168 B2
Langham Rd
Altrincham WA14 ...119 C2
Oldham OL8 ......66 D3
Salford M6 ......154 F2
Standish WN6 .....19 E2
Stockport SK4 ....168 B1
Langham St
■ Ashton-u-L OL7 ...85 A5
Wigan WN5 ......36 C1
Langholm Cl WN3 ....54 D3
Langholm Dr BL2 ....42 F6
Langholme Cl M15 ...162 D7
Langholme PI M30 ...79 B2
Langholme Way OL10 ..28 F1
Langland Cl
Manchester,Charlestown
M9 ....64 E4
Manchester,North Reddish
M19 ....99 D2
Langland Dr M30 .....95 C7
Langley Ave
Hazel Grove SK7 ....124 B1
Middleton M24 .....46 E4
Ince-le-Wd Ct WA12 ...89 C1
Oldham OL4 ......67 A7
Prestwich M25 .....63 B6
Langley Cl Golborne WA3 .74 E1
Standish WN6 .....19 E2
Urmston M41 ......95 C4
Langley Cres M25 ....63 B6
Langley Ct Hadfield SK13 .104 A5
■ Manchester M7 ...81 B5
Langley Dr ■ Bolton BL3 .144 C5
Boothstown M28 ....77 F6
Handforth SK9 ....131 E3
Langley Gdns M25 ....63 B6
Langley Grange M25 ..63 B6
Langley Hall Rd M25 ..63 B6
Langley Ho ■ M24 ....46 F1
Langley La M24,OL10 ..46 D4
Langley Platt La M29,
M46 ....76 D8
Langley Rd
Manchester M14 ....98 D1
Manchester,Charlestown
M6,M27 ......80 F7

Langley Rd continued
Prestwich M25 .....63 A5
Sale M33 ....107 E4
Langley Rd S M6,M27 ..81 A5
Langley St WN5 .....54 D6
Langness St ■ M11 ...83 C1
Lango St ■ M16 .....97 C4
Langport Ave M12 ...164 E6
Langroyd Wlk ■ M8 ..155 F7
Langset Ave ■ M22 ...56 D6
Langside Ave
■ Gamesley SK13 ...171 D1
Salford M6 ....80 C3
Langsett Gn ■ SK13 ..171 D1
Langsett Gr ■ SK13 ..171 D1
Langsett La SK13 ....171 D1
Langsett Terr ■ SK13 .171 D1
Langshaw Rd BL3 ....144 C5
Langshaw St
Manchester M16 ....97 C4
Salford M5,M6 .....154 F1
Langshaw Wlk BL3 ...144 C5
Langside Ave M9 ....64 E4
Langside Dr BL3 .....40 C4
Langston St M3 .....158 F3
Langstone Cl BL6 .....22 B3
Langthorne St M19 ...111 B8
Langthorne Wlk BL3 ..145 D5
Langton Ave WN6 ....19 E1
Langton Cl
Newton-le-W WA12 ...89 A4
Oldham M35 ......84 C8
Langton Gn SK7 ....124 A1
Langton PI WN6 ....19 F1
Langton St Heywood OL10 .29 D3
Middleton M24 .....65 A8
Salford M6 ......154 E2
Langton Terr OL11 ....30 E4
Langtree Cl M28 .....78 B8
Langtree La WN6 .....19 D3
Langworthy Ave M38 ..60 B4
Langworthy Rd
Manchester M40 .....83 A7
Salford M6 ......154 F3
Langworthy Road Prim Sch
M6 ....154 F3
Langworthy Sta M5 ..154 F1
Lanhill Dr M8 .....156 C6
Lankro Way M30,M17 ..79 F1
Lanreath Wlk ■ M8 ..156 B6
Lansbury Ho ■ M16 ...97 D3
Lansbury St WN5 .....54 A6
Lansdale Gdns M19 ..111 B8
Lansdale St Eccles M30 ..95 A8
Walkden M28 .....60 D5
Lansdown Cl SK8 ....132 C7
Lansdowne WA3 ......91 E2
Lansdowne Ave
Droylsden M34 .....84 C1
Romiley SK6 ......113 D2
Lansdowne Cl
■ Bolton BL2 ......25 B1
Ramsbottom BL0 ...138 B5
Lansdowne Ct OL9 ..152 B6
Lansdowne Dr M28 ...60 C2
Lansdowne Ho M20 ..110 B2
Lansdowne Rd
Altrincham WA14 ...119 D6
Bolton BL2 ......25 B2
Chadderton OL9 ....152 C6
Eccles M30 ......79 D3
Flixton M41 ......106 E8
Manchester M8 .....64 F5
Over Hulton M46 ....58 F5
Sale M33 ....108 A6
Lansdowne Rd N M41 ..94 E1
Lansdowne St ■ OL11 ..30 C5
Lanstead Dr M40 ....160 E2
Lantern View SK22 ...127 B1
Lapwing Cl
Newton-le-W WA12 ...89 C3
Rochdale OL11 .....29 E7
Lapwing Ct ■ SK15 ...86 A4
Lapwing La ■ M20 ...110 A5
Larch Ave Cheadle SK8 .123 A1
Brinnington SK5 ....112 C6
Manchester M20 ....110 A5
Larch Ave Cheadle SK8 .123 A1
Radcliffe M26 .....44 B1
Stretford M32 .....96 D1
Swinton M27 ......79 C6
Wigan WN5 ......54 A6
Larch Cl Billinge WN5 ..71 D5
Failsworth M35 .....83 F6
Golborne WA3 .....90 F6
Marple SK6 ......125 E5
Poynton SK12 .....133 F3
Rawtenstall BB4 .....2 E8
Sale M33 ....108 A4
Larch Gr Atherton M46 ..58 C4
Chadderton OL9 ....152 B8
Oldham OL4 ......67 E8
Swinton M27 ......61 B2
Larch Rd Eccles M30 ...79 A4
Leigh WN7 ......75 C5
Partington M31 ....105 E3
Larch St Bury BL9 ...141 B2
Oldham OL8 ......66 E3
Larch Way SK13 ....116 F8
Larches The OL5 .....68 E1
Larchview Rd M24 ....65 C8
Larchway Bramhall SK7 .132 C7
High Lane SK6 .....134 F7

Larchway continued
Milnrow OL16 ....31 D7
Larchwood
Chadderton OL9 ....65 E8
Cheadle SK8 ....122 D6
Larchwood Ave M9 ......157 F7
Larchwood Cl M33 ......107 C4
Larchwood Dr
Wigan WN1 ....37 B4
Wilmslow SK9 ....137 E8
Larchwood St BL1 ......143 F2
Larden Wlk ⓵ M8 ......155 F6
Larel Trad Est OL2 ......49 A2
Largs Wlk ⑦ M23 ......120 F6
Lark Hill Farnworth BL4 ..60 E7
Stalybridge SK15 ....86 A4
Lark Hill Com Prim Sch
M6 ....154 F2
Lark Hill Ct M24 ....65 A8
Lark Hill La OL3 ....51 A4
Lark Hill Pl OL12 ....14 E1
Lark Hill Prim Sch SK3 ..123 C8
Lark Hill Rd
Stockport SK3 ....123 C8
Uppermill OL3 ....51 A3
Lark St Bolton BL1 ......145 F8
Farnworth BL4 ....60 D7
Oldham OL1 ....49 D3
Larkfield Ave
Walkden M38 ....59 F5
Wigan WN1 ....37 B4
Larkfield Cl
Ashton-u-L OL7 ....85 B7
Ramsbottom BL8 ....10 F1
Larkfield Gr Bolton BL2 ..148 B8
Walkden M38 ....59 F5
Larkhill Ave M40 ....36 F8
Larkhill Cl WA15 ....120 B6
Larkhill Rd SK8 ....123 C5
Larkhill Rise M22 ......121 E5
Larkhill Wlk ⑧ M8 .....156 B6
Larks Rise M43 ....84 D3
Larkside Ave M28 ....60 E3
Larkspur Cl M7 ....75 F3
Larkswood Dr SK2 .....124 F5
Larkwood Cl SK15 ......86 E7
Larmuth Ave M21 .....109 C6
Larne Ave Stockport SK3 .123 B7
Larne St M11 ....165 A8
Larwood Ave SK4 ......168 B1
Lascar Ave M5 ....161 A8
Lashbrook Cl M40 .....160 D4
Lassell Fold SK14 .....102 B6
Lassell St M11 ....99 F7
Lassington Ave M11 ....99 D8
Last Drop Village The*
BL7 ....9 A1
Lastingham St M40 .....83 C6
Latchford St OL7 ......166 A4
Latchmere Rd M14 ....110 C8
Latham Ave WA12 ....89 C4
Latham Cl SK6 ....112 F5
Latham Ho WA12 ....89 B4
Latham La WN5 ....54 A8
Latham Rd BL6 ....21 C3
Latham St Bolton BL1 ...143 F2
Droylsden M11 ....99 F7
Lathbury Rd M40,M9 ...157 D6
Lathom Gr M33 ....108 A3
Lathom Hall Ave OL4 ....68 A7
Lathom Rd Irlam M44 ..105 F8
Manchester M20 ....110 D7
Lathom St ⑥ BL9 ......141 A4
Latimer Cl ② WN5 ......53 F7
Latimer St OL4 ....67 A6
Latrigg Cres M24 ....46 C2
Latrobe St M43 ....100 A8
Lauderdale Cres M13 ..163 C6
Launceston Cl OL8 ......67 C4
Launceston Dr SK7 ....132 F7
Launceston Rd
Hindley WN2 ....57 C3
Radcliffe M26 ....43 D5
Laundry St M6 ....154 F4
Laura St BL9 ....11 C2
Laureate Way M34 .....113 A7
Laureate's Pl OL4 ....68 B7
Laurel Ave Chadderton OL9 .65 E8
Cheadle SK8 ....122 D6
Manchester M14 ....98 A2
Newton-le-W WA12 ......89 D3
Laurel Bank Hyde SK14 .113 C8
Stalybridge SK15 ......102 B8
Laurel Bank Gdns M9 ...64 D3
Laurel Cres WN2 ....57 A3
Laurel Ct Manchester SK4 .168 B4
⑱ Rochdale OL16 ....31 B6
Laurel Dr
Altrincham WA15 ......120 B4
Walkden M38 ....60 A4
Laurel End La SK4 .....168 A3
Laurel Gn M34 ....101 A2
Laurel Gr
Ashton-in-M WN4 ....73 B4
Golborne WA3 ....87 F7
Leigh WN7 ....75 E8
Salford M5 ....80 C2
Laurel Ho SK4 ....168 B4
Laurel St Bolton BL1 ...144 C7
Bury BL9 ....141 B2
Bury,Tottington BL8 ....26 F6
⑥ Oldham OL4 ....67 B6

Laurel St continued
Stockport SK4 ....169 E2
Wigan WN5 ....54 F7
Laurel Way SK8 ....132 C8
Laurel Wlk M31 ....105 E2
Laurels Dr OL15 ....15 F2
Laurels The
② Bolton BL1 ....145 F8
Mossley OL5 ....68 D1
Laurence Cl M12 ......165 B6
Laurence Lowry Ct ②
M27 ....61 F1
Lauria Terr BL2 ....26 D1
Laurie Pl ② OL12 ....14 F1
Laurieston Ct SK8 ....122 C5
Lausanne Rd
Manchester M20 ....110 B7
Stockport SK7 ....123 E3
Lavender Cl
Altrincham M23 ....108 E1
Sale M33 ....107 C5
Lavender Hill BB4 ....1 F8
Lavender Rd
Farnworth BL4 ....42 A1
Oldham OL4 ....67 A6
Wigan WN6 ....36 F3
Lavender St M26 ....43 D3
Lavender Wlk
Downall Green WN4 ......72 D5
Partington M31 ....105 E2
Lavenders Brow SK1 ...169 F1
Lavenham Ave M11 ......83 D1
Lavenham Cl
Hazel Grove SK7 ....133 E8
Whitefield BL9 ....44 F3
Laverton Cl BL9 ....28 E1
Lavington Ave SK8 ....123 A6
Lavington Gr M18 ......99 D4
Lavinia St M30 ....79 B2
Lavister Ave M19 ......110 E3
Law St Rochdale OL11 ...30 C4
Walsden OL14 ....6 B7
Lawefield Cres M27 ....61 D4
Lawers Ave OL9 ....152 A8
Lawflat OL12 ....15 C5
Lawler Ave M5 ....161 B6
Lawn Cl OL8 ....67 C3
Lawn Dr
Altrincham WA15 ......119 E6
Swinton M27 ....79 F7
Lawn St BL1 ....143 D1
Lawnbank Cl M24 ....46 E1
Lawndale Cl M26 ....44 B2
Lawnfield Cl SK7 ......123 D2
Lawnfold SK13 ....171 E4
Lawngreen Ave M21 ...109 A7
Lawnhurst Trad Est SK3 .123 B5
Lawns Ave WN5 ....53 C5
Lawns The
Altrincham WA14 ......119 C3
Hindley WN2 ....56 C5
Wilmslow SK9 ....136 E4
Lawnside Mews M20 ...110 A5
Lawnswood OL13 ....30 C3
Lawnswood Dr
Pendlebury M27 ....80 B6
Tyldesley M29 ....59 D1
Lawnswood Park Rd M27 .80 B6
Lawrence Cl OL12 ....14 A1
Lawrence Ct WN2 ....74 B8
Lawrence Pl SK12 .....133 D2
Lawrence Rd
Altrincham WA14 ......119 C6
Hazel Grove SK7 ....124 E3
Urmston M41 ....94 E3
Lawrence St Bury BL9 ..44 F1
Stockport SK1 ....169 E1
Lawrie Ave BL0 ....138 B6
Lawson Ave Gatley SK8 .122 B5
Leigh WN7 ....75 E1
Lawson Cl Middleton M24 .47 A4
Swinton M27 ....79 C7
Lawson Dr WA15 ....120 A6
Lawson Gr M33 ....108 A6
Lawson Rd Bolton BL1 ..142 C2
Horwich BL6 ....22 C4
Lawson St ② Bolton BL1 .143 E1
Manchester M9 ....64 C2
Lawson Wlk M34 ....113 A8
Lawton Ave SK7 ....132 E8
Lawton Cl Culcheth WA3 .91 E3
Romiley SK6 ....112 F1
Lawton Fold OL4 ....68 B7
Lawton Moor Rd M23 ..109 A1
Lawton St OL6 ....166 C3
Lawton Sq OL3 ....50 F4
Lawton St Delph OL3 ....50 F4
Droylsden M43 ....84 B2
Hyde SK14 ....167 E3
Manchester M11 ....99 D7
Rochdale OL11 ....15 A1
② Stalybridge SK15 .....86 B1
Laxey Ave M40 ....83 B7
Laxey Cres WN7 ....75 C7
Laxey St M40 ....83 B7
Laxfield Dr M41 ....94 D3
Laxford Gr BL3 ....40 E6
Layard St OL6 ....166 B3
Laycock Ave Bolton BL2 .25 B6
Stalybridge SK15 ....86 E4
Laycock Cres ④ M35 ...83 F7
Laycock Dr SK16 ......102 A7
Laycock Gr M35 ....83 F7
Laycock St OL16 ....15 D3
Laycock Way M34 .....112 F8
Layfield Cl M26 ....26 D7
Layland Ave M9 ....91 E4
Laystall St M1 ....159 B1

Laythe Barn Cl OL16 ....31 E6
Layton Ave SK14 ......101 C2
Layton Cl SK1 ....124 A8
Layton Dr Kearsley BL4 .60 F6
Romiley SK6 ....113 C3
Layton St M40 ....160 D2
Lazenby Cres WN2 ......38 F3
Lazonby Ave WN2 ....38 F3
Lazonby Wlk ⑦ M13 ....98 F4
Le Bas Ho M20 ....109 F6
Le Gendre St BL2 ....25 B2
Le Mans Cres BL1 .....145 F7
Lea Ct Failsworth M35 ..83 E7
Manchester SK4 ....168 B4
Lea Dr M9 ....64 F3
Lea Gate Cl Bolton BL2 ..25 D5
Wigan WN3 ....54 E3
Lea Mount Dr BL9 ....28 D4
Lea Rd Gatley SK8 .....122 B1
Manchester SK4 ....168 B4
Lea St M34 ....150 A7
Lea Vale Cl M38 ....59 F4
Lea View Royton OL2 ....48 C3
Wigan WN1 ....37 F1
Leabank St ⑤ M19 ......99 A2
Leabrook Dr M40 ....83 E8
Leaburn Dr M19 ....110 E4
Leach Cl OL16 ....15 C2
Leach St Bolton BL3 ...145 E5
④ Farnworth BL4 ....42 E1
Manchester M18 ....165 B6
Milnrow OL16 ....31 F5
Prestwich M25 ....62 F4
Rochdale OL16 ....31 B6
Shaw OL2 ....149 C6
Leach Wlk OL4 ....67 E8
Leaches Rd BL0 ....11 D8
Leaconfield Dr M28 .....78 F7
Leacroft WN4 ....72 F6
Leacroft Ave BL2 ....42 D5
Leacroft Rd M21 ....109 D5
Leadale Cl WN6 ....19 D1
Leadale Rise OL4 ....68 A6
Leader St
Wigan,Norley WN5 ......54 C6
Wigan,Scholes WN1 ....151 E8
Leader Williams Rd M44 .93 F1
Leaf St Bolton BL3 .....148 C5
Manchester M15 ....162 F6
Reddish SK5 ....111 E7
Leafield M29 ....59 C1
Leafield Ave M20 ......110 D4
Leafield Cl M26 ....43 E3
Leafield Dr Cheadle SK8 .131 F6
Worsley M28 ....78 A6
Leafield Rd SK12 ......135 C6
Leaford Ave M34 ....100 D4
Leaford Cl M34 ....100 D4
Leagate M41 ....95 E1
League St OL16 ....31 A5
Leah St OL15 ....16 B5
Leaholme Cl M40 ....83 F5
Leak St M40 ....161 C6
Leal Holme Ave M22 ....38 A3
Leam St OL6 ....85 D4
Leamington Ave Bury BL9 .27 E8
Manchester M20 ....109 F4
Newton-le-W WA12 ......89 C3
Leamington Ct ③ SK5 ..111 E7
Leamington Rd
Eccles M30 ....79 B3
Reddish SK5 ....111 E7
Urmston M41 ....95 C3
Leamington St
Manchester M11 ....99 D7
Oldham OL4 ....67 A6
Rochdale OL12 ....139 E8
Leamore Wlk ⑨ M9 .....64 E2
Leander Cl M9 ....64 E2
Leander Dr OL11 ....30 D1
Leas The WA15 ....120 C3
Leaside Ave OL1 ....48 B2
Leaside Cl OL12 ....14 D2
Leaside Dr M20 ....110 D5
Leaside Gr M28 ....60 E3
Leaside Way SK9 ......137 C6
Leaton Ave M23 ....121 A6
Leavengreave Ct OL12 ...4 D4
Leaway Ince-in-M WN2 .151 F7
Wardle OL12 ....15 C6
Lecester Rd M8 ....156 A6
Leckenby Cl ② M28 .....78 A6
Leconfield Dr M9 ....64 E4
Leconfield Rd M30 ......78 F1
Lecturers Cl BL3 ......145 F5
Ledbrooke Cl M5 ......161 B8
Ledburn Cl M15 ....162 D6
Ledburn Ct M15 ....162 D6
Ledbury Ave M41 ....95 D4
Ledbury Cl M24 ....65 A6
Ledbury Rd M35 ....83 E7
Ledbury St Leigh WN7 ..75 F6
Ledbury Wlk M9 ....64 E5
Ledge Ley SK8 ....131 E8
Ledmore Gr WN4 ....72 D3
Ledsham Ave M9 ....64 A5
Ledson Rd M23 ....120 F5
Ledward La WA14 ......119 B2
Lee Ave Altrincham WA14 .119 C2
Bolton BL3 ....147 D3
Lee Bank BL5 ....58 B8
Lee Cres M32 ....96 E2
Lee Cross M32 ....96 C2
Lee Dale Cl M34 ....101 A2
Lee Fold M29 ....77 C7
Lee Gate BL2 ....25 D5

Lee Gr BL4 ....59 F8
Lee Head SK13 ....115 C5
Lee Ho M22 ....121 E8
Lee La Abram WN2 ......74 B8
Horwich BL6 ....22 B4
Lee Mount SK13 ....116 C7
Lee Rd Bacup OL13 ......3 E8
Manchester M9 ....157 D8
Lee Side OL3 ....51 D4
Lee St Atherton M46 ....58 D2
Bury BL9 ....27 F8
Littleborough OL15 .....16 B6
Middleton M24 ....46 F3
Oldham OL8 ....153 E5
Stockport SK1 ....169 F1
Uppermill OL3 ....69 B8
Lee Vale Dr SK13 .....115 C2
Lee's St OL13 ....4 C8
Leech Ave OL6 ....85 E5
Leech Brook Ave M34 ..100 C5
Leech Brook Cl M34 ...100 C6
Leech St Hyde SK14 ...167 F7
Stalybridge SK15 ....86 A1
Leedale St M12 ....99 A2
Leeds Cl M26 ....45 B3
Leeds St WN3 ....150 B7
Leeds St Ind Est WN3 .150 B7
Leefields Cl OL3 ....69 B8
Leegate Cl SK4 ....110 F4
Leegate Dr M9 ....64 F4
Leegate Gdns SK4 .....168 A4
Leegate Rd SK4 ....168 A4
Leegrange Rd M9 ....64 E1
Leek St M26 ....43 E3
Leemans Hill St BL8 ....27 A5
Lees Ave M34 ....100 E3
Lees Brook Pk OL4 .....67 D6
Lees Cotts BL7 ....9 C2
Lees Gr OL4 ....67 D5
Lees Hall Cres M14 ...110 D8
Lees Hall Ct ⑨ M14 ...110 D8
Lees La WN8 ....35 B6
Lees New Rd OL4,OL6 ..67 D2
Lees Park Ave M43 .....84 C2
Lees Park Way M43 ....84 C2
Lees Rd Adlington PR6 ..21 B8
Ashton-u-L OL6 ....85 D7
Bramhall SK7 ....132 D5
Oldham OL4 ....67 C6
Lees Row SK13 ....104 C5
Lees St ② Abram WN2 ..74 B8
Ashton-u-L OL6 ....166 A4
Droylsden M43 ....84 B2
Manchester M11,M18 ....99 E6
Middleton M24 ....65 D7
② Mossley OL5 ....68 C2
Oldham OL8 ....85 A8
Shaw OL2 ....149 B7
⑥ Stalybridge SK15 .....86 A2
Swinton M27 ....61 F1
Lees St OL2 ....149 C7
Leesfield OL6 ....166 A4
Leeside SK4 ....168 A1
Leesstone Rd M22 .....121 E6
Leesway OL4 ....67 E5
Leesway Dr M34 ....101 A2
Leeswood Ave M21 ....109 C6
Leewood M27 ....61 D4
Leff Bank M3 ....158 E1
Legh Ct M33 ....108 E3
Legh Dr Droylsden M34 .84 B1
Romiley SK6 ....113 B6
Legh Rd High Lane SK12 .135 A6
Sale M33 ....108 E3
Salford M7 ....155 D8
Legh St Ashton-in-M WN4 .73 B2
Eccles M30 ....79 C1
Golborne WA3 ....90 A8
Newton-le-W WA12 ......89 A3
Salford M7 ....155 D7
Leghorn Wlk ⑭ M11 ...160 F1
Legion Gr M7 ....155 E6
Legwood Ct M41 ....95 C2
Leicester Ave
Denton M34 ....100 F1
Droylsden M43 ....83 F3
Hindley WN2 ....56 F6
Horwich BL6 ....22 A3
Sale M33 ....120 A8
Salford M7 ....155 F8
Leicester Ct M7* 63 F1
Leicester Dr SK13 .....116 F8
Leicester Rd
Altrincham WA15 ......119 F2
Failsworth M35 ....84 A6
Sale M33 ....108 B5
Salford M7 ....155 F8
Tyldesley M29 ....59 A2
Whitefield M45 ....44 D1
Leicester St
Ashton-u-L OL7 ....166 B4
Reddish SK5 ....99 F2
Rochdale OL11 ....31 A5
Leigh Arc ④ WN1 ......150 C8
Leigh Ave Marple SK6 ..125 E6
Swinton M27 ....79 D5
Leigh Bsns Pk WN7 .....76 B8
Leigh CE Inf Sch WN7 ..75 E5
Leigh CE Jun Sch WN7 .75 E5
Leigh Cl Bury BL8 ....26 F2
Poynton SK12 ....133 E4
Leigh Comm BL5 ....39 E1
Leigh Commerce Pk
WN7 ....76 B2
Leigh Fold SK14 ....101 E5

Leigh Infmy WN7 ....76 A6
Leigh La BL8 ....27 B3
Leigh Prim Sch SK14 ..167 F2
Leigh Rd
Altrincham WA15 ......119 E2
Atherton M46 ....58 B2
Hindley WN2 ....57 B2
Leigh WN7 ....75 E6
Westhoughton BL5 ......57 F6
Westhoughton BL5 ......57 F8
Wilmslow SK9 ....136 D5
Worsley M28 ....78 C6
Leigh St Aspull WN2 ....38 F3
Bury BL8 ....27 B3
Farnworth BL4 ....60 D8
① Heywood OL10 ....29 C2
Hyde SK:4 ....167 E2
Leigh WN2 ....57 B1
Westhoughton BL5 ......31 D7
Wigan WN1 ....151 D7
Leigh St Peters CE Jun Sch
WN7 ....75 C5
Leigh Westleigh Meth Prim
Sch WN7 ....75 D8
Leighbrook Rd M14 ....110 B8
Leighs Cotts WA15 ....120 C4
Leighton Ave
Atherton M46 ....58 B3
Bolton BL1 ....144 B8
Littleborough OL15 .....15 F2
Leighton Dr
Golborne WN7 ....75 B1
Marple SK6 ....126 C8
Leighton Rd M16 ......97 C4
Leighton St Atherton M46 .58 B3
Manchester M40 ....83 A8
Leinster Rd M27 ....79 E7
Leinster St BL4 ....60 C7
Leith Ave M33 ....108 E4
Leith Rd M33 ....108 E4
Lemnos St OL1 ....67 A7
Lemon St M29 ....76 F8
Lemonpark Ind Est OL10 .46 E8
Len Cox Wlk ⑧ M4 ....159 B2
Lena St Bolton BL1 ....143 F2
Manchester M1 ....159 B1
Lench Rd BB4 ....2 D8
Lench St BB4 ....2 F8
Lenfield La OL1 ....48 E1
Lenham Ave M30 ....83 D5
Lenham Cl SK5 ....112 B6
Lenham Gdns BL2 ......42 E6
Lenham Twrs SK5 .....112 B6
Lenham Wlk M22 ......130 D8
Lennox Gdns BL3 ....40 F5
Lennox St OL6 ....166 C3
Lennox Wlk OL10 ....28 F1
Lenora St BL3 ....146 B4
Lenten Gr OL10 ....46 E7
Lenthall Wlk ⑳ M8 ....155 F7
Lentmead Dr M40 ......65 A1
Lenton Gdns M22 .....121 E5
Leominster Dr M22 ....121 F2
Leominster Rd M24 .....65 B6
Leonard St WN7 ....75 B4
Leonard St Bolton BL3 .147 E3
Rochdale OL11 ....30 C1
Leonardin Cl OL2 ....48 F8
Leopold Ave M20 ......110 A5
Leopold St
Rochdale OL11 ....139 D7
Wigan WN5 ....54 C5
Lepp Cres BL8 ....27 C5
Lepton Gr M9 ....64 E2
Lerryn Dr SK7 ....123 D1
Lesley Rd M32 ....96 A1
Leslie Gr WA15 ....120 A6
Leslie Hough Way M6 ...81 B4
Leslie St Bolton BL3 ...155 B3
Manchester M14 ....98 B3
Lessingham Ave WN1 ...37 B3
Lester Rd M38 ....59 E5
Lester St M32 ....96 D2
Letchford Ave ② OL11 .31 A5
Letchworth St M14 .....98 B3
Letcombe Ct WN7 ......75 F7
Letham St OL8 ....68 F2
Letitia St BL6 ....22 A3
Levedale Rd M9 ....64 E4
Leven Cl BL4 ....61 B5
Leven Wlk Whitefield M45 .63 C8
② Wythenshawe M23 ..121 F2
Levengreave Cl WN2 ....57 C3
Levenhurst Rd M8 ....155 F7
Levens Cl SK8 ....122 B4
Levens Dr BL2 ....25 E1
Levens Pl Ince-in-M WN2 .56 A4
Levens St Manchester M40 .83 A7
Salford M6 ....80 A4
Levens Wlk
Chadderton OL9 ....152 A5
Wigan WN1 ....37 B4
Levenshulme High Sch
M19 ....111 A7
Levenshulme Rd M18 ...99 D4
Levenshulme Sta M19 ..99 D1
Levenshulme Terr ⑧
M19 ....99 A1
Levenshulme Trad Est
M19 ....99 C2
Lever Ave M27 ....80 B8
Lever Bridge Pl BL3 ....42 D5

Lever Cl **7** M29 ....58 F1
Lever Dr BL3 ....147 F4
Lever Edge La BL3 ....147 E3
Lever Edge Prim Sch
BL3 ....147 E2
Lever Gr BL2 ....148 A3
Lever Hall Rd BL2 ....42 D7
Lever Park Ave BL6 ....22 B5
Lever Park Sch BL6 ....22 C5
Lever St Bolton BL3 ....147 F4
Hazel Grove SK7 ....124 D3
Heywood OL10 ....29 D3
Little Lever BL3 ....43 A4
Manchester M1 ....159 B1
Middleton M24 ....47 A1
Radcliffe M26 ....43 F5
Ramsbottom BL0 ....138 C6
Tyldesley M29 ....58 F1
Westhoughton BL5 ....39 E3
Lever Wlk M24 ....64 F7
Leverett Cl WA14 ....119 A5
Leverhulme Ave BL3 ....42 A3
Levi St BL1 ....23 F1
Levington Dr OL8 ....85 A8
Lewes Ave M34 ....100 F1
Lewes Wlk OL9 ....152 B6
Lewis Ave Manchester M9 .....64 E1
Urmston M41 ....95 D5
Lewis Cl Adlington PR7 ....20 E6
Wigan WN3 ....150 A5
Lewis Dr OL10 ....46 A6
Lewis Rd Droylsden M43 ....83 E2
Reddish SK5 ....99 F1
Lewis St Eccles M30 ....79 D1
Heywood OL10 ....29 E3
Manchester M40 ....160 D3
Shaw OL2 ....149 B5
Lewis Street Prim Sch
M30 ....79 D1
Lewisham Ave M40 ....83 B4
Lewisham Cl OL2 ....48 B3
Lewtas St M30 ....79 E1
Lexton Ave M8 ....64 B2
Ley Cres M29 ....77 B6
Ley Dr OL10 ....46 E7
Ley Hey Ave SK6 ....125 F7
Ley Hey Ct SK6 ....125 F7
Ley Hey Rd SK6 ....125 F7
Ley La SK6 ....126 D8
Ley Rd M29 ....77 A7
Leybourne Ave M19 ....99 B2
Leybourne St BL1 ....143 E2
Leybrook Rd M22 ....121 C3
Leyburn Ave Royton OL2 ....48 D4
Stretford M32 ....96 C3
Urmston M41 ....95 A1
Leyburn Cl Whitefield M45 .....62 E8
Wigan WN1 ....151 F8
Leyburn Gr
2 Farnworth BL4 ....42 D1
Romiley SK6 ....113 C2
Leyburn Ho **2** M13 ....98 E4
Leyburn Rd M40 ....65 C2
Leyburne Rd SK2 ....124 D6
Leycett Dr M23 ....109 A1
Leycroft St
Manchester M1 ....159 B1
Manchester M1 ....163 B8
Leyden Wlk M23 ....121 A4
Leyfield Ave SK6 ....113 C2
Leyfield Rd OL16 ....31 E6
Leygate View SK22 ....127 B1
Leyland Ave Gatley SK8 ....122 B6
Hindley WN2 ....56 C3
Irlam M44 ....94 B4
Manchester M20 ....110 C3
Leyland Green Rd WN4 ....72 C5
Leyland Mill Farm WN1 ....37 D4
Leyland Mill La WN1 ....37 C3
Leyland St Abram WN2 ....56 B1
Bury BL9 ....44 F4
Hindley WN2 ....56 C4
Stockport SK1 ....169 E1
Leylands La SK14 ....114 F7
Leys Rd WA14 ....119 E8
Leyton Ave M40 ....83 B7
Leyton Cl Farnworth BL4 ....147 F1
2 Wigan WN5 ....54 D5
Leyton Dr BL9 ....44 F5
Leyton St **2** OL12 ....15 A2
Leywell Dr OL1 ....49 D3
Leywell Rd M9 ....157 F8
Libra St BL1 ....143 D2
Library La OL9 ....153 D8
Library St
Westhoughton BL5 ....57 F8
Wigan WN1 ....150 C8
Lichens Cres OL8 ....67 A3
Lichfield Ave
Altrincham WA15 ....120 C3
Ashton-u-L OL6 ....85 D8
Bolton BL2 ....25 B2
Golborne WA3 ....90 D8
Reddish SK5 ....111 E8
Tyldesley M29 ....77 C7
Lichfield Cl Farnworth BL4 .....60 A8
Radcliffe M26 ....43 D5
Lichfield Dr Bury OL8 ....140 D4
Chadderton OL9 ....48 A1
Manchester,Cheetham Hill
M8 ....63 C2
Manchester,Sedgley Park
M25 ....79 F6
Swinton M27 ....79 F6
Lichfield Gr WN4 ....73 C2
Lichfield Rd Eccles M30 ....79 E1
Radcliffe M26 ....43 D5
Urmston M41 ....95 D3

Lichfield St Salford M6 ....81 B5
Wigan WN5 ....54 C5
Lichfield Terr OL16 ....31 C4
Lichfield Wlk SK6 ....113 A1
Lidbrook Wlk M12 ....164 E5
Liddington Hall Dr BL0 ....11 B4
Lidgate Cl WN3 ....54 D3
Lidgate Gr
2 Farnworth BL4 ....60 C8
7 Manchester M20 ....110 A3
Lidgett Cl M38 ....60 C5
Lidiard St M8 ....64 A1
Lido Ho OL4 ....68 A6
Lieutenant Wlk M5 ....161 B8
Liffey Ave M22 ....121 E3
Lifton Ave M40 ....160 E4
Light Alders La SK12 ....135 A6
Light Oaks Inf & Jun Sch
M6 ....80 B4
Light Oaks Rd
Fowley Common WA3 ....92 C6
Salford M6 ....80 C4
Lightborne Rd M33 ....107 E4
Lightbounds Rd BL1 ....23 F3
Lightbourne Ave M27 ....79 F7
Lightbowne Rd M40 ....65 C2
Lightburn Ave OL15 ....15 E4
Lightbourne Ave
Bolton BL1 ....144 B7
Leigh WN7 ....75 E3
Lightfoot Wlk **6** M11 ....160 F1
Lighthorne Ave SK3 ....122 F7
Lighthorne Gr SK3 ....122 F7
Lighthorne Rd SK3 ....122 F7
Lighthouse OL15 ....6 C1
Lightowlers La OL15 ....16 D7
Lightshaw La WA3 ....74 B4
Lightwood M28 ....78 B8
Lightwood Cl **7** BL4 ....42 E1
Lignum Ave OL9 ....152 B8
Lila St M9 ....57 F7
Lilac Ave Bury BL9 ....44 D7
Downall Green WN4 ....72 D5
Hyde SK14 ....113 D8
Leigh WN7 ....75 E7
Newhey OL16 ....80 A8
Pendlebury M27 ....80 A8
Wigan WN6 ....37 A3
Lilac Cres **5** M46 ....81 A2
Lilac Gdns WN3 ....55 F4
Lilac Gr Billinge WN5 ....71 D4
Chadderton OL9 ....152 B8
Manchester M40 ....65 A1
Prestwich M25 ....63 A6
Lilac La OL8 ....66 D2
Lilac Rd Altrincham WA15 .....120 A3
Golborne WA3 ....74 A1
Rochdale OL11 ....30 F2
Lilac St SK2 ....170 F6
Lilac Terr **6** OL2 ....3 D8
Lilac View Cl OL2 ....49 D6
Lilac Wlk M31 ....105 E3
Liley St OL16 ....31 A7
Lilford Cl M12 ....165 A6
Lilford St Atherton M46 ....58 B2
Leigh WN7 ....75 E4
Lilian Dr WN6 ....37 A3
Lilian St M6 ....97 C4
Lillian Gr SK5 ....111 F8
Lilly St Bolton BL1 ....145 D8
Hyde SK14 ....113 F8
Lilmore Ave M40 ....83 C6
Lilstock Wlk **10** M9 ....64 E3
Lily Ave Farnworth BL4 ....42 B1
Lily Cl SK3 ....170 D5
Lily Hill St M45 ....44 E2
Lily La Ashton-in-M WN4 ....73 F7
Manchester M40 ....65 A2
Platt Bridge WN2 ....56 A1
Lily Lane Jun & Inf Sch
M40 ....83 A8
Lily Lanes OL6 ....85 E8
Lily Pl WN4 ....73 E5
Lily St Ashton-in-M WN4 ....73 E5
Eccles M30 ....79 B1
Middleton M24 ....65 C8
Milnrow OL16 ....31 F6
Oldham OL1 ....48 E1
Royton OL2 ....48 F4
Lily Thomas Ct **3** M11 ....99 F2
Lima St BL9 ....141 B3
Limbert Circ M8 ....64 C1
Lime Ave Leigh WN7 ....75 E8
New Mills SK22 ....127 D1
Swinton M27 ....79 C6
Urmston M41 ....95 B2
Whitefield M45 ....144 D8
Lime Bank St M12 ....164 D8
Lime Cl Abram Brow WN2 ....74 C7
Dukinfield SK16 ....101 D6
Hollinfare WA3 ....105 A2
Salford M6 ....81 A3
Lime Cres M16 ....97 B4
Lime Ct M6 ....81 A3
Lime Gate OL8 ....66 C2
Lime Gdns
Dukinfield SK16 ....101 B8
Middleton M24 ....64 E8
Lime Gr Altrincham WA15 .....120 B7
Ashton-u-L OL6 ....85 C5
Bury BL9 ....44 C7
Cheadle SK8 ....122 D6
Denton M34 ....100 F4
Dukinfield SK15 ....101 E8
Golborne WA3 ....90 E6
Heywood OL10 ....29 C3

Lime Gr continued
Hindley WN2 ....56 F3
Littleborough OL15 ....15 F6
Manchester M16 ....97 B4
Prestwich M25 ....63 A6
Ramsbottom BL0 ....11 D7
Royton OL2 ....48 D6
Walkden M28 ....60 D1
Lime Green Rd OL8 ....80 F8
Lime Kiln La SK6 ....126 A5
Lime La M35 ....84 C7
Lime Pl SK16 ....101 B8
Lime Rd M32 ....96 D1
Lime St Atherton M46 ....57 F3
Bury BL9 ....27 F6
Chadderton OL9 ....48 C1
Dukinfield SK16 ....101 B8
Eccles M30 ....79 D1
Farnworth BL4 ....60 E8
Rochdale OL11 ....30 C4
Romiley SK6 ....112 E4
Tyldesley M29 ....58 F1
Wigan WN1 ....151 D8
Lime Tree Cl M41 ....95 E1
Lime Tree Gr M35 ....84 B7
Lime Tree Prim Sch
M33 ....108 E3
Lime Vale WN3 ....55 F4
Lime Vale Rd WN5 ....71 C3
Lime Wlk
6 Handforth SK9 ....131 D1
Partington M31 ....105 D3
Limebrook Cl M11 ....99 E7
Limedrich Rd M35 ....84 A8
Limefield Middleton M24 ....64 E8
Milnrow OL16 ....31 E7
Mossley OL5 ....68 B2
1 Wigan WN1 ....151 D8
Limefield Ave BL4 ....42 D1
Limefield Brow BL9 ....27 F7
Limefield Cl BL1 ....142 B4
Limefield Ct M7 ....63 D1
Limefield Rd Bolton BL1 ....142 B4
Bury BL9 ....27 F7
Manchester M7 ....63 D1
Radcliffe M26 ....43 E3
Limefield Terr M19 ....99 A1
Limehurst Ave
8 Ashton-u-L OL7 ....85 A6
Manchester M20 ....109 F8
Limehurst Ct CT OL8 ....66 D1
Limehurst Prim Sch OL8 ....84 D8
Limehurst Rd OL7 ....85 A6
Limekiln La M12 ....164 D8
Limers Gate OL12 ....14 F5
Limerston Dr M40 ....83 A5
Limes Ave WN6 ....37 B6
Limes The Culcheth WA3 ....91 D4
Golborne WA3 ....90 D6
Mossley,Micklehurst OL5 ....68 E1
Mossley,Mossley Cross OL5 ....68 B1
Standish WN6 ....37 A6
Stockport SK3 ....170 D7
Limesdale Cl BL2 ....43 B5
Limeside Prim Sch OL8 ....66 D1
Limeside Rd OL8 ....66 C1
Limestead Ave M8 ....156 A8
Limetrees Rd M24 ....64 F8
Limewood Cl BB4 ....1 A7
Limewood Mdw M29 ....77 C6
Limley Dr M21 ....109 C7
Linacre Ave BL3 ....147 E2
Linacre Way SK13 ....116 F7
Linbeck Gr WA3 ....74 E1
Linby St M15 ....162 E7
Lincoln Ave Denton M34 ....100 F1
Droylsden M43 ....84 A3
Gatley SK8 ....131 B7
Golborne WA3 ....74 D1
Little Lever BL3 ....43 B3
Manchester M19 ....99 B1
Urmston M41 ....95 C4
Lincoln Cl Ashton-u-L OL6 ......85 D8
Golborne WN7 ....91 C8
Rochdale OL11 ....31 A6
Swinton M27 ....59 A2
Lincoln Close Ind Est **2**
OL11 ....31 A6
Lincoln Ct Failsworth M40 ......83 B4
14 Manchester M7 ....63 E1
Lincoln Dr
Altrincham WA15 ....120 B5
Ashton-in-M WN4 ....73 D2
Aspull WN2 ....38 C5
7 Bury BL9 ....44 F8
Littleborough OL15 ....16 A3
Manchester M25 ....63 C2
Lincoln Gn SK5 ....112 C6
Lincoln Gr Atherton M46 ....58 B3
Bolton BL2 ....25 E4
Manchester M13 ....163 C5
Sale M33 ....108 F4
Lincoln Leach Ct M26 ....144 C6
Lincoln Mill (Ent Ctr)
M23 ....108 F2
Lincoln Pl WN5 ....54 D5
Lincoln Rd Bolton BL1 ....144 B8
Failsworth M35 ....84 A6
Handforth SK9 ....131 A1
Hindley WN2 ....56 D2
Middleton M24 ....65 C5
7 Swinton M27 ....79 F7
Lincoln Rise SK6 ....112 F2
Lincoln St Eccles M30 ....79 C1
Manchester M13 ....98 F4

Lincoln St continued
Oldham OL9 ....152 C5
Rochdale OL11 ....31 A6
Lincoln Way SK13 ....116 F8
Lincoln Wlk OL10 ....29 A2
Lincroft Rd WN2 ....57 A3
Lind St M40 ....160 E2
Lindale Dr SK7 ....124 D2
Lindale SK14 ....101 C5
Lindale Ave Bolton BL1 ....40 F8
Chadderton OL9 ....152 A6
Failsworth M40 ....65 D2
Royton OL2 ....48 C8
Urmston M41 ....94 F3
Whitefield BL9 ....45 A3
Lindale Cl M28 ....77 E7
Lindale Dr M24 ....46 E3
Lindale Rd M28 ....77 E7
Lindale Rise OL2 ....49 D7
Linden Ave
Altrincham WA15 ....119 E5
Ashton-in-M WN4 ....72 F5
Atherton M46 ....58 B2
Denton M34 ....100 D7
Little Lever BL3 ....43 A5
Oldham OL4 ....67 D8
Orrell WN5 ....53 E6
Pendlebury M6 ....80 E6
Ramsbottom BL0 ....11 D6
Sale M33 ....107 F4
Swinton M27 ....79 D7
Linden Cl Denton M34 ....101 A3
Edenfield BL0 ....1 D2
Lymm WA13 ....117 A4
Linden Ct WN5 ....53 E6
Linden Dr M5 ....161 A8
Linden Gr Billinge WN5 ....71 C3
Bramhall SK7 ....132 D4
Leigh WN7 ....75 F7
Manchester M14 ....110 D8
Orrell WN5 ....53 E6
Stockport SK2 ....124 B4
Linden Lea Rawtenstall BB4 ....1 F8
Sale M33 ....108 B2
Linden Mews M20 ....77 F6
Linden Pk M19 ....111 A8
Linden Rd Boothstown M28 ....77 F6
Cheadle SK8 ....123 A3
Denton M34 ....101 A3
Hindley WN2 ....56 E7
Manchester M20 ....110 A4
Stalybridge SK15 ....102 D7
Linden Road Prim Sch
M34 ....101 A3
Linden St WN5 ....54 C5
Linden Way SK6 ....135 A7
Linden Wlk Bolton BL2 ....25 B5
Orrell WN5 ....53 E6
Lindenwood OL9 ....65 E8
Lindeth Ave M18 ....99 D4
Lindfield Dr BL1 ....143 E1
Lindfield Est S SK9 ....137 A6
Lindfield Est S SK9 ....137 A6
Lindinis Ave M6 ....81 B2
Lindisfarne **17** OL12 ....139 E8
Lindisfarne Ave WA3 ....91 C8
Lindisfarne Cl M33 ....108 B2
Lindisfarne Dr SK12 ....133 D4
Lindisfarne Pl BL2 ....25 C2
Lindisfarne Rd OL7 ....84 E5
Lindley Ave WN5 ....53 C5
Lindley Gr SK3 ....170 D5
Lindley St Kearsley BL4 ....61 B8
Little Lever BL3 ....43 B3
Lindleywood Rd M14 ....110 E8
Lindon Park Rd BB4 ....1 C7
Lindon Way SK14 ....103 A8
Lindop Rd WA15 ....119 F1
Lindow Cl BL8 ....27 B6
Lindow Ct Romiley SK6 ....112 D3
4 Sale M33 ....108 B2
Wilmslow SK9 ....136 E8
Lindow Fold Dr SK9 ....136 C6
Lindow La SK9 ....136 E6
Lindow Par SK9 ....136 F6
Lindow Prim Sch SK9 ....136 D3
Lindow Rd M16 ....97 C2
Lindow St Leigh WN7 ....75 D6
Sale M33 ....108 F3
Lindrick Ave M45 ....62 D6
Lindrick Cl M40 ....83 D7
Lindrick Terr BL3 ....145 D5
Lindsay Ave
Bramhall SK8 ....123 B1
Manchester M19 ....98 F1
Swinton M27 ....79 C6
Lindsay Cl OL4 ....49 D2
Lindsay Rd M19 ....110 F8
Lindsay St Horwich BL6 ....22 C5
Stalybridge SK15 ....86 B1
Lindsay Terr WN7 ....38 E5
Lindsell Rd WA14 ....119 C8
Lindsgate Dr WA15 ....120 B7
Lindside Wlk **3** M9 ....157 D8
Lindum Ave M16 ....97 C4
Lindum Ct OL10 ....29 D2
Lindum St M14 ....98 B3
Lindwall Cl M23 ....109 B2
Linear View WA12 ....89 C1
Lineholme OL1 ....48 A1
Lineholme La SK15 ....86 E3
Linen Ct M3 ....158 D2
Lines Rd Droylsden M43 ....84 B1
Irlam M44 ....105 F4

Linfield St M11 ....83 B1
Linford Ave M40 ....65 C2
Ling Dr M46 ....58 D2
Lingard Cl M34 ....100 C8
Lingard La SK6 ....112 D5
Lingard Rd M22 ....109 D1
Lingard St Leigh WN7 ....76 B4
Reddish SK5 ....111 F8
Lingard Terr M34 ....100 C8
Lingards La M29 ....77 A4
Lingards La WN7 ....77 A4
Lingcrest Rd M19 ....111 C7
Lingdale Rd SK8 ....132 E2
Lingdale Wlk M40 ....83 A7
Lingfield Ave
Hazel Grove SK7 ....124 F2
Sale M33 ....107 B2
Lingfield Cl **7** BL8 ....27 C7
Lingfield Cres WN6 ....36 E3
Lingfield Rd M11 ....83 C2
Lingfield Wlk OL9 ....152 C1
Lingholme Dr M24 ....46 C2
Lingmell Ave WA11 ....71 C1
Lingmell Cl Bolton BL1 ....40 F8
Middleton M24 ....46 D2
Urmston M41 ....95 A4
Lingmoor Cl
Middleton M24 ....46 C2
Wigan WN3 ....55 A1
Lingmoor Dr M29 ....77 B7
Lingmoor Rd BL1 ....23 F1
Lingmoor Wlk **8** M15 ....162 F6
Lings Wlk M22 ....121 E1
Linguard Bsns Pk **6**
OL16 ....31 A6
Linhope Cl SK4 ....110 E3
Link Ave M41 ....95 E4
Link La OL8 ....66 E2
Link Rd Oldham OL4 ....67 F7
Sale M33 ....107 D2
Link The Brinnington SK5 ......112 D3
Handforth SK9 ....131 D3
Oldham OL2 ....48 F8
Link Wlk M31 ....105 D2
Linkfield Dr M28 ....77 F6
Links Ave M35 ....83 F5
Links Cres M25 ....63 E2
Links Dr BL6 ....40 B7
Links Pl OL6 ....85 E6
Links Rd
Bolton,Harwood BL2 ....26 A3
Bolton,Lostock Junction BL6 ...40 B7
Heywood OL10 ....46 D8
Marple SK6 ....125 F4
Romiley SK6 ....113 D2
Wilmslow SK9 ....136 E4
Links Rise M41 ....95 A4
Links View M40 ....119 E3
Manchester M25 ....63 A1
Rochdale OL11 ....30 A6
Oldham OL9 ....152 C8
Lindfield Est S SK9 ....137 A6 (?)
Linkside Ave OL2 ....48 D5
Linksview Ct M45 ....122 A4
Manchester M25 ....63 A2
Pendlebury M27 ....80 A6
Linkway Dr Cl SK4 ....111 A5
Linksway SK9 ....45 B3
Linkway Ave WN4 ....73 E5
Linkway The BL6 ....39 D8
Linley Ave M26 ....44 E5
Linley Cl WN6 ....36 C4
Linley Dr OL4 ....49 C2
Linley Gr BL0 ....11 A2
Linley Rd Cheadle SK8 ....132 B8
Sale M33 ....108 B5
Wigan WN5 ....54 E5
Linn St M8 ....64 A1
Linnell Dr OL11 ....29 B6
Linnet Cl Droylsden M34 ....84 C1
Hazel Grove SK2 ....124 F5
Manchester M12 ....98 F4
Newton-le-W WA12 ....89 C3
Linnet Dr Bury BL9 ....141 B4
Irlam M44 ....94 A3
Leigh WN7 ....76 B5
Linnet Hill OL11 ....30 C6
Linnet's Wood Mews
M28 ....60 E3
Linney La OL2 ....149 C7
Linney Rd SK7 ....123 D2
Linney Sq WN1 ....151 E8
Linnyshaw Ind Est M28 ....60 F3
Linsford Ct SK3 ....123 B8 (?)
Linslade Gdns BL3 ....145 E5
Linslade Ho **10** M5 ....161 B8
Linslade Wlk **7** M9 ....157 D7
Linsley St M3 ....158 F2
Linstead Dr M8 ....155 F6
Linthorpe Wlk BL3 ....147 E4
Linthorpe Wlk BL3 ....147 E4
Linton Ave Bury BL3 ....27 F5
Golborne WA3 ....73 F2
Reddish M34 ....100 A3
Linton Cl M4 ....160 C2
Linton Rd M33 ....108 C6
Linton St M4 ....61 A8 (?)
Linton Wlk M7 ....80 F8
Linwood Cl **9** WN2 ....56 C4
Linwood Gr M12 ....99 A3
Linwood St M35,M40 ....83 C6
Lion Brow M9 ....64 D3

Lion Fold La M9 ....64 D3
Lion La BL6 ....21 C2
Lion St M9 ....64 D2
Lions Dr M27 ....80 A7
Liptrot St WN5 ....54 F7
Lisbon St 17 OL12 ....14 C1
Lisburn Ave
  Manchester M16,M21 .....97 C1
  Sale M33 ....108 A3
Lisburn Rd M40 ....83 A8
Lisburne Ave SK2 ....124 D7
Lisburne CI SK2 ....124 D6
Lisburne La SK2 ....124 D6
Lisburne Sch SK2 ....124 E6
Liscard Ave M14 ....98 B1
Liscard St M6 ....58 B3
Lisetto Ave 1 OL4 ....67 B5
Liskeard Ave OL2 ....48 F4
Liskeard CI OL16 ....15 C1
Liskeard Dr SK7 ....132 F7
Lisle St 3 OL12 ....31 A8
Lismore WA15 ....119 F2
Lismore Ave Bolton BL3 ..40 F6
  Stockport SK3 ....123 B8
Lismore Rd SK16 ....101 D7
Lismore Way M41 ....95 B5
Lismore Wlk M22 ....130 E8
Lissadel St M6 ....81 B4
Lisson Gr WA15 ....119 E2
Lister Rd M24 ....64 B6
Lister St 1 BL3 ....146 B3
Litcham CI SK16 ....101 F8
Litcham Cl M1 ....163 B7
Litchfield CI OL3 ....33 C2
Litchfield Ct M7 ....64 C7
Litchfield Gr M28 ....79 A7
Litherland Ave M22 .....121 E2
Litherland Rd Bolton BL3 .147 E2
  Sale M33 ....108 A3
Little 66 BL9 ....45 B7
Little Ancoats St M1,M4 .159 B2
Little Bank St 6 OL4 ...67 B6
Little Bollington CE Prim Sch
  WA14 ....118 B2
Little Brook Rd M33 ....107 C1
Little Brow BL7 ....25 A7
Little Church St 3 WN5 .54 B6
Little Clegg Rd OL15 ....15 F2
Little David St M1 .....163 A8
Little Ees La M33 ......107 F7
Little Egerton St SK1 ..170 D7
Little Factory St M29 ..58 F1
Little Flatt OL12 ....14 B1
Little Harwood Lee BL2 ..25 E3
Little Heath La WA14 ...118 D5
Little Heaton CE Prim Sch
  M24 ....46 C7
Little Hey St OL2 ....49 B4
Little Holme St M44 ....160 D1
Little Holme Wlk BL3 ...147 F4
Little Howarth Way 1
  OL12 ....15 C4
Little John St M3 ......158 E1
Little La WN3,WN5 ......54 A6
Little Lever Sch (Specialist
  Language Coll) BL3 ....42 F3
Little Lever St
  Manchester M1 ....159 A1
  8 Manchester M1,M4 ....159 B2
Little London 2 WN1 ...37 C1
Little Mdws BL7 ....24 F7
Little Meadow Rd WA14 ..119 B1
Little Moor Clough BL7 ..8 E2
Little Moor La OL4 ......67 C8
Little Moss La M27 ......79 E6
Little Nelson St 1 M4 ..159 A3
Little Oak CI OL4 ....67 E6
Little Pasture WN7 ......75 D7
Little Peter St M15 ....162 E7
Little Pitt St M1 ......159 B1
Little Quay St M3 ......158 E1
Little Scotland BL6 .....21 B2
Little St SK1 ....124 B8
Little Stones Rd BL7 ....8 E2
Little Town OL8 ....66 C4
Little Underbank SK1 ...169 F1
Littleborough Coach House &
  Heritage Ctr* WN5 .....16 B5
Littleborough Com Prim Sch
  OL15 ....16 B7
Littleborough Sta OL15 ..16 B5
Littlebourne Wlk BL1 ....25 A6
Littlebrook CI
  Cheadle SK8 ....123 C4
  Hadfield SK13 ....104 A4
Littledale St OL12 .....139 E8
Littlefields SK14 ......103 A4
Littlegate BL5 ....57 C2
Littlegreen Gdns M6 ...154 F3
Littleham Wlk M18 .....165 C5
Littlehaven CI M12 .....164 E5
Littlehills CI M24 .....46 E1
Littlemoor Cotts SK1 ...124 B8
Littlemoor CI 1 SK13 ..116 C8
Littlemoor Ho 11 OL4 ..67 C8
Littlemoor La OL3 ......67 A5
Littlemoor Prim Sch OL4 .67 C8
Littlemoor Rd SK14 ....103 A4
Littlemoss Bsns Pk M43 ..84 C3
Littlemoss High Sch for Boys
  M43 ....84 C4
Littlemoss Rd M43 .....84 C3
Littler Ave M21 ....109 C5
Littlers Point* M17 ....96 D5
Littleton Gr WN6 ....19 E2

Littleton Rd M6,M7,M25 ..81 A6
Littlewood OL2 ....49 A4
Littlewood Ave 1 BL9 ...27 F5
Littlewood Rd M22 ......121 D6
Littlewood St M6 ....154 E2
Litton Bank 12 SK13 ....171 E1
Litton CI SK13 ....171 E1
Litton Gdns 11 SK13 ....171 E1
Litton Mews SK13 ....171 E1
Littondale CI OL2 ......48 E5
Liverpool CI SK5 ....111 E7
Liverpool Rd
  Ashton-in-M WN4 ....73 A3
  Eccles M30 ....79 C1
  Garswood WA11,WN4 ....72 D2
  Irlam M30,M44 ....94 D4
  Irlam,Cadishead M44 ..105 D4
  Manchester M3 ....162 E8
  Platt Bridge WN2 ......56 C3
Liverpool St
  7 Reddish SK5 ....111 E7
  Salford M5 ....81 B1
Liverstudd Ave SK5 .....111 F8
Liverton Ct M9 ....64 B5
Livesey St
  Manchester M4 ....159 C3
  Manchester,Levenshulme
    M19 ....111 B8
  Oldham OL1 ....67 C8
Livingstone Ave 2 OL5 .68 C1
Livingstone Pri M16 ....161 B5
Livingstone Prim Sch
  OL5 ....86 C8
Livingstone St
  2 Ashton-in-M WN4 ....73 A5
  Oldham,County End OL4 .68 A6
  Oldham,Lees OL4 ......67 E5
Livsey La OL10 ....29 A2
Livsey St Rochdale OL16 .31 A7
  Whitefield M45 ....62 F8
Liza St WN7 ....75 E8
Lizard St M1 ....159 B1
Lizmar Terr M40,M9 ....157 F8
Llanberis Rd SK8 ......122 E1
Llanfair Rd 7 SK3 .....123 C8
Lloyd Ave SK8 ....122 A6
Lloyd Ct M14 ....118 B2
Lloyd Gdns WA14 ....119 D3
Lloyd Rd M19 ....111 B7
Lloyd Sq 6 WA14 ......119 D4
Lloyd St
  Altrincham WA14,WA15 .119 D4
  Heywood OL10 ....29 D1
  Manchester M2 ....158 F1
  Rochdale OL11 ....139 D5
  Stockport SK4 ....169 D3
  Whitworth OL12 ....4 C1
Lloyd St N M14,M15 ....163 A5
Lloyd St S M14 ....98 A2
Lloyd's Ct WA14 ....119 D4
Lobden Cres OL12 ......14 D8
Lobelia Ave BL4 ....42 A1
Lobelia Wlk 6 M31 ....105 E2
Lobley CI OL12 ....15 B2
Local Board St WN2 ....151 F7
Loch St WN5 ....54 B6
Lochawe CI OL10 ....29 A1
Lochinver Gr OL10 .....29 A1
Lochmaddy CI SK7 ......124 F1
Lock CI OL10 ....46 E8
Lock Flight Bldgs WN3 ..54 F2
Lock Keepers Mews M27 ..80 D8
Lock La Bolton BL3,BL6 ..40 D3
  Partington M31 ....105 E3
Lock Rd WA14 ....119 C6
Locke Ind Est BL6 .....22 B3
Locker La WN4 ....73 F4
Lockerbie PI WN3 ......54 E2
Lockett Gdns M3 ....158 D2
Lockett Rd WN4 ....73 C6
Lockett St
  Manchester M8 ....158 E4
  Salford M6 ....81 A5
Lockhart CI M12 ....165 A5
Lockhart St OL16 ......31 B5
Locking Gate Rise OL4 ..49 E1
Lockingate St OL6 .....85 A5
Locklands La M44 ......94 A2
Locks View WN1 ....151 F8
Lockside SK6 ....126 A6
Lockside View OL5 .....68 E3
Locksley CI SK4 ....168 C2
Lockton CI
  Manchester M1 ....163 B7
  Reddish SK5 ....111 E6
Lockton Ct M1 ....163 B7
Lockwood St 7 M12 ....99 B3
Locomotion Ind Est BL6 .22 B2
Lodden Wlk 21 M9 .....157 E8
Lodge Ave M41 ....95 C2
Lodge Bank
  Hadfield SK13 ....104 A6
  Horwich BL6 ....21 F2
Lodge Bank Est BL6 ....21 F3
Lodge Bank Rd OL15 ...15 F3
Lodge Brow M26 ....40 E2
Lodge CI Dukinfield SK16 .101 E7
  Lymm WA13 ....117 B4
Lodge Ct Manchester SK4 .110 F2
  Mottram-in-L SK14 ...103 A4
Lodge Dr Culcheth WA3 .91 F3
  Tyldesley M29 ....77 B6
Lodge Farm CI SK7 ....123 E2
Lodge Fold M43 ....84 B2
Lodge Gn SK16 ....101 E7
Lodge Gr M46 ....58 E1
Lodge La Delph OL3 ....50 E5

Lodge La continued
  Dukinfield SK16 ......101 E8
  Haydock WA11,WA12,WN4 .89 B8
  Hyde SK14 ....167 D4
  Leigh WN7 ....76 E4
  Tyldesley M46 ....58 D1
Lodge Mill La BL0 .....2 A1
Lodge Rd Orrell WN5 ...53 E4
  Radcliffe M26 ....64 B2
  Tyldesley M46 ....58 D1
Lodge Rise M43 ....84 B2
Lodge St Ashton-u-L OL7 .84 F1
  Dukinfield SK14 ......101 E5
  Littleborough OL15 ...16 B5
  Manchester M40 ....157 E5
  Manchester M24 ....47 A1
  Ramsbottom BL0 ......138 C6
  Ramsbottom,Shuttleworth
    BL0 ....11 E8
  Wardle OL12 ....15 C6
Lodge The SK13 ....104 A6
Lodge View Cvn Pk BL2 .148 A8
Lodgepole CI M30 .....94 F8
Lodgeside CI M43 .....84 B2
Loeminster PI WN2 ....151 F7
Loen Cres BL1 ....142 C3
Logan Ave M22 ....121 E2
Logan St BL1 ....24 E5
Logan Wlk M22 ....121 E2
Loganberry Ave M6 ....81 A3
Logwood Ave Bury BL8 .140 D3
Logwood Ho WN5 ......54 E8
Logwood PI WN5 ......54 E8
Loire Dr WN5 ....54 F8
Loisine CI OL11 ......10 B3
Lok Fu Gdns M8 ....155 E5
Lomas CI M19 ....110 E3
Lomas St Failsworth M35 .66 A1
  Manchester M24 ......47 B1
  Stockport SK3 ....170 D7
Lomax St Bolton BL1 ...143 E2
  Bury BL9 ....141 A3
  7 Farnworth BL4 .....42 C2
  Manchester M1,M4 ....159 C1
  4 Platt Bridge WN2 ..56 B2
  Ramsbottom BL8 ......10 F1
  Rochdale OL12,OL16 ...14 F1
  Whitefield M45 ....44 E2
Lomax's Bldgs BL2 ....145 F6
Lombard CI SK6 ....112 F4
Lombard Gr M14 ......110 C8
Lombard St Atherton M46 .58 B3
  Oldham OL1 ....153 E7
  Rochdale OL12 ....139 D8
Lombardy Ct 9 M6 ....81 A3
Lomond Ave
  Altrincham WA15 ......120 A3
  Stretford M32 ....96 D3
Lomond CI SK2 ....124 A3
Lomond Dr BL8 ....27 B4
Lomond PI BL3 ....40 E6
Lomond Rd M22,SK8 ...122 E1
Lomond Terr OL16 .....31 C4
London CI WN5 ....54 E8
London Fields WN5 ....71 E5
London PI SK1 ....169 F1
London Rd
  Alderley Edge SK9 ....137 A1
  Hazel Grove SK2,SK7 ..124 D3
  Manchester M1 ....163 B8
  Mossley SK10,SK12 ....133 C1
  Oldham OL1 ....49 B1
London Rd N SK12 ....133 E5
London Rd S SK12 ....133 D3
London Sq SK1 ....169 F1
London St Bolton BL3 ..147 E4
  Salford M6 ....81 B4
  Whitefield M45 ....62 F7
Long Acres Dr OL12 ...9 G2
Long Croft La SK8 ....122 F1
Long Cswy Farnworth BL4 .60 D7
  Leigh M46 ....76 B8
Long Grain PI SK2 ....124 D5
Long Hey WA15 ....120 A3
Long Heys or Back La
  WN8 ....35 A6
Long Hill OL11 ....30 D4
Long La Bolton BL2,BL3 ..42 E6
  Bury BL9 ....27 E7
  Charlesworth SK13 ....115 C7
  Hindley WN2 ....57 A4
  Oldham OL9 ....65 F3
  Uppermill OL3 ....65 A8
  Westhoughton BL5 .....39 D2
Long Marl Dr SK9 .....131 F4
Long Mdw Bolton BL7 ..25 C7
  Dukinfield SK14 ......101 F6
Long Meadow Pas
  SK14 ....167 D3
Long Millgate
  Manchester M3 ....158 F2
  Manchester M3,M4 ....159 A2
Long Row SK15 ....86 F7
Long Rushes OL2 ......48 F8
Long St Manchester M18 .99 E6
  Middleton M24 ....47 A1
  Swinton M27 ....79 F7
Long Wlk M31 ....105 D3
Longacre St M1,M4 ....159 C1
Longacres Rd WA15 ....129 D7
Longbow Ct M7 ....155 D5
Longbridge Rd M17 ....96 A6
Longbrook WN6 ....36 B7
Longbutt La WA13 .....117 A2
Longclough Dr SK13 ...116 A8

Longcrag Wlk 4 M15 ..163 A5
Longcroft WN7 ....76 E4
Longcroft Cotts BL9 ..11 F1
Longcroft Dr WA14 ....119 B4
Longcroft Gr
  Droylsden M34 ....100 B8
  Wythenshawe M23 .....120 F7
Longdale CI OL2 ......48 C4
Longdale Dr SK14 .....103 A3
Longdale Gdns SK14 ...103 A3
Longdell Wlk 4 M9 ...157 E8
Longden Ave OL4 ......49 E3
Longden Ct SK7 ....132 E5
Longden Rd
  Ashton-in-M M19 .....73 A3
  Manchester M19 ....99 B2
Longden St 11 BL1 ...144 C8
Longdendale High Sch
  SK14 ....103 C5
Longdendale Recn Ctr
  SK14 ....102 F3
Longfellow Ave BL3 ...146 B3
Longfellow CI WN3 ....150 A5
Longfellow Cres OL1 ..49 D4
Longfellow Wlk 5 M34 .113 A7
Longfield Ave
  Altrincham WA15 ......120 C6
  Gatley SK8 ....131 C7
  Urmston M41 ....95 C1
Longfield CI SK14 ....101 E6
Longfield Cres OL4 ...67 D8
Longfield Dr M41 .....95 B2
Longfield La 18 OL4 ..49 D1
Longfield PI OL2 .....149 A6
Longfield Rd Bolton BL3 .146 B3
  Rochdale OL11 ....30 D2
  Shaw OL2 ....149 A6
  Wythenshawe M23 .....120 F8
Longfield Sh Ctr M25 .63 A5
Longfield St 7 WN2 ..37 F2
Longford Ave Bolton BL3 .142 C2
  Stretford M32 ....96 F3
Longford CI M32 ......96 E3
Longford Cotts M32 ...96 F2
Longford Gdns BL3 ....147 E4
Longford Ho 4 M21 ...96 F2
Longford Park Sch M32 ..96 F2
Longford PI M14 ......98 C4
Longford Rd
  Manchester M21 ....97 A1
  Reddish SK5 ....96 E3
  Stretford M32 ....96 E3
  Manchester M21 ....99 E6
Longford Rd W
  Reddish SK5 ....99 E7
Longford St
  Heywood OL10 ....29 D2
  Manchester M18 ....99 C4
Longford Trad Est M32 .96 D3
Longham CI
  Bramhall SK7 ....123 D1
  Manchester M11 ....160 E1
Longhey Rd M22 ......121 E5
Longhill Wlk 3 M40 ..83 A6
Longhirst CI BL1 .....142 B3
Longhope Rd M22 .....121 D3
Longhurst La SK6 .....126 C6
Longhurst Rd
  Hindley WN2 ....57 A4
  Manchester M9 ....64 B5
Longland Dr M18 .....165 B6
Longlands Dr SK14 ....102 B3
Longlevens Rd M22 ...121 C3
Longley Dr M28 ......79 B6
Longley La 2 M22 ....121 E7
Longley Rd M28 ......60 D2
Longley St Oldham OL1 .153 F6
  Shaw OL2 ....149 B5
Longmead Ave
  Ashton-in-M WN4 .....73 C4
  Hazel Grove SK7 ......124 D1
Longmead Rd M6 ......154 D4
Longmead Way M24 ...47 B1
Longmeade Gdns SK9 .137 C6
Longmeadow SK13 .....115 B8
Longmeadow Gr M34 ..100 E2
Longmere Ave M22 ...121 D3
Longmoor Rd SK13 ....116 A7
Longnor Gr SK13 .....171 D2
Longnor Mews SK13 ...171 D2
Longnor Rd Gatley SK8 .131 D8
  Hazel Grove SK7 ......124 E1
Longnor Way 22 SK13 .171 D2
Longport Ave M20 ....110 A7
Longridge BL7 ....25 C8
Longridge Ave
  Stalybridge SK15 .....86 A4
  Standish WN6 ....36 F8
Longridge Cres BL1 ...23 F2
Longridge Dr Bury BL8 .44 A8
  Heywood OL10 ....29 E1
Longridge Way WN6 ..36 F8
Longshaw Ave
  Longshaw WN5 ....53 E1
  Swinton M27 ....61 F1
Longshaw Comm
  Billinge WN5 ....71 E8
  Longshaw WN5 ....53 E1
Longshaw Dr M28 .....60 A4
Longshaw Ford Rd BL1 .23 C3
Longshaw Old Rd WN5 .53 E1
Longshoot CI WN1 .....37 D1
Longshut La SK1,SK2 ..170 F7
Longshut La W SK2 ...170 F7
Longsight WA15 ......129 C7
Longsight La Bolton BL2 .25 D4
  Cheadle SK8 ....131 F6

Longsight Rd
  Manchester M18 ......99 B3
  Ramsbottom BL0,BL8 ..11 A2
Longson St BL1 ....25 A1
Longsons The SK5 ....169 F3
Longthwaite Cl 2 M24 .46 D2
Longton Ave
  Golborne WA3 ....90 C7
  Manchester M20 ......110 A5
Longton Rd
  Manchester M9 ....64 C4
  Salford M6 ....80 C5
Longton St Bury BL9 ..44 F4
  Hindley WN2 ....52 F4
Longtown Gdns 7 BL1 .143 E2
Longview Dr M27 .....62 C1
Longwall Ave M28 ....78 C8
Longwood Ave SK2 ....124 B6
Longwood CI SK6 .....113 E3
Longwood Rd
  Stretford M17 ....96 B6
  Wythenshawe M22 ....121 E3
Longworth Cl M41 ....94 E1
Longworth Clough BL7 .8 D2
Longworth La 8 ......8 C2
Longworth Rd Bolton BL7 .8 B3
  Horwich BL6 ....22 C4
Longworth St Bolton BL1 .148 C7
  Manchester M3 ....162 E8
Lonsdale Ave Leigh WN7 .75 D2
  Reddish SK5 ....99 F3
  Rochdale OL16 ....31 B5
  Swinton M27 ....79 D5
  Urmston M41 ....95 B4
Lonsdale Gr 8 BL4 ...60 C8
Lonsdale Rd Bolton BL1 .144 B8
  Manchester M19 ....99 B2
  Oldham OL8 ....66 B2
Lonsdale St Bury BL8 ..27 C2
  Failsworth M40 ....83 C6
Loom St M4 ....159 B2
Loonies Ct 1 SK1 ....170 F8
Lord Ave Bacup OL13 .3 C8
  2 Tyldesley M46 ....58 F1
Lord Byng St M50 ....154 F1
Lord Derby Rd SK14 ..113 E7
Lord Gr 18 M46 ......58 F1
Lord Kitchener Ct M33 .108 B5
Lord La M35 ....83 F6
Lord Lanes Mews M35 .83 F6
Lord Napier Dr M5 ...161 B7
Lord Sheldon Way OL7 .84 E2
Lord St Ashton-in-M WN4 .73 D4
  Ashton-u-L OL6 ......166 B4
  Bury BL9 ....140 F2
  Bury,Heap Bridge BL9 .141 C1
  Farnworth BL4 ....60 E8
  Glossop SK13 ....101 C5
  Hindley WN2 ....56 D4
  Hollingworth SK14 ...171 D4
  Horwich BL6 ....22 B4
  Ince-in-M WN2 ....56 A7
  Leigh WN7 ....75 F5
  Manchester M3,M4 ....43 B3
  Middleton M24 ....47 A2
  Newton-le-W WA12 ....89 A3
  Oldham OL1 ....153 F7
  Radcliffe M26 ....44 A3
  Reddish M34 ....100 A4
  Salford M7 ....81 C4
  Stalybridge SK15,SK16 .101 F8
  Stockport SK1 ....169 F1
  Tyldesley,Gin Pit M29 .76 F6
  Tyldesley,Hindsford M46 .58 E1
  Westhoughton BL5 ....39 E1
  Wigan WN1 ....37 C1
Lord St S WN7 ....76 A5
Lord Street Prim Sch
  BL6 ....22 B4
Lord's Ave M5 ....154 D2
Lord's St M44 ....105 C5
Lord's Stile La BL7 ..25 A7
Lords Coll BL2 ......148 A6
Lordsfields Ave OL7 ..166 B4
Lordship CI M9 ....64 F1
Lordship St M15 .....162 D6
Lordy Cl WN6 ....37 B7
Loreto Coll M15 .....162 D6
Loreto Gram Sch WA14 .119 C5
Loreto Prep Sch WA14 .119 C5
Loretto Rd M41 ......95 F1
Lorgill Cl SK3 ....123 F4
Loring St M40 ....83 C6
Lorland Rd SK3 ......123 B7
Lorna Gr SK8 ....123 B2
Lorna Rd SK8 ....123 C6
Lorne Ave OL13 ......3 C8
Lorne Gr Stockport SK3 .170 E6
  Urmston M41 ....95 E2
Lorne Rd M14 ....110 C8
Lorne St Bolton BL1 ..145 F7
  Eccles M30 ....95 B8
  Farnworth BL3,BL4 ...29 C1
  Manchester M13 ......163 C5
  Mossley OL5 ....68 C1
  Oldham OL8 ....66 C4
  Rochdale OL12 ....15 B3
  Wigan WN1 ....151 E8
Lorraine CI OL10 ....28 F1
Lorraine Rd WA15 ....119 E6
Lorton CI Boothstown M28 .77 F6
  Middleton M24 ....46 C2

Lorton Gr BL2 ....42 F8
Lostock Ave
　Hazel Grove SK7 ....124 B1
　7 Manchester M19 ...99 B1
　Poynton SK12 ....133 B4
　Sale M33 ....108 E4
　Urmston M41 ....95 B3
Lostock Cl Billinge WN5 ..71 E5
　Heywood OL10 ....29 B3
Lostock Coll M32 ....96 A3
Lostock Ct
　Handforth SK9 ....131 D4
　Urmston M32 ....95 F4
Lostock Dr BL9 ....27 F6
Lostock Gr M32 ....96 B3
Lostock Hall Prim Sch
　SK12 ....133 B3
Lostock Hall Rd SK12 ...133 B3
Lostock Ind Est BL6 .....39 E7
Lostock Junction La BL6 .40 C7
Lostock La BL5,BL6 ......39 E6
Lostock Park Dr BL6 .....40 C4
Lostock Prim Sch BL6 ....40 C6
Lostock Rd Four Gates BL5 .39 C4
　Poynton SK12 ....133 D2
　Salford M5 ....154 E2
　Urmston M41 ....95 D4
Lostock St M40 ....160 D3
Lostock Sta BL6 ....40 C6
Lostock Way SK9 ....131 D4
Lostock Wlk Leigh WN7 ...75 D6
　Whitefield M45 ....45 C1
Lothian Ave M30 ....79 B3
Lottery Row BL1 ....145 F7
Lottery St SK3 ....169 D1
Lottie St M27 ....80 A8
Loughborough Cl 3
　M33 ....107 D3
Loughfield M41 ....95 A2
Loughrigg Ave
　Billinge WA11 ....71 B1
　Royton OL2 ....48 C8
Loughrigg Cl M29 ....77 B7
Louis Ave BL9 ....140 F4
Louis St BL0 ....1 D5
Louisa St Bolton BL1 ....143 E2
　Manchester M11 ....99 D8
　Walkden M28 ....60 D4
Louise Cl OL12 ....15 C3
Louise Gdns
　Rochdale OL12 ....15 C3
　Westhoughton BL5 .....57 F6
Louise St M35 ....83 E7
Louvain St M35 ....23 F4
Louvoine Cl M18 ....99 E5
Lovalle St BL1 ....142 C1
Lovat Rd BL2 ....43 A7
Lovatt Ct WA13 ....117 B4
Love La Edenfield BL0 ....1 E1
　Stockport SK4 ....169 E2
Loveless Ho M46 ....58 D4
Lovell Ct M8 ....63 F2
Lovell Dr SK14 ....167 F4
Lovers La Atherton M46 ..58 A1
　Uppermill OL4 ....68 D6
Lovett Wlk M22 ....121 E8
Low Bank OL12 ....15 A8
Low Bank Rd WN4 ....72 F4
Low Crompton Rd OL2 ....48 E6
Low Gate La OL3 ....34 A1
Low Gn M46 ....58 E5
Low Grove La OL3 ....68 E5
Low Hall Com Prim Sch
　WN2 ....56 A3
Low Hall Gdns WN2 ....56 B3
Low Hill OL12 ....15 C3
Low Lea Rd SK6 ....126 B6
Low Mdws OL2 ....48 D6
Low Wood Cl SK7 ....123 C1
Low Wood Rd M34 ....100 A4
Low's Pl 3 OL12 ....15 A2
Lowcock St M7 ....158 E4
Lowcroft Cres OL40 ......65 F8
Lowcross Rd M40 ....83 A6
Lowe Ave M46 ....58 C5
Lowe Gn OL2 ....48 E5
Lowe Mill La WN2 ....56 D5
Lowe St Denton M34 .....100 B3
　Golborne WA3 ....90 A8
　Radcliffe M26 ....43 F4
　Stockport SK1 ....169 F2
Lower Albion St M1 .....163 B8
Lower Alma St SK16 .....166 C2
Lower Bamford Cl 7
　M24 ....47 A2
Lower Bank M25 ....116 D8
Lower Bank Cl SK13 .....171 F3
Lower Bank St BL9 ......140 E2
Lower Barn Rd SK13 .....171 E4
Lower Beechwood
　OL11 ....139 D5
Lower Bennett St SK14 ..101 C5
Lower Bents La SK6 .....112 F4
Lower Birches OL4 ....67 F4
Lower Blue Bell Cotts
　BL5 ....39 C4
Lower Bridgeman St
　BL2 ....148 A6
Lower Brook La M28 ......79 A5
Lower Brook St M1 .....163 B8
Lower Brooklands Par 5
　M8 ....63 E2
Lower Broughton Rd
　Salford M7 ....158 D4
　Salford M7 ....81 F1
Lower Bury St SK4 ......169 D2

Lower Byrom St M3 ......162 E8
Lower Calderbrook OL15 ..6 C1
Lower Carr La OL3 ....69 B6
Lower Carrs SK1 ....169 F1
Lower Chatham St M1 ...163 A7
Lower Clowes BB4 ....1 E8
Lower Clowes Rd BB4 ....1 E8
Lower Count Hill OL4 ....49 E2
Lower Crimble OL11 .....29 F4
Lower Croft M45 ....62 C6
Lower Crossbank OL4 ....67 F7
Lower Darcy St BL2 ....148 C5
Lower Dingle OL1 ....49 C4
Lower Drake Fold BL5 ...57 E5
Lower Edge Ave OL1 ....153 E8
Lower Falinge OL12 ....139 E8
Lower Fields OL3 ....51 A1
Lower Fields Rise OL42 .149 B8
Lower Fold Bolton BL2 ...25 F4
　Denton M34 ....101 A2
　Marple SK6 ....126 A3
Lower Fold Ave OL2 .....49 A4
Lower Frenches Dr OL3 ..67 A6
Lower Gates OL16 ......139 F7
Lower Gn Ashton-u-L OL6 .166 C4
　Middleton M8 ....64 C5
　3 Rochdale OL12 .....14 C1
Lower Goodwin Cl BL2 ...25 E2
Lower Green La M29 .....77 C3
Lower Greenshall La
　SK12 ....135 F6
Lower Hague SK22 ......135 E8
Lower Hardman St M3 ...158 E1
Lower Hey La OL5 ....68 E3
Lower Higham Visitors Ctr*
　SK14 ....114 A8
Lower Hillgate SK1 ....169 F1
Lower House Dr BL6 .....40 C7
Lower House La OL12 ....15 B7
Lower House St 7 OL1 ...67 B8
Lower House Wlk BL7 ....25 A8
Lower Jowkin La OL11 ...29 D7
Lower Kersall Com Prim Sch
　M7 ....81 B6
Lower Knoll Rd OL3 .....51 C5
Lower La OL16 ....31 D4
Lower Landedmans BL5 ..57 F5
Lower Leigh Rd BL5 .....57 F5
Lower Lime Rd OL8 ......84 C8
Lower Longshoot WN1 ...151 D8
Lower Lyndon Ave WN6 ..36 A6
Lower Makinson Fold 1
　BL6 ....22 D1
Lower Marlands BL7 .....24 F8
Lower Maw BL7 ....9 D6
Lower Mead BL7 ....8 F1
Lower Meadow Rd SK9 ...131 E4
Lower Moat Cl SK4 .....169 E3
Lower Monton Rd M30 ....79 F2
Lower Mosley St M1,M2 .162 F8
Lower Moss La
　Manchester M15 ......162 D7
　Whitefield M45 ....62 F8
Lower New Row M28 ......60 A1
Lower Ormond St M15 ...163 A7
Lower Park Cres SK12 ..133 C6
Lower Park Prim Sch
　SK12 ....133 C4
Lower Park Rd
　Manchester M14 ....98 C3
　Poynton SK12 ....133 B5
Lower Rawson St BL4 ....42 E1
Lower Rd BL0 ....11 E8
Lower Seedley Rd M6 ...154 E3
Lower Sheriff St OL12 ..139 E8
Lower Southfield BL5 ....57 E7
Lower Sq SK13 ....104 A7
Lower St Farnworth BL4 ..60 C7
　18 Rochdale OL16 .....31 A4
Lower St Stephen St 18
　WN6 ....37 A1
Lower Stones OL3 ....50 E3
Lower Strines Rd SK6 ..126 A5
Lower Sutherland St
　M27 ....79 E8
Lower Tenterfield OL11 ..13 D2
Lower Tong BL7 ....24 F7
Lower Turf La OL4 ......68 B8
Lower Tweedale St
　OL11 ....139 F6
Lower Vickers St M40 ..160 D3
Lower Victoria St OL9 ..152 B7
Lower Wharf St OL6 ....166 C2
Lower Wheat End OL16 ...31 B8
Lower Woodhill Rd BL8 .140 D3
Lower Wrigley Gn OL3 ...51 C3
Lowerbank M34 ....100 F5
Lowercroft Bsns Pk BL8 ..26 F3
Lowercroft Rd BL8 ......26 F2
Lowerfield Dr SK2 .....124 E5
Lowerfields OL8 ....67 B4
Lowerfold OL12 ....14 C4
Lowerfold Cres OL12 ...14 C4
Lowerfold Dr OL12 .....14 C4
Lowerfold Way OL12 ....14 C4
Lowerlea SK12 ....135 C6
Lower Market St M14 ..115 B8
Lowerplace Prim Sch
　OL16 ....31 B4
Lowerwood La 12 BL2 ....25 B1
Lowes Rd BL9 ....28 A6
Lowes The WA14 ....119 B1
Lowestead Rd M11 ....83 C2
Lowestoft St M14 ....98 B2
Loweswater Ave M29 ....77 A7

Loweswater Rd
　Farnworth BL4 ....59 E7
　Gatley SK8 ....122 B3
Loweswater Terr SK15 ...86 A4
Lowfell Wlk M18 ....99 D3
Lowfield Ave
　Ashton-u-L OL6 ....85 F5
　Droylsden M43 ....83 F3
Lowfield Gdns WN3 ......92 C7
Lowfield Rd SK2,SK3 ...170 E7
Lowfield Wlk 7 M9 ......64 E3
Lowhouse Cl OL16 ....32 A7
Lowick Ave BL3 ....42 A3
Lowick Cl SK7 ....124 D2
Lowick Gn SK6 ....112 F5
Lowland Gr OL7 ....85 A6
Lowland Rd SK2 ....124 B4
Lowlands Cl M24 ....65 C5
Lowndes Cl SK2 ....124 B7
Lowndes La SK1,SK2 ...124 B7
Lowndes St BL1 ....142 B1
Lowndes Wlk 5 M13 ....164 D5
Lowood Ave M41 ....94 F4
Lowood Cl OL16 ....31 F6
Lowood St WN7 ....75 D5
Lowrey Wlk 11 M9 .....157 F7
Lowry Ct M7 Marple SK6 .126 B8
　Swinton M27 ....61 F1
Lowry Gr SK14 ....103 A4
Lowry Ho Eccles M30 ....79 E2
　4 Manchester M14 ....110 D8
Lowry The
　5 Manchester M14 ...110 C8
　* Salford M50 ....96 E7
Lowry Wlk BL1 ....143 D1
Lows The OL4 ....67 B5
Lowside Ave Bolton BL1 ..40 C6
　Romiley SK6 ....113 C5
Lowside Dr OL4 ....67 B5
Lowstern Cl BL7 ....8 E1
Lowther Ave
　Altrincham WA15 ......120 A6
　Culcheth WA3 ....91 F4
　Manchester M18 ....99 F4
　Royton OL2 ....48 C8
Lowther Cl M25 ....63 F3
Lowther Cres M24 ......46 D1
Lowther Dr WN7 ....76 E7
Lowther Gdns M41 ......94 D3
Lowther Rd
　Manchester M8 ....64 A1
　Prestwich M25 ....62 F3
　Rochdale OL11 ....30 E4
Lowther St BL3 ....42 A4
Lowther Terr WN6 ......35 C8
Lowthorpe St M14 ......98 A2
Lowton Ave M9 ....157 F7
Lowton Bsns Pk WA3 ....91 A7
Lowton Com High Sch
　WA3 ....91 B8
Lowton Gdns WA3 ....90 B5
Lowton Jun & Inf Sch
　WA3 ....91 A7
Lowton Rd Golborne WA3 .74 C1
　Sale M33 ....108 A4
Lowton St 5 M26 ....44 A3
Lowton St Mary's CE Prim
　Sch WA3 ....91 A8
Lowton West Prim Sch
　WA3 ....90 D8
Loxford St M15 ....162 F6
Loxham St BL4 ....42 D2
Loxley Wlk M40 ....160 E4
Loxton Cres WN3 ....55 B3
Loynd St BL0 ....11 C8
Lubeck St M9 ....157 E8
Lucas Rd BL4 ....60 A2
Lucas St Bury BL9 .....141 A3
　Oldham OL4 ....67 B7
Lucas Wlk M11 ....160 F1
Lucerne Cl OL9 ....152 C6
Lucerne Rd SK7 ....123 E3
Lucien Cl M12 ....164 E5
Luciol Cl M29 ....77 A8
Lucknow St OL11 ......139 F5
Lucy St Bolton BL1 ....142 A1
　Manchester M15 ......161 C6
　Salford M7 ....155 D5
　Stockport SK3 ....170 E8
Ludford Gr M33 ....107 F1
Ludgate Hill M4 ....159 B3
Ludgate Rd
　Failsworth M40 ....83 C4
　Rochdale OL11 ....30 E4
Ludgate St M4 ....159 A3
Ludlow Ave Hindley WN2 .57 A4
　Prestwich M25,M45 ...63 B6
　Swinton M27 ....79 C7
Ludlow Dr WN7 ....76 E7
Ludlow Pk 2 OL4 ....67 D6
Ludlow Rd SK2 ....124 C8
Ludlow St WN6 ....19 D3
Ludovic Terr WN1 ......37 E3
Ludwell Wlk 11 M8 ....156 A6
Ludworth Prim Sch SK6 .126 B8
Lugano Rd SK7 ....123 E3
Luke Kirby Ct M27 ......61 F1
Luke Rd M43 ....84 B1
Luke St Ashton-in-M WN4 .73 D5
　17 Bacup OL13 ....3 C8
Luke Wlk M8 ....156 B6
Lullington Cl M22 .....121 E1
Lullington Rd M6 ......154 D4

Lulworth Ave M41 ....94 F2
Lulworth Cl BL8 ....27 C6
Lulworth Cres M35 .....84 B8
Lulworth Dr WN2 ....57 A7
Lulworth Gdns M23 ....120 F8
Lulworth Rd Bolton BL3 .146 A3
　Eccles M30 ....79 C3
　Middleton M24 ....47 A2
Lum Head Prim Sch
　SK8 ....122 B3
Lum St BL1 ....148 A8
Lumb Carr Ave BL0 .....11 A4
Lumb Carr Rd BL0,BL8 ...11 A4
Lumb Cl SK7 ....132 E6
Lumb Cotts BL0 ....1 B4
Lumb Flats BL0 ....1 B4
Lumb Holes La BB4 ......2 E7
Lumb La Bramhall SK7 ..132 E6
　Droylsden M43 ....100 C8
　Droylsden M43 ....84 C1
Lumber La M28 ....60 A3
Lumley Cl M14 ....98 B4
Lumn Hollow SK14 .....167 E2
Lumn Rd SK14 ....167 E2
Lumn St BL9 ....28 D4
Lumn's La M27 ....62 C1
Lumsden St BL3 ....145 E5
Lumwood BL1 ....142 B3
Luna St M4 ....159 B2
Lund Ave M26 ....42 B8
Lund St M16 ....161 C6
Lundale Wlk 18 M40 ....83 A6
Lundy Ave M21 ....109 C5
Lune Cl M45 ....45 A1
Lune Dr M45 ....63 A8
Lune Gr Heywood OL10 ...29 B3
　Leigh WN7 ....75 C5
Lune Rd WN2 ....56 A2
Lune St Oldham OL8 ....66 F4
　Tyldesley M29 ....76 F8
Lune Way SK5 ....111 F5
Lune Wlk Droylsden M43 .100 B8
　Whitefield M45 ....63 A8
Lunedale 7 M26 ....58 E2
Lunedale Gn SK2 ......124 E6
Lunehurst 18 WA3 ......90 E8
Lunn Ave M18 ....99 F6
Luntswood Gr WA12 .....89 A4
Lupin Ave BL4 ....42 A2
Lupin Cl OL1 ....49 E3
Lupton St Denton M34 ..100 F4
　Manchester M3 ....158 D2
Lurden Wlk OL9 ....66 B4
Lurdin La WN1,WN6 .....37 B7
Lurgan Ave M33 ....108 C3
Lutener Av WA14 ......119 D8
Luton Dr M23 ....121 A4
Luton Gr M46 ....58 B3
Luton Rd SK5 ....111 F8
Luton St Bolton BL3 ...42 A4
　3 Bury BL9 ....27 B1
Luxor Gr M34 ....99 F3
Luzley Brook Rd OL2 ..149 A5
Luzley Rd OL5,OL6 .....86 B7
Lyceum Pas 1 OL16 ....139 F7
Lyceum Pl M15 ....163 A7
Lychgate WN5 ....54 E5
Lychgate Ct M40 ......67 E4
Lychgate Mews
　Manchester,Chorlton-cum-Hardy
　M21 ....109 A8
　Manchester,Heaton Mersey
　SK4 ....110 C8
Lydbrook Cl BL1 ......145 E6
Lydden Ave M11 ....83 D3
Lydford OL11 ....139 E6
Lydford Gn WN6 ....36 F8
Lydford St M6 ....81 C4
Lydford Wlk M13 ......163 C6
Lydgate Ave BL2 ....42 E8
Lydgate Cl Denton M34 .101 B1
　Mossley SK15 ....86 E6
　Whitefield M45 ....45 A1
Lydgate Dr OL4 ....68 C5
Lydgate Fold OL4 ......68 C5
Lydgate Rd Droylsden M43 .83 E2
　Sale M33 ....108 C2
Lydgate The OL15 ......16 E6
Lydgate Wlk M45 ....45 A1
Lydiat La SK9 ....137 A1
Lydiate Cl BL3 ....147 D3
Lydney Ave SK8 ....131 C7
Lydney Rd M41 ....94 D3
Lyefield Ave WN1 ......37 F1
Lyefield Wlk 24 OL16 ..31 B6
Lymbridge Dr BL6 ......21 D1
Lyme Ave SK9 ....131 B1
Lyme Clough Way M24 ..46 F4
Lyme Gr
　Altrincham WA14 .....119 C4
　Droylsden M43 ....99 F8
　Marple SK6 ....126 B8
　Romiley SK6 ....113 D3
　Stockport SK4 ....170 F7
Lyme Park Ctry Pk*
　SK12 ....135 B1
Lyme Rd Hazel Grove SK7 .124 E1
　High Lane SK12 ......135 A6
　Poynton SK12 ....133 E1
Lyme St Hazel Grove SK7 .124 D3
　Manchester SK4 ......110 F7
　Newton-le-W WA12 ....89 C3
Lyme Terr 1 SK16 .....166 B1

Lymefield Dr M28 ....78 A7
Lymefield Gr SK2 ......124 B6
Lymefield Terr SK14 ...115 B7
Lymefield Visiter Ctr*
　SK13 ....115 B8
Lymewood Dr
　Disley SK12 ....135 C6
　Wilmslow SK9 ....137 E8
Lymington Cl M24 ......65 B5
Lymington Dr M23 .....108 D1
Lymm Cl Stockport SK3 .170 D6
　Walkden M28 ....60 A3
Lymm High Sch WA13 ...117 B3
Lymm Rd WA14 ....118 B5
Lymm Wlk SK8 ....123 A5
Lymn St WN2 ....56 B3
Lyn Gr OL10 ....29 A3
Lynbridge Cl WN5 .....53 E5
Lyncombe Cl SK8 ......132 B6
Lyndale Ave Reddish SK5 .99 F3
　Swinton M27 ....61 F7
Lyndale Dr OL15 ....16 A6
Lyndene Ave M28 ......79 A8
Lyndene Ct OL10 ......29 C3
Lyndene Gdns SK8 .....122 B6
Lyndene Rd M22 ....121 D5
Lyndhurst Ave
　Ashton-u-L OL6 ....85 B5
　Denton M34 ....100 E3
　Hazel Grove SK7 .....124 C1
　Irlam M44 ....94 B3
　Manchester M25 ......63 E3
　Oldham OL9 ....65 F5
　Romiley SK6 ....112 F4
　Sale M33 ....107 F3
　Trub OL11 ....47 D8
　Urmston M41 ....94 D3
Lyndhurst Cl SK9 .....136 D5
Lyndhurst Com Prim Sch
　SK16 ....166 C1
Lyndhurst Dr WA15 ....120 A2
Lyndhurst Prim Sch OL8 .66 D3
Lyndhurst Rd
　Manchester M20 ......110 B5
　Oldham OL8 ....66 D3
　Reddish SK5 ....99 E6
　Stretford M32 ....96 A3
Lyndhurst St M6 ......154 E2
Lyndhurst View SK16 ..166 C1
Lyndon Ave WN6 ....36 A7
Lyndon Cl Bury BL8 ....26 F6
　Oldham OL4 ....68 C8
Lyndon Croft OL8 .....66 D4
Lyndon Rd M44 ....93 F2
Lyne Ave SK13 ....116 A8
Lyne Edge Cres SK16 ..101 F7
Lyne Edge Rd SK14 ....102 A7
Lyne View SK14 ....101 F6
Lyneham Wlk
　3 Manchester M9 .....64 E5
　Salford M7 ....155 F6
Lyngard Cl SK9 ....131 E1
Lyngarth Ho 1 WA14 ..119 E6
Lyngate Cl SK1 ....124 A8
Lynham Dr OL10 ....46 D8
Lynmouth Ave
　Manchester M20 ......110 A6
　Oldham OL8 ....66 F3
　10 Reddish SK5 .....111 E7
　Royton OL2 ....48 C3
　Urmston M41 ....107 A8
Lynmouth Cl
　Chadderton OL9 ......47 E1
　Radcliffe M26 ....44 C4
　Wigan WN6 ....37 A2
Lynmouth Ct M25 ......62 F3
Lynn Ave M33 ....108 D6
Lynn Dr M43 ....84 A1
Lynn St OL9 ....66 C6
Lyne Cl SK13 ....116 F8
Lynnwood Dr OL11 .....30 B8
Lynnwood Rd M19 ......110 D2
Lynroyle Way OL11 ....30 D3
Lynside Wlk M22 ......130 E8
Lynsted Ave BL3 ......42 E3
Lynstock Way BL6 .....39 E6
Lynthorpe Ave M44 ....105 D6
Lynthorpe Rd M40 .....65 D2
Lynton Ave
　Hattersley SK14 .....102 C2
　Irlam M44 ....105 C2
　Oldham OL8 ....66 F3
　Rochdale OL13 ....30 B3
　Royton OL2 ....48 C3
　Swinton M27 ....61 F1
　Urmston M41 ....94 C2
　Wigan WN6 ....37 A3
Lynton Cl OL9 ....47 A1
Lynton Cres M28 ......78 D8
Lynton Dr 9 High Lane SK6 .134 E8
　Manchester M19 .....110 F7
　Prestwich M25 ....63 C6
Lynton Gr WA15 ....119 F5
Lynton La SK9 ....137 A2
Lynton Lea M26 ....44 C4
Lynton Mews SK9 .....137 A2
Lynton Park Rd SK8 ...131 F8
Lynton Rd Bolton BL3 ..146 C2
　Cheadle SK8 ....122 C5
　Hindley WN2 ....56 F6
　Manchester,Chorlton-cum-Hardy
　M21 ....97 A1
　Manchester,Heaton Chapel
　SK4 ....111 C5

Lynton Rd continued
Swinton M27 ....61 F1
Tyldesley M29 ....77 D8
Lynton St Leigh WN7 ...75 D5
Manchester M14 ....98 B2
Lynton Wlk SK14 ....102 C2
Lyntonvale Ave SK8 ...122 B6
Lynway Dr M20 ....110 B5
Lynway Gr M24 ....47 B2
Lynwell Rd M30 ....79 D2
Lynwood
Altrincham WA15 ....129 A8
Wilmslow SK9 ....137 A6
Lynwood Ave Bolton BL3 ..42 B2
Eccles M30 ....79 D2
Golborne WA3 ....90 E6
Manchester M16 ....97 C2
Lynwood Cl OL7 ....85 A7
Lynwood Ct M8 ....63 F2
Lynwood Dr OL4 ....67 E8
Lynwood Gr Atherton M46 ..58 B3
Bolton BL2 ....25 D4
Droylsden M34 ....84 C1
Reddish SK4 ....111 C6
Sale M33 ....108 C5
Lyon Gr M28 ....79 A8
Lyon Ind Est WA14 ....119 B7
Lyon Rd Altrincham WA14 ..119 C7
Kearsley BL4 ....60 E6
Wigan WN6 ....37 A2
Lyon St Ashton-in-M WN4 ..72 F7
Shaw OL2 ....149 B7
Swinton M27 ....79 F7
Wigan WN3 ....150 B7
Lyons Dr BL8 ....27 A1
Lyons Fold M33 ....108 B6
Lyons Rd M17 ....96 A7
Lyra Pl M7 ....81 C3
Lysander Cl M14 ....110 B8
Lyth St M14 ....110 D7
Lytham Ave M21 ....109 C7
Lytham Cl OL6 ....85 E6
Lytham Ct OL6 ....85 E6
Lytham Dr Bramhall SK7 ..133 A7
Heywood OL10 ....29 C1
Lytham Rd
Ashton-in-M WN4 ....72 F5
Gatley SK8 ....122 B1
Manchester M14,M19 .....98 F1
Urmston M41 ....94 C2
Lytham St Rochdale OL12 ..14 E3
Stockport SK3 ....170 F6
Lytherton Ave M44 ....105 E6
Lytton Ave M8 ....156 A6
Lytton Rd M43 ....84 A2
Lytton St BL1 ....143 D2

M

Mab's Cross Prim Sch
WN1 ....37 D1
Mabel Ave Bolton BL3 ...42 A3
Worsley M28 ....79 A7
Mabel Rd M35 ....66 A1
Mabel St 5 Bolton BL1 ..144 C8
Failsworth M40 ....83 D5
2 Rochdale OL12 ....14 D2
Westhoughton BL5 ....57 F6
Wigan WN5 ....54 E6
Mabel's Brow BL4 ......60 E7
Maberry Cl WN6 ....35 D7
Mabfield Rd M14 ....98 C1
Mableden Cl SK8 ....131 D8
Mabs Ct OL6 ....85 D2
Macaulay St
Rochdale OL11 ....30 D2
Royton OL2 ....48 E4
Macaulay Way 7 M34 ..113 A8
Macauley Cl SK16 ......102 A7
Macauley Pl WN3 ....54 F4
Macauley Rd
Manchester M16 ....97 B2
Reddish SK5 ....99 E1
Macclesfield Ct WN2 ...56 C5
Macclesfield Rd
Alderley Edge SK9 ......137 B1
Hazel Grove SK7 ....133 F8
Wilmslow SK9 ....137 D6
Macdonald Ave
Farnworth BL4 ....60 B7
Wigan WN3 ....90 B3
Macdonald Rd M44 .....105 E8
Macdonald St Oldham OL8 ..66 F4
Wigan WN5 ....54 B6
Macefin Ave M21 ....109 D4
Macfarren St M12 ....99 A3
Macintosh Way OL1 ....153 F7
Mackenzie Ave WN3 ...56 E8
Mackenzie Gr BL1 ......24 D5
Mackenzie Ind Pk SK3 ..123 B6
Mackenzie Rd M7 ....81 B6
Mackenzie St Bolton BL1 ..143 D4
Manchester M12 ....99 A3
Mackenzie Wlk OL1 ....153 F7
Mackeson Dr OL6 ....85 E4
Mackeson Rd OL6 ....85 E4
Maclaren Dr M8 ....63 E1
Maclure Rd OL11 ......139 F6
Macnair Cl SK6 ....126 A5
Macnair Mews SK6 .....126 A5
Madams Wood Rd M28 ..60 A3
Maddison Rd M43 ....99 F8
Madeira Pl M30 ....79 C2

Madeley Cl
Altrincham WA14 ......128 E8
Wigan WN3 ....54 E3
Madeley Dr OL9 ....152 B6
Madeley Gdns
Bolton BL1 ....143 E2
Rochdale OL12 ....14 C1
Maden St M29 ....76 F6
Maden Wlk OL9 ....152 B8
Madn's Sq 9 OL15 ......16 B5
Madison Apartments
M16 ....161 B5
Madison Ave
Cheadle SK8 ....123 A2
Droylsden M34 ....100 C8
Madison Gdns M35 ......83 E7
Madison St M40 ....78 E1
Madras Rd SK3 ....123 C7
Maesbrook Dr M20 .....77 A8
Mafeking Ave BL9 ......28 A5
Mafeking Pl WN4 ....73 C3
Mafeking Rd BL2 ....42 E7
Mafeking St OL8 ....66 C3
Magda Rd SK2 ....124 D6
Magdala St Heywood OL10 ..46 E8
Oldham OL1 ....153 E8
Magdalen Dr WN4 ......72 F4
Magenta Ave M44 ......105 E6
Magna Carta Ct M6,M27 ..80 B6
Magnolia Cl
5 Partington M31 .....105 E2
**Sale M33 ....107 C6
Magnolia Ct
6 Sale M33 ....107 C6
7 Salford M6 ....81 A2
Magpie Cl M43 ....84 C3
Magpie La OL4 ....67 E4
Magpie Wlk 8 M11 .....160 F1
Maguire Ave SK13 .....104 A6
Maher Gdns M15 ....97 E4
Mahogany Wlk 11 M33 ..107 C5
Mahood St SK3 ....170 D7
Maida St M12 ....99 B2
Maiden Cl
5 Ashton-u-L OL7 ....85 A6
Rawtenstall BB4 ....2 F8
Maiden Mews 4 M27 ....79 F7
Maidford Cl
Manchester M4 ....160 D1
Stretford M32 ....96 E2
Maidstone Ave M21 ....97 A1
Maidstone Cl WN7 ......57 C2
Maidstone Mews 2 M21 ..97 A1
Maidstone Rd SK4 .....110 D3
Maidstone Wlk 8 SK14 ..101 A1
Main Ave M19 ....110 F7
Main Dr OL11 ....48 D1
Main La WA3 ....90 F3
Main Rd Oldham OL9 ...152 C7
Swinton M27 ....62 C3
Main St Billinge WN5 ...71 E5
Hyde SK14 ....167 D4
Maine Rd M14 ....98 A3
Mainhill Wlk M40 ......83 C5
Mainprice Cl M6 ......154 F4
Mains Ave WN2 ....73 F7
Mainwaring Dr SK9 ...137 D8
Mainwaring Terr M23 ..109 A2
Mainway M24 ....64 F6
Mainway E M24 ....65 C6
Mainwood Rd WA15 ...120 C5
Maismore Rd M22 .....121 B1
Maitland Ave M21 .....109 D5
Maitland Cl Rochdale OL12 ..15 C3
Walsden OL14 ....6 A8
Maitland St
Stockport SK1 ....124 B7
Walsden OL14 ....6 A8
Maitland Wlk OL9 .....152 B8
Maizefield Cl M33 .....108 F4
Majestic Mews WN5 ....53 B5
Major St Manchester M1 ..163 A8
Milnrow OL16 ....31 F6
Ramsbottom BL0 ......138 B6
Wigan WN5 ....54 C6
Major Wlk M5 ....161 B8
Makants Cl
Over Hulton M46 ....58 F5
Tyldesley M29 ....77 E8
Makepeace Wlk M8 .....63 E2
Makerfield Dr M42 ......89 A5
Makerfield Way WN2 ...56 B7
Makin Cl OL10 ....29 D1
Makin St M1 ....163 A7
Makinson Arc 18 WN1 ..150 C8
Makinson Ave
Hindley WN2 ....56 E7
Horwich BL6 ....22 E1
Makinson La BL6 ....22 F4
Makkah Cl M40 ....83 A5
Malaga Ave M90 ......130 B7
Malakoff St SK15 ....85 E1
Malbrook Wlk 3 M13 ..163 C6
Malby St OL1 ....153 F8
Malcolm Ave M27 ......62 A3
Malcolm Dr M27 ....62 A2
Malden Gr M23 ....121 A7
Maldon Cl
Hazel Grove SK2 ......125 A6
Little Lever BL3 ....43 A3
Wigan WN2 ....37 F2
Maldon Cres M27 ......79 F6
Maldon Dr M30 ....79 F4
Maldon Rd WN6 ....36 F8
Maldon St OL11 ....139 F5
Maldwyn Ave Bolton BL3 ..146 C2

Maldwyn Ave continued
Manchester M8 ....64 A2
Maleham St M7 ....155 E6
Malgam Dr M20 ....122 B8
Malham Ave WN3 ......55 A2
Malham Cl Leigh WN7 ...75 C5
Royton OL2 ....48 D4
Whitefield M45 ....63 A8
Malham Ct SK2 ....124 D6
Malham St 4 BL3 .....146 A4
Malika Pl WN4 ....72 E6
Malimson Bourne M7 ..155 D6
Mall The Bury BL9 ....140 F2
5 Eccles M30 ....79 F2
Hyde SK14 ....167 D2
Sale M33 ....108 B5
Stalybridge SK15 ......102 E6
Mallaig Wlk M11 ......165 C8
Mallard Cl
Dukinfield SK16 ....101 E7
Hazel Grove SK2 ......125 A5
1 Oldham OL8 ....66 D2
Mallard Cres SK12 ....133 A4
Mallard Ct SK8 ....131 B8
Mallard Dr BL6 ....22 A3
Mallard Gn WA14 .....119 B8
Mallard St M1 ....163 A7
Mallards Reach SK6 ...113 A2
Mallet Cres BL1 ....23 F7
Malley Gdns OL5 ....68 C5
Malley Wlk 8 M9 ......64 E3
Malling Rd M23 ....121 A4
Mallison St BL1 ....143 F3
Mallory Ave OL7 ....85 B5
Mallory Ct WA14 ......119 C3
Mallory Dr WN7 ....76 C5
Mallory Rd SK14 ......102 A4
Mallory Wlk M23 ......120 D8
Mallow Croft OL16 .....31 C4
Mallow Wlk M31 ......105 F2
Mallowdale M28 ....78 B8
Mallowdale Ave 4 M14 ..110 B8
Mallowdale Cl BL1 ......40 D7
Mallowdale Rd SK2 ....124 E5
Malmesbury Cl SK12 ..133 D4
Malmesbury Rd SK8 ...132 B6
Malpas Ave WN1 ....37 E1
Malpas Cl Cheadle SK8 ..123 A4
Handforth SK9 ....131 E1
Malpas Dr WA14 ......107 E1
Malpas St
Manchester M12 ......165 A6
Oldham OL1 ....153 F7
Malrae WA15 ....119 E1
Malsham Rd M23 ......108 F2
Malt St M15 ....162 D7
Malta Cl M24 ....65 D8
Malta St Manchester M4 ..160 D1
Oldham OL4 ....67 D6
Maltby Dr BL3 ....146 C3
Maltby Rd M23 ....120 F6
Maltings La 7 OL11 .....30 C2
Malton Ave Bolton BL3 ..146 A4
Golborne WA3 ....90 E7
Manchester M21 ....109 B8
Whitefield M45 ....44 F2
Malton Cl Chadderton OL9 ..47 F1
Leigh WN7 ....75 C6
1 Whitefield M45 ....44 F2
Malton Dr
Altrincham WA14 ......119 A6
Hazel Grove SK7 ......133 D7
Malton Rd
Boothstown M28 ....77 E7
Manchester SK4 ....168 A4
Malton St OL8 ....153 D5
Malus Ct M6 ....81 A3
Malverley Dr WN7 ......76 C5
Malvern Ave
Ashton-u-L OL6 ....85 C7
Atherton M46 ....58 F5
Bolton BL1 ....142 A1
Bury BL9 ....27 F5
Droylsden M43 ....84 C2
Hindley WN2 ....57 A4
Urmston M41 ....95 B2
Wythenshawe SK8 ....121 F5
Malvern Cl
Ashton-in-M WN4 ....73 B4
2 Farnworth BL4 ....59 F8
Horwich BL6 ....22 C5
Milnrow OL16 ....32 A7
Pendlebury M27 ....80 D6
Prestwich M25 ....62 C3
Royton OL2 ....48 C3
5 Shaw OL2 ....48 F8
Stockport SK4 ....169 D3
Wigan WN3 ....54 C3
Malvern Cres WN3 ......55 F4
Malvern Dr
Altrincham WA14 ......119 B5
Pendlebury M27 ....80 D6
Malvern Gr
Manchester M20 ......110 A6
Salford M6 ....80 C3
Malvern Rd M24 ....65 A5
Malvern Rise SK13 ....104 A5
Malvern Row 1 M15 ..162 D6
Malvern St
Manchester M15 ......162 D6
Oldham OL8 ....153 D5
Malvern St E OL11 .....30 C7
Malvern St W OL11 .....30 C7
Malvern Terr WN7 ......75 F3

Malvern Way BB4 ....1 A7
Man Utd FC (Old Trafford)
M17 ....96 F5
Manby Rd M18 ....99 B4
Manby St M18 ....99 B4
Mancentral Trad Est
M3 ....158 D1
Manchester Acad M15 ..98 B4
Manchester Airport Sta
M90 ....130 B7
Manchester Bsns Sch
M15 ....163 A6
Manchester CE Cath*
M3 ....158 F2
Manchester Chambers
OL1 ....153 E7
Manchester City Art Gal*
M1 ....159 A1
Manchester Coll of Art &
Tech (St John's Ctr)
M3 ....158 E1
Manchester Coll of Arts &
Tech (Openshaw Campus)
M11 ....165 B7
Manchester Evening News
Arena* M3 ....158 F3
Manchester Gram Sch
M13 ....98 E2
Manchester High Sch for
Girls M14 ....98 C1
Manchester Ind Pk M40 ..157 F5
Manchester International
Airport M90 ....130 A7
Manchester Islamic High Sch
for Girls M21 ....97 A1
Manchester Jewish Mus*
M8 ....159 A4
Manchester Jewish Sch
M25 ....63 B3
Manchester Jun Girls Sch
M7 ....63 E1
Manchester Met Univ
Hollings Bldg M14 .....98 D2
Manchester Met Univ The
Manchester M1 ....163 B8
Manchester M15 ......163 A7
Manchester,Didsbury M20 ..110 B2
Manchester Metropolitan
Univ, Elizabeth Gaskell
Campus M13,M14 ....98 C4
Manchester Mus The*
M13 ....163 B6
Manchester New Rd
Middleton M24,M9 ......64 F6
Partington M31 ....105 F3
Manchester Old Rd
Bury BL9 ....140 E1
Middleton M24 ....64 D7
Manchester RC Cath*
M3 ....158 D2
Manchester Rd
Altrincham WA14 ......119 D7
Ashton-u-L M34,M43,OL7 ..84 E1
Bolton BL3 ....42 B4
Bury BL9 ....140 E1
Bury,Blackford Bridge BL9,
M45 ....44 F5
Carrington M31 ....106 B6
Cheadle M20,SK8 .....122 D7
Denton M34 ....100 C3
Diggle HD7,OL3 ....52 A8
Droylsden M34 ....100 B8
Dukinfield SK14 ....101 C3
Handforth SK9 ....131 C2
Haslingden BB4 ....1 A8
Heywood OL10 ....46 D7
Hollinfare WA3 ....105 A2
Hollinfare,Hollins Green
WA3 ....105 B3
Ince-in-M WN2,WN1 ....56 A7
Leigh M29,WN7 ....76 D4
Manchester M16,M21 ..97 B1
Manchester M21 ......109 A8
Mossley OL3,OL5,SK15 ..68 D3
Oldham OL8 ....66 C3
Pendlebury M27 ....80 B7
Ramsbottom BL0,BL9 ..11 E4
Reddish M34 ....99 B4
Rochdale OL11 ....30 C4
Scot Lane End BL6 .....38 E8
Shaw OL2 ....149 A5
Stockport SK4 ....169 E4
Swinton M27,M28 ......61 C2
Tintwistle SK13 ....104 A3
Tintwistle SK13 ....104 A7
Tyldesley M29 ....77 C8
Walkden M28 ....60 E2
Westhoughton BL5 .....40 B1
Manchester Rd E M38 ..60 A2
Manchester Rd N M34 ..100 D4
Manchester Rd S M34 ..100 D3
Manchester Rd W M38 ..59 E5
Manchester Road Prim Sch
M43 ....84 C2
Manchester Royal Infmy
M13 ....163 C5
Manchester Science Pk
M15 ....163 A5
Manchester St
Heywood OL10 ....29 E1
Manchester M16 ......161 C5
Oldham OL8,OL9 ......153 D6
Manchester United Mus*
M32 ....96 F5
Manchet St OL11 ....30 B1
Mancroft Ave BL3 ......147 D4

Mancroft Terr BL3 .....147 D4
Mancroft Wlk 1 M1 ....163 B7
Mancunian Rd M34 ....113 A8
Mancunian Way
Manchester M1,M12,M15 ..163 B7
Manchester M15 ......162 D7
Mandalay Gdns SK6 ...125 D7
Mandarin Gn WA14 ....119 B8
Mandarin Wlk 3 M6 .....81 A3
Manderville Cl WN3 .....54 D2
Mandeville St M19 .....111 B8
Mandeville Terr BL8 .....10 B2
Mandley Ave M40 ....65 D2
Mandley Cl BL3 ....43 A5
Mandley Park Ave M7 ..155 E7
Mandon Cl M26 ....43 E5
Manesty Cl M24 ....46 C2
Manet Cl M7 ....81 B8
Mangle St M1 ....159 B1
Mango Pl M6 ....81 A2
Manifold Dr SK6 ....134 F6
Manifold St M6 ....81 B5
Manilla Wlk 1 M11 ....160 F1
Manipur St M11 ....164 F8
Manley Ave Golborne WA3 ..73 F7
Swinton M27 ....61 E4
Manley Cl Leigh WN7 ...75 D4
Ramsbottom BL9 ....11 C2
Manley Cres BL5 ....40 B1
Manley Gr Bramhall SK7 ..132 E6
Mottram-in-L SK14 ....102 F3
Manley Park Jun Sch
M16 ....97 C3
Manley Park Prim Sch
M16 ....97 C3
Manley Rd
Manchester M16,M21 ..97 D1
Oldham OL8 ....66 E4
Rochdale OL11 ....30 C4
Sale M33 ....107 F1
Manley St Ince-in-M WN3 ..151 E6
Salford M7 ....155 D6
Manley Terr BL1 ......143 E4
Manley Way SK14 .....103 A3
Manley Units M16 ......97 E3
Manning Ave WN6 ......37 A2
Manningham Rd BL3 ...144 B5
Mannington Dr M9 ....156 C7
Mannion Ho WN1 ......151 D8
Mannock St OL8 ....153 D6
Manns OL3 ....68 F5
Manor Ave Golborne WA3 ..90 C8
Little Lever BL3 ....43 C3
Manchester M16 ....97 D2
Sale M33 ....107 D4
Urmston M41 ....95 B2
Manor Cl Chadderton OL9 ..152 C8
Cheadle SK8 ....123 C1
Denton M34 ....101 B2
Garswood WN4 ....72 C3
Uppermill OL4 ....68 E5
Shevington WN6 ......136 F8
Manor Ct Golborne WA3 ..90 C8
Sale M33 ....107 D4
5 Stockport SK1 ....112 A1
Stretford M32 ....96 B1
Manor Dr
Manchester M21 ......109 D4
Royton OL2 ....48 E3
Manor Farm Cl OL7 .....84 F5
Manor Farm Rise OL4 ..67 D7
Manor Gate Rd BL2 .....43 A8
Manor Gdns SK9 ......137 D7
Manor Gr Aspull WN2 ...38 B5
Leigh WN7 ....76 C3
Wigan WN5 ....54 B8
Manor Green Prim Sch
M34 ....113 A8
Manor High Sch M33 ..107 D5
Manor Hill Rd SK6 ....125 F7
Manor House Cl WA11 ..71 F8
Manor La OL3 ....51 E8
Manor Lo Bramhall SK8 ..123 C1
Pendlebury M27 ....80 D8
Manor Mill Cl OL12 ......15 D3
Manor Park Rd SK13 ..104 E1
Manor Park View SK13 ..104 E2
Manor Pk M41 ....95 D1
Manor Rd Bury BL9 ....141 A4
Manchester M19 ....99 B2
Marple SK6 ....125 F7
Middleton M24 ....65 A6
Oldham OL4 ....67 A5
Romiley SK6 ....113 B5
Sale M33 ....108 B5
Salford M6 ....154 D4
Shaw OL2 ....149 A6
Shevington WN6 ....36 A6
Stretford M32 ....96 A3
Swinton M27 ....79 F6
Tyldesley M29 ....77 C6
Wilmslow SK9 ....136 E8
Manor St Bolton BL1 ...145 F7
Bury BL9 ....141 A2
Denton M34 ....100 F7
Farnworth BL4 ....60 B8
Glossop SK13 ....104 D1
Golborne WA3 ....74 B1

Manor St *continued*
Kearsley BL4 61 B5
Manchester M12 163 C7
Middleton M24 47 A2
Mossley OL5 68 C2
Oldham OL2 49 A2
Ramsbottom BL0 138 B7
Wigan WN1 150 C8
Wigan,Worsley Hall WN5 54 F6
Manor View SK6 113 B5
Manor Way PR7 19 D8
Manor Wlk M34 100 F7
Manordale Wlk M40 156 C6
Manorfield Cl BL1 142 A1
Manorial Dr M38 59 E5
Mansart Cl WN4 73 D3
Manse Ave WN6 18 F5
Manse Gdns WA12 89 D4
Manse The OL5 86 C8
Mansell Way BL6 39 D8
Mansfield Ave
Denton M34 100 D5
Manchester M9 64 D4
Ramsbottom BL0 11 B2
Mansfield Cl
Ashton-u-L OL7 84 F1
Denton M34 100 D5
Mansfield Cres M34 100 D4
Mansfield Dr M9 64 E4
Mansfield Gr BL1 142 B1
Mansfield Grange OL11 30 C6
Mansfield Rd Hyde SK14 167 F1
Manchester M9 64 E4
Mossley OL5 68 E1
7 Oldham OL8 67 B5
Rochdale OL11 29 E7
Urmston M41 95 B1
Mansfield St
Ashton-u-L OL7 84 F1
Golborne WA3 73 F1
Mansfield View OL5 68 E1
Mansford Dr M40 157 F5
Manshaw Cres M34 100 A7
Manshaw Rd M11,M34 100 A7
Mansion Ave M45 44 E3
Manson Ave M15 162 D7
Manstead Wlk M40 160 E2
Manston Dr SK8 123 A2
Manswood Dr M8 156 A7
Mantell Wlk M40 83 A5
Manthorpe Ave M28 79 A7
Mantley La OL1,OL3 50 A7
Manton Ave
Manchester M9 65 B2
Reddish M34 100 A3
Manton Cl M7 155 F6
Manvers St SK5 169 E3
Manwaring St M35 83 E8
Manway Bsns Pk WA14 119 E8
Maple Ave
Altrincham WA15 120 E5
Atherton M46 58 B4
Bolton BL1 142 B1
Bury BL9 141 B2
Cheadle SK8 122 F2
Denton M34 100 E3
Droylsden M34 84 B1
Eccles M30 79 A4
Golborne WA3 90 F7
Hindley WN2 56 F3
Horwich BL6 22 E1
Ince-in-M WN2 151 F6
Manchester M21 109 B8
Marple SK6 125 F4
Newton-le-W WA12 89 D2
Poynton SK12 133 F3
Stalybridge SK15 101 F8
Stretford M32 96 D1
Whitefield M45 62 F6
Maple Cl Billinge WN5 71 D5
Chadderton OL9 48 B1
Kearsley BL4 60 F5
Middleton M24 65 D8
Sale M33 107 C4
Salford M6 154 F3
Shaw OL2 48 F8
Stockport SK2 124 B6
Maple Cres WN7 75 F7
Maple Ct SK4 168 C4
Maple Dr WN7 74 B7
Maple Gr Bury BL8 27 A5
Failsworth,Holt Lane End M35 83 E5
Failsworth,New Moston M40 65 F2
Prestwich M25 63 A6
Ramsbottom BL0 11 D6
Walkden M28 78 D8
Wigan WN6 37 A3
Maple Lo M23 120 C8
Maple Rd
Alderley Edge SK9 137 B3
Bramhall SK7 132 E6
Chadderton OL9 48 B1
Farnworth BL4 60 A8
Partington M31 105 E3
Sale M23 108 C1
Swinton M27 79 E6
Maple Rd W M23 120 C8
Maple St Ashton-in-M WN4 73 A6
Bolton BL3 145 D5
Bolton,Bradshaw BL2 25 C5
Oldham OL8 66 C3
Rochdale OL11 139 D6
Walsden OL14 6 A7
Maple Wlk M23 120 C8
Maplecroft SK1 124 B8
Mapledon Rd M9 157 F8
Maplefield Dr M28 78 B7
Maples SK9 136 F6
Maplewood Cl Royton OL1 48 C2
Stalybridge SK15 86 C3
Maplewood Gdns BL1 143 F2
Maplewood Ho BL1 143 E1
Maplewood Rd SK9 137 E8
Mapley Ave M22 121 D8
Maplin Cl M13 163 C7
Maplin Dr SK2 125 A5
Marble St
Manchester M2 159 A1
Oldham OL1 67 B8
Marbury Ave M14 98 B1
Marbury Cl Cheadle SK3 123 A7
Urmston M41 94 D3
Marbury Dr WA14 107 E1
Marbury Gr WN6 36 E8
Marbury Rd
Handforth SK9 131 B1
Reddish SK4 111 D7
Marcer Rd M40 160 D2
March Ave SK4 168 B2
March Dr BL8 27 D5
March St OL16 31 A7
Marchbank WN2 38 A2
Marchbank Dr SK8 122 C6
Marches Cl OL2 49 B4
Marchioness St 6 M18 99 F6
Marchmont Cl M13 164 D6
Marchwood Ave M21 97 D1
Marcliff Gr SK4 168 B2
Marcliffe Dr Reddish M19 99 C1
Rochdale OL11 30 B6
Marcliffe Ind Est SK7 124 E1
Marcroft Pl 6 OL11 31 A4
Marcus Garvey Ct M16 97 E2
Marcus Gr M14 98 C3
Marcus St BL1 142 B1
Mardale Ave
Manchester M20 110 C5
Royton OL2 48 C8
Swinton M27 61 C2
Urmston M41 94 F3
Mardale Cl Atherton M46 58 C5
Bolton BL2 25 F1
Prestwich M25 63 C7
Stalybridge SK15 86 A3
Mardale Dr 1 Bolton BL2 25 F1
Gatley SK8 122 B6
Middleton M24 46 E1
Mardale Rd M27 79 D6
Marden Rd M23 121 A5
Mardyke OL12 139 E8
Marfield Ave OL9 152 A5
Marfield St M9 64 E1
Marford Cl M22 121 D6
Marford Cres M33 107 F2
Margaret Ashton Cl M9 157 F7
Margaret Ave
Rochdale OL16 31 C7
Wigan WN6 36 C4
Margaret Ho 5 OL6 166 A2
Margaret Rd
Denton M34 101 A4
Droylsden M43 83 E2
Margaret St
Ashton-u-L OL6 166 A2
Ashton-u-L OL7 166 A1
3 Bury BL9 140 F1
Heywood OL10 29 B2
Hindley WN2 56 D6
Oldham OL8 66 B2
Reddish SK5 111 E7
Shaw OL2 149 B6
Wigan WN6 37 A1
Margaret Terr OL6 166 A2
Margate Ave M40 83 B5
Margate Rd SK5 111 F7
Margrove Chase BL6 40 C5
Margrove Cl M35 84 C7
Margrove Rd M6 80 C4
Margroy Cl OL12 15 A2
Marguerita Rd M40 83 D4
Marham Cl
Dukinfield SK14 101 D6
Manchester M21 109 E6
Maria St BL1 143 E2
Marie Cl M34 100 F2
Marie St M7 155 E7
Marigold St
Rochdale OL11 139 F5
Wigan WN5 54 D7
Marigold Terr M24 65 D7
Mariman Dr M8 64 A2
Marina Ave M34 101 A1
Marina Cl SK9 131 D5
Marina Cres M11 83 B3
Marina Dr Marple SK6 125 C7
Wigan WN5 54 D5
Marina Rd Droylsden M43 84 B2
Romiley SK6 112 E4
Marine Ave M31 105 D3
Marion Pl WN2 73 F8
Marion St Farnworth BL3 42 C2
Oldham OL8 66 F3
Maritime Cl WA12 89 C5
Maritime Ct 5 M33 107 F4
Marjorie Cl M18 165 B6
Mark Ave M6 81 B4
Mark Jones Wlk M40 83 B5
Mark La OL2 49 D6
Mark St Bacup OL13 3 C8
Boothstown M28 77 F7
Oldham OL9 153 D7
Rochdale OL12 15 B1
Markenfield Dr OL2 48 F7
Market App WN4 73 B3
Market Arc 8 SK13 104 C1
Market Ave OL6 166 B3
Market Chambers BL0 138 C7
Market Par BL9 140 F2
Market Pl Adlington PR7 21 A7
Ashton-u-L OL6 166 B3
13 Atherton M46 58 D3
Bury BL9 140 E2
Edenfield BL0 1 D3
Farnworth BL4 60 D8
Heywood OL10 29 D2
Hyde SK14 167 D2
Leigh WN7 75 F5
Middleton M24 47 A1
Mottram-in-L SK14 103 A3
Oldham OL1 153 E7
Ramsbottom BL0 138 C7
Romiley SK6 114 A2
Standish WN6 19 E1
Stockport SK1 169 F2
Wigan WN1 150 C8
Market Pl The BL1 145 F8
Market Prec BL4 60 D8
Market Sq OL2 48 D4
Market St Adlington PR7 21 A6
Altrincham WA14 119 D4
Ashton-u-L OL6 166 B3
Atherton M46 58 C3
Bolton BL1 145 F7
Broadbottom SK14 115 A8
Bury BL9 140 F1
Bury,Gigg BL9 44 F8
Bury,Tottington BL8 26 F6
Denton M34 100 F3
Disley SK12 135 D6
Droylsden M43 84 B1
Edenfield BL0 1 D4
Farnworth BL4 42 D1
7 Glossop SK13 104 C1
Heywood OL10 29 C2
Hindley WN2 56 D5
Hollingworth SK14 103 D5
Hyde SK14 167 D2
Kearsley M26 61 B8
Leigh WN7 75 F5
Little Lever BL3 43 B3
Manchester M1 159 A1
Manchester M4 158 F2
Marple SK6 125 F6
6 Middleton M24 46 F1
Mossley OL5 68 C1
Mottram-in-L SK14 103 A4
Newton-le-W WA12 89 A3
5 Rawtenstall BB4 2 F8
Shaw OL2 149 B6
Stalybridge SK15 86 A2
Standish WN6 19 E1
Swinton M27 62 A1
Tyldesley M29 58 F1
Westhoughton BL5 57 E8
Whitworth OL12,OL13 4 D4
Wigan WN1 150 C8
Market Street Sta M1 159 A1
Market Way
Rochdale OL16 139 F8
Salford M6 154 F3
Market Wlk M33 108 B4
Marketgate Sh Ctr WN1 150 C8
Markfield Ave M13 164 D5
Markham Cl M12 164 E8
Markham St SK14 101 D5
Markington St M14 98 A3
Markland Ct WN6 150 A8
Markland Hill BL1 40 E8
Markland Hill Cl BL1 23 F1
Markland Hill La BL1 23 F1
Markland Hill Prim Sch BL1 40 F8
Markland St
6 Bolton BL3 145 F6
Hyde SK14 167 E1
Ramsbottom BL0 138 C6
Wigan WN1 151 E8
Marklands Rd
Horwich BL6 22 E5
Tyldesley M29 77 A4
Marks St M26 44 A3
Markwood OL3 50 F4
Marl Gr WN5 53 D4
Marland Ave
Cheadle SK8 122 F2
Oldham OL8 67 A1
Rochdale OL11 30 B4
Marland Cl OL11 30 B5
Marland Cres SK5 111 F8
Marland Fold OL11 30 B5
Marland Fold Com Specl Sch OL8 67 A1
Marland Fold La OL8 66 F1
Marland Gn OL11 30 B4
Marland Hill Com Prim Sch OL11 30 C5
Marland Hill Rd OL11 30 C5
Marland Old Rd OL11 30 B4
Marland St OL9 66 A3
Marland Way M32 96 D3
Marlands Sq 15 M29 58 F1
Marlborough Ave
Alderley Edge SK9 137 B2
Bramhall SK8 123 B2
Ince-in-M WN3 55 F4
Manchester M16 97 C2
Marlborough Cl
Ashton-u-L OL7 100 E8
Denton M34 100 F3
Marple SK6 125 D7
Ramsbottom BL0 11 C3
Whitworth OL12 14 C7
Marlborough Ct BL1 23 E2
Marlborough Dr
Failsworth M35 83 E6
Reddish SK4 169 D4
Marlborough Gdns 3 BL4 59 F8
Marlborough Gr M43 84 C2
Marlborough Rd
Altrincham WA14 119 D2
Atherton M46 58 F4
Hyde SK14 113 E8
Irlam M44 94 B3
Manchester M7,M8 155 F6
Royton OL2 48 E2
Sale M33 108 B4
Salford,Ellesmere Park M30 80 A4
Salford,Higher Broughton M7 155 F7
Stretford M32 96 C3
Urmston M41 94 F2
Marlborough Rd Prim Sch M7 155 F6
Marlborough St
12 Ashton-u-L OL7 84 F1
5 Ashton-u-L OL7 84 F1
Bolton BL1 145 D8
Heywood OL10 46 E8
Oldham OL4 67 A6
14 Rochdale OL12 14 C1
Marlbrook Dr BL5 57 E5
Marlbrook Wlk BL3 147 F4
Marlcroft Ave SK4 168 B2
Marld Cres BL1 23 F2
Marle Ave OL5 68 E1
Marle Croft M45 62 C6
Marle Rise OL5 68 E1
Marled Hey BL7 9 D5
Marler Rd SK14 167 E4
Marley Cl WA15 119 F7
Marley Dr M33 108 A6
Marley Rd
Manchester M19 111 B8
Poynton SK12 133 E2
Marleyer Cl M40 83 C7
Marleyer Rise SK6 125 A8
Marlfield Ct M41 94 E1
Marlfield Rd
Altrincham WA15 129 D7
Shaw OL2 48 E8
Marlhill Cl SK2 124 E5
Marlhill Ct SK2 124 E5
Marlinford Dr M40 83 C5
Marloes WA14 119 B2
Marlor Ct OL10 29 B2
Marlor St M34 100 E4
Marlow Brow SK13 104 A4
Marlow Cl 2 Bolton BL2 25 F1
Cheadle SK8 122 F2
Urmston M41 95 B4
Marlow Ct PR7 20 F6
Marlow Dr
Altrincham WA14 118 F2
Handforth SK9 131 C5
Irlam M44 94 A3
Swinton M27 79 E6
Marlow Ho 9 M5 154 F1
Marlow Rd M9 64 F1
Marlow St SK13 104 A5
Marlowe Cl WN3 150 A5
Marlowe Dr M20 110 B4
Marlowe Wlk 15 M34 113 A7
Marlowe Wlks SK6 112 F2
Marlton Wlk M9 64 E4
Marlwood Cl OL1 48 C2
Marlwood Rd BL1 23 F2
Marmion Cl WA3 74 E1
Marmion Dr M21 109 A8
Marne Ave Ashton-u-L OL6 85 F5
Wythenshawe M22 121 E5
Marne Cres OL11 30 C7
Marnland Gr BL3 40 E4
Marnock Cl WN2 74 F8
Maroon Rd M22 130 F7
Marple Ave BL1 25 A4
Marple Cl Oldham OL8 66 D2
Shevington Moor WN6 19 B2
Marple Ct SK1 124 A7
Marple Gr M32 96 C3
Marple Hall Dr SK6 125 D7
Marple Hall Sch SK6 125 C7
Marple Old Rd SK2 125 A6
Marple Rd
Charlesworth SK13 115 B5
Stockport SK2 124 E6
Marple St M15 162 D5
Marple Sta SK6 126 A7
Marquis Ave BL9 140 E4
Marquis Dr SK8 131 D7
Marquis St M19 99 D1
Marrick Ave SK8 122 C5
Marrick Cl WN3 55 A2
Marriott St
Manchester M20 110 B6
Stockport SK1 170 F8
Marriott's Ct M2 159 A1
Marron Pl M2 162 F8
Marryat Ct M12 164 F6
Mars Ave BL3 146 C3
Mars St Edgworth BL7 9 E6
Oldham OL9 152 C7
Marsden Cl
Ashton-u-L OL7 84 E5
Mossley OL5 68 B1
Royton OL16 48 C8
Marsden Dr WA15 120 C6
Marsden Rd Bolton BL1 145 E7
Romiley SK6 113 C3
Marsden St
Boothstown M28 77 F6
Bury BL9 140 F3
Eccles M30 79 C3
Hadfield SK13 104 A4
Ince-in-M WN3 55 F4
13 Manchester M2 158 F1
Middleton M24 65 C7
Walkden M28 61 B2
Westhoughton BL5 57 E8
Wigan WN1 150 C8
Wigan,Worsley Hall WN5 54 F6
Marsett Cl OL12 14 A1
Marsett Wlk 9 M23 108 F2
Marsh Brook Fold BL5 57 A7
Marsh Cl SK3 170 D6
Marsh Fold La BL1 144 C8
Marsh Gn WN5 36 D1
Marsh Green Prim Sch WN5 54 D8
Marsh Hey Cl M38 59 F6
Marsh La Ashley WA16 128 A4
Farnworth BL4 60 A8
Little Lever BL3 43 B4
Wigan WN1 150 C8
Marsh Rd Little Lever BL3 43 B4
Walkden M38 60 B4
Marsh Row WN2 57 A4
Marsh St 12 Bolton BL1 143 E2
Horwich BL6 22 A4
Walkden M28 60 F2
Westhoughton BL5 39 E1
Marshall Ct
6 Ashton-u-L OL6 85 D2
1 Oldham OL1 153 E8
Marshall Rd M19 99 A1
Marshall St Denton M34 100 E4
Leigh WN7 75 E4
Manchester M4 159 B2
Manchester,Brunswick M12 163 C6
Rochdale OL16 31 C7
Marshall Stevens Way M17 96 B5
Marsham Cl
7 Manchester M13 98 E4
Oldham OL4 68 B5
Marsham Dr SK6 126 A5
Marsham Rd
Hazel Grove SK7 124 C1
Westhoughton BL5 57 F6
Marshbank 16 BL5 39 E1
Marshbrook Cl WN2 57 A6
Marshbrook Dr M9 64 C2
Marshbrook Rd 1 M41 95 C3
Marshdale WN7 75 D6
Marshdale Rd BL1 40 F8
Marshfield Rd WA15 120 C6
Marshfield Wlk 13 M13 163 C6
Marshway Dr WA12 89 B5
Marsland Ave WA15 120 B8
Marsland Cl M34 100 B3
Marsland Green La M29 76 E3
Marsland Rd
Altrincham WA15 120 B6
Marple SK6 125 D7
Sale M33 108 B3
Marsland St
Hazel Grove SK7 124 D2
Stockport SK1 169 F2
Marsland St N M7 155 F7
Marsland St S M7 155 F7
Marsland Street Ind Ctr SK7 124 E2
Marsland Terr SK1 124 B8
Marslands OL3 51 B3
Marston Cl Failsworth M35 84 C6
Horwich BL6 39 F8
Whitefield M45 63 C8
Marston Dr M44 94 B1
Marston Ho 8 M5 154 F1
Marston Rd Salford M7 155 E8
Stretford M32 96 F2
Marston St M40 157 D5
Martens Rd M44 105 E5
Martha St 8 Bolton BL3 147 D4
Oldham OL1 153 D8
Martha's Terr OL16 15 C3
Marthall Dr M33 108 E1
Marthall Way 8 SK9 131 E5
Martham Dr SK2 125 A6
Martin Ave Farnworth BL4 59 F7
Little Lever BL3 43 C3
Newton-le-W WA12 89 C5
8 Oldham OL4 67 C6
Martin Cl Denton M34 100 F5
Hazel Grove SK2 124 F5
Martin Dr M44 94 A4
Martin Gr BL4 60 F7
Martin Ho M14 98 D3
Martin La OL12 14 B1
Martin Rd M27 62 B2
Martin St 8 Atherton M46 58 D3
Bury BL9 28 D3
Denton M34 100 F7
Edgworth BL7 9 D4
Hyde SK14 167 E2
Salford M5 154 E2
Martindale Cl OL2 48 E5
Martindale Cres
Manchester M12 164 E5
Middleton M24 46 D3
Wigan WN5 54 F6
Martindale Gdns BL1 143 E2
Martindale Rd WA11 71 C2

Martingale Cl M26 ....44 A5
Martingale Ct M8 ....156 A7
Martingale Way M43 ....84 D2
Martins Ct WN2 ....57 A6
Martins Field OL12 ....13 F1
Martinsclough BL6 ....40 C6
Martinscroft Rd M23 ....121 B5
Martland Ave
  Golborne WA3 ....90 E7
  Shevington WN6 ....35 F5
Martland Cres WN6 ....36 E3
Martland Mill La WN5 ....36 D2
Martlesham Wlk 5 M4 ....159 A2
Martlet Ave Disley SK12 ....135 C6
  Rochdale OL11 ....29 F7
Martlet Cl M14 ....98 B1
Martlew Dr M46 ....58 F4
Martock Ave M22 ....121 E3
Marton Ave Bolton BL2 ....148 C8
  Manchester M20 ....110 C2
Marton Cl WA3 ....91 E4
Marton Dr M46 ....58 E4
Marton Gn SK3 ....170 D5
Marton Gr SK4 ....111 E6
Marton Grange M25 ....63 E3
Marton Pl M33 ....108 A4
Marton St WN1 ....37 C1
Marton Way 5 SK9 ....131 E5
Marus Ave WN3 ....54 F3
Marus Bridge Prim Sch
  WN3 ....54 E2
Marvic Ct M13 ....98 E3
Marwick Ct WN6 ....19 D2
Marwood Cl
  Altrincham WA14 ....119 B6
  Kearsley M26 ....61 A8
Marwood Dr M23 ....120 F3
Mary France St M15 ....162 E6
Mary Hutton Ct BL5 ....58 A8
Mary St Cheadle SK8 ....122 D6
  Denton M34 ....101 A4
  Droylsden M43 ....84 B1
  Dukinfield SK16 ....166 B1
  Farnworth BL4 ....60 D7
  Heywood OL10 ....29 C2
  Hyde SK14 ....167 D3
  Manchester M3 ....158 F3
  Ramsbottom BL0 ....138 B5
  Rochdale OL16 ....15 D4
  Stockport SK1 ....112 A2
  Wigan WN3 ....77 A8
Mary St E BL6 ....22 E4
Mary St W BL6 ....22 A4
Maryfield Cl WA3 ....90 A7
Maryland Ave BL2 ....42 D7
Marylebone Cl WN1 ....37 D3
Marylebone Pl WN1 ....37 D3
Marylon Dr M22 ....121 E8
Masboro St M8 ....155 F7
Masbury Cl BL1 ....24 E7
Masefield Ave Leigh WN7 ....75 D7
  Prestwich M25 ....62 F3
  Radcliffe M26 ....43 E4
  Wigan WN5 ....54 A6
Masefield Cl SK16 ....102 B7
Masefield Cres M43 ....84 A1
Masefield Dr
  Farnworth BL4 ....60 B7
  Stockport SK4 ....168 A2
  4 Wigan WN3 ....54 F5
Masefield Gr SK5 ....99 E1
Masefield Prim Sch BL3 ....43 B4
Masefield Rd
  Droylsden M43 ....84 A1
  Little Lever BL3 ....43 B4
  Oldham OL1 ....49 B2
Mason Cl WN4 ....73 D4
Mason Gdns BL3 ....147 E4
Mason La M46 ....58 E2
Mason Row BL7 ....8 E2
Mason St Abram WN2 ....74 B8
  8 Ashton-u-L OL7 ....84 F1
  Bolton BL7 ....8 E1
  Bury BL9 ....141 A2
  Heywood OL10 ....29 B2
  Horwich BL6 ....22 B3
  Manchester M4 ....159 B2
  Rochdale OL16 ....139 F7
  Wigan WN3 ....150 B7
Mason St Ind Est WN3 ....150 B7
Masons Gr SK13 ....104 A6
Massey Ave
  Ashton-u-L OL6 ....85 C6
  Failsworth M35 ....84 B8
Massey Croft OL12 ....14 C8
Massey Rd
  Altrincham WA15 ....119 E4
  Sale M33 ....108 E4
Massey St
  8 Alderley Edge SK9 ....137 A1
  Bury BL9 ....141 B3
  Salford M5 ....81 C1
  Stockport SK1 ....169 F1
Massey Wlk M22 ....121 F1
Massie St SK8 ....122 D6
Matchmoor La BL6 ....23 A4
Matham Wlk M15 ....163 A7
Mather Ave Eccles M30 ....79 E2
  Golborne WA3 ....90 E6
  Manchester M25 ....63 C1
  Whitefield M45 ....44 F1
Mather Cl BL3 ....144 C5
Mather Fold Rd M28 ....60 B1
Mather La WN7 ....76 A4
Mather Rd Bury BL9 ....27 F7

Mather Rd continued
  Eccles M30 ....79 E2
Mather St
  2 Atherton M46 ....58 D3
  Bolton BL3 ....145 E6
  Failsworth M35 ....83 E7
  Farnworth BL4 ....60 E8
  Radcliffe M26 ....44 A3
Mather Street Prim Sch
  M35 ....83 D7
Mather Way 4 M6 ....81 A3
Matheson Dr WN5 ....54 E8
Matisse Way M7 ....81 B8
Matley Cl SK14 ....102 B5
Matley Gn SK5 ....112 C6
Matley La SK14,SK15 ....102 D6
Matley Park La SK15 ....102 D6
Matlock Ave
  Ashton-u-L OL6 ....85 F6
  Denton M34 ....113 A8
  Salford M7 ....81 A7
  Urmston M41 ....107 B8
Matlock Bank 16 SK13 ....171 E1
Matlock Cl Atherton M46 ....58 D2
  Farnworth BL4 ....42 E1
  Sale M33 ....108 C4
Matlock Dr SK7 ....133 E8
Matlock Gdns 15 SK13 ....171 E1
Matlock La 15 SK13 ....171 E1
Matlock Mews WA14 ....119 E5
Matlock Pl 14 SK13 ....171 E1
Matlock Rd Gatley SK8 ....131 C2
  Reddish M32 ....100 A1
  Stretford M32 ....96 A3
  Wilmslow M33 ....95 C8
Matson Wlk 4 M22 ....121 A2
Matt Busby Cl M27 ....80 B7
Matterdale Terr SK15 ....86 A4
Matthew Cl Oldham OL8 ....67 C4
Matthew Moss High Sch
  OL11 ....30 B4
Matthew Moss La OL11 ....30 B4
Matthew's St SK12 ....164 F7
Matthews Ave BL4 ....60 F7
Matthews La M12,M19 ....99 B2
Matthias Ct M3 ....158 D1
Mattison St M11 ....99 E7
Maud St Bolton BL2 ....25 C5
  Rochdale OL12 ....15 A2
Maudsley St BL9 ....140 E1
Mauldeth Cl SK4 ....168 A3
Mauldeth Rd
  Manchester M14,M19,
  M20 ....110 D7
  Manchester,Burnage M19 ....110 F6
  Manchester,Heaton Moor
  SK4,M19 ....168 A3
  Stockport M19,SK4 ....110 F4
Mauldeth Rd W
  Manchester M20,M21 ....109 D8
  Manchester,Withington
  M20 ....110 B8
Mauldeth Road Prim Sch
  M20 ....110 E7
Maunby Gdns 11 M38 ....60 C3
Maureen Ave M8 ....156 A8
Maureen St OL12 ....15 A2
Maurice Cl SK16 ....101 E8
Maurice Dr M6 ....154 F4
Maurice Pariser Wlk
  M8 ....155 F7
Maurice St M6 ....154 F4
Maveen Ct SK2 ....124 A4
Maveen Gr SK2 ....124 A4
Mavis Gr OL16 ....32 A6
Mavis St OL11 ....30 C1
Mawdsley Dr M8 ....156 C8
Mawdsley St BL1 ....145 F7
Max Woosnam Wlk 3
  M14 ....98 A3
Maxwell Ave SK2 ....124 C5
Maxwell St Bolton BL1 ....143 E4
  Bury BL9 ....141 B3
May Ave Abram Brow WN2 ....74 C7
  Cheadle SK8 ....123 B5
  Leigh WN7 ....75 D6
  Stockport SK4 ....168 C2
May Ct 16 M16 ....97 D3
May Dr M19 ....110 F6
May Gr M19 ....111 B8
May Pl 9 OL11 ....31 A6
May Rd Cheadle SK8 ....132 B6
  Manchester M16 ....97 D3
  Pendlebury M27 ....80 B6
May St Bolton BL2 ....148 A7
  Eccles M30 ....79 C4
  Edgworth BL7 ....9 E6
  Failsworth M40 ....83 C5
  Golborne WA3 ....74 B2
  Heywood OL10 ....46 E8
  Leigh WN7 ....75 C5
  Oldham OL8 ....66 C4
  Radcliffe M26 ....44 A3
May Tree Dr WN1 ....37 B4
May Wlk 2 M31 ....105 E3
Mayall St E 8 OL4 ....67 C7
Mayan Ave M7 ....158 D2
Maybank St BL3 ....145 D5
Mayberth Ave M8 ....64 A2
Maybrook Wlk 11 M9 ....157 D8
Mayburn Cl M24 ....65 C5
Maybury Cl BL0 ....138 B5

Maybury St M18 ....99 E6
Maycroft SK5 ....112 B6
Maycroft Ave M20 ....110 C5
Mayer St SK2 ....124 C7
Mayes Gdns M4 ....160 D1
Mayes St M4 ....159 A2
Mayfair Horwich BL6 ....22 D3
  1 Manchester M7 ....63 C1
Mayfair Ave Radcliffe M26 ....43 D4
  Salford M6 ....80 B3
  Urmston M41 ....95 B2
  Whitefield M45 ....62 F7
Mayfair Cl
  Dukinfield SK16 ....102 A8
  Haslingden BB4 ....1 A7
  Poynton SK12 ....133 E4
  Stalybridge SK16 ....101 F8
Mayfair Cotts WN1 ....20 C1
Mayfair Cres M35 ....84 B8
Mayfair Ct
  Altrincham WA15 ....120 B7
  3 Manchester,Fallowfield
  M14 ....110 C8
  Manchester,West Didsbury
  M20 ....109 F3
  Irlam M44 ....94 A2
  Pennington Green WN2 ....38 D2
  Royton OL2 ....48 D2
  Sale M33 ....107 E2
  Wigan WN5 ....54 F2
Mayfair Gdns
  Rochdale OL11 ....139 D5
  Whitefield M45 ....62 F7
Mayfair Gr M45 ....62 F7
Mayfair Rd M22 ....121 E4
Mayfair The M20 ....110 B5
Mayfield Bolton BL2 ....25 D5
  Radcliffe M26 ....43 E2
Mayfield Ave
  Adlington PR6 ....21 A7
  Bolton BL3 ....42 B3
  2 Denton M34 ....113 A7
  Farnworth BL4 ....60 C7
  Oldham OL4 ....68 A7
  Reddish M45 ....111 F5
  Sale M33 ....108 E4
  Stretford M32 ....96 B1
  Swinton M27 ....79 C6
  Walkden M28 ....60 D3
Mayfield Cl
  Altrincham WA15 ....120 B6
  Ramsbottom BL0 ....11 A2
Mayfield Ct WN5 ....54 B8
Mayfield Gr
  Manchester M18 ....99 F3
  Reddish M45 ....111 F5
  Wilmslow SK9 ....136 E5
Mayfield Ind Est M44 ....94 C3
Mayfield Mans M16 ....97 E3
Mayfield Prim Sch OL1 ....49 B1
Mayfield Rd
  Altrincham WA15 ....120 B6
  Bramhall SK7 ....132 E4
  Manchester,Broughton Park
  M7 ....63 C1
  Manchester,Whalley Range
  M16 ....97 E3
  Oldham OL1 ....49 B1
  Ramsbottom BL0 ....11 A2
  Romiley SK6 ....114 B1
  Up Holland WN8 ....53 B7
  Wigan WN5 ....54 B8
Mayfield St
  Ashton-in-M WN4 ....73 A3
  Atherton M46 ....58 C2
  Denton M34 ....100 E5
  Rochdale OL16 ....15 B1
Mayfield Terr OL16 ....15 B1
Mayflower Ave M5 ....161 B8
Mayflower Cotts WN1 ....37 C8
Mayford Rd M19 ....99 B2
Maygate OL9 ....153 D8
Mayhill Dr Salford M6 ....80 A4
Worsley M28 ....79 A8
Mayhurst Ave M21 ....109 D3
Mayo St M12 ....164 D8
Mayor St Bolton BL1 ....145 D6
  Bury BL8 ....27 C3
  Chadderton OL9 ....152 C7
Mayor's Rd WA15 ....119 E4
Mayorlowe Ave SK5 ....112 C4
Maypole Ind Est WN2 ....74 C7
Maypool Dr SK5 ....111 F6
Mayrick Cl WA12 ....89 A3
Maysmith Mews M7 ....155 D6
Mayton St M11 ....165 A8
Mayville Dr M20 ....110 B5
Maywood Ave M20 ....122 B8
Maze St BL3 ....42 D5
Mc Naught St 10 OL16 ....31 B6
McCall Wlk M11 ....83 B2
McConnell Rd M40 ....83 A7
McCormack Dr M1 ....151 D8
McCready Dr M5 ....161 B8
McDonna St BL1 ....142 C3
McDonough Cl OL8 ....67 A3
McEvoy St 6 BL1 ....143 F2
McKean St BL3 ....42 A4
Mckie Cl OL8 ....67 A3
McLaren Ct M21 ....97 A1
McLean Dr M44 ....94 B4
Meachin Ave M21 ....109 C5
Mead The
  Manchester M21 ....109 B7
  Salford M5 ....154 D2
Mead Way M34 ....112 F8

Meade Cl M41 ....95 C2
Meade Gr M13 ....98 F3
Meade Hill Rd M25,M8 ....63 E3
Meade Manor M21 ....109 B7
Meade The Bolton BL3 ....147 E2
  Wilmslow SK9 ....137 C8
Meadfoot Ave M25 ....63 C3
Meadland Gr BL1 ....143 F4
Meadow Ave
  Altrincham WA15 ....120 B3
  Swinton M27 ....62 B1
Meadow Bank
  Altrincham WA15 ....120 A7
  Glossop SK13 ....115 F7
  Hollingworth SK14 ....103 D6
  Manchester M21 ....109 A7
  Romiley SK6 ....112 F3
  Stockport SK4 ....168 B2
Meadow Bank Cl OL4 ....67 E4
Meadow Bank Ct M22 ....96 B1
Meadow Brook Way
  SK8 ....123 B4
Meadow Brow SK9 ....137 A2
Meadow Cl
  Altrincham WA15 ....120 B3
  Denton M34 ....113 A7
  Heywood OL10 ....29 C2
  Leigh WN7 ....75 E2
  Little Lever BL3 ....43 B2
  Mossley OL5 ....68 E3
  Romiley SK6 ....113 A5
  Stretford M32 ....96 E1
  Wilmslow SK9 ....136 E4
Meadow Cotts OL12 ....4 D3
Meadow Croft
  Hazel Grove SK7 ....124 E4
  Whitefield M45 ....62 C6
Meadow Ct
  2 Altrincham WA15 ....120 D6
  Salford M6 ....80 B3
  Stretford M21 ....108 F8
  7 Wigan WN6 ....37 A1
Meadow Fold OL3 ....69 C8
Meadow Head Ave OL12 ....14 D6
Meadow Ind Est SK1 ....169 F3
Meadow La Bolton BL2 ....43 A7
  Denton M34 ....113 A7
  Disley SK12 ....135 D6
  Dukinfield SK16 ....101 D8
  Eccles M28 ....78 F5
  Oldham OL8 ....66 E2
Meadow Pit La WN2 ....37 F8
Meadow Pk BL0 ....1 C4
Meadow Rd
  Manchester M24 ....64 C6
  Salford M7 ....81 C3
  Urmston M41 ....95 D1
Meadow Rise
  Glossop SK13 ....115 F7
  Shaw OL2 ....32 A1
Meadow St Adlington PR7 ....21 A6
  Hyde SK14 ....167 E1
  Stockport SK2 ....124 C8
Meadow The Bolton BL6 ....40 C7
  Delph OL3 ....50 F5
Meadow View OL12 ....14 A1
Meadow Wlk
  Altrincham WA15 ....120 B3
  Blackrod BL6 ....21 E1
  Bury BL8 ....26 E6
  Coppull PR7 ....19 D8
  Edgworth BL7 ....9 E6
  Manchester M40 ....65 A1
  Wilmslow SK9 ....136 E4
Meadow Wlk
  Farnworth BL4 ....60 A8
  Littleborough OL15 ....15 F5
  Romiley SK6 ....112 F3
  Tyldesley M29 ....77 C6
Meadowbank BL7 ....8 B3
Meadowbank Ave M46 ....58 E5
Meadowbank Cl M35 ....84 A6
Meadowbank Gdns WA3 ....92 C7
Meadowbank Prim Sch
  M46 ....58 D4
Meadowbank Rd BL3 ....146 B2
Meadowbrook Cl
  Bolton BL6 ....40 B3
  Bury BL9 ....44 F8
Meadowburn Nook M30 ....79 B4
Meadowcroft
  Ashton-in-M WN4 ....72 F6
  Mottram-in-L SK14 ....103 A4
  Radcliffe M26 ....43 F5
  Westhoughton BL5 ....57 F7
Meadowcroft La
  1 Oldham OL11 ....49 B1
  Rochdale OL11 ....29 F6
Meadowfield Bolton BL6 ....31 B3
  Oldham OL11 ....49 B1
  Up Holland WN8 ....53 A7
Meadowfield Cl SK13 ....171 F3
Meadowfield Ct SK14 ....167 D4
Meadowfield Dr M28 ....78 B6
Meadowgate
  Urmston M41 ....95 D1
  Worsley M28 ....78 F8
Meadowgate Rd M6 ....80 C3
Meadows Cl
  Hazel Grove SK7 ....124 E3
  4 Hindley WN2 ....56 D5
Meadows Rd
  Cheadle SK8 ....131 F8
  Gatley SK8 ....122 B1

Meadows Rd continued
  Reddish SK4 ....111 C6
  Sale M33 ....108 C6
  Manchester,Sch The M9 ....64 F4
Meadows St WN6 ....37 A1
Meadows The
  Glossop SK13 ....116 E8
  Irlam M44 ....105 E6
  Middleton M24 ....65 B6
  Oldham OL4 ....68 A6
  Prestwich M25 ....63 E5
  Radcliffe M26 ....43 E5
  Rochdale OL12 ....13 A4
  Romiley SK6 ....113 B4
  Uppermill OL3 ....69 B7
  Whitworth OL12 ....4 C1
Meadowside
  Bramhall SK7 ....123 C2
  Rochdale OL16 ....32 C3
Meadowside Ave
  Ashton-in-M WN4 ....73 A8
  Bolton BL2 ....148 C5
  Irlam M44 ....94 A2
  Walkden M28 ....60 E4
  Wythenshawe M22 ....121 E4
Meadowside Cl M26 ....44 A5
Meadowside Gr M28 ....60 E3
Meads Gr Farnworth BL4 ....59 E8
  Tyldesley M29 ....77 C8
Meads The OL9 ....152 A6
Meadscroft Dr SK9 ....136 F1
Meadway Bramhall SK7 ....132 E5
  Bury BL9 ....44 F6
  Dukinfield SK16 ....101 E7
  Failsworth OL9 ....65 E2
  Golborne WA3 ....90 D8
  High Lane SK6 ....134 F8
  Ince-in-M WN2 ....151 F7
  Poynton SK12 ....133 B4
  Ramsbottom BL0 ....1 C1
  Rochdale OL11 ....30 C4
  Sale M33 ....107 E2
  Stalybridge SK15 ....102 E6
  Tyldesley M29 ....59 D1
Meadway Cl Horwich BL6 ....22 D3
  Sale M33 ....107 E2
Meadway Rd SK8 ....123 B3
Meal St SK4 ....169 E3
Mealhouse Brow SK1 ....169 F1
Mealhouse Ct M46 ....58 C3
Mealhouse La
  Atherton M46 ....58 C3
  Bolton BL1 ....145 F7
Meanley Rd M29,WN7 ....76 F7
Meanley St 10 M29 ....59 A1
Meanwood Brow 18
  OL12 ....14 C1
Meanwood Fold OL12 ....139 D8
Meanwood Prim Sch
  OL12 ....14 C1
Measham Mews M1 ....163 A4
Meburn Wlk M14 ....98 B4
Mechinoh Sch M7 ....63 E1
Meddings Cl SK9 ....136 F1
Medina Cl SK8 ....123 B4
Medlar Way WN4 ....72 F5
Medley St OL12 ....14 D1
Medlock Dr OL4 ....60 B8
Medlock Ho 1 M15 ....162 D7
Medlock Prim Sch M13 ....163 C2
Medlock Rd M35 ....84 B5
Medlock Sports Ctr M43 ....84 B2
Medlock St Droylsden M43 ....84 B2
  Manchester M15 ....162 F7
Medlock Vale* M35 ....84 E6
Medlock Valley High Sch
  M11 ....160 E1
Medlock Valley Visitor Ctr*
  OL6 ....67 C2
Medlock Way Oldham OL4 ....67 E6
  Platt Bridge WN2 ....56 A2
  Whitefield M45 ....63 C8
Medowell Wlk M8 ....64 B2
Medway Cl
  Ashton-in-M WN4 ....72 F6
  Golborne WN7 ....131 D2
  Handforth SK9 ....131 D2
  Oldham OL8 ....66 C3
  Salford M5 ....154 D3
Medway Cres WA14 ....119 C6
Medway Dr Horwich BL6 ....22 D3
  Kearsley BL4 ....61 B5
Medway Pl WN5 ....54 D7
Medway Rd Culcheth WA3 ....92 A2
  Oldham OL8 ....66 C3
  Shaw OL2 ....149 B8
Medway Wlk
  Manchester M40 ....160 D3
  Wigan WN5 ....54 D7
Mee's Sq M30 ....95 D8
Meech St OL11 ....165 C8
Meek St OL1 ....49 A2
Meerbrook Rd SK3 ....123 A8
Megfield BL5 ....57 E6
Megna Cl OL3 ....153 D7
Melandra Castle Rd
  SK13 ....171 D2
Melandra Cres SK14 ....102 E2
Melandra Rd SK13 ....171 E3
Melanie Cl BL6 ....38 A6
Melanie Dr SK5 ....111 F8
Melba St M11 ....99 E8
Melbecks Wlk 5 M23 ....108 F2

Melbourne Ave
Chadderton OL9 152 B7
Stretford M32 96 D2
Wythenshawe M90 130 A8
Melbourne Cl
Horwich BL6 22 C3
Rochdale OL11 31 B2
Melbourne Gr BL6 22 C3
Melbourne Mews
Chadderton OL9 152 B7
Salford M7 155 E5
Melbourne Rd
Bolton BL3 144 B5
Bramhall SK7 132 F5
Rochdale OL11 31 A2
Melbourne St
Chadderton OL9 152 B7
Denton M34 100 E2
Manchester M15 162 E7
Manchester,Harpurhey M9 157 E8
Pendlebury M27 80 B8
Reddish SK5 111 F8
Salford M7 155 E5
Stalybridge SK15 86 A1
Melbourne St N OL6 166 C4
Melbourne St S OL6 166 C3
Melbury Ave M20 110 D4
Melbury Dr BL6 39 F8
Melbury Rd SK8 132 B6
Meldon Rd M13 98 E2
Meldreth Dr M12 98 F4
Meldrum St OL8 66 F4
Meldrum Wlk OL8 67 A4
Melford Ave M40 65 E1
Melford Dr
Ashton-in-M WN4 73 A4
Orrell WN5 53 D3
Melford Gr OL4 67 D6
Melford Rd SK7 124 F1
Melfort Ave M32 96 E1
Meliden Cres Bolton BL1 142 B1
Wythenshawe M22 121 E3
Melksham Cl 4 M5 81 B2
Mellalieu St
Middleton M24 46 F1
Royton OL2 48 E2
Melland Ave M21 109 C5
Melland High Sch M18 99 D2
Melland Rd M18 99 C3
Meller Rd M13 98 F2
Melling Ave
Chadderton OL9 47 E1
Reddish SK4 111 E6
Melling Cl Adlington PR6 21 B7
Leigh WN7 75 F1
Melling Rd OL4 67 C6
Melling St
Manchester M12 99 A4
Wigan WN5 54 E5
Melling Way WN3 54 D1
Mellings Ave WN5 53 E1
Mellington Ave M20 122 C8
Mellodew Dr OL1 49 D4
Mellor Brook Dr WN2 56 A2
Mellor Brow OL10 29 C2
Mellor Cl Ashton-u-L OL6 85 E2
Standish WN6 19 E2
Mellor Ct SK2 124 E6
Mellor Dr Bury BL9 44 D7
Walkden M28 60 C1
Mellor Gr BL1 142 B1
Mellor Prim Sch SK6 126 C6
Mellor Rd
Ashton-u-L,Higher Hurst
OL6 85 F4
Ashton-u-L,Stamford Park
OL6 85 E3
Cheadle SK8 123 B1
New Mills SK6,SK22 127 C3
Mellor St Droylsden M43 83 F1
Eccles M30 79 D1
Failsworth M35 83 D6
Manchester,Ardwick M12 163 C8
Manchester,MilesPlatting
M40 160 D3
Oldham OL4 67 E6
Prestwich M25 62 F4
2 Radcliffe M26 44 B2
Rochdale OL11,OL12 139 D7
Royton OL2 48 D5
Stretford M32 96 E4
Mellor Way OL9 66 B4
Mellors Rd M17 96 B7
Mellowstone Dr M21 109 F8
Melloy Pl M8 159 A4
Melmerby Cl WN4 72 F3
Melmerby Ct M5 154 F1
Melon Pl 7 M6 81 B2
Melrose 18 OL12 139 E8
Melrose Ave Bolton BL1 142 A1
Bury BL8 27 C3
Cheadle SK3 122 F7
Eccles M30 79 B4
Heywood OL10 29 C3
Leigh WN7 57 D1
Littleborough OL15 16 A7
Manchester M20 110 C3
Sale M33 108 B4
Melrose Cl 6 M45 44 F2
Melrose Cres
Altrincham WA15 120 B1
Garswood WN4 72 C3
Poynton SK12 134 D5
Stockport SK3 123 D4
Melrose Ct
Chadderton OL9 66 A4
15 Handforth SK9 131 E1
Melrose Dr WN3 54 D3
Melrose Gdns M26 43 E5
Melrose Rd
Little Lever BL3 42 F3
Radcliffe M26 43 E5
Melrose St Failsworth M40 83 C5
3 Oldham OL1 49 B1
Ramsbottom BL9 11 B2
Rochdale OL11 139 D7
Melsomby Rd M23 109 A2
Meltham Ave M20 110 A6
Meltham Cl SK4 110 E1
Meltham Pl 7 BL3 147 D4
Meltham Rd SK4 110 E1
Melton Ave Reddish M34 100 A3
Urmston M41 94 D3
Melton Cl Heywood OL10 29 B1
Tyldesley M29 77 B8
Walkden M28 60 C2
Melton Dr BL9 45 A5
Melton Rd M8 63 E1
Melton Row M26 43 F4
Melton St Heywood OL10 29 B1
Manchester M9 64 F1
Radcliffe M26 43 F4
Reddish SK5 169 F4
Melton Way M26 43 F4
Melton Wlk M26 43 F4
Melverley Rd M9 64 A5
Melverley St WN3 150 A7
Melville Cl M11 99 E7
Melville Ct 3 M20 110 A2
Melville Rd Irlam M44 105 C5
Kearsley BL4 60 F6
Stretford M32 96 B3
Melville St
Ashton-u-L OL6 166 B3
Bolton BL3 42 A4
Oldham OL4 67 E5
Rochdale OL11 30 D1
Salford M3 158 D2
Melvin Ave M22 121 E4
Melyncourt Dr SK14 102 E3
Memorial Rd M28 60 D2
Menai Gr SK8 123 A6
Menai Rd SK3 170 E6
Menai St BL3 146 B4
Mendip Ave Wigan WN3 54 C3
Wythenshawe M22 121 F4
Mendip Cl Bolton BL2 43 A7
Chadderton OL9 152 A5
Gatley SK8 131 B7
Horwich BL6 22 C5
Royton OL2 48 C3
Stockport SK4 169 E3
Mendip Cres BL8 27 B3
Mendip Ct SK4 169 E3
Mendip Dr Bolton BL2 43 A6
Milnrow OL16 32 A7
Mendip Rd OL8 66 D3
Mendips Cl 3 OL2 48 F8
Menston Ave M40 65 E1
Mentmore Rd OL16 31 D8
Mentone Cres M22 121 E4
Mentone Rd SK4 168 C3
Mentor St M13 98 F3
Menzies Ct M21 97 B1
Mercer Cres BB4 1 A8
Mercer La OL11 29 E8
Mercer Rd M18 99 D5
Mercer St Droylsden M43 84 B2
Manchester M19 99 B1
Newton-le-W WA12 89 D4
Mercer's Rd OL10 46 D7
Merchants Cres WA3 74 E1
Merchants Quay M50 161 A6
Mercia St BL3 144 C5
Mercian Mall OL6 166 B3
Mercian Way SK3 170 E7
Mercury Bldgs M1 159 B1
Mercury Pk M41 95 F5
Mercury Way M41 95 F6
Mere Ave Droylsden M43 99 E8
Leigh WN7 75 D5
Middleton M24 65 A6
Salford M6 154 E2
Mere Bank Cl M28 60 C3
Mere Cl Reddish M34 100 B2
Sale M33 108 F3
Whitefield BL9 45 B5
Mere Dr Manchester M20 110 B4
Swinton M27 62 A2
Mere Fold M28 60 B3
Mere Gdns BL1 145 E8
Mere Gr WA11 71 B1
Mere Ho SK4 110 E1
Mere La OL11 139 F5
Mere Oaks Sch WN1 37 B5
Mere Rd Ashton-in-M WN4 73 C4
Newton-le-W WA12 89 F4
Mere Side SK15 85 F4
Mere St 7 Leigh WN7 75 D5
Rochdale OL11 139 F6
Wigan WN5 54 F6
Mere The Ashton-u-L OL6 85 E6
Cheadle SK8 123 A4
Mere Wlk BL1 145 E8
Merebank Cl OL11 29 E8
Mereclough Ave M28 60 F1
Meredew Ave M27 79 E6
Meredith Ct 6 M15 163 A6
Meredith St Bolton BL3 147 F3
Manchester M14 110 D7
Merefield Ave OL11 139 E5
Merefield Cl WN2 56 E4
Merefield Rd WA15 120 C5
Merefield St OL11 139 E5
Merefield Terr OL11 139 E5
Merefold BL6 21 F3
Merehall Cl BL1 145 E8
Merehall Dr BL1 145 E8
Merehall St BL1 143 E1
Mereland Ave M20 110 C4
Mereland Cl WN5 53 E6
Meremanor M28 60 F1
Merepool Cl SK6 125 C7
Mereside Cl SK8 122 F4
Mereside Gr M28 60 E3
Mereside Wlk 12 M15 162 D6
Merewood Ave M22 121 D6
Meriden Cl M26 43 F6
Meriden Gr BL6 40 D6
Meridian Pl M20 110 A4
Merinall Cl OL16 31 C7
Meriton Rd SK9 131 D4
Meriton Wlk M18 99 B4
Merlewood BL0 1 E3
Merlewood Ave
6 Droylsden M34 84 B1
Reddish M19 111 C7
Uppermill OL3 69 B8
Merlewood Dr
Swinton M27 79 C6
Tyldesley M29 77 B8
Merlin Cl
Hazel Grove SK2 125 A6
Littleborough OL15 16 A2
Oldham OL8 85 A8
Merlin Gr BL1 142 B1
Merlin Ho 3 M19 110 D4
Merlin Rd Irlam M44 94 A4
Milnrow OL16 31 F6
Merlyn Ave Denton M34 100 E2
Manchester M20 110 C4
Sale M33 108 C6
Merlyn Ct M20 110 C4
Merrick Ave M22 121 E4
Merrick St OL10 29 E1
Merridale The WA15 129 A8
Merridge Wlk 5 M8 155 F6
Merrill St M4 160 D1
Merriman St M16 97 E4
Merrion St BL4 42 C2
Merrow Wlk M1 163 B7
Merrybent Cl SK2 124 D4
Merrybower Rd M7 155 E8
Merrydale Ave M30 79 E4
Merryman Hall OL16 15 B2
Mersey Cl Hindley WN2 57 C3
Whitefield M45 45 B1
Mersey Cres M20 109 D3
Mersey Dr
Partington M31 106 A4
Whitefield M45 45 B1
Mersey Drive Com Prim Sch
M45 45 C2
Mersey Ind Est
Manchester SK4 110 E1
Oldham M35 66 B1
Mersey Mdws M20 109 F3
Mersey Rd
Manchester,Heaton Mersey
SK4 110 F2
Manchester,West Didsbury
M20 109 F3
Orrell WN5 53 F7
Platt Bridge WN2 55 F2
Sale M33 108 B6
Mersey Rd N M35 66 B1
Mersey Sq Stockport SK1 169 E1
Whitefield M45 45 B1
Mersey St Droylsden M11 99 E7
Leigh WN7 75 C5
Stockport SK1 112 A2
Mersey Vale Prim Sch
SK4 168 A1
Mersey Valley Visitor Ctr*
M33 108 F6
Merseybank Ave M21 109 D4
Merseyway SK1 169 E2
Merston Dr M20 122 C8
Merton Ave
Hazel Grove SK7 133 F8
Oldham OL8 66 D3
Romiley SK6 113 A4
Merton Cl BL3 144 C5
Merton Dr M43 83 E1
Merton Gr
Altrincham WA15 120 B6
Failsworth OL9 65 D3
Tyldesley M29 77 C6
Merton Rd Prestwich M25 63 C5
Sale M33 108 A6
5 Stockport SK3 123 B8
Wigan WN3 54 C4
Merton St BL8 140 D3
Merton Wlk 14 M9 157 E7
Merville Ave M40 64 F1
Mervyn Pl WN3 55 B4
Mervyn Rd M7 81 B6
Merwell Rd M41 94 E1
Merwood Ave SK8 131 D8
Merwood Gr M14 98 E4
Meshaw Cl M23 108 E2
Mesne Lea Gr M28 78 E8
Mesne Lea Prim Sch
M28 60 E1
Mesne Lea Rd M28 60 E1
Mesnefield Rd M7 81 A8
Mesnes Ave WN3 150 A5
Mesnes Park Terr 9
WN1 37 C1
Mesnes Rd Wigan WN1 150 C8
Wigan,Whitley WN1 37 C3
Mesnes St WN1 150 C8
Mesnes Terr WN1 37 C1
Metal Box Way BL5 40 A2
Metcalf Mews OL3 69 B8
Metcalf Terr BL2 26 D1
Metcalfe Ct Romiley SK6 113 B2
Walkden M38 59 F4
Metcalfe Dr SK6 113 B2
Metfield Pl 8 BL1 144 C8
Metfield Wlk 19 M40 65 D2
Methodist Cotts BL5 39 D3
Methuen St 6 M12 99 B3
Methwold St BL3 146 C4
Metron Rd SK12 133 B4
Mevagissey Wlk 3 OL4 67 C8
Mews The Bolton BL1 144 B8
Gatley SK8 122 B5
12 Hindley WN2 56 D5
Manchester M40 160 E3
Prestwich M25 63 B3
Sale M33 108 C3
Whitefield M45 62 D8
Wilmslow SK9 130 D4
Worsley M28 78 E6
Mexborough St 7 OL4 67 D8
Meyer St SK2,SK3 170 F6
Meynell Dr WN7 75 F2
Meyrick Cl WN3 54 C2
Meyrick Rd M6 81 A3
Meyrick St WN5 54 F6
Miall St OL11 139 F6
Micawber Rd SK12 133 E2
Michael Ct M19 110 D2
Michael St 3 M24 64 F8
Michael Wife La
Edenfield BL0 1 F2
Edenfield BL0 1 F3
Michaels Hey Par M23 120 C8
Michigan Ave M50 96 F8
Mickleby Wlk M40 160 D3
Micklehurst All Saints' CE
Prim Sch OL5 68 E1
Micklehurst Ave M20 109 E4
Micklehurst Gn SK2 124 E5
Micklehurst Rd OL5 68 E1
Mickleton M46 58 E4
Midbrook Wlk 6 M22 121 B1
Middle Field OL11 13 E1
Middle Gate OL8 66 E2
Middle Gn OL6 166 C4
Middle Hill OL12 14 F4
Middle Hillgate SK1 170 F8
Middle Newgate OL15 16 B8
Middle St OL12 4 D1
Middle Turn BL7 9 D7
Middle Wood La OL15 15 E6
Middlebourne St M6 154 E2
Middlebrook Dr BL6 40 D6
Middlecot Cl WN5 53 E5
Middlefield OL8 85 A8
Middlefields SK8 123 B4
Middlegate M40 65 D3
Middleham St M14 98 A2
Middlesex Dr 8 BL9 44 F8
Middlesex Rd
Brinnington SK5 112 C6
Manchester M9 64 D2
Middlesex Wlk OL9 153 D6
Middlestone Dr M9 157 D7
Middleton Ave M35 83 F7
Middleton Central Ind Est
M24 64 F8
Middleton Cl M26 43 F7
Middleton Dr BL9 44 F3
Middleton Old Rd M9 64 D2
Middleton Parish CE Prim
Sch M24 46 F2
Middleton Rd
Chadderton,Chadderton Park
OL9 65 F8
Chadderton,Westwood
OL9 152 B7
Heywood OL10 46 E7
Manchester M8,M9 63 F3
Middleton M24 64 A6
Reddish SK5 99 F2
Royton OL2 48 C3
Middleton Tech Sch M24 65 C8
Middleton View M24 65 B8
Middleton Way M24 64 F8
Middleway OL4 68 B5
Middlewich Wlk M18 165 C5
Middlewood WA3 90 E8
Middlewood Ct OL9 152 A8
Middlewood Dr SK4 168 A1
Middlewood Gn OL9 152 A8
Middlewood Rd
Hazel Grove SK7,SK12 134 C7
High Lane SK6 134 D7
Poynton SK12 134 B4
Middlewood St M5 158 D1
Middlewood Sta SK12 134 D6
Middlewood Wlk M9 157 D7
Midford Ave M30 79 B2
Midford Dr BL1 24 E7
Midford Wlk 12 M8 156 A6
Midge Hall Dr OL11 30 A6
Midge Hill OL5 68 D4
Midgley Ave M18 99 E6
Midgley Cres OL6 85 E4
Midgley Dr OL16 31 C2
Midgley St M27 79 D6
Midgrove OL3 50 F3
Midgrove La OL3 50 F4
Midhurst Ave M40 83 B4
Midhurst Cl
1 Bolton BL1 143 E1
Cheadle SK8 131 F8
Midhurst St OL11 139 F5
Midhurst Way OL9 152 B6
Midland Cl WN7 75 C6
Midland Rd Reddish SK5 99 F2
Stockport SK7 123 E3
Midland St M12 164 D7
Midland Wlk SK7 123 E3
Midlothian St M11 83 B2
Midmoor Wlk 5 M9 64 E3
Midville Rd M11 83 C3
Midway SK8 132 B5
Midway St M12 99 A2
Milan St M7 155 E7
Milbourne Rd BL9 27 F6
Milburn Ave M23 109 B2
Milburn Dr BL2 42 F8
Milbury Dr OL15 16 A2
Milden Cl M20 110 C4
Mildred Ave
Manchester M25 63 C1
Oldham OL4 68 B5
Royton OL2 48 E2
Mildred St M7 81 C5
Mile End La SK2 124 B6
Mile La BL8 26 F1
Miles Ave OL13 3 D8
Miles La
Appley Bridge WN6 35 E6
Shevington WN6 36 A6
Miles St 4 Bolton BL1 143 D2
Farnworth BL4 60 C8
Hyde SK14 167 F2
Manchester M12 165 A7
Oldham OL1 67 B8
Milford Ave 2 OL8 66 C2
Milford Brow OL4 67 E7
Milford Cres OL15 16 B6
Milford Dr M19 111 C7
Milford Gr SK2 124 C7
Milford Rd
Bolton,Harwood BL2 25 F4
Bolton,Lever Edge BL3 147 E3
4 Wigan WN2 37 F2
Milford St Ince-in-M WN3 151 E6
Manchester M9 64 B4
6 Rochdale OL12 14 F1
Salford M6 154 E2
Milk St Hyde SK14 167 D2
Manchester M2 159 A1
2 Oldham OL4 67 C7
Ramsbottom BL0 138 B5
Rochdale OL11 139 F6
Tyldesley M29 59 A1
Wigan WN3 150 C7
Milking Green Ind Est
OL4 67 F5
Milkstone Pl OL11 139 F6
Milkstone Rd OL11 139 F6
Milkwood Gr 2 M18 99 D4
Mill Bank
Appley Bridge WN6 35 D7
Radcliffe M26 44 B2
Mill Beck Gr BL3 147 E4
Mill Brook Ind Est M23 120 E6
Mill Brow Chadderton OL1 48 A2
Manchester M9 64 C2
Mottram-in-L SK14 115 A8
Oldham OL6,OL8 67 C2
Worsley M28 78 F6
Mill Brow Rd SK6 126 E8
Mill Croft Bolton BL1 145 D8
Shaw OL2 149 C6
Mill Croft Cl OL12 13 C2
Mill Ct M41 95 E2
Mill Fold Gdns OL15 16 A4
Mill Fold Rd M24 64 F8
Mill Gate Oldham OL8 66 D2
Rochdale OL16 15 C2
Mill Green Sch WA12 89 E3
Mill Green St M12 164 D8
Mill Hill M38 59 E6
Mill Hill Ave SK12 133 D7
Mill Hill Gr SK14 102 F2
Mill Hill Hollow SK12 133 D7
Mill Hill St BL2 148 A8
Mill Hill Way 3 SK14 102 F2
Mill House Cl OL12 15 D4
Mill House View WN8 53 C7
Mill La Altrincham WA15 129 E4
Appley Bridge WN6 35 D7
Ashton-u-L OL6 166 B2
Aspull WN2 38 F3
4 Bury BL8 27 B4
Cheadle SK8 122 D6
Cheadle,Cheadle Hulme
SK8 123 B3
Denton M34,SK14 101 B2
Failsworth M35 83 C7
Hazel Grove SK7 133 F8
Horwich BL6 22 D4
Leigh WN7 76 B4
Lymm WA13 117 C4
Marple SK6 125 B7
Mossley OL5 68 C2
Newton-le-W WA12 89 E3
Oldham OL9 66 C4
Reddish,North Reddish SK5 99 F1
Reddish,Reddish Vale SK5 112 B8
Romiley SK6 113 A5
Royton OL2 48 C4
Up Holland WN8 53 A8
Uppermill OL4 50 D1
Westhoughton BL5 57 E5
Wythenshawe M22 109 E1
Mill Mdw
Newton-le-W WA12 89 E3
Wigan WN1 151 D7
Mill Nook OL12 14 F3

Mill Pond Ave SK22 127 D1
Mill Rd Bury BL9 27 F8
Orrell WN5 53 D5
Wilmslow SK9 137 B7
Mill St Adlington PR6 21 B8
Altrincham WA14 119 E5
Ashton-in-M WN4 73 C2
9 Bolton,Cox Green BL7 24 F8
Bolton,Mill Hill BL1 148 A8
Bury BL8 26 F8
Dukinfield SK14 101 E5
Failsworth M35 83 D7
Farnworth BL4 60 C8
Glossop SK13 104 D1
Golborne WA3 90 A8
Hazel Grove SK7 124 D3
Hindley WN2 56 D5
Leigh WN7 76 A4
Manchester M11 165 A8
Mossley OL5 86 C8
Radcliffe M26 44 B2
Ramsbottom BL0 11 A4
Royton OL2 48 D4
Salford M6 81 A4
Stalybridge SK15 86 C1
Tyldesley M46 58 E1
Uppermill OL3 69 B8
Westhoughton BL5 57 F8
Wigan WN3 150 B7
Wilmslow SK9 137 B7
Worsley M28 78 A6
Mill Yd BL9 141 A3
Millais St M40 83 A8
Millar Barn La BB4 2 F8
Millard St OL9 152 A7
Millard Wlk 4 M18 99 D4
Millbank Ct OL10 29 B2
Millbank St Heywood OL10 29 B2
Manchester M1,M4 159 C1
Millbeck Ct 4 M24 46 D2
Millbeck Farm WN5 54 D5
Millbeck Gr WA11 71 B2
Millbeck Rd M24 46 D2
Millbeck St 5 M15 163 A6
Millbrae Gdns OL2 48 F7
Millbrook SK14 103 E6
Millbrook Ave
Atherton M46 58 E5
Denton M34 100 D1
Millbrook Bank OL11 13 D1
Millbrook Cl
Fowley Common WA3 92 C5
Shaw OL2 49 D6
Millbrook Fold SK7 133 F8
Millbrook Gr 1 SK9 131 D1
Millbrook Ho BL4 60 E8
Millbrook Prim Sch
Mossley SK15 86 E5
Shevington WN6 36 B6
Millbrook Rd M23 121 A4
Millbrook St SK1 170 F8
Millcrest Cl M28 77 F5
Millcroft Ave WN5 53 D5
Millcroft La OL3 51 A7
Milldale Cl Atherton M46 58 C3
Bolton BL6 40 B7
Milldale Rd WN7 75 B1
Miller Meadow Cl OL2 149 C8
Miller Rd OL8 66 E3
Miller St Ashton-u-L OL6 166 C4
Bolton BL1 143 E4
Heywood OL10 29 D2
Manchester M4 159 A2
Radcliffe M26 43 F6
Ramsbottom BL9 11 C2
Scot Lane End BL6 38 E7
Miller's La Atherton M46 58 D1
Platt Bridge WN2 56 A2
Millers Brook Cl OL10 29 D3
Millers Cl M23 109 A3
Millers Ct M5 80 A2
Millers La WA13 117 B5
Millers Nook WN8 53 B7
Millers St M30 79 C2
Millers Wharf SK15 86 B2
Millersdale Ct SK13 104 F1
Millet Terr BL9 28 E7
Millett St Bury BL9 140 D2
Ramsbottom BL0 11 D7
Millfield Ct WA15 119 E2
Millfield Dr M28 78 B6
Millfield Gr OL16 31 B6
Millfield La WN4,WA11 72 E1
Millfield Rd BL2 43 A7
Millfield Wlk 2 M40 65 C2
Millfold OL12 4 D2
Millford Ave M41 94 E2
Millford Gdns M41 94 E2
Millgate Bolton BL7 8 D2
Delph OL3 50 F4
Stockport SK1 169 F2
Wigan WN1 150 C8
Millgate La M20 110 B1
Millgate Terr OL12 4 E5
Millgreen Cl WN8 53 A7
Millhall Cl M15 162 E5
Millhead Ave M40 160 E2
Millhouse Ave M23 121 A4
Millhouse St BL0 11 E8
Milliner Ct SK2 124 D7
Milling St M1 162 F8
Millingford Ave WA3 73 F2
Millingford Gr WN4 73 B3
Millingford Ind Est WA3 90 A8
Millington Wlk 9 M15 162 D6
Millom Ave M23 109 B1
Millom Cl OL16 15 C1
Millom Dr BL9 45 A2
Millom Pl SK8 122 B3
Millow St M4 159 A3
Millpool Wlk 1 M9 157 D8
Millrise OL1 153 E8
Mills Farm Cl OL8 67 A1
Mills Hill Com Prim Sch
OL9 65 E8
Mills Hill Rd M24 65 D8
Mills Hill Sta M24 47 D1
Mills St Heywood OL10 29 B2
Whitworth OL12 4 D1
Millstone Cl
Poynton SK12 133 F5
Romiley SK6 113 A3
Millstone Rd BL1 23 F1
Millstream La M40 83 E4
Milltown SK13 104 D1
Milltown Cl 3 M26 44 B2
Milltown St M26 44 B3
Millwall Cl M18 99 D5
Millway WA15 129 C7
Millway Wlk 19 M40 83 C5
Millwell La 5 BL1 145 F7
Millwood Cl
Ashton-in-M WN4 73 A5
4 Cheadle SK8 131 E8
Millwood Ct BL9 44 F6
Millwood Prim Specl Sch
BL9 44 F6
Millwood Terr 3 SK14 167 D2
Millwright St M40 83 C5
Milne Cl M12 165 A6
Milne St Chadderton OL9 152 B7
Chadderton OL9 48 C1
Haslingden BL0 1 C5
Oldham OL9 152 C5
Oldham,Higginshaw OL1 49 A2
Rochdale OL11 30 C2
Shaw OL2 149 B6
Milner Ave
Altrincham WA14 119 B7
Bury BL9 27 F5
Milner St Manchester M16 97 D4
Pendlebury M27 80 A8
Radcliffe M26 43 E3
Whitworth OL12 14 C8
Whitworth OL12 4 C1
Milnes Ave WN7 75 F2
Milngate Cl OL16 31 C3
Milnholme BL1 142 B3
Milnrow Cl M13 163 B7
Milnrow Parish CE Prim Sch
OL16 31 F6
Milnrow Rd
Littleborough OL15 16 A2
Rochdale OL16 31 B7
Shaw OL2 149 B7
Shaw,Jubilee OL16,OL2 32 C2
Shaw,Small Brook OL2 149 C8
Milnrow Sta OL16 31 F5
Milnthorpe Rd BL2 42 F8
Milnthorpe St M6 81 B5
Milnthorpe Way M12 164 E6
Milo St M9 64 D3
Milsom Ave BL3 146 C3
Milstead Wlk M40 83 A5
Milston Wlk M8 156 A6
Milton Ave Bolton BL3 146 B4
Droylsden M43 84 A1
Irlam M44 105 E6
Little Lever BL3 43 B4
Newton-le-W WA12 89 B3
Salford M5 154 D2
Stalybridge SK15 86 E4
Milton Cl Atherton M46 58 D5
Dukinfield SK16 102 B7
Haslingden BB4 1 A7
Marple SK6 125 F4
Stretford M32 96 E3
Milton Cres Cheadle SK8 122 C5
Farnworth BL4 60 B6
Milton Ct Bramhall SK7 132 F6
5 Manchester,Broughton Park
M7 63 E1
Manchester,Green End
M19 110 E4
Milton Dr
Chadderton OL9 152 A6
Poynton SK12 133 D4
Sale M33 108 B6
Sale,Brooklands WA15 108 A1
Milton Gr Longshaw WN5 53 D1
Manchester M16 97 C4
Orrell WN5 53 F6
Sale M33 108 A6
Wigan,Marylebone WN1 37 C3
Wigan,Redwood WN5 54 A6
Milton Ind Ct SK6 112 F5
Milton Lo M16 97 C2
Milton Mount 1 M18 99 D4
Milton Pl M6 81 B3
Milton Rd Bramhall SK7 132 E7
Coppull PR7 19 E8
Droylsden M34 84 D1
Golborne WA3 90 D7
Prestwich M25 63 C5
Radcliffe M26 43 E4
Stretford M32 96 E3
Swinton M27 61 D1
Milton St Denton M34 100 E4
Eccles M30 79 D2
Hyde SK14 167 D4
Leigh WN7 75 E5
Middleton M24 46 F1
Mossley OL5 68 C2
Milton St *continued*
Ramsbottom BL0 138 B6
Rochdale OL16 139 F7
Royton OL2 48 E4
Salford M7 158 E4
Milton St John's CE Prim Sch
OL5 68 C2
Milton Street Day Hospl
OL2 48 E4
Milton View OL5 68 D2
Milverton Ave SK14 102 C2
Milverton Cl BL6 40 D5
Milverton Dr SK7 132 B5
Milverton Rd M14 98 D3
Milverton Wlk SK14 102 C2
Milwain Dr SK4 111 C6
Milwain Rd
Manchester M19 111 A8
Stretford M32 96 C1
Mimosa Dr M27 61 F2
Mincing St 2 M4 159 A3
Minden Cl Bury BL8 27 B2
Manchester M20 110 D4
Minden Par BL9 140 F2
Minden St M6 80 E6
Mine St OL10 29 D4
Minehead Ave
Hindley WN7 57 D2
Manchester M20 109 F6
Urmston M41 107 B8
Minerva Rd
Ashton-u-L OL6,SK16 166 C2
Farnworth BL4 42 A2
Minford Cl M40 83 B6
Minnie St Bolton BL3 146 B3
Whitworth OL12 4 D2
Minoan Gdns M7 81 C5
Minor St Failsworth M35 66 A1
Rochdale OL11 30 C1
Minorca Ave M11 83 D2
Minorca Cl OL11 29 E8
Minorca St BL3 147 E4
Minshull St M1 159 A1
Minshull St S M1 163 B8
Minsmere Cl 1 M8 156 A6
Minsmere Wlks SK2 124 F4
Minstead Cl SK14 102 A1
Minstead Wlk M22 121 B2
Minster Cl Bolton BL2 25 C2
Dukinfield SK16 101 D6
Minster Dr
Altrincham WA14 128 A8
Cheadle SK8 123 A5
Urmston M41 95 A3
Minster Gr M29 77 B7
Minster Rd Bolton BL2 25 C2
Manchester M9 157 F8
Minster Way OL9 48 A1
Minsterley Par M22 121 C1
Minstrel Cl
Abram Brow WN2 74 B7
Swinton M27 79 D7
Mint St BL0 1 C2
Minto St OL7 166 A4
Minton St Failsworth M40 83 C8
Oldham OL4 67 A5
Mintridge Cl 9 M11 99 E7
Mirabel St M3 158 F3
Miranda Ct M5 161 C8
Mirfield Ave
Manchester M9 64 D4
Oldham OL8 66 E4
Stockport SK4 168 B2
Mirfield Cl WA3 90 D7
Mirfield Dr Eccles M30 79 D4
Middleton M24 46 F1
Urmston M41 95 C4
Mirfield Rd M9 64 D4
Miriam Gr WN7 76 A4
Miriam St 9 Bolton BL3 146 B4
Failsworth M35 83 D5
Miry La Westhoughton BL5 57 E6
Wigan WN3,WN6 150 A8
Missenden Ho 12 M5 154 F1
Mission St OL10 29 C2
Missouri Ave M50 154 E1
Mistletoe Gr M3 158 D3
Mistral Ct M30 79 E3
Mitcham Ave M9 65 A3
Mitchell Cl SK8 121 F6
Mitchell Gdns M22 121 E4
Mitchell Hey OL12 139 E7
Mitchell Rd WN5 71 E5
Mitchell St
Ashton-in-M WN4 73 C2
Bury BL8 27 C4
Eccles M30 79 C3
Failsworth M40 83 B5
Golborne WA3 90 A8
Ince-in-M WN2 56 A7
Leigh WN7 75 B5
Manchester M11 164 F8
Oldham OL1 153 E8
Rochdale,Greengate OL16 15 C3
Rochdale,Spotland Bridge
OL12 139 D8
Wigan WN5 54 E6
Mitchells Quay M35 83 E7
Mitcheson Gdns M6 154 F3
Mitford Rd M14 110 C7
Mitford St M32 96 C1
Mitre Rd M12,M13 98 F4
Mitre St Bolton BL1 143 E4
Failsworth M35 83 F8
Mitton Cl Bury BL8 26 F2
Culcheth WA3 91 E5
Heywood OL10 28 F2
Mizpah Gr BL8 27 B2
Mizzy Rd OL12 14 F1
Moadlock SK6 113 C4
Moat Ave M22 121 C5
Moat Gdns M22 121 C4
Moat Hall Ave M30 95 A8
Moat House St WN2 56 A7
Moat Rd M22 121 C4
Moat Wlk SK5 112 C7
Mobberley Cl M19 110 E4
Mobberley Rd
Ashley WA14,WA15,WA16 128 E3
Bolton BL2 42 E8
Wilmslow SK9 130 D1
Mocha Par M7 158 D3
Modbury Cl SK7 124 A1
Modbury Wlk 13 M8 156 A6
Mode Hill La M45 45 C1
Mode Hill Wlk M45 63 C8
Mode Wheel Circ M17 96 C7
Mode Wheel Rd M5,
M50 154 D1
Mode Wheel Rd S
Salford M50 154 D1
Stretford M50 96 D8
Mode Wheel Wkshp M50 96 D8
Modwen Rd M5 161 B6
Moelfre Dr SK8 132 C7
Moffat Cl BL2 42 F6
Moggie La SK10 133 F1
Moisant St BL3 147 D3
Moison Ho SK2 124 A6
Mold St Bolton BL1 143 E3
Oldham OL1 153 E8
Molesworth St OL16 31 A7
Mollets Wood M34 101 A5
Mollington Rd M22 130 E8
Mollis Gr OL1 49 E3
Molyneux Rd Reddish M19 99 C1
Westhoughton BL5 40 B1
Molyneux St
Rochdale OL12 139 D8
Wigan WN1 151 D8
Mona Ave Cheadle SK8 122 D1
Stretford M32 96 C3
Mona St Hyde SK14 167 E2
Salford M6 81 A4
Wigan WN1 150 B8
Monaco Dr M22 109 D2
Monarch Cl Irlam M44 105 E6
Royton OL2 48 E2
Monart Rd M9 64 E1
Moncrieffe St Bolton BL3 145 F6
Bolton BL4 148 A5
Mond Rd M44 94 B4
Monde Trad Est M17 96 A6
Money Ash Rd WA15 119 E3
Monfa Ave SK2 124 A4
Monica Ave M8 63 F2
Monica Gr M19 110 F8
Monica Terr WN4 73 B2
Monks Cl Manchester M8 64 B2
Milnrow OL16 31 E6
Monks Ct M5 80 B2
Monks Hall Gr M30 79 F2
Monks La BL2 25 D2
Monks' Rd SK13 116 A3
Monksdale Ave M41 95 B2
Monkswood OL1 153 E7
Monkton Ave M18 99 C3
Monkwood Dr 3 M9 157 E8
Monmouth Ave Bury BL9 27 F5
Sale M33 107 F5
Monmouth Cres WN4 73 D2
Monmouth Rd SK8 123 B1
Monmouth St
2 Manchester M18 99 E6
Middleton M24 65 C8
Oldham OL9 152 C5
Rochdale OL11 139 F6
Monroe Cl Salford M6 154 E4
Wigan WN3 55 A3
Mons Ave OL11 30 C8
Monsal Ave Salford M7 81 A7
Stockport SK2 124 D7
Monsall Cl BL9 45 A2
Monsall Rd M40,M9 157 E6
Monsall St
Manchester M40 157 D5
Oldham OL8 66 E3
Montagu Rd SK2 124 D8
Montagu St SK6 114 B2
Montague Ho SK3 170 D8
Montague Rd
Ashton-u-L OL6 85 D3
Manchester M16 161 A5
Sale M33 108 B4
Montague St BL3 146 B3
Montague Way SK15 86 A2
Montana Sq M11 99 E7
Montcliffe Cres M16 97 F2
Monteagle St M9 64 B4
Montford Rise WN2 38 A2
Montford St M50 96 F8
Montfort Cl BL5 57 D6
Montgomery OL11 139 E6
Montgomery Dr BL9 45 B2
Montgomery Ho OL8 66 B1
Montgomery Rd M13 98 F2
Montgomery St
Oldham OL8 66 B1
Rochdale OL11 30 C4
Montgomery Way M26 43 C5
Montmano Dr M20 109 F6
Monton Ave M30 79 E3
Monton Bridge Ct M30 79 C4
Monton Gn M30 79 D4
Monton Green Prim Sch
M30 79 E4
Monton Ho SK5 112 B4
Monton La M30 79 E2
Monton Mews 4 WN1 37 B3
Monton Prep Sch M30 79 D3
Monton Rd
Brinnington SK5 112 C4
Eccles M30 79 D3
Monton St Bolton BL3 147 E3
Manchester M14 98 A4
Radcliffe M26 43 F3
Monton Village Sch M30 79 D3
Montondale M30 79 C3
Montonfields Rd M30 79 C3
Montonmill Gdns M30 79 C3
Montpellier Mews 10 M7 63 E1
Montpellior Rd M22 121 D2
Montreal St
Abram Brow WN7 74 E4
3 Manchester M19 99 B1
Oldham OL8 66 F4
Montrey Cres WN4 72 C3
Montrose 2 M30 79 E2
Montrose Ave Bolton BL2 25 C1
Dukinfield SK16 101 C7
2 Manchester M20 110 A5
Ramsbottom BL0 11 A2
Stockport SK2 124 A3
Stretford M32 96 B2
Wigan WN5 54 D7
Montrose Cres 3 M19 99 A1
Montrose Dr BL7 25 B7
Montrose Gdns OL2 48 F4
Montrose Sch WN5 54 D7
Montrose St OL11 30 C1
Montserrat Brow BL1 23 D2
Montserrat Rd BL1 23 E2
Monument Mans 6 WN1 37 C2
Monument Rd WN1 37 D2
Monyash Ct 18 SK13 171 D1
Monyash Gr 19 SK13 171 D1
Monyash Lea 20 SK13 171 D1
Monyash Mews SK13 171 D1
Monyash Pl 17 SK13 171 D1
Monyash View WN2 56 F3
Monyash Way 18 SK13 171 E1
Moody St WN6 19 E1
Moon Gr M14 98 D3
Moon St OL9 152 C7
Moor Allerton Sch M20 109 F4
Moor Ave WN6 35 E8
Moor Bank La OL16 31 E3
Moor Cl M26 43 E5
Moor Cres OL3 51 B3
Moor Edge Rd OL5,SK15 86 F8
Moor End M22 121 D8
Moor End Ave M7 81 C8
Moor End Ct M7 81 C8
Moor End Rd SK6 127 A5
Moor Gate BL2 25 D5
Moor Gate La OL15 15 E7
Moor Hill OL11 29 F8
Moor La Bolton BL1,BL3 145 E6
Bramhall SK7 132 E3
Leigh WN7 75 E8
Manchester M7 63 C1
Rochdale OL12 13 F3
Salford M7,M25 81 B8
Uppermill OL3 51 C2
Urmston M41 95 A3
Wilmslow SK9 136 D5
Wilmslow SK9 136 E5
Wythenshawe M23 109 A2
Moor Lo SK4 168 B4
Moor Nook M33 108 D3
Moor Park Ave OL11 30 B2
Moor Park Rd M20 122 C8
Moor Platt M33 108 D3
Moor Platt Cl BL6 22 F3
Moor Rd Haslingden BB4 1 A5
Littleborough OL15 6 C1
Orrell WN5 53 E6
Ramsbottom BL8 138 A6
Wythenshawe M23 120 E8
Moor Side La BL0 12 A7
Moor St Bury BL9 140 F3
Eccles M30 79 B1
Heywood OL10 29 B2
Oldham OL1 67 B7
Shaw OL2 149 A6
Swinton M27 79 F7
Moor Top Pl SK4 168 B3
Moor View Bacup OL13 3 B7
Rawtenstall BB4 2 F6
Moor View Cl OL12 13 F2
Moor Way BL8 10 C3
Moorbottom Rd BL8 10 E5
Moorby Ave M19 110 E4
Moorby St 7 OL1 67 A8
Moorby Wlk BL3 145 F5
Moorclose St M24 65 C8
Moorcock Ave M27 80 B8
Moorcot Ct M23 120 F7
Moorcroft Edenfield BL0 1 D2
Rochdale OL11 30 F3
Moorcroft Dr M19 110 F4
Moorcroft Rd M23 108 F1
Moorcroft Sq SK14 101 E6
Moorcroft St
1 Droylsden M43 84 B1
Oldham OL8 66 C2
Moorcroft Wlk M19 110 F4
Moordale Ave OL4 49 E1
Moordale St M20 110 A5
Moordown Cl M8 156 B6
Moore Gr WA13 117 B5
Moore Ho M30 95 D8
Moore St Rochdale OL16 139 F7
Wigan WN1 37 E1

Moore St E WN1 ....37 E1
Moore Wlk 10 M34 ......113 A7
Moore's Ct 8 BL1 ....144 C8
Mooredge Terr OL2 ....48 E2
Moores La WN6 ....19 D2
Moorfield Boothstown M28 .77 F6
  Edgworth BL7 ....9 D6
  Manchester M7 ....63 C1
  Radcliffe M26 ....43 E4
  Swinton M28 ....78 F8
Moorfield Ave
  Denton M34 ....101 A2
  Littleborough OL15 ....16 A7
  Manchester M14 ....110 C7
  Stalybridge SK15 ....102 D7
Moorfield Chase BL4 ....60 D7
Moorfield Cl
  8 Eccles M30 ....79 D1
  Irlam M44 ....94 B3
  Swinton M27 ....79 D6
Moorfield Com Prim Sch
  M44 ....94 A3
Moorfield Cres WA3 ....91 A7
Moorfield Dr
  Dukinfield SK14 ....101 E5
  Wilmslow SK9 ....136 E5
Moorfield Gr Bolton BL2 .....25 B1
  Manchester SK4 ....168 B4
  Sale M33 ....168 B4
Moorfield Hamlet OL2 ....48 F7
Moorfield Hts SK15 ....86 E7
Moorfield Inf Sch SK7 ......124 C1
Moorfield Jun Sch SK7 .....124 C1
Moorfield Mews OL2 ....64 A7
Moorfield Par M44 ....94 B3
Moorfield Pl 8 OL12 ....14 F1
Moorfield Prec OL14 ....103 D5
Moorfield Rd Irlam M44 ......94 B3
  Manchester M20 ....109 F4
  8 Oldham OL8 ....66 B2
  Salford M6 ....80 D5
  Swinton M27 ....79 C6
Moorfield St
  Hollingworth SK14 ....103 D5
  8 Manchester M20 ....110 B7
  Platt Bridge WN2 ....56 B3
Moorfield Terr
  Hollingworth SK14 ....103 D5
  Mossley SK15 ....86 E7
Moorfield Wlk M41 ....95 D2
Moorgate BL9 ....141 A3
Moorgate Ave
  Manchester M20 ....109 F6
  Rochdale OL11 ....30 A7
Moorgate Ct 2 BL2 ....25 B1
Moorgate Dr
  Mossley SK15 ....86 E6
  Tyldesley M29 ....77 C5
Moorgate Mews SK15 ....86 E7
Moorgate Prim Sch BL2 ...148 B8
Moorgate Rd
  Mossley SK15 ....86 E7
  Radcliffe M26 ....43 F8
Moorgate St OL3 ....69 B8
Moorhead St M4 ....159 B3
Moorhey Rd M38 ....59 F6
Moorhey Sch OL4 ....67 B6
Moorhill Ct 7 M7 ....63 C1
Moorhouse Com Prim Sch
  OL16 ....31 E6
Moorhouse Farm OL16 ......31 E6
Moorhouse Fold OL16 ....31 E6
Moorings Cl WN1 ....151 F8
Moorings Rd M17 ....96 B8
Moorings The
  Disley SK12 ....135 E6
  Mossley OL5 ....68 E3
  Worsley M28 ....79 A5
Moorland Ave
  Droylsden M43 ....83 E1
  Manchester M8 ....63 F2
  Milnrow OL16 ....32 A6
  Rochdale OL11 ....29 F8
  Sale M33 ....108 C3
  Uppermill OL3 ....50 F2
  Whitworth OL12 ....14 C7
Moorland Cres OL12 ....14 C7
Moorland Dr
  Cheadle SK8 ....131 F8
  Horwich BL6 ....22 F3
  Walkden M38 ....60 A6
Moorland Fold SK15 ....102 E7
Moorland Gr BL1 ....142 A2
Moorland Rd
  Hindley WN2 ....56 C5
  Manchester M20 ....110 B3
  Mossley SK15 ....86 E5
  Stockport SK2 ....124 B4
Moorland St
  Littleborough OL15 ....16 C7
  Rochdale OL12 ....14 E1
Moorland Terr OL12 ....14 A1
Moorlands Ave Leigh WN7 ..75 F3
  Urmston M41 ....95 B3
Moorlands Cres OL5 ....68 D1
Moorlands Dr OL5 ....68 E3
Moorlands Jun Sch
  M33 ....108 E5
Moorlands St OL2 ....149 C7
Moorlands View
  Bolton BL3 ....146 A2
  Edenfield BL0 ....1 D5
Moorlea M35 ....83 F8
Moorsbrook Gr 9 SK9 .....131 E1
Moorsholme Ave 8 M40 ....83 A7

Moorside
  Littleborough OL15 ....16 D6
  Rochdale OL11 ....30 F3
Moorside Ave
  Ainsworth BL2 ....26 D1
  Bolton BL1 ....142 A1
  Droylsden M43 ....84 C2
  Farnworth BL4 ....84 C2
  Horwich BL6 ....22 C2
Moorside Cl SK13 ....116 B7
Moorside Cres M43 ....84 C2
Moorside Ct Denton M34 ...101 A4
  Sale M33 ....108 B4
Moorside High M27 ....79 D7
Moorside Ho WA15 ....120 C7
Moorside La M34 ....101 A4
Moorside Lo M27 ....79 D8
Moorside Prim Sch
  Droylsden M43 ....84 B1
  Swinton M27 ....79 D7
Moorside Rd Bury BL8 ....26 E5
  Manchester M8 ....64 A1
  Salford M7 ....81 C8
  Stockport SK4 ....168 A2
  Swinton M27 ....79 D8
  Urmston M41 ....94 E3
  Urmston M41 ....95 A3
Moorside St M43 ....84 C2
Moorside Sta M27 ....61 D1
Moorside View Bury BL8 ....26 F6
  Shaw OL2 ....149 C8
Moorside Wlk WN5 ....54 B8
Moorsley Dr M9 ....90 C4
Moorsview BL0 ....2 A2
Moorton Ave M19 ....110 F7
Moorton Pk M19 ....110 F7
Moortop Cl M9 ....64 C6
Moorville Rd M6 ....80 C5
Moorway Dr M9 ....65 A4
Morden Ave
  Ashton-in-M WN4 ....73 B3
  17 Droylsden M11 ....83 C2
Morecambe Cl M40 ....83 B6
Morelands The BL1 ....144 A7
Morely St OL4 ....49 E1
Moresby St WN7 ....75 D5
Moresby Dr M20 ....122 B8
Moreton Ave
  Bramhall SK7 ....132 E5
  Sale M33 ....107 F3
  Stretford M32 ....96 D2
  Whitefield M45 ....44 F1
Moreton Cl
  Dukinfield SK16 ....101 D6
  Golborne WA3 ....73 F1
Moreton Dr Bury BL8 ....27 B3
  Handforth SK9 ....131 E3
  Leigh WN7 ....75 E1
  Poynton SK12 ....123 C5
Moreton Ho WA14 ....119 B4
Moreton La SK2 ....124 C7
Moreton St OL9 ....65 F8
Moreton Way SK14 ....102 F3
Moreton Wlk SK2 ....124 D7
Morgan Pl SK5 ....169 F4
Morgan St OL15 ....16 B5
Morillon Rd M44 ....94 A4
Morland Rd M16 ....97 C4
Morley Ave
  Manchester M14 ....98 A1
  Swinton M27 ....79 E6
Morley Green Rd SK9 .....130 C1
Morley Ho M22 ....121 E8
Morley Rd M26 ....43 D4
Morley St Atherton M46 ....58 C2
  Bolton BL3 ....145 D6
  Bury BL9 ....44 F8
  Glossop SK13 ....116 D8
  Rochdale OL16 ....15 B1
  Whitefield M45 ....44 F1
Morley's La Tyldesley M29 ..76 F3
  Tyldesley M29 ....77 A3
Morna Wlk M12 ....164 D8
Morningside WA14 ....119 B5
Morningside Cl
  Droylsden M43 ....100 A4
  22 Rochdale OL16 ....31 B6
Morningside Dr M20 ......122 C8
Mornington Ave SK8 ......122 D4
Mornington Cres M14 ....110 B8
Mornington Ct 5 OL1 .....153 E8
Mornington Rd
  Adlington PR6 ....21 B8
  Bolton BL1 ....144 B8
  Cheadle SK8 ....122 D4
  Hindley WN2 ....56 F5
  Over Hulton M46 ....58 F6
  Rochdale OL11 ....14 A4
Morpeth Cl Ashton-u-L OL7 .84 E4
  Manchester M12 ....164 E5
Morpeth St M27 ....79 E6

Morrell Rd M22 ....121 E8
Morris Ct 8 M14 ....110 C8
Morris Fold Dr BL6 ....40 C6
Morris Gn BL3 ....146 C2
Morris Gr M41 ....106 E8
Morris Green Bsns Pk
  BL3 ....146 C4
Morris Green La BL3 ......146 C2
Morris Green St BL3 ......146 C2
Morris Ho WN1 ....151 D8
Morris Rd WN6 ....53 A7
Morris St Bolton BL1 ......148 A7
  1 Hindley WN2 ....56 D5
  Ince-in-M WN3 ....55 E4
  Manchester M20 ....110 B7
  Oldham OL4 ....67 A6
  Radcliffe M26 ....44 E5
  Tyldesley M29 ....58 F1
  Wigan WN1 ....151 D8
Morrison St BL3 ....147 E3
Morrowfield Ave M8 ....155 F7
Morse Rd M40 ....83 B5
Morston Cl M28 ....78 B8
Mort Fold M38 ....60 A5
Mort La M28,M29,M38 .....59 E2
Mort St Farnworth BL4 .....60 B8
  Hindley WN2 ....22 B4
  Horwich BL6 ....21 E2
  8 Tyldesley M29 ....58 F1
  Wigan WN6 ....37 A1
Mortar St Oldham OL4 ......67 C7
  Oldham OL4 ....67 C8
Mortfield Gdns BL1 ....145 D8
Mortfield La BL1 ....145 D8
Mortimer Ave M9 ....64 E4
Mortimer St OL1 ....67 A8
Mortlake Cl M28 ....59 F3
Mortlake Dr M40 ....83 B5
Morton Ave WN3 ....54 D3
Morton Cl WN3 ....54 D3
Morton St Failsworth M35 ..83 C6
  Middleton M24 ....47 A1
  Radcliffe M26 ....44 B2
  Stockport SK4 ....169 E4
Morton Terr
  18 Denton M34 ....101 A1
  Romiley SK6 ....113 B5
Mortons The BL5 ....39 E2
Morven Ave SK7 ....124 F3
Morven Dr M23 ....121 A5
Morven Gr BL2 ....42 F7
Morville Dr WN3 ....54 C4
Morville Rd M21 ....97 D1
Morville St M11 ....163 C8
Moschatel Wlk M31 ......106 A3
Moscow Rd SK3 ....170 D7
Moscow Rd E SK3 ....170 D7
Mosedale Ave WA11 ....71 B1
Mosedale Cl
  Tyldesley M29 ....77 C6
  Wythenshawe M23 ....120 E6
Mosley Ave Bury BL9 ....27 F5
  Ramsbottom BL0 ....11 B2
Mosley Cl WA15 ....119 F7
Mosley Common Rd M28,
  M29 ....77 F7
Mosley Rd
  Altrincham WA15 ....120 B6
  Stretford M17 ....96 C6
Mosley St
  Manchester M1,M2 ......159 A1
  Radcliffe M26 ....43 F4
Mosley Street Sta M1 ....159 A1
Moss (PRU) The BL2 ......42 F6
Moss Ave Leigh WN7 ....76 B5
  Orrell WN5 ....53 D3
  Rochdale OL16 ....15 B1
Moss Bank Bramhall SK7 ..132 C5
  Manchester M8 ....156 A8
Moss Bank Ave M43 ....84 B2
Moss Bank Cl BL1 ....143 E4
Moss Bank Ct M43 ....84 C2
Moss Bank Gr M27 ....61 D2
Moss Bank Ho BL1 ....142 A3
Moss Bank Rd
  Billinge WA11 ....71 B2
  Swinton M27 ....61 D2
Moss Bank Way
  Bolton,Doffcocker BL1 ......23 E1
  Bolton,Smithills BL1 ......142 B3
Moss Bridge Rd OL16 ......31 B5
Moss Brook Dr M9 ....157 E7
Moss Cl Haslingden BB4 .....1 A8
  Radcliffe M26 ....44 A3
Moss Colliery Rd M27 ......61 E4
Moss Croft Cl M41 ....94 E3
Moss Farm Cl M24 ....64 A8
Moss Field Com Sch
  OL10 ....29 C3
Moss Gate Rd OL2 ....32 A1
Moss Gn M31 ....106 F6
Moss Gr Lymm WA13 .....117 B4

Moss Gr continued
  Shaw OL2 ....31 E1
  Standish WN6 ....36 E8
Moss Grange Ave M16 ......97 D4
Moss Grove Ct 2 M15 .....97 E4
Moss Hall Rd BL9,OL10 .....45 F7
Moss Hey M23 ....109 B1
Moss Hey Prim Sch
  SK7 ....132 C5
Moss Hey St OL2 ....149 C6
Moss House La M28 ....78 A5
Moss House Terr M9 ....64 C1
Moss Ind Est
  Golborne WN7 ....75 B1
  Rochdale OL16 ....31 B5
Moss La
  Alderley Edge SK9 ....137 B1
  Altrincham WA14,WA15 ...119 E4
  Altrincham WA15 ....119 F7
  Altrincham WA15 ....120 A5
  Appley Bridge WN6 ....7 D6
  Ashton-u-L OL7 ....84 E2
  Bolton BL1 ....142 B3
  Bramhall SK7 ....132 C5
  Fowley Common WA3 ....92 D5
  Golborne WA3 ....90 B5
  Horwich BL6 ....21 F2
  Irlam M44 ....61 B5
  Kearsley BL4 ....60 C5
  Middleton M9 ....64 F5
  Mottram-in-L SK14 ....114 F8
  Partington M31 ....105 F3
  Partington M31 ....106 A2
  Rochdale,Castleton OL11 ...46 B2
  Rochdale OL16 ....31 A6
  Royton OL2 ....49 A3
  Sale M33 ....107 B3
  Sale M33 ....107 E4
  Swinton M27 ....61 D2
  Tyldesley M29 ....59 D1
  Urmston M41 ....94 F3
  Walkden M28 ....60 E4
  Whitefield M45 ....62 F8
  Wilmslow SK9 ....136 A4
  Wythenshawe M23 ....130 E6
Moss La E M14,M15,M16 ...98 A4
Moss La W M15,M16 ....97 E4
Moss Lea BL1 ....143 D4
Moss Lodge La OL7 ....84 E1
Moss Manor M33 ....107 E3
Moss Mdw BL5 ....39 E2
Moss Meadow Rd M6 ....80 C4
Moss Mill St OL16 ....31 B5
Moss Park Jun & Inf Sch
  M32 ....96 B2
Moss Park Rd M32 ....96 B2
Moss Pit Row WN2 ....38 B4
Moss Pl 5 BL9 ....44 E8
Moss Rd
  Alderley Edge SK9 ....137 C2
  Irlam M44 ....105 C7
  Irlam M44 ....93 B1
  Kearsley BL4 ....60 C5
  Orrell WN5 ....53 D3
  Stretford M32 ....96 C3
  Stretford M33 ....107 B3
  Stretford M33 ....107 E4
  Swinton M27 ....61 D2
  Tyldesley M29 ....59 D5
  Urmston M41 ....94 E3
  Walkden M28 ....60 E4
  Whitefield M45 ....62 F8
  Wilmslow SK9 ....136 A4
  Wythenshawe M23 ....130 E6
Moss Rose SK9 ....137 B2
Moss Row Bury BL9 ....140 F1
  Rochdale OL11 ....13 D1
Moss Shaw Way M26 ....43 E5
Moss Side La
  Hollinfare WA3 ....105 A2
  Rochdale OL16 ....31 C5
Moss Side Rd M44 ....93 B1
Moss Side St OL12 ....4 E5
Moss St Bury BL8 ....140 E2
  Droylsden M43 ....84 B1
  Droylsden M43 ....84 B2
  2 Farnworth BL4 ....42 E1
  5 Heywood OL10 ....29 C2
  Hollingworth SK14 ....103 D5
  Ince-in-M WN3 ....55 F3
  Oldham OL4 ....67 C8
  Platt Bridge WN2 ....56 A3
  Ramsbottom BL9 ....11 D2
  Salford M7 ....158 D3
  Wigan,Redwood WN5 ......54 B6
  Wigan,Springfield WN6 .....37 A1
Moss St E OL6 ....166 B3
Moss St W OL7 ....84 F2
Moss Terr
  Ashton-u-L OL6 ....166 A2
  8 Wigan WN5 ....54 B5
  Wilmslow SK9 ....137 F8
Moss The M24 ....65 B6
Moss Vale Cres M32 ....95 F3
Moss Vale Rd M41 ....95 E2
Moss View Com Sch
  M31 ....106 A3
Moss View Rd Bolton BL2 ...42 E8
  Partington M31 ....106 A3
Moss Way M33 ....107 E4
Mossack Ave M22 ....121 D1
Mossbank Cl SK13 ....171 E4
Mossbank Gr OL10 ....29 C2
Mossbray Ave M19 ....110 D4
Mossbrook Ct M40 ....159 C4
Mossbrook Dr M38 ....59 E6
Mossclough Ct M9 ....157 F2
Mosscot Wlk M13 ....163 B7
Mossdale Ave BL1 ....40 D7
Mossdale Rd
  Sale M33 ....107 F1
  Wythenshawe M23 ....108 F1
Mossdown Rd OL2 ....49 A3

Mossfield Cl Bury BL9 .....141 B4
  Stockport SK4 ....168 B2
Mossfield Ct BL1 ....145 E8
Mossfield Dr M9 ....65 A4
Mossfield Gn M30 ....94 C4
Mossfield Prim Sch M27 ...61 F1
Mossfield Rd
  Altrincham WA15 ....120 D6
  Farnworth BL4 ....60 B8
  Kearsley BL4 ....60 F5
  Swinton M27 ....61 F2
Mossford St M11 ....99 D8
Mossgate Rd SK9 ....119 F6
Mosshall Cl M15 ....162 D6
Mossland Cl OL10 ....46 D8
Mossland Gr BL3 ....40 D2
Mosslea Ave M8 ....63 F3
Mossley Hollins High Sch
  OL5 ....68 E1
Mossley Rd
  Ashton-u-L OL6 ....166 C3
  Ashton-u-L,Higher Hurst
  OL6 ....85 E4
  Uppermill OL4 ....68 D5
Mossley Sta OL5 ....68 C1
Mossmere Rd SK8 ....123 A4
Mossway M24,M9 ....64 F5
Mosswood Pk M20 ....122 B8
Mosswood Rd SK9 ....131 E1
Mossy Lea Fold WN6 ....19 A3
Mossy Lea Rd WN6 ....18 F5
Mossylea Cl M24 ....65 B5
Moston Bank Ave M9 .....157 F7
Moston La
  Manchester M9,M40 ......157 F8
  Manchester,Moston M40 ...65 D2
Moston La E M9,M40 ....65 E1
Moston Lane Com Prim Sch
  M9 ....157 F8
Moston Rd M24 ....65 D5
Moston St Reddish SK5 ...111 F8
  Salford M7 ....155 F7
Moston Sta M40 ....65 D2
Mostyn Ave Bury BL9 ......27 F5
  Cheadle SK8 ....122 E1
  Manchester M14 ....110 E8
  Mostyn St SK14 ....124 C1
  Mostyn St SL15,SK14 .....101 F8
Motcombe Farm Rd
  SK8 ....122 B1
Motcombe Gr SK8 ....122 A3
Motcombe Rd SK8 ....122 A3
Motherwell Ave 2 M19 .....99 A1
Mottershead Ave BL3 ......43 A4
Mottershead Rd M22 .....121 C4
Mottram CE Prim Sch
  SK14 ....103 A3
Mottram Cl SK8 ....123 A5
Mottram Dr
  Altrincham WA15 ....120 A5
  Wigan WN3 ....150 B5
Mottram Fold SK1 ....170 F6
Mottram Mews 6 SK1 .....22 B4
Mottram Moor SK14 .....103 B4
Mottram Old Rd
  Hyde SK14 ....114 B8
  Stalybridge SK15 ....102 D7
Mottram Rd
  Alderley Edge SK9 ....137 D1
  Hattersley SK14 ....102 C3
  Mottram-in-L SK14 ....115 A8
  Sale M33 ....108 F3
  Stalybridge SK15 ....102 F7
Mottram St Horwich BL6 ....22 B4
  8 Stockport SK1 ....170 F6
Mough La OL9 ....65 E3
Mouldsworth Ave
  Manchester M20 ....110 A7
  Reddish SK4 ....111 D6
Moulton St M8 ....158 E4
Moulton St Prec M8 ......158 E4
Mouncey St M1 ....163 A7
Mount Ave
  Littleborough OL15 ....16 A7
  Rawtenstall BB4 ....2 F8
  Rochdale OL12 ....15 C7
Mount Carmel Cres M5 ...161 C7
Mount Carmel Ct M5 .....161 C7
Mount Carmel RC Prim Sch
  M9 ....64 D2
Mount Cres WN3 ....53 F6
Mount Dr Marple SK6 .....125 F5
  Urmston M41 ....94 E3
Mount Fold M24 ....65 B7
Mount La SK9 ....121 F6
Mount La OL3 ....50 E1
Mount Pleasant
  Adlington PR6 ....21 A8
  18 Bacup OL13 ....3 A8
  Bolton BL3 ....148 C5
  Edgworth BL7 ....7 D5
  Hazel Grove SK7 ....124 D3
  Middleton,Rhodes M24 ....64 C8
  Middleton,Sinister M25 ....63 F8
  Ramsbottom BL9 ....11 F3
  Wilmslow SK9 ....137 B8
Mount Pleasant Bsns Ctr
  OL16 ....67 B7
Mount Pleasant Rd
  Denton M34 ....100 F2
  Farnworth M38 ....59 F8

234 Mou – New

Mount Pleasant St
Ashton-u-L OL6 ...166 C3
Denton M34 ...100 F7
2 Horwich BL6 ...22 D1
Oldham OL4 ...67 B7
Mount Pleasant Trad Est OL6 ...166 C4
Mount Pleasant Wlk M26 .44 A4
Mount Rd
Manchester M18,M19 ...99 C3
Middleton M24 ...65 A7
Prestwich M25 ...63 C6
Romiley SK14 ...114 A6
Stockport SK4 ...168 C2
Mount Sion Rd M26 ...43 E2
Mount Skip La M38 ...60 A4
Mount St Bolton BL1 ...143 E1
Denton M34 ...101 B1
Eccles M30 ...95 C8
Glossop SK13 ...116 C8
Heywood OL10 ...29 D1
Horwich BL6 ...22 D2
Hyde SK14 ...167 E2
Leigh WN7 ...75 C4
Manchester M2 ...162 F8
Ramsbottom BL0 ...138 B6
Rochdale OL12 ...139 E8
Rochdale,Castleton OL11 ...30 C1
Royton OL2 ...48 E3
Salford M3 ...158 D3
Swinton M27 ...79 F7
Mount St Joseph Sch BL4 ...42 A2
Mount St Joseph's Rd BL3 ...144 B5
Mount Terr M43 ...83 E3
Mount The
Altrincham WA14 ...119 D5
Altrincham,Hale WA15 ...129 C8
Ashton-u-L OL6 ...85 D3
Brinnington SK5 ...112 B4
Mount View
Ince-in-M WN3 ...151 D5
Uppermill OL3 ...69 B8
Mount View Rd OL2 ...49 D6
Mount Zion Rd BL9 ...44 F5
Mountain Ash OL12 ...14 B3
Mountain Ash Cl
Rochdale OL12 ...14 B3
9 Sale M33 ...107 C5
Mountain Ash Cotts OL3 .33 D1
Mountain Gr M28 ...60 C4
Mountain Rd PR7 ...19 E8
Mountain St
Failsworth M40 ...83 D4
Mossley OL5 ...68 C1
Stockport SK1 ...112 A2
Walkden M28 ...60 C4
Mountbatten Ave SK16 ..101 F6
Mountbatten Cl BL9 ...45 C2
Mountbatten St M18 ...165 C5
Mountfield M25 ...63 B4
Mountfield Ct WN5 ...53 F7
Mountfield Rd
Bramhall SK7 ...132 E5
Stockport SK3 ...123 C7
Mountfield Wlk
5 Bolton BL1 ...143 E1
11 Manchester M11 ...160 F1
Mountford Ave M8 ...63 F2
Mountheath Ind Pk M25 ..63 B1
Mountmorres Cl BL5 ...59 A7
Mountroyal Cl SK14 ...102 A5
Mountside Cl OL12 ...14 F2
Mountside Cres M25 ...62 F4
Mousell St M8 ...159 A4
Mouselow Cl SK13 ...171 F3
Mow Halls La OL3 ...51 A1
Mowat Ct M14 ...110 D8
Mowbray Ave
Manchester M25 ...63 C1
Sale M33 ...108 C3
Mowbray St
Ashton-u-L OL7 ...166 A2
Bolton BL1 ...142 B1
5 Oldham OL1 ...153 F6
Rochdale OL11 ...30 B3
Stockport SK1 ...170 F8
Mowbray Wlk 4 M24 ...46 E2
Moxley Rd M8 ...63 F1
Moxon Way WN4 ...73 D4
Moyse Ave BL8 ...26 F5
Mozart Cl M4 ...159 C2
Mudhurst La SK12 ...135 E3
Muirfield Ave SK6 ...113 A4
Muirfield Cl Bolton BL3 ...40 F3
Failsworth M40 ...83 C7
Heywood OL10 ...29 D1
Prestwich M25 ...63 B5
Wilmslow SK9 ...137 D8
Muirfield Dr M29 ...77 C7
Muirhead Ct M6 ...81 A5
Mulberry Ave WA3 ...90 F7
Mulberry Cl Gatley SK8 ..131 C7
Rochdale OL11 ...139 E5
Wigan WN5 ...54 D6
Mulberry Ct
Altrincham WA14 ...119 D6
8 Horwich BL6 ...22 D1
7 Salford M6 ...81 A3
Urmston M41 ...95 E2
Mulberry Mews SK4 ...169 E2
Mulberry Mount St SK3 .170 E8
Mulberry Rd M6 ...81 A3
Mulberry St
2 Ashton-u-L OL6 ...166 C3
Manchester M2 ...158 F1
Mulberry Wlk
Droylsden M43 ...99 E8
Sale M33 ...107 D6
Mule St BL2 ...148 A7
Mulgrave Rd M28 ...79 A8
Mulgrave St Bolton BL3 ..146 C2
Swinton M27 ...61 D1
Mulgrove Wlk 29 M9 ...64 E3
Mull Ave M12 ...164 F5
Mullacre Rd M22 ...121 D6
Mulliner St 1 BL1 ...143 F1
Mullineux St M28 ...60 D2
Mullins Ave WA12 ...89 C5
Mullion Cl M19 ...99 D2
Mullion Dr WA15 ...119 E6
Mullion Wlk M8 ...156 B6
Mulmount Cl OL8 ...66 C3
Mumps OL1 ...67 A7
Munday St M4 ...160 D1
Municipal Cl 2 OL10 ...29 D2
Munn Rd M9 ...64 C5
Munro Ave Orrell WN5 ...53 E6
Wythenshawe M22 ...121 F2
Munslow Wlk M9 ...64 F3
Munster St M4 ...159 A3
Muriel St Heywood OL10 ..29 E2
Rochdale OL16 ...31 B5
Salford M7 ...155 D5
Murieston Rd WA15 ...119 E2
Murphy Cl WN3 ...150 A5
Murray Rd BL9 ...140 F2
Murray St Atherton M46 ..58 B2
Manchester M4 ...159 C2
Salford M7 ...155 D6
Murrayfield OL11 ...29 E6
Murrow Wlk 3 M9 ...157 D8
Murton Terr BL1 ...143 F4
Mus of Science & Ind* M60,M3 ...162 E8
Mus of Science & Ind (Air & Space Gal)* M3 ...162 E8
Musbury Ave SK8 ...123 B2
Musden Ave BB4 ...1 A7
Musden Wlk SK4 ...111 D7
Museum of the Manchesters The* OL6 ...166 B3
Museum of Transport* M8 ...156 B6
Museum St M2 ...162 F8
Musgrave Gdns BL1 ...144 C8
Musgrave Rd Bolton BL1 .144 C8
Wythenshawe M22 ...121 D3
Muslin St M5 ...81 C1
Mustard La WA3 ...91 B1
Muter Ave M22 ...121 F2
Mutual St OL10 ...29 E3
My St M5 ...154 E1
Mycroft Cl WN7 ...75 E8
Myerscroft Cl M40 ...65 E1
Myrrh St BL1 ...143 E2
Myrtle Ave
Ashton-in-M WN4 ...72 F6
Leigh WN7 ...75 E7
Newton-le-W WA12 ...89 C2
Myrtle Bank M25 ...63 A1
Myrtle Cl OL8 ...153 E5
Myrtle Gdns BL9 ...141 B2
Myrtle Gr Billinge WN5 ...71 D4
Droylsden M43 ...84 C2
Manchester M25 ...63 B2
Reddish M34 ...99 F3
Whitefield M45 ...44 D2
Myrtle Pl M7 ...81 C4
Myrtle Rd Middleton M24 ..47 C2
Partington M31 ...105 D3
Myrtle St Bolton BL1 ...145 D8
Manchester,Beswick M11 ..164 F8
3 Manchester,Old Trafford M16 ...97 C4
Stockport SK3 ...123 B8
Wigan WN1 ...150 B8
Myrtle St N BL9 ...141 B2
Myrtle St S BL9 ...141 B2
Myrtleleaf Gr M5 ...154 D2
Mytham Gdns BL3 ...43 B2
Mytham Prim Sch BL3 ...43 B3
Mytham Rd BL3 ...43 B2
Mythorn Wlk M40 ...83 B5
Mythorne Ave M44 ...105 C3
Mytton Rd BL1 ...142 B4
Mytton St M15 ...162 F5

N

Nabbs Fold BL8 ...10 F3
Nabbs Way BL8 ...11 A1
Naburn Cl SK5 ...112 C6
Naburn Dr WN5 ...53 E5
Naburn St M13 ...98 D4
Nada Lo M8 ...63 F1
Nada Rd M8 ...63 F1
Naden Wlk M45 ...63 A8
Nadin St 1 OL8 ...66 E3
Nadine St M6 ...154 E3
Nailgate OL16 ...31 C2
Nailsworth Wlk 5 M13 .163 C5
Nairn Cl Manchester M40 .160 E3
Standish WN6 ...19 D1
Nall St Manchester M19 ...111 B7
Milnrow OL16 ...31 E6
Nameplate Cl M30 ...79 B2
Nan Nook Rd M23 ...108 F1
Nancy St M15 ...162 D6
Nandywell BL3 ...43 B3
Nangreave Rd SK2 ...124 B6
Nangreave St M5 ...158 D1
Nangreaves St WN7 ...75 C5
Nansen Ave M30 ...79 C3
Nansen Cl M32 ...96 E4
Nansen Rd SK8 ...122 A4
Nansen St
Manchester M11 ...164 E8
Salford M6 ...154 E2
Stretford M32 ...96 E4
Nansmoss La SK9 ...130 D1
Nantes Ct BL1 ...143 D2
Nantwich Ave OL12 ...14 F3
Nantwich Cl SK8 ...123 A5
Nantwich Rd M14 ...98 A1
Nantwich Way 6 SK9 ...131 E5
Nantwich Wlk BL3 ...147 E4
Napier Ct
Manchester,City Park M15 .161 C6
Manchester,Heaton Moor SK4 ...168 B3
Napier Gn M5 ...161 B7
Napier Ho OL14 ...6 A8
Napier Rd Eccles M30 ...79 C3
Manchester,Chorlton-cum-Hardy M21 ...109 B8
Manchester,Heaton Moor SK4 ...168 B3
Napier St
Hazel Grove SK7 ...124 D3
Hyde SK14 ...167 E1
Shaw OL2 ...149 B8
Swinton M27 ...79 D7
Napier St E OL8 ...153 D5
Napier St W OL8 ...153 D5
Naples Rd SK3 ...123 B7
Naples St M4 ...159 A3
Narbonne Ave M30 ...80 A4
Narborough Cl WN2 ...56 E4
Narbuth Dr M8 ...155 F7
Narcissus Ave BB4 ...1 A8
Narcissus Wlk 6 M28 ...59 F3
Narrow La SK10 ...134 A1
Narrows The WA14 ...119 C4
Naseby Ave M9 ...64 F4
Naseby Ct M25 ...63 C5
Naseby Pl M25 ...63 C5
Naseby Rd SK5 ...99 F1
Naseby Wlk M45 ...63 C8
Nash Rd M17 ...95 F8
Nash St M15 ...162 E6
Nasmyth Ave M34 ...101 A4
Nasmyth Bsns Ctr M30 ...79 C2
Nasmyth Rd M30 ...95 C8
Nasmyth St Horwich BL6 ..22 C3
Manchester M8 ...156 C5
Nately Rd M16 ...97 A2
Nathan Dr M3 ...158 E2
Nathaniel Ct WN2 ...56 B3
Nathans Rd M22 ...121 C4
National Cycling Ctr M11 .83 A2
National Dr M5 ...161 A8
National Squash Ctr M11 ...160 F2
National Trad Est SK7 ..124 C3
Naunton Ave WN7 ...75 C5
Naunton Rd M24 ...65 B7
Naunton Wlk 24 M9 ...157 E8
Naval St M4 ...159 C2
Navenby Ave M16 ...97 C4
Navenby Rd WN3 ...55 A2
Navigation Cl WN7 ...75 E4
Navigation Ho WN7 ...76 A4
Navigation Prim Sch WA14 ...119 D6
Navigation Rd WA14 ...119 D6
Navigation Road Sta WA14 ...119 E6
Naylor Ave WA3 ...90 B8
Naylor Ct 19 M40 ...159 C3
Naylor St Atherton M46 ..58 C2
Manchester M40 ...160 D3
Oldham OL1 ...153 E7
Naylorfarm Ave WN6 ...35 F5
Nazarene Theological Coll The M20 ...110 A3
Naze Ct 3 OL1 ...153 E8
Naze Wlk SK5 ...112 C6
Nazeby Wlk OL9 ...152 C5
Neal Ave Ashton-u-L OL6 ..85 D3
Gatley SK8 ...122 A1
Neale Ave OL3 ...69 B5
Neale Rd M21 ...109 B7
Near Birches Par OL4 ...67 E4
Near Hey Cl M26 ...43 E3
Nearbrook Rd M22 ...121 C4
Nearcroft Rd M23 ...121 B7
Nearmaker Ave M22 ...121 C4
Nearmaker Rd M22 ...121 C4
Neary Way M41 ...95 C5
Neasden Gr 6 BL3 ...144 C5
Neath Ave M22 ...121 D7
Neath Cl Poynton SK12 ...133 D5
Prestwich M45 ...63 C7
Neath Fold BL3 ...147 D3
Neath St OL9 ...153 D7
Nebo St BL3 ...147 D4
Nebraska St BL1 ...143 E1
Neden Cl M11 ...165 B8
Needham Ave M21 ...109 B8
Needwood Cl M40 ...157 D5
Needwood Rd SK6 ...113 C5
Neenton Sq M12 ...165 A7
Neild Gdns WN7 ...75 E4
Neild St Manchester M1 ..163 B8
Oldham OL8 ...66 F4
Neill St M8 ...158 E4
Neilson Cl M24 ...65 C7
Neilson Ct M23 ...121 A6
Neilston Ave M40 ...83 B7
Nel Pan La WN7 ...75 D8
Nell Carrs BL0 ...11 E8
Nell La M20,M21 ...109 D6
Nell St BL1 ...143 F4
Nellie St OL10 ...29 B2
Nelson Ave Eccles M30 ...79 D3
Poynton SK12 ...134 A3
Nelson Cl SK12 ...134 A3
Nelson Ct
Manchester,Miles Platting M40 ...160 D4
Manchester,Old Trafford M15 ...97 E4
Nelson Dr Droylsden M43 ..83 E2
Ince-in-M WN2 ...56 A8
Irlam M44 ...105 E6
Nelson Fold M27 ...62 A1
Nelson Mandela Ct 9 M16 ...97 E3
Nelson Rd M9 ...64 D5
Nelson Sq BL1 ...145 F7
Nelson St Atherton M46 ..58 B3
Atherton M46 ...58 B4
Bacup OL13 ...4 C8
Bolton BL3 ...148 A5
6 Bury BL9 ...44 F8
Denton M34 ...100 F4
Denton,Hooley Hill M34 ..100 F6
Eccles M30 ...79 D2
Farnworth BL4 ...60 E8
Hazel Grove SK7 ...124 F4
Heywood OL10 ...29 D1
8 Hindley WN2 ...56 D6
Horwich BL6 ...22 D3
Hyde SK14 ...167 E2
Little Lever BL3 ...43 B3
7 Littleborough OL15 ...16 B5
Manchester,Brunswick M13 ...163 B5
Manchester,Miles Platting M40 ...160 E4
Middleton M24 ...65 C7
Newton-le-W WA12 ...89 A3
Oldham OL4 ...67 E5
Rochdale OL16 ...139 F7
Salford,Lower Broughton M7 ...155 D5
Salford,Weaste M5 ...154 E1
Stretford M32 ...96 D1
Tyldesley M29 ...77 B8
Walsden OL14 ...6 A8
Nelson Way OL9 ...66 B4
Nelstrop Cres SK4 ...111 D6
Nelstrop Rd SK4 ...111 D6
Nelstrop Rd N M19,SK4, SK5 ...111 C8
Nelstrop Wlk SK4 ...111 C6
Nene Gr WN2 ...56 E4
Nepaul Rd M9 ...64 E1
Neptune Gdns 11 M7 ...81 C5
Nesbit St BL2 ...25 B3
Nesfield Rd M23 ...108 F2
Neston Ave Bolton BL1 ...24 F5
Manchester M20 ...110 A6
Sale M33 ...108 E2
Neston Cl OL2 ...49 D7
Neston Gr SK3 ...170 D5
Neston Rd Bury BL8 ...26 F5
Rochdale OL16 ...31 C4
Neston St M11 ...99 F7
Neston Way SK9 ...131 D3
Neswick Wlk 4 M23 ...108 F2
Nether Hey St OL8 ...67 B4
Nether St Hyde SK14 ...113 F8
Manchester M12 ...163 C8
Netherbury Cl M18 ...99 C3
Netherby Rd WN6 ...37 A3
Nethercote Ave M23 ...121 B6
Nethercott Ct M29 ...58 E1
Nethercroft OL11 ...13 E1
Nethercroft Ct WA14 ...119 C5
Nethercroft Rd WA15 ...120 C5
Netherfield Cl OL8 ...66 C4
Netherfield Rd BL3 ...147 E2
Netherfields WN7 ...75 D7
Netherhey La OL1 ...48 C2
Netherhouse Rd OL2 ...149 A7
Netherland St M5 ...161 A8
Netherlees OL4 ...67 D5
Netherley Rd PR7 ...19 E8
Netherlow Ct SK14 ...167 E2
Netherton Gr BL4 ...42 B2
Netherton Rd M14 ...98 A1
Nethervale Dr M9 ...157 E7
Netherwood M35 ...84 B8
Netherwood Ct WN6 ...36 A6
Netherwood Rd M22 ...121 C7
Netley Ave OL12 ...14 F3
Netley Gdns M26 ...43 E5
Netley Rd M23 ...121 A4
Nettlebarn Rd M22 ...121 C5
Nettleford Rd M16 ...109 E8
Nettleton Gr M9 ...64 F1
Network Ctr M27 ...80 E7
Nevada St 18 BL1 ...143 E1
Nevendon Dr M23 ...120 F4
Nevern Cl BL1 ...40 F8
Nevile Ct M7 ...81 B8
Nevile Rd M7 ...81 B8
Nevill Rd SK7 ...123 E2
Nevill Road Inf Sch SK7 .123 E2
Nevill Road Jun Sch SK7 ...123 E2
Neville Cardus Wlk 12 M14 ...98 C3
Neville Cl BL1 ...145 E8
Neville Dr M44 ...94 A4
Neville St
Chadderton OL9 ...152 C7
Hazel Grove SK7 ...124 D3
Newton-le-W WA12 ...89 A3
Platt Bridge WN2 ...56 A3
Nevin Ave SK8 ...122 E1
Nevin Cl Bramhall SK7 ...133 A7
5 Oldham OL8 ...66 B2
Nevin Rd M40 ...65 D1
Nevis Gr BL1 ...24 D5
Nevis St OL11 ...31 A2
Nevy Fold Ave BL6 ...22 F3
New Allen St M4,M40 ...159 C3
New Bailey St M3 ...158 E1
New Bank St
1 Hadfield SK13 ...104 A5
Manchester M12 ...164 F5
Tyldesley M29 ...77 A8
New Barn Haslingden BB4 ...1 B6
Shaw OL3 ...50 C6
New Barn Ave WN4 ...73 C3
New Barn La Leigh WN7 ...75 E2
Rawtenstall BB4 ...2 A8
Rochdale OL11 ...30 E4
New Barn Rd OL8 ...67 A2
New Barn St Bolton BL1 ..142 B1
11 Rochdale OL16 ...31 A5
Shaw OL2 ...149 A7
New Barns Ave M21 ...109 D6
New Barton St M6 ...80 C5
New Beech Rd SK4 ...110 E2
New Beech St SK14 ...167 D3
New Bridge La SK1 ...112 A2
New Bridge St M3 ...158 F3
New Briggs Fold BL7 ...8 E2
New Broad La OL16 ...31 C3
New Broadcasting House (BBC) M1 ...163 A7
New Brunswick St BL6 ...22 B3
New Buildings Pl 4 OL16 ...139 F8
New Cathedral St M1 ...158 F2
New Chapel La BL6 ...22 F2
New Church Ct M45 ...62 F7
New Church Rd BL1 ...23 F2
New Church St M26 ...44 B3
New City Rd M28 ...78 A8
New Collier's Row BL1 ...23 E6
New Court Dr BL7 ...8 E3
New Croft Com Specl High Sch M6 ...154 F3
New Cross M4 ...159 B2
New Cross St
Pendlebury M27 ...80 A7
Salford M5 ...80 C2
New Drake Gn BL5 ...57 E5
New Earth St Mossley OL5 .68 D2
Oldham OL4 ...67 C5
New Elizabeth St M8 ...156 A5
New Ellesmere App M28 .60 D4
New Elm Rd M3 ...162 D8
New Field Cl
Radcliffe M26 ...43 E3
Rochdale OL16 ...31 B8
New Fold WN5 ...53 C4
New Forest Rd M23 ...120 C8
New Gate BL5 ...146 A1
New George St 8 BL8 ...27 C3
New Gn BL2 ...25 E6
New Hall Ave Gatley SK8 .131 B7
Salford M7 ...155 D8
New Hall La Bolton BL1 ..144 A8
Culcheth WA3 ...92 A2
Culcheth,Wigshaw WA3 ...91 E1
New Hall Mews BL1 ...23 D1
New Hall Pl BL1 ...144 A8
New Hall Rd Bury BL9 ...28 E4
Sale M33 ...108 F4
Salford M7 ...155 D8
New Herbert St M6 ...80 C5
New Hey Rd Cheadle SK8 .122 E6
Denshaw HD7 ...34 F8
New Hey Sta OL16 ...32 B3
New Heys Way BL2 ...25 D6
New Ho OL4 ...68 C8
New Holder St BL1 ...145 E7
New Islington M4 ...159 C2
New Kings Head Yd M3 ..158 F2
New La Bolton BL2 ...25 E2
Eccles M30 ...79 B1
Middleton M24 ...47 A1
Royton OL2 ...48 D4
New Lane Ct BL2 ...25 E2
New Lane End WA3 ...91 A2
New Lawns SK5 ...100 A1
New Lees St OL6 ...85 D5
New Lester Cl M29 ...59 B1
New Lester Way M38 ...59 E4
New Line OL13 ...4 B8
New Lodge WN1 ...37 D2
New Market M2 ...158 F1
New Market La M1,M2 ..159 A1
New Market St WN1 ...150 C8
New Mdw BL6 ...40 C7
New Miles La WN6 ...35 F5
New Mill St OL15 ...16 A5
New Mills Rd SK13 ...115 B4
New Moor La SK7 ...124 D3
New Moss Rd M44 ...105 D6
New Moston Prim Sch M40 ...65 E2
New Mount St 5 M4 ...159 A3
New Oak Cl M35 ...84 C8
New Park Rd M5 ...161 B7
New Quay St M3 ...158 E1
New Radcliffe St OL1 ...153 E7
New Raven Ct BL3 ...43 A3

New Rd Adlington PR6 . . . . .21 D8
Aspull WN2 . . . . .38 A5
Littleborough OL15 . . . . . .15 F5
Oldham OL8 . . . . .66 E4
Radcliffe M26 . . . . .44 B2
Tintwistle SK13 . . . . .104 A7
Whitworth OL12 . . . . .1 B1
New Ridd Rise SK14 . . . . .13 D8
New Rock BL5 . . . . .57 F5
New Royd Ave OL4 . . . . . .67 F8
New Smithfield Mkt
M18 . . . . .165 C7
New Springs BL1 . . . . . .142 B3
New St Altrincham WA14 . .119 D4
Ashton-in-M WN4 . . . . . . .73 C4
Blackrod BL6 . . . . .21 D2
Bolton BL1 . . . . .145 E6
Bury BL8 . . . . .26 F6
Droylsden M43 . . . . .100 A8
Eccles M30 . . . . .79 C1
Littleborough OL15 . . . . . .15 F4
Manchester M40 . . . . . . .160 E4
Milnrow OL16 . . . . .32 A5
Mottram-in-L SK14 . . . . . .115 A8
Oldham OL4 . . . . .67 E6
Platt Bridge WN2 . . . . . . .56 A2
Radcliffe M26 . . . . .44 B2
Rochdale OL12 . . . . .14 E2
Stalybridge SK15 . . . . . . .102 A8
Swinton M27 . . . . .62 A1
Uppermill OL3 . . . . .69 B8
Wigan WN5 . . . . .54 B5
Wilmslow SK9 . . . . .136 E5
New Summerseat House Sch
BL0 . . . . .11 B2
New Tame OL3 . . . . .50 C7
New Tempest Rd BL6 . . . .40 C4
New Terr SK14 . . . . .101 F5
New Thomas St M6 . . . . .81 A4
New Tong Field BL7 . . . . .24 F7
New Union St M4 . . . . . . .159 C2
New Vernon St BL9 . . . .140 F4
New Viaduct St M11,
M40 . . . . .160 E2
New Vine St M15 . . . . . .162 F6
New Wakefield St M1 . . .163 A7
New Way OL12 . . . . .4 C1
New Welcome St M15 . . .162 F6
New York BL3 . . . . .40 F5
New York St OL10 . . . . . .29 B2
New Zealand Rd SK1 . . .112 B2
Newall Gr WN7 . . . . .75 F6
Newall Green High Sch
M23 . . . . .120 F3
Newall Green Jun & Inf Sch
M23 . . . . .121 B4
Newall Rd M23 . . . . .120 F3
Newall St
Littleborough OL15 . . . . . .16 B6
Oldham OL9 . . . . .66 B2
Walsden OL14 . . . . .6 A8
Newark Ave
Little Lever M26 . . . . .43 C5
■ Manchester M14 . . . . . .98 B3
Newark Park Way OL2 . . .48 C6
Newark Rd Hindley WN2 . .56 C4
Reddish SK5 . . . . .111 F5
Rochdale OL12 . . . . .14 F3
Swinton M27 . . . . .62 B2
Newark Sq OL12 . . . . . . .14 F3
Newark St WN6 . . . . .36 F1
Newbank Chase OL9 . . . .152 A8
Newbank Cl M24 . . . . .65 C7
Newbank Twrs M3 . . . . . .158 E3
Newbarn Cl OL2 . . . . . . .149 A7
Newbeck Cl BL6 . . . . .22 D1
Newbeck St ■ M4 . . . . . .159 A2
Newberry Gr SK3 . . . . . . .170 D5
Newbold Moss OL16 . . . . .31 B8
Newbold St Bury BL8 . . . .27 C2
Rochdale OL16 . . . . .31 C7
Newbold Wlk M15 . . . . . .162 F6
Newboult Rd SK8 . . . . . .122 E6
Newbourne Cl SK7 . . . . . .124 D3
Newbreak Cl ■ OL4 . . . . .67 D8
Newbreak St ■ OL4 . . . . .67 D8
Newbridge OL9 . . . . .86 D8
Newbridge Cl BL4 . . . . . . .42 E2
Newbridge Gdns BL2 . . . .25 E4
Newbrook Ave M21 . . . . .109 D4
Newbrook Rd BL5,M46 . . . .58 F6
Newbrook Sch M20 . . . . .109 F5
Newburn Ave M9 . . . . .64 F4
Newburn Cl WN3 . . . . .54 E4
Newbury Ave M33 . . . . . .107 C4
Newbury Cl SK8 . . . . .132 A6
Newbury Ct SK9 . . . . .137 A6
Newbury Dr Eccles M30 . . .79 B3
Urmston M41 . . . . .95 C5
Newbury Gr OL10 . . . . .46 C8
Newbury Pl M7 . . . . .155 E7
Newbury Rd Gatley SK8 . .131 C7
Little Lever BL3 . . . . .42 F3
Newbury Wlk Bolton BL1 . .143 E1
Chadderton OL9 . . . . .152 C7
Manchester M9 . . . . .157 D6
Newby Cl BL9 . . . . .45 A7
Newby Dr
Altrincham WA14 . . . . . . .119 D6
Gatley SK8 . . . . .122 A6
Middleton M24 . . . . .46 F3
Sale M33 . . . . .108 C3
Newby Rd Bolton BL2 . . . .25 F2
Hazel Grove SK7 . . . . . . .124 D2
Stockport SK4 . . . . .168 C2
Newby Road Ind Est
SK7 . . . . .124 D2
Newby Sq WN5 . . . . .54 B5

Newcastle St ■ M15 . . . . .162 F7
Newcastle Wlk ■ M34 . . .101 A1
Newchurch OL8 . . . . .85 A8
Newchurch Com Prim Sch
WA3 . . . . .91 E2
Newchurch Cl ■ M26 . . . .44 B3
Newchurch La WA3 . . . . . .91 F2
Newchurch Pl OL11 . . . . . .30 C1
Newchurch Rd Bacup OL13 . .3 C8
Rawtenstall BB4,OL13 . . . . .2 F8
Newchurch St
Manchester M11 . . . . . . .164 F8
Rochdale OL11 . . . . .30 D1
Newchurch Wlk ■ M26 . . .44 B3
Newcliffe Rd M9 . . . . .64 F4
Newcombe Cl M11 . . . . . .160 F1
Newcombe Ct ■ M33 . . . .107 F4
Newcombe Dr M38 . . . . . .59 F6
Newcombe Rd BL0 . . . . . .11 B2
Newcombe St M3 . . . . . .158 F3
Newcroft M35 . . . . .84 B6
Newcroft Cres M41 . . . . . .95 F1
Newcroft Dr
Stockport SK3 . . . . .170 D6
Stretford M41 . . . . .96 A1
Newcroft Rd M41 . . . . . . .95 F1
Newdale Rd M12 . . . . .99 C3
Newearth Rd M28 . . . . . . .78 B8
Newendon Rd WN1 . . . . . .37 B4
Newfield Cl WA13 . . . . . .117 A5
Newfield Head La OL16 . . .32 B5
Newfield View OL16 . . . . . .32 A6
Newgate Rochdale OL16 . .139 F7
Wilmslow SK9 . . . . .136 D7
Newgate Ave M46 . . . . . . .35 E8
Newgate Dr M38 . . . . .60 A6
Newgate Rd M33 . . . . . . .107 C1
Newhall Ave Eccles M30 . .95 A7
Little Lever BL2 . . . . .43 B6
Newhall Dr M23 . . . . . . .109 B2
Newhall Rd SK5 . . . . . . .100 A2
Newham Ave M11 . . . . . . .83 B2
Newham Dr BL8 . . . . .27 B1
Newhart Gr M28 . . . . .60 C2
Newhaven Ave
Droylsden M11 . . . . .99 F7
Leigh WN7 . . . . .75 F8
Newhaven Bsns Pk M40 . .79 E1
Newhaven Cl
Bramhall SK8 . . . . .123 C2
Bury BL9 . . . . .27 C7
Newhaven Wlk ■ BL2 . . . .25 B1
Newhey Ave M22 . . . . . . .121 D5
Newhey Com Prim Sch
OL16 . . . . .32 A4
Newhey Rd Milnrow OL16 . .32 A5
Wythenshawe M22 . . . . . .121 D5
Newholme Ave
Manchester M20 . . . . . . .110 C6
Stretford M32 . . . . .96 E2
Newholme Gdns M8 . . . . .60 C3
Newholme Rd M20 . . . . . .109 F5
Newhouse Cl OL12 . . . . . .15 C6
Newhouse Cres OL11 . . . .29 E8
Newhouse Dr WN3 . . . . . .54 D1
Newhouse Rd OL10 . . . . . .46 D8
Newhouse St OL12 . . . . . .15 C6
Newick Wlk ■ M9 . . . . . . .64 E3
Newington Ave M8 . . . . . .63 F3
Newington Dr WA14 . . . . .119 B3
Newington Dr
Bolton BL1 . . . . .143 F1
Bury BL8 . . . . .27 A1
Newington Wlk ■ BL1 . . .143 F1
Newland Ave WN5 . . . . . . .54 D5
Newland Dr BL5 . . . . .58 F8
Newland Mews WA3 . . . . . .91 E5
Newland St M8 . . . . .64 B1
Newlands M35 . . . . .83 E4
Newlands Ave Bolton BL2 . .25 E4
Cheadle SK8 . . . . .132 A7
Eccles M30 . . . . .94 F7
Irlam M44 . . . . .94 A2
Tyldesley M29 . . . . .77 A6
Whitefield M45 . . . . .44 E1
Newlands Cl
Cheadle SK8 . . . . .132 A7
Rochdale OL12 . . . . .14 F3
Newlands Dr
Golborne WA3 . . . . .90 D8
Manchester M20 . . . . . . .122 C8
Pendlebury M27 . . . . .60 C6
Prestwich M25 . . . . .63 A5
Scot Lane End BL6 . . . . . .38 E7
Wilmslow SK9 . . . . .136 E5
Newlands Rd
Cheadle SK8 . . . . .122 D6
Leigh WN7 . . . . .75 F3
Wythenshawe M23 . . . . . .120 F8
Newlands Wlk M24 . . . . . .46 E3
Newlea Cl BL1 . . . . .142 C2
Newlyn Ave SK15 . . . . . . .86 D3
Newlyn Cl SK7 . . . . .124 D1
Newlyn Dr
Ashton-in-M WN4 . . . . . . .73 B1
Romiley SK6 . . . . .113 A3
Sale M33 . . . . .108 C1
Newlyn St M14 . . . . .98 B2
Newman Ave WN6 . . . . . . .37 A2
Newman Cl M23 . . . . .56 C6
Newman St
Ashton-u-L OL6 . . . . .166 A3
Hyde SK14 . . . . .167 E3
Rochdale OL16 . . . . .15 C3
Wigan WN1 . . . . .37 E2
Newmarket Cl M33 . . . . .107 B2

Newmarket Gr OL7 . . . . . .84 E5
Newmarket Mews M7 . . .155 D6
Newmarket Rd
Ashton-u-L OL7 . . . . .84 F5
Little Lever BL3 . . . . .43 A2
Newmill St ■ M8 . . . . . . .156 A6
Newmarsh St BL1 . . . . . .143 F4
Newpark Wlk ■ M8 . . . . .156 A6
Newport Ave SK5 . . . . . . .111 E7
Newport Mews BL4 . . . . . .60 D7
Newport Rd Bolton BL3 . . .42 A3
Denton M34 . . . . .113 B8
Manchester M21 . . . . .97 A1
Newport St
Bolton BL1,BL3 . . . . .145 F6
Bury BL9 . . . . .27 A5
Farnworth BL4 . . . . .60 D7
Manchester M14 . . . . .98 B3
Middleton M24 . . . . .47 C1
Oldham OL8 . . . . .66 C3
Salford M6 . . . . .154 E2
Newquay Ave
Ainsworth BL2 . . . . .26 D1
Reddish SK5 . . . . .111 E7
Newquay Dr SK7 . . . . . . .132 F7
Newquay Ho ■ OL9 . . . . .48 A1
Newquay Rd M30 . . . . .95 E8
Newry St BL1 . . . . .143 D3
Newry Wlk M9 . . . . .64 B3
Newsham Cl BL3 . . . . . . .145 D5
Newsham Rd SK3 . . . . . .170 E6
Newsham Wlk
■ Manchester M12 . . . . . .99 B3
Wigan WN6 . . . . .36 F1
Newsholme Cl WA3 . . . . . .91 F3
Newsholme St M8 . . . . . .155 F7
Newstead ■ OL12 . . . . . .139 E8
Newstead Ave
Ashton-u-L OL6 . . . . .85 C7
Manchester M20 . . . . . . .110 D5
Newstead Cl SK12 . . . . . .133 D5
Newstead Dr BL3 . . . . . . .146 A2
Newstead Gr SK6 . . . . . . .112 F3
Newstead Rd
Urmston M41 . . . . .95 E3
Wigan WN3 . . . . .54 F3
Newstead Terr WA15 . . . .119 F7
Newton Ave
Manchester,Longsight M12 . .98 F4
Manchester,Withington
M20 . . . . .110 A6
Newton Bsns Pk SK14 . . .102 A5
Newton Cl WN1 . . . . .37 D2
Newton Comm Hospl
WA12 . . . . .89 B2
Newton Cres M24 . . . . . . .46 D3
Newton Dr BL8 . . . . .11 A1
Newton for Hyde Sta
SK14 . . . . .167 F4
Newton Gn SK14 . . . . . . .101 F5
Newton Hall Ct SK14 . . . .101 C5
Newton Hall Rd SK14 . . . .101 C5
Newton Heath Upper Sch
M40 . . . . .157 F5
Newton Ho M14 . . . . .110 D8
Newton La WA12 . . . . .89 E6
Newton Moor Ind Est
SK14 . . . . .101 A5
Newton Park Dr WA12 . . . .89 F3
Newton Rd
Altrincham WA14 . . . . . . .119 E7
Billinge WN5,WA9,WN4 . . .71 F6
Failsworth M35 . . . . .83 F5
Golborne,Lowton Common
WA3,WN7 . . . . .91 A8
Golborne,Town of Lowton
WA12,WA3 . . . . .90 D5
Handforth SK9 . . . . .131 A1
Manchester M24 . . . . .64 B6
Urmston M41 . . . . .95 C2
Newton St
Ashton-u-L OL6 . . . . .166 C3
Bolton BL1 . . . . .143 E2
Bury BL9 . . . . .27 F6
Droylsden M43 . . . . .84 C3
Failsworth M40 . . . . .83 C5
Hyde SK14 . . . . .167 D4
Leigh WN7 . . . . .75 F5
Manchester M1 . . . . .159 B1
Rochdale OL16 . . . . .31 A5
■ Stalybridge SK15 . . . . . .85 F2
Stretford M32 . . . . .96 D1
Newton Terr
■ Dukinfield SK16 . . . . . .166 B1
Newton Westpark Prim Sch
WN7 . . . . .75 C8
Newton Wlk BL1 . . . . .143 E2
Newton Wood Rd SK16 . .101 B6
Newton-le-Willows Com
High Sch WA12 . . . . .89 D5
Newton-le-Willows Prim Sch
WA12 . . . . .89 D3
Newton-le-Willows Sta
WA12 . . . . .89 E3
Newtondale Ave ■ OL2 . . .48 C4
Newtonhurst SK14 . . . . . .102 A5
Newtonmore Wlk M11 . . . .83 B1
Newtown Ave M34 . . . . . .100 F2
Newtown Cl
Manchester M11 . . . . . . .165 B8
Swinton M27 . . . . .61 C7
Newtown Ct
Manchester M40 . . . . . . .159 C4
Prestwich M25 . . . . .63 C4

Newtown St
Prestwich M25 . . . . .63 C4
Shaw OL2 . . . . .149 B6
Newville Dr M20 . . . . . . .110 D5
Ney St OL7 . . . . .84 F6
Neyland Cl BL1 . . . . .40 F7
Niagara Ho SK2 . . . . .124 A6
Niagara St SK2 . . . . .124 A6
Nicholas Croft M4 . . . . . .159 A2
Nicholas Owen Cl M11 . . .165 C8
Nicholas Rd OL8 . . . . .66 E4
Nicholas St Bolton BL2 . . .148 A8
Manchester M1,M2 . . . . .159 A1
Nicholas Varley Com Sch
M40 . . . . .160 E4
Nicholls St M12 . . . . .164 D7
Nichols St M6 . . . . .81 B3
Nicholson Sq SK16 . . . . .101 B8
Nicholson St Oldham OL4 . .67 E6
Rochdale OL11 . . . . .139 F5
Stockport SK4 . . . . .169 E2
Nickleby Rd SK12 . . . . . . .133 E3
Nicol Mere Dr WN4 . . . . .73 A5
Nicol Mere Sch WN4 . . . . .73 A5
Nicol Rd WN4 . . . . .73 B5
Nicola St BL7 . . . . .24 E8
Nicolas Rd M21 . . . . .97 A1
Nield Rd M34 . . . . .100 F3
Nield St OL5 . . . . .68 B2
Nield's Brow WA14 . . . . .119 C2
Nield's Way SK6 . . . . .126 D4
Nigel Rd M9 . . . . .157 F7
Nigher Moss Ave OL16 . . .31 C6
Nightingale Cl SK9 . . . . . .131 B1
Nightingale Ct ■ WN6 . . . .37 A1
Nightingale Dr M34 . . . . . .84 C1
Nightingale Rd M23 . . . . .109 A1
Nightingale St BL6 . . . . . .21 C3
Nightingale St ■ PR6 . . . .21 A8
Nightingales Wlk ■
BL3 . . . . .147 F3
Nile St Ashton-u-L OL7 . . .100 F8
Bolton BL3 . . . . .145 F5
Oldham OL1 . . . . .153 E8
Rochdale OL16 . . . . .31 A8
Nile Terr M7 . . . . .155 D5
Nimble Nook OL9 . . . . . . .152 A5
Nina Dr M40 . . . . .65 C3
Nine Acre Ct M5 . . . . .161 B2
Nine Acre Dr M5 . . . . . . .161 B7
Ninehouse La BL3 . . . . . .147 F4
Ninfield Rd M23 . . . . .121 B4
Ninian Ct ■ M24 . . . . .46 F1
Ninian Gdns M28 . . . . . . .60 D3
Ninth Ave OL8 . . . . .66 D1
Nipper La M45 . . . . .44 E2
Nisbet Ave M22 . . . . .121 E3
Niven St M12 . . . . .163 C7
Nixon Rd BL3 . . . . .146 C3
Nixon Rd S BL3 . . . . .146 C3
Nixon St Failsworth M35 . . .83 E7
Rochdale OL11 . . . . .30 B3
Stockport SK3 . . . . .170 F6
No 11 Pass M20 . . . . . . .109 F5
No 2 Pas SK3 . . . . .169 D1
Noahs Ark La WA16 . . . . .136 A1
Noble Mdw OL12 . . . . .15 D4
Noble St Bolton BL3 . . . . .145 E5
■ Leigh WN7 . . . . .76 A5
Oldham OL8 . . . . .66 E4
Noel Dr M33 . . . . .108 D4
Noel St BL1 . . . . .145 E7
Nolan St M9 . . . . .157 E8
Nona St M6 . . . . .154 E3
Nook Farm Ave OL12 . . . .14 F3
Nook Fields BL2 . . . . .25 E3
Nook La Ashton-u-L OL6 . . .85 C8
Golborne WA3 . . . . .90 B8
Tyldesley M29 . . . . .77 D2
Nook The
Appley Bridge WN6 . . . . . .35 E7
Bramhall SK7 . . . . .132 D5
Eccles M30 . . . . .79 A4
Urmston M41 . . . . .94 F2
Noon Ct WA12 . . . . .89 B1
Noon Sun Cl OL3 . . . . . . .69 A4
Noon Sun St OL12 . . . . . .14 F1
Norbet Wlk ■ M9 . . . . . . .157 E7
Norbreck Ave
Cheadle SK8 . . . . .123 A6
Manchester M21 . . . . . . .109 B7
Norbreck Cres WN6 . . . . .37 A2
Norbreck Gdns BL2 . . . . .148 C8
Norbreck St BL2 . . . . .148 C8
Norburn Rd M13 . . . . .98 F2
Norbury Ave Billinge WN5 . .71 D5
Hyde SK14 . . . . .167 D2
Marple SK6 . . . . .125 E6
Sale M33 . . . . .107 F4
■ Salford M6 . . . . .80 C3
Uppermill OL4 . . . . .68 C6
Norbury Cl M40 . . . . .160 D4
Norbury Cres SK7 . . . . . .124 D2
Norbury Dr SK6 . . . . .125 E6
Norbury Gr Bolton BL2 . . .147 F4
Swinton M27 . . . . .61 E1
Norbury Hall Prim Sch
SK7 . . . . .124 E1
Norbury Ho ■ OL4 . . . . . .67 B8
Norbury Hollow Rd SK7 . .134 B8
Norbury La OL8 . . . . .66 F3
Norbury Mews SK6 . . . . .125 E6
Norbury St Leigh WN7 . . . .75 D5
Rochdale OL16 . . . . .31 B4

Norbury St continued
Salford M7 . . . . .155 E6
Stockport SK1 . . . . .169 F1
Norbury Way ■ SK9 . . . .131 D5
Norcliffe Wlk M18 . . . . . . .99 B4
Norcot Wlk ■ M15 . . . . . .162 D6
Norcross Cl SK2 . . . . .124 C5
Nordale Pk OL12 . . . . .13 D2
Nordek Cl OL2 . . . . .48 D5
Nordek Dr OL2 . . . . .48 C5
Norden Ave M20 . . . . .110 A6
Norden Cl OL11 . . . . .13 C2
Norden Com Prim Sch
OL12 . . . . .13 F2
Norden Ct BL3 . . . . .147 E4
Norden Rd OL11 . . . . .29 E6
Norden Way OL11 . . . . . . .13 D2
Nordens Dr OL9 . . . . .47 F1
Nordens Rd OL9 . . . . .65 F8
Nordens St OL9 . . . . .152 A8
Noreen Ave M25 . . . . .63 C5
Norfield Cl SK16 . . . . .101 C8
Norford Way OL16 . . . . . . .31 F8
Norfolk Ave
Droylsden M43 . . . . .83 F3
Heywood OL10 . . . . .29 A2
Manchester M18 . . . . .99 C4
Reddish,Debdale M34 . . . .99 F3
Reddish,Heaton Chapel
SK4 . . . . .111 C6
Whitefield M45 . . . . .63 A8
Norfolk Cl Hindley WN2 . . .57 A6
Irlam M44 . . . . .105 C5
Little Lever BL3 . . . . .43 B4
Littleborough OL15 . . . . . . .6 C1
Norfolk Cres M35 . . . . . . .83 E6
Norfolk Dr BL4 . . . . .42 D1
Norfolk Gdns M41 . . . . . . .94 D3
Norfolk Ho
■ Manchester M7 . . . . . . .63 E1
■ Sale M33 . . . . .108 D4
Norfolk Rd Atherton M46 . .58 C5
Longshaw WN5 . . . . .53 E1
Manchester M18 . . . . .99 C4
Norfolk St Glossop SK13 . .104 D1
Hyde SK14 . . . . .167 D2
Manchester M2 . . . . .159 A1
Oldham OL4 . . . . .67 C8
Rochdale OL16 . . . . .139 F6
Salford M6 . . . . .81 A5
Walkden M28 . . . . .60 D6
Wigan,Springfield WN6 . . .37 A2
■ Wigan,Worsley Hall
WN5 . . . . .54 F6
Norfolk Way OL2 . . . . . . .48 D2
Norford Way OL16 . . . . . .29 E7
Norgate St M20 . . . . .110 B3
Norlan Ave M34 . . . . .100 F2
Norland Wlk M40 . . . . .83 A5
Norleigh Rd M22 . . . . . . .121 D8
Norley Ave M32 . . . . .96 F3
Norley Cl OL1 . . . . .49 C1
Norley Dr Manchester M19 . .99 C2
Sale M33 . . . . .108 C4
Norley Hall Ave WN5 . . . . .54 C6
Norley Rd Leigh WN7 . . . . .75 B4
Wigan WN5 . . . . .54 C7
Norman Ave
Haydock WA11 . . . . .89 A7
Hazel Grove SK7 . . . . . . .124 C3
Newton-le-W WA12 . . . . . .89 E3
Norman Cl M24 . . . . .47 C1
Norman Gr
Manchester M12 . . . . .99 A4
Reddish SK5 . . . . .111 E7
Norman Rd
Altrincham WA14 . . . . . . .119 C6
Ashton-u-L OL6 . . . . .85 C6
Manchester,Heaton Norris
SK4 . . . . .168 B3
Rochdale OL11 . . . . .139 D6
Sale M33 . . . . .108 B3
Salford M7 . . . . .155 E7
Stalybridge SK15 . . . . . . .85 F2
Norman Rd W M9 . . . . . .157 F7
Norman St Bury BL9 . . . . .141 B4
Failsworth M35 . . . . .66 A1
Hyde SK14 . . . . .167 E2
Middleton M24 . . . . .65 B5
Middleton M24 . . . . .47 B1
Oldham OL1 . . . . .153 D8
Radcliffe M26 . . . . .44 B4
Norman Weall Ct ■ M24 . .47 A2
Norman's Pl WA14 . . . . . .119 D4
Normanby Chase WA14 . .119 B4
Normanby Gr M27 . . . . . . .61 E1
Normanby Rd Bolton BL3 . .146 C2
Swinton M27 . . . . .61 E1
Wigan WN5 . . . . .54 E6
Normanby St
■ Manchester M14 . . . . .142 A1
Swinton M27 . . . . .61 E1
Wigan WN5 . . . . .54 E6
Normandy Cres M26 . . . . .43 F3
Normanhurst M25 . . . . . . .80 C3
Normanton Ave M6 . . . . . .80 C4
Normanton Cl WN6 . . . . . .36 F4
Normanton Dr M9 . . . . . . .64 E5
Normanton Rd SK3,SK8 . .123 A6
Normington Cl ■ OL4 . . . .67 C7
Norreys Ave M41 . . . . .94 E3
Norreys St ■ OL16 . . . . . .31 A8
Norris Ave SK4 . . . . .168 C1
Norris Bank Prim Sch
SK4 . . . . .168 B3
Norris Bank Terr SK4 . . . .168 C1

Norris Hill Dr SK4 168 C2
Norris Rd M33 108 D2
Norris St Bolton BL3 145 E5
Farnworth BL4 60 D7
Little Lever BL3 43 A3
Tyldesley M29 77 A8
Norris Twrs SK4 169 E2
North Area Coll SK4 111 B5
North Ave Farnworth BL4 60 B8
Golborne WN7 74 F4
Leigh WN7 76 C3
Manchester M19 110 F7
Ramsbottom BL8 10 F1
Stalybridge SK15 86 A3
Uppermill OL3 69 B5
Whitefield BL9 45 B4
North Back Rock BL9 140 F2
North Blackfield La M7 81 C8
North Bolton Sixth Form Coll BL1 142 C4
North Brook Rd SK13 171 E4
North Broughton St M3 158 E2
North Butts St WN7 76 B3
North Cestrian Gram Sch WA14 119 C5
North Chadderton Sch OL9 48 A2
North Chadderton Sch (Lower) OL9 152 A8
North Cheshire Jewish Prim Sch SK8 122 C2
North Circ M45 63 A6
North Cl SK13 103 F7
North Clifden La M7 155 E6
North Cres Droylsden M11 83 D3
Failsworth M40 65 D3
North Croft OL8 67 A3
North Dean St M27 62 A1
North Downs Rd SK8 122 F3
North Dr
Appley Bridge WN6 18 C2
Droylsden M34 84 C1
Pendlebury M27 80 B7
North Edge WN7 76 B6
North End Rd SK15 86 B2
North Gate OL8 66 E2
North George St M3 158 D2
North Gr
Manchester M13 164 D5
Urmston M41 95 C2
Walkden M28 60 C3
North Grecian Street Prim Sch M7 81 C5
North Heaton Prim Sch SK4 111 C6
North Hill St M3 158 D3
North La Rochdale OL12 139 F8
Tyldesley M29 77 A6
North Lonsdale St M32 96 E4
North Manchester General Hospl M8 64 B1
North Manchester High Sch for Boys M9 65 B3
North Manchester High Sch for Girls M40 65 A1
North Mead M21 109 B7
North Nook OL4 67 F8
North Par Newhey OL16 32 C4
Sale M33 108 D2
North Park Rd SK7 123 E3
North Pl SK1 169 F1
North Quarry Bsns Pk WN6 18 D1
North Rd
Altrincham WA15 129 A8
Atherton M46 58 B5
Carrington M31 106 E4
Droylsden M34 84 D1
Droylsden,Clayton M11 83 C2
Glossop SK13 104 C3
Prestwich M25 62 F5
Stretford M17 96 C5
Stretford,Mossfield M32 96 B4
North Reddish Inf Sch SK5 99 F1
North Reddish Jun Sch SK5 99 F1
North Rise OL3 69 B5
North St Ashton-in-M WN4 73 D5
Ashton-u-L OL6 166 A2
Heywood OL10 29 B2
Leigh WN7 76 B4
Manchester M8 159 A4
Middleton M24 47 A2
Radcliffe M26 44 C4
Ramsbottom BL0 1 C2
Rochdale OL16 31 A8
Royton OL2 48 D3
1 Royton OL2 48 D4
Whitworth OL12 4 C1
North Stage M50 96 F8
North Star Dr M3 158 D1
North Trafford Coll of F Ed M32 96 F4
North Vale Rd WA15 119 F6
North Veiw M45 44 E2
North View Mossley OL5 68 E1
Ramsbottom,Higher Summerseat BL9 11 B2
Ramsbottom,Strongstry BL0 1 C2
North View Cl OL4 68 C5
North Walkden Prim Sch M28 60 C5
North Way Bolton BL1 25 B4
Brinnington SK5 112 C6
North Way *continued*
Hyde SK14 167 E2
North Western St
Manchester M1,M12 163 C8
Manchester,Ardwick M12 164 D7
Manchester,Levenshulme M19 111 A8
North Woodley 6 M26 44 C1
Northallerton Rd M7 81 B6
Northampton Rd M40 157 F6
Northampton Way 1 M34 101 A1
Northavon Cl M30 80 A1
Northbank Gdns M19 110 E6
Northbank Ind Pk M44 105 F6
Northbank Wlk M20 109 D3
Northbourne St M6 154 E2
Northbrook Ave M8 63 F4
Northcliffe Rd SK2 124 C8
Northcombe Rd SK3 170 E5
Northcote Rd SK7 132 F7
Northcroft WN1 37 F1
Northdale Rd M9 64 B5
Northdene Dr OL11 29 F6
Northdown Ave
Manchester M15 162 D6
Romiley SK6 113 C5
Northdowns Rd OL2 48 F8
Northen Gr M20 109 F4
Northenden Prim Sch M22 109 D1
Northenden Rd
Gatley SK8 122 A6
Sale M33 108 C4
Sale M33 108 E3
Northenden View M20 110 B2
Northern Ave M27 62 C3
Northern Gr BL1 142 C1
Northfield Ave M40 65 F2
Northfield Ct WN3 74 C1
Northfield Dr SK9 137 D8
Northfield Rd Bury BL9 27 F6
Failsworth M40 65 F2
Northfield St BL3 144 C5
Northfleet Rd M30 94 F8
Northgate OL12 14 C7
Northgate Cl BL6 22 C1
Northgate La OL1 49 E3
Northgate Rd SK3 123 C8
Northland Rd Bolton BL1 24 F6
Manchester M9 65 A3
Northlands M26 43 E5
Northleach Cl BL8 27 B3
Northleigh Dr M25 63 D3
Northleigh Ho 1 M16 97 B2
Northleigh Rd M16 97 B3
Northmoor Rd M12 99 A3
Northolme Gdns M19 110 E5
Northolt Ave WN7 75 F8
Northolt Ct M11 83 D2
Northolt Dr BL3 147 F4
Northolt Fold OL10 46 E7
Northolt Rd M23 108 F1
Northridge Rd M9 64 D6
Northside Ave M41 94 F1
Northstead Ave M34 101 B2
Northumberland Ave OL7 166 B4
Northumberland Cl M16 161 C5
Northumberland Cres M16 161 C5
Northumberland Rd
Brinnington SK5 112 B6
Manchester M16 161 C5
Partington M31 105 E2
Northumberland St
Salford M7 155 E7
Wigan WN1 37 E1
Northumberland Way M22 121 E6
Northumbria St 9 BL3 144 C5
Northurst Dr M8 63 F3
Northward Rd SK9 136 F6
Northway
Altrincham WA14 119 E6
Droylsden M43 100 A8
4 Eccles M30 79 F2
Wigan WN1 37 C1
Northways WN6 19 D2
Northwell St 2 WN7 75 E8
Northwold Cl WN3 54 D3
Northwold Dr Bolton BL1 40 E8
Manchester M9 65 B3
Northwood BL2 25 D4
Northwood Ave WA12 89 F3
Northwood Cres BL3 144 C5
Northwood Gr M33 108 B4
Norton Ave
Manchester M12 99 B3
Reddish M34 100 A3
Sale M33 107 D6
Urmston M41 95 D4
Norton Gr SK4 168 B1
Norton Grange M25 63 D3
Norton Rd
Boothstown M28 77 E7
Rochdale OL12 14 F3
Norton St Bolton BL1 143 F3
14 Manchester M1 159 C1
Manchester,Miles Platting M40 160 E4
Manchester,Old Trafford M16 97 D4
Salford M3 158 F2
Salford,Higher Broughton M7 155 E7
Norview Dr M20 122 B8
Norville Ave M40,M9 65 D3
Norway Gr SK5 169 F4
Norway St Bolton BL1 143 D2
Salford M6 154 E2
Stretford M32 96 E3
Norweb Way WN7 76 B3
Norwell Rd M22 121 E5
Norwich Ave
Ashton-in-M WN4 73 D3
Chadderton OL9 48 A1
Denton M34 100 F1
Golborne WA3 90 D8
Rochdale OL11 30 B7
Norwich Cl Ashton-u-L OL6 85 D8
Dukinfield SK16 102 A7
Norwich Dr BL8 140 D3
Norwich Rd M32 95 F3
Norwich St OL11 31 A5
Norwick Cl BL3 40 E4
Norwood M25 63 B2
Norwood Ave
Ashton-in-M WN4 72 F6
Bramhall SK7 132 D5
Cheadle SK8 123 A3
Golborne WA3 90 F7
High Lane SK6 134 D7
Manchester M20 110 D4
Salford M7 81 B8
Tyldesley M29 77 B6
Wigan WN6 37 A3
Norwood Cl Adlington PR6 21 A8
Shaw OL2 149 A8
Walkden M28 78 E8
Norwood Cres OL2 48 E2
Norwood Ct M32 96 E1
Norwood Dr
Altrincham WA15 120 D5
Swinton M27 79 D7
Norwood Gr Bolton BL1 144 C8
Royton OL2 48 E2
Norwood Ho 6 WA14 119 D5
Norwood Lo M7 81 B8
Norwood Pk WA14 119 C5
Norwood Rd Gatley SK8 122 B6
Stockport SK2 124 B4
Stretford M32 96 E2
Noseby Ct M25 63 C5
Nostell Rd WN4 73 A5
Nottingham Ave SK5 112 C6
Nottingham Cl SK5 112 C5
Nottingham Dr
Ashton-u-L OL6 85 B7
Bolton BL1 143 E1
Failsworth M35 84 A6
Nottingham Pl WN1 37 E1
Nottingham Way 3 M34 101 A1
Nowell Ct M24 47 A3
Nowell Ho M24 47 A3
Nowell Rd M24 47 A3
Nudger Cl OL3 50 F2
Nudger Gn OL3 51 A2
Nuffield Rd M22 121 E4
Nugent House Sch WN5 71 D4
Nugent Rd BL3 147 E3
Nugget St OL4 67 B6
Nuneaton Dr M40 160 D3
Nuneham Ave M20 110 C7
Nunfield Cl M40 65 B2
Nunnery Rd BL3 146 B4
Nunthorpe Dr M8 156 C8
Nursery Ave WA15 128 E8
Nursery Cl Glossop SK13 116 C8
Sale M33 108 D4
Stockport SK2 124 D7
Nursery Dr SK12 133 D4
Nursery Gr M31 105 F4
Nursery La Cheadle SK3 123 A7
Wilmslow SK9 136 F5
Nursery Rd Cheadle SK8 123 A1
Failsworth M35 84 A7
Prestwich M25 63 A6
Stockport SK4 168 C2
Urmston M41 95 A4
Nursery St
Manchester M16 97 F3
Salford M6 154 F3
Nuthatch Ave M28 78 D8
Nuthurst Rd M40 65 D1
Nutsford Vale M12,M18 99 B4
Nutt La M25 63 E8
Nutt St WN1 37 E2
Nuttal Ave M45 62 F8
Nuttal Mews M45 62 F8
Nuttall Ave Horwich BL6 22 A3
Little Lever BL3 43 C3
Whitefield M45 62 F8
Nuttall Cl BL0 138 C5
Nuttall Hall Cotts BL0 11 D5
Nuttall Hall Rd BL0 11 D5
Nuttall La BL0 138 B5
Nuttall Mews M45 62 F8
Nuttall Rd BL0 11 D4
Nuttall Sq BL9 44 F5
Nuttall St Atherton M46 58 E3
Bury BL9 141 A1
Irlam M44 105 E6
Manchester M11 165 A7
Manchester,City Park M16 161 C5
Oldham OL8 67 B4
Rochdale OL16 31 A7
Nutwood Ct SK5 111 E7

O

O'Kane Ho 10 M30 79 D1
Oadby Cl M12 99 A4
Oadby Pl 1 SK5 99 F2
Oak Ave Abram Brow WN2 74 C7
Cheadle SK8 123 A2
Golborne WA3 90 B8
Hindley WN2 57 A3
9 Horwich BL6 22 E1
Irlam M44 105 D5
Little Lever BL3 43 B3
Manchester M21 109 B8
Manchester,Heaton Norris SK4 168 B2
Middleton M24 65 A7
Newton-le-W WA12 89 D3
Ramsbottom BL0 11 A2
Reddish M18 99 F4
Romiley SK6 113 C2
Royton OL2 48 D6
Standish WN6 36 F8
Whitefield M45 62 F7
Wilmslow SK9 136 F5
Oak Bank Manchester M9 157 D8
Prestwich M25 62 F1
Oak Bank Ave M9 64 F1
Oak Bank Cl M45 63 B8
Oak Brow Cotts SK9 130 E4
Oak Cl Mottram-in-L SK14 103 A4
Whitworth OL12 4 D4
Wilmslow SK9 136 F6
Oak Coppice BL1 144 A7
Oak Cotts SK9 130 E4
Oak Ct SK6 113 A5
Oak Dr Cheadle SK7 132 C7
Manchester M14 98 D1
Marple SK6 125 D6
Reddish M34 100 A4
Oak Gates BL7 8 E1
Oak Gr Ashton-u-L OL6 85 D6
Cheadle SK8 122 E5
Eccles M30 79 B1
Poynton SK12 133 D4
Urmston M41 95 E2
Oak Grove Prim Sch SK8 131 C7
Oak Hill OL15 15 F5
Oak Hill Cl WN1 37 B4
Oak La Whitefield M45 63 B8
Wilmslow SK9 136 F6
Oak Lea Ave SK9 137 A5
Oak Lo SK7 132 F7
Oak Mews SK9 131 C1
Oak Rd Altrincham WA15 119 E3
Cheadle SK8 122 E5
Failsworth M35 83 F6
Manchester M20 110 B5
Oldham OL8 66 D2
Partington M31 105 D2
Sale M33 108 D4
Salford M7 81 C5
Oak Shaw Cl M9 64 D2
Oak St Atherton M46 58 A1
Denton M34 100 F6
Eccles M30 79 D1
Glossop SK13 104 C1
Hazel Grove SK7 124 D3
Heywood OL10 29 B3
Hyde SK14 167 E4
Leigh WN7 75 F3
Littleborough OL15 16 C5
Manchester M4 159 A2
2 Manchester M4 159 B2
Middleton M24 65 D7
Newhey OL16 32 B4
2 Radcliffe M26 44 C1
Ramsbottom BL0 138 B5
Rochdale OL16 139 F7
Shaw OL2 149 C7
Stockport SK3 123 B8
Swinton M27 62 A1
Tyldesley M29 59 A1
Whitworth OL12 4 D5
Wigan WN1 151 E7
Oak Terr Littleborough OL15 6 D2
Rawtenstall BB4 1 E8
Oak Tree Cl Atherton M46 58 A1
Hyde SK14 102 A2
Stockport SK2 124 D8
Oak Tree Cres SK15 102 B8
Oak Tree Dr SK16 101 F7
Oak View Oldham OL1 48 D1
Whitworth OL12 4 D4
Oak View Rd OL3 69 B5
Oak Wood View OL5 86 C6
Oakbank WN2 56 B3
Oakbank Ave OL9 65 F8
Oakbank Dr BL1 24 D6
Oakbarton BL6 40 C4
Oakcliffe Rd OL12 15 D4
Oakcroft SK15 102 E8
Oakcroft Way M22 121 E6
Oakdale BL2 25 E4
Oakdale Cl M45 62 D8
Oakdale Ct
Altrincham WA14 119 C5
Delph OL3 50 E3
Stalybridge SK15 86 B2
Oakdale Dr Gatley SK8 122 B2
Manchester M20 110 C1
Tyldesley M29 77 C6
Oakdale Sch SK16 101 E6
Oakdene M27 79 B6
Oakdene Ave Gatley SK8 131 C7
Reddish SK4 111 D5
Oakdene Cres SK6 125 F7
Oakdene Gdns SK6 125 F7
Oakdene Rd Marple SK6 125 F7
Middleton M24 65 C8
Sale WA15 120 B8
Oakdene St M9 157 F8
Oaken Bank Rd M24 47 A5
Oaken Clough 3 OL7 85 A6
Oaken Clough Dr 1 OL7 85 A6
Oaken Clough Terr OL7 84 F6
Oaken St OL7 85 A6
Oakenbottom Rd BL2 42 D7
Oakenclough 1 OL1 153 E7
Oakenclough Cl SK9 131 D2
Oakenclough Dr BL1 23 F2
Oakenclough Prim Sch SK9 131 D1
Oakenden Cl WN4 73 A6
Oakengates WN6 19 F1
Oakenrod Hill OL11 30 C6
Oakenrod Prim Sch OL11 139 D7
Oakenshaw Ave OL12 14 C6
Oakenshaw View OL12 14 C6
Oaker Ave M20 109 E4
Oaker Pl M20 109 E4
Oakes St BL4 60 F7
Oakfield Dukinfield SK16 101 E6
Manchester M25 63 D3
Sale M33 108 A5
Oakfield Ave
Atherton M46 58 C4
Cheadle SK8 122 E6
Droylsden M43 83 F1
Golborne WA3 73 F1
Manchester,Firswood M16 97 A3
Manchester,Whalley Range M16 97 D3
Mossley SK15 86 E6
Oakfield Cl
Alderley Edge SK9 137 B3
Bramhall SK7 132 E4
Horwich BL6 22 F2
Oakfield Cres WN2 38 C5
Oakfield Ct WA15 119 F6
Oakfield Dr M38 59 E5
Oakfield Gr Farnworth BL4 60 C6
Manchester M18 99 D4
Oakfield Mews
1 Sale M33 108 A4
Stockport SK3 170 F5
Oakfield Prim Sch SK14 101 E5
Oakfield Rd
Alderley Edge SK9 137 B2
Altrincham WA15 119 E4
Dukinfield SK14 101 E5
Hadfield SK13 171 E3
Manchester M20 110 A3
Poynton SK12 133 F4
Stockport SK3 170 F5
Oakfield St
Altrincham WA15 119 E5
Manchester M8 156 A6
Oakfield Terr OL11 30 C8
Oakfield Trad Est WA15 119 E5
Oakfold Ave OL6 85 D6
Oakford Ave M40 159 C3
Oakford Wlk BL3 146 C4
Oakham Cl BL8 27 D5
Oakham Mews M7 63 D1
Oakham Rd M34 101 A1
Oakhead WN7 76 C3
Oakhill Cl BL2 43 A7
Oakhill Ct M7 155 E7
Oakhill Trad Est M28 60 C6
Oakhill Way M8 155 F7
Oakhouse Dr M21 109 B7
Oakhurst Chase SK9 137 A2
Oakhurst Dr SK3 123 B5
Oakhurst Gr BL5 57 C7
Oakington Ave 10 M14 98 B3
Oakland Ave
Manchester M19 110 E4
Salford M6 80 B4
Stockport SK2 124 D6
Oakland Ct SK12 133 D4
Oakland Gr BL1 142 A2
Oakland Terr OL11 30 C1
Oaklands BL1 40 F7
Oaklands Ave
Cheadle SK8 123 A2
Marple SK6 126 C8
Oaklands Cl SK9 131 E1
Oaklands Dene SK14 102 A2
Oaklands Dr
Hazel Grove SK7 124 E1
Hyde SK14 102 A2
Prestwich M25 63 B4
Sale M33 108 A5
Oaklands Ho M14 98 C1
Oaklands Hospl The M6 80 B4
Oaklands Inf Sch SK9 131 E1
Oaklands Pk OL4 68 F5
Oaklands Rd Edenfield BL0 1 D2
Golborne WA3 90 F7
Royton OL2 48 E2
Salford M7 81 A8
Swinton M27 79 D6
Uppermill OL4 68 F5
Oaklea 1 Manchester M16 97 C3
Shevington Moor WN6 19 A2
Oaklea Rd M33 107 E5
Oakleigh Manchester SK4 168 B3
4 Stockport SK3 123 F4
Oakleigh Ave
Altrincham WA15 120 A7
Bolton BL3 42 A2
1 Manchester M19 110 F7
Oakleigh Cl OL10 46 E7
Oakleigh Rd SK8 131 E8
Oakley Ave WN5 71 E6
Oakley Cl Failsworth M40 83 C5
Radcliffe M26 62 A8
Oakley Dr Oldham OL1 49 D4

Oakley Dr *continued*
Wigan WN5 . . . . .54 E6
Oakley Pk BL1 . . . . .40 F7
Oakley St OL15 . . . . .15 E4
Oakley Villas SK4 . . . . .168 B3
Oaklings The WN2 . . . . .57 A3
Oakmere Ave M30 . . . . .79 C4
Oakmere Cl M22 . . . . .121 D4
Oakmere Rd Cheadle SK8 .122 F4
Handforth SK9 . . . . .131 D5
Oakmoor Dr M7 . . . . .81 B8
Oakmoor Rd M23 . . . . .121 A6
Oakridge Wlk ☑ M9 . . . .157 D7
Oaks Ave BL2 . . . . .25 C4
Oaks La BL2 . . . . .25 B4
Oaks Prim Sch The BL1 . . .24 F6
Oaks The Gatley SK8 . . . .122 A2
Glossop SK13 . . . . .116 A7
Hyde SK14 . . . . .102 A3
Oakshaw Dr OL12 . . . . .14 A1
Oakside Cl SK8 . . . . .122 E6
Oaktree Cotts SK8 . . . . . .122 F3
Oakville Cl OL3 . . . . .122 D5
Oakville Dr M6 . . . . .80 A4
Oakville Terr ☑ M40 . . . . .64 F1
Oakway Manchester M20 .122 C8
Middleton M24 . . . . .46 F4
Oakwell Dr
Manchester M7 . . . . .63 E1
Whitefield BL9 . . . . .45 B3
Oakwell Mans M7 . . . . .63 E1
Oakwood Chadderton OL9 .65 E7
Glossop SK13 . . . . .115 F8
Sale M33 . . . . .107 C4
Oakwood Ave
Ashton-in-M WN4 . . . . .73 A2
Denton M34 . . . . .100 E7
Failsworth M40 . . . . .65 D1
Gatley SK8 . . . . .122 B5
Shevington WN6 . . . . .35 F5
Swinton M27 . . . . .61 E4
Walkden M28 . . . . .60 F2
Wilmslow SK9 . . . . .136 E6
Oakwood Cl BL8 . . . . .27 B3
Oakwood Ct WA14 . . . . . .128 B8
Oakwood Dr Bolton BL1 . . .40 F8
Leigh WN7 . . . . .75 E1
Salford M6 . . . . .80 B5
Walkden M28 . . . . .60 F2
Oakwood Est M5 . . . . . . .154 D1
Oakwood high sch M6 . . . .80 C5
Oakwood La WA14 . . . . . .119 B1
Oakwood Mews M24 . . . . . .65 C8
Oakwood Rd Disley SK12 .135 D6
Romiley SK6 . . . . .113 C2
Oakworth Croft OL4 . . . . . .49 F4
Oakworth Dr BL1 . . . . .24 D5
Oakworth St M9 . . . . .64 C3
Oat St SK1 . . . . .124 A7
Oatlands Rd M22 . . . . .121 C2
Oban Ave Failsworth M40 . .83 A4
Oldham OL1 . . . . .49 B1
Oban Cres SK3 . . . . .123 D4
Oban Dr Garswood WN4 . . .72 C4
Sale M33 . . . . .108 E3
Oban Gr BL1 . . . . .24 E5
Oban St BL1 . . . . .143 D3
Oban Way WN2 . . . . .38 D5
Oberlin St Oldham OL4 . . . .67 D7
Rochdale OL13 . . . . .139 D5
Oberon Cl M30 . . . . .79 D2
Occlestone Cl M33 . . . . . .108 E1
Ocean St WA14 . . . . .119 B6
Ocean Street Trad Est
WA14 . . . . .119 B6
Ocean Wlk M15 . . . . .162 F5
Ockendon Dr M9 . . . . .157 E7
Octavia Dr M40 . . . . .83 C4
Odell St M11 . . . . .165 B7
Odessa Ave M6 . . . . .80 B4
Odette St M18 . . . . .99 C4
Off Grove Rd SK15 . . . . . . .86 D4
Off Ridge Hill La ☑ SK15 .85 F2
Off Stamford St SK15 . . . . .86 D4
Offerton Dr SK2 . . . . .124 D6
Offerton Fold SK2 . . . . . . .124 C7
Offerton Gn SK2 . . . . .124 F6
Offerton Hall Prim Sch
SK2 . . . . .124 E6
Offerton High Sch SK2 . . .124 E8
Offerton Ind Est SK1,
SK2 . . . . .124 C7
Offerton La SK1,SK2 . . . .124 C8
Offerton Rd SK1,SK7 . . . .125 A4
Offerton St Horwich BL6 . . .22 A3
Stockport SK1 . . . . .112 B2
Ogbourne Wlk ☑ M13 . . .163 C6
Ogden Cl Haslingden BB4 . . .1 A7
Heywood OL10 . . . . .29 A2
Whitefield M45 . . . . .45 A1
Ogden Ct SK14 . . . . .167 E2
Ogden Gdns SK16 . . . . . . .101 E8
Ogden Gr SK8 . . . . .121 F4
Ogden La Manchester M11 .99 D7
Newhey OL16 . . . . .32 D5
Ogden Rd Bramhall SK7 . .132 D5
Failsworth M35 . . . . .83 F6
Ogden St Chadderton OL9 .152 C8
Ⓓ Manchester M20 . . . .110 B3
Middleton M24 . . . . .65 A8
Mottram-in-L SK14 . . . . . .115 D8
Ⓢ Oldham OL4 . . . . .67 C6
Prestwich M25 . . . . .63 B4
Rochdale OL11 . . . . .30 C2
Swinton M27 . . . . .79 F7
Ogden Wlk M45 . . . . .63 A8

Ogmore Wlk M40 . . . . .65 C2
Ogwen Dr M25 . . . . .63 B5
Ohio Ave M50 . . . . .96 F8
Okehampton Cl M26 . . . . . .43 C5
Okehampton Cres M33 . .107 D5
Okell Gr WN7 . . . . .75 D6
Okeover Rd M7 . . . . .155 D8
Olaf St ☑ BL2 . . . . .25 B1
Old Bank Cl SK6 . . . . .113 A3
Old Bank St M2 . . . . .158 F1
Old Bank The M15 . . . . . . .163 A6
Old Bank View OL1 . . . . . . .49 C4
Old Barn Rd BL7 . . . . .25 A8
Old Barton Rd M17,M30 . . .95 C7
Old Bedions Sports Ctr
M20 . . . . .122 A8
Old Bent La OL12 . . . . .15 A7
Old Birley St M15 . . . . . . .162 F5
Old Boston WA11 . . . . .89 A7
Old Boston Trad Est
WA11 . . . . .89 B8
Old Broadway M20 . . . . . .110 B5
Old Brook Cl OL2 . . . . .49 D8
Old Brow OL5 . . . . .68 C1
Old Brow La OL16 . . . . .15 C3
Old Brown Ct OL5 . . . . .86 C8
Old Chapel St SK3 . . . . . .170 D7
Old Church Mews ☑
SK16 . . . . .101 E8
Old Church St
Failsworth M40 . . . . .83 C6
Oldham OL1 . . . . .153 F7
Old Clay Dr OL12 . . . . .15 D4
Old Clough La M28 . . . . . . .60 F1
Old Colliery Yd WN4 . . . . . .72 C3
Old Court St SK14 . . . . . .167 D2
Old Croft Mews SK1 . . . .124 B7
Old Crofts Bank M41 . . . . . .95 C3
Old Cross St OL6 . . . . .166 C3
Old Ctyd The M22 . . . . . . .121 F5
Old Dairy Mews SK14 . . .101 D5
Old Delph Rd OL11 . . . . . . .13 F1
Old Doctors St BL8 . . . . . . .26 F7
Old Eagley Mews BL1 . . . . .24 F6
Old Edge La OL2 . . . . .48 E2
Old Elm St M12,M13 . . . . .163 C6
Old Engine Ho The BL0 . .138 C6
Old Engine La BL0 . . . . . . .11 D6
Old Farm Cres M43 . . . . . . .99 F8
Old Farm Dr SK2 . . . . .124 F6
Old Fold Eccles M30 . . . . . .79 C4
Ⓩ Wigan WN5 . . . . .54 B6
Old Fold Rd Aspull WN2 . . .38 D5
Westhoughton BL5 . . . . .57 C7
Old Garden The WA15 . . .120 B7
Old Gardens St ☑ SK1 . .170 F8
Old Gn Bolton BL3 . . . . .25 E6
Ramsbottom BL8 . . . . .10 F1
Old Greenwood La BL6 . . .22 D1
Old Ground St BL0 . . . . . .138 C6
Old Hall Cl Bury BL8 . . . . . .27 B2
Old Hall Clough BL6 . . . . . .40 C7
Old Hall St Sale M33 . . . .108 E4
Whitefield M45 . . . . .62 C7
Old Hall Dr
Ashton-in-M WN4 . . . . .73 A2
Manchester M18 . . . . .99 D4
Stockport SK2 . . . . .124 E6
Old Hall Drive Prim Sch
M18 . . . . .99 D4
Old Hall Farm BL3 . . . . .42 E4
Old Hall La Bolton BL1,BL6 .23 C1
Manchester,Rusholme M13,
M14,M19 . . . . .98 E2
Marple SK6 . . . . .126 C5
Mottram-in-L SK14 . . . . . .103 A5
Westhoughton BL5 . . . . .57 E6
Whitefield M45 . . . . .62 C6
Woodford SK7 . . . . .132 D1
Worsley M28 . . . . .78 E7
Old Hall Mill La M46 . . . . . .58 A6
Old Hall Prim Sch BL8 . . . .27 B7
Old Hall Rd
Failsworth M40 . . . . .83 B7
Gatley SK8 . . . . .122 A6
Manchester M7 . . . . .63 D1
Sale M33 . . . . .108 D3
Stretford M32 . . . . .96 A4
Whitefield M45 . . . . .62 C7
Old Hall Sq ☑ SK13 . . . .104 A5
Old Hall St
Dukinfield SK16 . . . . .101 A7
Farnworth BL4 . . . . .60 E7
Hazel Grove WN3 . . . . .151 E6
Ⓢ Manchester M11 . . . . . .99 E7
Middleton M24 . . . . .47 A1
Old Hall St N BL1 . . . . . . .145 F7
Old Hey Wlk M12 . . . . .89 C1
Old Heyes Rd WA15 . . . . .120 B8
Old House Terrs OL6 . . . . . .85 E5
Old Kiln OL3 . . . . .3 DB
Old Kiln La Bolton BL1 . . . . .23 D1
Oldham OL4 . . . . .68 A4
Old La Bury BL9 . . . . .27 F8
Glossop SK13 . . . . .116 A7
Horwich BL6 . . . . .22 D2
Manchester M11 . . . . .99 D7
Oldham OL9 . . . . .66 B4
Shevington WN6 . . . . .36 A6
Uppermill OL3 . . . . .51 B2
Uppermill,Ladcastle OL3 . . .68 E6
Walkden M38 . . . . .59 F6
Westhoughton BL5 . . . . .57 B4
Whitworth OL12,OL13 . . . . .4 E6
Wigan WN1 . . . . .37 B4

Old Lansdowne Rd M20 .110 A4
Old Lees St OL6 . . . . .85 D5
Old Links Cl BL1 . . . . .23 E2
Old Lord's Cres BL6 . . . . . .22 B5
Old Manor Pk M46 . . . . . . .58 A2
Old Market Pl ☑ WA14 .119 D5
Old Market St M9 . . . . .64 D2
Old Meadow Dr M34 . . . .100 F5
Old Meadow La WA15 . . .120 B5
Old Medlock St M3 . . . . . .162 E8
Old Mill Cl M27 . . . . .80 B8
Old Mill Ho OL4 . . . . .68 A5
Old Mill La
Hazel Grove SK7 . . . . .134 A8
Oldham OL4 . . . . .68 A5
Old Mill St M4 . . . . .159 C1
Old Mills Hill M24 . . . . .47 D1
Old Moat Com Prim Sch
M20 . . . . .110 A7
Old Moat La M20 . . . . .110 B7
Old Moss La WA3 . . . . .92 E6
Old Mount St M4 . . . . .159 B2
Old Nans La BL2 . . . . .25 F2
Old Nursery Fold BL2 . . . . .25 E4
Old Oak Cl BL2 . . . . .43 B5
Old Oak Dr M34 . . . . .101 A3
Old Oak St M20 . . . . .110 B3
Old Oake Cl M28 . . . . .60 F2
Old Orch SK9 . . . . .137 A7
Old Orch The WA15 . . . . .120 B8
Old Pack Horse Rd BL8 . . .51 B6
Old Packhorse Rd OL15 . . .16 F6
Old Park La M17 . . . . .95 C6
Old Parrin La M30 . . . . .79 B3
Old Pasture Cl SK2 . . . . . .124 E7
Old Pepper La WN6 . . . . . . .19 B2
Old Quarry La BL7 . . . . .8 F1
Old Rake BL6 . . . . .22 E5
Old Rd Ashton-in-M WN4 . .73 A4
Ashton-u-L OL6 . . . . .86 A6
Bolton BL1 . . . . .143 E3
Cheadle SK8 . . . . .122 F6
Dukinfield SK16 . . . . .166 C1
Failsworth M35 . . . . .83 E8
Handforth SK9 . . . . .131 D3
Hyde SK14 . . . . .167 D4
Manchester M9 . . . . .157 F8
Mottram-in-L SK14 . . . . . .102 F5
Rochdale OL16 . . . . .15 E4
Stockport SK5 . . . . .169 E3
Tintwistle SK13 . . . . .104 A7
Wilmslow SK9 . . . . .137 B8
Old Rectory Gdns SK8 . . .122 F5
Old River Cl M44 . . . . .94 A2
Old School Cl BL5 . . . . .58 C7
Old School Ct Eccles M30 .79 D4
Manchester M9 . . . . .64 C2
Old School House The
OL15 . . . . .15 F6
Old School La
Adlington PR7 . . . . .20 E5
Cheadle SK8 . . . . .132 A8
Old School Mews
☑ Bacup OL13 . . . . .3 C8
Ⓓ Dukinfield SK15,SK16 .101 E8
Old School Pl WN4 . . . . . . .73 C4
Old School Rooms The ☑
BL1 . . . . .145 F6
Old Shaw St M5 . . . . .161 B8
Old Sirs BL5 . . . . .57 F5
Old St Ashton-u-L OL6 . . .166 B3
Manchester M11 . . . . .99 E8
Oldham OL4 . . . . .67 D5
Stalybridge SK15 . . . . .86 A2
Old Stables The M34 . . . .100 F6
Old Station St ☑ M30 . . . .79 C1
Old Swan Cl BL7 . . . . .8 E2
Old Swan Cotts BL7 . . . . . . .8 E2
Old Tannery The SK14 . . .113 F8
Old Thorn La OL3 . . . . .69 D6
Old Towns Cl BL8 . . . . .26 F3
Old Trafford Com Sch
M16 . . . . .161 C6
Old Vicarage Sta M16 . . . . .97 A4
Old Vicarage Gdns BL5 . . .57 E5
Old Vicarage Mews BL5 . . .57 E5
Old Vicarage Rd BL6 . . . . . .22 F3
Old Wargrave Rd WA12 . . .89 C2
Old Well Wlk M33 . . . . . . .107 C2
Old Wellington Rd M30 . . .79 F2
Old Wells Cl M38 . . . . .60 A6
Old Wells La BL6 . . . . .22 D6
Old Wool La SK8 . . . . .122 F4
Old York St M15 . . . . .162 E6
Oldbridge Dr M9 . . . . .56 D6
Oldbrook Fold WA15 . . . . .120 B4
Oldbury Cl Heywood OL10 .46 D7
Manchester M40 . . . . .160 D2
Oldcastle Ave M20 . . . . . .110 A8
Oldcott Cl OL4 . . . . .77 F5
Oldcroft OL4 . . . . .68 A6
Oldershaw Dr M9 . . . . . . .157 E7
Oldfield Brow Prim Sch
WA14 . . . . .119 A5
Oldfield Cl BL5 . . . . .57 F6
Oldfield Dr WA15 . . . . . . .119 F6
Oldfield Gr BL5 . . . . .57 F6
Oldfield La WA14 . . . . .118 F4
Oldfield Mews WA14 . . . . .119 A5
Oldfield Rd
Altrincham WA14 . . . . .119 B5
Prestwich M25 . . . . .63 A4
Sale M33 . . . . .108 C5
Salford M5 . . . . .161 C8
Oldfield St M11 . . . . .83 C1

Oldgate Wlk ⓘ M15 . . . .162 D6
Oldhall Cres SK9 . . . . .131 E3
Oldham Art Gal & Mus*
OL1 . . . . .153 F6
Oldham Ave SK1 . . . . .112 B1
Oldham Coll The OL9 . . . .153 E7
Oldham Dr ⓘ M40 . . . . . .159 C3
Oldham Dr SK8 . . . . .113 A4
Oldham Mumps Sta OL4 . .67 A6
Oldham Rd Ashton-u-L OL7 .85 A5
Delph OL3 . . . . .50 D2
Failsworth M35,M40 . . . . . .83 D6
Middleton M24 . . . . .65 A8
Rochdale OL11,OL16 . . . . .31 A3
Royton OL1,OL2 . . . . .48 E3
Shaw OL1,OL4 . . . . .50 B7
Shaw,Shaw Side OL2 . . . .149 B5
Uppermill OL4,OL3 . . . . . . .68 D6
Oldham Sixth Form Coll
OL8 . . . . .153 E6
Oldham St Denton M34 . .100 C3
Droylsden M43 . . . . .84 B2
Hyde SK14 . . . . .167 D2
Manchester M1,M4 . . . . . .159 B2
Ⓑ Manchester SK9 . . . . .131 F2
Salford M5 . . . . .158 D1
Oldham Study Ctr & Natural
History Mus* OL8 . . . . .153 D5
Oldham Way OL1,OL4,
OL8,OL9 . . . . .153 E6
Oldham Werneth Sta
OL9 . . . . .153 D6
Oldham West Bsns Ctr
OL9 . . . . .152 B7
Oldhams Bsns Ctr OL4 . .153 F6
Oldhams Prim Sch BL1 . . .24 C5
Oldhams Terr BL1 . . . . . . .143 D4
Oldhams Rd SK6 . . . . .126 A6
Oldmill St OL12 . . . . .139 F8
Oldmoor Rd SK6 . . . . .112 E5
Oldstead Gr BL3 . . . . .40 F3
Oldstead Wlk M9 . . . . .157 D6
Oldway Wlk M40 . . . . .83 B5
Oldwood La WA3 . . . . .91 A4
Oleo Terr M44 . . . . .94 C3
Olga St BL1 . . . . .143 D2
Olivant St M8 . . . . .159 B4
Olive Bank BL8 . . . . .27 B4
Olive Gr WN6 . . . . .36 F3
Olive Rd WA15 . . . . .120 A8
Olive Shapley Ave
M20 . . . . .110 B3
Olive St Bacup OL13 . . . . . . .3 E8
Bolton BL3 . . . . .147 D4
Failsworth M35 . . . . .83 E8
Heywood OL10 . . . . .29 E2
Radcliffe M26 . . . . .44 C2
Rochdale OL11 . . . . .30 C1
Olive Terr SK14 . . . . .115 A8
Oliver Cl OL15 . . . . .15 F5
Oliver St Atherton M46 . . . .58 D3
Ⓑ Bacup OL13 . . . . .3 E8
Manchester,Beswick M11 . .164 F8
Oldham OL1 . . . . .153 F6
Stockport SK1,SK3 . . . . . .170 F8
Olivia Ct M5 . . . . .161 C8
Olivia Gr M14 . . . . .98 D3
Ollerbarrow Rd WA15 . . .119 E2
Ollerbrook Ct ⓘ BL1 . . . .143 F2
Ollersett Ave SK22 . . . . . .127 D1
Ollersett La SK22 . . . . . . .127 E1
Ollerton ⓘ OL12 . . . . . . .139 E8
Ollerton Ave
Manchester M16 . . . . .97 C3
Sale M33 . . . . .107 D5
Ollerton Cl WN2 . . . . .38 A2
Ollerton Dr M35 . . . . .83 F6
Ollerton Rd SK9 . . . . .131 E5
Ollerton St
Ⓘ Adlington PR6 . . . . .21 A8
Bolton BL1 . . . . .145 F8
Ollier Ave M12 . . . . .99 B2
Olney OL11 . . . . .139 E6
Olney Ave M22 . . . . .121 D6
Olney St M13 . . . . .98 D4
Olsberg Cl M26 . . . . .44 C4
Olwen Ave M12 . . . . .165 A5
Olwen Cres SK5 . . . . .111 F8
Olympia ☑ M44 . . . . .94 C2
Olympic Ct M50 . . . . .96 F8
Omer Ave M19 . . . . .98 F2
Omer Dr M19 . . . . .110 F7
Onchan Ave M11 . . . . .67 B6
One Ash Cl OL12 . . . . .14 D3
One Oak Ct SK7 . . . . .123 D2
One Oak La SK9 . . . . .137 F7
Ongar Wlk M9 . . . . .157 D6
Onslow Ave M40 . . . . .65 C1
Onslow Cl OL1 . . . . .153 E8
Onslow Rd SK3 . . . . .123 C8
Onslow St OL11 . . . . .30 D1
Onward St SK14 . . . . .167 D2
Onyx Gr OL15 . . . . .16 B4
Oozewood Rd M2,OL2 . . . .48 B5

Oram St BL9 . . . . .141 A4
Orama Ave M6 . . . . .80 A4
Orange Hill Rd M25 . . . . . .63 C5
Orange St M6 . . . . .81 A3
Orbital Way M34 . . . . .100 D3
Orchard Ave Bolton BL1 . .143 F3
Partington M31 . . . . .105 F4
Reddish M18 . . . . .99 E4
Worsley M28 . . . . .78 B7
Orchard Brow WA3 . . . . . .105 A2
Orchard Cl Cheadle SK8 . .132 C7
Leigh WN7 . . . . .75 F7
Poynton SK12 . . . . .133 E3
Shevington WN6 . . . . .36 A7
Wilmslow SK9 . . . . .136 F5
Orchard Ct SK2 . . . . .124 D6
Orchard Dr
Altrincham WA15 . . . . .120 A3
Gamesley SK13 . . . . .171 E1
Handforth SK9 . . . . .131 E2
Orchard Gdns BL2 . . . . . . .25 D3
Orchard Grs SK9 . . . . .137 B1
Orchard Gr
Manchester M20 . . . . .109 F5
Shaw OL2 . . . . .149 A2
Orchard Ind Est M6 . . . . . .81 A5
Orchard La WN7 . . . . .76 A7
Orchard Pl Poynton SK12 .133 D4
Sale M33 . . . . .120 B7
Ⓓ Sale M33 . . . . .108 B5
Orchard Rd
Altrincham WA15 . . . . .119 C5
Failsworth M35 . . . . .83 F7
Lymm WA13 . . . . .117 B5
Romiley SK6 . . . . .114 B2
Orchard Rd E M22 . . . . . .109 E2
Orchard Rd W M22 . . . . . .109 D2
Orchard Rise SK14 . . . . . .113 F7
Orchard St
Ashton-in-M WN4 . . . . .73 C3
Heywood OL10 . . . . .29 E3
Hyde SK14 . . . . .167 E2
Manchester M20 . . . . .81 A4
Stockport SK1 . . . . .169 F1
Wigan WN1 . . . . .151 D8
Orchard The Disley SK12 .135 D6
Oldham OL4 . . . . .67 C3
Urmston M41 . . . . .95 C1
Ⓢ Westhoughton BL5 . . . .39 E1
Orchard Trad Est M6 . . . . .80 F5
Orchard Vale SK3 . . . . . . .123 C6
Orchards The
Heywood OL10 . . . . .29 E2
Orrell WN5 . . . . .53 B8
Orchid Ave BL4 . . . . .42 B1
Orchid Cl Irlam M44 . . . . .105 E8
Oldham OL1 . . . . .48 D1
Up Holland WN8 . . . . .53 B6
Orchid Dr BL9 . . . . .45 A4
Orchid St M9 . . . . .157 D7
Orchid Wlk ⓘ M9 . . . . . . .64 E3
Ordsall Ave M30 . . . . .60 B8
Ordsall District Ctr M5 . . .161 B8
Ordsall Dr M5 . . . . .161 B7
Ordsall Hall Mus* M5 . . .161 B7
Ordsall La M5 . . . . .161 C8
Oregon Ave OL1 . . . . .48 E1
Oregon Cl M13 . . . . .163 C6
Orford Ave SK12 . . . . .135 D6
Orford Cl SK6 . . . . .134 E7
Orford Ct WN7 . . . . .76 B8
Orford Rd Failsworth M40 . .83 C5
Prestwich M25 . . . . .63 B5
Organ St Hindley WN2 . . . .57 B3
Leigh WN7 . . . . .75 E5
Organ Way SK14 . . . . .103 D5
Oriel Ave OL8 . . . . .66 E3
Oriel Bank High Sch
SK2 . . . . .170 F5
Oriel Cl Chadderton OL9 . .152 A5
Stockport SK2 . . . . .124 B6
Oriel Rd Ashton-in-M WN4 . .72 F4
Manchester M20 . . . . .110 A4
Rochdale OL11 . . . . .139 F5
Orient Rd M6 . . . . .80 B4
Orient St M7 . . . . .155 F7
Oriole Cl M28 . . . . .78 C8
Oriole Ho ☑ M19 . . . . . . .110 D4
Orion Bsns Pk SK3 . . . . . .123 B5
Orion Pl M7 . . . . .81 C4
Orkney Cl Radcliffe M26 . . .44 B4
Wythenshawe M23 . . . . . .121 A4
Orkney Dr M41 . . . . .95 D5
Orlanda Ave M6 . . . . .80 B4
Orlando Dr M7 . . . . .155 F6
Orlando St BL3 . . . . .148 A3
Orleans Way OL1 . . . . . . .153 E7
Orley Wlk OL1 . . . . .48 D1
Orme Ave Middleton M24 . .65 A7
Salford M6 . . . . .80 B4
Orme Cl Manchester M11 . .165 A8
Urmston M41 . . . . .95 C2
Orme St
Alderley Edge SK9 . . . . . .137 A1
Oldham OL4 . . . . .67 B7
Ⓘ Manchester M14 . . . . . .98 B3
Ormerod Ave OL2 . . . . .48 E5
Ormerod Cl SK6 . . . . .113 A3
Ormond St BL9 . . . . .28 E1
Ormonds St Bolton BL3 . . .42 D5
Bury BL9 . . . . .141 A3
Ormonde Ave M6 . . . . .80 B4

Ormonde Ct OL6 ....166 C4
Ormonde St OL6 ....166 C4
Ormrod St Bolton BL3 ...145 E6
Bolton,Hall I' th' Wood
BL2 ....25 C4
Bury BL9 ....141 A2
🔟 Farnworth BL4 ......60 C8
Ormrods The BL9 ....28 F5
Orms Gill Pl SK2 ....124 E6
Ormsby Ave M18 ....99 B4
Ormsby Cl Standish WN6 ..19 E2
Stockport SK3 ....123 E4
Ormsgill Cl M15 ....162 F6
Ormsgill St M15 ....162 F6
Ormside Cl WN2 ....57 C4
Ormskirk Ave M20 ......109 F6
Ormskirk Cl BL8 ....44 A8
Ormskirk Rd
2 Reddish SK5 ....111 F6
Up Holland WN8 ....53 A7
Wigan WN5 ....54 D6
Ormston Ave BL6 ....22 C5
Ornston Gr WN7 ....75 F7
Ornatus St BL2 ....24 F5
Ornhill Rd 1 M15 ......97 F4
Ornsey Wlk 12 M11 .....83 C1
Oronsay Gr M5 ....154 E1
Orphanage St SK4 .....169 E3
Orpington Dr BL8 .....27 B1
Orpington Rd 2 M9 ...157 E7
Orpington St WN5 ....54 C6
Orrel Sta WN5 ....53 A3
Orrell Arc 3 WN1 .....150 C8
Orrell Gdns WN5 ......53 F6
Orrell Hall Cl WN5 ...54 B8
Orrell Holgate Prim Sch
WN5 ....53 E5
Orrell Lamberhead Green
Com Prim Sch WN5 ...53 D4
Orrell Newfold Com Prim Sch
WN5 ....53 D4
Orrell Rd WN5 ....53 E7
Orrell St Bury BL8 ...140 D3
Manchester M11 ......99 D8
Wigan WN1 ....151 D7
Orrell Sta WN5 ......53 A3
Orrell Water Pk* WN5 ..53 E4
Orrishmere Prim Sch
SK8 ....123 A3
Orrishmere Rd SK8 ...122 F3
Orron St OL15 ....16 A5
Orsett Cl M40 ....159 C3
Orthes Gr SK4 ....111 D5
Orton Ave M23 ....109 A1
Orton Rd M23 ....109 A1
Orton Way M11 ....72 F3
Orvietto Ave M6 .....80 B4
Orville Dr M19 ......110 F7
Orwell Ave Reddish M34 ..100 A3
Wythenshawe M22 ....121 D6
Orwell Cl Bury BL8 ..140 D4
Handforth SK9 ......131 D2
Orwell Rd BL1 ......142 B2
Osborne Ave WA12 ...89 C3
Osborne Ct M46 .....58 C3
Osborne Dr M27 .....80 C7
Osborne Gr Bolton BL1 ..142 C1
Gatley SK8 ....122 A3
Leigh WN7 ....76 D6
Osborne Ho M30 ....79 C2
Osborne Ind Est OL9 ..152 E8
Osborne Pl SK13 ...104 A5
Osborne Rd
Altrincham WA15 ...119 E5
Ashton-in-M WN4 ...73 A4
Denton M34 ....100 F4
Golborne WA3 ......49 B7
Hyde SK14 ....167 E1
Manchester, Levenshulme
M19 ....99 A1
3 Manchester,Harpurhey
M9 ....157 E7
Oldham OL8 ....153 D5
Salford M6 ....80 A2
Stockport SK2 ......170 F2
Osborne St Heywood OL10 ..29 D1
Manchester M40 ....159 C4
Manchester,Didsbury M20 ..110 A3
Oldham OL9 ....152 D5
Rochdale OL11 .....139 F5
Romiley SK6 ....112 D3
Salford M6 ....154 F2
Shaw OL2 ....149 B6
Osborne Terr Bacup OL13 ..3 D8
Sale M33 ....108 B4
Osbourne Cl
Farnworth BL4 .....42 D1
Wilmslow SK9 ......137 D6
Osbourne Pl 7 WA14 ..119 D4
Osbourne Wlk M26 ...43 E3
Oscar St Bolton BL1 ..142 D2
Manchester M40 ...83 A7
Oscott Ave M38 ....60 A6
Oscroft Cl M8 .....155 F6
Oscroft Wlk M11 ..110 D7
Osmond St OL4 ....67 C7
Osmund Ave BL2 ...25 E5
Osprey Ave BL5 ...57 D6
Osprey Cl Dukinfield SK16 ..101 E7
Manchester M15 ...162 E5
Osprey Ct M15 ....162 E5
Osprey Dr Droylsden M43 ..84 C3
Irlam M44 ....94 A3
Wilmslow SK9 .....137 C8
Osprey Wlk M13 ...163 C6

Ospreys The WN3 ......54 C4
Ossington Ct M23 ....109 A3
Ossington Wlk M23 ...109 A2
Ossory St M14 ....98 B3
Osterley Rd M9 ......65 A3
Ostlers Gate M43 ....84 D2
Ostrich La M25 ......63 C3
Oswald Cl M6 ....81 A5
Oswald La M21 ....97 B1
Oswald Rd M21 ....97 A1
Oswald Road Prim Sch
M21 ....97 A1
Oswald St Bolton BL3 ..146 C4
Manchester M4 ......159 A3
Manchester M4 ......160 D1
Oldham OL9 ....153 D8
Reddish SK5 ....99 F3
Rochdale OL16 ......31 B8
Shaw OL2 ....149 A8
Oswestry Cl BL8 ....26 F8
Otago St 2 OL4 .....49 C1
Othello Dr M30 .....79 C2
Otley Ave M6 ....80 C3
Otley Cl OL9 ....152 B6
Otley Gr SK3 ....123 D4
Otmoor Way OL2 ....49 A4
Otranto Ave M6 ....80 B3
Otter Dr Manchester M8 ..155 E5
Whitefield BL9 .....45 B4
Otterburn Pl SK2 ..124 E6
Otterbury Cl BL8 ..26 F2
Otterham Wlk M40 ..83 C5
Otterspool Rd SK6 ..125 B8
Otterwood Sq WN5 ..36 C2
Ottery Wlk 1 M40 ..65 D2
Ottowa Cl M23 .....120 F4
Oughtrington Com Prim Sch
WA13 ....117 B4
Oughtrington Cres
WA13 ....117 B4
Oughtrington La WA13 ..117 A2
Oughtrington View
WA13 ....117 B4
Oulder Hill OL11 ...30 B7
Oulder Hill Com Sch
OL11 ....30 B7
Oulder Hill Dr OL11 ..30 B7
Oldfield Cl 22 OL16 ..31 B6
Oulton Ave M33 ....108 E5
Oulton Cl 5 WN7 ...76 A4
Oulton St BL1 ......25 A5
Oulton Wlk M40 ....160 D3
Oundle Cl M14 .....98 C3
Our Lady & Lancashire
Martyrs RC Prim Sch
M28 ....60 A3
Our Lady & St Anselm's RC
Prim Sch OL12 ....4 D2
Our Lady & St Paul RC Prim
Sch OL10 ....28 F1
Our Lady of Grace RC Prim
Sch M25 ....63 A6
Our Lady of Lourdes RC Prim
Sch
Bury BL8 ....27 C6
Farnworth BL4 .....60 A8
Partington M31 ....105 A3
Our Lady of the Rosary RC
Prim Sch
Leigh WN7 ....75 B5
Urmston M41 ....95 C4
Our Lady's RC High Sch
Manchester M9 .....64 D5
Royton OL2 ....48 D3
Our Lady's RC Prim Sch
Aspull WN2 ....38 C5
Manchester M16 ...97 D3
Oldham OL4 ....49 E3
Stockport SK3 .....170 E8
Ouse St M50 ....80 C1
Outham Mews OL3 ...51 B1
Outram Cl SK6 .....125 F4
Outram Sq M43 ....100 A8
Outrington Dr M11 ..165 A8
Outterside St PR7 ..21 A6
Outwood Dr SK8 ...131 A8
Outwood Gr BL1 ...24 E5
Outwood La M90 ...130 C7
Outwood La W M90 ..130 B8
Outwood Prim Sch M26 ..131 D7
Outwood Rd Gatley SK8 ..131 A7
Radcliffe M26 .....44 A1
Oval Dr SK16 ......101 B7
Oval The Gatley SK8 ..131 A8
Shevington WN6 ...35 F5
Over Hey BL7 ......9 B6
Over Town La
Rochdale OL12 .....13 A3
Rochdale,Wolstenholme
OL12 ....13 C3
Overbeck Cl WN6 ..37 A4
Overbridge Rd M7,M8 ..158 F4
Overbrook Ave M40 ..156 C5
Overbrook Dr M25 ..63 B3
Overcombe Wlk 1 M40 ..156 C5
Overdale 1 Marple SK6 ..125 F4
Pendlebury M27 ...80 A6
Overdale Cl OL1 ..48 E1
Overdale Cres M41 ..94 F2
Overdale Dr Bolton BL1 ..144 A7
Glossop SK13 ......116 B8
Overdale Rd
New Mills SK12 ....135 F6
Romiley SK6 ....125 A8
Wythenshawe M22 ..121 D5

Overdell Dr OL12 ..14 C4
Overdene Cl BL6 ...40 C6
Overens St OL4 ....67 B7
Overfield Way OL12 ..14 F2
Overgreen BL2 .....25 E3
Overhill Dr SK9 ...137 E7
Overhill La SK9 ...137 E7
Overhill Rd
Chadderton OL9 ...65 F8
Wilmslow SK9 .....137 D7
Overhill Way WN3 ..54 D3
Overlea Dr M19 ...110 E5
Overlinks Dr M6 ..80 B5
Overshores Rd BL7 ..9 B8
Overstone Dr M8 ..155 F7
Overt St OL11 ....139 F5
Overton Ave M22 ..121 D5
Overton Cl M26 ...44 B1
Overton Cres
Hazel Grove SK7 ..124 E4
Sale M33 ....107 D1
Overton Rd M22 ..121 D5
Overton St WN7 ...75 E4
Overton Way 2 SK9 ..131 D5
Overwood Rd M22 ..121 D8
Ovington Wlk 8 M40 ..156 C5
Owen Fold OL4 ....67 F7
Owen St Eccles M30 ..79 B1
2 Leigh WN7 ......75 D5
Oldham OL1 ....49 E3
Salford M6 ....81 A5
Stockport SK3 ....170 F8
Owen's Row BL6 ..22 C3
Owenington Gr M38 ..60 A5
Owens Cl OL9 .....65 E8
Owens Farm Dr SK2 ..124 E7
Owler La OL9 .....65 E3
Owlerbarrow Rd BL8 ..27 A3
Owlsfield WA12 ...89 A4
Owlwood Cl M38 ..59 E3
Owlwood Dr M38 ..59 E3
Owsten Ct BL6 ....21 F3
Ox Gate BL2 ......25 D5
Ox Hey Cl La Denshaw OL3 ..33 E1
Horwich BL6 ......39 F7
Ox St BL0 ....138 B5
Oxbow Way M45 ..63 A8
Oxbridge Cl 3 M33 ..107 D3
Oxburgh Rd WN3 ..55 F4
Oxendale Dr M24 ..46 D1
Oxendon Ave M11 ..83 B3
Oxenhurst Gr SK2 ..124 E5
Oxford Ave Droylsden M43 ..83 F3
Rochdale OL11 ....30 A6
Sale M33 ....107 D4
Whitefield M45 ...63 A8
Oxford Cl BL4 ....59 F8
Oxford Ct Manchester M2 ..162 F8
3 Manchester,Hulme
M15 ....162 F6
Manchester,Old Trafford
M16 ....162 D5
Wigan WN1 ....37 D1
Oxford Dr Middleton M24 ..47 C2
Romiley SK6 ......113 C4
Irlam M44 ....105 C6
Oxford Grove Prim Sch
BL1 ....142 C1
Oxford Ho OL9 ...152 C6
Oxford Pl Manchester M14 ..98 C4
14 Rochdale OL16 ..31 A5
Oxford Rd
Altrincham WA14 ..119 B4
Atherton M46 .....58 B5
Dukinfield SK16 ..101 D8
Horwich BL6 ......39 F8
Hyde SK14 ....113 E8
Little Lever BL3 ..42 B6
Manchester M1,M13 ..163 B6
Manchester M9 ...80 B4
Oxford Rd Sta M1 ..162 F7
Oxford Road Sta M1 ..163 A7
Manchester M1,M13 ..163 A5
Bolton BL1 ....141 A1
Bury BL9 ....141 A1
Eccles M30 ....79 E1
Hindley WN2 ......56 F7
Leigh WN7 ....75 F7
Manchester M1,M60,M2 ..163 A8
Manchester M16 ..162 D5
Newton-le-W WA12 ..89 B3
Oldham OL1 ....152 C5
Shaw OL2 ....149 B7
Stalybridge,Copley SK15 ..86 C1
Stalybridge,Millbrook SK15 ..86 D4
Oxford Sd E OL7 ..166 A1
Oxford Sd W OL7 ..100 F8
Oxford Way Rochdale OL12 ..14 E2
Stockport SK4 ...169 D3
Oxford Wlk 4 M34 ..101 A1
Oxhill Wlk 7 M40 ..65 D2
Oxhouse Rd WN5 ..53 A6
Oxlea Gr BL5 .....57 E7
Oxney Rd M14 ....98 C4
Oxted Wlk 8 M8 ..156 A6
Oxton Ave M22 ...121 C4
Oxton St M11 ....99 F7
Oyu Lubavitch Girls Sch
M7 ....63 D1
Ozanam Ct M7 ....155 D7

P

Pacific Rd WA14 ...119 A6

Pacific Way M50 ..96 C8
Pack Horse Yd 6 OL10 ..139 F7
Packer St 1 Bolton BL1 ..142 C2
Rochdale OL16 ....139 F7
Packwood Chase OL9 ..65 F8
Padbury Cl M41 ...94 D3
Padbury Ho 7 M6 ..154 F1
Padbury Way BL2 ..25 E1
Padbury Wlk M40 ..157 F5
Padden Brook SK6 ..113 B2
Padden Brook Mews
SK6 ....113 B2
Paddington Ave M40 ..83 B5
Paddington Cl M6 ..81 A2
Paddison St 2 M27 ..79 E7
Paddock Chase SK12 ..133 F6
Paddock Cl M46 ...58 E5
Paddock Hill La WA16 ..136 A3
Paddock La
Failsworth M35 ...83 F5
Lymm WA13 ....117 C7
Partington WA13,WA14 ..118 B5
Paddock Rd SK14 ..113 D8
Paddock Rise WN6 ..36 E3
Paddock St M12 ..163 C7
Paddock The
Altrincham WA15 ..120 B4
Ashton-in-M WN4 ..72 F6
Bramhall SK7 .....123 D1
Cheadle SK8 ......122 E5
Hadfield SK13 ....103 F5
Handforth SK9 ...131 D4
Hollingworth SK14 ..103 E8
Lymm WA13 ....117 C4
Ramsbottom BL0 ..138 B7
Uppermill OL3 ....68 F4
Worsley M28 .....78 E7
Paddocks The SK3 ..124 A4
Paderborn Ct BL1 ..145 E6
Padfield Com Prim Sch
SK13 ....104 B5
Padfield Cl M13 ..116 D7
Padfield Main Rd SK13 ..104 C5
Padiham Cl Bury BL9 ..44 D7
Leigh WN7 ....76 A5
Padstow Cl SK14 ..113 D8
Padstow Dr SK7 ..132 F7
Padstow Pl 2 OL9 ..48 A1
Padstow St M40 ..160 E3
Padstow Wlk SK14 ..102 D3
Padworth Wlk M22 ..120 D8
Pagan St OL16 ...139 F8
Pagefield Cl 13 WN6 ..37 A1
Pagefield Ind Est WN6 ..36 F1
Pagefield St WN6 ..37 A1
Paget St M40 .....157 D5
Pagnall Ct OL9 ..152 B5
Paignton Ave
Hattersley SK14 ..102 D2
Manchester M19 ..110 F8
Paignton Cl WN5 ..71 E8
Paignton Dr M33 ..107 D5
Paignton Gr SK5 ..111 E7
Paignton Wlk SK14 ..102 C2
Pailin Dr M43 ....84 C2
Pailton Cl BL6 ...40 D6
Painswick Rd M22 ..121 B1
Paisley Pk BL4 ...42 D1
Paiton St BL1 ....144 C1
Palace Arc WN4 ..73 B3
Palace Ct 8 BL1 ..145 F8
Palace Gdns OL12 ..15 C4
Palace Gr WN7 ...76 D6
Palace Rd Ashton-u-L OL6 ..85 E5
Sale M33 ....108 A5
Palace St Bolton BL1 ..145 F8
Bury BL9 ....141 A2
Oldham OL1 ......152 C7
Palatine Ave
Manchester M20 ..110 B6
Rochdale OL11 ...30 A8
Wigan WN3 ....54 E4
Palatine Cres M20 ..110 B5
Palatine Dr BL9 ..27 F8
Palatine Ho 4 SK3 ..170 E8
Palatine Rd
Manchester M20 ..110 B6
Rochdale OL11 ...30 A8
Wythenshawe M20,M22 ..109 E2
Palatine St 4 Bolton BL1 ..143 F1
Denton M34 ......100 E4
Ramsbottom BL0 ..138 C6
Rochdale OL16 ...31 C7
Palatine Terr OL11 ..30 A8
Palewood Cl WN1 ..37 E1
Paley St BL1 .....145 F7
Palfrey Pl M12 ..163 C7
Palgrave Ave M40 ..157 D5
Palin St WN1 ....57 B3
Palin Wood Rd OL3 ..50 F5
Pall Mall M2 .....158 F1
Pallotine Wlk OL11 ..139 D5
Palm Bsns Ctr OL9 ..152 B7
Palm Cl M33 .....107 D5
Palm Gr Chadderton OL9 ..152 B7
Wigan WN5 ....54 D6
Palm St Bolton BL1 ..143 F3
Droylsden M43 ...83 E2
Manchester M13 ..98 F3
Oldham OL4 ......67 B7
Palma Ave M90 ..130 B8
Palmer Ave SK8 ..122 F6
Palmer Cl Manchester M8 ..64 B2
Oldham OL8 ......66 F4
Palmer Gr WN7 ..57 E1

Palmer St
Dukinfield SK16 ..166 B1
6 Sale M33 ....108 A4
Salford M7 ....81 C5
Palmerston Ave M16 ..97 D2
Palmerston Cl
Hindley WN2 ......56 C4
Ramsbottom BL0 ..11 C4
Reddish M34 .....100 B3
Palmerston Rd
Reddish M34 .....100 B3
Stockport SK2 ...124 B3
Palmerston St M12 ..160 E1
Pandora St M20 ..110 A5
Panfield Rd M22 ..121 D4
Pangbourne Ave M41 ..95 E3
Pangbourne Cl SK3 ..123 C6
Pankhurst Wlk 11 M14 ..98 B3
Panmure St OL8 ..66 F4
Pansy Rd BL4 ....60 A8
Panton St BL6 ...22 D1
Paper Mill Rd BL7 ..25 A7
Parade Rd M90 ..130 C7
Parade The
1 Alderley Edge SK9 ..137 A1
Culcheth WA3 ....91 E3
Romiley SK6 .....113 A1
Swinton M27 .....79 F8
2 Whitefield M45 ..44 F2
Paradise St Denton M34 ..100 F7
Hadfield SK13 ...104 A5
Ramsbottom BL0 ..138 C2
Paragon Ind Est OL15 ..15 F3
Parbold Ave M20 ..110 A6
Parbrook Cl M40 ..157 D5
Parbrook La WN6 ..36 B7
Parchments The WA12 ..89 D4
Pardoners Ct M5 ..80 B2
Pargate Chase OL11 ..30 A8
Parham Wlk 9 M9 ..64 E3
Paris Ave Salford M5 ..161 B7
Wigan WN3 ....54 C3
Paris St BL3 .....146 B4
Parish Church CE Jun Sch
The OL1 ....153 F8
Parish View M5 ..161 B8
Park Ave
Altrincham WA14 ..119 C8
Altrincham WA15 ..119 F1
Bolton BL1 ....143 E4
Bramhall SK7 ....132 D5
Chadderton OL9 ..48 B1
Cheadle SK8 .....122 F1
Cheadle,Cheadle Health
SK3 ....122 F7
Failsworth M35 ..83 D8
Golborne WA3 ....73 F2
Hyde SK14 ....167 D4
Longshaw WN5 ...53 E1
Manchester,Levenshulme
M19 ....99 A1
Manchester,Old Trafford
M16 ....161 C5
Pendlebury M27 ..80 A7
Prestwich M25 ...133 E4
Radcliffe M26 ...44 D4
Ramsbottom BL0 ..11 D6
Romiley SK6 .....113 C2
Sale M33 ....108 A6
Salford M7 ....155 F8
Shevington WN6 ..35 C2
Urmston M41 .....95 C2
Whitefield M45 ..62 D6
Wilmslow SK9 ...137 C8
Park Ave N WA12 ..89 C2
Park Ave S WA12 ..89 C2
Park Bank M46 ..58 F6
Park Bglws 8 SK6 ..125 F5
Park Bridge Rd
Oldham OL7,OL8 ..85 A8
Oldham,Park Bridge OL6 ..67 B1
Park Brow Cl M21 ..109 C7
Park Cl Altrincham WA14 ..119 F8
Chadderton OL9 ..104 D2
Glossop SK13 ....104 D2
Stalybridge SK15 ..85 F3
Whitefield M45 ..62 F6
Park Cotts Shaw OL2 ..48 F8
Uppermill OL3 ...68 E5
Park Court Mews SK8 ..122 E4
Park Cres Ashton-u-L OL6 ..85 D3
Bacup OL13 ....3 F8
Chadderton OL9 ..47 F1
Glossop SK13 ....104 B3
Handforth SK9 ...131 B1
Manchester M14 ..98 C3
Wigan WN1 ....37 B1
Park Cres W WN1 ..37 B1
Park Ct Manchester M25 ..162 F2
Rochdale OL11 ...139 F6
Sale M33 ....108 A5
Wythenshawe M22 ..121 D3
Park Dean Com Specl Sch
OL8 ....67 B2
Park Dene Dr SK13 ..104 C2
Park Dr Altrincham WA15 ..
Altrincham,Timperley
WA15 ....120 A7
Eccles M30 ......79 D4
Hyde SK14 ....167 D4
Manchester M14 ..98 C2
Stockport SK4 ...168 B2
Park Edge BL5 ...58 A7
Park Field Rd M20 ..110 A6
Park Gate Ave M20 ..110 B6
Park Gate Cl SK6 ..112 C5
Park Gates Ave SK8 ..123 C1

Park Gates Dr SK8 .....123 C1
Park Gr Manchester M19 ...99 A2
Manchester,Heaton Moor
SK4 .....168 B4
Radcliffe M26 .....43 F4
Walkden M28 .....78 D8
Park Grange WN2 .....56 E4
Park Hey Dr WN6 .....35 E7
Park Hill Cl Manchester M25 ..63 D2
21 Rochdale OL12 .....14 F1
Park Hill Cl SK22 .....127 C1
Park Hill Dr M45 .....62 E8
Park Hill Rd WA15 .....120 A1
Park Hill St BL1 .....145 D8
Park Ho Manchester M20 ..110 A4
Manchester,Levenshulme
M19 .....99 A1
Sale M33 .....120 C7
Droylsden M43 .....100 A8
Park House Bridge Est
M6 .....80 F7
Park House Bridge Rd
M6 .....80 E6
Park Ind Est WN4 .....72 E3
Park La Altrincham WA15 ..120 A1
Dukinfield SK16 .....101 C8
Golborne WN2,WN7 .....74 D6
Horwich BL6 .....22 D3
Leigh WN7 .....76 C4
Little Bollington WA14 ...118 B2
Oldham OL8 .....66 F2
Pendlebury M27 .....80 D6
Poynton SK12 .....133 F3
Rochdale OL16 .....139 F8
Royton OL2 .....48 D4
Royton OL2 .....48 D5
Salford M7 .....155 D8
Salford,Irlams o' th' Height
M6 .....80 C5
Stockport SK1 .....124 B8
Uppermill OL3 .....69 C5
Whitefield M45 .....62 D7
Park La W M27 .....80 D7
Park Lane Ct Salford M7 ..155 D8
Whitefield M45 .....62 D7
Park Lo 1 M19 .....99 A1
Park Lodge Cl SK8 .....122 E4
Park Mdw BL5 .....58 A8
Park Mews M14 .....98 A3
Park Mill Ind Est OL5 ...68 D3
Park Mount SK8 .....122 A5
Park Par Ashton-u-L OL6 ..166 B2
Shaw OL2 .....32 C1
Park Par Ind Est OL6 ...166 A2
Park Pl Manchester SK4 ..110 F2
Manchester,Strangeways
M4 .....159 A3
Prestwich M25 .....63 C5
Salford M6 .....80 A3
Park Range WN2 .....98 D3
Park Rd Adlington PR7 ...20 F6
Altrincham, Bowdon Heath
WA15 .....119 F1
Altrincham,Bowden WA14 ..119 A2
Altrincham,Timperley
WA15 .....120 A7
Bolton BL1 .....144 C7
Bramhall SK8 .....123 C1
Bury BL9 .....140 E4
Cheadle SK8 .....122 E6
Denton M34 .....100 E3
Droylsden M34 .....100 D8
Eccles M30 .....79 D4
Edgworth BL7 .....9 E5
Golborne WA3 .....90 A7
Hadfield SK13 .....104 B8
High Lane SK12 .....134 F6
Hindley WN2 .....56 E3
Hyde SK14 .....167 D4
Little Lever BL3 .....42 F4
Longshaw WN5 .....53 F1
Manchester M25,M8 .....63 E2
Manchester,Heaton Moor
SK4 .....111 B5
Middleton M24 .....65 A8
Oldham OL8 .....153 F5
Oldham,Glodwick OL4,OL8 ..67 A5
Partington M31 .....106 A3
Partington,Warburton
WA13 .....117 C8
Ramsbottom BL0 .....10 F3
Rochdale OL12 .....15 A1
Romiley SK6 .....113 C3
Sale,Ashton upon Mersey
M33 .....108 A6
Sale,Timperley WA15 ...120 B7
Salford M6 .....80 A3
Stalybridge SK3,SK16 ...85 D1
Standish WN6 .....36 E8
Stretford M17,M32 .....96 C3
Stretford M32 .....96 C3
Walkden M28 .....60 D1
Westhoughton BL5 .....57 A6
Wigan,Redwood WN5 .....54 B6
Wigan,Springfield WN6 ..37 A1
Wilmslow SK9 .....136 F7
Wythenshawe SK8 .....121 F5
Park Rd N
Newton-le-W WA12 .....89 E4
Urmston M41 .....95 C2
Park Rd S
Newton-le-W WA12 .....89 D2
Urmston M41 .....95 C2
Park Rise SK6 .....113 C3
Park Road Prim Sch
Altrincham WA14 .....119 E8
Sale M33 .....108 A6

Park Row 3 Bolton BL1 ...24 F6
Manchester M14 .....110 F2
Park Seventeen M45 .....44 F1
Park Side Ave OL2 .....149 C8
Park Sq Ashton-u-L OL6 ..85 E4
Park St Ashton-u-L OL7 ..166 A2
Ashton-u-L OL7 .....166 B2
Atherton M46 .....58 E4
Bolton BL1 .....145 D8
Denton M34 .....100 D3
Droylsden M43 .....84 D2
Farnworth BL4 .....42 D1
Heywood OL10 .....46 E8
Manchester M3 .....158 F3
Mossley OL5 .....86 C8
Oldham OL8 .....153 E5
Oldham OL8 .....153 E6
Pendlebury M27 .....80 A7
Prestwich M25 .....63 C4
Radcliffe M26 .....44 C4
Rochdale OL16 .....139 F6
Romiley SK6 .....112 F3
Royton OL2 .....48 E4
Salford M3 .....158 D1
Salford,Broughton Park
M7 .....155 D8
Shaw OL2 .....149 C7
Stalybridge SK15 .....86 B1
Stockport SK1 .....169 F2
Wigan WN3 .....150 B8
1 Tyldesley M29 .....59 A1
Park Terr Heywood OL10 ..29 D3
Mossley OL5 .....86 C8
Westhoughton BL5 .....39 F1
Whitefield M45 .....62 D7
Park The Stretford M32 ...96 E4
Uppermill OL3 .....69 C5
Uppermill,Lydgate OL4 ...69 D6
Park View Abram WN2 ...56 B1
Ashton-in-M WN4 .....73 B2
2 Bolton BL1 .....24 F6
Chadderton OL9 .....48 B1
Cheadle SK3 .....122 E7
Droylsden M34 .....100 D8
Farnworth BL4 .....42 D1
Gatley SK8 .....122 A6
Hazel Grove SK7 .....134 B8
Ince-in-M WN3 .....56 B7
Kearsley BL4 .....60 F7
Little Bollington WA14 ...118 B2
Littleborough OL15 .....16 B6
Manchester,Burnage M14 ..110 E7
7 Manchester,Longford Park
M21 .....96 F1
Manchester,Moss Side M14 ..98 A4
Newton-le-W WA12 .....89 E3
Romiley SK6 .....112 C3
Stockport SK1 .....124 B7
Park View Ct
Poynton SK12 .....133 E4
Prestwich M25 .....63 B3
Romiley SK6 .....112 C3
Park View Prim Sch M25 ..63 B3
Park View Rd Bolton BL3 ..146 C4
Prestwich M25 .....63 B3
Park View Rise SK22 ...127 C1
Park Way Eccles M17,M41 ..96 A6
Urmston M32,M41 .....95 F5
Parkbridge Wlk M13 ...163 B6
Parkbrook Rd M23 .....121 B7
Parkdale Chadderton OL9 ..48 B1
Tyldesley M29 .....77 B5
Parkdale Ave
Denton M34 .....100 D7
Manchester M18 .....165 C5
Parkdale Rd BL2 .....25 C1
Parkdene Cl BL2 .....25 D4
Parkend Dr WN7 .....75 D2
Parkend Rd M23 .....121 A5
Parker St Bolton BL9 ...141 A2
Manchester M1 .....159 A1
Parkfield Chadderton OL9 ..48 B1
1 Middleton M24 .....64 F8
Salford M5 .....154 D2
Shevington WN6 .....36 B7
Parkfield Ave
Farnworth BL4 .....60 C7
Manchester M14 .....98 B3
Manchester,Sedgley Park
M25 .....63 D3
Marple SK6 .....125 F6
2 Oldham OL8 .....66 B2
Tyldesley M29 .....77 B6
Urmston M41 .....95 B1
Parkfield Cl Leigh WN7 ...76 A7
Tyldesley M29 .....77 B6
Parkfield Ct WA14 .....119 C4
Parkfield Dr
Middleton M24 .....64 E8
Tyldesley M29 .....59 D1
Parkfield Ind Est M24 ...64 F8
Parkfield Lo M20 .....110 A4
Parkfield Prim Sch M24 ..64 E8
Parkfield Rd
Altrincham WA14 .....119 C4
Bolton BL3 .....147 F3
Cheadle SK8 .....122 F1
Parkfield Rd N M40 .....65 F1
Parkfield Rd S M20 .....110 A4
Parkfield St
Manchester M14 .....98 B3
Manchester M14 .....98 B4
Rochdale OL16 .....31 B2
Parkfields
Abram Brow WN2 .....74 C6
Stalybridge SK15 .....86 F2

Parkgate
Altrincham WA14 .....119 B4
Bury BL8 .....26 F5
Chadderton OL9 .....48 B1
Parkgate Dr Bolton BL1 ..25 A5
Pendlebury M27 .....80 A7
Stockport SK2 .....124 B4
Parkgate Way
7 Handforth SK9 .....131 D4
Shaw OL2 .....49 D7
Parkham Cl BL5 .....57 F6
Parkhill Ave M8 .....63 F7
Parkhills Cl Bl.9 .....44 F8
Parkhills Rd BL9 .....44 F8
Parkhouse St M11 .....165 B8
Parkhurst Ave M40 .....65 E1
Parkin Cl SK16 .....101 C8
Parkin St M12 .....99 A3
Parkinson St Bolton BL3 ..144 C5
Bury BL9 .....27 F5
Parklake Ave M7 .....155 E8
Parkland Ave SK22 .....127 C1
Parklands Royton OL2 ...48 C7
Sale M33 .....108 C5
Shaw OL2 .....49 D8
Whitefield M45 .....61 E8
Parklands Dr Aspull WN2 ..38 C6
Sale M33 .....107 D2
Parklands High Sch
M22 .....121 C3
Parklands Rd M23 .....120 F7
Parklands The
Kearsley M26 .....61 B7
Stockport SK4 .....169 E4
Parklands Way SK12 ...133 E4
Parklea Ct 6 M7 .....63 E1
Parklee Com Sch M46 ...58 D2
Parkleigh Dr M40 .....65 E7
Parkmount Rd M9 .....64 E1
Parks Nook BL4 .....60 C7
Parks The WA12 .....73 B1
Parks Yd BL9 .....140 E2
Parkside Hindley WN2 ...56 E6
Parkside Ind Est OL2 ...48 E4
Parkside La M33 .....126 C6
Parkside Rd
Golborne WA12,WA2 .....90 B2
Manchester M14 .....98 A2
Sale M33 .....108 D3
Parkside St BL2 .....25 C1
Parkside Wlk Bury BL9 ..140 F1
Stockport SK7 .....123 E3
Parkstead Dr M9 .....157 D6
Parkstone Ave
Droylsden M18 .....99 F6
Whitefield M45 .....62 E8
Parkstone Dr M27 .....80 B6
Parkstone La M28 .....78 F4
Parkstone Rd M44 .....94 A3
Parksway
Manchester,Higher Blackley
M9 .....64 B6
Manchester,Sedgley Park
M25 .....63 C2
Pendlebury M27 .....80 C6
Parkview Ct M32 .....96 E1
Parkview Pk WA13 .....117 D1
Parkville Rd
Manchester M20 .....110 C5
Prestwich M25 .....63 C6
Parkway Chadderton OL9 ..48 A1
Cheadle SK8 .....122 F7
Denton M34 .....100 C3
New Mills SK22 .....127 C1
Rochdale OL11 .....30 B8
Shevington Moor WN6 ...19 F2
Stockport SK3 .....123 E2
Walkden M38 .....59 F4
Westhoughton BL5 .....57 D6
Wilmslow SK9 .....137 B6
Parkway Bsns Ctr M14 ..97 F2
Parkway Circ M17 .....96 A6
Parkway Four Ind Est
M17 .....96 A6
Parkway Gr M38 .....59 E4
Parkway Ind Est M17 ...96 A6
Parkway Trad Est M32 ...96 A5
Parkwood 8 .....2 D2
Parkwood Cl WN3 .....151 E6
Parkwood Dr BL5 .....58 F7
Parkwood Rd M23 .....121 C7
Parlane St M4 .....159 B3
Parliament Pl BL9 .....140 E1
Parliament St Bury BL9 ..140 E1
Ince-in-M WN3 .....151 E6
Up Holland WN8 .....53 C7
Parndon Dr SK2 .....124 C7
Parnell Ave M22 .....121 D8
Parnell St M29 .....77 B5
Parnham Ct M44 .....94 B8
Parochial CE Prim Sch
OL6 .....85 D3
Parr Cl BL4 .....60 B8

Parr Fold BL9 .....45 B2
Parr Fold Ave M28 .....60 C1
Parr Ho OL8 .....153 F5
Parr La BL9,M45 .....45 B2
Parr St Droylsden M11 ...99 E7
Eccles M30 .....79 C2
Tyldesley M29 .....76 F8
Parrbrook Cl M45 .....45 A1
Parrbrook Wlk M45 .....45 B1
Parrenthorn High Sch
M25 .....63 D7
Parrenthorn Rd M25 .....63 C7
Parrfield Rd M28 .....79 A7
Parrin La M30 .....79 C3
Parrot St Bolton BL3 .....145 E5
Droylsden M11 .....83 C1
Parrs Ct M44 .....93 F2
Parrs Mount Mews SK4 ..110 F2
Parrs Wood Ave M20 ...110 C2
Parrs Wood Entertainment
Ctr M20 .....110 D1
Parrs Wood La M19,M20,
SK4 .....110 D1
Manchester,Burnage M20 ..110 D4
Manchester,East Didsbury
M20 .....122 B8
Parrs Wood Tech Coll
M20 .....110 D1
Parry Mead SK6 .....113 A4
Parry Rd M12 .....99 A4
Parry Wlk 11 OL6 .....166 C3
Parslow Ave M8 .....156 A8
Parson's La BL9 .....140 F3
Parson's Wlk WN1 .....37 B1
Parsonage M3 .....158 F1
Parsonage Brow WN8 ...53 A7
Parsonage Ct Bury BL9 ..141 A3
Salford M5 .....161 C8
Up Holland WN8 .....53 A7
Parsonage Ct
Manchester,Heaton Moor
SK4 .....168 B4
5 Manchester,Withington
M20 .....110 B6
Parsonage Dr M28 .....60 C2
Parsonage Gdns SK6 ...126 A4
Parsonage La M3 .....158 F2
Parsonage Rd
Kearsley M26 .....61 C7
Manchester,Heaton Moor
SK4 .....168 C4
Manchester,Withington
M20 .....110 C2
Urmston M41 .....94 E1
Walkden M28 .....60 C2
Parsonage Ret Pk WN7 ..75 F5
Parsonage St Bury BL9 ..141 A3
Hyde SK14 .....167 D1
Manchester,Crumpsall M8 ..63 F1
Radcliffe M26 .....44 A3
Stockport SK4 .....169 E2
Parsonage Way
Cheadle SK8 .....123 B5
Leigh WN7 .....75 E6
Parsons Dr M24 .....46 F2
Parsons St OL9 .....152 C6
Part St BL5 .....39 E2
Parth St BL9 .....28 D1
Partington Cl
Farnworth BL4 .....42 C1
Glossop SK13 .....104 F1
Partington La M27 .....79 E7
Partington Pk
Glossop SK13 .....104 C3
Trub OL11 .....47 C8
Partington Pl 3 M33 ...108 B5
Partington Prim Sch
M31 .....105 F3
Partington St Bolton BL3 ..146 C2
Eccles M30 .....79 D3
Failsworth M35 .....83 F7
Heywood OL10 .....29 A2
Manchester M40 .....157 F5
4 Oldham OL11 .....67 A7
Rochdale OL11 .....30 B2
Swinton M28 .....79 C8
Wigan WN5 .....54 C6
Partridge Ave M23 .....121 C6
Partridge Cl Irlam M44 ...94 A4
Partridge Ct SK2 .....124 B5
Partridge Rd M35 .....84 C6
Partridge Rise M43 .....84 D3
Partridge St M32 .....96 F5
Partridge Way OL9 .....65 E8
Parvet Ave M43 .....83 F3
Pascal St M19 .....111 A8
Pass St OL9 .....153 D6
Pass The OL16 .....31 A8
Passmonds Cres OL11,
OL12 .....14 B1
Passmonds Way OL12 ...14 B1
Paston Rd M22 .....121 D7
Pasture Cl
Ashton-in-M WN4 .....72 E6
Heywood OL10 .....29 B2
Pasture Field Rd M22 ...121 F1
Pasturefield Cl 1 M33 ..108 F3
Pasturegreen Way M44 ..94 B3
Pastures La OL4 .....68 B8
Patch Croft Rd M22 .....121 F1
Patch La SK7 .....132 D5
Patchett St
Manchester M12 .....164 F6

Patchett St continued
9 Tyldesley M29 .....59 A1
Pateley Sq 2 WN6 .....37 B3
Patey St M12 .....99 A3
Pathfield Wlk 2 M9 ...157 D8
Patience St 11 OL12 ...14 C1
Patmos St M3 .....11 D6
Paton Ave BL3 .....42 A3
Paton Ct M7 .....63 E1
Paton Mews 5 BL3 .....42 A3
Paton St Manchester M1 ..159 B1
Rochdale OL12 .....14 D3
Patricia Dr M28 .....60 E2
Patrick Roddy Ct M18 ..165 C5
Patricroft Rd WN2 .....151 F6
Patricroft Sta M30 .....79 C2
Patten St M20 .....110 B6
Patterdale Ave
Ashton-u-L OL7 .....84 F5
Urmston M41 .....95 B4
Patterdale Cl Oldham OL1 ..49 A1
Rochdale OL11 .....30 B8
Stalybridge SK15 .....86 A3
Patterdale Dr Bury M24 ..44 E7
Middleton M24 .....46 E2
Patterdale Pl WN2 .....56 E7
Patterdale Rd
Ashton-in-M WN4 .....73 A8
Ashton-u-L OL7 .....84 F5
Bolton BL2 .....25 F4
Leigh WN7 .....76 C4
Partington M31 .....105 E3
Romiley SK6 .....113 B4
Stockport SK1 .....124 B7
Woodley SK6 .....113 A3
Patterdale Wlk WA15 ...120 D5
Patterson Ave M21 .....97 A1
Patterson St Bolton BL3 ..146 A4
Denton M34 .....100 F4
Newton-le-W WA12 .....89 B3
Westhoughton BL5 .....57 B7
Patting Cl M44 .....94 C3
Pattishall Cl M4 .....160 D1
Pattison Cl OL12 .....14 D3
Patton Cl BL9 .....45 B2
Paul Ct 6 SK1 .....112 A1
Paul Row OL15 .....6 C1
Paulden Ave Oldham OL4 ..49 E1
Wythenshawe M23 .....121 B6
Paulden Dr M35 .....84 A7
Paulette St 143 E2
Paulhan Rd M20 .....110 D4
Paulhan St BL3 .....147 E3
Pauline St WN2 .....57 B1
Pavilion Cl OL12 .....14 F2
Pavilion Dr OL6 .....85 D5
Pavilion Ho M20 .....110 A4
Pavilion Sq BL5 .....57 E8
Pavilion Wlk M26 .....43 F3
Pavilions The SK8 .....122 D4
Paxford Pl SK9 .....137 A5
Paythorne Sq M14 .....91 F3
Paythorne Gn SK2 .....124 E5
Peabody St BL3 .....147 E4
Peace St Atherton M46 ...58 E3
Bolton BL3 .....145 D5
3 Failsworth M35 .....66 A1
Tyldesley M29 .....76 F7
Peacefield SK6 .....125 E5
Peaceful Prim Sch
SK6 .....125 E5
Peacehaven Ct 12 M11 ..83 C2
Peaceville Rd M19 .....98 F1
Peach Bank M24 .....65 A8
Peach Bank Ho M24 .....65 A8
Peach St OL4 .....49 D1
Peach St M25 .....63 C5
Peach Tree Cl M7 .....155 F6
Peach Tree Ct M6 .....81 A2
Peacock Ave Gatley SK8 ..131 B6
Salford M6 .....80 D5
Peacock Cl
Hadfield SK13 .....171 E4
Manchester M18 .....165 C6
Peacock Fold WN7 .....75 D5
Peacock Gr M18 .....99 D4
Peacock Way 5 SK9 ...131 D5
Peak Bank SK6 .....113 B3
Peak Cl OL4 .....49 F4
Peak Ho 8 SK13 .....104 A5
Peak St Bolton BL1 .....143 D2
Manchester M1 .....159 B1
Oldham OL9 .....152 C6
Stockport SK1 .....112 A1
Peakdale Ave
Manchester M8 .....156 B8
Peakdale Rd
Droylsden M43 .....83 D3
Hadfield SK13 .....171 E3
Marple SK6 .....126 A4
Peaknaze Cl
Glossop SK13 .....116 B8
Pendlebury M27 .....80 B8
Pear Ave BL9 .....141 C3
Pear Cl M24 .....65 B6
Pear Ind Est SK6 .....112 C2
Pear Tree Cl
Hadfield SK13 .....171 E4
Marple SK6 .....126 A8
Salford M6 .....81 A2
Pear Tree Ct Aspull WN2 ..52 A1
3 Salford M6 .....81 A2
Pear Tree Dr SK15 .....86 B2
Pear Tree Gr M29 .....59 E1

Pear Tree Wlk 10 M33 ...107 C5
Pearl Ave M7 ...63 E1
Pearl Brook Ind Est BL6 ..22 B3
Pearl Mill Cl OL8 ...67 B4
Pearl St Denton M34 ...100 E3
Hazel Grove SK7 ...124 E4
Rochdale OL11 ...30 C8
Wigan WN6 ...37 B3
Pearl Way SK14 ...103 A2
Pearly Bank OL1 ...49 D4
Pearn Ave M19 ...110 F5
Pearn Rd M19 ...110 F5
Pearson Cl Milnrow OL16 ..31 F7
Partington M31 ...106 A3
Pearson Gr 7 OL4 ...67 E6
Pearson Ho M30 ...95 D8
Pearson Mews SK16 ...101 C6
Pearson St Bury BL9 ...141 B3
Dukinfield SK16 ...101 C6
Reddish SK5 ...169 F3
Rochdale OL16 ...31 C8
Peart Ave SK6 ...113 C6
Peart St M34 ...100 E3
Peartree Ct OL10 ...46 A8
Peartree Wlk M22 ...121 B4
Peary St M4 ...159 B3
Peaslake Cl SK6 ...113 D2
Peatfield Ave M27 ...61 E2
Peatfield Wlk M15 ...162 F5
Pebble Cl SK15 ...86 A4
Pebworth Cl M24,M9 ...64 F5
Peckford Dr M40 ...83 A5
Peckforton Cl SK8 ...122 A5
Peckforton Wlk 11 SK9 ..131 E1
Peckmill Cl SK9 ...131 E2
Pedder St BL1 ...142 C1
Pedler Brow La OL12 ...15 E6
Pedley Wlk M13 ...163 B7
Peebles Cl WN4 ...72 C4
Peebles Dr M40 ...83 D4
Peel Ave
Altrincham WA14 ...119 D2
Ramsbottom BL0 ...138 A5
Peel Brow BL0 ...11 D6
Peel Brow Sch BL0 ...11 D6
Peel Cl M46 ...58 E3
Peel Cnr M29 ...77 B8
Peel Cott St OL14 ...6 A8
Peel Cottage Rd OL14 ...6 A8
Peel Cross Rd M5 ...81 A1
Peel Ct SK2 ...124 A6
Peel Ctr The SK1 ...112 A2
Peel Dr Sale M33 ...108 E4
Walkden M38 ...59 F4
Peel Gr Manchester M12 ...99 A4
Worsley M28 ...78 F8
Peel Green Rd M30 ...95 C8
Peel Green Trad Est M30 .95 B8
Peel Hall Ave M29 ...59 B1
Peel Hall Prim Sch
Walkden M38 ...59 F3
Wythenshawe M22 ...121 F3
Peel Hall Rd
Ramsbottom BL0,BL9 ...11 B2
Wythenshawe M22 ...121 F2
Peel Ind Est BL9 ...140 E3
Peel La Heywood OL10 ...29 B3
Manchester M8 ...159 B4
Tyldesley M29 ...77 C4
Walkden M28,M38 ...59 F3
Peel Moat Ct SK4 ...111 B5
Peel Moat Rd SK4 ...111 B5
Peel Moat Sports Ctr
SK4 ...111 B5
Peel Mount
Ramsbottom BL0 ...11 A4
Salford M6 ...81 B3
Peel Park Cres M38 ...59 F4
Peel Rd WA15 ...119 E3
Peel Sq M18 ...99 D5
Peel St Adlington PR6 ...21 B8
Ashton-u-L OL6 ...166 B3
Chadderton OL9 ...152 B7
Denton M34 ...100 E4
Denton,Audenshaw M34 ...100 E6
Droylsden M43 ...99 F8
Dukinfield SK16 ...166 C1
Eccles M30 ...79 F2
Failsworth M35 ...83 D6
Farnworth BL4 ...60 E8
Hadfield SK13 ...104 C5
Heywood OL10 ...29 B2
Hyde SK14 ...167 F1
Leigh WN7 ...75 E5
Littleborough OL15 ...16 B5
Newton-le-W WA12 ...89 A3
Platt Bridge WN2 ...56 A2
1 Radcliffe M26 ...44 B2
Rochdale OL12 ...139 E8
Stalybridge SK15 ...85 F1
Stockport SK2 ...170 F6
Westhoughton BL5 ...39 E1
Peel Terr 19 SK16 ...166 B1
Peel Twr* BL8 ...10 F5
Peel View BL8 ...27 A6
Peel Way BL9 ...140 E2
Peelgate Dr SK8 ...122 A2
Peels Ave OL4 ...68 A7
Peelwood Ave M38 ...60 A4
Peelwood Gr M46 ...58 E2
Peerglow Pk Est WA14 ..119 E8
Peers Cl M41 ...94 D4
Peers St BL8 ...27 C2
Pegamoid St BL2 ...25 B1
Pegasus Ct Rochdale OL11 .30 C6
Pegasus Ct *continued*
Sale M33 ...108 D5
Pegasus Sq M7 ...81 C3
Pegwell Dr M7 ...155 E5
Pekin St OL6 ...166 C4
Pelham Pl M8 ...64 B2
Pelham St Ashton-u-L OL7 ..84 E1
Bolton BL3 ...146 C3
Oldham OL8 ...66 F2
Pellowe Rd OL8 ...66 E4
Pelton Ave M27 ...61 D2
Pelton Wlk M40 ...157 D5
Pemberlei Rd WN2 ...38 D2
Pemberton Com High Sch
WN5 ...54 C7
Pemberton Ho OL2 ...149 B8
Pemberton Prim Sch
WN5 ...54 C6
Pemberton Rd WN3,WN5 .54 B2
Pemberton St
Bolton BL1 ...143 E4
Manchester M16 ...97 C4
3 Rochdale OL11 ...30 C2
Walkden M38 ...60 B4
Pemberton Sta WN3 ...54 D4
Pemberton Way OL2 ...149 B8
Pembridge Fold M24 ...65 C8
Pembridge Rd M9 ...64 F4
Pembroke Ave
Eccles M30 ...79 D2
Sale M33 ...107 F5
Pembroke Cl Horwich BL6 .22 A4
Manchester M13 ...164 D6
Pembroke Ct
Hazel Grove SK7 ...124 E2
Pendlebury M27 ...80 B8
14 Rochdale OL12 ...14 F1
Romiley SK6 ...112 F2
Pembroke Dr Bury BL9 ...44 E7
Oldham OL4 ...49 E4
Pembroke Gr M44 ...105 C6
Pembroke Ho 3 SK3 ...170 E8
Pembroke Rd
Hindley WN2 ...57 C3
Wigan WN5 ...36 D1
Pembroke St Bolton BL1 .145 D8
Littleborough OL15 ...16 B6
Oldham OL8 ...153 D6
Salford,Higher Broughton
M7 ...155 E6
3 Salford,Seedley M6 ...154 E1
Pembroke Way 6 M34 ..101 A1
Pembry Cl SK5 ...112 B5
Pembury Cl M22 ...121 C3
Penarth Rd Bolton BL3 ...146 B4
Wythenshawe M22 ...121 D8
Penbeen Cl M22 ...121 E1
Penbury Rd WN1 ...37 B5
Pencarrow Cl M20 ...109 F3
Pencombe Cl M12 ...165 A5
Pencroft Way M15 ...163 A5
Pendeen Cl M29 ...77 A7
Pendennis 2 OL11 ...139 E6
Pendennis Ave BL6 ...40 D5
Pendennis Cl M26 ...43 C5
Pendennis Cres WN2 ...57 A3
Pendennis Rd SK4 ...168 C3
Pendle Ave BL1 ...24 E6
Pendle Cl Bury BL8 ...27 B3
Oldham OL4 ...67 D5
Wigan WN5 ...54 D5
Pendle Ct BL1 ...143 D3
Pendle Dr BL6 ...22 C5
Pendle Gdns WA3 ...91 E2
Pendle Gr OL2 ...48 C3
Pendle Rd Denton M34 ...100 F2
Golborne WA3 ...74 C1
Pendle Wlk SK5 ...112 A4
Pendlebury Cl M25 ...62 F2
Pendlebury Ct SK3 ...124 A4
Pendlebury Fold BL3 ...40 D2
Pendlebury La WN1,WN2 .37 D6
Pendlebury Rd
Gatley SK8 ...122 B6
Swinton M27 ...79 F8
Pendlebury St BL1 ...143 F3
Pendlebury Twrs SK5 ...169 F3
Pendlecroft Ave M27 ...80 C7
Pendlegreen Cl M11 ...164 F8
Pendleton Coll M6 ...154 D4
Pendleton Coll (De La Salle
Ctr) M6 ...80 C3
Pendleton Gn 3 M6 ...154 F3
Pendleton Way M6 ...154 F3
Pendleway M27 ...62 A1
Pendragon Pl M35 ...84 A7
Pendrell Wlk 32 M9 ...64 E3
Penelope Rd 4 M6 ...80 D5
Penerly Dr M9 ...157 D6
Penfair Cl M11 ...83 A1
Penfield Cl M1 ...163 B7
Penfold Wlk M12 ...164 F6
Pengarth Rd BL6 ...22 C4
Pengham Wlk M23 ...109 A1
Pengwern Ave 3 BL3 ...146 B4
Penhale Mews SK7 ...132 F7
Penhall Wlk M40 ...83 A5
Peninsula M7 ...81 B7
Penistone Ave
Manchester M9 ...65 A3
Rochdale OL16 ...31 C6
Salford M6 ...80 C3
Penketh Ave
Manchester M18 ...99 B4
Tyldesley M29 ...77 B6
Penketh St WN6 ...37 B2
Penleach Ave WN7 ...76 B5
Penmere Gr M33 ...107 E1
Penmoor Chase SK7 ...124 B1
Penmore Cl OL2 ...49 D7
Penn Gn SK8 ...123 B1
Penn House Cl SK7 ...132 E8
Penn St Farnworth BL4 ...60 C8
Heywood OL10 ...29 D1
Horwich BL6 ...22 C3
Manchester M40 ...157 F8
Oldham OL8 ...153 D5
Rochdale OL16 ...139 F8
Pennant Dr M25 ...63 A5
Pennant St OL1 ...67 B8
Pennant Street Ind Est 9
OL1 ...67 B8
Pennell Dr 3 WN3 ...54 F5
Pennell St M11 ...83 D1
Pennine Ave
Chadderton OL9 ...152 A5
Wigan WN3 ...54 C2
Pennine Bsns Pk OL10 ...46 B8
Pennine Cl Bury BL8 ...27 B3
Horwich BL6 ...22 C5
Manchester M9 ...64 F4
Pennine Ct
3 Oldham OL4 ...67 A6
Stalybridge SK15 ...86 D3
Swinton M27 ...62 A1
Pennine Dr
Altrincham WA14 ...119 B5
Ashton-u-L OL6 ...85 E4
Milnrow OL16 ...32 A6
Wardle OL12 ...15 C6
Pennine Gr Ashton-u-L OL6 .85 E6
Leigh WN7 ...75 C8
Pennine La WA3 ...74 C1
Pennine Prec 3 OL16 ...31 F5
Pennine Rd
Glossop SK13 ...116 A8
Horwich BL6 ...22 C5
Romiley SK6 ...113 C6
Stockport SK7 ...124 B1
Pennine Sq OL1 ...48 D1
Pennine Terr 2 SK16 ...166 C1
Pennine Vale OL2 ...149 C8
Pennine View
Denton M34 ...100 E5
Littleborough OL15 ...6 D2
Mossley OL5 ...68 D1
Royton OL2 ...48 E4
Stalybridge SK15 ...86 C4
Pennine Wlk WN2 ...56 B2
Pennington Ave WN7 ...75 E3
Pennington Cl
Pennington Green WN2 ...38 E2
Walkden M38 ...59 E4
Pennington Ct WN7 ...75 B1
Pennington Dr WA12 ...89 E3
Pennington Flash Ctry Pk*
WN7 ...75 B3
Pennington Gdns WN7 ...75 E3
Pennington Green La
WN2 ...38 E2
Pennington La
Ince-in-M WN2 ...56 A8
Standish WN2 ...37 E8
Pennington Mews WN7 ...75 E2
Pennington Rd
Bolton BL3 ...147 F3
Leigh WN7 ...75 F3
Pennington St Bury BL8 ...26 F4
7 Hindley WN2 ...56 D6
Manchester M12 ...99 A2
Oldham OL9 ...66 B3
1 Walkden M28 ...60 E2
Pennon Cl M7 ...155 E6
Penny Black Chambers
M28 ...78 F5
Penny Bridge La M41 ...95 A2
Penny Brook Fold SK7 ...124 F3
Penny La Haydock WA11 ...89 A7
Stockport SK5 ...169 F3
Penny Mdw OL6 ...166 C3
Pennygate Cl WN2 ...56 D6
Pennyhurst St WN3 ...150 B7
Pennymoor Dr WA14 ...119 B6
Penrhos Ave SK8 ...121 F4
Penrhyn Ave
Cheadle SK8 ...122 E1
Middleton M24 ...65 A7
Penrhyn Cres SK7 ...133 C8
Penrhyn Dr
Hazel Grove SK7 ...124 D1
Prestwich M25 ...63 B4
Penrhyn Gr M46 ...58 C5
Penrhyn Rd SK3 ...123 C8
Penrice Cl M26 ...43 D5
Penrice Fold M28 ...78 B7
Penrith Ave
Ashton-u-L OL7 ...84 F5
Bolton BL1 ...142 A1
Droylsden M11 ...83 B3
Oldham OL8 ...66 C4
Prestwich M45 ...63 B7
Reddish SK5 ...99 F1
Sale M33 ...108 C2
Walkden M28 ...60 F2
Penrith Cl M31 ...105 E4
Penrith Cres WN4 ...73 B4
Penrith St OL11 ...139 F5
Penrod Pl M6 ...81 B4
Penrose Gdns M24 ...47 B1
Penrose St BL2 ...148 C7
Penrose Wlk M24 ...47 A4
Penroy Ave M20 ...109 D3
Penroyson Cl M12 ...164 F6
Penruddock Wlk 4 M13 ...98 F4
Penry Ave M44 ...105 E6
Penryn Ave Royton OL2 ...48 F3
Penryn Ave *continued*
Sale M33 ...108 C1
Penryn Ct M7 ...63 D1
Pensarn Ave M14 ...110 E8
Pensarn Gr SK5 ...169 F4
Pensby Cl M27 ...80 C7
Pensby Wlk M40 ...157 D5
Pensford Ct BL2 ...25 E6
Pensford Rd M23 ...120 F3
Penshaw Ave WN3 ...55 B3
Penshurst Rd SK5 ...112 B6
Penshurst Wlk 20 M34 ..101 A1
Penson St WN1 ...37 D2
Penswick Rd WN2 ...57 C3
Penthorpe Dr OL2 ...48 F3
Pentland Ave M40 ...65 C2
Pentland Cl SK7 ...124 B1
Pentland Terr BL1 ...143 E1
Pentland Way SK14 ...102 B6
Pentlands Ave M7 ...155 D5
Pentlands The 4 OL2 ...48 F8
Pentwyn Gr M23 ...121 B7
Penydarren View 9 BL4 ..42 C2
Penzance Pl 3 OL9 ...48 A1
Penzance St M40 ...160 E3
Peoples History Mus*
M3 ...158 E1
Peover Ave M33 ...108 E4
Peover Rd SK9 ...131 E5
Peover Wlk SK8 ...123 A5
Pepler Ave M23 ...109 B2
Peploe Wlk M23 ...108 D1
Pepper Ct SK9 ...137 A6
Pepper La WN6 ...19 B3
Pepper Mill La WN1 ...151 D7
Pepper Rd SK7 ...124 B2
Pepper St WA16 ...128 F1
Pepperhill Rd M16 ...97 F4
Peppermint Cl OL16 ...32 C4
Pepperwood Dr WN3 ...54 E2
Pepys Pl WN3 ...55 A4
Perceval Way WN2 ...56 D4
Perch St 4 WN1 ...37 E1
Perch Wlk 4 M4 ...159 C1
Percival Cl M8 ...155 F6
Percival Rd M43 ...84 B1
Percival Wlk OL2 ...48 E3
Percy Dr M5 ...161 B7
Percy Rd M34 ...100 E2
Percy St Bolton BL1 ...143 F2
Bury BL9 ...141 B3
Farnworth BL4 ...60 E7
Manchester M15 ...162 D6
Oldham OL4 ...67 C7
Ramsbottom BL0 ...138 B5
Rochdale OL16 ...31 B5
Stalybridge SK15 ...86 B2
Stockport SK1 ...169 F2
Whitworth OL12 ...4 E6
Peregrin Dr WN7 ...76 B5
Peregrine Cres M43 ...84 C3
Peregrine Dr M44 ...94 A3
Peregrine Rd SK2 ...125 A4
Peregrine St M15,M16 ...162 F5
Perendale Rise BL1 ...143 E4
Periton Wlk 8 M9 ...64 E3
Perivale Dr OL8 ...67 B4
Perkins Ave M7 ...155 E5
Pernham St OL4 ...67 C7
Perrin St SK14 ...167 D2
Perry Ave SK14 ...102 A4
Perry Brook Com Prim Sch
WN4 ...73 A7
Perry Cl OL11 ...139 D5
Perry Rd WA15 ...120 B6
Perrybrook Wlk WN4 ...73 D4
Perrygate Ave M20 ...110 A6
Perrymead M25 ...63 C6
Perryn Pl WN6 ...19 F1
Pershore 8 OL12 ...139 E8
Pershore Rd M24 ...47 A3
Perth 4 M30 ...79 E2
Perth Ave Chadderton OL9 .66 A4
Ince-in-M WN2 ...56 A8
Perth Cl SK7 ...132 F5
Perth Rd OL11 ...31 B2
Perth St Bolton BL3 ...146 C3
Royton OL2 ...49 A4
Swinton M27 ...79 D7
Peru St M3 ...158 D2
Peter Martin St 2 BL6 ...22 B4
Peter Moss Way M19 ...99 C1
Peter St
Altrincham WA14 ...119 D3
Ashton-in-M WN4 ...73 C3
Bury BL9 ...140 F3
Denton M34 ...101 A3
Eccles M30 ...79 D1
Golborne WA3 ...90 A8
Hadfield SK13 ...104 A6
Hazel Grove SK7 ...124 D3
Hindley WN2 ...56 D5
Leigh WN7 ...76 B4
Manchester M2,M3 ...162 F8
Oldham OL1 ...153 F6
Stockport SK1 ...112 A2
14 Tyldesley M29 ...58 F1
Westhoughton BL5 ...57 A7
Wigan WN5 ...54 B8
Peterborough Cl OL6 ...85 B6
Peterborough Dr 10
BL1 ...143 F1
Peterborough St 1 M18 ..99 F6
Peterborough Wlk BL1 ..143 E1
Peterchurch Wlk M11 ...165 C8
Peterhead Cl BL1 ...143 D1
Peterhead Wlk 4 M5 ...81 A1
Peterhouse Gdns SK6 ...113 C4
Peterhouse Wlk WN4 ...72 F4
Peterloo Ct 5 M5 ...154 E2
Peterloo Terr 8 M24 ...47 A2
Peters Ct WA15 ...120 D5
Petersburg Rd SK3 ...170 D6
Petersfield Dr M23 ...120 D7
Petersfield Gdns WA3 ...91 E4
Petersfield Wlk 1 BL1 ..145 E8
Peterswood Cl M22 ...121 B3
Peterwood Gdns M32 ...96 A1
Petheridge Dr 3 M22 ...121 B1
Petrel Ave SK12 ...133 B4
Petrel Cl Droylsden M43 ...84 C3
Rochdale OL11 ...29 F7
Stockport SK3 ...170 D6
Tyldesley M29 ...77 A8
Petrie Ct M6 ...81 B4
Petrie St OL12 ...139 F8
Petrock Wlk 5 M40 ...83 C5
Petticoat La WN2 ...56 B7
Petts Cres OL15 ...16 A6
Petunia Wlk 8 M28 ...59 F3
Petworth Ave WN3 ...54 D2
Petworth Cl M22 ...121 E5
Petworth Rd OL9 ...152 B6
Pevensey Ct M9 ...65 A2
Pevensey Rd M6 ...80 E5
Pevensey Wlk OL9 ...152 B6
Peveril Ave SK22 ...127 C1
Peveril Cl M45 ...63 C7
Peveril Cres M21 ...97 A2
Peveril Ct SK13 ...116 F8
Peveril Dr SK7 ...133 F8
Peveril Rd
Altrincham WA14 ...119 C7
Oldham OL1 ...49 C1
Salford M5 ...154 D2
Peveril St BL3 ...146 C3
Peveril Terr SK14 ...113 F8
Pewfist Gn BL5 ...57 E6
Pewfist Spinney The BL5 .57 D7
Pewfist The BL5 ...57 E7
Pewsey Rd M22 ...121 F3
Pexhill Ct SK4 ...168 A2
Pexwood OL1 ...47 E1
Pheasant Cl M28 ...78 B6
Pheasant Dr M21 ...109 D7
Pheasant Rise WA14 ...119 D1
Phelan Cl M40 ...156 C5
Phethean St Bolton BL2 ..148 A7
Farnworth BL4 ...42 C2
Philip Ave M34 ...100 E5
Philip Cl 6 WN5 ...54 D5
Philip Dr M33 ...108 B2
Philip Howard Ct 2 BL4 ..60 C8
Philip Howard Rd SK13 .116 C8
Philip St Bolton BL3 ...145 D5
Eccles M30 ...79 D1
Oldham OL4 ...67 C8
Rochdale OL11 ...139 F5
Philips Ave BL4 ...60 D7
Philips Dr M45 ...62 D6
Philips High Sch M45 ...62 E8
Philips Park Rd
Manchester M11 ...160 E2
Whitefield M45 ...62 D6
Whitefield M45 ...62 F6
Phillimore St OL4 ...67 E5
Phillip Way 1 SK14 ...102 E1
Phillips Pl M45 ...62 F7
Phillips St WN7 ...75 E8
Phipps St M28 ...60 C4
Phoebe St 5 Bolton BL3 .146 C4
Salford M5 ...161 B8
Phoenix Cl OL10 ...29 F1
Phoenix Ind Est M35 ...84 A8
Phoenix Park Ind Est
OL10 ...29 F1
Phoenix Pl OL4 ...67 F7
Phoenix St Bolton BL1 ...148 A8
Bury BL9 ...140 E2
Farnworth BL4 ...60 D7
Littleborough OL15 ...16 B6
Manchester M2 ...159 A1
Oldham OL1 ...153 F6
Oldham,County End OL4 ...67 F7
Rochdale OL12 ...14 C1
Phoenix Way
Radcliffe M26 ...44 A2
Urmston M41 ...95 E6
Phyllis St Middleton M24 ..65 C7
Rochdale OL12 ...14 B1
Picadilly WN5 ...71 E5
Piccadilly Manchester M1 .159 B1
Stockport SK1 ...169 F1
Piccadilly Gdns M1 ...159 A1
Piccadilly Gdns Sta M1 .159 A1
Piccadilly Plaza M1 ...159 A1
Piccadilly Sta M1 ...163 B8
Piccadilly Trad Est M1 ..163 C8
Piccadilly Village* M1 159 C1
Pickering Cl
Altrincham WA15 ...120 A7
Bury BL8 ...27 B5
Kearsley M26 ...61 A8
Urmston M41 ...95 B2
Pickford Ave BL3 ...43 C3
Pickford Ct M15 ...162 E5
Pickford La SK16 ...101 C8
Pickford Mews SK16 ...101 C8
Pickford St M4 ...159 B2
Pickford Wlk OL2 ...48 E3
Pickford's Brow SK1 ...169 F1
Pickhill La OL3 ...69 B8
Pickhill Mews OL3 ...69 B8
Pickley Gn WN7 ...57 E1
Pickmere Ave M20 ...110 B8

Pickmere Cl
4 Droylsden M43 ....84 B1
Stockport SK3 ....123 C6
Wythenshawe M33 ....108 F2
Pickmere Ct 10 SK9 ....131 D5
Pickmere Gdns SK8 ....122 F4
Pickmere Mews OL3 ....69 B8
Pickmere Rd SK9 ....131 D5
Pickmere Terr 2 SK16 ....166 B1
Picksley St WN7 ....76 B4
Pickthorn Cl WN2 ....56 B3
Pickup St Ince-in-M WN2 ....151 F7
Rochdale OL16 ....31 A7
Pickwick Rd SK12 ....133 D3
Picton Cl M3 ....158 E2
Picton Dr SK9 ....131 E2
Picton Sq 4 OL4 ....67 A6
Picton St Ashton-u-L OL7 ....85 A6
Salford M7 ....158 D3
Picton Wlk 5 M16 ....97 F3
Pictor Sch WA15 ....120 A7
Pierce St OL1 ....49 C1
Piercy Ave M7 ....158 D4
Piercy St Failsworth M35 ....83 E7
Manchester M4 ....160 D2
Pierpoint St WA3 ....90 A7
Piethorne Cl OL16 ....32 C4
Pigeon St M1 ....159 B1
Piggott St BL4 ....60 C7
Pigot St 2 WN5 ....54 B6
Pike Ave Atherton M46 ....58 A2
Failsworth M35 ....84 C6
Pike Fold La M9 ....64 C3
Pike Fold Prim Sch M9 ....64 C3
Pike Nook Wkshp BL3 ....145 D5
Pike Rd BL3 ....147 D4
Pike St OL11 ....139 F5
Pike View BL6 ....22 D4
Pike View Cl OL4 ....67 B5
Pike's La SK13 ....116 B8
Pikehouse Cotts OL15 ....16 D7
Pikes Lane Prim Sch
BL3 ....145 D6
Pilgrim Dr M11 ....160 F1
Pilgrims Way WN6 ....37 A7
Pilkington Dr M45 ....45 B2
Pilkington Rd
Kearsley BL4 ....60 F6
Manchester M9 ....65 A3
Radcliffe M26 ....43 F4
Pilkington St Bolton BL3 ....145 E5
Hindley WN2 ....56 D6
Middleton M24 ....47 C1
Ramsbottom BL0 ....138 B5
Pilkington Way M26 ....44 A2
Pilling Field BL7 ....8 E1
Pilling St Bury BL8 ....27 C3
Denton M34 ....100 F3
Leigh WN7 ....75 D5
3 Rawtenstall BB4 ....2 F8
Rochdale OL12 ....139 D8
Pilling Wlk OL9 ....152 A6
Pilning St BL3 ....42 A4
Pilot Ind Est BL3 ....42 B4
Pilot St BL9 ....140 F1
Pilsley Cl WN5 ....36 A1
Pilsworth Cotts BL9 ....45 C5
Pilsworth Rd OL10 ....46 A8
Pilsworth Way BL9 ....45 A6
Pimblett St Golborne WA3 ....90 A7
Manchester M3 ....158 F3
Pimbo La WN8 ....53 A4
Pimhole Rd BL9 ....141 A2
Pimlico Cl M7 ....155 D6
Pimlott Gr
Dukinfield SK14 ....101 D5
Prestwich M25 ....62 F2
Pimlott Rd BL1 ....25 B3
Pimmcroft Way M33 ....109 A3
Pin Mill Brow M12 ....164 D8
Pincher Wlk 14 M11 ....83 C1
Pinder Wlk 5 M15 ....162 F6
Pine Ave
Newton-le-W WA12 ....89 D2
Whitefield M45 ....62 F6
Pine Cl Denton M34 ....100 E6
Marple SK6 ....125 E4
Pine Ct Manchester M20 ....110 A4
Stockport SK7 ....123 D2
Pine Gr Denton M34 ....101 A3
Eccles M30 ....79 E4
Farnworth BL4 ....60 B8
Golborne WA3 ....90 C8
Manchester M13,M14 ....98 E4
Prestwich M45 ....63 A6
Royton OL2 ....48 D6
Sale M33 ....107 D6
Stalybridge SK16 ....101 F8
Swinton M27 ....79 D7
Westhoughton BL5 ....57 E7
Worsley M28 ....78 E8
Pine Lo SK7 ....132 F7
Pine Mdw M26 ....61 C6
Pine Rd Bramhall SK7 ....132 F8
Dukinfield SK15 ....101 E8
Manchester M20 ....110 B4
Poynton SK12 ....133 F3
Wigan WN5 ....54 E6
Pine St Ashton-u-L OL6 ....166 B4
Bolton BL1 ....143 F2
Bury BL9 ....141 B2
Chadderton OL9 ....152 A8
Dukinfield SK16 ....101 D5
Heywood OL10 ....29 D2
Littleborough OL15 ....16 B6
Manchester M1 ....159 A1
Middleton M24 ....65 C7
Newhey OL16 ....32 B4
Pine St *continued*
Radcliffe M26 ....44 B4
Rochdale OL16 ....31 B7
Romiley SK6 ....113 B5
5 Tyldesley M29 ....59 A1
Pine St N BL9 ....141 B3
Pine St S BL9 ....141 B3
Pine Tree Rd OL8 ....66 D1
Pine View WN3 ....54 B1
Pine Wlk 1 M31 ....105 E3
Pineapple St SK7 ....124 E2
Pinehurst Rd M40 ....157 E5
Pinelea WA15 ....119 F4
Pines The WN7 ....75 F3
Pinetop Cl M21 ....109 D7
Pinetree St M18 ....165 C5
Pinevale WN6 ....37 A7
Pineway OL4 ....67 F6
Pinewood
Altrincham WA14 ....119 A2
Ashton-in-M WN4 ....73 A2
Chadderton OL9 ....65 E7
Sale M33 ....107 D4
Pinewood Cl
Abram Brow WN2 ....74 C7
30 Bolton BL1 ....143 E2
Dukinfield SK16 ....166 C1
Manchester SK4 ....168 A3
Pinewood Cres
Ince-in-M WN2 ....151 F6
Orrell WN5 ....53 E6
Ramsbottom BL0 ....11 B2
Pinewood Ct
Altrincham WA14 ....119 E1
Sale M33 ....108 D5
Pinewood Rd
Manchester M21 ....109 A7
Wilmslow SK9 ....137 E8
Pinewoods The SK6 ....113 B5
Pinfold Hadfield SK13 ....171 E4
Rochdale OL11 ....139 E6
Pinfold Ave M9 ....65 A2
Pinfold Cl
Altrincham WA15 ....129 D7
Westhoughton BL5 ....57 D5
Pinfold Ct 4 M32 ....96 C1
Pinfold Dr Cheadle SK8 ....123 A1
Prestwich M25 ....62 F5
Pinfold La Romiley SK6 ....113 E4
Whitefield M45 ....62 F8
Wythenshawe M90,WA15 ....129 F6
Pinfold Prim Sch SK14 ....102 E1
Pinfold Rd M28 ....60 C1
Pinfold St WN2 ....56 A7
Pingate Dr SK8 ....132 A6
Pingate La SK8 ....132 A6
Pingate La S SK8 ....132 A6
Pingle La OL3 ....50 E5
Pingot OL2 ....32 D1
Pingot Ave M23 ....109 B1
Pingot Ct 6 WN7 ....75 D5
Pingot La SK14 ....103 B1
Pingot Rd WN5 ....71 E5
Pingot The Irlam M44 ....94 B3
Leigh WN7 ....75 D5
Pingott La 5 SK13 ....104 A5
Pinhigh Pl M6 ....80 B6
Pink Bank La M12 ....99 A4
Pinnacle Dr BL7 ....8 E2
Pinner Pl M19 ....111 A6
Pinners Cl BL0 ....138 B7
Pinnington La M32 ....96 D2
Pinnington Rd M18 ....99 D6
Pintail Ave SK3 ....170 D6
Pintail Cl 5 OL12 ....14 B2
Pinwood Ct 13 SK9 ....131 E1
Pioneer Cl BL6 ....22 C4
Pioneer Ct OL7 ....166 A1
Pioneer Ind Est WN5 ....54 E6
Pioneer Rd M27 ....62 D2
Pioneer St Droylsden M11 ....83 B2
Horwich BL6 ....22 C4
4 Littleborough OL15 ....16 B5
Walsden OL14 ....6 A7
Pioneers St 4 OL11 ....31 A6
Pioneers Villa OL16 ....32 E4
Piper Hill High Sch
M23 ....109 B2
Piperhill Ave M22 ....109 D2
Pipers Cl OL11 ....29 D8
Pipers Ct M44 ....94 C3
Pipers The WA3 ....90 F8
Pipewell Ave M18 ....165 C5
Pipit Ave WA12 ....89 C3
Pipit Cl M34 ....84 C2
Pirie Wlk 4 M40 ....83 C6
Pit La OL16,OL2 ....31 D1
Pit St M34 ....100 F3
Pitcairn Ho 12 M30 ....79 D1
Pitchcombe Rd M22 ....121 B2
Pitcombe Cl BL1 ....24 D7
Pitfield Gdns M23 ....120 F7
Pitfield La BL2 ....25 F4
Pitfield St BL2 ....148 B7
Pitman Cl M11 ....165 A8
Pitmore Wlk 3 M40 ....65 D2
Pits Farm Ave OL11 ....30 C7
Pitsford Rd M40 ....157 E5
Pitshouse OL12 ....13 E2
Pitshouse La OL12 ....13 E2
Pitt St Denton M34 ....100 F6
Heywood OL10 ....29 C2
Hyde SK14 ....167 D3
Ince-in-M WN3 ....151 D6
Oldham OL4 ....67 A5
Radcliffe M26 ....43 E3
Rochdale OL12 ....139 F8
Stockport SK3 ....170 D8
Pitt St *continued*
Wigan WN3 ....150 B7
Pitt St E OL4 ....67 B5
Pittbrook St M12 ....164 D7
Pixmore Ave BL1 ....25 B4
Place Rd WA14 ....119 C6
Place The M1 ....159 B1
Plain Pit St SK14 ....101 C5
Plainsfield St 8 M16 ....97 E4
Plane Ave WN5 ....54 E7
Plane Ct 4 M6 ....81 A2
Plane Rd M35 ....83 F5
Plane St OL4 ....67 C7
Plane Tree Cl SK6 ....125 D5
Plane Tree Gr WA11 ....89 A7
Plane Tree Rd M31 ....105 D3
Planet Way M34 ....100 E5
Planetree Rd WA15 ....120 A2
Planetree Wlk M23 ....120 C8
Plank La WN7 ....75 B4
Plant Cl M33 ....108 A5
Plant Hill High Sch M9 ....64 C4
Plant Hill Rd M9 ....64 D4
Plant St M1 ....159 B1
Plantagenet Wlk M40 ....83 D4
Plantation Ave M28 ....60 C4
Plantation Gates WN1 ....37 E2
Plantation Gr BL9 ....45 C4
Plantation Ind Est OL6 ....85 D2
Plantation Rd BL7 ....9 F7
Plantation St
Ashton-u-L OL6 ....85 D2
Bacup OL13 ....3 C8
Manchester M18 ....99 E5
Plantation View BL9 ....11 C3
Plasden Ct M23 ....121 A5
Plate St OL1 ....153 F7
Plato St OL9 ....153 D7
Platt Ave OL6 ....85 C6
Platt Cl OL16 ....32 A5
Platt Croft WN7 ....76 C4
Platt Ct M14 ....98 C2
Platt Fold Rd WN7 ....76 A6
Platt Fold St WN7 ....76 A5
Platt Hill Ave BL3 ....146 A4
Platt La Hindley WN2 ....56 D5
Manchester M14 ....98 B2
Standish WN1 ....20 B3
Uppermill OL3 ....50 F2
Westhoughton BL5 ....58 B7
Wigan WN1 ....37 E1
Platt St Cheadle SK8 ....122 E6
Dukinfield SK16 ....101 A7
Hadfield SK13 ....104 B5
Leigh WN7 ....75 F6
8 Oldham OL4 ....67 F6
Platt Bridge WN2 ....56 A2
Platt Wlk M34 ....100 E1
Plattbrook Cl M14 ....98 B1
Platting La OL11 ....31 A4
Platting Rd OL4 ....68 C7
Platts Dr M44 ....94 A2
Plattwood Wlk 16 M15 ....162 D6
Playfair Cl OL10 ....46 E7
Playfair St Bolton BL1 ....24 F6
Manchester M14 ....98 B4
Pleachway SK4 ....110 F2
Pleasance Way WA12 ....89 D4
Pleasant Ct 5 OL11 ....30 C2
Pleasant Gdns BL1 ....145 E8
Pleasant Rd M30 ....79 E1
Pleasant St Bury BL8 ....26 F4
Heywood OL10 ....29 C4
Manchester M9 ....157 D7
Rochdale OL11 ....30 C2
Pleasant Terr 6 SK16 ....166 C1
Pleasant View Bacup OL13 ....3 C7
Radcliffe M26 ....62 B8
Romiley SK6 ....114 B3
Pleasant Way SK8 ....132 C6
Pleasington Dr Bury BL8 ....26 E2
Failsworth M40 ....65 C2
Plevna St BL2 ....148 A7
Plodder La BL4,BL5 ....59 D8
Plodder La Prim Sch BL4 ....60 B8
Plough Cl M41 ....94 C1
Plough Fields M28 ....78 A5
Plough St 6 SK16 ....101 D8
Ploughbank Dr M21 ....109 D7
Ploughfields BL5 ....39 E3
Plover Cl
Newton-le-W WA12 ....89 C3
Rochdale OL11 ....29 F7
Plover Dr
Altrincham WA14 ....119 B8
Bury BL9 ....141 B4
Irlam M44 ....94 A4
Plover Terr M21 ....109 D7
Plover Way WA3 ....90 E8
Plowden Ave BL3 ....146 C3
Plowden Rd M22 ....121 B2
Plowley Cl M20 ....110 B2
Plucksbridge Rd SK6 ....126 B3
Plum St OL8 ....153 D5
Plum Tree Cl M30 ....79 E2
Plum Tree Ct 2 M5 ....81 A2
Plumbley Dr M16 ....97 C3
Plumbley St 11 M11 ....99 E7
Plumley Cl SK3 ....170 F5
Plumley Rd SK9 ....131 D5
Plummer Ave M21 ....109 B6
Plumpton Cl OL1,OL2 ....48 E1
Plumpton Dr BL9 ....27 E6
Plumpton Rd OL11 ....48 C8
Plumpton Wlk 6 M13 ....98 F4
Plunge Rd BL0 ....1 E3
Pluto Cl M6 ....81 C4
Plymouth Ave M13 ....164 E5
Plymouth Cl OL6 ....85 C7
Plymouth Dr
Bramhall SK7 ....132 F7
1 Farnworth BL4 ....59 F8
Plymouth Gr
Manchester M13 ....164 D5
Radcliffe M26 ....43 D5
Standish WN6 ....37 A7
Stockport SK3 ....123 B7
Plymouth Gr W M13 ....164 E5
Plymouth Grove Prim Sch
M13 ....164 E5
Plymouth Ho M13 ....163 C6
Plymouth Rd M33 ....107 D5
Plymouth St OL8 ....66 F4
Plymouth View M13 ....163 C6
Plymouth Village M12 ....164 D5
Plymtree Cl M8 ....63 E2
Pobgreen La OL3 ....51 D1
Pochard Dr
Altrincham WA14 ....119 B7
Poynton SK12 ....133 A4
Pochin St M40 ....160 E3
Pocket Nook La WA3 ....91 B7
Pocket Nook Rd BL6 ....40 B3
Pocket Wkshps The
BL3 ....144 C6
Pocklington Dr M23 ....120 F7
Podnor La SK6 ....127 A6
Podsmead Rd M22 ....121 B2
Poet's Nook WN7 ....75 E4
Point Ret Pk The OL16 ....31 A7
Poise Brook Dr SK2 ....124 F5
Poise Brook Rd SK2 ....124 F5
Poise Cl SK7 ....125 A3
Poke St 1 WN5 ....54 B6
Poland St
1 Ashton-u-L M34 ....100 E8
Manchester M4 ....159 C2
Poland Street Ind Est
M4 ....159 C2
Polden Cl OL8 ....66 E3
Polden Wlk 1 M9 ....64 F1
Polding St WN3 ....55 E4
Pole La Failsworth M35 ....83 F8
Whitefield BL9,M45 ....45 C2
Whitefield M45 ....45 D1
Pole Lane Ct BL9 ....45 C3
Pole St Ashton-u-L OL7 ....166 B4
Bolton BL2 ....25 B1
Standish WN6 ....19 E1
Poleacre La SK6 ....113 C6
Polebrook Ave M12 ....164 D6
Polefield App M25 ....63 B6
Polefield Circ M25 ....63 B6
Polefield Gdns M25 ....63 B6
Polefield Gr M25 ....63 B6
Polefield Grange M25 ....63 B6
Polefield Hall Rd M25 ....63 B6
Polefield Rd
Manchester M9 ....64 E2
Prestwich M25 ....63 C6
Polegate Dr WN2 ....57 D2
Polesworth Cl M12 ....165 A6
Police St
1 Altrincham WA14 ....119 D5
Eccles M30 ....79 C2
Manchester M2 ....158 F1
Pollard Ct 4 OL1 ....153 E8
Pollard Gr OL15 ....16 C8
Pollard Ho BL3 ....146 B2
Pollard Sq M31 ....106 A3
Pollard St M4 ....160 D1
Pollard St E M4,M40 ....160 D2
Pollards La BL9 ....11 C2
Polldean Ho SK8 ....122 D3
Pollen Cl M33 ....108 D2
Pollen Rd WA14 ....119 C6
Polletts Ave SK5 ....112 C6
Pollit Croft SK6 ....112 F1
Pollitt Ave OL6 ....85 C5
Pollitt Cl M12 ....164 F6
Pollitt St M26 ....44 C3
Pollitts Cl M30 ....79 B2
Polly Gn OL12 ....14 F3
Polonia Ct OL8 ....66 C3
Polperro Cl OL2 ....49 A4
Polperro Wlk SK14 ....102 D3
Polruan Rd M21 ....97 A2
Polruan Wlk SK14 ....102 E3
Polworth Rd M9 ....64 E1
Polygon Ave M12,M13 ....163 C6
Polygon Rd M8 ....63 F1
Polygon St M13 ....163 C7
Polygon The Eccles M30 ....80 A2
Salford M7 ....81 C5
Pomfret St
Manchester M12 ....165 A6
Salford M6 ....80 C5
Pomona Cres M5 ....161 B7
Pomona St OL11 ....139 F5
Pomona Sta M5,M16 ....161 B6
Pomona Strand M16,M5 ....161 B6
Pond St WA3 ....91 A8
Ponds Cl M21 ....97 B1
Pondwater Cl M28 ....60 A3
Ponsford Ave M9 ....65 A3
Ponsonby Rd M32 ....96 D3
Pontefract Cl M27 ....80 B7
Pool Bank St M24 ....64 B7
Pool Fold M35 ....84 A6
Pool House Rd SK12 ....134 D5
Pool Rd WA3 ....105 A3
Pool St Bolton BL1 ....145 E7
Bolton BL1 ....145 E8
Hindley WN2 ....56 D4
Oldham OL8 ....66 F4
Wigan WN3 ....150 B6
Pool Terr BL1 ....142 A2
Poolbank Cl WN2 ....57 C3
Poolcroft M33 ....108 F3
Poole Cl SK7 ....123 D1
Pooley Cl M24 ....46 B1
Poolfield Cl M26 ....43 E3
Poolstock WN3 ....150 B6
Poolstock La WN3 ....55 A4
Poolton Rd M9 ....64 B4
Poot Hall OL12 ....14 F3
Pope Way 9 M34 ....113 A8
Poplar Ave
Altrincham WA14 ....119 E6
Bolton,Astley Bridge BL1 ....24 F5
Bolton,Bradshaw BL2 ....25 C6
Bury BL9 ....141 B3
Culcheth WA3 ....91 F3
Downall Green WN4 ....72 D5
Horwich BL6 ....22 E1
Manchester M19 ....111 B7
New Mills SK22 ....127 D1
Newton-le-W WA12 ....89 D3
Oldham OL8 ....66 D2
4 Rochdale OL12 ....14 C1
Uppermill OL4 ....68 C4
Wigan WN5 ....54 E6
Wilmslow SK9 ....136 F5
Poplar Cl SK8 ....122 B5
Poplar Ct Denton M34 ....100 F7
Manchester M14 ....98 D1
Poplar Dr M25 ....63 A2
Poplar Gr Ashton-u-L OL6 ....85 C5
Hindley WN2 ....57 B3
Irlam M44 ....105 D6
Manchester M18 ....99 D4
Ramsbottom BL0 ....11 D7
Sale M33 ....108 B3
Stockport SK2 ....124 C4
Tyldesley M29 ....77 A8
Urmston M41 ....95 E2
Westhoughton BL5 ....57 E8
Poplar Rd
Dukinfield SK16 ....101 F7
Eccles M30 ....79 E4
Manchester M19 ....110 D3
Stretford M32 ....108 C8
Swinton M27 ....79 D7
Walkden M28 ....60 E1
Poplar St Denton M34 ....100 F7
Failsworth M35 ....83 D6
Golborne WA3 ....74 B1
Leigh WN7 ....75 F4
Manchester SK4 ....110 F2
Middleton M24 ....65 D7
Tyldesley M29 ....59 A1
Poplar St Prim Sch
M34 ....100 E6
Poplar Way SK6 ....135 A7
Poplar Wlk
Chadderton OL9 ....152 B8
Partington M31 ....105 D3
Poplars Rd SK15 ....86 D3
Poplars The Adlington PR7 ....20 F6
Golborne,Bank Heath WA3 ....74 B1
Golborne,Wash End WN7 ....91 C8
Mossley OL5 ....68 E1
Poplin Dr M3 ....158 E3
Poppy Cl Chadderton OL9 ....65 E7
Sale M33 ....108 E1
Poppyfield View OL11 ....29 E8
Poppythorn La M25 ....63 A5
Porchester Dr M26 ....43 C5
Porchfield Sq M3 ....162 E8
Porlock Ave
Droylsden M34 ....100 C8
Hattersley SK14 ....102 C2
Porlock Cl
Platt Bridge WN2 ....56 A1
Stockport SK1 ....124 C8
Porlock Rd Urmston M41 ....107 B8
Wythenshawe M23 ....121 B6
Porlock Wlk SK14 ....102 C2
Porritt Cl OL11 ....29 E6
Porritt St Bury BL9 ....141 A4
Bury BL9 ....141 B4
Porritt Way BL0 ....138 C7
Port Soderick Ave M5 ....81 A1
Port St Manchester M1 ....159 B1
Oldham OL8 ....66 F4
Stockport SK1 ....169 E2
Portal Ct M24 ....65 C8
Portal Gr M34 ....101 B1
Portal Wlk 9 M9 ....157 D8
Porter Ave WA12 ....89 C5
Porter Dr M40 ....157 D6
Porter St Bury BL9 ....140 F4
Oldham OL9 ....152 C5
Porterfield Dr M29 ....77 A8
Porters Wood Cl WN5 ....54 B7
Portfield Cl BL1 ....40 F8
Portfield Wlk 18 M40 ....83 A6
Portgate Wlk M13 ....164 D5
Porthleven Cres M29 ....77 C8
Porthleven Dr M23 ....120 E6
Porthtowan Wlk SK14 ....102 E3
Portinscale Cl BL8 ....27 B3
Portland Basin Mus*
OL7 ....166 A1
Portland Cl Abram WN2 ....74 A8
Hazel Grove SK7 ....124 B1
Platt Bridge WN2 ....56 A1
Portland Cres M13 ....164 D5
Portland Ct M20 ....110 B3
Portland Gr SK4 ....168 B4

Portland Ho
3 Ashton-u-L OL6 .....166 A2
Salford M6 .....80 A3
Marple SK6 .....125 E5
Portland Ind Est BL9 .....141 A4
Portland Pl
Ashton-u-L OL7 .....166 A2
Horwich BL6 .....22 C3
Portland Rd
Altrincham WA14 .....119 D3
Manchester M13 .....98 F3
New Mills SK22 .....127 D1
Pendlebury M27 .....80 B7
Salford M30 .....80 A4
Stretford M32 .....96 E4
Walkden M28 .....60 C5
Portland St Bolton BL1 .....143 E2
Bury BL9 .....141 A4
6 Leigh WN7 .....75 F5
Manchester M1 .....159 A1
Rochdale OL16 .....139 F8
Wigan WN5 .....54 E6
Portland St N OL6 .....166 A3
Portland St S OL6,OL7 .....166 A2
Portland Terr M9 .....166 A3
Portland The 10 M14 .....110 D8
Portloe Rd SK8 .....131 B7
Portman Rd M16 .....97 E3
Portman St OL5 .....68 C1
Porton Wlk 1 M22 .....121 E1
Portrea Cl SK3 .....170 F5
Portree Cl OL10 .....29 A1
Portree Ct OL10 .....79 B2
Portrush Rd M22 .....121 E2
Portside Cl M28 .....78 B5
Portslade Wlk M23 .....120 F4
Portsmouth Cl M7 .....155 D5
Portsmouth St M13 .....163 B5
Portstone St 11 M16 .....97 E4
Portugal Rd M25 .....80 A2
Portugal St Ashton-u-L OL7 .....84 F1
Bolton BL2 .....148 B7
Manchester M4 .....159 C4
10 Manchester M4 .....159 C3
Portugal St E M1 .....163 C8
Portville Rd M19 .....99 A2
Portway M22 .....121 C1
Portwood Ind Est SK1 .....112 B2
Portwood Pl SK1 .....169 F2
Portwood Wlk 9 M9 .....157 D7
Posnett St SK3 .....123 C8
Post Office St WA14 .....119 D5
Post St SK13 .....104 B5
Postal St M1 .....159 B1
Postbridge Cl M13 .....163 C6
Pot Gn BL0 .....11 A3
Pot Hill OL6 .....166 C4
Pot Hill Sq OL6 .....166 C4
Potato Wharf M3 .....162 D8
Pott St M27 .....61 F2
Potter Ho OL8 .....153 F5
Potter St SK13 .....171 E3
Potter St Bury BL9 .....141 A3
Radcliffe M26 .....44 D4
Potterdale Cl OL1 .....49 A1
Potters La M9 .....157 F7
Pottery La M11,M12 .....165 A7
Pottery Rd WN3 .....150 B7
Pottery Terr WN3 .....150 B7
Pottinger St
Ashton-u-L OL7 .....100 F8
Ashton-u-L OL7 .....84 F1
Poulton Ave BL2 .....42 E7
Poulton Dr 7 WN4 .....72 F5
Poulton St M11 .....99 E7
Poundswick La M22 .....121 D3
Powell Ave SK14 .....167 E3
Powell Ct 8 BL9 .....140 F3
Powell Dr WN5 .....71 D3
Powell St Abram WN2 .....56 B1
Bury BL8 .....27 B1
Droylsden M11 .....83 D2
Manchester M16 .....97 D4
10 Wigan WN1 .....37 C1
Powicke Dr SK6 .....112 F1
Powicke Wlk SK6 .....113 A1
Powis Rd M41 .....94 C1
Pownall Ave
Bramhall SK7 .....132 F7
4 Manchester M20 .....110 A4
Pownall Ct SK9 .....136 E8
Pownall Green Prim Sch
SK7 .....132 E7
Pownall Hall Sch SK9 .....136 F8
Pownall Rd
Altrincham WA14 .....119 D3
Cheadle SK8 .....123 A5
Wilmslow SK9 .....136 F8
Pownall St
Hazel Grove SK7 .....124 D3
Leigh WN7 .....76 A4
Powys St M46 .....58 E1
Poynings Dr M22 .....121 C1
Poynt Chase M28 .....78 B6
Poynter St OL1 .....49 D4
Poynter Wlk OL1 .....49 D4
Poynton Ind Est M22 .....110 C6
Poynton Sta SK12 .....133 E4
Poynton Information Ctr*
SK12 .....133 E4
Poynton St Bury BL9 .....141 A4
Manchester M15 .....162 F6
Poynton Sta SK12 .....133 C4
Praed Rd M7 .....96 C6
Pratt Wlk 21 M11 .....160 F1

Precinct The
Cheadle SK8 .....123 A2
Rochdale OL11 .....29 E7
Stockport SK2 .....124 D6
Preece Cl SK14 .....102 A4
Presall Ave SK8 .....131 B8
Presall Cl BL8 .....26 F1
Prefect Pl WN5 .....54 C8
Premier Rd M8 .....158 F4
Premier St M16 .....97 D4
Prentice Wlk M11 .....83 A1
Prenton St M11 .....99 E8
Prenton Way BL8 .....26 F5
Presall St 2 BL2 .....148 C8
Presbury Ct 1 M20 .....110 A2
Presbyterian Fold 6
M9 .....56 D6
Prescot Ave Atherton M46 .....58 E5
Tyldesley M29 .....59 D1
Prescot Cl BL9 .....141 A1
Prescot Rd
Altrincham WA15 .....119 F2
Manchester M9 .....157 D7
Prescott Ave WA3 .....73 F2
Prescott La WN5 .....54 B8
Prescott Rd SK9 .....131 B1
Prescott St Bolton BL3 .....146 C4
Golborne WA3 .....74 A1
Hindley WN2 .....56 D5
Leigh WN7 .....75 F6
Rochdale OL16 .....15 C2
Walkden M28 .....60 B3
Wigan WN3,WN1,WN6 .....150 B8
Prescott Wlk M34 .....101 B1
Press St M11 .....99 D7
Prestage St
Manchester,Levenshulme
M12 .....99 B2
Manchester,Old Trafford
M16 .....97 D4
Salford M16 .....161 C5
Prestbury Ave
Manchester WA15 .....119 E6
Manchester M14 .....97 F1
Wigan WN3 .....54 E2
Prestbury Cl Bury BL9 .....141 A1
Stockport SK2 .....124 D4
Prestbury Ct 1 M28 .....60 D2
Prestbury Dr Oldham OL1 .....48 D1
Romiley SK6 .....112 E3
Prestbury Rd Bolton BL1 .....25 A5
Wilmslow SK9 .....137 E5
Prestfield Rd M45 .....44 E1
Presto Gdns BL3 .....146 B4
Presto St Bolton BL3 .....146 B4
Farnworth BL4 .....60 E8
Prestolee Ct M27 .....80 E8
Prestolee Prim Sch M26 .....61 B8
Prestolee Rd
Kearsley M26 .....43 B1
Little Lever BL3 .....43 B4
Preston Ave Irlam M44 .....105 F7
Salford M30 .....80 A3
Preston Cl M30 .....80 A3
Preston Rd
Manchester M19 .....111 A8
Standish PR7,WN6 .....19 D5
Preston St 2 Bolton BL3 .....42 B4
Manchester M18 .....165 C6
Middleton M24 .....65 A8
Oldham OL4 .....67 A6
12 Rochdale OL12 .....14 C1
Prestwich Ave
Culcheth WA3 .....91 E3
Leigh WN7 .....76 B5
Prestwich Cl SK2 .....124 B7
Prestwich Com High Sch
M25 .....63 B5
Prestwich Forest Pk*
M25 .....62 E3
Prestwich Hills M25 .....62 F5
Prestwich Hospl M25 .....62 F5
Prestwich Ind Est M25 .....58 B4
Prestwich Park Rd S
M25 .....63 A3
Prestwich Prep Sch M25 .....63 C5
Prestwich St
Atherton M46 .....58 B3
4 Denton M34 .....100 F7
Prestwichts Sta M25 .....63 A5
Prestwich Wlk 1 M40 .....65 C2
Prestwood Cl BL1 .....143 D1
Prestwood Dr BL1 .....143 D1
Prestwood Rd
Farnworth BL4 .....42 A1
Salford M6 .....80 C4
Pretoria Rd
Ashton-u-M WN4 .....73 B4
Bolton BL2 .....42 E8
Oldham OL8 .....66 C3
Pretoria St 2 OL12 .....14 C1
Price St Bury BL9 .....141 A1
Dukinfield SK16 .....101 C8
Farnworth BL4 .....42 D1
Manchester M4 .....160 D1
Prichard St WA12 .....96 D2
Prickshaw OL12 .....14 B6
Prickshaw La OL12 .....14 B6
Pride Cl WA12 .....89 E2
Priest Ave SK8 .....122 A4
Priest St SK1 .....170 F7
Priestley Rd M27,M28 .....79 C8
Priestley Way OL2 .....49 D7
Priestnall Cl SK4 .....110 F3
Priestnall Rd SK4 .....110 F3
Priestnall Rec Ctr SK4 .....110 F3
Priestnall Sch SK4 .....110 F3

Priestners Way WN7 .....75 E6
Priestwood Ave OL4 .....49 F4
Primary Cl M44 .....105 D5
Primley Wlk 8 M9 .....157 E8
Primrose Ave
Farnworth BL4 .....42 A1
Hyde SK14 .....113 D8
Marple SK6 .....125 E6
Uppermill OL3 .....142 A1
Urmston M41 .....95 D2
Walkden M28 .....60 B2
Primrose Bank
2 Altrincham WA14 .....119 C1
1 Bacup OL13 .....3 C8
Bury BL8 .....26 E7
Oldham OL8 .....153 E5
Uppermill OL3 .....69 B5
Walkden M28 .....60 B2
Primrose Cl Bolton BL2 .....26 A4
Salford M6 .....154 F2
Primrose Cotts 1
WA14 .....119 C1
Primrose Cres
Glossop SK13 .....116 B8
Hyde SK14 .....113 D8
Primrose Dr Bury BL9 .....28 D4
Droylsden M43 .....84 C3
Primrose Gr WN5 .....54 F7
Primrose Hill SK13 .....116 B8
Primrose La
Glossop SK13 .....116 B8
New Mills SK6,SK22 .....127 A3
Standish WN6 .....19 D2
Primrose St 9 Bacup OL13 .....3 C8
Bolton BL1 .....143 F4
4 Leigh WN7 .....75 F5
Manchester M4 .....159 B2
Rochdale OL12 .....139 D8
Tyldesley M29 .....59 A1
Primrose St N M29 .....59 A1
Primrose St S M29 .....77 A8
Primrose Terr
Glossop SK13 .....116 B8
Urmston M41 .....95 C6
Primrose View WN4 .....73 C2
Primrose Wlk
Marple SK6 .....125 E6
Oldham OL8 .....153 E5
Primula Dr WA3 .....90 D8
Primula St BL1 .....24 F5
Prince Albert Ave 4
M19 .....99 A2
Prince Charlie St OL1 .....67 C8
Prince Edward Ave
Denton M34 .....100 F2
7 Denton M34 .....100 F2
Prince George St 3 OL1 .....49 C1
Prince of Wales Bsns Pk
OL1 .....67 C8
Prince Rd SK12 .....134 C5
Prince St
Ashton-u-M WN4 .....73 A5
Bacup OL13 .....4 D7
Bolton BL1 .....145 D6
Heywood OL10 .....29 D2
6 Oldham OL1 .....67 A7
Ramsbottom BL0 .....138 C6
Rochdale OL16 .....31 B5
Prince Way OL2 .....48 C6
Prince's Ave
Little Lever BL3 .....43 B4
Manchester M20 .....110 C4
Romiley SK6 .....113 A3
Tyldesley M29 .....77 B6
Prince's Dr SK6 .....125 E7
Prince's Pk WN6 .....35 F4
Prince's Rd SK14 .....113 A3
Prince's St SK1 .....169 E2
Princedom St M9 .....157 E8
Princes Ave M44 .....94 C3
Princes Ct M33 .....108 D3
Princes Dr M33 .....108 D3
Princes Gdns WN7 .....76 C5
Princes Rd
Altrincham WA14 .....119 D6
Manchester SK4 .....168 A4
Sale M33 .....108 A3
Princess Ave
Ashton-u-M WN4 .....73 C3
Atherton M46 .....58 D7
Cheadle SK8 .....123 A3
Denton M34 .....100 E3
Haydock WA11 .....89 A7
Kearsley BL4 .....60 F6
Manchester M25 .....63 C2
Rochdale OL12 .....15 C4
Princess Christian Coll
M14 .....98 C1
Princess Cl
Dukinfield SK16 .....101 D8
Heywood OL10 .....29 D2
Mossley OL5 .....86 E8
Princess St M15 .....162 D6
Princess Dr M24 .....46 F2
Princess Gr BL4 .....60 D8
Princess Par BL9 .....141 A2
Princess Parkway M20,
M23 .....109 C2
Princess Rd Adlington PR6 .....21 B8
Ashton-in-M WN4 .....73 C3
Bolton BL3 .....146 B4
Failsworth OL9 .....65 E3
Manchester,Moss Side M14,
M16 .....97 F4
Manchester,West Didsbury
M14,M20,M21,M16 .....109 E6

Princess Rd continued
Milnrow OL16 .....31 D7
Prestwich M25 .....63 C4
Shaw OL2 .....149 A6
Urmston M41 .....95 B2
Wigan WN5 .....36 C4
Wilmslow SK9 .....136 F5
Princess St
Altrincham WA14 .....119 C8
Ashton-u-L OL6 .....85 D4
Bolton BL1 .....145 F7
Eccles M30 .....79 C2
Failsworth M35 .....83 E7
Glossop SK13 .....116 C8
Hindley WN2 .....56 C5
Hyde SK14 .....167 E2
5 Leigh WN7 .....76 A5
Manchester,St George's
M15 .....162 D6
Oldham OL4 .....67 C6
Pendlebury M27 .....80 A7
Radcliffe M26 .....43 E3
Salford M6 .....81 A4
Whitworth OL12 .....14 C8
Wigan WN3 .....150 C7
Princess Wlk SK7 .....133 A7
Princethorpe Cl BL6 .....40 D6
Princeton Cl 1 M6 .....80 F4
Prinknash Rd M22 .....121 D1
Printer St Droylsden M11 .....99 D8
Oldham OL1 .....153 F6
Printers Dr SK15 .....87 A6
Printers Fold SK14 .....103 D5
Printers La BL2,BL7 .....25 C6
Printers St M11 .....99 E8
Printon Ave M9 .....64 B3
Printshop La M46 .....58 E1
Printworks La M19 .....99 C1
Printworks Rd SK15 .....86 C3
Printworks The M4 .....159 A2
Prior St OL8 .....67 B5
Priorsleigh SK14 .....110 F2
Priory Ave Leigh WN7 .....57 D1
Manchester M21 .....109 B8
Salford M7 .....81 C6
Priory Cl Dukinfield SK16 .....101 D6
Oldham OL8 .....66 D3
Sale M33 .....108 D6
1 Wigan WN5 .....53 C8
Priory Ct
5 Altrincham WA14 .....119 C1
Eccles M30 .....79 E2
Reddish SK5 .....111 E8
Priory Gdns M20 .....110 B4
Priory Gr Chadderton OL9 .....66 A4
Salford M7 .....81 C6
Priory La SK5 .....111 E8
Priory Nook WN8 .....53 C7
Priory Pl BL2 .....25 C6
Priory Rd
Altrincham WA14 .....128 B8
Ashton-in-M WN4 .....72 F5
Cheadle SK8 .....123 A5
Sale M33 .....108 D5
Swinton M27 .....79 E8
Up Holland WN8 .....53 C7
Wilmslow SK9 .....136 F3
Priory St WA14 .....119 C1
Priory The M7 .....81 C6
Pritchard St M1 .....163 A7
Private La BB4 .....1 C8
Privet St OL4 .....49 D1
Proctor Cl WN5 .....36 E1
Proctor St BL2 .....148 C8
Proctor Way M30 .....94 F7
Prodesse Ct WN2 .....56 C4
Proe's Ct WN1 .....150 B8
Progress Ave M34 .....100 F6
Progress St
Ashton-u-L OL6 .....166 A3
Bolton BL1 .....143 F1
Hindley WN2 .....56 D5
Rochdale OL11 .....30 C1
Promenade St OL10 .....29 C2
Propps Hall Dr M35 .....83 E6
Propps Jun & Inf Sch
M35 .....83 E6
Prospect Ave Bolton BL2 .....26 A3
Farnworth BL4 .....60 C7
Irlam M44 .....105 D4
Prospect Cotts WN2 .....38 A6
Prospect Ct BL3 .....26 F7
Prospect Dr
Failsworth WA15 .....129 D8
Failsworth M35 .....83 F5
Prospect Hill BL2 .....25 F4
Prospect Ho M9 .....157 E7
Prospect Ind Ctr 15 WN2 .....56 D5
Prospect Pl
Ashton-u-L OL6 .....85 D5
Farnworth BL4 .....60 C7
Oldham OL1 .....29 D3
Prospect Rd
Ashton-u-L OL6 .....85 C5
Dukinfield SK16 .....101 D5
Irlam M44 .....105 D4
Oldham OL9 .....152 C7
Standish WN6 .....19 D2
Prospect St Bolton BL3 .....143 F1
Heywood OL10 .....46 B8
Hindley WN2 .....56 D5
Littleborough OL15 .....16 B6
Rochdale OL11 .....30 E4
Tyldesley M29 .....58 E1
Prospect Terr Bacup OL13 .....3 F7
Bury BL8 .....140 D4

Prospect Vale SK8 .....122 B1
Prospect Vale Prim Sch
SK8 .....122 B1
Prospect Villas M9 .....64 E1
Prosperity M27 .....77 D8
Prosser Ave M44 .....58 A2
Protector Way M44 .....105 F8
Prout St M12 .....99 A3
Providence Ho OL4 .....67 E8
Providence St
8 Ashton-u-L OL6 .....85 D4
Bolton BL3 .....145 F5
Denton M34 .....100 F7
Manchester M4 .....160 D1
Walsden OL14 .....6 A7
Provident Ave M19 .....99 C1
Provident St OL2 .....149 B7
Provident Way WA15 .....120 A7
Provis Rd M21 .....109 B7
Prubella Ave M34 .....100 C5
Pryce Ave WN2 .....151 F7
Pryce St BL1 .....143 D1
Pryme St M15 .....162 E7
Pudding La SK14 .....102 C3
Puffin Ave SK12 .....133 B4
Puffingate Cl SK15 .....86 E7
Pugin Wlk M9 .....157 D6
Pulborough Cl BL8 .....27 B7
Pulford Ave M21 .....109 D4
Pulford Rd M33 .....108 D2
Pullman Cl M18 .....111 B8
Pullman Dr M32 .....95 F3
Pullman St OL11 .....139 F5
Pulman Ct BL3 .....148 A5
Pump St 10 Hindley WN2 .....56 D5
Manchester M4,M12 .....160 E2
12 Oldham OL9 .....66 B2
Punch La BL3 .....40 D2
Punch St BL3 .....145 D6
Pungle The BL5 .....57 D5
Purbeck Cl M22 .....121 C1
Purbeck Dr Bury BL8 .....27 B1
Horwich BL6 .....39 F8
Purbeck Way M29 .....77 B7
Purcell Cl BL1 .....143 D1
Purcell St M12 .....99 A3
Purdon St BL9 .....27 F6
Purdy Ho OL8 .....153 E5
Puritan Wlk 7 M40 .....156 C5
Purley Ave M23 .....109 B1
Purley Dr M44 .....105 C5
Purple St BL1 .....145 F7
Purslow Cl M12 .....160 E1
Purton Wlk 9 M9 .....157 E7
Putney Cl OL1 .....48 E1
Puzzletree Ct SK2 .....124 C7
Pye Cl WA11 .....89 B8
Pyegrove SK13 .....104 F1
Pyegrove Rd SK13 .....104 E1
Pyke St WN1 .....37 D1
Pym St Eccles M30 .....79 D1
Heywood OL10 .....29 D1
Manchester M40 .....157 F8
Pymgate Dr SK8 .....122 A2
Pyramid Ct M7 .....155 D6
Pyrus Cl M30 .....94 F8
Pytha Fold Rd M20 .....110 D5

Q

Quadrant The
Droylsden M43 .....83 F1
Manchester M9 .....65 A3
Romiley SK6 .....113 A2
Stockport SK1 .....112 B1
Quail Dr M44 .....94 A3
Quail St OL4 .....67 C6
Quainton Ho 5 M5 .....154 F1
Quakerfields BL5 .....57 D7
Quakers Field BL8 .....26 F8
Quakers Terr WN6 .....19 D3
Quakers' Pl WN5 .....19 E1
Quantock Cl
Stockport SK4 .....169 E2
Wigan WN3 .....54 C2
Quantock Dr OL8 .....66 F3
Quantock St 7 M16 .....97 E4
Quariton Dr BL8 .....10 F2
Quarmby Rd M18 .....99 F4
Quarry Bank Mill* SK9 .....130 F2
Quarry Bank Rd SK9 .....130 D8
Quarry Cl SK13 .....104 D8
Quarry Clough SK15 .....102 D8
Quarry Hill OL12 .....14 E3
Quarry Hts BL8 .....11 A4
Quarry Pl WN1 .....151 E8
Quarry Pond Rd M28 .....59 F3
Quarry Rd Kearsley BL4 .....61 A7
New Mills SK22 .....127 B5
Romiley SK6 .....113 B2
Quarry Rise Romiley SK6 .....113 B3
Stalybridge SK15,SK16 .....101 F8
Quarry St 6 Radcliffe M26 .....44 B3
Ramsbottom BL0 .....11 D6
Rochdale OL16 .....15 A1
Romiley SK6 .....113 B5
Stalybridge SK15 .....85 F1
4 Whitworth OL12 .....14 C8
Quarry Wlk 8 M11 .....160 F1
Quay St Heywood OL10 .....29 C1
Manchester M2 .....158 E1
Salford M3 .....158 E2
Quays The M50 .....96 E2
Quayside WN7 .....75 A4
Quayside Cl M28 .....78 B5

Quebec Pl BL3 ....145 D5
Quebec St
Abram Brow WN2,WN7 ...74 E5
Bolton BL3 ....145 D5
Denton M34 ....100 E4
Oldham OL9 ....153 D8
Queen Alexandra Cl M5 .161 C8
Queen Ann Cl BL9 .....45 C4
Queen Ann Dr M28 .....78 B7
Queen Anne Ct SK9 ...137 C6
Queen Sq OL6 ....85 D3
Queen St Ashton-u-L OL6 .166 C3
⑤ Bacup OL13 ....3 C8
Bolton BL1 ....145 E7
Bury,Pimhole BL9 .....141 A2
Bury,Tottington BL8 ...27 A5
Cheadle SK8 ....122 F6
Denton M34 ....100 E4
Denton,Hooley Hill M34 .100 E4
Dukinfield SK16 ......166 B1
Failsworth M35 ....83 E7
Farnworth BL4 ....60 D8
Glossop SK13 ....116 B8
Golborne WA3 ....90 B8
Hadfield SK13 ....104 A4
Heywood OL10 ....29 D2
⑤ Hindley WN2 ....56 D6
Horwich BL6 ....22 B3
Hyde SK14 ....167 E1
Leigh WN7 ....76 A5
Littleborough OL15 ....16 B5
Manchester M2 ....158 F3
Marple SK6 ....126 A6
Middleton M24 ....65 C8
Mossley OL5 ....68 C1
Newton-le-W WA12 .....89 B3
Oldham OL1 ....153 F6
⑩ Oldham,County End OL4 .67 F6
Platt Bridge WN2 ......56 A2
Radcliffe M26 ....44 C2
Ramsbottom BL0 ......138 B6
Rochdale OL12 ....139 F8
Royton OL2 ....48 D4
Salford M3 ....158 E2
Salford,Triams o' th' Height
M6 ....80 D5
Shaw OL2 ....149 B6
Stalybridge SK15 .....86 A2
Stockport SK1 ....112 A2
Walkden M38 ....60 B3
Westhoughton BL5 .....39 D4
Wigan WN3 ....150 C7
Wigan,Norley WN5 .....54 B6
Wigan,Pemberton WN5 ..54 D5
Queen St W M20 ....110 B7
Queen Victoria St
Eccles M30 ....79 C2
Rochdale OL11 ....31 A4
Queen's Ave
Ashton-in-M WN4 ......73 B3
Atherton M46 ....58 C5
Bolton BL7 ....25 A7
Glazebury WA3 ....92 C7
Little Lever BL3 ......43 A4
Romiley SK6 ....113 A3
Queen's Cl M7 ....60 D3
Queen's Ct
③ Manchester M21 .....97 B2
Manchester,Withington
M20 ....110 A4
Marple SK6 ....126 A6
Queen's Dr Glossop SK13 .104 F1
Manchester SK4 ....168 A2
Manchester,Sedgley Park
M25 ....63 C2
Queen's Gdns SK8 ....122 E6
Queen's Gr M12 ....99 A4
Queen's Park Rd OL10 ..29 D3
Queen's Rd
Altrincham WA15 ......119 F3
Ashton-in-M WN4 ......73 B4
Ashton-u-L OL6 ....85 D5
Cheadle SK8 ....122 F4
Hazel Grove SK7 ......124 E3
⑩ Littleborough OL15 ...16 B5
Romiley SK6 ....113 A3
Urmston M41 ....95 D1
Wilmslow SK9 ....137 A6
Queen's Terr
⑦ Dukinfield SK16 .....166 B1
Queenhill Dr SK14 ....102 A5
Queenhill Rd M22 .....109 E1
Queens Ave
Manchester M18 ......165 B5
Rochdale OL12 ....15 C4
Queens Cl
Boothstown M28 ......77 F7
Hyde SK14 ....113 E7
Manchester SK4 ......168 A2
Queens Ct
Manchester SK4 ......168 A3
Manchester,Collyhurst
M40 ....157 D5
Urmston M41 ....94 E2
Queens Dr Cheadle SK8 .123 A4
Golborne WA3 ....90 C8
Hyde SK14 ....113 F7
Newton-le-W WA12 .....89 C5
Rochdale OL12 ....15 C4
Queens Gdns WN7 .....76 C5
Queens Pl BL9 ....11 C2
Queens Rd Bolton BL3 .146 B4
Chadderton OL9 ......152 A7
Haydock WA11 ....89 A7
Manchester,Cheetham Hill
M8,M9 ....156 B6

Queens Rd continued
Manchester,Collyhurst
M40,M9 ....157 D5
Oldham OL8 ....67 A5
Orrell WN5 ....53 C5
Sale M33 ....107 F5
Queens Road Prim Sch
SK8 ....123 A3
Queens Terr SK9 ......131 D3
Queens View OL15 .....16 A3
Queens Wlk M43 ....84 A1
Queensbridge Prim Sch
BL4 ....60 D8
Queensbrook BL1 .....145 E7
Queensbury Cl Bolton BL1 .24 D5
⑯ Handforth SK9 ......131 D1
Wilmslow SK9 ....137 D8
Queensbury Ct M40 ...160 E3
Queensbury Par M40 ..160 E3
Queenscroft M30 ......79 F3
Queensferry St M40 ...83 C6
Queensgate Bolton BL1 .144 C8
Bramhall SK7 ....132 E5
Queensgate Dr OL2 ...48 C6
Queensgate Prim Sch
SK7 ....132 E4
Queensland Rd M18 ...165 B5
Queenston Rd M20 ....110 A4
Queensway
Dukinfield SK16 ......101 F7
Gatley SK8 ....131 C8
Ince-in-M WN2 ....56 A8
Irlam M44 ....63 F3
Kearsley BL4 ....60 F5
Leigh WN7 ....76 D6
Manchester M19 ......110 D2
Mossley OL5 ....86 D8
Partington M31 ......108 C4
Poynton SK12 ....133 D3
Rochdale OL11 ....30 E3
Shevington WN6 ....35 F4
Swinton M27 ....62 A2
Uppermill OL3 ....69 B6
Urmston M41 ....95 E4
Walkden M28 ....78 C8
Wigan WN1 ....37 B2
Queensway Com Prim Sch
OL11 ....30 F3
Quenby St M15 ....162 D7
Quendon Ave M7 .....158 E4
Quick Edge La OL4 ....68 A2
Quick Rd OL4,OL5 .....68 D4
Quick View OL5 ....68 E3
Quickedge Rd OL4,OL5 .68 C3
Quickmere Ct ⑥ OL5 ..68 C2
Quickwood OL5 ....68 D2
Quill Ct M44 ....149 B8
Quilter Gr M9 ....64 C2
Quinn St M11 ....83 A1
Quinney Cres M16 ....97 F4
Quinton ⑩ OL4 ......139 E8
Quinton Wlk M13 .....163 B6
Quintrell Brow BL7 ...25 A8

R

Rabbit La SK14 ....103 A6
Rabden Cl OL10 ....29 A2
Raby St M14,M16 ......97 F4
Race The SK9 ....131 C2
Racecourse Pk SK9 ...136 F6
Racecourse Rd SK9 ...136 E6
Racecourse Wlk M26 ..43 F4
Racefield Hamlet OL2 .48 A4
Racefield Rd WA14 ...119 C4
Rachel Rosing Wlk M8 .155 F8
Rachel St M12 ....163 C8
Rack House Prim Sch
M23 ....109 A1
Rackhouse Rd M23 ....109 B1
Radbourne Cl M12 ....165 A6
Radburn Gr BL3 ....40 F4
Radcliffe Ave WA3 ....91 E3
Radcliffe Gr WN7 ......75 F7
Radcliffe Hall CE/Meth Prim
Sch M26 ....44 A4
Radcliffe High Sch M26 .44 A3
Radcliffe Inf Sch M26 .43 E4
Radcliffe Jun Sch M26 .43 E4
Radcliffe Moor Rd BL2,
M26 ....43 C5
Radcliffe Park Cres M6 .80 C5
Radcliffe Park Rd M6 ..80 C5
Radcliffe St
Bolton,Darcy Lever BL2,BL3 .42 D5
Bolton,Springfield BL2 .148 B7
Bury BL9 ....44 E7
Oldham OL4 ....49 D2
Radcliffe St
Oldham,Cold Hurst OL1 .153 F8
Oldham,Grotton OL4 ...68 A6
Royton OL2 ....48 E7
Radcliffe Sta M26 .....44 B3
Radclyffe Com Sec Sch
(Upper) The OL9 .....65 F7
Radclyffe Prim Sch M5 .161 A7
Radclyffe Sch The OL9 .152 A6
Radclyffe St
Chadderton OL9 ......152 C8
Middleton M24 ....47 A2
Radclyffe Terr M24 ...47 A2
Radelan Gr M26 ....43 D4
Radford Cl SK2 ....124 E7
② Manchester M9 .....157 E8

Radford Ho SK2 ......124 E7
Radford St M7 ....81 C8
Radium St M4 ....159 C2
Radlet Dr WA15 ......120 A8
Radlett Wlk ⑨ M13 ..163 C5
Radley Cl Bolton BL1 .142 A1
⑦ Sale M33 ....107 D3
Radley St Droylsden M43 .99 E8
Manchester M16 ......97 F3
Radnor Ave M34 ......100 B3
Radnor Cl WN2 ....57 A3
Radnor Dr WN7 ....75 C5
Radnor St
Manchester,Gorton M18 .99 C4
Manchester,Moss Side M15 .97 F4
Oldham OL9 ....152 C5
Stretford M32 ....96 B1
Radnormere Dr SK8 ..123 A4
Radstock Cl Bolton BL1 .24 E7
Manchester M14 ......98 B1
Radstock Rd M32 .....96 C2
Radway M29 ....59 C1
Rae St SK3 ....123 C8
Raeburn Dr SK6 ......126 B8
Raglan Ave
Prestwich M25,M45 ...63 B7
Swinton M27 ....62 B2
Raglan Cl M11 ....160 F1
Raglan Dr WA14 .....119 E8
Raglan Rd Sale M33 ..108 A3
Stretford M32 ....96 B3
Raglan St Bolton BL1 .143 D2
Hyde SK14 ....101 C2
Rochdale OL11 ....30 C1
Raglan Wlk ⑥ M15 ..162 F6
Ragley Cl M27 ....133 F4
Raikes Clough Ind Est
BL3 ....42 C4
Raikes La BL3 ....42 B4
Raikes Lane Ind Est BL3 .42 C5
Raikes Rd BL3 ....42 D5
Raikes Way BL3 ......42 D5
Rail Pl ⑧ M15 ....163 A6
Railgate OL13 ....4 C8
Railside Terr M30 ....80 A2
Railton Ave M16 ......97 D3
Railton Terr M9 ......157 F7
Railway App ⑪ OL11 ..30 C2
Railway Bank SK14 ...101 C2
Railway Brow OL11 ...30 C1
Railway Cotts
Hollinfare WA3 ....105 B5
Romiley SK6 ....112 F4
Railway Rd
Adlington PR6,PR7 ....21 A7
Golborne WA3 ....74 B1
Leigh WN7 ....75 E5
Oldham OL9 ....152 C6
Oldham,Factory Fold OL9 .66 A2
Stockport SK1,SK3 ...170 E8
Stretford M32 ....96 F5
Urmston M41 ....95 E2
Railway St
Altrincham WA14 .....119 D4
Atherton M46 ....58 B4
Bacup OL13 ....3 B8
Dukinfield SK16 ......166 B1
Farnworth BL4 ....42 E1
Glossop SK13 ....104 C1
Hadfield SK13 ....104 A5
Heywood OL10 ....29 D2
Hindley WN2 ....56 E7
Hyde SK14 ....167 D2
Littleborough OL15 ....16 B5
Manchester M18 ......99 D6
Newhey OL16 ....32 B4
Newton-le-W WA12 ....89 B3
Radcliffe M26 ....44 A3
Ramsbottom,Summerseat
BL9 ....11 C2
Rochdale OL16 ....31 A6
Stockport SK4 ....169 E2
Wigan WN6 ....37 A1
Railway Street Ind Est
M18 ....99 D6
Railway Terr Bury BL8 .27 C1
Disley SK12 ....135 D6
Entwistle BL7 ....9 B8
⑤ Manchester M21 ...97 B2
Railway View
⑨ Oldham OL4 ....67 F6
Shaw OL2 ....149 C8
Raimond St BL1 ......142 C3
Rainbow Cl M21 ......109 B7
Rainbow Dr M46 ......58 D5
Raincliff Ave M13 ....98 F2
Raincourt Cl OL16 ....32 A6
Rainford Ave
Altrincham WA15 .....120 A6
Manchester M20 .....110 A8
Rainford Ho ⑤ BL1 ..145 F8
Rainford Rd WA11,WN5 .71 F1
Rainford St BL2 ....25 B3
Rainham Dr Bolton BL1 .143 E1
Manchester M8 ......156 A7
Rainham Gr ⑧ BL1 ..143 E1
Rainham Way
Brinnington SK5 ......112 B6
Chadderton OL9 ......152 B6
Rainhill Wlk M40 .....83 D4
Rainow Dr SK12 ......134 A2
Rainow Ave M43 ....83 E1
Rainow Rd SK3 ......123 C6
Rainow Way ⑩ SK9 ..131 E1
Rainshaw St Bolton BL1 .143 F4
⑪ Oldham OL4 ....67 D8

Rainshaw St continued
Royton OL2 ....48 D4
Rainsough Ave M25 ...63 A1
Rainsough Brow M25 ..62 F1
Rainsough Cl M25 ....63 A1
Rainton Wlk ⑥ M40 ..65 D2
Rainwood OL9 ....65 A3
Raithby Dr WN3 ......55 A3
Raja Cl M8 ....156 B7
Rake OL11 ....29 D8
Rake Fold BL8 ....138 A6
Rake Head Barn La OL14 .6 A8
Rake Head La OL13 ....3 B8
Rake La M27 ....62 B2
Rake St BL9 ....140 F4
Rake Terr OL15 ....16 C6
Rakehead Wlk M15 ...162 F5
Rakewood Dr OL4 .....49 E4
Rakewood Rd OL15 ...16 C2
Raleigh Cl
Manchester M20 .....110 A5
Oldham OL1 ....153 F8
Raleigh Gdns OL15 .....6 C1
Raleigh St Reddish SK5 .169 E4
Stretford M32 ....96 E2
Ralli Courts M3 ......158 E1
Ralph Ave M14 ....113 E7
Ralph Green St OL9 ...66 A3
Ralph Sherwin Ct OL12 .15 D4
Ralph St Bolton BL1 ..143 D2
Droylsden M11 ....83 D1
Rochdale OL12 ....15 A1
Ralphs La SK16 ......101 C7
Ralston Cl M7 ....155 F8
Ralstone Ave OL8 ....66 F4
Ram St M38 ....59 F5
Ramage Wlk M12 ....160 E1
Rames Ave SK8 .....123 C1
Ramillies Hall Sch SK8 .123 C2
Ramp Ed E M90 .....130 C7
Ramp Rd S M90 .....130 C7
Ramp Rd W M90 .....130 B7
Ramsay Ave BL4 ......60 B7
Ramsay Pl OL16 ......31 A8
Ramsay St Bolton BL1 .143 E4
Rochdale OL16 ....31 A8
Ramsay Terr ⑲ OL16 .31 A8
Ramsbottom Cottage Hospl
BL0 ....138 C5
Ramsbottom Heritage Ctr
Mus* BL0 ....138 C6
Ramsbottom La BL0 ..138 C7
Ramsbottom Rd
Hawkshaw BL8,BL7 ....10 A3
Horwich BL6 ....22 C3
Ramsbottom Sta BL0 .138 C6
Ramsbury Dr M40 .....65 D2
Ramsdale Rd SK7 ....132 E8
Ramsdale St OL9 .....152 A7
Ramsden Cl
Glossop SK13 ....104 D2
Oldham OL1 ....153 E7
Wigan WN3 ....150 A5
Ramsden Cres OL1 ...153 E8
Ramsden Fold M27 ....61 F2
Ramsden La OL14 ......6 A8
Ramsden Rd OL12 .....15 C6
Ramsden St
Ashton-u-L OL6 ......166 B4
Bolton BL3 ....42 D5
Oldham OL1 ....153 E7
Walsden OL14 ....6 A7
Ramsden Wood Rd OL14 .6 A7
Ramsey Ave M19 .....99 D1
Ramsey Cl
Ashton-in-M WN4 .....73 B2
Atherton M46 ....58 E2
Ramsey Gr BL8 ......27 B2
Ramsey Mill OL9 .....152 B5
Ramsey St
Chadderton OL9 .....152 B5
⑤ Leigh WN7 ....76 A4
Manchester M40 ......83 B7
Oldham OL1 ....67 B8
Ramsgate Rd
Failsworth M40 ....83 C4
Reddish SK5 ....111 F7
Ramsgate St M7,M8 ..155 F5
Ramsgill Cl M23 .....108 F1
Ramsgreave Cl BL9 ...44 D7
Ramwell Gdns BL3 ...145 D5
Ramwells Brow BL7 ...25 A8
Ranby Ave M9 ....64 F4
Rand St BL3 ....49 D1
Randal St BL3 ....146 C4
Randall Ave WN6 .....36 A5
Randall Gr BL9 ....45 A2
Randall Wlk ⑳ M11 ..160 F1
Randerson St M12 ...163 C7
Randle St ⑦ M8 .....156 A6
Randlesham St M25 ...63 C4
Randolph Pl SK3 .....170 E7
Randolph Rd BL4 .....60 F7
Randolph St Bolton BL3 .145 D6
Manchester M19 ......99 B2
Oldham OL8 ....66 C2
Rands Clough Dr M28 ..78 B6
Ranelagh Rd M27 .....80 C7
Ranelagh St M11 ......83 B2
Raneley Gr OL11 ......31 A2
Ranford Rd M19 .....111 A8
Range Dr SK6 ....126 B7
Range Hall Ct ⑦ SK1 .112 A1
Range La OL3 ....69 D3
Range Rd Dukinfield SK16 .102 B7
Manchester M16 ......97 E3
Stalybridge SK15 .....102 B8

Range Rd continued
Stockport SK3 ....170 E7
Range St Bolton BL3 ..147 D4
Manchester M11 ......165 C8
Rangemore Ave M22 .121 D8
Ranicar St WN2 ....57 C3
Rankine Terr BL3 ....145 D5
Ranmore Ave
Garswood WN4 ....72 D4
Manchester M11 ......99 D8
Rannoch Rd BL2 ......43 A7
Ransfield Rd M21 .....97 B1
Ranulph Ct ⑪ M6 .....80 D5
Ranworth Ave SK4 ...110 F2
Ranworth Cl Bolton BL1 .25 A6
Manchester M11 ......161 C8
Raper St OL4 ....67 C8
Rapes Highway OL3 ...33 F5
Raphael St BL1 ......143 D2
Rappax Rd WA15 ....129 A8
Rasbottom St BL3 ...145 E6
Raspberry La M44 ....94 A5
Rassbottom Brow ⑥
SK15 ....85 F2
Rassbottom Ind Est SK15 .85 F2
Rassbottom St SK15 ..85 F1
Rassey Cl WN6 ....37 A7
Rastell Wlk ㉘ M9 ...64 E3
Ratcliffe Ave M44 ....94 A2
Ratcliffe Rd WN2 ....38 C6
Ratcliffe St Leigh WN7 .75 F6
Manchester M19 ......99 B1
⑥ Stockport SK1 .....170 F8
Tyldesley M29 ....59 B1
Ratcliffe Terr OL5 ....86 C8
Rath Wlk ⑭ M40 .....83 C5
Rathan Rd M41 ....95 C4
Rathbone St OL16 ....31 C7
Rathbourne Ave M9 ..64 D4
Rathen Ave WN2 ......56 A8
Rathen Rd M20 ......110 C5
Rathmel Rd M23 ....108 F2
Rathmell Cl WA3 ......91 E3
Rathmore Ave M40 ..157 E5
Rathvale Dr M22 ....130 C8
Rathybank Cl ⑰ BL1 .142 C2
Rattenbury Ct M6 ....80 C5
Raveden Cl BL1 .....142 C3
Raveley Ave M14 ....110 D3
Ravelston Dr M9 .....157 D7
Raven Ave
Chadderton OL9 .....152 A5
Haslingden BB4 ....1 A7
Raven Cl M43 ....84 C3
Raven Croft BB4 ....1 B8
Raven Ct M15 ....162 E5
Raven Dr M44 ....94 A3
Raven Ho M6 ....81 A5
Raven Pk BB4 ....1 B8
Raven Rd Bolton BL3 .146 A4
Sale WA15 ....120 B8
Raven St Bury BL9 ...140 F4
Manchester M12 ......163 C8
Rochdale OL16 ....13 E1
Raven Terr ⑧ SK16 ..166 C1
Raven Way Salford M6 .154 F3
⑤ Salford,Pendleton M6 .81 A3
Ravendale Cl OL12 ....14 A1
Ravenfield Gr ⑩ BL1 .145 D8
Ravenhead Cl ⑱ M14 .110 D8
Ravenhead Dr WN8 ...53 A7
Ravenhead Sq SK15 ..86 E5
Ravenhurst M7 ....63 E1
Ravenhurst Dr BL1 ...40 D6
Ravenna Ave M23 ...120 D7
Ravenoak Ave M19 ..111 C8
Ravenoak Park Rd SK8 .132 B8
Ravenoak Rd
Cheadle SK8 ....132 B8
Stockport SK2 ....124 A4
Ravens Cl M25 ....63 E2
Ravens Holme BL1 ....40 E7
Ravens Wood BL1 .....40 E7
Ravensbury Com Prim Sch
M11 ....83 B2
Ravensbury St M11 ...83 B2
Ravenscar Cres M22 .130 D8
Ravenscar Wlk BL4 ...60 D7
Ravenscraig Rd M38 ..60 B6
Ravensdale Gdns M30 .79 E3
Ravensdale Rd BL1 ...40 E7
Ravensdale St M14 ...98 C3
Ravensfield Ind Est
SK16 ....166 B1
Ravenside Pk OL9 ...152 A5
Ravenside Ret Pk BL2 .148 A6
Ravenstone Dr Diggle OL3 .51 C3
Sale M33 ....108 C2
Ravenstones Dr OL2 ..48 E5
Ravenswood 63 D2
Ravenswood M40 ....109 F4
Ravenswood Ave
Stockport SK4 ....168 A1
Wigan WN3 ....54 D3
Ravenswood Ct ⑤ SK3 .123 F4
Ravenswood Dr
Bolton BL1 ....40 E7
Cheadle SK8 ....132 B8
Hindley WN2 ....56 E7
Manchester M9 ....64 E3
Ravenswood Rd
Stretford M32 ....96 F4
Wilmslow SK9 ....136 E4

Ravenwood OL9 ....65 D7
Ravenwood Dr
  Altrincham WA15 .....129 D7
  Denton M34 ....100 E6
Ravine Ave M9 ....157 F7
Rawcliffe Ave BL2 .....42 F7
Rawcliffe St M14 ......98 B3
Rawdon Cl **8** M19 ...99 B1
Rawkin Cl M15 ....162 E5
Rawlinson St **12** BL6 ..22 B4
Rawlyn Rd BL1 ....142 A2
Rawpool Gdns M23 ....121 A7
Rawson Ave BL1 ....142 C1
Rawson Rd BL1 ....142 C1
Rawson St BL4 ....142 C1
Rawsons Rake BL0,BL8 .138 A6
Rawsthorne Ave BL0 ....1 D2
Rawthorne St
  Bolton BL1 ....143 E2
  Tyldesley M29 ....77 D8
Rawstron St OL12 ....4 C1
Rawthey Pl WN2 ....55 F2
Rayburn Way M8 ......156 A5
Raycroft Ave M9 ......65 A2
Raydale Cl WA3 ....74 E1
Rayden Cres BL5 ......57 E6
Raydon Ave M40 ......157 D5
Rayleigh Ave M11 .....99 F7
Raymond Ave Bury BL9 .27 F5
  Oldham OL9 ....66 B4
Raymond Rd M23 .....109 B2
Raymond St M27 ......61 F1
Rayner La
  Ashton-u-L M34,M43,OL7 .84 E2
  Ashton-u-L OL7 ......84 F3
Rayner St SK4 ....124 B8
Rayners Cl SK15 ......85 F1
Raynham Ave M20 ....110 B3
Raynham St OL6 .....166 C3
Rayson Hill Dr M9 ....64 C2
Rayson St M9 ....64 C2
Reabrook Ave M12 ...164 F6
Reach The M28 ....60 E2
Read Cl BL9 ....44 D7
Read St SK14 ....101 C3
Read St W SK14 .....101 C3
Reade Ave M41 ....94 F1
Reade Ho M41 ....94 F1
Reading Cl M11 ......165 C8
Reading Dr M33 .....107 D4
Reading St M6 ....81 B5
Reading Wlk **1** M34 ..100 F1
Readitt Wlk M11 ......83 B2
Reaney Wlk M12 .....165 A6
Reather Wlk M40 ....159 C3
Rebecca St M8 ....156 A8
Recreation Ave WN4 ..73 D4
Recreation Dr WN5 ...71 C5
Recreation Rd M35 ...66 B1
Recreation St Bolton BL3 .147 E4
  Bolton,Harwood Lee BL2 ..25 E5
  Prestwich M25 ......63 C4
Rectory Ave
  Golborne WA3 ....90 C8
  Manchester M8 ......64 A1
  Prestwich M25 ......63 B4
Rectory CE Prim Sch
  WN4 ....72 D5
Rectory Cl Denton M34 .101 A2
  Radcliffe M26 ....44 D4
Rectory Ct **3** SK6 ...125 F5
Rectory Fields SK1 ...112 A1
Rectory Gdns
  Prestwich M25 ......63 B4
  Westhoughton BL5 ...57 E5
Rectory Gn Prestwich M25 .63 B4
  Stockport SK1 ......112 A1
Rectory Gr M25 ......63 B3
Rectory Hill BL9 .....28 D4
Rectory La Bury BL9 ..28 D4
  Prestwich M25 ......63 B4
  Radcliffe M26 ....44 B5
  Standish WN1,WN6 ...20 A1
Rectory Rd
  Downall Green WN4 ..72 D5
  Manchester M8 ......63 F1
Rectory St M24 ......46 F1
Red Bank Bury BL9 ...28 B6
  Manchester M4,M8 ..159 A3
Red Bank Ave WA12 ..89 F1
Red Barn Rd M26 .....43 C6
Red Bridge BL2 ......26 A1
Red Brook St OL11 ..139 D7
Red Gables OL7 ......84 A4
Red Hall **5** OL4 .....67 C6
Red Hill Way WN2 ....56 D6
Red House La WA14 .118 E8
Red La Bolton BL2 ...25 E1
  Disley SK12 ....135 C5
  Rochdale OL10 ......15 B2
Red Lane Prim Sch BL2 .25 F1
Red Lion St M4 .....159 A2
Red Lumb St OL12 ...13 A3
Red Pike Wlk **2** OL1 ..67 A8
Red Rock Brow WN1 ..37 C8
Red Rock La Kearsley M26 .61 E6
  Standish WN1,WN2 ...37 D8
Red Rose Cres M19 .111 C7
Red Rose St M33 ...108 B6
Red Rose Gdns M38 ..60 A4
Red Rose Ret Pk M5 .161 B8
Red Rose Wks OL2 ...48 F4
Red Row SK7 ....134 B8
Red Waters WN7 .....76 A6

Redacre SK12 ....133 F6
Redacre Rd M18 .....99 E5
Redbarn Cl SK6 .....112 F4
Redbourne Dr M41 ...94 F4
Redbrick Ct **8** OL7 .166 A1
Redbridge Gr M21 ..109 A8
Redbrook Ave M40 ..157 E5
Redbrook Cl **6** BL4 ..42 E1
Redbrook Gr **2** SK9 .131 D1
Redbrook Rd
  Altrincham WA15 ...120 D5
  Ince-in-M WN3 .....151 E6
  Partington M31 ....105 E2
Redburn Rd M23 ....121 B7
Redby St M11 ......165 B7
Redcar Ave
  Manchester M20 ...110 B6
  Urmston M41 ....95 A4
Redcar Cl
  Hazel Grove SK7 ...125 A1
  Oldham OL1 ....49 B1
Redcar Rd Bolton BL1 .142 B4
  Little Lever BL3 .....43 A3
  Pendlebury M27 .....80 C7
Redcar St OL12 .....139 E8
Redcliffe Ct M25 ....63 B2
Redcliffe Ave M14 ...98 C3
Redclyffe Rd Eccles M41 .95 D7
  Manchester M20 ...110 A5
Redcot Cl M45 ......62 C7
Redcote St M40 .....83 A8
Redcroft Gdns **2** M19 .110 E4
Redcroft Rd M33 ...107 C6
Redcross St
  Rochdale OL12 .....14 F1
  Rochdale,Town Head OL12 .139 F8
Redcross St N OL12 ..14 F1
Reddaway Cl M6 ....81 A5
Reddish Cl BL2 ......25 E6
Reddish La Lymm WA13 .117 A5
  Reddish M18,SK5 ...99 E4
Reddish North Sta SK5 .99 F2
Reddish South Sta SK5 .111 F6
Reddish Vale Ctry Pk*
  SK5 ....112 B7
Reddish Vale Ctry Pk Visitor
  Ctr* SK5 ....112 B7
Reddish Vale Rd SK5 .112 A7
Reddish Vale Tech Coll
  SK5 ....111 F7
Reddy La WA14 .....118 B1
Reddyshore Brow OL15 .16 C8
Reddyshore Scout Gate
  OL14 ....6 C5
Redesmere Cl
  Altrincham WA15 ...120 D6
  Droylsden M43 .....84 B1
Redesmere Dr
  Alderley Edge SK9 ..137 A1
  Cheadle SK8 ....123 C6
Redesmere Pk M41 .107 B8
Redesmere Rd SK9 .131 D5
Redfearn Wood OL12 .14 B2
Redfern Ave M33 ...108 E3
Redfern Cl SK13 ....104 A6
Redfern Cotts OL11 ..13 D1
Redfern Ho SK6 ....113 A2
Redfern St M4 .....159 A2
Redfern Way OL11 ..13 D1
Redfield Cl M11 ....160 F1
Redford Cl WN7 .....76 A5
Redford Dr SK7 ....124 A2
Redford St BL8 ......27 C3
Redgate Hadfield SK13 .104 C4
  Hyde SK14 ....113 D8
Redgate La
  Manchester M12 ....99 A4
  Manchester,Longsight
  M12 ....164 F5
Redgate Rd WN4 ....73 B6
Redgate Way BL4 ..147 F1
Redgrave Pas OL4 ...67 D8
Redgrave Rise WN3 ..54 D3
Redgrave Wlk M19 ..99 C1
Redhill Dr SK6 .....112 E3
Redhill Gr BL1 .....143 E1
Redhill St M4 ......159 C2
Redhouse La Disley SK12 .135 E7
  Romiley SK6 ....113 A4
Redington Cl M28 ...78 A5
Redisher Cl BL0 .....10 F3
Redisher Croft BL0 ..10 F3
Redland Ave M14 ..110 E8
Redland Cl OL15 ....16 B6
Redland Cres M21 .109 B6
Redland Ct WN2 ....56 A2
Redlynch Wlk M8 ..156 A6
Redmain Gr WA3 ...90 E8
Redmayne Cl WA12 ..89 B4
Redmere Dr BL0 ....10 A4
Redmere Gr M14 ...110 C8
Redmire Mews SK6 .101 F7
Redmires Ct **7** M5 ..81 A1
Redmond Cl M34 ...100 E4
Redmoor Sq **3** M13 .163 B7
Redmoss Row M27 ..80 D8
Rednal Wlk WN3 ...150 B6
Redpol Ave WN7 ....76 B5
Redpoll Cl M28 .....78 B6
Redruth St M14 .....98 B2
Redruth Wlk **4** OL9 ..48 A1
Redscar Wlk M24 ....46 E1

Redshank Cl WA12 ..89 C4
Redshank Gr WN7 ...76 A6
Redshaw Ave BL2 ...25 B6
Redshaw St M4 .....48 C3
Redstart Cl **7** WA3 ...90 E8
Redstart Gr M28 ....78 D8
Redstock Cl BL5 ....40 B1
Redstone Rd M19 ..110 D3
Redthorn Ave **2** M19 .110 F7
Redvale Rd M7 .....155 E6
Redvales Rd BL9 ....44 E1
Redvers St OL1 ....153 D8
Redwater Cl **9** M28 ..78 A6
Redwing Ctr M17 ...96 C6
Redwing Rd BL8 ....10 F2
Redwood Chadderton OL9 .65 D7
  Sale M33 ....107 C4
  Shevington WN6 ....36 B6
  Westhoughton BL5 ..57 C8
Redwood Ave Wigan WN5 .54 A6
  Wigan,Beech Hill WN6 ..36 F3
Redwood Cl OL12 ...14 B3
Redwood Dr Denton M34 .100 E6
  Manchester M8 ....156 B5
  Rawtenstall BR4 .....1 F8
  Romiley SK6 ....112 F3
Redwood Ho M22 ..109 C1
Redwood La OL4 ....67 E7
Redwood Park Gr OL16 .31 D7
Redwood Rd OL3 ...69 C7
Redwood St M6 .....81 A4
Reece Cres SK16 ..101 D8
Reece Ct WN3 ......55 A4
Reed Cl **8** OL1 ....153 E8
Reed Hill OL16 .....14 D4
Reed St Manchester M18 .99 D6
  9 Oldham OL1 .....67 A8
Reedbank M26 ......62 A8
Reedham Cl BL1 ...144 C8
Reedham Wlk
  Manchester M40 ...160 D4
  Oldham OL9 ....66 B4
Reedley Dr M28 .....78 C8
Reedmace Cl M28 ...78 B6
Reedmaker Pl M27 ..79 D8
Reedshaw Bank SK2 .124 D5
Reedshaw Rd M9 ..156 C6
Reedsmere Cl WN5 ..54 F6
Reeman Cl SK6 ....113 A4
Reeman Ct SK9 ....131 B2
Reeve Cl SK2 ......124 F5
Reeve St WA3 ......91 B8
Reeves Ct M5 ......80 A2
Reeves Rd M21 ...109 B7
Reeves St WN7 .....75 F6
Reevey Ave SK7 ...124 C2
Reform St Rochdale OL16 .15 A1
Reform Wlk M11 ...165 B8
Refuge St OL2 .....149 B6
Regaby Gr WN2 ....57 A5
Regal Cl M45 ....63 B8
Regal Fold OL12 ....15 B4
Regal Wlk M40 .....65 E1
Regan Ave M21 ...109 D7
  5 Radcliffe M26 ...44 B2
Regatta Cl OL9 .....66 A3
Regatta St M6 ......80 B8
Regency Chambers BL9 .140 E2
Regency Cl
  Glossop SK13 .....104 D1
  Manchester M40 ...157 D5
  Oldham OL8 ....66 D4
Regency Ct
  Altrincham WA15 ...120 C3
  Cheadle SK8 ....123 A2
  Rochdale OL11 .....29 F7
  Sale M33 ....107 F4
  Stockport SK2 .....124 A6
  Wigan WN1 ....151 D8
Regency Gdns
  Cheadle SK8 ....131 E8
  Hyde SK14 ....167 F4
Regency Lo M25 ....63 A3
Regency St BL8 ....136 F5
Regency Wharf WN7 .76 C4
Regent Ave
  Ashton-in-M WN4 ...72 F5
  Manchester M14 ....98 A2
  Walkden M38 ....60 C4
Regent Bank SK9 ..136 F5
Regent Cl Bramhall SK7 .132 D4
  Cheadle SK8 ....123 C4
  Heywood OL10 .....29 B1
  Wilmslow SK9 .....136 F5
Regent Cres
  Failsworth M35 .....83 E6
  Oldham OL12 ....48 D2
Regent Ct
  Altrincham WA15 ...119 D4
  Altrincham,Hale WA15 .129 C8
  Manchester SK4 ...111 C5
  Manchester,Broughton Park
  M7 ....63 D1
Regent Dr Bolton BL6 ..80 D7
  Denton M34 ....100 D1
  Leigh WN7 ....76 D7
Regent Ho M14 .....98 A3
Regent Pl M14 .....98 C4
Regent Rd
  Altrincham WA14 ...119 D4
  Bolton BL6 ....40 B6
  Platt Bridge WN2 ..56 A3
  Salford M5 ....161 A1
  Stockport SK2 .....124 A6
Regent Road Cvn Site
  M6 ....154 F4
Regent Sq M5 .....161 B8

Regent St Bury BL9 ..140 F4
  Eccles M30 ....79 F2
  Failsworth M40 ....83 D5
  Glossop SK13 .....104 D1
  Hadfield SK13 .....104 B5
  Heywood OL10 .....29 B2
  8 Hindley WN2 ....56 D5
  Littleborough OL15 .16 B5
  Middleton M24 .....54 A3
  Newton-le-W WA12 ..89 A3
  Oldham OL1 ....67 A7
  Ramsbottom BL0 ....11 A4
  Rochdale OL12,OL16 .15 A1
  Shaw OL2 ....149 B7
  Tyldesley M46 .....58 E2
Regent Terr M5 ...158 D1
Regents Dr OL5 ....86 D8
Regents Hill BL6 ...40 C6
Regents The SK9 ..137 C8
Regina Ave SK15 ...86 A2
Regina Cres WN7 ..76 E6
Regina St M6 ......80 A4
Reginald Latham Ct
  M40 ....160 D3
Reginald St Bolton BL3 .146 A2
  2 Droylsden M11 ..99 F7
  Eccles M30 ....79 C3
  Swinton M27 ....61 D1
Reid Cl M34 ....113 A8
Reigate Cl WA14 ..119 B1
Reigate Rd M41 ...106 E8
Reilly St M15 ......162 F6
Reins Lee Ave OL8 ..67 A2
Reins Lee Rd OL7 ..85 A6
Reliance St M40 ...83 C6
Reliance Street Ent Pk 1
  M40 ....83 C6
Reliance Street Trad Est
  M40 ....83 C6
Rembrandt Wlk OL2 .49 D4
Rena Cl SK4 ....169 D3
Rena Ct SK4 ......169 D3
Rendel Cl
  Newton-le-W WA12 ..89 D2
  Stretford M32 .....96 D2
Renfrew Cl WN3 ....55 A3
Renfrew Dr BL3 ....40 F3
Renfrew Rd WN2 ...38 C8
Rennie Cl M32 .....96 E2
Renshaw Dr M30 ...79 D1
Renshaw Ave BL9 .141 C3
Renshaw St
  Altrincham WA14 ...119 E5
  Eccles M30 ....79 D1
Renton Rd Bolton BL3 .146 B3
  Stretford M32 .....96 D1
Renwick Gr BL3 ...146 C3
Renwick Sq WN4 ...72 F3
Repton Ave
  Droylsden M43 .....83 D3
  Failsworth M40 ....65 E1
  Hyde SK14 ....167 E3
  Ince-in-M WN3 .....55 F4
  Oldham OL8 ....66 D3
  Reddish M34 ......100 A3
  Urmston M41 ......94 D2
Repton Cl **6** M33 .107 D3
Reservoir Rd SK3 .170 D7
Reservoir St Aspull WN2 .38 F6
  Rochdale OL16 .....15 C1
  Salford M3 ....158 E3
  Salford,Seedley M6 .80 D3
Restormel Ave WN2 .38 D5
Retford Ave OL16 ...31 B4
Retford Cl BL8 .....27 C3
Retford St OL4 .....67 B5
Retiro St OL1 .....153 F6
Retreat The SK6 ..113 C1
Reuben St SK4 ....169 E4
Revers St BL8 .....140 C3
Rex Bldgs SK9 ....137 B6
Reynard Ct **8** M14 ..98 E4
Reynard Rd M21 ..109 B7
Reynard St SK14 ..167 D3
Reynell Rd M13 ....98 F2
Reyner St Ashton-u-L OL6 .85 E2
  Manchester M1 ....163 A8
Reynold St SK14 ..167 D2
Reynolds Cl BL3 ..147 F4
Reynolds Dr
  Manchester M18 ....99 D6
  Marple SK6 ....126 A5
  Over Hulton BL5 ...58 F7
Reynolds Mews SK9 .137 E8
Reynolds Rd M16 ..97 C4
Rhine Cl BL8 ....26 F7
Rhine Dr M8 ......155 E6
Rhiwlas Dr BL9 ....44 F8
Rhode Hos SK6 ...113 B5
Rhode St BL8 ......26 F6
Rhodes Ave Haslingden BB4 .1 A7
  Oldham OL4 ....67 D8
  Uppermill OL3 .....51 C1
Rhodes Bank OL1 ..67 A7
Rhodes Cres OL11 ..30 F3
Rhodes Dr BL9 .....45 A2
Rhodes Gn M24 ....64 B8
Rhodes Hill OL4 ...67 D8
Rhodes St
  Dukinfield SK14 ...101 C3
  Hadfield SK13 .....104 B5
  Oldham,County End OL4 .67 C7
  Oldham,Mumps OL1 .67 A7
  Rochdale OL12 .....15 B3

Rhodes St continued
  Royton OL2 ....49 A3
Rhodes St N SK14 .101 C3
Rhodeswood Dr SK13 .104 A6
Rhos Ave Cheadle SK8 .122 E1
  Manchester M14 ...110 E8
  Middleton M24 .....65 A7
Rhos Dr SK7 ......124 D1
Rhosleigh Ave BL1 .143 E4
Rialto Gdns M7 ...155 E6
Ribbesford Rd WN3 .54 C4
Ribble Ave Bolton BL2 .42 E7
  Chadderton OL9 ...67 F8
  Littleborough OL15 .15 F6
Ribble Cl WA3 .....91 F2
Ribble Cres WN5 ...71 C3
Ribble Dr Boothstown M28 .77 F6
  Bury BL9 ....27 F8
  Kearsley BL4 ......60 E8
  Whitefield M45 ....45 A1
  Wigan WN5 ....54 C7
Ribble Drive Com Prim Sch
  M45 ....45 A1
Ribble Gr Heywood OL10 ..29 A3
  Leigh WN7 ....75 C5
Ribble Rd Oldham OL8 .66 D2
  Platt Bridge WN2 ..56 A2
  Shevington Moor WN6 .19 B2
Ribble St Bacup OL13 ..4 A8
  Rochdale OL11 .....30 E4
Ribble Wlk M43 ...100 A8
Ribblesdale Cl OL10 .66 E7
Ribblesdale Dr M40 .156 C5
Ribblesdale Rd BL3 .147 D4
Ribbleton Cl BL8 ...26 F1
Ribchester Dr BL9 ..44 D7
Ribchester Gdns WA3 .92 A3
Ribchester Gr BL2 ..25 E1
Riber Bank SK13 ..171 E1
Riber Cl **3** SK13 ..171 E1
Riber Fold **6** SK13 .171 E1
Riber Gn **20** SK13 .171 E1
Ribston St M15 ...162 E6
Rice St M3 ....162 E8
Richard Burch St 3
  BL9 ....140 F3
Richard Gwyn Cl BL5 .57 D6
Richard Reynolds Ct
  M44 ....105 E6
Richard St Failsworth M35 .83 F7
  Ince-in-M WN3 ....151 D6
  Radcliffe M26 .....43 F3
  Ramsbottom BL0 ...11 E7
  Rochdale OL11 ....139 F6
  Stockport SK1 ....169 F2
Richards Cl M34 ..100 F6
Richards Rd WN6 ..19 B3
Richardson Cl M45 .44 F1
Richardson Rd M30 .79 E2
Richardson St
  8 Manchester M11 ..99 E7
  Stockport SK1 ....124 A7
Richbell Cl M44 ...105 F7
Richborough Cl M7 .155 E5
Richelieu St BL3 ...42 A4
Richmond Ave
  Chadderton OL9 ...66 A4
  Handforth SK9 ....131 D4
  Manchester M25 ...63 C1
  Royton OL2 ....48 D4
  Urmston M41 ......95 E2
Richmond Cl Bury BL8 .26 F6
  Culcheth WA3 .....91 D4
  Dukinfield SK16 ...101 D6
  Hadfield SK13 .....104 A5
  Lymm WA13 ....117 B4
  Mossley OL5 ....86 E8
  Rochdale OL16 .....31 C3
  Sale M33 ....108 F3
  Shaw OL2 ....149 B5
  Stalybridge SK15 ...86 A1
  Standish WN1 .....37 B7
  Whitefield M45 ....62 D7
Richmond Cres OL5 .86 E8
Richmond Ct
  Altrincham WA14 ...119 B2
  Cheadle SK8 ....122 C6
  Denton M34 ....100 C4
  1 Manchester M13 .98 F4
  Stockport SK2 .....124 D5
Richmond Dr Leigh WN7 .76 D7
  Lymm WA13 ....117 B4
  Swinton M28 ......79 C3
Richmond Gdns
  Bolton BL3 ....42 B3
  Newton-le-W M22 ..89 C2
Richmond Gn WA14 .119 B2
Richmond Gr
  Cheadle SK8 ....122 F1
  Eccles M30 ....79 E3
  Farnworth BL4 ....42 A1
  Leigh WN7 ....76 E6
  Manchester M13 ....98 E4
Richmond Gr E M12 .164 E5
Richmond Hill
  Hyde SK14 ....167 F1
  Wigan WN5 ....54 C6
Richmond Hill Rd SK8 .122 C6
Richmond Ho **7** SK15 .86 A1
Richmond Park Sch
  M12 ....164 E5
Richmond Prim Sch
  OL9 ....153 D6
Richmond Rd
  Altrincham WA14 ...119 D5
  Altrincham,Rosehill WA14 .119 C2
  Ashton-in-M WN4 ..72 F5

Richmond Rd continued
Boothstown M28 . . . . **77** E7
Dukinfield SK16 . . . . **101** D6
Eccles M17 . . . . **96** A7
Failsworth M35 . . . . **84** B8
Hindley WN2 . . . . **57** A3
Manchester M14 . . . . **110** D8
Manchester,Heaton Mersey
SK4 . . . . **110** F2
Reddish M34 . . . . **100** A3
Romiley SK6 . . . . **113** C3
Richmond St
Ashton-u-L OL7 . . . . **84** F3
Atherton M46 . . . . **58** C2
Bury BL9 . . . . **44** E8
Denton M34 . . . . **100** F6
Droylsden M43 . . . . **84** C2
Horwich BL6 . . . . **22** B3
Hyde SK14 . . . . **167** A2
Manchester M1 . . . . **163** A8
Salford M3 . . . . **158** E3
Stalybridge SK15 . . . . **86** C2
Wigan WN1 . . . . **150** B8
Wigan,Worsley Mesnes
WN3 . . . . **150** A5
Richmond Terr SK6 . . . . **126** B1
Richmond Wlk
Oldham OL9 . . . . **153** D6
Radcliffe M26 . . . . **43** E6
Ricroft Rd SK6 . . . . **114** B3
Ridding Ave M22 . . . . **121** E3
Ridding Cl SK2 . . . . **124** D6
Ridding Ct WA15 . . . . **119** F8
Riddings Rd
Altrincham WA15 . . . . **119** F2
Sale WA15 . . . . **120** A8
Riddle Ct M5 . . . . **80** C2
Ridge Ave
Altrincham WA15 . . . . **129** D6
Marple SK6 . . . . **126** A4
Standish WN1 . . . . **37** B7
Ridge Cl Hadfield SK14 . . . . . **171** E3
Romiley SK6 . . . . **113** F2
Ridge Cres Marple SK6 . . . . . **126** A3
Marple SK6 . . . . **63** B8
Ridge Danvers Coll
Cheadle SK8 . . . . **122** F3
Marple SK6 . . . . **125** E5
Marple SK6 . . . . **125** F5
Ridge End Fold SK6 . . . . **126** A2
Ridge Gr M45 . . . . **63** B8
Ridge Hill La SK15 . . . . **86** A3
Ridge Hill Prim Sch SK15 . . . **85** F3
Ridge La OL3 . . . . **51** D5
Ridge Rd SK6 . . . . **132** D6
Ridge Pk SK7 . . . . **132** D6
Ridge Wlk M9 . . . . **64** E3
Ridgecroft OL7 . . . . **85** B6
Ridgedale Ctr ☑ SK6 . . . . **125** F6
Ridgedales The OL1 . . . . **49** E4
Ridgefield M2 . . . . **158** F1
Ridgefield St M35 . . . . **83** E6
Ridgegreen M28 . . . . **78** A5
Ridgemont Ave M45 . . . . **168** B2
Ridgemont Wlk ☑ M23 . . . . **108** F2
Ridgeway Golborne WA3 . . . . . **90** E7
Swinton M27 . . . . **62** B2
Wilmslow SK9 . . . . **137** F7
Ridgeway Gates ☑ BL1 . . . . **145** F7
Ridgeway Rd WA15 . . . . **120** C5
Ridgeway The SK12 . . . . **135** C6
Ridgewell Ave ☑ WA3 . . . . . . **90** D8
Ridgewood Ave
Chadderton OL9 . . . . **65** E8
Manchester M40 . . . . **157** D5
Ridgewood Cl WN2 . . . . **57** C3
Ridgmont Dr
Boothstown M28 . . . . **77** F6
Horwich BL6 . . . . **22** F3
Ridgmont Rd SK7 . . . . **132** E5
Ridgway St M40 . . . . **160** D2
Ridgway The SK6 . . . . **114** A1
Riding Cl M29 . . . . **77** D7
Riding Fold M43 . . . . **84** D3
Riding Fold La M28 . . . . **79** A5
Riding Gate BL2 . . . . **25** E6
Riding Gate Mews BL2 . . . . . . **25** E6
Riding Head La BL0 . . . . **11** F8
Riding La WN4 . . . . **73** B5
Ridings St M40 . . . . **158** E1
Ridings Ct OL3 . . . . **51** A2
Ridings Rd SK13 . . . . **103** F5
Ridings St
Manchester M40 . . . . **157** F5
Manchester,Openshaw
M11 . . . . **165** B8
Ridings Way OL9 . . . . **152** B6
Ridley Dr WA14 . . . . **107** E1
Ridley Gr M33 . . . . **108** F3
Ridley St OL4 . . . . **67** A6
Ridley Wlk M15 . . . . **163** A5
Ridling La SK14 . . . . **167** E2
Ridsdale Ave M20 . . . . **110** A6
Ridsdale Way M6 . . . . **81** A5
Ridyard St
Platt Bridge WN2 . . . . **56** B3
Walkden M38 . . . . **59** F5
Walkden M38 . . . . **54** C7
Riefield BL1 . . . . **142** B3
Rifle Rd M21,M33 . . . . **108** F5
Rifle St OL1 . . . . **153** F8
Riga Rd M14 . . . . **98** C1
Riga St M4 . . . . **159** A2
Rigby Ave Blackrod BL6 . . . . . **21** C2

Rigby Ave continued
Radcliffe M26 . . . . **44** C5
Rigby Ct Bolton BL3 . . . . **147** F4
Rochdale OL12 . . . . **13** E2
Rigby Gr M38 . . . . **59** E4
Rigby La BL2 . . . . **25** C5
Rigby St
Altrincham WA14 . . . . **119** D3
Ashton-in-M WN4 . . . . **73** A3
Bolton BL3 . . . . **147** F4
Golborne WA3 . . . . **90** A8
Hindley WN2 . . . . **56** E6
Salford M7 . . . . **155** D5
Rigby Wlk M7 . . . . **155** E6
Rigby's Yd ☑ WN5 . . . . **54** B6
Rigel Pl M7 . . . . **81** C3
Rigel St M4 . . . . **159** C3
Rigton Cl M12 . . . . **165** A5
Riley Cl M33 . . . . **107** B1
Riley Ct ☑ BL1 . . . . **143** F1
Riley La WN2 . . . . **38** B7
Riley Sq WN1 . . . . **151** D8
Riley St M46 . . . . **58** A1
Riley Wood Cl SK6 . . . . **112** F1
Rilldene Wlk OL11 . . . . **29** D8
Rilston Ave WA3 . . . . **91** D3
Rimington Ave WA3 . . . . **74** C1
Rimington Cl WA3 . . . . **91** E3
Rimington Fold M24 . . . . **46** D3
Rimmer Cl M11 . . . . **160** E1
Rimmington Cl M9 . . . . **65** A2
Rimsdale Cl SK8 . . . . **122** A3
Rimsdale Wlk BL3 . . . . **40** E5
Rimworth Dr M40 . . . . **159** C4
Rindle Rd M29 . . . . **93** C8
Ring Lows La OL12 . . . . **15** A4
Ring-o-Bells La SK12 . . . . . . **135** D6
Ringcroft Gdns M40 . . . . **65** B1
Ringford Wlk M40 . . . . **157** E5
Ringley Ave WA3 . . . . **73** F1
Ringley Chase M45 . . . . **62** E8
Ringley Cl M45 . . . . **62** D8
Ringley Ct M27 . . . . **80** E8
Ringley Dr M45 . . . . **62** E7
Ringley Gr BL1 . . . . **24** E5
Ringley Hey M45 . . . . **62** D8
Ringley Mdws M26 . . . . **61** C7
Ringley Old Brow M26 . . . . . . **61** C7
Ringley Pk M45 . . . . **62** E8
Ringley Rd Kearsley M45 . . . . . **61** D8
Kearsley M45 . . . . **61** D8
Whitefield M45 . . . . **62** C7
Ringley Rd W M26 . . . . **61** E8
Ringley St M9 . . . . **157** D8
Ringlow Ave M27 . . . . **79** C7
Ringlow Park Rd M27 . . . . **79** C7
Ringmer Dr ☑ M22 . . . . **121** C1
Ringmere Ct ☑ OL1 . . . . **153** F8
Ringmore Rd SK7 . . . . **124** A2
Rings Cl M35 . . . . **83** F6
Ringstead Cl SK9 . . . . **131** D1
Ringstead Dr
Manchester M40 . . . . **159** C3
☑ Handforth SK9 . . . . **131** D1
Ringstone M25 . . . . **63** A3
Ringway Ave WN7 . . . . **75** F8
Ringway Gr M33 . . . . **108** E2
Ringway Rd M22,M90 . . . . . . **130** D7
Ringway Rd W M22,M90 . . . . **130** B8
Ringway Trad Est M22 . . . . **130** E8
Ringwood Ave
Droylsden M34 . . . . **84** C1
Hazel Grove SK7 . . . . **124** B1
Hyde SK14 . . . . **102** A1
Manchester M12 . . . . **99** B3
Radcliffe M26 . . . . **44** B1
Ramsbottom BL0 . . . . **11** A4
Ringwood Way OL9 . . . . **152** C8
Rink St M14 . . . . **110** D7
Ripley Ave Cheadle SK8 . . . . **132** B5
Stockport SK2 . . . . **124** B4
Ripley Cl Hazel Grove SK7 . . **133** E8
Manchester M4 . . . . **164** D8
Ripley Cres M41 . . . . **94** F5
Ripley Dr Leigh WN7 . . . . **75** F7
Wigan WN3 . . . . **54** C4
Ripley St BL2 . . . . **25** B4
Ripley Way M34 . . . . **112** F8
Ripon Ave Bolton BL1 . . . . **23** F1
Golborne WA3 . . . . **90** D8
☑ Wigan WN6 . . . . **37** B3
Ripon Cl
Altrincham WA15 . . . . **120** C1
Chadderton OL9 . . . . **152** B6
Little Lever BL3 . . . . **42** F3
Newton-le-W WA12 . . . . **89** C5
Radcliffe M26 . . . . **44** B5
Stockport SK1 . . . . **170** F8
☑ Whitefield M45 . . . . **44** F2
Ripon Cres WN2 . . . . **56** B3
Ripon Dr Ashton-in-M WN4 . . . **73** D2
Bolton BL1 . . . . **23** F1
Ripon Hall Ave BL0 . . . . **11** B4
Ripon Ho M14 . . . . **98** E4
Ripon Rd M32 . . . . **95** F3
Ripon St Ashton-u-L OL6 . . . . **166** C3
Manchester M15 . . . . **163** A5
Oldham OL1 . . . . **153** D8
Ripon Wlk SK6 . . . . **113** A1
Rippenden Ave M21 . . . . **97** A2
Rippingham Rd M20 . . . . **110** B7
Rippleton Rd M22 . . . . **121** E4
Ripponden Rd
Denshaw OL3 . . . . **33** D3
Oldham OL1,OL4 . . . . **49** E3
Ripponden St ☑ OL1 . . . . **49** C1
Ripton Wlk M9 . . . . **64** B4

Risbury Wlk ☑ M40 . . . . **83** C6
Rise The Oldham OL4 . . . . **67** F7
Wigan WN6 . . . . **36** C3
Rises The SK13 . . . . **103** F5
Rishton Ave BL3 . . . . **147** F2
Rishton La BL3 . . . . **147** F3
Rishworth Cl SK2 . . . . **124** D5
Rishworth Dr M40 . . . . **83** E8
Rishworth Rise OL2 . . . . **32** A1
Rising La OL8 . . . . **66** E2
Rising Lane Cl OL8 . . . . **66** E2
Rising The SK22 . . . . **127** B1
Risley Ave M9 . . . . **64** E3
Risley St OL1 . . . . **153** F8
Rissington Ave M23 . . . . **121** B6
Rita Ave ☑ M14 . . . . **98** B3
Ritson Cl M18 . . . . **165** B6
Riva Rd M19 . . . . **110** D2
River La M31 . . . . **105** F4
River Pl Manchester M15 . . . . **162** E7
Milnrow OL16 . . . . **31** F6
River St
Bury,Blackford Bridge BL9 . . . . . **44** F4
Bury,Heap Bridge BL9 . . . . **141** C2
Heywood OL10 . . . . **29** D3
Manchester M15 . . . . **162** F7
Manchester,Ardwick M12 . . . . . **163** C8
Radcliffe M26 . . . . **44** B2
Rochdale OL16 . . . . **139** F7
Stockport SK1 . . . . **112** B3
Wilmslow SK9 . . . . **137** B8
River View SK5 . . . . **112** A7
River View Cl M25 . . . . **62** F2
River Way WN1 . . . . **150** C8
Riverbank OL3 . . . . **50** F1
Riverbank Dr BL8 . . . . **140** D3
Riverbank Lawns M3 . . . . **158** E3
Riverbank The M26 . . . . **61** A8
Riverbank Twr M3 . . . . **158** E3
Riverbank Way SK13 . . . . **116** F7
Riverbank Wlk M20 . . . . **109** E4
Riverbanks BL2 . . . . **148** C5
Riverdale Cl WN6 . . . . **36** D4
Riverdale Rd M9 . . . . **64** B3
Rivermead OL12 . . . . **14** D4
Rivermead Ave WA15 . . . . . . **129** C7
Rivermead Cl M34 . . . . **113** A7
Rivermead Rd M34 . . . . **113** B7
Rivermead Way M45 . . . . **63** A8
Riverpark Rd M40 . . . . **83** A3
Rivers Edge The OL12 . . . . **4** C1
Rivers La M41 . . . . **95** C5
Rivers St WN5 . . . . **53** E6
Riversdale Dr OL8 . . . . **67** A1
Riversdale Rd SK8 . . . . **122** C5
Riversdale View SK6 . . . . **113** A5
Riversdale Ct M25 . . . . **63** A3
Rivershill M33 . . . . **108** A6
Rivershill Dr OL10 . . . . **29** B2
Rivershill Gdns WA15 . . . . . . **129** D6
Riverside Bolton BL1 . . . . **25** A2
Chadderton OL9 . . . . **47** E1
Dukinfield SK16 . . . . **166** C1
Salford M7 . . . . **158** D3
Riverside Ave Irlam M44 . . . . . **94** F3
Manchester M21 . . . . **109** D3
Wigan WN1 . . . . **37** D1
Riverside Bsns Pk SK9 . . . . . **137** B7
Riverside Cl SK13 . . . . **104** D1
Riverside Ct
Manchester M20 . . . . **109** F3
Marple SK6 . . . . **126** B8
Whitworth OL12 . . . . **4** D4
Riverside Dr Kearsley M26 . . . **61** B8
Ramsbottom BL0 . . . . **11** B2
Rochdale OL16 . . . . **15** C2
Urmston M41 . . . . **107** B8
Riverside Gdns M33 . . . . **108** A6
Riverside Ho OL3 . . . . **51** A2
Riverside Mews M15 . . . . **162** E7
Riverside Rd M26 . . . . **44** D4
Riverside Wlk BB4 . . . . **1** A7
Riverside Works BL2 . . . . **148** B8
Riversleigh Cl BL1 . . . . **23** F3
Riversmeade Bolton BL7 . . . . . **25** C7
Leigh WN7 . . . . **75** E6
Riverstone Bridge OL15 . . . . . **16** B5
Riverstone Dr M23 . . . . **120** D7
Riverton Rd M20 . . . . **122** B8
Riverview M7 . . . . **158** C4
Riverview Cotts SK13 . . . . **116** C7
Riverview Ct M7 . . . . **81** C8
Riviera Ct OL12 . . . . **13** C2
Rivington Ave
Bickershaw WN2 . . . . **74** F8
Bury BL8 . . . . **27** A1
Shaw OL2 . . . . **49** D7
Up Holland WN8 . . . . **53** C7
Rivington Gr
Droylsden M34 . . . . **100** C8
Irlam M44 . . . . **105** D6
Rivington Hall Cl BL0 . . . . **11** C4
Rivington La
Adlington PR6 . . . . **21** D6
Horwich BL6 . . . . **22** A7

Rivington Pl PR7 . . . . **19** D6
Rivington Rd
Altrincham WA15 . . . . **119** F2
Oldham OL4 . . . . **68** A7
Salford M6 . . . . **80** C4
Rivington St Atherton M46 . . . . **58** B2
Blackrod BL6 . . . . **21** D2
Oldham OL1 . . . . **48** F1
Rochdale OL12 . . . . **14** F1
Rivington Way WN6 . . . . **36** F8
Rivington Wlk M12 . . . . **164** F5
Rix St BL1 . . . . **143** E2
Rixson St OL4 . . . . **67** D6
Rixton Ct M16 . . . . **97** B3
Rixton Dr M29 . . . . **77** B8
RL Hughes Prim Sch
WN4 . . . . **73** A3
Roach Cl WN1 . . . . **159** C4
Roach Gn WN1 . . . . **37** E1
Roach Pl OL16 . . . . **31** A8
Roach St
Bury,Blackford Bridge BL9 . . . . . **44** F4
Bury,Heap Bridge BL9 . . . . **141** C2
Roach Vale OL16 . . . . **15** C2
Roaches Ind Est OL5 . . . . **68** B3
Roaches Mews OL5 . . . . **68** D3
Roaches Way OL5 . . . . **68** E3
Roachill Cl WA14 . . . . **119** B5
Roachwood Cl OL9 . . . . **65** E7
Road La OL12 . . . . **14** D4
Roading Brook Rd BL2 . . . . . . **26** B3
Roads Ford Ave OL16 . . . . **31** F7
Roadside Ct WA3 . . . . **90** C8
Roaring Gate La WA15 . . . . . **120** E2
Rob La WA12 . . . . **89** E5
Robe Wlk ☑ M18 . . . . **99** D6
Robert Hall St M5 . . . . **161** B8
Robert Lawrence Ct M41 . . . . . **95** A1
Robert Malcolm Cl M40 . . . . . **157** D5
Robert Owen Gdns M22 . . . . **121** D8
Robert Owen St M43 . . . . **84** C2
Robert Salt Ct WA14 . . . . **119** E6
Robert Saville Ct OL11 . . . . . . **30** C6
Robert St Bolton BL2 . . . . **25** F3
Bury BL8 . . . . **27** C3
Dukinfield SK16 . . . . **101** B8
Dukinfield,Kingston SK14 . . . . . **101** C3
☑ Failsworth M35 . . . . **66** A1
Heywood OL10 . . . . **46** E8
Manchester M3 . . . . **158** E3
Oldham OL8 . . . . **66** B3
Platt Bridge WN2 . . . . **56** A3
Prestwich M25 . . . . **63** C4
Radcliffe M26 . . . . **44** A4
Ramsbottom BL0 . . . . **1** C1
☑ Sale M33 . . . . **108** B6
Sale M33 . . . . **108** B6
Tyldesley M46 . . . . **58** E1
Roberts Ave M14 . . . . **98** B4
Roberts St M30 . . . . **79** D1
Robertscroft Cl M22 . . . . **121** C3
Robertshaw Ave M21 . . . . **109** B6
Robertshaw St WN7 . . . . **75** F7
Robeson Way M22,SK8 . . . . . **121** F6
Robin Cl BL4 . . . . **59** F7
Robin Croft SK5 . . . . **112** D3
Robin Dr M44 . . . . **94** A3
Robin Hill Dr WN6 . . . . **19** B2
Robin Hill La WN6 . . . . **19** C3
Robin Hood La WN6 . . . . **118** B3
Robin Hood St M8 . . . . **155** F8
Robin Park Rd WN5 . . . . **54** F7
Robin Rd BL9 . . . . **11** B2
Robin St OL1 . . . . **153** E8
Robin's La Billinge WA11 . . . . . **71** A8
Bramhall SK7 . . . . **132** D7
Robina Cl M30 . . . . **94** F8
Robins Cl Bramhall SK7 . . . . . **132** E7
Droylsden M43 . . . . **84** C3
Robins La WA3 . . . . **91** D2
Robinsbay Rd M22 . . . . **130** E8
Robinson St Pk SK15 . . . . **85** E1
Robinson St
Ashton-u-L OL6 . . . . **166** B4
Chadderton OL9 . . . . **152** B6
Dukinfield SK15 . . . . **101** E8
☑ Horwich BL6 . . . . **22** B4
Hyde SK14 . . . . **167** F3
☑ Oldham OL1 . . . . **153** F6
Stockport SK3 . . . . **170** D7
☑ Tyldesley M29 . . . . **59** A1
Robinsway WA14 . . . . **119** C1
Robinswood Rd M22 . . . . **121** D2
Robinwood Lo SK13 . . . . **171** E1
Robson Ave M41 . . . . **95** F2
Robson Pl WN2 . . . . **74** B8
Robson St OL1 . . . . **153** F6
Robson Way ☑ WA3 . . . . **90** F8
Roby Cl M1 . . . . **159** B1
Roby Mill WN8 . . . . **35** B3
Roby Rd M30 . . . . **94** D8
Roby St M1 . . . . **159** B1
Roby Well Way WN5 . . . . **71** D5
Roch Ave OL10 . . . . **29** A2
Roch Cres M45 . . . . **45** C1
Roch Mills Cres OL11 . . . . **30** C5
Roch Mills Gdns OL11 . . . . . . **139** D5
Roch Pl WN7 . . . . **75** F7
Roch St OL16 . . . . **31** A8
Roch Vale Cvn Pk OL16 . . . . . **31** A7
Roch Valley Way OL11 . . . . . . **30** C5
Roch Way M45 . . . . **45** B1
Roch Wlk M45 . . . . **45** C1
Rochbury Cl OL11 . . . . **29** F6

Rochdale AFC (Spotland Stadium) OL11 . . . . **30** C8
Rochdale Ho M15 . . . . **162** E7
Rochdale Infmy OL12 . . . . **14** F1
Rochdale La
Heywood OL10 . . . . **29** D2
Royton OL2 . . . . **48** D5
Rochdale Old Rd BL9 . . . . **28** B4
Rochdale Pioneers Mus*
OL12 . . . . **139** F8
Rochdale Rd Bacup OL13 . . . . . **4** B8
Bury BL9 . . . . **141** B2
Denshaw OL3 . . . . **33** B3
Edenfield BL0 . . . . **1** F2
Heywood OL10 . . . . **29** D2
Littleborough HX6,OL15 . . . . **7** E1
Manchester M9 . . . . **64** D3
Manchester,Collyhurst
M40,M8,M9 . . . . **157** D6
Middleton M24,OL11 . . . . **47** C4
Milnrow OL16 . . . . **31** E7
Oldham OL1 . . . . **49** A4
Oldham,Cold Hurst OL1 . . . . . . **153** E8
Ramsbottom BL0 . . . . **12** B7
Royton OL2 . . . . **48** D6
Shaw OL2 . . . . **149** B7
Shaw,High Crompton OL2,
OL16 . . . . **48** F8
Walsden OL14,OL15 . . . . **6** B6
Rochdale Rd E OL10 . . . . **29** F3
Rochdale Sta OL11 . . . . **139** F6
Roche Gdns SK8 . . . . **132** B6
Roche Rd OL3 . . . . **50** E5
Rochester Ave Bolton BL2 . . . . **25** E1
Manchester M21 . . . . **109** C6
Manchester,Sedgley Park
M25 . . . . **63** C2
Walkden M28 . . . . **60** C1
Rochester Cl
Ashton-u-L OL6 . . . . **85** C7
Dukinfield SK16 . . . . **102** A7
Golborne WA3 . . . . **90** A8
Rochester Dr WA14 . . . . **107** E1
Rochester Gr SK7 . . . . **124** E3
Rochester Rd M41 . . . . **95** D4
Rochester Way OL9 . . . . **152** B6
Rochford Ave
Whitefield M45 . . . . **62** D7
Wythenshawe M22 . . . . **130** D8
Rochford Cl M45 . . . . **62** D7
Rochford Ho M34 . . . . **100** E6
Rochford Rd M30 . . . . **94** F8
Rock Ave BL1 . . . . **142** C2
Rock Fold BL7 . . . . **8** F1
Rock Gdns SK14 . . . . **113** E2
Rock Nook OL15 . . . . **6** D1
Rock Rd Urmston M41 . . . . **95** F2
Worsley M28 . . . . **78** B2
Rock St Ashton-u-L OL7 . . . . . . **85** A5
Droylsden M11 . . . . **99** E8
Golborne WA3 . . . . **74** A2
☑ Heywood OL10 . . . . **29** E1
Hyde SK14 . . . . **113** B3
Oldham OL1 . . . . **153** F7
Radcliffe M26 . . . . **44** B2
Ramsbottom BL0 . . . . **11** F7
Salford M7 . . . . **155** D6
Rock Terr Bolton BL7 . . . . **8** F1
Mossley OL5 . . . . **68** D3
Rock The Bury BL9 . . . . **140** F3
Bury BL9 . . . . **140** F3
Rockall Wlk M11 . . . . **160** F1
Rockbourne Ct ☑ WN2 . . . . . . **56** A4
Rockdove Ave M15 . . . . **162** F7
Rocket Way M3 . . . . **158** D1
Rockfield Dr ☑ M9 . . . . **157** E8
Rockhampton St M18 . . . . **99** E5
Rockhaven Ave BL6 . . . . **22** C4
Rockhouse Cl M30 . . . . **95** C8
Rockingham Cl
Manchester M12 . . . . **164** D6
Shaw OL2 . . . . **48** B8
Rockingham Dr WN7 . . . . **76** C4
Rockland Wlk ☑ M40 . . . . **65** C2
Rockley Gdns M6 . . . . **81** B4
Rocklyn Ave M40 . . . . **65** C2
Rocklynes SK6 . . . . **113** B2
Rockmead Dr M9 . . . . **64** E3
Rocky Bank Terr WN3 . . . . . . **151** E5
Rocky La M27,M30 . . . . **79** D4
Roda St M9 . . . . **157** F7
Rodborough Rd M23 . . . . **121** A3
Rodenheath Cl SK9 . . . . **137** D7
Rodenhurst Dr ☑ M40 . . . . **83** A7
Rodepool Cl SK9 . . . . **131** D2
Rodgers Cl BL5 . . . . **57** E6
Rodgers Way BL5 . . . . **57** E6
Rodmell Ave M40 . . . . **157** D5
Rodmell Cl BL7 . . . . **9** C2
Rodmill Ct M14 . . . . **98** C1
Rodmill Dr SK8 . . . . **122** A4
Rodney Ct ☑ M4 . . . . **159** C3
Rodney Dr SK6 . . . . **113** A5
Rodney St Ashton-u-L OL7 . . . . **84** F1
Atherton M46 . . . . **58** C2
Manchester M4 . . . . **159** C2
Rochdale OL11 . . . . **139** D6
Salford M3 . . . . **158** D1
Wigan WN1 . . . . **150** C7
Roe Cross Gn SK14 . . . . **102** F3
Roe Cross Ind Est SK14 . . . . **103** A5
Roe Cross Rd SK14,SK15 . . . **102** F5
Roe Gn M28 . . . . **79** A8
Roe Green Ave M28 . . . . **79** A8

Roe La OL4 ....67 D5
Roe St Manchester M4 ....159 C3
  Rochdale OL12 ....14 C1
Roeacre Bsns Pk OL10 ......29 E2
Roeacre St OL10 ....29 E2
Roebuck Gdns [5] M33 .....108 A4
Roebuck La Oldham OL4 ....50 A3
  Sale M33 ....108 A4
Roebuck St WN2 ....57 C3
Roeburn Wlk M45 ....63 C8
Roecliffe Cl WN3 ....150 B6
Roedean Gdns M41 ....94 D2
Roefield Terr OL12 ....30 B8
Rogate Dr M23 ....121 A5
Roger Byrne Cl M40 ....83 B5
Roger Cl SK6 ....112 F2
Roger Hay SK8 ....123 A2
Roger St M8 ....159 A3
Rogerson Cl WA15 ....120 C7
Rogerstead BL3 ....144 C6
Rogerton Cl WN7 ....26 B4
Rokeby Ave Golborne WA3 ..74 D1
  Stretford M32 ....96 D1
Rokeden WA12 ....89 D4
Roker Ave M13 ....98 F2
Roker Ind Est OL1 ....67 B7
Roker Park Ave M34 ....100 D7
Roland Rd [2] Bolton BL3 ...146 C4
  Reddish SK5 ....111 F7
Rolla St M3 ....158 E2
Rollesby Cl BL8 ....27 D5
Rolleston Ave M40 ....160 D2
Rollins La SK6 ....114 A1
Rolls Cres M15 ....162 E5
Rollswood Dr M40 ....83 A6
Roman Cl
  Newton-le-W WA12 ....89 C2
  Wigan WN3 ....54 F4
Roman Ct M7 ....155 D5
Roman Rd
  Ashton-in-M WN4 ....73 A5
  Manchester M25 ....63 A1
  Oldham M35,OL8 ....66 B1
  Royton OL2 ....48 E3
  Stockport SK4 ....169 E2
Roman St Ashton-u-L OL7 ..166 A1
  Manchester M44 ....159 A2
  Mossley OL5 ....68 D3
  Radcliffe M26 ....43 E3
Romans Cl SK15 ....86 C3
Rome Rd M40 ....159 C3
Romer Ave M40 ....65 E1
Romer St BL2 ....148 C7
Romford Ave
  Denton M34 ....101 A4
  Leigh WN7 ....75 F6
Romford Cl OL8 ....153 E5
Romford Pl WN2 ....56 E5
Romford Rd M33 ....107 E6
Romford St WN2 ....56 E5
Romford Wlk M9 ....64 A2
Romiley Cres BL2 ....42 D8
Romiley Dr BL2 ....42 D8
Romiley Prec SK6 ....113 C2
Romiley Prim Sch SK6 ......113 C2
Romiley Sq WN6 ....36 E8
Romiley St Salford M6 ....80 D5
  Stockport SK1 ....112 B3
Romiley Sta SK6 ....113 C2
Romley Rd M41 ....95 D4
Romney Ave OL11 ....30 F2
Romney Chase BL1 ....143 E4
Romney Rd BL1 ....23 E2
Romney St
  Ashton-u-L OL6 ....166 C3
  Manchester M40 ....83 A8
  Salford M6 ....81 B5
Romney Twrs SK5 ....112 B6
Romney Way
  Brinnington SK5 ....112 B6
  Wigan WN1 ....37 B3
Romney Wlk OL9 ....152 B6
Romsey Ave M41 ....46 F3
Romsey Dr SK8 ....132 C6
Romsey Gdns M23 ....121 A6
Romsey Gr WN3 ....54 D2
Romsley Cl M12 ....165 A6
Romsley Dr BL3 ....146 C3
Rona Wlk M12 ....164 F5
Ronald St
  Droylsden M11,M43 ....83 D1
  Oldham OL4 ....67 C7
  Rochdale OL11 ....30 C1
Ronaldsay Gdns M5 ....154 E1
Ronan Ct SK4 ....168 B4
Rondin Cl M12 ....164 E2
Rondin Rd M12 ....164 E8
Ronnis Mount OL7 ....85 A7
Ronton Wlk M8 ....156 C8
Roocroft Cl BL1 ....143 D1
Roocroft Sq BL6 ....21 C2
Rooden Ct M25 ....63 C4
Roods La OL11 ....13 C1
Rook St Manchester M15 ...162 E5
  Oldham OL4 ....67 C5
  Ramsbottom BL0 ....13 A6
Rooke St M30 ....95 A8
Rookery Ave
  Appley Bridge WN6 ....35 E8
  Ashton-in-M WN4 ....73 B2
  Droylsden M18 ....99 F6
Rookery Cl SK15 ....102 E7
Rookery The WA12 ....139 D4
Rookerypool Cl SK9 ....131 D2

Rookfield M33 ....108 C5
Rookfield Ave M33 ....108 C5
Rookley Wlk [11] M14 ....98 C3
Rookswood Dr OL11 ....30 B3
Rookway M24 ....65 A7
Rookwood OL1,OL9 ....47 E1
Rookwood Ave M23 ....120 F7
Rookwood Hill SK7 ....123 E1
Rooley Moor Rd
  Bacup OL12,OL13 ....3 C4
  Rochdale OL12 ....14 A3
  Rochdale,Spotland Fold
  OL12 ....14 C1
Rooley St OL11,OL12 ....14 C1
Roosevelt Rd BL4 ....60 F7
Rooth St SK4 ....169 D2
Rope St OL12 ....139 F8
Rope Wlk M6 ....162 B6
Ropefield Way LE12 ....14 E3
Ropley Wlk [4] M9 ....64 F1
Rosa Gr M7 ....155 D6
Rosalind Ct M5 ....161 C8
Rosamond Dr M3 ....158 D2
Rosamond St BL3 ....146 C4
Rosamond St W M13,
  M15 ....163 A6
Rosary Rd OL8 ....67 A1
Roscoe Ave WA12 ....89 E3
Roscoe Ct BL5 ....57 F7
Roscoe Lowe Brow PR6 .....21 D7
Roscoe Pk E st WA14 ....119 E8
Roscoe Rd M44 ....93 E1
Roscoe St Oldham OL1 ....67 A6
  Stockport SK3 ....170 D8
  Wigan WN1 ....151 E7
Roscow Ave BL2 ....42 E8
Roscow Fold Prim Sch
  BL2 ....42 E8
Roscow Rd BL4 ....61 A7
Rose Acre M28 ....78 B7
Rose Ave
  Abram Brow WN2 ....33 A5
  Farnworth BL4 ....42 C1
  Irlam M44 ....93 F1
  Littleborough OL15 ....15 F3
  Rochdale OL11 ....13 D2
  Wigan WN6 ....37 A4
Rose Bank Cl
  Hollingworth SK14 ....103 D5
  Wigan WN1 ....37 B4
Rose Bridge High Sch
  WN1 ....151 B8
Rose Cottage Rd M14,
  M20 ....110 B8
Rose Cotts [4] M14 ....110 D8
Rose Cres M44 ....93 F1
Rose Ct WN1 ....151 F8
Rose Gr Bury BL8 ....27 A2
  Kearsley BL4 ....60 F7
Rose Hey La M35 ....83 E4
Rose Hill Bolton BL2 ....148 A5
  Delph OL3 ....50 F4
  Denton M34 ....100 E3
  Ramsbottom BL0 ....138 B6
  Stalybridge SK15 ....102 A3
Rose Hill Ave
  Failsworth M40 ....83 B4
  Wigan WN5 ....54 C6
Rose Hill Cl
  Ashton-u-L OL6 ....85 F5
  Bolton BL7 ....25 A7
Rose Hill Cres OL6 ....85 F5
Rose Hill Dr BL7 ....25 A7
Rose Hill Marple Sta
  SK6 ....125 E6
Rose Hill Rd OL6 ....85 F5
Rose Hill St OL10 ....29 E2
Rose Hill View WN4 ....72 F7
Rose La M41 ....125 E6
Rose Lea BL2 ....25 E4
Rose Leigh M41 ....95 D2
Rose Mount M24 ....46 F2
Rose St Bolton BL2 ....148 A5
  Chadderton OL9 ....66 A3
  Hindley WN2 ....56 F1
  Middleton M24 ....65 C8
  Reddish SK5 ....169 F3
  Wigan WN1 ....151 F8
Rose Terr SK15 ....86 A1
Rose Thorns Cl M24 ....46 F4
Rose Vale SK8 ....122 B1
Rose Wlk Marple SK6 ....125 E6
  [5] Partington M31 ....105 E3
Rose Wood M34 ....100 D3
Roseacre Cl BL2 ....148 C8
Roseacre Dr SK8 ....122 C1
Rosebank Bolton BL6 ....40 C7
  Edenfield BL0 ....1 D1
Rosebank Cl BL2 ....26 C1
Rosebank Rd
  Failsworth M40 ....83 B4
  Irlam M44 ....105 C4
Roseberry Ave [4] OL1 ....69 B7
Roseberry Cl BL0 ....11 C3
Roseberry Rd WN4 ....73 A5
Roseberry St Bolton BL3 ...146 C4
  Oldham OL8 ....153 D6
Rosebery St
  Manchester M14 ....97 F3
  Stockport SK3 ....124 D4
  Westhoughton BL5 ....57 F8
Rosebridge Ct WN1 ....151 F7
Rosebridge Way WN1 ....151 F7
Rosebury Ave WN7 ....76 B5
Rosecroft Cl SK3 ....123 E4
Rosedale Ave
  Atherton M46 ....58 D3
  Bolton BL1 ....24 E5

Rosedale Ave continued
  Golborne WA3 ....90 C7
Rosedale Cl OL1 ....49 B1
Rosedale Ct M34 ....100 E3
Rosedale Dr WN7 ....76 C5
Rosedale Rd
  Manchester M14 ....98 A2
  Reddish SK4 ....111 D5
  Reddish SK4 ....169 D4
Rosedale Way SK16 ....101 C6
Rosefield Cl WN3 ....170 E5
Rosefield Cres OL16 ....31 C7
Rosegarth Ave M20 ....109 D4
Rosehay Ave M34 ....100 F2
Rosehill Cl M6 ....154 F2
Rosehill Cl Oldham OL4 ......67 E8
  Salford M6 ....154 F2
Rosehill Methodist Com Prim
  Sch OL6 ....85 F6
Rosehill Rd M27 ....61 F2
Roseland Ave M20 ....110 B4
Roseland Dr M25 ....63 C6
Roselands Ave M33 ....107 F2
Roseleigh Ave WN3 ....110 F7
Rosemary Ave WN1 ....37 D2
Rosemary Dr Hyde SK14 ...113 D7
  Littleborough OL15 ....15 F6
  Newton-le-W WA12 ....89 F3
Rosemary Gr M7 ....81 C5
Rosemary La
  Over Hulton BL5 ....59 B6
  Stockport SK1 ....112 A1
Rosemary Rd OL9 ....65 E8
Rosemary Wlk M31 ....105 F2
Rosemead [5] SK5 ....111 F6
Rosemount SK14 ....101 D5
Rosemount Cres SK14 ......101 D5
Rosen Sq OL9 ....152 B7
Roseneath SK7 ....123 D1
Roseneath Ave M19 ....99 C1
Roseneath Gr BL3 ....147 D3
Roseneath Rd
  Bolton BL3 ....147 D3
  Urmston M41 ....95 C2
Rosette Wlk [3] M27 ....79 F7
Rosevale Ave M19 ....110 E5
Rosevale Cl [8] WN2 ....56 D4
Roseway SK7 ....123 F2
Rosewell Cl M40 ....160 D4
Rosewood Rochdale OL11 ...13 E1
  Westhoughton BL5 ....57 D6
Rosewood Ave Bury BL8 .....27 A6
  Droylsden M43 ....84 C3
  Stockport SK4 ....168 A1
Rosewood Cl
  Abram Brow WN2 ....74 B7
  Dukinfield SK16 ....101 D6
Rosewood Cres OL9 ....48 B1
Rosewood Ct SK2 ....124 C5
Rosewood Gdns
  [6] Sale M33 ....108 F3
  Wythenshawe SK8 ....121 F6
Rosewood Wlk M23 ....120 C8
Rosford Ave M14 ....98 B2
Rosgill Cl M18 ....165 C5
Rosgill Wlk M18 ....165 C5
Rosina Cl WN4 ....72 F6
Rosina St M11 ....99 F8
Roslin Gdns BL1 ....142 C3
Roslin St M11 ....83 D2
Roslyn Ave M41 ....94 E1
Roslyn Rd SK3 ....170 E5
Ross Ave Manchester M19 ...98 F1
  Oldham OL9 ....65 F4
  Stockport SK3 ....170 E5
  Whitefield M45 ....62 F6
Ross Cl Billinge WN5 ....71 E6
  Wigan WN2 ....37 F2
Ross Gr M41 ....95 C2
Ross Lave La M34 ....100 C1
Ross St OL8 ....153 D5
Rossall Ave
  [5] Radcliffe M26 ....44 C1
  Stretford M32 ....96 C3
Rossall Cl BL2 ....148 C8
Rossall Cres WN7 ....76 A3
Rossall Rd Bolton BL2 ....148 C8
  Rochdale OL12 ....15 A2
Rossall St [1] BL2 ....148 C8
Rossall Way M6 ....81 A3
Rossdale Gr WN6 ....36 F4
Rossenclough Rd SK9 ......131 D1
Rossendale Ave M9 ....64 F1
Rossendale Cl OL2 ....49 D7
Rossendale Rd SK8 ....131 C8
Rossendale Sch BL0 ....12 A7
Rossendale Way OL2 ....149 B8
Rossett Ave Sale WA15 .....120 A8
  Wythenshawe M22 ....130 D8
Rossett Cl WN3 ....55 A3
Rossett Dr M41 ....95 A4
Rossetti Wlk [2] M34 ....113 A7
Rosshill Wlk M15 ....162 D6
Rossington St M40 ....160 E1
Rossini St BL1 ....143 D3
Rosslare Rd M22 ....121 E2
Rosslyn Gr WA15 ....120 A6
Rosslyn Rd Cheadle SK8 ...122 D1
  Manchester M16 ....97 B1
  Manchester,Moston M40 ......65 A1
Rossmere Ave OL11 ....30 B6
Rossmill La WA15 ....129 B7
Rosthorne Ave
  Golborne WA3 ....90 D8

Rostherne Ave continued
  High Lane SK6 ....134 E8
  Manchester M14 ....98 A1
  Manchester M16 ....97 C3
Rostherne Ct WA14 ....119 D3
Rostherne Gdns BL3 ....146 B4
Rostherne Rd Sale M33 ....108 F3
  Stockport SK3 ....170 E5
  Wilmslow SK9 ....136 F4
Rostherne St
  [1] Altrincham WA14 ....119 D3
  [1] Salford M6 ....154 E1
Rosthernemere Rd SK8 .....122 F4
Rosthwaite Cl
  Middleton M24 ....46 C1
  Wigan WN3 ....55 A2
Rosthwaite Gr WA11 ....71 B1
Roston Ct M7 ....155 E8
Roston Rd M7 ....155 E8
Rostrevor Rd SK3 ....170 E5
Rostron Ave M12 ....164 E6
Rostron Rd BL0 ....138 B6
Rostron St M19 ....99 B1
Rothay Cl Bolton BL2 ....25 F1
Rothay Dr Middleton M24 ....46 F3
  Reddish SK5 ....111 F8
Rothay St M7 ....76 B4
Rothbury Ave OL7 ....84 E5
Rothbury Cl BL8 ....26 F2
Rothbury Ct BL3 ....146 B3
Rotherby Rd M22 ....121 E5
Rotherdale Ave WA15 ....120 D5
Rotherhead Cl BL6 ....21 E7
Rothermere Wlk [5]
  M23 ....120 E7
Rotherwood Ave M32 ....96 E3
Rotherwood Rd SK9 ....136 D6
Rothesay Ave SK16 ....101 C7
Rothesay Cres M33 ....107 C2
Rothesay Rd Bolton BL3 ....146 B3
  Manchester M8 ....156 A6
  Oldham OL1 ....49 C1
  Pendlebury M27 ....80 B7
Rothesay Terr OL16 ....31 C4
Rothiemay Rd M41 ....94 E2
Rothley Ave M22 ....121 D5
Rothman Cl M40 ....83 C6
Rothwell Cres M38 ....59 E5
Rothwell La M38 ....59 E5
Rothwell Rd Adlington PR6 ..21 B7
  Golborne WA3 ....74 C1
Rothwell St Bolton BL3 ......145 E6
  Failsworth M35 ....83 F7
  Failsworth,Newton Heath
  M40 ....83 C6
  Rochdale OL12 ....15 B1
  Walkden M28 ....60 F3
Rottingdene Dr [3] M22 ....121 C1
Rough Hill La BL9 ....28 C8
Roughey Gdns M22 ....121 D4
Roughlea Ave WA3 ....91 D4
Roughlee Ave M27 ....79 D7
Roughtown Ct OL5 ....68 D2
Roughtown Rd OL5 ....68 D2
Round Hey OL5 ....68 C8
Round Hill Cl SK13 ....171 F3
Round House Ave WN7 ....37 E1
Round Thorn Rd M24 ....46 E5
Roundcroft SK6 ....113 E3
Roundham Wlk [27] M9 ....157 E8
Roundhey SK8 ....131 C8
Roundhill Way OL4 ....49 E1
Roundmoor Rd WN6 ....37 A7
Roundthorn Bsns Pk
  M23 ....120 E5
Roundthorn Ind Est
  M23 ....120 E6
Roundthorn La BL5 ....57 C5
Roundthorn Rd
  Oldham OL4 ....67 C5
  Wythenshawe M23 ....120 F6
Roundthorn Wlk [9]
  M23 ....120 E6
Roundway SK7 ....132 D6
Roundwood High Sch
  M22 ....121 D7
Roundwood Rd M22 ....121 D7
Rousden Cl M40 ....157 D5
Rouse St OL11 ....30 C4
Routledge Wlk M9 ....157 E8
Rowan Ave Golborne WA3 ...90 F7
  [2] Horwich BL6 ....22 E1
  Manchester M16 ....97 C3
  Sale M33 ....108 B3
  Urmston M41 ....95 D3
  Wigan WN6 ....36 F3
Rowan Cl Failsworth M35 ....83 F6
  Rochdale OL12 ....14 B3
  [6] Sale M33 ....108 B3
Rowan Cres SK16 ....101 C7
Rowan Ct Hyde SK14 ....167 D4
  Wilmslow SK9 ....137 B7
Rowan Dr Bury BL9 ....141 B3
  Cheadle SK8 ....123 B5
Rowan Lo SK7 ....132 F7
Rowan Pl M25 ....63 E8
Rowan St SK14 ....167 F1
Rowan Tree Dr M33 ....108 B3
Rowan Tree Rd OL8 ....66 D1

Rowan Wlk
  Hadfield SK13 ....171 E4
  Partington M31 ....105 E2
Rowanhill WN1 ....37 D1
Rowans St BL8 ....27 C4
Rowans The
  [6] Adlington PR6 ....21 A8
  Bolton BL1 ....40 F7
  Mossley OL5 ....68 D1
Rowanside Dr SK9 ....137 E8
Rowanswood Dr SK14 ......102 A3
Rowanwood OL9 ....65 E7
Rowany Cl M25 ....63 A3
Rowarth Ave
  Denton M34 ....113 A8
  [10] Gamesley SK13 ....171 D2
Rowarth Bank [5] SK13 ....171 D2
Rowarth Cl [5] SK13 ....171 D2
Rowarth Fold [9] SK13 .....171 D2
Rowarth Rd M23 ....121 A2
Rowarth Way [8] SK13 .....171 D2
Rowbottom Sq WN1 ....150 C8
Rowbottom Wlk OL8 ....153 E5
Rowcon Cl M34 ....100 A8
Rowdell Wlk M23 ....109 B2
Rowden Rd OL4 ....67 E4
Rowe Gn M34 ....100 F2
Rowe St M29 ....77 B8
Rowena St BL3 ....42 C2
Rowendale St M1 ....162 F8
Rowfield Dr M23 ....120 F3
Rowland Ave M41 ....95 E3
Rowland St [17] OL16 ....31 B6
Rowland St Atherton M46 ....58 D3
  [16] Rochdale OL16 ....31 B6
  Salford M5 ....161 A8
Rowland St S M46 ....58 D3
Rowland Way OL4 ....67 E7
Rowlands Rd BL9 ....11 D2
Rowlandsway M22 ....121 D2
Rowley Bd SK7 ....133 E8
Rowley St OL6 ....85 D6
Rowood Ave
  Manchester M8 ....156 B6
  Reddish SK5 ....99 F2
Rowrah Cres M24 ....46 C1
Rowsley Ave Bolton BL1 ....142 A1
  Manchester M20 ....109 E4
Rowsley Cl [27] SK13 ....171 E2
Rowsley Gr [24] SK13 ......171 E2
Rowsley Gr
  [30] Gamesley SK13 ....171 E2
  Reddish SK5 ....171 E1
Rowsley Mews SK13 ....171 E2
Rowsley Rd Eccles M30 ......95 C8
  Stretford M32 ....96 A3
Rowsley St
  Manchester M11 ....160 F1
  Salford M6 ....81 B5
Rowsley Wlk [8] SK13 ......171 E2
Rowson Dr M44 ....105 D6
Rowton Rise WN1 ....37 B8
Rowton St BL2 ....148 C8
Roxalina St BL3 ....147 E4
Roxburgh St [5] M18 ....99 D5
Roxbury Ave OL4 ....67 D5
Roxby Cl M28 ....60 B3
Roxby Dr [18] M40 ....65 D2
Roxholme Wlk M22 ....130 C8
Roxton Cl BL6 ....22 B5
Roxton Rd SK4 ....111 C6
Roxwell Wlk M9 ....157 D8
Roy Grainger Ct [8] M16 ....97 E3
Roy Ho OL2 ....48 D6
Roy St Bolton BL3 ....146 B4
  Royton OL2 ....48 D6
Royal Albert Edward Infmy
  WN1 ....37 C2
Royal Arc [5] WN1 ....150 C8
Royal Ave Bury BL9 ....27 F5
  Droylsden M43 ....84 B2
  Heywood OL10 ....29 D1
  Urmston M41 ....95 C3
Royal Bolton Hospl BL4 ....147 F1
Royal Court Dr BL1 ....145 D8
Royal Cres SK8 ....122 C2
Royal Dr WN7 ....76 E6
Royal Eye Hospl M13 ....163 B5
Royal Gdns
  Altrincham WA14 ....118 F2
  Ramsbottom BL0 ....11 A3
Royal George Cotts OL3 .....68 E5
Royal George St SK1,
  SK3 ....170 F8
Royal Manchester Children's
  Hospl M27 ....80 C7
Royal Northern Coll of Music
  M13 ....163 A4
Royal Oak Ind Est SK1 ......170 F7
Royal Oak Rd M23 ....121 A7
Royal Oak Yd SK1 ....170 F7
Royal Oldham Hospl The
  OL1 ....48 D1
Royal Par OL1 ....48 D1
Royal Pl SK12 ....135 D5
Royal Schools for the Deaf &
  Communication Disorders
  SK8 ....131 D6
Royce Ave WN5 ....131 C5
Royce Ct SK16 ....131 C3
Royce Rd M15 ....162 E6
Royce Cres Prim Sch
  M15 ....162 E6
Royce Ct [22] M15 ....162 D6

Royce Rd M15 ....162 E6
Royce Trad Est M17 ....95 F7
Royd St OL8 ....66 C4
Roydale St M40 ....160 E3
Royden Ave Irlam M44 .105 F8
Manchester M9 ....64 D5
Wigan WN3 ....55 A2
Royden Cres WN5 ......71 E5
Royden Rd WN5 ....71 E5
Roydes St M24 ....47 B2
Royds Cl Bury BL8 ......27 A5
Manchester M13 ....164 D5
Royds Pl 16 OL6 ....31 A5
Royds Rd OL13 ....3 A7
Royds St
Bury,Tottington BL8 ....26 F7
Bury,Woodgate Hill BL9 .28 D4
Littleborough OL15 .....16 C5
Milnrow OL16 ....32 A5
Rochdale OL16 ....31 B5
Royds St W OL16 ....31 A5
Royland Ave BL3 ....42 A3
Royland Ct BL3 ....147 F3
Royle Ave SK13 ....104 D1
Royle Barn Rd OL11 ....30 C3
Royle Cl Oldham OL8 ....66 F3
Stockport SK2 ....124 A5
Royle Green Rd M22 ...121 E8
Royle Pennine Trad Est
OL11 ....30 D3
Royle St OL13 ....30 D3
Royle St Denton M34 ..100 F5
Manchester M14 ....110 D7
Salford M6 ....154 F1
Stockport SK1 ....170 F7
Walkden M28 ....41 C7
Roylelands Bglws OL10 .30 C3
Royles Sq 2 SK9 .....137 A1
Royley OL2 ....48 C3
Royley Carr Flats SK6 .113 A3
Royley Cres OL2 ....48 C3
Royley Ho OL2 ....48 C3
Royley Rd OL8 ....66 E4
Royley Way OL2 ....48 C3
Roynton Rd BL6 ....22 B7
Royon Dr SK3 ....123 B7
Royston Ave Bolton BL2 148 C8
Manchester M16 ....97 D3
Reddish M34 ....100 A3
Royston Cl
2 Golborne WA3 ......90 E8
Ramsbottom BL8 ....10 F1
Royston Ct 5 M16 .....97 D3
Royston Rd
Manchester M16 ....97 B3
Urmston M41 ....95 E3
Royton & Crompton Sch
OL2 ....49 A4
Royton Ave OL3 ....108 E2
Royton Hall Wlk OL2 ...48 E4
Rozel Sq M3 ....162 E8
Ruabon Cres WN2 ......57 A4
Ruabon Rd M20 ....110 C2
Rubens Cl SK6 ....126 C8
Ruby Gr WN7 ....75 E4
Ruby St Bolton BL1 ....143 F3
Denton M34 ....100 E3
Manchester M13 ......163 A6
Ramsbottom BL9 ....11 C3
Rudcroft Cl M13 ......163 B6
Rudd St M40 ....83 A7
Rudding St OL2 ....49 A2
Ruddpark Rd M22 .....121 D1
Rudford Gdns BL3 .....147 F4
Rudgwick Dr BL8 ....27 C7
Rudheath Ave M20 ....110 A7
Rudman Dr M5 ....161 C8
Rudman St OL12 ....14 E2
Rudolph St BL3 ....147 F3
Rudston Ave M40 ......65 B2
Rudyard Ave
Middleton M24 ....47 C3
Standish WN6 ....19 E2
Rudyard Gr Reddish SK4 111 D6
Rochdale OL11 ....30 F2
Sale M33 ....107 E2
Rudyard Rd M6 ....80 C5
Rudyard St M7 ....155 D6
Ruecroft Cl WN6 ......35 D8
Rufford Ave Hyde SK14 167 F2
Rochdale OL11 ....30 C3
Rufford Cl Ashton-u-L OL6 .85 C7
Shaw OL2 ....48 F7
Whitefield M45 ....45 A2
Rufford Dr BL3 ....147 D2
Whitefield M45 ....44 F2
Rufford Pl Reddish M18 .99 F4
Tyldesley M29 ....76 F4
Rufford Rd M16 ....97 D3
Rufford St 4 WN4 .....72 F5
Rufus M14 ....110 E7
Rugby Dr Orrell WN5 ...53 F8
Sale M33 ....108 A2
Rugby Rd High WN7 ...107 F5
Rochdale OL12,OL16 ...15 A1
Salford M6 ....80 A3
Rugby Rd Ind Est OL16 .15 A1
Rugby St M7,M8 ....158 E4
Rugeley St M6 ....81 B5
Ruins La BL2 ....25 E4
Ruislip Ave M40 ......157 E5
Ruislip Cl OL8 ....67 B4
Rumbles La OL3 ....50 F4
Rumbold St 6 M18 .....99 E6
Rumworth Rd BL6 .....40 C6
Rumworth St BL3 .....147 D4
Runcorn St M15 ......161 C7

Runger La M90,WA15 ..129 F8
Runhall Cl M12 ....165 A6
Running Hill Farm OL3 .51 D2
Running Hill Gate OL3 .51 D1
Running Hill La OL3 ....51 D2
Runnymeade M6,M27 ...80 B5
Runnymede Ct SK3 ...123 C6
Runnymede Ct
Bolton BL3 ....145 D5
Royton OL2 ....48 E4
Stockport SK3 ....123 C6
Runshaw Ave WN6 .....35 E8
Rupert St Bolton BL3 ..147 F3
Failsworth M40 ....83 E4
Radcliffe M26 ....44 B1
Reddish SK5 ....111 E7
Rochdale OL12 ....14 C1
Wigan WN1 ....151 E7
Rupert Terr 5 SK5 ....111 E7
Ruscombe Fold M24 ....46 D3
Rush Acre Cl M26 ......43 E3
Rush Bank OL2 ....48 F8
Rush Gdns WA13 ......117 A4
Rush Gr OL3 ....69 B7
Rush Hill Rd OL3 ....69 B7
Rush Mount OL2 ....48 F8
Rush St SK16 ....101 F8
Rushall Wlk M23 ......120 F2
Rushbrooke Ave 1 M11 .83 C2
Rushbury Dr OL2 ....49 A4
Rushcroft Ct M9 ....65 A2
Rushcroft Prim Sch
OL2 ....149 B8
Rushcroft Rd OL2 ......48 F8
Rushden Rd M19 ....99 B2
Rushdene WN3 ....54 E3
Rushen St 8 M11 ......83 C1
Rushes Mdw WA13 ....117 B5
Rushey Ave M22 ......121 C6
Rushey Cl WA15 ......129 D7
Rushey Field BL7 ......24 F8
Rushey Fold Ct 23 BL1 .143 E2
Rushey Fold La BL1 ...143 D2
Rushey Rd M22 ....121 C6
Rusheylea Cl BL1 .....142 C2
Rushfield Dr M13 ......98 F3
Rushfield Rd SK8 .....132 A6
Rushford Ave M19 .....99 A2
Rushford Ct 1 M19 ....99 A2
Rushford Gr BL1 ......143 F4
Rushford St M12 ....99 A3
Rushgreen Rd WA13 ..117 A4
Rushill Terr OL3 ....69 B7
Rushlake Dr BL1 .....143 E1
Rushleigh Gdns OL11 ..85 E6
Rushley Ave M7 ....81 B7
Rushmere Ashton-u-L OL6 .85 E6
Glossop SK13 ....116 E8
Rushmere Ave M19 ....99 B1
Rushmere Dr BL8 ......27 C5
Rushmere Wlk M16 ...162 D5
Rushmoor Ave WN4 ....73 E4
Rushmoor Cl M44 ......94 A2
Rusholme Gdns 3 M14 .98 C2
Rusholme Gr M14 ......98 C3
Rusholme Pl M14 ......98 C4
Rushside Rd SK8 .....132 A6
Rushton Ave Leigh WN7 .75 D8
Newton-le-W WA12 ....89 A8
Rushton Cl SK6 ....126 A5
Rushton Dr Marple SK6 125 F5
Romiley SK6 ....113 C3
Stockport SK7 ....123 D3
Rushton Gdns SK7 ...123 D2
Rushton Gr
Manchester M11 ....99 E7
Oldham OL4 ....49 E3
Rushton Rd Bolton BL1 142 B1
Cheadle SK8 ....132 A6
Stockport SK3 ....123 B7
Rushton St 5 Bacup OL13 .3 E8
Manchester M20 ......110 B2
Walkden M28 ....60 D2
Rushwick Ave M40 ...157 E5
Rushworth Bldgs OL13 ..3 C8
Rushworth Ct SK4 ....111 C5
Rushy Hill View 18 OL12 .14 C1
Rushy View WA12 .....89 A4
Rushycroft SK14 ......103 A4
Rushyfield Cres SK6 ..113 D3
Ruskin Ave Denton M34 100 E1
Kearsley BL4 ....60 F7
Manchester M14 ....98 B4
Newton-le-W WA12 ....89 C4
Oldham OL9 ....65 F3
Ruskin Cres Abram WN2 .56 B1
Prestwich M25 ....62 F3
Ruskin Dr M33 ....107 D4
Ruskin Gdns SK6 .....113 A3
Ruskin Gr SK6 ....113 A3
Ruskin Rd Droylsden M43 .84 A2
Little Lever BL3 ....43 B6
Manchester M16 ....97 C3
Prestwich M25 ....62 F3
Reddish SK5 ....99 E1
Rochdale OL11 ....30 F2
Ruskin St Oldham OL1 .153 D8
Radcliffe M26 ....44 C4
Ruskington Dr M9 ....157 D7
Rusland Ct Manchester M9 .65 A3
Sale M33 ....108 A5
Rusland Dr BL2 ....25 E2
Rusland Wlk 8 M22 ..121 C2
Russel St OL11 ....139 E5
Russeldene Rd WN3 ...54 E1

Russell Ave
High Lane SK6 ....134 E7
Manchester M16 ....97 D2
Sale M33 ....108 D5
Russell Cl BL1 ....144 C8
Russell Ct Farnworth BL4 .60 E7
Manchester M16 ....97 C3
Walkden M38 ....60 C3
Russell Dr M44 ....94 A2
Russell Gdns SK4 ....168 B1
Russell Pl 1 M33 .....108 B5
Russell Rd
Manchester M16 ....97 D3
Partington M31 ....106 A3
Salford M6 ....80 B5
Russell Scott Prim Sch
M34 ....100 E4
Russell St
6 Ashton-u-L OL6 .....85 C4
Atherton M46 ....58 C3
Bolton BL1 ....145 D8
5 Bury BL9 ....140 F4
Chadderton OL9 ....153 F7
Denton M34 ....100 F3
Dukinfield SK16 ......101 C8
Eccles M30 ....79 F2
Farnworth BL4 ....60 E8
Heywood OL10 ....29 E1
Hindley WN2 ....57 C2
Hyde SK14 ....167 E2
Ince-in-M WN2 ....56 A8
Manchester M158 F4
Moss Side M16 ....97 F3
Mossley OL5 ....68 C1
Prestwich M25 ....63 C4
Romiley SK6 ....113 A3
Stockport SK2 ....124 A6
Swinton M27 ....61 E1
Walkden M38 ....60 C3
Russet Rd M9 ....64 D1
Russet Wlk BL1 ......143 E4
Rustons Wlk 2 M40 ...65 E1
Ruth St Bolton BL1 ...145 E8
10 Bury BL9 ....140 F4
Edenfield BL0 ....1 D2
Manchester M18 ....99 D3
Oldham OL1 ....153 F8
Whitworth OL12 ....14 C8
Rutherford Ave 2 M14 .98 B3
Rutherford Cl SK14 ..167 D2
Rutherford Dr BL5 .....58 F7
Rutherford Way M17 ..167 D2
Rutherglade Cl M40 ..156 C6
Rutherglen Dr BL3 ....147 D4
Ruthergien Wlk M40 ..157 E5
Ruthin Ave Cheadle SK8 122 E2
Manchester M9 ....64 C5
Middleton M24 ....65 A6
Ruthin Cl Oldham OL8 ..66 B2
Salford M6 ....81 A2
Ruthin Ct M6 ....81 A2
Rutland OL12 ....139 E6
Rutland Ave Denton M34 101 B2
Golborne WA3 ....90 D7
Manchester,Firswood M16 .97 A3
Manchester,Withington
M20 ....110 A6
Over Hulton M46 .....109 C6
Swinton M27 ....61 F2
Urmston M41 ....95 E3
Rutland Cl
6 Ashton-u-L OL6 .....85 C2
Gatley SK8 ....122 B6
Little Lever BL3 ....43 B4
Rutland Cres SK5 ....100 E4
Rutland Ct Stockport SK2 124 A5
Stockport,Heavily SK2 .124 B7
Rutland Dr
Ashton-in-M WN4 ......73 C4
Bury BL9 ....45 A8
Salford M7 ....81 C5
Rutland Gr Bolton BL1 .142 C1
Farnworth BL4 ....60 C7
Rutland La M33 ....108 F4
Rutland Rd
Altrincham WA14 .....119 D6
Droylsden M43 ....83 E2
Eccles M30 ....79 F3
Hazel Grove SK7 .....133 E8
Hindley WN2 ....56 F6
Irlam M44 ....105 D5
Partington M31 ....105 E2
Tyldesley M29 ....58 F2
Walkden M28 ....60 D1
Rutland St Ashton-u-L OL6 .85 C2
Bolton BL3 ....147 D4
Droylsden M43 ....100 B8
Dukinfield SK14 ......101 C5
Failsworth M35 ....83 F8
Heywood OL10 ....29 E1
Leigh WN7 ....76 E4
4 Manchester M18 .....99 D6
Oldham OL9 ....152 C5
Swinton M27 ....61 E1
Rutland Way OL2 .....149 C7
Rutland Wlk BB4 ....1 A8
Rutter's La SK7 ......124 C2
Ryall Ave M5 ....161 B8
Ryall Ave S M5 ......161 B8
Ryan St BL1 ....99 E7
Ryburn Sq OL11 ....29 E6
Rydal Ave Chadderton OL9 .47 F1
Droylsden M43 ....83 E1
Dukinfield SK14 ......101 C5
Eccles M30 ....79 B4
Hazel Grove SK7 .....124 C3
High Lane SK6 ....134 E7

Rydal Ave continued
Hindley WN2 ....56 E5
Middleton M24 ....64 F6
Orrell WN5 ....53 F8
Royton OL2 ....48 C8
Sale M33 ....107 F5
Urmston M41 ....107 A8
Rydal Cl Ashton-in-M WN4 .73 C4
Blackrod BL6 ....21 C3
Bury BL9 ....44 E8
Gatley SK8 ....122 B4
Reddish M34 ....100 B2
Tyldesley M29 ....77 A7
Rydal Cres Swinton M27 .79 F7
Walkden M28 ....60 E1
Rydal Dr WN15 ....129 D8
Rydal Gr Ashton-u-L OL7 .84 F2
Farnworth BL4 ....59 F7
Heywood OL10 ....46 D8
Whitefield M45 ....63 A8
Rydal Ho 4 M28 ......60 E2
Rydal Pl Abram WN2 ..74 B8
Ince-in-M WN2 ....56 B8
Rydal Rd Bolton BL1 ..144 A8
Haslingden BB4 ....1 C8
Little Lever BL3 ....43 A3
Stretford M32 ....96 D3
Rydal St Leigh WN7 ...75 E5
Newton-le-W WA12 ....89 C3
Rydal Wlk Oldham OL4 .67 D7
Stalybridge SK15 ......86 A3
Wigan WN5 ....54 C7
Ryde Ave Denton M34 .113 D8
Manchester SK4 ......168 B2
Ryde St Bolton BL3 ...146 A4
Wigan WN5 ....54 E6
Ryder Ave WA14 .....119 E2
Ryder Brow M18 ....99 D4
Ryder Brow Sta M18 ..99 D4
Ryder Gr WN7 ....76 C2
Ryder St Bolton BL1 ..143 F4
Heywood OL10 ....29 D2
Manchester M40 ......160 D4
Ryderbrow Rd M18 ....99 D4
Rydings La OL12 ......15 A5
Rydings Rd OL12 ......15 A4
Rydings Specl Sch OL12 .15 A4
Rydley St BL2 ....148 B6
Rye Bank Rd M16 ......97 B3
Rye Croft M45 ....62 C7
Rye Croft Ave M6 .....80 C3
Rye Hill BL5 ....57 F8
Rye St OL10 ....29 E3
Rye Wlk Chadderton OL9 .47 E6
Manchester M13 ......163 C5
Ryebank Gr OL6 ....85 D5
Ryebank Mews 3 M21 .96 F1
Ryebank Rd M21 ......96 F1
Ryeburn Ave M22 ....121 D3
Ryeburn Dr BL2 ....25 B5
Ryeburn Wlk M41 .....94 F4
Ryeburne St OL4 ......67 C7
Ryecroft Ave Bury BL8 .26 F6
Golborne WA3 ....74 E1
Heywood OL10 ....29 A2
Ryecroft Cl OL9 ....65 F3
Ryecroft Dr BL5 ....40 E1
Ryecroft Gr M23 .....121 A7
Ryecroft Ho OL1 ......166 A1
Ryecroft La Denton M34 100 F7
Eccles M28 ....78 F4
Ryecroft Rd M22 ......96 C1
Ryecroft St OL7 ....84 F1
Ryecroft View M34 ...100 C8
Ryedale Ave M40 .....157 D5
Ryefield M6 ....80 D6
Ryefield Cl SK4 ......168 B3
Ryefield Cl WA15 ....120 C5
Ryefield Rd M33 .....107 C2
Ryefield St BL1 ....25 A1
Ryefields Rochdale OL11 .30 A6
OL12 ....15 D4
Ryefields Dr OL3 ......51 B1
Ryeford Cl WN3 ......151 F6
Ryeland Cl OL16 ....31 B4
Ryelands WA3 ....74 D8
Rygate Wlk 3 M8 ....155 F6
Rylance Rd WN3 ......54 D1
Rylance St M11 ......164 E8
Ryland Cl SK5 ....99 F1
Rylands Ave WN6 .....37 A2
Rylands Ho M7 ....110 D8
Rylands St M18 ......99 E6
Rylane Wlk M40 .....157 D5
Rylatt Ct 1 BL3 ......147 F5
Ryley Ave BL3 ....144 B5
Ryley St 4 BL3 ......144 C6
Ryleys La SK9 ....136 F1
Ryleys Sch The SK9 ..136 F1
Rylstone Ave M21 ...109 D3
Ryther Gr M9 ....64 B5
Ryton Ave M18 ....99 C3
Ryton Cl WN3 ....150 B6

Sack St 4 SK14 ......101 D5
Sackville Cl OL2 ......32 A1
Sackville St
Ashton-u-L OL6 ......166 B3
2 Bolton BL2 ....148 C7
Manchester M1 ......163 A8
6 Rochdale OL11 .....30 C2
Salford M3 ....158 E2
Sacred Heart RC Inf Sch
M18 ....99 D4
Sacred Heart RC Jun & Inf
Sch OL1 ....49 C2
Sacred Heart RC Jun Sch
M18 ....99 C4
Sacred Heart RC Prim Sch
Hindley WN2 ....57 B3
Leigh WN7 ....75 E5
Rochdale OL16 ....31 C6
Tyldesley M46 ....58 E1
Westhoughton BL5 ....39 F1
Wigan WN6 ....36 F2
Wythenshawe M23 ...120 F6
Saddle Cote M28 ......79 A4
Saddle Gr M43 ....84 D3
Saddle St BL2 ....25 B2
Saddleback Cl 3 M28 ..78 B6
Saddleback Cres WN5 .54 B6
Saddleback Rd WN5 ...54 B7
Saddlewood Ave M19 .110 D2
Saddleworth Bsns Ctr
OL3 ....50 F4
Saddleworth Fold OL3 .51 C1
Saddleworth Mus & Art
Gall* OL3 ....69 B8
Saddleworth Prep Sch
OL4 ....68 C8
Saddleworth Sch OL3 .51 B1
Sadie Ave M32 ....96 A4
Sadler Ct M15 ....162 E5
Sadler St Bolton BL3 ..42 A4
Middleton M24 ....46 F1
Safflower Ave M27 ....79 D8
Saffron Cl WA3 ....90 E8
Saffron Dr OL4 ....49 D2
Saffron Wlk
Partington M31 ....105 F2
8 Wythenshawe M22 .121 D1
Safton Ct BL9 ....27 B6
Sagar St M8 ....158 F4
Sagars Rd Handforth SK9 131 D4
Handforth SK9 ....131 C3
SS Osmund & Andrew RC
Prim Sch BL2 ....148 A7
SS Simon & Jude's CE Prim
Sch BL3 ....42 A3
Saintsbridge Rd M22 .121 C2
St Aelred's RC Tech Coll
WA12 ....89 D4
St Agnes CE Prim Sch
Manchester M13 ......98 F3
Oldham OL4 ....68 A4
St Agnes Rd M13 .....98 F2
St Agnes St SK5 ......99 F3
St Aidan & St Oswald's RC
Sch OL2 ....48 E3
St Aidan's CE Prim Sch
WN5 ....71 E5
St Aidan's Cl Billinge WN5 .71 E6
Rochdale OL11 ....139 D5
St Aidan's Gr M7 .....81 B6
St Aidan's RC Prim Sch
WN3 ....54 D2
St Aidans Rd Prim Sch
M23 ....109 B1
St Alban's Ave WN4 ..111 C5
St Alban's Ct OL11 ...139 E6
St Albans Cl SK16 ...139 E6
St Alban's Terr
Manchester M8 ......155 F5
Rochdale OL11 ....139 E6
St Albans Ave
Ashton-u-L OL6 ....85 C7
Failsworth M40 ....83 B5
St Albans Cl
Haydock WA11 ....89 A7
Oldham OL4 ....66 F4
St Albans Cres WA14 119 C8
St Aldates SK6 ....112 F2
St Aldwyn's Rd M20 ..110 C4
St Alphonsus RC Prim Sch
M16 ....162 D5
St Ambrose Barlow RC High
Sch M27 ....79 F7
St Ambrose Barlow RC Prim
Sch M28 ....77 A5
St Ambrose Coll WA15 129 B8
St Ambrose Gdns M6 .154 F2
St Ambrose RC Prim Sch
Manchester M21 ......109 D4
Stockport SK3 ....170 E5
St Ambrose Rd
Oldham OL4 ....49 C1
Tyldesley M29 ....77 A5
St Andrew's Ave
Altrincham WA15 .....119 F7
Droylsden M43 ....83 E1
St Andrew's CE Prim Sch
Eccles M30 ....79 E1
Manchester M19 .....111 B8
Radcliffe M26 ....43 F6
Ramsbottom BL9 .....138 B5
Wigan WN6 ....36 F2

S

Sabden Brook Dr WN2 .55 F2
Sabden Cl Bury BL9 ...27 F7
Manchester M40 ......160 E3
Sabden Rd BL1 ....143 D2
Sabina St M7 ....81 C8

St Andrew's CE Prim Sch
continued
Worsley M28 . . . . .78 A6
St Andrew's Cl
Ramsbottom BL0 . . . . .138 C5
Romiley SK6 . . . . .113 B1
St Andrew's Cres WN2 . . . .56 D5
St Andrew's Rd
Heywood OL10 . . . . .29 D1
Wigan WN6 . . . . .36 F2
St Andrew's Rd
Radcliffe M26 . . . . .43 F6
Wigan WN2 . . . . .96 B2
St Andrew's Sq M1 . . . . .163 C8
St Andrew's St
Manchester M1 . . . . .163 C8
Radcliffe M26 . . . . .43 F6
St Andrew's View M26 . . . .43 F6
St Andrews Ave M30 . . . . .79 E1
St Andrews CE Prim Sch,
  Over Hulton BL5 . . . . .59 A8
St Andrews Cl
Manchester SK4 . . . . .168 B4
Rochdale OL15 . . . . .15 E4
Sale M33 . . . . .107 C1
St Andrews Ct
Altrincham WA15 . . . . .119 F3
Hadfield SK13 . . . . .104 A4
Stockport SK1 . . . . .112 A1
St Andrews Dr
Heywood OL10 . . . . .46 D8
Leigh WN7 . . . . .76 C5
St Andrews Meth Prim Sch
  M28 . . . . .60 B3
St Andrews Rd Bolton BL6 . .40 B7
Gatley SK8 . . . . .122 C1
Manchester SK4 . . . . .168 B4
St Ann St Bolton BL1 . . . . .143 E1
Manchester M2 . . . . .158 F1
St Ann's Pas M2 . . . . . . .158 F1
St Ann's RC Prim Sch
  M32 . . . . .96 D2
St Ann's Rd
Hazel Grove SK7 . . . . .124 C1
Prestwich M25 . . . . .63 A3
Rochdale OL16 . . . . .31 D8
St Ann's Rd N SK8 . . . . . .122 B2
St Ann's Rd S SK8 . . . . . .131 C8
St Ann's Sq Gatley SK8 . . .131 C8
Manchester M2 . . . . .158 F1
St Ann's St WN7 . . . . .79 E8
St Anne's Way Royton OL2 . .48 E3
Salford M6 . . . . .154 E3
Tyldesley M46 . . . . .58 E1
St Anne's CE Jun & Inf Sch
  OL2 . . . . .48 E3
St Anne's CE Lydgate Prim
  Sch OL4 . . . . .68 C6
St Anne's CE Prim Sch
Sale M33 . . . . .108 D4
Wigan WN6 . . . . .36 D3
St Anne's Cres OL4 . . . . . .68 D5
St Anne's Ct Denton M34 .100 E4
Sale M33 . . . . .108 C4
Shevington WN6 . . . . .35 F5
St Anne's Dr Denton M34 .101 A4
Shevington WN6 . . . . .36 A5
St Anne's Fulshaw CE Prim
  Sch SK9 . . . . .136 F6
St Anne's Gdns OL10 . . . .29 F2
St Anne's Hospl WA14 . . . .119 C3
St Anne's Prim Sch
  M34 . . . . .101 A4
St Anne's RC Prim Sch
Droylsden M34 . . . . .100 A4
Manchester M4 . . . . .160 D1
Manchester M8 . . . . .156 A8
Oldham OL4 . . . . .67 C7
St Anne's Rd M34 . . . . . . .101 A4
St Anne's St Bury BL9 . . .140 F4
Manchester M40 . . . . .157 F5
St Annes Mdw BL8 . . . . . .26 F7
St Annes RC High Sch
  SK4 . . . . .169 D4
St Annes Rd Denton M34 .100 E4
Horwich BL6 . . . . .22 C4
Manchester M21 . . . . .109 B7
St Annes Sq OL3 . . . . .50 F4
St Annes St SK14 . . . . . . .115 A8
St Anns Cl M25 . . . . .63 A3
St Anns St M33 . . . . .108 F3
St Anthony's RC Prim Sch
  M22 . . . . .121 D1
St Anthonys Dr OL5 . . . . . .68 B2
St Antony's RC Coll M41 . .95 F2
St Asaph's Dr M7 . . . . . . .155 F8
St Asaphs Dr OL6 . . . . . . .85 B6
St Aubin's Rd BL2 . . . . . .148 B6
St Aubyn's Rd WN1 . . . . . .37 C4
St Augustine of Canterbury
  RC High Sch OL8 . . . . . . .66 D3
St Augustine St
Bolton BL1 . . . . .143 D2
Manchester M40 . . . . .157 E5
St Augustine's CE Prim Sch
Manchester M40 . . . . .157 E5
Pendlebury M27 . . . . .80 B8
St Augustine's Ct 27
  BL2 . . . . .25 B1
St Augustine's Rd SK3 . .123 B8
St Austell Ave M29 . . . . . .77 C8
St Austell Dr Gatley SK8 . .132 B1
Ramsbottom BL8 . . . . .10 F2
St Austell Ho M16 . . . . . . .97 E1
St Austell Pl OL9 . . . . .48 B1

St Austell Rd M16 . . . . . . .97 E1
St Austell's Dr M27 . . . . . .80 C7
St Austells Dr M25 . . . . . .63 B5
St Barnabas Sq M11 . . . .165 B8
St Barnabas' CE Prim Sch
  M11 . . . . .165 B8
St Barnabas's Dr OL15 . . .16 A6
St Bartholomew St 4
  BL3 . . . . .42 A4
St Bartholomew's CE Prim
  Sch OL2 . . . . .14 C8
St Bartholomew's Dr
  M5 . . . . .161 C8
St Bede CE Prim Sch
  BL3 . . . . .146 C2
St Bede's Ave BL3 . . . . . .146 B2
St Bede's Coll M16 . . . . . .97 E3
St Bees Cl Gatley SK8 . . . .122 B3
Manchester M14 . . . . .98 A4
St Bees Rd BL2 . . . . .25 C2
St Bees Wlk 9 M14 . . . . . .98 A4
St Benedict's RC Prim Sch
  SK9 . . . . .131 E3
St Benedict's Sq M12 . . . .164 F6
St Benedicts Ct RC Prim Sch
  WN2 . . . . .56 C6
St Bernadett's RC Prim Sch
  WN6 . . . . .36 A6
St Bernadette's CE Prim Sch
  Brinnington SK5 . . . . .112 B4
Whitefield M45 . . . . .44 F2
St Bernard's Ave 1 M6 . . .81 C5
St Bernard's Cl M6 . . . . . .81 B5
St Bernard's Dr
Bolton BL3 . . . . .40 E5
Manchester M19 . . . . .110 F6
St Boniface RC Prim Sch
  M7 . . . . .81 C6
St Boniface Rd M7 . . . . . . .81 C4
St Brannock's Rd M21 . . . .97 C1
St Brannocks Rd SK8 . . . .132 B7
St Brelades Dr M7 . . . . . .155 F8
St Brendan's Rd
  M20 . . . . .25 E4
St Brendan's Rd N M20 . .110 B7
St Bride St M16 . . . . .162 D5
St Brides Cl BL6 . . . . .22 A4
St Brides Way M16 . . . . . .162 D5
St Brigid's RC Prim Sch
  M11 . . . . .165 A8
St Catherine's CE Prim Sch
  BL6 . . . . .22 A3
St Catherine's RC Prim Sch
Golborne WA3 . . . . .90 E7
Manchester M20 . . . . .110 C3
St Catherines Rd M20 . . .110 B7
St Catherines Dr BL4 . . . . .59 F8
St Catherines Prep Sch
  SK6 . . . . .126 B7
St Chad's Ave SK6 . . . . . .113 C2
St Chad's CE Prim Sch
  OL3 . . . . .51 C1
St Chad's Cl OL16 . . . . . .139 F7
St Chad's Ct OL16 . . . . . .139 F7
St Chad's Gr SK6 . . . . . . .113 C2
St Chad's Rd M20 . . . . . . .110 D7
St Chad's St M4,M8 . . . . .159 A4
St Chads Cres
Oldham OL8 . . . . .66 D1
Uppermill OL3 . . . . .69 C8
St Chads RC Prim Sch
  M8 . . . . .156 A5
St Charles Cl SK13 . . . . . .103 F5
St Charles's RC Prim Sch
  M27 . . . . .79 D8
St Christopher's Ave OL6 . .85 E6
St Christopher's Dr SK6 . .113 A2
St Christopher's RC Prim Sch
  Ashton-u-L OL6 . . . . .85 E6
Romiley SK6 . . . . .113 A2
St Christopher's Rd OL6 . . .85 E6
St Chrysostom's CE Prim Sch
  M13 . . . . .164 D5
St Clair Rd BL8 . . . . .10 F3
St Clare Terr BL6 . . . . .39 F8
St Clare's RC Prim Sch
  M9 . . . . .64 C5
St Clement's Ct
  2 Irlam M44 . . . . .94 B3
Oldham OL8 . . . . .153 F5
Prestwich M25 . . . . .63 C4
Wigan WN3 . . . . .150 A5
St Clement's Dr M5 . . . . . .161 B7
St Clement's Egerton CE Prim
  Sch M5 . . . . .161 B7
St Clement's Rd
Manchester M21 . . . . .109 A8
Wigan WN1 . . . . .37 C4
St Clement's St WN3 . . . . .55 F4
St Clements Ct OL11 . . . . . .30 C8
St Clements Fold M41 . . . . .95 E2
St Columba's RC Prim Sch
  BL2 . . . . .25 B4
St Cuthbert's RC High Sch
  OL16 . . . . .31 B1
St Cuthbert's RC Prim Sch
Manchester M20 . . . . .110 C6
Wigan WN5 . . . . .54 D6
St Cuthberts Fold OL8 . . . .67 A1

St Damian's RC Science Coll
  OL6 . . . . .85 E7
St David Haigh & Aspull CE
  Prim Sch WN2 . . . . .38 B7
St David's Ave SK6 . . . . . .113 B2
St David's Cl OL6 . . . . .85 D7
St David's Cres WN2 . . . . .38 B8
St David's Ct M8 . . . . .156 A5
St David's Rd SK7 . . . . . . .124 C1
St Davids Cl M33 . . . . . . .108 A3
St Davids Rd SK8 . . . . . . .123 A6
St Davids Wlk M32 . . . . . . .96 A3
St Domingo St OL9 . . . . . .153 E6
St Dominics Mews BL3 . . .146 B3
St Dominics Way M24 . . . .65 A7
St Dunstan's RC Prim Sch
  M40 . . . . .83 A8
St Dunstan Wlk 10 M40 . . .83 A6
St Edmund Arrowsmith RC
  High Sch WN4 . . . . .73 B2
St Edmund Hall Cl BL0 . . . .11 C4
St Edmund St BL1 . . . . . .145 E7
St Edmund's RC Prim Sch
  M38 . . . . .60 B4
St Edmund's Rd M40 . . . . .157 E6
St Edmunds Sch
  M40 . . . . .157 E6
St Edward's RC Prim Sch
Manchester M14 . . . . .98 B2
Wigan WN5 . . . . .54 F7
St Edward's RC Sch OL4 . . .67 E7
St Edwards CE Prim Sch
  OL11 . . . . .30 C2
St Elisabeth's CE Prim Sch
  SK5 . . . . .111 E8
St Elisabeth's Way SK5 . .111 E8
St Elizabeth Pk* M34 . . . .100 D3
St Elizabeth's RC Prim Sch
  M22 . . . . .121 E2
St Elizabeth's Rd WN2 . . .38 B5
St Elmo Ave SK2 . . . . . . .124 D7
St Elmo Pk SK12 . . . . . . .134 C4
St Ethelbert's Ave BL3 . . .144 B5
St Ethelbert's RC Prim Sch
  BL3 . . . . .144 B5
St Francis RC Prim Sch
  M12 . . . . .165 B6
St Gabriel Cl WN8 . . . . . . .35 C3
St Gabriel's CE Prim Sch
  M24 . . . . .65 D7
St Gabriel's Cl OL11 . . . . . .30 D1
St Gabriel's RC High Sch
  BL9 . . . . .140 D1
St Gabriels Hollow
Leigh WN7 . . . . .76 E7
Rochdale OL11 . . . . .30 D1
St George's Ave
Sale WA15 . . . . .120 A8
Westhoughton BL5 . . . . .57 E6
St George's CE Inf Sch
  M46 . . . . .58 B4
St George's CE Jun Sch
  M46 . . . . .58 C4
St George's Cres
Hyde SK14 . . . . .167 D1
Mossley OL5 . . . . .68 B1
Salford M6 . . . . .81 A5
Stockport SK2 . . . . .170 F6
St George's Ct
Altrincham WA14 . . . . .119 B7
16 Bolton BL1 . . . . .145 E8
10 Bolton BL1 . . . . .145 F8
3 Stretford M32 . . . . .96 C1
Whitefield BL9 . . . . .45 C3
St George's Dr M40 . . . . . .83 B7
St George's Gdns M34 . . .101 A1
St George's Pl
Atherton M46 . . . . .58 B4
Salford M6 . . . . .81 A5
St George's Rd
Bolton BL1 . . . . .145 E8
Carrington M31 . . . . .106 D6
Droylsden M43 . . . . .83 F3
Manchester M14 . . . . .110 E7
Rochdale OL11 . . . . .29 F8
St George's Sq
9 Bolton BL1 . . . . .145 F8
Failsworth OL9 . . . . .83 B6
St George's St
Bolton BL1 . . . . .145 E8
Stalybridge SK15 . . . . .86 A3
Tyldesley M29 . . . . .76 F8
St George's Terr BB4 . . . . . .3 A6
St George's Way M6 . . . . . .81 A4
St Georges CE Prim Sch
  BL5 . . . . .57 D7
St Georges Ct
Hyde SK14 . . . . .167 E2
Manchester M15 . . . . .162 D7
Tyldesley M47 . . . . .76 F8
St Georges Dr SK14 . . . . .167 D1
St Georges Rd
Stretford M32 . . . . .96 C1
Whitefield BL9 . . . . .45 C4
St Germain St BL4 . . . . . . .60 C8
St Gilbert's RC Prim Sch
  M30 . . . . .94 E1
St Giles Dr SK14 . . . . .167 F2
St Gregory's RC Prim Sch
  BL4 . . . . .60 E8

St Gregorys Cl BL4 . . . . . . .60 C8
St Gregorys Rd M12 . . . . .163 C7
St Helena Rd BL1 . . . . . . .145 E7
St Helens Cl WA3 . . . . . . .103 B3
St Helens Coll Newton
  Campus WA12 . . . . .89 B4
St Helens Rd
Bolton BL3,BL5 . . . . .146 B3
Golborne WN7 . . . . .75 C1
Leigh WN7 . . . . .75 E2
St Helier Sq M19 . . . . . . .110 F6
St Helier's Dr M7 . . . . . . .155 F8
St Heliers St BL3 . . . . . . .147 D4
St Herberts Cl M19 . . . . . .152 B7
St Herberts RC Sch OL9 . .152 A7
St Hilda's CE Prim Sch
Manchester M16 . . . . .97 E2
Oldham OL1 . . . . .153 D8
Prestwich M25 . . . . .63 C4
St Hilda's Cl M22 . . . . . . .109 E1
St Hilda's Dr OL1 . . . . . . .153 D8
St Hilda's Rd Denton M34 .100 F6
Manchester M16 . . . . .97 E2
Whitefield M22 . . . . .109 D1
St Hilda's View M34 . . . . .100 E5
St Hugh of Lincoln RC Prim
  Sch M32 . . . . .95 F3
St Hugh's CE Prim Sch
  OL4 . . . . .67 E3
St Hugh's Cl WA14 . . . . . .119 E8
St Hugh's RC Prim Sch
  WA15 . . . . .119 F8
St Ignatius Wlk
  M13 . . . . .163 C6
St Ignatius Wlk M5 . . . . .161 B8
St Ives Ave SK8 . . . . .123 A6
St Ives Cres M33 . . . . . . .108 A1
St Ives Rd M14 . . . . .98 B2
St Jame's Cl OL2 . . . . .48 C8
St James Ave BL2 . . . . . . .42 E7
St James CE Prim Sch
Farnworth BL4 . . . . .60 C7
Manchester,Rusholme M14 . .98 D2
Wardle OL12 . . . . .15 C6
St James CE Prim Sch Daisy
  Hill BL5 . . . . .57 F5
St James Cl
Glossop SK13 . . . . .116 C7
Newton-le-W WA12 . . . . .89 B3
St James Cres M20 . . . . . .74 F8
St James Ct
Altrincham WA15 . . . . .119 E4
Cheadle SK8 . . . . .131 F6
Manchester M20 . . . . .122 B8
4 Oldham OL4 . . . . .67 C8
Standish WN6 . . . . .19 D2
St James Dr M33 . . . . . . .108 A3
St James Gr WN3 . . . . . . .150 B6
St James Lo SK3 . . . . . . .124 A4
St James Rd SK4 . . . . . . .111 B5
St James St
Ashton-u-L OL6 . . . . .85 D2
Eccles M30 . . . . .79 E2
Farnworth BL4 . . . . .60 B7
Heywood OL10 . . . . .29 C2
Manchester M1 . . . . .163 A8
Milnrow OL16 . . . . .31 F6
Shaw OL2 . . . . .149 B7
Westhoughton BL5 . . . . .57 F5
St James' Ave BL8 . . . . . . .27 B4
St James' CE Prim Sch
Ashton-u-L OL6 . . . . .166 C3
Glossop SK13 . . . . .116 B8
Manchester M18 . . . . .99 D5
Wigan WN3 . . . . .54 F5
St James' Ct
1 Hattersley SK14 . . . . . . .102 D3
Salford M6 . . . . .80 B3
St James' Dr SK9 . . . . . . .137 A6
Orrell WN5 . . . . .53 D4
St James' RC High Sch
  Hattersley SK14 . . . . .102 D3
Manchester M19 . . . . .110 F6
St James' Rd WN5 . . . . . . .53 D4
St James' St BL2 . . . . .28 E8
St James' Way SK8 . . . . . .131 F6
St James' CE Sec Sch
  BL4 . . . . .60 A8
St James's Gr WA14 . . . . .107 F1
St James's RC Prim Sch
  M6 . . . . .154 F3
St James's Rd M7 . . . . . . .155 E6
St James's Sq 3 M2 . . . .158 F1
St James's St OL1 . . . . . . .67 B7
St James's Terr OL10 . . . . .29 C2
St John Bosco RC Prim Sch
  M9 . . . . .65 A3
St John Fisher RC High Sch
  WN6 . . . . .36 B4
St John Fisher RC Prim Sch
Denton M34 . . . . .101 B1
Middleton M24 . . . . .47 B3
Wythenshawe M22 . . . . . . .121 D4
St John Rigby RC Sixth Form
  Coll WN5 . . . . .35 F7
St John Southworth's RC
  Prim Sch WN4 . . . . .73 D4
St John St Atherton M46 . . .58 D3
Dukinfield SK16 . . . . .101 E8
1 Eccles M30 . . . . .79 D1
Horwich BL6 . . . . .22 B3
Irlam M44 . . . . .94 A2
Manchester M3 . . . . .162 E8
Newton-le-W WA12 . . . . .89 A3
6 Oldham OL4 . . . . .67 F6

St John St continued
Pendlebury M27 . . . . .80 D6
Walkden M28 . . . . .60 D4
Wigan WN5 . . . . .54 B6
St John the Baptist CE Sch
  WN2 . . . . .37 F3
St John the Evangelist RC
  Prim Sch BL7 . . . . .24 F8
St John Vianney Lower Sch
  SK4 . . . . .168 B2
St John Vianney Upper Sch
  M16 . . . . .97 B2
St John with St Michael CE
  Prim Sch OL12 . . . . .4 E5
St John's Ave
Droylsden M43 . . . . .84 B2
Westhoughton BL5 . . . . .39 D3
St John's CE Inf Sch
Failsworth M35 . . . . .83 F8
Leigh WN7 . . . . .75 F6
St John's CE Jun Sch
  M35 . . . . .84 A7
St John's CE Mosley Common
  Prim Sch M28 . . . . .77 F7
St John's CE Prim Sch
  BL9 . . . . .140 F4
St John's CE Prim Sch
Coppull PR7 . . . . .19 D6
Dukinfield SK16 . . . . .101 E8
Farnworth BL4 . . . . .60 E8
Hindley WN2 . . . . .57 B3
Manchester M13 . . . . .98 E4
Manchester,Heaton Mersey
  SK4 . . . . .110 C3
Radcliffe M26 . . . . .44 B1
Slattocks M24 . . . . .47 C6
Wigan WN5 . . . . .54 B6
St John's Cl
Dukinfield SK16 . . . . .101 E8
Romiley SK6 . . . . .113 B2
St John's Ct
5 Abram WN2 . . . . .56 B1
Altrincham WA14 . . . . .119 D3
Hyde SK14 . . . . .167 F3
Radcliffe M26 . . . . .44 C2
4 Rochdale OL16 . . . . .31 B6
Salford M7 . . . . .81 B5
St John's Dr Hyde SK14 . . .167 F3
6 Rochdale OL16 . . . . .31 B6
St John's Gdns OL5 . . . . . .68 D2
St John's Ind Est OL4 . . . . .67 E6
St John's Mews BL8 . . . . . .26 F7
St John's Pass M3 . . . . . .162 E8
St John's Pl SK4 . . . . .110 C3
St John's RC Prim Sch
Manchester M21 . . . . .97 A1
Rochdale OL11 . . . . .139 F6
St John's Rd
Altrincham WA14 . . . . .119 D3
Aspull WN2 . . . . .38 B5
Bolton BL3 . . . . .40 B4
Broadbottom M28 . . . . .77 F7
Denton M34 . . . . .100 F5
Hazel Grove SK7 . . . . .124 B1
Manchester M13 . . . . .98 F4
Manchester M16 . . . . .97 C4
Manchester,Heaton Mersey
  SK4 . . . . .110 C3
Wilmslow SK9 . . . . .136 E3
St John's St Abram WN2 . . .74 B8
Farnworth BL4 . . . . .60 E8
Oldham OL9 . . . . .152 C6
Radcliffe M26 . . . . .44 B2
Rawtenstall BB4 . . . . .2 F8
Salford M7 . . . . .155 D6
St Johns CE Prim Sch
  M27 . . . . .80 C6
St Johns Ct OL4 . . . . .67 F7
St Johns Sq M3 . . . . .158 D2
St Johns Wlk 3 SK3 . . . . .123 B8
St Johns Wood BL6 . . . . . . .40 B4
St Joseph & St Bede RC Prim
  Sch BL9 . . . . .141 B4
St Joseph St BL1 . . . . . . .143 D2
St Joseph's Con Ctr WN8 . .35 B2
St Joseph's Dr
Rochdale OL16 . . . . .31 B4
Salford M5 . . . . .161 B8
St Joseph's RC High Sch
  OL10 . . . . .29 C1
St Joseph's RC High Sch &
  Sports Coll BL6 . . . . .22 E1
St Joseph's RC Inf Sch
  SK5 . . . . .111 E8
St Joseph's RC Jun & Inf Sch
  OL2 . . . . .149 C5
St Joseph's RC Jun Sch
  SK5 . . . . .111 E8
St Joseph's RC Prim Sch
Adlington PR6 . . . . .21 B8
Bacup OL13 . . . . .3 D8
Heywood OL10 . . . . .29 C1
Leigh WN7 . . . . .76 A4
Manchester M13 . . . . .98 E4
Mossley OL5 . . . . .68 C1
Ramsbottom BL0 . . . . .138 B6
Sale M33 . . . . .108 B4
Shevington Moor WN6 . . . . .19 A3
Stockport SK1 . . . . .169 F1
Walkden M38 . . . . .60 A5
St Joseph's The Worker RC
  Prim Sch M45 . . . . .94 A3
St Josephs Ave M45 . . . . .63 C7
St Josephs Cl OL2 . . . . . .149 C8

St Jude's RC Prim Sch
WN3 ....54 F5
St Katherines Dr BL6 ......21 C3
St Kentigern's RC Prim Sch
M14 ....98 A1
St Kilda Ave BL4 ....60 F6
St Kilda's Ave M43 ....83 F3
St Kilda's Dr M7 ....155 F8
St Lawrence Quay M50 ....96 F7
St Lawrence Rd M34 ......101 A3
St Leonard's Ave BL6 ......22 F1
St Leonard's Ct **4** M43 ..107 F4
St Leonard's St M24 ......111 D5
St Leonard's Sq **8** M24 ....47 A1
St Leonards Dr WA15 ....119 F6
St Lesmo Ct SK3 ....123 C7
St Lesmo Rd SK3 ....123 C7
St Lewis RC Prim Sch
WA3 ....91 B1
St Luke Cld Prim Sch BL9 ..44 F8
St Luke St OL11 ....139 F5
St Luke's Ave WA3 ....90 D8
St Luke's CE Prim Sch
Glossop SK13 ....104 C1
Golborne WA3 ....90 E7
Heywood OL10 ....29 D3
Manchester M12 ....164 E5
Salford M5 ....154 D1
St Luke's Cres SK16 ......101 C8
St Luke's Dr WN5 ....53 E4
St Luke's RC Prim Sch
M6 ....80 C5
St Luke's Rd M6 ....154 E2
St Lukes Cres CE Prim Sch
OL9 ....152 A7
St Lukes Ct Bolton BL1 ..144 C8
Chadderton OL9 ....152 A7
St Lukes Ho WN4 ....73 D4
St Lukes Wlk **15** M40 ......83 A6
St Malachy's RC Prim Sch
M40 ....156 C5
St Malo Rd WN1 ....37 C4
St Margaret Mary's RC Prim
Sch M40 ....65 D3
St Margaret Ward RC Prim
Sch M33 ....107 C2
St Margaret's Ave M19 ..110 F6
St Margaret's CE Jun & Inf
Sch OL8 ....66 B2
St Margaret's CE Prim Sch
Heywood OL10 ....29 A1
Manchester M16 ....97 D2
Prestwich M25 ....63 D7
St Margaret's Cl
Altrincham WA14 ....119 C4
Bolton BL1 ....144 B8
St Margaret's Gdns OL8 ..66 C3
St Margaret's RC Prim Sch
SK13 ....115 D8
St Margaret's Rd
Altrincham WA14 ....119 C3
Bolton BL1 ....144 B8
Cheadle SK8 ....123 A6
Failsworth M24,M40 ....65 D3
Prestwich M25 ....63 C6
St Maries RC Prim Sch
BL9 ....140 F1
St Maries Ho Prim Sch
WN6 ....19 E2
St Mark St SK16 ....166 B1
St Mark's Ave
Altrincham WA14 ....119 A5
Royton OL2 ....49 A4
Wigan WN5 ....54 F7
St Mark's CE Prim Sch
Bury BL9 ....141 A4
Manchester M40 ....160 D3
Romiley SK6 ....113 A4
Worsley M28 ....78 F6
St Mark's Cl OL2 ....49 A4
St Mark's Cres M28 ....60 D1
St Mark's Ct OL10 ....152 B8
St Mark's La M7,M8 ......155 F8
St Mark's RC Prim Sch
M27 ....62 A2
St Mark's Sq **11** BL9 ......140 F4
St Mark's St Bolton BL3 ..145 F5
Reddish M19 ....99 C1
Romiley SK6 ....113 A4
St Mark's View BL3 ....145 F5
St Mark's Wlk BL3 ....147 E4
St Marks CE Prim Sch
WN5 ....54 F6
St Martin's Ave SK4 ......168 C2
St Martin's CE Jun & Inf Sch
OL8 ....67 B2
St Martin's Cl
Droylsden M43 ....83 F3
Hyde SK14 ....167 F2
St Martin's Dr M7 ....155 F8
St Martin's Rd
Marple SK6 ....126 A6
Oldham OL8 ....67 B2
St Martin's St OL11 ....30 D1
St Martins Rd M33 ....107 E6
St Mary & St John RC Prim
Sch WN1 ....37 D1
St Mary's Ave
Billinge WN5 ....71 C4
Bolton BL3 ....144 B5
Denton M34 ....113 A8
St Mary's CE Jun & Inf Sch
M16 ....97 E4
St Mary's CE Prim Sch
Bolton BL3 ....146 A4
Droylsden M43 ....84 B1

St Mary's CE Prim Sch
continued
Failsworth M40 ....65 C1
Hawkshaw BL8 ....10 C2
Irlam M44 ....105 C5
Prestwich M45 ....63 A4
Reddish SK5 ....112 A6
Rochdale OL11 ....31 A4
Sale M33 ....108 A4
Urmston M41 ....95 B4
St Mary's CE Prim Sch High
Crompton OL2 ....48 F8
St Mary's Cl Aspull WN2 ....38 B5
Atherton M46 ....58 E2
Rochdale OL16 ....31 B4
Stockport SK1 ....112 A1
St Mary's Crest OL3 ....69 C5
St Mary's Ct
Failsworth M40 ....83 B8
Golborne WA3 ....91 B8
St Mary's SK14 ....103 D5
St Mary's Dr
Manchester M8 ....63 F1
Prestwich M25 ....63 A4
St Mary's Dr Cheadle SK8 122 F6
Reddish SK5 ....111 F6
Uppermill OL3 ....69 C5
St Mary's Gate
Manchester M8 ....158 F2
Rochdale OL12,OL16 ......139 E8
Shaw OL2 ....149 B7
Uppermill OL3 ....69 C5
St Mary's Hall Rd M8 ......63 F1
St Mary's Hospl M13 ....98 C4
St Mary's Ind Pk SK14 ..102 A6
St Mary's Parsonage
M3 ....158 F1
St Mary's Pk M25 ....63 A4
St Mary's RC Prim Sch
Billinge WN5 ....71 D4
Denton M34 ....100 E3
Dukinfield SK16 ....101 E6
Eccles M30 ....79 E1
Glossop SK13 ....116 D8
Horwich BL6 ....22 D2
Littleborough OL15 ....16 A5
Manchester M19 ....111 A8
Marple SK6 ....126 B7
Middleton M24 ....65 A6
Radcliffe M26 ....44 A4
Stockport SK4 ....169 E2
Swinton M27 ....79 F8
St Mary's Rd
Altrincham WA14 ....119 C3
Aspull WN2 ....38 C5
Disley SK12 ....135 D5
Dukinfield SK14 ....101 F5
St Mary's RC **11** Eccles M40 ..79 F2
Failsworth M40 ....83 B7
Glossop SK13 ....116 C8
Prestwich M25 ....63 B4
Sale M33 ....107 F5
Walkden M28 ....60 C5
St Mary's St
Manchester M15 ....162 E5
Manchester M3 ....158 F1
St Mary's Way
2 Leigh WN7 ....75 F5
Oldham OL1 ....153 F7
Stockport SK1 ....112 A2
St Marys Ct M25 ....63 A4
St Marys Rd OL1 ....153 F8
St Marys View **3** SK14 ..101 F5
St Matthew's CE Inf Sch
M24 ....47 F2
St Matthew's CE Prim Sch
Bolton BL3 ....143 E1
Little Lever BL3 ....43 A3
Stockport SK4 ....170 E8
St Matthew's Cl WN3 ......54 C4
St Matthew's Dr OL1 ......48 A2
St Matthew's RC High Sch
Failsworth M40 ....65 C2
Manchester M9 ....64 F1
St Matthew's Rd SK3 ....170 D8
St Matthew's Terr **8**
BL1 ....143 E1
St Matthew's Terr M40 ..170 D8
St Matthew's Wlk BL3 ..143 E1
St Matthews Ct **9** M32 ..96 C1
St Mawes Ct M26 ....43 A3
St Maxentius CE Prim Sch
BL2 ....25 D5
St Michael's Ave
Atherton M46 ....58 A1
Bolton BL3 ....42 B2
Bramhall SK7 ....132 E8
St Michael's Bamford CE
Prim Sch OL10 ....29 C5
St Michael's CE Prim Sch
Atherton M46 ....58 B2
Bolton BL3 ....42 C3
Middleton M24 ....65 A5
Urmston M41 ....94 F1
St Michael's Ct
Eccles M30 ....95 A8
8 Wigan WN1 ....37 C2

St Michael's RC Prim Sch
M45 ....45 B1
St Michael's Rd SK14 ....102 A2
St Michael's Sq
6 Ashton-u-L OL6 ......166 C3
Manchester M8 ....159 A3
St Michaels Cl BL8 ....43 F8
St Michaels Ct M33 ......107 E6
St Michaels Gdns M45 ....45 B1
St Modwen Rd M32 ....96 A5
St Monica's RC High Sch
M25 ....63 C3
St Monica's RC Prim Sch
M41 ....94 E2
St Nathaniel's CE Prim Sch
WN2 ....56 B3
St Nicholas Rd
Golborne WA3 ....75 A1
Manchester M15 ....162 E6
St Osmund's Dr BL2 ....42 E7
St Osmund's Gr BL2 ......42 E7
St Oswald's Ave
Ashton-in-M WN4 ....73 B3
Coppull PR7 ....19 D8
St Oswald's Dr M19 ....90 B2
St Oswalds Rd M46 ....73 A2
St Quen Ctr M28 ....60 D3
St Patrick St WN1 ....151 D8
St Patrick's CE High Sch
M30 ....79 B2
St Patrick's RC Prim Sch
Manchester M4 ....159 C3
Oldham OL8 ....153 D6
Rochdale OL16 ....15 A1
Wigan WN1 ....151 D8
St Patricks Way WN1 ....151 D7
St Paul's Ave WN3 ....54 F4
St Paul's CE Prim Sch
Bolton BL1 ....143 F3
Brinnington SK5 ....112 B4
Bury BL9 ....141 B4
Manchester M20 ....110 B6
Royton OL2 ....48 C3
St Paul's CE Prim Sch
Stalybridge SK15 ....86 C2
Walkden M28 ....60 F2
Wigan WN3 ....54 F3
St Paul's Ct M26 ....44 A1
St Paul's Gdns SK14 ......167 E3
St Paul's Hill SK14 ....102 A2
St Paul's Hill Rd
Hyde SK14 ....102 A2
Hyde SK14 ....167 F2
St Paul's Pl **1** BL1 ......142 C3
St Paul's RC High Sch
M23 ....121 B4
St Paul's RC Prim Sch
Hyde SK14 ....167 F4
Poynton SK12 ....133 E2
St Paul's Rd
Manchester,Heaton Moor
SK4 ....168 B4
Manchester,Sedgley Park
M7 ....63 C1
Manchester,Withington
M20 ....110 C6
St Paul's Rise **4** M7 ......63 C1
St Paul's St Bury BL9 ....141 A3
Hyde SK14 ....167 E3
Ramsbottom BL0 ....138 C6
Stalybridge SK15 ....86 C2
Stockport SK1 ....112 A3
St Paul's Villas BL9 ......141 A3
St Pauls CE Prim Sch
Salford M5 ....81 B1
St Pauls Cl SK15 ....86 C2
St Pauls Ct
1 Manchester M7 ....63 C1
2 Walkden M28 ....60 D2
St Pauls Ho **6** BL9 ......141 A3
St Pauls Ho **2** OL2 ......48 D7
St Pauls Peel CE Prim Sch
M38 ....59 F5
St Pauls Rd M28 ....60 E2
St Pauls Trad Est SK15 ....86 C2
St Peter & St John RC Prim
Sch M3 ....158 D2
St Peter Smithills Dean CE
Prim Sch BL1 ....142 B4
St Peter's Ave BL1 ....142 A2
St Peter's CE Prim Sch
Ashton-u-L OL7 ....166 A1
Bury BL9 ....44 E6
Farnworth BL4 ....60 D7
Hindley WN2 ....56 C5
Newton-le-W WA12 ....89 E4
Rochdale OL16 ....31 B5
Swinton M27 ....79 E8
St Peter's Ct WA13 ....117 A4
St Peter's Dr M33 ....96 E3
St Peter's Dr SK14 ....167 F2
St Peter's Gate OL14 ......6 B8
St Peter's RC High Sch
Droylsden M11 ....99 A4
Manchester M12 ....99 A4
Orrell WN5 ....53 F7
St Peter's RC Prim Sch
Hazel Grove SK7 ....124 D1
Middleton M24 ....65 A7
Stalybridge SK15 ....86 A1
Wythenshawe M23 ....121 A3
St Peter's Rd Bury BL9 ....44 F6

St Peter's Rd continued
Swinton M27 ....79 E8
St Peter's Sq
Manchester M1 ....162 F8
Stockport SK1 ....169 F1
St Peter's Sq Sta M2 ......162 F8
St Peter's St
6 Ashton-u-L OL6 ......166 A2
Rochdale OL16 ....31 B6
St Peter's Terr BL4 ....60 D7
St Peter's Way
Bolton BL1 ....145 F8
Bolton BL1,BL2,BL3,BL4 ..42 B4
St Petersgate SK1 ....169 F1
St Philip Howard RC Sch
SK13 ....116 B8
St Philip's Ave BL3 ....147 D4
St Philip's CE Prim Sch
Atherton M46 ....58 E3
Salford M3 ....158 D1
St Philip's Pl M3 ....158 D2
St Philip's Rd M18 ....99 D4
St Philips CE Prim Sch
M15 ....162 F6
St Philips Sq M3 ....158 D2
St Phillip's Dr OL1,OL2 ....48 E1
St Raphael's RC Prim Sch
SK5 ....86 E4
St Richard's Cl M46 ....58 C4
St Richard's RC Jun & Inf Sch
M46 ....58 C4
St Richard's RC Prim Sch
M12 ....99 B3
St Saviour CE Prim Sch
M26 ....61 C7
St Saviour's Com Prim Sch
OL13 ....4 A8
St Saviour's Rd SK2 ......124 C5
St Sebastian's RC Prim Sch
M6 ....81 A5
St Simon St M3 ....158 E3
St Simons CE Prim Sch
SK7 ....124 E3
St Simons Ct M23 ....124 C8
St Stephen & All Martyrs CE
Inf Sch OL11 ....153 F8
St Stephen & All Martyrs' CE
Sch BL2 ....148 C5
St Stephen Ho
6 Oldham OL1 ....67 A8
Salford M3 ....158 E2
St Stephen's Ave
Ashton-u-L M34 ....100 E8
Wigan WN1 ....37 E2
St Stephen's CE Prim Sch
Bury BL8 ....27 B1
Hazel Grove SK2 ....124 F4
Kearsley BL4 ....61 A6
Tyldesley M29 ....77 B6
Wigan WN1 ....37 E2
St Stephen's Cl
Bolton BL2 ....148 C5
Manchester M13 ....164 D5
St Stephen's Gdns
Kearsley BL4 ....61 A6
10 Middleton M24 ....47 A2
St Stephen's Rd WN6 ......19 C1
St Stephens Cl M29 ....77 A5
St Stephens View M43 ....84 A2
St Teresa's RC Prim Sch
Irlam M44 ....105 E3
Manchester M16 ....97 A3
Up Holland WN8 ....35 B1
St Teresa's RC Prim Sch
Manchester M16 ....97 A3
St Teresa's Rd M16 ....97 A4
St Thomas Aquinas RC High
Sch (Upper Sch) M21 ..109 D7
St Thomas CE Jun & Inf Sch
OL4 ....67 E6
St Thomas CE Prim Sch
Ashton-in-M WN4 ....73 C3
Leigh WN7 ....76 B4
Oldham OL8 ....153 D5
Westhoughton BL5 ....40 B1
St Thomas Cl **1** BL9 ....141 A2
St Thomas Hospl SK3 ....170 E8
St Thomas Mooreside CE Prim
Sch OL1 ....48 A4
St Thomas More RC High Sch
Denton M34 ....100 F2
Wigan WN5 ....54 F7
St Thomas More RC Prim Sch
M24 ....65 A5
St Thomas of Canterbury
Prim Sch M7 ....155 E6
St Thomas of Canterbury RC
Prim Sch BL1 ....144 A8
St Thomas Par OL4 ....67 E6
St Thomas St Bolton BL1 143 D2
Wigan WN3 ....150 C7
St Thomas St N OL8 ......153 D5
St Thomas St S OL8 ......153 E5
St Thomas the Martyr CE
Prim Sch WN6 ....53 B7
St Thomas' CE Prim Sch
Bury BL9 ....141 B1
Newhey OL16 ....32 B4
Reddish SK4 ....111 C6
St Thomas' CE Prim Sch
SK1 ....170 F8
St Thomas' Cl M26 ....44 A3

St Thomas' Com Prim Sch
M8 ....156 C8
St Thomas' Pl M8 ....159 A4
St Thomas's CE Prim Sch
BL1 ....143 D2
St Thomas's Circ OL8 ....153 D5
St Thomas's Ct WN8 ......53 C7
St Thomas's Pl SK11 ....170 F8
St Veronica's RC Prim Sch
BB4 ....1 B7
St Vincent RC Jun & Inf Sch
OL12 ....14 A1
St Vincent St M4 ....159 C2
St Vincent's RC Inf Sch
WA15 ....119 E5
St Vincent's RC Jun Sch
WA15 ....119 E5
St Werburgh's Rd M21,
M16 ....109 C8
St Wilfred's Dr OL12 ......14 D4
St Wilfred's CE Jun & Inf Sch
M40 ....83 C3
St Wilfrid's Ent Ctr M15 162 E6
St Wilfrid's RC Prim Sch
M15 ....162 E6
St Wilfrid's Rd WN6 ....19 F1
St Wilfrid's Way WN6 ....19 E1
St Wilfrids CE Prim Sch
M22 ....121 E8
St Wilfrids St M15 ....162 E6
St William's RC Prim Sch
WN2 ....151 F7
St Williams Ave BL3 ......147 E3
St Williams' RC Prim Sch
BL3 ....147 E3
St Willibrord's RC Prim Sch
M11 ....83 C3
St Winifred's Pl **2** SK15 ..85 F7
St Winifred's RC Prim Sch
SK4 ....168 A2
Salcombe Ave BL2 ....26 D1
Salcombe Cl Sale M33 ....107 E5
Wigan WN1 ....37 E2
Salcombe Gr BL2 ....42 F6
Salcombe Rd
Droylsden M11,M43 ....99 D8
Stockport SK2 ....124 C8
Salcot Wlk **8** M40 ......159 C3
Sale Gram Sch M33 ......108 C3
Sale Heys Rd M33 ....107 F3
Sale La M29 ....77 D8
Sale Rd M23 ....109 B2
Sale St OL15 ....16 B6
Sale Sta M33 ....108 B4
Sale Water Pk* M33 ......108 E7
Salem Gr OL4 ....67 D6
Sales's La BL9 ....12 B3
Salesbury Way WN3 ....55 A3
Salford App M3 ....158 F2
Salford Art Gallery & Mus*
M6 ....81 C2
Salford Central Sta M3 ..158 E1
Salford Coll (Quays Campus)
M5 ....161 A7
Salford Coll (Wardley
Campus) M27 ....61 C2
Salford Coll (Worsley
Campus) M28 ....60 D1
Salford Crescent Sta M6 ..81 B2
Salford Foyer M6 ....154 F3
Salford Quays Sta M50 ..161 A7
Salford Rd BL5 ....59 C7
Salford St Bury BL9 ......141 A4
Oldham OL4 ....67 C5
Salik Gdns OL11 ....139 F5
Salisbury Ave
Heywood OL10 ....46 C8
Hindley WN2 ....56 E6
Salisbury Cres OL6 ....85 D7
Salisbury Dr
Dukinfield SK16 ....102 A2
Manchester M25 ....63 C2
Salisbury Ho M3 ....158 E2
Salisbury Rd
Altrincham WA14 ....119 D7
1 Ashton-in-M WN4 ......73 A5
Horwich BL6 ....22 F1
Manchester M21 ....97 C1
Oldham OL4 ....67 B6
Radcliffe M26 ....43 B5
Salford M30 ....80 A4
Swinton M27 ....79 E7
Urmston M41 ....95 D4
Whitefield M45 ....62 E8
Salisbury St Bolton BL3 ..145 D6
Golborne WA3 ....90 A8
Hadfield SK13 ....104 A5
Manchester M14 ....98 A4
Middleton M24 ....47 B1
Reddish SK5 ....111 F8
Shaw OL2 ....48 F8
Salisbury Terr BL3 ....43 C3
Salisbury Way M29 ....77 D8
Salix Ct M6 ....81 A3
Salkeld Ave WN4 ....72 F3
Salkeld St OL11 ....139 F5
Sallowfields WN5 ....53 D5
Sally Barn Cotts BB4 ....3 C5
Salmon Fields OL2 ....48 F3
Salmon St
Manchester M4 ....159 A2
1 Wigan WN1 ....37 E1
Salsbury Hall Cl BL0 ....11 B4
Salop St Bolton BL2 ......148 A6

Salop St continued
Salford M6 ....81 A4
Saltash Cl M22 ....121 D1
Saltburn Wlk 26 M9 .157 E8
Saltdene Rd 2 M22 ...121 C1
Salter Rake Gate OL14 ...6 B8
Saltergate BL3 ....40 F4
Saltergate Mews M5 ...81 A1
Salters Ct M46 ....58 D3
Saltersbrook Gr 12 SK9 .131 E1
Salterton Dr Bolton BL3 .146 A2
   Bolton BL3 ....40 F2
Salterton Wlk 17 M40 ...83 A7
Salteye Rd M30 ....79 A1
Saltford Ave M4 ....159 C2
Saltford Ct M4 ....160 D2
Salthill Ave OL10 ....46 E7
Salthill Dr M22 ....121 E2
Saltire Gdns M7 ....155 E8
Saltram Cl M26 ....43 C5
Saltram Rd M23 ....54 C4
Saltrush Rd M22 ....121 D1
Salts Dr OL15 ....16 A6
Salts St OL2 ....149 B7
Saltwood Dr BL1 ....143 F1
Salutation St 10 M15 .162 F6
Salvin Cl WN4 ....73 D3
Salvin Wlk 27 M9 ....64 E3
Salwick Cl WN3 ....54 E4
Sam Cowan Cl M14 ...98 A3
Sam Rd OL3 ....51 C5
Sam Swire St M15 ....162 F5
Samian Gdns M7 ....81 C5
Samlesbury Cl
   Manchester M20 ....109 C3
   Shaw OL2 ....48 F7
Sammy Cookson Cl M14 .98 A3
Samouth Cl M40 ....160 D3
Sampson Sq M14 ....99 A4
Samson St OL16 ....31 C8
Samuel La OL2 ....48 E8
Samuel Laycock Sch
   SK15 ....85 F4
Samuel St Bury BL9 ....141 A3
   Failsworth M35 ....83 F8
   Hollingworth SK14 ....103 C4
   Manchester M19 ....111 B8
   Middleton M24 ....47 A2
   Rochdale OL11 ....30 C2
   Stockport SK4 ....169 D3
   Tyldesley M46 ....58 F1
Samwoods Ho WN4 ....73 A5
Sanby Ave M18 ....99 C4
Sanby Rd M18 ....99 C4
Sanctuary Cl M15 ....163 B5
Sanctuary The M15 .....162 E6
Sand Banks BL1 ....24 F6
Sand Beds La BL0,BB4 ...2 E5
Sand Hole La
   Rochdale OL11 ....30 F1
   Rochdale,Bamford OL11 ...29 E5
Sand Hole Rd BL4 ....61 A6
Sand St Manchester M40 .159 C4
   Stalybridge SK15 ....101 F8
Sandace Rd M23 ....121 B7
Sandal St M40 ....160 E3
Sandalwood BL5 ....57 D6
Sandalwood Dr WN6 ...36 F3
Sandbach Ave M14 ...109 F8
Sandbach Rd Reddish SK5 .99 E2
   Sale M33 ....108 F3
Sandbach Wlk SK8 ...123 A4
Sandbank Gdns OL12 ...4 C2
Sandbed La Delph OL3 ...51 A5
   Mossley OL5 ....68 C2
Sandbrook Gdns WN5 .53 D5
Sandbrook Rd WN5 ...53 C5
Sandbrook Way
   Denton M34 ....101 A3
   Rochdale OL16 ....30 E4
Sandby Dr SK6 ....126 B8
Sanderling Cl BL5 ....57 D6
Sanderling Dr WN7 ...76 A6
Sanderling Rd
   Hazel Grove SK2 ....125 A4
   Newton-le-W WA12 ....89 C4
Sanderson Ave M40 ...157 E5
Sanderson Cl M28 ....79 B7
Sanderson Ct M40 .....157 E5
Sanderson La PR7 ....18 A8
Sanderson St Bury BL9 .141 A3
   Leigh WN7 ....75 D5
   Manchester M40 ....157 E5
Sanderson's Croft WN7 ...64 E3
Sanderstead Dr M9 ...64 E3
Sandfield Cl 3 WA3 .....90 E8
Sandfield Cres WA3 ...92 C7
Sandfield Dr BL6 ....40 C6
Sandfield Rd OL16 ....31 B5
Sandfold SK5 ....99 E3
Sandford Ave 3 M18 ...99 F6
Sandford Cl BL2 ....25 E4
Sandford Rd
   Sale M33 ....108 F3
Sandford St Orrell WN5 ...53 C5
   Manchester M26 ....44 D4
Sandgate Ave
   Droylsden M11 ....83 D2
   Kearsley M26 ....61 C7
Sandgate Dr WN7 ....75 F6
Sandgate Dr M41 ....95 C4
Sandgate Rd
   Chadderton OL9 ....152 B6

Sandgate Rd continued
   Prestwich M45 ....63 B7
Sandham St BL3 ....147 E4
Sandham Wlk BL3 ....147 F4
Sandheys M34 ....100 F5
Sandheys Gr M18 ....99 E4
Sandhill Cl BL3 ....147 E4
Sandhill La SK6 ....114 E1
Sandhill St SK14 ....146 F7
Sandhill Wlk M22 ....121 B2
Sandhurst Ave M20 ...110 A6
Sandhurst Cl BL8 ....27 B3
Sandhurst Ct BL2 ....42 E6
Sandhurst Dr Bolton BL2 .42 E6
   2 Wilmslow SK9 ....137 C8
Sandhurst Rd
   Manchester M20 ....110 C2
   Stockport SK2 ....124 B5
Sandiacre WN6 ....36 E8
Sandilands Jun & Inf Sch
   M23 ....120 D8
Sandilands Rd M23 ...120 D7
Sandilea Ct M7 ....63 A1
Sandileigh Ave
   Altrincham WA15 ....119 F3
   Brinnington SK5 ....112 B4
   Cheadle SK8 ....123 A6
   Manchester M20 ....110 B6
Sandileigh Dr WA15 ...119 F3
Sandimoss Ct 1 M33 .107 F4
Sandiway Glossop SK13 .116 F7
   Heywood OL10 ....29 E2
   Irlam M44 ....94 A2
   Romiley SK6 ....112 F3
   Stockport SK4 ....123 E2
Sandiway Cl SK6 ....125 F8
Sandiway Dr M20 ....110 A3
Sandiway Pl WA14 ....119 D5
Sandiway Rd
   Altrincham WA14 ....119 D6
   Handforth SK9 ....131 D5
   Sale M33 ....107 F4
Sandley Dr WA3 ....74 A2
Sandmere Wlk 28 M9 ...64 E3
Sandon St BL3 ....147 D4
Sandown Ave M6 ....154 E2
Sandown Cl Culcheth WA3 .91 F4
   8 Oldham OL1 ....49 A1
   Wilmslow SK9 ....137 D8
Sandown Cres
   Little Lever BL3 ....43 A2
   Manchester M18 ....99 D3
Sandown Dr
   Altrincham WA15 ....129 D6
   Denton M34 ....113 B8
   Sale M33 ....107 E3
Sandown Gdns M41 ...95 A2
Sandown Rd Bolton BL2 ...25 E3
   Hazel Grove SK7 ....125 A2
   Stockport SK3 ....123 B8
   Whitefield BL9 ....45 A2
   Wigan WN6 ....36 E3
Sandown St M18 ....99 F6
Sandpiper Cl
   Dukinfield SK16 ....101 E7
   Farnworth BL4 ....59 F7
   Newton-le-W WA12 ....89 C4
Sandpiper Dr SK3 ...170 D6
Sandpits Bsns Pk SK14 .102 E3
Sandra Dr WA12 ....89 E3
Sandray Cl BL3 ....40 F5
Sandray Gr M5 ....154 E1
Sandridge Cl BL4 ....60 E8
Sandridge Wlk M40 ...164 E6
Sandringham Ave
   Denton M34 ....100 D6
   Reddish M34 ....100 A3
   Stalybridge SK15 ....86 A3
Sandringham Cl
   Adlington PR7 ....20 E6
   Altrincham WA14 ....118 F1
   Wigan WN3 ....54 E5
Sandringham Ct
   Golborne WA3 ....90 E7
   5 Wilmslow SK9 ....137 A6
Sandringham Dr
   Dukinfield SK16 ....101 F7
   Leigh WN7 ....76 E7
   Milnrow OL16 ....32 A6
   Poynton SK12 ....133 D3
   Ramsbottom BL8 ....11 A1
   Stockport SK4 ....168 A1
Sandringham Grange
   M25 ....63 E3
Sandringham Rd
   Cheadle SK8 ....123 A3
   Hazel Grove SK7 ....124 F2
   Hindley WN2 ....56 E4
   Horwich BL6 ....22 E2
   Hyde SK14 ....113 E7
   Romiley SK6 ....112 D3
   Worsley M28 ....78 A6
Sandringham St M18 ...99 C4
Sandringham Way
   Royton OL2 ....48 C6
   6 Wilmslow SK9 ....137 A6
Sands Ave M24,OL9 .....47 D1
Sands Cl SK14 ....102 D1
Sands Wlk SK14 ....102 D1
Sandsend Cl M8 ....155 E5
Sandsend Rd M41 ....95 C3
Sandstone Rd
   Milnrow OL16 ....31 F7
   Wigan WN3 ....54 F4
Sandstone Way M21 ...109 D6

Sandway WN6 ....36 F2
Sandwell Dr M33 ....108 B6
Sandwich Rd M30 ....79 F3
Sandwich St M28 ....60 D2
Sandwick Cres BL3 ...145 D5
Sandwith Cl WN3 ....55 B2
Sandwood Ave BL3 .....40 E6
Sandy Acre OL5 ....86 C8
Sandy Bank OL2 ....48 F8
Sandy Bank Ave SK14 .102 D1
Sandy Bank Rd
   Edgworth BL7 ....9 D5
   Manchester M8 ....155 F8
Sandy Brow M9 ....64 D2
Sandy Brow La WA3 ...90 E2
Sandy Cl BL9 ....44 F4
Sandy Ct WN7 ....75 F1
Sandy Gr Dukinfield SK16 .101 D8
   Salford M6 ....154 E3
   Swinton M27 ....79 F8
Sandy Haven Cl SK14 .102 D1
Sandy Haven Wlk SK14 .102 D1
Sandy La Adlington PR7 ...20 F6
   Charlesworth SK13 ....115 A4
   Cheadle WA3 ....91 A1
   Droylsden M43 ....84 A2
   Dukinfield SK16 ....101 D8
   Golborne WA3 ....89 F8
   Golborne,Aspull Common
      WA3 ....75 A1
   Irlam M44 ....94 A2
   Lymm WA13 ....117 B4
   Manchester M21 ....109 C8
   Middleton M24 ....65 C8
   Orrell WN5 ....53 D4
   Prestwich M25 ....63 A2
   Reddish SK4,SK5 ....169 E3
   Rochdale OL11 ....30 C7
   Romiley SK6 ....113 D3
   Royton OL2 ....48 D4
   Salford M6 ....154 E3
   Stretford M32 ....96 C1
   Tyldesley M29 ....77 A4
   Tyldesley,Town Lane M29 ...77 A4
   Uppermill OL3 ....51 B2
   Wilmslow SK9 ....136 E8
   Wythenshawe M23 ....120 C7
Sandy Meade M25 ....63 A3
Sandy Pk WN2 ....57 A6
Sandy Way WN2 ....57 A6
Sandy Wlk M24 OL2 .....48 D4
Sandy Wood M6 ....154 E3
Sandyacre Cl BL5 ....59 A6
Sandybank Cl SK13 ...171 E4
Sandybrook Cl BL8 .....40 A2
Sandycroft Ave 8 WN1 ...37 C1
Sandygate Cl M27 ....79 E7
Sandyhill Rd M9 ....64 B3
Sandyhills BL3 ....147 E4
Sandylands Dr M25 ...63 A1
Sandyshot Wlk 4 M22 .121 F3
Sandyway WA3 ....106 A8
Sandyway BL3 ....63 A3
Sandyway Cl BL3 ....57 D8
Sandywell Cl M11 ....99 D7
Sandywell St M11 ....99 D8
Sanfold La M19 ....99 C2
Sangster Ct M5 ....161 A8
Sankey Gr M9 ....64 B3
Sankey St Bury BL9 ...140 D2
   Golborne WA3 ....90 A8
   Newton-le-W WA12 ....89 A3
Sankey Valley Ind Est
   WA12 ....89 A2
Santiago St M14 ....98 B3
Santley St M12 ....99 A3
Santon Ave M14 ....110 E8
Santon Dr WA3 ....90 E8
Sapling Gr M33 ....107 D2
Sapling Rd Bolton BL3 .146 C2
   Swinton M27 ....79 D5
Sarah Butterworth Ct 11
   OL16 ....31 B6
Sarah Butterworth St
   OL16 ....31 B6
Sarah St Bacup OL13 ...4 C8
   1 Eccles M30 ....79 B1
   Edenfield BL0 ....1 E3
   Hindley WN2 ....57 B2
   Manchester M11 ....164 F8
   Middleton M24 ....64 F8
   2 Oldham OL8 ....66 D2
   5 Rochdale OL11 ....31 A6
   Shaw OL2 ....149 A5
Sargent Dr M16 ....97 E4
Sargent Rd SK6 ....112 D2
Sark Rd M21 ....97 A2
Sarn Ave M22 ....121 D4
Sarnesfield Cl M12 .....99 A4
Sarnia Ct M7 ....155 D7
Sarsfield Ave 1 WA3 ...90 D8
Satinwood Cl WN4 .....72 F2
Satinwood Wlk M3 ...158 F1
Saturn Gr M6 ....81 C4
Saunton Ave BL2 ....25 F3
Saunton Rd M11 ....99 D8
Sautridge Cl OL11 ...47 D7
Savernake Rd SK6 ...113 C5
Saville Cl BL9 ....45 A2
Saville Rd Gatley SK8 ...122 B6
   Radcliffe BL9 ....44 E3
Saville St Bolton BL2 ...148 A6
   Middleton M24 ....65 B2
Savio Way M24 ....65 A7
Saviour CE Prim Sch
   M40 ....156 C5
Saviours Terr BL3 .....144 C5
Savoy Ct M45 ....44 E2

Savoy Dr OL2 ....48 D2
Savoy St Oldham OL4 ...67 B5
   Rochdale OL11 ....30 C8
Saw Mill Way 5 OL15 ...16 A5
Saw St BL3 ....143 E2
Sawley Ave Golborne WA3 .74 D1
   Littleborough OL15 ....16 A7
   Oldham OL4 ....67 D4
   Whitefield M45 ....44 F2
   Wigan WN6 ....36 F2
Sawley Cl M33 ....92 A2
Sawley Dr SK8 ....132 C6
Sawley Rd M40 ....160 E4
Sawmill The BL9 ....140 F1
Sawpit St WA13,WA14 ...118 A6
Sawston Wlk M40 ....65 C3
Sawyer Brow SK14 ...167 F4
Sawyer Dr WN4 ....72 D3
Sawyer St Bury BL8 ...27 B4
   5 Rochdale OL12 ....14 F1
Saxbrook Wlk 3 M22 .121 F3
Saxby Ave BL7 ....24 F8
Saxby St M6 ....80 C5
Saxelby Dr M8 ....156 B7
Saxfield Dr M23 ....121 C6
Saxholme Wlk 5 M22 .121 C2
Saxon Ave
   Dukinfield SK16 ....101 C8
   Manchester M8 ....64 A2
Saxon Cl BL8 ....27 B2
Saxon Dr Chadderton OL9 ...65 E8
   Denton M34 ....100 E7
   Droylsden M43 ....84 B2
Saxon Hall L Ctr OL16 ...31 C8
Saxon Ho 8 M16 ....97 D3
Saxon Rd OL5 ....68 D3
Saxon St Denton M34 .100 F3
   Droylsden M43 ....84 B2
   Manchester M40 ....160 E3
   Middleton M24 ....65 B8
   Oldham OL4 ....67 C7
   Radcliffe M26 ....43 F3
Saxonholme Rd OL11 ...47 C7
Saxthorpe Cl
   8 Sale M33 ....107 D5
   Wigan WN3 ....54 D3
Saxthorpe Wlk M12 ...164 E5
Saxwood Ave M9 ....64 D1
Saxwood Cl OL12 ....13 F1
Sayle Ave OL7 ....84 F4
Scafell Cl High Lane SK6 .134 E8
   Oldham OL1 ....48 F1
Scafell Dr WN5 ....54 B6
Scafell Gr WN2 ....56 B2
Scalby Wlk 2 M22 .....121 D1
Scale St M5 ....81 A1
Scarborough St M40 ...83 A8
Scarcroft Rd M12 .....165 A5
Scardale Ave BL1 .....142 A1
Scarfield Dr OL11 .....13 E1
Scargill Cl 1 M14 .....110 C8
Scargill Rd BL3 ....146 A4
Scarisbrick Ave M20 .110 D3
Scarisbrick Rd M19 ...110 F8
Scarisbrick St 3 WN1 ...37 C1
Scarr Ave M26 ....44 C2
Scarr La OL12 ....49 D7
Scarr Terr OL12 ....4 D2
Scarsdale Rd M14 .....98 E4
Scarsdale St M6 ....81 A3
Scarthwood Cl BL2 ...25 E5
Scawfell Ave BL2 ....25 B2
Scawton Wlk M9 ....64 B5
Sceptre Cl WA12 ....89 A3
Schofield Gdns WN7 ...75 F3
Schofield Hall Rd M46 .57 F3
Schofield La M46 ....57 F3
Schofield Rd
   Droylsden M43 ....84 B1
   Eccles M30 ....79 A1
Schofield St
   Droylsden M11 ....83 C2
   Failsworth M35 ....83 F8
   Haslingden BB4 ....1 A6
   Heywood OL10 ....29 D1
   Leigh WN7 ....75 E4
   Littleborough OL15 ....16 C6
   Littleborough,Summit OL15 ...16 D2
   Milnrow OL16 ....32 A5
   Oldham OL8 ....66 F3
   Radcliffe M26 ....44 B4
   Rawtenstall BB4 ....2 E8
   Rochdale OL11 ....31 A6
   Royton OL2 ....48 D5
Scholars Dr M20 ....110 A7
Scholars St 11 M12 ...99 A4
Scholars Way 05 M24 .46 F1
Scholefield La WN1 ...151 E8
Scholes WN1 ....151 D8
Scholes Bank BL6 ....22 A5
Scholes Cl M7 ....155 F8
Scholes Dr M40 ....65 C1
Scholes La M25 ....63 C3
Scholes St Bury BL8 ...27 C3
   Chadderton OL9 ....66 A1
   Failsworth M35 ....66 A1
   Oldham OL1 ....153 F6
   Pendlebury M27 ....80 A8
   Swinton M27 ....61 D1
Scholes The Wlk M25 ...63 C3
Scholey St BL2 ....148 A5
Scholfield Ave M41 ...95 F1
School Ave
   Ashton-u-L OL6 ....85 D6
   Stretford M32 ....96 C1
   Wigan WN1 ....37 D2
School Brow Billinge WN5 .71 E5

School Brow continued
   Bury BL9 ....140 E3
   Bury BL9 ....140 F2
   Romiley SK6 ....113 A2
   Worsley M28 ....78 F6
School Cl SK12 ....133 F3
School Court No 1 M4 .159 B3
School Cres SK15 ....86 A4
School Ct Bolton BL7 .....8 E2
   Edenfield BL0 ....1 D2
   Manchester M4 ....159 B3
   Stockport SK3 ....170 F6
School Dr Billinge WN5 ...71 E5
   Dukinfield SK16 ....101 E6
School Gr
   Manchester M20 ....110 D6
   Prestwich M25 ....63 A2
School Gr W M20 ......110 C6
School Hill BL1 ....145 E8
School House Flats 1
   OL8 ....66 C2
School La Aspull WN2 ...37 E7
   Bury BL9 ....27 E8
   Carrington M31 ....106 D6
   Edgworth BL7 ....9 D8
   Garswood WN4 ....72 C3
   Hollinfare WA3 ....105 A2
   Hyde SK14 ....113 E7
   Irlam M44 ....105 D5
   Irlam,Springfield M44 ....93 F2
   Manchester M9 ....64 C2
   Manchester,Didsbury M19,
      M20 ....110 C3
   Mossley SK15 ....86 E7
   Partington WA14 ....118 D5
   Poynton SK12 ....133 F4
   Reddish SK4 ....111 C5
   Rochdale OL11 ....29 C8
   Rochdale OL16 ....139 F7
   Romiley SK6 ....114 B4
   Standish WN6 ....19 D1
   Up Holland,WN5,WN8 ...53 C7
   Up Holland,Roby Mill WN8 .35 B3
   Wigan WN1 ....151 D8
School Mews
   Bramhall SK7 ....132 E7
   Newhey OL16 ....32 B4
School Rd
   Altrincham WA15 ....119 F3
   Eccles M30 ....95 C8
   Failsworth M35 ....83 F7
   Handforth SK9 ....131 D4
   Oldham OL8 ....66 B2
   Sale M33 ....108 A5
   Sale M33 ....108 B5
   Stretford M32 ....96 C2
School St
   Ashton-in-M WN4 ....73 D5
   Atherton M46 ....58 B2
   Bacup OL13 ....3 B8
   Bolton BL7 ....24 F7
   Bury BL9 ....141 B1
   Eccles M30 ....79 B3
   Golborne WA3 ....90 A8
   Hazel Grove SK7 ....124 E2
   Heywood OL10 ....29 C2
   Horwich BL6 ....22 C3
   Ince-in-M WN2 ....151 F7
   Leigh WN7 ....75 E8
   Little Lever BL3 ....43 B3
   Littleborough OL15 ....15 E5
   Manchester M4 ....159 B3
   Newton-le-W WA12 ....89 B3
   Oldham OL8 ....153 D5
   Oldham,Grotton OL4 ....68 A6
   Radcliffe M26 ....44 E4
   Ramsbottom BL0 ....138 B5
   Rochdale OL12 ....14 C3
   Salford M7 ....158 E4
   Tyldesley M29 ....76 F8
   Tyldesley,Gin Pit M29 ...76 F7
   Uppermill OL3 ....69 B8
   Westhoughton BL5 ....57 E8
   Wigan WN1 ....151 D8
School Street Ind Est
   SK7 ....124 E2
School Terr Golborne WA3 ...90 A8
   Whitworth OL12 ....4 D1
School View BL7 ....9 D8
School Way WN5 ....54 C6
School Wlk M16 ....162 D5
Schoolhouse M17 ....96 D5
Schools Hill SK8 ....122 D3
Schools Rd M18 ....99 E5
Schoolside Cl M8 ....156 A6
Schoolside La M24 ...64 E7
Schuster Rd M14 ....98 D3
Schwabe St M24 ....64 C8
Scobell St BL8 ....27 A5
Scoles Prec WN1 ....151 D8
Scoltock Way OL1 .....153 F7
Score St M11 ....83 D1
Scorton Av BL2 ....42 F7
Scorton St BL1 ....144 C8
Scorton Wlk 28 M40 ...65 D2
Scot La Aspull WN2 .....38 E6
   Wigan,Marsh Green WN5,
      WN6 ....36 E1
   Wigan,Worsley Hall WN5 .54 F7
Scot Lane End CE Prim Sch
   WN5 ....54 F7
Scotforth Cl M15 ....162 E7
Scotia Wlk 1 WA3 .....90 F8
Scotland M4 ....159 A3
Scotland Hall Rd M40 ...83 C4
Scotland La BL8 ....28 D8

Scotland Pl BL0 ....138 C6
Scotland St
Ashton-u-L OL6 ....166 C2
Failsworth M40 ....83 C5
Scott Ave Bury BL9 ....44 F6
Eccles M30 ....79 C3
Hindley WN2 ....56 E6
Manchester M21 ....97 B2
Scott Cl SK5 ....169 F4
Scott Dr Altrincham WA15 .119 F4
Marple SK6 ....126 B8
Scott Gate M34 ....100 F7
Scott Ho Manchester M19 .99 A2
Walsden OL14 ....6 A8
Scott House (Childrens Orthopaedic) Hospl
OL11 ....29 D8
Scott Rd Denton M34 ....100 E1
Droylsden M43 ....84 A1
Golborne WA3 ....74 D2
Prestwich M25 ....62 F3
Scott St Kearsley M26 ....61 D7
Leigh WN7 ....75 D5
Tyldesley M29 ....77 C4
Walsden OL14 ....6 A8
Westhoughton BL5 ....39 E2
Wigan WN6 ....37 B1
Scott Wlk WA12 ....89 C1
Scottfield OL8 ....153 F5
Scottfield Rd OL8 ....153 F5
Scottia Rd M30 ....95 C8
Scotts Ind Est OL16 ....31 A6
Scout Dr M23 ....120 F4
Scout Rd M28 ....47 A3
Scout Rd Bolton BL1,BL7 .24 B7
Edenfield BL0 ....2 A2
Scout View BL8 ....27 A6
Scovell St M7 ....155 D6
Scowcroft La OL2 ....155 C6
Scowcroft St OL1 ....25 B1
Scroggins La M31 ....105 F4
Scropton St M40 ....157 D6
Seabright Wlk M12 M11 .160 F1
Seabrook Cres M41 ....95 D4
Seabrook Rd M40 ....83 C4
Seacombe Ave M14 ....98 A1
Seacombe Gr Sk3 ....123 B8
Seaford Rd Bolton BL2 ....25 E6
Salford M6 ....81 B4
Seaford Wlk
Chadderton OL9 ....152 B6
Manchester M9 ....64 C3
Seaforth Ave M46 ....58 C4
Seaforth Rd BL1 ....24 E5
Seaham Dr BL8 ....27 C5
Seaham Wlk M14 ....98 B3
Seal Rd SK7 ....133 A7
Sealand Cl M33 ....108 E2
Sealand Dr M30 ....95 A8
Sealand Ho M25 ....63 C5
Sealand Rd M23 ....108 F2
Sealand Way SK9 ....131 D4
Seale Ave M34 ....100 D7
Sealey Wlk M40 ....160 E4
Seaman Way WN2 ....56 A6
Seamon's Dr WA14 ....119 B6
Seamon's Rd WA14 ....119 A6
Seamons Wlk WA14 ....119 B5
Searby Rd M18 ....99 B4
Searness Rd M24 ....46 D2
Seascale Ave M11 ....83 B3
Seascale Cres WN1 ....37 C3
Seascales Wlk M24 ....46 E2
Seathwaite Cl M29 ....77 A7
Seathwaite Rd BL4 ....59 F7
Seathwaite Wlk M18 .165 C5
Seatoller Cl OL2 ....48 E4
Seatoller Dr M24 ....46 C1
Seatoller PI WN5 ....54 E2
Seaton Cl SK7 ....124 D1
Seaton Mews OL7 ....84 F4
Seaton Rd BL1 ....142 C2
Seaton Way M14 ....98 A4
Sebastian Cl SK6 ....126 B7
Second Ave Atherton M46 .58 D4
Bolton BL1 ....144 B7
Bury BL9 ....28 D4
Droylsden M11 ....83 D2
Little Lever BL3 ....42 F4
Mossley SK15 ....86 E5
Oldham OL8 ....66 D1
Poynton SK12 ....133 D1
Stretford M17 ....96 F6
Swinton M27 ....79 D5
Tyldesley M29 ....77 B4
Wigan WN6 ....37 A2
Second St BL1 ....23 F4
Section St M3 BL3 ....145 F6
Sedan Cl M5 ....81 A1
Sedburgh Cl M33 ....107 D3
Sedbury Cl M23 ....120 F1
Seddon Ave
Manchester M18 ....99 D6
Radcliffe M26 ....44 D5
Seddon Gdns M44 ....105 E6
Seddon House Dr WN6 .36 E3
Seddon La M26 ....61 A8
Seddon Rd M44 ....119 D2
Seddon St Little Lever BL3 .43 B3
Manchester M12 ....164 E6
Radcliffe M26 ....44 A3
Walkden M38 ....59 F5
Westhoughton BL5 ....39 E3
Seddons Ave BL8 ....44 A8
Sedge Cl SK5 ....112 A8
Sedgeborough Rd M16 ..97 E3

Sedgefield Cl M5 ....81 A2
Sedgefield Dr
Bolton BL1 ....142 B3
Wigan WN6 ....36 E3
Sedgefield Pk 1 OL4 ....67 D6
Sedgefield Rd M26 ....62 A8
Sedgefield Wlk 3 M23 .108 E2
Sedgeford Cl SK9 ....131 D1
Sedgeford Rd M40 ....157 D5
Sedgely M9 ....37 A7
Sedgemoor Cl SK8 ....123 B2
Sedgemoor Vale BL2 ....25 F2
Sedgemoor Way OL1 .153 E7
Sedgley Ave
Manchester M25 ....63 C2
Prestwich M25 ....62 F5
Rochdale OL16 ....31 B4
Sedgley Cl M24 ....65 C7
Sedgley Dr BL5 ....57 E5
Sedgley Park Com Prim Sch
M25 ....63 D2
Sedgley Park Rd M25 ....63 C2
Sedgley Park Trad Est
M25 ....63 B1
Sedgley Rd M8 ....156 A8
Sedgley St M24 ....65 C7
Sedwyn St 7 WN1 ....37 E1
Seed St BL1 ....144 C7
Seedfield Rd BL9 ....27 F5
Seedley Ave M38 ....60 B4
Seedley Park Rd M6 ....154 E2
Seedley Prim Sch M6 .154 E2
Seedley Rd M6 ....154 F3
Seedley St M14 ....98 B3
Seedley Terr M6 ....154 E3
Seedley View Rd M6 .154 E2
Seel St OL5 ....68 B1
Sefton Ave Atherton M46 ..58 C5
Orrell WN5 ....53 D5
Sefton Cl
Manchester M13 ....163 B6
Middleton M24 ....64 E8
Orrell WN5 ....53 D5
Sefton Cres M33 ....108 B6
Sefton Ct 8 Bolton BL1 .145 E8
Bury BL9 ....27 F6
Sefton Dr Bury BL9 ....28 A6
Handforth SK9 ....131 C2
Swinton M27 ....79 A6
Tyldesley M29 ....77 B6
Sefton Fold Dr WN5 ....71 D5
Sefton Fold Gdns WN5 ..71 D5
Sefton La BL6 ....22 D1
Sefton Rd
Ashton-in-M WN4 ....72 F6
Bolton BL1 ....142 B2
Manchester M21 ....109 B8
Middleton M24 ....64 E8
Orrell WN5 ....53 D5
Sale M33 ....108 B5
Swinton M27 ....61 F1
Wigan WN3 ....54 F4
Sefton St Bury BL9 ....27 F6
Glossop SK13 ....116 C8
Heywood OL10 ....29 E1
Leigh WN7 ....75 F5
Manchester M8 ....156 A8
Oldham OL9 ....66 B2
Radcliffe M26 ....44 C1
Whitefield M45 ....62 F4
Sefton View WN5 ....53 D5
Segal Cl M7 ....155 D7
Selborne Rd M21 ....97 B1
Selbourne Cl Reddish SK5 .99 E2
Westhoughton BL5 ....40 A1
Selbourne St M7 ....155 C7
Selby Ave Chadderton OL9 .47 F1
Whitefield M45 ....44 F2
Selby Cl Milnrow OL16 ....31 E6
Poynton SK12 ....133 D5
Radcliffe M26 ....44 D5
Stretford M32 ....96 A3
Selby Dr Salford M6 ....80 D3
Urmston M41 ....94 F5
Wigan WN3 ....54 C4
Selby Gdns M3 ....132 C6
Selby Rd Middleton M24 .46 F3
Stretford M32 ....96 A3
Selby St Manchester M11 .165 A8
Reddish SK4 ....99 D4
Rochdale OL16 ....31 B8
Selby Wlk BL8 ....26 F1
Selden St OL8 ....153 D5
Selham Wlk M13 ....163 C7
Selhurst Ave M11 ....83 C2
Selkirk Ave
Garswood WN4 ....72 D4
Oldham OL8 ....66 D4
Selkirk Dr M9 ....64 F3
Selkirk Gr WN5 ....54 C8
Selkirk PI OL10 ....29 A1
Selkirk Rd Bolton BL1 ....24 D5
Chadderton OL9 ....66 A4
Sellars Sq M43 ....84 A1
Sellers Way OL9 ....166 A3
Selsby Ave M30 ....79 B2
Selsey Ave Cheadle SK3 .122 F7
Sale M33 ....107 F3
Selsey Dr M20 ....122 C8
Selside Wlk 2 M14 ....110 C8
Selstead Rd M22 ....121 C1
Selston Rd M9 ....64 B4
Selworth Ave M33 ....108 E4

Selworth Cl 6 WA15 ....119 E6
Selworthy Rd M16 ....97 E4
Selwyn Ave
Manchester M9 ....157 D8
Manchester M9 ....64 D1
Selwyn Cl
Newton-le-W WA12 ....89 B5
Oldham OL8 ....153 E5
Selwyn Dr SK8 ....132 C7
Selwyn Dr Bolton BL2 .148 A6
Leigh WN7 ....75 F6
Oldham OL8 ....153 E5
Semple Way OL9 ....65 B1
Senecar Cl WN2 ....38 B2
Senior Ave M14 ....110 E7
Senior Rd M30 ....95 A8
Senior St M3 ....158 E3
Sennicar La Aspull WN2 .37 E6
Wigan WN1 ....37 C5
Sepal Cl SK5 ....100 A1
Sephton Ave WA3 ....91 E3
Sephton St WN3 ....151 F6
Sepia Gr M7 ....46 F1
Sequoia St M9 ....157 E8
Sergeants La M45 ....62 C7
Serin Cl Hazel Grove SK2 .124 F5
Newton-le-W WA12 ....89 C3
Service St SK3 ....123 B8
Sesame Gdns M44 ....94 C3
Set St SK15 ....85 F1
Setantii - Tales of Tameside
(Mus)* OL6 ....166 B3
Settle St Bolton BL3 .147 E3
Little Lever BL3 ....43 C3
Settstones La OL3 ....51 D1
Seven Acres La OL12 ....13 E2
Seven Oaks WN7 ....76 A6
Seven Stiles Dr SK6 .125 E7
Sevenacres OL3 ....50 F5
Sevenoaks Ave
Manchester SK4 ....111 A5
Urmston M41 ....95 D3
Sevenoaks Dr Bolton BL3 .147 E3
Pendlebury M27 ....80 A6
Sevenoaks Rd SK8 .122 B6
Sevenoaks Wlk 3 M13 .163 C5
Sevenside Trad Est M17 ..96 B5
Seventh Ave OL8 ....66 D1
Severn Cl
Altrincham WA14 ....119 C6
Billinge WN5 ....71 D3
Bury BL9 ....27 F7
Severn Dr Bramhall SK7 .132 C6
Hindley WN2 ....57 C3
Milnrow OL16 ....32 A6
Wigan WN5 ....54 D7
Severn Rd
Ashton-in-M WN4 ....73 E5
Chadderton OL9 ....65 F8
Culcheth WA3 ....91 F2
Heywood OL10 ....29 A3
Oldham OL6 ....66 C1
Severn St M7 ....76 B4
Severn Way Kearsley BL4 ..61 B6
Reddish SK5 ....111 F5
Seville St Royton OL2 ....48 E2
Shaw OL2 ....149 A5
Seville's Bldgs OL5 ....68 C2
Sewell Way M38 ....59 F3
Sewerby St M16 ....97 F4
Sexa St M11 ....99 D8
Sexton St Heywood OL10 .29 C2
Tintwistle SK13 ....103 F7
Seymour Ave M11 ....83 D2
Seymour Cl M16 ....161 C5
Seymour Ct
Manchester SK4 ....110 E2
2 Radcliffe M26 ....44 B3
Salford M7 ....155 F8
Seymour Dr BL2 ....25 C6
Seymour Gr
Altrincham WA15 ....120 A5
Farnworth BL4 ....42 A1
Manchester M16 ....97 F4
Marple SK6 ....125 E6
Rochdale OL16 ....31 B3
Sale M33 ....108 B4
Seymour Ho 10 SK9 ....131 E1
Seymour Park Prim Sch
M16 ....97 B4
Seymour Rd Bolton BL1 .143 F3
Cheadle SK8 ....132 A8
Manchester M7,M8 ....63 F1
Stockport SK2 ....124 B5
Seymour Rd S M11 ....83 D2
Seymour Road Prim Sch
M11 ....83 D2
Seymour St Bolton BL2 .25 C6
Denton M34 ....100 D4
Heywood OL10 ....29 C1
Radcliffe M26 ....44 B3
Seymour Wlk 4 M26 ....44 B3
Shackleton Ct M40 ....83 C4
Shackleton Gr BL1 ....23 E2
Shackleton St M30 ....79 C3
Shackliffe Rd M40 ....65 B2
Shaddock Ave OL12 ....13 F1
Shade Ave OL4 ....67 F5
Shade Terr SK6 ....134 F7
Shadowbrook Ave SK10 ..138 A2
Shadowbrook Cl OL1 ....48 E1
Shadowmoss Rd M22 .130 E8
Shadows La OL5 ....68 E4
Shadows Mews OL5 ....68 E4
Shadwell St E OL10 ....29 E3

Shadwell St E OL10 ....29 E3
Shadwell St W OL10 ....29 D3
Shadworth Cl OL5 ....68 E4
Shady La Bolton BL7 ....25 B7
Wythenshawe M23 ....120 D7
Shady Oak Rd SK2 ....124 F6
Shaftesbury Ave
Altrincham WA15 ....120 C6
Bramhall SK8 ....123 C1
Eccles M30 ....95 C8
Horwich BL6 ....39 F8
Littleborough OL15 ....15 F3
Shaftesbury Cl BL6 ....39 F8
Shaftesbury Dr OL12 ....15 D6
Shaftesbury Gdns M41 ..94 D2
Shaftesbury Rd
Cheadle SK8 ....123 B6
Manchester M8 ....156 A7
Swinton M27 ....79 F7
Shafton Wlk 22 M40 ....65 D2
Shaftsbury Ct 20 BL1 .143 E1
Shaftsbury Dr OL10 ....46 C8
Shaftsbury Dr WN5 ....54 A8
Shaftsbury St M6 ....36 F3
Shakerley CE Prim Sch
M29 ....59 A2
Shakerley La M46,M29 ....58 F4
Shakerley Rd M29 ....58 F1
Shakespeare Ave
Bury BL9 ....44 F6
Denton M34 ....112 F8
Radcliffe M26 ....43 E4
Stalybridge SK15 ....86 A4
Shakespeare Cl OL15 ....6 C1
Shakespeare Cres
Droylsden M43 ....84 A2
Eccles M30 ....79 D2
Shakespeare Dr SK8 ....122 F6
Shakespeare Gr WN3 ....55 A4
Shakespeare Rd
Droylsden M43 ....84 A2
Oldham OL1 ....49 C2
Prestwich M25 ....62 F3
Romiley SK6 ....112 F2
Swinton M27 ....79 E8
Shakespeare Wlk M13 .163 C6
Shakleton Ave M9 ....65 A3
Shalbourne Rd M28 ....60 C3
Shaldon Dr M40 ....83 E4
Shalfleet Cl BL2 ....25 F5
Shalford Dr M22 ....130 D8
Shandon Ave M22 ....109 D1
Shanklin Ave 2 M41 ....95 C2
Shanklin Cl Denton M34 .113 B8
Manchester M21 ....97 A1
Shanklin Ho 4 M21 ....97 A1
Shanley Ct OL9 ....152 C6
Shannon Cl OL10 ....29 A3
Shannon Rd M22 ....121 E4
Shap Ave WA15 ....120 D5
Shap Cres M28 ....60 F1
Shap Dr M28 ....60 F1
Shap Gate WN5 ....54 B7
Shapwick Cl 8 M9 ....64 E3
Sharcott Cl 3 M16 ....97 F4
Shardlow Cl M40 ....160 D4
Shared St WN1 ....151 D7
Shargate Cl SK9 ....131 C1
Sharman St BL3 ....148 B5
Sharnbrook Wlk
8 Bolton BL2 ....25 B1
4 Manchester M8 ....63 E2
Sharnford Cl BL2 .148 B6
Sharnford Sq M12 ....165 A6
Sharon Ave OL4 ....68 E5
Sharon Cl OL7 ....84 E1
Sharp St Bury BL8 ....27 B4
Ince-in-M WN3 ....151 E6
Manchester M4 ....159 B3
Middleton M24 ....65 A8
Prestwich M25 ....63 A4
Walkden M28 ....60 E3
Sharples Ave BL1 ....24 E6
Sharples Dr BL8 ....27 A3
Sharples Gn BL7 ....9 D6
Sharples Hall 9 BL1 ....24 F6
Sharples Hall Dr BL1 ....24 F6
Sharples Hall Fold BL1 ..24 F5
Sharples Hall Mews BL1 .24 F6
Sharples Mdw BL7 ....9 D6
Sharples Pk BL1 ....143 D4
Sharples Prim Sch BL1 ..25 A5
Sharples St SK4 ....169 E3
Sharraw Wlk M9 ....157 E7
Sharrington Dr M23 ....120 D6
Sharrow Wlk M9 ....157 D7
Sharston Ind Area M22 .121 E7
Sharston Rd M22 ....121 E7
Shaving La M28 ....60 D1
Shaw & Crompton Sta
OL2 ....149 C6
Shaw Ave M14 SK14 ....113 F8
Shaw Hall Ave SK14 ....102 B5
Shaw Hall Bank Rd OL3 .68 F5
Shaw Head Dr M35 ....83 F6
Shaw Heath SK2,SK3 ....170 E7
Shaw Heath View OL3 ....68 F4
Farnworth BL4 ....60 D7
Shaw Hill St OL1 ....153 F8
Littleborough OL15,OL16 .16 A1
Shaw Moor Ave SK15 ....86 C1
Shaw Rd Horwich BL6 ....22 B5

Shaw Rd continued
Manchester SK4 ....168 B4
Newhey OL16 ....32 B3
Oldham OL1 ....67 A2
Royton OL2 ....48 F4
Royton,Buersil Head OL16 .31 B1
Shaw Rd S SK3 ....170 E6
Shaw St Ashton-in-M WN4 .73 B5
Ashton-u-L OL6 ....85 D3
Bolton BL3 ....145 E5
Bury BL9 ....141 B3
Culcheth WA3 ....92 A3
Farnworth BL4 ....42 D2
Glossop SK13 ....116 C8
Manchester M3 ....158 F3
Mottram-in-L SK14 ....103 A4
Oldham OL1 ....153 F8
Oldham,Grotton OL4 ....68 A6
Rochdale OL12 ....15 B2
Royton OL2 ....48 E4
Uppermill OL3 ....69 B6
Wigan WN1 ....37 C1
Shaw Terr 5 SK16 ....166 C1
Shaw The SK13 ....171 F3
Shaw's Rd WA14 ....119 D4
Shawbrook Ave M28 ....78 B8
Shawbrook Rd M19 ....111 A5
Shawbury Cl BL6 ....21 D1
Shawbury Gr M33 ....107 F2
Shawbury Rd M23 ....121 B4
Shawbury St M24 ....65 C7
Shawclough Cl OL12 ....14 D3
Shawclough Com Prim Sch
OL12 ....14 E3
Shawclough Dr OL12 ....14 D3
Shawclough Rd OL12 ....14 D3
Shawclough Way OL12 ..14 D3
Shawcroft Cl OL2 ....149 A5
Shawcross Fold SK1 ....169 F2
Shawcross La M22 ....121 E8
Shawcross St Hyde SK14 .113 F8
Salford M6 ....154 F1
Stockport SK1 ....124 A8
Shawdene Rd M22 ....121 D8
Shawe Hall Ave M41 ....107 A8
Shawe Hall Cres M41 ....107 A8
Shawe Rd M41 ....95 A2
Shawe View M41 ....95 A2
Shawes Dr PR6 ....21 C7
Shawfield Cl M14 ....110 A8
Shawfield Ct SK2 ....124 D5
Shawfield Gr OL12 ....13 F2
Shawfield La
Rochdale OL12 ....14 A2
Rochdale,Norden OL12 ....13 F2
Shawfield Rd SK13 ....171 F3
Shawfields SK15 ....86 D3
Shawfold OL2 ....149 B2
Shawford Cres M40 ....65 C2
Shawford Rd M40 ....65 C2
Shawgreen Cl M15 ....162 D6
Shawgrove Sch M20 ....109 F5
Shawheath Cl M15 ....162 D6
Shawhill Wlk M40 ....160 E2
Shawlea Ave M19 ....110 E6
Shaws Fold SK9 ....130 F3
Shaws La OL3 ....69 C7
Shay Ave WA15 ....120 E1
Shay La WA15 ....120 D1
Shayfield Ave
Chadderton OL9 ....65 E8
Wythenshawe M22 ....121 D5
Shayfield Dr M22 ....121 D5
Shayfield Rd M22 ....121 D5
Sheader Dr M5 ....80 C2
Sheaf Field Wlk M26 ....44 A4
Sheard Ave OL6 ....85 D6
Sheardhall Ave SK12 ....135 E5
Shearer Way M27 ....80 E7
Shearing Ave OL12 ....13 F1
Shearsby Cl M15 ....162 E5
Shearwater Ave M29 ....77 A8
Shearwater Dr
Walkden M28 ....60 C3
Westhoughton BL5 ....57 D6
Shearwater Gdns M30 ..95 A8
Shearwater Rd SK2 ....124 A5
Shed St OL12 ....4 D1
Sheddings The BL3 ....42 A4
Sheep Gap OL12 ....14 B1
Sheep Gate Dr BL8 ....26 E5
Sheepfoot La
Manchester M25,M8 ....63 E3
Oldham OL1 ....48 D1
Sheepfoot Wlk OL1 ....48 D1
Sheerness St M18 ....99 D5
Sheffield Rd
Glossop SK13 ....104 F1
Hyde SK14 ....167 F4
Hyde,Godley SK14 ....102 A3
Sheffield St
Manchester M1 ....163 C8
Stockport SK4 ....169 E3
Shefford Cl M11 ....164 F8
Shefford Cres WN3 ....54 C2
Sheiling Ct WA14 ....119 C4
Sheilings The WA3 ....90 F8
Shelbourne Ave BL1 ....142 B1
Shelburne Dr WN2 ....56 C4
Shelderton Cl 5 M40 ....83 A7
Sheldon Ave
Standish WN6 ....19 E2
Urmston M41 ....95 B2

Sheldon Cl Farnworth BL4 .42 B2
8 Gamesley SK13 ....171 D1
Partington M31 ....105 E3
Sheldon Ct OL7 ....85 B5
Sheldon Fold 9 SK13 ...171 D1
Sheldon Pl 8 SK13 .....171 D1
Sheldon Rd
 Hazel Grove SK7 ....133 E8
 Poynton SK12 ....134 C2
Sheldon St M11 ....83 D2
Sheldrake Cl SK16 ......101 E7
Sheldrake Rd WA14 ....119 B8
Sheldwich Cl WN7 ....75 F3
Shelfield OL11 ....13 F1
Shelfield Cl OL11 ....13 F1
Shelfield La OL11 ....13 F1
Shelford Ave M18 ....99 B4
Shellbrook St 8 SK9 ...131 D1
Shelley Ave M24 ....47 B3
Shelley Cl PR7 ....19 F8
Shelley Ct SK8 ....123 A1
Shelley Dr Abram WN2 ...56 B1
 Wigan WN5 ....54 A6
Shelley Gr Droylsden M43 .84 A1
 Dukinfield SK14 ....101 D5
 Stalybridge SK15 ....86 E4
Shelley Rd Oldham OL9 ...65 F3
 Oldham,Broadbent OL1 .49 C1
 Prestwich M25 ....62 F3
 Reddish SK5 ....99 E1
 Swinton M27 ....79 E8
Shelley Rise SK16 ......102 B7
Shelley St Failsworth M40 .83 C8
 Leigh WN7 ....75 D7
Shelley Way M34 ....112 F8
Shelley Wlk Atherton M46 .58 D5
 Bolton BL1 ....143 D1
Shellingford Cl WN6 .....35 D7
Shelmerdine Cl 6 SK14 .102 F2
Shelmerdine Gdns M6 ...80 C4
Shelton Ave M33 ....107 D4
Shenfield Wlk M40 .....160 D3
Shenhurst Cl SK9 ....136 E4
Shenton Park Ave M33 .107 C2
Shenton St SK14 ....101 C4
Shentonfield Rd M22 ...121 E6
Shepherd Cross St BL1 .142 C1
Shepherd Cross St Ind Est
 BL1 ....143 D2
Shepherd Ct 1 OL16 ....31 B6
Shepherd St Bury BL8 ....26 F8
 Heywood OL10 ....29 C2
 Manchester M9 ....64 E1
 Rochdale,Norden OL11 ..13 D1
 Rochdale,Town Head OL12 139 F8
 Royton OL2 ....48 E3
 Royton OL2 ....48 E4
Shepherd Wlk M34 .....112 F8
Shepherd's Brow WA14 .119 A3
Shepherd's Dr BL6 ....23 A3
Shepherds Cl
 Blackrod BL6 ....21 C3
 Ramsbottom BL8 ....10 F1
Shepherds Gn OL3 ....69 D5
Shepherds Way OL16 ....31 F5
Shepley Ave BL3 ....144 C5
Shepley Cl
 2 Dukinfield SK16 .....101 D8
 Hazel Grove SK7 ....133 D8
Shepley Dr SK7 ....124 E1
Shepley La Marple SK6 .125 F3
 Marple SK6 ....125 F4
Shepley Lane Ind Est
 SK6 ....125 F3
Shepley North Ind Est
 M34 ....101 A7
Shepley Rd M34,SK16 ...100 F6
Shepley South Ind Est
 M34 ....101 A6
Shepley St Denton M34 .100 F7
 Failsworth M35 ....66 A1
 Glossop SK13 ....104 F2
 Hadfield SK13 ....171 E3
 Hyde SK14 ....167 E2
 Manchester M1 ....163 B8
 4 Oldham OL4 ....67 E6
 Stalybridge SK15 ....86 A2
Shepton Ave WN2 ....56 A1
Shepton Cl BL1 ....24 D7
Shepton Dr M23 ....121 A2
Sheraton Cl WN5 ....36 B1
Sheraton Rd OL8 ....66 E4
Sherborne Ave WN2 .....57 A5
Sherborne Ho M24 ....47 A3
Sherborne Rd
 Cheadle SK3 ....123 A7
 Middleton M24 ....47 A3
 Urmston M41 ....95 E3
 Wigan WN5 ....54 A8
Sherborne St M3,M8 ...158 F4
Sherborne St W M3 .....158 E3
Sherborne Trad Est M8 .158 E4
Sherbourne Cl
 Cheadle SK8 ....132 B6
 Oldham OL8 ....67 C4
 Radcliffe M26 ....43 D5
Sherbourne Ct M25 ......63 A4
Sherbourne Dr OL10 .....29 A3
Sherbourne Pl WN3 ....151 E5
Sherbourne Rd BL1 .....142 A1
Sherbourne St M25 ......63 A4
Sherbrook Cl M33 ......107 F3
Sherbrook Rise SK9 ....137 C6

Sherbrooke Ave OL3 .....51 C1
Sherbrooke Rd SK12 ...135 D6
Sherdley Cl M8 ....64 A1
Sherdley Rd M8 ....64 A1
Sherford Cl SK7 ....124 A2
Sheri Dr WA12 ....89 E2
Sheridan Ave WA3 ....90 D7
Sheridan Ct M40 ....157 E5
Sheridan Way
 Chadderton OL9 ....65 E8
 Denton M34 ....112 F8
Sheriff St Bolton BL2 ....25 B1
 Milnrow OL16 ....32 A5
 Rochdale OL12 ....139 E8
 Rochdale OL12 ....14 C2
Sheriffs Dr M29 ....59 D1
Sheringham Dr Bury BL8 .27 D5
 Hyde SK14 ....102 A3
 Swinton M27 ....79 F6
Sheringham Pl BL3 .....145 D5
Sheringham Rd M14 ....110 D7
Sherlock St M14 ....110 D7
Sherratt St M4 ....159 B2
Sherrington St M12 ....99 A3
Sherway Dr WA15 ....120 C6
Sherwell Rd M9 ....64 B3
Sherwin Way OL11 ....30 D1
Sherwood Ave
 Ashton-in-M WN4 ....73 C4
 Cheadle SK8 ....122 F2
 Droylsden M43 ....84 C2
 Manchester M14 ....110 C8
 Radcliffe M26 ....43 F8
 Sale M33 ....108 D5
 Salford M7 ....81 B7
 Stockport SK4 ....168 A1
 Tyldesley M29 ....77 A6
Sherwood Bsns Pk OL11 .30 D2
Sherwood Cl
 Ashton-u-L OL6 ....85 C7
 Bury BL8 ....26 F7
 Marple SK6 ....125 F4
 Salford M5 ....154 D3
Sherwood Cres
 Platt Bridge WN2 ....56 A2
 Wigan WN5 ....54 D7
Sherwood Dr
 Pendlebury M27 ....80 B7
 Wigan WN5 ....54 D6
Sherwood Fold SK13 ...115 D7
Sherwood Gr Leigh WN7 .76 B2
 Wigan WN5 ....54 D7
Sherwood Ind Pk OL11 ..30 D2
Sherwood Rd
 Reddish M34 ....100 B3
 Romiley SK6 ....113 B5
Sherwood St Bolton BL1 .143 F3
 Manchester M14 ....110 C8
 Oldham OL1 ....153 D8
 Rochdale OL12 ....30 D2
 Sherwood Way OL2 .....48 E8
Shetland Rd M40 ....160 D3
Shetland Way
 Radcliffe M26 ....44 A5
 Urmston M41 ....95 D5
Shevington Com Prim Sch
 WN6 ....35 F6
Shevington Gdns M23 .109 B1
Shevington High Sch
 WN6 ....36 B7
Shevington La WN6 ......36 B7
Shevington Moor WN6 ...19 A2
Shevington Vale Prim Sch
 WN6 ....35 B8
Shiel St M28 ....60 D3
Shield Cl OL8 ....153 E6
Shield Dr M28 ....79 C8
Shield St SK3 ....170 E8
Shieldborn Dr M9 ....157 E7
Shiers Dr SK8 ....122 D2
Shiffnall St BL2 ....148 A6
Shildon Cl WN2 ....37 F2
Shilford Dr M4 ....159 C3
Shillingford Rd BL4 ......60 C8
Shillingstone Cl BL2 .....26 A3
Shillington 1 M28 ....59 F3
Shiloh La OL1,OL4 ....68 A3
Shiloh Rd SK6 ....127 B6
Shilton Gdns BL3 ....145 E5
Shilton St BL0 ....138 B5
Shilton Wlk 21 M40 .....65 D2
Ship Canal Ho M15 ....162 E8
Ship La OL3,OL4 ....50 B5
Shipgates 1 BL1 ....145 F7
Shipham Cl WN7 ....75 D8
Shipla Cl OL9 ....153 E7
Shipley Ave M6 ....80 C3
Shipley View M41 ....94 F5
Shipper Bottom La BL0 ..11 D5
Shippey St M14 ....110 D7
Shipston Cl BL8 ....27 B3
Shipton St BL1 ....142 B1
Shirburn 8 OL11 ....139 E6
Shire Gdns M26 ....43 F4
Shire Hill Hospl SK13 ...104 E3
Shire Way SK13 ....104 E3
Shirebrook Dr
 Glossop SK13 ....116 F8
 Radcliffe M26 ....44 B4
Shireburn Ave BL2 .....148 C8
Shiredale Cl SK8 ....123 B4
Shiredale Dr M9 ....157 D7
Shiregreen Ave M40 ...156 C5
Shirehills M25 ....63 A3
Shireoak Rd M20 ....110 D7
Shires Cl WN2 ....56 E4
Shires The Droylsden M43 .84 D3

Shires The continued
 Radcliffe M26 ....44 A5
Shirewell Rd WN5 ....53 E5
Shirley Ave
 Droylsden M34 ....100 C8
 Dukinfield SK14 ....101 D5
 Eccles M30 ....95 C8
 Failsworth OL9 ....65 E2
 Gatley SK8 ....131 C6
 Marple SK6 ....125 E6
 Pendlebury M27 ....80 C7
 Reddish M34 ....99 F3
 Salford M7 ....81 A7
 Stretford M32 ....96 F3
Shirley Cl SK7 ....124 C2
Shirley Cl M33 ....108 C4
Shirley Gr SK3 ....170 E5
Shirley Rd M8 ....156 A7
Shirley St OL11 ....30 C2
Shoecroft Ave M34 .....100 E2
Shoemaker Gdns WN2 ...38 C5
Sholver Hey La OL1 ......49 D4
Sholver Hill Cl OL1 ....49 E4
Sholver La OL1 ....49 D4
Shone Ave M22 ....121 F2
Shopping City M6 ....154 F3
Shore Ave OL2 ....32 C1
Shore Fold OL15 ....15 F6
Shore Gn M23 ....121 A3
Shore Hill OL15 ....16 C6
Shore Lea OL15 ....15 F6
Shore Mount OL15 ....15 F6
Shore Rd OL15 ....15 F7
Shore St Milnrow OL16 ..31 F6
 Oldham OL1 ....67 A7
Shoredich Cl SK4 ....111 B5
Shorefield Cl OL16 ....31 F7
Shorefield Mount BL7 ...24 E8
Shoreham Cl 5 M16 ....97 E4
Shoreham Wlk OL9 .....152 A6
Shoreswood BL1 ....24 D5
Shorland St M27 ....79 C7
Shorrocks St BL8 ....26 F3
Short Ave M43 ....99 F8
Short St Bacup OL13 ......3 B8
 Golborne WA3 ....74 B1
 Hazel Grove SK7 ......124 D8
 Heywood OL10 ....29 B1
 Manchester ML 159 A1
 Salford M7 ....158 E3
 Stockport SK4 ....169 E3
 3 Tyldesley M46 ....58 F1
 12 Wigan WN5 ....54 B6
Short St E SK1 ....169 E3
Shortcroft St M15 ......162 F7
Shortland Cres M19 ....110 D3
Shortland Pl WN2 ....75 A8
Shortlands Ave BL9 ......44 F8
Shortwood Cl 17 M40 ...83 A6
Shottery Wlks SK6 .....112 F3
Shotton Wlk 8 M14 .....98 C3
Shottwood Fold OL15 ...16 C8
Shrewsbury Cl WN2 .....56 F6
Shrewsbury Ct M16 ....162 D5
Shrewsbury Gdns SK8 .132 C6
Shrewsbury Rd
 Bolton BL1 ....144 B8
 Droylsden M43 ....84 A3
 Prestwich M25 ....63 A3
 Sale M33 ....108 A2
Shrewsbury St
 Glossop SK13 ....104 C1
 Manchester M16 ....162 D5
 Manchester M16 ....97 D4
 Oldham OL4 ....67 C8
Shrewsbury Way 7
 M34 ....101 A1
Shrigley Cl SK9 ....131 D1
Shrigley Rd SK10,SK12 .134 C2
Shrigley Rd N SK12 ....134 C3
Shrivenham Wlk M23 ...120 F7
Shropshire Ave M5 .....112 C6
Shropshire Dr SK13 ....116 F8
Shropshire Rd M35 ......84 A6
Shropshire Sq M12 ....164 F6
Shrowbridge Wlk M12 .165 A6
Shrub St BL3 ....147 D5
Shrubbery The BL6 ......40 C7
Shudehill M4 ....159 A2
Shudehill Rd M28 ....60 A1
Shudehill Sta M4 ....159 A2
Shurdington Rd BL5,M46 .58 F6
Shurmer St BL3 ....146 C4
Shutt La OL3 ....49 C1
Shuttle Hillock Rd WN2 ..74 F7
Shuttle St 6 Eccles M30 ..79 F2
 Hindley WN2 ....56 E6
 Radcliffe M26 ....44 C1
 Tyldesley M29 ....59 A1
Shuttleworth Cl M21 ...109 D8
Shutts La SK15 ....102 D8
Siam St M11 ....164 F8
Sibley Ave WN4 ....73 D4
Sibley Rd SK4 ....168 B3
Sibley St M18 ....99 D5
Siblies Wlk 7 M22 .....121 B1
Sibson Ct 3 M21 ....97 A1
Sibson Rd
 Manchester M21 ....97 A1
 Sale M33 ....108 A4
Sickle St
 Manchester M1,M2 ....159 A1
 Oldham OL4 ....67 A5
Siddall St M29 ....56 C5
Sidbury Rd M21 ....109 C8
Sidcup Rd M23 ....120 F5
Siddal Moor Sports Coll
 OL10 ....46 D7

Siddall St Heywood OL10 ..46 E8
 Manchester M12 ....99 A2
 Oldham OL1 ....153 F8
 2 Radcliffe M26 ....44 A4
 Shaw OL2 ....149 B7
Siddeley St WN7 ....75 D5
Siddington Ave
 Manchester M20 ....110 A7
 Stockport SK3 ....170 D6
Siddington Rd
 Handforth SK9 ....131 D5
 Poynton SK12 ....133 F2
Siddow Comm WN7 ......76 A4
Side Ave WA14 ....119 C1
Side St Droylsden M11 ...83 B2
 Oldham OL8 ....66 C2
Sidebottom St SK6 .....112 F4
Sidebottom St
 Droylsden M43 ....83 F1
 Oldham OL4 ....67 E8
 Stalybridge SK15 ....86 A2
Sidford Cl BL3 ....147 D3
Siding St OL13 ....3 C8
Sidings The Bacup OL13 ...4 A8
 Bury BL9 ....140 E1
 Worsley M28 ....79 A5
Sidley Ave M9 ....64 F4
Sidley Pl SK14 ....167 F3
Sidley St SK14 ....167 F3
Sidmouth Ave M41 ....94 E3
Sidmouth Dr M9 ....64 D2
Sidmouth Gr
 Cheadle SK8 ....131 F7
 Wigan WN3 ....54 E3
Sidmouth Rd M33 ......107 D5
Sidmouth St Denton M34 .100 D7
 Oldham OL9 ....152 B5
Sidney Rd M9 ....64 D1
Sidney St Bolton BL3 ...145 F5
 Leigh WN7 ....76 A5
 Manchester M1 ....163 A7
 8 Manchester M3 ......158 F1
 Oldham OL1 ....49 A1
 Salford M3 ....158 D2
Sidwell Wlk M4 ....160 D1
Siemens Rd Irlam M44 ..105 E5
 Manchester M20 ....110 B5
Siemens St BL6 ....22 C2
Sienna Cl M44 ....105 E6
Sighthill Wlk M9 ....157 D8
Signal Cl M30 ....79 B2
Signal Dr M40 ....157 E6
Signet Wlk M8 ....156 B6
Silas St M16 ....85 D5
Silburn Way M2,M9 ....64 F7
Silbury Wlk M8 ....155 F5
Silchester Dr M40 .....157 D6
Silchester Way BL2 .....25 E1
Silchester Wlk 3 OL1 .153 F7
Silcock St WA3 ....74 A1
Silfield Cl M11 ....160 E1
Silk Mill SK12 ....133 C4
Silk St Eccles M30 ....79 F1
 Failsworth M40 ....83 C6
 Glossop SK13 ....104 E1
 Leigh WN7 ....75 F5
 Manchester M4 ....159 C2
 Manchester M4 ....64 F8
 Middleton M24 ....64 B8
 Rochdale OL11 ....30 C4
 Salford M3 ....158 D3
 Westhoughton BL5 ....39 E1
Silkhey Gr M28 ....60 D1
Silkin Cl M13 ....163 B7
Silkin Ct M13 ....163 B7
Silkstone St M11 ....165 C7
Sillavan Way M3 ....158 E2
Sillitoe Dr WN6 ....37 A1
Silsbury Dr WN6 ....37 A8
Silsden Ave Golborne WA3 .91 B8
 Manchester M9 ....64 B5
Silsden Wlk M7 ....80 F8
Silton St M9 ....157 F8
Silver Birch Gr
 Ashton-in-M WN4 ....73 A5
 Pendlebury M27 ....80 B6
Silver Birch Mews SK16 .101 E7
Silver Birches M34 ....101 B1
Silver Ct SK16 ....101 B7
Silver Ct 3 M45 ....44 E1
Silver Hill OL15 ....31 F7
Silver Hill Rd SK14 ....167 E1
Silver Jubilee Wlk 4
 M4 ....159 B2
Silver Spring SK14 .....113 F8
Silver St Bury BL9 .....140 E2
 Irlam M44 ....94 B3
 Manchester M1 ....159 A1
 Manchester M1 ....163 A8
 Oldham OL1 ....153 E6
 5 Platt Bridge WN2 .....56 B2
 Ramsbottom BL0 ....138 C4
 Rochdale OL12 ....139 D8
 Walsden OL14 ....6 A7
 Whitefield M45 ....44 E1
Silver Terr M11 ....161 D7
Silverbirch Cl M33 ....107 D2
Silverbirch Way 8 M35 .83 F7
Silvercroft St M15 .....162 E7
Silverdale
 Altrincham WA14 ....119 C4
 5 Romiley SK6 ....112 F3
 Swinton M27 ....62 A2
 Wigan WN1 ....37 C2
Silverdale Ave
 Chadderton OL9 ....152 A6
 Denton M34 ....101 A2
 Ince-in-M WN2 ....56 A8
 Irlam M44 ....94 B3

Silverdale Ave continued
 Manchester M25 ....63 E2
 Walkden M38 ....60 A5
Silverdale Cl Bury BL9 ...45 A8
 High Lane SK6 ....134 E8
Silverdale Ct WN1 .....151 D8
Silverdale Dr Oldham OL4 .67 F6
 Wilmslow SK9 ....137 A4
Silverdale Rd Bolton BL1 .144 C7
 Farnworth BL4 ....42 A1
 Gatley SK8 ....122 B4
 Hindley WN2 ....56 F5
 Manchester M21 ....97 C1
 Manchester SK4 ....168 C4
 Newton-le-W WA12 .....89 B4
 Wigan WN5 ....54 B8
Silverdale St M11 ....99 F8
Silverdale Vocational Ctr
 M27 ....62 B1
Silverlea Dr M9 ....64 C2
Silvermere OL6 ....85 E6
Silvermere Cl BL0 .....138 B5
Silverstone Dr M40 ......83 D4
Silverton Cl SK14 ......102 E2
Silverton Gr Bolton BL1 .143 F4
 Middleton M24 ....46 D4
Silverton Ho M6 ....80 A3
Silverwell La BL1,BL2 ..145 F7
Silverwell St Bolton BL1 .145 F7
 Failsworth M40 ....83 D5
 Horwich BL6 ....22 B4
Silverwood OL9 ....65 E7
Silverwood Ave M21 ...109 B8
Silvester St BL6 ....21 D2
Silvington Way WN2 .....38 A2
Simeon St
 Manchester M4 ....159 B3
 Milnrow OL16 ....31 F6
 Walsden OL14 ....6 A8
Simfield Cl WN6 ....19 D1
Simister Dr BL9 ....45 A2
Simister Gn M25 ....63 E8
Simister La
 Middleton M24,M25 ....46 A1
 Middleton M25 ....63 E8
Simister Rd M35 ....83 F7
Simister St 10 M9 ......157 E8
Simm's Sq WN2 ....38 D4
Simmondley Gr SK13 ...116 A8
Simmondley La SK13 ...116 A8
Simmondley New Rd
 SK13 ....116 A7
Simmondley Prim Sch
 SK13 ....116 A8
Simms Cl M3 ....158 D2
Simon Cl M33 ....108 A3
Simon Freeman Cl M19,
 SK4 ....111 C6
Simon La M24 ....46 A2
Simonbury Cl BL8 ....26 F2
Simons Cl SK13 ....116 A7
Simonsway M22,SK8 ...121 D2
Simpkin St WN2 ....56 B1
Simpson Ave M27 ....78 A6
Simpson Gr M28 ....78 A6
Simpson Hill Cl OL10 ...29 F3
Simpson Rd M28 ....78 A6
Simpson Sq OL9 ....66 C3
Simpson St Droylsden M11 .83 A1
 Hyde SK14 ....167 D2
 Manchester M4 ....159 B3
 Manchester M4 ....64 F8
 Wilmslow SK9 ....136 F6
Sinclair Pl WN5 ....54 E8
Sinclair St OL11 ....30 D3
Sinderland La WA14 ...106 D1
Sinderland Rd
 Altrincham WA14 ....119 C8
 Partington M31,WA14 .106 C2
Sindsley Cl M27 ....61 D1
Sindsley Gr BL3 ....147 E3
Sindsley Rd M27 ....61 D2
Singapore Ave M90 ....130 A8
Singleton Ave Bolton BL2 .42 F7
 Horwich BL6 ....22 F5
Singleton Cl M7 ....63 C1
Singleton Gr BL5 ....40 B1
Singleton Lo M7 ....63 D1
Singleton Rd
 Manchester M7 ....63 D1
 Manchester,Heaton Moor
 SK4 ....168 B4
Singleton St M26 ....43 D4
Sion St BL3 ....147 D3
Sir Matt Busby Way M17 .96 F5
Sir Richard Fairey Rd
 SK4 ....111 B7
Sir Williams Ct M23 ...117 B6
Sir William St M11 ......99 F8
Sirius Pl M7 ....158 D3
Siskin Cl Leigh WN7 .....76 B5
 Newton-le-W WA12 .....89 C3
Siskin Rd SK2 ....124 F5
Sisley St M7 ....81 B8
Sisson St M35 ....83 F7
Sisters' St M43 ....100 A8
Sitch La SK22 ....127 F3
Sittingbourne Rd WN1 ...37 C4
Sixpools Gr 6 M28 ....78 C8
Sixth Ave Bolton BL1 ...144 B7
 Bury BL9 ....28 D4
 Little Lever BL3 ....42 F8
 Oldham OL8 ....66 C1
Sixth St M17 ....96 D5
Size House Pl 7 WN7 ....76 A4
Size St OL12 ....4 D1

Skagen BL1 ...143 E1
Skagen Ct BL1 ...143 E1
Skaife Rd M33 ...108 E4
Skarratt Cl M12 ...164 F6
Skegness Cl BL8 ...27 D5
Skelton Green La SK10 ...133 F1
Skelton Gr Bolton BL2 ...42 F8
  Manchester M13 ...98 F2
Skelton Rd
  Altrincham WA14 ...119 E7
  Stretford M32 ...96 D3
Skelton St WN4 ...72 F6
Skelwith Ave BL3 ...147 F2
Skelwith Cl M41 ...95 A4
Skerry Cl M13 ...163 B7
Skerton Rd M16 ...97 B4
Skiddaw Pl WN5 ...54 C6
Skilgate Wlk 10 M40 ...83 C6
Skip Pl M3,M4 ...159 A3
Skipton Ave
  Chadderton OL9 ...47 F1
  Failsworth M40 ...65 D1
  Hindley WN2 ...57 A4
Skipton Cl Bury BL8 ...26 F2
  Hazel Grove SK7 ...133 C8
  Reddish SK5 ...111 F8
Skipton Dr M41 ...94 F5
Skipton St Bolton BL2 ...148 C8
  Oldham OL8 ...67 B4
Skipton Wlk BL2 ...148 C7
Skull House La WN6 ...35 D8
Skye Cl OL10 ...28 F1
Skye Croft SK6 ...113 D3
Skye Rd M41 ...95 D5
Skye Wlk M23 ...121 A4
Skyes Cres WN3 ...54 C1
Skyes Ct 8 OL16 ...31 B6
Slack Fold La BL4 ...147 D1
Slack Gate OL12 ...14 E8
Slack Gate La OL3 ...50 D8
Slack Hall OL4 ...67 F8
Slack La Bolton BL2 ...25 E7
  Delph OL3 ...50 D6
  Swinton M27 ...79 C6
  Westhoughton BL5 ...39 F3
Slack Rd M9 ...64 D1
Slack St Hyde SK14 ...167 F4
  Rochdale OL16 ...139 F7
Slackcote OL3 ...50 C7
Slackcote La OL3 ...50 C7
Slackey Brow BL4 ...42 C6
Slackey Fold WN2 ...57 B1
Slade Gr M13 ...98 F3
Slade Hall Rd M12 ...99 A2
Slade La M13,M19 ...98 F2
Slade Mount M19 ...110 F8
Slade St BL3 ...43 A3
Sladen Fold OL15 ...16 D8
Sladen Ct OL12 ...14 F1
Slades View Cl OL3 ...51 C5
Slag La WA3 ...74 F2
Slaidburn Ave BL2 ...42 F6
Slaidburn Cl
  6 Milnrow OL16 ...31 F5
  Wigan WN3 ...55 A2
Slaidburn Cres WA3 ...73 F2
Slaidburn Dr BL2 ...26 F3
Slaithwaite Dr 5 M11 ...83 C2
Slant Cl SK13 ...116 E8
Slate Ave 7 M4 ...159 C1
Slate La Ashton-u-L OL7 ...100 E8
  Ashton-u-L OL7 ...84 E1
  Droylsden M34 ...100 C8
Slate Wharf M15 ...162 D7
Slateacre Rd SK14 ...113 F7
Slatelands Ave SK13 ...116 B8
Slatelands Rd SK13 ...116 B8
Slater Ave BL6 ...22 C4
Slater La BL1 ...25 A1
Slater St Bolton BL1 ...143 F1
  Eccles M30 ...79 B2
  Failsworth M35 ...65 F1
  Farnworth BL4 ...60 D8
  Oldham OL9 ...153 E6
Slater St N WN7 ...75 D5
Slater Way 2 SK14 ...102 E3
Slater's Nook 14 BL5 ...39 E1
Slaterfield BL3 ...145 E5
Slaunt Bank OL12 ...13 D2
Slawson Way OL10 ...29 F3
Sleaford Cl Bury BL8 ...27 D5
  Manchester M40 ...160 D3
Sledbrook St WN5 ...54 D3
Sleddale Cl SK2 ...124 D5
Sledmere Cl Bolton BL1 ...143 F2
  Droylsden M11 ...83 A1
Sledmoor Rd M23 ...108 F1
Sliimbridge Cl BL2 ...26 A1
Sloane Ave OL4 ...67 F8
Sloane St
  5 Ashton-u-L OL6 ...166 C3
  Bolton BL3 ...146 B3
  Droylsden M11 ...83 A2
Slough Ind Ctr M5 ...161 C8
Smallbridge Cl 5 M8 ...78 C8
Smallbridge Prim Sch
  OL12 ...15 B3
Smallbrook La WN7 ...57 E3
Smallbrook Rd OL2 ...32 C1
Smalldale Ave M16 ...97 F3
Smalley St Rochdale OL11 ...30 C2
  Standish WN6 ...19 F1
Smallfield Dr M9 ...157 D8
Smallridge Cl M40 ...160 D3
Smallshaw OL12 ...14 A4
Smallshaw Fold OL6 ...85 B5
Smallshaw La OL6 ...85 C5
Smallshaw Rd OL12 ...14 A4

Smallshaw Sq OL6 ...85 B5
Smallwood St M40 ...83 C6
Smart St M12 ...99 A3
Smeaton Cl M32 ...96 E2
Smeaton St Horwich BL6 ...22 C2
  Manchester M8 ...156 C6
Smedley Ave Bolton BL3 ...42 A3
  Manchester M8 ...156 C6
Smedley La
  Manchester M8 ...156 B6
  Manchester M8,M9 ...156 B7
Smedley Rd M40,M8 ...156 C6
Smedley St M8 ...156 B6
Smethurst Hall Pk WN5 ...53 C2
Smethurst Hall Rd BL9 ...28 F4
Smethurst La
  Bolton BL3,BL4 ...146 B2
  Wigan WN5 ...54 C5
Smethurst Rd WN5 ...53 C2
Smethurst St 7 Bury BL8 ...27 C4
  Heywood OL10 ...29 B2
  Manchester M9 ...64 D1
  Middleton M24 ...65 D7
  Wigan WN5 ...54 C5
Smith Ave WN5 ...54 B8
Smith Brow BL6 ...21 C3
Smith Fold La M28 ...60 A3
Smith Hill OL16 ...32 A6
Smith La Ashley WA16 ...128 E1
  Bolton BL7 ...8 F1
Smith St Adlington PR7 ...20 F6
  Ashton-u-L OL7 ...84 F1
  Aspull WN2 ...38 A6
  Atherton M46 ...58 C3
  Bury BL9 ...141 A3
  Cheadle SK8 ...122 F6
  Denton M34 ...100 F2
  Dukinfield SK14 ...101 D5
  Dukinfield SK16 ...101 A8
  4 Heywood OL10 ...29 D2
  Leigh WN7 ...76 A5
  6 Littleborough OL15 ...16 B5
  Manchester M16 ...161 C6
  Mossley OL5 ...68 B2
  Oldham OL4 ...67 B8
  Ramsbottom BL0 ...138 B5
  Rochdale OL16 ...139 F7
  Walkden M28 ...60 D3
Smith's La WN2 ...75 B8
Smith's Pl 11 M46 ...58 D3
Smith's Rd BL3 ...42 D3
Smithies Ave M24 ...47 A2
Smithies St OL10 ...29 E2
Smithill's Hall (Mus)*
  BL1 ...142 B4
Smithills Country Pk*
  BL1 ...24 B5
Smithills Croft Rd BL1 ...142 B4
Smithills Dean Rd BL1 ...142 B4
Smithills Dr BL1 ...23 F7
Smithills Hall Cl BL0 ...138 C5
Smithills Sch BL1 ...142 C4
Smithills Lawn SK9 ...137 A5
Smithwood Ave WN2 ...56 F6
Smithy Bridge Prim Sch
  OL15 ...15 F3
Smithy Bridge Rd OL15,
  OL16 ...15 F3
Smithy Bridge Sta OL15 ...15 F3
Smithy Brow WN6 ...18 C8
Smithy Cl SK13 ...104 D1
Smithy Croft BL7 ...24 F8
Smithy Fold
  Glossop SK13 ...104 D1
  Rochdale OL12 ...14 C1
Smithy Fold Rd 8 SK14 ...167 E1
Smithy Gn Cheadle SK8 ...132 A8
  Newhey OL16 ...32 E4
  Romiley SK6 ...113 B5
Smithy Gr OL6 ...166 C4
Smithy Hill BL3 ...146 A4
Smithy La
  Altrincham WA14 ...118 D3
  Flixton SK6 ...114 F1
  Hyde SK14 ...167 E1
  4 Manchester M3 ...158 F1
  Partington M31 ...105 F3
  Uppermill OL3 ...69 B8
Smithy Nook OL15 ...6 C1
Smithy St
  Hazel Grove SK7 ...124 D3
  Leigh WN7 ...75 F4
  Ramsbottom BL0 ...138 C6
  Westhoughton BL5 ...39 E3
Smock La WN4 ...72 C4
Smyrna St Heywood OL10 ...29 C1
  7 Oldham OL4 ...67 B6
  Radcliffe M26 ...43 F4
  Salford M5 ...154 E1
Smyrna Wlk BL3 ...43 F4
Snape St BL3 ...42 D3
Snapebrook Gr 6 SK9 ...131 E1
Snell St M4 ...160 D1
Snipe Ave OL11 ...30 F8
Snipe Cl SK12 ...133 A4
Snipe Rd OL8 ...67 B2
Snipe Ret Pk OL7 ...100 D8
Snipe St BL3 ...147 F4
Snipe Way OL7 ...100 D8
Snowber Wlk M31 ...105 E3
Snowden Ave
  Urmston M41 ...107 B8
  Wigan WN3 ...55 A4
Snowden St Bolton BL1 ...145 E8
  Heywood OL10 ...46 E8

Snowden St continued
  1 Oldham OL8 ...66 F4
Snowden Wlk 4 M40 ...65 C2
Snowdon Dr BL6 ...22 C5
Snowdon Rd M30 ...80 A3
Snowdon St OL11 ...31 A2
Snowdrop Cl BB4 ...1 A8
Snowdrop Wlk M7 ...155 D6
Snowshill Dr WN3 ...54 C4
Snydale Cl BL5 ...40 B2
Snydale Way BL3,BL5 ...40 C1
Soane St WN4 ...73 D3
Soap St M4 ...159 A2
Soapstone Way M44 ...106 A8
Society St OL2 ...149 B7
Sofa St BL1 ...142 B1
Soham Cl WN2 ...56 E4
Soho St Bolton BL3 ...145 F6
  Oldham OL4 ...67 B7
Sola St WN1 ...159 A2
Sole St WN1 ...37 E1
Solent Ave M8 ...64 A2
Solent Dr BL3 ...42 D5
Solness St BL9 ...27 F6
Solway Cl
  Ashton-in-M WN4 ...73 A4
  Bolton BL3 ...147 D3
  Oldham OL8 ...153 E5
  Swinton M27 ...61 E4
Solway Rd M22 ...121 E4
Somerdale Ave BL1 ...144 A7
Somerfield Rd M9 ...64 D1
Somerford Ave M20 ...110 A8
Somerford Way 3 SK9 ...131 E5
Somers Rd SK5 ...99 F1
Somers Wlk M9 ...64 B3
Somersby Ct SK7 ...123 E3
Somersby Dr BL7 ...24 F8
Somersby Wlk BL3 ...145 F5
Somerset Ave Shaw OL2 ...48 F7
  Tyldesley M29 ...58 F3
Somerset Cl
  Brimington SK5 ...112 C4
  Irlam M44 ...105 D6
Somerset Dr BL9 ...44 F8
Somerset Gr OL11 ...30 A8
Somerset Pl M33 ...108 B6
Somerset Rd
  Altrincham WA14 ...119 D6
  Atherton M46 ...58 C5
  Bolton BL1 ...144 B8
  Droylsden M43 ...84 A3
  Failsworth M35 ...83 E6
  Salford M30 ...80 A4
  Wigan WN5 ...54 C7
Somerset Wlk BB4 ...1 A8
Somerton Ave Sale M33 ...108 C3
  Wythenshawe M22 ...121 C3
Somerton Ct M9 ...65 A3
Somerton Rd BL2 ...43 A6
Somerville Ave WN5 ...37 C3
Somerville Gdns WN1 ...37 C3
Somerville Sq BL1 ...142 C3
Somerville St BL1 ...142 C3
Somerwood Wlk M12 ...164 F6
Sommerville Ct M7 ...155 D8
Sonning Dr BL3 ...146 A2
Sonning Wlk M8 ...156 B6
Sopwith Dr M14 ...98 B1
Sorby Rd M44 ...106 A7
Sorrel Bank M6 ...154 F4
Sorrel Dr OL15 ...15 F6
Sorrel St M15 ...162 E6
Sorrel Way OL4 ...49 E2
Sorrell Bank SK5 ...100 D2
Sorton St SK1 ...163 A7
Soudan Rd SK2 ...124 A6
Soudan St M24 ...47 C1
Sougher's La WN4 ...72 F7
Sougher's Lane End WN4 ...72 E6
Sound The OL3 ...50 F4
Source Code SK15 ...86 B3
Source Rd SK9 ...131 D3
South Ave Golborne WN7 ...74 F4
  Heywood OL10 ...29 B2
  Kearsley M47 ...60 F6
  Leigh WN7 ...76 C3
  Manchester M19 ...110 F7
  Swinton M27 ...79 C6
  Uppermill OL3 ...69 B6
  Whitefield M45 ...44 E1
South Back Rock 1
  BL9 ...140 F2
South Bank SK13 ...137 B2
South Bank Rd SK9 ...140 E1
South Bolton Sixth Form Coll
  BL3 ...146 C2
South Chadderton Sch
  OL9 ...65 F3
South Cliffe St 1 M11 ...99 F7
  Whitefield BL9 ...45 A3
South Cres Droylsden M11 ...83 D2
  Failsworth M40 ...83 C7
South Croft OL8 ...66 C2
South Cross St Bury BL9 ...140 F2
  Bury BL9 ...141 A2
South Croston St M16 ...97 D4
South Ct OL16 ...31 A8
South Downs Cl 2 OL2 ...48 F8
South Downs Dr WA14 ...119 D1
South Downs Rd WA14 ...119 D1

South Dr
  Altrincham WA15 ...120 A7
  Appley Bridge WN6 ...18 C2
  Bolton BL2 ...25 E3
  Gatley SK8 ...122 A4
  Manchester M21 ...109 B6
  Wilmslow SK9 ...137 B6
South Failsworth Com Prim
  Sch M35 ...84 A7
South Field Ind Est M17 ...96 C6
South Gr
  9 Alderley Edge SK9 ...137 A1
  Manchester M13 ...164 D5
  Sale M33 ...108 B3
  Walkden M28 ...60 C2
South Hall St M5 ...161 C8
South Hey WN7 ...75 C5
South Hill OL4 ...67 F5
South Hill St OL4 ...67 A6
South King St Eccles M30 ...79 B2
  Manchester M2 ...158 F1
South La M29 ...77 A5
South Lancashire Ind Est
  WN4 ...73 B6
South Langworthy Rd
  Salford M50 ...154 F1
  Salford M50 ...96 E8
South Lonsdale St M32 ...96 E3
South Marlow St SK13 ...104 A4
South Mead SK12 ...133 B5
South Meade
  Altrincham WA15 ...120 A7
  Manchester M21 ...109 B7
  Manchester,Sedgley Park
    M25 ...63 D2
  Swinton M27 ...79 E6
South Meadway SK6 ...114 A1
South Mesnefield Rd M7 ...81 A8
South Oak La SK9 ...137 A1
South Par Rochdale OL16 ...139 F7
  Stockport SK7 ...123 F2
South Park Dr SK12 ...133 E5
South Park Rd SK8 ...122 B6
South Pine St BL9 ...141 A1
South Pl 1 BL9 ...31 A8
South Pump St M1 ...163 B8
South Radford St M7 ...81 A7
South Rd
  Altrincham,Ashley Heath
    WA14 ...128 E8
  Altrincham,Hale WA14 ...119 C2
  Manchester M20 ...110 B2
  Stretford M32 ...96 B4
  Swinton M27 ...62 D2
South Ridge M34 ...100 F5
South Row M25 ...62 F1
South Royd St BL8 ...26 F7
South Side SK14 ...113 F8
South St
  Alderley Edge SK9 ...137 A1
  Ashton-u-L OL7 ...100 E8
  Bolton BL3 ...147 E3
  Heywood OL10 ...29 B2
  Manchester M11 ...165 C7
  Manchester,Longsight
    M12 ...164 E5
  Oldham OL8 ...66 B2
  Ramsbottom BL0 ...11 D6
  Rochdale OL16 ...31 A8
  Tyldesley M46 ...58 E1
South Terr
  12 Alderley Edge SK9 ...137 A1
  Bury BL9 ...44 D7
  Ramsbottom BL0 ...1 C2
South Terrace Ct 12
  OL16 ...31 A5
South Trafford Coll
  WA14 ...119 D8
South Vale Cres WA15 ...119 F5
South View Atherton M46 ...58 C3
  2 Manchester M14 ...98 C2
  Mossley SK15 ...86 F6
  Reddish SK5 ...99 F3
  Rochdale OL11 ...29 E6
  Romiley SK6 ...113 C6
South View Gdns SK8 ...122 C3
South View Rd
  Glossop SK13 ...116 F7
  Rochdale OL12 ...15 E3
South View St BL2 ...148 C7
South View Terr OL16 ...15 E4
South Villa Ct WN6 ...36 E8
South Way OL8 ...66 D4
South William St M3 ...158 D1
Southall St M3 ...158 F4
Southam St M7 ...155 F7
Southampton Cl M7 ...155 D5
Southbank Rd M19 ...110 D5
Southbourne Ave M41 ...95 F2
Southbourne St M6 ...154 E2
Southbrook Ave M8 ...63 F3
Southbrook Cl SK13 ...171 E4
Southbrook Gr BL3 ...147 F3
Southchurch Par M40 ...159 C4
Southcliffe Rd SK5 ...111 F6
Southcombe Wlk M15 ...97 E4
Southcourt WN7 ...76 B4
Southcross Rd M18 ...99 D3
Southdene Ave M20 ...109 E4
Southdown Cl
  Rochdale OL16 ...30 C5
  Stockport SK1 ...169 E2
Southdown Cres
  Cheadle SK8 ...131 F8
  Manchester M9 ...65 A2
Southdown Dr M28 ...77 F6
Southdowns Cl OL2 ...149 A8
Southend Ave M15 ...162 D6

Southend St BL3 ...146 C3
Southern App M27 ...62 C2
Southern Cl Denton M34 ...112 F8
  Stockport SK7 ...123 F1
Southern Cres SK7 ...123 F1
Southern Ho 4 BL1 ...143 D1
Southern Ind Est M28 ...60 D5
Southern Rd M33 ...108 A6
Southern St
  Manchester M3 ...162 E8
  Salford M6 ...154 E2
  Walkden M28 ...60 D5
  Wigan WN5 ...54 D5
Southern's Fold WN2 ...38 A3
Southernby Cl 9 M13 ...98 F4
Southery Ave WN3 ...54 D3
Southey Cl OL15 ...15 E2
Southey Ct 8 M34 ...113 A8
Southey Wlk 8 M34 ...113 A7
Southfield M21 ...56 B2
Southfield Ave BL9 ...27 F6
Southfield Cl
  Dukinfield SK16 ...101 D6
  Handforth SK9 ...131 C3
Southfield Dr BL5 ...57 E7
Southfield Rd BL0 ...11 A2
Southfield St 15 BL3 ...42 A4
Southfields Ave M11 ...83 C2
Southfields Dr WA15 ...120 B7
Southgarth Rd M6 ...154 E3
Southgate Bolton BL2 ...25 E4
  Manchester M3 ...158 F1
  Manchester,Chorlton-cum-Hardy
    M21 ...109 B7
  Manchester,Heaton Chapel
    SK4 ...111 C5
  Urmston M41 ...107 B8
  Whitworth OL12 ...14 C7
Southgate Ave M40 ...83 A4
Southgate Cl M33 ...108 C5
Southgate Ind Pk OL10 ...29 E1
Southgate Mews SK4 ...111 C5
Southgate Rd
  Failsworth OL9 ...65 E3
  Whitefield BL9 ...44 F3
Southgate St OL9 ...153 F6
Southgate Way 11 OL2 ...166 A1
Southgrove Ave BL1 ...24 E6
Southlands Ave
  Eccles M30 ...95 A8
  Standish WN6 ...36 E8
Southlawn St WN5 ...137 A5
Southlea Rd M19,M20 ...110 D6
Southleigh Dr BL2 ...43 A6
Southlink OL4 ...67 A6
Southlink Bsns Pk OL4 ...67 A4
Southlink Wkshps OL4 ...67 A6
Southmill St M2 ...162 F8
Southmoor M23 ...120 E7
Southmoor Pk M23 ...120 E7
Southmoor Rd M23 ...120 F6
Southmoor Wlk BL3 ...145 E5
Southolme St SK5 ...57 E6
Southpoint SK4 ...168 A2
Southpool Cl SK7 ...124 A2
Southport Cl St M11 ...99 D7
Southridge St SK6 ...112 E6
Southview Wlk OL4 ...49 E1
Southward Rd M11 ...89 A7
Southwark Dr SK16 ...101 D6
Southway
  Altrincham WA14 ...119 E6
  Ashton-u-L OL7 ...85 B6
  Droylsden M43 ...100 A8
  7 Eccles M30 ...79 F2
  Failsworth OL9 ...65 F2
Southwell Cl
  15 Bolton BL3 ...145 D8
  Golborne WA3 ...90 C8
Southwell Gdns WA3 ...113 A1
Southwell St M9 ...157 E7
Southwold Cl M19 ...99 C1
Southwold Cl M13 ...147 F3
Southwood Cl SK8 ...64 A5
Southwood Dr M9 ...64 A5
Southworth Ct M3 ...158 D2
Southworth Rd WA12 ...89 F4
Southyard St M19 ...111 B8
Sovereign Ent Pk M50 ...161 C1
Sovereign Fold Rd WN7 ...57 E1
Sovereign Hall Cvn Pk
  OL5 ...68 F5
Sovereign Rd WN1 ...151 D7
Sovereign St M6 ...81 A4
Sowerby Cl BL8 ...26 F2
Sowerby Wlk M9 ...64 B4
Spa Cl SK5 ...111 E8
Spa Cres M38 ...59 E6
Spa Gr M38 ...60 A6
Spa La Oldham OL4 ...67 C5
  Walkden M38 ...60 A6
Spa Rd Atherton M46 ...58 D5
  Bolton BL1 ...145 E7
Spade St M13,M15 ...163 B5
Spark Rd M23 ...120 F7
Sparkford Ave M23 ...108 D1
Sparkle St M1 ...163 B8
Sparrow Cl SK5 ...99 E2

Sparrow Hill
Appley Bridge WN6,WN8 . . . .18 A2
Rochdale OL16 . . . . .139 F7
Sparrow Hill Com Prim Sch
OL16 . . . . .139 E7
Sparrow Hill Com Prim Sch
(Annexe) OL11 . . . . .139 F6
Sparrow St OL2 . . . . .48 E2
Sparrowfield Cl SK15 . . . . . .86 E7
Sparta Ave M28 . . . . .60 D2
Spath Wlk M11 . . . . .165 A8
Sparth Bottoms Rd
OL11 . . . . .139 D6
Sparth Ct SK4 . . . . .169 D3
Sparth Hall SK4 . . . . .169 D3
Sparth La SK4 . . . . .169 D3
Sparth Rd M40 . . . . .83 D5
Sparthfield Ave OL11 . . . . .139 E5
Sparthfield Rd SK4 . . . . . .169 D3
Spath Holme M20 . . . . . . .110 A3
Spath La SK8 . . . . .131 F5
Spath La E SK8 . . . . .132 B5
Spath Rd M20 . . . . .110 A3
Spath Wlk SK8 . . . . .132 B5
Spathfield Ct SK4 . . . . .169 D3
Spaw St M3 . . . . .158 E2
Spawell Cl WA3 . . . . .90 E8
Speakman Ave Leigh WN7 . .76 B5
Newton-le-W WA12 . . . . .89 C5
Speakmans Dr WN6 . . . . . . .35 C6
Spean Wlk M11 . . . . .83 D2
Spear St M1,M4 . . . . .159 B2
Spectator St M4 . . . . .160 D2
Specton Wlk M12 . . . . .99 B3
Speedwell SK13 . . . . .103 F7
Speedwell Cl
Golborne WA3 . . . . .90 E8
Tintwistle SK13 . . . . .103 F7
Speke Wlk M34 . . . . .100 E1
Spelding Dr WN6 . . . . .36 E4
Spen Fold Bury BL8 . . . . . . .44 A8
Littleborough OL15 . . . . .16 A4
Spencer Ave
Dukinfield SK14 . . . . .101 D5
Little Lever BL3 . . . . .43 C3
Manchester M16 . . . . .97 C2
Whitefield M45 . . . . .44 E2
Spencer La OL11 . . . . .29 E5
Spencer St WN7 . . . . .37 C3
Spencer Rd W WN6 . . . . . . .37 A3
Spencer St Bury BL8 . . . . . .27 C3
Spey Cl Altrincham WA14 . .119 C6
Standish WN6 . . . . .19 D1
Spey Ho SK5 . . . . .99 F2
Speyside Cl M45 . . . . .63 A8
Spilsby Sq WN3 . . . . .55 A2
Spindle Ave SK15 . . . . .86 C5
Spindle Croft BL4 . . . . .60 D8
Spindle Ct OL2 . . . . .48 E4
Spindle Hillock WN4 . . . . . .72 D4
Spindle Point Prim Sch
BL4 . . . . .61 B5
Spindle Wlk BL5 . . . . .39 F2
Spindlepoint Dr M28 . . . . . .78 C8
Spindles Sh Ctr The
OL1 . . . . .153 E6
Spindles The OL5 . . . . .86 D8
Spindlewood Cl SK15 . . . . . .86 D2
Spindlewood Rd WN3 . . . . .151 F6
Spinks St OL4 . . . . .67 B5
Spinnerbottom SK22 . . . . .127 F2
Spinnerette Cl WN7 . . . . . . .76 A5
Spinners Gdns OL12 . . . . . . .15 C4
Spinners Gn OL12 . . . . .14 F2
Spinners La SK12 . . . . .133 C4
Spinners Mews BL1 . . . . . .145 E8
Spinners Way OL4 . . . . .49 E4
Spinney Cl Glossop SK13 . .104 C2
Handforth SK9 . . . . .131 C3
Spinney Dr Bury BL9 . . . . . .27 E6
Sale M33 . . . . .107 D2
Spinney Gr M34 . . . . .100 F5
Spinney Nook BL2 . . . . .25 D2
Spinney Rd M23 . . . . .121 B7
Spinney The Bolton BL1 . . .144 B7
Chapeltown BL7 . . . . .9 C2
Cheadle SK8 . . . . .122 E3
Oldham OL4 . . . . .68 A8
Rochdale OL12 . . . . .14 D3
Urmston M41 . . . . .95 A2
Whitefield M45 . . . . .62 C7
Wigan WN5 . . . . .54 E5
Spinning Gate Sh Ctr
WN7 . . . . .75 F4
Spinning Jenny Way
WN7 . . . . .75 F4

Spinning Jenny Wlk 2
M4 . . . . .159 C2
Spinning Mdw BL1 . . . . . . .145 D8
Spinningdale M38 . . . . .59 D6
Spinningfield M3 . . . . .158 F1
Spinningfield Way OL10 . . .46 D7
Spinningfields BL1 . . . . . . .143 D4
Spinnings The BL9 . . . . .11 C3
Spion Kop WN4 . . . . .73 A3
Spire Hollin SK13 . . . . .104 C2
Spire Hollin SK13 . . . . .104 C2
Spire Wlk M12 . . . . .164 D8
Spiredale Dr WN6 . . . . .19 F2
Spirewood Gdns SK6 . . . . .113 A2
Spod Rd OL12 . . . . .14 D1
Spodden Cotts OL12 . . . . . .4 D2
Spodden Fold OL12 . . . . . . .14 C8
Spodden St OL12 . . . . .139 D8
Spodden Wlk M45 . . . . .45 C1
Spodegreen La WA14 . . . . .118 C1
Spokeshave Way OL16 . . . . .15 C2
Spooner Rd 8 M30 . . . . .79 C1
Sportside Ave M28 . . . . .60 E4
Sportside Cl M28 . . . . .60 E4
Sportside Gr M28 . . . . .60 E4
Sportsman St WN7 . . . . .75 D5
Sportsmans Dr OL8 . . . . . . .67 A2
Spotland Bridge Ind Ctr
OL11 . . . . .30 C8
Spotland Prim Sch
OL12 . . . . .139 D8
Spotland Rd OL12 . . . . .139 E8
Spotland Tops OL12 . . . . . .14 B1
Spreadbury St 7 M40 . . . . .83 A7
Spring Ave Hyde SK14 . . . . .113 F8
Whitefield M45 . . . . .44 E2
Spring Bank
Altrincham WA14 . . . . .119 D3
Appley Bridge WN6 . . . . .35 C8
Salford M6 . . . . .154 E3
Stalybridge SK15 . . . . .102 B8
Whitworth OL12 . . . . .14 D4
Spring Bank Ave
Ashton-u-L OL6 . . . . .85 B5
Denton M34 . . . . .100 D7
Spring Bank La
Rochdale OL11 . . . . .29 E8
Stalybridge SK15 . . . . .86 C5
Spring Bank Pl SK1 . . . . . .170 E8
Spring Bank Rd SK22 . . . . .127 C1
Spring Bank St OL8 . . . . . . .66 C4
Spring Bank Terr M34 . . . . .100 C7
Spring Bottom OL14 . . . . . . .5 F7
Spring Brook Sch OL9 . . . . .65 F7
Spring Cl Ashton-u-L OL7 . . .85 A6
Bury BL8 . . . . .26 E6
Ramsbottom BL0 . . . . .138 B6
Spring Clough M28 . . . . .79 B6
Spring Clough Ave M28 . . . .60 F2
Spring Clough Dr
Oldham OL8 . . . . .67 C4
Walkden M28 . . . . .60 F2
Spring Cotts 7 OL5 . . . . . . .68 C2
Spring Garden St 10 OL2 . . .48 D4
Spring Gardens St 4 BB4 . . .2 F8
Spring Gdns
Altrincham WA15 . . . . .120 C5
Atherton M46 . . . . .58 D3
Bolton BL2 . . . . .25 F4
Hadfield SK13 . . . . .104 A5
Haslingden BB4 . . . . .1 A8
Horwich BL6 . . . . .22 B4
Hyde SK14 . . . . .167 D4
Manchester M1,M2 . . . . .159 A1
Middleton M24 . . . . .47 A1
Rawtenstall BB4 . . . . .2 F6
Royton OL2 . . . . .48 D4
Salford M6 . . . . .81 A3
Stockport SK1 . . . . .112 A1
Wigan WN1 . . . . .150 B8
Spring Gr Uppermill OL3 . . . .69 B5
Whitefield M45 . . . . .44 E2
Wigan WN1 . . . . .151 D7
Spring Hall Rise OL4 . . . . . .49 F4
Spring Hill Ct 5 OL4 . . . . . .67 D8
Spring Hill High Sch
OL16 . . . . .31 B5
Spring La Lymm WA13 . . . . .117 F3
Oldham OL4 . . . . .67 E5
Radcliffe M26 . . . . .44 A4
Spring Meadow La OL3 . . . .69 C8
Spring Mill Cl 4 BL3 . . . . . .147 E4
Spring Mill Wlk OL16 . . . . . .15 C2
Spring Pl OL12 . . . . .4 D3
Spring Rd
Altrincham WA14 . . . . .119 D2
Orrell WN5 . . . . .53 F8
Poynton SK12 . . . . .133 F2
Wigan WN5 . . . . .36 A1
Spring Rise
Glossop SK13 . . . . .115 F7
Shaw OL2 . . . . .32 A1
Spring Side
Rawtenstall BB4 . . . . .2 F6
Whitworth OL12 . . . . .4 D4
Spring Side Cotts BL7 . . . . . .8 A2
Spring St Bolton BL3 . . . . . .145 F5
Bury BL9 . . . . .140 F1
Bury,Tottington BL8 . . . . .26 F7
Bury,Walshaw BL8 . . . . .26 F4
Farnworth BL4 . . . . .42 B4
Glossop SK13 . . . . .104 B1
Hollingworth SK14 . . . . .103 C5
Horwich BL6 . . . . .22 B4
Ince-in-M WN3 . . . . .55 E4
Manchester M12 . . . . .99 A2
Mossley OL5 . . . . .68 C2

Spring St continued
Mottram-in-U SK14 . . . . . . .115 A8
Oldham OL4 . . . . .67 C8
Oldham,County End OL4 . . . .68 A6
Ramsbottom,Bank La BL0 . . .11 D7
Ramsbottom,Tanners BL0 . . .138 B6
Stalybridge SK15 . . . . .85 F2
Uppermill OL3 . . . . .69 B8
Wigan WN1 . . . . .151 D7
Wilmslow SK9 . . . . .137 A7
Spring Terr 4 Bacup OL13 . . .3 D8
Bury BL8 . . . . .26 F7
Chadderton OL9 . . . . .152 A7
Newhey OL16 . . . . .32 B3
Rochdale OL11 . . . . .14 A1
Spring Vale
Hazel Grove SK7 . . . . .124 E2
Middleton M24 . . . . .47 B1
Prestwich M25 . . . . .63 A2
Spring Vale Dr BL8 . . . . . . .26 E6
Spring Vale St BL8 . . . . . . .26 F6
Spring Vale Terr OL15 . . . . .16 B5
Spring Vale Way OL2 . . . . .149 A5
Spring Water Dr SK13 . . . . .171 E3
Spring Wood St BL0 . . . . . .138 B7
Springbank
Chadderton OL9 . . . . .152 A7
Hadfield SK13 . . . . .103 F5
Springbank Cl
Manchester M8 . . . . .63 F1
Romiley SK6 . . . . .113 B5
Springbank Gdns WA13 . . .117 B5
Springbank Ind Est WN2 . . .56 B3
Springbank Rd SK6 . . . . . . .113 C6
Springbourne WN6 . . . . .36 F2
Springbridge Rd M16 . . . . . .97 F1
Springburn Cl
Horwich BL6 . . . . .22 D1
Worsley M28 . . . . .78 A6
Springburn Gdns M20 . . . .110 A3
Springfield
Charlesworth SK13 . . . . .115 C6
Kearsley M26 . . . . .61 C6
Urmston M41 . . . . .95 C2
Springfield Ave
Golborne WA3 . . . . .74 D8
Hazel Grove SK7 . . . . .124 D3
Littleborough OL15 . . . . .16 A7
Lymm WA13 . . . . .117 B5
Marple SK6 . . . . .125 F6
Reddish SK5 . . . . .111 E7
Springfield Cl
Failsworth M35 . . . . .83 F8
Hadfield SK13 . . . . .171 E4
Heywood OL10 . . . . .29 B1
Springfield Dr SK9 . . . . . . .136 D5
Springfield Gdns BL6 . . . . . .61 A6
Springfield Ind Est M35 . . . .83 E8
Springfield La Irlam M44 . . .93 F2
Rochdale OL16 . . . . .15 D3
Royton OL2 . . . . .48 C7
Salford M3 . . . . .158 E3
Springfield Prim Sch
M33 . . . . .108 B4
Springfield Rd
Altrincham WA15 . . . . .120 C5
Altrincham WA14 . . . . .119 D5
Atherton M46 . . . . .58 E4
Bolton BL1 . . . . .24 E7
Coppull PR7 . . . . .19 E8
Droylsden M43 . . . . .83 F3
Farnworth BL4 . . . . .42 A1
Gatley SK8 . . . . .122 B5
Hindley WN2 . . . . .56 C6
Horwich BL6 . . . . .22 D1
Kearsley BL4 . . . . .60 F6
Middleton M24 . . . . .46 F2
Ramsbottom BL0 . . . . .11 A2
Sale M33 . . . . .108 B4
Wigan WN6 . . . . .37 A2
Springfield Rd N PR7 . . . . . .19 E8
Springfield St
Ashton-u-L OL6 . . . . .85 E5
18 Bolton BL3 . . . . .42 A4
Heywood OL10 . . . . .29 A2
Wigan WN1 . . . . .37 D2
Springhead Ave
Manchester M20 . . . . .110 A7
Oldham OL4 . . . . .68 A5
Springhead Inf Sch OL4 . . .68 A6
Springhill OL2 . . . . .149 A8
Springhill Ave OL3 . . . . .3 D8
Springhill Villas OL13 . . . . . .3 D8
Springlawn BL1 . . . . .40 F8
Springlees Ct 7 OL4 . . . . . .67 F6
Springmeadow SK13 . . . . . .115 D7
Springmount WA3 . . . . .90 F8
Springpool WN3 . . . . .54 B2
Springs Brow PR7 . . . . .19 D5
Springs La SK15 . . . . .85 F3
Springs Rd M24,OL9 . . . . . .65 C6
Springs The
Altrincham WA14 . . . . .119 B2
Rochdale OL11 . . . . .29 E7
Springside Ave M28 . . . . . . .60 E3
Springside Cl M28 . . . . .60 E3
Springside Gr M28 . . . . .60 E3
Springside Prim Sch BL9 . . .27 E2
Springside Rd BL9 . . . . .27 D2
Springside Wlk 20 M15 . . . .162 D6
Springvale Cl OL14 . . . . .84 F5
Springvale Ct M24 . . . . .65 B8
Springville Ave M9 . . . . . . .157 F7

Springwater Ave BL0 . . . . . .11 A3
Springwater St BL2 . . . . . . .25 E3
Springwater La M45 . . . . . . .44 E2
Springwell Cl 1 M6 . . . . . .154 E2
Springwell Gdns M45 . . . . .102 E1
Springwell Way 2
SK14 . . . . .102 E1
Springwood Delph OL3 . . . . .50 E5
Glossop SK13 . . . . .115 F8
Springwood Ave
Chadderton OL9 . . . . .47 E1
Pendlebury M27 . . . . .80 B6
Springwood Cres SK6 . . . . .113 E2
Springwood Hall OL7 . . . . . .85 A7
Springwood Hall Rd OL8 . . .67 A2
Springwood La SK6 . . . . . . .113 F3
Springwood Prim Sch
Pendlebury M27 . . . . .80 A7
Romiley SK6 . . . . .113 E2
Springwood Way OL7 . . . . . .85 A6
Sprodley Dr WN6 . . . . .18 B2
Spruce Ave BL9 . . . . .141 B2
Spruce Cl WA3 . . . . .90 F7
Spruce Cres 2 BL9 . . . . .27 F7
Spruce Ct 1 M6 . . . . .81 B2
Spruce Lo SK8 . . . . .122 D6
Spruce Rd WN6 . . . . .36 E3
Spruce St
Manchester M15 . . . . .162 E6
Ramsbottom BL0 . . . . .138 B5
Rochdale OL16 . . . . .31 B6
Spruce Wlk 7 Sale M33 . . .107 C6
Walsden OL14 . . . . .6 A8
Handforth SK9 . . . . .131 A1
Spur The OL8 . . . . .67 A3
Spur Wlk M8 . . . . .155 F7
Spurn La OL3 . . . . .51 B4
Square Rd OL14 . . . . .6 A8
Square St BL0 . . . . .138 C6
Square The
Altrincham WA15 . . . . .129 C8
Bury BL9 . . . . .140 F2
Hyde SK14 . . . . .167 D2
Stockport SK4 . . . . .168 C3
Swinton M27 . . . . .79 E5
Uppermill OL3 . . . . .69 B5
Square View OL14 . . . . .6 B8
Squire Rd M8 . . . . .155 F7
Squires Ct M5 . . . . .80 A2
Squires La M46 . . . . .76 E8
Squirrel Dr WA14 . . . . .119 C8
Squirrel La BL6 . . . . .22 E3
Squirrel's Jump SK9 . . . . . .137 C1
Stable Fold M26 . . . . .44 A4
Stable La SK9 . . . . .137 C1
Stablefold Eccles M28 . . . . .79 A5
Mossley OL5 . . . . .86 C8
Stableford Ave M30 . . . . . . .79 C4
Stables The
Droylsden M43 . . . . .84 D3
Prestwich M25 . . . . .63 C3
4 Sale M33 . . . . .108 A4
Whitworth OL12 . . . . .14 D5
Stablings The SK9 . . . . .137 A5
Stack La OL13 . . . . .4 B8
Stadium Way
Wigan,Marsh Green WN5 . . . .36 E1
Wigan,Wallgate WN5,
WN6 . . . . .150 A7
Stafford Cl SK13 . . . . .116 F8
Stafford Ct 2 OL16 . . . . . . .15 E4
Stafford Rd Eccles M30 . . . .79 F3
Failsworth M35 . . . . .84 A5
Swinton M27 . . . . .79 F8
Walkden M28 . . . . .60 C1
Stafford St Bury BL8 . . . . . .140 D4
Hindley WN2 . . . . .56 C5
Ince-in-M WN3 . . . . .55 E4
New Mills SK22 . . . . .127 C1
Oldham OL9 . . . . .66 C4
Stafford Wlk 12 M34 . . . . .101 A1
Stag Ind Est WA14 . . . . .119 B6
Stag Pasture Rd OL8 . . . . . .66 E1
Stage La WA13 . . . . .117 C4
Stage The M50 . . . . .96 F8
Stainburn Cl WN6 . . . . .35 E6
Stainburn Rd M11 . . . . .165 B8
Stainburne Rd SK2 . . . . . . .124 D6
Staindale OL4 . . . . .67 D6
Stainer St M12 . . . . .99 A3
Stainer St M12 . . . . .99 A3
Stainforth Cl Bury BL8 . . . . .26 F7
Culcheth WA3 . . . . .91 D4
Stainforth St M11 . . . . .164 F8
Stainmoor Ct SK2 . . . . .124 D6
Stainmore Ave OL6 . . . . .85 D7
Stainsbury St BL3 . . . . .146 C4
Stainton Ave M18 . . . . .99 E4
Stainton Cl M26 . . . . .43 F3
Stainton Dr M24 . . . . .46 D3
Stainton Rd M26 . . . . .43 F5
Stairgate WN1 . . . . .150 C8
Staithes Rd M22 . . . . .130 D8
Stakeford Dr M8 . . . . .156 C8
Stakehill Ind Est M24 . . . . . .47 D4
Stakehill La M24 . . . . .47 D4
Staley Cl SK15 . . . . .86 C2
Staley Hall Cres SK15 . . . . .86 C3
Staley Hall Rd SK15 . . . . . . .86 C3
Staley Rd OL5 . . . . .86 E8
Staley St 18 Oldham OL4 . . .67 F6
Oldham,Moorhey OL4 . . . . . .67 F6
Stalham Cl M40 . . . . .160 D3
Stalmine Ave SK8 . . . . .131 B8
Stalybridge Ctry Pk*
SK15 . . . . .87 A2
Stalybridge Rd SK14 . . . . . .103 A4

Stalybridge Sta SK15 . . . . . .85 F2
Stalyhill Dr SK15 . . . . .102 E7
Stalyhill Inf Sch SK15 . . . . .102 E7
Stalyhill Jun Sch SK15 . . . .102 D7
Stamford Arc 2 OL6 . . . . . .166 C3
Stamford Ave
Altrincham WA14 . . . . .119 A5
Ashton-u-L SK15 . . . . .85 E2
Stamford Cl SK15 . . . . .85 E2
Stamford Ct
3 Ashton-u-L OL6 . . . . .85 D2
Manchester M13 . . . . .98 F3
Stamford Dr
Failsworth M35 . . . . .84 B6
Stalybridge SK15 . . . . .85 F2
Stamford Gr SK15 . . . . .85 F2
Stamford Grange 1
WA14 . . . . .119 C4
Stamford High Sch OL6 . . . .85 E4
Stamford New Rd
WA14 . . . . .119 D4
Stamford Park Inf Sch
WA15 . . . . .119 E3
Stamford Park Jun Sch
WA15 . . . . .119 E3
Stamford Park Rd
WA15 . . . . .119 E3
Stamford Pl M33 . . . . .108 C4
Stamford Rd
Alderley Edge SK9 . . . . .137 B1
Altrincham WA14 . . . . .119 C2
Carrington M31 . . . . .106 D7
Denton M34 . . . . .100 D6
Handforth SK9 . . . . .131 A1
Little Bollington WA14 . . . . .118 B2
Manchester M13 . . . . .98 F3
Oldham OL4 . . . . .67 F7
Salford M7 . . . . .81 B6
Urmston M41 . . . . .95 B2
Stamford Sq
8 Altrincham WA14 . . . . . . .119 D5
Ashton-u-L SK15 . . . . .85 D2
Stamford St
Altrincham WA14 . . . . .119 D5
Atherton M46 . . . . .58 E4
Heywood OL10 . . . . .29 E1
Manchester M16 . . . . .97 D4
Stamford St Central
OL6 . . . . .166 B2
Stamford St Ctrl OL6 . . . . .166 C3
Stamford St E OL6 . . . . .85 D2
Stamford St W OL6 . . . . . . .166 A2
Stamford Way 2 WA14 . . . .119 D5
Stampstone St OL1 . . . . .67 B8
Stan Jolly Wlk M11 . . . . . . .165 C8
Stanage Ave M9 . . . . .64 F4
Stanbank St SK4 . . . . .169 E4
Stanbridge Ct SK4 . . . . . . .143 F4
Stanbrook St M19 . . . . .111 C8
Stanbury Cl BL9 . . . . .28 D1
Stanbury Dr SK16 . . . . .101 D8
Stanbury Wlk M40 . . . . . . .160 D3
Stancliffe Gr WN2 . . . . .38 C6
Stancliffe Rd M22 . . . . .121 E5
Stancross Rd M23 . . . . .120 C8
Stand Ave M45 . . . . .44 E1
Stand Cl M26,M45 . . . . .62 C8
Stand La M26,M45 . . . . .44 C1
Stand Rise M26 . . . . .62 B8
Standedge Foot Rd OL3 . . . .51 D8
Standedge Rd OL3 . . . . .51 C5
Standedge St M11 . . . . .83 D2
Standedge Wlk SK15 . . . . . .86 E6
Standell Wlk M9 . . . . .64 E1
Standfield Ctr 8 M28 . . . . . .78 A6
Standfield Dr M28 . . . . .78 A7
Standish Ave WN5 . . . . .71 E5
Standish Com High Sch
WN6 . . . . .19 C2
Standish Gallery 13
WN1 . . . . .150 C8
Standish Ho SK14 . . . . .167 E2
Standish Rd M14 . . . . .110 D8
Standish St M29 . . . . .77 D3
Standish St Wilfred's CE Prim
Sch WN6 . . . . .19 F1
Standish Wlk M34 . . . . .100 E1
Standish Wood La WN6 . . . .36 E5
Standishgate WN1 . . . . .150 C8
Standmoor Ct M45 . . . . .62 D7
Standmoor Rd M45 . . . . .62 D7
Standon Wlk M40 . . . . .65 D2
Standrick Hill Rise SK15 . . .86 E5
Standring Ave BL8 . . . . .44 A8
Stanedge Cl BL0 . . . . .11 C4
Stanedge Gr WN3 . . . . .55 B2
Stanedge Rd M26 . . . . .61 C7
Stanford Hall Cres BL0 . . . . .11 B4
Stanhope Ave
Denton M34 . . . . .100 E5
Prestwich M25 . . . . .63 A5
Stanhope Cl Denton M34 . . .100 E5
Wilmslow SK9 . . . . .137 D8
Stanhope Rd
Altrincham WA14 . . . . .119 A2
Salford M6 . . . . .80 E5
Stanhope St
Ashton-u-L OL6 . . . . .85 D4

Stanhope St *continued*
Denton M34 ... 100 E5
Leigh WN7 ... 75 D6
Manchester M19 ... 99 B1
Mossley OL5 ... 86 C8
Reddish SK5 ... 111 E7
Rochdale OL11 ... 139 F5
Stanhope Way M35 ... 83 E8
Stanhorne Ave M8 ... 64 A2
Stanier Ave M30 ... 79 D3
Stanier Pl BL6 ... 22 C2
Stanier St M9 ... 157 E8
Stanion Gr SK16 ... 101 D8
Stanlaw M30 ... 79 E1
Stanley Ave
Hazel Grove SK7 ... 124 D3
Hyde SK14 ... 167 E4
Manchester M14 ... 98 D3
Marple SK6 ... 125 D7
Stanley Ave N M25 ... 63 A6
Stanley Ave S M25 ... 63 A6
Stanley Cl
Manchester M16 ... 161 C5
Westhoughton BL5 ... 57 F7
Whitefield M45 ... 44 F1
Stanley Ct M16 ... 161 C5
Stanley Dr
Altrincham WA15 ... 120 A5
Gatley SK8,SK9 ... 131 D6
Leigh WN7 ... 75 D8
Whitefield M45 ... 62 F6
Stanley Gr Horwich BL6 ... 22 D1
Manchester M21 ... 109 A8
Manchester,Belle Vue M12, M18 ... 99 B4
Manchester,Heaton Moor SK4 ... 168 B4
Urmston M41 ... 95 D2
Stanley Green Ind Est SK8 ... 131 E5
Stanley Green Ret Pk SK8 ... 131 F6
Stanley Grove Com Prim Sch M12 ... 99 A4
Stanley Hall La SK12 ... 135 C6
Stanley Ho M16 ... 97 E2
Stanley La WN2 ... 38 C7
Stanley Mews BL2 ... 42 D7
Stanley Mount M33 ... 108 A3
Stanley Park Wlk BL2 ... 148 C8
Stanley Pl Rochdale OL12 ... 139 E8
Wigan WN1 ... 151 E8
Stanley Rd Aspull WN2 ... 38 C6
Bolton BL1 ... 142 B1
Eccles M30 ... 95 C8
Farnworth BL4 ... 59 E8
Handforth SK8,SK9 ... 131 E6
Manchester SK4 ... 168 B3
Manchester,Old Trafford M16 ... 161 C5
Manchester,Whalley Range M16 ... 97 E2
Oldham OL9 ... 66 B4
Pendlebury M27 ... 80 A8
Platt Bridge WN2 ... 56 A3
Radcliffe M26 ... 43 E6
Reddish M34 ... 100 B3
Salford M7 ... 155 E8
Up Holland WN8 ... 53 B7
Walkden M28 ... 60 D2
Whitefield M45 ... 44 F1
Stanley Road Prim Sch OL9 ... 66 B4
Stanley Sq SK15 ... 85 F1
Stanley St Atherton M46 ... 58 C3
Chadderton OL9 ... 152 B8
Heywood OL10 ... 29 D2
Manchester M11 ... 99 E7
Manchester M40 ... 157 F5
Manchester M8 ... 159 A4
Newton-le-W WA12 ... 89 A3
Oldham OL4 ... 68 A6
Oldham,Nether Lees OL4 ... 67 E5
Prestwich M25 ... 63 C4
Ramsbottom BL0 ... 138 B5
Rochdale OL12 ... 139 E8
Salford M3 ... 158 E1
3 Stalybridge SK15 ... 85 F1
Stockport SK1 ... 112 A2
Tyldesley M29 ... 59 A1
Whitefield M45 ... 44 F1
Wigan WN5 ... 54 F6
Stanley St S BL3 ... 145 E6
Stanmoor Dr WN2 ... 38 D6
Stanmore Ave M32 ... 96 B2
Stanmore Dr BL3 ... 144 C5
Stannard Rd M30 ... 79 A1
Stanney Cl OL16 ... 31 E5
Stanney Rd OL16 ... 31 B8
Stanneybrook Cl OL16 ... 31 B8
Stanneylands Cl SK9 ... 131 C2
Stanneylands Dr SK9 ... 131 B2
Stanneylands Rd SK9 ... 131 B2
Stannybrook Rd M35,OL8 .84 D6
Stanrose Cl BL7 ... 8 E1
Stansbury Pl SK2 ... 124 E6
Stansby Gdns M12 ... 164 E6
Stansfield Cl WN7 ... 76 C2
Stansfield Dr OL11 ... 13 F1
Stansfield Hall OL15 ... 6 C1
Stansfield Hall CE/Free Church Prim Sch OL15 ... 16 D8
Stansfield Rd Bolton BL2 ... 148 B8
Failsworth M35 ... 84 A8
Hyde SK14 ... 167 E4
Rawtenstall BB4 ... 2 E8
Stansfield Road Jun & Inf Schs M35 ... 84 A8
Stansfield St
2 Bacup OL13 ... 3 C8
Chadderton OL9 ... 152 B5
Droylsden M11 ... 99 D8
Failsworth M40 ... 83 D4
Oldham OL1 ... 153 E8
Stanstead Cl WN2 ... 37 F2
Stansted Wlk M23 ... 108 D1
Stanthorne Ave M20 ... 110 A7
Stanton Ave
Manchester M20 ... 109 E4
Salford M7 ... 81 B7
Stanton Cl WN3 ... 55 B3
Stanton Ct M32 ... 96 D4
Stanton Gdns
Manchester M20 ... 109 E4
Stockport SK4 ... 168 B1
Stanton St Droylsden M11 .. 83 C2
Oldham OL9 ... 66 B3
Stretford M32 ... 96 D4
Stanway Ave 8 BL3 ... 145 D6
Stanway Cl
6 Bolton BL3 ... 145 D6
Middleton M24 ... 65 B6
Stanway Dr WA15 ... 119 F3
Stanway Rd M45 ... 63 B8
Stanway St
Manchester M9 ... 157 E8
Stretford M32 ... 96 D4
Stanwell Rd
Failsworth M40 ... 65 C1
Swinton M27 ... 79 F7
Stanwick Ave M9 ... 64 A4
Stanworth Ave BL2 ... 42 E6
Stanworth Cl 6 M16 ... 97 E3
Stanyard Ct M5 ... 161 A8
Stanycliffe La M24 ... 47 B3
Stanyforth St SK13 ... 104 A4
Stapelton Ave BL1 ... 23 E1
Stapleford Cl
Over Hulton BL5 ... 59 A6
Sale M33 ... 108 E5
Wythenshawe M23 ... 120 F4
Stapleford Gr BL8 ... 27 A2
Stapleford Wlk M34 ... 100 E1
Staplehurst Cl WN7 ... 57 C2
Staplehurst Rd M40 ... 83 A4
Staplers Wlk 9 M14 ... 98 C3
Stapleton Ave BL1 ... 40 E8
Stapleton Rd M6 ... 80 C5
Stapleton St WN2 ... 56 A2
Star Bank OL13 ... 3 D7
Star Gr M7 ... 155 E6
Star Ind Est OL8 ... 153 F5
Star La BL6 ... 21 F3
Starbeck Cl BL8 ... 26 F2
Starcliffe St BL3,BL4 ... 42 D2
Starcross Wlk M40 ... 83 B6
Starfield Ave OL15 ... 15 F2
Starkey St OL10 ... 29 D3
Starkie Rd BL2 ... 25 B1
Starkie St M28 ... 79 A8
Starkies BL9 ... 44 E7
Starling Cl Droylsden M43 .84 D3
Wythenshawe M22 ... 121 E5
Starling Dr BL4 ... 59 F7
Starling Rd M26 ... 43 E8
Starmoor Dr M8 ... 156 A6
Starmount Cl BL2 ... 43 B6
Starring La OL15 ... 15 E5
Starring Rd OL15 ... 15 F5
Starring Way OL15 ... 15 F5
Startham Ave WN5 ... 71 D3
Starting Chair OL4 ... 68 C8
Stash Gr M23 ... 121 B7
Statford Ave M30 ... 95 C8
Statham Cl M34 ... 101 A3
Statham Fold SK14 ... 102 A4
Statham St M6 ... 81 B2
Statham Wlk 2 M13 ... 163 B7
Station App
Manchester M1 ... 163 A8
Manchester M1 ... 163 B8
Manchester,East Didsbury M20 ... 110 C1
Station Approach Bsns Ctr OL11 ... 139 F6
Station Ave Leigh WN2 ... 56 D1
Orrell WN5 ... 53 D5
Station Bridge M41 ... 95 D2
Station Cl 1 SK14 ... 167 D2
Station Cotts SK8 ... 123 B2
Station La OL4 ... 68 B5
Station Lofts OL7 ... 166 B2
Station Mews WN4 ... 72 D3
Station Rd Adlington PR7 ... 21 A6
Blackrod BL6 ... 21 E1
Chapeltown BL7 ... 9 C4
Cheadle SK8 ... 123 B1
Diggle OL3 ... 51 D5
Eccles M30 ... 79 D1
Garswood WN4 ... 72 C3
Hadfield SK13 ... 104 A5
Handforth SK9 ... 131 A4
Handforth SK9 ... 131 D3
Haslingden BB4 ... 1 A7
Hyde SK14 ... 102 B2
Irlam M44 ... 105 E7
Kearsley BL4 ... 61 A7
15 Littleborough OL15 ... 16 B5
Manchester SK4 ... 110 E1
Manchester,Crumpsall M8 ... 64 A1
Marple SK6 ... 125 F6
Marple,Strines SK6,SK22 .. 126 D1
Milnrow OL16 ... 31 F5
Mossley OL5 ... 68 D1
Oldham OL4 ... 68 A5
Partington WA14 ... 118 B5
Station Rd *continued*
Ramsbottom BL8 ... 10 F1
Reddish SK5 ... 99 E2
Rochdale OL11 ... 139 F6
Romiley SK6 ... 113 B5
Stockport SK1 ... 169 E1
Stretford M32 ... 96 D3
Swinton M27 ... 61 F1
Uppermill OL3 ... 69 B8
Urmston M41 ... 95 D2
Whitworth OL12 ... 4 D3
Whitworth,Broadley OL12 ... 14 C5
Wigan WN1 ... 150 C8
Wilmslow SK9 ... 137 B7
Station St Bolton BL3 ... 145 F6
Dukinfield SK16 ... 166 B1
Glossop SK13 ... 104 D1
Hazel Grove SK7 ... 124 D2
Oldham OL4 ... 67 F6
Station View 11 M19 ... 99 A1
Stationers Entry 4 OL16 ... 139 F7
Staton Ave BL2 ... 148 C8
Staton St M11 ... 165 C8
Statter St BL9 ... 45 A4
Staveleigh Mall OL6 ... 166 B3
Staveley Ave Bolton BL1 ... 24 E6
Stalybridge SK15 ... 86 A3
Staveley Cl Middleton M24 .46 E2
Shaw OL2 ... 49 D6
Stavely Wlk 8 OL2 ... 48 E4
Staverton Cl M13 ... 163 C7
Stavesacre WN7 ... 75 F3
Staveton Cl SK7 ... 124 A3
Stavordale 11 OL12 ... 139 E8
Staycott St M16 ... 97 F4
Stayley Dr SK15 ... 86 C2
Stayley Rd OL5 ... 86 D8
Stead St BL0 ... 138 C6
Steadway OL3 ... 69 C5
Stedman Cl M11 ... 160 E1
Steele Gdns BL2 ... 42 E5
Steeles Ave SK14 ... 167 E3
Steeple Cl M8 ... 155 F5
Steeple Dr M5 ... 161 A8
Steeple View OL2 ... 48 D4
Stein Ave WA3 ... 90 E8
Stelfox Ave
Manchester M14 ... 98 A1
Sale WA15 ... 120 C7
Stelfox La M34 ... 100 E7
Stelfox St M30 ... 95 B8
Stella Maris RC Jun Sch SK4 ... 110 E2
Stella St M9 ... 64 B4
Stelling St M18 ... 99 D5
Stenbury Cl M14 ... 98 C3
Stenner La M20 ... 110 B1
Stenson Sq 1 M11 ... 99 D7
Stephen Cl 7 BL8 ... 27 C2
Stephen Lawry Wlk 1 M40 ... 83 A7
Stephen St Bury BL8 ... 27 C2
Manchester M3 ... 158 F4
Platt Bridge WN2 ... 56 A2
Stockport SK1 ... 124 B8
Urmston M41 ... 95 E2
Stephen St S BL8 ... 27 C1
Stephen Wlk SK1 ... 124 B8
Stephen's Way WN3 ... 54 E5
Stephens Rd
Manchester M20 ... 110 D6
Stalybridge SK15 ... 85 F4
Stephens St BL2 ... 42 D8
Stephens Terr 6 M20 ... 110 B3
Stephenson Ave M43 ... 84 A1
Stephenson Rd
Newton-le-W WA12 ... 89 D2
Stretford M32 ... 96 E2
Stephenson Sq OL12 ... 15 C3
Stephenson St
Abram WN2 ... 74 B8
Failsworth M35 ... 66 A1
Horwich BL6 ... 22 B2
4 Oldham OL4 ... 67 D8
Stepping Hill Hospl SK2 ... 124 C4
Steps Mdw OL12 ... 15 D4
Steptoe Dr OL1 ... 48 D1
Sterling 6 M30 ... 79 E2
Sterling Pl OL10 ... 28 F1
Stern Ave M5 ... 161 A8
Sterndale Ave WN6 ... 19 E2
Sterndale Rd
Boothstown M28 ... 77 F6
Romiley SK6 ... 113 B1
Stockport SK3 ... 170 E5
Sterratt St BL1 ... 145 D6
Stetchworth Dr M28 ... 78 B7
Steven Ct M21 ... 109 C8
Stevens St SK9 ... 137 A1
Stevenson Cl WN3 ... 150 B5
Stevenson Ct BL4 ... 60 E7
Stevenson Dr OL1 ... 49 E4
Stevenson Pl M1 ... 159 B1
Stevenson Rd M27 ... 61 E1
Stevenson Sq M1 ... 159 B1
Stevenson St Salford M3 .158 D1
Walkden M28 ... 60 B3
Stewart Ave BL4 ... 60 B7
Stewart Rd WN3 ... 55 A3
Stewart St Ashton-u-L OL7 .84 F2
Bolton BL1 ... 143 E2
Bury BL8 ... 27 B3
Bury BL8 ... 27 C4
Newhey OL16 ... 32 B3
Stewerton Cl WA3 ... 73 F2
Steynton Cl BL1 ... 40 F8
Stile Cl M41 ... 94 C2
Stiles Ave SK6 ... 125 F7
Stiles Cl SK13 ... 103 E5
Stilton Dr M11 ... 165 A8
Stirling Ave
Hazel Grove SK7 ... 124 D1
Ince-in-M WN2 ... 56 A8
Manchester M20 ... 109 F8
6 Marple SK6 ... 125 F5
Stirling Cl Leigh WN7 ... 76 D6
Stockport SK3 ... 123 C6
Stirling Dr Garswood WN4 .72 D4
Stalybridge SK15 ... 86 A3
Stirling Gr M45 ... 63 A8
Stirling Rd Bolton BL1 ... 24 E5
Hindley WN2 ... 56 F4
Oldham OL9 ... 65 F4
Stirling St Oldham OL9 ... 152 C7
Wigan WN1 ... 37 C2
Stirrup Brook Gr M28 ... 77 F5
Stitch La SK4 ... 169 D3
Stitch-Mi-Lane BL2 ... 25 F2
Stiups La OL16 ... 31 B4
Stobart Ave M25 ... 63 C2
Stock Cl OL12 ... 14 E2
Stock Gr OL16 ... 31 F7
Stock La OL9 ... 152 B6
Stock St BL8 ... 27 E5
Stockburn Dr M35 ... 84 C7
Stockbury Cl 6 BL1 ... 143 F1
Stockdale Ave SK3 ... 170 F5
Stockdale Gr BL2 ... 25 F2
Stockdale Rd M9 ... 64 E4
Stockfield Mount OL9 ... 152 B6
Stockfield Rd OL9 ... 152 B7
Stockholm Rd SK3 ... 170 E6
Stockholm St M11 ... 83 B2
Stockland Cl M13 ... 163 B7
Stockley Ave BL2 ... 25 E2
Stockley Dr WN6 ... 35 E8
Stockley Wlk 20 M15 ... 162 D6
Stockmar Grange BL1 ... 40 E8
Stockport Air Raid Shelters Mus* SK1 ... 169 E1
Stockport Coll of F & H Ed SK1 ... 170 F8
Stockport Gram Sch SK2 ... 124 A5
Stockport Hat Mus* SK4 ... 169 E1
Stockport Mus* SK1 .. 112 B2
Stockport Rd
Altrincham WA15 ... 119 F5
Altrincham,Timperley WA15 ... 120 B6
Ashton-u-L OL7 ... 100 F8
Cheadle SK8 ... 122 E6
Denton M34 ... 100 F2
Hattersley SK14 ... 102 E2
Hyde SK14 ... 113 D7
Manchester M12,M13, M19 ... 164 D5
Marple SK6 ... 125 E6
Mossley OL5 ... 68 C2
Romiley SK6 ... 113 B2
Uppermill OL4 ... 68 C5
Stockport Rd E SK6 ... 112 F4
Stockport Rd W SK6 ... 112 D3
Stockport Sch SK2 ... 124 B5
Stockport Sta SK3 ... 170 E8
Stockport Trad Est
Stockport SK3 ... 168 B1
Stockport SK4 ... 123 B8
Stocks Brow SK13 ... 104 A7
Stocks Gdns SK15 ... 86 C1
Stocks Ind Est M30 ... 79 C2
Stocks La SK15 ... 86 C1
Stocks Park Dr BL6 ... 22 C3
Stocks St
Manchester M4,M8 ... 159 A4
Rochdale OL11 ... 30 B2
Stocks St E M4,M8 ... 159 A4
Stocks The SK13 ... 104 A7
Stocksfield Dr
3 Manchester M9 ... 64 E3
Walkden M38 ... 59 F5
Stocksgate OL12 ... 14 B2
Stockton Ave 4 SK3 ... 123 B8
Stockton Dr BL8 ... 27 B5
Stockton Pk OL4 ... 67 D6
Stockton Rd
Manchester M21 ... 109 A8
Wilmslow SK9 ... 136 F4
Stockton St
Farnworth BL4 ... 42 C2
Littleborough OL15 ... 16 A5
4 Manchester M16 ... 97 E4
3 Swinton M27 ... 79 E7
Stockwell Cl WN3 ... 54 D3
Stockwood Wlk M9 ... 157 D7
Stoke Abbott Cl SK7 ... 132 E7
Stokes St M11 ... 83 D1
Stokesay Cl Bury BL9 ... 44 F5
Royton OL2 ... 49 A4
Stokesay Dr SK7 ... 124 C1
Stokesay Rd M33 ... 107 E5
Stokesby Gdns BL6 ... 40 B8
Stokesley Wlk BL3 ... 147 E3
Stokoe Ave WA14 ... 119 A6
Stonall Ave M15 ... 162 D7
Stone Breaks Rd OL4 ... 68 B7
Stone Cl BL0 ... 11 A4
Stone Cross La N WA3 ... 90 C7
Stone Cross La S WA3 ... 90 C6
Stone Cross Pk WA3 ... 90 B7
Stone Gdns WN7 ... 76 A5
Stone Hall La WN8 ... 35 A5
Stone Haven WN3 ... 54 D2
Stone Hill La OL12 ... 14 A2
Stone Hill Rd BL4 ... 60 D6
Stone House Rd WN5 ... 36 D2
Stone Mead SK6 ... 113 E3
Stone Mead Ave WA15 .. 129 C7
Stone Meadow Cvn Pk M31 ... 106 E7
Stone Pale M45 ... 62 F7
Stone Pit Cl WA3 ... 74 F1
Stone Pit La WA3 ... 90 F2
Stone Pits BL0 ... 1 E3
Stone Pl M14 ... 98 C3
Stone Row Marple SK6 ... 126 A6
Wigan WN2 ... 38 A3
Stone St Bolton BL2 ... 25 B1
Manchester M3 ... 162 E8
Milnrow OL16 ... 31 F5
Rawtenstall BB4 ... 2 F8
Stoneacre BL6 ... 39 F8
Stoneacre Ct M27 ... 79 F7
Stoneacre Rd M22 ... 121 C2
Stonebeck Ct BL5 ... 58 F8
Stonebeck Rd M23 ... 120 F5
Stonebridge Cl BL6 ... 40 C6
Stonechat Cl
Droylsden M43 ... 84 C3
10 Golborne WA3 ... 90 E8
Walkden M28 ... 78 B8
Stonechurch BL3 ... 145 D5
Stonecliffe Ave SK15 ... 86 A2
Stonecliffe Terr SK15 ... 86 A3
Stoneclough Rd BL4,M26 .61 A7
Stonecroft 2 OL1 ... 153 E7
Stonecroft Ct M20 ... 110 A4
Stonecrop WN6 ... 18 D2
Stonedelph Cl BL2 ... 26 D1
Stonefield M29 ... 59 C1
Stonefield Dr M8 ... 155 E5
Stonefield St 1 OL16 ... 31 F5
Stoneflat Ct OL12 ... 139 D8
Stonehaven BL3 ... 40 F3
Stonehead St M9 ... 157 F7
Stonehewer St M26 ... 44 B2
Stonehill Cres OL12 ... 14 A3
Stonehill Dr OL12 ... 14 B3
Stonehill Rd OL12 ... 14 B3
Stonehouse BL7 ... 25 B7
Stonehouse Wlk 3 M23 ... 120 E7
Stonehurst Cl M12 ... 165 A6
Stonelands Way OL4 ... 68 A4
Stoneleigh Ave M33 ... 107 E5
Stoneleigh Dr M26 ... 61 B7
Stoneleigh Mews SK4 ... 111 C5
Stoneleigh Prim Sch OL1 .49 B2
Stoneleigh Rd OL4 ... 68 A7
Stoneleigh St OL1 ... 67 B8
Stonelow Cl M15 ... 162 F6
Stonely Dr OL14 ... 6 A7
Stonemead Cl BL3 ... 147 F4
Stonemill Terr SK5 ... 169 F3
Stonepail Cl SK8 ... 121 F5
Stonepail Rd SK8 ... 122 A5
Stoner Rd PR7 ... 20 F7
Stoneridge SK13 ... 103 F5
Stones Bank Rd BL7 ... 8 B5
Stonesby Cl M16 ... 97 D4
Stonesdale Cl OL2 ... 48 E5
Stonesteads Dr BL7 ... 25 A8
Stonesteads Way BL7 ... 25 A8
Stoneswood Dr OL5 ... 68 D2
Stoneswood Rd OL3 ... 50 F4
Stonethwaite Cl WN3 ... 55 A2
Stoney Bank M26 ... 61 C7
Stoney Brow WN8 ... 35 B1
Stoney Knoll M7 ... 155 D6
Stoney La Adlington PR7 ... 20 E4
Delph OL3 ... 50 D7
Wilmslow SK9 ... 136 F5
Stoneycroft Ave BL6 ... 22 D4
Stoneycroft Cl BL6 ... 22 D5
Stoneyfield SK15 ... 86 A4
Stoneyfield Cl M16 ... 97 F2
Stoneygate La WN6 ... 18 B2
Stoneygate Wlk M11 ... 99 D7
Stoneyhurst Cres WA3 ... 91 D5
Stoneyroyd OL12 ... 4 D1
Stoneyside Ave M28 ... 60 E4
Stoneyside Gr M28 ... 60 E4
Stoneyvale Ct OL11 ... 30 F4
Stonie Heyes Ave OL12 ... 15 B2
Stonyford Rd M33 ... 108 D4
Stonyhurst Ave Bolton BL1 .24 F5
Ince-in-M WN3 ... 151 D6
Stopes Rd BL3,M26 ... 43 C3
Stopford Ave OL15 ... 15 E4
Stopford St Droylsden M11 .99 F7
Ince-in-M WN2 ... 151 F7
Stockport SK3 ... 170 D8
Stopford Wlk M34 ... 100 F3
Stopforth St WN6 ... 37 A1
Stopley Wlk M11 ... 165 A8
Store St Ashton-u-L OL7 ... 85 A6
Horwich BL6 ... 22 C4
Manchester M1,M4 ... 159 C1
Manchester M11 ... 165 B7
Radcliffe M26 ... 44 D4
Rochdale OL11 ... 13 E1
Shaw OL2 ... 149 C8
Stockport SK2 ... 124 C4
Stores St M25 ... 63 C4
Storeton Cl M22 ... 121 E2
Stortford Dr M23 ... 109 B2
Storth Bank SK13 ... 115 F7

Storth Meadow Rd
SK13 . . . . .115 F7
Stothard Rd M32 . . . . .96 C1
Stott Dr M41 . . . . .94 D1
Stott Ho OL8 . . . . .153 E5
Stott La Bolton BL2 . . . . . .25 B1
Middleton M24,OL10 . . . . .46 F5
Salford M6,M5 . . . . .80 B2
Stott Milne St OL9 . . . . . .152 B5
Swinton M27 . . . . .79 D6
Stott St Failsworth M35 . . .83 D6
Milnrow OL16 . . . . .31 F4
Rochdale OL12 . . . . .14 F1
7 Rochdale,Hurstead
OL16 . . . . .15 D4
Stott's La M35 . . . . .83 D6
Stottfield OL2 . . . . .48 B3
Stour Cl WA14 . . . . .119 C6
Stour Rd M29 . . . . .77 B7
Stourbridge Ave M38 . . . .60 A6
Stourport Cl SK6 . . . . . . .113 A1
Stourport St OL1 . . . . .67 A8
Stout St WN7 . . . . .75 C4
Stovell Ave M12 . . . . .99 A2
Stovell Rd M40 . . . . .83 A8
Stow Cl BL8 . . . . .27 D5
Stow Gdns M20 . . . . .110 A6
Stowell Ct BL1 . . . . .143 E1
Stowell Ho 7 M5 . . . . . . .154 E1
Stowell St Bolton BL1 . . . .143 E1
Salford M5 . . . . .154 E1
Stowell Tech Ctr
Salford M5 . . . . .161 A8
Stretford M50 . . . . .96 F8
Stowfield Cl M9 . . . . .64 B4
Stracey St M40 . . . . .160 E3
Stradbroke Cl
Golborne WA3 . . . . .91 A7
Manchester M18 . . . . . . .165 C5
Strain Ave M9 . . . . .64 D4
Straits The M29 . . . . .77 C6
Strand Ave WN4 . . . . .73 B4
Strand Ct M32 . . . . .108 C8
Strand The
Ashton-in-M WN4 . . . . . . .73 B4
Horwich BL6 . . . . .22 D3
Rochdale OL11 . . . . .30 F2
Strand Way OL1,OL2 . . . . .48 D2
Strang St BL0 . . . . .138 C6
Strange Rd WN4 . . . . .72 D3
Strange St WN7 . . . . .75 B4
Strangford St M26 . . . . . . .43 D4
Stranraer Rd WN5 . . . . . . .36 D1
Stranton Dr M28 . . . . .79 C8
Stratfield Ave M23 . . . . . .108 D1
Stratford Ave Bolton BL1 . .42 A4
Bury BL9 . . . . .27 E8
Manchester M20 . . . . . . .109 F5
Oldham OL8 . . . . .66 F3
Rochdale OL11 . . . . .139 E5
Stratford Cl BL4 . . . . .147 F1
Stratford Gdns SK6 . . . . .112 F3
Stratford Rd M24 . . . . .65 B5
Stratford Sq SK8 . . . . . . .131 C7
Stratford St WN6 . . . . .37 A1
Strathaven Pl OL10 . . . . . .28 F1
Strathblane Cl 3 M20 . . .110 B7
Strathfield Dr 8 M11 . . . .83 C2
Strathmere Ave M32 . . . . .96 D3
Strathmore Ave
Ashton-in-M WN4 . . . . . . .73 A5
Denton M34 . . . . .101 B2
4 Manchester M16 . . . . .97 B2
Strathmore Cl BL0 . . . . . . .11 C4
Strathmore Rd BL2 . . . . . .25 E1
Stratton Dr WN2 . . . . .55 F1
Stratton Gr BL6 . . . . .22 B5
Stratton Rd
Manchester M16 . . . . .97 B2
Stockport SK2 . . . . .124 C8
Swinton M27 . . . . .61 F1
Strawberry Bank M6 . . . . .81 B3
Strawberry Cl WA14 . . . . .119 B7
Strawberry Hill M6 . . . . . .81 B3
Strawberry Hill Rd BL2 . .148 B5
Strawberry La
Uppermill OL5 . . . . .68 C4
Wilmslow SK9 . . . . .136 E6
Strawberry Rd M6 . . . . . . .81 B3
Stray St M11 . . . . .99 E8
Stray The BL1 . . . . .25 B4
Stream Terr SK1 . . . . .112 B1
Streamside Cl WA15 . . . . .120 B4
Street Bridge Rd OL1,OL2 .48 A2
Street La M26 . . . . .43 F8
Street Lo OL11 . . . . .30 B1
Streetgate M38 . . . . .59 F5
Streethouse La OL3 . . . . . .50 F1
Stretford Gram Sch M32 . .96 E1
Stretford High Sch M32 . . .96 F4
Stretford Ho 7 M32 . . . . . .96 C1
Stretford Meml Hospl
M16 . . . . .97 B3
Stretford Motorway Est
M32 . . . . .96 A5
Stretford Rd
Manchester M15,M16 . . . .162 E6
Urmston M41 . . . . .95 D1
Stretford Sta M32 . . . . . . .96 D1
Stretton Ave Billinge WN5 . .71 E5
Golborne WA3 . . . . .90 F7
Manchester M20 . . . . . . .110 C3
Sale M33 . . . . .107 E4
Stretford M32 . . . . .96 A3

Stretton Cl
Manchester M40 . . . . . . .157 D5
Standish WN6 . . . . .36 E8
Stretton Rd Bolton BL3 . . .146 B4
Ramsbottom BL0 . . . . .11 A2
Stretton Way 8 SK9 . . . .131 D5
Striding Edge Wlk 1
OL1 . . . . .49 A1
Strines Cl WN2 . . . . .56 D6
Strines Ct SK14 . . . . .167 E4
Strines Rd Marple SK6 . . .126 B3
New Mills SK6 . . . . .135 D8
Strines St OL14 . . . . .6 A7
Strines Sta SK22 . . . . . . .126 D1
Stringer Ave OL15 . . . . . .102 F2
Stringer Cl SK14 . . . . . . .102 F2
Stringer St Leigh WN7 . . . .75 F5
Stockport SK1 . . . . .112 A2
Stringer Way SK14 . . . . .102 F2
Stroma Gdns M41 . . . . . . .95 C5
Stromness Gr OL10 . . . . . .28 F1
Strong St M7 . . . . .158 E4
Strongstry Rd BL0 . . . . . . .1 C2
Strontian Wlk 9 M11 . . . .83 C1
Stroud Ave M30 . . . . .79 B3
Stroud Cl Middleton M24 . . .65 A5
Wigan M40 . . . . .37 F2
Stuart Ave Bacup OL13 . . . .3 D8
Hindley WN2 . . . . .57 C3
Irlam M44 . . . . .93 F2
Stuart Cres WN5 . . . . .71 E5
Stuart Dr SK6 . . . . .125 C7
Stuart Ho M43 . . . . .100 A8
Stuart Rd
Altrincham WA14 . . . . . . .119 B7
Bloxton SK6 . . . . .112 D6
Stretford M32 . . . . .96 D3
Stuart St Droylsden M11 . . .83 A2
Middleton M24 . . . . .65 C8
Oldham OL8 . . . . .153 E5
Rochdale OL16 . . . . .31 A6
Rochdale OL16 . . . . .31 B6
Stuart St E M11 . . . . .83 A2
Stuart Wlk M24 . . . . .64 F7
Stubbins Cl M23 . . . . .108 E1
Stubbins La BL0 . . . . .138 C8
Stubbins Prim Sch BL0 . . . .1 D1
Stubbins St BL0 . . . . .1 C1
Stubbins Vale Rd BL0 . . . . .1 C1
Stubbins Vale Terr BL0 . . . .1 B1
Stubbs Cl M7 . . . . .81 B8
Stubbylee La OL13 . . . . . . .3 F8
Stubley Gdns 8 OL15 . . . .16 A5
Stubley La OL15 . . . . .15 F4
Stubley Mill Rd
Littleborough OL15 . . . . . .16 A5
Littleborough,Dearnley
OL15 . . . . .15 F4
Studforth Wlk 3 M15 . . . .163 A5
Studland Rd M22 . . . . . . .121 F3
Studley Cl OL2 . . . . .49 A4
Studley Ct M29 . . . . .58 F1
Sturton Ave WN3 . . . . .54 E3
Styal Ave Reddish SK5 . . .111 F6
Stretford M32 . . . . .96 A3
Styal Cross SK9 . . . . .130 E4
Styal Ctry Pk* SK9 . . . . .130 E3
Styal Gn SK9 . . . . .130 F3
Styal Gr SK8 . . . . .122 A3
Styal Ho M22 . . . . .121 F7
Styal Prim Sch SK9 . . . . .130 E4
Styal Rd
Gatley M22,SK8,SK9 . . . . .122 A3
Wilmslow SK9 . . . . .137 B8
Wythenshawe M22 . . . . .130 F7
Styal St BL1 . . . . .144 B8
Styal Sta SK9 . . . . .131 A4
Styal View SK9 . . . . .131 B2
Styhead Dr M24 . . . . .46 D3
Style St M4 . . . . .159 A3
Styperson Way SK12 . . . .133 B1
Sudbrook Cl WA3 . . . . . . .90 E8
Sudbury Cl
Manchester M16 . . . . . . .161 C5
Wigan WN3 . . . . .55 B2
Sudbury Dr Bolton BL6 . . . .40 C6
Gatley SK8 . . . . .131 C8
Sudbury Rd SK7 . . . . .133 E8
Sudden St OL11 . . . . .30 C4
Sudell St M4,M40 . . . . . . .159 B3
Sudell Street Ind Est
M4 . . . . .159 B3
Sudley Rd OL11 . . . . .139 D5
Sudlow St OL16 . . . . .31 A8
Sudren St BL8 . . . . .26 F3
Sue Patterson Wlk M40 . .156 C5
Suez St WA12 . . . . .89 B3
Suffield St M24 . . . . .65 A8
Suffield Wlk 1 M22 . . . . .121 D1
Suffolk Ave M43 . . . . .84 A3
Suffolk Cl Little Lever BL4 . .43 B5
Standish WN1 . . . . .37 B8
Suffolk Dr
Brinnington SK5 . . . . .112 C6
Handforth SK9 . . . . .131 C1
Suffolk Gr WN7 . . . . .75 C5
Suffolk St Oldham OL9 . . . .66 B4
Rochdale OL11 . . . . .139 F6
Salford M6 . . . . .81 A5
Sugar La OL3 . . . . .51 A2
Sugden Sports Ctr M1 . . .163 A7
Sugden St OL6 . . . . .85 D3
Sulby Ave M41 . . . . .95 C2
Sulby St Kearsley M26 . . . .61 B7
Manchester M40 . . . . .83 A8
Sulgrave Ave SK12 . . . . .133 F4
Sullivan St M12 . . . . .99 A3

Sullivan Way WN1 . . . . . . .37 D1
Sultan St BL9 . . . . .44 F8
Sulway Cl M27 . . . . .80 A7
Sumac St M11 . . . . .83 D2
Sumbland Ho M27 . . . . . . .62 B2
Summer Ave M41 . . . . .95 E2
Summer Castle OL16 . . . . .31 A7
Summer Pl 7 M14 . . . . . . .98 C2
Summer St Horwich BL6 . . .22 B4
Rochdale OL16 . . . . .31 A7
Summerbottom SK14 . . . .115 A8
Summercroft OL9 . . . . .66 B4
Summerdale Dr BL0 . . . . . .11 B2
Summerfield Ave M43 . . . . .83 E3
Summerfield Ct 2 M21 . . .96 F1
Summerfield Dr
Middleton M24 . . . . .47 C1
Tyldesley M29 . . . . .77 B8
Summerfield Pl SK9 . . . . .137 A5
Summerfield Rd
Bolton BL3 . . . . .42 B4
Worsley M28 . . . . .79 A8
Wythenshawe M22 . . . . .121 C2
Summerfield View OL8 . . . .67 C3
Summerfields PR7 . . . . . . .19 F7
Summerfields Ctr 11
SK9 . . . . .131 D1
Summerlea SK8 . . . . .132 B8
Summers Ave SK15 . . . . . .86 C2
Summers St OL9 . . . . . . .152 C7
Summersales Ind Est
WN3 . . . . .54 C4
Summerseat Cl
Oldham OL4 . . . . .68 A7
Salford M5 . . . . .161 A8
Summerseat La BL0 . . . . . .11 A2
Summerseat Meth Prim Sch
BL9 . . . . .11 D2
Summerseat Sta BL9 . . . . .11 C2
Summersgill Cl OL10 . . . . .29 E1
Summershades La OL4 . . . .68 D6
Summershades Rise OL4 . .68 D6
Summerton Ho 3 M5 . . . . .81 A1
Summerville Ave M9 . . . . .157 F7
Summerville Prim Sch
M6 . . . . .80 D5
Summerville Rd M6 . . . . . .80 D5
Summit Cl BL0 . . . . .28 F4
Summit St OL10 . . . . .28 F3
Sumner Ave BL2 . . . . .26 D1
Sumner Rd M6 . . . . .80 D5
Sumner St Aspull WN2 . . . .38 D5
Atherton M46 . . . . .58 C3
Bolton BL3 . . . . .146 B2
Glossop SK13 . . . . .116 C8
Shaw OL2 . . . . .149 B5
Sumner Way M41 . . . . .95 D2
Sumners Pl SK13 . . . . . . .104 B1
Sun Gate OL15 . . . . .15 F1
Sun Inn Mews OL3 . . . . . .33 D7
Sun St Mossley OL5 . . . . . .68 C1
Ramsbottom BL0 . . . . . . .138 B7
Sun Vale Ave OL14 . . . . . . .6 B7
Sunadale Cl BL3 . . . . .144 B5
Sunbank Cl OL12 . . . . .14 D2
Sunbank La WA15 . . . . . . .129 E6
Sunbeam St WA12 . . . . . . .89 C3
Sunbeam Wlk 10 M11 . . .160 F1
Sunbury Cl
Handforth SK9 . . . . .131 E2
Stalybridge SK16 . . . . . . .101 F8
Sunbury Dr M40 . . . . .83 D4
Sundance Ct M50 . . . . .96 E8
Sunderland Ave OL6 . . . . .166 C4
Sunderland Pl M5 . . . . .36 D1
Sundew Pl M24 . . . . .65 D7
Sundial Cl SK14 . . . . .102 D3
Sundial Rd SK2 . . . . .124 D7
Sundial Wlk SK14 . . . . . . .102 D3
Sundridge Cl BL4 . . . . .60 B8
Sunfield SK6 . . . . .113 C3
Sunfield Ave OL4 . . . . .49 E4
Sunfield Cres OL2 . . . . . . .48 E3
Sunfield Dr OL2 . . . . .48 F3
Sunfield Est OL3 . . . . .51 C4
Sunfield La OL3 . . . . .51 C4
Sunfield Rd OL1 . . . . .153 E8
Sunfield Way OL4 . . . . .67 F7
Sunflower Mdw M44 . . . . . .94 B3
Sunhill Cl OL16 . . . . .31 B2
Sunk La M24 . . . . .65 A7
Sunlaws St SK13 . . . . . . .116 B8
Sunleigh Rd WN2 . . . . .56 E6
Sunlight Rd BL1 . . . . .144 C7
Sunning Hill Prim Sch
BL3 . . . . .147 D4
Sunning Hill St 13 BL3 . .147 D4
Sunningdale Ave
Droylsden M11 . . . . .83 B2
Radcliffe M26 . . . . .43 A8
Sale M33 . . . . .108 E3
Whitefield M45 . . . . .62 C7
Sunningdale Cl Bury BL8 . .44 A8
Dukinfield SK14 . . . . .101 F5
Sunningdale Ct
Reddish M34 . . . . .100 B4
Sale M33 . . . . .108 E3
Sunningdale Dr
Bramhall SK7 . . . . .133 A7
Glossop SK13 . . . . .104 E1
Heywood OL10 . . . . .46 D8
Irlam M44 . . . . .93 F3
Prestwich M25 . . . . .63 B5
Salford M6 . . . . .80 B5
Sunningdale Gr WN7 . . . . .76 D7
Sunningdale Rd
Denton M34 . . . . .101 B1
Urmston M41 . . . . .95 B1

Sunningdale Wlk 1
BL3 . . . . .145 D5
Sunninghey Ct SK9 . . . . .136 F2
Sunny Ave BL9 . . . . .27 F5
Sunny Bank Kearsley M26 . .61 A8
Oldham OL4 . . . . .67 C5
Wilmslow SK9 . . . . .136 D4
Sunny Bank,Fulshaw Park
SK9 . . . . .137 B6
Sunny Bank Ave M43 . . . . .83 F1
Sunny Bank Cl BB4 . . . . . . .1 A6
Sunny Bank Prim Sch
BL9 . . . . .45 A3
Sunny Bank Rd
Altrincham WA14 . . . . . . .128 C8
Droylsden M43 . . . . .83 F1
Haslingden BB4 . . . . .1 A6
Manchester M13 . . . . .98 E3
Whitefield BL9 . . . . .45 A3
Sunny Banks SK13 . . . . . .116 B8
Sunny Bower St BL8 . . . . . .26 F6
Sunny Brow Rd
Manchester M18 . . . . .99 C4
Middleton M24 . . . . .64 E8
Sunny Dr Orrell WN5 . . . . . .53 F6
Prestwich M25 . . . . .62 F4
Sunny Garth BL5 . . . . .57 E8
Sunny Lea Mews SK9 . . . .137 A6
Sunny Side M32 . . . . .96 F2
Sunny Side Cotts OL12 . . .13 B2
Sunnybank Ave
Eccles M30 . . . . .79 F3
Manchester SK4 . . . . .110 F4
Sunnybank Cl WA12 . . . . . .89 C4
Sunnybank Rd
Bolton BL1 . . . . .142 C2
Tyldesley M29 . . . . .77 B6
Sunnyfield Rd
Manchester WN3 . . . . . . .110 F3
Prestwich M25 . . . . .63 C7
Sunnyfields WN3 . . . . .54 C7
Sunnylea Ave M19 . . . . . .110 E5
Sunnymead Ave BL1 . . . . .143 F4
Sunnymede Vale BL0 . . . . .11 A3
Sunnyside OL7 . . . . .84 F5
Sunnyside Ave M43 . . . . . .83 F4
Sunnyside Cres 8 OL6 . . .85 D2
Sunnyside Ct
Droylsden M43 . . . . .83 F3
Manchester M20 . . . . . . .110 C3
Sunnyside Gr OL6 . . . . . . .85 D2
Sunnyside Rd
Ashton-in-M WN4 . . . . . . .72 F7
Droylsden M43 . . . . .84 A3
Sunnywood Dr BL8 . . . . . . .27 A6
Sunnywood La BL8 . . . . . . .27 A6
Sunset Ave M22 . . . . .109 D2
Sunwell Terr SK6 . . . . . . .125 F3
Surbiton Rd M40 . . . . .83 B8
Surma Cl Oldham OL9 . . . .153 D7
Rochdale OL16 . . . . .31 B5
Surrey Ave Droylsden M43 . .83 F3
Leigh WN7 . . . . .76 E4
Shaw OL2 . . . . .48 F7
Surrey Cl BL3 . . . . .43 B4
Surrey Dr BL9 . . . . .44 F8
Surrey Park Cl OL2 . . . . . .149 B8
Surrey Rd M9 . . . . .64 D2
Surrey St Ashton-u-L OL6 . .85 D5
Glossop SK13 . . . . .104 C1
Manchester M9 . . . . .64 C2
Oldham OL9 . . . . .52 E3
Surrey Way SK5 . . . . .112 C4
Surtees Rd M23 . . . . .109 A2
Sussex Ave Heywood OL10 .28 E1
Manchester M20 . . . . . . .110 B4
Sussex Cl
Chadderton OL9 . . . . .152 B6
Hindley WN2 . . . . .57 A5
Standish WN1 . . . . .20 B1
Swinton M27 . . . . .62 A2
Sussex Dr Bury BL9 . . . . . .44 F8
Droylsden M43 . . . . .84 A3
Haslingden BB4 . . . . .1 B8
Sussex Pl SK14 . . . . .101 E5
Sussex Rd Irlam M44 . . . . .105 C6
Partington M31 . . . . .105 E2
Stockport SK3 . . . . .123 B8
Sussex St Leigh WN7 . . . . .76 E4
12 Manchester M2 . . . . .158 F1
Rochdale OL11 . . . . .139 F6
Salford M7 . . . . .158 D4
Sutch La WA13 . . . . .117 B8
Sutcliffe Ave M12 . . . . .99 B2
Sutcliffe St Ashton-u-L OL7 . .84 F1
Bacup OL13 . . . . .4 C8
Bolton BL1 . . . . .143 E2
Littleborough OL16 . . . . . .16 B6
Middleton M24 . . . . .46 F8
Oldham OL8 . . . . .153 E5
Royton OL2 . . . . .49 A3
Sutcliffes Pl 3 OL11 . . . . .31 A4
Sutherland Cl OL8 . . . . . . .66 F1
Sutherland Gr BL4 . . . . . . .60 B8
Sutherland Rd
Bolton BL1 . . . . .142 A1
Heywood OL10 . . . . .28 F1
Manchester M16 . . . . .97 A3
Wigan WN3 . . . . .55 A3
Sutherland St
Ashton-u-L OL6 . . . . .85 E3
Eccles M30 . . . . .79 B3
3 Farnworth BL4 . . . . . .60 C8
Hindley WN2 . . . . .56 C5
Swinton M27 . . . . .61 E1
1 Wigan WN5 . . . . .54 F6
Suthers St Oldham OL9 . . .152 C6

Suthers St continued
Radcliffe M26 . . . . .44 C1
Sutton Ave WA3 . . . . .91 F4
Sutton Cl BL8 . . . . .44 B8
Sutton Dr M43 . . . . .83 E3
Sutton Ho 5 M6 . . . . .154 F3
Sutton La PR6 . . . . .21 B8
Sutton Manor 1 M21 . . . . .97 A1
Sutton Rd
Alderley Edge SK9 . . . . . .136 F2
Bolton BL3 . . . . .40 F4
Manchester M18 . . . . .99 C3
Manchester,Heaton Norris
SK4 . . . . .168 C3
Poynton SK12 . . . . .134 A2
Sutton Way
Hadfield SK13 . . . . .104 A5
1 Handforth SK9 . . . . . .131 E5
Salford M5 . . . . .154 F3
Suttons La SK6 . . . . .126 A5
Swailes St 8 OL4 . . . . . . .153 D7
Swain St OL12 . . . . .14 E1
Swaindrod La OL15 . . . . . .16 F7
Swaine St SK3 . . . . .169 E1
Swale Dr WA14 . . . . .119 C6
Swalecliff Ave M23 . . . . . .108 D1
Swaledale Cl OL2 . . . . .48 E5
Swallow Bank Dr OL11 . . . .30 B3
Swallow Cl SK15 . . . . .86 F7
Swallow Ct SK1 . . . . .169 E4
Swallow Dr Bury BL9 . . . . .141 B4
Irlam M44 . . . . .94 A3
Rochdale OL11 . . . . .29 F7
Swallow La SK15 . . . . .86 F6
Swallow St
Manchester M12 . . . . .99 A4
Manchester,Bradford M11 .160 F1
Oldham OL8 . . . . .66 D2
Stockport SK1 . . . . .112 D1
Swallowfield WN7 . . . . .76 A5
Swan Cl SK12 . . . . .133 B4
Swan Ct OL2 . . . . .149 B6
Swan La Bolton BL3 . . . . . .147 D4
Hindley WN2 . . . . .57 B4
Swan Meadow Rd WN3 . . .150 B7
Swan Rd Ramsbottom BL8 . .10 F2
Sale WA15 . . . . .108 A1
Swan St Ashton-u-L OL6 . .166 C3
Manchester M4 . . . . .159 B2
Wilmslow SK9 . . . . .137 B7
Swanage Ave Sale M23 . . .108 D3
Stockport SK2 . . . . .124 D6
Swanage Cl BL8 . . . . .27 C6
Swanage Rd M30 . . . . .79 B3
Swanbourne Gdns SK3 . . .123 C6
Swanfield Wlk WA3 . . . . . . .73 F2
Swanhill Cl 2 M18 . . . . . . .99 F6
Swanley Ave M40 . . . . . . .157 E5
Swann Gr SK8 . . . . .123 B1
Swann La SK8 . . . . .123 B1
Swanton St M43 . . . . .150 B7
Swansea St OL8 . . . . .67 B4
Swanton Wlk 17 M8 . . . . .155 F6
Swarbrick Dr M25 . . . . .62 F2
Swayfield Ave M13 . . . . . . .98 F3
Swaylands Dr M33 . . . . . .108 B1
Sweet Briar Cl OL12 . . . . . .14 E2
Sweet Briar La OL12 . . . . . .14 E2
Sweetbriar Cl OL2 . . . . . . .149 B7
Sweetloves Gr BL1 . . . . . . .24 E5
Sweetloves La BL1 . . . . . . .24 E5
Swettenham Rd SK9 . . . . .131 D5
Swift Cl SK6 . . . . .113 C5
Rochdale OL11 . . . . .29 F7
Swift St Ashton-u-L OL6 . . . .85 D5
Wigan WN5 . . . . .150 A7
Swift Wlk 8 M40 . . . . .83 C5
Swiftsure Ave M3 . . . . . . .158 D1
Swinbourne Gr M20 . . . . .110 C2
Swinburn Gr WN5 . . . . .53 D1
Swinburn St M9 . . . . .64 F1
Swinburne Ave M43 . . . . . .84 A3
Swinburne Gr OL5 . . . . . . .99 D1
Swinburne Way M34 . . . . .113 A7
Swindells St Hyde SK14 . . .167 E1
Swindell's St 6 M11 . . . . . .99 E7
Swindells St OL14 . . . . .6 B1
Swindon Cl M18 . . . . .99 D5
Swinfield Ave M21 . . . . . . .108 F8
Swinford Gr OL2 . . . . .149 A5
Swinford Wlk 8 M9 . . . . . .64 E3
Swinley Chase SK9 . . . . . .131 F1
Swinley La WN1 . . . . .37 C2
Swinley St WN1 . . . . .37 C2
Swinside WN1 . . . . .37 F1
Swinside Cl M24 . . . . .46 C2
Swinside Rd BL2 . . . . .42 F8
Swinstead Ave M40 . . . . . .157 E5
Swinton Cres BL9 . . . . .45 A1
Swinton Gr M13 . . . . .163 C5
Swinton Hall Rd M27 . . . . .80 A8
Swinton High Sch The
M27 . . . . .61 F1
Swinton Park Rd M6 . . . . . .80 B5
Swinton St Bolton BL2 . . . . .42 E7
Oldham OL4 . . . . .67 C5
Swinton Sta M27 . . . . .61 F1
Swiss Hill SK9 . . . . .137 B1
Swithemby St BL6 . . . . . . .22 A4
Swithin Rd M22 . . . . .130 E8
Swythamley Cl SK3 . . . . . .123 A8
Swythamley Rd SK3 . . . . .123 A8
Sybil St OL15 . . . . .16 A6

Sycamore Ave
Altrincham WA14 ....119 A5
Denton M34 ....100 F2
Golborne WA3 ....74 A1
Heywood OL10 ....46 E8
Hindley WN2 ....56 F3
Newhey OL16 ....32 A3
Newton-le-W WA12 ....89 C3
Oldham,Greenacres OL4 ..67 D8
Oldham,White Gate OL9 ..65 F3
Radcliffe M26 ....61 F8
Tyldesley M29 ....59 D1
Wigan WN6 ....36 F3

Sycamore Cl
Ashton-u-L OL6 ....85 E2
Handforth SK9 ....131 B2
Littleborough OL15 ....15 F5
Manchester M20 ....110 C7
New Mills SK22 ....127 E1
Stalybridge SK16 ....101 F8

Sycamore Cotts OL3 ....50 F1

Sycamore Cres
Ashton-u-L OL6 ....85 C5
Hollinfare WA3 ....105 A2

Sycamore Ct
🅱 Manchester M16 ....97 D3
Manchester,Miles Platting
M40 ....160 E3
🅱 Sale M33 ....107 C6
🅱 Salford M6 ....81 A3

Sycamore Dr 🅱 Bury BL9 ..27 F7
Radcliffe M26 ....44 A5
Wigan WN3 ....54 C2

Sycamore Gr M35 ....84 B7
Sycamore Lo SK7 ....132 F7
Sycamore Pl M45 ....62 F6

Sycamore Rd
Atherton M46 ....58 E3
Bury BL8 ....26 F5
Eccles M30 ....79 A4
New Mills SK22 ....127 F2
Partington M31 ....105 E3
Romiley SK6 ....113 A4
Sycamore St Sale M33 ...108 E4
Stockport SK3 ....123 B8

Sycamore Wlk
Cheadle SK8 ....122 D6
🅱 Horwich BL6 ....22 E1

Sycamores The
Hadfield SK13 ....171 F3
Kearsley M26 ....61 B6
Mossley OL5 ....68 E1
Oldham OL4 ....67 E8
Stalybridge SK15 ....102 B8
Sydall St M34 ....100 F3
Syddal Cl SK7 ....132 D5
Syddal Cres SK7 ....132 D4
Syddal Gn SK7 ....132 D5
Syddal Park Prep Sch
SK7 ....132 D5
Syddal Park Sch SK7 ...132 D5
Syddal Rd SK7 ....132 D5
Syddall St SK14 ....167 D2
Sydenham St 🅱 OL1 .....49 B1
Sydenham Terr OL12 ....14 D3
Syderstone Cl WN2 .....56 E4
Sydney Ave Eccles M30 ..79 C2
Leigh WN7 ....75 C2
Wythenshawe M90 ......130 A8
Sydney Gdns OL5 ....6 C1
Sydney Jones Ct M40 ...65 C1
Sydney Rd SK7 ....132 F5
Sydney St Failsworth M35 .83 E7
Mossley OL5 ....86 D8
Platt Bridge WN2 ....56 B3
Salford M6 ....154 E2
Stockport SK2 ....124 C2
Stretford M32 ....96 D2
Swinton M27 ....79 D7
Syke La OL12 ....14 F4
Syke Rd Littleborough OL15 .16 C2
Rochdale OL12 ....14 F4
Sykefield Cl WN2 ....57 C3
Sykes Ave BL9 ....45 B4
Sykes Cl OL3 ....69 B5
Sykes Mdw SK3 ....170 D6
Sykes St Bury BL9 .....141 A3
Hyde SK14 ....167 F1
Newhey OL16 ....32 A4
Reddish SK5 ....111 F8
🅱 Rochdale OL16 ....31 B6
Sykes Wlk 🅱 SK5 ......111 F8

Sylvan Ave
Altrincham WA15 ....119 F8
Failsworth M35 ....83 E5
Manchester M16 ....97 D3
Sale M33 ....108 C3
Urmston M41 ....95 D3
Wilmslow SK9 ....136 F5
Sylvan Cl M24 ....46 D2
Sylvan Gr WA14 ....119 D5
Sylvan St OL9 ....152 C7
Sylvandale Ave M19 ....99 A1
Sylvester Cl SK1,SK2 ...124 B7
Sylvester Cl SK14 ......102 E2
Sylvester Way
🅱 Denton M34 ....113 A7
🅱 Hattersley SK14 ....101 E7
Sylvia Gr 🅱 SK5 ....111 E7
Symond Rd M9 ....64 E5
Symons Rd M33 ....108 B5
Symons St M7 ....155 E7
Syndall Ave M12 ....164 D6
Syndall St M12 ....164 D6
Synergy Ho M15 ....163 A5
Syresham St 🅱 WN2 ....56 B2

T

Taberner Cl WN6 ....19 F1
Taberner St 🅱 WN2 .....56 B2
Tabley Ave M14 ....98 B2
Tabley Gdns
🅱 Droylsden M43 ....84 B1
Marple SK6 ....126 A4
Tabley Gr Manchester M13 .98 F2
Reddish SK5 ....111 E7
Sale WA15 ....120 A8
Tabley Mere Gdns SK8 ..122 F3
Tabley Mews 🅱 WA14 ...119 D5
Tabley Rd Bolton BL3 ...146 B4
Handforth SK9 ....131 D5
Sale M33 ....108 E4
Tabley St Dukinfield SK16 .101 E8
Mossley OL5 ....86 D8
Salford M6 ....81 B5
Tabor St M24 ....46 F2
Tackler Cl M27 ....79 F7
Tadcaster Wlk OL1 .....153 F7
Taddington Pl 🅱 SK13 ..171 E1
Tadlow Wlk 🅱 M40 .....159 C3
Tadman Gr WA14 ....119 A6
Tadmor Cl M38 ....59 F4
Tagore Cl M13 ....98 E4
Tahir Cl M8 ....156 B7
Tait Mews SK4 ....110 F2
Talavera St M7 ....155 D5
Talbenny Cl BL1 ....40 F8
Talbot Ave BL3 ....43 A4
Talbot Cl Oldham OL4 ...67 C8
Rawtenstall BL0 ....1 E5
Talbot Ct BL1 ....143 F4
Talbot Gr BL9 ....28 A6
Talbot Pl M16 ....161 B5

Talbot Rd
Alderley Edge SK9 ....137 B1
Altrincham WA14 ....119 B2
Dukinfield SK14 ....101 F5
Glossop SK13 ....104 C2
Manchester M14 ....110 E7
Sale M33 ....108 E4
Stretford M16,M32,M15 ..96 F3
Talbot St Ashton-u-L OL6 .166 A3
Eccles M30 ....79 E1
Glossop SK13 ....104 C2
Golborne WA3 ....90 A8
Hazel Grove SK7 ....124 E4
Middleton M24 ....47 A2
Rochdale OL11 ....139 F6
Stockport SK1,SK4 .....169 E1
Talford Gr M20 ....110 A5
Talgarth Rd M40 ....159 C4
Talkin Dr M24 ....46 E3
Tall Trees OL2 ....63 D1
Tall Trees Cl OL2 ......48 C4
Tall Trees Pl SK2 ......124 C6
Talland Wlk M13 ....164 D5
Tallarn Cl M20 ....110 A1
Tallis St M12 ....99 A3
Tallow Way M44 ....106 A8
Tallyman Way M27 ......80 E7
Talman Gr WN4 ....73 D3
Tamar Cl Kearsley BL4 ...61 B5
Whitefield M45 ....63 A8
Tamar Ct 🅱 M15 ....162 D6
Tamar Dr M23 ....121 A4
Tamar Way OL10 ....29 A3
Tamarin Cl M27 ....61 C1
Tame Barn Cl OL16 .....32 A6
Tame Cl SK15 ....86 C3
Tame La OL3 ....50 D7
Tame St Denton M34 ...100 F4
Denton,Guide Bridge M34 .100 F7
Manchester M4 ....160 D1
Mossley OL5 ....68 E3
Stalybridge SK15,SK16 ...85 E1
Uppermill OL3 ....69 B8
Tame Valley Cl OL5 .....68 E3
Tame Valley Prim Sch
SK5 ....112 C2
Tame View OL5 ....68 C2
Tame Water Villas OL3 ..50 F1
Tame Wlk 🅱 SK9 ....131 D2
Tamebank OL3 ....68 D3
Tamer Gr WN7 ....75 C8
Tamerton Dr M8 ....156 A6
Tameside Coll OL6 .....85 D3
Tameside Coll (The Hyde Ctr)
SK14 ....113 D7
Tameside Coll of Tech
SK14 ....167 E2
Tameside Ct
Dukinfield SK16 ....101 B8
🅱 Hattersley SK14 ......102 E2
Tameside General Hospl
OL6 ....85 E4
Tamworth Ave
Prestwich M45 ....63 B7
Salford M5 ....161 B8
Tamworth Ave W M5 ...161 A8
Tamworth Cl
Hazel Grove SK7 ....133 D8
Manchester M15 ....162 E5
Tamworth Ct M15 ......162 E5
Tamworth Dr Bury BL8 ...27 C5
Wigan WN2 ....56 E3
Tamworth St
Manchester M15 ....97 E4
Newton-le-W WA12 ......89 A3
Oldham OL9 ....66 J3
Stockport SK3 ....112 B2
Tamworth Wlk M5 ......161 B8
Tan House Dr WN3 ......54 C2

Tan House La WN3 ......54 C2
Tan Pit Cotts WN8 ......35 C4
Tan Pits Cl M29 ....77 C7
Tan Yard Brow M18 ......99 E5
Tandis Ct M6 ....80 A4
Tandle Hill Ctry Pk★
OL2 ....48 A6
Tandle Hill Rd OL2 ......48 B6
Tandlewood Mews 🅱
M40 ....83 C5
Tandlewood Pk OL10 ....48 B6
Tanfield Dr M26 ....61 B7
Tanfield Rd M20 ....122 B8
Tanfield Sch M20 ....122 B8
Tang The SK6 ....113 B1
Tangmere Ave OL10 ......46 E7
Tangmere Cl M16 ....65 C3
Tangmere Ct M16 ....97 D3
Tanhill Cl SK2 ....124 C6
Tanhill La OL8 ....67 A2
Tanhouse Ave M29 ......77 D7
Tanhouse Rd M41 ....94 D3
Tanner Brook Cl BL3 ...147 E4
Tanner Cl SK14 ....167 D3
Tanner's La WA3 ....90 B8
Tanners Croft BL0 ......138 B6
Tanners Fold OL7 ....67 A2
Tanners Gn M46 ....154 F3
Tanners St Droylsden M18 .99 E5
Ramsbottom BL0 ....138 B6
Tannery Way WA14 .....119 E7
Tannock Ct SK7 ....124 F1
Tannock Rd SK7 ....124 F1
Tanpit Wlk 🅱 M22 .....121 C2
Tanpits Rd BL9 ....40 E3
Tansey Gr M7 ....155 F7
Tansley Ave PR7 ....19 D8
Tansley Cl BL6 ....22 C2
Tansley Rd M8 ....64 B2
Tansley Sq WN5 ....54 D5
Tanworth Wlk 🅱 BL1 ...143 E2
Tanyard Dr WA15 ....129 C8
Tanyard Gn SK5 ....111 F5
Tanyard La WA15 ....129 A5
Tape St BL0 ....138 B6
Taper St BL0 ....138 B6
Tapley Ave SK12 ....133 E2
Taplin Dr M18 ....105 C5
Taplow Gr SK8 ....122 F2
Taplow Wlk M14 ....98 E3
Tarbet Dr BL2 ....42 F7
Tarbet Rd SK16 ....101 C7
Tarbet Wlk M8 ....155 F6
Tarbolton Cres WA15 ...120 C3
Tariff St M1 ....159 B1
Tarleton Ave M46 ......58 B5
Tarleton Cl BL8 ....26 F1
Tarleton Ho 🅱 M6 ......80 C4
Tarleton Pl BL3 ....146 A3
Tarleton Wlk M13 ......164 D6
Tarn Cl WN4 ....73 B3
Tarn Dr BL9 ....44 E6
Tarn Gr M28 ....60 F1
Tarnbrook Cl M45 ....63 C8
Tarnbrook Dr WN2 ......38 B5
Tarnbrook Wlk M15 ....163 A5
Tarnrigg Cl WN3 ....54 E3
Tarns The SK8 ....122 B3
Tarnside Cl
Hazel Grove SK2 ....124 F6
Rochdale OL16 ....15 C3
Tarnside Fold SK13 ....116 A7
Tarnside Rd WN5 ....53 E6
Tarnway WA3 ....74 C1
Tarporley Ave M14 .....110 A8
Tarporley Cl SK3 ......170 D5
Tarporley Wlk SK9 .....131 E2
Tarran Gr M34 ....101 B1
Tarran Pl WA14 ....119 E6
Tarrant Cl WN3 ....54 D2
Tarrington Cl M12 .....165 A5
Tartan St M11 ....83 B2
Tarves Wlk M11 ....83 B1

Tarvin Ave
Manchester M20 ....110 A7
Reddish SK4 ....111 D7
Tarvin Cl WA3 ....90 E7
Tarvin Dr SK6 ....125 E6
Tarvin Rd SK8 ....123 A4
Tarvin Way 🅱 SK9 .....131 D5
Tarvin Wlk BL1 ....143 E2
Tasle Alley M2 ....158 F1
Tatchbury Rd M35 ......84 A7
Tate St OL8 ....66 F4
Tatham Cl 🅱 M13 ......98 F3
Tatham Gr WN3 ....54 D1
Tatland Dr M22 ....121 F3
Tatlock Cl WN5 ....71 E5
Tattenhall Wlk 🅱 M14 .110 D8
Tattersall Ave BL1 .....23 E2
Tattersall St OL1 ......153 D6
Tatton Cl Cheadle SK8 ..123 A4
Hazel Grove SK7 ....124 F4
Tatton Ct
🅱 Handforth SK9 ....131 E5
🅱 Manchester M14 ......110 D8
Manchester SK4 ....168 C4
Tatton Fold M22 ....109 E1
Tatton Gdns SK6 ....113 D5
Tatton Gr M20 ....110 B6
Tatton Mews SK9 ......131 E5
Tatton Pl Manchester M13 .98 E4
Sale M33 ....108 B5
Tatton Rd Denton M34 ..101 A1

Tatton Rd continued
Handforth SK9 ....131 E5
Sale M33 ....108 B5
Tatton Rd N SK4 ....111 C5
Tatton Rd S SK4 ....168 C4
Tatton St Hyde SK14 ...113 E7
Manchester M15 ....162 D7
Salford M5 ....161 B8
Stalybridge SK15 ....85 C1
Stockport SK1 ....169 F1
Tatton Terr 🅱 SK16 ...166 B1
Tatton View M20 ....110 B6
Tattonmere Gdns SK8 ..123 A4

Taunton Ave
Ashton-u-L OL7 ....166 A4
Brinnington SK5 ....112 C5
Eccles M30 ....79 B3
Hindley WN7 ....57 D2
Rochdale OL11 ....30 B7
Urmston M41 ....107 B8
Taunton Brook La OL7 ...84 E5
Taunton Cl Bolton BL1 ..142 C1
Hazel Grove SK7 ....125 A2
Taunton Dr BL4 ....147 F1
Taunton Gn OL7 ....84 F5
Taunton Gr M45 ....63 A6
Taunton Hall Cl OL7 .....84 F5
Taunton Lawns OL7 .....85 A5
Taunton Pl OL7 ....84 F5

Taunton Rd
Ashton-u-L OL7 ....166 A4
Chadderton OL9 ....48 A1
Sale M33 ....107 D4
Taunton St M4 ....160 D1
Manchester 🅱 M34 ....101 A1
Taurus St OL4 ....67 C8
Tavern Court Ave M35 ...84 B7
Tavern Ct M35 ....84 B7
Tavern Rd SK13 ....171 E3
Tavery Cl M4 ....159 C2
Tavistock Cl SK14 .....102 E2
Tavistock Dr OL9 ....47 F1
Tavistock Rd Bolton BL1 .145 D6
Hindley WN2 ....57 A4
Rochdale OL11 ....30 F2
Sale M33 ....107 D5
Tavistock Sq M9 ....157 D7
Tavistock Way M46 ......58 B4
Tawton Ave SK14 ....102 E3
Taxi Rd M90 ....130 B7
Tay Cl OL8 ....153 E5
Tayfield Rd M22 ....121 C2
Taylor Ave OL11 ....29 F8
Taylor Bldgs BL4 ....60 B7
Taylor Bsns Pk WA3 ....91 F1
Taylor Gr WN2 ....57 C3
Taylor Green Way OL4 ...67 F7
Taylor Ho BL8 ....27 C5
Taylor Holme Ind Est OL13 .3 B8
Taylor La M34 ....100 D4

Taylor Rd
Altrincham WA14 ....119 A5
Hindley WN2 ....57 C3
Urmston M41 ....95 E2
Taylor St 🅱 Bolton BL3 .145 F6
Bury BL9 ....141 A3
Chadderton OL9 ....152 A7
Denton M34 ....84 A1
Droylsden M43 ....84 A1
Golborne WN3 ....74 C1
Heywood OL10 ....29 C2
Hollingworth SK14 .....171 D4
Horwich BL6 ....22 B3
Hyde SK14 ....75 D8
Leigh WN7 ....75 D8
Manchester M18 ....165 C6
Middleton M24 ....65 A8
Oldham OL1 ....67 C8
🅱 Oldham,Lees OL4 ....67 E6
Prestwich M25 ....44 A3
Radcliffe M26 ....14 F1
Rochdale OL12 ....14 F1
Royton OL2 ....48 D5
Stalybridge SK15 ....86 B1
Whitworth OL12 ....14 D8
Wigan WN3 ....150 B8
Taylor Terr 🅱 SK16 ....166 B1
Taylor's La Ainsworth BL2 .43 B7
Ince-in-M WN3 ....55 F3
Taylor's Rd M32 ....96 E3
Taylors Pl 🅱 OL12 .....14 F1
Taylorson St M5 ....161 B7
Taylorson St S M5 .....161 A6
Tayton Cl M29 ....60 D2
Taywood Rd BL3 ....61 D4
Teak Dr BL4 ....61 D4
Teak St BL9 ....141 B2
Teal Ave SK12 ....133 A4
Teal Cl Altrincham WA14 .119 B8
Hazel Grove SK2 ....124 F5
Wigan WN3 ....54 E6
Teal Ct OL11 ....29 F7
Teal St BL3 ....147 F4
Tealby Ave M16 ....97 C4
Tealby Ct M21 ....97 C1
Tealby Rd M18 ....99 B4
Tealdale Cl OL9 ....48 A4
Teasdale Cl OL9 ....48 A4
Tebbutt St M4 ....159 B3
Tebworth Dr WN7 ....56 E4
Ted Jackson Mlk M11 ..164 F8
Tedburn Wlk 🅱 M40 ....65 D2
Tedder Cl BL9 ....45 B2
Tedder Dr M22 ....130 F7
Teddington Rd M40 .....65 C2
Teer St M4 ....160 D2
Tees St OL16 ....31 B6
Tees Wlk OL8 ....153 E5

Teesdale Ave M41 ......95 A4
Teesdale Cl SK2 ....124 E6
Teesdale Dr WN7 ....76 C5
Teesdale Wlk 🅰 M9 ....64 E3
Teignmouth Ave M40 ...159 C4
Teignmouth St M40 ....159 C4
Telfer Ave M13 ....98 E2
Telfer Rd M13 ....98 E2
Telford Cl M34 ....100 F7
Telford Cres WN7 ....75 D8
Telford Mews OL3 ......69 B8
Telford Rd SK6 ....125 F5
Telford St Atherton M46 ..58 A2
Horwich BL6 ....22 D2
Manchester M8 ....156 C5
Telford Way OL11 ....31 A2
Telford Wlk M16 ....97 D4
Tell St OL12 ....139 D7
Tellers Cl M46 ....58 D6
Telford St Atherton M46 ..80 D6
Tellson Cres M6 ....80 D6
Telryn Wlk M8 ....156 C8
Temperance Sq SK14 ...103 A4
Temperance St
Bolton BL3 ....145 E5
🅱 Manchester M1,M12 ..163 C8
Manchester M12 ....164 D7
Mottram-in-L SK14 .....115 A8
Tempest Chase BL6 .....40 C4
Tempest Rd
Alderley Edge SK9 .....137 C1
Bolton BL3 ....40 C4
Tempest St BL3 ....146 B4
Temple Cl OL4 ....67 E8
Temple Dr Bolton BL1 ..142 C3
Pendlebury M27 ....80 B7
Temple La OL15 ....6 D1
Temple Moor Inf Sch
M33 ....108 E4
Temple Prim Sch M8 ...156 B6
Temple Rd Bolton BL1 ..142 C3
Sale M33 ....108 D4
Temple Sq M8 ....156 B6
Temple St Hadfield SK13 .104 C5
Heywood OL10 ....29 D2
Middleton M24 ....47 B1
Oldham OL1 ....67 B7
Templecombe Dr BL1 ....24 E7
Templegate Cl WN6 .....19 F2
Templeton Cl
Altrincham WA14 ....119 B6
Westhoughton BL5 ......57 E8
Templeton Rd WN2 ......56 B2
Ten Acre Cl M45 ....62 D7
Ten Acre Dr M45 ....62 D7
Ten Acres La M40 ....83 A4
Ten Foot Cl SK13 ......104 B2
Ten Ho OL8 ....67 C2
Tenax Circ M17 ....96 B8
Tenax Rd M17 ....96 B7
Tenbury Cl M6 ....154 F3

Tenbury Dr
Ashton-in-M WN4 ....73 A4
Middleton M24 ....65 A5
Tenby Ave Bolton BL1 ..142 A1
Manchester M20 ....110 B6
Stretford M32 ....96 E4
Tenby Cl M15 ....161 C6
Tenby Dr Cheadle SK8 ..123 B1
Pendlebury M6 ....80 D5
Tenby Gr 🅱 OL2 ....14 C1
Tenby Rd Oldham OL8 ...66 B2
Stockport SK3 ....123 B7
Tenby St OL12 ....14 C1
Tenement La SK7,SK8 ...123 C3
Tenement St WN2 ....56 A5
Teneriffe St M7 ....155 D5
Tenham Wlk 🅱 M9 ......64 E3
Tennis St Bolton BL1 ...143 D3
Manchester M16 ....97 B4
Tennyson Ave Bury BL9 ..44 F6
Denton M34 ....113 A7
Dukinfield SK16 ....102 A7
Leigh WN7 ....75 C8
Radcliffe M26 ....43 E4
Tennyson Cl SK4 ....168 B2
Tennyson Dr
Longshaw WN5 ....53 D1
Wigan WN1 ....37 C3
Tennyson Gdns M25 ....62 F3

Tennyson Rd
Cheadle SK8 ....122 F6
Droylsden M43 ....84 A2
Farnworth BL4 ....60 B6
Middleton M24 ....47 B2
Reddish SK5 ....99 D1
Swinton M27 ....79 B8
Tennyson St Bolton BL1 .143 D1
Manchester M13 ....163 C5
Oldham OL1 ....31 A5
🅱 Rochdale OL11 ....31 A5
Tennyson Wlk 🅱 BL1 ...143 E2
Tensing Ave
Ashton-u-L OL7 ....85 B5
Manchester M46 ....58 C5
Tensing St OL8 ....85 A4
Tenter Dr WN6 ....37 F2
Tentercroft Oldham OL1 .153 F7
Rochdale OL12 ....139 E7
Tenterden St M46 ......154 D3
Tenterden Wlk M22 ....121 C3
Tenters St 🅱 BL9 ......140 E2
Teer St M4 ....160 D2
Tenterheads BB4 ....2 F7
Tenterhill La OL11 .....13 D2

Syc–Ten 257

Tenters St BL9 .... 140 D2
Tenth St M17 .... 96 D6
Terence St M40 .... 83 D5
Terminal Rd E M90 .... 130 C7
Terminal Rd N M90 .... 130 B7
Terminal Rd S M90 .... 130 B7
Tern Ave BL4 .... 59 F8
Tern Cl Altrincham WA14 .. 119 B8
Dukinfield SK16 .... 101 E7
Rochdale OL11 .... 29 F7
Tern Dr SK12 .... 133 B4
Ternhill Ct BL4 .... 60 D8
Terrace St 10 Oldham OL4 .. 67 B7
Oldham OL4 .... 67 B7
Terrace The M25 .... 63 B3
Terrington Cl M21 .... 109 E7
Tetbury Cl WN5 .... 36 D1
Tetbury Dr BL2 .... 43 A8
Tetbury Rd M22 .... 121 B1
Tetlow Gr M30 .... 79 C1
Tetlow La M7 .... 155 E8
Tetlow St Dukinfield SK14 .. 101 E5
Failsworth M40 .... 83 D5
Middleton M24 .... 65 A8
Oldham OL9 .... 153 D6
Tetsworth Wlk 16 M40 .... 65 D2
Teviot St 8 M13 .... 98 E4
Tewkesbury Ave
Altrincham WA15 .... 120 C3
Ashton-u-L OL6 .... 85 C7
Chadderton OL9 .... 48 A2
Droylsden M43 .... 84 A3
Middleton M24 .... 46 F3
Urmston M41 .... 95 D4
Tewkesbury Cl
Cheadle SK8 .... 132 B6
Poynton SK12 .... 133 D4
Tewkesbury Dr M25 .... 63 C2
Tewkesbury Rd
Cheadle SK3 .... 123 B6
Golborne WA3 .... 90 B8
Manchester M40 .... 160 D3
Texas St OL6 .... 166 C2
Textile St M12 .... 165 A7
Textilose Rd M17 .... 96 B5
Teynham Wlk 5 M22 .... 121 C1
Thackeray Cl M8 .... 156 A6
Thackeray Gr M43 .... 84 A2
Thackeray Pl WN3 .... 150 A5
Thackeray Rd OL1 .... 49 C1
Thames Ave WN7 .... 75 F1
Thames Cl Bury BL9 .... 27 F7
Manchester M11 .... 165 B8
Thames Ct 2 M15 .... 162 D6
Thames Dr WN5 .... 53 F7
Thames Ind Est M12 .... 164 D7
Thames Rd Culcheth WA3 .. 92 A2
Milnrow OL16 .... 32 B6
Thames St OL1 .... 67 A8
Thames Steet OL16 .... 31 B6
Thames Trad Ctr M44 .... 105 F7
Thanet Cl M7 .... 155 E5
Thanet Gr WN7 .... 76 A5
Thankerton Ave M34 .... 84 D1
Thatch Leach OL9 .... 65 F5
Thatch Leach La M45 .... 63 A7
Thatcher Cl WA14 .... 119 C1
Thatcher St OL8 .... 67 A4
Thaxmead Dr M40 .... 83 D4
Thaxted Cl SK2 .... 125 A5
Thaxted Dr SK2 .... 125 A5
Thaxted Pl BL1 .... 144 C8
Thaxted Wlk M22 .... 130 C8
Theatre St OL1 .... 153 F7
Thekla St OL9 .... 153 D8
Thelma St BL0 .... 138 B6
Thelwall Ave Bolton BL2 .. 42 D8
Manchester M14 .... 110 A8
Thelwall Cl
3 Altrincham WA15 .... 119 E6
Leigh WN7 .... 75 B4
Thelwall Ct M14 .... 110 A8
Thelwall Rd M33 .... 108 E3
Theobald Rd WA14 .... 119 D1
Theta Cl M11 .... 83 B2
Thetford 12 OL12 .... 139 E8
Thetford Cl Bury BL8 .... 27 D5
Hindley WN2 .... 56 E4
Thetford Dr M8 .... 156 B7
Thicketford Brow BL2 .... 25 D1
Thicketford Cl BL2 .... 25 C2
Thicketford Rd BL2 .... 25 C1
Thicknesse Ave WN6 .... 36 F3
Thimble Cl OL12 .... 15 D4
Thimbles The OL12 .... 15 D4
Third Ave Bolton BL1 .... 144 B7
Bury BL9 .... 28 D4
Droylsden M11 .... 83 C3
Little Lever BL3 .... 42 F4
Mossley SK15 .... 86 E6
Oldham OL8 .... 66 D1
Poynton SK12 .... 133 D1
Stretford M17 .... 96 D6
Swinton M27 .... 79 E5
Tyldesley M29 .... 77 B4
Wigan WN6 .... 37 A2
Third St BL1 .... 23 F4
Thirkhill Pl 2 M30 .... 79 F2
Thirlby Dr M22 .... 121 D1
Thirlemere Rd SK1 .... 124 B7
Thirlmere Ave
Abram WN2 .... 74 B8
Ashton-in-M WN4 .... 73 C4
Ashton-u-L OL7 .... 84 F4
Haslingden BB4 .... 1 C8
Thirlmere Ave *continued*
Horwich BL6 .... 22 C2
Ince-in-M WN2 .... 56 B7
1 Orrell WN5 .... 53 F7
Pendlebury M27 .... 80 A7
Standish WN6 .... 37 A7
Stretford M32 .... 96 C3
Tyldesley M29 .... 77 A7
Up Holland WN8 .... 53 B7
Thirlmere Cl
Adlington PR6 .... 21 B8
Alderley Edge SK9 .... 136 F1
Stalybridge SK15 .... 86 A4
Thirlmere Dr Bury BL9 .... 44 E7
Middleton M24 .... 46 E2
Walkden M38 .... 60 A5
Thirlmere Gr
Farnworth BL4 .... 59 E8
Royton OL2 .... 48 D6
Thirlmere Mews M24 .... 46 E2
Thirlmere Rd
Blackrod BL6 .... 21 C3
Golborne WA3 .... 74 C1
Hindley WN2 .... 56 E5
Over Hulton BL5 .... 58 F7
Partington M31 .... 105 E4
Rochdale OL11 .... 30 B4
Urmston M41 .... 94 E3
Wigan WN5 .... 54 C7
Wythenshawe M22 .... 121 B2
Thirlmere St WN7 .... 75 E5
Thirlspot Cl BL1 .... 24 E6
Thirlstone Ave OL4 .... 49 F4
Thirsfield Dr 6 M11 .... 83 C2
Thirsk Ave Chadderton OL9 .. 47 F1
Sale M33 .... 107 C3
Thirsk Cl BL8 .... 27 B5
Thirsk Mews M7 .... 155 D6
Thirsk Rd BL3 .... 43 A2
Thirsk St M12 .... 163 C7
Thistle Bank Cl M9 .... 64 C1
Thistle Cl SK15 .... 102 E7
Thistle Gn OL16 .... 31 E7
Thistle Sq M31 .... 105 E2
Thistle Way OL4 .... 49 D2
Thistle Wlk 4 M31 .... 105 E2
Thistledown Cl
Eccles M30 .... 95 D8
Wigan WN6 .... 37 A2
Thistleton Rd BL3 .... 40 F3
Thistlewood Dr SK9 .... 137 D8
Thistley Fields SK14 .... 113 C8
Thomas Chambers
SK13 .... 116 C7
Thomas Cl M34 .... 101 A4
Thomas Ct M15 .... 162 D7
Thomas Dr BL3 .... 145 D5
Thomas Garnet Ct 1
BL4 .... 60 C8
Thomas Gibbon Cl 5
M32 .... 96 C1
Thomas Henshaw Ct
OL11 .... 30 C4
Thomas Ho 1 OL2 .... 48 E4
Thomas Holden St BL1 .. 145 E8
Thomas Johnson Cl 4
M30 .... 79 C1
Thomas More Cl BL4 .... 60 F6
Thomas Regan Ct 4
M18 .... 99 D6
Thomas St
Altrincham WA15 .... 119 E4
Aspull WN2 .... 38 B6
Atherton M46 .... 58 D3
Bolton BL3 .... 145 D5
Farnworth BL4 .... 60 E7
Farnworth BL4 .... 60 E8
Glossop SK13 .... 104 E1
Golborne WA3 .... 90 A8
Hindley WN2 .... 57 B3
Manchester M4 .... 159 A2
Manchester M8 .... 155 F8
Oldham OL4 .... 67 E5
Radcliffe M26 .... 44 B3
8 Rochdale OL16 .... 31 A8
Rochdale,Dearnley OL15 .... 15 E4
Romiley SK6 .... 113 A3
Romiley,Compstall SK6 .... 114 B2
Royton OL2 .... 49 A3
Shaw OL2 .... 149 C6
Stockport SK1 .... 170 F7
Stretford M32 .... 96 D3
Westhoughton BL5 .... 39 E3
Whitworth OL12 .... 4 D2
Thomas St W SK1,SK2 .... 170 F7
Thomas Telford Basin 11
M1 .... 159 C1
Thomason Fold BL7 .... 9 D6
Thomasson Cl 7 BL1 .... 143 E1
Thomasson Meml Sch
BL1 .... 144 B7
Thompson Ave
Ainsworth BL2 .... 26 D1
Culcheth WA3 .... 91 E3
Whitefield M45 .... 63 A7
Thompson Cl
Newton-le-W WA12 .... 89 C1
Reddish M34 .... 100 B3
Thompson Ct
Reddish M34 .... 100 B3
Stalybridge SK15 .... 85 F2
Thompson Dr BL9 .... 141 C3
Thompson Fold SK15 .... 85 F2
Thompson Ho M46 .... 58 C3
Thompson La OL9 .... 66 A4
Thompson Rd
Bolton BL1 .... 142 B1
Reddish M34 .... 100 B3
Thompson Rd *continued*
Urmston M17 .... 95 E8
Thompson St
Ashton-in-M WN4 .... 73 D4
Bolton BL3 .... 145 F5
Horwich BL6 .... 22 A3
Leigh WN7 .... 75 B5
Manchester M4 .... 159 B2
Manchester M40 .... 157 F5
Manchester,Strangeways
M3 .... 158 F3
Wigan,Longshoot WN1 .... 37 E1
Wigan,Worsley Mesnes
WN3 .... 55 A4
Thomson Rd M18 .... 99 C4
Thomson St
Manchester M13 .... 163 C6
Stockport SK3 .... 170 E8
Thor Gr M5 .... 161 C8
Thoralby Cl M12 .... 165 A5
Thorburn Dr OL12 .... 14 B7
Thorburn Ho WN5 .... 54 C7
Thorburn La WN5 .... 54 D8
Thorburn Rd WN5 .... 54 D6
Thoresby Cl
Little Lever M26 .... 43 C5
Wigan WN3 .... 54 E3
Thoresway Rd
Manchester M13 .... 98 E3
Wilmslow SK9 .... 136 F5
Thorgill Wlk 10 M40 .... 83 A7
Thoriby Rd WA3 .... 91 F3
Thorley Cl OL9 .... 65 E2
Thorley Dr
Altrincham WA15 .... 120 B5
Urmston M41 .... 95 D2
Thorley La
Altrincham WA15 .... 120 B4
Wythenshawe M22,WA15 .. 121 A1
Thorley Mews SK7 .... 132 F7
Thorley St M35 .... 83 F8
Thorn Ave M35 .... 83 F6
Thorn Cl OL10 .... 29 B3
Thorn Ct 2 M6 .... 81 B2
Thorn Dr M22 .... 131 A8
Thorn Gr
Altrincham WA15 .... 119 E3
Cheadle SK8 .... 132 A7
Manchester M14 .... 110 D8
Sale M33 .... 108 B4
Thorn Grove Prim Sch
SK8 .... 132 A7
Thorn Lea Atherton M46 .... 58 E2
Bolton BL2 .... 25 D4
Thorn Lea Cl BL1 .... 40 F7
Thorn Rd Bramhall SK7 .. 132 E5
Oldham OL8 .... 67 C3
Swinton M27 .... 79 E6
Thorn St Bolton BL1 .... 143 F2
Hindley WN2 .... 56 D4
Ramsbottom BL9 .... 11 C3
Thorn View BL9 .... 141 C3
Thorn Well BL5 .... 57 E7
Thorn Wlk M31 .... 105 E2
Thornaby Wlk M9 .... 157 D6
Thornage Dr M40 .... 159 C4
Thornbank BL3 .... 144 C6
Thornbank Cl OL10 .... 46 E7
Thornbeck Dr BL1 .... 23 F1
Thornbeck Rd BL1 .... 23 F1
Thornbridge Ave M21 .... 109 B8
Thornbury 9 OL11 .... 139 E6
Thornbury Ave
Golborne WA3 .... 90 E7
Hattersley SK14 .... 102 E2
Thornbury Cl
3 Bolton BL1 .... 145 E8
Bramhall SK8 .... 123 C1
Thornbury Rd M32 .... 96 E4
Thornbury Way M18 .... 165 C5
Thornbush Cl WA3 .... 74 E1
Thornbush Way OL16 .... 31 C8
Thornby Wlk 8 M23 .... 121 A5
Thorncliff Ave OL8 .... 66 E3
Thorncliffe Ave
Dukinfield SK16 .... 101 C7
Royton OL2 .... 48 C6
Thorncliffe Gr M19 .... 99 C1
Thorncliffe Pk OL2 .... 48 C6
Thorncliffe Rd BL1 .... 24 E5
Thorncombe Rd 1 M16 .... 97 E3
Thorncross Cl M15 .... 161 C7
Thorndale Cl OL2 .... 48 E5
Thorndale Gr WA15 .... 120 A5
Thornden Rd M40 .... 160 D4
Thorne Ave M41 .... 95 A3
Thorne Ho M14 .... 98 D2
Thorne St BL4 .... 42 C1
Thornecliffewood SK14 .. 103 D5
Thorneside M34 .... 100 F5
Thorney Dr SK8 .... 132 C6
Thorney Hill Cl 10 OL4 .... 67 A6
Thorneycroft WN7 .... 76 C5
Thorneycroft Ave M21 .. 109 C5
Thorneycroft Cl WA15 .. 120 B5
Thorneycroft Rd WA15 .. 120 B5
Thorneyholme Cl BL6 .... 40 C6
Thorneylea OL12 .... 4 D1
Thornfield SK9 .... 137 A4
Thornfield Ave 8 BB4 .... 2 F8
Thornfield Cl WA3 .... 90 C8
Thornfield Cres M38 .... 59 F5
Thornfield Ct SK4 .... 168 A3
Thornfield Dr 4 M27 .... 79 E7
Thornfield Gr
Cheadle SK8 .... 123 A2
Walkden M38 .... 59 F5
Thornfield Hey SK9 .... 137 E8
Thornfield Rd Bury BL8 .... 26 E7
Manchester SK4 .... 168 A3
Manchester,Green End
M19 .... 110 E5
Thornfield Sch SK4 .... 168 A3
Thornfield St M5 .... 154 D1
Thornfield Terr OL6 .... 166 C2
Thornford Wlk 14 M40 .... 65 D2
Thorngate Rd M8 .... 156 A5
Thorngrove Ave 1 M23 .. 120 D7
Thorngrove Dr SK9 .... 137 C6
Thorngrove Hill SK9 .... 137 C6
Thorngrove Ho 4 M23 .. 120 D7
Thorngrove Rd SK9 .... 137 C6
Thornham Cl BL8 .... 27 C6
Thornham Ct OL16 .... 48 C8
Thornham Dr BL1 .... 25 A6
Thornham La
Royton OL16,OL2 .... 48 C8
Slattocks M24,OL11,OL2 .... 47 E6
Thornham New Rd OL11,
OL16 .... 47 E8
Thornham Old Rd M24,
OL2 .... 48 B7
Thornham Rd Sale M33 .. 107 F3
Shaw OL2 .... 48 E8
Thornham St James CE Prim
Sch OL2 .... 48 C8
Thornhill Cl Bolton BL1 .. 142 C3
Reddish M34 .... 100 A2
Thornhill Dr M28 .... 60 E1
Thornhill Rd
Droylsden M43 .... 84 B2
Garswood WN4 .... 72 C4
Manchester SK4 .... 110 F2
Ramsbottom BL0 .... 11 A1
Thornholme Cl M18 .... 99 B3
Thornholme Rd SK6 .... 125 F4
Thorniley Brow M4 .... 159 A2
Thornlea M43 .... 83 E1
Thornlea Ave Oldham OL8 .. 66 C1
Swinton M27 .... 79 D6
Thornlea Dr OL12 .... 14 B2
Thornlee Ct OL4 .... 68 B5
Thornleigh Rd M14 .... 98 B1
Thornleigh Salesian Coll
BL1 .... 143 D4
Thornley Ave BL1 .... 142 C2
Thornley Cl OL4 .... 68 A5
Thornley Cres
Oldham OL4 .... 68 A5
Romiley SK6 .... 113 A4
Thornley La OL4 .... 68 A5
Thornley La N M34,SK5 .... 99 F3
Thornley La S M34,SK5 .. 100 A2
Thornley Mews BL1 .... 142 C2
Thornley Park Rd OL4 .... 68 A5
Thornley Rd Denton M34 .. 101 A4
Prestwich M25 .... 63 C7
Thornley St Hyde SK14 .. 167 E1
Middleton M24 .... 47 B1
Radcliffe M26 .... 44 B2
Thornmere Cl M27 .... 61 C2
Thorns Ave BL1 .... 143 D3
Thorns Cl BL1 .... 143 D3
Thorns Clough OL3 .... 51 C5
Thorns Rd BL1 .... 143 D3
Thorns The M21 .... 109 B7
Thorns Villa Gdns M28 .... 78 A5
Thornsett SK22 .... 127 E2
Thornsett Cl 11 M9 .... 157 E8
Thornsett Prim Sch
SK22 .... 127 E3
Thornsett Trad Est
SK22 .... 127 E2
Thornsgreen Rd M22 .... 130 D8
Thornton Ave Bolton BL1 .. 23 F1
Droylsden M34 .... 100 C8
Urmston M41 .... 95 A2
Thornton Cl
Ashton-in-M WN4 .... 72 F4
Boothstown M28 .... 77 E7
Farnworth BL4 .... 60 B7
Golborne WA3 .... 75 A1
Leigh WN7 .... 75 F1
Little Lever BL3 .... 43 C3
Thornton Cres M25 .... 62 F5
Thornton Ct M16 .... 161 C5
Thornton Dr SK9 .... 131 D3
Thornton Gate SK8 .... 122 A6
Thornton Pl SK4 .... 168 B4
Thornton Rd
Boothstown M28 .... 77 E7
Gatley SK8 .... 131 C8
Manchester M14 .... 98 A2
Thornton St
1 Bolton BL2 .... 148 A7
Manchester M40 .... 160 D4
Oldham OL4 .... 153 F5
Rochdale OL11 .... 139 F5
Thornton St N M40 .... 157 D5
Thorntree Cl M9 .... 157 E7
Thorntree Pl 2 OL12 .... 139 E8
Thornvale WN2 .... 74 C7
Thornway Bramhall SK8 .. 132 C7
High Lane SK6 .... 134 F7
Walkden M28 .... 78 A8
Thornwood Ave M18 .... 99 E4
Thornydyke Ave BL1 .... 24 E5
Thorold Gr M33 .... 108 E4
Thorp Prim Sch OL2 .... 48 C5
Thorp Rd Manchester M40 .. 83 A6
Royton OL2 .... 48 D4
Thorp St Eccles M30 .... 95 B8
Whitefield M45 .... 44 E1
Thorp View OL2 .... 48 C6
Thorpe Ave Radcliffe M26 .. 44 D5
Swinton M27 .... 61 E1
Thorpe Cl
Altrincham WA15 .... 120 C7
Denton M34 .... 100 F4
Oldham OL4 .... 68 A8
Thorpe Gr SK4 .... 111 D6
Thorpe Hall Gr SK14 .... 101 F6
Thorpe La Denton M34 .. 100 F5
Oldham OL4 .... 68 A8
Thorpe St Bolton BL1 .... 143 D2
Glossop SK13 .... 104 E2
Manchester M16 .... 97 C4
Middleton M24 .... 64 C7
Ramsbottom BL0 .... 138 B5
Walkden M28 .... 60 D4
Thorpebrook Rd M40 .... 83 A6
Thorpeness Sq M18 .... 99 D6
Thorsby Ave SK14 .... 167 F2
Thorsby Cl Bolton BL7 .... 24 F8
Droylsden M18 .... 99 E5
Thorsby Rd WA15 .... 119 E5
Thorsby Way 16 M34 .... 101 A1
Thorverton Sq M40 .... 83 C8
Thrapston Ave M34 .... 84 D1
Threadfold Way BL7 .... 24 F7
Threadmill La M27 .... 79 D8
Threaphurst La SK7 .... 125 C1
Threapwood Rd M22 .... 121 E1
Three Acre Ave OL2 .... 49 A4
Three Acres Dr SK5 .... 111 E5
Three Lane Ends OL10 .... 45 F7
Three Sisters Rd WN4 .... 73 B7
Three Sisters Recn Area*
WN4 .... 73 C7
Threlkeld Cl M24 .... 46 C1
Threlkeld Rd Bolton BL1 .. 24 D6
Middleton M24 .... 46 C1
Thresher Cl 3 M33 .... 108 F3
Threshfield Cl BL9 .... 27 F7
Threshfield Dr WA15 .... 120 C7
Throstle Bank St SK14 .. 101 C4
Throstle Ct 3 OL2 .... 48 D4
Throstle Gr Bury BL8 .... 27 C5
Marple SK6 .... 125 E5
Throstle Hall Ct 1 M24 .. 46 F1
Throstle Nest Ave WN6 .... 37 A2
Throstle St OL14 .... 6 B6
Throstles Cl M43 .... 84 C3
Thrum Fold OL12 .... 14 D3
Thrum Hall La
Rochdale OL12 .... 14 D3
Rochdale OL12 .... 14 E3
Thrush Ave BL4 .... 59 F8
Thrush Dr BL9 .... 141 B4
Thrush Ho M6 .... 81 A5
Thrush St OL12 .... 14 C1
Thruxton Cl 4 M16 .... 97 E3
Thurland Rd OL4 .... 67 C6
Thurland St OL9 .... 65 E8
Thurlby Ave M9 .... 64 E5
Thurlby Cl WN4 .... 73 D4
Thurlby St M13 .... 98 D4
Thurleigh Rd M20 .... 110 B4
Thurlestone Ave BL2 .... 26 D1
Thurlestone Dr
Stockport SK7 .... 124 B2
3 Urmston M41 .... 95 C3
Thurlestone Rd WA14 .. 119 B6
Thurloe St M14 .... 98 C3
Thurlow WA3 .... 90 E7
Thurlow St Salford M50 .. 154 F1
Stretford M50 .... 96 F8
Thurlston Cres M8 .... 156 B7
Thurlwood Ave M20 .... 110 A7
Thurnham St BL3 .... 146 C3
Thursby Ave M20 .... 110 A6
Thursby Ho WN5 .... 54 C7
Thursby Wlk M24 .... 46 C2
Thursfield St M6 .... 81 B5
Thursford Gr BL6 .... 21 D1
Thurstan St WN3 .... 55 E4
Thurstane St BL1 .... 142 C2
Thurston Ave WN3 .... 55 B3
Thurston Cl BL9 .... 45 A2
Thurston Clough Rd OL3,
OL4 .... 50 D2
Thurston Gn SK9 .... 137 A1
Thurstons OL3 .... 51 D6
Thynne St Bolton BL3 .... 145 F5
Farnworth BL4 .... 42 C2
Tib La M2 .... 158 F1
Tib St Denton M34 .... 101 A2
Manchester M1,M4 .... 159 A2
Ramsbottom BL0 .... 138 B5
Tiber Ave OL8 .... 66 C1
Tideswell Ave
Manchester M40 .... 160 D3
Wigan WN5 .... 36 A1
Tideswell Bank 8 SK13 .. 171 E1
Tideswell Cl SK8 .... 131 D8
Tideswell Rd
Droylsden M43 .... 83 E3
Hazel Grove SK7 .... 133 E8
Tideswell Way M34 .... 113 A8
Tideswell Wlk 7 SK13 .. 171 E1
Tideway Cl M7 .... 80 F8
Tidworth Ave M4 .... 160 D2
Tiefield Wlk M21 .... 109 E6
Tiernan Lo 14 WN6 .... 37 A1
Tiflis St OL12 .... 139 E8
Tig Fold Rd BL4 .... 59 E8
Tilbury Gr WN6 .... 35 D7
Tilbury St OL1 .... 153 E8
Tilby Cl M41 .... 94 E2
Tildsley St BL3 .... 147 E4
Tile St BL9 .... 140 F3
Tilehurst Ct M7 .... 81 B7
Tilgate Wlk 17 M9 .... 64 E3
Tillard Ave SK3 .... 123 B8

Tillhey Rd M22 ...121 D2
Tillington Cl BL1 ...143 E3
Tilney Ave M32 ...96 E1
Tilshead Wlk M13 ...163 C6
Tilside Gr BL6 ...40 B7
Tilson Rd M23 ...120 F5
Tilstock Wlk M23 ...120 E8
Tilston Wlk 5 SK9 ...131 E1
Tilton St OL1 ...49 C1
Timberbottom BL2 ...25 C4
Timbercliffe OL15 ...6 D1
Timberhurst BL9 ...28 D2
Timbersbrook Gr 5
SK9 ...131 D2
Times Ret Pk OL10 ...29 C2
Times St M24 ...65 B8
Timothy Cl M6 ...80 B3
Timperley Cl OL8 ...67 B2
Timperley Fold OL6 ...85 C6
Timperley La WN7 ...76 B2
Timperley Rd OL6 ...85 C6
Timperley St M11 ...165 C8
Timperley Sta WA15 ...119 F8
Timpson Rd M23 ...120 E7
Timsbury Cl BL2 ...42 F5
Timson St 2 M35 ...83 F7
Tin St BL3 ...145 E5
Tindall St Eccles M30 ...95 B8
Reddish SK5 ...99 F3
Tindle St M28 ...60 F3
Tinkersfield WN7 ...75 D7
Tinline St BL9 ...141 A2
Tinningham Cl M11 ...99 E7
Tinsdale Wlk M24 ...46 C1
Tinshill Cl M12 ...165 A5
Tinsley Cl M40 ...160 E2
Tinsley Gr BL2 ...148 B8
Tintagel Ct
Little Lever M26 ...43 C5
Stalybridge SK15 ...85 F2
Tintagel Rd WN2 ...57 A4
Tintagel Wlk SK14 ...102 E3
Tintern Ave
Ashton-in-M WN4 ...73 D3
Bolton BL2 ...25 B2
Heywood OL10 ...29 C4
Littleborough OL15 ...16 A7
Manchester M20 ...109 F5
Rochdale OL12 ...14 E2
Tyldesley M29 ...77 C7
Urmston M41 ...107 A8
Whitefield M45 ...62 F8
Tintern Cl SK12 ...133 D5
Tintern Ct M20 ...109 F5
Tintern Dr WA15 ...120 C2
Tintern Gr SK1 ...112 B1
Tintern Pl OL10 ...29 C4
Tintern St M14 ...98 B2
Tintwhistle CE Prim Sch
SK13 ...103 F6
Tinwald Pl WN1 ...37 F1
Tipperary St SK15 ...86 E5
Tipping St
Altrincham WA14 ...119 D3
Wigan WN3 ...150 B6
Tipton Cl Cheadle SK8 ...123 B4
Radcliffe M26 ...43 D5
Tipton Dr M23 ...109 B2
Tiptree Wlk 18 M9 ...157 E8
Tirce Cl SK7 ...124 F1
Tirza Ave M19 ...110 F8
Tissington Bank 15
SK13 ...171 D1
Tissington Terr 16 SK13 ...171 D1
Titchfield Rd OL8 ...67 C4
Tithe Barn Cl OL12 ...15 D4
Tithe Barn Cres BL1 ...25 B4
Tithe Barn Ct SK4 ...110 F4
Tithe Barn Prim Sch
SK4 ...168 A3
Tithe Barn Rd SK4 ...110 F4
Tithe Barn St 6 BL5 ...39 E1
Tithebarn Rd
Altrincham WA15 ...129 C8
Garswood WN4 ...72 D2
Tithebarn St 3 Bury BL9 ...140 F2
Radcliffe M26 ...44 D4
Up Holland WN8 ...53 B7
Titian Rise OL1 ...49 A3
Titterington Ave M21 ...97 B2
Tiverton Ave Hindley WN7 ...57 D2
Sale M33 ...107 F3
Tiverton Cl
Little Lever M26 ...43 C5
Tyldesley M29 ...77 D7
Tiverton Dr
Handforth SK9 ...131 D1
Sale M33 ...107 F3
Tiverton Ho M6 ...80 A3
Tiverton Pl OL7 ...85 A5
Tiverton Rd M41 ...95 E3
Tiverton Wlk BL1 ...142 C1
Tiviot Dale SK1 ...169 F2
Tiviot Way SK1,SK4,SK5 ...169 F3
Tivoli St M3 ...158 E1
Tixall Wlk 3 M8 ...63 E2
Toad La OL12 ...139 F8
Toad Pond Cl M27 ...79 C6
Tobermory Cl M11 ...83 D1
Tobermory Rd SK8 ...122 C1
Todd St Bury BL9 ...140 F4
Glossop SK13 ...116 D8
Heywood OL10 ...29 A2
Manchester M3 ...159 A2
Rochdale OL11 ...31 A7
Salford M7 ...155 D6

Todd's Pl M9 ...64 C1
Toddington La WN2 ...38 B8
Todmorden Rd OL15 ...16 C7
Toft Rd M18 ...99 C4
Toft Way SK9 ...131 E4
Toledo St M11 ...83 D1
Toll Bar Bsns Pk 11 OL13 ...3 D8
Toll Bar St M1 ...164 E6
Toll Gate Cl M13 ...98 E4
Radcliffe M26 ...43 E4
Toll Green Cl WN2 ...56 D7
Toll St Platt Bridge WN2 ...56 A1
Radcliffe M26 ...43 E4
Tolland La WN3 ...128 F8
Tolland Ave M40 ...157 D5
Tollard Cl SK8 ...132 B6
Tollbar St SK1 ...170 F8
Tollemache Cl SK14 ...103 A5
Tollemache Rd SK14 ...103 A5
Tollesbury Cl M40 ...160 D4
Tollgate Way OL16 ...31 C8
Tolver St M18 ...156 B7
Tom Lomas Wlk M11 ...83 B2
Tom Shepley St SK14 ...167 E2
Tomcroft La M34 ...100 D2
Tomlin Sq 7 BL2 ...148 C7
Tomlinson Cl OL8 ...153 E5
Tomlinson St Horwich BL6 ...22 B3
Manchester M40 ...65 C3
Manchester,Hulme M15 ...162 E6
Rochdale OL11 ...30 C3
Tommy Browell Cl 9
M14 ...98 A3
Tommy Johnson Wlk 7
M14 ...98 A3
Tommy La BL2 ...25 C5
Tommy Taylor Cl 1 M40 ...83 C5
Tonacliffe Prim Sch
OL12 ...14 C6
Tonacliffe Rd OL12 ...14 C6
Tonacliffe Terr OL12 ...14 C7
Tonacliffe Way OL12 ...14 C6
Tonbridge Cl BL8 ...27 C7
Tonbridge Pl 9 BL2 ...25 B1
Tonbridge Rd
Manchester M19 ...111 B8
Reddish SK5 ...111 F8
Tong End OL12 ...4 C2
Tong Head Ave BL1 ...25 B4
Tong La Bacup OL13 ...4 C8
Whitworth OL12 ...4 D1
Tong Rd BL3 ...43 A5
Tong St BL4 ...61 C5
Tonge Bridge Way BL2 ...148 B8
Tonge Cl M45 ...45 B1
Tonge Clough BL7 ...24 F8
Tonge Ct M24 ...65 B8
Tonge Fold Rd BL2 ...148 C7
Tonge Hall Cl M24 ...65 B8
Tonge Moor Prim Sch
BL2 ...25 B1
Tonge Old Rd BL2 ...25 B2
Tonge Park Ave BL2 ...25 C1
Tonge Roughs M24 ...65 D8
Tonge St Heywood OL10 ...29 D2
Manchester M12 ...164 D7
Oldham M24 ...65 E6
Rochdale OL16 ...31 A6
Tongfields BL7 ...24 F8
Tongley Wlk 18 M40 ...65 D2
Tonman St M3 ...162 E8
Tontine WN5 ...53 C5
Tontine WN5,WN8 ...53 C6
Tooley La WN6 ...18 D6
Tooley Ho M30 ...95 D8
Toon Cres BL8 ...27 C6
Tootal Dr M5,M6 ...80 C3
Tootal Drive Prim Sch
M6 ...80 C3
Tootal Gr M5 ...80 C2
Tootal Rd M5 ...154 D2
Toothill Cl WN4 ...73 B5
Top o'th' Brow Prim Sch
BL2 ...25 E2
Top o' th' Gn OL12 ...66 C4
Top o' th' La BL2 ...42 D5
Top o' th' Meadows La
OL4 ...50 A1
Top O'Th' Close Rd OL14 ...6 D6
Top Of Heap OL10 ...28 F2
Top of Wallsuches BL6 ...22 F4
Top Schwabe St M24 ...64 E8
Top St Middleton M24 ...46 F1
Oldham OL4 ...67 E5
Topaz St M19 ...99 A1
Topcliffe Rd WN2 ...56 F6
Topcroft Cl M22 ...121 E8
Topfield Rd M22 ...121 C4
Topham St BL9 ...45 A8
Topley St M40 ...157 D6
Topp St BL4 ...60 E7
Topp Way BL1 ...145 E8
Topping Fold Rd BL9 ...141 C3
Topping St Bolton BL1 ...143 E1
Bury BL9 ...141 A3
Toppings Gn BL7 ...25 A7
Toppings The SK6 ...113 A3
Topsham Wlk M40 ...83 D5
Topside OL1 ...48 E1
Tor Ave BL8 ...10 F2
Tor End Rd BB4 ...1 A6
Tor Hey Mews BL8 ...10 F2
Tor View Sch SK84 ...1 D8
Torah St M8 ...159 A4
Torbay Cl 1 BL3 ...144 C5

Torbay Dr SK2 ...124 B7
Torbay Rd
Manchester M21 ...109 C8
Urmston M41 ...95 E1
Torbrook Gr 1 SK9 ...131 D2
Torcross Rd M9 ...64 B5
Torkington Ave M27 ...61 F1
Torkington La SK6,SK7 ...125 E3
Torkington Prim Sch
SK7 ...125 A2
Torkington Rd
Gatley SK8 ...122 B5
Hazel Grove SK7 ...125 B3
Hazel Grove,Torkington Park
SK7 ...124 F2
Wilmslow SK9 ...137 D6
Torkington St SK3 ...170 D8
Torksey Wlk M9 ...64 C5
Torness Wlk M11 ...83 B1
Toronto Ave M90 ...130 B7
Toronto Rd SK2 ...124 A6
Toronto St BL2 ...42 E8
Torpoint Wlk M40 ...65 C1
Torquay Cl 2 M13 ...163 C5
Torquay Gr SK2 ...124 B4
Torquay Rd M33 ...108 C4
Torra Barn Cl BL7 ...8 C3
Torrax Cl M6 ...80 B6
Torre Cl M24 ...47 A3
Torrens St M6 ...80 D5
Torridon Cl WN6 ...37 A3
Torridon Rd BL2 ...42 F7
Torrin Wlk 1 M22 ...121 C1
Torrin Cl SK3 ...170 F5
Torrington Ave
Bolton BL1 ...143 E3
Manchester M9 ...65 A2
Torrington Dr SK14 ...102 E2
Torrington Rd M27 ...80 B6
Torrington St OL10 ...46 E8
Torrisdale Cl BL3 ...144 B5
Torside Cl WN2 ...56 D6
Torside Way
Hadfield SK13 ...104 A5
Swinton M27 ...61 F2
Torver Cl WN3 ...55 A2
Torver Dr Bolton BL2 ...42 F8
Middleton M24 ...46 D2
Torver Wlk M22 ...121 B2
Totland Gr OL9 ...47 E1
Totland Cl M12 ...99 B3
Totley Ave 1 SK13 ...171 D1
Totley Gn 33 SK13 ...171 D1
Totley Lanes 34 SK13 ...171 D1
Totley Mews SK13 ...171 D1
Totley Pl 35 SK13 ...171 D1
Totnes Ave
Chadderton OL9 ...47 F1
Stockport SK7 ...124 A2
Totnes Rd
Manchester M21 ...109 C8
Sale M33 ...108 C4
Totridge Cl SK2 ...124 D5
Tottenham Dr M23 ...120 E7
Tottington Ave OL4 ...67 F7
Tottington High Sch BL8 ...26 F6
Tottington La M25 ...62 F5
Tottington Prim Sch BL8 ...26 F5
Tottington Rd
Bolton BL7,BL8 ...9 F2
Bolton,Harwood Lee BL2 ...25 F6
Bury BL8 ...27 C4
Tottington St 18 M11 ...83 C2
Totton Ho BL1 ...144 C7
Totton Rd M35 ...83 F7
Touchet Hall Rd M24 ...47 D4
Touchstones* OL16 ...139 E7
Toulston Rd WN6 ...36 F2
Tours Ave M23 ...109 A2
Towcester Cl M4 ...160 D1
Tower Ave BL0 ...138 A5
Tower Ct BL7 ...9 C4
Tower Farm BL8 ...10 D4
Tower Gr WN7 ...76 D6
Tower Grange M7 ...155 E8
Tower Hill Rd WN8 ...53 B6
Tower Nook WN8 ...53 A5
Tower Sq M13 ...163 C6
Tower St Chapeltown BL7 ...9 C4
Heywood OL10 ...29 C2
Hyde SK14 ...167 D1
Radcliffe M26 ...44 D4
Stalybridge SK16 ...85 D1
Tower View Ho BL4 ...21 C3
Towers Ave BL3 ...146 A4
Towers Ct SK12 ...133 F5
Towers Rd SK12 ...133 F5
Towers St 2 OL4 ...49 D1
Towey Cl M18 ...99 D6
Town Fields Cl BL9 ...140 F1
Town Fold SK6 ...126 B7
Town Gate Dr M41 ...94 C2
Town Hall La 2 M2 ...158 F1
Town Hall Sq OL16 ...139 F7
Town House Rd OL15 ...16 B6
Town La
Charlesworth SK13 ...115 D6
Coppull PR7 ...19 B8
Denton M34 ...100 E2
Dukinfield SK16 ...101 C8
Town Mill Brow OL12 ...139 E7
Town Sq M33 ...108 A4
Town Square Sh Ctr
OL1 ...153 F6
Town St SK6 ...113 B7
Town's View SK15 ...86 B1

Towncliffe Wlk 18 M15 ...162 D6
Towncroft M34 ...101 A4
Towncroft Ave M24 ...46 F2
Towncroft La BL1 ...40 E8
Townend St SK14 ...167 E2
Townfield M41 ...95 B1
Townfield Gdns WA14 ...119 D5
Townfield La WA13 ...117 B7
Townfield Rd WA14 ...119 D5
Townfield St 4 OL4 ...67 B7
Townfield Wlk 18 M15 ...162 D6
Townfields WN4 ...73 A3
Towngate Bsns Ctr M38 ...59 E5
Townley Fold SK14 ...102 B6
Townley Rd OL16 ...32 A6
Townley St
Manchester M8 ...155 F5
Manchester,Beswick M11 ...164 F8
Middleton M24 ...65 A8
Townrow St OL10 ...29 E2
Townscliffe La SK6 ...126 C6
Townsend Rd M27 ...61 F1
Townsfield Rd BL5 ...57 F7
Townside Row BL9 ...140 F1
Townsley Gr OL6 ...85 E5
Townson Dr WN7 ...75 F1
Towton St M9 ...157 E8
Towyn Ave M5 ...81 A2
Toxhead Cl BL6 ...22 A3
Toxteth St M11 ...99 F7
Tracey St M8 ...64 A1
Tracks La WN5 ...53 D3
Tracy Dr WA12 ...89 E3
Traders Ave M41 ...95 E6
Trafalgar Ave
Droylsden M34 ...100 C7
Poynton SK12 ...134 A3
Trafalgar Bsns Pk M8 ...158 E4
Trafalgar Ct M11 ...97 E2
Trafalgar Gr M7 ...155 D5
Trafalgar Ho M34 ...100 C7
Trafalgar Pl M14 ...110 C8
Trafalgar Rd Hindley WN2 ...56 D5
Sale M33 ...108 C6
Salford M6 ...80 A3
Wigan WN1 ...37 C1
Trafalgar Sq
Ashton-u-L OL7 ...84 F1
3 Ashton-u-L OL7 ...84 F1
Trafalgar St
Ashton-u-L OL7 ...84 F1
Oldham OL1 ...153 E8
Rochdale OL16 ...31 A8
Salford M7 ...155 E5
Trafalgar Wlk
Manchester M11 ...165 B8
Manchester M15 ...162 E5
Trafford Bank Rd M16 ...161 C5
Trafford Bar Sta M16 ...161 B5
Trafford Ctr 2 M17 ...94 A6
Trafford Ctr M17 ...95 D6
Walkden M38 ...60 B5
Trafford General Hospl
M41 ...95 A3
Trafford Gr Farnworth BL4 ...42 E1
Stretford M32 ...96 E3
Trafford Mans 2 M16 ...97 B2
Trafford Park Rd M17 ...96 C5
Trafford Park Sta M32 ...96 C5
Trafford Pk Rd M17 ...161 A5
Trafford Pl
Manchester M15 ...162 D6
Wilmslow SK9 ...137 D6
Trafford Rd
Alderley Edge SK9 ...137 B1
Eccles M30 ...79 D1
Handforth SK9 ...131 B1
Hindley WN2 ...56 C5

Traylen Way OL12 ...14 A1
Trecastell Cl WN1 ...37 F1
Tredcroft St SK13 ...116 B8
Tredgold St BL6 ...22 C2
Tree Ave M43 ...84 A3
Tree Cl OL4 ...67 D8
Tree House Ave 2 OL7 ...85 A6
Tree Tops BL7 ...25 C6
Tree Wlk M32 ...96 C1
Treelands Wlk M5 ...161 B6
Treen Rd M29 ...77 C8
Treetop Cl OL3 ...50 F1
Treetops Ave BL0 ...11 A3
Trefoil Way OL15 ...15 F6
Tregaer Fold M24 ...65 C8
Tregaron Gr WN2 ...57 A3
Tremain Wlk 10 M9 ...157 D7
Trenam Pl M5 ...81 B2
Trenant Rd M6 ...154 D4
Trenchard Ct M11,M43 ...83 D2
Trenchard Dr M22 ...130 F7
Trencherbone M26 ...43 E5
Trengrove St 7 OL12 ...14 C1
Trent Ave Chadderton OL9 ...65 E8
Heywood OL10 ...29 A3
Milnrow OL16 ...32 A6
Trent Cl Bramhall SK7 ...132 C6
Brimington SK5 ...112 C5
Trent Ct Manchester M15 ...162 D6
Stockport SK3 ...170 D7
Trent Dr Bury BL9 ...27 F8
Trent Gr WN7 ...75 C4
Trent Ind Est OL2 ...149 B8
Trent Rd Ashton-in-M WN4 ...73 E5
Billinge WN5 ...71 D3
Shaw OL2 ...149 A8
Wigan WN5 ...54 C4
Trent St OL16 ...31 B6
Trent Way BL4 ...42 A3
Trentham Ave
Farnworth BL4 ...42 C1
Manchester SK4 ...110 F4
Trentham Cl BL4 ...42 C1
Trentham Gr M40 ...65 A1
Trentham Lawns M6 ...81 B4
Trentham Rd M16 ...97 A3
Trentham St
Farnworth BL4 ...42 C1
Salford M15 ...161 C7
Swinton M27 ...61 E1
Tresco Ave M32 ...96 E1
Trescott Mews WN6 ...36 F8
Treswell Ct WN3 ...150 A6
Trevarrick Ct Horwich BL6 ...22 E2
2 Oldham OL4 ...67 C8
Trevelyan Dr WN5 ...53 D1
Trevelyan St M30 ...80 A2
Trevor Ave Bolton BL3 ...147 D3
Sale M33 ...107 F2
Trevor Dr M40 ...65 E2
Trevor Gr SK1 ...124 A8
Trevor Rd Eccles M30 ...79 B3
Swinton M27 ...79 E6
Urmston M41 ...95 A2
Trevor St Manchester M11 ...99 E7
Rochdale OL11 ...30 B3
Triangle The WA15 ...120 B7
Tribune Ave WA14 ...119 B7
Trident Rd M30 ...94 F7
Trillo Ave BL2 ...148 B6
Trimdon Cl M11 ...83 B2
Trimingham Dr BL8 ...27 D5
Trimley Ave M40 ...157 C5
Tring Wlk M9 ...64 B3
Trinity Ave M33 ...108 D4
Trinity Bldgs OL5 ...68 C2
Trinity CE High Sch
M15 ...163 A6
Trinity Cl SK16 ...101 E8
Trinity Cres M28 ...60 E3
Trinity Ct Ashton-u-L OL6 ...166 A3
Salford M3 ...158 D2
Trinity Gdns
Ashton-in-M WN4 ...72 F4
Stockport SK3 ...123 F3
Trinity Gn BL0 ...11 B2
Trinity Ho OL1 ...153 E8
Trinity Rd M33 ...108 D4
Trinity Ret Pk BL2 ...145 F5
Trinity St Bacup OL13 ...3 C8
Bolton BL3 ...145 F6
Bury BL9 ...140 F1
Marple SK6 ...125 F6
2 Middleton M24 ...64 F8
Rochdale OL12 ...13 E2
Stalybridge SK15 ...86 A1
Trinity Way M3 ...158 D2
Trinity Wlk 18 M11 ...98 B3
Trippier Rd M30 ...94 F8
Tripps Mews M20 ...109 F4
Triscombe Way M16 ...97 E3
Tristam Ct M11 ...163 C7
Trojan Gdns 7 M7 ...81 C5
Trongate Wlk 18 M9 ...157 E8
Troon Cl Bolton BL3 ...40 F3
Bramhall SK7 ...133 A7
Troon Dr SK8 ...122 C1
Troon Rd M23 ...120 F3
Trough Gate OL8 ...66 D2

Troutbeck Ave M4 ....160 D2
Troutbeck Cl BL8 ....10 B2
Troutbeck Dr
  Ramsbottom BL0 ....138 C7
  Tyldesley M29 ....77 A7
Troutbeck Gr WA11 ....71 B2
Troutbeck Rd
  Altrincham WA15 ....120 D5
  Ashton-in-M WN4 ....73 C5
  Gatley SK8 ....122 B3
Troutbeck Rise WN5 .....54 B6
Troutbeck Wlk ⑤ OL2 ...48 E4
Troutbeck Way OL11 .....30 B4
Trowbridge Dr M40 ....6 C1
Trowbridge Rd M34 .....101 A1
Trows La OL11 ....30 D1
Trowtree Ave M12 ......164 E6
Troy Wlk M5 ....161 B7
Troydale Dr M40 ....83 B6
Trumpet St M1 ....5 E2
Truro Ave Ashton-u-L OL6 ...85 D7
  Brinnington SK5 ....112 C5
  Stretford M32 ....96 E2
Truro Cl Bramhall SK7 ..132 F7
  Bury BL8 ....140 D3
Truro Dr M33 ....107 D4
Truro Rd Chadderton OL9 ...48 A1
  Tyldesley M29 ....77 C8
Truro Wlk M34 ....100 F1
Trust Rd M18 ....99 C3
Tucana Ave M7 ....81 C3
Tucker's Hill Brow WN2 ...21 B1
Tudbury Way M3 ....158 D2
Tudor Ave Bolton BL1 ...144 B7
  Failsworth M35 ....65 D3
  Farnworth BL4 ....60 B7
  Manchester M9 ....64 E1
  Stalybridge SK15 ....86 D3
Tudor Cl OL5 ....68 E1
Tudor Ct Bolton BL3 ....145 E8
  Manchester,Old Trafford
  M16 ....161 C5
  Manchester,Sedgley Park
  M25 ....63 C3
  Rochdale OL12 ....15 B1
Tudor Gn SK9 ....131 E1
Tudor Grange SK14 ......54 E2
Tudor Hall St OL11 ......30 C2
Tudor Ind Est SK14 ....101 D7
Tudor Rd
  Altrincham WA14 ....119 B7
  Handforth SK9 ....131 E1
Tudor St ⑨ Bolton BL3 .146 C4
  Middleton M24 ....65 B8
  Oldham OL8 ....153 D5
  Oldham OL8 ....153 E5
  Wigan WN7 ....59 B7
Tuer St M13 ....163 A6
Tuffley Rd M23 ....121 A3
Tufton Wlk M9 ....157 D7
Tugford Cl ⑨ M16 ....97 E4
Tuley St M11 ....164 F7
Tulip Ave Farnworth BL4 ...42 A1
  Kearsley BL4 ....60 F5
  Sale M33 ....107 C4
Tulip Cl Chadderton OL9 ...65 E7
  Stockport SK3 ....170 D5
Tulip Dr Altrincham WA15 ...119 F6
  Wigan WN6 ....36 F3
Tulip Gr OL12 ....14 E3
Tulip Rd M31 ....105 E2
Tulip Wlk M40 ....158 D4
Tulketh Street Ind Est
  Manchester M40 ....157 F8
  Manchester M40 ....83 A8
Tulle Ct M25 ....63 A4
Tully St M7 ....158 D7
Tully St S M7 ....155 E6
Tulpen Sq OL9 ....152 B7
Tulworth Rd SK12 .....133 D4
Tumblewood Dr SK8 ...122 E4
Tumbling Bank Terr OL4 ...67 F5
Tumbling Wlk M9 ....64 D3
Tunbridge Sq M5 ....81 A2
Tunicliffe's New Row
  WN7 ....75 C5
Tunley La WN5 ....18 E5
Tunley Moss WN6 ....18 E4
Tuns Rd OL8 ....67 B2
Tunshill Gr OL16 ....32 A6
Tunshill La WN5 ....54 D5
Tunstall Rd OL4 ....67 C6
Tunstall St
  ② Manchester M11 ......99 E7
  Stockport SK4 ....169 E2
Tunstead Ave M20 ....109 F6
Tunstead La OL3 ....69 D5
Tunstead Mill Terr ③
  OL13 ....3 B8
Tunstead Rd OL13 ....3 C8
Turbary Wlk OL16 ......31 D6
Turf Cl OL2 ....48 B8
Turf Hill Rd OL16 ......31 C4
Turf House Cl OL15 .....15 F7
Turf La Chadderton OL9 ...66 A3
  Royton OL2 ....48 F3
Turf Lea Rd SK6 ....126 B1
Turf Pit La OL4 ....49 F4
Turf St M26 ....43 D4
Turf Terr OL15 ....16 A6

Turfland Ave OL2 ....48 F3
Turfton Rd OL2 ....48 F3
Turk St ⑥ BL1 ....144 C8
Turks Rd M26 ....43 E5
Turley St M8 ....156 B6
Turn Moss Rd M21,M32 ...96 F1
Turn Rd BL0 ....11 E8
Turn St OL6 ....85 D4
Turnberry BL3 ....40 F3
Turnberry Cl M29 ......77 C8
Turnberry Dr SK9 .....137 D8
Turnberry Rd SK8 ....122 C1
Turnberry Wlk M8 ....156 C8
Turnbull Ave M25 ......63 C7
Turnbull Rd
  Manchester M13 ....98 F2
  Reddish M18 ....99 F4
Turnbury Cl M33 ......108 B6
Turnbury Rd M22 .....121 E5
Turncliff Cres SK6 ...125 D7
Turncroft La SK1 .....112 B1
Turncroft Way M28 ....77 F7
Turnditch Cl WN6 ......37 A4
Turnell Way M28 ....79 A5
Turner Ave Failsworth M35 ...83 E6
  Irlam M44 ....94 A3
  Leigh WN2 ....56 E1
Turner Bridge Rd BL2 .148 C8
Turner Dr M41 ....95 F2
Turner Gdns SK14 ....167 E4
Turner La Ashton-u-L OL6 ...166 B4
  Brinnington SK6 ......112 F6
  Hyde SK14 ....167 F4
Turner Rd SK6 ....125 F5
Turner St Ashton-u-L OL6 ...166 B4
  ③ Bacup OL13 ....3 C8
  Bolton BL1 ....148 A8
  Denton M34 ....100 E5
  Droylsden M11 ....83 C1
  Hindley WN7 ....56 D7
  Leigh WN2 ....76 A4
  Manchester M4 ......159 A2
  Manchester,Gorton M18 ...99 D5
  Manchester,Old Trafford
  M16 ....161 C6
  Oldham OL4 ....67 E8
  Rochdale OL12 ....14 E1
  Salford M7 ....155 E7
  Westhoughton BL5 .....57 E5
  Wigan WN1 ....37 D1
Turner's Pl OL12 ....3 C8
Turnerford Cl BL7 ......8 A4
Turnfield Cl OL16 ......15 D3
Turnfield Rd SK8 .....122 D3
Turnfield Rd SK8 .....122 D3
Turnhill Rd OL16 ....31 B3
Turnhill Dr WN4 ....73 B2
Turnlee Cl SK13 ......116 C7
Turnlee Dr SK13 ......116 C7
Turnlee Rd SK13 .....116 C7
Turnough Rd OL16 .....31 F7
Turnpike Cl OL3 ....51 A5
Turnpike Ct ⑦ M16 ....97 C3
Turnpike Gn ⑥ M6 ...154 F3
Turnpike The SK6 ....125 D7
Turnpike Wlk M11 ....160 F1
Turnstone Ave WA12 ...89 C4
Turnstone Cl WN7 .....76 A6
Turnstone Rd
  ⑧ Bolton BL2 ....148 A6
  Hazel Grove SK2 .....125 A6
Turret Hall Dr ① WA3 ...90 E8
Turriff Gr WN2 ....44 E7
Turton & Edgworth CE Prim
  Coll BL7 ....9 D5
Turton Ave BL3 ....43 A4
Turton Cl Bury BL8 ....44 A8
  Heywood OL10 ....29 A2
Turton High Sch Media Arts
  Coll BL7 ....25 B7
Turton Hts BL2 ....25 B6
Turton La M25 ....62 F5
Turton Rd Bolton BL2,BL7 ...25 C5
  Bury BL8 ....26 D8
Turton St Bolton BL1 ...148 A8
  Golborne WA3 ....90 A8
  Manchester M11 ....99 D7
Turton's Terr* BL7 .....9 C3
Turves Rd SK8 ....122 F1
Turville Ho SK3 ......131 D2
Turvin Rd HX6,OL11 ....7 D2
Tuscan Rd M20 ....122 B8
Tuscany View M7 ......81 B8
Tutbury St M4 ....160 D1
Tuxford Wlk M40 ....157 D5
Tweed Cl
  Altrincham WA14 .....119 C6
  Oldham OL8 ....153 E5
Tweedale Ave M9 ......64 C4
Tweedale St OL11 ....139 C6
Tweedale Way OL9 ....65 C4
Tweedle Hill Rd M9 ...64 C4
Tweedsdale Cl M45 ....45 B1
Tweenbrook Ave M23 .121 A3
Twelve Apostles RC Prim Sch
  M7 ....75 D8
Twelve Yards Rd M44 .93 E6
Twigworth Rd M22 ...121 C2
Twillbrook Dr M3 ....158 E3
Twin St OL10 ....29 E1
Twinegate OL12 ....14 E3
Twining Brook Rd SK8 ...123 B3
Twining Rd M17 ....95 E8
Twinnies Ct SK9 .....131 B1
Twinnies Rd SK9 ....131 B1

Twirl Hill Rd OL6 .....85 E8
Twiss Green Com Prim Sch
  WA3 ....91 E4
Twiss Green Dr WA3 ...91 E4
Twiss Green La WA3 ...91 E4
Twisse Rd BL2 ....42 F7
Twist Ave WA3 ....90 C8
Twist La WN7 ....75 E5
Two Acre Dr OL2 .....48 F7
Two Acre La OL4 .....50 B3
Two Bridges Rd OL16 ...32 C3
Two Brooks La BL8 ...10 D3
Two Porches Sch M46 ...58 D4
Two Trees Com High Sch
  M34 ....101 A1
Two Trees La M34 ...101 A1
Twoacre Ave M22 ...121 C5
Twyford Cl M20 ......109 F3
Tybyrne Cl M28 ....77 F7
Tydden St OL8 ....66 F3
Tydeman Wlk ② OL16 ...32 A5
Tyersall Cl M30 ......79 F7
Tyldesley Arc ⑪ WN1 ..150 C8
Tyldesley Old Rd M46 ...58 E2
Tyldesley Pas ⑤ M29 ...58 E1
Tyldesley Prim Sch M29 ...77 B7
Tyldesley Rd M46 ....58 E2
Tyldesley St M14 .....98 A3
Tyldesley St George's Central
  CE Prim Sch M29 .....59 A1
Tyler St SK9 ....137 A1
Tyler Wlk ② M9 ......90 F8
Tymm St M40 ....83 C8
Tyndall Ave M40 .....65 A1
Tyne Ct M28 ....60 C3
Tyne St ⑧ OL4 ....67 C7
Tynedale Cl SK5 ....111 F5
Tynesbank M28 ....60 C2
Tynesbank Cotts M28 ...60 C3
Tyntesfield Prim Sch
  M33 ....107 E1
Tynwald St OL4 ......67 C7
Tynwell Wlk ⑧ M40 ..156 C5
Tyrer Ave WN3 ....54 F5
Tyrol Wlk M11 ....164 F8
Tyrone Cl M23 ......120 D8
Tyrone Dr OL11 ......29 F5
Tyrrell Gr SK14 .....102 A1
Tysoe Gdns M3 ......158 D2
Tyson St M8 ....155 F8
Tytherington Dr M19 ...99 D1

Union Rd continued
  Marple SK6 ....125 F6
  Rochdale OL12 ....15 E4
Union St Ashton-u-L OL6 ...166 C3
  Bacup OL13 ....3 C8
  Bolton BL7 ....26 D8
  Bury BL9 ....140 F2
  Glossop SK13 ....116 C8
  Hyde SK14 ....167 E2
  Ince-in-M WN2 ....56 A8
  Leigh WN7 ....75 F5
  Manchester M12 ......163 C7
  Manchester M14 ......98 B3
  Manchester M24 ......47 A1
  Manchester,Abbey Hey M18 ...99 E6
  Middleton M24 ....47 A1
  Oldham OL1 ....153 F6
  Oldham,County End OL4 ...67 E6
  Oldham,Mumps OL1 ....67 A7
  Ramsbottom BL0 ....138 C6
  Rochdale OL12,OL16 ...139 F8
  Royton OL2 ....48 D3
  Salford M6 ....81 A4
  Stockport SK1 ......170 F8
  Swinton M27 ....62 A1
  Swinton M27 ....79 E8
  Tyldesley M29 ......58 F1
  Whitworth OL12 ....14 C8
Union St W OL8 .....153 E6
Union Terr M7 ......155 F8
United Rd M17 ....96 E7
United Trad Est M17 ...96 F5
Unity Cl OL10 ....29 B1
Unity Cres OL10 ....29 B1
Unity Dr M7 ....155 F6
Unity St Heywood OL10 ...29 B1
  Walsden OL14 ....6 A8
Univ of Manchester (Lab)
  M30 ....94 D6
Univ of Manchester Inst of
  Science & Tech M1 ...163 B8
Univ of Manchester The
  Manchester M13 .....163 B6
  Manchester M15 .....163 A5
Univ of Salford
  Salford M3 ....158 D2
  Salford M6 ....81 C3
Univ of Salford, Irwell Valley
  Campus M6 ....81 B4
University Rd M5,M6 ...81 B1
University Rd W M5 ...81 B2
Unsworth Ave
  Golborne WA3 ....74 E1
  Tyldesley M29 ......77 C8
Unsworth Prim Sch BL9 ...45 A2
Unsworth St Bacup OL13 ...3 D7
  ② Hindley WN2 ......56 A4
  Leigh WN7 ....75 E7
  Radcliffe M26 ......43 F4
  Tyldesley M29 ......59 B1
Unsworth Terr WN2 ...56 C5
Unsworth Way OL1 ...153 E8
Unwin Ave M18 ......99 D4
Up Holland High Sch
  WN5 ....53 C4
Upavon Ct M8 ....155 F6
Upavon Rd M22 .....121 F3
Upcast La SK9 .....136 E3
Upholland Rd WN5 ...53 E3
Upholland Roby Mill CE Prim
  Sch WN8 ....35 B3
Upland Dr
  Ashton-in-M WN4 ....73 D4
  Walkden M38 ....59 F6
Upland Rd OL8 ......67 A4
Uplands M24 ....65 A7
Uplands Ave M26 ....43 F4
Uplands Rd Flixton M41 ...106 E8
  Glossop SK13 ......116 D8
  Romiley SK14 ......114 A6
Uplands The OL5 ....68 D1
Upper Brook St M13 ...163 B6
  Stockport SK1 .....170 F8
Upper Broom Way BL5 ...40 A2
Upper Camp St M7 ...155 D5
Upper Campfield Mkt
  M3 ....162 E8
Upper Chorlton Rd M16 ...97 C3
Upper Cliff Hill OL12 ...32 C1
Upper Conran St M9 ...157 E8
Upper Cyrus St M40 ...160 E2
Upper Dicconson St
  WN1 ....37 C1
Upper Downs WA14 ...119 C3
Upper George St
  ⑳ Rochdale OL16 ...14 F1
  Tyldesley M29 .....58 E2
Upper Gloucester St M6 ...81 A3
Upper Hayes Cl OL16 ...31 C8
Upper Helena St M40 ...160 E2
Upper Hibbert La SK6 ...125 F4
Upper Kent Rd M14 ...98 E3
Upper Kirby St M4 ..159 C1
Upper Lees Dr BL5 ...40 A1
Upper Lloyd St M14 ...98 A3
Upper Mead OL7 ......8 A1
Upper Medlock St M15 ...162 F7
Upper Monsall St M40 ...157 F6
Upper Moss La M15 ...162 E6
Upper Park Rd
  Manchester M14 ....98 C4
  Manchester,Broughton Park
  M7 ....63 E1

Upper Passmonds Gr
  OL11 ....30 B8
Upper St Stephen St
  WN6 ....150 B8
Upper Stone Dr OL16 ...31 D6
Upper West Gr M13 ...164 D5
Upper Wharf St M5 ...81 C1
Upper Wilton St M25 ...63 C4
Uppermill Dr M19 ...110 E3
Uppingham Dr M38 ...138 B7
Upton OL11 ....139 E6
Upton Ave Cheadle SK8 ...132 A8
  Manchester SK4 ....110 E4
Upton Cl Golborne WA3 ...90 D8
  Middleton M24 .....65 A5
Upton Dr WA14 .....119 E8
Upton La M29 ....77 C8
Upton Rd M46 ......58 E4
Upton St M1 ....159 B1
Upton Way Bury BL8 ...26 F5
  ⑰ Handforth SK9 ...131 D5
Upton Wlk ⑩ OL7 ...166 A1
Upwood Rd WA3 .....90 D7
Upwood Wlk ㉛ M9 ...64 E3
Urban Ave WA15 ...119 E4
Urban Rd WA15 ....119 E4
Urban Rd
  Altrincham WA15 ...119 E4
  Sale M33 ....108 A4
Urbis* ① M3,M4 ...159 A2
Urmston St OL8 ....66 F3
Urmston Ave WN2 ...89 B5
Urmston Gram Sch M41 ...95 C2
Urmston Inf Sch M41 ...95 C2
Urmston Jun Sch M41 ...95 C2
Urmston La M32,M41 ...96 B1
Urmston Pk M41 ....95 C2
Urmston St WN7 ...75 D5
Urmston Sta M41 ...95 B2
Urwick Rd SK6 ....113 B2
Usk Cl M45 ....63 C7
Uttley St Bolton BL1 ...143 D2
  Rochdale OL11 .....30 C4
Uvedale Ho M30 ....79 D1
Uxbridge Ave ⑯ M11 ...83 C2
Uxbridge St OL6 ...166 A3

Vaal St OL8 ....66 C3
Valance Cl M12 ...165 A6
Valdene Cl BL4 ....60 D7
Valdene Dr Farnworth BL4 ...60 D7
  Walkden M28 ....78 D8
Vale Ave Bury BL9 ...44 D7
  Horwich BL6 ....22 A3
  Kearsley M26 ......61 C7
  Sale M33 ....108 E5
  Swinton M27 ....62 A1
  Urmston M41 ....94 E1
Vale Cl Appley Bridge WN6 ...35 E8
  Hazel Grove SK7 ...125 A2
  Manchester SK4 ...110 F2
  Romiley SK6 ......113 F2
Vale Coppice Horwich BL6 ...22 A3
  Ramsbottom BL0 ...11 C3
Vale Cotts
  Dukinfield SK14 ...101 C4
  Horwich BL6 ....21 F2
  Littleborough OL15 ...16 A5
Vale Cres SK8 ....122 F2
Vale Croft WN8 ....53 A6
Vale Dr Oldham OL9 ...153 D6
  Prestwich M25 ....63 A2
Vale Edge M26 ....44 A5
Vale Head SK9 ...131 D2
Vale House Dr SK13 ...104 A5
Vale La M35 ....83 A8
Vale Park Ind Est M8 ...156 C7
Vale Rd Altrincham WA15 ...120 B5
  Altrincham,Rosehill WA14 ...119 B1
  Droylsden M43 ....84 B3
  Manchester SK4 ...110 F1
  Mossley SK15 .....86 E6
  Romiley SK6 ......113 F2
  Shaw OL2 ....49 D6
  Wilmslow SK9 .....136 E8
Vale Side OL5 ....86 C8
Vale St Ashton-u-L OL7 ...85 A6
  Bolton BL2 ....43 A7
  Droylsden M11 ....29 E2
  Heywood OL10 .....29 E2
  Middleton M24 ....65 B8
Vale The
  Appley Bridge WN6 ...35 D8
  Mossley SK15 .....86 C8
Vale Top Ave M9 ...157 F7
Vale View
  ③ Altrincham WA14 ...119 C1
  ⑥ Bolton BL7 .....24 F7
Vale Works M4 ....159 A3
Valemount SK13 ...104 A5
Valencia Rd M7 ....81 B6
Valentia Rd M9 ....64 D4
Valentine St
  Failsworth M35 ...83 E7
  Oldham OL4 ....67 C6
Valentines Rd M46 ...58 A1
Valerie Wlk ① M15 ...162 F7
Valetta Cl M14 ....110 D8
Valewood Ave SK4 ...168 A1
Valiant Rd WN5 ...54 D8
Valiant Wlk ① M40 ...65 E1
Valletts La BL1 ...142 C1
Valletts S BL1 ....142 C1
Valley Ave BL8 ....27 B4

Valley Cl Cheadle SK8 . . . . . . **122** E3
Mossley OL5 . . . . **68** B2
Valley Com Prim Sch The
BL1 . . . . **143** F2
Valley Cotts OL3 . . . . **69** C4
Valley Dr SK9 . . . . **131** C3
Valley Gdns SK14 . . . . **114** E8
Valley Gr M34 . . . . **101** B2
Valley New Rd OL2 . . . . **48** E3
Valley Rd Bramhall SK7 . . . . . . **123** F1
Cheadle SK8 . . . . **122** E3
Glossop SK13 . . . . **115** F8
Hattersley SK14 . . . . **114** E8
Middleton M24 . . . . **47** D2
Romiley SK6 . . . . **112** D4
Royton OL2 . . . . **48** E3
Stockport SK4 . . . . **168** A1
Urmston M41 . . . . **94** D4
Wigan WN5 . . . . **54** D5
Valley Rd S M41 . . . . **94** C2
Valley Rise OL2 . . . . **32** A1
Valley St SK7 . . . . **132** C5
Valley View Bolton BL7 . . . . . . **25** A7
Dukinfield SK14 . . . . **102** A4
Newton-le-W WA12 . . . . **89** B1
Whitworth OL12 . . . . **4** D4
Valley Way SK15 . . . . **86** C1
Valley Wlk M11 . . . . **160** F1
Valpy Ave BL2 . . . . **25** B3
Vanbrugh Gr M16 . . . . **36** B1
Vancouver Quay M50 . . . . **96** F7
Vane St M30 . . . . **79** D2
Vanguard Cl M30 . . . . **94** F7
Vannes Gr SK14 . . . . **102** F3
Vant St OL8 . . . . **67** C4
Vantomme St BL1 . . . . **143** E4
Varden Gr SK3 . . . . **170** D5
Varden Rd SK12 . . . . **133** E3
Vardon Dr SK9 . . . . **137** D6
Varey St M18 . . . . **99** D5
Varley Rd BL3 . . . . **146** A4
Varley St M40 . . . . **160** D3
Varna St M11 . . . . **99** D7
Varna Street Prim Sch
M11 . . . . **99** D6
Vauban Dr M6 . . . . **80** B3
Vaudrey Dr Cheadle SK8 . . . . . **123** A2
Hazel Grove SK7 . . . . **124** E2
Sale WA15 . . . . **27** D8
Vaudrey La M34 . . . . **101** A2
Vaudrey Rd SK7 . . . . **113** A5
Vaudrey St SK15 . . . . **86** A1
Vaughan Ave M40 . . . . **83** A8
Vaughan Gr OL4 . . . . **67** E6
Vaughan Ind Est M12 . . . . **164** F7
Vaughan Rd
Manchester SK4 . . . . **169** D3
Manchester,Chorlton-cum-Hardy
M21 . . . . **109** D8
Vaughan St Eccles M30 . . . . . . **79** B3
Manchester M12 . . . . **164** F7
Royton OL2 . . . . **48** E3
Vauxhall Ct M40 . . . . **159** C4
Vauxhall Ind Est SK5 . . . . . . **111** E6
Vauxhall St WN1 . . . . **151** D8
Vauxhall St M40 . . . . **159** B4
Vauze Ave BL6 . . . . **21** D1
Vavasour Ct BL6 . . . . **21** D2
Vavasour St OL16 . . . . **31** B6
Vawdrey Dr ⑤ M23 . . . . **108** F2
Vaynor ⑱ OL12 . . . . **139** E8
Vega St M8 . . . . **158** E4
Vela Wlk M7 . . . . **81** C3
Velmere Ave M9 . . . . **64** A5
Velour Cl M3 . . . . **158** E2
Velvet Cl M1 . . . . **163** A8
Vendale Ave M27 . . . . **79** D6
Venesta Ave M6 . . . . **80** B4
Venetia St M40 . . . . **83** C5
Venice St Bolton BL3 . . . . **146** C4
Manchester M1 . . . . **163** A8
Venlow Gdns SK8 . . . . **123** B3
Ventnor Ave Bolton BL1 . . . . . . **143** F3
Manchester M19 . . . . **111** C8
Sale M33 . . . . **108** B6
Whitefield BL9 . . . . **45** A3
Ventnor Cl M34 . . . . **113** B8
Ventnor Rd
Manchester SK4 . . . . **168** A2
Manchester,Didsbury M20 . . . . **110** C3
Ventnor St
Manchester M9 . . . . **157** E8
Rochdale OL11 . . . . **139** F5
Salford M6 . . . . **81** A4
Ventor St M9 . . . . **157** D8
Ventura St M14 . . . . **98** A1
Ventura St SK22 . . . . **127** D1
Venture Scout Way M8 . . . . . **155** F6
Venture Way SK12 . . . . **133** F3
Venwood Rd M25 . . . . **62** F2
Verbena Ave BL4 . . . . **42** A1
Verbena Cl M31 . . . . **105** F3
Verda St WN7 . . . . **74** B8
Verdant La M30 . . . . **94** F8
Verdon St M4 . . . . **159** A3
Verdun Ave M6 . . . . **80** B3
Verdun Cres OL11 . . . . **30** C8
Verdun Rd M30 . . . . **79** B4
Verdure Ave Bolton BL1 . . . . . . **40** E8
Sale M33 . . . . **108** C1
Verdure Cl M35 . . . . **84** B7
Vere St M6 . . . . **154** F3
Verity Cl Manchester M20 . . . . **110** C4
Royton OL2 . . . . **48** D3
Verity Wlk M9 . . . . **64** B3

Vermont St BL1 . . . . **145** D8
Salford M3 . . . . **158** D2
Verne Ave M27 . . . . **79** E8
Verne Dr OL1 . . . . **49** E5
Verne Wlk WN4 . . . . **73** D3
Verney Rd OL2 . . . . **48** E2
Vernham Wlk BL3 . . . . **147** E4
Vernon Ave Eccles M30 . . . . . . **79** C3
Stockport SK1 . . . . **112** B2
Stretford M32 . . . . **96** D1
Vernon Cl Cheadle SK8 . . . . . . **122** E1
Poynton SK12 . . . . **133** D2
Vernon Ct ⑧ M7 . . . . **63** C1
Vernon Dr Marple SK6 . . . . **125** D7
Prestwich M25 . . . . **63** A2
Vernon Gr M33 . . . . **108** C4
Vernon Inf Sch SK12 . . . . **133** E3
Vernon Jun Sch SK12 . . . . **133** E3
Vernon Park Prim Sch
SK1 . . . . **112** A1
Vernon Pk WA15 . . . . **120** A7
Vernon Rd Droylsden M43 . . . . **83** E2
Manchester M7 . . . . **63** C1
Poynton SK12 . . . . **133** E2
Ramsbottom BL8 . . . . **11** A1
Romiley SK6 . . . . **112** E3
Vernon St
Ashton-u-L OL6 . . . . **166** C4
Bolton BL1 . . . . **145** E8
Bury BL9 . . . . **140** F4
Farnworth BL4 . . . . **42** E1
Hazel Grove SK7 . . . . **124** D3
Hyde SK14 . . . . **167** E2
Leigh WN7 . . . . **75** F5
Manchester M16 . . . . **162** D5
Manchester,Harpurhey M9 . . . . **157** E7
Mossley OL5 . . . . **68** C2
Salford M7 . . . . **155** D5
Stockport SK1 . . . . **169** F2
Vernon View ③ SK6 . . . . **112** F3
Vernon Wlk
⑤ Bolton BL1 . . . . **145** E8
Stockport SK1 . . . . **169** E1
Verona Dr M40 . . . . **83** C4
Veronica Rd M20 . . . . **110** C3
Verra St BL0 . . . . **138** C6
Verrill Ave M23 . . . . **109** C1
Verwood Wlk ⑨ M23 . . . . **121** A5
Vesper St M35 . . . . **84** A8
Vesta St Manchester M4 . . . . . **159** C1
Ramsbottom BL0 . . . . **138** B7
Vestris Dr M6 . . . . **80** B3
Vetch Cl WA3 . . . . **105** B5
Viaduct Rd WA14 . . . . **119** D7
Viaduct St
Manchester M12 . . . . **164** E8
Newton-le-W WA12 . . . . **89** A3
Salford M3 . . . . **158** E1
Stockport SK1 . . . . **169** E1
Vicar's Dr OL16 . . . . **139** F6
Vicar's Gate OL16 . . . . **139** F7
Vicarage Ave SK8 . . . . **132** B7
Vicarage Cl Adlington PR6 . . . . **21** A8
Bolton BL3 . . . . **27** E8
Dukinfield SK16 . . . . **101** E8
Oldham OL4 . . . . **67** F7
Platt Bridge WN2 . . . . **56** A2
Salford M6 . . . . **80** B3
Vicarage Cres OL6 . . . . **85** D5
Vicarage Ct ③ M23 . . . . **120** D6
Vicarage Dr
Dukinfield SK16 . . . . **101** E8
Rochdale OL12,OL16 . . . . **15** C3
Vicarage Gdns
Hyde SK14 . . . . **167** F2
Stockport SK3 . . . . **170** D8
Vicarage Gr M30 . . . . **79** F2
Vicarage La
Altrincham WA14 . . . . **119** C1
Middleton M24 . . . . **65** D7
Poynton SK12 . . . . **133** E5
Shevington WN6 . . . . **36** A5
Vicarage Rd Abram WN2 . . . . . **56** B1
Ashton-in-M WN4 . . . . **73** B2
Ashton-u-L OL7 . . . . **85** B5
Blackrod BL6 . . . . **21** C2
Golborne WN7 . . . . **74** B1
Irlam M44 . . . . **94** A2
Orrell WN5 . . . . **53** D4
Stockport SK3 . . . . **170** E6
Swinton M27 . . . . **79** E8
Urmston M41 . . . . **95** B4
Walkden M28 . . . . **60** C4
Vicarage Rd N OL11 . . . . **30** C1
Vicarage Rd S OL11 . . . . **30** C1
Vicarage Rd W BL6 . . . . **21** C2
Vicarage Sq WN7 . . . . **75** F5
Vicarage St Bolton BL3 . . . . . **145** D5
Oldham OL8 . . . . **66** C3
⑪ Radcliffe M26 . . . . **44** A3
Shaw OL2 . . . . **149** B7
Vicarage View OL11 . . . . **30** D1
Vicarage Way OL2 . . . . **149** A6
Vicars Hall Gdns M28 . . . . **77** F5
Vicars Hall La M28 . . . . **77** F4
Vicars Rd M21 . . . . **109** A8
Vicars St M30 . . . . **79** F2
Viceroy Ct M20 . . . . **110** B2
Vicker Cl M27 . . . . **61** F2
Vicker Gr M20 . . . . **109** F5
Vickerman St BL1 . . . . **143** D2
Vickers Row BL4 . . . . **60** B8
Vickers St Bolton BL3 . . . . **145** E5
Manchester M40 . . . . **160** E4
Victor Ave BL9 . . . . **140** E4
Victor Cl WN5 . . . . **54** D8
Victor Mann St M11 . . . . **100** A7
Victor St Heywood OL10 . . . . . . **46** E8
Manchester M40 . . . . **159** C4

Victor St continued
Salford M3 . . . . **158** D2
Victoria Ave
Altrincham WA15 . . . . **119** F7
Cheadle SK8 . . . . **123** A2
Eccles M30 . . . . **79** F3
Hadfield SK13 . . . . **104** A5
Hazel Grove SK7 . . . . **124** E3
Leigh WN7 . . . . **56** E1
Manchester M19 . . . . **111** A8
Manchester M20 . . . . **110** A3
Manchester,Higher Blackley
M9 . . . . **64** C5
Pendlebury M27 . . . . **80** A8
⑦ Romiley SK6 . . . . **112** F3
Whitefield M45 . . . . **63** A8
Wigan WN6 . . . . **37** A1
Victoria Ave E M24,M40,
M9 . . . . **65** B4
Victoria Avenue Com Prim
Sch M9 . . . . **64** C5
Victoria Bridge St M3 . . . . **158** F2
Victoria Cl Aspull WN2 . . . . **38** B6
Bramhall SK7 . . . . **132** D6
Hyde SK14 . . . . **167** E2
⑥ Worsley M28 . . . . **78** A6
Victoria Cres Eccles M30 . . . . . **79** F3
Standish WN6 . . . . **36** E8
Victoria Ct
⑤ Ashton-u-L OL7 . . . . **166** A1
Bury BL8 . . . . **27** A3
Farnworth BL4 . . . . **42** C2
Horwich BL6 . . . . **22** C3
⑦ Manchester M20 . . . . **110** A3
Manchester,Openshaw
M11 . . . . **165** C8
Stretford M32 . . . . **96** C2
Victoria Dr M33 . . . . **108** B6
Victoria Gdns Hyde SK14 . . . . **167** F4
Shaw OL2 . . . . **149** B7
Victoria Gr Bolton BL1 . . . . . . **142** C1
Manchester M14 . . . . **110** C7
Reddish SK4 . . . . **111** D5
Victoria Grange M20 . . . . **110** A4
Victoria Ho
Manchester M11 . . . . **165** C8
Salford M6 . . . . **80** A4
Victoria Ind Est WN7 . . . . **75** E7
Victoria Ind Est The M4 . . . . . **160** D1
Victoria La Swinton M27 . . . . . . **79** D8
Whitefield M45 . . . . **62** F7
Victoria Lo M7 . . . . **81** C5
Victoria Mews
⑤ Dukinfield SK16 . . . . **101** C6
Whitefield BL9 . . . . **45** B2
Victoria Mill M40 . . . . **160** D3
Victoria Mkt SK15 . . . . **86** A1
Victoria Par
Rawtenstall BB4 . . . . **2** E8
Urmston M41 . . . . **95** D2
Victoria Park Jun Sch
M32 . . . . **96** D2
Victoria Pk SK1 . . . . **124** B8
Victoria Rd
Altrincham WA15 . . . . **119** D3
Altrincham,Timperley
WA15 . . . . **120** A6
Bolton BL1 . . . . **40** D8
Dukinfield SK16 . . . . **101** C6
Eccles M30 . . . . **79** E3
Garswood WN4 . . . . **72** D8
Irlam M44 . . . . **93** F1
Kearsley BL4 . . . . **61** A6
Manchester M19 . . . . **98** F1
Manchester,Fallowfield
M14 . . . . **110** B8
Manchester,Whalley Range
M16 . . . . **97** D2
Newton-le-W WA12 . . . . **89** C3
Platt Bridge WN2 . . . . **56** A2
Sale M33 . . . . **108** D3
Salford M6 . . . . **80** A4
Stockport SK4 . . . . **169** E3
Stretford M32 . . . . **96** D1
Urmston M41 . . . . **95** B2
Wilmslow SK9 . . . . **137** A6
Wythenshawe M22 . . . . **121** D8
Victoria Sq Bolton BL1 . . . . . . **145** F7
Manchester M4 . . . . **159** B2
Manchester M60 . . . . **23** D1
Victoria St Ainsworth BL2 . . . . **26** E1
Altrincham WA14 . . . . **119** D5
Ashton-u-L OL7 . . . . **166** A1
Bacup OL13 . . . . **3** D8
Blackrod BL6 . . . . **21** D2
Bury BL8 . . . . **140** D2
Bury BL8 . . . . **140** D3
Bury,Tottington BL8 . . . . **26** E7
Chadderton OL9 . . . . **152** C8
Denton M34 . . . . **100** F3
Dukinfield SK16 . . . . **101** D8
Failsworth M35 . . . . **83** D6
⑥ Farnworth BL4 . . . . **42** E2
Glossop SK13 . . . . **116** C8
Heywood OL10 . . . . **29** E1
Leigh WN7 . . . . **75** F5
Littleborough OL15 . . . . **16** B5
Manchester,Openshaw
M11 . . . . **165** C8
Middleton M24 . . . . **65** B8
Oldham OL8 . . . . **84** F8
Oldham,Lees OL4 . . . . **67** A6
Oldham,Mumps OL4 . . . . **67** A6
Stockport SK2 . . . . **170** F6
Violet Way M24 . . . . **65** D7

Victoria St continued
Ramsbottom BL0 . . . . **138** B6
Rawtenstall BB4 . . . . **2** E8
⑫ Rochdale OL12 . . . . **14** F1
Shaw OL2 . . . . **149** B7
Stalybridge,Millbrook SK15 . . . . **86** D4
⑥ Stalybridge,Stamford Park
SK15 . . . . **85** F2
Westhoughton BL5 . . . . **57** F8
Whitworth OL12 . . . . **14** C8
Wigan WN5 . . . . **54** F6
Worsley M28 . . . . **78** A6
Victoria St E OL7 . . . . **166** A2
Victoria Sta M3 . . . . **159** A3
Victoria Station App
M3 . . . . **159** A2
Victoria Terr
Bickershaw WN2 . . . . **74** F8
Heywood OL10 . . . . **29** C4
Manchester M13 . . . . **98** C4
Manchester,Longsight M12 . . . . **98** F4
Milnrow OL16 . . . . **32** A5
Victoria The M50 . . . . **96** F7
Victoria Trad Est OL9 . . . . **66** B3
Victoria Way
Bramhall SK7 . . . . **132** D6
Leigh WN7 . . . . **75** F7
Royton OL2 . . . . **48** C6
Victoria Wlk OL9 . . . . **48** C1
Victoria Works Ind Est
M46 . . . . **58** B4
Victory Cl M34 . . . . **100** C7
Victory Rd Irlam M44 . . . . **105** C4
Little Lever BL3 . . . . **43** B4
Victory St Bolton BL1 . . . . **144** C8
Manchester M14 . . . . **98** C3
Victory Trad Est BL3 . . . . **148** A5
Vienna Rd SK3 . . . . **170** D6
Vienna Rd E SK3 . . . . **170** E6
View St BL3 . . . . **147** E4
Viewfield Wlk ⑯ M9 . . . . **157** E7
Viewlands Dr SK9 . . . . **131** D2
Vigo Ave BL3 . . . . **146** B3
Vigo St Heywood OL10 . . . . **29** E1
Oldham OL4 . . . . **67** D5
Viking Cl M11 . . . . **160** F1
Viking St Bolton BL3 . . . . **42** A4
Rochdale OL11 . . . . **30** C8
Villa Ave WN6 . . . . **37** A4
Villa Rd OL8 . . . . **66** F4
Villa The SK14 . . . . **103** A5
Village Circ M17 . . . . **96** D6
Village Ct
⑧ Handforth SK9 . . . . **131** D1
Stretford M17 . . . . **96** C6
Village Gn OL3 . . . . **69** B8
Village Gr M7 . . . . **81** C5
Village The M41 . . . . **106** F8
Village View Billinge WN5 . . . . . **71** E5
⑫ Leigh WN7 . . . . **76** B4
Village Way ⑫ SK9 . . . . **131** D1
Village Way (Ashburton Rd E)
M17 . . . . **96** C6
Village Wlk ⑪ M11 . . . . **83** C1
Villdale Ave SK2 . . . . **124** C7
Villiers Ct M45 . . . . **63** A6
Villiers Dr OL8 . . . . **66** F4
Villiers St Ashton-u-L OL6 . . . . **85** D2
Bury BL9 . . . . **141** A3
Hyde SK14 . . . . **167** F2
Salford M6 . . . . **154** F4
Vinca Gr M7 . . . . **155** D6
Vincent Ave Eccles M30 . . . . . . **79** D4
Manchester M21 . . . . **97** A1
Oldham OL4 . . . . **67** C8
Vincent Ct BL3 . . . . **147** E3
Vincent St Bolton BL3 . . . . **145** D6
Hyde SK14 . . . . **113** F8
Littleborough OL15 . . . . **16** A6
Manchester M11 . . . . **165** C8
Middleton M24 . . . . **47** A2
⑰ Rochdale OL16 . . . . **31** A5
Salford M7 . . . . **155** E7
Vincent Way WN5 . . . . **54** D8
Vine Ave M27 . . . . **80** B8
Vine Cl Sale M33 . . . . **107** C5
Shaw OL2 . . . . **149** B7
Vine Ct Rochdale OL16 . . . . **31** B6
Stretford M32 . . . . **96** D1
Vine Fold M40 . . . . **65** F1
Vine Gr Stockport SK2 . . . . **124** C6
Wigan WN3 . . . . **150** C7
Vine Pl OL11 . . . . **139** F5
Vine St Eccles M30 . . . . **79** C1
Hazel Grove SK7 . . . . **124** E3
Hindley WN2 . . . . **56** D6
Manchester M11,M18 . . . . **99** E6
Oldham OL9 . . . . **66** B3
Prestwich M25 . . . . **63** C5
Salford M7 . . . . **81** C8
Wigan WN1 . . . . **37** D1
Vinery Gr M34 . . . . **100** E3
Vineyard Cl OL12 . . . . **15** C7
Vineyard St OL4 . . . . **67** E8
Viola St Bolton BL1 . . . . **143** E3
Viola St Bolton BL1 . . . . **83** D2
Droylsden M43 . . . . **83** D2
Violet Ave BL4 . . . . **42** E2
Violet Ct M22 . . . . **121** D1
Violet Hill Ct OL4 . . . . **67** E8
Violet St Ashton-in-M WN4 . . . . **73** B2
Droylsden M18 . . . . **99** F6
Ince-in-M WN3 . . . . **151** E6
Stockport SK2 . . . . **170** F6
Violet Way M24 . . . . **65** D7
Vip Centre Ind Est OL1 . . . . . . **49** C1

Val – Wal	**261**

Virgil St M15 . . . . **162** D6
Virginia Chase SK8 . . . . **131** F8
Virginia Cl M23 . . . . **120** D7
Virginia St Bolton BL3 . . . . **146** B4
Rochdale OL11 . . . . **30** E4
Virginia Way WN5 . . . . **54** D8
Viscount Dr Gatley SK8 . . . . . . **131** D7
Wythenshawe M90 . . . . **129** F7
Viscount Rd WN5 . . . . **54** D8
Viscount St M14 . . . . **98** C3
Vista Ave WN12 . . . . **89** A4
Vista Rd WA11,WA12 . . . . **89** A4
Vista The M44 . . . . **105** C4
Vista Way WA12 . . . . **89** A4
Vivian Cl WN6 . . . . **98** E4
Vivian St OL11 . . . . **139** E5
Vixen Cl M21 . . . . **109** E7
Voewood Ho SK1 . . . . **124** B8
Voltaire Ave M6 . . . . **80** B3
Vorlich Dr OL9 . . . . **65** F8
Vulcan Cl WA12 . . . . **89** C1
Vulcan Dr WN1 . . . . **151** D7
Vulcan Ind Est WA12 . . . . **89** D1
Vulcan Rd WN5 . . . . **54** D8
Vulcan St OL1 . . . . **49** B1
Vyner Gr M33 . . . . **107** F6

W

Wadcroft Wlk ⑲ M9 . . . . **157** E8
Waddicor Ave OL6 . . . . **85** E6
Waddington Cl Bury BL8 . . . . . **26** E2
Golborne WA3 . . . . **74** B8
Waddington Fold OL16 . . . . **31** C2
Waddington Rd BL1 . . . . **142** A1
Waddington St OL9 . . . . **152** C8
Wade Bank BL5 . . . . **57** F8
Wade Hill La OL3 . . . . **68** E8
Wade Ho ⑥ M30 . . . . **79** D1
Wade Row OL3 . . . . **69** B8
Wade St ⑦ Bolton BL3 . . . . . . **147** F3
Middleton M24 . . . . **65** D6
Wade Wlk M11 . . . . **165** A8
Wadebridge Ave M23 . . . . **120** D7
Wadebridge Cl ③ BL2 . . . . **25** B1
Wadebrook Dr SK9 . . . . **131** D1
Wadeford Cl M4 . . . . **159** C3
Wadesmill Wlk M13 . . . . **163** B7
Wadeson Rd M13 . . . . **163** C7
Wadham Gdns SK6 . . . . **113** C5
Wadham Way WA15 . . . . **119** F1
Wadhurst Wlk ⑥ M13 . . . . . . **163** C5
Wadlow Cl M3 . . . . **158** E3
Wadsworth Cl SK9 . . . . **131** E3
Wadsworth Dr WN6 . . . . **36** F2
Wadsworth Ind Pk BL3 . . . . . **147** E4
Wadsworth Mews M43 . . . . **83** F1
Waggon Rd Bolton BL2 . . . . **42** D8
Bolton BL2 . . . . **66** C8
Waggoners Ct ② M27 . . . . **79** F7
Wagner St BL1 . . . . **143** D3
Wagstaffe Dr M35 . . . . **83** F7
Wagstaffe St M24 . . . . **47** A2
Wagtail Cl M28 . . . . **78** D8
Wain Cl M30 . . . . **79** B2
Wain Stones Gn SK2 . . . . **124** E6
Waincliffe Ave M20,M21 . . . . . **109** D4
Wainfleet Cl WN3 . . . . **54** E2
Waingap Cres OL12 . . . . **14** D8
Waingap Rise OL12 . . . . **14** E4
Waingap View OL12 . . . . **14** E4
Wainman St M6 . . . . **81** B5
Wainscot Cl M27 . . . . **77** B7
Wainwright Ave M34 . . . . **99** F3
Wainwright Cl
Oldham OL4 . . . . **68** A7
Stockport SK2 . . . . **124** A7
Wainwright Rd WA14 . . . . **119** C5
Wainwright St
Oldham OL8 . . . . **153** E5
Stalybridge SK15 . . . . **85** D1
Waithlands Rd OL16 . . . . **31** B6
Wakefield Cres
Romiley SK6 . . . . **113** A1
Standish WN6 . . . . **37** A6
Wakefield Dr
Chadderton OL2 . . . . **48** C1
Swinton M27 . . . . **61** D4
Wakefield Mews BL7 . . . . **24** F7
Wakefield Rd SK15 . . . . **86** B3
Wakefield St
Golborne WA3 . . . . **90** A7
⑤ Manchester M1 . . . . **163** A7
Wakefield Wlk M34 . . . . **101** A1
Wakeling Rd M34 . . . . **112** E8
Walcot Pl WN3 . . . . **54** F2
Walcott Cl M13 . . . . **164** E5
Wald Ave M14 . . . . **110** C7
Waldeck St BL1 . . . . **145** D8
Waldeck Wlk ⑦ M9 . . . . **64** E3
Walden Ave OL4 . . . . **49** C2
Walden Cl M14 . . . . **110** A8
Walden Cres SK7 . . . . **124** C3
Waldon Ave SK8 . . . . **122** D5
Waldon Cl BL3 . . . . **146** C4
Hindley WN2 . . . . **56** F4
Waldorf Cl WN3 . . . . **54** D2
Wales St OL1 . . . . **49** D1
Walford Rd WN4 . . . . **73** C3
Walford St BL1 . . . . **24** F4
Walk Mill Cl OL12 . . . . **15** D4
Walk The Atherton M46 . . . . . . **58** F3
⑤ Rochdale OL16 . . . . **139** F7

Walkdale Brow SK13 ....**116** B7
Walkden Ave WN1 .....**37** B2
Walkden Ave E WN1 ....**37** C2
Walkden Ct M28 ....**60** C4
Walkden High Sch M28 ...**60** E1
Walkden Market Pl 🏠
  M28 ....**60** D3
Walkden Rd Walkden M28 **.60** D1
  Worsley M28 ....**78** E7
Walkden Sta M28 ....**60** D2
Walkdene Dr M28 ....**60** B3
Walkdens Ave M46 ......**58** A2
Walker Ave Bolton BL3 ..**147** F3
  Failsworth M35 ....**84** B6
  Prestwich M25,M45 ......**63** A6
  Stalybridge SK15 ....**86** C2
Walker Cl Hyde SK14 ...**167** F2
  Kearsley BL4 ....**61** A6
Walker Fold SK14 .....**167** F2
Walker Fold Rd BL1 ....**23** D4
Walker Gn M30 ....**79** B5
Walker Ho 🏠 M30 ......**79** D1
Walker La SK14 ....**167** F2
Walker Rd Eccles M30 ...**79** A4
  Failsworth OL9 ....**65** F2
  Irlam M44 ....**93** F1
  Manchester M9 ....**64** E4
Walker St Bolton BL1 ...**145** D6
  🏠 Bury BL9 ....**44** E8
  Denton M34 ....**100** E4
  Hadfield SK13 ....**104** A4
  Heywood OL10 ....**29** C1
  Middleton M24 ....**64** C7
  Oldham OL8 ....**153** D6
  🏠 Radcliffe M26 ....**44** C1
  Rochdale OL16 ....**31** A7
  Stockport SK1 ....**169** E1
  Westhoughton BL5 ....**57** E8
Walker's Croft M3 ....**158** F2
Walker's La OL4 ....**68** A3
Walker's Rd OL4 ....**66** C2
Walkers Cl OL3 ....**69** B8
Walkers Ct Farnworth BL4 **.60** D8
  Oldham OL4 ....**68** A6
Walkers Dr WN7 ....**76** A5
Walkerwood Dr SK15 ...**86** D2
Walkmill OL3 ....**50** F1
Walkway The BL3 ....**40** F5
Wall Hill Rd OL3 ....**50** E2
Wall St Oldham OL8 ....**153** F5
  Salford M6 ....**154** F2
  Wigan WN6 ....**36** F1
Wall Way M18 ....**99** E4
Wallace Ave M14 ....**98** D3
Wallace La WN1 ....**37** E1
Wallace St 🏠 OL8 ......**66** F4
Wallasey Ave M14 ......**98** A1
Wallbank Dr OL12 ......**14** C7
Wallbank Rd SK7 ......**124** A1
Wallbrook Ave WN5 ....**53** E1
Wallbrook Cres M38 ....**60** B6
Wallbrook Gr BL4 ......**42** B2
Walled Gdn The
  Manchester M16 ....**97** E2
  Swinton M27 ....**79** D6
Waller Ave M14 ....**110** C8
Walley St BL1 ....**143** E3
Wallgarth Cl WN3 ......**54** C2
Wallgate WN3 ....**150** B7
Wallhead Rd OL16 ......**31** D7
Wallingford Rd
  Handforth SK9 ....**131** C5
  Urmston M41 ....**95** E3
Wallis St Chadderton OL9 **.66** A4
  Failsworth M40 ....**83** C5
Walls St WN7 ....**57** C2
Wallshaw Pl OL1 ....**67** A7
Wallshaw St OL1 ....**67** A7
Wallsuches BL6 ....**22** F4
Wallwork Cl OL11 ......**13** E1
Wallwork Rd M29 ......**77** D6
Wallwork St
  Droylsden M11 ....**99** E8
  Radcliffe M26 ....**44** A4
  Reddish SK5 ....**99** F2
Wallworth Ave M18 ....**99** D5
Wallworth Terr SK9 ....**136** E8
Wally Sq M7 ....**155** E6
Walmer Dr SK7 ....**124** A1
Walmer Rd WN2 ....**57** A5
Walmer St
  Manchester M14 ....**98** C3
  Manchester,Abbey Hey M18 **.99** E6
Walmer St E M14 ......**98** C3
Walmersley Ct 🏠 SK6 ..**125** F1
Walmersley Old Rd BL9 .**27** F7
Walmersley Rd WN7 ....**75** E5
  Failsworth M40 ....**65** E1
Walmesley Ave WN3 ...**150** C6
Walmesley Dr WN7 .....**56** B7
Walmesley Rd WN7 .....**75** E5
Walmley Gr BL3 ....**146** C3
Walmsley Ave OL15 ....**15** F3
Walmsley CE Prim Sch
  BL7 ....**8** E1
Walmsley Gr M41 ....**95** D2
Walmsley St 🏠 Bury BL8 **.27** B4
  Newton-le-W WA12 ......**89** D4
  Reddish SK5 ....**169** F3
  Stalybridge SK15 ....**102** A8
Walney Rd Wigan WN3 ...**54** D2
  Wythenshawe M22 ....**121** D4
Walnut Ave Bury BL9 ...**141** C3

Walnut Ave continued
  Oldham OL4 ....**67** D8
  Wigan WN1 ....**37** D2
Walnut Cl Hyde SK14 ...**102** A2
  Swinton M27 ....**61** D4
  Wilmslow SK9 ....**137** E8
Walnut Gr Leigh WN7 ...**75** F8
  Sale M33 ....**108** A4
Walnut Rd Eccles M30 ...**79** A4
  Partington M31 ....**105** D3
Walnut St Bolton BL1 ...**143** F2
  🏠 Manchester M18 ......**99** D5
Walnut Tree Rd SK3 ...**123** A8
Walnut Wlk 🏠 M32 .....**96** C1
Walpole Ave WN3 ......**54** F3
Walpole St OL16 ....**31** A7
Walsall St M6 ....**81** A5
Walsden Est OL14 ......**6** B7
Walsden St M11 ....**83** C2
Walsh Ave M9 ....**64** D2
Walsh Cl WA12 ....**89** C5
Walsh Fold BL7 ....**9** D2
Walsh Ho M46 ....**58** D4
Walsh St Chadderton OL9 **.152** B6
  Horwich BL6 ....**22** B4
  🏠 Manchester M9 ......**157** D8
Walshaw Brook Cl BL8 ...**26** F4
Walshaw Dr M27 ....**79** F7
Walshaw La BL8 ....**26** F4
Walshaw Rd BL8 ....**27** B4
Walshaw Wlk BL8 ......**26** F5
Walsh Way BL3 ....**140** D2
Walsingham Ave
  Manchester M20 ....**109** F4
  Middleton M24 ....**65** A5
Walter Scott Ave WN1 ...**37** B5
Walter Scott St 🏠 OL1 ..**67** B8
Walter St
  Ashton-in-M WN4 ....**73** D4
  Droylsden M18 ....**99** E6
  Leigh WN7 ....**75** B5
  Manchester M16 ....**97** C4
  Manchester M9 ....**157** D8
  Prestwich M25 ....**62** F4
  Radcliffe M26 ....**43** F6
  Walkden M28 ....**60** D2
  Wigan WN5 ....**54** D6
Walters Dr OL8 ....**67** A3
Walters Green Cres WA3 **.74** A2
Waltham Ave
  Glazebury WA3 ....**92** C7
  Wigan WN6 ....**36** F2
Waltham Dr SK8 ....**132** B6
Waltham Gdns M26 .....**43** E5
Waltham Rd M16 ....**97** E1
Waltham St OL4 ....**67** C6
Walthew La WN5 ....**36** B1
Walthew La
  Platt Bridge WN2 ....**56** A2
  Wigan WN5 ....**36** D2
Walton Cl Heywood OL10 .**46** D8
  Middleton M24 ....**46** C1
Walton Ct BL3 ....**147** F4
Walton Dr Bury BL9 .....**27** E8
  Marple SK6 ....**125** D7
Walton Ho M35 ....**83** F8
Walton Pl BL4 ....**60** E7
Walton Rd
  Altrincham WA14 ....**119** B5
  Culcheth WA3 ....**91** F3
  Manchester M9 ....**64** D5
  Sale M33 ....**108** A4
Walton Way M34 ....**101** B1
Walworth Cl M26 ....**61** C7
Walworth Dr 🏠 WN2 ...**96** E1
Wanborough Ct WN7 .....**75** F5
Wandsworth Ave M11 ...**83** D2
Wanley Wlk 🏠 M9 ......**64** E3
Wansbeck Cl M32 ....**96** E1
Wansbeck La M6 ....**81** C3
Wansbeck Rd M32 ....**96** E1
Wansfell Wlk M4 ....**160** D2
Wansford St M14 ....**98** A3
Wanstead Ave M9 ....**65** B3
Wapping St BL1 ....**143** D2
War Office Rd OL11 .....**30** B2
Warbeck Cl Hindley WN2 .**56** E3
  Reddish SK5 ....**100** A2
Warbeck Rd M40 ....**65** D2
Warbreck Dr BL8 ....**108** D3
Warburton Bridge Rd
  WA13,WA3 ....**105** A1
Warburton Dr WA15 ...**129** D6
Warburton La
  Partington M31 ....**105** F4
  Partington M31 ....**105** E2
Warburton St Bolton BL1 **.143** F2
  Eccles M30 ....**79** C1
  🏠 Manchester M20 ....**110** B3
  Salford M5 ....**161** B6
Warburton View WA15 ..**120** C7
Warcock Rd OL4 ....**67** C7
Ward La Diggle OL3 .....**51** F5
  Disley SK12 ....**135** F4
Ward Rd M43 ....**84** B1

Ward St Chadderton OL9 **.152** C7
  Hindley WN2 ....**56** E7
  Hyde SK14 ....**167** E2
  Manchester,Didsbury
  🏠 Manchester,Didsbury
    M20 ....**110** B3
  Oldham OL1 ....**153** D8
  Romiley Sk6 ....**112** F3
  Stockport SK1 ....**124** A7
Warde St M15 ....**162** E6
Warden La M40 ....**83** B6
Warden St M40 ....**83** B6
Wardend Cl M38 ....**60** A6
Wardens Bank BL5 ......**57** E5
Wardham Cl BL5 ....**57** F5
Wardle Brook Ave SK14 .**102** D2
Wardle Brook Wlk
  SK14 ....**102** D3
Wardle Cl Radcliffe M26 .**43** E5
  Stretford M32 ....**96** E2
Wardle Ct M33 ....**108** C4
Wardle Edge OL12 ......**15** B4
Wardle Fold OL12 ......**15** C7
Wardle Gdns OL12 ......**15** C3
Wardle High Sch OL12 ...**15** D5
Wardle Rd Rochdale OL12 .**15** C4
  Sale M33 ....**108** C4
Wardle St Bacup OL13 ....**3** D8
  Bolton BL2 ....**148** C5
  Littleborough OL15 ......**16** A6
  Manchester M40 ....**160** E3
Wardley Ave
  Manchester M16 ....**97** E1
  Walkden M28 ....**60** B3
Wardley CE Prim Sch
  M27 ....**61** C2
Wardley Dr BL1 ....**144** A7
Wardley Hall La M29 ...**79** A8
Wardley Hall Rd M27,M28 **.61** B1
Wardley Ho 🏠 M6 ......**80** C4
Wardley Ind Est M28 ....**61** C1
Wardley Rd M29 ....**77** D8
Wardley Sq M29 ....**77** D8
Wardley St Swinton M27 .**79** F8
  Wigan WN5 ....**54** B6
Wardlow Ave
  🏠 Gamesley SK13 ......**171** D1
  Wigan WN5 ....**36** A1
Wardlow Fold 🏠 SK13 ..**171** D1
Wardlow Gdns 🏠 SK13 .**171** D1
Wardlow Gr 🏠 SK13 ....**171** D1
Wardlow Mews SK13 ....**171** D1
Wardlow St BL3 ....**146** B4
Wardlow Wlk 🏠 SK13 ...**171** D1
Wardour St Atherton M46 .**58** C2
  Atherton M46 ....**58** D2
Wards 🏠 M13 ....**163** B6
Wardsend Wlk 🏠 M15 ..**162** D6
Ware Cl WN4 ....**73** D4
Wareham Gr M30 ....**79** C3
Wareham St M8 ....**64** B1
Wareing St M29 ....**76** F8
Wareing Way BL3 ......**145** E6
Wareings Yd 🏠 OL11 ....**31** A4
Warfield Wlk 🏠 M9 .....**64** E3
Warford Ave SK12 .....**134** A2
Warford La WA16 ......**136** B1
Warford St M4 ....**159** A3
Warford Terr WA16 ....**136** B2
Wargrave CE Prim Sch
  WA12 ....**89** C1
Wargrave House Sch
  WA12 ....**89** C1
Wargrave Mews WA12 ...**89** C1
Wargrave Rd WA12 .....**89** C2
Warham St SK9 ....**137** B7
Warke The M28 ....**78** F6
Warlands End Gate OL14 .**6** D5
Warley Cl SK8 ....**122** E6
Warley Gr SK16 ....**101** C8
Warley Rd M16 ....**97** A3
Warley St OL15 ....**16** B6
Warlingham Cl BL8 .....**27** B1
Warlow Crest OL3 ....**69** A4
Warlow Dr Leigh WN7 ....**57** D1
  Uppermill OL3 ....**69** A4
Warmarsh Gr OL5 ....**68** D2
Warmington Dr M12 ....**164** E6
Warminster Gr WN3 ....**54** D2
Warmley Rd M23 ......**120** D8
Warncliffe St 🏠 WN5 ...**54** D5
Warne Ave M43 ....**84** C2
Warner Wlk 🏠 M11 ....**160** F1
Warnford Cl M40 ....**83** C4
Warp Wlk 🏠 M4 ....**159** C2
Warre St OL6 ....**166** B3
Warren Ave SK8 ....**122** D5
Warren Bank M9 ....**64** D3
Warren Bruce Rd M17 ...**96** D5
Warren Cl Atherton M46 .**58** E5
  Denton M34 ....**100** D2
  Poynton SK12 ....**133** B4
  Stockport SK12 ....**123** D2
Warren Dr
  Altrincham WA15 ......**129** D7
  Bacup OL13 ....**4** C8
  Newton-le-W WA12 ......**89** F4
  Swinton M27 ....**79** D5
Warren Hey SK9 ....**137** E8
Warren La OL8 ....**67** B4
Warren Lea
  Poynton SK12 ....**133** E5
  Romiley SK6 ....**113** A4
Warren Rd Cheadle SK8 .**123** B2
  Stockport SK3 ....**170** E6
  Stretford M17 ....**96** B6

Warren Rd continued
  Walkden M28 ....**60** E3
Warren St 🏠 Bury BL8 ...**27** B1
  Manchester M9 ....**64** C2
  Salford M7 ....**155** F8
  Stockport SK1 ....**169** F2
Warren Wood Prim Sch
  SK2 ....**125** A6
Warrener St M33 ......**108** D4
Warrington La
  Broomedge WA13 ......**117** E2
  Wigan WN1 ....**151** D7
Warrington Rd
  Abram Brow WN2 ....**74** B7
  Ashton-in-M WN4 ....**73** B2
  Fowley Common WA3,WN7 **.92** C5
  Golborne WA3,WA12 .....**90** A6
  Ince-in-M WN3 ....**151** E6
  Leigh WN7 ....**76** B3
  Manchester M9 ....**64** C4
  Platt Bridge WN2 ....**56** A1
  Wigan WN3,WN5 ....**54** F3
Warrington St
  Ashton-u-L OL6 ....**166** B3
  🏠 Oldham OL4 ....**67** E6
  Stalybridge SK15 ....**86** B1
Warsall Rd M22 ....**121** E7
Warslow Dr M33 ....**108** E1
Warsop Ave M22 ......**121** E5
Warstead Wlk 🏠 M13 ..**163** C5
Warth Fold Rd M26 .....**44** C4
Warth La BB4 ....**2** D8
Warth Rd BL9 ....**44** D7
Warthenbury Wlk M13 ...**98** E3
Warton Cl Bramhall SK7 .**133** A7
  Bury BL8 ....**26** F1
Warton Dr M23 ....**121** A5
Warwick Ave
  Ashton-in-M WN4 ....**73** D2
  Denton M34 ....**100** F1
  Manchester M20 ....**109** F4
  Newton-le-W WA12 ......**89** E2
  Prestwich M45 ....**63** B7
Warwick Cl Bury BL8 ....**27** B4
  Cheadle SK8 ....**123** A4
  Dukinfield SK16 ....**101** C6
  Glossop SK13 ....**116** F8
  Manchester SK4 ....**168** A3
  Prestwich M45 ....**63** A7
  Ramsbottom BL8 ....**11** A1
  Shaw OL2 ....**48** F7
Warwick Ct
  Altrincham WA15 ......**119** F1
  Hazel Grove SK7 ....**124** D1
  Hindley WN2 ....**56** F6
  Sale M33 ....**108** D4
  Urmston M41 ....**95** B3
Warwick Gdns BL3 .....**146** B2
Warwick Ho SK4 ....**100** C8
Warwick Ho
  🏠 Sale M33 ....**108** D4
  🏠 Manchester M19 .....**99** A2
Warwick Mall SK8 .....**122** D6
Warwick Rd
  Altrincham WA15 ......**119** E1
  Ashton-u-L OL6 ....**85** C5
  Aspull WN2 ....**38** C5
  Failsworth M35 ....**84** A5
  Irlam M44 ....**105** D8
  Manchester M21 ....**97** B1
  Manchester,Firswood M16,
    M17 ....**97** A4
  Manchester,Heaton Norris
    SK4 ....**168** C3
  Middleton M24 ....**65** B6
  Radcliffe M26 ....**43** F6
  Romiley SK6 ....**113** A2
  Tyldesley M29 ....**77** B3
  Walkden M28 ....**60** C1
Warwick Rd S M16 ......**97** A3
Warwick St Adlington PR7 **.20** F6
  Bolton BL1 ....**143** E4
  Leigh WN7 ....**76** E3
  🏠 Manchester,M1,M4 ..**159** B2
  Oldham OL9 ....**152** C5
  🏠 Oldham OL9 ....**66** C4
  Prestwich M25 ....**62** F4
  Rochdale OL12 ....**15** B2
  Urmston M41 ....**95** B3
Wasdale Ave Bolton BL2 ..**25** F1
  Urmston M41 ....**95** B3
Wasdale Dr Gatley SK8 ..**122** B3
  Middleton M24 ....**46** C6
Wasdale Rd WN4 ....**73** A8
Wasdale St OL11 ....**30** C1
Wasdale Terr SK15 ......**86** A4
Wasdale Wlk 🏠 OL1 ....**67** A8
Wash Fold BL8 ....**27** B5
Wash La Bury BL9 ......**141** B2
  Leigh WN7 ....**76** A4
Washacre BL5 ....**57** B5
Washacre Cl BL5 ....**57** B5
Washacre Prim Sch BL5 ..**57** F7
Washbrook OL9 ....**66** C4
Washbrook Ave M28 .....**60** B1
Washbrook Dr M32 ......**96** B2
Washbrook Ho OL9 ......**66** C4
Washbrook Cl BL5 ......**57** F7
Washford Dr M23 ......**120** D8

Washington Cl SK8 .....**131** F8
Washington Ct 🏠 BL9 ...**140** F3
Washington Ctr The M50 ..**96** E8
Washington St
  🏠 Bolton BL3 ....**144** C6
  Oldham OL9 ....**152** C7
Washway Rd M33 ......**107** F2
Washwood Cl M38 ....**60** B6
Wasnidge Wlk M15 ....**162** F5
Wasp Ave OL11 ....**31** A3
Wastdale Ave BL9 ......**45** A3
Wastdale Rd M23 ......**121** A4
Waste St 🏠 OL1 ....**67** A7
Wastwater St 🏠 OL1 ....**49** A1
Watburn Rd SK22 ......**127** D1
Watchgate Cl M24 ....**46** D3
Water Dr WN6 ....**37** B7
Water Gate OL3 ....**69** B8
Water Grove Rd SK16 ...**101** F7
Water La Droylsden M43 ..**83** E1
  Edenfield BL0 ....**1** D2
  Farnworth BL4 ....**60** E7
  Hollingworth SK14 .....**103** D5
  Milnrow OL16 ....**32** A5
  Radcliffe M26 ....**43** F3
  Wilmslow SK9 ....**137** A7
Water Lane St M26 ......**43** F3
Water Mill Clough OL1 ..**48** C2
Water Rd SK15 ....**85** F2
Water St Adlington PR7 ...**21** A6
  Ashton-u-L OL6 ....**166** B3
  Bolton BL4 ....**144** B6
  Bolton BL1 ....**145** F7
  Denton M34 ....**100** F7
  Glossop SK13 ....**104** E3
  Hyde SK14 ....**167** D2
  Manchester M3 ....**158** E1
  🏠 Middleton M24 ......**46** F1
  Newton-le-W WA12 .....**89** C4
  Radcliffe M26 ....**44** A3
  Ramsbottom BL0 ....**138** B5
  Rochdale OL16 ....**31** A7
  Royton OL2 ....**49** A4
  Stalybridge SK15 ....**86** A2
  Stockport SK1 ....**169** F3
  Whitworth OL12 ....**14** C8
  Wigan WN1 ....**150** C8
Water''s Reach SK6 ...**134** E7
Water's Edge BL4 ....**42** A2
Water's Nook Rd BL5 ....**58** A4
Water's Reach M17 ......**96** F6
Waterbarn La OL13 ....**3** F1
Waterbeck Cl WN1 ....**37** E1
Waterdale Cl M28 ....**78** B6
Waterdale Dr M45 ....**63** A8
Waterfield Way M35 ....**84** A6
Waterfold La BL9 ......**141** C1
Waterfoot Cotts SK14 ..**103** A4
Waterfoot Prim Sch BB4 ..**2** F8
Waterford Ave
  Manchester M20 ....**109** D3
  Reddish SK5 ....**113** F2
Waterford Pl SK8 ......**131** B8
Waterfront Quay M50 ..**161** A7
Waterfront The M11 .....**83** A2
Watergate M34 ....**100** C8
Watergate Dr BL5 ....**59** C7
Watergate La BL4,BL5 ...**59** C7
Watergate Milne Ct 🏠
  OL4 ....**67** D8
Waterhouse Cl OL12 .....**15** C6
Waterhouse Nook BL6,
  PR7 ....**21** A5
Waterhouse Rd M18 .....**99** E4
Waterhouse St OL12 ...**139** F8
Waterloo Ct Bury BL9 ....**44** E8
  🏠 Oldham OL9 ....**110** A5
  🏠 Stalybridge SK15 ...**86** A2
Waterloo Gdns OL6 .....**85** E5
Waterloo Ind Pk BL1 ....**25** A1
Waterloo La 🏠 SK1 ....**112** A7
Waterloo Prim Sch OL7 ..**85** A5
Waterloo Rd
  Ashton-u-L OL6 ....**85** B5
  Bramhall SK7 ....**132** F8
  Manchester M8 ....**155** E3
  Poynton SK12 ....**134** A2
  Stalybridge SK15 ....**86** A2
  Stockport SK1 ....**169** F1
Waterloo St
  Ashton-u-L OL6 ....**85** C4
  Bolton BL3 ....**143** F1
  Bury BL8 ....**27** B4
  Manchester M1 ....**163** A8
  Manchester,Blackley M8,M9 **.64** C1
  Oldham OL9 ....**153** D8
  🏠 Wigan WN6 ....**37** A1

Waterpark Hall 🔟 M7 ....63 E1
Waterpark Rd M7 ......155 E8
Waters Edge Marple SK6 .126 B8
 Uppermill OL3 ....69 A5
 Walkden M28 ....60 F2
Waters Edge Fold OL1 ..49 C4
Waters Meeting Rd
 Bolton BL1 ....143 F1
 Bolton BL1 ....143 F3
 Bolton BL1 ....25 A2
Waters Reach
 Poynton SK12 ....133 F5
 Wigan WN1 ....151 F8
Watersedge Cl SK8 .....123 B3
Watersfield Cl SK8 .....131 F8
Watersheddings Prim Sch
 OL1 ....49 C1
Watersheddings St 🔟 ...49 D1
Watersheddings Way 🔟
 OL4 ....49 D1
Waterside Disley SK12 ..135 E7
 Hadfield SK13 ....104 A6
 Hattersley SK14 ....102 D2
 Marple SK6 ....125 F5
 Sale M33 ....108 C5
 Stretford M17 ....96 F6
 Uppermill OL3 ....69 C4
Waterside Ave 🔟 SK6 ..125 F5
 SK13 ....103 F6
Waterside Dr
 Hattersley SK14 ....102 D2
 Manchester M21 ......109 D4
 Oldham OL11 ....49 C4
 Radcliffe M26 ....44 D4
Waterside Cotts OL3 ....69 C4
Waterside Ct SK14 .....102 D2
Waterside Dr SK13 .....150 B7
Waterside La OL16 .....31 B8
Waterside Rd
 Disley SK12 ....135 F7
 Ramsbottom BL9 ....11 C3
Waterside Trad Est 🔟
 WN7 ....76 B4
Waterside Wlk 🔟 SK14 .102 D2
Waterslea M30 ....79 C2
Waterslea Dr BL1 ....40 F8
Watersmead Cl BL1 ....143 F2
Watersmead St BL1 ....143 F2
Watersmeet M32 ....96 D4
Waterson Ave M40 ......83 A7
Waterton Ave OL5 ....68 B2
Waterton La OL5 ....68 B2
Waterview Cl OL16 ......32 B3
Waterview Pk WN7 ......75 E4
Waterworks Rd
 Delph OL3 ....51 A6
 Oldham OL4 ....49 E1
Watfield Wlk 🔟 M9 ....157 D7
Watford Ave M14 ....98 B2
Watford Bridge Ind Est
 SK22 ....127 D1
Watford Bridge Rd
 SK22 ....127 D1
Watford Cl 🔟 BL1 ......143 E2
Watford La M27 ....127 C2
Watford Rd
 Manchester M19 ......111 A6
 New Mills SK22 ......127 C2
Watkin Ave SK13 ....171 E4
Watkin Cl M13 ....163 C6
Watkin St
 Dukinfield SK14 ....102 A5
 Rochdale OL16 ....31 B4
 Salford M3 ....158 D3
 Wigan WN1 ....150 C8
Watkins Dr M25 ....63 F3
Watling St Bolton BL8 ...26 B7
 Bury BL8 ....26 F1
 Littleborough OL15 ....15 F5
Watlington Cl OL1 ....49 D3
Watson Ave
 Ashton-in-M WN4 ......73 C3
 Golborne WA3 ....73 F1
Watson Gdns M22 ......14 D2
Watson Rd BL4 ....59 F8
Watson St Denton M34 .101 B3
 Eccles M30 ....79 C2
 Manchester M2,M3 ...162 F8
 Oldham OL4 ....67 C8
 Radcliffe M26 ....44 A4
 Swinton M27 ....79 F8
Watton Cl M27 ....61 F2
Watts St Chadderton OL9 .152 B7
 Horwich BL6 ....22 C2
 Manchester M19 ......111 B8
 Oldham OL8 ....153 E6
 Rochdale OL12 ....31 A8
Waugh Ave M35 ....83 F7
Wavell Dr BL9 ....45 A1
Wavell Rd M22 ....121 D2
Waveney Dr
 Altrincham WA14 .....119 C6
 Handforth SK9 ....131 D2
Waveney Rd Shaw OL2 .149 A8
 Wythenshawe M22 ...121 E4
Waverley
 🔟 Heywood OL10 .....29 C2
 🔟 Rochdale OL12 ...139 E8
Waverley Ave
 Failsworth M35 ....60 F6
 Stretford M32 ....96 F3
Waverley Cres M43 ......84 A3
Waverley Ct WN3 ....54 D3
Waverley Dr SK8 ....132 B7
Waverley Gr WN7 ....76 D6
Waverley Rd Bolton BL1 .143 E3

Waverley Rd continued
 Golborne WA3 ....74 D1
 Hindley WN2 ....56 C5
 Hyde SK14 ....113 D8
 Manchester M9 ....157 F7
 Middleton M24 ....47 A3
 Pendlebury M27 ....80 C7
 Sale M33 ....108 C6
 Stockport SK3 ....123 C7
 Walkden M28 ....60 B1
Waverley Rd W M9 .....157 F7
Waverley Sq BL4 ....60 C6
Waverley St Oldham OL1 .49 C1
 Rochdale OL11 ....30 C1
Waverton Ave SK4 .....111 D7
Waverton Rd M14 ....98 A1
Wavertree Ave M46 ......58 C4
Wavertree Ct 🔟 BL1 ...145 E8
Wavertree Rd M9 ....64 C4
Waybridge Ind Pk M50 ..96 C8
Wayfarers Dr
 Newton-le-W WA12 ....89 E2
 Tyldesley M29 ....77 A8
Wayfarers Way M27 .....79 F7
Wayfaring BL5 ....39 F2
Wayford Wlk M9 ....156 C7
Wayland Rd M18 ....99 E4
Wayland Rd S M18 ......99 D3
Wayne Cl M43 ....84 C4
Wayne St M11 ....99 E8
Wayoh Croft BL7 ....9 D6
Wayside Dr SK12 ......133 C4
Wayside Gdns SK7 ....125 A2
Wayside Gr M28 ....60 E4
Weald Cl M13 ....163 C6
Wealdstone Gr BL2 ......25 B2
Weardale Rd M9 ....64 B5
Wearhead Cl WA3 ....89 F7
Wearhead Row M5 .....154 F1
Wearish La BL5 ....57 C6
Weaste Ave M38 ....60 B4
Weaste Dr M5 ....154 D3
Weaste La M5,M6 .....154 D3
Weaste Rd M5 ....154 D1
Weaste Sta M5 ....154 D1
Weaste Trad Est M6 ...154 D2
Weatherall St N M7 ....155 F7
Weatherley Cl OL8 ......67 A1
Weatherley Dr SK6 ....125 D6
Weaver Ave M28 ....60 A2
Weaver Cl WA14 ....119 C1
Weaver Ct M15 ....162 D6
Weaver Dr BL9 ....27 F8
Weaver Gr WN7 ....75 C4
Weaver Ho 🔟 M7 ....81 C5
Weaver Rd WA3 ....92 A2
Weaver Wlk 🔟 M11 .....99 D7
Weaverham Way SK9 ...131 E4
Weaverham Wlk M33 ...108 E3
Weavers Ct Bolton BL3 .145 E5
 🔟 Middleton M24 ....46 F1
 Mottram-in-L SK14 ...103 A4
Weavers Gn BL4 ....60 D8
Weavers La SK7 ....132 C6
Weavers Rd M24 ....46 F1
Webb Gr SK14 ....102 F1
Webb La SK1 ....124 A8
Webb St Bury BL8 .....140 D3
 Horwich BL6 ....22 C3
Webb Wlk SK14 ....102 F1
Webdale Dr M40 ....83 A7
Weber Dr BL3 ....145 D5
Webster Gr M25 ....62 F2
Webster Prim Sch M15 ..98 A4
Webster St Bolton BL3 .148 B5
 🔟 Mossley OL5 ....68 C2
 Oldham OL8 ....153 F5
Webster's St WN7 ....56 A3
Wedgewood Dr WN6 ....36 D3
Wedgwood St M40 .....160 F4
Wedgwood Rd M27 ......62 C2
Wedhurst St OL4 ....67 C7
Wedlock St OL11 ....67 A7
Wednesbough SK14 ...103 C5
Wedsdall Ave M5 ....161 A6
Weeder Sq OL7 ....49 E8
Weedon Ave WA12 ......89 B5
Weedon St OL16 ....31 B8
Weeton Ave BL2 ....42 F7
Weft Wlk 🔟 M4 ....159 C1
Weighbridge Ct M44 ....94 C3
Weint The WA3 ....105 B3
Weir Rd M24 ....46 E1
Weir St M15 ....162 E5
Welbeck Ave
 Failsworth OL9 ....65 D3
 Littleborough OL15 ...16 A6
 Newton-le-W WA12 ....89 D2
 Urmston M41 ....95 F3
Welbeck Cl Milnrow OL16 .31 D6
 Whitefield M45 ....44 F7
Welbeck Gr M7 ....155 E7
Welbeck Ho 🔟 OL6 ...166 A2
Welbeck Rd
 Ashton-in-M WN4 ......73 C4
 Bolton BL1 ....144 A8
 Eccles M30 ....79 E4
 Hyde SK14 ....167 F2
 Reddish SK5 ....111 F8
 Rochdale OL16 ....31 B4
 Swinton M28 ....59 E3
 Wigan WN3 ....54 E3
Welbeck St M18 ....99 E6
Welbeck St N OL6 .....166 A2
Welbeck St S OL6,OL7 .166 A2
Welbeck Terr OL6 .....166 A2
Welburn Ave M22 .....121 E3

Welburn Cl WN5 ....53 E5
Welburn St OL11 ......139 F5
Welbury Rd M23 ....108 F1
Welby St M13 ....98 D4
Welch Hill St WN7 ....75 E4
Welch Rd SK14 ....167 E1
Welcomb Cl SK6 ......112 F4
Welcomb St M11 ......165 B7
Welcomb Wlk M45 ......62 F7
Welcome Par OL8 ....67 D3
Welcroft St SK1 ....170 F8
Weld Rd M20 ....110 B3
Welden Ave BL3 ....146 A2
Weldon Cres SK3 .....123 E4
Weldon Dr M9 ....64 D5
Weldon Gr WN1 ....37 E2
Weldon Rd WA14 .....119 D6
Welfold Ho 🔟 OL4 .....67 B5
Welford Ave WA3 ....94 D1
Welford Cl SK9 ....137 E8
Welford Gn SK5 ....111 F5
Welford Rd M9 ....63 F3
Welford St M6 ....81 B4
Welkin Rd SK6 ....112 C3
Welkin Rd Ind Est SK6 .112 C3
Well Gate SK13 ....104 E2
Well Gr M45 ....44 E2
Well Green Prim Sch
 WA15 ....120 C2
Well i' th' La OL11 ....31 A4
Well La M45 ....44 F2
Well Mdw SK14 ....167 D4
Well Mead SK6 ....112 E3
Well Meadow Cl SK4 ..167 D4
Well Meadow La OL3 ...69 C8
Well Rd WN7 ....57 D1
Well Row SK14 ....115 A8
Well St Ainsworth BL2 ..26 C1
 Bolton BL1 ....148 A7
 Heywood OL10 ....29 E1
 Manchester M4 ....159 A2
 🔟 Rochdale OL11 ....31 A5
 Tyldesley M29 ....77 A8
Well St W BL0 ....1 C2
Well St W BL0 ....138 B5
Well-i-Hole Rd OL3 ......68 F4
Wellacre Ave M41 ....94 D2
Wellacre Tech Coll M41 .94 D2
Welland Ave OL10 ....29 A3
Welland Cl M15 ....162 D6
Welland Ct 🔟 M15 ....162 D6
Welland Rd
 Ashton-in-M WN4 ......73 E5
 Handforth SK9 ....131 E2
 Shaw OL2 ....149 A8
Welland St Droylsden M11 .99 D8
 Reddish SK5 ....99 F1
Welland The BL5 ....57 E8
Wellbank SK15 ....102 D8
Wellbank Ave OL6 ......85 E6
Wellbank Cl
 Little Lever BL3 ....43 B3
 Oldham OL8 ....67 A4
Wellbank St BL8 ....26 F6
Wellbank St BL8 ....26 F6
Wellbank View OL12 ....13 F2
Wellbrooke Cl WN4 .....73 C3
Wellbrow Terr OL12 ....14 D2
Wellbrow Wlk 🔟 M9 ....64 E3
Wellburn Cl BL3 ....40 F2
Wellcross Rd WN8 .....53 B6
Wellens Way M24 ....64 C7
Weller Ave
 Manchester M21 .....109 D7
 Poynton SK12 ....133 D2
Weller Cl SK12 ....133 D2
Weller Gdns M21 ......109 D7
Wellesbourne Dr M23 .120 F7
Wellesley Ave M18 .....99 D6
Wellesley Cl
 Newton-le-W WA12 ....89 B5
Wellfield Cl BL9 ....44 E6
Wellfield Gdns WA15 ..120 C3
Wellfield Inf Sch M33 ..107 F6
Wellfield Jun Sch M33 .107 F6
Wellfield La WA15 .....120 C3
Wellfield Pl 🔟 OL11 ....31 A5
Wellfield Rd Bolton BL3 .147 A4
 Culcheth WA3 ....91 F4
 Hindley WN2 ....57 A4
 Manchester M8 ....156 A8
 Stockport SK2 ....124 C6
 Wigan WN6 ....37 A3
 Wythenshawe M23 ...121 A7
Wellfield St OL11 ....31 A4
Wellgate Ave M19 .....111 B8
Wellgreen Cl WA15 ....120 C3
Wellgreen Lo WA15 ....120 C3
Wellham Rd WN3 ....55 B3
Wellhead Cl M15 ......162 F5
Wellhouse Dr M40 ......65 C3
Welling Rd M40 ....83 E4
Welling St 🔟 BL2 ....25 B1
Wellington Ave
 Newton-le-W WA12 ....89 A3
 Sale M33 ....108 C6
Wellington Clough 🔟
 OL7 ....85 A6
Wellington Cres M16 ...97 C3
Wellington Ct
 🔟 Bury BL8 ....27 B1
 Oldham OL8 ....66 D4
Wellington Dr M29 ......59 E1

Wellington Gdns
 Bury BL8 ....27 B1
 Newton-le-W WA12 ....89 A3
Wellington Gr
 Ince-in-M WN3 ....151 D5
 Manchester M15 .....162 D6
 Stockport SK2 ....170 F7
Wellington Lo OL15 .....16 B6
Wellington Mews BL7 ....9 D4
Wellington Mill SK4 ...169 E1
Wellington Par SK16 ..166 B1
Wellington Pl
 Altrincham WA14 .....119 D4
 🔟 Rochdale OL16 ......31 A8
Wellington Rd
 Altrincham WA15 .....119 F6
 Ashton-u-L OL6 ......166 B3
 Bury BL9 ....140 F1
 Chapeltown BL7 ....9 D4
 Eccles M30 ....79 F2
 Hazel Grove SK7 .....134 B8
 Manchester M8 ......156 B8
 Manchester,Fallowfield
 M14,M20 ....110 C8
 Manchester,Whalley range
 M16 ....97 E2
 Oldham OL8 ....153 E5
 Over Hulton M46 ....58 F5
 Swinton M27 ....79 F8
 Uppermill OL3 ....69 B6
Wellington Rd N M19,
 SK3,SK4 ....169 D3
Wellington Rd S SK1,
 SK2 ....170 F8
Wellington Sch WA15 .119 F6
Wellington Sq 🔟 BL8 ...27 B1
Wellington St
 Ashton-u-L OL6 ......166 B2
 Bolton BL3 ....145 E6
 Bury BL8 ....140 D1
 Chadderton OL9 .....152 B8
 Denton M34 ....100 F6
 Dukinfield SK14 ......101 C3
 🔟 Failsworth M35 ......66 A1
 Farnworth BL4 ....60 D8
 Hazel Grove SK7 ....124 F3
 🔟 Littleborough OL15 ..16 B5
 Manchester M18 ....99 D5
 Milnrow OL16 ....32 A6
 Newton-le-W WA12 ....89 A3
 Oldham OL4,OL8 .....153 F6
 🔟 Radcliffe M26 ....44 C4
 🔟 Rochdale OL12 ....14 F1
 Salford M3 ....158 D2
 Stockport SK1 ....169 F1
 Stretford M32 ....96 C1
 Westhoughton BL5 .....39 D1
 Wigan WN1 ....151 D8
Wellington St E 🔟 M7 .155 E7
Wellington St W M7 ...155 D6
Wellington Terr
 🔟 Dukinfield SK16 ...166 B1
 Salford M5 ....154 D2
Wellington Wlk BL3 ...145 E6
Wellmead Cl M8 ......155 F5
Wellock St M40 ....157 F5
Wellpark Wlk 🔟 M40 ...83 C5
Wells Ave Billinge WN5 ..71 D6
 Chadderton OL9 ....48 A1
 Manchester M25 ......63 C2
Wells Cl Droylsden M43 .99 F2
Gatley SK8 ....131 C7
Middleton M24 ....64 C7
 Tyldesley M29 ....77 C8
Wells Ct SK16 ....101 C6
Wells Dr Dukinfield SK16 .101 C6
 Manchester SK4 ......110 C2
 Wigan WN2 ....37 F2
Wells Pl WN1 ....151 E8
Wells Rd OL1 ....49 E5
Wells St BL9 ....140 E1
Wellside Wlk 🔟 M8 ...156 A6
Wellstock La M38 ....59 F6
Wellwood Dr 🔟 M40 ....83 C5
Wellyhole St OL4 ....67 D6
Welman Way WA15 ...119 F4
Welney Rd M16 ....97 B3
Welshpool Cl M23 .....109 B2
Welshpool Way 🔟 M34 .101 A1
Welton Ave M20 ....110 C2
Welton Cl Leigh WN7 ...76 C5
 Wilmslow SK9 ....136 F4
Welton Dr SK9 ....136 E4
Welton Gr SK9 ....136 E4
Welwyn Cl M41 ....95 B5
Welwyn Dr M6 ....80 A5
Welwyn Wlk M40 ......160 D2
Wembley Gr M14 ......110 C8
Wembley Rd M18 ....99 C3
Wembury St M9 ....157 E8
Wembury St N M9 .....157 E8
Wembury Wlk SK14 ...102 E3
Wemsley Gr 🔟 BL2 ....42 D8
Wemyss Ave SK5 ....99 F1
Wendlebury Cl WN7 ....75 E1
Wendlebury Gn 🔟 OL2 .149 A5
Wendon Rd M23 ....121 B5
Wendover Dr BL3 ....40 E5
Wendover Rd
 Urmston M41 ....95 C2
 Wythenshawe M23 ...120 D8
Wenfield Dr M9 ....65 B3
Wenlock Ave OL6 ....85 E6
Wenlock Cl
 Hazel Grove SK2 .....125 A6
 Horwich BL6 ....22 C6

Wenlock Ct M12 ....164 F6
Wenlock Gr 🔟 WN2 .....56 D4
Wenlock Rd Hindley WN2 .56 D5
 Leigh WN7 ....75 E2
 Sale M33 ....108 A2
Wenlock St
 🔟 Hindley WN2 ....56 D5
 Swinton M27 ....79 D8
Wenlock Way M12 ....164 F6
Wenning Cl M45 ....45 C1
Wenning Wlk 🔟 WN2 ...56 A2
Wensley Ct M7 ....63 A1
Wensley Dr
 Hazel Grove SK7 .....133 D7
 Manchester M20 .....110 B5
Wensley Rd Cheadle SK8 .122 C6
 Golborne WA3 ....90 E7
 Manchester M7 ....63 A1
 Reddish SK5 ....169 F4
Wensley Way OL16 ......31 C6
Wensleydale Ave SK8 .122 C6
Wensleydale Cl
 Royton OL2 ....48 C5
 Whitefield BL9 ....45 A3
 Wythenshawe M23 ...120 F3
Wensleydale Rd WN7 ...76 C5
Wentbridge Rd BL1 ...145 D8
Wentworth Ave
 Altrincham WA15 .....120 A6
 Bury BL8 ....27 B4
 Farnworth BL4 ....60 C7
 Heywood OL10 ....46 D8
 Irlam M44 ....94 A3
 🔟 Manchester M18 .....99 E6
 Salford M6 ....80 C3
 Whitefield M45 ....62 D7
Wentworth Cl
 Marple SK6 ....125 F8
 Middleton M26 ....64 E8
 Radcliffe M26 ....43 D4
Wentworth Ct
 Failsworth M35 ....83 F6
 Whitefield M45 ....62 E8
Wentworth Dr
 Bramhall SK7 ....133 A7
 Sale M33 ....107 F5
Wentworth High Sch
 M30 ....79 F4
Wentworth Rd
 Reddish SK5 ....99 F1
 Salford M30 ....80 A4
 Swinton M27 ....79 D6
Wentworth Wlk 🔟 SK14 .101 F5
Wenworth Ave M41 .....95 B1
Werneth Ave Hyde SK14 .113 F8
 Manchester M14 ....98 B2
 Hazel Grove SK7 .....124 E4
Werneth Cl Denton M34 .100 F7
 Hazel Grove SK7 .....124 E4
Werneth Cres OL8 ......66 C4
Werneth Ct SK14 ......167 E1
Werneth Hall Rd OL8 ..153 D5
Werneth Hollow SK6 ...113 B6
Werneth Inf Sch OL8 ..153 E5
Werneth Jun Sch OL8 .153 E5
Werneth Low Ctry Pk
 SK14 ....114 A7
Werneth Low Rd SK14,
 SK6 ....113 E5
Werneth Prep Sch OL8 .153 D5
Werneth Rd
 Glossop SK13 ....116 A3
 Hyde SK14 ....167 F2
 Romiley SK6 ....113 C5
 Werneth Rise SK14 ..113 F2
Werneth St Denton M34 .100 F5
 Stockport SK1 ....112 B3
Werneth Wlk M34 .....100 F7
Wescoe Cl WN5 ....53 E5
Wesley Cl Rochdale OL12 .15 C3
Wesley Ct
 🔟 Bury BL8 ....26 E7
Wesley Ct Bury BL8 .....26 E7
 Manchester SK4 ......110 F2
 Walkden M28 ....60 D4
 Westhoughton BL5 .....39 E2
Wesley Dr Ashton-u-L OL6 .85 D6
 Worsley M28 ....78 F8
Wesley Gn M5 ....161 B8
Wesley Methodist Prim Sch
 M26 ....43 F5
Wesley Mews 🔟 BL2 ..148 B2
Wesley Sq M41 ....95 A2
Wesley St Atherton M46 .58 E3
 Bolton BL3 ....145 E5
 Bolton,Toppings BL7 ..25 F2
 Bury BL8 ....26 E7
 Eccles M30 ....79 C2
 Failsworth M35 ....66 A1
 Farnworth BL4 ....60 E7
 Glossop SK13 ....104 E2
 Hadfield SK13 ....104 E2
 Hazel Grove SK7 .....124 E3
 Heywood OL10 ....29 C2
 Manchester M11 .....165 A8
 Milnrow OL16 ....31 E6
 🔟 Rochdale OL12 ....15 B3
 Royton OL2 ....48 E3
 Stockport SK1 ....169 F1
 Stretford M32 ....96 F2
 Swinton M27 ....79 F8
 Westhoughton BL5 .....39 E2
 Wigan WN5 ....54 D5
Wesleys The 🔟 BL4 .....59 F8
Wessenden Bank E SK2 .124 D5

Wessenden Bank W
SK2 . . . . .124 D5
Wessex CI WN1 . . . . .20 B1
Wessex Park Cl OL2 . . .149 B8
Wessex Rd WN5 . . . . .36 D1
Wessington Bank 12
SK13 . . . . .171 E2
Wessington Fold 14
SK13 . . . . .171 E2
Wessington Gn 16 SK13 .171 E2
Wessington Mews SK13 .171 E2
West Ashton St M50 . . .154 F1
West Ave
Altrincham WA14 . . . . . .119 A5
Droylsden M18 . . . . .99 E5
Failsworth M40 . . . . .65 D1
Farnworth BL4 . . . . .60 B8
Gatley SK8 . . . . .122 C1
Golborne WA3 . . . . .74 B1
Leigh WN7 . . . . .76 C3
Manchester M19 . . . . . . .110 F7
Rochdale OL12 . . . . .15 C3
Stalybridge SK15 . . . . .86 A3
Walkden M28 . . . . .60 C3
Whitefield M45 . . . . .44 E2
West Bank M11 . . . . . . .100 A7
West Bank St Salford M5 .161 C8
Tyldesley M46 . . . . .58 E1
West Bridgewater St
WN7 . . . . .75 F4
West Central Dr M27 . . . .80 B7
West Charles St M5 . . . . .81 B1
West Church St 9 OL10 .29 C2
West CI M46 . . . . .58 E1
West Cotts OL3 . . . . .68 F5
West Craven St M5 . . . .161 B7
West Cres M24 . . . . .64 F7
West Croft Ind Est M24 .64 C7
West Crown Ave M5 . . .161 B8
West Dean St M5 . . . . . . .81 C1
West Downs Rd SK8 . . .122 F3
West Dr Bury B19 . . . . .27 E5
Droylsden M43 . . . . .83 F1
Gatley SK8 . . . . .122 A4
Pendlebury,Irlams o' th' Height
M6 .80 E6
Pendlebury,Swinton Park
M27 . . . . .80 B7
Tintwistle SK13 . . . . .103 F7
West Duke St M5 . . . . . .158 D1
West Egerton St M5 . . . .81 B1
West End Ave SK8 . . . . .122 A6
West End St OL9 . . . . . . .153 D7
West Gdns 1 OL13 . . . . . .3 B8
West Gn M24 . . . . .64 B7
West Gr Manchester M13 .164 D5
1 Mossley OL5 . . . . .68 C1
Sale M33 . . . . .108 B3
Westhoughton BL5 . . . . . .57 E6
West High St M5 . . . . . . .81 A2
West Hill OL11 . . . . .139 E6
West Hill Cl SK15 . . . . . . .85 F2
West Hope St M5 . . . . . . .81 B1
West King St M3 . . . . . .158 E2
West Lea M34 . . . . .99 F4
West Marwood St M7 . .155 E6
West Mdw SK5 . . . . .100 A1
West Meade Bolton BL3 .147 D2
Manchester,Chorlton-cum-Hardy
M21 . . . . .109 A7
Manchester,Sedgley Park
M25 . . . . .63 D2
Swinton M27 . . . . .79 E6
West Mosley St M2 . . . .159 A1
West Mount Orrell WN5 . . .53 F6
Wigan WN1 . . . . .37 D2
West Oak Pl SK8 . . . . . .122 F1
West One Ret Pk M50 . . .80 A1
West Over M6 . . . . .113 A1
West Par M33 . . . . .107 C3
West Park Ave
Denton M34 . . . . .101 B2
Poynton SK12 . . . . .133 A4
West Park Rd
Stockport,Bramhall Park
SK7 . . . . .123 D2
Stockport,Portwood SK1 .112 B2
West Park St M5 . . . . . .161 B7
West Pk SK14 . . . . .113 E6
West Pl M19 . . . . .110 F7
West Point Lo 1 M19 . .110 F8
West Rd
Altrincham WA14 . . . . . .119 C2
Prestwich M25 . . . . .62 F6
Stretford M32 . . . . .96 A4
Urmston M41 . . . . .95 F7
West Row M25 . . . . .62 F1
West St
Alderley Edge SK9 . . . . .137 A1
Ashton-u-l OL6 . . . . .166 B3
Bolton BL1 . . . . .144 C7
Droylsden M11 . . . . .83 B2
Dukinfield SK14 . . . . .101 D5
Dukinfield SK16 . . . . .166 B1
Failsworth M35 . . . . .83 F7
Farnworth BL4 . . . . .42 E1
Heywood OL10 . . . . .29 D2
Hindley WN2 . . . . .56 A8
Ince-in-M WN2 . . . . .56 A8
Littleborough OL15 . . . . . .16 C5
Middleton M24 . . . . .47 A2
Milnrow OL16 . . . . .31 D7
Oldham OL1 . . . . .153 E7

West St continued
Oldham OL9 . . . . .153 D6
Oldham,Nether Lees OL4 . .67 E5
2 Radcliffe M26 . . . . .44 A3
Ramsbottom BL0 . . . . . . .138 B5
Rawtenstall BB4 . . . . .2 E8
Rochdale OL16 . . . . .31 A8
Stalybridge SK15 . . . . .85 F2
Stockport SK3 . . . . .169 D1
Tintwistle SK13 . . . . .103 F7
Tyldesley M46 . . . . .58 E1
Wigan WN6 . . . . .37 B1
West Starkey St OL10 . .29 C3
West Thorpe WA14 . . . .119 B2
West Towers St M6 . . . .154 F1
West Vale M26 . . . . .44 A5
West Vale Rd WA15 . . . .119 F6
West View Bacup OL13 . . . .3 B8
Denton M34 . . . . .100 E7
Haslingden BB4 . . . . .1 A7
Littleborough OL15 . . . . . .16 C5
Ramsbottom BL0 . . . . .1 C2
Shaw OL3 . . . . .50 C6
West View Ct M22 . . . .121 F8
West View Gr M45 . . . . . .62 F6
West View Rd M22 . . . .121 E8
West Way Bolton BL1 . . . .25 B3
Walkden M38 . . . . .60 A5
West Wlk BL7 . . . . .8 D2
West Works Rd M17,M32 .96 C5
Westage Gdns M23 . . . .121 A7
Westbank Rd Bolton BL6 . .40 D6
Manchester M20 . . . . . . .110 D5
Westbourne BB4 . . . . .1 A8
Westbourne Ave
Bolton BL3 . . . . .42 B3
Leigh WN7 . . . . .75 E7
Swinton M27 . . . . .75 F7
Swinton M27 . . . . .61 D5
Whitefield M45 . . . . .44 D1
Westbourne Dr
Ashton-u-l OL7 . . . . .166 A4
17 Handforth SK9 . . . . . .131 D1
Westbourne Gr
Manchester M9 . . . . .157 D8
Manchester,Withington
M20 . . . . .110 A6
Reddish SK5 . . . . .111 F8
Sale M33 . . . . .108 A4
Westbourne Pk M41 . . . .95 D2
Westbourne Range M18 . .99 F4
Westbourne Rd
Denton M34 . . . . .100 E2
Eccles M30 . . . . .79 B4
Manchester M14 . . . . . . .110 D8
Urmston M41 . . . . .95 D2
Westbourne St OL9 . . . .153 D7
Westbridge Mews WN1 .150 C7
Westbrook Cl OL11 . . . . .47 D8
Westbrook Ct BL2 . . . . .148 A6
Westbrook Rd
Stretford M17 . . . . .96 D7
Swinton M27 . . . . .79 E7
Westbrook Sq M12 . . . .165 A6
Westbrook St BL2 . . . . .148 A6
Westbrook Wlk 3 M20 .110 A8
Westbury Ave Sale M33 .107 C1
Wigan WN3 . . . . .54 D2
Westbury Cl Bury BL8 . . . .27 A1
Westhoughton BL5 . . . . . .40 A2
Westbury Dr SK6 . . . . . .125 E6
Westbury Rd M8 . . . . . . .64 B1
Westbury St
Ashton-u-l OL6 . . . . .166 C3
Dukinfield SK14 . . . . .101 C5
Westbury Street Ind Est
SK14 . . . . .101 C5
Westbury Way OL,OL2 . .48 D2
Westby Cl SK7 . . . . .133 A7
Westby Gr BL2 . . . . .148 C8
Westchapel Mews BL5 . .39 E3
Westcliffe Ho 3 OL12 . . .15 D4
Westcliffe Rd BL1 . . . . . .24 F6
Westcombe Dr BL8 . . . . .27 C5
Westcott Ave M20 . . . . .110 A6
Westcott Cl BL2 . . . . .25 E5
Westcott Ct M15 . . . . . .162 D7
Westcott Dr WN3 . . . . . . .54 C4
Westcott Gr OL2 . . . . . .149 A5
Westcourt Rd
Bolton BL3 . . . . .147 D3
Sale M33 . . . . .108 A6
Westcraig Ave M40 . . . . .65 C3
Westcroft Rd M19,M20 . . .99 B2
Westdale Gdns M19 . . . .111 A5
Westdean Cres M19 . . . .110 F5
Westdown Gdns 1 OL2 . .48 F8
Westend Ave PR7 . . . . . .19 D8
Westend St BL4 . . . . .60 B8
Wester Hill Rd OL8 . . . . .67 A1
Westerdale 1 OL4 . . . . . .67 C6
Westerdale Dr M29 . . . . .77 B8
Westerdale Dr
Bolton BL2 . . . . .144 A5
Royton OL2 . . . . .48 C5
Westerham Ave M5 . . . . .81 A1
Westerham Cl BL8 . . . . . .27 C7
Westerling Way M16 . . . .97 E3
Western Ave M27 . . . . . .62 D2
Western Circ M19 . . . . . .110 F6
Western Ct OL13 . . . . .3 B8
Western Rd Bacup OL13 . .3 C8
Urmston M41 . . . . .94 E1
Western St
Manchester M18 . . . . .99 E6
Salford M6 . . . . .154 E3
Westerton Ct BL3 . . . . . .145 D5

Westfield
Altrincham WA14 . . . . . .119 C3
Salford M6 . . . . .154 E4
Westfield Ave
Ashton-in-M WN4 . . . . . . .73 A4
Middleton M24 . . . . .65 A7
Westfield Cl OL11 . . . . . .13 F1
Westfield Dr
Romiley SK6 . . . . .113 C5
Uppermill OL4 . . . . .68 E5
Westfield Gr Denton M34 .100 E5
Wigan WN1 . . . . .37 B3
Westfield Rd Bolton BL3 .146 B2
Cheadle SK8 . . . . .131 F8
Droylsden M43 . . . . .83 E2
Manchester M21 . . . . .97 B1
Tyldesley M46 . . . . .58 E1
Westfield St
Chadderton OL1,OL9 . . . .48 C1
Chadderton OL9 . . . . . . .152 C8
Manchester M7 . . . . .63 D1
Westfields WA15 . . . . . .128 F8
Westgate
Altrincham WA15 . . . . . .119 E2
Sale M33 . . . . .108 A1
Urmston M41 . . . . .95 B1
Whitworth OL12 . . . . .14 B7
Wilmslow SK9 . . . . .137 A5
Westgate Ave
Bolton BL1 . . . . .144 C7
Bury BL9 . . . . .140 E1
Manchester M9 . . . . .64 C2
Ramsbottom BL0 . . . . .11 A2
Westgate Cl OL12 . . . . . .14 B7
Westgate Dr Orrell WN5 . .53 D5
Swinton M27 . . . . .79 F6
Tyldesley M29 . . . . .77 C6
Westgate Ho OL8 . . . . . .66 D2
Westgate Rd M6 . . . . . . .80 D4
Westgate St OL7 . . . . . . .166 A1
Westgrove Ave BL1 . . . . .24 E6
Westhead Ave WA3 . . . . .74 E1
Westhide Wlk 5 M9 . . . . .64 F1
Westholm Ave SK4 . . . . .111 B7
Westholme Cl SK9 . . . . .137 A2
Westholme Rd
Manchester M20 . . . . . . .110 B5
Prestwich M25 . . . . .63 C7
Westhorne Fold 1 M8 . . .63 E2
Westhoughton High Sch
BL5 . . . . .57 F8
Westhoughton Parochial CE
Prim Sch BL5 . . . . .57 E8
Westhoughton Prim Sch
BL5 . . . . .39 F1
Westhoughton Rd PR6,
PR7 . . . . .20 F8
Westhoughton Sta BL5 . .39 E2
Westhulme Ave OL1 . . . . .48 D1
Westhulme St OL1 . . . . . .48 D1
Westhulme Way OL1 . . . .48 C1
Westinghouse Cl WN6 . .150 A8
Westinghouse Rd M17 . . .96 B5
Westlake Gr WN2 . . . . . . .57 B4
Westlake St M11 . . . . . .165 C7
Westland Ave Bolton BL1 .142 A1
Farnworth BL4 . . . . .60 C6
Stockport SK1 . . . . .112 B1
Westland Dr M9 . . . . .64 D4
Westlands M45 . . . . .62 F6
Westlands The M27 . . . . .80 C6
Westlea Dr M18 . . . . .99 D3
Westleigh Dr M25 . . . . . .63 D3
Westleigh High Sch
WN7 . . . . .57 D1
Westleigh La WN7 . . . . . .57 D1
Westleigh Meth Prim Sch
WN7 . . . . .57 D1
Westleigh St M9 . . . . . . .157 D8
Westleigh St Paul's CE Prim
Sch WN7 . . . . .75 E8
Westleigh View WN7 . . . .75 E8
Westlock WN3 . . . . .150 C6
Westmarsh Cl 4 BL1 . . .143 E1
Westmead M46 . . . . .36 E8
Westmead Dr WA15 . . . .120 B7
Westmeade Rd M28 . . . . .60 C5
Westmere Dr M9 . . . . . . .156 C6
Westminster Ave
Ashton-u-l OL6 . . . . .85 D7
Farnworth BL4 . . . . .60 C8
Manchester M16 . . . . .97 D4
Radcliffe M26 . . . . .43 D4
Reddish SK5 . . . . .111 E7
Royton OL2 . . . . .48 C6
Whitefield M45 . . . . .62 F6
Westminster Cl
Marple SK6 . . . . .125 D7
Sale M33 . . . . .107 D3
Shaw OL2 . . . . .48 E8
Westminster Dr
Cheadle SK8 . . . . .132 B6
Leigh WN7 . . . . .75 D6
Wilmslow SK9 . . . . .137 A4
Westminster Ho M3 . . . .158 E3
Westminster Rd
Altrincham WA15 . . . . . .120 A2
Bolton BL1 . . . . .24 E5
Eccles M30 . . . . .79 F3
Failsworth M35 . . . . .84 B8
Urmston M41 . . . . .95 A4
Walkden M28 . . . . .60 D2
Westminster St
Bury BL9 . . . . .140 E1
Farnworth BL4 . . . . .60 C8
5 Manchester M19 . . . . .99 B1
Oldham OL1 . . . . .153 D8
Rochdale OL11 . . . . .139 D5
Salford M15 . . . . .161 C7
Swinton M27 . . . . .61 E1

Westminster St continued
Wigan WN5 . . . . .54 F6
Westminster Way SK16 .101 D6
Westminster Wlk 4 BL4 . .60 C8
Westmoor Gables SK4 .168 A4
Westmoorland St 3
WN1 . . . . .37 E1
Westmoreland Cl
Altrincham WA14 . . . . . .128 B8
Bury BL9 . . . . .44 E6
Westmorland Ave
Ashton-u-l OL7 . . . . .166 B4
Dukinfield SK16 . . . . .101 E8
Westmorland Cl SK5 . . .112 C6
Westmorland Dr
Brinnington SK5 . . . . . . .112 C6
Wardle OL12 . . . . .15 D6
Westmorland Prim Sch
SK5 . . . . .112 C6
Westmorland Rd
Manchester M20 . . . . . . .110 A2
Partington M31 . . . . .105 E2
Sale M33 . . . . .108 C2
Westmorland Wlk 2 OL2 .48 E4
Westmount Cl M40 . . . . .156 C6
Weston Ave
Failsworth M40 . . . . .65 E1
Rochdale OL16 . . . . .31 B4
Swinton M27 . . . . .61 A4
Urmston M41 . . . . .95 B1
Weston Ct M14 . . . . .98 D2
Stockport SK8 . . . . .123 D4
Weston Gr Reddish SK4 .111 C6
Wythenshawe M22 . . . . .121 E8
Weston Pk WN6 . . . . .36 A5
Weston Rd 3 Irlam M44 . .94 A2
Wilmslow SK9 . . . . .137 E6
Weston St Atherton M46 . .58 E4
Bolton BL3 . . . . .42 A4
Manchester M4 . . . . .160 D2
Milnrow OL16 . . . . .31 E6
Oldham OL8 . . . . .67 C4
Reddish SK5 . . . . .169 E4
Westonby Ct WN4 . . . . . .73 D3
Westover Rd M41 . . . . . . .95 C3
Westover St M27 . . . . . . .61 F1
Westpark BL1 . . . . .144 C7
Westpoint Ent Pk M17 . .95 F7
Westray Cres M5 . . . . . .154 E1
Westray Rd M13 . . . . .98 E2
Westrees WN7 . . . . .76 A7
Westville Gdns M19 . . . .110 E5
Westward Ho OL16 . . . . . .31 B4
Westward Rd SK9 . . . . . .136 F6
Westway Droylsden M43 .100 A8
Oldham OL1 . . . . .67 E5
Shaw OL2 . . . . .149 B6
Westwell Gdns 8 BL1 . .143 F1
Westwell Gr 8 WN7 . . . . .75 E8
Westwell St WN7 . . . . . . .75 E8
Westwick Terr 17 BL1 . .143 E2
Westwood Ave
Altrincham WA15 . . . . . .119 F7
Failsworth M40 . . . . .65 E1
Hyde SK14 . . . . .102 B3
Salford M7 . . . . .155 E8
Urmston M41 . . . . .95 F1
Walkden M28 . . . . .60 A3
Westwood Bsns Ctr
OL9 . . . . .153 D6
Westwood Cotts 6 M16 .97 F4
Westwood Cres M30 . . . .79 B4
Westwood Dr
Oldham OL9 . . . . .153 D7
Pendlebury M27 . . . . .80 C6
Sale M33 . . . . .108 B2
Westwood Ind Est OL9 .152 C7
Westwood La WN5 . . . . .151 D5
Westwood Lo WA15 . . . .119 F7
Westwood Park Com Prim
Sch M30 . . . . .79 B3
Westwood Pk WN3 . . . . .150 C6
Westwood Prim Sch
OL9 . . . . .153 D7
Westwood Rd
Bolton BL1 . . . . .144 C8
Gatley SK8 . . . . .131 B8
Stockport SK2 . . . . .124 B4
Stretford M32 . . . . .96 B2
Wigan WN3 . . . . .150 C6
Westwood St M14 . . . . . .97 F4
Westwood Terr WN3 . . . .151 E5
Westwood Trad Est SK6 .125 E5
Westwood Way OL1 . . . . .48 D1
Wetherall St M19 . . . . . . .99 B1
Wetherby Cl WA12 . . . . . .89 C5
Wetherby Dr
Hazel Grove SK7 . . . . . . .125 A2
Royton OL2 . . . . .48 D5
Wetherby St M11 . . . . . . .99 E7
Wexford Wlk M22 . . . . . .121 E2
Wexham Gdns WN2 . . . . .56 A3
Wey Gates Dr WA15 . . . .129 C7
Weybourne Ave M9 . . . . .65 A2
Weybourne Dr
Romiley SK6 . . . . .112 F4

Weybourne Dr continued
Wigan WN3 . . . . .54 E3
Weybourne Gr BL2 . . . . . .25 B4
Weybridge Cl 4 BL1 . . . .145 E8
Weybridge Rd M4 . . . . . .159 C2
Weycroft Cl BL2 . . . . .43 A6
Weyhill Rd M23 . . . . .121 A5
Weylands Gr M6 . . . . .80 B5
Weymouth Dr WN2 . . . . . .57 A4
Weymouth Ho 6 OL9 . . . .48 A1
Weymouth Rd
Ashton-u-l OL6 . . . . .85 F6
Eccles M30 . . . . .79 B3
Weymouth St BL1 . . . . . .143 E2
Weythorne Dr
Bolton BL1 . . . . .143 F4
Bury BL9 . . . . .28 F4
Whalley Ave Bolton BL1 . . .2 C3
Glazebury WA3 . . . . .92 C7
Littleborough OL15 . . . . . .16 A6
Manchester,Chorlton-cum-Hardy
M21 . . . . .109 C7
Manchester,Levenshulme
M19 . . . . .99 B2
Manchester,Whalley Range
M16 . . . . .97 D3
Sale M33 . . . . .108 C5
Urmston M41 . . . . .95 E3
Whalley Cl
Altrincham WA15 . . . . . .119 E8
Milnrow OL16 . . . . .31 D6
Whitefield M45 . . . . .44 F1
Wigan WN3 . . . . .55 A2
Whalley Dr BL8 . . . . .26 F2
Whalley Gdns OL12 . . . . .14 B1
Whalley Gr Ashton-u-l OL6 .85 C7
Leigh WN7 . . . . .57 D1
Manchester M16 . . . . .97 D2
Whalley Range High Sch
M16 . . . . .109 F8
Whalley Rd
Altrincham WA15 . . . . . .120 A2
Heywood OL10 . . . . .29 A2
Manchester M16 . . . . .97 D3
Middleton M24 . . . . .46 F3
Ramsbottom BL0 . . . . .11 C7
Rochdale OL12 . . . . .14 B1
Stockport SK2 . . . . .124 C7
Whitefield M45 . . . . .44 F1
Wham Bar Dr OL10 . . . . .29 B3
Wham Bottom La OL12 . .14 D4
Wham La OL3 . . . . .33 D1
Wham St OL10 . . . . .29 B2
Wharf Cl
Altrincham WA14 . . . . . .119 D7
Manchester M1 . . . . .159 B1
Wharf Cotts OL1 . . . . . . .68 D1
Wharf End M17 . . . . .161 A6
Wharf Rd
Altrincham WA14 . . . . . .119 D7
Sale M33 . . . . .108 B5
Wharf St Dukinfield SK16 .166 C1
Oldham OL3 . . . . .66 B3
Stockport SK4,SK5 . . . . .169 E3
Wharf The OL3 . . . . .51 B2
Wharfdale 2 WN7 . . . . . . .76 A4
Wharfedale Ave M40 . . . .65 A1
Wharfedale Rd SK5 . . . .111 E8
Wharfside Ave M30 . . . . .95 D8
Wharfside Bsns Ctr M17 .96 F6
Wharfside Way (Trafford
Park Rd) M17 . . . . .96 E6
Wharmton Rise OL4 . . . . .68 E6
Wharmton School Cotts
OL3 . . . . .50 F1
Wharmton View
Mossley OL5 . . . . .68 E3
Uppermill OL3 . . . . .69 A6
Wharncliffe Cl SK13 . . . .171 E4
Wharncliffe St 5 WN2 . . .56 D5
Wharton Hall OL1 . . . . . . .67 A7
Wharton Hall Cl M29 . . . .59 B1
Wharton La M38 . . . . .59 D4
Wharton Lo M38 . . . . .59 D4
Wharton Prim Sch M38 . .59 E5
Wheat Cl M13 . . . . .163 C5
Wheat Croft SK3 . . . . . . .170 F5
Wheatcroft SK13 . . . . . . .171 E4
Wheater's Cres M7 . . . . .158 D4
Wheater's St M7 . . . . . . .158 D4
Wheatfield SK15 . . . . . . .102 E2
Wheatfield Cl Bury BL9 . . .27 F7
Romiley SK6 . . . . .113 A4
Wheatfield Cres OL2 . . . .48 D3
Wheatfield Ho OL2 . . . . . .48 D3
Wheatfield St BL2 . . . . . .148 C5
Wheathill St 4 OL16 . . . . .31 A4
Wheatlea Ind Est WN3 . .54 F1
Wheatlea Rd WN3 . . . . . . .54 F2
Wheatley Ave WA12 . . . . .89 C5
Wheatley Rd M27 . . . . . . .61 D2
Wheatley Wlk M12 . . . . .165 A6
Wheatsheaf Ctr The
OL16 . . . . .139 F8
Wheatsheaf Ind Est M27 .62 B1
Wheatsheaf Wlk WN6 . . .19 D1
Wheeldale OL4 . . . . .67 C6
Wheeldale Cl BL1 . . . . . .143 E2
Wheeldon St M14 . . . . . . .98 A3
Wheelock Cl SK9 . . . . . .131 D1
Wheelton Cl BL8 . . . . .27 A1
Wheelwright Cl
Marple SK6 . . . . .125 F8
Rochdale OL11 . . . . .30 B4

Wheelwright Dr OL16 . . . . . . .15 C3
Whelan Ave BL9 . . . . .44 E7
Whelan Cl BL9 . . . . .44 E7
Wheler St WM1,M43 . . . . .99 E8
Whelley WN1,WN2 . . . . .37 E2
Whelley Hospl (General)
WN1 . . . . .37 E2
Whernside Ave
Ashton-u-L OL6 . . . . .85 C7
Manchester M40 . . . . .65 A1
Whernside Cl SK4 . . . . .169 E3
Whernshurst Rd SK6 . . . . . .126 E4
Whetstone Hill Cl OL1 . . . . . .49 B2
Whetstone Hill La
6 Oldham OL1 . . . . .49 C1
Oldham OL1 . . . . .49 C1
Whetstone Hill Rd OL1 . . . . .49 B1
Whewell Ave M45 . . . . .44 E5
Whewell St 14 M29 . . . . .59 A1
Whickham M14 . . . . .98 B3
Whiley St M13 . . . . .98 F4
Whimberry Cl M5 . . . . .161 C7
Whimberry Dr SK15 . . . . .86 E5
Whimberry Way M20 . . . . . .110 D6
Whimbrel Ave WA12 . . . . .89 C3
Whimbrel Rd
Hazel Grove SK2 . . . . .125 A5
Tyldesley M29 . . . . .77 C7
Whinberry Rd WA14 . . . . . . .119 B7
Whinberry Way OL4 . . . . .49 F4
Whinberry Way WA12 . . . . . . .89 C4
Whinchat Cl
Golborne WA3 . . . . .90 E7
Hazel Grove SK2 . . . . .125 A4
Whinfell Dr M24 . . . . .46 C1
Whingroves Wlk 11 M40 . . .83 A6
Whinmoor Wlk M40 . . . . .83 B7
Whins Ave BL4 . . . . .59 E8
Whins Crest BL6 . . . . .40 C7
Whinslee Dr BL6 . . . . .40 C7
Whinslee Dr BL6 . . . . .40 C7
Whinstone Way OL1,OL9 . . . .47 E1
Whipney La BL8 . . . . .10 E1
Whipp St OL10 . . . . .29 B3
Whirley Cl SK4 . . . . .111 D5
Whistlecroft Ct WN3 . . . . . .151 F6
Whistley St M 56 B3
Whiston Dr BL2 . . . . .148 C6
Whiston Rd M8 . . . . .64 B1
Whit La Manchester M6 . . . . . .80 F6
Salford M6 . . . . .81 A5
Whitaker St M24 . . . . .64 F8
Whitbeam Gr WN2 . . . . .56 E2
Whitbrook Way M24 . . . . .47 C5
Whitburn Ave M13 . . . . .98 E2
Whitburn Cl 11 Bolton BL3 . .98 E4
Garswood WN4 . . . . .72 D4
Whitburn Dr BL8 . . . . .27 C5
Whitburn Rd M23 . . . . .121 A4
Whitby Ave Heywood OL10 . .29 C3
Manchester M14 . . . . .110 E8
Manchester,Whalley Range
M16 . . . . .97 D3
Salford M6 . . . . .80 C3
Urmston M41 . . . . .95 E2
Whitby Cl Bury BL8 . . . . .26 F2
Cheadle SK8 . . . . .122 C6
Poynton SK12 . . . . .133 D4
Whitby Rd
Manchester M14 . . . . .110 E8
Oldham OL8 . . . . .67 C4
Rochdale OL11 . . . . .31 A5
Whitchurch Dr M16 . . . . . . .162 D5
Whitchurch Gdns 8
BL1 . . . . .143 E2
Whitchurch Rd M20 . . . . .110 A7
Whitchurch St M3 . . . . .158 E3
White Bank Ave SK5 . . . . . . .112 C4
White Bank Rd OL8 . . . . .66 E1
White Birk Cl M 10 F2
White Brook La
Uppermill OL3 . . . . .69 C8
Uppermill OL3 . . . . .69 D6
White Broom WA13 . . . . .117 B4
White Carr La BL9 . . . . .12 E4
White City Ret Pk M16 . . . . .161 A5
White City Way M16 . . . . . . .161 A5
White Hart Mdw 3 M24 . . . .47 A2
White Hart St SK14 . . . . .167 D4
White Hill Cl OL12 . . . . .14 D4
White Horse Cl BL6 . . . . .22 C5
White Horse Gr BL5 . . . . .40 D4
White Horse Mdws OL16 . . . .31 C2
White House Ave M8 . . . . .63 F3
White House Cl OL10 . . . . .46 D7
White Lady Cl 2 M28 . . . . . . .59 E3
White Lion Brow BL1 . . . . . .145 E7
White Lodge Dr WN4 . . . . .73 D4
White Moss Ave M9 . . . . .65 A2
White Moss Rd M9 . . . . .64 F3
White Rd SK22 . . . . .127 C2
White Slack Gate OL14 . . . . . .6 A6
White St Bury BL8 . . . . .27 B4
Leigh WN7 . . . . .76 C4
Salford M6 . . . . .154 E1
8 Wigan WN6 . . . . .37 A1
White Swallows Rd M27 . . . .80 B6
White Swan Ind Est 9
OL1 . . . . .67 C8
Whiteacre WN6 . . . . .19 A2
Whiteacre Rd OL6 . . . . .85 D4
Whiteacre Wlk M15 . . . . . . .162 E5
Whiteacres M27 . . . . .79 D7

Whitebeam Cl
Altrincham WA15 . . . . .120 E5
Newhey OL16 . . . . .32 A3
Salford M6 . . . . .81 A3
Whitebeam Ct M6 . . . . .81 A3
Whitebeam Wlk
1 Sale M33 . . . . .107 D5
Westhoughton BL5 . . . . .39 F2
Whitebeck Ct M9 . . . . .65 A4
Whitebrook Rd M14 . . . . .98 B1
Whitecar Ave M40 . . . . .65 E1
Whitecarr La M23,WA15 . . . .120 E3
Whitechapel Cl BL2 . . . . .42 E7
Whitechapel St M20 . . . . . . .110 B3
Whitecliff Cl M14 . . . . .98 C3
Whitecroft Ave
Golborne WA3 . . . . .74 E1
Shaw OL2 . . . . .49 D7
Whitecroft Dr BL8 . . . . .26 F2
Whitecroft Gdns 3
M9 . . . . .110 E4
Whitecroft Rd
Bolton BL1 . . . . .142 A1
Marple SK6 . . . . .126 C1
Wigan WN6 . . . . .55 B2
Whitecroft St 12 OL1 . . . . . . .49 C1
Whitefield
Lymm WA13 . . . . .117 A4
Manchester SK4 . . . . .169 D3
Pendlebury M6 . . . . .80 D6
Whitefield Ave
Newton-le-W WA12 . . . . .89 E2
Rochdale OL11 . . . . .29 F8
Whitefield Cl
Golborne WA3 . . . . .90 A8
Lymm WA13 . . . . .117 A5
Whitefield Com Prim Sch
M45 . . . . .63 A8
Whitefield Gr WA13 . . . . . . .117 A4
Whitefield Rd Bury BL9 . . . . .44 D7
Romiley SK6 . . . . .112 E4
Sale M33 . . . . .108 A5
Whitefield Sta M45 . . . . .44 F1
Whitefriar Ct M3 . . . . .158 E3
Whitefriars Wlk M22 . . . . . . .130 D8
Whitegate Bolton BL3 . . . . . . .40 C2
Rochdale OL15 . . . . .15 E4
Whitegate Ave
Culcheth WA3 . . . . .91 F2
Oldham OL9 . . . . .65 F4
Whitegate Dr M40 . . . . .65 E1
Whitegate Dr Bolton BL1 . . .143 F4
Swinton M27 . . . . .62 D2
Whitegate End Prim Sch
OL9 . . . . .65 E3
Whitegate La 6 Oldham OL9 .66 A4
Whitegate Pk M41 . . . . .94 E2
Whitegate Rd OL9 . . . . .65 E3
Whitegates Rd
Cheadle SK8 . . . . .122 D5
Middleton M24 . . . . .47 C4
Whitegates St SK15 . . . . . . .120 B5
Whitegates La OL4 . . . . .50 B2
Whitegates Rd
Cheadle SK8 . . . . .122 D5
Middleton M24 . . . . .47 C4
Whitehall Ave WN6 . . . . .35 E8
Whitehall Cl SK9 . . . . .137 A5
Whitehall La Blackrod BL6 . . .21 D3
Bolton BL1 . . . . .24 D6
Oldham OL4 . . . . .49 F4
Whitehall Rd
Manchester M20 . . . . .110 C3
Sale M33 . . . . .108 B3
Whitehall St
Ince-in-M WN3 . . . . .151 E6
Oldham OL1 . . . . .153 F8
Rochdale OL12 . . . . .14 F1
Whitehaven Gdns M20 . . . . .110 A2
Whitehaven Pl SK14 . . . . . . .101 C5
Whitehead Cres Bury BL8 . . .27 C5
Kearsley M26 . . . . .61 C7
Whitehead Rd
Stretford M21 . . . . .108 F8
Swinton M27 . . . . .62 B2
Whitehead St
Denton M34 . . . . .100 F7
Middleton M24 . . . . .47 C1
Milnrow OL16 . . . . .31 E6
Oldham OL9 . . . . .32 D4
Shaw OL2 . . . . .48 F8
Walkden M28 . . . . .60 D4
Whitehill Cotts BL7 . . . . .24 D6
Whitehill Dr M40 . . . . .83 A7
Whitehill Ind Est SK4,
SK5 . . . . .111 E5
Whitehill Prim Sch SK4 . . . .169 E4
Whitehill St SK4,SK5 . . . . . . .111 E5
Whitehill St W SK4 . . . . .169 E4
Whiteholme Ave M21 . . . . . .109 D4
Whitehouse Ave 4 OL4 . . . . .67 C6
Whitehouse Dr
Altrincham WA14 . . . . .129 A8
Northenden M23 . . . . .121 A5
Whitehouse La WA14 . . . . . .118 D8
Whitehurst Rd SK4 . . . . .110 F4
Whitekirk Cl M13 . . . . .163 B6
Whitelake Ave M41 . . . . .94 F2
Whitelake View M41 . . . . .94 F3
Whiteland Ave BL3 . . . . .144 C5
Whitelands
Ashton-u-L OL6,SK15 . . . . .85 D2
Ashton-u-L OL6,SK15 . . . . .85 D3
Whitelands Terr OL6 . . . . . . .166 C2
Whitelea Dr SK3 . . . . .170 D5
Whitelees Rd OL15 . . . . .16 A5
Whitelegge St BL8 . . . . .27 B4
Whiteley Dr M24 . . . . .65 C7

Whiteley Pl WA14 . . . . .119 D6
Whiteley St
Droylsden M11 . . . . .83 C2
Manchester OL9 . . . . .66 B4
Whiteley's Pl 6 OL12 . . . . . .139 E8
Whitelow Rd
Manchester M21 . . . . .109 A8
Manchester,Heaton Moor
SK4 . . . . .168 A3
Ramsbottom BL0 . . . . .11 E5
Whitemoss OL12 . . . . .14 B2
Whitemoss 8 SK6 . . . . .125 E7
Whiteoak Ct M14 . . . . .110 C8
Whiteoak Rd M14 . . . . .110 C8
Whiteoak View BL3 . . . . .42 D5
Whiteside Ave
Hindley WN2 . . . . .56 E7
2 Wigan WN6 . . . . .37 A1
Whiteside Fold OL12 . . . . .14 A1
Whitesmead Cl SK12 . . . . . . .135 D5
Whitestone Cl BL6 . . . . .40 D6
Whitestone Ho 16 OL1 . . . .153 E8
Whitethorn Cl M23 . . . . .163 D5
Whitethorn Ave
Manchester M19 . . . . .110 F7
1 Manchester,Whalley Range
M16 . . . . .97 D3
Whitethorn Cl SK6 . . . . .125 E7
Whitewater Dr M7 . . . . .80 F8
Whitewell Cl BL9 . . . . .141 C3
Whitewell Cl Bury BL9 . . . . . .44 D7
Rochdale OL16 . . . . .31 C8
Whitewillow Cl M35 . . . . .84 A6
Whitewood Cl WN4 . . . . .73 A6
Whitfield Ave SK13 . . . . .116 C7
Whitfield Brows OL15 . . . . . . .16 C7
Whitfield Cres OL16 . . . . .32 B3
Whitfield Cross SK13 . . . . . .116 D7
Whitfield Dr OL16 . . . . .31 E5
Whitfield Pk SK13 . . . . .116 C7
Whitfield Rise OL2 . . . . .32 A1
Whitfield St Leigh WN7 . . . . .76 C4
Manchester M3 . . . . .159 A4
Whitford Wlk M40 . . . . .160 D3
Whiting Gr BL3 . . . . .40 E6
Whitlea Cl WN2 . . . . .57 C3
Whitland Ave BL1 . . . . .40 D8
Whitland Dr OL8 . . . . .66 B2
Whitle Rd SK22 . . . . .127 C1
Whitledge Gn WN4 . . . . .73 A5
Whitledge Rd WN4 . . . . .73 A5
Whitley Cres
Abram Brow WN2 . . . . .74 B7
Wigan WN1 . . . . .37 C4
Whitley Gdns WA15 . . . . . . .120 C7
Whitley Pl WA15 . . . . .120 C7
Whitley Rd
Manchester M40 . . . . .159 C4
Manchester,Heaton Moor
SK4 . . . . .168 B3
Up Holland WN8 . . . . .35 D3
Whitley St BL3 . . . . .42 D2
Whitlow Ave
Altrincham WA14 . . . . .119 B8
Golborne WA3 . . . . .74 F1
Whitman St M40,M9 . . . . . . .157 F8
Whitmore Rd M14 . . . . .98 B1
Whitnall St
Dukinfield SK14 . . . . .101 D5
Manchester M16 . . . . .97 E4
Whitsand Rd M22 . . . . .121 E5
Whitsbury Ave
Hindley WN2 . . . . .56 D4
Manchester M18 . . . . .99 D3
Whitstable Cl OL10 . . . . .46 D8
Whitstable Rd M40 . . . . .65 D1
Whitsters Hollow BL1 . . . . . .142 B2
Whitsundale BL5 . . . . .39 F2
Whitswood Cl 2 M16 . . . . . . .97 F3
Whittaker Dr OL15 . . . . .15 F2
Whittaker La
Littleborough OL15 . . . . .16 E4
Prestwich M25 . . . . .63 C4
Rochdale OL11 . . . . .13 D1
Whittaker Moss Prim Sch
OL11 . . . . .13 F3
Whittaker St
Ashton-u-L OL6 . . . . .85 D5
Manchester M40 . . . . .83 A8
Radcliffe M26 . . . . .44 B4
Rochdale OL11 . . . . .13 E1
Whittingham Dr BL0 . . . . .11 C3
Whittingham Gr OL1 . . . . . . .153 D8
Whittington St OL7 . . . . .166 A1
Whittle Bank Rd SK22 . . . . .127 B2
Whittle Ct WN3 . . . . .54 E2
Whittle Dr Shaw OL2 . . . . . . .49 D8
Walkden M28 . . . . .60 B3
Whittle Gr Bolton BL1 . . . . . .142 B1
Walkden M28 . . . . .60 B3
Whittle Hill BL7 . . . . .8 E3
Whittle St Bury BL9 . . . . .27 C3
Littleborough OL15 . . . . .15 F5
Manchester M4 . . . . .159 B2
Swinton M27 . . . . .79 E7
Walkden M28 . . . . .60 B3
Whittle's Croft M1 . . . . .159 B1
Whittle's Croft Wharf
M1 . . . . .159 B1
Whittle's Terr 1 OL15 . . . . .39 E1
Whittlebrook Gr OL10 . . . . . . .46 F7
Whittles Ave M34 . . . . .101 A4
Whittles St OL13 . . . . .4 B8
Whittles Terr OL16 . . . . .31 F6
Whittles Wlk M34 . . . . .101 A2
Whitton Mews 5 BL6 . . . . . . .22 B4

Whitwell Bank 4 SK13 . . . . .171 D2
Whitwell Cl
3 Gamesley SK13 . . . . .171 D2
Standish WN6 . . . . .19 D2
Whitwell Fold 1 SK13 . . . . .171 D2
Whitwell Gdns BL6 . . . . .22 B5
Whitwell Gn SK13 . . . . .171 E2
Whitwell Lea 2 SK13 . . . . . .171 D2
Whitwell Way M18 . . . . .165 C5
Whitwell Wlk 4 M13 . . . . .98 E4
Whitworth Art Gall*
M15 . . . . .98 B4
Whitworth Com High Sch
OL12 . . . . .14 C8
Whitworth La M14 . . . . .98 D1
Whitworth Park Mans
M14 . . . . .98 A4
Whitworth Rake OL12 . . . . . . .14 D8
Whitworth Rd OL12 . . . . .14 F2
Whitworth Sq OL12 . . . . .14 C8
Whitworth St
Manchester M11 . . . . .163 A8
Manchester M11 . . . . .165 B8
Milnrow OL16 . . . . .31 F6
Rochdale OL16 . . . . .15 C2
Whitworth St E M11 . . . . . . .165 C4
Whitworth St W M1,M3 . . . .162 F8
Whitworth Water Ski Ctr*
OL12 . . . . .14 C8
Whixhall Ave M12 . . . . .164 E6
Whoolden St BL4 . . . . .42 C1
Whowell Fold BL1 . . . . .142 C3
Whowell St BL3 . . . . .145 E6
Wibbersley Pk M41 . . . . .94 F2
Wibsey Cotts OL3 . . . . .33 D2
Wichbrook Rd 8 M28 . . . . . . .59 F3
Wicheaves Cres M28 . . . . .60 A3
Wicheries The M28 . . . . .59 F3
Wicken Bank OL10 . . . . .46 E7
Wicken St SK2 . . . . .124 C7
Wickenby Dr M33 . . . . .108 A5
Wickentree Holt OL12 . . . . . . .14 A1
Wickentree La M35 . . . . .66 A1
Wicker La WA15 . . . . .129 C8
Wicket Gr M27 . . . . .61 E4
Wickham Terr 11 M24 . . . . . .47 A2
Wickliffe St 16 BL1 . . . . .145 E8
Wicklow Ave SK3 . . . . .123 B7
Wicklow Dr M22 . . . . .121 E2
Wicklow St 3 OL8 . . . . .66 E3
Wickmere Wlk M8 . . . . .155 F6
Widcombe Dr BL2 . . . . .42 F5
Widdop St SK12 . . . . .153 D7
Widdow's St WN7 . . . . .76 B4
Widdrington Rd WN1 . . . . .37 D2
Widecombe Cl M41 . . . . .95 B4
Widford Wlk BL6 . . . . .21 E1
Widgeon Cl
Manchester M14 . . . . .110 B8
Poynton SK12 . . . . .133 B4
Widgeon Rd WA14 . . . . .119 B8
Widnes St M11 . . . . .165 C7
Widworth La BL9 . . . . .27 F5
Wiend The
Ashton-in-M WN4 . . . . .73 A5
Aspull WN2 . . . . .38 B4
Atherton M46 . . . . .58 E5
Billinge WN5 . . . . .71 F7
Bolton BL3 . . . . .144 B5
Bolton BL3 . . . . .145 A6
Golborne WA3 . . . . .74 B3
Leigh WN7 . . . . .75 D7
Shevington WN6 . . . . .36 B5
Westhoughton BL5 . . . . .57 C6
Wigan Sq WN1 . . . . .150 C8
Wigan St WN2 . . . . .56 B8
Wigan Wallgate Sta
WN1 . . . . .150 C8
Wiggins Wlk 13 M14 . . . . .98 C3
Wigginton Ave M45 . . . . .63 A7
Wighurst Wlk 6 M22 . . . . . .121 D1
Wigley St M12 . . . . .164 E7
Wigmore Rd M8 . . . . .156 B7
Wigmore St 15 OL6 . . . . .85 D4
Wigsby Ave M40 . . . . .65 D1
Wigsey La WA13 . . . . .117 A7
Wigshaw Cl M33 . . . . .108 A4
Wigshaw La WA3 . . . . .91 D2
Wigwam Cl SK12 . . . . .133 C4
Wike St BL8 . . . . .140 C2
Wilberforce Cl M15 . . . . .162 F5
Wilbraham Prim Sch
M14 . . . . .98 A1
Wilbraham Rd
Manchester M14,M16,M21 . . .97 C1

Wilbraham Rd continued
Walkden M28 . . . . .60 E3
Wilbraham Regency Ct 5
M21 . . . . .97 A1
Wilbraham St Leigh WN7 . . .75 C5
Westhoughton BL5 . . . . .57 E8
Wilburn St M5 . . . . .162 D8
Wilby Ave BL3 . . . . .43 B5
Wilby Cl BL8 . . . . .27 D5
Wilby St M8 . . . . .156 B6
Wilby Rd WA11 . . . . .89 B8
Wilcock St
Manchester M16 . . . . .97 E4
Wigan WN5 . . . . .150 A7
Wilcockson Ho 4 BL4 . . . . . .60 D8
Wilcott Dr Sale M33 . . . . .107 E5
Wilmslow WN5 . . . . .136 F4
Wilcott Rd SK8 . . . . .122 A5
Wild Arum Cl 8 M31 . . . . . . .90 E8
Wild Bank Com Sch
SK15 . . . . .86 C2
Wild's Pas WN7 . . . . .75 F4
Wild's Sq 8 OL5 . . . . .68 C2
Wildbank Chase SK15 . . . . .102 E7
Wildbrook Cl M38 . . . . .59 E3
Wildbrook Cres OL8 . . . . .67 A2
Wildbrook Gr M38 . . . . .59 E3
Wildbrook Terr OL8 . . . . .67 A2
Wildcroft Ave M40 . . . . .65 A1
Wilde St WM4 . . . . .100 F3
Wilders Moor Rd 3 M28 . . . .78 C8
Wilderswood Ave BL6 . . . . . . .22 C4
Wilderswood Cl M20 . . . . . . .110 C5
Wilderswood Ct BL6 . . . . .22 D4
Wildhouse La OL16 . . . . .31 F8
Wilding St WN3 . . . . .151 E6
Wildman La BL4 . . . . .59 F8
Wildmoor Ave OL4 . . . . .67 E4
Wilds Pl BL0 . . . . .138 B5
Wildwood Cl
Ramsbottom BL0 . . . . .11 A4
Stockport SK2 . . . . .124 A5
Wilford Ave M33 . . . . .108 A2
Wilfred Dr BL9 . . . . .141 A4
Wilfred St Eccles M30 . . . . . . .95 A8
Manchester M40 . . . . .83 D8
Manchester M40 . . . . .83 A7
Oldham OL4 . . . . .67 C6
Salford M7 . . . . .158 E4
Wigan WN5 . . . . .54 F7
Wilfrid St M27 . . . . .61 F1
Wilfrid's Pl WN6 . . . . .19 F1
Wilham Ave M30 . . . . .79 D1
Wilkes St 1 OL1 . . . . .49 D3
Wilkesley Ave WN6 . . . . .36 D8
Wilkin Croft SK8 . . . . .122 E1
Wilkins La SK9 . . . . .130 E5
Wilkinson Ave BL3 . . . . .43 A5
Wilkinson Rd BL1 . . . . .24 D5
Wilkinson St
Ashton-u-L OL6 . . . . .166 A2
Leigh WN7 . . . . .75 E5
Stockport SK4 . . . . .169 E2
Wilks Ave M22 . . . . .121 F3
Will Griffith Wlk M11 . . . . .99 E7
Will Moor Wood Cl SK15 . .86 D5
Willan Ent Ctr
Chadderton OL9 . . . . .152 B7
Stretford M17 . . . . .96 C6
Willan Ind Est M50 . . . . .154 F1
Willan Rd Eccles M30 . . . . . . .79 E2
Manchester M9 . . . . .64 E2
Willand Cl BL2 . . . . .43 A6
Willand Dr BL2 . . . . .43 A6
Willard St WN5 . . . . .53 D3
Willard St WN7 . . . . .124 D3
Willaston Cl M21 . . . . .109 A7
Willaston Way 8 SK9 . . . . . .131 D5
Willbutts La OL11 . . . . .30 C8
Willdale Cl M11 . . . . .83 A2
Willdor Gr SK3 . . . . .123 B6
Willenhall Rd M23 . . . . .109 C2
Willerby Rd M8 . . . . .155 E5
Willesden Ave M13 . . . . .98 E3
William Chadwick Cl 1
M40 . . . . .159 C3
William Cl M41 . . . . .95 C2
William Coates Ct 6
M16 . . . . .161 C5
William Ford Ho SK14 . . . . .103 A4
William Greenwood Cl
. . . . .29 C2
William Henry St 2
OL11 . . . . .31 A4
William Hulme's Gram Sch
M16 . . . . .97 F1
William Hulme's Gram Sch
Prep Dept M21 . . . . .97 E1
William Jessop Ct 10
M1 . . . . .159 C1
William Kay Cl M16 . . . . .97 E4

William Lister Cl M40 . . . .**83** D4
William St
Ashton-u-L OL7 . . . .**166** A1
Ashton-u-L OL7 . . . .**84** F2
Bacup OL13 . . . .**4** C8
Failsworth M35 . . . .**66** A1
Hindley WN2 . . . .**56** E5
Horwich BL6 . . . .**22** A3
Ince-in-M WN3 . . . .**151** D6
5 Leigh WN7 . . . .**76** A5
Leigh WN7 . . . .**76** A5
Littleborough OL15 . . . .**16** A5
5 Manchester M41 . . . . .**163** A7
Manchester,Ardwick M12 . .**164** D8
Manchester,Disbury M20 . .**110** B3
Middleton M24 . . . .**65** B8
Radcliffe M26 . . . .**44** B4
Ramsbottom BL0 . . . .**1** C1
Rochdale OL11 . . . .**139** F6
Rochdale,Wuerdle OL16 . . .**15** D4
Salford M3 . . . .**158** E2
Whitworth OL12 . . . .**4** C1
William Way WN7 . . . . . .**75** B1
William Wlk 2 WA14 . . . .**119** D3
Williams Ave WA12 . . . . .**89** C5
Williams Cres OL9 . . . . . .**65** F3
Williams Rd
Failsworth M40 . . . .**83** C7
Manchester M18 . . . .**165** C5
Williams St
Little Lever BL3 . . . .**43** B3
Manchester M18 . . . .**165** C5
Williamson Ave
Radcliffe M26 . . . .**43** F6
Romiley SK6 . . . .**113** A4
Williamson La M43 . . . .**100** B8
Williamson St
Ashton-u-L OL6 . . . .**166** B3
Manchester M35 . . . .**159** B3
Reddish SK5 . . . .**111** F7
Williamson's Yd 6 OL1 . .**67** B7
Willingdon Cl BL8 . . . . . .**27** C7
Willingdon Dr M25 . . . . . .**63** B5
Willis Rd SK3 . . . .**170** E6
Willis St BL3 . . . .**146** C4
Williton Wlk 6 M22 . . . .**121** F3
Willock St M7 . . . .**155** F6
Willoughby Ave M20 . . . .**110** C4
Willoughby Cl M33 . . . . .**108** A5
Willow Ave Cheadle SK8 .**122** F2
Middleton M24 . . . .**65** C8
Newton-le-W WA12 . . . . . .**89** E4
Reddish SK5 . . . .**169** H4
Tyldesley M29 . . . .**77** A6
Urmston M41 . . . .**95** E2
Willow Bank
Altrincham WA15 . . . .**120** A6
Cheadle SK8 . . . .**132** A6
Manchester,Fallowfield
M14 . . . .**110** C8
1 Manchester,Harpurhey
M9 . . . .**157** E7
Oldham OL4 . . . .**67** D4
Willow Bank Cl SK2 . . . .**124** D7
Willow Bank Cl M20 . . . .**122** B8
Willow Bank Est WA12 . .**89** F4
Willow Cl Adlington PR6 . .**21** B8
Bolton BL3 . . . .**146** B4
Dukinfield SK16 . . . .**101** F7
Poynton SK12 . . . .**133** E3
Whitefield BL9 . . . .**45** B3
Willow Cres WN7 . . . .**75** E8
Willow Ct Gatley SK8 . . .**122** A6
Manchester M14 . . . .**98** D1
Manchester,Fallowfield
M14 . . . .**110** C8
Marple SK6 . . . .**125** F5
Sale M33 . . . .**108** A2
Standish WN6 . . . .**19** E2
Willow Dr Handforth SK9 .**131** D3
Hindley WN2 . . . .**56** F3
Sale M33 . . . .**107** E2
Whitefield BL9 . . . .**45** B2
Willow Fold M43 . . . . . .**100** B8
Willow Gr
Ashton-in-M WN4 . . . .**73** E5
Chadderton OL9 . . . .**152** B8
Denton M34 . . . .**100** E3
Golborne WA3 . . . .**74** A1
Manchester M18 . . . .**99** E4
Marple SK6 . . . .**125** F5
Willow Hill Rd M8 . . . . . .**64** A1
Willow Lawn SK8 . . . . . .**123** A2
Willow Lo 1 WN2 . . . . . .**56** B1
Willow Pk M14 . . . .**110** C8
Willow Rd Eccles M30 . . .**79** A4
High Lane SK6 . . . .**134** F7
Newton-le-W WA12 . . . . . .**89** E4
Partington M31 . . . .**105** E2
Prestwich M25,M45 . . . . . .**63** A3
Wigan WN6 . . . .**37** A3
Willow Rise OL15 . . . .**16** A7
Willow St 2 Abram WN2 . .**56** B1
Atherton M46 . . . .**58** C4
Bury BL9 . . . .**141** B3
Droylsden M11 . . . .**83** A1
Heywood OL10 . . . .**29** D2
Manchester M8 . . . .**158** E4
Oldham OL1 . . . .**67** A7
Rawtenstall BB4 . . . .**2** E8
Swinton,Chorlton Fold M27 .**79** D5
Swinton,Hazelhurst M28 . . .**79** C7
Willow Tree Cl WN1 . . . . .**37** B4

Willow Tree Ct
1 Eccles M30 . . . .**79** C1
Sale M33 . . . .**108** B3
Willow Tree Mews SK8 . .**122** B1
Willow Tree Rd WA14 . . .**119** D3
Willow Way
Bramhall SK7 . . . .**132** D7
Manchester M20 . . . .**110** C3
Willow Wood Cl OL6 . . . . .**85** E3
Willowbank M26 . . . .**61** F8
Willowbank Ave BL2 . . . .**148** B6
Willowbrook Ave M40 . . . .**83** A7
Willowbrook Dr WN6 . . . . .**36** B7
Willowbrook Gdns M22 . .**121** C4
Willowcroft Ave WN2 . . . . .**38** F3
Willowdale WA12 . . . .**89** E3
Willowdene Cl Bolton BL7 . .**24** F8
3 Manchester M40 . . . . .**156** C5
Willowfield Gr WN4 . . . . . .**73** A2
Willowfield Rd OL4 . . . . . .**49** D2
Willowmead Way OL12 . . .**14** A2
Willows Ave OL28 . . . .**60** F1
Willows Cl WN9 . . . .**136** F6
Willows Cotts OL16 . . . . . .**31** E6
Willows Dr M35 . . . .**83** F5
Willows End SK15 . . . .**86** D3
Willows La Bolton BL3 . . .**146** A4
Milnrow OL16 . . . .**31** E6
Willows Prim Sch
WA15 . . . .**120** A6
Willows Prim Sch The
M22 . . . .**121** C2
Willows Rd M5 . . . .**154** D2
Willows The
5 Atherton M46 . . . .**58** D3
Coppull PR7 . . . .**19** E8
Little Lever BL3 . . . .**43** A5
Manchester SK4 . . . .**168** A3
Manchester,Barlow Moor
M21 . . . .**109** A7
Mossley OL5 . . . .**68** E1
Partington M31 . . . .**105** F3
Sale M33 . . . .**107** D2
Whitworth OL12 . . . .**14** C5
Wilma Ave M9 . . . .**64** C4
Wilmans Wlk SK13 . . . . .**104** A6
Wilmcote Cl BL6 . . . .**40** D6
Wilmcote Gdns 2 SK6 . . .**112** F3
Wilmcote Rd M40 . . . . . .**159** C4
Wilmers OL15 . . . .**6** D2
Wilmington Rd M32 . . . . . .**96** B2
Wilmot Dr WA3 . . . .**89** F7
Wilmot St BL1 . . . .**142** C3
Wilmott St
Manchester M15 . . . .**162** F7
Manchester M15 . . . .**163** A6
Wilmslow Ave BL1 . . . .**24** E5
Wilmslow Ct SK9 . . . .**131** D3
Wilmslow Grange Prim Sch
SK9 . . . .**131** C4
Wilmslow High Sch SK9 .**137** B6
Wilmslow Old Rd M90 . . .**130** A6
Wilmslow Park Way SK9 .**137** D7
Wilmslow Prep Sch
SK9 . . . .**137** C2
Wilmslow Rd
Alderley Edge SK9 . . . . . .**137** A2
Cheadle SK8 . . . .**122** D3
Cheadle SK8 . . . .**122** D5
Gatley SK8,SK9 . . . .**131** C6
Handforth SK9 . . . .**131** D4
Manchester M20 . . . .**110** B1
Manchester M20 . . . .**110** C1
Manchester,Rusholme M14 .**98** C2
Manchester,Withington
M14,M20 . . . .**110** B5
Woodford SK7 . . . .**132** C1
Wythenshawe M90,SK9,
WA15 . . . .**130** A6
Wilmslow Sta SK9 . . . . . .**137** C7
Wilmslow Ave Salford M7 .**155** C6
Whitefield M45 . . . .**62** F8
Wilpshire Ave 8 M12 . . . .**99** B3
Wilsford Cl WA3 . . . .**74** B1
Wilsham Rd WN5 . . . .**53** E5
Wilshaw Gr OL7 . . . .**85** B6
Wilshaw La OL7 . . . .**85** A5
Wilson Ave Heywood OL10 .**29** A2
Swinton M27 . . . .**62** B2
Wigan WN6 . . . .**37** B2
Wilson Cres OL6 . . . .**85** E4
Wilson Fold Ave BL6 . . . . .**39** F8
Wilson Rd
Manchester,Blackley M9 . . .**64** D1
Manchester,Heaton Moor
SK4 . . . .**168** C5
Wilson St 8 Bolton BL3 . .**145** F6
Bury BL9 . . . .**141** A1
Farnworth BL4 . . . .**60** E8
Horwich BL6 . . . .**22** A4
Hyde SK14 . . . .**167** E2
Manchester,Brunswick
M12,M13 . . . .**163** C6
Oldham OL8 . . . .**66** E4
Radcliffe M26 . . . .**43** F4
Rochdale OL12 . . . .**139** F8
2 Sale M33 . . . .**108** B5
Stretford M32 . . . .**96** E4
Uppermill OL3 . . . .**69** A6
Wilson Way OL1 . . . .**153** F8
Wilson's Terr SK13 . . . . .**116** B8
Wilsons Pk M40 . . . .**157** E5
Wilton Ave Gatley SK8 . . .**122** A5
Manchester,Firswood M16 . .**97** A3
Manchester,Sedgley M25 . . .**63** D2

Wilton Ave continued
Pendlebury M27 . . . .**80** C7
Wigan WN2 . . . .**37** F2
Wilton Cotts WA3 . . . .**75** A2
Wilton Cres SK9 . . . .**136** F2
Wilton Ct Middleton M25 . .**63** E8
Reddish M34 . . . .**100** A4
Wilton Dr
Altrincham WA15 . . . .**129** C8
Whitefield BL9 . . . .**45** A5
Wilton Gdns M26 . . . .**44** C5
Wilton Gr Heywood OL10 . .**29** D1
Reddish M34 . . . .**100** A4
Wilton La WA3 . . . .**91** B5
Wilton Paddock M34 . . . .**100** A4
Wilton Pl M3 . . . .**158** D2
Wilton Rd Bolton BL1 . . . . .**24** E5
Manchester M21 . . . .**109** B8
Manchester,Crumpsall M8 . .**64** A2
Salford M6 . . . .**80** B4
Shevington WN6 . . . .**36** A6
Wilton St
Ashton-in-M WN4 . . . .**73** A6
Denton M34 . . . .**143** F3
Heywood OL10 . . . .**29** C2
Middleton M24 . . . .**47** B3
Oldham OL9 . . . .**66** A4
Prestwich M25 . . . .**63** C4
Reddish SK5 . . . .**99** F2
Whitefield M45 . . . .**62** F7
Wigan WN1 . . . .**151** D7
Wilton Terr OL12 . . . .**139** E8
Wiltshire Ave SK5 . . . . . .**112** C4
Wiltshire Cl BL9 . . . .**45** A8
Wiltshire Dr
Chadderton OL9 . . . .**152** B5
Failsworth M35 . . . .**84** A6
Partington M31 . . . .**105** E2
Wiltshire Pl WN5 . . . .**54** C6
Wiltshire Rd
Chadderton OL9 . . . .**152** B5
Failsworth M35 . . . .**84** A6
Partington M31 . . . .**105** E2
Wiltshire St M7 . . . .**155** E6
Wimberry Hill Rd BL5 . . . .**39** D3
Wimbledon Dr
Rochdale OL11 . . . .**139** D5
Stockport SK3 . . . .**123** C7
Wimbledon Rd M35 . . . . . .**84** A8
Wimborne Ave
Chadderton OL9 . . . .**48** A1
Urmston M41 . . . .**95** D3
Wimborne Cl
Cheadle SK8 . . . .**123** C4
Reddish M34 . . . .**22** F1
Wimborne Rd WN5 . . . . . .**54** A8
Wimpenny Ho OL8 . . . . . .**153** E5
Wimpole St
Ashton-u-L OL6 . . . .**166** C3
4 Oldham M11 . . . .**49** A1
Wimpory St M11 . . . .**99** D7
Winbolt St SK2 . . . .**124** C4
Winby St **5** OL11 . . . .**31** A4
Wincanton Ave M23 . . . . .**120** D8
Wincanton Dr BL1 . . . .**24** D7
Wincanton Pk OL4 . . . .**67** D6
Wince Cl M24 . . . .**65** C6
Winchcombe Cl M33 . . . .**162** D6
Wincham Rd M33 . . . . . .**107** E2
Winchcombe Cl WN7 . . . . .**75** E1
Winchester Ave
Ashton-in-M WN4 . . . .**73** A3
Ashton-u-L OL6 . . . .**85** D8
Chadderton OL9 . . . .**47** F1
Denton M34 . . . .**100** F1
Heywood OL10 . . . .**46** C8
Manchester M25 . . . .**63** C2
Tyldesley M29 . . . .**77** C7
Winchester Cl Bury BL8 . .**27** C7
4 Orrell WN5 . . . .**53** F7
Rochdale OL11 . . . .**30** A7
Wilmslow SK9 . . . .**137** A6
Winchester Dr Sale M33 .**107** D4
Stockport SK4 . . . .**168** B2
Winchester Gr WN3 . . . . .**151** D6
Winchester Pk M20 . . . . .**109** F3
Winchester Rd
Altrincham WA15 . . . .**120** C1
Ashton-in-M WA11 . . . .**72** E1
Dukinfield SK16 . . . .**102** A7
Longshaw WN5 . . . .**53** D2
Radcliffe M26 . . . .**43** D5
Salford M30 . . . .**80** A4
Swinton M30 . . . .**80** C4
Urmston M41 . . . .**95** E3
Winchester Way BL2 . . . . .**25** D1
Wincle Ave SK12 . . . .**134** A2
Wincombe St M14 . . . .**98** B2
Windale M28 . . . .**78** E5
Windcroft Cl M11 . . . .**165** A8
Winder Dr M4 . . . .**159** C2
Winder St BL1 . . . .**145** F8
Windermere Ave
Atherton M46 . . . .**58** C5
Little Lever BL3 . . . .**43** A4
Pendlebury M27 . . . .**80** A7
Reddish M34 . . . .**100** B2
Sale M33 . . . .**108** D2
Windermere Cl
Manchester M11 . . . .**165** A8
Prestwich M25 . . . .**63** B1
Stretford M32 . . . .**96** C3
Windermere Cres OL7 . . . .**84** F5
Windermere Dr
Adlington PR6 . . . .**21** B8
Alderley Edge SK9 . . . . . .**137** B2
Bury BL9 . . . .**44** F7
Ramsbottom BL0 . . . .**138** C7

Windermere Gr WN7 . . . . .**75** E6
Windermere Ho 3 M28 . . .**60** E2
Windermere Mews M24 . . .**46** E3
Windermere Rd
Abram WN2 . . . .**74** B8
Dukinfield SK14 . . . .**101** C5
Farnworth BL4 . . . .**59** E7
Handforth SK9 . . . .**131** C4
High Lane SK6 . . . .**134** E8
Hindley WN2 . . . .**56** E5
Ince-in-M WN2 . . . .**56** B7
Leigh WN7 . . . .**75** E5
Middleton M24 . . . .**46** D3
Orrell WN5 . . . .**53** F8
Royton OL2 . . . .**48** D6
Stalybridge SK15 . . . .**86** A4
Stockport SK1 . . . .**124** B7
Urmston M41 . . . .**95** C1
Windermere St
Bolton BL1 . . . .**143** F2
5 Wigan WN1 . . . .**37** E1
Windermere Wlk 6 OL4 . . .**67** C7
Winders Way M6 . . . .**81** B4
Windfields Cl SK8 . . . . . .**123** B3
Windgate Rise SK15 . . . . .**86** D5
Windham St OL16 . . . .**15** C3
Windle Ave M9 . . . .**63** F3
Windle Ct SK2 . . . .**124** C5
Windlehurst Dr M28 . . . . . .**78** B7
Windlehurst Hall SK6 . . . .**125** F1
Windlehurst Old Rd
SK6 . . . .**125** F2
Windlehurst Rd SK6 . . . . .**125** C2
Windleshaw St WN3 . . . . .**151** E6
Windley St BL2 . . . .**148** A8
Windmill Ave M5 . . . .**161** B7
Windmill Cl Denton M34 . .**100** C2
Walkden M28 . . . .**60** C5
Wigan WN1 . . . .**151** D8
Windmill Ct 2 OL16 . . . . . .**31** B6
Windover Cl BL5 . . . .**59** A7
Windover St BL3 . . . .**146** A4
Windrush Ave BL0 . . . .**11** A2
Windrush Dr
Manchester M9 . . . .**157** D7
Westhoughton BL5 . . . .**39** F1
Windrush The OL12 . . . . . .**14** C4
Windsor Ave
Adlington PR7 . . . .**20** F6
Chadderton OL9 . . . .**66** A4
Failsworth M35 . . . .**84** B8
Gatley SK8 . . . .**122** A5
Heywood OL10 . . . .**29** B1
Irlam M44 . . . .**94** B3
Little Lever BL3 . . . .**43** A3
Manchester SK4 . . . .**168** A3
Newton-le-W WA12 . . . . . .**89** D2
Swinton M27 . . . .**62** A2
Tyldesley M29 . . . .**77** A6
Urmston M41 . . . .**94** F2
Walkden M38 . . . .**60** A5
Whitefield M45 . . . .**63** A7
Wilmslow SK9 . . . .**137** A6
Windsor Cl Poynton SK12 .**133** D4
Ramsbottom BL8 . . . .**11** A1
Windsor Cres Aspull WN2 .**38** D5
Manchester M25 . . . .**63** B3
Windsor Ct Bolton BL3 . . .**107** F5
Windsor Dr
Ashton-u-L OL6 . . . .**118** F1
Altrincham WA14 . . . .**119** F8
Ashton-u-L OL7 . . . .**84** F4
Bury BL8 . . . .**44** B8
Droylsden M34 . . . .**84** D1
Dukinfield SK16 . . . .**101** F7
Haydock WA11 . . . .**89** B6
Horwich BL6 . . . .**22** E2
Marple SK6 . . . .**125** E5
Stalybridge SK15 . . . .**86** A3
Windsor Gr
Ashton-u-L OL6 . . . .**85** C7
Bolton BL1 . . . .**142** C1
Cheadle SK8 . . . .**123** B7
Hindley WN2 . . . .**57** B3
Kearsley M26 . . . .**61** B7
Romiley SK6 . . . .**113** C2
Windsor Rd
Ashton-in-M WN4 . . . .**73** C1
Billinge WN5 . . . .**25** A7
Droylsden M43 . . . .**83** E1
Failsworth M40 . . . .**83** E4
Golborne WA3 . . . .**90** C8
Hazel Grove SK7 . . . .**124** F2
Hyde SK14 . . . .**113** E7
Leigh WN7 . . . .**76** E6
Manchester M25 . . . .**63** B3
Manchester,Harpurhey M9 .**157** E7
Manchester,Levenshulme
M19 . . . .**99** A1
Oldham OL8 . . . .**66** D4
Reddish M34 . . . .**100** A3
Romiley SK6 . . . .**113** C3
Up Holland WN8 . . . .**53** A6
Windsor St Failsworth M40 .**83** E4

Windsor St continued
Failsworth,Holt Lane End
M35 . . . .**84** A8
Manchester M18 . . . .**99** C4
Rochdale OL11 . . . .**31** A5
Salford M5 . . . .**81** B1
Stockport SK2 . . . .**124** A6
Tyldesley M46 . . . .**58** E2
Wigan WN1 . . . .**37** D1
Windsor Terr
Milnrow OL16 . . . .**31** E6
Rochdale OL16 . . . .**31** C7
Stockport SK2 . . . .**124** A6
Windsor Wlk SK2 . . . .**170** F6
Windy Bank Ave WA3 . . . .**90** E8
Windy Harbour La BL7 . . . .**25** B8
Windybank M9 . . . .**64** C5
Winfell Dr M40 . . . .**146** A3
Winfield Ave M20 . . . .**110** D6
Winfield Dr M18 . . . .**99** E6
Winfield Gr SK6 . . . .**114** B1
Winfield St SK14 . . . .**167** F2
Winfield St M9 . . . .**157** E8
Wingate Ave BL8 . . . .**27** B2
Wingate Dr
Altrincham WA15 . . . .**120** B5
Manchester M20 . . . .**110** C2
Whitefield M45 . . . .**44** E1
Wingate Rd
Manchester SK4 . . . .**168** C4
Walkden M38 . . . .**60** B4
Wingate St OL11 . . . .**13** E1
Wingates Gr BL5 . . . .**39** D3
Wingates Ind Est BL5 . . . .**39** D2
Wingates La BL5 . . . .**39** D5
Wingates Rd WN1 . . . .**37** C4
Wingates Sq BL5 . . . .**39** D3
Wingfield Ave SK9 . . . . . .**136** E6
Wingfield Cl WN6 . . . .**37** B1
Wingfield Dr
Pendlebury M27 . . . .**80** A6
Wilmslow SK9 . . . .**136** E6
Wingfield Gr SK13 . . . . . .**116** F7
Wingfield St M32 . . . .**96** D4
Wingfield Villas OL15 . . . .**16** C7
Wingrove Ho 3 M6 . . . . .**154** F2
Wings Gr OL10 . . . .**46** D7
Winhill Rd SK22 . . . .**127** C1
Winifred Ave BL9 . . . .**28** F4
Winifred Rd
Failsworth M40 . . . .**83** B7
Farnworth BL4 . . . .**42** A1
Manchester M20 . . . .**110** B3
Stockport SK2 . . . .**124** A6
Winifred St 4 Eccles M30 .**79** B1
Hyde SK14 . . . .**113** E7
Ince-in-M WN3 . . . .**151** E6
Ramsbottom BL0 . . . .**138** B5
Rochdale OL12 . . . .**14** B1
Winmarith Dr WA15 . . . . .**129** D7
Winmarleigh Cl BL8 . . . . . .**27** B3
Winmarleigh Gdns WN7 . . .**75** E3
Winnall Wlk 3 M40 . . . . .**83** C6
Winnard St WA3 . . . .**74** B2
Winnats Cl SK13 . . . .**116** F8
Winnie St M40 . . . .**83** A8
Winning Hill Cl M18 . . . . . .**99** D4
Winnington Gn SK2 . . . . .**124** D6
Winnington Rd SK6 . . . . .**125** F7
Winnipeg Quay M50 . . . . . .**96** F7
Winnows The M34 . . . . . .**100** D3
Winscar Rd WN2 . . . .**56** D6
Winscombe Dr M40 . . . . .**159** C4
Winsfield Rd SK7 . . . .**133** E8
Winsford Dr OL11 . . . .**29** C5
Winsford Gr BL3 . . . .**40** F5
Winsford Rd M14 . . . .**98** A1
Winsford Wlk M33 . . . . . .**108** E3
Winskill Rd M44 . . . .**106** A8
Winslade Cl Oldham OL4 . . .**49** D2
Stockport SK7 . . . .**123** A2
Winsley Rd M23 . . . .**108** F2
Winslow Ave SK14 . . . . . .**103** A2
Winslow Pl M19 . . . .**110** F6
Winslow St BL3 . . . .**40** D3
Manchester M11 . . . .**165** A8
Winsmoor Dr M40 . . . .**56** E4
Winson Cl BL3 . . . .**147** E4
Winstanley Cl 6 M6 . . . . .**80** C5
Winstanley Coll WN5 . . . . .**53** F3
Winstanley Com Prim Sch
WN3 . . . .**54** C2
Winstanley Rd M33 . . . . .**151** E6
Winstanley Rd
Ashton-in-M WN2 . . . .**73** F8
Garswood WN4,WN5 . . . . .**72** B6
Manchester M40 . . . .**160** D3
Orrell WN5 . . . .**53** F3
Sale M33 . . . .**108** C5
Winster Ave
Manchester M20 . . . .**109** E4
Salford M7 . . . .**81** B6
Stretford M32 . . . .**96** A3
Winster Cl 2 Bolton BL2 . . .**25** F1
Whitefield M45 . . . .**63** B8
Winster Dr
3 Middleton M24 . . . .**46** E2
Platt Bridge WN2 . . . .**55** F2
Winster Gn M30 . . . .**95** B8
Winster Gr SK2 . . . .**124** A6
Winster Mews 17 SK13 . .**171** E2
Winster Rd M30 . . . .**95** B8
Winstone Ave
Little Lever BL3 . . . .**43** C3

Winston Ave *continued*
Newton-le-W WA12 . . . . .89 C3
Rochdale OL11 . . . . .29 E6
Winston Cl Marple SK6 . .125 D7
Radcliffe M26 . . . . .43 E5
Winston Rd
Manchester M40,M9 . . . . . .157 F8
Manchester M9 . . . . .64 F1
Sale M33 . . . . .107 F5
Winswell Cl M11 . . . . .83 B2
Winter Hey La BL6 . . . . .22 B3
Winter St BL1 . . . . .143 D3
Winterbottom Gr SK14 . .102 F2
Winterbottom St O9 . . . . .153 D7
Winterbottom Wlk 4
SK14 . . . . .102 F2
Winterburn Ave
Bolton BL2 . . . . .25 B6
Manchester M21 . . . . .109 D4
Winterburn Gr SK14 . . . . .124 E5
Winterburnlee Gr OL14 . . . .6 A8
Winterdyne St M9 . . . . . . .157 E7
Winterfield Dr BL3 . . . . . .146 A3
Winterford Ave M13 . . . . .164 D5
Winterford Rd
Manchester M7,M8 . . . . . . .155 F7
Mossley OL5 . . . . .68 E1
Wintergreen Wlk 3
M31 .105 F3
Wintermans Rd M19 . . . . .109 E7
Winterslow Ave M23 . . . .108 D1
Winterton Cl BL5 . . . . .40 A1
Winterton Rd SK5 . . . . . . .100 A1
Winthrop Ave M40 . . . . . . .157 D5
Winton Ave Denton M34 .100 D7
Failsworth M40 . . . . .65 D1
Wigan WN5 . . . . .54 D5
Winton Cl SK7 . . . . .123 D1
Winton Ct WA14 . . . . .119 C2
Winton Gn BL6 . . . . .22 F1
Winton Gr BL3 . . . . .40 E4
Winton Rd
Altrincham WA14 . . . . .119 C2
Golborne WA3 . . . . .90 E6
Pendlebury M6 . . . . .80 D5
Winton St Ashton-u-L OL6 .166 B3
Littleborough OL15 . . . . .16 B5
3 Stalybridge SK15 . . . . . . .86 B1
Winward St Bolton BL3 . .146 A4
Leigh WN7 . . . . .75 B5
18 Westhoughton BL5 . . . . .39 E3
Winwick La WA3 . . . . .90 E3
Winwick Rd WA12 . . . . .89 F1
Winwood Dr M24 . . . . .47 B1
Winwood Fold M24 . . . . . . .46 F4
Winwood Rd M20 . . . . .122 C8
Wirral Cl Culcheth WA3 . . .91 E4
Swinton M27 . . . . .62 A2
Wirral Cres SK3 . . . . .123 A8
Wirral Dr WN3 . . . . .54 C2
Wisbech Dr M23 . . . . .108 F1
Wisbeck Rd BL2 . . . . .148 C8
Wiseley St M11 . . . . .164 E8
Wiseman Terr M25 . . . . . . .63 C4
Wishaw Sq M21 . . . . .109 F7
Wisley Cl SK5 . . . . .112 A8
Wistaria Rd M18 . . . . .99 D5
Witham Ave M22 . . . . .121 E5
Witham Cl Heywood OL10 . .29 A3
Standish WN6 . . . . .19 D1
Witham St OL6 . . . . .85 D4
Withenfield Rd M23 . . . . . .120 F8
Withens Gn SK2 . . . . .124 E6
Withern 18 OL10 . . . . .29 C2
Withill Wlk 4 M40 . . . . . . .73 A5
Withington Ave WA3 . . . . . .92 A4
Withington Dr M29 . . . . . . .77 C7
Withington Girls Sch
M14 .110 C8
Withington Gn M24 . . . . . . .47 A4
Withington Hospl M20 . . .109 F5
Withington La WN2 . . . . . . .38 C2
Withington Rd M16,M21 . . .97 D2
Withington St
Heywood OL10 . . . . .46 E8
Salford M6 . . . . .81 B2
Withins Ave M26 . . . . .44 C5
Withins Cl BL2 . . . . .42 E8
Withins Dr BL2 . . . . .42 E8
Withins Gr BL2 . . . . .42 E8
Withins Hall Rd M35 . . . . . .84 B6
Withins La Bolton BL2 . . . . .42 E8
Radcliffe M26 . . . . .44 C5
Withins Rd Culcheth WA3 . .91 F3
Oldham OL8 . . . . .66 B2
Withins Sch BL2 . . . . .25 E2
Withins Sports Ctr BL2 . . .25 E2
Withins St M26 . . . . .44 C4
Withnell Dr BL8 . . . . .27 A1
Withnell Rd M19 . . . . .110 D3
Withy Gr M4 . . . . .159 A2
Withy Tree Gr 1 M34 . . . .101 A2
Withycombe Pl M6 . . . . . . .81 A5
Withypool Dr SK2 . . . . .124 E5
Witley Dr M33 . . . . .107 D6
Witley Rd OL16 . . . . .31 B7
Witney Cl 15 BL1 . . . . .143 E2
Wittenbury Rd SK4 . . . . . .168 B2
Wittenham Ho SK9 . . . . . .131 D2
Witterage Cl M12 . . . . .164 F6
Woburn Ave Bolton BL2 . . .25 C3
Leigh WN7 . . . . .57 D1
Newton-le-W WA12 . . . . .89 D2
Woburn Cl
3 Manchester M16 . . . . . . .97 F3
Milnrow OL16 . . . . .31 E6

Woburn Ct SK12 . . . . .133 F4
Woburn Dr
Altrincham WA15 . . . . .120 B2
Bury BL9 . . . . .44 F5
Woburn Rd M16 . . . . .97 A2
Woden's Ave M5 . . . . .161 C7
Woden's Ave M5 . . . . .161 C7
Woking Rd SK8 . . . . .132 A7
Woking Terr BL1 . . . . .143 E1
Wolfenden Gn BB4 . . . . .2 F8
Wolfenden St BL1 . . . . . . .143 E2
Wolfenden Terr 25 BL1 . .143 E2
Wolford Dr M29 . . . . .59 E7
Wolfreton Cres M27 . . . . . .62 A3
Wolfson Sq WN4 . . . . .72 F4
Wollaton Wlk M34 . . . . . . .100 E1
Wolmer St WN4 . . . . .73 A4
Wolseley Ho M33 . . . . .108 C6
Wolseley Pl M20 . . . . .110 B5
Wolseley Rd M33 . . . . .108 C6
Wolseley St 1 Bury BL8 . . .27 B1
Newhey OL16 . . . . .32 B4
Wolsey Cl
Ashton-in-M WN4 . . . . .73 A5
Radcliffe M26 . . . . .44 F3
Wolsey Dr WA14 . . . . .119 A1
Wolsey St Heywood OL10 . .29 C1
Radcliffe M26 . . . . .44 A3
Wolstenholme Ave BL9 . . .27 F6
Wolstenholme Coalpit La
OL11,OL12 . . . . .13 B2
Wolstenholme La OL11,
OL11,OL12 . . . . .13 C2
Wolstenvale Cl M24 . . . . . .47 B1
Wolver Cl M38 . . . . .60 B6
Wolverton Ave OL8 . . . . . . .66 D3
Wolverton Dr SK9 . . . . . . .131 D1
Wolvesey OL11 . . . . .139 E6
Wood Bank Rd OL15 . . . . . .16 A3
Wood Bank Terr OL5 . . . . . .68 D2
Wood Brook La OL4 . . . . . . .68 B7
Wood Brook Rd OL4 . . . . . .68 B7
Wood Cottage Cl 4 M28 . .78 F7
Wood Cots SK6 . . . . .113 A6
Wood Edge Cl BL4 . . . . .42 C2
Wood Fold BL7 . . . . .25 C6
Wood Fold Prim Sch
WN6 . . . . .36 D8
Wood Gdns SK9 . . . . .137 B2
Wood Gr Denton M34 . . . . .100 F4
Romiley SK6 . . . . .113 A5
Whitefield M45 . . . . .44 F3
Wood Hey Cl M26 . . . . .43 D3
Wood Hey Gr
2 Denton M34 . . . . .101 A2
Rochdale OL12 . . . . .14 F4
Wood La
Altrincham WA15 . . . . .120 B5
Altrincham WA15 . . . . .129 D1
Ashton-u-L OL6,OL7 . . . . .85 B5
Edenfield BL0 . . . . .1 D2
Marple SK6 . . . . .125 B7
Middleton M24 . . . . .47 A5
Partington M31 . . . . .105 D3
Wrightington Bar WN6 . . . . . .18 E8
Wood La N SK10 . . . . .134 B1
Wood La W SK10 . . . . .133 F1
Wood Lea Bank 9 BB4 . . . .2 F8
Wood Lea Rd BB4 . . . . .2 F8
Wood Mount WA15 . . . . . .120 B5
Wood Rd Manchester M16 . .97 D3
Sale WA15 . . . . .108 B1
Wood Rd N M16 . . . . .97 C3
Wood Road La
Bury BL8,BL9 . . . . .27 B8
Ramsbottom BL9 . . . . .11 C1
Wood Sorrel Way WA3 . . . .90 E8
Wood Sq Droylsden M43 . .100 A8
Uppermill OL3 . . . . .69 B6
Wood St
Altrincham WA14 . . . . .119 D4
Ashton-u-L OL6 . . . . .166 B3
Atherton M46 . . . . .58 B4
Bolton BL1 . . . . .145 F7
Bury BL8 . . . . .140 D2
Bury BL8 . . . . .27 C3
Cheadle SK8 . . . . .122 D6
Denton M34 . . . . .100 F4
Dukinfield SK16 . . . . .101 C6
Eccles M30 . . . . .79 F1
Glossop SK13 . . . . .116 C8
Golborne WA3 . . . . .90 B8
Hindley WN2 . . . . .57 B3
Hollingworth SK14 . . . . .103 D5
Horwich BL6 . . . . .22 C3
Hyde SK14 . . . . .167 E2
Littleborough OL15 . . . . .16 B5
Manchester M11 . . . . .165 B8
Manchester M3 . . . . .158 F1
Middleton M24 . . . . .64 F8
Newhey OL16 . . . . .32 C4
Oldham OL1 . . . . .67 B8
Radcliffe M26 . . . . .61 E8
Ramsbottom BL0 . . . . .138 B5
Rochdale OL16 . . . . .31 A6
Shaw OL2 . . . . .48 F8
7 Stalybridge SK15 . . . . . . .85 F2
Stockport SK3 . . . . .169 D1
Tyldesley M29 . . . . .77 B8
Westhoughton BL5 . . . . .57 D8
Wigan WN3 . . . . .150 C7
Wigan,Parson's Meadow
WN5 . . . . .54 F7
Wood Terr BL2 . . . . .26 D1
Wood Top Ave OL11 . . . . . .29 F5
Wood Top Cl SK2 . . . . .124 E7

Wood View Heywood OL10 . .29 C4
Shevington WN6 . . . . .36 B5
Wythenshawe M22 . . . . .109 D1
Wood's Hospl SK13 . . . . . .104 C3
Wood's La WN4 . . . . .73 C5
Woodacre M16 . . . . .97 E1
Woodacre Cl M33 . . . . .108 A2
Woodacres Ct SK9 . . . . . . .136 F6
Woodall Cl M33 . . . . .108 D4
Woodark Cl OL4 . . . . .67 F5
Woodbank
Alderley Edge SK9 . . . . .137 A2
Bolton BL2 . . . . .25 D2
Stockport SK1 . . . . .112 B1
Woodbank Ave
Romiley SK6 . . . . .112 C3
Stockport SK1 . . . . .124 C8
Woodbank Ct M41 . . . . .95 B3
Woodbank Dr BL8 . . . . .27 C4
Woodbank Works Ind Est
SK1 . . . . .112 B1
Woodbine Ave M44 . . . . . .105 D4
Woodbine Cres SK2 . . . . . .170 F7
Woodbine Rd Bolton BL3 .146 C3
Lymm WA13 . . . . .117 B4
Woodbine St
Manchester M14 . . . . .98 A4
Rochdale OL16 . . . . .31 A5
Woodbine St E OL16 . . . . . .31 B5
Woodbine Terr 1 M44 . . . .94 A2
Woodbourne Ct M33 . . . . .108 B2
Woodbourne Rd
Manchester M14 . . . . .111 C6
Sale M33 . . . . .108 A2
Woodbray Ave M19 . . . . . .110 E5
Woodbridge Ave M34 . . . .100 E7
Woodbridge Dr BL2 . . . . . . .25 B1
Woodbridge Gdns OL12 . . .14 C2
Woodbridge Gr M23 . . . . . .109 A1
Woodbridge Rd M41 . . . . . .94 D3
Woodbrook Ave
Hyde SK14 . . . . .167 F2
Oldham OL4 . . . . .68 B7
Woodbrook Dr WN3 . . . . . . .54 D4
Woodbrook Rd SK9 . . . . . .137 C1
Woodburn Dr BL1 . . . . .142 B3
Woodburn Rd M22 . . . . . . .121 D8
Woodburn Row M29 . . . . . .77 C3
Woodbury Cres SK16 . . . . .101 B7
Woodbury Rd SK3 . . . . . . .123 B7
Woodchurch WN1 . . . . .37 F1
Woodchurch Cl 8 BL1 . . . .143 E1
Woodchurch Wlk
Chadderton OL9 . . . . .152 B6
7 Sale M33 . . . . .108 F3
Woodcock Cl
Droylsden M43 . . . . .84 C3
Rochdale OL11 . . . . .29 F7
Woodcock Dr M22 . . . . .56 B2
Woodcock Gr SK13 . . . . . .104 E1
Woodcock Ho WN1 . . . . . . .151 D8
Woodcote Ave SK7 . . . . . . .123 C2
Woodcote Rd
Sale M14,M31 . . . . .107 A2
Sale M14 . . . . .107 D1
Woodcote View SK9 . . . . . .131 F1
Woodcote Wlk M8 . . . . . . .156 C8
Woodcott Bank BL1 . . . . . .143 E4
Woodcott Gr 3 SK9 . . . . . .131 E1
Woodcourt Wigan WN3 . . .150 B6
Wythenshawe M23 . . . . .120 C8
Woodcroft
Appley Bridge WN6 . . . . .35 E6
Stockport SK2 . . . . .124 D6
Woodcroft Ave M19 . . . . . .110 E4
Wooddagger Cl WN2 . . . . . .56 F5
Woodeaton Cl OL2 . . . . .49 A4
Wooded Cl BL9 . . . . .27 F5
Woodedge Dr WN6 . . . . .73 A3
Woodend Shaw OL2 . . . . . .149 C8
Stockport SK7 . . . . .123 D2
Woodend Ct SK14 . . . . .167 D1
Woodend Dr SK15 . . . . .102 D6
Woodend La
Altrincham WA14 . . . . .129 C1
Hyde SK14 . . . . .167 D1
Stalybridge SK15 . . . . .102 D6
Wardle OL12 . . . . .15 D6
Woodend Mill OL5 . . . . .68 D2
Woodend Mills Ind Est
OL4 . . . . .67 F5
Woodend Rd
Stockport SK3 . . . . .123 F4
Wythenshawe M22 . . . . .121 D4
Woodend St Oldham OL4 . . .67 F5
Oldham,Oldham Edge OL1 . . .48 E1
Woodend View OL12 . . . . . .68 D2
Woodfield M22 . . . . .121 D3
Woodfield Ave
Hyde SK14 . . . . .113 D8
Rochdale OL12 . . . . .14 E2
Romiley SK6 . . . . .113 A4
Woodfield Cl
Hadfield SK13 . . . . .103 F5
Oldham OL8 . . . . .66 C4
Woodfield Cres
Ashton-in-M WN4 . . . . .73 A4
Romiley SK6 . . . . .112 F2
Woodfield Ct SK2 . . . . .124 E6
Woodfield Dr M28 . . . . .78 B6
Woodfield Gr Eccles M30 . . .79 C1
Farnworth BL4 . . . . .60 C6
Sale M33 . . . . .108 A6
Woodfield Mews SK14 . . .113 D8
Woodfield Prim Sch
WN1 . . . . .37 C4

Woodfield Rd
Altrincham WA14 . . . . .119 C6
Cheadle SK8 . . . . .132 B7
Manchester M24 . . . . .64 C6
Manchester,Crumpsall M8 . . .64 A1
Salford M6 . . . . .154 D4
Woodfield St Bolton BL3 . . .42 A3
Wigan WN2 . . . . .38 A3
Woodfield Terr OL10 . . . . . .29 E3
Woodfields Ret Pk BL9 . . .140 F3
Woodfold Ave M19 . . . . .99 A2
Woodfold Rd M35 . . . . .84 A7
Woodford Aerodrome
SK7 . . . . .133 A1
Woodford Ave
Denton M34 . . . . .101 A4
Eccles M30 . . . . .79 B2
Golborne WA3 . . . . .90 D7
Shaw OL2 . . . . .49 D7
Woodford Cl
Droylsden M43 . . . . .100 B8
3 Hindley WN2 . . . . .56 E6
Woodford Dr M27 . . . . .61 E2
Woodford Gdns M20 . . . . .110 A2
Woodford Gr BL3 . . . . .146 C4
Woodford Rd
Bramhall SK7 . . . . .133 B6
Bramhall SK7 . . . . .132 E4
Woodford St
4 Hindley WN2 . . . . .56 E6
8 Wigan WN5 . . . . .54 B6
Woodgarth Ave M40 . . . . . .83 D5
Woodgarth Dr M27 . . . . . . .79 E6
Woodgarth La M28 . . . . .78 F5
Woodgate Ave Bury BL9 . . .28 D4
Rochdale OL11 . . . . .30 A6
Woodgate Cl SK6 . . . . .112 F3
Woodgate Dr M25 . . . . .63 C6
Woodgate Hill Rd
Bury,Fern Grove BL9 . . . . . .141 C4
Bury,Woodgate Hill BL9 . . . .28 D4
Woodgate Rd M16 . . . . .97 E3
Sale M33 . . . . .108 B1
Woodgate St BL3 . . . . .42 A3
Woodgrange Cl M6 . . . . . . .154 E2
Woodgreen 6 WN2 . . . . . . .56 D4
Woodgreen Dr M26 . . . . . . .62 A8
Woodhall Ave
Manchester M20 . . . . .110 A7
Whitefield M45 . . . . .62 D6
Woodhall Cl Bolton BL2 . . .25 C3
Bramhall SK7 . . . . .132 E3
Bury BL8 . . . . .27 D5
Woodhall Cres SK5 . . . . . .112 A4
Woodhall Rd SK5 . . . . .169 F4
Woodhall St M35 . . . . .83 F8
Woodham Rd M23 . . . . .108 F1
Woodham Wlk BL3 . . . . . . .145 D5
Woodhays St M6 . . . . .154 F2
Woodhead Cl Oldham OL4 . .67 E7
Ramsbottom BL0 . . . . .11 C4
Woodhead Dr WA15 . . . . . .119 F1
Woodhead Gr WN3 . . . . .55 B2
Woodhead Rd
Altrincham WA14 . . . . .119 F1
Glossop SK13 . . . . .104 D4
Tintwistle SK13 . . . . .104 B8
Woodhead St 6 M16 . . . . . .97 E4
Woodhey Cl M33 . . . . .132 A4
Woodhey High Sch BL0 . . .11 A3
Woodhey Rd BL0 . . . . .11 A3
Woodhey St M6 . . . . .154 F2
Woodheys Dr M33 . . . . .107 D1
Woodheys Prim Sch
M33 .107 E2
Woodheys Rd OL15 . . . . . . .16 A2
Woodheys St 1 M5 . . . . . .154 F1
Woodhill OL2 . . . . .46 F2
Woodhill Cl
Manchester M12 . . . . .99 B4
Middleton M24 . . . . .46 F2
Woodhill Dr M25 . . . . .63 B3
Woodhill Fold BL8 . . . . .27 B2
Woodhill Rd Bury BL8 . . . .140 D3
Woodhill St BL8 . . . . .140 D4
Woodhill Vale BL8 . . . . . . .140 D4
Woodhill Works BL8 . . . . . .140 D4
Woodhouse Ct M41 . . . . . . .95 A4
Woodhouse Dr M24 . . . . . . .36 E2
Woodhouse Farm Cotts
OL12 . . . . .13 D2
Woodhouse Knowl OL3 . . . .50 F4
Woodhouse La
Partington WA14 . . . . .118 C4
Rochdale OL15 . . . . .13 E3
Sale M33 . . . . .107 C2
Sale M33 . . . . .107 D2
Wigan WN6 . . . . .36 E3
Wigan WN6 . . . . .36 F2
Wythenshawe M90 . . . . .130 D7
Wythenshawe,Benchill
M22 .121 D4
Woodhouse La EWA15 . . .108 A1
Woodhouse Park Prim Sch
M22 .130 D8
Woodhouse Rd Shaw OL2 . .32 C1
Urmston M41 . . . . .94 F4
Wythenshawe M22 . . . . .130 D8
Woodhouse St
Atherton M46 . . . . .58 D2
Manchester M18 . . . . .99 E5

Woodhouses Prim Sch
M35 . . . . .84 C6
Woodhurst Dr WN6 . . . . . . .19 D1
Wooding Cl M31 . . . . .106 A4
Woodlake Ave M21 . . . . . . .109 C4
Woodland Ave Bolton BL3 . .42 B2
Hazel Grove SK7 . . . . .124 E1
Hindley WN2 . . . . .57 A3
Lymm WA13 . . . . .117 A2
Newton-le-W WA12 . . . . .89 F3
Reddish M18 . . . . .99 E4
Woodland Cres M25 . . . . . .63 B2
Woodland Dr
Ashton-in-M WN4 . . . . .73 B5
Lymm WA13 . . . . .117 A2
Standish WN6 . . . . .19 E2
Woodland Gr Bolton BL7 . . . .8 C2
Wigan WN1 . . . . .37 D2
Woodland Pk OL2 . . . . .48 B6
Woodland Rd
Heywood OL10 . . . . .29 E3
Manchester M19 . . . . .111 A7
Reddish M18 . . . . .99 E4
Rochdale OL12 . . . . .14 C2
Tyldesley M29 . . . . .77 B7
Woodland St
Heywood OL10 . . . . .29 D2
Manchester M12 . . . . .165 B5
Rochdale OL12 . . . . .15 A2
Woodland Terr BL7 . . . . .25 B8
Woodland Way M24 . . . . . . .64 F6
Woodlands
Failsworth M35 . . . . .83 E4
Swinton M41 . . . . .95 C3
Woodlands Ave
Cheadle SK8 . . . . .123 A4
Eccles M30 . . . . .95 A8
Ince-in-M WN3 . . . . .151 F6
Irlam M44 . . . . .94 A3
Leigh WN7 . . . . .75 F3
Rochdale OL11 . . . . .30 A6
Romiley SK6 . . . . .113 A5
Stretford M32 . . . . .96 D2
Swinton M27 . . . . .79 D6
Urmston M41 . . . . .94 C2
Whitefield M45 . . . . .44 E1
Woodlands Cl
Broadbottom SK14 . . . . .102 F1
Cheadle SK8 . . . . .132 A8
Stalybridge SK15 . . . . .102 D7
Tintwistle SK13 . . . . .103 F6
Worsley M28 . . . . .78 E7
Woodlands Ct
Altrincham WA15 . . . . .119 E5
Stockport SK2 . . . . .124 D8
Woodlands Dr
Over Hulton M46 . . . . .58 F5
Romiley SK6 . . . . .113 A5
Sale M23,M33 . . . . .108 C1
Shevington WN6 . . . . .35 F4
Stockport SK2 . . . . .124 D8
Woodlands Gr
Broadbottom SK14 . . . . .102 F1
Bury BL8 . . . . .27 B3
Woodlands Heald Est 28 . .92 C6
Woodlands Ind Est WA12 . .89 C6
Woodlands La WA15 . . . . .119 C5
Woodlands Park Rd
SK2 . . . . .124 D8
Woodlands Parkway
WA15 . . . . .119 E6
Woodlands Rd
Altrincham WA14,WA15 . . .119 E5
Ashton-u-L OL6 . . . . .85 E6
Edenfield BL0 . . . . .1 D2
Handforth SK9 . . . . .131 E3
High Lane SK6 . . . . .134 D5
Manchester,Cheetham Hill
M8 . . . . .156 B7
Manchester,Heaton Mersey
SK4 . . . . .110 C2
Manchester,Whalley Range
M21 . . . . .97 E1
Milnrow OL16 . . . . .31 F5
Sale M33 . . . . .108 C4
Stalybridge SK15 . . . . .102 D7
Wilmslow SK9 . . . . .130 F1
Worsley M28 . . . . .78 F7
Woodlands Road Sta
M8 . . . . .156 A8
Woodlands St M8 . . . . .156 A8
Woodlands The
Bolton BL6 . . . . .40 C8
Bury BL8 . . . . .140 D4
Heywood OL10 . . . . .46 E8
Pendlebury M27 . . . . .80 B7
Wigan WN1 . . . . .37 D3
Woodlands View OL16 . . . . .31 C8
Woodlark Cl M3 . . . . .158 D1
Woodlawn Ct M16 . . . . .97 C3
Woodlea
Altrincham WA15 . . . . .119 F4
Oldham OL9 . . . . .65 D7
Worsley M28 . . . . .78 E8
Woodlea Ave M19 . . . . .110 E6
Woodlea Rd WA13 . . . . . . .116 E6
Woodleigh WA14 . . . . .119 A5
Woodleigh Ct
Alderley Edge SK9 . . . . .137 A2
Bury BL8 . . . . .26 F1
Woodleigh Dr M43 . . . . .84 C4
Woodleigh Rd OL4 . . . . .68 A7
Woodleigh St M9 . . . . .64 F1
Woodley M30 . . . . .79 C4
Woodley Ave M26 . . . . .44 B1

Woodley Cl SK2 .....124 D7
Woodley Gr WN7 ......75 D5
Woodley Inf Sch SK6 .113 C5
Woodley Jun Sch SK6 .113 C5
Woodley Prec SK6 ...113 A5
Woodley St BL9 ......44 F8
Woodley Sta SK6 ....113 B6
Woodliffe St M16 ...161 C5
Woodlinn Wlk M9 ....157 D7
Woodman Dr BL9 .....27 E6
Woodman St SK1 ....169 E2
Woodmeadow Ct 10 OL5 .68 C2
Woodmere Dr M9 ....64 E3
Woodmount Cl SK6 ..113 F2
Woodnook Rd WN6 ...35 E8
Woodpark Cl OL8 ....67 A3
Woodpecker Pl M28 ..78 D8
Woodridings WA14 ..119 B3
Woodrow Way M44 ..105 F8
Woodroyd Wlk M12 ..164 F6
Woodroyd Cl SK7 ...123 D1
Woodroyd Dr BL9 ...141 C3
Woodruff Wlk 7 M31 .105 F3
Woodruffe Gdns SK6 .125 A8
Woodrush Rd WN6 ...36 D3
Woods The
 2 Altrincham WA14 .119 E6
 Oldham OL4 ....68 B6
 Rochdale OL11 .....30 C3
Woodseats La SK13 .115 B6
Woodsend Circ M41 ..94 D3
Woodsend Crescent Rd
 M41 ....94 D2
Woodsend Rd M41 ...94 D3
Woodsend Prim Sch
 M41 ....94 D3
Woodsend Rd M41 ..94 E3
Woodsend Rd S M41 .94 E1
Woodshaw Gr 2 M28 .78 C8
Woodside
 Manchester SK4 ...110 F1
 Newhey OL16 ......32 C5
 Shaw OL2 ....49 D8
Woodside Ave
 Ashton-in-M WN4 ...73 A8
 Manchester M19 ...110 F5
 Walkden M28 ......60 F2
Woodside Cl Oldham OL4 .67 E6
 Up Holland WN8 ...53 C8
Woodside Dr
 High Lane SK6 ....134 F7
 Hyde SK14 ....167 E1
 Ramsbottom BL0 ..138 A5
 2 Salford M6 .....80 C3
Woodside La SK12 ..133 E4
Woodside Mews SK7 .123 C2
Woodside Pl BL2 ...148 C5
Woodside Rd
 Lymm WA13 ....117 B1
 Manchester M16 ...97 B2
Woodside Sq BL2 ..148 C5
Woodside St SK15 ...86 E6
Woodsley Rd BL1 ...223 E3
Woodsmoor La SK2,SK3 .124 A4
Woodsmoor Rd M27 .79 D7
Woodsmoor Sta SK2 .124 B4
Woodstock Ave
 Cheadle SK8 ......132 A7
 Newton-le-W WA12 .89 D2
 Reddish SK5 ......111 F5
Woodstock Cl
 Heywood OL10 .....29 E2
 Leigh WN7 ....75 E1
Woodstock Cres SK6 .113 A5
Woodstock Dr
 Bolton BL1 ......142 A1
 Bury BL8 ....26 D7
 Pendlebury M27 ...80 B6
 Worsley M28 ......79 A6
Woodstock Gn
 Oldham OL8 ....67 A3
 Reddish SK5 .....112 A5
Woodstock Rd
 Altrincham WA14 .119 C8
 Failsworth M40 ....65 C1
 Manchester M16 ...97 B3
 Romiley SK6 .....113 A5
Woodstock St
 Oldham OL4 ......153 F6
 7 Rochdale OL12 ..14 C1
Woodthorpe Cl M25 .63 D2
Woodthorpe Dr SK8 .123 A2
Woodthorpe Grange
 M25 ....63 D2
Woodvale
 Altrincham WA14 .119 C2
 Middleton M24 ....47 A4
Woodvale Ave Aspull WN2 .38 F3
 Atherton M46 .....58 B5
 Bolton BL3 ....147 D2
Woodvale Dr Bolton BL3 .147 D2
Woodvale Gr BL3 ..147 D2
Woodvale Rd M26 ...44 B2
Woodvale Wlk 18 M11 .160 F1

Woodview Ave M19 ..110 F5
Woodville Dr Marple SK6 .125 E4
 Sale M33 ....108 A5
 Stalybridge SK15 ..86 D3
Woodville Gr SK5 ..111 F6
Woodville Rd
 Altrincham WA14 .119 C3
 Ince-in-M WN3 ....55 F4
 Sale M33 ....108 A5
Woodville Terr 10 M40 .64 F1
Woodward Cl BL9 ...27 F5
Woodward Ct M4 ..160 D2
Woodward Pl M4 ..159 C2
Woodward Rd M25 ..62 F2
Woodward St M4 ..159 C2
Woodwards Rd BL5 ..57 F6
Woodville La M23 ..108 E1
Woodyates St SK9 .108 A7
Wool Rd OL3 ....51 B2
Woolden Rd M44,WA3 .105 B8
Woolden St Eccles M30 .79 B3
 8 Wigan WN5 .....54 F6
Wooler Gr WN1 .....56 D2
Woolfall Cl M12 ..164 F6
Woolfold Trad Est BL8 .27 B4
Woollacott St 2 OL1 .153 F6
Woollam Pl M3 ....162 D8
Woolley Ave SK12 .133 D2
Woolley Bridge Rd
 SK13 ....103 E5
Woolley Cl SK14 ..171 D4
Woolley La
 Hollingworth SK14 .103 D6
 Hollingworth SK14 .171 D4
Woolley Mill La SK13 .103 E7
Woolley St M8 ....158 F4
Woolley Terr 8 SK14 .166 B1
Woolmore Ave OL1 ..48 E1
Woolpack Gn 2 M6 .154 F3
Woolston Dr 2 M6 ..77 C8
Woolston Ho 8 M6 ..80 C4
Woolton Cl
 Ashton-in-M WN4 ..72 F5
 8 Failsworth M40 ..65 C2
Wootton St SK14 ..167 D4
Worcester Ave
 Brinnington SK5 ..112 C5
 Denton M34 ......101 A1
 Golborne WA3 .....90 B8
 Hindley WN2 ......56 F6
Worcester Cl
 Ashton-u-L OL6 ...85 D8
 Bury BL9 ....45 A8
 Romiley SK6 .....113 A1
 Salford M6 ....80 C4
Worcester Gr SK13 .116 F8
Worcester Rd
 Cheadle SK8 .....123 A4
 Little Lever BL3 ..42 F3
 Middleton M24 ....64 F5
 Sale M33 ....107 D3
 Salford M6 ....80 C4
 Swinton M27 ......61 D2
Worcester St
 19 Bolton BL1 ...143 E1
 Bury BL8 ....140 D4
 Oldham OL9 ......152 B5
 Rochdale OL11 ....30 E4
 Salford M7 ......155 E6
Wordsworth Ave
 Atherton M46 .....58 E5
 Bury BL9 ....44 F6
 Droylsden M43 ....84 A2
 Farnworth BL4 ....60 B7
 Leigh WN7 ....75 D7
 Longshaw WN5 ....53 D1
 Manchester M8 ...156 A6
 Orrell WN5 ....53 F6
 Radcliffe M26 ....43 E4
 Wigan WN5 ....37 C3
Wordsworth Cl SK16 .102 A7
Wordsworth Cres
 Ashton-u-L OL7 ...84 E5
 Littleborough OL15 .15 F2
Wordsworth Gdns M25 .62 F3
Wordsworth Ind Est
 BL1 ....143 D2
Wordsworth Rd
 Denton M34 ......113 A7
 Manchester M16 ...97 B3
 Middleton M24 ....47 B2
 6 Oldham OL1 .....49 D1
 Reddish SK5 ......99 D1
 Swinton M27 ......61 E1
 Walkden M38 .....60 B5
Wordsworth St BL1 .143 D2
Wordsworth Way OL11 .29 E6
Workesleigh St 9 M40 .83 C5
Works Bsns Ctr The
 M12 ....163 C7
World Freight Ctr M16 .96 E1
World Way M90 ...130 B8
Worrall St Failsworth M40 .83 A6
 8 Rochdale OL12 ..14 D2
 Salford M5 ......161 C7
Worrell Cl M26 ....43 F4
Worsbrough Ave M28 .60 C2
Worsefold St M40 ..83 A8
Worsel St BL3 ....146 C4
Worsley Ave
 Manchester M40 ...65 A1
 Walkden M28 ......60 A2
Worsley Brow M28 ..78 F6
Worsley Bsns Pk M28 .77 F8
Worsley Cl WN5 ....54 F5
Worsley Cres SK2 .124 B7
Worsley Ct 4 M14 ..98 C2

Worsley Gn WN5 ....54 B5
Worsley Gr
 Manchester M19 ...99 A1
 Walkden M28 ......60 A2
Worsley Mesnes Com Prim
 Sch WN3 ....55 A4
Worsley Mesnes Dr
 WN3 ....150 A5
Worsley Pl Rochdale OL16 .31 B7
 Shaw OL2 ....149 A6
Worsley Rd Bolton BL3 .146 A4
 Eccles M30 ....79 B3
 Farnworth BL4 ....60 D7
 Swinton M27,M28 .79 C6
Worsley Rd N M28 ..60 D5
Worsley St Bolton BL3 .145 E5
 Bury BL8 ....26 E7
 Golborne WA3 .....90 A8
 Manchester M3 ...162 E8
 Manchester,St George's
  M15 ....162 D7
 Oldham OL8 ....67 B5
 Pendlebury M27 ...80 A7
 Rochdale OL16 ....31 B7
 Salford M3 ......158 E2
 Swinton M27 ......61 F2
 Wigan WN5 ....54 B5
Worsley Terr WN1 ..37 C1
Worston Ave BL1 ...23 F3
North Prim Sch SK12 .133 F2
Worth's La M34 ...102 E2
Worthing Cl SK2 ..124 D6
Worthing Gr M46 ...58 B3
Worthing St M14 ...98 B2
Worthington Ave
 Heywood OL10 .....46 E7
 9 Partington M31 .105 F3
Worthington Cl
 Ashton-u-L OL7 ...85 A5
 7 Hattersley SK14 .102 E2
Worthington Ct M33 .108 E4
Worthington Dr M7 .63 D1
Worthington Fold M28 .58 B3
Worthington Prim Sch
 M33 ....108 F4
Worthington Rd
 Denton M34 ......101 B1
 Sale M33 ....108 F4
Worthington St
 Ashton-u-L OL7 ...85 A5
 4 Bolton BL2 .....146 C3
 Failsworth M40 ...83 C8
 Hindley WN2 ......56 D6
 Manchester M16 ...97 C4
 Stalybridge SK15 ..85 F1
Worthington Way WN3 .54 F2
Wortley Ave M6 ....80 C3
Wortley Gr M40 ....65 B2
Wotton Dr WN4 ....73 D3
Wragby Cl BL8 .....27 D5
Wrath Cl BL2 ......25 B5
Wraxhall Cres WN7 .57 E6
Wray Pl OL16 ......31 C6
Wray St WN1 .....151 E8
Wraysbury Wlk 15 M40 .83 A7
Wrayton Lo M33 ..108 B3
Wrekin Ave M23 ..121 A3
Wren Ave M27 .....62 B2
Wren Cl Droylsden M34 .84 C1
 Farnworth BL4 ....59 F8
 Hazel Grove SK2 .124 F5
 Wigan WN5 ....36 B1
Wren Dr Bury BL9 .141 B4
 Irlam M44 ....94 A4
Wren Gdns M24 ...46 F1
Wren Gn OL16 .....31 B6
Wren Nest Rd SK13 .104 B1
Wren Nest Terr SK13 .104 C1
Wren St OL4 ......67 C6
Wren's Nest Ave OL2 .149 C8
Wrenbury Ave M20 .109 F7
Wrenbury Cl 8 WN5 .54 B5
Wrenbury Cres SK3 .123 C6
Wrenbury Dr
 5 Bolton BL7 .....24 F6
 Cheadle SK8 .....122 E6
 Rochdale OL16 ....31 C4
Wrenbury Wlk M33 .108 E3
Wrenswood Dr BL8 .28 C8
Wrexham Cl OL8 ...66 B2
Wrigglesworth Cl BL8 .26 F3
Wright Robinson Cl
 M11 ....164 B8
Wright Robinson Sports Coll
 M18 ....99 F6
Wright St
 Abram Brow WN2 ..74 B7
 Ashton-in-M WN4 ..73 A6
 Ashton-u-L M34 ..100 E8
 13 Ashton-u-L OL6 .85 D4
 Chadderton OL9 ..152 B5
 Failsworth M35 ...83 F8
 Horwich BL6 ......22 B4
 Manchester M16 ..161 C6
 12 Oldham OL1 ....67 A7
 Platt Bridge WN2 ..56 A3
 Radcliffe M26 ....43 F3
 6 Wigan WN1 .....37 E1
Wright St W 3 BL6 .22 B4
Wright Tree Villas M44 .105 E5
Wrightington Hospl
 WN6 ....18 D2
Wrightington Mossy Lea Prim
 Sch WN6 ....18 F6
Wrightington St WN1 .37 C1
Wrights Bank N SK2 .124 E5
Wrights Bank S SK2 .124 E5
Wrigley Cres M35 ..84 C6

Wrigley Fold M24 ..46 D3
Wrigley Head M35 ..83 F8
Wrigley Head Cres M35 .83 F8
Wrigley Pl OL15 ...15 F3
Wrigley Sq 1 OL4 ..67 F6
Wrigley St
 Ashton-u-L OL6 ..166 B4
 Oldham,County End OL4 .67 F6
 Oldham,Greenacres Moor
  OL4 ....67 B7
 Oldham,Wood Brook OL4 .68 B8
Wrington Cl WN7 ...75 D8
Wroe St Bolton OL4 .158 D2
 Salford M3 ......158 D2
 Swinton M27 ......61 F3
Wroe Terr M27 ....61 F3
Wrotham Cl 2 M5 ..81 A1
Wroxeter Wlk M12 .164 F6
Wroxham Ave
 Reddish M34 .....100 A3
 Urmston M41 .....95 B3
Wroxham Cl BL8 ...27 C5
Wroxham Rd M9 ...64 B3
Wuerdle Cl OL16 ..15 E4
Wuerdle Farm Way 3
 OL16 ....15 E4
Wuerdle Pl OL16 ..15 E4
Wuerdle St 1 OL16 .15 E4
Wyatt Ave M5 ....161 C7
Wyatt Gr WN4 .....73 D3
Wyatt St Dukinfield SK16 .101 D8
 Stockport SK4 ...169 E2
Wybersley Rd SK6 .135 A8
Wych Fold SK14 ..113 E7
Wych St OL6 .....166 B2
Wychbury St M6 ..154 E2
Wychelm Rd M31 ..105 F3
Wycherley Rd OL12 .14 B2
Wychwood WA14 ..119 B1
Wychwood Cl M40 .65 B7
Wycliffe Ave SK9 .137 A7
Wycliffe Ct M41 ...95 C2
Wycliffe Rd M41 ...95 C2
Wycliffe St Eccles M30 .79 C1
 Stockport SK4 ...169 D2
Wycombe Ave M18 .99 E6
Wycombe Cl M41 ..95 C5
Wycombe Dr M29 ..77 B7
Wye Ave M35 .....83 F7
Wye St OL8 ......153 D5
Wyecroft Cl WN3 .113 B5
Wyke Pk OL4 .....67 D6
Wykeham Cl WN3 .151 F6
Wykeham Gr OL12 .14 B1
Wykeham Mews BL1 .144 A7
Wykeham St M14 ..98 A3
Wylam Wlk 8 M12 .99 B3
Wylde The BL9 ...140 E2
Wynard Ave WN1 ..37 C1
Wynchgate Rd SK7 .125 A3
Wyndale Dr M35 ..83 F5
Wyndale Rd OL8 ..66 F3
Wyndcliff Dr M41 ..94 E1
Wyndham Ave
 Bolton BL3 ......146 A3
 Swinton M27 ......61 F3
Wyndham Cl SK7 ..132 E7
Wyne Cl SK7 .....125 A3
Wynfield Ave M22 .130 F7
Wynford Sq M50 ..154 F1
Wyngate Rd
 Altrincham WA15 .128 F8
 Cheadle SK8 .....122 F1
Wynne Ave M27 ...62 A3
Wynne Cl Denton M34 .100 F1
 Manchester M11 ..164 F8
Wynne Gr M34 ...100 F1
Wynne St Bolton BL1 .143 E2
 Salford M6 ....81 B3
 Tyldesley M29 ....58 F1
 Walkden M38 .....60 A4
Wynnstay Gr M14 .110 C8
Wynnstay Rd M33 .108 C5
Wynton Cl WN7 ...75 E2
Wynyard Cl BL2 ..108 D2
Wynyard Rd M22 .121 C3
Wyre Ave WN2 ....56 A2
Wyre Cl M45 ......45 B1
Wyre Dr M28 .....78 B7
Wyre St Manchester M1 .163 B8
 Mossley OL5 ......68 B1
Wyresdale Rd BL1 .144 C8
Wyrevale Gr WN4 .73 C3
Wythall Ave M38 ..60 A6
Wythburn Ave
 Bolton BL1 ......144 A1
 Manchester M8 ...156 C6
 Urmston M41 .....95 B3
Wythburn Rd
 Middleton M24 ....46 E3
 Stockport SK1 ...124 B7
Wythburn St M6 ..154 E2
Wythens Rd SK8 ..131 B8
Wythenshawe Ctr M22 .121 D2
Wythenshawe Hall (Art Gall &
 Mus)* M23 ......121 B8
Wythenshawe Hospl
 M23 ....120 F5
Wythenshawe Rd
 Sale M33 ....108 F4
 Wythenshawe M23 .109 B1
Wythop Gdns M5 ..81 A1
Wyvern Ave SK5 ..111 E5
Wyverne Rd M21 ..109 D8
Wyville Cl SK7 ...125 A3
Wyville Dr Manchester M9 .64 B6
 Salford M6 ......154 F3
 Swinton M27 ......79 E6

Wyvis Cl OL9 .....48 A1

X
Xaverian Coll M14 ..98 C3

Y
Yale St BL7 ....9 D4
Yarburgh St M16 ..97 E3
Yardley Ave M32 ..96 A2
Yardley Cl M32 ...96 A2
Yare St 7 BB4 ......2 F8
Yarmouth Dr M23 .109 B1
Yarn Croft M29 ...77 B8
Yarn Wlk 8 M4 ..159 C1
Yarnton Cl OL2 ..149 A5
Yarrow Cl OL11 ..119 F5
Yarrow Gr BL6 ....22 B4
Yarrow Pl BL1 ...143 E1
Yarrow St WN2 ...56 C4
Yarrow Wlk M45 ..45 C1
Yarwell 28 OL12 .139 E8
Yarwood Ave M23 .120 F7
Yarwood Cl OL10 ..29 E3
Yarwood St
 Altrincham WA14 .119 D3
 Bury BL9 ....141 A2
Yasmin Gdns OL1 ..48 D1
Yates Dr M29 .....60 A3
Yates Gr WN6 .....36 F4
Yates St Bolton BL2 .25 A1
 Leigh WN7 ....75 E7
 Middleton M24 ....64 C7
 Oldham OL1 ....49 B1
 Stockport SK1 ...150 A7
 3 Stockport SK1 ..168 C1
Yattendon Ave M23 .120 D8
Yea Fold OL15 ....15 E3
Yeadon Rd M18 ...99 D3
Yealand Ave SK4 .169 D3
Yealand Cl OL11 ..30 B6
Yealand Gr WN2 ..57 A5
Yeardsley Cl SK7 .123 E3
Yeargate Ind Est BL9 .28 D2
Yellow Brook Cl WN2 .38 C6
Yellow Lodge Dr BL5 .40 B1
Yendale Dr M35 ..84 C8
Yeoford Dr WA14 .119 B6
Yeoman Cl SK7 ...124 D3
Yeoman Wlk M11 .160 F1
Yeoman's Cl OL16 .31 F7
Yeomanry Ct 3 M16 .97 D3
Yeovil St M14 ....97 F3
Yesoiday Hatorah Sch
 M25 ....63 B2
Yew Cl BL3 ......146 B4
Yew Cres OL4 ....67 D8
Yew Ct OL12 .....15 B2
Yew Dale Gdns OL11 .30 B4
Yew St Ashton-u-L OL7 .85 A6
 Denton M34 ......100 F5
 Heywood OL10 ....29 B2
 Manchester M15 ..162 E5
 Salford M7 ....81 C6
 Stockport SK4 ...168 C1
Yew Tree Ave
 Hazel Grove SK7 .124 F1
 Manchester M14 ...98 A2
 7 Manchester,Levenshulme
  M19 ....99 A1
 Newton-le-W WA12 .89 A4
 Wythenshawe M22 .109 D1
Yew Tree Cl
 Ashton-u-L OL7 ...85 A6
 Marple SK6 ......125 E5
 Wilmslow SK9 ...137 D7
Yew Tree Com Prim Sch
 SK16 ....101 E6
Yew Tree Com Sch OL9 .66 A4
Yew Tree Cres M14 .98 B1
Yew Tree Ct OL4 ...6 A8
Yew Tree Dr Bolton BL6 .40 B6
 Chadderton OL9 ...65 D7
 Prestwich M25 ....63 B4
 Romiley SK6 .....112 D3
 Sale M33 ....108 B4
 Manchester M22 ..109 D1
Yew Tree Farm Trad Est
 WA11 ....89 A8
Yew Tree Gr Gatley SK8 .122 A3
 Rawtenstall BL0 ...1 F8
Yew Tree La Bolton BL1 .25 A4
 Dukinfield SK16 ..101 F7
 Wythenshawe M23 .109 B2
Yew Tree Park Rd SK8 .132 B6
Yew Tree Rd
 Denton M34 ......100 E1
 Manchester M14 ...98 B2
 Wardsend SK10 ..134 B1
Yew Tree Way WA3 .90 B7
Yew Wlk 1 M31 ..105 E2
Yewbarrow Cl M29 .77 B7
Yewbarrow Rd 1 OL1 .67 A8
 Swinton M27 ......62 B1
Yewdale
 Billinge WA11 .....71 B1
 Bolton BL2 ....25 F2
Yewdale Cres 3 WN1 .37 B3
Yewdale Dr M24 ..46 E1
Yewdale Gdns BL2 .25 F2

Yewdale Rd
Ashton-in-M WN4 ....**73** A7
Stockport SK1 ....**124** B7
Yewlands Ave M9 ....**64** D5
Yewtree Ave M46 ....**58** C4
Yewtree La SK12 ....**133** F3
York Ave
Culcheth WA3 ....**91** F2
Haslingden BB4 ....**1** B8
Little Lever BL3 ....**43** A3
Manchester M16 ....**97** C2
Manchester,Sedgley Park
M25 ....**63** D2
Oldham OL8 ....**66** D4
Rochdale OL11 ....**30** A6
Sale M33 ....**108** B5
Swinton M27 ....**61** D2
Tyldesley M29 ....**59** A2
Urmston M41 ....**95** E3
York Cl
Cheadle SK8 ....**123** A5
Denton M34 ....**100** F4
York Cres SK9 ....**137** D8

York Dr Altrincham WA14 ..**119** D1
Hazel Grove SK7 ....**125** A2
Ramsbottom BL0 ....**11** A4
Wythenshawe M90 ....**129** F7
York Pl Adlington PR6 ....**21** A8
Ashton-u-L OL6 ....**166** A2
Manchester M13 ....**98** C4
York Rd Altrincham WA14 ..**119** C1
Ashton-in-M WN4 ....**73** C3
Chadderton OL9 ....**65** F8
Denton M34 ....**100** F4
Droylsden M43 ....**83** F3
Hindley WN2 ....**56** F6
Hyde SK14 ....**113** E8
Irlam M44 ....**105** D5
Manchester M21 ....**109** B8
Manchester,Heaton Moor
SK4 ....**111** B5
Sale M33 ....**108** A5
York Rd E M24 ....**65** C5
York Rd S WN4 ....**73** C2
York Rd W M24 ....**65** C5
York Sq G OL2 ....**48** D4

York St
Altrincham WA15 ....**119** E3
Ashton-u-L M34 ....**100** E8
Atherton M46 ....**58** D3
Bury BL9 ....**141** A2
Farnworth BL4 ....**60** E8
Glossop SK13 ....**104** E1
Golborne WA3 ....**74** A1
Heywood OL10 ....**29** D2
Leigh WN7 ....**76** D4
Manchester M1 ....**163** A8
Manchester M1,M13 .....**163** A7
Manchester M1,M2 .....**159** A1
Manchester M15 ....**162** E7
Manchester M19 ....**111** A8
Manchester M9 ....**157** E8
Manchester,Didsbury M20 .**110** B3
Oldham OL9 ....**153** E6
Radcliffe M26 ....**44** D5
Rochdale OL16 ....**31** B6
Stockport SK3 ....**170** E8
Whitefield M45 ....**62** F8
Wigan WN3 ....**150** B8

York Terr G Bolton BL1 ..**143** E2
Glossop SK13 ....**116** C8
Sale M33 ....**108** A4
Yorkdale Rd OL4 ....**67** D6
Yorkshire Rd M31 ....**105** E2
Yorkshire St
Ashton-u-L OL6 ....**166** B3
Oldham OL1 ....**153** F7
Rochdale OL12,OL16 .....**31** A8
Rochdale OL16 ....**139** F8
Salford M3 ....**158** E2
Yorkshire Terr OL5 ....**68** C1
Yorkshire Way SK13 ....**116** F8
Youd St WN7 ....**75** F5
Youlgreave Cres SK13 ...**171** D1
Young St Farnworth BL4 ..**60** E7
Leigh WN7 ....**76** E4
Manchester M3 ....**158** E1
Radcliffe M26 ....**43** F5
Ramsbottom BL0 ....**138** B6
Yulan Dr M33 ....**107** C4
Yule St SK3 ....**170** D8
Yvonne Cl WN4 ....**73** D5

Yew – Zyb **269**

Z

Zama St BL0 ....**11** A4
Zealand St OL4 ....**67** C8
Zebra St M7 ....**155** F7
Zedburgh G OL12 ....**139** E8
Zeta St M9 ....**157** F7
Zetland Ave BL3 ....**146** B2
Zetland Ave N BL3 .....**146** B2
Zetland Rd M21 ....**109** B8
Zetland St SK16 ....**166** B1
Zinda Dil OL8 ....**153** E5
Zinnia Dr M44 ....**105** E8
Zion Cres M15 ....**162** E6
Zion Terr OL12 ....**13** E2
Zulu St BL2 ....**148** B7
Zurich Gdns SK7 ....**123** E3
Zyburn Ct M6 ....**80** A3

07761 38 22 38

Name and Address	Telephone	Page	Grid reference
38 Rosewood Avenue	M43 7HW		

NG	NH	NJ	NK
NM	NN	NO	NP
NR	NS	NT	NU
NX	NY	NZ	
SC	SD	SE	TA
SH	SJ	SK	TF	TG
SM	SN	SO	SP	TL	TM
SR	SS	ST	SU	TQ	TR
SW	SX	SY	SZ	TV

Any feature in this atlas can be given a unique reference to help you find the same feature on other Ordnance Survey maps of the area, or to help someone else locate you if they do not have a Street Atlas.

The grid squares in this atlas match the Ordnance Survey National Grid and are at 500 metre intervals. The small figures at the bottom and sides of every other grid line are the National Grid kilometre values (**00** to **99** km) and are repeated across the country every 100 km (see left).

To give a unique National Grid reference you need to locate where in the country you are. The country is divided into 100 km squares with each square given a unique two-letter reference. Use the administrative map to determine in which 100 km square a particular page of this atlas falls.

The bold letters and numbers between each grid line (**A** to **F**, **1** to **8**) are for use within a specific Street Atlas only, and when used with the page number, are a convenient way of referencing these grid squares.

Example   The railway bridge over DARLEY GREEN RD in grid square B1

Step 1: Identify the two-letter reference, in this example the page is in **SP**

Step 2: Identify the 1 km square in which the railway bridge falls. Use the figures in the southwest corner of this square: Eastings **17**, Northings **74**. This gives a unique reference: **SP 17 74**, accurate to 1 km.

Step 3: To give a more precise reference accurate to 100 m you need to estimate how many tenths along and how many tenths up this 1 km square the feature is (to help with this the 1 km square is divided into four 500 m squares). This makes the bridge about **8** tenths along and about **1** tenth up from the southwest corner.

This gives a unique reference: **SP 178 741**, accurate to 100 m.

Eastings (read from left to right along the bottom) come before Northings (read from bottom to top). If you have trouble remembering say to yourself "Along the hall, THEN up the stairs"!

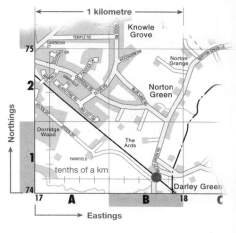